M000195988

ITALY

ALEXEI J. COHEN

Contents

Discover Italy

Imagine the world without Italy. No pizza, no month of August, and no *Mona Lisa*. It's hard to even consider. Fortunately travelers don't have to. Italy is the fifth most-visited country in the world and one of the most fascinating and stimulating places to visit. The numbers are impressive: 3,100 years of written language, a dozen golden ages, more than 100,000 historic monuments, and 41 UNESCO World Heritage sites. No other country can compete.

Dig deep into Italy's many layers and unearth a land that has influenced everything from the alphabet to the Hollywood Western. Seeing it all would take a lifetime – yet it's impossible to resist trying.

For such a relatively small country, Italy has a tremendous range of landscapes. It's hard to imagine that the peaks of the Italian Alps are on the same continent as the rocky coastlines of Sardinia. Spectacular countryside surrounds the vibrant Italian cities where Romanesque, Renaissance, and Baroque were born. Wildflowers bloom in spring along Alpine valleys and Sicilian ridges, while dark-green olive groves stretch into the Puglian horizon. The sea gleams invitingly along an endless coast and wraps itself around steaming volcanic islands and remote archipelagos.

Italy's culinary specialties are just as diverse as its landscapes – and just as worth savoring. Homogenization hasn't yet conquered Italy, and each region has at least one pasta shape to call its own. Flavors

change from hillside to hillside, and wine is varied with vines in every corner of the country. A decent sommelier could identify his location from the aroma alone.

Italy is overflowing with artistic and architectural heritage as well. Italian artists and architects broke the mold. This is where cement came of age and the arch revolutionized entrances. No two duomos are alike, no two frescoes contain the same shades, and no two sculptures portray the same emotion.

Light strikes Italy the way Michelangelo painted. Every hour, pastel houses and marble facades change color. The granite, limestone, and tufa stone used in one hill town are never identical to the next. The Greek temples in Paestum are a different shade of ivory than those standing in Agrigento.

Whether you've come to Italy for the food, the art, the architecture, or on a whim, all of your senses will be stimulated. There's no shortage of beautiful things to see, and the ingenuity of it all never fails to astound.

Planning Your Trip

▶ WHERE TO GO

Rome and Lazio

Rome, Italy's capital and largest city, is the most visited destination in the country. Each cobblestone is soaked in history, and the historic center features one breathtaking monument after another—from the Pantheon to the Sistine Chapel. The countryside around the city is a day-tripper's dream, with volcanic lakes, the tombs of Cerveteri, and the Gulf of Gaeta.

Florence and Tuscany

Many of Italy's trademark sights exist in this region, including the Leaning Tower of Pisa and Michelangelo's statue *David*. Florence, in the center of the region, features the world-class Galleria degli Uffizi, and Siena has one of the country's best preserved medieval centers. Between these cities are rolling hills and cypress-lined roads leading to countless fortified castles and hill towns that haven't changed since the 15th century.

IF YOU HAVE...

- **ONE WEEK:** Visit Rome, Ostia Antica, Florence, and Fiesole.
- **TWO WEEKS:** Add Pisa, Elba, Siena, and Chianti.
- **THREE WEEKS:** Add Verona, Venice, and the Dolomites.
- **FOUR WEEKS:** Add Naples, Capri, the Amalfi Coast, and Sicily.

Vittoriano Emanuele monument in Piazza Venezia, Rome

Liguria

Known as the Italian Riviera, this region features small pastel-colored fishing villages in the Cinque Terre, where coastal paths provide an endless series of spectacular views. Genova, the only city in the region, boasts some of the finest collections of paintings and sculptures in northern Italy and the largest aquarium in Europe.

Piedmont and Aosta Valley

Turin, the capital of Piedmont, hosted the Winter Olympics in 2006 and is home to the Museo Egizio, which houses the world's sec-

detail of the Leaning Tower of Pisa

The Vatican's Basilica di San Pietro is the largest church in the world.

ond-largest collection of Egyptian artifacts. Beyond the city is breathtaking countryside and Italy's first national park. The smallest region of Italy, Aosta Valley, offers winter sports and summer hiking among magnificent mountain backdrops.

Milan, Lombardy, and the Lakes

Italy's largest and most stunning lakes, including Lake Maggiore and Lake Como, are accessible here. The region's cosmopolitan city, Milan, is Italy's financial and fashion capital. Leonardo da Vinci's The Last Supper is visible inside Milan's Santa Maria delle Grazie.

Trentino-Alto Adige

Formed by two distinct provinces, Trentino-Alto Adige is an entirely mountainous region with the Dolomite Mountains as a continuous backdrop. The small towns scattered along the tree-lined valleys exude an Alpine charm and offer an ideal base for exploring the region's infinite trails and ski slopes.

Venice, Veneto, and Friuli-Venezia Giulia

Venice is the unmistakable star of the region, with its maze of canals and vaporetto boats that ferry legions of tourists from San Marco to dozens of small towns around the lagoon. Inland, Verona is the site of the third-largest Roman arena in the world, and Friuli is full of Roman, Venetian, and Hapsburg influences. Italy's most popular ski resort, Cortina, is an ideal base during the hiking season.

Emilia Romagna

Emilia Romagna has a reputation for producing some of the finest food in the country, and Bologna is a good place to sample the local dishes. The piazzas in Piacenza and Parma are renowned for their inventive use of stone, Ravenna's mosaics recall the days when the city overshadowed Rome, and the Po River provides a wonderful habitat for many species. The region is also home to Europe's longest beach in Rimini, where Fellini was inspired.

Le Marche

A rural region along the Adriatic, Le Marche boasts a long culinary tradition and some of the best-preserved medieval towns in Italy, such as Urbino, San Leo, and San Marino. The landscape is varied here, from the Monti Sibillini to the secluded inlets and bays along the region's

the town of Scanno overlooking Lago di Scanno in Abruzzo

extensive coastline. Pesaro is the largest resort here and Conero Riviera possesses some of the most pristine beaches.

Umbria

Umbria combines verdant green countryside and rugged terrain with enchanting towns. Examples of medieval architecture can be easily reached from the regional capital of Perugia, and exploring the steep narrow streets of Gubbio and Todi is the best way to walk off the region's smoked ham, truffle, and lentil specialties. Events such as Umbria Jazz and Eurochocolate provide cultural dynamism.

Abruzzo and Molise

Undiscovered Italy starts in these once-united regions. Abruzzo has more acres of parkland than any other region in Europe. Pescara, Abruzzo's most densely populated city, is the center of an active beach scene. Molise is wild and sparsely populated, with stunning mountain views.

Naples and Campania

Naples, a major metropolis and the largest city in Southern Italy, is best known for its opera offerings. After Naples, Benevento is the region's most important center for contemporary art. The ruins of Pompeii are just one of the many archeological parks in Campa-

nia that reveal ancient temples, mosaics, and other Roman treasures. The islands of Capri, Ischia, and Procida and the Amalfi Coast feature some of Italy's most spectacular coastal scenery and its most charming hotels.

Puglia

Greek influence is strong in Italy's easternmost region, and many of the fortified towns lining the Adriatic and Ionic coasts—including Bari, the region's capital—have inherited temples and amphitheaters from antiquity. Brindisi is where Via Appia ends and Caesar embarked for his rendezvous with Cleopatra.

market stall in Palermo

A vivid past is equally present in the circular *trulli* houses lining the streets of Alberobello and the Baroque masterpiece city of Lecce.

Basilicata and Calabria

Like Sicily and Puglia, these southern regions share a strong Greek heritage. Basilicata provided a home for Byzantine religious refugees who left their mark in churches and caves carved into the soft tufa stone around Matera. Although tourists are generally attracted to Calabria's enchanting coastline, it is almost entirely covered by highlands and plateaus. Both regions boast unspoiled landscapes throughout their rugged interiors and deserted beaches.

Sicily

Italy's largest island could easily be mistaken for another country. The dialects are differ-ent, the food is spicier, and the vegetation is sub-tropical. Palermo, with its multiple Euro-Afro-Asian personality, is the best example of Sicily's cultural crossroads. Hills and mountains prevail here, with the highest running along the northern coast towards Mount Etna, a UNESCO World Heritage site.

Sardinia

Although often overlooked by visitors on a tight schedule, the island of Sardinia is arguably the best region in Italy and boasts some of the country's cleanest beaches and most postcard-perfect coastlines. There are few large towns here and culture takes a backseat to nature. Costa Smeralda features clear emerald waters that don't disappoint, and Arcipelago della Maddalena is a big draw for scuba divers.

▶ WHEN TO GO

Tourism is a year-round reality in Italy that peaks in August and during the Christmas and Easter holidays. There is no single best time to visit, and what period you choose depends on personal preferences regarding weather, costs, services, and elbow room.

Spring and fall are pleasant throughout the country. With the exception of Easter, there are fewer tourists waiting in line and hotels charge mid-season rates. Some resort towns, especially on islands, may be closed. Autumn is also harvest time, when *sagre* festivals celebrate everything from apples in Trentino to truffles in Tuscany. New vintages are bottled and wine flows freely in Chianti. By September, Italian schools have started again and beaches are virtually abandoned.

Summer is by far the most popular time to visit Italy, and hotels take advantage of the demand and raise their rates. Airlines also charge their highest fares in summer, so tick-

Tuscan countryside

ets should be purchased well in advance. Also keep in mind that the majority of Italians go on vacation in August and over 70 percent decide to remain within the country.

costumed revelers at Venice's Carnevale

Winter is packed with religious festivals, and if you want a white Christmas it's best to spend it in Aosta or Trentino. Carnevale in Venice also takes place during this time, and the Tuscan and Sardinian versions are equally festive. Winter is the best time to hit the slopes, and Italian ski resorts offer a variety of activities. Many Italians take a *settimana bianca* (winter break) in February, which means lift lines are longer than usual. There are fewer tourists during this time, so art lovers can spend quality time with their favorite paintings. Accommodations are also more affordable in winter, and last-minute travelers will have no problem finding a room.

▶ BEFORE YOU GO

Passports and Visas

Visitors from the United States and Canada do not need a visa to enter Italy; a valid passport is all that is required for stays under three months. EU travelers can enter the country with any valid ID.

Getting There

Rome Fiumicino, Milan Malpensa, and Pisa Galileo Galilei are the main international airports with daily flights from North America. You can transfer from all three to dozens of smaller airports around the country and the islands of Sicily and Sardinia.

Since the Schengen Agreement, traveling between EU countries has become hassle-free. Border controls are a thing of the past, and entering Italy by car from France, Switzerland, Austria, or Slovenia is a breeze. You may need to pay a toll when entering the country.

There are daily departures from Paris to Rome onboard the Artesia train service. There are also many trains from Northern

European cities to Milan, Turin, Venice, and Verona. Single tickets can be purchased through www.trenitalia.it; if you are on a European vacation and will be visiting many countries, it might be more cost-effective to purchase a railpass from Eurail or Rail Europe.

Bus service is the cheapest, but least comfortable, way to reach Italy. Eurolines operates service from many European capitals.

It's also possible to reach Italy by sea from many Mediterranean countries. During the summer, there are frequent links from the Greek ports of Corfu and Patras to Brindisi on the Adriatic coast. Ferries also operate from Spain, France, and Tunisia to Genova, Livorno, Cagliari, and Palermo.

Scooter rentals are a good option for getting around Italian cities.

Getting Around

Low-cost aviation within Italy provides the quickest way of getting from city to city. Rome–Milan is the busiest route and flights from both cities connect to many smaller destinations.

Eurostar (ES) trains are the fastest and connect major cities. Reservations are mandatory, but there are usually hourly departures from Rome to Florence and Naples. Intercity trains are slightly slower, but you can usually get a last-minute ticket without a problem. Direct and Inter-Regional trains are generally the most crowded as they make local stops; it can be worth buying a first-class ticket for a slightly larger seat and more legroom.

The no-hassle and low-risk way to guarantee yourself a car rental is to reserve one prior to departure. You'll need your passport and a driver's license if you plan on renting a car. An international license is not required, but it can avoid confusion if you are pulled over. It only costs $15 and is available from any AAA office in the United States.

Driving without insurance is a risk you don't want to take in Italy. However, Collision Damage Waiver insurance can often double the price of a rental and may already be provided by your credit card company. American Express and other cards offer coverage, so it's a good idea to check with your credit card issuer before your departure.

What to Take

Some formal clothes may be necessary if you plan on any fine dining or clubbing. Flip-flops are fine for the beach, but the Swiss Guard won't permit them inside the Vatican. Keep in mind that knees and shoulders must be covered when entering religious buildings.

Most hotels provide hairdryers, but if you are staying in a bed-and-breakfast or camping you may want to pack a small one. It should be adaptable to Italy's 220 voltage. A European plug converter is useful for recharging MP3 players, digital cameras, and cellular phones. Adapters can be hard to find in Italy and airports are usually the best place to pick them up.

Items like binoculars are helpful for observing the ceiling of the Sistine Chapel, church facades, and wildlife.

Explore Italy

▶ ## THE BEST OF ITALY

the Colosseum by moonlight

Tourism to Italy didn't start yesterday. You are following in the footsteps of Dickens, Stendhal, Goethe, and Twain. Since the 19th century, seeing the ancient and Renaissance sights has been a rite of passage. Artists and poets came here to be inspired, romanced, and thrilled. Although times have changed, most of the monuments haven't. A 12-day itinerary means you'll be seeing a lot in a little amount of time, but there's always room to cut out something or set out on a monumental mission. If this is your first trip to Italy, Rome, Florence, and Venice are must-see cities. Veteran travelers may want to avoid the crowds and seek out less-frequented destinations. This itinerary is intended for train travelers, but because of the relatively short distances between cities and the good highways it is feasible for drivers as well.

Day 1

After landing in Rome, give yourself a caffeine lift at the nearest bar. Walking is the best way to beat jet-lag, so head to the Colosseum and find out what all the fuss is about. Before

turning in, grab yourself a *cacio e pepe* pasta at any of the trattorias in Trastevere.

Day 2

If it's sunny, check out the Forum, take a lap around the Circus Maximus, and walk up the Vittorio Emanuele monument for a view of

FOLLOWING MICHELANGELO

Sculpture, painting, and architecture. Michelangelo Buonarroti could do it all. He was recognized as a genius nearly from the moment he picked up a chisel, and spent his long life executing high-profile commissions for cardinals, popes, and princes. Yet for someone with such a monumental reputation, he wasn't especially prolific; rather, he combined frenetic periods of non-stop creativity with long bouts of idleness. What he did produce has captivated viewers for half a millennium and has inspired generation after generation. The majority of his work is in Rome and Florence, which makes a Michelangelo pilgrimage possible.

The **Sistine Chapel** contains the mother of all ceilings and took Michelangelo four years to complete. It covers 8,600 square feet and recounts man's ascent to heaven. Two decades after the frescoes on the vault were finished, Pope Clement VII recalled the artist to paint **The Last Judgment** in the same chapel. It's a rare opportunity to compare Michelangelo's creative evolution and witness how changing politics had an influence on his brushstroke.

One of Michelangelo's earliest sculptures, the **Pietà,** is now behind glass after it was attacked by art terrorists in 1972. But the figure of the lifeless Christ in the arms of Mary still leaves an impression. Although commissioned as a funeral monument, it was moved to **Basilica di San Pietro** at the **Vatican.** It is the only work signed by the artist. Michelangelo wasn't just paid to decorate the Vatican, he also had a hand in its expansion. He was appointed chief architect in 1564 and spent most of his time planning the dome. Although he died before its completion, the designs he left behind served as the blueprint for what was eventually built.

To see a building that Michelangelo did complete, cross the Tiber and head to **Palazzo Farnese.** The third floor and elaborate cornice are all his handiwork, along with a renovation of the courtyard that can be seen upon request from the French embassy, which is now housed inside the building.

For Michelangelo fans, a trip to Florence is a must. **David** is probably the most recognizable statue in the world and was completed

interior dome of the Vatican's Basilica di San Pietro, Rome

before Michelangelo turned 30. This sculpture exceeded expectations and took four days to haul from the artist's studio to Piazza della Signoria. In 1873, it was moved to the **Galleria dell'Accademia,** where it was attacked by a hammer-wielding visitor. The damage allowed art historians to pinpoint the origin of the marble, and can still be seen on the toes of the left foot. The Galleria dell'Accademia also contains unfinished works by Michelangelo, offering visitors an opportunity to see the chisel marks left behind by the artist. The **Basilica di San Lorenzo** is also ripe with his creations, various drawings and his only painting in Florence are hanging in the **Galleria degli Uffizi,** and some of his earliest works are on display at the **Museo Nazionale del Bargello.** A visit to **Palazzo Vecchio** rounds out a Florence Michelangelo tour with youthful sketches and self-portraits of the artist.

the city. If it's raining, get in line early at the Musei Vaticani and head straight for the Sistine Chapel. Afterwards, visit the interior of St. Peter's and climb to the top if you still have the energy. At night, enjoy a bit of wine-bar hopping around Campo dei Fiori.

Day 3

Ride the Rome–Lido train out to Ostia Antica and have a stroll along the ancient baths, amphitheater, and fish shops. Once you're back in town, sample a slice of pizza and throw a couple of coins into the Fontana di Trevi to be on the safe side. After you've done enough window shopping along Via Condotti, scale the Spanish Steps and rest a moment under the pines in Villa Borghese. Grab a *panino* from one of the snack bars and take in the view or walk down to Gusto in Piazza Augusto Imperatore for a buffet lunch. Make sure not to miss the Giotto sculptures in the Museo e Galleria Borghese nearby.

Day 4

Catch an early Eurostar train to Florence. Get a good look at the baptistery doors and marble interior of the Duomo. If you skipped the Vatican climb, make sure to slog it out to the top of Brunelleschi's dome.

Fontana di Trevi, Rome

Afterwards have a look at the city from the nearby fort, and on your way back over the Ponte Vecchio check with the tourist office to see what concerts are scheduled inside the city's churches. Enjoy a *bistecca Fiorentina* at Il Cibreo and leave room for an ice-cream from Gelateria Cavini. End the evening with a cosmopolitan and dancing at Full Up.

a close look at Ghiberti's panels on the north baptistery doors of Florence's Duomo

Day 5

Get to the Galleria degli Uffizi as early as possible and take a long gaze at Botticelli's *Birth of Venus*. Stop for a cappuccino at the museum bar on your way out and do some people-watching from the terrace above Piazza della Signoria. After lunch at Mercato Centrale, head for Galleria dell'Accademia to view Michelangelo's *David,* the most famous statue in the world. Later ride the local train to Pisa and visit the Campo dei Miracoli to catch a glimpse of the Leaning Tower of Pisa. Before returning to Florence, have dinner under the arcades at Vineria di Piazza.

Day 6

Get behind the wheel of a car rental and drive south along the scenic SS1 to the Cinque Terre. Head to Corniglia and start off walking south on the lower trail toward Manarola and Riomaggiore. There are plenty of places along the way to enjoy a picnic, as well as pleasant churches in both towns and several traditional trattoria with enjoyable views. You can catch the ferry or follow the more demanding high trail back to Corniglia.

Day 7

If your legs have recovered, hike north towards Vernazza, the Cinque Terre's wealthiest town. There are also frequent ferries to Vernazza that might save you a blister or two. Explore the defensive walls that are still in place and have a look inside Castello Doria, which protected residents from marauding pirates in the Middle Ages. It's another 45 minutes by foot to Monterosso, where you'll be glad you brought your swimsuit. Before diving in, have a look at the gothic church of San Giovanni Battista. You can rent an umbrella and deck chair from one of the *stabilimenti* that also offer light snacks and mixed drinks. Take the ferry back to Corniglia and savor your last fish dinner before returning to Florence.

Ponte Rialto on the Grand Canal, Venice

Day 8

Take a last look at the Arno before catching the Eurostar to Verona. If you don't fancy train food, stock up on cheese, cold cuts, and bread at Norcineria Bucchi. Check in to one of the convenient bed-and-breakfasts near the train station. The tourist office sells opera tickets during the summer and can provide you with a map for exploring Veneto's second-largest town.

Day 9

Take one of the local trains that leave every half-hour to Venice. If you want to travel light, you can leave whatever you don't need locked up at the station. Cross the Ponte Rialto and let your instincts guide you through the maze of streets. Eventually you'll stumble across the Grand Canal and the Piazza San Marco. Pizzeria Marciana, behind the duomo, is a reliable lunch option.

Day 10

In the morning join a walking tour with City Museums or CHORUS that lead small groups around the city's palazzos and churches. At lunch, make sure to sample some fried lagoon fish or hearty *brodo di pesce* at Vecio Fritolin. Afterwards ride a *vaporetto* out to the islands of Murano and Burano. Browse the linen stalls and have a look at the glassblowers demonstrating their skills in dozens of workshops. Celebrate the journey with a glass of Prosecco at Harry's Dolci.

Day 11

Take the Eurostar back to Rome. If you catch an early train you can make it to Termini before 2 P.M. Jump on the Archeobus and stretch your legs with a walk down the Via Appia Antica. If the weather isn't good, go underground into the catacombs of San Callisto; otherwise, rent a bike and ride out to the aqueducts that run through the nearby park. Afterwards stop by Casa del Jazz for an open-air concert or head straight to the Pantheon and enjoy your last night at Eau Vive.

Day 12

Most hotels will let you leave your luggage at the front desk after check-out time. You can then wander the streets of the *centro storico* and do some last-minute souvenir shopping. Take a couple of minutes for a final cappuccino at Bar della Pace before heading to Fiumicino airport.

▶ THE GOLDEN TRIANGLE

Milan, Turin, and Genova aren't just known for the factories that fueled Italy's post-war recovery. They are all surrounded by remarkable landscapes that have helped shape their history. Milan is striking distance from a half-dozen lakes, Turin is surrounded by the Alps, and Genova sits proudly on the sea. When you combine the three you get a memorable visit. Milan's international airport makes it a good place to start, and although the cities are connected by rail, car is the recommended mode of travel as it allows you to discover many of the smaller destinations along the way.

Day 1

Head for the Duomo in the center of Milan. The Gothic facade should be clear of scaffolding and on a sunny day there's an excellent view of the city from the rooftop terrace. The weather can be unpredictable in Milan, and Galleria Vittorio Emanuele II is a good way of avoiding the rain while on your first shopping excursion. Enjoy the pastry creations of Ernst Knam at the Gucci Caffè in between purchases. End the day with dinner at Arturosa la Latteria.

MANGIA, MANGIA

Fresh ingredients prepared simply are the secret to eating well in Italy.

You can admire castles and gaze at frescoes, but to truly understand an Italian town and its residents you'll need to taste the food. What you taste depends on the season and the latitude. *Pandoro* and panettone cakes make their appearance around December and April, while frappe pastries are only served during Carnevale. Some regions are renowned for certain ingredients; If tripe is on the menu you're probably in Rome, while if you see polenta, the Alps can't be far.

NORTHERN ITALY

Pasta isn't the only first course option in Piedmont and Lombardy, where **risotto** and **polenta** are equally popular. Fish dominates nearly every course around the lakes and throughout Veneto. *Brodo di pesce* (fish soup) is served up and down the coast, and once you've sampled a few bowls you should be able to distinguish the Friuli version that's flavored with saffron from the spicier Venetian variety. The farther north you go, the heartier the food gets – and butter often replaces oil as French and Austrian influences become evident. **Pesto** was born in Genova and no one should leave Milan without tasting *costolette alla Milanese* (breaded veal cutlets served with lemon). The abundance of mountain pastures translates to some of the best goat and cow cheeses on the peninsula. A slice of **gorgonzola, taleggio,** or **fontina** from the Aosta Valley and a loaf of bread makes an unforgettable lunch.

CENTRAL ITALY

Trademark ingredients like **Mortadella** and **Parma ham** form the basis of many appetizers in this region. **Modena's balsamic vinegar** is used to flavor soups, stews, and salads, and the **boar** that run wild in the forests of Le Marche are frequently added to *ragù* sauces. Bologna is the undisputed capital of **tortellini** stuffed with meat. Cheeses are harder here than they are in the north and **parmesan** and **pecorino** go hand in hand with many of the pastas of the area. Central Italy is also famous for **black truffles** – a sprinkle is all it takes to change the flavor of a dish. Meat-and-potato types should stick with *bistecca alla Fiorentina* (steak served on the bone and seasoned with rosemary and local oil). *Torta di Riso* (rice cake) is the traditional Tuscan way of ending a meal and can be served with any number of seasonal fruits.

SOUTHERN ITALY

Meals last longer in the south, and once you've tasted a grilled swordfish steak you'll understand why diners aren't in a hurry. **Olive groves** cover a large portion of Puglia and are a staple of many recipes, along with oregano, capers, and sun-dried tomatoes. **Pasta is hand-rolled** in many village trattorias, and *orecchiette* (little ears) are one of the hundreds of original pasta shapes to look out for. **North African flavors** have reached the shores of Sicily, where couscous is common, while Sardinians prefer roasted lamb. Less adventurous appetites can always rely on **pizza,** which varies in thickness from Naples to Brindisi. Desserts, such as the **ricotta-stuffed cannoli** from Palermo and **Cagliari's nougat** flavored with nuts or chocolate, are often linked with religious festivals.

shop the Galleria Vittorio Emanuele II

Day 2

If you forgot to make a reservation to see Leonardo da Vinci's *The Last Supper,* the Pinacoteca di Brera gallery is the next best thing. Then explore the back streets of the Brera neighborhood and start window shopping on Via Montenapoleone. If you need a rest, board one of the tour barges that travel along the city's canals. Make sure to get back in time for happy hour at Moscatelli and get acquainted with Milan's risotto dishes at Bagutta.

Day 3

If you're traveling by car, pick up your rental at the train station or airport and head north on the N36 towards Lecco on Lake Como. On weekdays, the town is quiet and you'll have no problem finding an outdoor table at one of the restaurants lining the port. Afterwards catch a Navigazione Laghi boat that makes round-trips around the lake. Later drive along the scenic N583 to the fishing village of Pescallo and bunk down inside the former convent at La Pergola.

Day 4

Spend the morning hiking the green hills behind town or exploring the attractive, narrow streets of Bellagio. From here you can set off on another ferry ride or visit the numerous villas that dot the lakeside. Villa Melzi and Villa Serbelloni are the closest. In the evening, continue along the N583 towards Como. After visiting the Gothic duomo, dine on lake fish and have your nightcap overlooking the lake.

Day 5

If there's time before setting off to Lake Maggiore, ride the cable car up to Brunate. Then head for Stresa on the N33 for your first taste of Piedmont. There are dozens of gardens to visit in this town, but the real gems are the Borromean Islands just offshore. A Baroque palace that looks as if it's floating on water dominates Isola Bella. For a romantic stay, spend the night at Albergo Belvedere.

Day 6

On your way to Turin, stop for lunch in Vercelli (60 km south of Stresa), where rice is more popular than pasta, or save your appetite for a *bollito* at Turin's Dai Saletta. The Alps will come into view before you reach Italy's most aristocratic city. Have a walk under the arcades and pick up a hot chocolate or ice coffee from any of the cafés in Piazza San Carlo.

Day 7

Visit the former Savoy palaces and get a bird's-eye view of Turin from the Mole Antonelliana, which houses a first-rate cinema museum. If it happens to be Saturday, explore the vast flea market in the Quadrilatero Romano neighborhood, where much of the city's nightlife is also concentrated. You can stay up late listening to live music and sipping excellent cocktails at AB+.

the Gothic facade of Milan's Duomo

Day 8

Head west into the Val di Susa for a better view of the Alps. Take the slow road through the valley and stop at the Sacra di San Michele monastery for a steep climb. You might start to hear French by the time you reach Susa, less than 40 kilometers from the border. If you've been craving fondue, grab a checker-clothed table at Antica Trattoria la Stellina.

Day 9

Nearly every road into the mountains above Susa is scenic. Rent a bike in town and start pedaling. If you have time, get on the old Via Francigena pilgrim road that connected Northern Europe with Rome during the Middle Ages. Before setting off, grab some focaccia or *pan della Marchesa* and a bottle of wine for an Alpine picnic along the way.

Day 10

You can backtrack through the valley or take the slow route to Sestriere (small town 40 km south of Susa) and reach the A6 byway of the Valle del Chisone. You'll see the Ligurian Sea from a distance, and Savona is a good place to get accustomed with the new scenery. Have lunch at Vino e Farinata and try to detect the change in accents. Stick to the coastal road all the way to Genova for a scenic drive.

Day 11

After breakfast walk to the Porto Antico. Galata Museo del Mare recounts the city's maritime history and the aquarium is just plain fun. Make sure to try the pesto at Sa Pesta for lunch. Later you can explore the Strada Nuova streets. Spend the evening at Teatro Carlo Felice listening to Genova's symphony orchestra.

Day 12

Wake up early and take a ride on the local train through the hillsides to Casella or along the coast to the fishing village of Nervi. You'll be back after lunch and can reach Santa Margherita while everyone is still napping. Walk the scenic path five kilometers to Portofino and spend the afternoon nursing a martini on the little Piazza Martiri overlooking the port.

Day 13

Have a look at the boutiques and yachts in the morning and visit the lighthouse for the best view of the Ligurian coast. If you've packed a picnic, keep on hiking to the abbey of San Fruttuoso and catch a ferry back.

Since it's your last day, splurge on dinner—or at least a cocktail—at Hotel Splendido.

Day 14

Say goodbye to the sweet life and count on it taking a minimum of two hours to reach Milan on the A7. If your flight is in the evening make a last stop at Pavia to see the cathedral and mail those postcards.

▶ LA DOLCE VITA: NAPLES AND THE AMALFI COAST

Naples is a good base to explore the Amalfi Coast and ease into what Italians call *la dolce vita* ("the sweet life"). Before heading for the sea and sand take some time to enjoy the center of Naples, which offers stunning reminders of the city's golden Bourbon age, when it was the third largest city in Europe. Ferries regularly depart from the city's port for Capri and the miniature, pastel-colored towns along the Amalfi Coast. There's little hope of finding an untrod path in Ravello or Amalfi, but with views this good it really doesn't matter. Positano is the place to unpack your white linen shirts and ponder magnificent sunsets with a glass of *limoncello*.

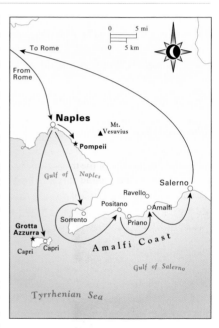

Day 1

You can drive to Naples from Rome, but the safest option is the train. The Eurostar from Rome takes under two hours and is convenient if you are traveling light. It's best to arrive during the day and avoid lingering around the station. Once you've dropped off any encumbering bags, head to Piazza del Plebiscito and enjoy a walk around the porticoes. If you want to see how the Bourbons lived, visit Palazzo Reale nearby and admire the frescoes and furnishings of the Royal apartments. Walk up Via Toledo,

which slices through the narrow streets of the old Spanish quarter. For a good view of the city and bay, ride the funicular to Castel Sant Elmo, otherwise hit the shops inside the glass-enclosed Galleria Umberto I. Place your lunch or dinner order at Antica Pizzeria di Matteo, where margherita and marinara are the only choices.

Day 2

Get an early start and imitate the locals by stopping into a bar for an espresso and *sfogliatelle* pastry. Find tranquility inside the old Franciscan complex of Santa Chiara. There are two cloisters here to explore and a cavernous church built out of volcanic rock. Naples has a surplus of chapels, and Cappella Sansevero is the one not to miss. After dinner, catch a show at Teatro San Carlo, and if you still have the energy, go dancing at Chez Moi.

Day 3

Head to the port and catch the ferry to Capri. Forty-five minutes later you'll be in heaven. Paradise isn't cheap, especially in summer, which makes the island a good day trip. After landing in Marina Grande, take the shuttle up to the village of Capri and observe the continuous bustle in the *piazzetta*. Hikers can move on to any of the scenic paths that circle the island; crowds thin the steeper you get. If you decide to spend the night then there's time to rent one of the traditional fishing boats and motor around the island. On the northwestern tip is the Grotta Azzurra,

which attracts swimmers with its famous aquamarine waters. Land-lovers can ride the bus or one of the distinctive convertible taxis to Anacapri and take the panoramic lift to the highest point on the island for an unforgettable view of the Amalfi Coast.

Day 4

Board the local train from Naples to Pompeii. Follow Via Marina towards the Stabian Baths and Teatro Grande. In the afternoon, visit Casa del Fauno, the largest and most luxurious villa in the area, or Villa dei Misteri. Back in Naples, enjoy some grilled calamari at La Cantina.

Day 5

Ferry service along the Amalfi Coast runs like clockwork and there's little reason to travel by car unless you enjoy hairpin curves and endless summer traffic. Hop on any boat sailing south and disembark in Sorrento. After polishing off the fish platter at Sant' Anna da Emilia, explore the streets that have retained their Roman pattern, visit the Coral Museum, and stroll along the port before making the long climb towards the Duomo. *Limoncello*

anchored sailboats in one of Capri's pristine inlets

Ravello on the Amalfi Coast

was born in Sorrento, and ordering a glass is mandatory; try one at Filou Club and then try to synchronize your departure for Positano with the sunset.

Day 6

After exploring Positano, walk down to the beach. Spiaggia Grande and Fornillo are the closest options. Spend the morning on a deck chair, taking periodic dips into the crystal clear water. During the summer, the town gets crowded and you may be better off heading down one of the footpaths that skirt the coast and lead to more secluded swimming options just outside of town. Stay near the beach for dinner or a nightcap at Bucca di Bacco.

Day 7

Enjoy a panoramic breakfast at Hotel Sirenuse then board the ferry for Praiano. Ten kilometers down the coast is the old maritime republic of Amalfi. Follow the narrow streets to the Arabic-influenced Duomo and climb the campanile for a bird's-eye view of the center. You can taste local specialties on the terrace at Da Gemma.

Day 8

Rent a moped from the port and drive six kilometers to Ravello, slightly inland. There are plenty of photo opportunities along the way and it's hard to resist pulling over. Park in the main square and walk up to Villa Cimbrone for a view that Gore Vidal dubbed the most beautiful in the world. There are surprisingly fewer tourists here than in other towns along the coast, and if you arrive in the summer you can catch one of the classical music concerts during Ravello Festival. Stop for lunch at Pasticceria Panza before heading back to Amalfi.

Day 9

Board the first ferry to Salerno. Start off in Piazza Cavour near the port and take a moment to stroll along the promenade. Via dei Mercanti is the main artery in the historic center and leads to a maze of narrow medieval streets full of artists' studios and family-owned shops like Antica Pasticceria Chianese dal 1860 where you can sample a delicious range of pastries. Anyone interested in the city's past can visit the Museo Archeologico Provinciale, which contains many well-preserved Roman relics. If you have the energy, climb the 300 meters to Castello di Arechi; otherwise settle for the Giardino delle Minerva, which contains 163 species and was the first botanical gardens in Europe. There are plenty of trattorias to choose from before settling into one of the plush red seats inside Teatro Verdi.

Day 10

All good things must come to an end, but the pastries baked at Café Bistrot can help make the return train journey to Rome less painful. Just point at whatever you like and Mario will wrap it up. Make sure to get a window seat on the left side of the train so you can enjoy one last look of the coast.

ROME AND LAZIO

Founded by orphaned twin brothers in 753 B.C., Rome has a unique and storied past. It's a city of firsts. First to have a population over one million, first to provide citizens with hot running water, and first to need a fire department. Standing still in the historic center offers more remarkable sights than a drive through most cities. That's not to say starting off with a bus tour isn't a bad idea. It's a good way of getting the lay of the land and discovering the landmarks that are indispensable to navigating the city.

Located 15 miles from the sea on the western coast of central Italy, Rome owes a great deal of its success to location. Fertile plains have fed its residents for centuries, hills have provided protection in the volatile early years, and the river Tiber, which divides the city, connected it to the outside world.

The seven famous hills of Rome now constitute the principal areas of interest. On the Capitoleum, formerly an ancient citadel when the city was barely a village, you'll find the museum of the same name and sumptuous artifacts that testify to the grandeur of the Republican and Imperial ages. From here you are within walking distance of photo opportunities with the Forum, Colosseum (Colosseo), Circus Maximus, and Palatine hill, where emperors lived and played.

Of course Rome isn't all ancient history, as you'll see when crossing any street corner. The Via del Corso, which runs from the Vittorio Emanuele monument on the Capitoleum to the Piazza del Popolo, is one of the principal

© ALEXEI J. COHEN

HIGHLIGHTS

Colosseo: The Colosseo is the Eternal City's most iconic sight and was ancient Rome's largest amphitheater. It stands defiantly as a reminder of its splendor (page 34).

Foro Romano: This small strip of land contains the highest concentration of ancient Roman treasures anywhere. Politics, commerce, and justice were all centered here in republican Rome (page 35).

Pantheon: Rome's largest temple has

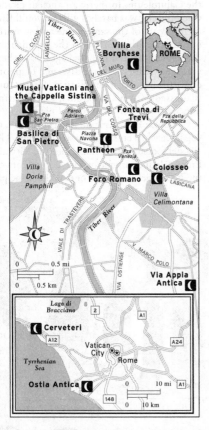

survived nearly 2,000 years without a wrinkle. The dome was the widest masonry span in the world until the New Orleans Superdome was built in 1961. The immense portico columns still influence architects today (page 43).

Fontana di Trevi: This high-Baroque fountain is one of Rome's most famous monuments. And if you believe in the legend, make sure to throw a coin into the fountain for a guaranteed return trip to Rome (page 44).

Villa Borghese: This former 17th-century residence is now the domain of walkers, bicyclists, and inline skaters. It features a world-class museum that contains two of Bernini's finest sculptures (page 45).

Basilica di San Pietro: The Vatican's Basilica di San Pietro is the largest church in the world and Rome's most heavily trafficked tourist sight. Bernini, Michelangelo, and Raphael all contributed their talents to the church's design (page 48).

Musei Vaticani and the Cappella Sistina: It could take days to see everything inside the Vatican Museums, but a visit to the Sistine Chapel is mandatory for any first-time visitor. The Sistine Chapel's 3,000 square feet of frescoes by Michelangelo is the world's most famous ceiling and arguably the most important work of art ever created (page 49).

Via Appia Antica: Walk or bike along this historic road in Rome's countryside on Sundays when it's closed to traffic. Take a tour of the monumental tombs along the way and the Circo di Massenzio arena (page 89).

Ostia Antica: This ancient city near the sea offers a vivid sense of what life was like in Roman antiquity. Ponder how the Romans once lived among baths, columns, temples, sculptures, mosaics, and frescoes (page 91).

Cerveteri: Etruscan civilization can be understood with a trip to Cerveteri. There are thousands of tombs waiting to be explored at the Necropoli della Bufoareccia (page 103).

LOOK FOR **(** TO FIND RECOMMENDED SIGHTS, ACTIVITIES, DINING, AND LODGING.

arteries of the city and is often clogged with visitors. Walking towards the Egyptian obelisk brought back by Cesare (Caesar) after visiting Cleopatra you'll find star attractions like the Trevi Fountain and the Spanish Steps. Partially pedestrianized streets like Via Condotti are ideal to window shop or place your bank account on life support. You can always choose to buy from the immigrant street merchants and their well-stocked array of Gucci imitations.

Late spring offers both warm, sunny days and elbow room from the crowds that flock to the capital during July and August. It makes walking up the Spanish Steps to the Villa Borghese much easier. From here you'll get one of the best views of Rome and a respite from the controlled chaos of the city below. The Villa, like many parks in Rome, features worthy sites, such as the Galleria Borghese, which houses Renaissance masters Raphael and Giotto, and the Casa del Cinema, where film classics are projected nightly.

On the left of Via del Corso, you'll find the oval-shaped Piazza Navona with its street artists eager to draw your caricature and no shortage of café tables from which to admire Bernini's Fontana dei Quattro Fiumi. You're also a short walk from the oldest intact building in Rome. The Pantheon never fails to impress with its size and intensity. The immense portico entry columns continue to influence architects today and may remind you of the courthouse back home. Piazza Farnese and Piazza Campo dei Fiori are nearby and the latter is a prime source of Roman nightlife. The maze of streets is exponential around here and GPS may be more useful than a map. Getting lost in Rome, however, can often be as rewarding as finding your way.

The city's 2.5 million residents seem unfazed by the beauty. They're too busy slaloming through traffic or enjoying an afternoon espresso to notice the Colosseum or Fontana di Trevi. What matters is a good meal and that trattoria on the Via Appia Antica that serves the best *cacia pepe* (cheese and pepper pasta) in town. Small talk revolves around food rather than the weather, which is generally good. No-

vember is the only exception and a profitable month for immigrants selling umbrellas outside subway stations. Even rain doesn't slow the mopeds down and Piazza Venezia remains hazardous to pedestrians 365 days a year. Clear blue skies return in time for Christmas, when shoppers huddle around department store windows along the Corso and super chic boutiques of Via Condotti.

Globalization hasn't put a dent in Rome's age-old routines. Shops close at 1 P.M., the Pope blesses pilgrims in St. Peters square on Sundays, and the daily market in Campo dei Fiori is still going strong.

Italy's capital and largest city is laid-back compared to Milan, where finance and fashion are king. There's always time to enjoy an *aperitivo* after work before facing the evening rush hour. With only two subway lines, congestion is guaranteed, but Rome's former popular mayor, Walter Veltroni, has initiated work on a third that will speed up getting to the stadium in time to see Rome's two football teams square off. Half of all the graffitti on city walls is sprayed by fans denigrating their rivals. Romans are more interested in getting a good night's sleep than staying up all night and restaurants outnumber bars or clubs. The best entertainment is sitting in a piazza gazing at *palazzi* and trying to guess what century you're in.

It's easy to focus on Rome and forget there is a region outside of the city. Although Lazio is often overlooked, that doesn't mean there's nothing to see. Both nature and culture compete for the visitor's attention and provide the key to understanding Rome. For it's here that the Etruscans reigned while Rome was still a backwater. The tombs of Cerveteri in Northern Lazio offer insight into this civilization, which was in many ways ahead of its time. The volcanic lakes glimpsed on the approach towards Leonardo da Vinci airport are the site of idyllic towns and provide a pleasant break from the pace of the capital. Further south are some of the area's cleanest beaches and a small archipelago off the coast that is a good introduction to Italy's many islands.

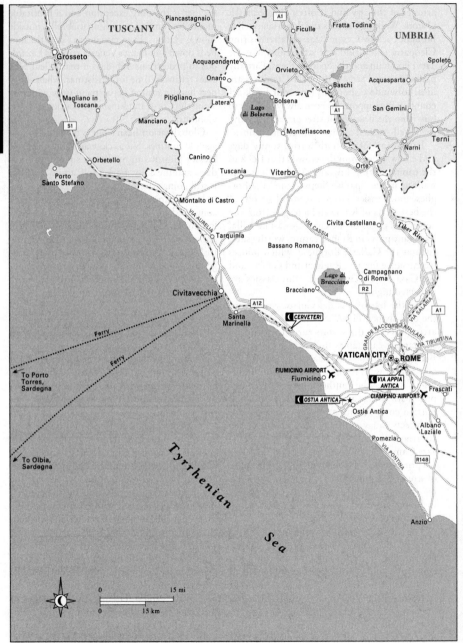

© AVALON TRAVEL

PLANNING YOUR TIME

Rome is deceptive. On a map it looks relatively compact, but once you hit the ground the density of the historic center can be overwhelming. Plan on three days to see the city's trademark sights with any additional time used to visit museums or explore the Lazio region. A full week could include a day trip to Cerveteri or Gaeta, a walk down the Appian Way, and a visit to Ostia Antica on the outskirts of Rome.

It's a good idea to approach the city neighborhood by neighborhood. You could do this chronologically, starting with the oldest parts first, or begin wherever you happen to be staying. There are no sharp divisions between neighborhoods and everything is within walking distance. That's not to say your feet won't hurt after a day on Roman cobblestones. They will, and the 110 tour bus is a relaxing alternative that provides a quick overview of the city. Public transportation is also convenient and a day pass gets you around the city relatively quickly.

Most areas can be covered in a long morning or afternoon with the chance to extend a visit by entering one of the many museums located in each neighborhood. The Roman Forum, for example, can be seen in a couple of hours, but is a natural one-two combo with the Museo Capitolino, where many of the site's artifacts are displayed.

Rome is one of the most visited cities in the world and tourists flock to nearly every square inch of the capital. Getting up early can help avoid tour groups that generally don't leave their hotels until mid-morning. Another way to escape the crowds is taking the 30-minute train ride to Ostia Antica or the bus to Appia Antica and EUR that are overlooked by tourists on a breakneck schedule.

Season can also make a difference in the lines outside the Vatican museums or for those waiting to stick their hands into the mouth of truth. Low season, November–March, however, is never that low. There are spikes at Christmas and Easter, and the city's population increases dramatically during the summer. August is a double-edged sword. Yes, there are thousands of tourists, but on the other hand many Romans leave the city and traffic is at its calmest. Many stores close during this period but there's also a wide range of outdoor concerts and cultural activities in parks and along the Tiber. It's the hottest time, when local newscasts start to warn residents about the risks of heatstroke and remind them to drink plenty of water and remain indoors.

Rome is generally a safe city and muggings and gun crime are rare. Still it's better to avoid Termini station after dark and be aware of pickpockets at all times. Most petty criminals operate in teams and can be quite young. Subways and anywhere large crowds gather is how most people "lose" their possessions; it's better to keep wallets and other valuables in a front pocket or locked in the hotel safe.

HISTORY

Rome didn't start out as the eternal city. It started out as a quiet place near a river with a few hills. It was an attractive spot for Iron Age settlers searching for food and safety. The first buildings were not the marble and travertine ruins of the Forum, but timber huts on the Palatino. Time passed, numbers grew, tribes merged, and before anyone knew it the area was thriving.

The first centuries were influenced by the Etruscans, who occupied the area of Northern Lazio and ruled the town until 509 B.C. when they were expelled and a Republic was founded. The next 500 years saw the steady growth of the city. One by one, the peoples of the Italian peninsula were conquered or absorbed before attention was turned overseas. It was during this period that Rome's first roads were built, the Punic Wars were waged and won against Carthage, and Spartacus' rebellion almost changed the course of history.

Cesare's assassination in 44 B.C. marked the beginning of a new age and it took 17 years of civil war before his adopted son Augusto eliminated the competition and declared himself emperor of Rome. The Empire increased the city's growth both in territory and splendor. The brick of the Republican age was replaced with marble and the city took on new dimensions. Subsequent emperors used architecture to influence public opinion and insured a legacy, which has survived up to this day.

No empire is eternal, however, and invading Goths and Vandals put an end to 1,200 years of glory in the 5th century A.D. The centuries that followed marked a drastic decline in population and prestige. Even the Papacy could do little to save the city from feuding families and recurring invasions. The city had to wait until the 16th century and the ideals of the Renaissance to rediscover itself. Popes and aristocrats began to recognize the city's potential and hired artists and architects to build churches and palaces. It was the beginning of a rebirth, which has continued to the present day.

Sights

Rome isn't easily divided into neighborhoods. There is no east side or west side, no left bank or right bank with distinct characteristics. Sights are scattered throughout a center where antiquity mixes with Renaissance and Baroque. Roman ruins are concentrated in the Fori (Forums) but temples are standing in the Jewish ghetto along the Tiber and near Piazza Navona. Via del Corso is the main thoroughfare leading to the Tridente, home to the Fontana di Trevi, Piazza di Spagna, as well as the city's most exclusive boutiques. Above the Spanish Steps is Villa Borghese, from where Rome's domes can best be observed. Across the rooftops is St. Peter's and to the left is Campo dei Fiori that transforms from a market during the day into one of Rome's liveliest squares at night. From there it's only a short walk to the narrow medieval streets of Trastevere on the other side of the Tiber. Outside the Aurelian walls that once encircled the city are Via Appia Antica and a glimpse of Roman countryside. The utopian neighborhood of EUR, with its artificial lake and symmetrical buildings, lies to the south while the 2,000-year-old town of Ostia Antica awaits near the sea.

Walking the cobblestone streets of Rome's historic center is like entering a time machine where ancient ruins mix with Middle Age neighborhoods, and Renaissance *piazze* flirt with Baroque fountains. From the terraces of Villa Borghese, the collage of domes and bell towers that have appeared over the centuries seem infinite. Diving into this maze of historic sights can be daunting and the secret is not to try to see it all or even pretend that you can.

Some of the best activities in Rome can be enjoyed at no cost and don't require much planning. Tossing coins into the Fontana di Trevi and hanging out on the Spanish Steps are free and can be enjoyed 24 hours a day.

There are only a few streets in Rome's *centro storico* (historic center) that are actually straight and it's not uncommon for locals to get lost. That's actually part of the fun and often more rewarding than struggling to find your location on a map. Signs aren't that helpful (except for major sights) and there's always a constant flow of travelers between Piazza Navona and the Pantheon. Landmarks such as the enormous Vittorio Emanuele monument in the center and the Tiber River that snakes its way through the city are helpful for staying on track.

FORI, PALATINO, AND CAPITOLINO

The Forum (Foro Romano) is one of the main highlights in this neighborhood. For nearly 1,000 years, this narrow stretch of former swamp and the adjacent hills was the center of the Western world. Here in the basilicas, temples, and stadiums deals were truck, senates convened, masses met, and triumphs displayed. Where to start is a tricky question, but an overview of the entire sight is a good beginning. From the Capitolino the entire Forum stretches

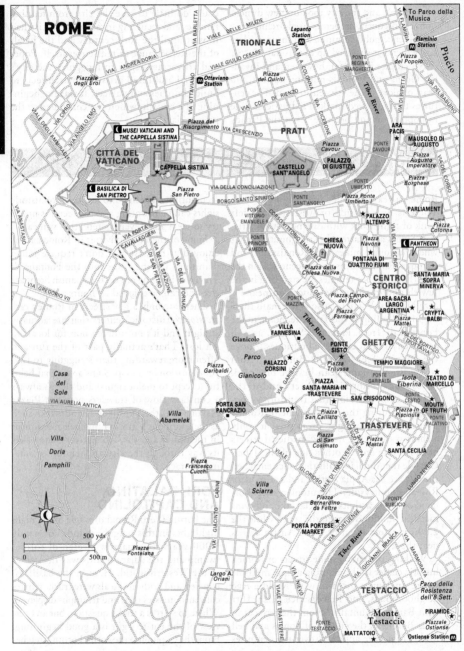

ROME

TRIONFALE

PRATI

CITTÀ DEL VATICANO

◐ MUSEI VATICANI AND THE CAPPELLA SISTINA

CAPPELLA SISTINA

◐ BASILICA DI SAN PIETRO

Piazza San Pietro

Piazzale degli Eroi

Ottaviano Station Ⓜ

Lepanto Station Ⓜ

Flaminio Station Ⓜ

Piazza del Popolo

Pincio

Piazza del Quiriti

Piazza del Risorgimento

Piazza Cavour

CASTELLO SANT'ANGELO

PALAZZO DI GIUSTIZIA

ARA PACIS ★

MAUSOLEO DI AUGUSTO ★

Piazza Augusta Imperatore

Piazza Borghese

PARLIAMENT

Piazza Colonna

CHIESA NUOVA ★

PALAZZO ALTEMPS ★

Piazza Navona

FONTANA DI QUATTRO FIUMI ★

◐ PANTHEON

SANTA MARIA SOPRA MINERVA ★

Piazza della Chiesa Nuova

Piazza Campo dei Fiori

Piazza Farnese

AREA SACRA LARGO ARGENTINA ★

CRYPTA BALBI ★

Piazza Mattei

CENTRO STORICO

VILLA FARNESINA ★

Gianicolo

Parco

PALAZZO CORSINI ★

Piazza Garibaldi

Gianicolo

PONTE SISTO ★

Piazza Trilussa

PIAZZA SANTA MARIA IN TRASTEVERE ★

SAN CRISOGONO ★

GHETTO

TEMPIO MAGGIORE ★

Isola Tiberina

TEATRO DI MARCELLO ★

MOUTH OF TRUTH ★

Piazza In Piscinula

Casa del Sole

Villa Abamelek

PORTA SAN PANCRAZIO ■

TEMPIETTO ★

Piazza San Callisto

Piazza di San Cosimato

Piazza Mastai

SANTA CECILIA ★

TRASTEVERE

Villa Doria Pamphili

Piazza Francesco Cucchi

Villa Sciarra

Piazza Bernardino da Feltre

PORTA PORTESE MARKET ★

Piazza Fonteiana

Largo A. Oriani

TESTACCIO

Monte Testaccio

Parco della Resistenza dell'8 Sett.

PIRAMIDE ★

Piazzale Ostiense

MATTATOIO ★

Ostiense Station Ⓜ

0 — 500 yds
0 — 500 m

To Parco della Musica

VIA FLAMINIA

VIALE DELLE MILIZIE

VIA BARLETTA

VIA ANDREA DORIA

VIALE GIULIO CESARE

VIA M. A. COLONNA

PONTE REGINA MARGHERITA

Tiber River

VIA DI RIPETTA

VIA DEL BABUINO

VIALE DEGLI AMMIRAGLI

VIA CIPRO

VIA ANGELO EMO

VIA COLA DI RIENZO

VIA CICERONE

VIA CRESCENZIO

PONTE CAVOUR

VIA DEL CORSO

VIA ANASTASIO

VIA PORTA CAVALLEGGERI

VIA DELLA STAZIONE DI SAN PIETRO

VIA DELLA CONCILIAZIONE

BORGO SANTO SPIRITO

PONTE SANT'ANGELO

PONTE UMBERTO

Piazza Ponte Umberto I

PALAZZO ALTEMPS ★

VIA DELLA SCROFA

VIA GREGORIO VII

PONTE VITTORIO EMANUELE II

PONTE PRINCIPE AMEDEO

CORSO VITTORIO EMANUELE

VIA GIULIA

PONTE MAZZINI

Tiber River

VIA DEL PORTICO D'OTTAVIA

PONTE GARIBALDI

PONTE CESTIO

PONTE PALATINO

Casa del Sole

VIA AURELIA ANTICA

VIA GARIBALDI

VIA DI SAN FRANCESCO A RIPA

VIALE DI TRASTEVERE

VIALE GLORIOSO

VIA GIACINTO CARINI

LUNGO TEVERE

PONTE SUBLICIO

VIA PORTUENSE

Tiber River

VIA GIOVANNI BRANCA

VIA MARMORATA

VIA NERVO

VIALE DI TRASTEVERE

PONTE TESTACCIO

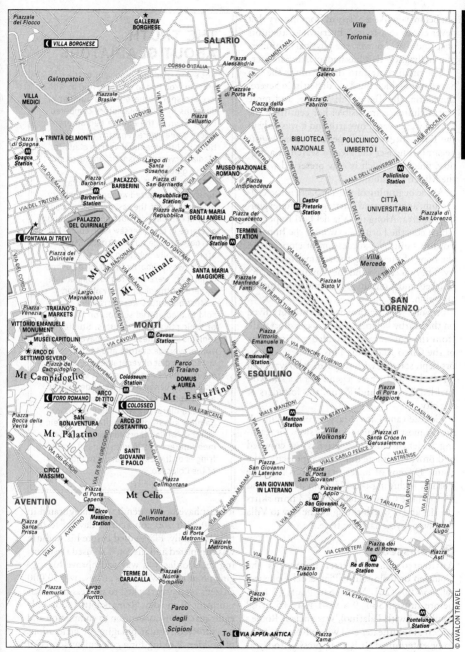

© AVALON TRAVEL

out before you like a postcard from history that never ceases to astound. Everywhere are hints of splendor and power, the physical reminders of a civilization that has had a lasting impact.

The main route into the Forum is the Via Sacra, from which the Arco di Settimio Severo, the Curia, the Tempio di Venere, and more recent churches are visible. For centuries, the Forum was covered by earth and it was only in the 17th century that Popes and archeologists began to uncover the area in search of antiquity, much of which is now preserved within the Museo Capitolino.

At the beginning of the Via Sacra is the Colosseum, another good starting point for exploring the area. Along the Via dei Fori Imperiali, which cuts the Forum in two, are the Imperial Forums built by a succession of emperors in the hope of preserving their names for posterity. They succeeded and the remains of Trajan's Markets and Column are testimony to Roman ambition.

Anyone who was anyone in antiquity lived on the nearby Palatino hill. It was a short walk from the Forum and provided a prime view of the Circo Massimo. This is where emperors slept, starting with Augusto, who was born on the hill and where legend has it a she-wolf suckled Romolo and Remo, the founders of the city.

Colosseo and Circo Massimo on the Linea B are the most convenient subway stops for reaching ancient Rome. The latter is less crowded and provides a more dramatic approach to the ruins. Dozens of buses make stops near the Forum, including the 175 from Termini and 85 from the Corso. The number 3 tram skirts the site and is worth riding all the way to Villa Borghese if you have the time.

〇 Colosseo

Anfiteatro Flavio, better known as the Colosseo or Colosseum (Piazza del Colosseo, tel. 06/700-4261, Mon.–Sat. 9 A.M.–1 hour before sunset, Sun. 9 A.M.–1 P.M., €5 or €8 combined with Palatino), was ancient Rome's largest amphitheater and where Romans came to be entertained. It is as impressive today as

THE TRUTH ABOUT GLADIATORS

Not every gladiator was sent to the Colosseum. You had to be good. And as with modern sports, there were a number of divisions in which gladiators competed. Every town in the empire had an arena where games were regularly held. Variations included: animal versus gladiator, gladiator versus prisoner, and gladiator versus gladiator.

There were 12 classes of gladiators, each with specialized weaponry. Contrary to popular belief, the vast majority of gladiatorial combats did not end in death and a referee in fact oversaw each contest. It has been calculated that 9 out of 10 gladiators actually survived the arena. The reason was primarily financial, as event organizers were required to compensate owners for the death of any gladiator.

Most gladiators were prisoners of war sold to gladiatorial schools on the basis of their physical attributes. Studies of remains show these men to have been of above-average stature and to have subsisted on a diet of vegetables, meats, and grains. They have also shown some particularly gruesome causes of death, like a trident to the skull. Tombstone epithets reveal a hierarchy with some gladiators gaining substantial wealth from their victories while others remained journeymen fighters destined to combat on the fringes of the empire far from the glory of the Colosseo.

it must have been when it was inaugurated in A.D. 80 with 100 consecutive days of festivities. Ironically, Flavio died before his stadium was completed and his son Tito used the opening ceremonies as a way to improve his sagging popularity. Within its arches, over 50,000 citizens regularly flocked to witness the entertainment of the day. Remarkably it took only eight years from conception to completion and has survived regular pillaging by generations of builders looking for a convenient source of stone. Its steady restoration began in the 19th century when pioneer archeologists and the Catholic Church began to recognize its historical significance. It was only in 1875, for instance, that the underground service passages were discovered.

Today the Colosseo teems with visitors and those hoping to make a euro off the masses. It costs €5 to pose with one of the modern-day gladiators circling the area and slightly more for a guided tour. Lines to see the interior, which served as a cow pasture in the Middle Ages and once housed a barbershop, are long. **RomaPass** allows quick access and it's also worth making early morning and evening visits when crowds thin and the stadium's travertine surface takes on different tones.

The Colosseo can be reached quickly via the Metro B stop, but makes more of an impression when approached from a distance along Via dei Fori Imperiali.

Three Arches

Whenever a consul, general, or emperor obtained a significant victory, it was customary to celebrate a "triumph." These could last weeks and were often accompanied by vows to build temples, libraries, or forums. Some edifices, such as columns and arches, also served as propaganda to remind citizens of an emperor's prowess. The **Arco di Constantino** (between Via di San Gregorio and Piazza del Colosseo) commemorates a victory over rival Maxentius at the Ponte Milvio in 312 B.C. and incorporates sculptures plundered from other monuments. It spanned the Via Triumphalis, where military processions once passed, and is now protected from overeager sightseers by an iron fence. Proximity to the Colosseo makes it appear small but stand close and its imposing stature becomes apparent.

Two other arches remain standing in the Forum. The **Arco di Tito** (Via Sacra, tel. 06/699-0110) was built by the Roman Senate to honor victories over the Jews. If you scan the sculptured relief carefully you'll spot the menorah and other spoils Tito brought back from Jerusalem. The **Arco di Settimio Severo** (Via Sacra) was built to celebrate Emporer Severo's 10th year in power. Above it there once rested a chariot pulled by four bronze horses. It's in excellent condition and provides a welcome bit of shade on hot summer days.

◖ Foro Romano

Foro Romano (Roman Forum) (Via dei Fori Imperiali, tel. 06/3996-7700, daily 9 A.M.–1 hour before sunset, free) was the center of ancient Rome and the place where all roads led to. It lies on both sides of the Via dei Fori Imperiali in the shadow of the Colosseum. The area is flat and can best be observed from the Palatino and Capitolino hills nearby. The highest concentration of Rome's archeological treasures are located here and there are several entrances to the site.

This was the Manhattan of the ancient world. It began as a chaotic mix of food stalls, temples, and civic buildings, and was gradually replaced by high-rise basilicas and monuments under the Empire. Subsequent leaders did their best to outdo themselves in a constant series of renovation and building projects. As land was scarce, they were forced to lay their foundations in the area now known as the **Fori Imperiali** (Imperial Forum). Cesare, Augusto, Traiano, and Constantino all immortalized themselves here.

What remains may look like a marble junkyard but all it takes is a little imagination to recreate the magnificence which once existed. If you want to see a scaled-down model of the entire ancient city, visit **Museo della Civiltà Romana** (EUR, Piazza G. Agnelli 10, tel. 06/592-6135, www.museociviltaromana. it, Tues.–Sun. 9 A.M.–2 P.M., €6.50). You can also watch a 5D reconstruction of the Forum at the **Time Elevator Cinema** (Via Santissimi Apostoli 20, tel. 06/9774-6243, daily 10:30 A.M.–7:30 P.M., €10).

The **Curia,** where the Roman Senate once met, lies at the northwestern edge of the Roman Forum. It's a faithful reconstruction of the building begun by Cesare after a fire destroyed its predecessor and was completed by his adopted son in A.D. 29. The replica is based

the remains of the Fori Imperiali

on Diocleziano's plans and although the original bronze doors were moved to the Basilica of San Giovanni in Laterano, the marble has remained and illustrates daily life during Traiano's dynasty. It's a good place to see what the Forum was like in its heyday, and many visitors miss the mosaics that are under their feet.

Cesare revolutionized the Forum, which had become cramped and overcrowded. First he had Cicerone (Cicero) purchase land for a small fortune then on the battlefield of Pharsalus in 48 B.C. he vowed to build the Tempio di Venere. What was initially intended as a simple addition soon laid the pattern for the Fori Imperiali, which are across the street from the Curia.

Foro Augusto (Forum of Augustus) is adjacent to Cesare's and was built to mark the defeat of his father's assassins, Bruto and Cassio. The centerpiece is a temple dedicated to Mars the Avenger, of which a short flight of stairs and four Corinthian columns are still visible. Nearby is the high wall he built to protect the forum from densely packed neighborhoods nearby and the ever-present menace of fire. The

area is not open to the public and can only be seen from the Via dei Fori Imperiali and a small footbridge that runs behind the site.

After successful military campaigns in Dacia, Emperor Traiano (Trajan) used his vast booty to build a forum next to the others. It was the last and greatest built designed by a Syrian architect who dispersed 30 million cubic feet of soil to make way for a vast square, semicircular market, the largest basilica ever built in ancient Rome, and Greek and Latin libraries. This forum became a center of political and administrative action where laws were adopted and funds distributed.

Traiano's Column (Trajan's Column) tells the story of the emperor's two campaigns in Dacia—from crossing the Danube to submission of the local chieftains—and includes over 60 portraits of the man himself. The statue of Traiano at the top however was removed by Pope Sixtus V and replaced with St. Peter. The column also marks the height of the hill, which was removed, to make way for **Traiano's Markets** (Trajan's Markets) and has survived nearly completely intact with the exception of the Emperor's gold funeral urn. If you look closely you'll see the small slits that allow light to enter the spiral staircase inside.

The **visitors center** (tel. 06/679-7702, Tues.–Sun. 9:30 A.M.–6:30 P.M.) in front of the church on Via dei Fori Imperiali organizes guided tours of the forum and provides audio guides. There's also a tourist information point out front where you can pick up a map and RomaPass.

Palatino

The Palatino, or Palatine (daily 9 A.M.–1 hour before sunset, €8), is one of Rome's seven hills and far less crowded than the Forum below. It's dominated by the remains of palaces where Rome's elite lived and is covered with wildflowers during spring. Some cats also call it home, and from the top there are views of the Forum on one side and the Circus Maximus on the other.

One of the most interesting houses is **Casa di Livia** in the center of the site, where Augusto and his wife lived. It is less grand than you might expect of Rome's first emperor and is one of the best-preserved dwellings on the Palatino. Time has raised the ground level above the house, which is reached by a short flight of steps. The original mosaic paving and religiously themed frescoes provide some insight on Roman decorating tastes. Many of the same colors and patterns seen here are still used throughout the city.

Nearby is the **stadium** Domiziano built inside his palace. The actual use of this particular model is unknown and may have served as a garden, riding track, or outdoor gym. In the 6th century, the Ostrogothic king Theodoric thought it might make a good place to run foot races and added the circular enclosure at the southern end of the complex. There's enough room to organize an impromptu 50-yard dash of your own, but the baths adjacent to the track have been out of order for a long time.

The Palatino can be reached from within the Foro Romano or Via San Gregorio beneath the arches of the aqueduct that fed the baths.

THE BEAUTY OF A BENCH

Been there, photographed this, tasted that. Walked up and down the city, risked a hand telling a lie, threw coins into a fountain and climbed a thousand steps. But how much have you really seen? It's not always the kilometers clocked or the route a tour bus takes that tells you about a city. Sometimes all it takes is a bench.

In an often overlooked corner of the Capitolino hill (through the first arch on your right after the long flight of steps and up a sloped gravel path) lies a good place to spend a few minutes just sitting still. From here you can see a symphony of rooftops, church domes, and monuments under a cloudless blue sky. The benches are marble and gleam white between the shade of the trees. Nearby couples meander hand in hand, children dash ahead of parents, and birds sing eternal songs.

Below, the city stretches silently into the distance and impressions of Rome grow between fragments of conversation and relaxed observation. This terrace is a natural place for contemplation, from here the world looks just fine.

Capitolino

The Capitolino is the smallest and most revered of Rome's seven hills. It is here that the Temple of Juno once stood and where Roman coins were minted. **Piazza del Campidoglio,** with its geometric marble paving designed by Michelangelo and Renaissance-era palazzos, is a sharp contrast to the ruins of the Forum. The three buildings that make up the square are Palazzo Nuovo, Conservatorio, and Senatorio, which contain the **Museo Capitolino** (Piazza del Campidoglio, tel. 06/3996-7800, daily 9 A.M.–8 P.M., www.museicapitolini. org, €6.50) and city hall. The facades are also the work of Michelangelo and the museum houses a collection of classical sculptures where you can see exactly what the Romans looked like, as well as the original bronze equestrian statue of Marcus Aurelius (the one outside in the square is a copy). Other highlights include the Hall of Philosophers, Mosaic of the Doves, and *Dying Gaul.*

The stairs to the right of Palazzo Nuovo (Marcus Aurelius is pointing to it) lead to the **Vittoriano** (Piazza Venezia) monument that was inaugurated in 1925 to honor the first king of the unified Italian state. Locals refer to it as "the wedding cake" and it's worth visiting more for the view rather than for any historic reason. There's also a pleasant bar with an outdoor terrace in the back that's a good place to take a breather.

AVENTINO AND TESTACCIO

Aventino is Rome's southernmost hill. Its location near the Tiber attracted foreign merchants who were not permitted to live within Rome's sacred boundary. Today it is a refuge for birds and a quiet residential neighborhood with a wonderful orange garden and famous keyhole view.

The original working-class grit is preserved in Testaccio, where generations of Romans have lived; their unique dialect prevails. The central market is stage to a constant flow of chatter between butchers, greengrocers, fishmongers, and enthusiastic clients. Browsing the artichokes in springtime is a particularly Roman pastime. Monte Testaccio, the small hill nearby, is an ancient dumping ground around which a ring of bars, clubs, and restaurants are now clustered.

Piramide station on the Linea B lies between the neighborhoods and is a good place to start a visit. Many buses terminate here and the 3 tram is another convenient option.

Circo Massimo

Sport was a part of Rome nearly from the beginning and horse racing at the Circo Massimo has been attributed to the city's founders. Today it is only a shadow of its former self, stripped of its travertine and marble. Yet it's easy to imagine 250,000 frenetic ancient Romans or one million modern ones celebrating their heroes (the Italian soccer team came here after winning the 2006 World Cup).

Circo Massimo should be walked. Follow in the path of the chariots, which were released from gates at the straight end near the Tiber and completed seven laps around the *spina* (central spine) in the middle. This long, low mound was once topped with extravagant obelisks and statues, which have since been moved to other parts of the city.

Charioteers competed in Ben-Hur-style and it was all over in less than 10 minutes, when the reds, greens, blacks, or whites chalked up yet another victory. From here you can see where the late emperors sat comfortably on the Palatino hill distracted by Christian uprisings or trouble in Dacia (modern-day Romania). The sight is open 24 hours a day and is worth returning to if possible. The tower at the far end is a medieval addition where the only original remains can be seen, as well as a distant view of the Vaticano. A smaller, better-preserved circus lies on the Via Appia Antica.

Terme di Caracalla

Hygiene was an important aspect of Roman culture and citizens visited public baths frequently. These were located throughout the city and could be used free of charge. Terme di Caracalla (Via delle Terme di Caracalla, tel. 06/3996-7700, daily 9 A.M.–6 P.M., €5) was completed by the emperor of the same name in A.D. 217 and many of the walls and elaborate mosaics are in good condition. Caracalla could accommodate up to 1,600 bathers who moved between hot, warm, and cold rooms. There were also changing facilities, libraries, and a courtyard for exercising. Guided tours with an archeologist can be arranged on weekend mornings but otherwise the lack of signage is frustrating. During the summer, opera concerts are held here.

Forum Boarium

Before the Foro Romano became the center of the ancient city, business was conducted in the Forum Boarium (Piazza della Bocca della Verità). This was where Rome's first port was located and explains the presence of the **Temples of Hercules and Portunus** that date from the Republican era. Portunus was the God of riv-

© ALEXEI J. COHEN

Arch of Giano, an example of Roman precision

ers and ports, and the rectangular structure shows the influence of Greek civilization on early Roman architecture. Neither of the temples can be visited; however, the rose garden in which they stand is a pleasant place to relax for a few moments.

Arch of Giano across the street is a four-faced arch erected in honor of Constantino or his successor during the 4th century. The statues of the Gods, which once adorned the 12 niches on either side, have disappeared, yet the monument has retained its sense of strength. It marked a busy crossroads where herders brought their cattle to market.

Santa Maria in Cosmedin (Piazza della Bocca della Verità 18, tel. 06/678-1419, daily 9 A.M.–1 P.M. and 2:30–6 P.M., free) is famous for the ancient drain cover that hangs in the portico and can supposedly distinguish between fact and fiction. There's usually a long line of people waiting to put their hand into the "mouth of truth"; many forget to even enter the church. That's too bad considering the quality of the mosaics of this 6th-cen-

tury building. What is immediately evident is the simplicity of the design. Ceilings are flat rather than arched (which was cheaper to build) and prayer seems more important than any embellishments. There's a small souvenir shop in the lobby where books and postcards are available. The entire sight was recently repainted but the probability of it remaining graffiti-free is very slim.

Santa Sabina and Garden

Santa Sabina (Piazza Pietro d'Illaria 1, tel. 06/574-3573, daily 10 A.M.–noon and 3:30–5:30 P.M.) is the most important church on the Aventino hill. But don't rush in or you'll miss the 5th-century doors that contain 18 carved panels recounting episodes from the New and Old Testaments. If the church looks new, it's due to a 20th-century restoration, which saved the 9th-century windows, marble frieze, and pulpit from ruin.

Rome specializes in romantic spots like the **Giardino degli Aranci** (orange garden) next to the church where couples regularly practice

PEACE UNDER THE PINES

Epitaphs are hard to write. It isn't easy to summarize a life, but if you've ever tried it may be worth visiting the **Protestant Cemetery** (Via Caio Cestio 6, Mon.-Sat. 9 A.M.-5 P.M., free). In this green oasis, surrounded by thick walls, you'll find graves of many ages and residents from all places. It's the final resting spot of diplomats, poets, bon vivants, architects, musicians, and actors – a cosmopolitan non-Catholic crowd banished outside city limits by the Pope and now kept company by gentle cats and occasional visitors seeking the tombs of Keats, Shelley, or Gramsci. Here the epitaphs speak of lives writ in water, loyal friends, and faithful wives. It is a romantic place with the scent of history and fading memories; strangers united in their choice of cemetery; This is a good spot to spend eternity or 30 minutes wandering the shaded paths. Afterwards life appears different, like a sudden dose of urgency or a new priority underneath umbrella pines and Roman skies.

their kissing. One could spend an afternoon here listening to the birds chatting away in the umbrella pines overhead and looking out over the rooftops. The terrace at the far end of the garden provides a view of Trastevere and San Pietro.

Piramide

Although the name Caius Cestio may have faded from memory, the Piramide di Cestio (Piazzale Ostiense) remains. Like the Egyptian models from which it was inspired, this pyramid is a monumental tomb and was incorporated into the Aurelian wall. Latin inscriptions indicate the structure was built in 333 days, as specified in Cestio's will. Nearby are the Porta San Paolo, which contains a small museum dedicated to the Via Ostiense, and the Protestant cemetery, where all non-Catholic foreigners were once buried. If you enter the cemetery

you can get a better look at the pyramid and avoid getting hit by any cars.

Monte Testaccio

Monte Testaccio (Via Galvani) is a fancy name for an antique dumping ground. This small hill stands 50 meters high and consists primarily of amphorae (vases) that were used to carry oil from Spain to the warehouses that once lined the river. Jars were smashed after being emptied and what remains is evidence of early globalization. The area is now a popular nighttime retreat for young Romans, who gather around the bars and restaurants that surround the hill.

TRASTEVERE

Rome is not only antiquity, it's also Trastevere, a medieval neighborhood awash with narrow streets that invite exploration. This side of Rome, however, hasn't escaped modernity and is often marred by traffic and third-rate graffiti. Even these offenses cannot remove the overall charm locals have managed to preserve. Unless your hotel is in the area, the best approach is over the **Ponte Sisto** bridge towards **Piazza Trilussa,** where you might begin with a walk along Via del Moro. Follow the smell of baked bread wherever it leads. The restaurants are abundant and choosing one is a unique pleasure.

Trastevere can be reached on the 23, 125, or 280 bus, or the 3 or 8 tram. Most streets are too narrow for public transportation and you'll need to walk to get to the center of the neighborhood.

Ponte Sisto

Ponte Sisto connects the Trastevere neighborhood with the rest of the city. It gets its name from Pope Sixtus IV, who opened the bridge in 1474 and financed the endeavor with taxes paid by prostitutes. The Renaissance years were boom times for those in the oldest profession, who numbered 6,800 in a city of only 50,000. Flooding destroyed previous bridges on this site and the remains of the Pons Auerelio were incorporated into the latest version. The round hole in the center serves as a flood alert. If water reaches that level, it's time to head for the hills. On most evenings, someone is playing an instrument on the bridge or selling fake Gucci bags.

San Crisogono

San Crisogono (Piazza Sonnino 44, tel. 06/581-8225, Mon–Sat. 7 A.M.–11 A.M. and 4–7 P.M., Sun. 8 A.M.–1 P.M.) is a welcome relief from the traffic on Viale Trastevere. It was built over a house where early Christians once worshipped. The church mixes Baroque with Romanesque and recycled Roman marble for its floors. To see the state of excavations, which have been ongoing since 1907, descend the steps near the sacristy at the far left end of the church. A small donation will get the lights turned on and reveal segments of the ancient church dating from the 8th century. You are likely to see as many parishioners as visitors coming and going throughout the day.

Santa Cecilia

Santa Cecilia (Piazza di Santa Cecilia, tel. 06/589-9289, daily 9 A.M.–1 P.M. and 2–7 P.M., €2) was commissioned by Pope Pascal I in 821 in honor of the martyred saint who resisted her torturers through song and was eventually beheaded. The church includes a convent, bell tower, cloister, and the immense *Last Judgment* fresco by Pietro Cavallini located in the choir of the nuns. It is one of the finest examples of Roman medieval painting in existence.

Santa Maria in Trastevere

Santa Maria in Trastevere (Piazza Santa Maria in Trastevere, daily 7:30 A.M.–1 P.M. and 4–7 P.M.) dates back to a dispute early Christians had with tavern keepers in the area. The matter reached the attention of the emperor Alexander Severus, who sided with the new religious order preferring faith over revelry. The present structure followed a familiar development cycle being built, rebuilt, and remodeled since the 3rd century. Its present form dates from Pope Innocent II in 1140. It is notable for the external mosaics, which were added in the 13th and 14th centuries and represent the Virgin Mary and child. The mosaics continue inside with a series illustrat-

ing the life of the Virgin Mary. The piazza in front of the church is the center of the neighborhood and the fountain in the middle is a popular meeting place. There are several outdoor cafés from where the church and street life can be admired.

Tempietto

The Tempietto (Piazza San Pietro in Montorio, tel. 06/581-3940, daily 8 A.M.–noon, 4–6 P.M.) was designed by Bramante between 1502–1507 and commemorates the site where Saint Peter was martyred. It set a new standard for proportions and became a model for countless other buildings in the 16th century. Gian Lorenzo Bernini built the entrance of the crypt over 100 years later. Inside stands a statue of the saint dating from the same period. The site hosts frequent exhibitions and events.

Palazzo Corsini

Before becoming the home of the **Galleria Nazionale d'Arte Antica,** Palazzo Corsini (Via della Lungara 10, tel. 06/6880-2323, Tues.–Fri. 9 A.M.–7 P.M., Sat.–Sun. 9 A.M.–1 P.M., €6) was the home of cardinals and noblemen, including Cardinal Neri Corsini for which it is named. Over the course of its long history it has hosted Michelangelo, Erasmus, and Queen Christina of Sweden. Today the gallery is filled with a first-rate collection of 17th- and 18th-century Italian art, as well as a smattering of Rubens and Van Dykes. The elaborate frescoed interiors are almost as interesting as the art hanging on the walls.

Villa Farnesina

When banker Agostino Chigi decided to build himself a villa, he didn't just want any villa. He wanted to set the standard. Villa Farnesina (Via della Lungara 230, tel. 06/6880-1767, Mon.–Sat. 9 A.M.–1 P.M., €5) did just that and the building's deceptively simple design of a central block with two projecting wings is enhanced through the paintings and imagination of its creator Baldassarre Peruzzi, who worked under Bramante and would later become Head of Work at San Pietro. His **Salone delle**

Prospettive creates the illusion of looking out on 16th-century Rome and alters depending on the viewer's perspective. Raffaello also had a hand in the decoration; the Loggia of Cupid and Psyche are his creations. Photography is strictly prohibited, but you can take pictures out in the formal gardens.

CAMPO DEI FIORI AND PIAZZA NAVONA

The streets in these neighborhoods flanking the Tiber are home to some of Rome's finest Renaissance and Baroque buildings. Both are vibrant and the market in Campo dei Fiori is better than going to the theater. You can watch the banter from the steps of the statue in the center and return in the evening when bars and restaurants keep the area animated until late.

The 116 electric bus is the best way of getting around Campo dei Fiori and Piazza Navona, although its diminutive size means seats are scarce. The 23 from Piramide and 64 from Termini make stops along Corso Vittorio Emanuele II, from where all the major sights are within walking distance.

Isola Tiberina

Whoever said "the more things change, the more they stay the same" was probably thinking of Rome, and the Isola Tiberina in particular. This small island of volcanic rock played a crucial role putting Rome on the map. It's here that Aesculapius, the God of medicine, was worshipped, where sick Romans waited to be healed outside his temple, and where a hospital was founded in 1548 that still operates today. The island itself was altered to resemble a ship in the 1st century A.D., the outlines of which are still visible. Ponte Fabrico, the bridge that connects the island to the Jewish Ghetto, is the oldest bridge in the city. The man playing saxophone is a regular and is oblivious to the pregnant women on their way to the hospital.

Ghetto

Jews have been living in Rome for over 2,000 years and have occupied the area opposite Isola Tiberina for nearly half that time. As religious hatred ebbed and flowed so did their fortunes. One century they were limited to selling fabrics, clothing, and second-hand iron, and the next they found themselves cramped behind high walls under the watchful eyes of the Swiss Guard. The character of the neighborhood and especially its inhabitants, renowned for being more Roman than the Romans, has survived. **Via del Portico di Ottavia** is the heart of the Ghetto and the place to give kosher Roman a try. The street has recently been recobbled and the benches are occupied by old-timers. Grab a seat if you can and enjoy the show.

Tempio Maggiore synagogue (Lungotevere Cenci, tel. 06/6840-0661, www.museoebraico. roma.it) down the block has Art Nouveau written all over it. There's a museum inside that features sacred objects and is the starting point for one-hour guided tours of the neighborhood in English or Italian (Associazione Culturale Le Cinque Scuole, tel. 06/558-0971, €3–7). The carabinieri police on duty are a relic from a terrorist attack in 1982.

Via della Reginella in the opposite direction became part of the neighborhood in 1823 when Pope Leo XIII allowed the Ghetto to be expanded. The air is medieval and the courtyards all around provide a clue of what the area once felt like. Further ahead is **Piazza Mattei** and the recently restored Fontana delle Tartarughe. Have a seat at one of the outside café tables and enjoy the graceful fountain modified and remodified over the decades.

Crypta Balbi (Via delle Botteghe Oscure, Tues.–Sun 9 A.M.–7 P.M., tel. 06/3996-7700, €3.50–7) around the corner is on a street named for the medieval craftsmen who once transformed pieces of repossessed marble into lime used for construction. The museum provides first-hand artifacts illustrating how the city has reinvented itself over the ages and helps sort out one era from the next.

Area Sacra dell'Argentina

Area Sacra dell'Argentina (Largo Argentina) is a large rectangular site in which four temples known simply as A, B, C, and D were discov-

At 2,000 years old, the Pantheon is the only Roman building still intact.

ered in the 1920s. Near temples C and D are the remains of Pompeii's Curia where the Senate convened and Cesare was murdered. Today the Area Sacra can only be visited by appointment and is the home of a cat refuge. A panel on one side provides details about the columns and stairs still standing and illustrates how the site once looked.

(Pantheon

Civilizations build reputations on buildings like the Pantheon (Piazza della Rotonda, tel. 06/6830-0230, daily 9 A.M.–6:30 P.M., free) and the fact that this one is still standing is further proof that the Romans knew a thing or two about construction. This former temple's first incarnation dates from 27 B.C., when it was dedicated to Jupiter, Mars, and Venus. Three Gods meant pulling out all the stops, and Emperor Adriano completely rebuilt the structure less than 100 years later. The 16 monolithic columns his architects used in the portico entrance are 12 meters high and dwarf the steady stream of visitors. The darkest col-

umn was recently traced to a hard labor camp the Romans operated in Egypt. The building was consecrated as a church in A.D. 663 and suffered only slight ravaging. Bronze tiles of the roof were removed as were bronze sheeting from the portico beams melted down to make canons for the Castello Sant'Angelo.

Years as a fortress, poultry market, and bell towers, added and later demolished, did not severely damage the building. The seven-meter thick walls are one of the keys to its longevity and they continue to support the largest dome ever built during antiquity. The only light enters through an oculus three meters in diameter, which is embedded in the vault. Most of the colored marble is original, as is Adriano's inscription on the frieze outside. It's no wonder Raffaello wanted to be buried here.

Campo dei Fiori

If you close your eyes and imagine a field of flowers you'll have an idea of what Campo dei Fiori (Piazza Campo dei Fiori) was like in the 14th century. Now add cardinals, noblemen, and fishmongers, who all animated the open area facing Pompeii's theater and the place starts to come alive. Today a flower and food market still thrives and a lively crowd gathers throughout the day and dangerously close to dawn. The hooded statue in the center is Giordano Bruno, who was burned here at the stake for being a little too ahead of the times.

Although only a short walk away, **Piazza Farnese** has little in common with its neighbor. Here order reigns, imposed by the palazzo built by the Farnese family and considered one of the finest in Rome. If you're wondering where the missing half of the Colosseo ended up, then Palazzo Farnese is partly to blame. The large fountains in the piazza on the other hand were commandeered from the baths of Caracalla. The palazzo itself has benefited from the designs of Michelangelo, who continued the project when the original architect died. He is responsible for the cornice, central balcony, and the third floor of the courtyard. The palazzo has belonged to the French government since 1635 and now serves as an embassy. Visits are free and may be arranged through the French consulate (Via Giulia 251, tel. 06/686-011).

Piazza Navona

Piazza Navona is not your typical square. In fact, it's not square at all since it inherited an oblong shape from the time of Domiziano's stadium. It can be entered by one of four streets and is entirely free of any automotive threats— which means fountains, churches, and street artists can be observed at leisure. Bernini's **Fontana di Quattro Fiumi** in the center of the piazza is the most intricate of the waterworks and was installed in 1651. Four mythical figures representing the Nile, Ganges, Danube, and Rio de la Plata support a Roman obelisk that once stood in Circo di Massenzio on the Via Appia Antica.

The church in front of the fountain is **Sant'Agnese** in Agone (Piazza Navona, tel. 06/6920-5401). According to legend, Agnese was stripped naked in an attempt to make her renounce her faith. The hair that miraculously grew to cover her is depicted in a marble relief near the altar. Boromini completed a restructuring of the church in 1657, which gave it a unique concave appearance topped by twin bell towers. The underground chambers can be reached through a passage on the right wall and lead to ruins of the stadium, a mosaic floor from the same period, and medieval frescoes from the church's first incarnation.

Palazzo Altemps

The 15th-century Palazzo Altemps (Piazza Sant'Appollinare 4, tel. 06/397-4990, Tues.– Sun. 9 A.M.–7:45 P.M.) is home of the **Museo Nazionale Romano** and houses Egyptian, Greek, and predominantly Roman sculptures. The most noteworthy is *Galata Suicida* (Galata's Suicide), commissioned by Cesare in the first century B.C. to commemorate his conquest of Gaul.

The Via del Governo Vecchio is named after the palazzo, which once housed the headquarters of the papal government. The street is lined with palazzos from the 15th and 16th centuries, including number 123, where it is believed Bramante once lived.

Chiesa Nuova

Chiesa Nuova (Piazza della Chiesa Nuova, tel. 06/687-5289, daily 7:30 A.M.–noon and 4:30–7 P.M.) may not look new, but it did replace a medieval church on the same site and the name stuck ever since it was completed in 1599. The idea for the church came from San Filippo Neri, who was an active participant in the Counter-Reformation and who had his wealthy followers wear rags and labor on the construction of the church. It took 20 years to complete the frescoes, which decorate the nave, dome, and apse. Three paintings by Rubens are present near the altar.

TRIDENTE

When viewed on Google Earth, it's clear where this part of the city gets its name. Whether the Tridente's urban planners had this in mind is unknown. What is certain is that ambitious popes and world leaders including Napoleon wished to redefine Rome in the 17th and 18th centuries and knocked down anything that got in their way. Medieval was replaced with **Piazza del Popolo,** the Spanish Steps, long vistas, imposing palazzos, and soul-stirring churches. Renaissance was born, Baroque blossomed, Rococo began, and the greatest artists ever known left their mark in less than a three-kilometer radius. There's a complex street pattern and understanding it soon becomes an obsession.

Spagna on the Linea A drops travelers off in the heart of the Tridente. For a more subtle approach to the area, try Barberini or Flaminio on the same line. The 2 tram lets passengers off at Piazza del Popolo and the Corso is always lined with buses.

◖ Fontana di Trevi

Fontana di Trevi, the Trevi Fountain (Piazza di Trevi), is a symbol of Baroque Rome. It resembles a large open-air theater, and the actors in this case are the four marble statues that represent the virtues of water. *Ocean* stands in

them overcame the lack of water pressure by sculpting a half-sunken boat that collects the water. The bees and suns that decorate the fountain are identical to those on Pope Urban VII's coat of arms and a reminder of who financed the project.

Trinità dei Monti

You won't be the only one searching for a seat on the **Spanish Steps.** These were actually built by the French owners of the Trinità dei Monti (Piazza della Trinità dei Monti, daily 7 A.M.–7 P.M.), who wished to connect the church with the square below in the 17th century. Wrangling between popes and French monarchs delayed the project until a design was found that satisfied all parties. The result is a stunning combination of terraces, curves, and balustrades that significantly raise the probability of ending up in someone else's photograph.

The view gets better with each step towards the Trinità dei Monti and reaches perfection from the platform in front of the entrance. The panorama, however, should not completely distract visitors from the 15th-century church, which was recently restored and whose interior includes paintings by Daniele da Volterra, who studied under Michelangelo. It was Volterra who covered up his master's *Last Judgment* nudes deemed too racy by the Pope. The muscled bodies in the *Deposition* show clear signs of his teacher's influence.

◖ Villa Borghese

An escape from the intensity of the city is only as far as the heights of Villa Borghese (Piazza del Popolo, tel. 06/8205-9127, www.villabor ghese.it, open 24 hours). From here the city's rooftops form an intricate tapestry and a stroll under umbrella pines can help rejuvenate spirits. Further up the hill is **Villa Medici** (Viale della Trinità dei Monti 1, tel. 06/676-11, hours vary). It was acquired by the Medici family in the 16th century and later gained the austere facade, which was popular at the time. The lightheartedness was reserved for the rear of the building, which is much more ornate and overlooks a park complete with hedged walks,

© ALEXEI J. COHEN

All it takes is a coin to guarantee a return visit to the Fontana di Trevi.

the center on a shell-shaped carriage pulled by seahorses and tritons. The small piazza gets crammed with visitors and sellers of cheap trinkets during afternoons in the middle of August. It's much more pleasant on early spring mornings or at night when the spirit of Mastroanni returns. It took Nicola Salvi 30 years to build his masterpiece. Water adds to the sense of movement and the stone nearly comes to life. To ensure a return trip to Rome all it takes is a coin. Rest assured that all the money is vacuumed out twice a month and donated to charity. For an original souvenir, you can always take a sample of the water back home.

Piazza di Spagna

Piazza di Spagna is a highlight for most visitors and has been since the time it was the headquarters of the Spanish embassy to the Holy See. Fortunately now you won't risk being conscripted into the Spanish army and may even get a glimpse of the **Fontana della Barcaccia,** believed to be either the work of Gian Lorenzo Bernini or his father. One of

It's hard to resist sitting on the Spanish Steps in front of the Trinità dei Monti.

© ALEXEI J. COHEN

secret gardens, and fountains. In 1804, Napoleon moved the French Academy into the villa and inspired such talents as Berlioz and Debussy. It continues to host a wide variety of cultural events.

Besides nature and history, the park offers one of the world's finest art collections. **Museo Borghese** (Piazzale Scipione Borghese 5, tel. 06/8424-1607, Tues.–Sat. 9 A.M.–10 P.M., Sun. 9 A.M.–8 P.M., €6.50) is so fine that entry must be reserved in advance. That's not as complicated as it may sound and allows you to visit the sculpture and picture galleries the art students outside are busy sketching.

Contemporary Italian art is less formal and you can show up unannounced at the **Museo Carlo Bilotti** (Viale Fiorello La Guardia, tel. 06/8205-9127, Tues.–Sun. 9 A.M.–7 P.M., www.museocarlobilotti.com, €4.50), also within the park. The former Aranciera houses an exposi-

tion space and small collection featuring Giorgio de Chirico.

Rome is a dense city. Maybe that's why the **Piazza del Popolo** is so refreshing. Here in this circular, cobblestone square commissioned by Napoleon, there is room to breathe in the city, to admire the twin Santa Maria churches or just sit on the steps under the Egyptian obelisk and watch the passersby.

Palazzo Barberini

Galleria Nazionale di Arte Antica (Via Barberini 18, tel. 06/481-4591, Tues.–Mon. 8:30 A.M.–7:30 P.M., €6) in Palazzo Barberini is a museum on the rise. It already hosts an impressive collection of paintings from Raffaello to Caravaggio but the transfer of the officer's club and hefty investment means it will soon get even better. When fully restored in 2009, it will rival Florence's Palazzo Pitti in size and

PASTA 101

Everyone cooks it, everyone eats it, but how much do you really know about Italy's greatest culinary legacy? If you can't tell bucatini from ziti, if al dente is a foreign concept, if you didn't know that pasta was first mentioned by an Arab scholar in A.D. 1154, that there are over 300 pasta shapes, and durum wheat is the secret ingredient, then forget the Foro: It's time to spend time at the **Museo Nazionale delle Paste Alimentari** (Piazza Scanderberg 117, tel. 06/699-1119, €5).

You'll be greeted by two lovely ladies and nine rooms of pasta history. An audio guide, included with entry fee, describes the objects around you, tracing pasta's evolution from handmade to industrial age. It's the story of kneading, rolling, pressing, cutting, and drying. It's also the impact of a revolutionary low-cost high-energy food on Italian

© PURESTOCK

culture and its yet-unrealized potential to feed the world.

You may start to get hungry around room seven. There are two restaurants within 20 meters of the museum and either one can satisfy your newly educated palate.

provide a permanent home to 1,500 artworks waiting to be displayed.

Mausoleo di Augusto

Emperors weren't just buried and forgotten; they left their physical imprint even after death. The Mausoleo di Augusto (Piazza Augusto Imperatore, tel. 06/6710-3431, call to arrange a visit) is one of several impressive examples of monumental tombs ancient Romans of wealth and distinction built for themselves. Like many, this one is circular and was once topped with poplar trees. It has been adapted by later ages that transformed it into fortress, palace, and prison. The interior can be visited by appointment only and renovation of the area is scheduled to be completed in 2012.

Ara Pacis

The museum that houses the Ara Pacis (Lungotevere in Augusta, Tues.–Sun. 9 A.M.–7 P.M., €6.50), completed in 2006, is the latest attraction in Rome. Although the Richard Meier–designed building has raised some eyebrows, visitors have proclaimed it a success. The Ara Pacis itself was commissioned by the senate in 13 B.C. to celebrate Augusto and mark a new beginning after years of civil war. It is part temple, part monumental arch adorned with figures recounting the history of the time. Each side of the monument's sculpted relief recalls specific events and legends of the past that are vividly deciphered by the museum's audio guide. The Imperial family, including Cesare, Tiberio, Augusto, and his wife Livia, are all preserved in stone.

VATICANO

Few cities offer the opportunity to leave with a single step, but Rome is one of them. The Vaticano is the smallest state in the world. Size, of course, doesn't matter when spirit is concerned and the Vaticano scores big on this count. Whether you are a believer or not, it's hard not to be moved by the grandeur of San Pietro, the view from its cupola, or the works on display within the museum. Waiting in line has never been so gratifying, but even this minor encumbrance can be avoided with foresight. Anyone can send a postcard from Italy but few take the trouble to mail theirs from the Vaticano post office.

Ottaviano on the Linea A is the fastest way to the Vatican, but the 23 bus from Piramide runs along the Tiber and is the most scenic. From Termini you can catch the 40.

◖ Basilica di San Pietro

The modern Vatican state dates from the Lateran Treaty of 1929 when its present boundaries were officially recognized. Although the population does not exceed 1,000, its religious and cultural importance is inestimable. Within the Vaticano walls lie the former papal residences—now converted into museums as well as gardens, a railway, radio station, and of course the Basilica di San Pietro, or the Basilica of Saint Peter (Piazza San Pietro, tel. 06/6988-4466, daily 7 A.M.–7 P.M.). Every Sunday morning, thousands of worshipers gather here to listen to the Pope deliver his message in a half-dozen languages.

The numbers are impressive: 11 chapels, 45 altars, 187 meters from entrance to apse, and 136 meters to the top of the cupola. Big is an understatement, but it didn't start out that way. Buried underneath the basilica are the remains of a Roman racetrack. Emperors enjoyed mixing sport with religious persecution and it's here that St. Peter was martyred in A.D. 64. Word spread quickly, pilgrims began to visit the site almost immediately, and early Christians were buried along the nearby road.

It was the obvious place, therefore, for the freshly converted emperor Constantino to build the first basilica in A.D. 324. That building lasted until 1503 when restoration proved impossible and Pope Julius II opted for demolition. Bramante was chosen to design a new basilica and the next century and a half saw the Vaticano undergo a succession of modifications as Popes and the artists they hired altered the original plans according to taste and architectural fashion. Michelangelo engineered the cupola, Carlo Maderno constructed the facade and Bernini designed the piazza. The result is

remarkably uniform considering how many different hands worked on the building.

The inside is as impressive as the outside. Popes didn't cut corners when it came to interior decoration and only the finest materials were used by the most talented craftsmen and artists. Immediately on the right behind bulletproof glass is Michelangelo's *Pietà* sculpture, which is his only signed work and was completed when he was barely 25. Below the dome is Bernini's *Baldacchino,* which towers above the Papal Altar and under which only Popes may celebrate mass. Nearby is the entrance to the grottoes, where relics of the original basilica can be seen, including fragments of Giotto's mosaic. This is also where Popes are buried and a steady stream of visitors pay their respects to John Paul II. The original Christian necropolis can be visited and provides insight into the origins of modern religion.

One of the greatest challenges of building San Pietro was the cupola. It needed to express the grandeur of the Pope's ambitions and withstand the laws of gravity. Michelangelo was a master of both expression and form. His reputation was already indisputable and when the Pope called he didn't hesitate to answer. The solution, which he never saw realized, actually consists of two domes—one fitted inside the other for the sake of maintaining proportions. Walking to the top is the best way to appreciate this structural marvel of engineering, which occupied 600 skilled workers for years. Although an elevator can take you part of the way up, you'll have to use your legs to reach the summit.

From the top of the cupola all of Rome is visible and the Piazza San Pietro below reveals its true shape. Bernini, who built the piazza for outdoor masses between 1656–1667, intended the space to symbolically embrace the world. The semicircular colonnades are made up of four rows of columns and topped with 140 statues of saints. Once you've returned to earth, you can stand on either of the marble discs near the fountains, from which the four lines of columns disappear into one. Pope

Sixtus V is responsible for the placement of the granite obelisk, which is the only visible reminder of Caligula's racetrack.

◖ Musei Vaticani and the Cappella Sistina

The Musei Vaticani, or Vatican Museums (Viale Vaticano, tel. 06/6988-4466 or 06/6988-3333, Mar.–Oct. Mon.–Fri. 8:45 A.M.–4:45 P.M. and Sat. 8:45 A.M.–1:45 P.M., Nov.–Feb. Mon.–Fri. 8:45 A.M.–1:45 P.M. and Sat. 8:45 A.M.–1:45 P.M.), is comprised of several museums, and visiting them all would require the stamina of an Olympic marathon runner. Various color-coded itineraries vary in length from 90 minutes to five hours. The favorite destinations are of course The Raffaello Rooms and the Cappella Sistina (Sistine Chapel), which takes 20 minutes to reach from the entrance without a single sideways glance or tourist jam.

Less crowded is the **Museo Pio-Clementino.** It contains Rome's first spiral staircase and such ancient sculptures as the *Laocoon*. This 1st century A.D. work was unearthed in Nero's villa near the Colosseo and depicts a Trojan priest punished for warning his fellow citizens about a large wooden gift horse. The Rooms of the Animals and Busts are filled with mosaics and the portraits of emperors who look surprisingly familiar.

The **Pinacoteca** contains a collection of paintings curators all over the world would beg for. Raffaello's vibrantly colored last work on oil *The Transfiguration* hangs near Leonardo da Vinci's unfinished *St. Jerome* and Caravaggio's *Descent from the Cross.* The Gallery of Maps and the Gallery of the Candelabra provide more breathing space, as well as a good view of the gardens.

Skipping the Cappella Sistina (Viale Vaticano, tel. 06/6988-4466, Mon.–Fri. 8:45 A.M.–3:20 P.M., Sat. and last Sun. of the month 8:45 A.M.–12:20 P.M.) is like leaving the Louvre without viewing the Mona Lisa. It's mandatory. When it comes to frescoes, this is it. Nothing is bigger, nothing is so closely associated with a single artist, and nothing is more impressive. The chapel, however, isn't just a ceiling but probably the most finely decorated room in the world. It was originally commissioned by Pope Sixtus IV between 1475–1481. He had the most talented artists of the time fresco the sidewalls and his successor, Julius II, asked Michelangelo to paint the altar and vault.

The ceiling took four years to complete and consists of over three hundred figures depicting the creation and fall of man. Every brushstroke was inspired from the Bible, beginning with Noah near the entrance and ending with the *Last Judgment* on the altar wall, which was completed in 1541 and provoked discussion until the nude figures were covered. Michelangelo worked alone for the most part on specially constructed scaffolding that allowed him to paint every corner of the 278 square meters. It's little wonder that this is where cardinals gather to elect new Popes and 15,000 visitors a day come to get a glimpse of genius.

While Michelangelo was busy on his chapel, Raffaello wasn't idling away. In fact, Julius II put him to work on his personal apartments that have since become known as **The Raffaello Rooms.** It took the artist 12 years to paint the four staterooms and he died before completing the project. What he left behind rivals the Cappella Sistina in brilliance and forever guaranteed him a place in art history. The Stanza Segnatura was the first room he painted and contains the most stunning works. *La Disputa* portrays saints, doctors, and laborers debating the meaning of the Bible while Christ offers himself as a sacrifice for sin. *The School of Athens* is a meeting of philosophers and includes Plato and Aristotle at the center of the fresco as well as a cameo of Raffaello himself on the extreme right next to his former teacher.

Vaticano Tours

The Vaticano has a lot to see and not all the sights are aboveground. Guided 75-minute tours (Reverenda Fabbrica di San Pietro, tel. 06/6988-5318, fax 06/6988-5518, uff.scavi@fabricsp.va) of the 1st century necropolis and remains of the original basilica must be booked in advance. Send a fax or email to the Ufficio degli Scavi indicating your preferred dates, the number of visitors, and the preferred language. You must also leave a contact number used to confirm the booking. The hotel where you are staying will do. Tours are run in small groups everyday but Sunday and cost €7.50 per person.

Borgo Pio

Pilgrims need a place to stay after an arduous journey and the Borgo Pio is where the first hostels and hospices began to appear. The word itself derives from the German *burg*, meaning town, and it was in fact a Saxon King bent on penance who set up the first colony here in A.D. 725. The long narrow streets parallel to Via della Conciliazione have retained their original function and are worth exploring.

Castello Sant'Angelo

Castello Sant'Angelo (Lungotevere Castello, tel. 06/681-9111, Tues.–Sun. 9 A.M.–7 P.M., €5) didn't start out as the castle, prison, or papal residence it would later become but as a mausoleum for emperor Adriano. Respect for the dead did not outlive the fall of the empire and the castle has had many roles since. In 1277 significant adjustments were made, walls enlarged, and the Vaticano Corridor added which allowed Popes to reach the castle from their palaces in times of unrest. The castle gets its name from the statue of the Archangel Michael, who allegedly appeared in A.D. 590 and whose sculpture now adorns the tower. Today the terrace provides a 360-degree view of the city and the rooftop bar is one of the more scenic places to stop for a drink.

The **Ponte Sant'Angelo** was built by Adriano to connect his mausoleum with the city. Pope Clement VII started adding the statues of Peter and Paul and Bernini lined the parapets with musically adept angels. Today itinerant salesmen hawk their wares to passing tourists. All it takes is a reservation to book a special visit. The payoff of seeing the Vaticano in a different light is far more rewarding than the standard itinerary.

Entertainment and Events

Rome doesn't have the reputation for nightlife the way Barcelona and Berlin do. Locals are not known for being the biggest drinkers on the block, but they are very social and enjoy chatting until the late hours in bars and clubs where young and old tend to mix. Nightlife is concentrated in several neighborhoods. Monte Testaccio is ringed with clubs and it's possible to enjoy a cocktail, listen to jazz, or dance the night away. The Ostiense neighborhood around Piramide is slightly more underground and has a gritty East Village ambiance. Piazza Navona is upscale and caters to foreign partygoers along with the Campo dei Fiori a stone's throw away. This is one of Rome's rowdiest squares along with Piazza Triulli across the river in Trastevere, where drinking is done outside and someone is usually playing the guitar or bongos. Along the river during the summer, dozens of temporary bars and restaurants are set up and remain busy well past midnight. Some establishments close June–August and relocate to Ostia where fires are lit on the beach and the dancing is done in the sand.

Parco della Musica has done wonders for the Roman music scene and the Renzo Piano built complex off Via Flaminia showcases the world's best classic, jazz, and contemporary music. Teatro dell'Opera may not be as famous as its Milanese or Venetian counterparts but the arias sound nearly as good and during the summer they move the sets to parks and gardens around the city. Churches are also another frequent venue and there's someone usually handing out fliers with upcoming events on the steps of the Pantheon. Otherwise La Repubblica publishes an entertainment supplement on Thursdays and the listings guide *Roma*

C'e comes out on Wednesdays. Both have English sections in the back and are available at all newsstands.

NIGHTLIFE
Live Music
Alexanderplatz (Via Ostia 9, tel. 06/3974-2171, daily 8:30 P.M.–3 A.M., €8) is the club of reference for Roman jazz musicians. Established players appear nightly in solo and combo arrangements. The club itself is comfortable and inviting. Dining is an option and the jazz menu recommended.

For over 10 years, **Big Mama** (Vicolo S. Francesco a Ripa 18, tel. 06/581-2551, Tues.–Sun. 9 P.M.–1:30 A.M., €10–15) has been an authentic home of top jazz and blues musicians searching for a groove in Trastevere. The small club is the most likely place to find a jam session in Rome.

Casa del Jazz (Viale di Porta Ardeatina 55, tel. 06/704-731, www.casajazz.it, €10–15) was converted from a mobster's villa to a home for jazz. It now regularly hosts local and international musicians in a 100-seat hall. A bookshop and bar have replaced bullets. The Sunday all-you-can-eat brunch (€25) is accompanied by a jazz trio in the restaurant's tranquil garden.

Don't let the distance put you off. **La Palma Club** (Via G. Mirri 35, tel. 06/4359-9029, Mon.–Sat. 8 P.M.–12:30 A.M., €5–10) is an oasis of musical experimentation housed in the vastness of a former *casale* (farmhouse). Every night features a standout concert, DJ set, or cultural event. Hosts and hostesses at the cocktail bar and restaurant are always welcoming.

The Place (Via Alberico II 27, tel. 06/6830-7137, Tues.–Sun. 8 P.M.–3 A.M., €10–15) vibrates with funk, Latin, and R&B. The reputation for fine music is deserved and the opportunity to accompany live acts with creative Mediterranean cuisine should be seized.

Piano bar enthusiasts won't want to miss a night at **Jonathan's Angels** (Via della Fossa 16, tel. 06/689-3426, daily, 4 P.M.–3 A.M., €5–10). Walls openly celebrate kitsch and the tables will all be taken unless you arrive early.

The **Folkstudio** (Via Frangipane 42, tel. 06/487-1063) has a 1960s pedigree that included concerts by Bob Dylan. The acoustic tradition remains alive with Irish folk, American country, and regional Italian music. There's a small fee to enter and it's strictly BYOB if you want to drink.

A recent influx of South Americans has fueled the success of clubs like **Berimbau** (Via dei Fienaroli 30, tel. 06/581-3249, concerts usually start at 10 P.M., €2 and up), where bossa nova and Latin groups entertain eager crowds.

The chances of hearing some variation of rock or jazz are about equal at **Villaggio Globale** (Lungotevere Testaccio, tel. 06/5730-0329, Wed.–Sun. hours vary per event, Fri. and Sat. concerts usually start around 9 P.M., DJs spin midnight–6 A.M., €5), which presents frequent live events within a former slaughterhouse. Show up early if you want to stand near the stage.

Dance Clubs
If you're searching for a party in Rome you'll find it. Discotheque is not a dirty word here and clubs present a range of nights. Whatever your style, you're likely to hear it or else discover a new genre spun by one of the Italian or International DJs who liven up the city's nocturnal hours. Even they need a rest and Monday nights are usually slow. Thursdays are up-tempo and weekends always pull a crowd. During the summer, many clubs relocate to the beaches of Ostia where patrons dance on sand. Many bars also have a house DJ and straddle the bar-disco divide.

Don't miss an evening mixing with beautiful people under the vaulted ceilings at the **Micca Club** (Via Pietro Micca 7, Esquilino, tel. 06/8744-0079). A small stage hosts regular musical events, including a burlesque show dedicated to Bettie Page. Weekends reverberate with lounge and chill-out and guest DJs with the latest Ibeza tracks are common.

Night owls will feel at home within **Akab's** (Via Monte Testaccio 69, tel. 06/578-2390, 11 P.M.–4 A.M. Tues.–Sun., €10–12) two floors of minimalist Japanese ambiance. The dancing is done to up-beat sounds. The cult evening is L-Ektrika and live performances are frequent.

Caffè Latino (Via Monte Testaccio 96, tel. 06/5728-8794, 10:30 P.M.–3 A.M. Tues.–Sun., €5–10) opened the way with wooden floors and throw pillows. It's a laid-back music café where DJs mix soul with progressive funk. Sunday is dedicated to Latin American music.

Hip-hop and house are the bread and butter of **Alpheus** (Via del Commercio 36, tel. 06/574-7826, Tues.–Sun. 10 P.M.–4 A.M., €5–10). Partygoers alternate between four dance floors and the garden is reserved for fresh air and conversation. Live rock is played on stage.

Gilda (Via Mario de Fiori 97, tel. 06/678-4838, Tues.–Sun. 11 P.M.–5 A.M., €15–20) is an old-school disco where ties outnumber nose rings. The crowd is mature and paparazzi are on the prowl for players, politicians, and showgirls.

Ethnic, industrial, vibrant. **Goa** (Via Libetta 13, tel. 06/574-8277, Tues.–Sun. 11 P.M.–3 A.M., €10–15) is *the* club in Rome and attracts faces from every continent. Thursday night Ultrabeat is not to be missed, along with the Sunday tea party.

If Gorgeous is in the house, you may want to be at **Classico Village** (Via Libetta 3, tel. 06/574-3364, daily 9 P.M.–3 A.M., €10–15). His nights are renowned for solid tracks and enthusiastic male crowds. Summer gives rise to outdoor dancing.

La Maison (Vicolo dei Granari 4, tel. 06/683-3312, Tues.–Sun. 11 P.M.–4 A.M., €10–15) is home to glamour. The vintage theater interior adorned with velvet and crystal helps. Sunday nights with DJ Flavia Lazzarini and artistic direction by Marco Longo makes finding this place worthwhile. Playlists vary from commercial to reggae with a heavy dose of experimental thrown into the mix.

Cool gets around and even Connecticut housewives have heard of the **Supper Club** (Via de Nari 14, tel. 06/686-4170, Mon.–Sat. 7 P.M.–2 A.M., €10–15). This ultra-hip lounge originated in Amsterdam and stimulates all the senses. The DJs and VJs here have all past their funky exams and long white leather sofas put listeners at ease.

Late happy hour, dancing, or both? It's your call at **Anima** (Via S. Maria dell'Anima 57, tel. 06/686-4021, Tues.–Sun. 8 P.M.–2 A.M., €8–12). The proximity to Navona has made this fun spot a destination for visitors who enjoy the futuristic bar and fruit buffet.

Rimini mixed with Ibiza equals tribal house harmony at **Alien** (Via Velletri 13, tel. 06/841-2212, Tues.–Sun. 11 P.M.–4 A.M., €10–15). The large space is filled with a youthful crowd transfering beats onto several dance floors.

Eat, drink, and dance on a two-story boat moored on the Tiber. **Baja** (Lungotevere A. da Brescia, tel. 06/3260-0118, Tues.–Sun. 7 P.M.–4 A.M., admission is free) is a floating party with an underground feel. Insomniacs will appreciate the DJs working overtime and the restaurant that serves until late.

Where **Bluecheese** will turn up next no one knows. Activate www.bluecheese.it to get the lowdown on this wandering party, which is followed faithfully and never grooves twice in the same location.

Wine Bars

Wine is as old as civilization and has been drunk in this town practically from the beginning. Roman wine bars, or *enoteche* as they're known in Italy, are a good place to cultivate or refine your palate. Menus offer local, regional, and international vintages, which makes the challenge of deciphering Chianti from Barolo all the more interesting. Food adds to the pleasure and most *enoteche* offer a selection of smoked meats and cheeses or a more extensive menu.

Cul de Sac (Piazza Pasquino 73, tel. 06/6880-1094, daily noon–4 P.M. and 6 P.M.–12:30 A.M., €5–10) is the perfect place to introduce taste buds to the art of the vine. The inexhaustible menu satisfies sommeliers and novices alike, who rub shoulders in an informal and genuine environment.

Enoteca Corsi (Via del Gesú 88, tel. 06/679-0821, daily 8:30 A.M.–8 P.M., €4–7) is an old-style wine bar with old-style prices. The flavor of nostalgia attracts a crowd that can count on a daily menu of Roman specialties handwritten in chalk.

A glass of red at **Vineria** (Campo dei Fiori 15, tel. 06/6880-3268, Mon.–Sat. 9 P.M.–1 A.M., €4–10) is a must for many Romans. The choice of bottles is wide and the recent renovation hasn't affected the charm of the place. Tables overlooking the piazza are hard to come by and should be savored.

Enoteca (Via della Croce 76b, tel. 06/679-0896, daily 10 A.M.–1 A.M.) was around long before the area was flooded with clothing boutiques. In fact, this is the perfect place to escape fashion and taste something timeless. The cellar has aged well and the food propositions are equally appetizing.

La Barrique (Via del Boschetto, 41b, tel. 06/4782-5953, Mon.–Sat. evening, €6–8) has divided its menu into regional specialties, which doesn't simplify things. It just makes you want to travel more.

Attention to design and an excellent selection of cured meats makes drinking a glass or two at **Cantina Castrocielo** (Via degli Astri 35, tel. 06/520-4979, Tues.–Sat. 7 P.M.–1 A.M., €6) memorable.

Appetizers and wine form a perpetual cycle at **Casa Bleve** (Via del Teatro 49, tel. 06/686-5970, www.casableve.it, Tues.–Sat. 11:30 A.M.–4 P.M., €6–10), which may be impossible to break. The cellar is notable for Lazio whites and Tuscan reds.

Palatium (Via Frattina 94, tel. 06/6920-2132, Mon.–Sat. 11 A.M.–late-night, €7–10) is the place to sample local dishes and local wines. Its central location and spacious, posh interior make it popular with the well-heeled, after-work crowd.

After being asked for the thousandth time, the owners of **Roscioli** (Via dei Giubbonari 21, tel. 06/687-5287, www.rosciolifinefood.com, Mon.–Sat. 12:30 P.M.–4 P.M. and 8 P.M.–midnight, €6–9) finally gave in. It's now possible to purchase the exceptional cheeses and wines on the extensive menu.

Tramonti & Muffati (Via Santa Maria Ausiliatrice 105, tel. 06/780-1342, Mon.–Sat. 7 P.M.–12:30 A.M., €5) may be one of the smallest wine bars in town but its passion is big. The selection tends towards lesser-known vineyards and clients are served with great attention.

If you're ready to pass from glasses of wine to bottles of top-quality regional labels, then the **Vino Garage** (Via di Monte Giordano 63, tel. 06/6830-0858, daily 6:30 P.M.–1 A.M., €6–9) is the place to make the transition. Champaignes are also well represented and a dozen different kinds of prosciuttos can be savored.

Pubs

Rome doesn't conjure up images of beer, but it does exist here. Peroni and Nastro are the local lagers greatly appreciated on scorching summer days or whenever the Scottish rugby team is in town. Pubs tend to cater to foreign residents and tourists while *birrerie* (beer halls) serve comfort food and have chalet-like decor and a strong local following.

The crisp cold beer on tap at **Antica Birreria Peroni** (Via S. Marcello 19, tel. 06/679-5310, Mon.–Sat. noon–midnight, €4–7) is perfect for washing down Tirolese dishes like sausage and sauerkraut. Drinkers are merry and the proximity of the dark wooden tables increases the opportunity to socialize.

Lowenhaus (Via della Fontanella 16b, tel. 06/323-0410, daily 1 P.M.–2 A.M., €5–8) is as close as you can get to Bavaria without boarding a plane. The German beer, goulash, and sausages add to the authenticity. Good weather means mugs are hoisted outside where music can erupt spontaneously.

If you've never eaten off a wooden plate then the **Birrerie Viennese** (Via delle Croce 21, tel. 06/679-5569, daily noon–2:30 P.M. and 7 P.M.–midnight, €7–11) is a must. Before you actually see the plate, however, there's a mound of food to get through and a stein to down.

Pint glasses filled to the rim, raucous barmen, and loud pop music are what have made **Trinity College** (Via del Collegio Romano 6, tel. 06678-6472, daily noon–3 A.M., €5–7) popular with locals and visitors alike. It's packed on weekends, when crowds overflow into the narrow streets and the small dance floor requires precision movements.

Those craving a Guinness can satisfy their thirst at the **Abbey Theatre** (Via del Governo Vecchio 51, tel. 06/686-1341, daily noon–2 A.M.). This cozy wood-paneled pub is fully equipped with Irish stouts and ales as well as some good bourbons. Flat-screen TVs make it a good place to watch *calcio* or rugby.

THE ARTS

Culture is king in Rome and the amount of music, dance, and theater experiences available each week provides no shortage of spectator opportunities. The quality of performances is high and many standout venues exist. The city attracts international artists of the finest caliber who perform in front of audiences who know when to applaud.

Performing Arts

Modern architecture and music harmonize at the **Parco della Musica** (Viale De Coubertin 30, tel. 06/4546-83900, www.auditorium. com). The three Renzo Piano–designed halls resemble metallic whales beached in the north of Rome. The auditorium regularly hosts classical, contemporary, and experimental performances of all types. This is what Michael Buble calls home and where Keith Jarrett does his finest improvisations. Acoustic connoisseurs will appreciate the modular wooden ceilings, which are adjusted according to the music being performed. The outdoor amphitheater holds summertime concerts and the restaurant/bar and café complement any evening.

The Orchestra Sinfonica di Rome performs regularly at the **Auditorium della Conciliazione** (Via della Conciliazione 4, tel. 06/6880-1044). They are often joined by guest conductors and international soloists in a varied symphonic program.

The **Teatro dell'Opera** (Via Firenze 62, tel. 06/481-601, €10–100) may not have the reputation of La Scala, but the lavish interior and persistently good productions will thrill both eyes and ears. The season runs November–January and generally includes the classics performed the way their creators intended them to be. During the summer, the stage

moves to the baths of Caracalla giving performances an entirely different meaning. A resident ballet company also performs within the opera house.

Teatro Olimpico (Piazza Gentile da Fabriano, tel. 06/320-1752) presents modern dance, ballet, and orchestral music. The theater is the permanent home of the Filarmonica, which generally presents one performance per week during the musical season.

Teatro del Vascello (Via G. Carini 72, tel. 06/588-1021) is committed to contemporary dance, and companies like Momix and Merce Cunningham have performed here in the past. Lesser-known names are given the chance to experiment and the RomaEuropa festival uses the theater as one of its venues. There are outdoor performances during the summer.

Classic productions are staged at **Teatro Argentina** (Largo Argentina 56, tel. 06/6880-4601), which inherited an opera house interior and houses one of the few permanent theater companies in the city. Famous Italian actors often make their debuts here.

The **Eliseo** (Via Nazionale 183, tel. 06/474-3431) and the **Piccolo Eliseo,** its sister theater next door, are as close as Rome gets to Broadway. Musicals and farce are regularly posted on the marquee outside.

Fringe and student productions with an experimental twist are performed at **Teatro Politecnico** (Via Tiepolo 13a, tel. 06/361-1501). There's a roughness to performances, and set design is often invigorating.

Shakespeare liked Italy so much he set many of his plays here. It's no surprise then to find a reconstruction of the **Globe Theater** (Via Valle Giulia, tel. 06/8205-9127, www.glo betheatreroma.com) in Villa Borghese that regularly presents the Bard's work in both English and Italian.

Regardless of the name, the **English Puppet Theater** (Piazza di Satiri, tel. 06/589-6201) doesn't always perform in English. Many of the traveling Neapolitan and Sicilian marionette companies are beyond translation anyway, and it's best to enjoy the performances in their original form.

Open-air comic performances are held July–September at the **Anfiteatro Quercia del Tasso** (Passeggiata del Gianicolo, tel. 06/575-0827) and at the Neapolitan puppet booth nearby.

Cinema

Many Roman cinemas offer a stark change from the multiplexes back home: several show films in their original language, a couple project outdoors in summer, and one is dedicated solely to children. March is the start of the city's month-long **Cin-Cin Cinema** promotion, when weekday tickets are reduced to €5.

Time Elevator (Via dei S.S. Apostoli 20, Piazza Venezia, tel. 06/9774-6243, daily 11 A.M.–8 P.M.) projects films in 5D. Besides the usual three dimensions, there are moving seats and multisensory effects. Films include one on the foundation and growth of Rome, which puts the city into instant historical perspective.

Movies are projected in their original language at the **Alcazar** (Via Merry del Val 14, tel. 06/588-0099), **Pasquino** (Vicolo del Piede 19, tel. 06/580-3622), and **Greenwich** (Via G. Bodoni, 59, tel. 06/574-5825). All three are independently owned and operated, which means the popcorn tastes better and isn't overpriced.

The **Nuovo Sacher** (Largo Ascianghi 1, tel. 06/581-8116) was the idea of an Italian director fed up with the films shown in most chain cinemas. Its single screen is dedicated to art rather than happy endings.

Galleries

It's hard to be a modern artist in Rome. The past is always present and it's impossible to top. Fortunately Roman artists aren't competing with Michelangelo but finding new ways of expressing themselves. The art scene has experienced a revival in recent years and new galleries have opened to meet the demand of a growing number of collectors ready to hang something different on their walls.

Art/Guide (tel./fax 06/854-1891, www.artguide.it) publishes a monthly list of events, exhibitions, and gallery locations that's available at all tourist information points.

Ta Matete (Via della Pilotta, tel. 06/679-1107, www.tamatete.com) is an open space where a regular rotation of artists explores the various shades of human emotion. **Il Gabbiano** (Via delle Frezze 51, tel. 06/322-7049, Mon.–Sun. 10 A.M.–1 P.M. and 4:30–7:30 P.M.) shows a lot of veteran artists and tends to concentrate on painting done on non-canvas materials like cardboard or wood. **Studio del Canova** (Via delle Colonnette 27, tel./fax 06/322-7162, daily 4–7:30 P.M.) organizes group exhibits of young artists working in a variety of styles.

Experimental video, photography, and some less traditional means of expression are on exhibit at **LaPortaBlu Gallery** (Arco degli Acetari 40, tel. 06/687-4106, Tues.–Sun. 5–8 P.M.). Nearby **Magazzino d'Arte Moderno** (Via dei Prefetti 17, tel. 06/687-5951, www.magazzinoartemoderna.com, Tues.–Sun. 11 A.M.–3 P.M. and 4–8 P.M.) continually pushes the envelope with one-artist shows that leave an impression.

Altri Lavori in Corso (Vicolo del Governo Vecchio 7, tel./fax 06/686-1719, www.altrilavoriincorso.com, daily 5–8 P.M.) spotlights international artists working in Rome and appointments for private visits can be made. **AAM** (Via dei Banchi Vecchi 61, first floor, tel. 06/6830-7537, www.aamgaleria.it, daily 4–8 P.M.) mixes architecture and art-inspired work from the likes of Roberto Caracciolo and Alan Fletcher. Established artists like Tracey Emin entrust their creative juices to **Lorcan O'Neill** (Via Orti d'Alibert 1e, tel. 06/6889-2980, daily noon–8 P.M.).

FESTIVALS AND EVENTS

The plane tickets are booked, a guide is purchased, and only later do you discover that the concert of a lifetime ended three days before your arrival. Events are what give the city a soul and what makes Rome a cultural capital as well as a political and spiritual one. The Colosseum is impressive but as a backdrop to a Sting or Billy Joel concert it's unforgettable.

Spring

Easter can fall in March or in April. What is certain is that pilgrims will have circled the date on their calendars. They'll be flocking to each of the basilicas, following the **Procession of the Cross** at 9 P.M. to the Colosseo on Good Friday, and attending the Pope's Sunday morning mass in Piazza San Pietro.

For two weeks starting in mid-May, Via dei Coronari rolls out the red carpet, candles are lit, and banners fly. It's time for the **Antiques Fair**, when the dealers who occupy nearly every shop on the street bring out their best merchandise and prospective buyers put on their poker faces.

The **International Tennis Championships** (Viale dei Gladiatori 31, tel. 06/3685-4200, www.internazionalibnlditalia.it) held in late May in the Foro Italico, is the last big clay court tournament before Roland Garros; most top players attend. Tickets are easily available for early rounds and sitting in the Monte Mario stands prevents sunburn.

Summer

The **Estate Romana** (www.estateromana. comune.roma.it) lasts the entire summer and brings entertainment and art to unexpected places. An outdoor cinema projects films nightly on the Isola Tiberina, world-reknowned authors recite their works in the Foro, and concerts are held in the Circo Massimo.

In July, **Musica nel Verde** (tel. 06/686-8441) frees music from its traditional confines and places it within the verdant scenery of Rome's botanical garden. The program varies between jazz, folk, and classical—all performed near an artificial lake and the Baroque splendor of Palazzo Corsini.

In the same month, the Terme di Caracalla becomes the backdrop for the **Rome Opera Summer Series** (tel. 06/687-6448), when such classics as *Aida* and *Madame Butterfly* are performed within the ancient baths.

According to legend, it snowed heavily in Rome on August 14 many years ago. Ever since, the **Festa della Madonna delle Neve** has been held at Santa Maria Maggiore, where white petals are thrown from the dome of the cathedral.

Festival Jazz (Villa Celimontana, Via della Navicella, tel. 06/589-7807, www.vil lacelimontanajazz.com) in Villa Celimontana presents two months of nightly concerts in one of Rome's most beautiful parks moments from the Colosseo. Prices rarely exceed €10 and the intimate outdoor ampitheater is bordered by an assortment of bars and restaurants.

Fall

Fall is a great time to visit the city and offers one great event after another. Besides the film festival and RomaEuropa, there's La Notte Bianca, when the eternal city transforms itself into the city that doesn't sleep. Throughout Rome, musical, cultural, and artistic events take center stage for 24 hours. Locals and visitors alike turn out in mass.

Festa Internazionale di Roma (www .romacinemafest.com) was launched in 2006 and became a major film festival from the first reel it projected. Stars turn out to walk the red carpets at the Auditorium and Casa del Cinema, as do locals eager to see dozens of world premiers. Booking tickets in advance is a must.

RomaEuropa Festival (tel. 800/795-525, www.romaeuropa.net) is a three-month-long cultural event dedicated to all facets of the arts. Performances are held in venues throughout the city and feature an international selection of artists, dancers, and musicians.

For Rome, the longest night of the year falls on a Saturday in September. **La Notte Bianca** (tel. 06/0606, www.lanottebianca.it) starts at 9 P.M. on the Capitolino. Every minute after that it spreads itself into the piazze, villas, museums, theaters, and shops of the city. Traffic comes to halt, subways continue as usual, and hundreds of thousands take to the streets. Each neighborhood provides signature moments: fireworks here, acrobats there, and enthusiasm everywhere. Musical, theatrical, and cultural events continue throughout the night, offering locals and visitors alike a chance to experience Rome in an entirely different light. Not everyone lasts until dawn, but the city never looks the same for those who do.

Winter

Christmas isn't the end of the holiday festivities for Italian children. For them there is still *la Befana,* which falls every year on January 6. The good are rewarded with sweets and the others get coal delivered to them from a wart-nosed witch. Mostly everyone's been good and the market held in Piazza Navona gives parents a final chance to treat children before schools reconvene.

Confetti-strewn streets are a sign that **Carnevale** has arrived. The other more edible indication are the *frappe* (fried or baked dough covered in sugar), which only appear in February and March and are the perfect companion to a cappuccino.

The **Equilibrio** festival is held throughout February at the Parco della Musica (tel. 06/8024-1281) and presents a spectrum of contemporary dance companies and soloists from around the world pushing the boundaries of movement a little further each year.

The numbers of joggers increases after New Year's Eve and it has little to do with resolutions. They're preparing for the **Rome Marathon** (tel. 06/406-5064, www.maratonadiroma.it). It takes place in March and attracts nearly 20,000 runners to the starting and finishing line beneath the Colosseo.

Shopping

Italy has its own unique rhythm, and nowhere is that more evident than in its shops. The only shops that remain open 24 hours a day are the florists, which means that it's never too late for love. Most family-owned clothing stores and small businesses close at 1 P.M. for lunch and re-open around 3 P.M. Don't let that frustrate you: Just accept it and adapt to the Italian schedule as quickly as you can or stick with larger shops in the center that operate non-stop hours.

Shopping also has its own special etiquette. Customers entering a small boutique or bar nearly always greet assistants with *"buongiorno"* or *"buonasera"* (good morning or good afternoon). Making a sale is never a life or death matter in Italy and most owners are happy to let shoppers browse to their heart's content. When leaving remember to utter *"arrivederci"* (goodbye) thus completing the cycle.

January and September are the best times to shop in Rome. All stores begin the sale season in unison during these months and windows are plastered with discounts on the previous season's stock. Each price tag should contain original and sales price. Check items carefully before buying and don't hesitate to try clothes on, as sizes generally run smaller and are cut differently than in North America. Don't worry if something catches your eye that won't fit in a suitcase. Roman stores, especially those selling furniture and housewares, are accustomed to tourists and can arrange for shipment directly to your door. Expect to pay up to 10 percent of the purchase price for home delivery.

Although you're unlikely to find a discarded Modriano in Rome's flea markets, collectors with patience will be rewarded. There's a great variety to rummage through and the city's major markets have something for everyone. Once you've found that something, it's time to practice your negotiating skills and discover the thrill of bartering.

Finally remember price is a theoretical concept at souvenir stands, flea markets, and antique stalls. If it sounds high, it probably is and should be negotiated. Instead of naming your price and revealing your cards ask sellers if they can lower theirs. They usually will.

FORI, PALATINO, AND CAPITOLINO

The shops that once lined Trajan's Forum went out of business a long time ago. Today the sales continue behind those ruins in Monti, which

© ALEXEI J. COHEN

The shops that once lined Trajan's Forum comprised the world's first shopping center.

competes with Trastevere and Testaccio for the title of most Roman neighborhood. There is something a little edgier here though and the boutiques aren't run of the mill. You'll find young designers and old hands practicing age-old crafts side by side. Traditionalists can also browse the windows along Via Nazionale, which is the Roman version of the Champs-Élysée.

Arts and Crafts

Via del Boschetto is the focal point for many of the area's craft and specialty shops. **La Vetra** (Via del Boschetto 93) is where Domenico Passagrilli has been blowing glass into bowls, lamp bases, and other intriguing objects for nearly 30 years. His most beautiful creations serve no other purpose than pleasing the senses.

Rome has been trading with the Middle East and beyond since ancient freighters plowed the Mediterranean. **Zadiq** (Via dei Fienili 42, tel. 06/6992-5176, Mon.–Sat. 10 A.M.–8 P.M.) continues that tradition. Here antique ceramics, rustic farm implements, silk robes, and contemporary designs compete for

your attention. It's hard to walk away without buying something.

Specialty

Silver and gold are the ingredients of nearly every object within **Longobardi** (Via dei Fienili 43, tel. 06/678-1104, Mon. 3:30–7:30 P.M., Tues.–Sat. 9:30 A.M.–7:30 P.M.). Most of the handcrafted tableware, frames, and jewelry is produced in Italy. The shop gets its name from the owner who is always willing to discuss his favorite topic: the history of Rome.

Bookstores

Don't judge **Mel Bookstore** (Via Nazionale 252, tel. 06/488-5405, Mon.–Sat. 9 A.M.–8 P.M., Sun. 10 A.M.–1 P.M. and 4–8 P.M.) by the entrance. The nondescript front doors lead to a palatial hall filled with every sort of book imaginable. Used books are in the basement, travel and fiction are on the ground floor, and design and architecture are next to the bar on the second floor.

You won't find many bestsellers at **Gutenberg**

al **Colosseo** (Via S. Giovanni in Laterano 94, Tues.–Sat. 10 A.M.–1 P.M. and 4–8 P.M.). This used bookstore with personality specializes in classics and some editions date back 300 years. You'll also find randomly displayed prints of how the city looked centuries ago.

A little farther up the block is **Libreria Archeologica** (Via S. Giovanni in Laterano 46, tel. 06/7720-1395, Mon.–Fri. 10 A.M.–7 P.M., Sat. 10 A.M.–1:30 P.M.). Greek and Roman archeology books are in the majority, along with quality maps that make original souvenirs.

Clothing

The shrine of Italian vintage clothing is **Escat** (Via dell'Angeletto 10, tel. 06/474-5721, Tues.–Sun. 9 A.M.–1 P.M. and 4–8 P.M.). There's a good stock of 1960s and 1970s shirts and jackets in fabrics that are rarely seen without blushing.

M.A.S. (Via dello Statuto 11, tel. 06/4938-3011, Tues.–Sun. 9 A.M.–1 P.M. and 4–8 P.M.) sells clothes on an industrial scale for men, women, and children. Two floors of an entire block are crammed with everything from underwear to overcoats and will leave bargain hunters breathless.

What Olivia likes, she sells; after all it's **Olivia's Boutique** (Via Leonina 68, tel. 06/483-964, Tues.–Sun. 9 A.M.–1 P.M. and 4–8 P.M.). Luckily she has good taste and sells an eclectic range of fashions at reasonable prices.

It's worth visiting **Paola B** (Viale Manzoni 31/33, tel. 06/7047-5471, Tues.–Sun. 9 A.M.–1 P.M. and 4–8 P.M.) for the dressing rooms alone. Once you're inside, you might also enjoy trying on some lesser-known Italian labels like Scarpa, Rivamonti, and Branca.

Shoes and Accessories

If you like the idea of a shoe that breathes, then **Geox** (Via Nazionale 232, tel. 06/481-4518, Tues.–Sun. 9 A.M.–1 P.M. and 3:30–8 P.M.) is just the thing. This fast-expanding company produces patented casual and elegant models renowned for their comfort and durability.

Handbags, handbags, and more handbags are all you'll find displayed at **Alexia** (Via

Nazionale 76, tel. 06/488-4890, Tues.–Sun. 9 A.M.–1 P.M. and 3:30–8 P.M.). Fendissime, Coccinelle, and Moschino are just a few of the brands competing for the attention of prospective buyers across two floors.

Markets

La Soffitta (Piazzale dei Partigiani) is held every Saturday and Sunday in the underground garage under the Ostiense train station. Stands sell antiques, collectibles, crafts, and a lot of stuff that falls under the category of junk.

TRASTEVERE
Arts and Crafts

The **Bottega Artigiana** (Via Santa Dorotea 21, tel. 06/588-2079, Mon.–Sat. 9:30 A.M.–1:30 P.M. and 3:30–7:30 P.M.) displays all the ceramics Domenico and Lavinia Sarti produce in their Anzio studio. The small shop contains terra-cotta vases and urns, some of which might fit in a suitcase. There's also an interesting selection of light fixtures and wall hangings.

Nearby **Arte del Mosaico** (Vicolo del Cinque 30, tel. 06/581-4797, Tues.–Sun. 9 A.M.–1 P.M. and 4–8 P.M.) sells small reproductions of Roman mosaics. Newer designs can be custom ordered and shipped directly home.

For a wider selection of products from around Italy, visit **La Galleria** (Via della Pelliccia 30, tel. 06/581-6614, Tues.–Sun. 9 A.M.–1 P.M. and 4–8 P.M.). This large space tends towards the rustic, whether it be textile, ceramic, or sculpture.

Antiques

The cousins who run **Le Cugine** (Via dei Vascellari 19, tel. 06/589-4844, Tues.–Sun. 10 A.M.–8 P.M.) have put together an eclectic range of odds and ends. Most objects come from Roman homes, and Sabrina Alfonsini happily shows visitors around the birdcages, tableware, and furniture.

Named after the box, **Pandora** (Piazza Santa Maria in Trastevere 6, tel. 06/581-7145, Tues.–Sun. 9:30 A.M.–1 P.M. and 4–8 P.M.) sells

Murano glass, small antique furnishings, and fashion accessories.

Specialty
Time is the theme at **Polvere di Tempo** (Via del Moro 59, tel. 06/588-0704, Mon.–Sat. 9 A.M.–1 P.M. and 4 P.M.–8 P.M.). Sundials, hourglasses, and vintage style clocks put minutes and hours into a new perspective. It's also a break from the overload of clothing boutiques in the area.

Handmade paper feels different. **Officina della Carta** (Via Benedetta 26b, tel. 06/589-5557, Mon.–Sat. 9 A.M.–1 P.M. and 4–8 P.M.) transforms authentic fibers into miniature diaries and leather-bound photo albums perfect for storing Roman memories.

Bookstores
Cinemaphiles will feel at home at **Libreria del Cinema** (Via dei Fienaroli 31d, tel. 06/581-7724), where books, magazines, and DVDs dedicated to the seventh art are the main attraction. Italian producers, writers, and actors regularly meet at the comfortable bar.

The **Corner Bookshop** (Via del Moro 45, tel. 06/583-6942, daily 10 A.M.–1:30 P.M. and 3:30–8 P.M.) is a no-frills haven of English-language literature where it can easily take all afternoon to choose a novel.

Clothing
Choose the fabric and the model and the tailors at **Capitolo Primo** (Via Luciano Manara 58, tel. 06/581-3949, Mon.–Sat. 9 A.M.–1 P.M. and 4–8 P.M.) will have the latest addition to your wardrobe ready in no time. They also sell one-offs by young designers once a month as well as sophisticated bridalwear.

Those searching for that twenty-something Italian look will find it at **Latrofa** (Via Sprovieri 7, tel. 06/581-2102, Tues.–Sat. 9 A.M.–1 P.M. and 4–8 P.M, Mon. 4–8 P.M.). Major men's and women's labels as well as connoisseur brands like Full Circle and Vintage are on display.

Accessories
Antica Cappelleria (Viale di Trastevere 109, tel. 06/5833-3206, Mon.–Sat. 9 A.M.–1 P.M. and 3:30 –8 P.M.) has been selling and repairing hats since 1921. Prices range from €13 for a wool knit to €500 for a handmade Panama.

Beauty
Anyone can smell like Obsession, Opium, or Poison, but you won't sniff those scents at **Rome Store** (Via della Lungaretta 63, tel. 06/581-8789), which only carries unique perfumes from pure essences.

Markets
Porta Portese (Via Ippolito Nievo, daily 5 A.M.–2 P.M.) has the flavor of a souk where you can find anyone and anything. In recent years "Made in China" labels have replaced antiques and the crowds seem more interested in knock-offs than the authentic. Still this is an experience and the stretch near Piazza Ippolito Nievo is the best chance to spot a Roman coin, illustrated text, or vintage Leica.

CAMPO DEI FIORI AND PIAZZA NAVONA
Both neighborhoods are virtually chain free and full of original clothing and jewelry boutiques. Via dei Giubbonari is lined with shops from Piazza dei Fiori to Via Arenula and anyone interested in antiques can get their fill along Via dei Coronari. If you prefer your art fresh from the easel, the 50 painters in Piazza Navona have oil paintings and watercolors of every dimension waiting to be framed and mounted.

Arts and Crafts
The **Laboratorio Marani** (Via di Monte Giordano 27, tel. 06/6830-7866, Mon.–Sat. 9 A.M.–7 P.M.) is covered with a light coat of white powder. That's the price to pay for working with plaster and creating antique sculpture immitations that are hard to distinguish from the originals. The workshop is continually creating new objects and it's worth taking a moment to observe the process.

A few steps from the Napoleonic museum lies **Opificio Romano** (Via dei Gigli D'Oro, daily 9 A.M.–7 P.M.). Here hundreds of mosaics based on Greek and Roman models are on display. Sizes and colors vary widely and custom made designs can be ordered if time permits. **Nicola Arduini** (Via degli Specchi 12, tel. 06/614-4724, daily 9 A.M.–7 P.M.) spends her days banging steel and other metals into shape. It's a violent profession with surprisingly delicate results that can be admired in a dining room or kitchen.

Ilaria Miani uses found wood and pieces from discarded antique furniture in her **Laboratorio** (Via degli Orti di Albert 13, tel. 06/686-1366, daily 9 A.M.–7 P.M., closed Mon. morning) to create all sorts of objects that border on art but remain practical in function.

Antiques

The number of antique stores is especially high in this neighborhood, and Via Giulia and Via dei Coronari are the center of the trade. Don't expect many bargains and remember to ask for a discount if the price seems exhorbitant.

Antichità Cipriani (Via Giulia 122, tel. 06/6830-8344, Mon.–Fri. 9 A.M.–1 P.M. and 3:30–8 P.M.) is almost exclusively devoted to neoclassical furniture and paintings. The pieces are simple and elegant composed mostly of darkly stained wood that was built without the use of nails.

For a break from the Baroque pieces which dominate many shops try **Antiquariato Valligiano** (Via Giulia 193, tel. 06/686-9505, Mon.–Fri. 10 A.M.–1 P.M. and 3:30–8 P.M.). It's one of the only places to find 19th-century country furniture, which means the tables and chairs show scars of practical usage.

Importers of Chinese antiques are rare in Rome. **Yaky** (Via Santa Maria del Pianto 55, tel. 06/6880-7724, Mon.–Fri. 9 A.M.–1 P.M. and 4–8 P.M.), therefore, has become a mecca for collectors who also appreciate the contemporay line of furniture based on traditional designs.

If you're after limited-edition books, prints, and paintings from past centuries then **Antiquaria Sant'Angelo** (Via del Banco di S. Spirito, tel. 06/686-5944, Mon.–Fri. 10 A.M.–1 P.M. and 4–8 P.M.) is bound to oblige. This well-furnished store opposite the Ponte Sant'Angelo even has a selection of antique frames that will enhance any picture.

All the major auction houses conduct sales in Rome, but it's smaller houses like **DAM Auctions** (Via Fuga Giardini, 9:30 A.M.–1 P.M. and 4–8 P.M., auctions usually held at 6 P.M.) where sellers can walk away satisfied with quality and price. Items on the block are primarily 17th- and 18th-century paintings and furniture. Sales are held regularly and are open to the public.

Specialty

Anyone who wants to sketch or paint their way around Rome can pick up the necessary materials at **Ditta G. Poggi** (Via del Gesú 74 and Via Pie di Marmo 38, tel. 06/678-4477, daily 10 A.M.–7 P.M.). Whatever brush, pad, or color you're after you'll find it here. There are also chips and cement for creating mosaics.

Herbs aren't generally the first item on a shopping list but they may be after a visit to **Antica Erboristeria Romana** (Via Torre Argentina 15, tel. 06/687-9493, Mon.–Sat. 8:30 A.M.–7:30 P.M.). This emporium of dried plants has been selling spice since 1752. Noses will be grateful for a sniff.

Bookstores

How places like **Il Museo del Louvre** (Via della Reginella 28, Mon.–Fri. 10 A.M.–8 P.M.) stay in business is a delightful mystery. This combination gallery and secondhand bookstore specializes in Italian literature and no doubt has a following of eager collectors. The signed edition of Neruda is under glass and costs €1,200. Watch your step when exiting. Next door is the collection of 20,000 photographs organized by subject.

Blink too long and you'll miss **Aseq** (Via Sant'Eustachio 4, tel. 06/686-8400, Mon.–Sat. 9 A.M.–8 P.M.) and an eclectic selection of titles ranging from Asian cuisine to medieval alchemy.

Clothing

Strategic Business Unit (Via di Pantaleo 68, tel. 06/6880-2547, daily 9 A.M.–7 P.M.) doesn't sound like it would create comfortable men's clothing, but the originators of this Roman label obviously have a sense of irony—as well as a talent for designing sportswear in a variety of fabrics.

Three boutiques at one location is the advantage of **Civico 93** (Via del Governo Vecchio 72-93, tel. 06/687-6572, Mon.–Sat. 9 A.M.–7 P.M.). Each has its own style, starting from casual and moving to elegant. Clothes are on the minimal side and the brands are primarily Italian names including Mezzo, Diva, and Rossodisera.

Shoes and Accessories

If you forgot your favorite shoes or the ones you did pack are no match for the cobblestones of Rome, **Totem** (Via della Maddalena 45, tel.06/6978-1701, 9:30 A.M.–7 P.M.) can help. There are flats and high-heels of all styles and descriptions. Further proof that style and comfort can coexist.

Bags sounds so typical, but what **Sirni** (Via della Stelletta 33, tel. 06/6880-5248, Tues.–Sun. 9:30 A.M.–7 P.M.) carries is all created in high-quality leather that's transformed into every size and shape imaginable. If you don't find what you're looking for on the shelves it can be ordered and sent to your home.

Children

Zingone (Via di Campo Marzio 37, tel. 06/687-1335) is a mini-outlet for mini-people. Besides its own label, which looks great on infants and young children, it carries Baby Graziella, Ao, and Lili Goffre.

Home

If you're tired of your couch or want to add some interior design to your home, then **Spazio Sette** (Via dei Barbieri 7, tel. 06/686-9708, Mon.–Sat. 9 A.M.–7 P.M., closed Mon. morning) is the place to come. All the top Italian furniture and interior brands are presented within a stunningly rennovated palazzo. There's a gift for every room.

Art'e (Piazza Rondanini 32, tel. 06/683-3907, Mon.–Sat. 9:30 A.M.–1 P.M. and 3:30–7:30 P.M.) could easily be mistaken for a design museum. The products are sleek and

the kitchen is king. There are dozens of retro toasters, juicers, and espresso makers.

Souvenir

Ferrari is synonymous with Italy and the **Ferrari Store** (Via Tomacelli 147, tel. 06/689-2979, daily 10 A.M.–7:30 P.M.) is the obvious pit stop for souvenirs. Red is the only color from the t-shirts and hats, to the key chains and books recounting the legendary car that has turned heads for generations.

Markets

Small is beautiful at the tiny tented market in **Vicolo della Moretta** (tel. 06/372-0204), held on the second Sunday of each month. It hasn't been overrun with tourists yet and stall-holders take the time to recount the story behind the antiques and collectables they sell.

TRIDENTE

Designer boutiques are omnipresent these days and even the most exclusive ones turn up at airports. Still something has to be said for shopping at the source and seeing the Piazza di Spagna each time you exit a boutique beats any departure lounge. Via Condotti is the epicenter of fashion but the adjacent streets are equally worth exploring. Via Babuino is even twinned with Madison Avenue, which makes sense after seeing the many galleries, boutiques, and hotels.

Arts and Crafts

Gold and silver leafing is nothing new. What is original about **Natura and Argento** (Via del Vantaggio 41a, tel. 06/321-9384, Mon.–Sat. 9 A.M.–7 P.M.) are the objects that owner Silvana Papette covers in those metals. Everything is organic and preserved with a special technique she has perfected over the years, from the artichoke earrings to the silver sunflowers.

Antiques

Everything is strictly made in Italy at **Apolloni** (Via del Babuino 133, tel. 06/3600-2216, Mon.–Sat. 9:30 A.M.–1 P.M. and 3:30–7:30 P.M.) and it was all made hundreds of years ago.

Most of the high-quality furniture, paintings, and silver dates from the 17th century.

Specialty

What happens to Swiss guardsmen when they retire? Franz Steiner opened **Tulipani Bianchi** (Via dei Bergamaschi 59, tel. 06/678-5449, Tues.–Sat. 9 A.M.–1 P.M. and 3:30–7 P.M.) and now works tulips, poppies, and hazelnut branches into bouquets even the coldest hearts cannot resist.

Bookstores

Feltrinelli (Via del Babuino 39, tel. 06/3600-1873, Mon. 2 P.M.–7:30 P.M., Tues.–Sat. 10 A.M.–7:30 P.M.) has several locations across the city but this one is the most inspiring. The white interior and bucolic courtyard are condusive to browsing. A wall of shelves in the front is devoted to English fiction and books about Rome. Children's books and design titles are down the corridor in the rear of the store.

Clothing

You don't just become Armani. It takes talent and hard work for a name to become synonymous with style. Just ask Ennio Capasa, who has transformed **Costume National** (Via del Babuino 106, tel. 06/6920-0686, Mon.–Sat. 11:30 A.M.–7:30 P.M.) into a premier avant-garde label. Celebrity clients swear by the his-and-hers lines that include hard-to-resist accessories.

Wardrobe suffering from drab? **Abitart** (Via della Scala 7, tel. 06/534-4162, Tues.–Sat. 10:30 A.M.–midnight) can help add colors and geometric patterns that are closer to art than clothing. Multiple locations.

Major men's brands at discount prices are the bread and butter of **Cashmerestock** (Via delle Carrozze 67, tel. 06/679-1527, Tues.–Sat. 11 A.M.–8 P.M., Sun.–Mon. 3–8 P.M.), which is also a relief from the more formal stores in the area.

Shoes and Accessories

Any man with a secret dandy fantasy or penchant for walking canes will find happiness at **Radiconini** (Via del Corso 139, tel. 06/679-1807, Tues.–Sat. morning 9:30 A.M.–1:30 P.M. and 4–7:30 P.M.). Start with the hats that come in balsa boxes and work your way to the smoking jackets and ties synonymous with fireside chats and the smell of pipe tobacco.

Caleffi (Via della Colonna Antonina 53, tel. 06/679-3773, Tues.–Sat. 9 A.M.–7:30 P.M., Mon. 3:30–7:30 P.M., closed Sun.) is where Italian politicians go between sessions of parliament to get measured up for handmade ties.

When it comes to bags, **Dotti** (Via Belsiana 26, tel. 06/6992-0456, Mon.–Sat. 9 A.M.–7 P.M.) thinks outside of the box. Handles are given new meaning here and materials run the gamut from coconut skin to velvet. Don't worry about needing the right occasion; these bags can be used continuously morning, noon, and night.

Zeis House (Piazza del Poplolo 21, tel. 06/324-0908, 9 A.M.–7 P.M.) puts sneakers on the pedestal they deserve. Trend brands like Merrel, Dutch, and BikkeMbergs all compete for the attention of your feet.

Jewelry

If *Breakfast at Tiffany's* had been filmed in Rome it would have been called *Breakfast at Bulgari's* (Via dei Condotti 10, tel. 06/679-3876, Tues.–Sat. 10:30 A.M.–7 P.M.). This jewelry institution founded by a Greek immigrant has been adorning women since 1884 with timeless designs. Don't be intimidated. Pretend you're Hepburn or Peppard and have a look.

Children

Toddlers' clothes will never clash after a visit to **Clayeux** (Via della Croce 82, tel. 06/679-0221, Mon.–Sat. 10:30 A.M.–7 P.M.). Whatever the color of the season, there are dozens of shade variations all of which can be mixed and matched with ease.

To reward good behavior or risk parental sanity, head to **Galleria San Carlo** (Via del Corso 114, tel. 06/679-0571, Mon.–Sat. 10:30 A.M.–7 P.M.). This toy store puts the accent on variety and choosing something could be a pleasure or a nightmare depending on your age.

Home

You can have any color plate, coffee cup, or teapot you like at **La Porcellana Bianca** (Via delle Vite 33, tel. 06/6920-0745, Mon.–Fri. 10 A.M.–7 P.M.) as long as it's white. Purists will appreciate the endless selection of grade A porcelain made in Arezzo.

Markets

If it's magazine covers of Sophia Loren or old Piranesi prints of 17th-century Rome that you're searching for, then the jackpot is **Mercato delle Stampe** (Largo delle Fontanella di Borghese, Mon.–Sat. 7 A.M.–1 P.M.). Everything here looks as though it would be the perfect addition to that blank wall back home.

The indoor market above the Piazza di Spagna known as **The Underground** (Via Francesco Crispi 96, tel. 06/3600-5345, first Sun. of every month 10 A.M.–7:30 P.M.) is more upscale than the name might suggest. Small antiques constitute the heart of the market, although coins, medals, and tools are also on display.

Kitsch, curiosities, and the occasional gem are reason enough to visit **Il Mercatino del Borghetto** (Via Flaminio, tel. 06/581-7308, Sun. year-round 10 A.M.–7 P.M.). This flea market housed in a former bus depot is more about quantity than quality but there are bargains to be had.

It's good to arrive early to the **Mercato di Ponte Milvio** (Lungotevere Capoprati, tel. 06/907-7312, first Sunday of each month, 8:30 A.M.–6 P.M.). In summer the vintage objects on the stands that line the Tiber all go fast. The C2 bus from Termini gets you there in 30 minutes.

VATICANO

Shopping is a religion to some, so it's no surprise to find stores in the shadow of San Pietro. Via Cola di Renzo houses the majority of these including a branch of the Coin department store. The lack of any parks means the best place to take a break from spending is one of the historic cafés that line this long street.

Antiques

Galleria dei Cosmati (Via Vittoria Colonna 11, tel. 06/361-141, 9 A.M.–1 P.M. and 3–7 P.M.) is one of the oldest antique stores in Rome. It's also one of the largest, which means that surveying all the objects could take a while. The owners are happy to answer any questions and will readily appraise anything you may be looking to sell.

Arts and Crafts

Needle and thread don't always get the credit they deserve. Inside **Italia Garipoli** (Borgo Vittorio 91, tel. 06/6880-2196) it becomes clear that embroidery is an art form and the intricate patterns on napkins, tablecloths, and handkerchiefs make you wonder how it was created. The answer is decades of practice and a steady hand.

Small, very small, and even smaller mosaics are created at **Savelli** (Via Paolo VI 27, tel. 06/6830-7017). You can find out how these little gems are made by having a look in the studio where an assortment of religious objects are also under construction.

Bookstores

There are two kinds of readers: those who prefer buying their books from Feltrinelli and those who prefer **Mondadori** (Piazza Cola di Rienzo 81, tel. 06/322-0188, Mon.–Sat. 9:30 A.M.–8 P.M., Sun. 9 A.M.–1 P.M. and 4–7:30 P.M.). Find out what kind you are at this large media store with an extensive English section.

Clothing

Brique (Via Cola di Rienzo 315, tel. 06/3973-6896) is for women who are more concerned with comfort than keeping up with what's on Milan catwalks. Clothes combine creativity with simplicity.

Iron (Via Cola di Rienzo 50, tel. 06/321-6798) sells lesser-known brands for men and women in a spacious store that features a little of everything at reasonable prices.

Accessories

Before you buy a bag anywhere else, check out **Maxim** (Via Ottaviano 17, tel. 06/3972-3718). Popular labels like Coccinelle, Nannini, and Biasia are all here and they're priced for a lot less than at some of the other stores in the area.

Sports and Recreation

Sports in Italy is synonymous with *calcio* (soccer) and Romans are especially mad for the game. Anywhere there's grass there's someone kicking a ball and five-a-side fields the size of tennis courts are located in outlying neighborhoods. Good weather makes it possible to stay outdoors most of the year and Romans like to be in the open air. During summer weekends the beaches of Ostia 30 minutes from the center are crowded and parking is impossible after 11 A.M. Tennis is also popular and the game is mostly played on clay courts. Jogging and cycling are common pastimes and what the city lacks in bicycle lanes it makes up for in beautiful parks.

PARKS

Private gardens of the rich and famous were donated to the city over the centuries, leaving Romans with wonderful settings to spend their lunch breaks or take a Sunday afternoon stroll. The largest and most accessible of these is **Villa Borghese** (Piazzale Flaminio, tel. 06/8205-9127, www.villaborghese.it, dawn–dusk), where bikes can be rented at five locations. An hour costs €8 and a passport or ID must be left as collateral. The tandem and quad options are a fun way of exploring the tree-lined alleys that crisscross the park. Children can enjoy pony and carousel rides and the **Bioparco** (Piazzale del Giardino Zoologico 1, tel. 06/360-8211, daily 9:30 A.M.–6 P.M., €8.50), where they are encouraged to discover nature. The park is also home to the world's smallest movie theater for kids (Viale della Pineta 15, tel. 06/855-3485, €5), which runs features (in Italian) on Wednesday–Sunday afternoons.

On the other side of town above Trastevere, **Villa Doria Pamphilj** (Via di San Pancrazio, dawn–dusk) is where dog lovers take their pets for a stretch and is full of pick-up soccer games on weekends. The villa and fountains in the center were financed by Pope Innocent X and have been inspiring joggers to run that extra kilometer since the park was opened to the public. **Villa Celimontana** (Piazza della Navicella,

7 A.M.–dusk) is the smallest of the three and the perfectly manicured gardens are a short way from the Circus Maximus. During the summer a month-long jazz festival (www.villacelimontanajazz.com) is organized on the grounds and the gravel paths are lit by candlelight.

Rome's parks were made for **running** and anyone trying to jog off jet lag should head towards Pamphilj or Borghese. If knees are a problem, the synthetic athletic track near Terme di Caracalla can cushion the blows. Cross-country runners should keep going along the ruts and ruins of Via Appia Antica. If you want to add culture to your workout, **Sight Jogging** (tel. 347/335-3185, www.sightjogging.it, €70 for 1 hour, €100 for 2 hours) provides both and offers running commentary on a dozen itineraries around the city.

CYCLING

Pedaling around the city should be done with caution. Bike lanes are rare but one of the few routes that does exist is a 15-kilometer path that follows the Tiber from Castel Giubileo to Ponte Risorgimento near the center. Another scenic itinerary is Villa Borghese to Villa Ada.

Hourly and daily rentals are available from **Collati** (Via dei Pellegrino 82, tel. 06/6880-1084) near Campo dei Fiori and **Eco Move Rent** (Via Varese 48, tel. 06/4470-4518, €11 per day) close to Termini. Bikes can be transported on the first car of the Rome–Lido di Ostia railway on weekends. The last stop is a good place for a leisurly ride along the beach. **Biciebike** (tel. 339/715-5964, www.biciebike.net, €15 plus cost of rental) provides half-day tours of the city every Sunday. Riders meet outside the Colosseo metro station at 9:30 A.M.

TENNIS

Rome is a clay court town with no shortage of tennis clubs. Some do not require membership and anyone looking for a game can find it at **Circolo della Stampa** (Piazza Mancini 19, tel. 06/323-2454), where an hour of singles is

CALCIO CRAZY

Calcio, or soccer, is far and away the most popular sport in Italy. Rome has two teams that share the same stadium. Built for the 1960 Olympics and refurbished during the 1990 World Cup, the Olimpico is encircled by groves of umbrella pines where t-shirt vendors hawk their wares and men wrinkled from many seasons in the sun sell Borghetti espresso for €2 a pop. At the entrances, riot police conduct relaxed searches of the incoming crowd and expectation lingers in the air.

Anyone who has never attended a football game, who considers baseball exciting, or wonders what the Colosseum was like in its heyday will benefit from time at the stadium. On a Sunday afternoon, the eastern stands are bathed in sun while the rest of the stadium is shaded by a modern overhang. On the immaculate green pitch, players prepare themselves for another encounter as supporters make for their seats. Enclosed within a Plexiglas-bordered segment of stadium, visiting fans begin their chants. Flags fly and scarves wave as the team anthem is played and Romans erupt into a united chorus. Players are announced and the home crowd shouts the names of their favorites. Fumi-

gants are lit as the game begins and smoke obscures the early minutes of action.

Views are surprisingly good. From the curves behind either goal, players look like pieces in a giant chess set controlling possession of the ball and searching for the decisive pass. Sounds from the field float up to the stands, where fans urge their team on shouting advice to coach, players, and referee. Missed occasions are rued, heads are lowered, curses sworn, ovations paid, and cries of despair gasped.

Optimism builds again after halftime and visiting supporters start into another catchy tune. Substitutions are made, diving saves, blind passes, corner kicks, tempers raised, give and goes, counter attacks, and then, suddenly, *goal!* A collective burst of Roman energy rises to its feet and thousands of hands wave. Scarves are displayed, songs have renewed vigor, and the fumigants have fire fighters working overtime. At the final whistle, crowds disperse at incredible speed. Moods vary depending on results and the polemics of football spread up and down the city from Testaccio to Garbatella as thoughts turn to the next game at the Olimpico.

€10 and doubles cost €12. The night supplement is €2 and you can choose from one of six clay or synthetic surfaces. **Oasis di Pace** (Via degli Eugenii 2, tel. 06/718-4550) runs a similar service near the Via Appia Antica and courts should be booked in advance.

GOLF

Why not interrupt the sightseeing with a round of golf? Rome has six courses, many of which are immersed in countryside and lined with umbrella pines. All you need to play is a reservation.

At **Circolo del Golf Fioranello** (Via della Falcognana 61, tel. 06/7138-0800, fax 06/713-8212, €20), Fabrizio Ramaccia will be happy to show you around the clubhouse, restaurant/bar, driving range, and outdoor swimming pool. He'll even offer advice on the

18-hole, 72-par course, and if you want company just say the word. It's a 35-minute taxi ride from the center which should not exceed €40. Rome's oldest club is **Circolo Golf Roma** (Via Appia Nuova 716, tel. 06/780-3407, www.golfroma.it) and the newest is the **Sheraton Golf Hotel** (Viale Parco dei Medici 22, tel. 06/655-3477), where die-hard golfers can wake up with a view of the green.

SPECTATOR SPORTS
Soccer

Rome's two soccer teams play in Stadio Olimpico (Viale Gladiatore 2, tel. 06/36-851), which means there's a game on every weekend. The season runs from late August to late May and most matches are held on Sunday afternoons. Roma (yellow and red) is the more popular and more successful of the sides and their hardcore supporters live in Testaccio and Garbatella. Lazio (sky blue and white) won the Italian Serie A championship in 2000 and have languished in mid-table ever since. Tickets in *le curve* (behind the goals), where the most faithful fans sit, are €10, while comfortable seats in the tribunes cost €20 and up. Games aren't generally sold-out and tickets can be purchased at the gates or the Roma Store in Piazza Colonna.

Basketball

Virtus Roma (Palazzetto dello Sport, tel. 06/3600-2439) have struggled to lift themselves above average for years. Team chemistry includes local players, Eastern Europeans, and NBA journeymen hoping for a comeback. Games are held at the EUR Palalottomatica arena and become especially animated when perennial league leaders Bologna or Milan are in town. Tickets start at €8 for adults and €1 for children under 14.

Rugby

Italian rugby has come a long way in recent years. Although clubs remain amateurish, the national team is now respectable and doesn't lose by the margins it once did; it even manages to beat Scotland now and again. The **Six Nations** (tel. 0862/404-206, €22–50) tournament runs January–March and is the occasion to watch England, France, or Ireland compete at the Stadio Flaminio. Unlike soccer, rival fans don't require a restraining order and post-game celebrations go on for hours at pubs around the center.

Horse Racing

Horse racing is one of the oldest sports in Rome. Although the standing-room -only days of the Circo Massimo may be over, it's still possible to place a bet and feel the adrenaline of a photo-finish.

Rome has two major tracks: **Ippodromo delle Capannelle** (Via Appia Nuova 1255, tel. 06/716-771) for flat racing and steeplechase and **Ippodromo di Tor di Valle** (Via del Mare, tel. 06/780-3470) on the Roma-Ostia line for trotting. Major race days are held in June and November.

Horse enthusiasts will enjoy the annual **International Horse Show** at the end of April in Villa Borghese.

Accommodations

Customer service was one thing the Romans didn't invent and until recently nonchalance was the most you could expect from any front desk. Hotels have gone through a Renaissance in recent years though, and many of the faded carpets and soft mattresses have been replaced with more modern furnishings. Design hotels like the De Russie and Radisson SAS Es. have helped shake things up, as have bed-and-breakfasts, which were virtually unknown a decade ago. Doors are now starting to be opened and smiles have replaced the bored expressions that once greeted guests.

One thing that hasn't changed are the prices. It still costs an arm and a leg for the five- or even four-star treatment, which is concentrated around Via Veneto and Piazza di Spagna. Rates change throughout the year but in Rome, high season is nearly year-round. Prices do dip slightly November–March and many hotels offer a discount for multiple night stays. If budget is an issue, take the bed-and-breakfast route and rest assured you will not have to sacrifice comfort or service. There are also campsites and hostels on the outskirts of the city with dormitory and twin room options.

If you plan on spending over three nights in Rome and aren't weighed down by too much luggage, consider spending a couple of nights in one neighborhood and the rest in another. Otherwise to really do as the Romans do rent an apartment for a week and get the instant local feel.

TERMINI

This area seems like a good place to stay. It's near the train station and airport shuttles, and there are lots of hotels, but unless you are on a lightning tour of the city it's best to get closer to the historic center. Termini is popular with business travelers short on time and tour groups short on cash. At night there's little going on around Piazza dei Cinquecento except the occasional drug deal and homeless people bedding down for the night. Restaurants are all downhill and the walk back up can seem eternal. There are a few hotels that overcome the cons, and convenient transportation links within the city and beyond remain a significant advantage.

€100-200

Hotel Kennedy (Via Filippo Turati 64, tel. 06/446-5373, www.hotelkennedy.net, €90/159 s/d) was recently renovated and now consists of 51 medium-sized rooms. They added double-plated glass to keep the decibels down and traded the white walls for bright reds and yellows. Satellite TV and air-conditioning are standard and breakfast is an all-you-can-eat buffet served 7:15–9:30 A.M. There's a small library next to the downstairs bar where friendly staff help guests kick-start the day with a cappuccino.

The first thing you notice about **Hotel Columbia** (Via del Viminale, tel. 06/488-3509, www.hotelcolumbia.com, €218–235 s/d) is the flowers. They add elegance to this mid-size hotel with wood beams and terra-cotta floors remeniscent of Tuscany. Rooms are refreshingly simple in style and contain minibar, safe, and Wi-Fi. The Diletti family who operate the hotel mean it when they say "have a nice day" and it's hard not to after enjoying breakfast on the rooftop terrace that's open throughout the day.

Over €300

All the design stops were pulled at the **Radisson SAS Es.** (Via F. Turati 171, tel. 06/444-841, www.eshotel.it, €300 d), which maintains its sleekness from reception to rooftop bar. The 169 standard rooms are inspired by Robinson Crusoe with bed, shower, sink, and wardrobe stand all fitted on a raft-like structure in the center. Televisions are flat and climate control can be personalized. Two restaurants make eating-in a sound option and Zest serves an American breakfast until 10:30 A.M. Bar Zest is popular with trendy, late-night drinkers who come to hang out on the terrace and can soothe any hangovers at the spa.

FORI, PALATINO, AND CAPITOLINO
Under €100

Hotel Perugia (Via del Colosseo 7, tel. 06/679-7200, www.hperugia.it, €80–100 s/d) isn't likely to win any awards for beauty. The reason to stay here is price and location. The only closer you can sleep to the Colosseo is in a tent. Rooms in this small hotel are bare and decoration consists of a photograph or two. There's no elevator but there is a balcony and a decent view from a couple of doubles on the fourth floor. The couple who run the place are friendly and can arrange guides, airport pickup, or bus tickets.

Another high-value, low-luxury hotel near the Mouth of Truth is **Casa Kolbe** (Via di San Teodoro 44, tel. 06/679-4974, €90 s/d). Rooms in the back look out on a garden and are all equiped with TV and bathrooms. The hotel restaurant serves lunch and dinner in an unadorned dining room. Guests are primarily young Northern Europeans who have come to see the Pope.

€100-200

Hotels like the **Nardizzi** (Via Firenze 38, tel. 06/4890-3916, www.hotelnardizzi.it, €105–145 s/d) only exist in Italy. Where else is it a family business to make visitors feel at home? A few minutes on the terrace is all it takes to feel as Roman as the owners. Rooms are spacious and the service goes beyond the two stars listed at the entrance. A continental breakfast is included with the price and the shops of Via Nazionale are just around the corner.

Location and Danilo at the front desk make the **(€ Duca d'Alba** (Via Leoni 14, tel. 06/484-471, www.hotelducadalba.com, €130–180 s/d) a convenient choice. Antiquity is only minutes away and the vibrant Monti neighborhood will liven up the evening. Danilo can help quench any curiosity about the city or provide directions to your next destination. The 27 rooms are small but comfortable and each contains an electronic safe.

€200-300

The **Lancelot** (Via Capo d'Africa 47, tel. 06/7045-0615, www.lancelothotel.com, €125–200 s/d) is a bit of Britain in Rome. All the rooms in this small hotel could be the setting of an Agatha Christie novel with plush couches, gilded mirrors, and antique writing desks that are a sharp contrast to the city outside. Some rooms have balconies and all are bright and cheerful. Breakfast is served on round tables that make meeting fellow travelers easy. Many guests are repeat visitors and the majority are English-speaking. The garden is a pleasant place to plan the next sojourn and the hotel restaurant (€25 fixed-price) is a convenient alternative right on your doorstep. Airport transfers and car or scooter rental can be arranged upon request.

Situated in a restored 19th-century palazzo two blocks from the Colosseo, the **Hotel Celio** (Via dei Santi Quattro 35c, tel. 06/7049-5333, www.charmingrome.com, €280–300 s/d) makes an immediate impression. The lounge is elegant and the staff are unusually attentive in a city where customer service is often neglected. Michelangelo and Cesare are the most charming rooms, with high ceilings and comfortable beds. End a grueling day of sightseeing with a swim in the hotel pool.

Over €300

Sipping a cocktail on a rooftop terrace overlooking the Colosseo may seem like the best thing about the **Capo d'Africa** (Via Capo d'Africa 54, tel. 06/772-801, www.hotelcapodafrica.com, €330–390 s/d). It isn't. This modern 64-room hotel could double as an art gallery and colorful paintings cover most of the walls. The gym is open 24 hours a day in case you crave a midnight workout and a personal trainer can be arranged. Families, businesspeople, and newlyweds pass through the lobby where multilingual staff take service seriously. If the pillow is causing you problems they'll replace it with an allergy-free version.

AVENTINO AND TESTACCIO
€100-200

If you can handle 1980s decor in a Fascist-era building and manage to reserve a room facing the courtyard away from the traffic on Via Marmorata, then **Hotel Santa Prisca** (Largo M. Gelsomini 25, tel. 06/574-1917, hsprisca@hotelsantaprisca.it, €110–150 s/d) might grow on you. The medium-size hotel is owned by nuns who care less about innovation than providing a good night sleep at reasonable prices. That explains the linoleum flooring and odd patterns on the armchairs. Breakfast is included and the lunch and dinner prix-fixe options are a bargain. The Testaccio neighborhood nearby provides an instant nightlife and the Colosseo is only 15 minutes away on foot.

Surrounded by an attractive garden on a quiet residential street in Aventino, **Villa San Pio** (Via Santa Melania 19, tel. 06/578-3214, www.aventinohotels.com, €130–200 s/d) provides elegant and silent rooms with Baroque flair. All the furniture matches in color and style and much of it is antique. Bathrooms are all done up in black and white marble and equipped with hair dryers and hydromassage jets. A spacious restaurant with wide vaulted ceilings serves Italian and Roman specialties.

€200-300

Hotel S. Anselmo (Piazza S. Anselmo 2, tel. 06/570-057, www.aventinohotels.com, €220–270 s/d) is as memorable as Rome. Each of the 34 rooms in this four-star hotel has a name and personality of its own. The Camera con Vista benefits from a bucolic view, while the Renaissance room could save you a trip to Florence. Downstairs, old and new, black and white blend seamlessly into a timeless style that

PENSIONI AND HOSTELS

You don't have to be wealthy to find a bed in Rome. The city offers students and budget travelers comfortable options at a fraction of the five-star prices. In fact, before hotels became the norm, Italian travelers of the 18th and 19th centuries stayed in *pensioni*. These still exist today and are generally family operated and offer minimum service at low cost. What you get is a clean room or simply a bed and a smile. Hostels are even cheaper and attract enthusiastic backpackers from around the world.

Satisfied travelers have left their artwork and memories all over the walls of **Pensione Ottaviano Hostel** (Via Ottaviano 6, tel. 06/3973-8138, info@pensioneottaviano.com,

€18 per bed). The ambiance is youthful and friendly. Internet access is free after 8:30 P.M. and the Vaticano is next door.

Staying at Hotel Pensione Tizi is a little like visiting an average Roman family. Tiziana will lead you to one of the 25 silent rooms, some of which share bathrooms.

If budget is a concern and sleeping 20 minutes outside of Rome isn't a problem, then the **Litus Rome Hostel** (tel. 06/569-7275, www.litusroma.com, €30) could be the ticket. Located in Ostia by the sea in a 1916 vintage building, the hostel offers four floors of immaculate rooms. Cinema and dining hall are located within, while beach life and the ruins of Ostia Antica are nearby.

---

may never go out of fashion. The breakfast buffet includes smoked salmon, fresh fruit, and homemade cakes served inside or in the garden where a giant palm stands guard. Uniformed staff provide impeccable service and Ari at the bar knows every cocktail in the book.

TRASTEVERE
€100-200

Moments from the main neighborhood square **Hotel Trastevere Manara** (Via Luciano Manara 24a, tel. 06/581-4713, €98–103 s/d) is a small modern establishment with electronic safes in each room. Furniture is quaint but clean and the front desk can point you in the right direction. There's a tram three minutes away that gets you into the center quickly if you don't want to walk. Breakfast is croissants and coffee, and most guests seem to be thirty-somethings on a romantic getaway.

Hotel Cisterna (Via della Cisterna 7–9, tel. 06/581-7212, www.cisternahotel.it, €130 d) gets its name from the fountain in the nearby courtyard. There are 20 rooms and those on the upper floors have pitched ceilings and wooden beams. The side-street location keeps the hustle and bustle of Trastevere at a safe distance, but there are no lack of bars and restau-

rants within a 300-meter radius of the hotel. Don't expect posh, but clean and friendly. Breakfast is included in the price and served until 10 A.M.

Villa della Fonte (Via della Fonte d'Olio 8, tel. 06/580-3797, www.villafonte.com, €110–160 s/d) is a small five-room hotel run by a friendly mother/daughter team. Rooms are bright and inlcude minibar and satellite TV. Mattresses were recently replaced and are quite firm. Parking is available nearby for a small supplement and chocolate croissants from a neighborhood bakery are served in bed or on the sun-filled patio. The balconies are perfect for observing the Trastevere street scene down below and what the villa lacks in size it makes up for in charm.

€200-300

Think of Italy and the **★ Hotel Santa Maria** (Vicolo del Piede 2, tel. 06/589-4626, www.hotelsantamaria.info, €180–220 s/d) probably comes to mind. It's quaint with a capital Q and a stay here is like entering a small village miles from Rome. That feeling has to do with the building's 17th-century cloister past. All the bricks, beams, tiles, and cobblestones were recently restored and are in the right place. A buffet breakfast is included and may be eaten in the courtyard besides the orange trees or under the high, wooden ceiling of the dining room. The half-dozen rooms come in double, triple, and quadruple options that all look out on a lovely portico where some guests spend the afternoons sipping wine from the hotel wine bar.

CAMPO DEI FIORI AND PIAZZA NAVONA
€100-200

Tastefully decorated rooms and 15th-century charm await at **Hotel Navona** (Via dei Sediari 8, tel. 06/6821-1392, www.hotelnavona. com, €120–155 s/d). Gilt-framed paintings of the city hang above the beds and heavy green curtains keep the sunlight out of the 20 rooms. They also have several large apartments with frescoed ceilings and fully equipped kitchens where guests can spend a weekend or more five minutes from Rome's most famous square. Breakfast is served on a long table in the communal dining room that encourages conversation among the international travelers.

Hotel Teatro di Pompeo (Largo del Pallaro 8, tel. 06/6830-0170, €170 d) provides an extra thrill for lovers of antiquity, who can enjoy a continental breakfast under the original vaults of a Roman theater. The 12 rooms are spacious, clean, and convenient given that Piazza Navona, the Spanish Steps, and Fontana di Trevi are all within walking distance. Half face a courtyard and you'll have to stick your neck out the window to see the sky but they are are quiet and suited for late risers. The ones in front face a small square and have tiled flooring and dark wood ceilings. A bar near the entrance is open throughout the day and Internet access is free.

€200-300

It doesn't get much more central than **Hotel due Torre** (Vicolo del Leonatta 23, tel. 06/687-6983, www.hotelduetorriroma.com, €150–230 s/d). Parquet floors and a personal touch that includes many antiques give the hotel a distinctive and refined feeling. It's practically like staying in a museum or a 1970s time capsule. All 22 rooms and four apartments have air-conditioning, minibar, and paintings depicting how the neighborhood once looked. English-language newspapers are stacked in the marble-covered lobby that is a comfortable staging point before heading out into the thick of the city.

Falling in love is easy at **⟨ Locanda Cairoli** (Piazza Benedetto Cairoli 2, tel. 06/6880-9278, www.locandacairioli.it, €180–240 s/d). This small hotel mixes period furnishings that would make any great-grandparent feel at home with modern art and photographs of Ernest Hemingway. The hominess is reinforced by the Greek- and English-speaking owner who can organize shopping and cultural tours of the city. Breakfast is included and the satellite TV should remain switched off.

Over €300

There's something unique about leaving the **Sole al Pantheon** (Piazza della Rotonda 63, tel. 06/678-0441, www.hotelsolealpantheon. com, €260–400 s/d) and coming face to face with Rome's oldest intact building. The hotel has been providing that feeling of awe since 1467 and you can see the Pantheon from many of the rooms facing the square that remains lively at all hours of the day. It's been recently modernized without sacrificing any of the charm. Doubles are small but the whirlpool tub is a nice consolation and all rooms have canopy beds, marble-clad sinks, and safes. Staff always say hello and the extensive sweet and savory buffet has something new every day. Sartre and Simone de Beauvoir stayed here when they were in town.

Raphael (Largo Febo 2, tel. 06/682-831, www.raphaelhotel.com, €250–600 s/d) takes elegance and sophistication to new heights. The rooftop views of the historic center at this four-star hotel could be the best part of your stay in Rome. Richard Meier designed the suites on the third floor, which feature Bose Digital Sound and the minimilism he's famous for. Standard doubles are inspired from Renaissance paintings and are bright and colorful.

The fitness center could help work some of the pasta off but most guests prefer to enjoy feasting on the creative dishes prepared by Jean François Daridon in the restaurant. The uniformed concierges are always at attention in the lobby and can book tickets to musical events or arrange for guided tours of the city.

TRIDENTE
Under €100

Sober rooms at sober prices could be the slogan for **Pensione Panda** (Via della Croce 35, tel. 06/678-0179, www.hotelpanda.it, €88–93 s/d). So what if the decoration is dull? The beds are well made and guests come for the Piazza di Spagna, which is only moments away. Rooms are spread out on two floors of a 19th-century *palazzo* that has preserved some of its original frescoes. A couple have balconies overlooking a central courtyard and are quieter than those facing the street. Air-conditioning is extra and may be worth the euros if you're traveling in August.

€100-200

Anyone with an aversion to big hotels will appreciate the intimacy of **Casa Howard** (Via Capo delle Case 18, tel. 06/6992-4555, www.casahoward.com, €150 d). Each of the five rooms is neatly decorated, some benefiting from antiques the owner has brought from her Tuscan farmhouse. The Verde room is especially beautiful and provides the ideal escape from the crowds stalking the Piazza di Spagna. The standard of service is high and additional perks like massages are available upon request.

In the heart of Via Veneto, **◖ Daphnae Inn** (Via di San Basilio 55, tel. 06/4782-3529, www.daphne-rome.com, €180 d) provides 15 refined rooms at two locations minutes from the Barberini subway stop. The Italo-American couple who run the place are extremely helpful and have good taste in furniture. Guests can choose between shared or en suite bathrooms. All rooms are soothing on the eye and linens and comforters match the dark, hardwood floors. There's a computer in the sitting room with Internet access and cell phones are provided for free.

A romantic hotel located on Purification Street seems like a contradiction, but once inside the **Barocco** (Via della Purificazione 4, Barberini, tel. 06/487-2001, www.hotelbarocco.com, €150–210 s/d) it all starts to make sense. This is the essence of elegance, where falling in love with service and refinement is possible. Some of the 41 rooms have balconies overlooking Rome's rooftops. Interiors are on the flowery side with primary colors favored throughout and lots of marble in the large bathrooms. Digital safes, air-conditioning, and satellite TV are standard, and the sound-proofed windows guarantee traffic won't interfere with your dreams.

€200-300

No room is the same at **Hotel Locarno** (Via della Penna 22, tel. 06/361-0841, www.hotellocarno.com, €210–240 s/d), where a view of the Tiber is only as far as the roof terrace. You may never want to leave the enchanting garden on the ground floor with its miniature fountain and overflowing vegetation. All 60 rooms have high ceilings and rustic fittings. Room 201 is especially comfortable, as are the two deluxe rooms on the sixth floor. Bicycles are provided for free.

One vine-covered entrance on a quiet street moments from Piazza di Spagna leads to two hotels: **Hotel Manfredi** (Via Margutta 61, tel. 06/320-7676, www.hotelmanfredi.it, €170–240 s/d) and **Hotel Forte** (tel. 06/3207625, www.hotelforte.com, €160–230 s/d) both offer comfortable chic that's not overdone and makes no attempt to be trendy. Each provides large beds in silent curtained rooms and professional three-star service. Breakfast can be eaten in bed or in either of the pleasant breakfast rooms.

Mozart (Via dei Greci 236, tel. 06/3600-1915, www.hotelmozart.com, €180–250 s/d) passes the white-glove test with flying colors. Rooms are immaculate and the hotel provides extras like airport connections at reasonable rates and Internet for free. Located on a cobblestone street near Piazza del Popolo and Piazza di Spagna.

Housed in a neoclassical building near the Parco della Musica, **Hotel Astrid** (Largo A. Sarti 4, tel. 06/323-6371, www.hotelastrid. com, €210–250 s/d) offers a refined escape from the historic center. The 48 rooms spread out on five floors are bright and many have a view of the Tiber. All the interiors are non-smoking, carpeted, and have a free minibar. Trams whisk passengers to Piazza del Popolo in under 10 minutes and the symphony orchestra is within walking distance.

VATICANO
Under €100

Travelers looking to make friends from all over the world should book a room at the **Alimandi** (Via Tunisi 8, tel. 06/3972-3948, €70–90 s/d). The low cost attracts a youthful crowd who can survive without luxury. Rooms are clean and conversations can go on for hours on the spacious rooftop terrace.

A night at **Residenza Madri Pie** (Via Alcide de Gasperi 4, tel. 06/631-967, www.residenzamadripie.it, €77–123 s/d) is a good way to prepare for the Vaticano, which is only 150 meters away. Many of the 73 rooms have views of Saint Peter's and all of them have pictures of saints hanging over the beds. The residence is favored by student travelers and pilgrims who congregate in the small chapel throughout the day. There's also a lovely garden out back that's cool in the summer and makes up for the lack of air-conditioning.

€100-200

After facing the crowds of the Piazza San Pietro the tranquility of **Santa Anna** (Borgo Pio 133-4, tel. 06/6880-1602, www.hotelsantanna.com, €160–200 s/d) is a godsend. All it takes is a few moments in the garden of this small hotel for serenity to return and if that doesn't work the minibar in each room should do the trick. Vatican colors of yellow and white predominate. Breakfast is included and rooms on the third floor have a terrace.

Hotel Giulio Cesare (Via degli Scipioni 287, tel. 06/321-0751, www.hotelgiuliocesare. com, €170–210 s/d) is as majestic as the name suggests. The lounge and entrance are decorated with antiques and tapestries. A hearty breakfast is served in the garden and there's free parking. The fireplace is lit in winter and the leather high-backed chairs in the lounge are perfect for reflecting on the day's events.

Amalia (Via Germanico 66, tel. 06/3972-3354, www.hotelamalia.com, €150–190 s/d) has cleanliness and convenience going for it. The 30 rooms on three floors are immaculate and the Ottaviano subway station two blocks away makes excursions to other parts of the city simple. It's popular with business and leisure travelers who appreciate the extra space and king-size beds.

It's hard to beat the **Ara Pacis** (Via Vittorio Colonna 11, tel. 06/320-4446, €165–195 s/d) on coziness. This quiet hotel near the Cavour bridge is tastefully decorated and a filling breakfast is included in the price.

€200-300

Before **《 Hotel Columbus** (Via della Conciliazione 33, tel. 06/686-5435, www.hotelcolumbus.net, €210–250 s/d) became a hotel it was the home of medieval princes and cardinals. The 15th-century pedigree still shows and most rooms have vaulted ceilings, wooden beams, and decoration fit for an aristocrat. Internet access and modern concessions to comfort have been made but should be used in moderation. The restaurant in the veranda looks out on a romantic courtyard.

After gazing on the Cappella Sistina, the ceilings of the **Arcangelo** (Via Boezio 15, tel. 06/687-4143, www.hotelarcangelo.com, €220–270 s/d) won't seem half bad. If it's charm you're after the fireplace usually does the trick. Stomachs will be seduced by the buffet breakfast that has enough calories to keep you going until dinner.

A new addition to the area's four-star hotel scene, the **Dei Consoli** (Via Varrone 2d, tel. 06/6889-2972, www.hoteldeiconsoli.com, €200–300 s/d) distinguishes itself with professionalism, modern furnishings, and the fact they welcome pets. The 26 rooms are divided into superior, deluxe, and junior suites where whirlpool tubs help weary guests recuperate. Everyone else can count on power showers and lots of Spanish porcelain in the bathrooms.

Over €300

The shops of Via Condotti and grottoes of the Vaticano are only a short walk away from **Hotel dei Mellini** (Via Muzio Clementi 81, tel. 06/324-771, www.hotelmellini. com, €370–430 s/d). This four-star hotel on a quiet residential street puts an emphasis on comfort and elegance. There's a non-smoking floor, roof garden, and small bar for winding down an evening. The 80 rooms are decorated in earth tones and feature Art Deco–inspired furniture.

Food

Food is as important as soccer in Rome and everyone has an opinion on the best restaurant or way to prepare *cacio pepe* (cheese and pepper pasta). Ingredients are locally grown and dishes rooted in a country tradition that aims to fill. Menus change with the seasons and are divided into antipasto (appetizers), *primo* (first), and *secondo* (second) courses. Must-try dishes include: *fiori di zucca* (fried zucchini flowers), *carciofi alla romana* (fried artichokes), and *saltimbocca alla romana* (veal wrapped in Parma ham). Lunch usually starts at 1 P.M. and restaurants don't get crowded until 8:30 P.M.

There are many levels of dining, from humble and homey to elaborate and refined. Locally inspired trattorias, *osteria,* and *ristoranti* are in the majority but regional, international, and fusion cooking can also be found. It may seem sacrilegious to stray from a strictly Italian diet when in Rome but you can always deviate towards Japanese, Indian, or French if the urge strikes.

Still more options arise when pizza is concerned. The Roman version is thin-crusted and comes with or without tomato sauce (*rosso* or *bianco*). *Pizzerie* (pizzerias) often serve a variety of starters, including such Roman favorites as fried cod and *suppli,* a fried rice ball with a melted mozzarella center.

FORI, PALATINO, AND CAPITOLINO

Besides the café at the top of the Vittorio Emanuele monument and the snack bars lining Via del Foro Romani, choices in the immediate vicinity are limited. It's better to avoid the restaurant at the entrance to the Colosseo subway stop. The view may be good but the food is likely to have been frozen 10 minutes before reaching your table. Head north towards the Monti neighborhood or east into San Giovanni to increase your stomach's chance of being satisfied.

Bakeries

Bread is nearly a religion in Rome and few places take it more seriously than **Panificio Panella** (Largo Leopardi 2, tel. 06/487-2344, Tues.–Sun. 7 A.M.–5 P.M.). This is where to try traditional local loaves like the rose-shaped buns known as *rosetta,* as well as cakes, tarts, and Italian-style doughnuts. The bar turns out some of the creamiest cappuccino in town.

Roman

If you want to eat like the ancient Romans ate, then **Magna Roma** (Via Capo d'Africa 26, tel. 06/700-9800, daily noon–2 P.M. and 8:30–11:30 P.M., www.maganroma.com, €15) is the place to do it. Potatoes, tomatoes, and even pasta are off the menu. Instead archeologist Franco Nicastro introduces palates to the flavors of the past using original recipes and one of the world's oldest cookbooks. Guests can choose from several 10-course meals that change weekly and are served by waiters in full toga regalia.

When you've been serving food for over 100 years in a working-class neighborhood the pasta can't be bad. That's the case with **La Carbonara** (Via Panisperna 214, tel. 06/482-5176, www.lacarbonara.it, Tues.–Sun. 12:30 P.M.–3 P.M. and 7–10:30 P.M., €10–13) and the restaurant's namesake is the first dish to try.

Indecision between seafood or steak can be resolved at **Il Covo** (Via del Boschetto 91, tel. 06/481-5871, Tues.–Sun. 7–11 P.M., €12–15). Risotto with cuttlefish or a hefty Chateaubriand will satisfy any craving. Two lines of tables fill a long room decorated with light wood and warm colors.

A couple that cooks together stays together, which explains the longevity of **Agata e Romeo** (Via Carlo Alberto 45, tel. 06/446-6115, Mon.–Fri. noon–3 P.M. and 7–11 P.M., €16–20). The couple in question have been serving *fusilli con radicchio e speck* and *risotto zizzania* to locals for over 30 years. The atmosphere does not distract from the food, which has a reputation for freshness and large portions. A tasting menu is available with many of the fine cheeses and wines from the cellar.

Regional

If Rome is your only stop in Italy, then at least let your stomach travel to **Trattoria Monti** (Via San Vito 13a, tel. 06/446-6573, Tues.–Sat. 12:30 P.M.–3 P.M. and 7–10:30 P.M., €12). The Camerucci clan have brought the flavors of the Le Marche region to Rome and one taste of the *tortello di rosso d'uovo* or stuffed rabbit and roast potatoes cooked in truffle oil is almost as good as being there. Like most good things, it comes in a small package; find it tucked in between Santa Maria Maggiore and Piazza Vittorio.

Seafood

Crab (Via Capo d'Africa 2, 06/7720-3636, closed Mon. lunch, Sun., and Aug., €22) is a good address for fish lovers. Quality ingredients have a price and in this case it's worth paying.

International

Not everyone likes Italian food, in which case **Maharajah** (Via dei Serpenti 124, tel.

06/474-7144, Mon.–Sat. 12:30–2:30 P.M. and 7:30–11:30 P.M., closed Sun. lunch) will be a welcome sight. All the Indian favorites like *rogan josh* and chicken tikka are on the menu as well as a variety of North Indian specialties and prix-fixe options.

Sushi has made inroads in Rome and **Hasekura** (Via dei Serpenti 27, tel. 06/483-648, Mon.–Sat. noon–2:30 P.M. and 7–10 P.M., €12–18) was one of the first to introduce sashimi and tempura to Italian palates. There's table and counter service; from counter seats you can watch chef Kimiji Ito demonstrate his knife-wielding skills. The lunch menu is light on both stomach and wallet.

Quick Bites

Panini (sandwiches) are a mainstay of the Italian lunch hour and **Fienile** (Via del Fienili 54, tel. 06/679-0849, Mon.–Tues. 8 A.M.–7:30 P.M., €5) makes a wide selection—all of which can be heated-up and eaten on the outdoor tables facing the Capitolino. This is the place for a light lunch after exploring the Forums or simply enjoying some sun with a cappuccino and pastry.

Pizza

La Gallina Bianca (Via Antonio Rosmini 9, tel. 06/474-3777, daily until late, €8–12) is a back-to-basics pizzeria where exotic toppings are frowned upon and mozzarella matters most. Pies are of the Neapolitan variety with a thick crust that is hard to resist. The house antipasto is enough food for two and makes a good starter.

Cafés

When Karol Wotila was studying theology at the Angelicum University, he took his coffee breaks at **Caffe Brasile** (Via dei Serpenti 23, tel. 06/488-2319, Mon.–Sat. 6 A.M.–8:30 P.M., Sun. noon–8 P.M.). The future Pope recognized a good roast and must have appreciated the unpretentious service.

Late-night espresso cravings can be filled at **Antico Caffe Santamaria** (Piazza di

APERITIVO

When six o'clock hunger strikes, it's time to discover happy hour Roman-style. Elegant locales present a tantalizing array of finger foods to cocktail-wielding locals – the Italian answer to tapas. The beauty of *aperitivo* is that hors d'oeuvres are included in the price of a drink and can often replace dinner.

COLOSSEO
The *aperitivo* at **Matermatuta** (Via Milano 47, tel. 06/4782-5746, Tues.-Sun., €6) starts when the sun goes down and provides Mediterranean snacks. There are over 400 types of wines available and bottles are uncorked until late.

AVENTINO AND TESTACCIO
The exotic interior and low lighting at **Ketumbar** (Via Galvani 24, tel. 06/5730-5338, daily, €8) is perfect for a romantic tête-à-téte. Well-prepared cosmopolitans become the precursor to a tantalizing cross-continental dinner.

Restaurants and bars now proliferate the post-industrial area where Testaccio meets Ostiense. **Nazca** (Via del Gazometro 40, tel. 06/574-7638, Tues.-Sun. 6:30 P.M.-2 A.M., €6-9) is one of the best. The mixed-style interior and refined happy hour are always in sync with the house DJ.

TRASTEVERE
Ombre Rosse (Piazza Sant'Egidio 12, tel. 06/588-4155, daily 7 A.M.-2 A.M. except Sun. morning, €5-8) changes throughout the day according to the hunger and thirst of its regulars. Outdoor tables await year-round along with a fine selection of whiskey, grappa, and cognac.

CAMPO DEI FIORI AND PIAZZA NAVONA
A stone's throw from the Pantheon, **Salotto 42** (Piazza di Pietra 42, tel. 06/678-5804,

daily, €7) presents an appetizing ethnic-inspired buffet in a warm reflective atmosphere. Nearby you'll also find **Caffe Universale** (Via delle Coppelle 16, tel. 06/6839-2065, daily, €8), which could easily be categorized under reading space, restaurant, or spa. Original interior design and Virginie Berre's obsession for quality ingredients satisfy both stomach and mind.

Fluid provides a dose of high tech in addition to a buffet and DJ set. The house cocktail is a safe bet and the youthful crowd linger until late. **Bar del Fico** (Piazza del Fico 26, tel. 06/686-5205, daily 9 A.M.-2 A.M., €5-8) is a good place to kick-off an evening. The Art Deco interior and extensive cocktail list provide proper sustenance for the night ahead. Drinking outdoors should be mandatory at **Bartaruga** (Piazza Mattei 18, tel. 06/689-2299, daily 3 P.M.-2 A.M., €5-8). The intimacy of the piazza and fountain is the perfect setting for falling in love.

TRIDENTE
Perhaps the most soothing place to sip a cocktail is within the enchanting garden of the **Hotel de Russie** (Via del Babuino 9, tel. 06/328-881, €10-15). Any shopping stress soon vanishes and the fragrance of the plants is reinvigorating. **Enojazz** (Via Bertolini 1b, tel. 06/808-8546, Mon.-Sat. 6 P.M.-2 A.M., €10) is 200 square meters of music, culture, and food that has energized the Roman scene. During *aperitivo*, the bar transforms into a super-buffet accompanied by wine and frozen drinks.

VATICANO
For an afternoon cocktail and up-close view of San Pietro, there's only one address. **Hotel Columbus** (Via della Conciliazione 33, tel. 06/686-5435, €10-12) provides instant tranquility from the crowds outside and service that's on par with any Swiss guard.

Santa Maria Maggiore 7a, tel. 06/446-5863), which also produces its own baked goods early every morning.

Delicacies

Your sweet tooth will smile the moment you enter **La Bottega del Cioccolato** (Via Leonina 83, tel. 06/482-1473, Mon.–Sat. 9:30 A.M.–12:30 P.M. and 3–7 P.M.). This small boutique dedicated to producing cacao in novel shapes and flavors is the place for finding an edible gift. The chocolate Colosseo beats a postcard any day.

If Italian food is famous, it's partly due to shops like **Polica Carlo** (Via dei Serpenti 150, tel. 06/488-0501, Mon.–Sat. 9 A.M.–7 P.M., closed Thurs. afternoooon), which has been selling the finest cheese, prosciutto, and pasta since 1928. For food aficionados, this place rivals the Pantheon.

AVENTINO AND TESTACCIO

Aventino is one of Rome's nicest residential neighborhoods and entirely lacking in restaurants except for what's on offer in the hotels. Visitors are better off walking downhill towards Testaccio where fifth-generation Romans live and trattorias serve the same classic dishes day in and day out. The neighborhood isn't on most people's must-see lists, so fellow diners are likely to be local and restaurants have to survive on repeat business. The area around the central market is a good place to start browsing menus.

Roman

Agustarella (Via G. Branca 98, tel. 06/574-6585, Mon.–Sat. noon–11 P.M., closed Sun., €12) is a classic Roman *osteria* in a quintessential Roman neighborhood. Adventurous palates will give the *trippa alla romana* (tripe) a try while the *rigatoni alla pajata* (rigatoni with intestines) is a safe bet for pasta lovers.

Perilli (Via Marmorata 39, tel. 06/574-2415, Thurs.–Tues. 12:30 P.M.–3 P.M. and 7:30–11 P.M., €10–14) doesn't need publicity. The owner won't answer many questions and the welcome may not be especially warm, but people who know their gnocchi from their rigatoni swear by this place and the immense portions. Large murals on the walls offer something to contemplate when conversation runs dry.

It doesn't get much more local than **Luna Piena** (Via Luca della Robbia 15, tel. 06/575-0279, Thurs.–Tues. noon–3 P.M., €8–12). The flavors are no different than what's being prepared in kitchens nearby and further proof that artichokes are underrated. No cut goes to waste and *coda alla vaccinara* (oxtail) is a delicacy here. Two dining rooms decorated with period photographs provide good atmosphere and only reservations can guarantee a table.

Historic isn't appetizing unless trattorias like **Da Felice** (Via Mastro Giorgio 29, tel. 06/574-6800, €12) are concerned. Expect to eat well, pay little, and come away satisfied.

Attention to detail is evident at **Letico** (Via Galvani 64, tel. 06/5725-0539, Tues.–Sun. 12:30 P.M.–2:30 P.M. and 7:30 P.M.–11 P.M., €9–11) from the layout of the bar to the bacon and broccoli flan. The kitchen's secret is simple: Innovate using traditional ingredients. Veal, pear, and prune au gratin is one of many successful combinations. The extensive wine list was chosen specifically to match the menu and is divided by region.

Pizza

Acqua e Farina (Piazza Orazio Giustiniani 2, tel. 06/574-1382, daily noon–12:30 A.M., €7–10) is a good place to start the search for Rome's best pizza. The "mini" option is the chance to get a taste of many toppings in a single sitting. Starters include *crostini di patate,* which uses sliced potatoes as a base for mushrooms, mozzarella, and *tartufo* (truffle). A line generally forms on weekends, but the activities on the *piazza* help time pass quickly.

Il Regno di Re Ferdinando (Via di Monte Testaccio, tel. 06/578-3725, Tues.–Sun. 7–11:30 P.M.) was one of the first Neapolitan pizzerias in the capital and continues to turn out thick-crusted pies. First-courses alternate depending on the day of the week; Saturday is devoted to lasagna. The well-manicured dining room is filled with a vivacious crowd and live music accompanies meals on some weekends. Good preparation for a night of dancing in the bars and clubs nearby.

Delicacies

Window shopping at **E. Volpetti** (Via Marmorata 47, tel. 06/574-2352, Mon.–Sat. 8 A.M.–2 P.M. and 5–8:15 P.M.) will affect your appetite. This gourmet emporium covers nearly every food group from thick-crusted breads and cured meats to freshly made pasta and dessert. Immaculately dressed attendants serve a steady stream of regulars, but don't feel obliged to buy. The smell alone is worth the visit.

TRASTEVERE

Restaurants line nearly every street in Trastevere and the wide choice can be confusing. Most serve classic Roman fare and it's hard to go wrong. Nevertheless don't stop at the first trattoria you see and don't be rushed into choosing by an over-zealous waiter.

Bakeries

Michele Tricarico (Vicolo del Cinque 35, 06/580-3886) bakes a salt-free loaf you won't find anywhere else but you'll wish you could. The secret he says is preparing the dough the night before and refreshing it the morning after like they did in the old days.

All it takes to make mouths water is stoneground wheat from an antique mill outside of Rome and an oven heated with hazelnut shells. That's the recipe **La Renella** (Via del Moro 15, tel. 06/581-7265) has been using for 130 years and the saliva hasn't stopped since.

Don't worry about the language barrier. Just point to one of the loaves of bread or array of chocolate confections and they'll understand. A bakery like **Valzani** (Via del Moro 37, tel. 06/580-3792) is never lost in translation.

Roman

Italians have a way of putting people at ease and it doesn't take long for **Da Giovanni** (Via della Lungara 41a, tel. 06/686-1514, Mon.–

PIZZA AND WATER

Finding a pizzeria in Rome is as easy as finding a cab in New York City. But like taxi drivers, some pizza is better than others. The first indication of quality is smell. The aroma of a wood-burning oven is a good sign. Then there is sight. Pizzas should be behind glass laid out in trays that have been pulled straight from the oven. There may be dozens of varieties. Simply choose the one you'd like and the approximate size of the cut. Sign language works well here, even for the locals. Your slice will be weighed as price is determined by weight. *Margherita* (tomato and mozzarella) is the cheapest and more elaborate varieties cost slightly more. You can eat your pizza on a tray within the establishment or say *"per portare via"* if you prefer take-away. Once you've found a good pizzeria, don't hesitate to return again and again.

Water is also plentiful and no one goes thirsty in Rome. It flows constantly under the city as it has for thousands of years. Here fountains can be found on nearly every street corner. Don't hesitate to stop for a drink or fill up a bottle. This water has age-old properties and fountains provide an oasis on hot summer days when the walk from Pantheon to Piazza Navona seems endless. Don't forget to splash some on your neck and face. Get refreshed before your next encounter with the city.

Sat. 7–10:30 P.M., €8–10) to feel like a second home. The menu reads pretty much like all the rest of the Roman trattorias in the neighborhood, but tastes slightly better—especially after the bill arrives. The small dining room is ungarnished of anything fashionable, which gives it instant charm.

The menu at **Da Lucia** (Vicolo del Mattonato 2, tel. 06/580-3601, Tues.–Sun. 7–11 P.M., €12–15) may seem limited but then again it's better to perfect a few age-old dishes than master none. Daily specials include *gnocchi al pomodoro* on Thursdays and regular helpings of *coniglio alla cacciatora* (roasted rabbit). The trattoria has been satisfying locals since 1938 and the street is one of the most photographed in Trastevere.

The piazza has been refurbished but **Galeone Corsetti** (Piazza San Cosimato 27, tel. 06/581-6311, Tues.–Sun. noon–3:30 P.M. and 7:30 P.M.–midnight, €12–17) remains unchanged. It's still run by the same family and still serving *bucatini all'amatriciana* using a recipe from 1927. *Spaghetti alla Corsetti* is prepared with a secret seafood sauce waiters are reluctant to discuss.

Asinocotto (Via dei Vascellari 48, tel. 06/589-8985, Tues.–Sun. 7:30–11:30 P.M., €14–18) succeeds in creating new flavors by combining ingredients generally segregated from each other. Shrimp, bacon, and avocado shish kebab with garlic soup is a case in point. The chocolate decadence dessert offers a surprise to jaded taste buds. Decor is reminiscent of Scandinavia and the tranquility inside is conducive to conversation.

Seafood

How a former rugby player switched from scrum to oven is uncertain. What is known is that the move produced one of the best fish restaurants in Rome. Fans of **Alberto Ciarla** (Piazza San Cosimo 1, tel. 06/588-4377, daily 7–11:30 P.M., €18–22) swear by the shrimp salad and spaghetti with bass.

Quick Bites

Come for the books and conversation, stay for the food at **Bibli Caffè** (Via dei Fienaroli 28, tel. 06/588-4097, closed Mon. lunch) where the offer changes throughout the day. Buffet at lunch, tea and pasticcini in the afternoon, and Roman finger food during the early evening for happy hour.

Pizza

Regulars call ◖ **Ai Marmi** (Viale Trastevere 53-57, tel. 06/580-0919, Thurs.–Tues. noon–2:30 A.M., €6–8) "the morgue" in reference to the white marble tables. The pizza is blue-chip Roman with a thin crust that doesn't disappoint. Starters include *suppli* (mozzarella-filled rice balls), fried olives, and cold platters. A large board is the only menu and displays everything available. Waiters move about frenetically and getting their attention can be a challenge.

Gelato

You can ask the gelato man at **Bar Cecere** (Via S. Francesco a Ripa 151, tel. 06/5833-2404) but all he'll tell you is that the *zabaione* is an old family recipe. It's one heirloom you can lick and it tastes even better surrounded by an almond waffle cone.

CAMPO DEI FIORI AND PIAZZA NAVONA

Rome's highest concentration of eateries are in these two neighborhoods. Restaurants around Campo dei Fiori are loud and boisterous and it's been a while since an Italian stepped into those lining Piazza Navona. Authenticity usually has some relation to the width of the street and if you want to taste the Jewish contribution to Roman cooking, head to the Ghetto where you can decide if you prefer artichokes *alla romana* (stir fried) or *alla guidea* (deep fried).

Roman

Roscioli (Via dei Giubbonari 34, tel. 06/687-5287, Mon.–Sat. 12:30–4 P.M. and 8:15 P.M.–midnight, €10–14) started out as a deli counter selling the finest cheeses and hams from France, Spain, and Italy. A good thing got better when they opened a restaurant in the back and began serving wine. Sample as much as possible.

Touristy isn't always bad, especially when classic dishes are served amidst elegant and spacious decor. That's the hallmark of **Pierluigi** (Piazza de' Ricci 144, tel. 06/686-1302, Tues.–Sun. noon–2:30 P.M. and 7 P.M.–11 P.M., €9–13) and an opportunity to discover artichokes prepared in both the Roman and Jewish styles.

Most restaurants stopped making their own bread a long time ago. That's not the case at **Ditirambo** (Piazza della Cancelleria 74, tel. 06/687-1626, daily noon–11:30 P.M., closed for lunch Mon., €15), where fresh loaves appear nightly and form a natural partnership with the wide selection of pasta dishes. It's little wonder reservations are recommended at this rustic establishment.

◖ **Sora Margherita** (Piazza delle Cinque Scole 30, tel. 06/686-4002, Mon.–Fri. 12:30–3 P.M., Fri. 8–11:30 P.M., closed Mon. winter, €8) has been written up before and they have the reviews mounted on the walls to prove it. Owners Lucia, Mario, and Ivan haven't let the attention go to their heads. This is a popular restaurant where the menu is handwritten every day and the decor won't distract you from your plate. Thursday is dedicated to gnocchi, Friday is *baccalà,* and *pasta e fagioli* remains on heavy rotation.

It would be hard to find a more historic location than **Da Giggetto** (Via del Portico di Ottavia, tel. 06/686-1106, Tues.–Sun. noon.–3 P.M. and 7:30–11 P.M., €15), where Lidia and her husband have been greeting customers with a smile for the last 50 years. Inside is a maze of spacious rooms where uniformed waiters whisk fried zucchini flowers, fish soup, and *carciofi alla giudea* from table to table.

For a sample of kosher fast food, visit **MKosher** (Via S. Maria del Pianto 64-65, tel. 06/6819-2968). Kebabs and falafel are the mainstays and taste even better when eaten on one of the nearby piazze.

Seafood

The father/son team behind **Monserrato** (Via Monserrato 96, tel. 06/687-3386, Tues.–Sun. noon–3 P.M. and 6:30 P.M.–12 A.M.) have made seafood their specialty. Romans have taken notice and the two intimate bottle-lined dining rooms fill up regularly with fish lovers.

London has fish and chips and Rome has **Filetti di Baccalà** (Largo dei Librari 88, tel. 06/686-4081, Mon.–Sat. 5 P.M.–10:30 P.M., closed Aug., €10). Here the fried cod is served

with *puntarelle* (a traditional Roman green) and the environment so refreshingly simple only cash is accepted.

International

The austere interior of **Eau Vive** (Via Monterone 85, Pantheon, tel. 06/6880-1095, Mon.–Sat. 12:30–2:30 P.M. and 7:30–10:30 P.M., €16) probably has something to do with the nuns who manage the restaurant and wished to preserve that 15th-century feeling. The menu favors exotic dishes and a moment of prayer accompanies every meal.

The chef at **L'Altro Mastai** (Via G. Giraud 53, tel. 06/6830-1296, Tues.–Sat. 7:30–11:15 P.M., €60) assisted Heinz Beck at La Pergola and it shows. The translucent stones and white flowers on the tables provide a hint of the food to come, which is unforgettable. If there's a special occasion, this is where to celebrate.

Quick Bites

Le Pain Quotidien (Via Tomacelli 24, tel. 06/6880-7727, Tues.–Sun. noon–3 P.M. and 7:30–11 P.M.) prepares a Roman version of brunch every weekend with homemade breads and eggs any way you like them. Pastries are available for lighter snacks, and stomachs suffering from jet lag will appreciate the kitchen being open until midnight seven days a week.

For a taste of quality Italian franchise food, **SquiSito** (Piazza Barberini, Tues.–Sun. noon.–3 P.M. and 7:30 P.M.–11 P.M., €12) is the answer. This is dependable Neapolitan pizza with a wide selection of self-service buffet options. While most Italian restaurants may not always operate the same hours as your stomach, SquiSito is open every day from lunch to dinner, including Christmas. Big screens display Italian soccer and international sporting events.

Pizza

Don't expect privacy at **Baffetto** (Via del Governo Vecchio 114, tel. 06/686-1617, daily 12:30–11 P.M.), where crowds wait to enjoy thin-crust pizza served by waiters with character.

COFFEE AND GELATO

One of the beautiful things about Rome is that no matter how hard you look you won't find a Starbucks. Coffee isn't about comfortable sofas and wireless Internet. It's taken seriously. The rule of thumb is pay first and drink later. Most coffee bars have a dedicated cashier who takes orders and keeps barmen focused on dispensing caffeine. Prices are posted and sitting down costs more than drinking at the counter. Romans drink coffee ritually morning, lunch, and afternoon. Espresso is the favorite style, **macchiato** does not come in a jumbo cup, **latte macchiato** is a glass of milk with a dash of coffee, and *marocchino* contains cacao and a little foam. Variations are endless, though the basic Italian roast has a consistent flavor from coast to coast. Caffeine rush hours are the best time to observe Italians with a habit.

Gelaterie are almost as common a sight in Rome as bars and pizzerias. The best will prepare their gelato in-house daily using fresh

© PURESTOCK

ingredients and offer original cream- and fruit-based flavors. Gelato can be ordered in various sizes of cones or cups with or without *panna* (whipped cream). In crowded *gelaterie* the pay-first rule may apply.

Pizza skeptics may turn their noses up at the thought of an electric oven, but that's what **Lo Zozzone** (Via del Teatro Pace 32, tel. 06/6880-8575, daily 12:30–11 p.m.) uses to produce white pizza with startling toppings. The *pizzaolo* working the dough are all veterans. Wrapped slices are good for taking away to the benches of Piazza Navona, although a few tables line the street outside.

Another takeaway option with a considerable reputation is **Il Forno di Campo dei Fiori** (Campo dei Fiori 22, tel. 06/6880-6662, Mon.–Sun. 12:30–11 p.m.). A tray of simple white or red pizza is continually being pulled fresh from the oven and salivation starts upon entrance to this small establishment. Breads are also a highlight and loaves can be cut to satisfy any appetite.

Gelato

Fresh tubs of gelato are prepared each morning at **Frigidarium** (Via del Governo Vecchio,

Navona, daily noon–2 a.m.). Pistachio and chocolate lovers should taste the Mozart flavor with *panna*. Sweet and savory crêpes are served in winter.

Lack of flavors isn't always a bad sign. What **Ciampini Lucini** (Piazza San Lorenzo in Lucina 29, tel. 06/687-3620, Tues.–Sun. noon–3 p.m. and 7:30–11 p.m.) does make it makes well and as long as the *zabaglione* (hazelnut-flavored chocolate) is plentiful there's no reason to taste anything else.

Cafés

Antico Caffè della Pace (Via della Pace 5, tel. 06/686-1216, daily 8 a.m.–9 p.m.) is a Roman institution frequented by local artists and personalities as well as visitors who fall for the beauty of its ivy-clad walls and delightful outdoor setting. Strong, aromatic coffee is standard fare at **Tazza d'Oro** (Via Degli Orfani 84, tel. 06/678-9792, Mon.–Sat. 7 a.m.–8 p.m.), where the house blend may be purchased and *granita al caffe* (iced coffee) is served during the summer months. Coffee tastes different at **Caffè Sant'Eustachio** (Piazza Sant'Eustachio 82, tel. 06/6880-2048, daily 8 A.M.–9 P.M.). The interior however hasn't changed since 1938 and neither has the unique blend prepared locally. Try the Gran Caffè (served already sweetened) or the Monachella (served with chocolate and whipped cream).

Delicacies

The specialty of **L'Antico Forno del Ghetto** (Piazza Costaguti 31, tel. 06/6880-3012, Tues.–Sun. 9 A.M.–6 P.M.) is *pane azzimo,* which is made from pizza dough and has a serious crunch to it. A variety of pastas are also available.

TRIDENTE
Roman

What **Matricianella** (Via del Leone 4, tel. 06/683-2100, Tues.–Sun. noon–3:30 P.M. and 7:30–11 P.M., €8–10) lacks in space it makes up for in wine. There are over 700 kinds, which makes choosing one of the roasted lamb dishes seem simple.

At **Maccheroni** (Piazza delle Coppelle 44, tel. 06/6830-7895, www.ristorantemaccheroni.com, daily noon–3 P.M. and 8 P.M.–midnight, €10–12), the name says it all. Expect pasta in all its Roman forms prepared within a glass-enclosed kitchen.

Fiaschetteria Beltramme (Via della Croce, Mon.–Sat. 7–11 P.M., €10–15) mixes the best of Lazio with a dash of Tuscany. The *tagliolini* and penne dishes are worth the risk of a stain and the meats are cooked in almost every way imaginable. The Rinascimento interior fills up quickly and the lack of a telephone makes showing up early or late a necessity.

There are many *osteria* with the word "Da" (of) in their name, but **Da Mario** (Vicolo Rosini 4, tel. 06/687-3434, Tues.–Sun. 12:30–3 P.M. and 7:15–10:30 P.M., closed August, €8–10) is one to look out for. The limited selection is actually a good sign and don't be surprised if your waiter forgets to bring a menu. *Pasta e ceci* (chickpea pasta) is usually served on Tuesdays and with any luck the

pollo con peperoni (chicken with peppers) will have been prepared that morning.

Regional

Tullio (Via San Nicola da Tolentino 26, tel. 06/475-8564, Mon.–Sat. noon–3 P.M. and 7–11:30 P.M.), near Piazza Barberini, is one of the best Tuscan restaurants in Rome—with the regulars to back it up. Waiters are efficient and there's an excellent price-to-quality ratio.

Watching chef Stefano Galbiati operate in the open kitchen puts a stomach immediately at ease. The ingredients he combines vary depending upon the season, but the result is always delicious at **Trattoria** (Via del Pozzo delle Cornacchie 25, tel. 06/6830-1427, Mon.–Sat. 6–11 P.M., closed Sun. €25), a modern eatery that has become a hit on the Roman gastronomic scene. The wine list is dominated by emerging Sicilian vineyards.

◖ Gusto (Piazza Augusto Imperatore 9, tel. 06/322-6273, www.gusto.it, daily noon–midnight, €8) is greater than the sum of its parts, which includes a trattoria, pizzeria, restaurant, and bookstore. The buffet brunch is the perfect break between Ara Pacis and Piazza di Spagna. The Enoteca regularly features live jazz and Brazilian evenings and the cheese bar is well stocked in Italian and French varieties served with honey and fruit.

Obikà (Piazza di Firenze, tel. 06/683-2630, daily 8 A.M.–midnight, €5 and up) is perhaps the world's first mozzarella bar with an Italian style brunch on weekends.

Tad (Via del Babuino 155a, tel. 06/326-9511, daily) isn't just a restaurant, it's also a concept store. That means a new way of shopping and a lot of attractive things to buy for the home, closet, or stereo. Rest assured the food is as tasty as the decor, and anyone concerned about healthy eating will appreciate ingredients prepared with simple flare.

Seafood

What the **Riccioli Cafè** (Piazza delle Coppelle 10a, tel. 06/6821-0313, daily until 1 A.M., €20) lacks in pasta, it makes up in oysters imported daily from Brittany. Main course options include sushi and barely cooked tuna, salmon, and trout. Indecision regarding what wine to drink can be quickly resolved with the help of the house sommelier.

Few restaurants score higher on the view-per-chew scale than **Porto Maltese** (Via di San Sebastianello 6a, 05/678-0546, www .portomaltese.com, 12:30–3 P.M. and 7:30–11 P.M., €11–14). Fortunately the seafood is as satisfying as the collage of city rooftops below, and even the check leaves a pleasant aftertaste. Walk off lunch or dinner with a stroll through the Villa Borghese.

International

If the urge for goulash and spaezle strikes there is only one place to go. The **Birreria Viennese** (Via della Croce 21, tel. 06/679-5569, daily until midnight, €12) successfully reproduces all the classic Austrian dishes within a lodge-like setting that includes a stuffed boar's head and hunting trophies.

Pizza

PizzaRè (Via di Ripetta 13, tel. 06/321-1468, daily noon–midnight, €6–10) serves some of the best Neapolitan pies in town. The large dining room is perpetually full of people eyeing the wood-burning oven with anticipation. Fried starters are excellent and if you have any room left, try one of the traditional desserts like *cassata napoletana* or *torta caprese*. Reservations are a good idea on weekends.

Pizzeria Il Leoncino (Via Del Leoncino 28, tel. 06/687-6306, daily noon–3:30 P.M. and 7–11:30 P.M., €8) bakes quality Roman-style pizza at affordable prices.

Gelato

If you're serious about gelato, sooner or later you'll be standing outside **S. Crispino** (Via della Panetteria 42, tel. 06/679-3924, daily in summer 11 A.M.–11 P.M.). The owners only serve the flavors they like, so expect lots of honey, cinnamon, and ginger. Two or three scoops can be combined, so don't forget a scoop of hazelnut.

There are almost as many *gelaterie* as bars and pizzerias in Rome.

© PURESTOCK

Giolitti (Via Uffici del Vicario 40, tel. 06/699-1243, daily in summer 11:30 A.M.–9:30 P.M.) has pioneered gelato since the early 20th century and has never strayed from the policy of fresh ingredients in every scoop.

Café

Caffè Greco (Via dei Condotti 86, tel. 06/679-1700, Tues.–Sat. 9 A.M.–7:30 P.M., Sun.–Mon. 10:30 A.M.–7 P.M.) was around long before the designer boutiques which now surround it. This is where Grand Tour stalwarts like Goethe and Stendhal drank their coffee, and portraits of many famous drinkers can be seen in the room farthest from the entrance.

VATICANO
Roman

Cacio e Pepe (grated cheese and pepper) is a classic Roman dish that sounds easy to prepare. Getting the balance and texture right, however, is an art that Italo-Indian chef Ajid Kumar has mastered and recreates nightly at **L'Arcangelo**

(Via G.G. Belli 59, tel. 06/321-0992, Mon.–Sat. 1–2:30 P.M. and 8–11:30 P.M., closed Sat. lunch, €9–12).

It's all about taste at **La Tradizione** (Via Cipro 8, tel. 06/3973-0349, 1 P.M.–2:30 P.M. and 8 P.M.–11:30 P.M., closed Sat. lunch, €10–14), where owners Valentino Belli and Renzo Fantucci go out of their way to reintroduce forgotten flavors into the daily diets of Romans.

International
Ask 100 food critics what the best restaurant is in Rome and 97 won't hesitate to name **La Pergola** (Via Cadlolo 101, Monte Mario, tel. 06/3509-2152, Tues.–Sat. 6 P.M.–midnight, closed Sun. and Mon., €75). The reason is the Mediterranean magic of Heinz Beck, who dis-penses with spices, onions, and garlic and lets the flavors of his ingenious ingredients speak for themselves. It's a feast for all senses, and includes a view from the top of the Hilton. The menu includes three prix-fixe options and a grand dessert that deserves applause. All of this comes at a price worth paying at least once in a lifetime.

Gelato
The hazelnut is good but it's the fruit flavors that have kept **Pellacchia** (Via Cola di Rienzo 103, tel. 06/321-0807, Tues.–Sun. 6 A.M.–1 A.M.) on the map. Lemons are delivered each week from the Amalfi coast and everything is made without adding an ounce of milk.

Information and Services

TOURIST INFORMATION
Azienda Di Promozione Turistica Di Roma (Via Parigi 11, tel. 06/488-991, www.aptroma.com, Mon.–Sat. 9 A.M.–7 P.M.) runs a dozen Tourist Information Points (TIPs) strategically located around the city. Each is open daily 9 A.M.–6 P.M. and operated by multilingual staff. TIP kiosks are where to pick up a free official map of the city, purchase the RomaPass, and receive a list of the month's top cultural events.

TIP locations include: Stazione Termini (Piazza dei Cinquecento), Colosseo (Piazza Tempio della Pace), Trastevere (Piazza Sonnino), Fontana di Trevi (Via Minghetti), Castel S.Angelo (Piazza Pia), and Fiumicino Airport (Terminal B).

The city's main tourist information line is 06/0608 and operates daily 9 A.M.–7 P.M. The call center provides details in English on events, shopping, restaurants, and transportation.

Consulates
If you misplace your passport, lose a friend, or need to declare a birth abroad, your consulate can help. The **United States consulate** (Via Veneto 119a/121, tel. 06/467-41) is located near the center, while the **Canadian consulate** (Via Zara, tel. 06/445-981) has a more down-to-earth location in the northwest of the city.

Lost and Found
Rome is a big city full of honest people but a wallet stuffed with euros could tempt even a saint. If you've lost something on a bus call 06/581-6040 between 7 A.M. and 6 P.M. Each line of the subway has its own lost and found office: Metro A (tel. 06/487-4309, daily 9:30 A.M.–12:30 P.M.) and Metro B (tel. 06/575-4295, daily 9 A.M.–6 P.M.).

EMERGENCIES AND POLICE
Dialing 118 in Italy equals 911 in the United States. Call that number if you break something while frolicking in the Fontana di Trevi. An ambulance with a unique siren will be on the scene in minutes.

There are a lot of uniforms on the streets of Rome. The white ones issue parking tickets, the blue ones chase criminals, and the ones carrying machine guns are after terrorists. The *vigili urbani* (white, tel. 06/888-7620) are the most common in the city and can direct you to the Colosseo, the *polizia* (blue, tel. 113) will listen to you recount how your iPod was stolen, and the *carabiniere* (blue with red stripes, tel. 112) shouldn't be disturbed.

HOSPITALS AND PHARMACIES

For less urgent matters, there are dozens of hospitals in the city center. The **Rome American Hospital** (Via Emilio Longoni 69, tel. 06/225-51) has no shortage of English-speaking doctors. **Policlinico Umberto I** (Viale del Policlinico 155, tel. 06/446-2341) is one of the largest and cures everything from hangovers to club foot.

Italian pharmacies are firmly in the 21st century and the place to find a toothbrush or something to ease the pain. They are recognizable by the green cross and operate throughout the day. To find out which ones are open on weekends or during the night, call 06/228-941.

You'll find well-equipped pharmacies on Via Cola di Rienzo 213/215 (tel. 06/324-4476), Piazza Risorgimento 44 (tel. 06/397-38166), Piazza Barberini 49 (tel. 06/487-1195), Via Nazionale 228 (tel. 06/488-0754), and Viale Trastevere 229/229a (tel. 06/588-2273).

BANKS AND CURRENCY EXCHANGE

Italian banks are generally open weekdays 8:30 A.M.–1:30 P.M. and 2:30–4:30 P.M. The lockers at the entrance are for storing keys, coins, and anything else that might activate the metal detectors and prevent you from entering. Fortunately most banks have cash dispensers on the outside where credit and ATM cards can be used to withdraw money. Fees vary and it is worth consulting your financial institution prior to departure.

There are basically three ways to obtain euros. You can exchange before you leave, upon arrival, or periodically whenever the need arises. Which method provides the best rate is the million euro question. Banks offer good rates but charge commission, while hotels

charge low commission but offer poor rates. **American Express** (Piazza di Spagna 38, tel. 800/874-333) does well on both counts. Don't worry too much, but do shop around if there are several exchange desks in the area.

Automatic exchange machines operate 24 hours a day at Fiumicino Airport and outside many bank branches in central Rome. Look for the *cambio* (exchange) sign in the window. Dedicated exchange offices like Thomas Cooke in Piazza Barberini are another option as are post offices in the city center.

MEDIA AND COMMUNICATIONS

There's nothing quite like sitting in a Roman square and reading the sports page of an American newspaper. Baseball takes on new meaning when contemplated in the shadow of Bernini or Bramante. *The International Herald Tribune* and *USA Today* are common sights within Italian newspaper kiosks, as are magazines like *Time* and *Newsweek.*

Most three-star or higher hotels come equipped with satellite television. Channels include CNN, BBC, and pay-per view films in English.

Internet

Internet cafés are common. The cost for one hour of surfing is about €3 and the most popular Internet point is the **EasyInternet** on Piazza Barberini. You can also log on at **Internet Point** (Via Gaeta 25, tel. 06/4782-3862) and **TreviNet Place** (Via in Arcione 103, tel. 06/6992-2320).

Rome has also gone wireless and anyone with a Wi-Fi-equipped laptop or PDA device can access the Internet throughout Villa Borghese. The plan is to spread coverage throughout the city in the future.

Telephone

Traditional coin-operated phones are nearly extinct in Rome and those that remain are in Termini station, subways, and the occasional bar. Today most public phones accept phone cards available in various denominations which can be purchased at *tabacchi* shops, recognizable by their distinctive black "T" sign, newsstands, and post offices. Local numbers have a 06 prefix and cost €0.10 per minute. Numbers starting with 3 are cellular and costs are higher. When calling the United States or Canada, dial 001 followed by the area code and number. To make a collect call to Canada, dial 172-1001; for the U.S., use 172-1011 (AT&T), 172-1022 (MCI), or 172-1877 (Sprint).

Cellular phone rental is another option, but prices are high and if you expect to make many local and international phone calls it is worth buying one. Reasonably priced mod-els can be purchased at electronics stores like UniEuro or Euronics or directly from network operators such as Vodaphone, Wind, and 3. Cellular service is pay-as-you-go, with cards available at newsstands or directly through ATM machines.

Postal Services

Francobolli (stamps) for standard-size postcards and letters can be purchased at *tabacchi*. Larger packages will require a trip to the post office. These are open Monday–Friday 8 A.M.–2 P.M. and Saturday 8:30 A.M.–midnight. Take a numbered ticket at the entrance and prepare for a short wait.

Getting There

BY AIR

Rome has two international airports. **Leonardo Da Vinci** (Via dell'Aeroporto di Fiumicino 320, tel. 06/65951, www.adr.it), also known as Fiumicino, is located near the sea 26 kilometers from the city. It is the main intercontinental entry point into the country with three terminals and scheduled non-stop flights to and from a dozen North American cities. Alitalia is the Italian national carrier and provides services to many of these.

The following airlines operate direct flights to Italy: Alitalia, American, Continental, Delta, Northwest, and United.

If you don't mind a brief stop in Amsterdam, Paris, or Zurich, the following airlines also fly to Rome and may be worth investigating: Air France, British Airways, Lufthansa, Swiss, or KLM.

Two train services connect the airport with the city. One is a direct link to Termini station that departs every half-hour 6:37 A.M.–11:37 P.M. and makes the return trip 5:52 A.M.–10:52 P.M. The trip takes 30 minutes. Express tickets cost €9.50 and may be purchased at the station counter or automatic ticket machines. The second train makes several stops including Ostiense, which is con-venient for anyone staying in Aventino or those who wish to avoid the crowds of Termini. The journey lasts 45 minutes and tickets cost €5. For further details consult the airport website (www.adr.it).

Ciampino (Via Appia Nuova, tel. 06/6595-9515, www.adr.it) is the smaller airport and used by charter and low-cost airlines flying to Italian and European destinations. It is simple to navigate and buses outside the arrivals hall shuttle back and forth between Termini station in Rome every 30 minutes 6 A.M.–11 P.M. Tickets cost €8 and the journey time is 35 minutes. Travelers in groups of three or four may find it worth taking a taxi. Rides into the city are fixed at €30, plus one euro per bag.

BY TRAIN

Trenitalia (www.trenitalia.com) operates the Italian rail network and runs local, intercity, and Eurostar services. The difference is speed and destination. Local trains are slow and make the most stops. Intercity and Eurostar trains are newer and link major Italian cities rapidly. All types generally have a first- and second-class option and arrive at Termini station (www.romatermini.it), which is the hub of the rail network. The station itself was remodeled in 1999 and now contains many shops and eating facilities. The large number of travelers attracts some less-than-savory characters and only train-spotters should linger. The A and B lines of the subway are downstairs and the main bus terminal is on Piazza dei Cinquecento outside.

BY CAR

If you arrive from the north on the A1 highway, exit at Rome Nord. If arrive from the south, exit at Rome Est. Both lead to the **Grande Raccordo Anulare** (GRA), or ring road, from where the center can be easily reached via the Aurelia, Flaminia, or Columbo. The GRA also leads to both of the city's airports.

Getting Around

WALKING

Rome is an immensely walkable city and the proximity of interesting sights makes this form of transportation the most convenient and rewarding. Many streets in the center are now pedestrian-only and drivers must have a permit to enter the historic center during the day. Although pedestrians do have the right of way at crosswalks, it's better to play it safe and beware of mopeds and motorcycles.

PUBLIC TRANSPORTATION

Rome offers a complete spectrum of mass transit options, including subway, trams, buses, and trains serving destinations throughout the city. The subway system is made up of two lines, Metro A and B, which intersect at Termini. Daily service begins at 5:30 A.M. and the last train departs at 11:30 P.M. (12:30 A.M. on Sat.). Six trams and hundreds of bus lines also operate day and night.

There are a variety of travel options. A single BIT ticket costs €1 and allows unlimited transfers between subway, bus, and tram for a period of 75 minutes. A full day of unlimited transfers costs €4. A three-day pass is €11. Tickets can be purchased at the automated machines within subway stations and at many *tabacchi*. They must be validated upon entry into the network.

Most of stations on Metro B are equipped with elevators, which isn't the case with Metro A; however, bus 590 follows the same route as this line and is wheelchair accessible (www.atac.roma.it, tel. 800/431-784).

The city has also recently launched **RomaPass**, which includes a map, two free entries to the museum of your choice, a program of events, and unlimited travel for three days—all for €18. The pass pays for itself and helps you avoid lines at Musei Capitolini and the Colosseo. Getting on and off city buses and trams gives you the freedom to follow your instinct and discover the city from a comfortable perspective. Try to avoid the morning and evening commuter rushes (7–9 A.M. and 5–7 P.M.).

TAXIS

If you hear drivers grumbling, it's because the mayor has made improving service a priority. A new code was established in 2007 that makes payment by credit card, air-conditioning, multilingual tariff guidelines, and smiling standard. Cabs can be useful, especially at night, and may be ordered by phone (tel. 06/8822 or 06/4994) or picked up at stands located within the larger piazze. They are not generally hailed NYC-style, but that shouldn't stop you from trying.

Journeys between Leonardo Da Vinci airport and the center are fixed at €40. Trips within the city are determined by a time-of-day/location/speed equation that even Einstein couldn't solve. A 10-minute journey from Termini to the Colosseum shouldn't cost more than €7. To contend a fare, make sure to get the receipt that specifies the route, taxi number, and amount paid.

ROME ON TWO WHEELS

All it takes is a few minutes in Rome to realize that the scooter is king. No form of transportation is as synonymous with a city and once you've experienced Rome's rush hours, narrow streets, and unexpected vistas you'll understand why. Getting from one place to another quickly is everyone's ambition here – something that Enrico Piaggio realized in 1946 with the launch of the Vespa and which Romans have embraced ever since.

Unless you're particularly adventurous, you might think scooters strictly for the natives. You'd be seriously mistaken and missing out on one of Rome's greatest thrills. For it's one thing to spend the day meandering through medieval streets on foot admiring cultural legacies, and something else entirely to feel the wind in one's face as history fades in and out of view.

Approaching the Colosseum and slowly following the long curve around Vespasiano's gift to the city or cruising along the Lungo Tevere on a warm summer evening, it soon becomes evident public transport and automobiles cannot compete. For the great advantage of the scooter lies in the access it provides. Unlike cars, which are restricted from many parts of the city center, scooterists are free to roam the narrowly veined *vias* that make up the heart of Rome. Here you can stop to admire a marvelously crafted fountain, there you can gaze upon lifelike sculptures, and a cappuccino is always just a moment away.

Of course not everything is so leisurely, and the scooter above all is practical. Everyday it gets nearly a quarter of Rome to work. Renting is a straight-forward affair for anyone with a driver's license; the real dilemma is choosing what type of scooter to saddle. Purists will shout "Vespa!" and there is good reason to believe the Piaggio originator of the phenomenon is the best option. After all, it's what Gregory Peck chose to drive Audrey Hepburn around on and is legendary enough to have spawned fan clubs from Mumbai to Buenos Aires.

Scooters, however, are never entirely without risk and riders must be wary of distracted motorists, oblivious pedestrians, cobblestones, and slick streets. Still these are nothing common sense and defensive driving cannot overcome and as any Roman scooterist will tell you a small price for such a great pleasure. As long as you avoid excessive use of the front brake, refrain from slaloming through traffic, and start slowly, you'll soon be swept into the ebb and flow of Roman traffic and enjoying a new dimension to the eternal city.

Rentals can be found at **Roma in Scooter** (Corso Vittorio Emanuele II 204, tel. 06/687-6922), **Joy Ride** (Via Cavour 199, tel. 06/481-5926), **Roma Rent** (Vicolo de' Bovari 7a, tel 06/689-6555), and **Sforza** (Via dei Caudini 2a, tel. 06/445-3691, www.sforzarent.com).

© PURESTOCK

Scooters, or *motorini,* are the most practical way of navigating the narrow streets.

DRIVING

Driving is one of the most challenging transportation options and probably more suited for leaving rather than entering the city. Cars offer little gratification unless you have hired a patient driver as well. Finding parking is a time-consuming, expensive ordeal. Anyone determined to experience life in the slow lane, however, can rent a vehicle at Termini (Platform 1, Via Marsala 29) or directly from either airport.

Options include Avis (tel. 06/481-4373), Europcar (tel. 06/488-2 854), Maggiore (tel. 06/488-0049), and Sixt (tel. 06/474-0014).

GUIDED TOURS

Many tour operators run double-decker hop-on/hop-off service, which is a good way to get an overall impression of Rome and guarantees a seat. Costs vary but the **110open,** which the city operates, is €13 per day and includes audio information in eight languages. Tickets may be purchased on-board, online (for a 10 percent discount), at TIP offices, and at Termini, where buses leave every 10 minutes on the two-hour loop.

The alternative is the **Archeobus,** which explores the origins of Rome through the Appia Antica park. Services are similar to the 110open and leave from Termini every 40 minutes. Tickets cost €8 or you may choose one of the various combination offers explained in the official map of Rome available free at information centers.

ALTERNATIVES

Before Rome became infested with cars, the horse and buggy ruled the streets. Today they've been relegated to tourist attractions and await clients near the Piazza di Spagna and Colosseo. Prices are negotiated with the driver and tours vary depending on interest. A 50-minute visit of ancient sites costs roughly €100 and can be split between up to four passengers.

If you always wanted to try a Segway, like the idea of riding a tandem, or fancy steering an electric car through narrow streets, then Rome can oblige. Many forms of alternative transport exist from unicycle to golf cart. The price isn't always a bargain but turning heads may compensate for what you spend.

Vicinity of Rome

◖ VIA APPIA ANTICA

If you start from anywhere in Rome then start on the Via Appia Antica (the Appian Way). Leave the hotel and close your eyes. Don't be distracted by traffic or Baroque. Ask to be dropped off where the Via Appia Antica passes Ciampino airport. Open your eyes. Now walk to the Circo Massimo. Soon the rough stone will make you glad you wore lightweight hiking shoes and shorts. That's assuming the weather is good, which it usually is. This is the Roman countryside pretty much as it would have been 2,000 years ago. You will notice broken bits of column, ancient plaques, and large artifacts. Roads were cemeteries in antiquity where citizens of a certain wealth and even freed slaves could erect a monument to themselves or their families. For a quick souvenir, make a char-

coal rubbing of one of monuments and have it translated when you get back.

Sights

Ancient Romans buried their dead outside the city walls and tombs are still visible along the Via Appia Antica. Early Christians followed the same practice but were laid to rest underground in passageways and galleries dug out of the soft volcanic rock. **San Callisto** (Via Appia Antica 110, tel. 06/5130-1580, Thurs.–Tues. 8:30 A.M.–noon and 2:30–5 P.M., €5) was discovered in 1849 and is the first of several catacombs in the area. It consists of five levels where 16 popes, 50 martyrs, and thousands of everyday believers spent a good part of eternity. A staircase from the church leads down to Crypt of Santa Cecilia that is decorated in

5th-century frescoes. Guides lead groups through a small section of the 19-kilometer-long network and point out urns of interest with the beams of their flashlights. It's advisable not to stray down any unlit corridors and avoid the catacombs altogether if you suffer from claustrophobia. A visit lasts approximately 40 minutes.

The first eye-openers are **Torre Selce** and **Villa dei Quintili,** where the wealthy once lived. Stop and gaze at the aqueducts. Some of the 14 thirst quenchers the Romans built are still in operation. Interesting tombs offer a foretaste of the Etruscans. **Cecilia Metella** (tel. 06/3996-7700, daily 9 A.M.–7 P.M., guided tours Sat. 10 A.M.–noon, €2 or €6 combo ticket) is the first of many monumental tombs in Rome and like the others has been transformed over the ages according to the whims of demand. Now it's a museum where the interior of an ancient grave can be examined. Further on is the **Circo di Massenzio** (€2). Private sponsorship of stadiums is another Roman innovation and this one is in better condition than its much larger cousin, the Circo Massimo. Here 10,000 regularly stood cheering their favorite charioteers.

If walking isn't your thing, hire a bicycle at the park office (Via Appia Antica 42, tel. 06/512-6314, www.parcoappiaantica.org) near Porta di San Sebastiano, where a guide and map of the area are also available. For a condensed overview, ride the Archeobus, leaving from Termini every 40 minutes. If you've made it to Via Appia Antica, you've made it to Rome and the city awaits.

Food

A bottle of wine, a loaf of bread, cold cuts, cheese, and clementines are the ingredients for a picnic. Let the Appia Antica do the rest.

There are also several restaurants lining the road. **Antica Hosteria L'Archeologia** (Via Appia Antica 139, Fri.–Wed. 12:30 P.M.–3 P.M. and 7:30 P.M.–11:30 P.M., €11–16) near the Catacombe di S. Sebastiano is one of the oldest and is a good way to start or finish a day on the Appia Antica.

GARBATELLA

Garbatella is like a village that has survived an urban onslaught. The neighborhood was conceived in the 1920s and 1930s as a working-class area with low-rise housing interconnected by extensive garden paths. Residents don't speak Italian, they speak Roman—and colorful murals demonstrate their affection to the local soccer team.

Garbatella has no sights in the traditional sense of the word and it's unlikely to show up in many guides. Sure there's a piazza based on fascist aesthetics, but the character of the people and the Roman cooking are what make it worth spending time walking these winding streets.

Food

(**Moschino** (Piazza Benedetto Brin 5, tel. 06/513-9473, Mon.–Sat. 12:30 P.M.–3 P.M. and 8 P.M.–11 P.M., €12–15) is ideally located in front of a pleasant square with a fountain where Italian teenagers idle away the hours. The interior is small and decorated with framed photos of horses and jockeys. Tables are covered in patented red-checkered tablecloths and the menu is whatever the cook happened to prepare that evening. Typical dishes include oxtail, rabbit, lentils, and artichokes *alla Romana*—simple trattoria food that's filling and will make you wish you had an Italian grandmother. After dinner, stroll through the archway next to the restaurant and along the picturesque streets of the neighborhood.

Getting There and Around

Take Metro B (direction Laurentina) or the train from Piramide to the Garbatella station. Turn right at the exit and keep walking. The scenery gets better as you move away from the modern apartment blocks and within 10 minutes you are passing under palm trees and umbrella pines. By bus take the 30 express on Via Colombo and get off at the Lazio Regional headquarters (you'll see it about five minutes after passing under the Aurelian walls). From there Via Genocchi leads to the heart of the neighborhood. The 23 bus from the Vaticano and Trastevere also works.

EUR

EUR is a suburb six kilometers south of the center that Benito Mussolini started in the 1930s. The acronym stands for the Universal Exposition of Rome, which was planned for 1942. Unfortunately the world had other priorities at the time and Il Duce's utopian dream neighborhood wasn't completed until after World War II. Buildings are monumental and covered in white marble that has aged well. In the center there's an artificial lake and the arena built for the 1960 Olympics where Rome's basketball team now play.

Sights

Palazzo della Civiltà del Lavoro (Piazza G. Agnelli) is the symbol of the area and was one of the first buildings completed. You'll understand very quickly why Romans call it the Colosseo Quadrato (square colosseum). Funny enough, the number of vertical and horizontal windows corresponds with the letters in a certain dictator's name. From the front steps there's an architecturally uniform view towards the **Palazzo dei Congressi** (Piazza John Kennedy 1, tel. 06/5451-3705), which hosts expositions and events. It's also where Rome Marathon participants pick up their numbers. The **Museo della Civiltà Romana** (Piazza G. Agnelli 10, tel. 06/592-6135, Tues.–Sun. 9 A.M.–2 P.M., €6.20) is a must for die-hard fans of antiquity and contains both a scale model of Imperial Rome and a replica of Trajan's column. The artificial lake and shops of Viale Europa are a pleasant break for anyone with time to spare.

Shopping

There is a weekly Sunday market during the summer that sells food, antiques, clothing, and knick-knacks. All the boutique stores are on Viale Europa and are likely to satisfy her rather than him.

Food

Opposite the Museo della Civiltà Romana, **Tata** (Piazza Guglielmo Marconi 11, tel. 06/592-0105, daily noon–3 P.M. and 7–midnight, €6–10) brings guests back to the present with a pleasing interior and excellent pizza. Good beer on tap.

Jet Set (Piazza Terracini, tel. 06/591-3743, daily, €9–14) on the lake serves Mediterranean at reasonable prices. Passing crew teams and kayakers provide the scenery.

Getting There and Around

EUR is 20 minutes from Termini on Metro B (direction Laurentina). The neighborhood has three stops. EUR Magliana is the first and most convenient for visiting Palazzo della Civiltà del Lavoro. The EUR Fermi and EUR Palasport stops are next to the lake and shops. The Rome–Ostia train leaves from Piramide every 15 minutes and stops at EUR Magliana. Most 700 bus lines terminate in EUR day and night. The 714 express departs from Termini and provides a different view of Rome. Once in EUR, all the sights are within walking distance, and there is a taxi stand on Viale Europa if necessary. Guided tours of the neighborhood are available with **Suerte Itinerarte** (tel. 06/4434-0160, www.suerteitinerarte.it).

◖ OSTIA ANTICA

Ostia Antica (Viale dei Romagnoli 717, tel. 06/5635-8899, winter Tues.–Sun. 9 A.M.–4 P.M., summer Tues.–Sun. 9 A.M.–6 P.M., museum daily 9 A.M.–1 P.M., €8) provides an instant sense of how the Romans lived. Unlike the ruins downtown, these are more extensive and it's easy to imagine oneself on the way to the forum.

The town was founded as a fort at the mouth of the Tiber to protect Rome from invaders. When threats faded it evolved into a major port where Egyptian grain and other materials from across the empire were stored. Ostia Antica contains many warehouses, apartment buildings, shops, temples, and one of Europe's oldest synagogues. At its peak, the population numbered nearly 100,000 and might have continued growing if the river hadn't silted up and a second port been built. The consequence was a slow decline and gradual burial that has yet to be full excavated.

There is much to ponder among the columns, sculptures, mosaics, and ancient frescoes. The

© ALEXEI J. COHEN

Ostia Antica's amphitheater

best thing to do is wander and discover. If the weather is good, a picnic among the ruins can only enhance the visit. The museum contains many of the artifacts discovered over years of digging and offers further insight into daily Roman life. A snack bar and gift shop handle all food and postcard needs.

Sights

The entrance is on the Decamanus, the Roman main street that ran from east to west. Immediately on the left are dozens of stone sarcophagi and behind these small family burial chambers where the remains of cremated relatives were placed and frequently visited. Death, however, was kept outside the city walls and cemeteries ran along the major roads.

Farther along on the right is the first of several baths, a major component of every Roman city. Climb the steps to get a better view of the various rooms and the mosaics depicting Nep-

tune. Citizens came here once a day to wash, relax, exercise, or simply to socialize.

Even if actors weren't particularly respected in Roman times, the theater was popular and Greek-style plays regularly performed. Ostia's **amphitheater** is a short distance from the baths. It's surprisingly good condition is a result of restoration during the 1930s. The theater has a semi-circular shape; the three large masks on stage once formed part of the backdrop.

From the top rows the **Piazzale delle Corporazioni** is visible. This large complex once held the offices of importers and the various guilds responsible for keeping ships afloat. The mosaics in front of each doorway were similar to modern-day neon signs and indicated the origin and business of the traders inside.

Every Roman town had its forum where the Decumanus intersected with the Cardo to form the heart of the city. This is where citizens gathered on religious or civic occasions and where business was conducted. The temple in the center was built by Adriano in the 2nd century A.D.

Adjacent to the forum are the largest baths, which include a public latrine that could still function given the urgency. The apartments nearby include the **House of Diana,** which is lined with shops and a bar where antique happy hours once took place.

Food

It's easy working up an appetite exploring the past and **Il Monumento** (Piazza Umberto 18, tel. 06/565-0021, Tues.–Sun., €13–16) has the solution. The *spaghetti monumento* is the house dish for a reason and is served with a freshly made seafood sauce. There's outdoor dining in a well-tended garden.

Getting There and Around

The train from Piramide departs every 15 minutes and takes less than 30 minutes to reach the Ostia Antica station. From there it's a five-minute walk to the entrance. Guided tours may be booked in advance and automated audio guides are available at the ticket office.

Southern Lazio

Southern Lazio is the beginning of Southern Italy and thus an entirely different zeitgeist. Careful observers will soon discover that within less than 100 kilometers flavors, dialects, and mannerisms have all subtly changed. A different architecture prevails and trains may be five minutes late. The land is also different and towns like Sperlonga and Gaeta benefit from the cleanest waters in the Mediterranean. Even closer to Rome stand the snow-capped Colli Albani mountains, exquisite summer villas, and panoramic terraces perfect for walking off the effects of a *porchetta* lunch.

TIVOLI

At the height of the empire, Rome was a crowded, noisy city. Anyone with money didn't hesitate to get away from it all and Tivoli was the obvious choice. The air was clean, the water was pure, and having a villa here became a point of prestige for the Roman elite. The town continued to attract wealthy families during the Renaissance and the villas and gardens they built are the main draw today.

Sights

A good example of country living is **Villa Gregoriana** (Largo Massimo, tel. 06/3996-7701, daily 9:30 A.M.–sunset, €4). The steep gardens were built around the River Aniene, and the cascade that Pope Gregory XVI constructed falls an impressive 160 meters. There are various natural grottoes from which to view the waterfall, as well as two Republican era temples.

Las Vegas may have succeeded in reconstructing the Eiffel Tower and Piazza San Marco, but **Villa d'Este** (Piazza Trento, tel. 07/7431-2070, winter Tues.–Sun. 9 A.M.–4 P.M., summer Tues.–Sun. 9 A.M.–6:30 P.M., €6.50) remains beyond imitation. Cardinal Ippolito d'Este wanted a unique garden and he got one. From the loggia of the villa the number of fountains lining the terraced slopes is uncountable. Whichever graveled path you choose will feature intricate waterworks and fountains with a sense of humor. Bernini's Fontana del Bicchierone is the Tiber and Tiberina in miniature. Viale delle Cento Fontane is lined with 100 spitting gargoyles and other grotesque creatures covered in a thick layer of moss. The lowest level of the garden is planted with flowerbeds and is a peaceful place from which to admire the Roman countryside below.

If you haven't gotten your fill of antiquity, then it's time to take things to the next level. **Villa Adriana** (tel. 07/7453-0203, daily 9 A.M.–1 hour before sunset, €8.50) was the summer residence of one of the empire's most memorable men. Adriano was a poet, philosopher, and architect whose pet projects included the wall that bears his name in Northern England. No expense was spared when it came to building his own villa in A.D. 118–134. All the familiar elements are present: two immense baths, a stadium, and a swimming pool that has no comparison even by today's standards.

Although it suffered a similar plundering to that of the Colosseo, its sheer size meant much remained for archeologists to uncover. The **Teatro Greco** is perhaps the best conserved building of the complex and the luxury box where Adriano once sat and watched plays being performed still stands. The **Teatro Marittimo** devoted to aquatic performances nearby is surrounded by water and contains a small island the Emperor used for meditation.

The villa requires several hours to fully navigate and it's worth buying a map on sale at the ticket office. You may also want to study the scale model in the snack bar to become familiar with the site. There are several marked itineraries, which last 1–3 hours.

Festivals and Events

Ceramics, metallurgy, and carpentry are all actively practiced in Tivoli. **The Fiera dell'Artigianato di San Giuseppe** (tel. 07/7431-7278) on March 19 is the opportunity to learn about the skills needed to perform these crafts, as well as purchase some one-of-a-kind objects.

Two colorful processions celebrate the **Festa dell'Assunta** (tel. 07/731-7192) on August 14 and 15. One carries the sacred image of the Madonna and the other that of the Savior. After a number of ritual events around town, the two groups meet up in Piazza Duomo.

The **Sagra del Pizzutello** is held on the third Sunday in September. An assortment of breads is available in Piazza Garibaldi to be sampled. Each of the town's four *rione* (neighborhoods) takes part in an historic parade that includes acrobatics, folkdance, and the *palio* (horse race) which caps the day.

Shopping

A short distance from the center lies **L'Ape Artigiana** (Via Empolitana 238, tel. 07/7433-0956, hours and days of operation vary—call in advance) and thousands of hardworking bees. You'll find a range of honey and wax products all naturally made in organic hives the owner cares for personally.

Accommodations

Adriano (Via Villa Adriana 194, tel. 07/7438-2235, www.hoteladriano.com, €95–140 s/d) was an obvious name for this hotel located near the villa, and the Emperor would have approved of the service and atmosphere. Activities include tennis, art, and cooking classes. The restaurant provides a mix of tradition and innovation most notably demonstrated in the roast rabbit.

Food

In the heart of medieval Tivoli, **La Ronda** (Via D. Giuliani 22, tel. 07/7431-7243, Tues.–Sun. 7–11:30 P.M., €12–15) prepares creative dishes with a variety of fish options. Summer is the best time to appreciate the views from the terrace.

The Dedoni sisters aren't so concerned with decor; what matters at **Antica Hosteria De' Carrettieri** (Via D. Giuliani 55, tel. 07/7433-0159, Thurs.–Tues. 12:30–2:30 P.M. and 7:30–10:30 P.M., €9–13) is the food. What

is served has a Sardinian flavor, which means hearty pastas and roast pig. The blueberry pie is almost too good to share.

La Buca di S. Antonio (Vicolo Sant'Antonio 19, tel. 07/7431-8961, daily 12:30 P.M.–3 P.M. and 7–10 P.M., €7–11) serves classics like *pollo alla cacciatora* (roast chicken) at lunch and pizza in the evening. It's a relaxed, family-run trattoria that's hard to find without a map.

For an *aperitivo* or gelato, try **Loft** (Piazza Garibaldi, tel. 07/7431-1853, daily 11:30 A.M.–9 P.M.), which presents the modern side of Tivoli inside or on the terrace, from where all the action of the piazza is visible.

Information

The tourist office is in Piazza Garibaldi (tel. 07/7431-1249) and provides maps as well as information on upcoming cultural events held throughout the year.

Getting There and Around

Trains from Rome make the short journey from Termini and Tiburtina stations every half-hour and let passengers off at the Tivoli station on Viale Mazzini from which Villa Gregoriana and D'Este are a 15–20 minute walk away. Cotral buses leave from Ponte Mammolo Metro B direction Rebibbia and take under an hour to reach Largo Saragat in Tivoli. Villa Adriana is 6 kilometers outside of town and can be reached with local bus number 4.

FRASCATI AND THE CASTELLI ROMANI

You might not associate Rome with mountains, but just a short distance outside of the city perched high above the capital are the Castelli Romani and the town of Frascati, which lies at the center of the region. The Castelli are famous for crisp white wine, fabulous villas, and Popes who enjoy spending their summer holidays away from the heat of the city.

Sights

Frascati is the largest of the Castelli Romani towns and the closest to Rome. From the main square there is an unimpeded view of the plain below and the sea in the distance. The privileged position attracted wealthy families who built a succession of ornate villas. Many of these are now open to the public and **Villa Aldobrandini** (Piazzale G. Marconi, tel. 06/942-0331, Mon.–Fri. 9 A.M.–1 P.M. and 3–5 P.M., free admission) near the center includes an extensive garden.

Castel Gandolfo (Piazza della Libertà, www.castelgandalfo.org, closed to the public) is famous for being the Pope's summer residence. The **Palazzo Papale** where he stays benefits from the same status as the Vaticano and every Sunday morning in August he appears on the balcony to bless the faithful who converge on the town. The nearby streets benefit from a view of the Albano Lake and there is no shortage of restaurants serving the local white Marino wine and lake fish.

Nemi is one of the smallest towns in the Castelli and perhaps the most picturesque. It overlooks the lake of the same name and was possessed by religious orders, cardinals, and aristocrats. **Palazzo Baronale** and **Santuario del Crocefisso** are reminders of that past and worth a look. Equally interesting is the **Museo delle Navi** (Fiamicino, Via A. Guidoni 35, tel. 06/652-9192, Tues.–Sun. 9 A.M.–1:30 P.M. and 2:30–6:30 P.M., €2)that contains remains of several Roman ships Caligula had built for the celebrations that were once held on the lake.

Festivals and Events

The **Sagra delle Fragole** in Nemi is one of the most popular of the Castelli festivals and held on the first Sunday in June. Local girls in typical dress distribute two tons of strawberries that have been marinated in wine. Music and folk demonstrations are held throughout the day, which ends with a fireworks display over the lake.

Food

Innovation and over 80 years of cooking tradition go together at **Cacciani** (Via Diaz 15, Frascati, tel. 06/941-9415 or 06/942-0378, Tues.–Sun. 12:30–3 P.M. and 7:30 P.M.–11:30 P.M., €15). Waiters know what you want before you do and the cellar matches up well with the menu.

Zarazà (Viale Regina Margherita 45, Frascati, tel. 06/942-2053, Tues.–Sun. noon–2:30 P.M. and 7–11 P.M., €9–12) is family run and the menu changes according to what they feel like eating. There's a penchant for pasta and you can count on *gnocchi alla romana* every Thursday.

If you want to wash the view down with a little wine, **Enoteca Frascati** (Via Diaz 42, tel. 06/941-7449, Tues.–Sun. 7 P.M.–1 A.M., closed Aug., €8) will do the trick. There are over 400 wines and a range of light foods to enjoy in a rustic atmosphere.

Getting There and Around

Frascati is the best connected of the Castelli towns and visitors can choose between bus or train service. All Cotral buses to the area leave from Anagnina Metro A (direction Anagnina). Service to Frascati is frequent, while buses to Castel Gandolfo depart every two hours and Nemi several times per day.

PARCO NAZIONALE DEL CIRCEO

Southern Lazio really begins after Latina and once you've reached Circeo you know you've made it. Italy's smallest national park was founded in 1937 and offers unique natural and archeological delights. The 8,500 hectares includes four distinct habitats as well as the island of Zannone, populated by a colony of Moufflon goats and migratory birds.

Sights

Choosing what to do isn't easy and the best place to start is the **Centro Visitatori del Parco** (Via Carlo Alberto 107, tel. 07/7351-8106, www.parks.it/parco.nazionale.circeo, daily, hours vary according to the season, free) just outside the town of Sabaudia. The center has information on all the itineraries available, as well as a small museum (€1.55) and library. Tours and bike rental can be arranged.

Anyone who enjoys a good hike will find

Monte Circeo hard to resist. The 541-meter-tall mountain is covered in Mediterranean shrub and dwarf palms. Getting to the top takes over an hour and all the paths along the promontory are well marked. Many of these are quite steep and several lead down to the sea.

There are several guided tours of the area's 54 caves, including **Grotta Guattari,** where Neanderthal remains were discovered. Walks or bicycle rides along the 24 kilometers of sand dunes are another option and bird-watchers can expect to spot flamingos, falcons, and woodpeckers that inhabit Italy's last remaining plain forest.

Remains of emperor Domiziano's luxurious villa are also located within the park and a short boat ride from Sabaudia brings visitors to the lakeside retreat where first century VIPs once frolicked. Tours must be arranged in advance by calling the visitor center or **Coop Mela Cotogna** (Largo G. Cesare 12, Sabaudia, tel. 07/7351-1206).

Sabaudia was one of the new cities founded in Italy during the 1930s and 1940s. Its main attractions are the park, for which it provides a natural point of departure, and the rationalist architecture most evident in Piazza del Comune.

Festivals and Events

At the end of May, hundreds of cyclists participate in the **Ciclonatura** (tel. 07/7351-5046), a-round-the-park bicycle excursion along the most suggestive trails.

During the third week of June, a large oven is placed in Sabaudia's central square, and bakers demonstrate their bread-, pizza-, and dessert-making skills. Participants are encouraged to taste local products and to try making dough from scratch. It's not as easy as it may seem.

The **Vendemmiata** (tel. 07/7351-4258) in Borgo Vodice is held on the second Sunday in September. If you always wanted to know how wine was made in the past, this is your chance to find out. The day consists of following the traditional production process. Grapes are pressed and antique tools demonstrated. It's

also a time to taste local flavors and watch a bit of folk-dancing.

San Felice Circeo is the site of the **Sagra del Pesce Azzurro** during the second week of September. The peach celebrated is a local variety grown near the sea and easy to conserve. During the festival, large quantities are cooked in the main square and distributed freely along with the local Moscato wine. The festival is an opportunity to taste traditional seafood dishes. For one day, everything served is based around fish.

Sports and Recreation

Stabilimenti are what Italians call beach-front resorts that offer everything from chaise lounges and umbrellas to seafood and water sports. Kite surfing has become popular in recent years and practitioners are a common sight rising and falling above the waves. **Kite-surf** (Via Lungomare 10, tel. 340/593-7330) can help initiate beginners and provide everything veterans need to practice this sport.

Saporetti (Via Lungomare, Torre di Paola, 07/7359-6024, daily in summer) is a star among *stabilimenti* and caters to many interests. You can lie on the beach with a good book, dine on freshly grilled swordfish, or windsurf. What makes it memorable is a stunning location below Monte Circeo and a kitchen that values simplicity over anything too elaborate.

Accommodations

The **Mini Hotel Saporetti** (Corso Vittorio Emanuelle 120, tel. 07/7351-5987, www.saporetti.com, €71–122 s/d) is a family establishment minutes from the center of town. All rooms have air-conditioning and the restaurant serves breakfast to late risers.

If stress is the problem, the **Oasi di Kufra** (Lungomare km 29,800, tel. 07/735-191, www.oasidikufra.it, €200–260 s/d) is the solution. It's a big hotel with three restaurants and rooms on the sea have their own balconies. The fitness area includes a gym, sauna, and indoor pool.

Food

Mother, father, and children all participate in the smooth running of **La Colomba** (Via degli

Artiglieri 11, tel. 07/7351-5028, Wed.–Mon. 12:30–3 P.M. and 7–10:30 P.M., €12–15). Fish specials are all cooked *al sale* (in rock salt) and it's hard not to appreciate the beautiful garden with a view of the nearby lake.

The piazza outside **Al Vecchio Mercato** (Piazza S. Barbara 13, tel. 07/7351-8815, Tues.–Sun. 12:30–2:30 P.M. and 7–10:30 P.M., €13–18) is alive with concerts, markets, and other events during the summer. Inside, fish soups prevail and *rombo con patate* (turbot and roast potatoes) comes out of the kitchen nearly every five minutes.

Getting There
Cotral buses leave daily from Laurentina Metro B (direction Laurentina) 8:45 A.M.–7 P.M. and drop passengers off in Piazza Oberdan. The trip takes two hours and cost €3.80. Buses in the opposite direction operate 5:50 A.M.–6:25 P.M. Drivers should take the Pontina SS 148 and exit onto the SS 184 before Latina. Stay on this road for 25 kilometers until you see the signs for Sabaudia.

Around Parco Nazionale del Circeo
Not all villages are eternal. Some are simply abandoned, the last inhabitants pass away, and all that remains is stone. That's what happened to **Ninfa** (Doganella di Ninfa, tel. 07/7363-2231, giardini-ninfa@liberi.it, Apr.–Nov. 9 A.M.–6 P.M., opening days vary, €8). Fortunately the Caetani family members were dreamers and in 1921 they transformed the area into a botanical park. Today the town is alive with visitors admiring streams, waterfalls, and gardens framed by medieval ruins.

TERRACINA
Terracina marks the fine line between Northern and Southern Italy and for years was the border between the Vaticano and the Kingdom of Naples. Most of the points of interest are in the high part of town where Roman and medieval structures alternate in the **Piazza del Municipio**. The Republican forum once located here has been replaced by a medieval

tower and the Palazzo Venditti. Along the Via Appia Antica is the **Chiesa del Salvatore,** designed in a neoclassical style by the same hands responsible for Piazza del Popolo in Rome. The modern town located near the sea caters to visitors looking for a place to eat and lie on the beach.

Sights
The 11th-century **duomo** was built on the remains of a Roman temple and the original steps are still visible. Keep your eyes on the ground as the pavement mosaics that begin in the portico and continue along the nave are nearly perfectly preserved.

Across the way housed in the town hall is the **Museo Archeologico** (Piazza Municipio, tel. 07/7370-2220, Mon.–Sat. 9:30 A.M.–1:30 P.M. and 3–7 P.M., €3). The entire museum displays Greek and Roman finds from the area, including several sculptures from the hilltop temple nearby.

A panoramic route starts at the entrance of the old town and skirts the medieval walls and towers towards the top of Mount Sant Angelo, which rises 277 meters. From there you get an unobstructed view of the sea. Nearby are the remains of the **Giove Anxur temple** built in A.D. 78. Although only the foundation and 12 columned arches are still standing, the location remains impressive.

Entertainment and Events
A regular antiques market is held the third and fourth Sunday of each month in Piazza del Municipio. Prices are better than those in Rome and most of the furniture dates from the 1900s.

Accommodations
Torino (Via Lungolinea Pio VI 70, tel. 07/7370-4080, €57–114 s/d) is a centrally located three-star hotel. Rooms are large and give onto a pleasant palm-lined garden. Full board is available at a reasonable rate and the basketball court is a welcome surprise.

The **Fiordaliso** (Via Terracina-Circeo, km 10,800, tel. 07/7378-0897, www.hotelfiordaliso.it, €90–120 s/d) is just the right size: big enough to provide all the services necessary and small enough to keep the restaurant and pool from overcrowding. Most guests spend their time 200 meters away on the beach. A shuttle service connects the hotel with the center of Terracina.

Food

Bottega Sarra (Via Villafranca 34, tel. 07/7370-2045, Thurs.–Tues. 1–3 P.M. and 7–11 P.M., €10–13) is named after the owner, who spends most of the day in his kitchen preparing fish-based pastas. The restaurant is small, so it's better to be safe and make a reservation.

Il Caminetto Enoteca (Via Marconi, tel. 07/7370-2623) near Piazza Napoli is the place to try local wines before or after watching the sunset from the boardwalk.

L'Incontro da Baffone (Via Appia Antica, km 104.5, tel. 07/7372-6007, Apr.–Sept. daily noon–3 P.M. and 7 P.M.–midnight, €9–14) is located a couple of kilometers outside of town directly on the sea. Ask for a table by the window or outside if the weather is good and put your faith in the house wine meant to be drunk with the catch of the day.

Getting There

Terracina is the last stop for Cotral buses from Rome Laurentina Metro B (direction Laurentina). Service runs Monday–Saturday 10 A.M.–5:15 P.M. There are only two departures on Sunday at 8:15 A.M. and 9:45 A.M. The journey takes two hours and 20 minutes and costs €4.40. Train service from Termini is slightly more frequent and terminates at Monte S. Biago, a short way from the center of town. Drivers can choose between the Via Appia SS 7 or Pontina SS 148 and SS 184.

SPERLONGA

The first tourists to Sperlonga were the ancient Greeks, who were attracted by clear waters and pristine beaches. Roman emporers also saw the advantages of spending their summers here and Tiberio went so far as to build himself a luxury villa. The old town is full of narrow, sloped streets from which the sea can be occasionally glimpsed and where bars and restau-

rants outnumber anything else. On the shores below are dozens of *stabilimenti* (beach resorts) where swimmers enjoy some of the cleanest waters in Europe.

Sights

From the port with its typical fishing boats and old-timers discussing the weather you can make out the cave where archeologists discovered Tiberio's art collection. Much of it has been restored and placed in the **Museo Archeologico Nazionale** (Via Flacca, tel. 07/715-4028, daily 8:30 A.M.–7 P.M., €2), which borders the site.

Festivals and Events

The first weekend of September is the time to celebrate Sperlonga's patron saints. If it's been a good year, the **Festa di San Leone e San Rocco** will be a little more raucous than usual, if it hasn't the town still puts on a good show in the hope of better things to come.

The weekly vegetable and fruit market is held every Saturday and is the best way to understand the nature of the town's inhabitants.

Summer nights mean open-air dancing and the best places for that are **Valle dei Corsari,** located just outside of town near the Roman villa, and **Al Fortino** (Via Flacca, km 16,000) on Bazzano beach.

Shopping

The question at **Le Terraglie** (Via Tiberio 2, tel. 07/7154-8284) is not what can be recycled but what can't be recycled. They've managed to turn pretty much everything that is usually regarded as trash into something worth buying.

Ceramics south of Rome have a different character than those in the north. Here the Greek influence is stronger and objects are more practical than artistic. **Ceramica da Giulia** (Via Orticello, tel. 07/7154-9380) continues the tradition selling vases, cups, and plates that are equally suitable behind glass or on a dining table.

Sports and Recreation

The small lakes of S. Puoto and Lago Lungo near town are known as "the eyes of Sperlonga" and have become havens for water-skiers. All levels can get their feet wet with the **Associazione Sportiva Sci Nautico Laghetto** (Via Flacca, km 11, tel. 07/7154-9655), which organizes lessons for children and adults.

The white sands typical of the area stretch for 10 kilometers in either direction of town. To the north, the most notable beaches are Bambole, Capovento, and Bazzano. Southern beaches include Canzatora and Amyclae. Although it may seem like an odyssey choosing one, they all border a calm, crystalline sea. Most are reached by Via Flacca, which runs from Terracina to Sperlonga.

Accommodations

The **Marconi** (Via S. Rocco 24, tel. 07/7154-8006, www.hotelmarconi.com, €80–160 s/d) is a comfortable place to come back to after a day spent on the nearby beach. The family run hotel is covered in vegetation and eight rooms benefit from sea views.

Elegance is not an afterthought at the **Virgilio Grand Hotel** (Viale Primo Romita 33, tel. 07/7155-7600, www.virgiliograndhotel.it, €170–250 s/d). It's the first thing they think about, from the position of the complimentary soaps to the freshly pressed uniforms worn with a smile. Getting lost on the way to the beach is impossible considering the sea is only 200 meters from the hotel.

Hostels are not very common in this area especially ones this close to the sea. The **Marina Degli Ulivi** (Via Fiorelle, tel. 07/7155-7031) provides clean rooms some with their own bathrooms and a full-board option. The owners are friendly and eager to help in anyway they can.

Food

In the center of the old town, **Gli Archi** (Via Ottaviano 17, tel. 07/7154-8300, Thurs.–Tues. noon–2:30 P.M. and 7:30–10 P.M., €10–13) is surrounded on all sides by arches. This is where to sample the Mediterranean diet without any garnish. First courses are notable and the waiter who suggested *linguine alle telline* (linguini with clams) knew what he was talking about.

Any restaurant that started out as a place where fishermen cooked their own catch is worth knowing about. **(Grotta dei Delfini** (Via Angolo 24, tel. 07/7154-8027, daily in summer noon–3 P.M. and 7–11:30 P.M., €12–15) wears its authenticity with pride and the fish they serve are as fresh as it gets. Wine should not be an option here.

Getting There and Around

By train, take the Rome–Naples line from Termini to Fondi. There will be a bus waiting at the station that completes the remaining 15-minute journey to Sperlonga. Cotral bus service from Laurentina Metro B (direction Laurentina) goes as far as Terracina, from where a local bus departs every half-hour for Sperlonga. Drivers should continue past Terracina on the Via Flacca SS 213, which follows the coast. Parking is difficult during the summer beach invasion.

GAETA

The Golf of Gaeta is the last stretch of coast in Southern Lazio, where Ulysees and Enea once struggled to find their way home and where thousands flock today to the seven beaches that have rendered the area famous. The town itself was the last capital of the Kingdom of Naples before the unification of Italy in 1861 and contains many fine monuments.

Sights

The **duomo** rises along the *lungomare* (seafront) and is dedicated to S. Erasmo. The Romanesque structure is the result of renovation and expansion of a smaller church on the same sight in the 8th century. The interior features a Baroque altar, numerous paintings, and a variety of sacred treasures. The tower that flanks the building is a 13th-century addition built in a Norman style.

Although Gaeta's churches are impressive, it's nature that inspires the most awe. Several kilometers from the center is a place cliff divers dream about, although they would probably hesitate to jump. The **Montagna Spaccata** (Santuario della Trinità, tel. 07/7146-2068, daily 8:30 A.M.–noon and 3 P.M.–sunset) is literally a mountain split in two overlooking a vertiginous drop to the sea.

Festivals and Events

Pizza tastes different in Southern Lazio and the **Sagra della Tiella** is the best time to sample the local variety covered in onions, calamari, and *polipi* (octopus). It all happens on the last Sunday in May throughout the medieval neighborhoods of Piazza Traniello and Piazzetta del Leone.

The most important religious festival is dedicated to the town's patron, S. Erasmo, on June 2. Costumes are dusted off and a parade through the town ends with a collective feast.

Shopping

It always feels like Christmas inside **Costantino Buonomo's** (Via XI G. Caboto 9, tel. 07/7146-2457) store. In June or November, you'll find him thinking about the nativity and putting together detailed handmade scenes in all shapes and sizes.

Food

Sometimes good things are hard to find. Keep searching for **La Cianciola** (Vico, 2 Buonomo, 16, tel. 07/7146-6190, €12–14), which is hidden up a quiet side street. They serve great pastas with shellfish in an atmosphere that's conducive to romance.

Getting There

There is no direct rail or bus service to Gaeta from Rome. Travelers must take a local or Intercity train to Formia on the Rome–Naples line from Termini (€8). At the Stazione di Formia catch the local bus that leaves every 15 minutes for Gaeta. By car take either the A1 autostrada (€2) south and exit at Cassino on the SS 630 towards Formia or the slightly slower but more direct Pontina SS 148 and 184, which run parallel to the coast.

LE ISOLE PONZIANE

Le Isole Ponziane, or Pontine Islands, are a small archipelago 50 kilometers from Gaeta.

They were formed by volcanic eruptions and have been a popular summertime destination since Roman antiquity. The only inhabited islands are **Ponza** and **Ventotene,** where beaches and clear, clean water continue to attract visitors.

Ponza

Ponza is the larger of the two and ferry boats dock in the small town of the same name dominated by the lighthouse. Tourism dates from two millennia ago and today leisure is not lacking. The main attractions are connected with the sea. Wind and waves have carved out impressive caves and left sandy beaches. The longest and most crowded during the summer is **Chiaia di Luna.** Take a taxi (Giuseppe Feola, tel. 07/71808514 or 349/062-5220, €10) there or better yet rent a boat from one of the dozens of operators. If your nautical skills are above par, you could even make the five-kilometer journey to **Palmarola,** where the beaches have more of a deserted feel and service is limited to grilled fish during the summer.

Some of the best sights are below the sea and scuba excursions for all levels can be arranged. The **Aqualand Diving Center** (Via Dante, tel. 07/7180-9799, Mar.–Sept., €33 per diver) introduces divers to the colorful Mediterranean fauna below the surface.

A day trip is possible to Ponza, but you'd miss out on the sunset and the feeling that only comes from waking up on a small island. **Villaggio dei Pescatori** (Via Forna Grande, Le Forna, tel. 07/7180-9024, www.villagio-deipescatori-ponza.it, €190 d) helps cultivate that feeling. Full and half-board is available. The hotel minibus will pick you up at the port and the bar and restaurant will handle your gastronomic needs.

Ventotene

Ventotene is the wilder of the two islands. There is less of everything except nature. Fishing, sailing, diving, or simply relaxing are the options of the day. Novice sailors can learn how to tie knots at the **Circolo Velico Ventotene**

(Via Calarossano, tel. 07/718-5336) sailing school. The ancient Roman fish farm and cisterns dug into tolfa rock are reached by foot or from the surrounding sea, which was declared a natural reserve in 1999. Boats can be easily hired directly at the port and the island circumnavigated in under an hour or until you decide to set anchor in one of the hundreds of secluded coves. September 19 and 20 is Santa Candida, when dozens of hot-air balloons converge on the island.

Agave & Ginestre (Via Calabattaglia, www. ventotene.net, €110–160 s/d) is an out-of-the-way hotel on an out-of-the-way island. The private beach and gardens will relieve any residual stress. The restaurant serves the island's typical lentil and lobster dishes.

Getting There
Ferries, hovercraft, and catamarans to the islands leave from Anzio, Terracina, Circeo, and Formia in Lazio and Ischea and Naples in Campagnia. There is also a connection between the two islands. Service varies depending on the season, with most activity running March–September. Motor vehicles can also be transported on most ferries and year-round service departs from Formia. **Linea Caremar** (tel. 07/712-2710) leaves daily at 9 A.M. and 5:30 P.M. for Ponza (€13) and 9:15 A.M. (€10) for Ventotene. The journey takes around two hours and 20 minutes. **Linea Vetor** (tel. 07/7170-0710) makes the trip in half the time and at double the price. The islands' respective tourist offices operate during the summer (Ponza IAT, tel. 07/718-0031, Ventotene IAT, tel. 07/718-5257).

ITRI
It's said that the residents of Itri have one of the highest life expectancy rates in Italy. The inclined streets and excellent olive oil probably have something to do with that. The town sits on the slopes of the Arunci Mountains 10 kilometers from the sea. The rough terrain was a natural hideout and bandits made Itri famous in the 18th century. Today the medieval castle and nearby sanctuary are the main attractions.

Sights
Il Castello (tel. 07/717-321) is in good condition and looks like it could still withstand a siege. Two towers remain, one circular and the other square from which archers once aimed.

It's hard to believe Itri had any vital strategic importance during World War II, and yet it was bombed. **Santa Maria Maggiore** took a direct hit but fortunately the 12th-century bell tower survived.

Museo del Brigantaggio (Corso Appio Claudio 268, tel. 07/7172-1061, Tues.–Sun. 4–8 P.M., €2) recounts the town's bandit past, most of which centers around Michele Pezza, better known on wanted posters as Fra Diavolo. He was part patriot, part bad guy, and is still a topic of conversation.

Entertainment and Events
Two weeks before the **Festa di San Giuseppe** (Piazza Umberto 1, tel. 07/7172-1223), piles of wood start appearing around the streets of Itri. By March 19, everything flammable has been piled up into a huge mound that's lit late in the evening. There's singing, dancing, and drinking. The local *zeppole* dessert is served and when the flames go out the night ends with courageous leaps over glowing charcoals. It's also customary to save a bit of ash for use in the following year's bonfire.

On the second weekend in June, the **Infiorata Trana** (Via della Repubblica, tel. 07/7173-2107) transforms Itri into a giant bouquet. Streets are covered with petals depicting all sorts of scenes. A sampling of the local produce is also organized.

Itri olives taste different. They get their special flavor from the perpetually mild climate and calcium-rich soil. During the **Sagra della Oliva Itrana** on the second or third Sunday of August (tel. 07/7131-1057), they can be tasted in all their forms.

Accommodations
Hotel Il Grottone (Corso V. Emanuele II 2, tel. 07/7172-7014, €60 d), is a two-star hotel in the center of Itri, but if you've come all this

way you probably won't mind going a little further for something special. The ⟨ **Mandarita** (Mandra d'Itri, tel. 07/7172-9186, www.mandrarita.it, €56–92 s/d) is an *agriturismo* (farmhouse accommodation) where olive oil is produced and livestock raised. Guests can lend a hand or relax by the pool and wait for dinner to be served.

Food

Crime may not pay, but it does help build an appetite. The **Enoteca Sii pur Brigante** (Via Ripa 5, tel. 07/7172-1594, €8–12) frees your stomach from hunger with cheeses aged in olive oil and wine from the keg.

Getting There

Itri is on the Rome–Naples rail line and there are several departures each morning from Termini station. Drivers have the advantage of being able to explore the surrounding country, which gets less attention than the areas around the coast. Take the Pontina SS 148 through Terracina and the Via Appia SS 7 the rest of the way.

Around Itri

Twelve kilometers from Itri on the SS 82 is the **Santuario della Madonna della Civita** (tel. 07/7172-7116, daily 7:30 A.M.–12:30 P.M. and 3–7:30 P.M.). The sanctuary continues to attract pilgrims and visitors curious about the collection of ancient tablets and great views of the surrounding countryside.

CASSINO

Cassino is famous for its Benedectine abbey and the hard-fought World War II battle that was waged here over several months and completely devastated the area. The town's original name was Casinum and dates from A.D. 8, when the Osca tribes inhabited the area. The Romans eventually got wind of the healthy waters and tranquil setting and colonized the town in A.D. 309.

Sights

The **Abbey of Montecassino** (daily 8:30 A.M.–12:30 P.M. and 3:30–5 P.M., until 6 P.M. in summer, high mass at 9 A.M., 10:30 A.M., and noon) was founded in 529 by Saint Benedict and has been a spiritual center ever since. The compound was completely rebuilt after World War II and can be visited along with the Polish, English, and German military cemeteries that testify to the absurdity of war.

The archeological zone is southwest of the town and includes the **Cappella del Crocifisso** (inside the Parco Archeologico Casinum, Via Montecassino Km 0.800, tel. 07/7630-1168, daily 9 A.M.–5 P.M., €2), where the first interment was carried out in 107 B.C. Remains of 11th-century frescoes can still be seen. Nearby is the **Museo Archeologico Nazionale** (Statale Montecassino, tel. 07/7630-1168, daily 9 A.M.–7 P.M., €4) which contains both prehistoric and Roman artifacts gathered from the surrounding area. A Roman road leads to an amphitheater and second theater still used today for summer events.

Accommodations

They're happy to see you at **Alba** (Via G. Di Biasio 53, tel. 07/7627-0000, www.albahotel.it, €65–82 s/d) and it shows. The hotel restaurant serves simple food that tastes divine after a climb to the top of the Abbey.

Getting There

There's regular train service between Termini and Cassino several times a day. Drivers can reach the town in under two hours following the A1 south. The abbey is nine kilometers from the station and a local bus makes the journey frequently.

Northern Lazio

Before the Romans arrived on the Maremma plains, tolfa mountains and volcanic lakes of Northern Lazio were the home of the Etruscans. This peaceful civilization traded with ancient Greeks and provided the cultural foundation of early Rome. Today the most extraordinary remains of Etruria are found within several extensive burial grounds, which provide clues into how this fascinating people once lived.

All of the destinations in Northern Lazio are within three hours of Rome and make excellent day trips. Visitor numbers are far fewer than in the capital and small towns in the area are a respite from crowded Roman streets. More intensive exploration of the area is no less rewarding and Viterbo is a good base for anyone planning a longer stay.

◖ CERVETERI

During the Etruscan age, Cerveteri was a major maritime city. The town's necropolis is a reminder of a thriving past and is the largest and best-preserved cemetery in Lazio, featuring the oldest and most monumental tombs. The modern town contains pleasant cobblestoned streets and provides a foretaste of the Italian hilltop towns to come—including wrinkled faces that examine strangers from balcony windows.

Sights

Entering the **Necropoli della Bufoareccia** (tel. 06/994-0001, winter Tues.–Sun. 8:30 A.M.–4:30 P.M., summer 8:30 A.M.–7:30 P.M., €4 or €6.50 for combined entry with museum), it becomes obvious the Etruscans wanted their dead to rest in peace. Visitors are provided a map with which to navigate this complex network of 2,000 tombs built when calendars barely existed and time was told by observing the sky. On autumn days, salamanders outnumber sightseers and the tolfa rock in which the Etruscans dug their burial chambers provides a tranquil setting to reflect on life and death. The attractions can also be seen from the comfort of a small train, which leaves every half-hour from the visitors center.

The **Museo Nazionale Cerite** (Piazza Santa Maria, tel. 06/994-1354, same hours as necropolis, €4 or €6.50 combined entry with necropolis) contains many of the intricate earthenware discovered in the tombs. Vases, perfume bottles, cooking utensils, drinking cups, and jewelry give an idea of the everyday life of an Etruscan.

Festivals and Events

The last weekends of June, July, and August are each dedicated to the *sagra* (festival) of fish, beef, and olives. It's a chance to taste local ingredients and have some fun. Events include treasure hunts, horse and bicycle races, and period reenactments. The first Sunday in November is the *sagra del vino novello* (new wine festival), when wine is consumed in great quantities.

Food

The **Cavallino Bianco** (Piazza Risorgimento 7, tel. 06/994-0138, www.ilcavalinobianco.it, daily noon–2:30 P.M. and 7:30–10 P.M., €8–10) is located on the small piazza in the oldest part of town. Decoration is vintage 1950s and you can eat the freshly made fettuccine and *saltimbocca alla romana* inside or out. There's also good local wines at bargain prices. For takeaway pizza or roast chicken, try **Pezzi di Pizza** (Piazza Moro Aldo 6, tel. 06/995-1877, Mon.–Sat. noon–3:30 P.M. and 6–10 P.M., €5), on the main square where old women sit knitting and discussing the days events.

Getting There and Around

Cotral bus service to Cerveteri leaves from Cornelia station on the Metro A (direction Battistini). Buses depart 7 A.M.–9:20 P.M. every day. The trip lasts slightly over an hour and drops passengers off directly in Piazza Risorgimento. Train service is also available from Termini or Ostiense stations, but requires a bus transfer at Ladispoli. The town is also reachable by car

Etruscan burial grounds outside of Cerveteri

© ALEXEI J. COHEN

along the A12 highway, which begins near Fiumicino. The exit is clearly marked and tolls don't exceed €2 either way. For a slow drive take Via Aurelia.

A shuttle bus connects Piazza Risorgimento with the necropolis, but the journey can be made on foot in under 15 minutes. The tourist office across from the bus stop (tel. 06/9955-1971, www.etruriaguide.it) provides maps and information on guided tours.

Around Cerveteri

Travelers arriving by car may want to continue on the winding roads up the Tufo hills towards the borgo of **Ceri** (approx. 20 minutes, admission free), where a medieval wall protects the stunning remnants of 8th-century architecture.

LAKE BRACCIANO

Lake Bracciano is the second largest in Lazio and was formed from a prehistoric volcanic eruption. Its proximity to Rome makes it a popular weekend destination for water-sport enthusiasts and families out for a Sunday lunch. The lake's two largest towns, **Anguillara** and **Bracciano** (APT office, Piazza Mazzini 14, tel. 06/9980-2379, Tues.–Sat. 10 A.M.–12 P.M. and 3 P.M.–6 P.M., €7, guided tours last one hour), both share a medieval past and can be visited in a single day.

Sights

The town of Bracciano is dominated by the **Castello Orsini-Odescalchi,** which counts Tom Cruise among its famous guests. The two castle towers have a fairy-tale quality and are open to the public. A climb up the circular steps reveals a panoramic view of the lake. The castle is still owned by the Odescalchi family, who take special pride in the well-preserved 15th-century frescoes.

The **Museo Storico dell'Aeronautica Militare** (Anguillara, tel. 06/996-8415, Tues.– Sun. 9:30 A.M.–5:30 P.M., €4) is the most important aeronautic museum in Italy. Exhibits trace Italian flight from Da Vinci to transatlantic hydroplanes and Italy's first jets. A must for plane-spotters.

Festivals and Events

Wild boar is a big deal around Northern Lazio and is especially prevalent in these parts. The **Sagra del Cinghiale** (wild boar festival) in **San Giuliano** (southeast of the lake, tel. 06/998-4001) continues an ancient tradition during the first week of September. All types of boar-based products are sold, including irresistible roasted boar sandwiches.

An arts and crafts market (tel. 06/904-3374) is held in Bracciano on the second Sunday of each month in Piazza del Comune.

Sports and Recreation

Winds crossing the lake regularly reach 15 knots, making it a center of windsurfing and sailing activity. Optimist, Laser, and Flying Junior sailboats can be rented from **Planet Sail** (Via del Porticciolo 1, tel./fax 06/9980-5489). Instructors provide weekly lessons to children and adults that include theory, practice, and lunch.

There are five campgrounds around the lake ready to get you back in touch with nature. **Vigna di Valle** (Anguillara, Strada Provinciale, km 3,500, tel. 06/996-8645, €6.50 per adult) is open year-round. Tents are pitched within an 8,000-square-meter wooded compound. Fires are permitted for cooking, but if you prefer a table, the camp restaurant serves lunch and dinner. Two kilometers north of Bracciano, **Rome Flash** (Via Settevene Palo, km 19,800, tel. 06/9980-5458, www.romaflash.it, €7.50 per adult) is located right on the lake. It's clean and well managed. Bungalows can be rented and the camp store keeps supply lines open. Tours leave every day during the summer and destinations are posted at the front desk.

Accommodations

Located lakeside several kilometers from Bracciano, **Villa Clementina** (Traversa Quarto del Lago 12, tel. 06/998-6268, www.hotelvillaclementina.it, €135–175 s/d) is a peaceful spot to spend a few days. The artist owner encourages creativity and anyone with an itch to paint will find a canvas and easel ready. Relaxing by the pool is the other option.

Food

The area's restaurants are renowned for lake fish and local dishes like *pollo alla diavola* (devil's chicken). If the locally produced Castelbraccianese is on the wine list, order a bottle. **Vino a Camino** (Piazza Mazzini 11, tel. 06/9980-3433, Tues.–Sun. 12:30–2:30 P.M. and 7:30–11 P.M., €10–13) is a catapult away from the castle. Local specialties vary depending on the season, while the house wine remains consistently good. During the summer tables are available in the garden.

Game meats and country dishes are the twin pillars of **Piccola Trattoria** (Via Fioravanti 22, tel. 06/9980-4536, Tues.–Sun. 12:30–3 P.M. and 7–10:30 P.M., €9–12). This simple, rustic restaurant has not let popularity ruin the atmosphere. Prices are still as low as before the euro was introduced.

Getting There and Around

The town of Bracciano is reachable by rail or bus. It's a one-hour journey from Termini by train on the Rome-Viterbo line that leaves every hour. Cotral bus service departs from Rome Saxa Rubra and makes several stops around the lake. Drivers should take Via Claudia all the way to the ring road which circles the lake. Local public transportation is relatively efficient and regularly connects Bracciano with neigboring towns.

VITERBO

The longest conclave on record was held here in 1272. Unlike modern papal elections this one was no brief affair and it took the cardinals 33 months of wrangling to choose Gregorio X. It happened within the **Palazzo dei Papi**, built 17 years earlier when Viterbo briefly became the papal seat and experienced its golden age. The Palazzo dei Papi remains one of the finest examples of Gothic architecture in Central Italy.

The heart of Viterbo is the **San Pellegrino** district (think sparkling water), which has retained its medieval character and contains numerous Romanesque bell towers, piazze, and archways. In the Middle Ages, the numerous intricate fountains quenched the thirsts of pilgrims walking the Via Francigena to Rome.

Sights

Piazza del Plebiscito is the center of town and a good place to start. The main civic buildings include the **Palazzo dei Priori** (Via Ascenzia, tel. 04/613-481, daily 9 A.M.–1 P.M. and 3–6 P.M., free) and Torre dell'Orologio, under which stands the town's mascot. Stonework on the *palazzi* demonstrates the skill of medieval masons and the porticos, courtyards, and facades are all meticulously carved.

Via San Lorenzo connects the political hub with the religious one. Midway down the street is S. Maria Nuova. Inside on the left is the pulpit from which Tommaso d'Aquino once preached. Further on is **Piazza S. Lorenzo,** which lies above an ancient Etruscan necropolis and contains the town's most impressive buildings. The Duomo has a black and white striped bell tower reminiscent of Siena and there's a good view of surrounding countryside from the Palazzo Papale's finely crafted loggia.

A walk in the adjacent **San Pellegrino** quarter is a walk back in time. Imagine yourself a squire or a baron and explore the maze of narrow streets.

Festivals and Events

The cherry festival called **Sagra delle Ciliege** (tel. 07/6129-1000) is held on the first Sunday in June. The variety being celebrated is the Ravenna, which grows locally and was imported from the Black Sea by a Roman proconsule with an appetite for fruit. It's distributed generously throughout a day filled with theatrical and musical events.

The fall highlight is the **Festa di Santa Rosa** (tel. 07/6130-4795) on September 2. Festivities include a procession in medieval costume and the much-awaited Macchina di Santa Rosa, when 90 locals carry a 30-meter-tall bell tower weighing 4,000 kilograms from the Chiesa San Sisto to the Santa Rosa sanctuary. None of this should be attempted at home.

The annual antiques fair (tel. 07/6129-1003) is held in October.

Sports and Recreation

The thermal waters near Viterbo are famous for their therapeutic qualities and a dip in the warm pools will ease aches and pains. The **Terme dei Bagni** (Strada dei Bagni 12, tel. 07/613-501, www.termedeipapi.it, €12 and up) is a day spa and elegant hotel two kilometers outside of town, offering a variety of relaxing treatments and swimming.

Accommodations

A convenient location, 12th-century charm, and an extensive buffet breakfast makes the **B&B dei Papi** (Via del Ginnasio 8, tel. 07/6130-9039, €80 d) memorable. Only three rooms means reservations are essential.

The **Balletti Palace** (Via Umbria 8, 07/6134-4777, €80–90 s/d) is a modern hotel a short walk from the historic district. The price of a room includes breakfast and the restaurant offers a selection of local favorites.

Food

Porta Romana (Via della Bontà 12, tel. 07/6130-7118, Mon.–Sat. 1–3 P.M. and 7–11 P.M., €7.50–10) greets guests with open arms. The pasta is homemade and the meat locally raised. The winter dish of choice is *pignataccia,* a stew consisting of veal, beef, pork, celery, carrots, and potatoes.

If you're in the mood for medieval only, **◖ Il Richiastro's** (Via Della Marrocca 16, 07/6122-8009, Fri.–Sun. 1–3 P.M. and 7–10 P.M., €8–11) re-creates the same dishes peasants once ate. That means lots of thick bean soups and roasted meats. Giovanna Sappucci will happily recount the origin of all her antique recipes.

Nuns have been replaced with gourmet food at **La Zaffera** (Piazza Carluccio 7, tel. 07/6134-4265, Tues.–Sun. noon–3 P.M. and 7–11 P.M., €15–20), which inhabits a former convent. Presentation counts here and the dishes look as though they've gone to finishing school.

Getting There and Around

Viterbo is 70 kilometers north of Rome and a one-hour drive on the Cassia SS 2. For the scenic alternative, leave the Cassia at Monterosi and follow the secondary road across the hillsides past Lago di Vico. A faster approach is on the A1 and exit at Orte. Trains leave every hour from Rome's Ostiense station. The journey takes a little over two hours and a one-way ticket is €4.50. Cotral buses depart from Saxa Rubra.

Around Viterbo

Five kilometers to the east of Viterbo is what Edith Wharton described as the perfect garden. **Villa Lante** (Bagnaia, tel. 07/6128-8008, daily 8:30 P.M.–1 hr before sunset, €2) is the playful side of the Renaissance, where fountains strike without warning and 450-year-old plumbing has yet to leak.

TARQUINIA

The fortified interior of Tarquinia is made up of three areas. The Castello is the oldest and dates from the 7th century. It's also the calmest, where pigeons go about their business undisturbed and the gothic symmetry of **Santa Maria di Castello** can be sketched in peace. The Cornetto Vecchio marks a period of expansion beginning in the 10th century and is home to the main street, and archeological museum Nuovo represents the last historic building boom and contains the **Convento di S. Francesco.**

There are 13 churches in all and Sunday is the time to hear their bells echoing across the narrow cobblestoned streets. Hiking boots will save your feet and a scarf may be necessary in late autumn and early spring. The town is on a hill and overlooks rolling wheat fields, the same ones that Stendhal gazed upon when he spent time here.

Sights

Tarquinia started out as an Etruscan settlement and the remains can be found in the necropolis and museum. The **Museo Archeologico** (Piazza Cavour, tel. 07/6685-6036, Tues.–Sun.

the entrance to Tarquinia

© ALEXEI J. COHEN

8:30 A.M.–7:30 P.M., €4 or €6.50 combined entry with necropolis) is housed within the Palazzo Vitelleschi, which in itself is worth a visit. Inside are sculpted urns, traces of a nearly forgotten language, and four replicas of the nearby tombs.

Three kilometers outside of town is the **Necropoli Monterozzi** (Strada Provinciale Monterozzi Marina, tel. 07/6685-6308, Tues.–Sun. 8:30 A.M.–2 P.M., summer 8:30 A.M.–one hour before sunset, €4 or €6.50 combined entry with Museo Archeologico) where 6,000 tombs have thus far been uncovered. The deepest is the tomb of Tifone, with multiple chambers and columns dug into the rock. Nearby are the remains of Ara della Regina, a rectangular temple where Etruscans once worshipped.

Festivals and Events

Tarquinia transforms itself into the West during **La Merce e il Trofeo dei Butteri** (tel. 07/6685-6016). Cows take center stage on the first Sunday of April, when anyone with a gift for lassoing can become an instant celebrity.

Branding and equestrian competitions round out the day founded to educate citizens about local breeding techniques.

Italian towns excel at festivities devoted to specific foods. It's no surprise then that mushrooms are celebrated in Tarquinia on the last weekend of October. What is surprising is that the **Sagra del Fungo** (tel. 07/768-491) is devoted exclusively to the *ferlengo*. If you thought all mushrooms were equal, try this one with pasta or on slices of thick country bread at one of the many stands. Music and folklore are present throughout the event.

Shopping

Two shops that are likely never to become chain stores are **Marco Bocchio** (Via Giotto, tel. 07/6684-2674, Tues.–Sun. 9 A.M.–1 P.M. and 3:30–7 P.M.) and **Todine Sculture** (Via L. Da Vinci Lotto 29, tel. 07/6685-8294, Tues.–Sun. 9 A.M.–1 P.M. and 3:30–7 P.M.). The first sells handcrafted ceramics and the second transforms marble and other stones into a variety of decorative objects.

Accommodations

Tarquina is only five kilometers from the sea. **Velcamare** (Via degli Argonauti 1, Tarquinia Lido, tel. 07/6686-4380, www.velcamare. com, €80–110 s/d), a small hotel surrounded by greenery, has its own private beach where cocktails are served and lounging is the primary activity.

Food

Re Tarquinio (Via Alberata Dante Alighieri, tel. 07/6684-2125, daily noon–3 P.M. and 7 P.M.–midnight, €12–15) is a wine bar and restaurant with an intimate, cave-like atmosphere. There are several rooms on the ground floor and a rooftop terrace, which all vary in mood. The menu offers light snacks at the bar and fine dining at the elegantly set tables.

Getting There

Public transportation to Tarquinia is limited and involves more transfers than the trip is worth. The most viable option is by car. The

journey from Rome takes 1.5 hours on the A12, which becomes the Via Aurelia SS1 after Civitavecchia. The town makes a nice lunch stop for anyone heading towards Tuscany.

TUSCANIA

Like Rome, legend has it Tuscania was founded on seven hills; like the other towns in the province, it was founded by the Etruscans. In the 3rd century B.C., however, the settlement was absorbed by the Roman Republic and the newly built Via Claudia helped to expand trade. History fluctuated between good times and bad until the town gradually shifted to its present location. The medieval streets around Piazza Basile were never intended for cars and offer a warren of narrow alleys to explore.

Sights

A third era of prosperity began after the town became part of the Papal state in 787 B.C. Shortly after the churches of **Santa Maria Maggiore** and **San Pietro** were begun. Both were long-term projects located on the edge of town that took centuries to complete. The effort paid off and provides unique examples of Romanesque architecture using tufo for structural support and marble for the decorative work around the entrances and rose windows.

Shopping

In Roman times, terra-cotta was the equivalent of plastic. It could be molded into nearly any shape and was used for carrying everything from Egyptian grain to Greek oil. The Etruscan version was less practical and more refined. You can see the difference in **Marcello Barlozzini's** (Via Martana 4, tel. 07/6143-4386) studio and shop. His plates and bowls are all inspired from original designs and contain the customary black and deep red colors of the time.

Accommodations

Locanda di Mirandolina (Via del Pozzo Bianco 40, tel. 07/6143-6595, www.mirandolina. it, €45–65 s/d) is a family-owned inn with five rooms and a restaurant that serves the local flavors. Guests can expect large dose of tranquillity and simplicity.

Food

The view alone is worth a visit to **Al Gallo** (Via Del Gallo 22, tel. 07/6144-3388, www. algallo.it, Tues.–Sun. 12:30–2:30 P.M. and 7:30–10:30 P.M., €15–20) restaurant and hotel. Fortunately, local dishes with a twist and wine options make each plate as attractive as the panorama.

If one of the reasons you came to Italy was cheese, then a detour to **Caseificio Pannucci** (S. Savino, tel. 07/6143-5225) shouldn't be optional. The *pecorino* produced here follows the same ancient recipe Roman farmers did. The goat's milk comes from a nearby herd and after one taste the supermarket version becomes unedible.

Getting There

Not all roads lead to Tuscania. The town is a 24-kilometer drive from Tarquinia and that's what you'll have to do as bus service is limited. Roads get narrower as you approach and it is worth spending the night if you have the time.

MONTEFIASCONE

Montefiascone lies on the side of an exctinct volcano overlooking the Lago di Bolsena, Lazio's largest lake. This is what Romans think of when they talk of getting away from it all. It's famous for Est Est Est wine, which got its name from a passing German cardinal. He had his assistants write those words on the doors of the local inns that served the best grapes.

Sights

Santa Margherita is severely out of proportion. It dominates the town and the immense cupola is the second largest in Italy. **San Flaviano** is a combination of two Romanesque churches, one built over the other during the 12th century. Inside are 14th-century frescoes and the remains of Etruscan-inspired insignia.

Sports and Recreation

The nearby town of **Bolsena** is a center for many of the lake's naturalistic activities, including horseback riding, archeotrekking, and sailing. Boats can be rented from **Navigazione Alto Lazio** (Corso della Repubblica 60, tel. 07/6179-8033) and guided tours of the two small islands of Bisentina and Martana can be arranged with **Barche Tipiche del Lago** (tel. 800/135-464 or 338/846-869). A half-day tour that includes breakfast and a boat full of history costs €120 and may be divided by up to four people.

Anyone who wants to go fishing is in the right place and can pick up tackle and line in the port. The lake is well stocked with eel, carp, whitefish, and black bass. Locals say the best time to cast is late afternoon when the fish begin to feed.

Entertainment and Events

For the first two weeks of August, **Est Est Est** is on everyone's lips and the straw-colored wine made from Trebbiano grapes is the only drink in town. Fortunately its low alcohol content doesn't distract from the craft demonstrations and parades.

Accommodations

What the **Altavista** (Via Dante 16, tel. 07/6182-0123, www.altavillahotel.com, €60–70 s/d) lacks in style it makes up for in comfort. Rooms are spacious and silent with beds that guarantee a good night's sleep. The panoramic road to the lake is nearby and there is parking for anyone who has arrived by car.

Getting There and Around

It's a three-hour train journey from Rome on the Viterbo line. Passengers must get off at Zepponami and complete the two-kilometer journey by bus. Drivers can choose between the Cassia SS2 or the A1 highway north until Orte (€2). Local bus service connects Montefiascone with Bolsena and circumnavigates the entire lake.

FLORENCE AND TUSCANY

Imagine Tuscany and many of Italy's trademark images come to mind: the Leaning Tower of Pisa, the statue of *David,* and the soft, gentle hills that English poets described as the entrance to heaven. The region contains a fine assortment of well-preserved towns and cities to explore, from the miniature Pienza to the magnificent Florence.

For a while this was the center of the world, a place where new ideas were the currency of choice. During the golden age of the Renaissance, artists, architects, and aristocrats like Raffaello, Brunelleschi, and the Medicis brought innovation to nearly every endeavor they undertook. Traces of their extraordinary creativity can be experienced walking along the ramparts of Lucca or admiring the stained glass windows of Siena's cathedral. Tuscany is where Galileo studied the theory of motion and where Michelangelo was inspired.

Tuscany has always been a fruitful and magical place and there's evidence of that every time you sit down for a meal. Portions are generous and there's no shortage of red wine to choose from. Grapes, grains, and olives are visible along the winding roads where every curve is worth a snapshot. Florence, in the center of the region, is the city that kicked-off the golden age of the Renaissance, but there's more than just this one stunning city to explore in Tuscany. Pisa and Siena are worth a visit and if remote hill towns are more your thing, Tuscany is the region to lace up the hiking shoes and start walking.

It's no wonder Tuscany is crowded during the summer and it's nearly as common to hear

© ALEXEI J. COHEN

HIGHLIGHTS

◖ Santa Maria del Fiore: Santa Maria del Fiore is Europe's fourth-largest church and some say Italy's finest. Covered in lavish marble, this iconic sight features a 106-meter dome that is visible from most areas in the city. The interior of the remarkable dome is also a must-see (page 117).

◖ Battistero di San Giovanni: The Battistero di San Giovanni features beautiful Renaissance mosaics by Cimabue and Giotto and sculpted bronze doors by Ghiberti and Pisano (page 118).

◖ Galleria dell'Accademia: Michelangelo's *David* and other works by the artist are the main reason most people make a visit to this museum. The *David* sculpture gets an entire room to itself, but is easily visible regardless of the number of visitors (page 120).

◖ Galleria degli Uffizi: One of the most-visited museums in the world, the Galleria degli Uffizi houses a remarkable collection of Italian works from the 13th-18th centuries (page 121).

◖ Palio delle Contrade: This twice-yearly, historic bareback horse race around the Campo is one of Italy's most spectacular festivals. A small wager only heightens the excitement (page 149).

◖ San Gimignano: San Gimignano is a charming medieval town with a skyline comparable to Manhattan's. A law passed in 1282 declared that no house could be destroyed unless it was replaced by something better. Fortunately it is one law the citizens never broke (page 153).

◖ Leaning Tower of Pisa: There's more than one leaning tower in Italy, but it's the precarious structure in Pisa that gets all the attention. Italy's most photographed building, after the Colosseum, is actually better in person and the tourists swarming around Piazza dei Miracoli below are as much a part of the scenery as the tower itself (page 164).

◖ Lucca: The buildings may have changed, but the streets are exactly where the Romans planned them when they founded this independent-minded town in 180 B.C. A four-kilometer ring wall built in the 16th century has prevented modern urbanization and has transformed Lucca into a pedestrian dream where walkers can explore Romanesque churches, tiny piazze, and medieval palazzos (page 169).

◖ Viareggio Carnevale: Venice's Carnevale may be more famous, but Viareggio's festivities demand dusk-until-dawn stamina from thousands of revelers (page 172).

◖ Parco Naturale della Maremma: This park preserves one of Italy's last pristine stretches of coastline. It is home to wild boar, birds of prey, and flamingos with 10,000 hectares of marshland, dunes, and pine forests. Try balancing culture with a walk in this seaside park (page 176).

LOOK FOR ◖ TO FIND RECOMMENDED SIGHTS, ACTIVITIES, DINING, AND LODGING.

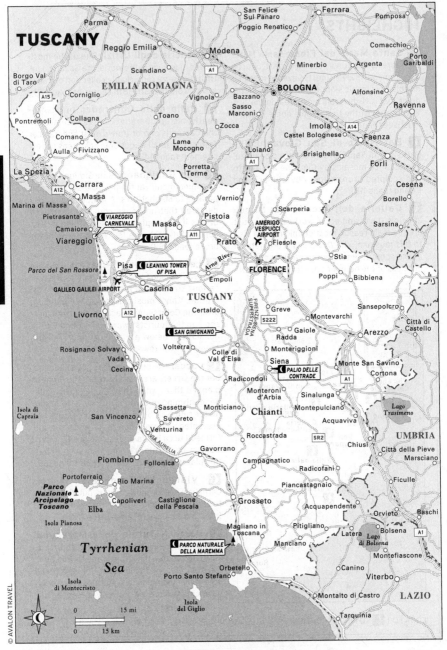

TUSCANY

San Felice
Sul Panaro
Poggio Renatico
Ferrara
Pomposa

Parma
Reggio Emilia
Modena
Comacchio
Porto
Garibaldi

Scandiano
A1
Minerbio
Argenta

Borgo Val
di Taro
Corniglio
EMILIA ROMAGNA
Vignola
Bazzano
BOLOGNA
Alfonsine
Ravenna

A15
Toano
Sasso
Marconi
Imola
A14
Faenza

Pontremoli
Collagna
Zocca
Castel Bolognese
Forlì

Comano
Lama
Mocogno
Loiano
Brisighella

Aulla
Fivizzano
A1
Cesena

La Spezia
Porretta
Terme
Vernio
Scarperia
Borello

Carrara
Sarsina

Massa
Pistoia
**AMERIGO
VESPUCCI
AIRPORT**

Marina di Massa
Pietrasanta
Massa
Prato
Fiesole
Stia

Camaiore
◖ **VIAREGGIO
CARNEVALE**
◖ **LUCCA**
A11
FLORENCE
Poppi
Bibbiena

Viareggio
Arno River
Parco del San Rossore
Pisa
◖ **LEANING TOWER
OF PISA**
Empoli
TUSCANY

GALILEO GALILEI AIRPORT
Cascina
Greve
Montevarchi
Sansepolcro

Livorno
A12
Pecciòli
Certaldo
S222
Gaiole
Arezzo
Città di
Castello

◖ **SAN GIMIGNANO**
Radda
Monte San Savino

Rosignano Solvay
Volterra
Colle di
Val d'Elsa
Monteriggioni
Cortona

Vada
Siena
◖ **PALIO DELLE
CONTRADE**

Cecina
Radicòndoli
A1

Isola di
Capraia
Monteroni
d'Arbia
Sinalunga
Lago
Trasimeno

Sassetta
Monticiano
Chianti
Montepulciano
UMBRIA

San Vincenzo
Suvereto
Acquaviva

Venturina
SR2
Chiusi
Città della Pieve

VIA AURELIA
Gavorrano
Roccastrada
Marsciano

Piombino
Campagnatico
Ficulle

Portoferraio
Follonica
Radicofani

**Parco
Nazionale
Arcipelago
Toscano**
Rio Marina
Piancastagnaio

Capoliveri
Castiglione
della Pescaia
Grosseto
Orvieto
Baschi

Elba
Acquapendente

Isola Pianosa
Magliano in
Toscana
Latera
Lago
di Bolsena
A1

_Tyrrhenian
Sea_
◖ **PARCO NATURALE
DELLA MAREMMA**
Pitigliano
Manciano
Montefiascone

Orbetello
Canino
Viterbo

Isola
di Montecristo
Porto Santo Stefano
Montalto di Castro
LAZIO

Isola
del Giglio
Tarquinia

0   15 mi

0   15 km

English, German, or French being spoken as Italian. But don't let that discourage you. Tuscany is relatively large and there is no limit to what can be discovered.

PLANNING YOUR TIME

Perhaps no question is tougher than what to do in Tuscany. The answer isn't simple and generally depends on how much time you have. Fortunately there is a direct flight between Pisa and New York several days a week. In eight hours you can go from crossing the Hudson to strolling the Arno. Starting your holiday in Tuscany means more time to explore a region that could keep you occupied for weeks.

Tuscany is on a lot of people's must-see lists. The word has been out for centuries now and the region has gained Holy Grail status for anyone interested in art, culture, or nature. Season and itinerary, therefore, are everything as cities like Florence and Siena can be a merry-go-round of tourists nearly all year long. August is crowded but there are hundreds of extraordinary events. Winters are mild and do little to discourage the flow of visitors. The best

NOVEMBER 4, 1966

The Arno River may look harmless as you pass over the Ponte Vecchio, but 40 years ago it wreaked havoc on Florence. Floodwaters rose above the embankments and spread to every corner of the city. Near Santa Croce, they reached nearly five meters above the piazzas and Cimabue's crucifix, along with thousands of other works of art, was severely damaged. Plaques in the neighborhood show exactly how high the water reached. The baptistery doors were swept off their hinges and Ghiberti's masterpiece was later found about 1.5 kilometers away. Streets resembled the canals of Venice and for nearly a week locals could only get around by boat. Nearly everyone has a story of how they were affected by the flood and how they later pitched in to make Florence beautiful again. The cleanup took years and occasionally led to old frescoes or Roman villas being accidentally uncovered. Some minor objects, however, are still waiting to be restored.

a view of Santa Maria del Fiore from Piazzale Michelangelo

© ALEXEI J. COHEN

MEDIEVAL GUILDS

Medieval guilds were a combination of union, governing body, and lobby group. They originated from the Societas Mercatorum in the 12th century and eventually split into Greater and Lesser Guilds. Your profession and your ability to afford the membership fees determined which guild you were in. After 1293, anyone who wanted to enter politics needed to belong to a guild but belonging didn't necessarily require being a skilled craftsman. Dante and Giotto, for example, were members of the Guild of Physicians and Apothecaries. The Guild of the Wool Weavers was the most important and over a third of the city was connected with the trade during the Renaissance.

Very little happened inside Palazzo Vecchio without their approval, and intrigue was guaranteed as Florence's ruling families vied for control of the city.

All guilds were headed by two consuls for renewable six-month terms. Besides the flow of raw material, they also regulated industry standards and the smooth operation of their trade. No one liked shoddy work and few corners were cut. Each guild had its own crest, many of which can still be spotted around the city today. Judges and notaries were represented by a star, while bankers adopted an eagle as their symbol. It's carved above many palazzo doorways.

thing to do is approach big towns from lesser-known angles, ditch the car in favor of bike or foot, and search for *agriturismo* accommodations. Certainly the classics like *David* and the Duomo are worth seeing, but there are many examples of beauty that still don't get the recognition they deserve.

HISTORY

Florence's history is a long one, and it involved the usual suspects. There were once Etruscans here, preceded by Iron Age tribes. The settlement along the Arno is one of the only ones on flat terrain. It proved a natural funnel for traffic coming down from Bologna and Venice. The sea was also close and the Mediterranean opened up markets for wool merchants and other trades that brought wealth to the town. With wealth came leisure and with leisure came art. Craftsmen became the best in the world and fine jewelers still line the Ponte Vecchio. It was only a small jump from creating beautiful ornaments to creating beautiful sculptures, frescoes, and eventually entire buildings.

The greatest geniuses of Italy—Giotto, Dante, Macchiavelli, Brunelleschi, Michelangelo, Donatello, Raffaello, and so on—resided in or had some connection with Florence. With minds like these and a wealthy political class, the result was explosive. They didn't call it the Renaissance then; to them, revitalizing the Western world was simply business as usual.

Florence

Unless you've traveled to Tuscany before, a visit to the region isn't complete without a stop in the capital. Firenze, as locals call their city, has a justified marble chip on its shoulder. After all, this is where civilization was given an injection of creativity after centuries of artistic stagnation. The Ponte Vecchio is still standing and the Uffizi remains the place to go for art. On the other side of town, Michelangelo's *David* waits to be examined and Brunelleschi's amazing dome is never far from view. The city hasn't lost its creative touch, although the Renaissance will always be a hard act to follow. Artisans pound away on the backstreets of the Oltrarno neighborhood and the wallets sold along Via de' Tornabuoni have a reassuring smell that is hard to resist.

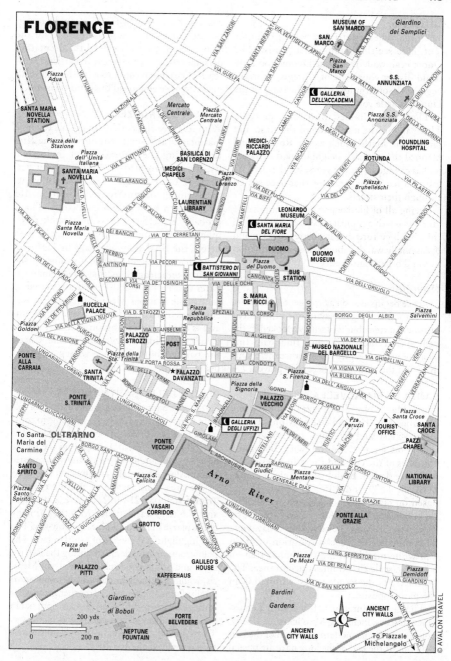

© AVALON TRAVEL

SIGHTS

The urge, whether arriving by car, train, or foot, is to see the Duomo first. Resist. The Duomo can wait. To see the Duomo too early could distort your view of Florence. Instead, begin with something lesser known and let the Duomo startle you suddenly.

The city is divided into four quarters. Three are on the north side of the Arno and one on the south, much as the Romans had planned things. Each neighborhood's character has changed over the years, yet they haven't lost that feeling of greatness that once soared through their streets.

Seeing all of Florence would seem possible given its relative compactness, yet the city is so thick with culture that it's better to relax and occasionally wander about with no destination in mind other than beauty.

Novella

Florence begins as soon as you get off the train. The station is the gateway to one of the city's historic quarters, but is often overlooked in the rush to the center. Here you'll find many fine palazzos where wealthy Renaissance merchants lived and the churches where they prayed.

SANTA MARIA NOVELLA

Santa Maria Novella (Piazza Santa Maria Novella, tel. 05/5264-5184, Mon.–Thurs. 9 A.M.–5 P.M. and Fri.–Sun. 1–5 P.M., €2.50) is a good first encounter with the many churches of the city and the principles of Renaissance design. Built by Dominican monks between 1279 and 1357 its iconic facade based on classic proportions was created by Leon Battista Alberti. Alberti was a man who greatly shaped how the city looks today. Here he combined the Tuscan tradition of green and white marble with a triumphal arch on a Roman scale that frames the entrance. The symmetry of the facade is best admired from the park opposite.

The Gothic interior is filled with Renaissance frescoes, including Massacio's *La Trinità*, noteworthy for its modern portrayal of the crucifixion. At the end of the long nave are several chapels where wealthy families could worship privately. Two of these were reserved for the Strozzi family, who financed the decoration personally and even selected the artists themselves. The church contains a cloister and small museum once employed by Spanish envoys.

PALAZZO STROZZI

With its three floors that are double the normal height and small windows on the first floor giving the impression of invincibility, the Palazzo Strozzi (Piazza Strozzi, tel. 05/5277-6461, daily 9 A.M.–8 P.M., www. fondazionepalazzostrozzi.it, €10) could be mistaken for a prison or fortress. That's probably the effect the wealthy banker Filippo Strozzi wanted. Unfortunately he died before the final stone was laid in 1536 and never had the chance to tie his horse to the original tethering rings that have remained. After relatives of the deceased attempted to assassinate Cosimo Medici, the palazzo was confiscated. Today it houses a small museum and is used as an exhibition space for blockbuster shows like *Cezanne in Florence*. Check the banners outside to see what's currently being shown.

PIAZZA DELLA SANTA TRINITÀ

Piazza della Santa Trinità is punctuated by a column removed from Caracalla in Rome to commemorate the Medici victory over the Sienesi at Marciano in 1554. Palazzos around the piazza have a reputation for elegance and were mostly commissioned by wealthy merchants who lived in the area. The facade of **Basilica Santa Trinità** (tel. 05/521-6912, daily 8 A.M.–noon and 4–6 P.M.) was designed with the harmony of the piazza in mind and is rather low-key. The real highlight is the work of Ghirlandaio. The painter was in great demand during the Renaissance and was in good standing with the Medicis, whom he kindly immortalized in his *Storie di San Francesco* frescoes. His other great work is the *Adorazione dei Pastori*. It is exceptional in both the realism of its subjects and landscape. The wrinkled, dirty faces he painted must surely have once lived and breathed.

VIA PORTA ROSSA

Along Via Porta Rossa are some of the oldest civic buildings in the city. The road stretches from Via Calzaiuoli to Via Tornabuoni near the Arno River. Along the way are **Palazzo Bartolini** (completed in 1500) and **Torre del Monaldi,** also called La Rognosa. Torre del Monaldi is one of the tallest and best-preserved towers in the city. Many of the *case torre* or tower houses were built to resist attack during the volatile years of the 13th century. Doors were easily defendable and ground floor windows were designed to repel attack. Holes on the higher stories of the towers were used to assemble temporary bridges from which to avoid any chaos down below.

PALAZZO DAVANZATI

Palazzo Davanzati (Via Porta Rossa 13, tel. 05/5238-8610, Tues.–Sun. 8:15 A.M.–1:50 P.M., free) is a stark contrast to the fortified towers along Via Porta Rossa. It was home to a family of wool merchants and later sold to a historian who added the loggia. After the last member of the Davanzati family jumped to his death, the palazzo was divided into apartments—and might have remained that way if Elia Volpi had not purchased the building and used it to display her private collection. In 1956, it was opened to the public as a museum dedicated to recreating the interior of a typical Florentine palazzo.

All the original fittings have been restored and period furniture installed to provide visitors with a glimpse of comfortable Renaissance life. The staircase in the courtyard leads to a kitchen on the top floor that's equipped with a system of running water. The toilets on each floor are also worth a peek and were a great luxury in a time when public latrines were hard to find.

PIAZZA DELLA REPUBBLICA

Piazza della Repubblica buzzes with life from morning until evening. The piazza is one of the rare open spaces in the city that has attracted crowds since it was built. Locals spend their afternoons in the elegant cafés that surround the square and street artists use it as their open-air studio. In winter, a carousel is set up in the center.

During the 19th century, the many cafés around the square were home to the city's intellectual set, led by Giovanni Papini, who encouraged the development of the Futurist movement, and Gabinetto Viesseux, who won a Nobel Prize for literature.

The piazza was once the location of the Roman Foro and streets in the vicinity have retained much of their antique patterns. Prior to the decision to build the present piazza in the late 19th century, it was the home of the Mercato Vecchio. This was the busiest market in the city, where everyone from doctors to charlatans set up their stalls. It was also the Jewish quarter. Although they suffered little persecution, Jews were required to wear a round piece of cloth sewn to their chest. From the Piazza the city opens up in many directions and new neighborhoods await.

San Giovanni

San Giovanni has been the heart of Florence since Roman legionnaires pitched their camp here 2,000 years ago. In the center of it all is the Duomo, capped with a cupola that symbolizes the city and the entire region. It's a natural tourist magnet. They know a good thing when they see it and fortunately there's a lot to see.

C SANTA MARIA DEL FIORE

Santa Maria del Fiore (tel. 05/5230-2885, Mon.–Fri. 8:30 A.M.–7 P.M. and Sat. 8:30 A.M.–5:40 P.M., €6), the Duomo for short, is Florence's most iconic sight and is a big draw for tourists. Every aspect of this grand church is the result of centuries of planning and the work of thousands of laborers, who handcrafted what many consider the finest church in Italy. It looms large over the city and comes in and out of view from nearly every neighborhood. From Piazzale Michelangelo and Fiesole it dominates the skyline and its 348-foot-high dome has never been superseded in Florence.

The cupola, or dome, may look like a simple matter of bricks, but it presented a huge

© ALEXEI J. COHEN

The Battistero di San Giovanni is where Dante was baptized.

dilemma in 1420 and it took the genius of Filippo Brunelleschi to complete the church. His solution relied on a double shell and eight ribs bound together by horizontal rings. All of this was built without scaffolding and is best appreciated with a walk to the top, where you'll come across some original Renaissance graffiti and get an unforgettable view of the city. Down below no expense was spared on the inlaid marble that was set in a series of intricate patterns (designed by Francesco da Sangolo in the 16th century). The marble on the facade is equally stunning but a lot newer than it looks. Although visitors love posing in front of it, most Florentines think it fails to live up to the dome. Don't miss the sides of the church, which are also clad in marble and where you can avoid the hordes of tour groups.

CAMPANILE

Giotto was made *capomastro* of the Duomo in 1334 and concentrated all his attention on the Campanile (Piazza del Duomo, daily 8:30 A.M.–7:30 P.M., €6). It was the first time

he had built anything this important. For this work, he used alternating layers of white Carrara, pink Siena, and green Prato marble. Only the first cornice was completed upon his death and two other architects worked on the project thereafter, leading to a discernable difference in style. At 85 meters the top of the Campanile offers a great view of the dome and the rest of the city.

The current marble Baroque facade of the Duomo was rebuilt 300 years after the Duomo was started and retained the style set by the adjacent Campanile. It did not receive rave reviews upon completion and modern Florentines often complain of its vulgarity.

◖ BATTISTERO DI SAN GIOVANNI

Questions remain regarding the origins of this baptistery (Piazza San Giovanni, tel. 05/5230-2885, Mon.–Fri. noon–7 P.M. and Sat.–Sun. 8:30 A.M.–2 P.M., €3). What is certain is that it rests on Roman foundations and was consecrated as a cathedral in 1059. It was rebuilt several centuries later with an octagonal shape and green marble siding. After 1129 it became a baptistery and Dante himself was christened here. Further additions included the pyramid-shaped roof and three sets of bronze doors.

The **baptistery doors** were originally made of wood but in 1328 it was decided they were not distinguished enough for such a building. Andrea Pisano was contracted to cast a new bronze set and it was 10 years before they were hinged. Ghiberti won the competition to build the second doors and broke away from Pisano's austere style. Each door contains 14 panels recounting the life of Christ. The variety of characters and expressions is remarkable, and binoculars would be useful to fully appreciate the level of craftsmanship. It took Ghiberti 25 years to complete the doors now located at the north entrance, and Florentines were so happy with the result they asked him to design the final set. This time he chose 10 episodes from the Old Testament, which were completed in 1452. Unobstructed views are rare but the originals can be seen at the **Museo dell'Opera del Duomo** (Piazza Duomo 9, tel. 05/5230-2885, Mon.–Fri. 9 A.M.–7:30 P.M. and Sat. and Sun. 9 A.M.–1:30 P.M., €6).

Building a church requires organization and the Opera del Duomo was established in 1296 to oversee the project. The building, which served as an administrative headquarters, now houses a museum. Many sculptures threatened by pollution have found a home inside and the first floor contains works by Arnolfo di Cambio and one of Michelangelo's last pieces. The *Pietà* would have ended up on his tomb if he hadn't grown frustrated with the poor quality of the marble and destroyed the left leg of Christ. Upstairs in the Brunelleschi rooms are models of the machinery created to complete the dome.

OSCURO MEDIOEVO

Any museum open until midnight must have something worth seeing. Oscuro Medioevo Fiorentino (Via Faenza 13r, tel. 05/528-2432, daily 11 A.M.–midnight, €8) presents the less attractive side of Florence and the effect the plague of 1348 had on the city. An interactive

audio guide recounts the life of average citizens struggling to survive. It's a far cry from the luxuries of Palazzo Davanzati.

BASILICA DI SAN LORENZO

Basilica di San Lorenzo (Piazza San Lorenzo, tel. 05/521-4042, daily 10 A.M.–5:30 P.M., €2.50) is one of the oldest churches in Florence and owes much to the Medicis. They purchased land for the expansion of the church in 1418 and entirely oversaw reconstruction of the building. The task was assigned to Brunelleschi, who put into practice Renaissance ideals of proportion and perspective.

The unfinished exterior is a stark contrast to the lavish interior, which demonstrates the wealth and power the Medicis had at their disposal. Many family members were buried here and Michelangelo built several of their tombs. Lorenzo Medici's final resting place in the new sacristy is covered by statues of *Crepuscolo* and *Aurora*, and as usual the artist portrayed his female subjects in muscular fashion.

In 1523 Michelangelo got the nod from Pope Clemente VII to build the Biblioteca Laurenziana adjacent to the cloister that forms part of the complex. He designed everything down to the vestibule steps leading to the bright reading room where the Medicis once perused their vast collection of Greek and Latin titles. The final addition to the church was the Cappella dei Principi. The last marble slab was set in 1962 and is so fanciful that it would have delighted Liberace.

PALAZZO MEDICI-RICCARDI

Cosimo il Vecchio was wary of public opinion and preferred that his friend Michelozzi design his residence rather than risk criticism with the more ambitious plans of Brunelleschi. Construction was completed in 1464 and the sober style of Palazzo Medici–Riccardi (Via Cavour 7, tel. 05/5276-0340, Thurs.–Tues. 9 A.M.–7 P.M., €5) instantly became a prototype of its genre throughout Tuscany. The palazzo remained in the Medici family until the mid-16th century when it was purchased by the Riccardi clan and greatly enlarged with little alteration to external appearance. Each of the floors is distinguished with a different material from the rough stone on the ground floor to an entirely smooth surface at the top. The shape of windows also varies and the twin bays separated by a single arch on the second and third floors is a break from Gothic. The residence includes a symmetrical courtyard and the *Corteo dei Magi* fresco covering an entire room on the second floor. The palazzo contains a museum and hosts frequent exhibitions.

◖ GALLERIA DELL'ACCADEMIA

If you're looking for *David,* you'll find him inside the Galleria dell'Accademia (Via Ricasoli 60, tel. 05/5238-8609, Tues.–Sun. 8:15 A.M.–6:50 P.M., €8.50). Michelangelo sculpted the masterpiece from an enormous piece of secondhand marble that had frustrated lesser artists. David was a popular subject and, like Donatello's version, this one is naked. Michelangelo, however, chose to capture the tense moments prior to the struggle with Goliath. The face is not relaxed but reveals the kind of apprehension you'd expect before facing a giant.

The statue gets an entire room to itself and is easily visible regardless of the number of visitors. Remember to walk around the statue and observe what many consider *David's* finest asset. The Accademia contains other works by Michelangelo, including four unfinished sculptures that were ordered for the tomb of Pope Julius II but remained embedded in stone. The effect is eerie and inspired future generations of sculptors to adopt this *nonfinite* technique.

Hanging next to Michelangelo isn't easy but the Accademia offers many other works that demonstrate the artistic accomplishments of the time. Although you may not have heard of Albertinelli or Granacci, an examination of these and other artists sheds light on the cultural changes occurring before and during the Renaissance.

MERCATO CENTRALE

Markets are a good place to observe a city and understand its inhabitants. Mercato Centrale (Via dell'Ariento 10/14, Mon.–Fri. 7 A.M.–2 P.M.

and Sat. 7 A.M.–5 P.M.) is housed in an art nouveau structure that must have shocked Florentine eyes when it was completed in 1874. The vast interior is filled with food stalls and a continuous chorus of buyers and sellers.

ORSANMICHELE

The name Orsanmichele (Via dei Calzaiuoli, tel. 05/5284-715, Tues.–Sun. 10 A.M.–5 P.M.) derives from the *orto* (garden) where an oratory once stood. The building was destroyed by the *comune* to make way for a grain market in 1240 and later burnt down by the Black Guelfs. After reconstruction, the building was transformed into a church and the guilds of the city decorated the outside with sculptures of their patron saints. Many of the originals by Ghilberti and Donatello have since been replaced with copies. Even so, a walk around the building remains impressive. The door on Via dei Calzaiuoli leads to a tranquil interior dominated by Andrea Orcagna's tabernacle. He spent 10 years perfecting his marble bas-relief of *The Death of the Virgin* and *Assumption.* On the other side is Bernardo Daddi's painting of *Virgin and Child,* completed during the plague of 1348.

Santa Croce

Santa Croce is the name of a neighborhood, a piazza, and a church. The name is a reminder of the oratory dedicated to the holy cross *(santa croce)* where Franciscan friars once preached. During the Middle Ages, merchants lived here along the banks of the Arno and it was a gathering spot whenever the city had something to celebrate. An early predecessor of *calcio* (soccer) was played in the 16th century and tournaments are still held in the square. On the neighborhood's eastern edge are the Galleria degli Uffizi and the Ponte Vecchio. There's also a tourist office (in Via Borgo S. Croce 29r) for anyone who would like a tour of the narrow streets in this part of Florence.

SANTA CROCE CHURCH

Florence was ripe territory for the Franciscans who founded the church of Santa Croce

(Piazza Santa Croce, tel. 05/5246-6105, Mon.–Sat. 9:30 A.M.–5:30 P.M., Sun. 1–5:30 P.M., €5) in 1218. A convent was built next door, where many of the city's wealthy families sent their children to be educated. Soon the church was overcrowded with worshippers and Arnoldo di Cambio was asked to enlarge the building. Construction took 150 years and upon consecration in 1443 the facade remained unfinished. The Quaratesi family offered to pay for the job but the Franciscans were firmly against sponsorship. It wasn't until an Englishman made a no-strings-attached donation in the 19th century that the building was completed.

The inside is spacious and was too wide for stone vaulting. Wooden roofs were cheaper to build and frequently used by Franciscans sworn to poverty. Ironically many of the city's most renowned citizens paid a lot of money to be buried here. Michelangelo, of course, didn't need to pay. He was nearly as famous then as he is now and his body lay in state for several days as citizens paid their final respects. He now rests under Vasari's sculpture in the first chapel on the right. Monuments to Machiavelli and Dante are located nearby.

Many artworks are now in the **Museo dell'Opera di Santa Croce** (Piazza Santa Croce 16, tel. 05/5246-6105, Mon.–Sat. 9:30 A.M.–5:30 P.M., €5). The entrance is immediately on the right of the church. Cimabue's *Crucifix,* destroyed during the flood of 1966, took several painstaking years to be restored. It is a landmark of Renaissance art and now looks as good as new. On the back wall of the museum are frescoes by Taddeo Gaddi, including his version of *The Last Supper.*

Borgo dei Greci is one of the oldest streets in the city and leads from Santa Croce to Palazzo Vecchio. Two thousand years ago Romans filled the amphitheater that stood nearby. At number three is Palazzo Peruzzi, which was home to a wealthy 14th-century family. They lost their fortune in 1343, however, after lending money to an English king bankrupted by continuous wars with the French.

MUSEO NAZIONALE DEL BARGELLO

The Museo Nazionale del Bargello (Via del Proconsolo 4, tel. 05/529-4883, daily 8:15 A.M.–6 P.M., closed 2nd and 4th Monday of each month, €4) has one of the highest concentrations of Renaissance sculpture in the world. Donatello, del Verrocchio, and Michelangelo are all well represented. The palazzo was built in 1255 as the headquarters for the Capitano del Popolo and was the first public building of the city. The tower rises 57 meters high and slightly exceeded the limit of the time. The present name derives from the palazzo's use as police headquarters and became a museum during Florence's brief stint as capital of Italy.

The museum covers three floors and it may be difficult to concentrate on a single sculpture with this much beauty around. The first room includes an early effort by Michelangelo that cemented his reputation as a genius. *Bacco Ebbro* (1497) catches the god of wine in full debauchery with the effects of drink clearly visible in the marble. Many of Michelangelo's works were never fully completed and it's possible to see the rough strokes left by his chisel.

PIAZZA DELLA SIGNORIA

Unlike most cities in Tuscany where religious and civic buildings stood side by side, Florence had a clear division between church and state. Piazza della Signoria was dedicated to political life and standards for its construction were higher than anywhere else. The piazza grew over the years as neighborhoods were pushed back and churches destroyed to make room for a rising elite. Rules were different here and prostitution and gambling prohibited.

Across from Palazzo Vecchio is the **Loggia dei Lanzi,** built in 1350 and initially used for public ceremonies. It was gradually turned into an outdoor sculpture gallery and houses Cellini's bronze *Perseus,* shown beheading Medusa. The statue took nearly a decade to complete and the final casting almost burned down the artist's house.

◖ GALLERIA DEGLI UFFIZI

Galleria degli Uffizi (Loggiata degli Uffizi 6, tel. 05/529-4883, Tues.–Sun. 8:15 A.M.–6:50 P.M.,

© ALEXEI J. COHEN

The Ponte Vecchio is Florence's oldest bridge.

€6.50) was built at the height of Florence's power when the city had reached preeminence in Tuscany and beyond. The building stretches from the Piazza della Signoria to the Arno river and once housed the magistrate offices, but soon became a repository for works of art. In 1584, Francesco I added a second story and Europe's first modern art gallery was born.

The remarkable collection contains works from the 13th–18th centuries; although the focus is on Florence, other Italian cities are well represented. Religious themes pervade much of the art and the second room contains several paintings of Madonna and child. Cimabue's version and Giotto's are light-years apart. Giotto's Virgin appears modern, her eyes look in two directions, and she is clearly feminine. They both, however, had problems painting babies. The red dots underneath many of the frames indicate that they have been restored.

Botticelli painted *Primavera* for the Medicis in 1481. The figures are weightless and float virtually on the canvas. Zephyr is chasing Chloris, Mercury is occupied with the clouds,

and the three Graces are engaged in a dance. There is little depth in the painting, giving it an unreal and dreamlike look that hypnotizes viewers.

The Uffizi is one of the most-visited museums in the world, yet smaller than similar institutions of its caliber. There are thick huddles around the pearls of the collection and little intimacy between artwork and observer. To avoid lines, purchase tickets in advance and arrive early. The bar at the exit of the museum is often crowded but the view from the balcony makes the wait bearable.

PONTE VECCHIO

The Ponte Vecchio (1345) is the oldest bridge in Florence, but the idea of lining it with houses and shops still seems revolutionary. These were originally rented out to butchers but the smell so infuriated Granduca Ferdinando I that he had them evicted in 1593. Since then the bridge has been occupied by jewelers. The Ponte Vecchio is open to pedestrians only. In the middle is a gap where the Arno River can be observed and trash was once dumped. Above is the Corridoio Vasariano, which links the Uffizi with Palazzo Pitti. Cosimo I used this route so he wouldn't have to walk the streets. The bridge was the only one spared by the Germans, who dynamited either side before their retreat in 1944. The effects of the explosions can still be seen on the shrapnel-scarred buildings nearby. It also survived the flood of 1966 that left shops waterlogged for months.

Santo Spirito

This quarter on the left bank of the Arno is commonly known as **Oltrarno** (beyond the Arno). Its location outside the immediate center has spared it much of the commercial exploitation of other neighborhoods. Streets are less crowded with visitors making it possible to catch a genuine glimpse of Florence's past. Highlights include Palazzo Pitti, Masaccio frescos, and a walk through the maze of streets where traditional handicrafts are still performed much the way they were during the Renaissance. Have a look at the goldsmiths, woodcarvers, and painters as they practice their art.

PALAZZO PITTI

The original nucleus of Palazzo Pitti, which gradually spread horizontally over the years, was built in the 14th century for the wealthy banker Luca Pitti. As a rival of the Medicis he wanted to express his power through architecture and flattened a large part of the existing neighborhood to get his wish. Pitti's fortunes turned rapidly and even before the palazzo was completed it fell into the hands of Cosimo I. It wasn't until the reign of the Regents of Lorraine, however, that the palazzo gained its present form.

Today the vast *casa museo* contains several museums. **Galleria Palatina** (Palazzo Pitti, tel. 05/5238-8611, Tues.–Sun. 8:15 A.M.–6:50 P.M., €8.50) originated as the personal collection of the Medicis and covers the entire second floor. Paintings hang just as the last residents of the palazzo had wanted; the lack of chronology would infuriate a curator. For everyone else, the haphazard display is refreshing and the gallery labels read like a who's who of the art world. Works by Botticelli, Tiziano, Perugino, and Veronese fill 11 finely decorated salons. One has only to look up at the ceiling frescoes to understand the supremacy of the Medicis. Rooms four and five are the showstoppers and it's easy to lose track of time admiring Raffaello's *Madonna della Seggiola.*

The entire collection owes its existence to Anna Maria Ludovica. She was the last Medici heir and had the forethought to devise a pact in 1737 that guaranteed the family collection would never be divided, sold, or leave the city.

Below the Palatina on the first floor is the **Museo degli Argenti** (Palazzo Pitti, tel. 05/5238-8709, Tues.–Sun. 8:15 A.M.–6:30 P.M., €6). The museum displays glassware and carpets, as well as fine jewelry greatly cherished by the Medicis. **The Royal Apartments** (Palazzo Pitti, tel. 05/5238-8614, Tues.–Sun. 8:15 A.M.–6:50 P.M., €6) provide further insight into the family's taste for luxury. The neoclassical design of the apartments was ordered by the Dukes of Lorraine, who lived in the palazzo until the 19th century. **Galleria d'Arte Moderna** (tel. 05/5238-8616, Tues.–Sun. 8:15 A.M.–6:50 P.M., €8.50), on the third floor, was opened in 1924 and is dedicated almost exclusively to Italian painters. There are a number of works by the group of Tuscan artists, known as the Macchiaioli or spot-makers, led by Diego Martelli.

It's easy to overdose on art in Florence and fortunately there are gardens like **Giardino di Boboli** (Palazzo Pitti, daily 8:15 A.M.–7:30 P.M. in summer and until 4:30 P.M. in winter, €6) in which to absorb everything. The garden blends an initial perfectly manicured section with a wilder natural park opened to the public in 1766. Art isn't entirely absent even here, though; the Viottolone alley is lined with sculptures.

FORTE BELVEDERE

Forte Belvedere (Via di San Leonardo, tel. 05/527–681, Wed.–Mon. 10 A.M.–7 P.M.) lies on the hill above Boboli and provides one of the best views of the city. It's a little harder to reach than **Piazzale Michelangelo,** whose convenient parking is a mandatory stop for busloads of camera-happy tourists. If you aren't planning on visiting Lucca or any of the other fortified towns in Tuscany, Belvedere's star-shaped ramparts are an excellent primer in military architecture. The fortress was built at the end of the 16th century and served as insurance for the Medicis, who were wary of attacks from outside the city and rebellions from within. It was also a reliable place to stash their treasure. Today you can walk around the terraces while admiring the city below.

SANTA MARIA DEL CARMINE
Santa Maria del Carmine (Piazza del Carmine, tel. 05/5276-8224, Tues.–Sat. 10 A.M.–5 P.M., Sun. 1–5 P.M.) is famous for its frescoes. You'll need to make a reservation to enter the chapel next door and pay €4 but it's worth the trouble. Masaccio started painting in 1424 and four years later had covered the room with scenes recounting the life of Saint Paul. The most memorable image however is Adam and Eve being forcefully escorted from the Garden of Eden. Masaccio died several years later at the age of 27 but in his short life helped shape the direction of Renaissance art.

ENTERTAINMENT AND EVENTS
Classical music can be heard any night of the week in Florence and the annual Maggio Musicale is a highlight of the musical calendar. Jazz is also well represented while rock, pop, and hip-hop enthusiasts may be slightly disappointed with the offerings. Theater picks up the slack and finding a happy hour in the center is easy. Discos open late and dance floors get crowded after midnight. Most clubs charge admission but there is generally someone handing out free passes along the busy streets and piazze.

Nightlife
LIVE MUSIC
Someone's always blowing their horn at the **Caruso Jazz Café** (Via Lambertesca, 14–16r, tel. 05/528-1940, daily noon–3 P.M.

and 7–11 P.M.). The legendary venue welcomes top musicians on weekends and the Burma Jazz Trio play the standards every Thursday night.

Concerts start at 10:15 P.M. at **Jazz Club** (Via Nuova dei Caccini 3, tel. 05/5247-9700, Tues.–Sat. 9 P.M.–2 A.M.). Jam sessions are on Tuesdays. Entrance is free with the purchase of a membership card at the door.

On May 14, Piazza Santissima Annunziata transforms itself into an open-air stage. **Jazz & Co** brings jazz, classical, ethnic, and lounge into one of Florence's most beautiful piazze for several weeks. Musicians start tuning at sunset and keep the notes reverberating off Renaissance facades until 2 A.M. There is no shortage of outdoor bars and cafés to enjoy the evening.

Churches are a good source of music in Florence and **Santa Margherita** (Via del Corso, tel. 05/521-5044) puts on a free organ concert at 9:15 P.M. every evening except Monday. If that sounds dull, you never heard an organ played in a Baroque church before. Concerts are also regularly organized by **Amici della Musica** at the Teatro della Pergola (Via Alamanni 39, tel. 05/521-0804).

NIGHTCLUBS AND DISCOS
If you like your discos big and brash, head to **Lo Space Electronic** (Via Palazzuolo 37, tel. 05/529-3082, Tues.–Sun. 10 P.M.–4 A.M.). The aquatic bar is a nice conversation piece but if you don't feel like talking, head to the second floor and dance with a young international crowd. Music varies between pop and hip-hop, and the entry fee depends on the evening.

Universale (Via Pisana 77r, tel. 05/5233-5495, Thurs.–Fri. 8 P.M.–3 A.M.) is a former cinema transformed into a spacious dance hall. The Sunday Aperichic evening is a good way to cap a weekend in Florence. If you get tired of the music you can change ambiences by entering the Casanova room.

During the summer, **Central Park** (Via del Fosso Macinante 1, tel. 05/535-9942, Thurs.–Sat. 9:30 P.M.–4 A.M.) and **Rio Grande** (Viale degli Olmi 1, tel. 05/535-2143, summer Tues.–Sat. 10 P.M.–3 A.M., winter Wed., Fri., Sat.

10 P.M.–3 A.M., €9.50 cover charge) both located in Parco delle Cascine near Ponte della Vittoria, feature outdoor dancefloors. Although the open-air spaces close in September, the clubs remain open year-round.

Maracanà (Via Faenza 4a/b, tel. 05/521-0298, Wed.–Sun. 8 P.M.–2 A.M.) is where Brazilians go to dance and everyone else tries to keep up. Evenings start with dinner and a floorshow that sets a carnival beat. Afterwards tables make way for the dance floor and the party doesn't stop until your legs do. Unlike the Maracanà, where the dress code is relaxed, **Yab Club** (Via Sassetti 5, tel. 05/521-5160, daily except Mon. and Sun. 10 P.M.–4 A.M.) prefers guests to be dressed as though it were their last night out. The music inside is chill-out, funk, hip-hop, and live. DJ Ravin from the Buddha Bar in Paris makes a monthly appearance.

For a dose of glamour in stylish surroundings head to **Full Up** (Via della Vigna Vecchia 23–25r, tel. 05/529-3006, Thurs.–Sat. 11 P.M.–3 A.M.). The club remains on the crest of the Florentine scene and provides an intimate space to dance, dine, or just sip a Cosmopolitan. Thursday is "Fruit Joy," when one of eight house DJs spins a mix of lounge and chill-out.

Tenax (Via Pratese 46, tel. 05/530-8160, Fri. 10:30 P.M.–4 A.M. and Sat. 10:30 P.M.–5 A.M.) is a little outside the city near the airport, but that hasn't stopped it from becoming one of Florence's most popular nighttime destinations. The club interior is ideal for concerts, and Thievery Corporation and Claude Challe have performed here in the past. "Nobody's Perfect" is Tenax's Saturday chill-out event. Upstairs is a small wine bar and lounge where the resident DJ works up a sweat on Fridays.

WINE BARS

All'Antico Vinaio (Via dei Neri 65, Mon.–Sat. 8 A.M.–3:30 P.M. and 5–9:30 P.M., €4) is a beacon for wine drinkers in Santa Croce. It's not so much the quantity but the quality that counts here. Red and white is sold by the bottle or glass at frugal prices. The selection of salami and authentic first courses are meant for anyone who prefers not to drink on an empty stomach.

Gianni Migliorini has turned **Casa del Vino** (Via dell'Ariento 16r, tel. 05/521-5609, Mon.–Fri. 9:30 A.M.–7 P.M. and Sat. 10 A.M.–3:30 P.M., €5) into a wine and tripe hall of fame. If you've never tasted the two together, then make this your first destination.

The wine list at **Enoteca Boccadama** (Piazza Santa Croce 25–26r, tel. 05/524-3640, Tues.–Sun. 9 A.M.–midnight, €6) is a delight for connoisseurs. Less refined palates can relax as it's hard to go wrong here and the real risk is going right.

I Fratellini (Via dei Cimatori 38r, tel. 05/5239-6096, daily 8 A.M.–8 P.M., €5) is literally a hole in the wall. The two owners serve their special panini and wine from inside a tiny room to eager patrons lining the street.

Le Volpi e L'Uva (Piazza dei Rossi 1r, tel. 05/5239-8132, Mon.–Sat. 10 A.M.–8 P.M., €5) is the place to decide once and for all who produces the best wine: France or Italy. Riccardo and Emilio make the taste test more interesting with a selection of cheeses and cold cuts. By the end of several glasses, it may be too close to call.

La Cantinetta Wine Bar (Via della Scala 7r, tel. 05/526-1870, daily 8 A.M.–midnight, €6) was opened in 2007 near Santa Maria Novella. The wood interior is faithful to Tuscan tradition and the tasting menu offers a chance to compare the flavors of different regions. Bottled beer from microbreweries around Europe are also available.

Past and present meet at **Angels Restaurant & Wine Bar** (Via del Proconsolo 29–31, tel. 05/5239-8762, €8). The contrast extends to a kitchen that prefers fusion over monotony. Come here for a great change of scenery just minutes from the Duomo.

The Arts
GALLERIES

If the Alinari brothers were alive today they would be Internet millionaires. Instead they lived in the first half of the 19th century. Photography was cutting-edge technology and the first cameras were being assembled in Europe. The brothers got their kicks from setting up their equipment all over Florence and capturing street life. The black and white photographs are a fascinating celluloid flashback to a past that doesn't exist anymore.

It's all at **Museo Nazionale Alinari della Fotografia** (Piazza Santa Maria Novella 14a r, tel. 05/521-6310, Thurs.–Tues. 9:30 A.M.–7:30 P.M., Sat. until 11:30 P.M., €9), which retraces the history and development of snapshots. Besides a permanent museum, there's an exhibition space that presents six photography and art shows a year. The Touch section is an innovative gallery designed specifically for the sight-impaired.

Galleria Masini (Piazza Goldoni 6r, tel. 05/529-4000, Mon.–Sat. 9 A.M.–1 P.M. and 3–7 P.M.) was opened in 1870 and is the oldest art gallery in Florence. Contemporary oil paintings are the mainstay of the gallery and landscapes dominate the walls. The art can be shipped anywhere in the world and the owner loves to practice his English.

Since the conversion of **Forte Belvedere** (Via di San Leonardo, Tues.–Sun. 2:30–7 P.M., often free) into an exhibition and gallery space, a number of excellent shows have been organized. The annual 15 X 15 event displays chosen works by 15 artists from 15 city galleries.

THEATER

The first performance inside **Teatro della Pergola** (Via della Pergola 18–32, tel. 05/5226-4335, www.teatrodellapergola.it, box office Tues.–Sat. 9:30 A.M.–6:45 P.M.) was staged in 1656. More recently many of Italy's top playwrights and composers developed their talents in this space. It was declared a national monument in 1925 and now dedicates itself entirely to prose. Recent plays included the work of Neil Simon, Luigi Pirandello, and Molière. A second smaller hall gives audiences the chance to see every expression. Gallery seats in the main theater are €14.50.

Teatro Verdi (Via Ghibellina 99, tel. 05/521-2320, www.teatroverdifirenze.it, box office Mon.–Fri. 3–7 P.M.) was built over the site of a former prison in the classic Italian style. All the velvet is red and box seats rise impressively on both sides of the theater. It is the frequent home of the Orchestra della Tuscany and presents opera, ballet, and jazz concerts, as well as classical chamber music.

Perhaps the most original theater in Florence is **Teatro del Sale** (Via de'Macci 111r, tel. 05/5200-1492, www.teatrodelsale.com), located in a 14th-century convent. It's dinner theater, to be more precise, operated in association with the Cibreo restaurant and serving dazzling dishes created by Fabio Picchi. The curtain rises in the early evening and performances range from classic, jazz, and blues to poetry readings and one-act plays. To enter this versatile locale you'll need to become a member. It's a formality practiced by many clubs in the city and in this case only costs €5. Reservations are a good idea.

Saschall (Via Fabrizio De André, tel. 05/5650-4112, www.saschall.it), inaugurated in 2002, is the newest theater in Florence and has quickly become a pillar of the city's cultural activity. From the outside it looks like a modern interpretation of the circus tent set up on the banks of the Arno. Inside hundreds of spectators gather regularly for a variety of musical and theatrical events. The street it's located on was recently renamed after one of Italy's most famous singers.

Vipertheater (Via Pistoiese/Via Lombardy, tel. 05/531-8056, www.viperclub.eu, Fri. and Sat. 9:30 P.M.–2 A.M.) is a multifunctional space in the suburb of Pistoiese. Depending on the evening you could find yourself watching a comic opera or partaking in a hard-jazz concert. It's also a popular stop for up-and-coming U.S. and European bands hoping to make it big in Florence. Concerts rarely cost over €15 and DJs keep the crowd warm. Take the Linea 35 or 56 from the train station towards Pistoiese 20.

CINEMA

If you feel like leaving Florence for a few hours and losing yourself in the world of the silver screen, there are a couple of cinemas projecting films in their original language. **Odeon** (Via Sassetti 1, Piazza Strozzi, tel. 05/521-4068) is a beautiful cinema that lets De Niro, Pitt, and Nicholson speak with their own voices on Monday and Tuesday nights. **Fulger** (Via Maso Finigurerra, tel. 05/5238-1881) gives English accents full reign on Thursdays. Don't be surprised if the projectionist takes a break mid-movie. That's your chance to grab a Magnum ice cream or to run to the restroom before the second reel. Most of the other cinemas in Florence project films dubbed in Italian.

SONAR International Short Film Festival (www.sonarfilmfestival.it) is held at the end of March in various theaters across the city. The program includes a selection of animated and experimental films.

Festivals and Events

Tradition has it that a new fire must be lit on the Saturday before Easter. Since 1764, a huge cart packed with firecrackers has been wheeled to the Duomo. Priests dressed as apostles carry the fire to the Archbishop, who intones the Gloria before lighting a long fuse. Several seconds later, all sound is drowned out by the roar of fireworks.

Taste (tel. 05/521-2622, www.taste firenze.it, Sat.–Sun. 10 A.M.–11 P.M., Mon. 10 A.M.–7 P.M., €8) is a voyage for gourmets across the gastronomic landscapes of Italy. The Pitti Immagine event held at Stazione Leopolda in mid-March provides a unique opportunity to sample the country's top oil, cheese, and wine products.

Whether the **Cricket Festival** originated as a rite of spring or as a means to save crops remains debatable. What is certain is that real insects aren't used anymore. Today the bugs are made of terra-cotta but they still live inside the traditional colorful cages Florentines once used to hunt insects in the 16th century. It makes an original souvenir. The vibrant festival is celebrated on May 28 in Parco delle Cascine.

Craft isn't dead in Florence. It's alive and well and celebrated every year during the **Mostra Internazionale dell'Artigianato** (Fortezza da Basso, Viale Strozzi 1, tel. 05/549-5969, www .mostraartigianato.it, late April or early May

daily 10 A.M.–9:30 P.M., €5). Artists from Florence, Tuscany, and around Italy rest their hands for one week and display the inventive spirit inside the city's premier exhibition space.

Each May music takes center stage during **Maggio Musicale** (Teatro Comunale, Via Solferino 15, tel. 05/521-3535, www.maggiofiorentino.com). Born as a means of exploring creative movements of the past, the festival proposes a new theme each year. In 2006 it was Romanticism, in 2007 Rossini. Contemporary interpretations are performed by the world's finest conductors, soloists, and singers. Tickets range from €15–120. The Teatro Comunale, which hosts the event, presents ballet and opera.

Popular belief says the English invented the beautiful game. Anyone who has seen Florentines play **Calcio Storico** knows where soccer, football, and rugby originated. "Reenactment" is the wrong word for describing the two teams of 27 costumed players squaring off against each other. This competition is as competitive now as it must have been in Dante's day. Don't look for a rulebook in Piazza Santa Croce in June when the tournament begins. What counts is scoring a *caccia* (goal) any way you can. Matches last 50 minutes and enthusiastic crowds fill the piazza and roar in support. The final match is played on June 24, the Feast Day of Florence's Patron Saint, St. John the Baptist.

Rificolone are paper lanterns illuminated with a candle and held aloft with a short pole. During the **Festa della Rificolona,** a celebration of the Virgin Mary's birth on the evening of September 8, they are set floating onto the Arno. The illumination of the river by thousands of colored lights is a spectacular sight.

Every guild has its day; for winemakers, it's the last Saturday of September. Since the 13th century, this has been the day to bring the new wine into town to be honored and blessed. Today the festival is mostly symbolic and recalls the role the surrounding countryside once played. The event begins with an afternoon procession from Piazza del Duomo through the surrounding streets. It's a colorful parade of heralds, flag wavers, and trumpeters, who return to the Piazza to perform traditional pageantry.

Later the *carro matto* (a great cart containing over 1,000 flasks of wine) is drawn into Piazza della Signoria, where festivities continue and the blessed wine is duly distributed.

SHOPPING

There's no shortage of places to shop in Florence. Although an influx of big-name boutiques has led to the closure of traditional stores, it remains possible to spend euros the old-fashioned way. Well-stocked antique shops are clustered in Via Maggio and Via dei Fossi and fine jewelry is still produced along the Ponte Vecchio in the bridge's characteristic workshops. On the other side, in Santo Spirito, many artisans continue to produce objects in wood, stone, and metal. The city's frequent craft markets are another way of discovering the skills of yesteryear. Handmade leather goods are concentrated in Santa Croce and it's best to browse rather than buy the first wallet you see. For chic clothing and accessories, visit the shops along Via Tornabuoni and Vigna Nuova.

If you spend over €155 in a single shop you are entitled to an instant VAT tax refund. Depending on the item, this could be 4 percent, 10 percent, or 20 percent of the purchase price. Look for the Cash Refund sign in participating stores.

As in many Italian cities, street vendors will try to tempt you with attractive contraband. Although it may seem like a good idea at the time, funding the black market has global consequences. It's also illegal and anyone caught buying a fake Gucci can expect a hefty fine.

Novella
CLOTHING

Prada (Via Tornabuoni 67r, tel. 05/526-7471, Mon.–Sat. 8:30 A.M.–8:30 P.M., Sun. 2–7 P.M.) may be synonymous with exclusive clothing and outlandish prices, but that doesn't mean you can't have a look. Check out the new patterns and colors of the season and find the equivalents nearby for less.

Men looking to recapture a little *dolce vita* can find it at **Emilio Pucci** (Via Tornabuoni 20–22r, tel. 05/5265-8082, Mon.–Sat. 8:30 A.M.–8:30 P.M.). Shirts have a nostalgic

cut that has been in vogue since this aristocratic family took up fashion in the 1950s.

ACCESSORIES

Anyone with a bag fetish can get their fix at **Furla** (Via della Vigna Nuova 47r, tel. 05/528-2779, daily 8:30 A.M.–8:30 P.M.). The boutique inside a former coach house also carries scarves, hats, and fine leather accessories.

Il Bisonte (Via del Parione 31r, tel. 05/521-5722, Mon.–Sat. 8:30 A.M.–8:30 P.M.) only uses *vacchetta* leather that gets better with age. Natural vegetable-tanned hides are transformed into handbags, briefcases, billfolds, and belts.

CHILDREN

Stylish parents dress their stylish children at **Ugo & Carolina** (Via delle Belle Donne 35r, tel. 05/528-7820, Mon.–Sat. 9 A.M.–8 P.M., closed Mon. morning). Both owners are mothers who understand the demands of toddlers and only sell quality brands. There are also jumpsuits for newborns and stretch clothes for expectant mothers.

BOOKS

The smell of old books is strong at **Alberto Cozzi** (Via del Parione 35r, tel. 05/529-4968, Tues.–Sat. 9 A.M.–1 P.M. and 2:30–7 P.M.). Paper is all locally made and artisans spend their days rebinding and restoring worn-out editions.

MARKETS

The best place to buy flowers is at the **Mercato delle Piante e dei Fiori** on Thursdays. The plant and flower market keeps Via Pellicceria smelling like roses 7 A.M.–7:30 P.M.

San Giovanni
ARTS AND CRAFTS

If Michelangelo were alive today, **Colorificio Poli** (Via Guelfa 45–49, tel. 05/521-6506, Mon.–Fri. 9 A.M.–1 P.M. and 3:30–7:30 P.M.) would be his art supply store. There are materials for painting and pigments for mixing colors as well as the materials for ceramic, porcelain, and restoration work.

CLOTHING

Florence is fashion. The season starts in January and February when designers start filling runways with haute couture. Recent shows have proven not all innovation is in Milan. The city is particularly strong in menswear and there is never a shortage of world premieres.

Gerard Loft (Via dei Pecori, 34–40r, tel. 05/528-2491, Mon. 2:30–7:30 P.M., Tues.–Sat. 10 A.M.–7:30 P.M.) sells cool. The shop stocks men, women, and children's brands that are a couple of seasons ahead of fashion. Labels include Munich Vintage 55, Swear, N.D.C., and limited-edition lines.

Gabs (Via S. Egidio 9r and Via S. Gallo 73r, tel. 05/5321-5343, Mon.–Sat. 9 A.M.–8:30 P.M.) is a new label founded by Franco Gabrielli for women tired of being dictated to by designers. It was an immediate success and the first boutique opened in Tokyo. The two Florence locations carry all their signature head-turners.

BOOKS

Bibliophiles and librarians will appreciate the amount of shelf space in the city. Anyone looking for secondhand editions and out-of-date manuscripts should browse the bookshops on **Via dei Servi** (Bartolini at 24–28r and Cornici Campani at 22r are worth a visit) or around the **Biblioteca Nazionale** (Piazza S. Ambrogio 2).

HOME

La Menagère (Via Ginori 8r, tel. 05/521-3875, Tues.–Sat. 9 A.M.–1 P.M. and 3–7 P.M.) can help replace everything from a wooden spoon to a hot plate. This welcoming shop with high ceilings and wooden floors sells porcelain and kitchen utensils that never cease to inspire cooks.

Santa Croce
ARTS AND CRAFTS

A walk down **Via de'Macci** reassures anyone who thought craft was extinct. Hammers and chisels continue to bang in this enclave where mass production could learn a thing or two. Carpenters work in a succession of small shops restoring furniture or assembling frames

as they have for centuries. **Osteria de'Macci** (Via de'Macci 77) is a good place to eat and listen to old timers recount how the neighborhood used to be.

CLOTHING

There's little chance **Babele** (Borgo Pinti 34r, tel. 05/524-4729, Tues.–Sat. 10 A.M.–1 P.M. and 3:30–7 P.M.) will start any worldwide trends but the one-style-fits-all dresses created by Angela Baldi have proven popular with locals.

HOME

Weaving is a Florentine skill that hasn't been lost at **Martini** (Via S. Veridiana 6r, tel. 05/5248-0612). All sorts of different natural straws are woven into baskets, carpets, trays, and household objects.

STATIONERY

Recycling is the keyword at **La Tartaruga** (Borgo Albizi 60r, tel. 05/5234-0845, Mon.–Sat. 9 A.M.–1 P.M. and 3–7 P.M.), where paper is transformed into everything imaginable. There are practical objects such as calendars and stationery as well as imaginative toys.

BEAUTY

Antica Officina del Farmacista (Borgo La Croce 44r, tel. 05/549-4537, Mon.–Sat. 8:30 A.M.–1 P.M. and 2:30 P.M.–7 P.M.) creates original scents for body and home. It's an olfactory souvenir that will keep the memory of Florence forever sweet.

MARKETS

A flea market is held in **Piazza dei Ciompi** every morning. On the last Sunday of the month, the same location hosts a large secondhand fair.

Mercato Nuovo del Porcellino is held daily 9 A.M.–8 P.M. on Via Porta Rossa. *Porcellino* means little pig and the market gets its name from a statue nearby. It's popular with tourists and there are plenty of bags, wallets, and woven goods for sale. This is a great market to find that special souvenir to take home with you.

Santo Spirito
ANTIQUES
Piumaccio d'Oro (Borgo San Frediano 65r, tel. 05/5239-8952, Mon.–Sat. 8:30 A.M.–1 P.M. and 2:30–7:30 P.M.) has been run by the Malenotti family for over 70 years. That's a lifetime of antique restoration and creation. The techniques practiced in the small workshop and displayed in the store result in one-of-a-kind tables, chests, chairs, and smaller objects found only here.

Giovanni Pratesi (Via Maggio 13, tel. 05/5239-6568, Mon.–Sat. 9 A.M.–1 P.M. and 3–7 P.M.) is all about Italian antiques. The small shop is filled with furniture, some paintings, sculpture, and decorative objects.

CLOTHING
Giuditta Blandini (Via dello Sprone 25r, tel. 05/5277-6275, www.organic-wear.it, Mon.–Sat. 9 A.M.–7:30 P.M.) combines ecology with style. Every stitch of her men's and women's lines respects the environment. All the cotton, linen, and wool is chemical-free and purchased from fair-trade markets that reward small farmers using biological methods of production. The result is comfortable clothing that looks great.

Any woman who isn't fixated with designer labels might fall in love with **Maçel** (Via Guicciardini 128r, tel. 05/528-7355). The clothes fit just as snugly as anywhere else and come from the same factories used by the big names.

ACCESSORIES
Angela Caputi Giuggiu (Via S. Spirito, 58r, tel. 05/521-2972, Tues.–Sat. 10 A.M.–1 P.M. and 3:30–7:30 P.M.) has been revolutionizing jewelry design since 1975. The collection is handcrafted from a variety of synthetic materials into unique colors, patterns, and shapes.

CHILDREN
If you're anywhere from being a newborn to eight years old, or know anyone in that circle **Mini Gold** (Via Maggio 7r, tel. 05/528-2098, Tues.–Sat. 10 A.M.–1 P.M. and 3:30–7:30 P.M.,

Mon. 10 A.M.–1 P.M.) should be on your map. Clothing here is designed to stand up to the rigors of childhood. A lot of the colorful collection is made in Denmark, where function is an obsession.

HARDWARE
You may not need a hammer, but if you want to know the difference between an American and an Italian hardware store you need to visit **SE-AR** (Via dei Serragli 43r, tel. 05/529-4114, Mon.–Fri. 8:30 A.M.–1 P.M. and 3:30–7:30 P.M.). A couple of minutes watching Riccardo and Massimo behind the old-time counter should do the trick. Besides all the usual goods, they also make spare sets of keys.

MARKETS
Piazza Santo Spirito hosts **Arti e Mestieri D'Oltrarno,** an arts and crafts market, on the second Sunday of every month except in July and August. The market is open 7 A.M.–7 P.M.

SPORTS AND RECREATION
Parks
Shelley liked to write poems in **Parco delle Cascine** and it's true there's something inspiring about the distant Duomo above the oak trees. It was a hit even among less romantic Florentines almost from inauguration day in the late 18th century.

Today this nearly rectangular park on the edge of Santa Maria Novella is where local joggers get a workout. There's an attractive racecourse and novice gamblers might try their luck in one of the frequent springtime races. A tennis club, swimming pool, and flying school are also located within the extensive grounds.

Golf
Professional golfers from around the world come to tee off on the **Ponte Vecchio Challenge** (tel. 800/385–078, www.ponte vecchiochallenge.it, 9:30 A.M.–6:30 P.M.). The unique two-day event requires power and finesse. Each team attempts to reach one of three

floating greens worth different points according to their distance. The competition is held in mid–December and best observed from Piazza Santa Maria Soprarno.

Circolo del Golf dell'Ugolino (Via Chiantigiana 3, tel. 05/5230-1009, www.golfugolino. it, summer daily 9 A.M.–7 P.M., €65) provides 18 holes across a wonderful Tuscan landscape. The course is south of Florence on the SS Chiantigiana, five kilometers after Grassina.

Skiing

The slopes of **Abetone** (tel. 05/736-0001, www.abetone.org) are 85 kilometers from Florence and have been a popular winter destination since resorts **Hotel Ristorante Excelsior** (Via Brennero 313, tel. 05/736-0010, €110 d) and **Albergo Regina** (Via Uccelliera 5, tel. 05/736-0007, www.albergoregina.com, €100 d) opened in the early 1900s. Today there are four valleys full of trails that keep downhill racers and cross-country enthusiasts occupied. Snowboarders can enjoy the new terrain park equipped with a half-pipe and three-meter jumps. The season officially opens on December 8 and artificial snow machines guarantee coverage whether nature feels like it or not. Renting equipment is convenient and accommodations plentiful if you decide to stay the night. **Copit** (tel. 05/521–463, www.copitspa. it) operates a daily bus service from Largo Alinari near Stazione SMN.

Soccer

Florentines cheer for purple. Their team, A.C. Fiorentina, has a successful past when heroes like Gabriel Battistuta and Rui Costa spent nearly a decade scoring goals in the Stadio Artemio Franchi. The most animated seats, where the singing never stops and the only danger is a hoarse voice, are in the *curva* Fiesole. Tickets can be purchased at Bar Marisa outside the stadium or any authorized *tabacchi*. The soccer season takes place during late-August–late-May. From the center of town take the 17, 10, 20, or 11 bus in the direction of Campo di Marte or follow the purple jerseys.

ACCOMMODATIONS
Novella
UNDER €100
Ostello Archi Rossi (Via Faenza 94r, tel. 05/529-0804, www.hostelarchirossi.com, €24 pp or €70 d) is five minutes from the train station and offers various-sized rooms with and without bathrooms. The lobby has a personality all its own and the brightly lit breakfast room encourages a lively communal spirit. Internet is free.

€100-200
Hotel Bellettini (Via dei Conti 7, tel. 05/521-3561, www.hotelbellettini.com, €100–140 s/d) is run by the Naldini sisters and their husbands. The family atmosphere includes comfortable rooms with traditional Tuscan furnishings. Rooms on the top floor have good views and there are several triple and quadruple options. Breakfast includes Gina's homemade cakes.

Art is everywhere at the **Albion** (Via Il Prato 22r, tel. 05/521-4171, www.hotelalbion.it, €129–167 s/d). Oil paintings fill the reception hall and small dining room, where breakfast is served 7:30–10:30 A.M. The neo-Gothic hotel is located near the Arno on a quiet side street.

€200-300
Once you sit on the rooftop terrace with a glass of Chianti in your hands, it may be hard to leave the **Antica Torre di Via Tornabuoni** (Via dei Tornabuoni, tel. 05/5265-8161, www.tornabuoni1.com, €200–290 s/d). Rooms 403 and 405 have equally good views of the Duomo and Jacopo d'Albasio's attention to detail makes staying here a pleasure. Luxury comes standard in all 11 rooms.

OVER €300
Rooms at **JK Place** (Piazza Santa Maria Novella 7, tel. 05/5264-5181, www.jkplace.com, €330 d) are anything but anonymous. Rooms feels more like home than a hotel and the four-poster beds, wall-to-wall carpeting, and LCD TV are welcoming after a day on the streets of Florence. *Aperitivo* is served on the rooftop

terrace and the restaurant on the ground floor gives Tuscan dishes the gourmet treatment.

San Giovanni
UNDER €100
Johanna II (Via Cinque Giornate 12, tel. 05/547-3377, www.johanna.it, €85–100 s/d) is on a quiet street in a small villa with a garden. Rooms are bright and inviting. An extensive breakfast buffet encourages late risers to start the day early. Parking is free and the owners of the residence operate three similar accommodations in the neighborhood.

€100-200
Located in the thick of medieval Florence near the Ponte Vecchio **Residenza Gli Apostoli** (Borgo SS. Apostoli 8, tel. 05/528-8432, www.residenzapostoli.it, €110–130 s/d) has a bare-bones elegance about it. The five rooms are on the first floor of a 13th-century palazzo and parking is available for a small fee.

Large rooms, frescoed ceilings, and Igino, Daniela, and Regis at the front desk are what make the **Cimabue** (Via Bonifacio Lupi 7, tel. 05/547-5601, www.hotelcimabue.it, €130–155 s/d) memorable. Room 22 is a good pick if you prefer a firm mattress. The hotel runs a variety of tours around the city and throughout the region.

Each of the rooms at the **C Antica Dimora Florence** (Via San Gallo 80, tel. 05/5463-3292, www.anticadimorafirenze.it, €125–150 s/d) is decorated in a different pastel shade and adorned with antique furniture you wish would fit in your luggage. The ambiance is peaceful and the living room is equipped with a small library. In the afternoons, tea and classical music are served. The bed-and-breakfast also has two apartments that are ideal for couples traveling together.

€200-300
A stay at **Residence Hilda** (Via dei Servi 40, tel. 05/528-8021, €230 d) gives you an idea of what it's like to live in Florence. The suites are all decorated in light tones with simple modern furniture. Each is equipped with a small

kitchen and there is a food delivery service if you don't feel like choosing your own tomatoes. Robiglio downstairs is the perfect coffee bar to start the day and all the major sights are within walking distance.

OVER €300
When E. M. Forster described his room with a view, he may have been thinking about the **Hotel degli Orafi** (Lungarno Archibusieri 4, tel. 05/526–622, www.hoteldegliorafi.it, €260–380 s/d). Although some of the decoration borders on flamboyant, the balconies overlooking the Arno are a romantic climax. Service is white glove and there is no request the concierge can't handle.

Santa Croce
UNDER €100
Bed & Breakfast Rovezzano (Via Aretina 507, tel. 05/569-0023, www.rovezzano.com, €62–78 s/d) is located in a residential area 10 minutes from the center. There's free parking and a swimming pool. Rooms are rustic and thick shutters block out all light.

€100-200
Hotel Liana (Via Alfieri 18, tel. 05/524-5303, www.hotelliana.com, €150–170 s/d) is 15 minutes from the Duomo in an elegant residential neighborhood near the botanical gardens. The 18th-century palazzo once housed the English consulate and has maintained an old-world atmosphere uncorrupted by bad taste. Each of the 24 rooms provides refined furnishings, from curtains to headboard.

€200-300
Every major sight is conveniently reachable from **Hotel Morandi** (Via Laura 50, tel. 05/5234-4747, www.hotelmorandi.it, €140–220 s/d). Minibar, safe, parking, and Wi-Fi are standard inside this historic building that's been transformed into a relaxing hotel.

Housed inside a former convent **J and J** (Via di Mezzo 20, tel. 05/526–312, www.cavalierehotels.com, €200–282 s/d) is a Martha Stewart dream come true. Spacious rooms with wood-burning fireplaces, hand-painted wallpaper, and oil paintings are the norm. Breakfast is served in an arched alcove where monks once dined. Guests receive discounts in a number of excellent restaurants nearby.

OVER €300

It's always nice to find fresh flowers and cold champagne in your room and that's exactly what you get at **Hotel Regency** (Piazza M. D'Azeglio 3, tel. 05/524-5247, www.regency-hotel.com, €365–430 s/d). Each of the 35 guestrooms is meticulously furnished with antique furnishings and tapestries, while the lounge and dining areas have that effortless five-star feeling.

Santo Spirito
UNDER €100

Hotel Boboli (Via Romana 63, tel. 05/5229-8645, www.hotelboboli.com, €65–85 s/d) is one of the best two-star establishments in the city. It's been recently refurbished and the bar downstairs remains open 8 A.M.–midnight. Breakfast is an Italian-style buffet with brioche, cake, and juice. Staff are friendly and available to advise guests 24 hours a day.

Antique furniture, wrought-iron beds, and parquet flooring are the hallmarks of **Hotel David** (Viale Michelangelo 1, tel. 05/5681-1695 www.davidhotel.it, €88–95 s/d). All rooms are soundproof and equipped with both shower and bath.

€100-200

Hotel Annalena (Via Romana 34, tel. 05/522-2402, www.hotelannalena.it, €115–175 s/d) is in a tranquil corner of Santo Spirito, minutes from Giardini Boboli. Rooms look out onto a garden ideal for planning the day's itinerary.

It's easy to forget you're in a city once you enter **Hotel Classic** (Viale Machiavelli 25, tel. 05/522-9351, www.classichotel.it, €133–166 s/d). Nature is all around this delightful villa. A continental breakfast is served in the vaulted dining room, garden, or in your room. Parking is available and the Ponte Vecchio is just 12 minutes away on foot.

€200-300

Palazzo Magnani Feroni (Borgo San Frediano 5, tel. 05/5239-9544, www.florencepalace.com, €280 d) takes spacious to new heights. Each of the suites has 20-foot-high ceilings and enough room for a good pillow fight. Bathrooms are decked out in precious marble and there are no hustlers in the billiard room downstairs. A rooftop terrace and bar provides postcard-perfect views.

FOOD

With so many visitors arriving to Florence every day, some chefs have gotten lazy. Tourist traps are everywhere and avoiding them requires a good nose and little observation. Locals won't accept a bad meal, so if you hear Italian that's generally a good sign.

Novella
TUSCAN

Il Latini (Via dei Palchetti 6r, tel. 05/210–916, Tues.–Sun. 12:30–2:30 P.M. and 7:30–10:30 P.M., €8–10) is a popular trattoria where the flavors haven't changed in 50 years. The two rooms get crowed and noisy, but that's part of the fun. Only Tuscan wines are featured in the extensive cellar and tables are assigned on a first come first serve basis.

There may be few tables at **Sostanza detto il Troia** (Via del Porcellana 25r, tel. 05/212–691, Mon.–Fri. noon–2:30 P.M. and 7:30–9:30 P.M., €8–11) but the ones they have managed to fit in this small restaurant are always full of reliable Tuscan fare like *pollo Fiorentina* (Florentine-style chicken) and *stracotto* (braised beef).

SEAFOOD

A Michelin star hasn't changed the way the four friends who founded **I Quattro Amici** (Via Degli Orti 29, tel. 05/215–413, daily 12:30–2:30 P.M. and 7:30–10:30 P.M., €15–20) operate. They still scour the markets looking for the freshest fish and serve it in a pleasant modern restaurant.

PIZZA

Words fail to describe the pizza served at **La Dantesca** (Via Panzani 57r, tel. 05/521-2287, daily 11:30 A.M.–11 P.M., €5.50–8), which overlooks Piazza Santa Maria Novella. The *pizzaiolo* must have inherited a thin slice of da Vinci's genius. The menu also includes some Tuscan favorites and an excellent *ribollita* (stew). Most tables provide a view of the medieval square.

Grotta di Leo (Via della Scala, 41–43r, tel. 05/521-9265, daily 11 A.M.–1 A.M.) serves mouthwatering pizzas in a pleasant interior or on the tables outside. The menu includes Tuscan and Mediterranean stalwarts.

APERITIVO

Lounge (Piazza Santa Maria Novella 9–10r, tel. 05/5264-5282, daily 9 A.M.–1 A.M.) is just that—and an opportunity to nurse a dry martini in a sophisticated modern room. This place is a must for anyone interested in cars, as it doubles as a dealership. A wide selection of breakfast items are offered in the mornings, as well as salads and other lunch options in the afternoon. In the summer you can sit outside overlooking the piazza.

CAFÉS

There are a handful of upscale cafés around Piazza della Repubblica in which to have a tea or espresso break. **Caffè Pazkowski** (Piazza della Rebubblica 6r, tel. 05/210–236, Tues.–Sun. 8 A.M.–1 P.M.) is a shrine to 1950s elegance. Seating is plentiful and it's a good place to rest while enjoying a selection of *mignon* (small pastries). A big band performs here regularly during the summer.

Writers and intellectuals used **Giubbe Rosse** (Piazza della Repubblica 14r, tel. 05/212–280, daily 7:30 A.M.–3 A.M.) as their home base for many years. A late closing hour and strong coffee make it a favorite with conversationalists.

San Giovanni

TUSCAN

The row of double-parked cars outside of **Mario's** (Via della Rosina 2r, tel. 05/521-8550, Mon.–Sat. 11 A.M.–3 P.M., closed Aug., €8) is one indication of how popular this trattoria has become. The restaurant is run by two huge

fans of the Florence soccer team who tend to seat guests next to strangers at the large tables. *Tortelli di patate* (ravioli-type pasta stuffed with potato) and *zuppa di fagioli* (bean soup) are excellent first courses. The house wine is drinkable, but refined palates may prefer something from the cellar.

Natural ingredients and traditional cooking go hand in hand at **ZàZà** (Piazza Mercato Centrale 26–27r, tel. 05/521–541, €12–15). This characteristic trattoria serves up great fish dishes and delicious desserts, as well as Florentine classics. Grab a table overlooking the market if any are free.

C Da Nerbone (Mercato Centrale, tel. 05/521-9949, Mon.–Sat. 7 A.M.–2 P.M., €10–15) has been around almost as long as the marketplace that houses it. In the morning you can try a tripe sandwich; lunchtime options include minestrone and *pappa al pomodoro* (tomato stew) eaten standing at the counter or one of the small tables. It's a Florentine fast-food experience. If you prefer a picnic all the ingredients are available nearby at **Baroni** (Mercato Centrale, Via Galluzzo, stands 256–258 and 277–280, Mon.–Sat. 7 A.M.–2 P.M.).

SPANISH

Posada (Via XX Settembre 33, daily 12:30–3:30 P.M. and 8 P.M.–1 A.M., €10–14) isn't just a taste of Spain, it's an entire mouthful of Spanish gastronomic culture. Dinner begins late with light tapas or a *paella alla catalana* (paella with chicken and beef in a potato base) that is better off shared. Sangria is the drink of choice and they won't let you leave until you've tasted the Santiago de Compostela pie à la mode made in-house.

PIZZA

Once you've decided on thick or thin, the next question is toppings. **Ristorante Il Grande Nuti** (Borgo San Lorenzo 22–26r, tel. 05/521-0145) proposes an original assortment and the adventurous should simply go with the house pizza. The ancient interior is minutes from the Duomo and equally famous for its excellent Tuscan dishes.

GELATO, A FLORENTINE INVENTION

Italy's culinary inventiveness extends way beyond pizza. Perhaps the most universal contribution to diets around the world is gelato, a type of ice cream. Credit for the discovery goes to the Florentine architect Bernardo Buontalenti, who was also employed by the Medicis as a master of ceremonies. One hot summer day in 1565 he was busy preparing a banquet for a group of Spanish diplomats and got more creative than usual. The new dessert that left everyone stunned was a concoction of egg yolks, honey, milk, butter, and sweet wine. Buontalenti knew how to freeze fats and it wasn't long before cream and fruit variations of his delicacy spread across Europe. Today *gelaterie* in the city sell a flavor named after the inventor that recreates the original recipe. Finding the best one is a unique Florentine pleasure.

APERITIVO

B. Gallo (Via del Proconsolo 75r, tel. 05/521-9251, daily noon–1 A.M.) in Piazza del Duomo mixes good food and drink with an up-close view of the Duomo. The cocktails are prepared with so much attention to detail that it's almost a shame to drink them. Stay on for a Tuscan dinner accompanied with an infinite possibility of wines or a nightcap in the second-floor lounge.

GELATO

Carabé (Via Ricasoli, 60r, tel. 05/528-9476, summer daily 11 A.M.–9 P.M., winter daily 11 A.M.–5 P.M.) serves a wide range of granitas and gelato. Flavors depend on what's in season and the Sicilian owners Antonio and Loredana celebrate their origins with a great cannoli, cassata, and brioche—the Sicilian ice-cream sandwich.

The flavors are too numerous to count at **Gelateria Cavini** (Piazza delle Cure 197r, tel. 05/558-7489, summer daily 11 A.M.–9 P.M., winter daily 11 A.M.–5 P.M.) and the lines of expectant customers are a good sign. It may seem like a long way to go for a gelato until the first lick of *nocciola* (hazelnut).

DELICACIES

Around the corner from the Mercato Centrale is an excellent place to stop for a mid-morning snack. **Pasticceria Sieni** (Via Sant'Antonio 54r, tel. 05/521-2830, Tues.–Sun. 7:30 A.M.–1 P.M. and 3:30 P.M.–8 P.M.) has preserved the art of confection and bakes mouth-watering *fedora* and *zuccotto* daily.

Norcineria Bucchi (Via Sant'Antonio 19, tel. 05/529-4859, daily 8 A.M.–8 P.M.) is nearly as popular with tourists as the Duomo, and for gourmets hunting Tuscan cheeses, *porchetta*, and smoked hams it is a rewarding destination. Service can be blunt, which just adds to the atmosphere.

Santa Croce
TUSCAN

Beware of the numerous restaurants around Piazza Santa Croce. Many of these were born simply to meet the demands of mass tourism and are as authentic as Milli Vanilli. If you care about your stomach and wallet, you're better off at **Del Fagioli** (Corso Tintori 47r, tel. 05/524-4285, Mon.–Fri. noon–3 P.M. and 7–11 P.M., €12–15). Start with some crostini appetizers and try the *ribollita* (stew) if you haven't already sampled this Florentine classic. Second courses are divided into grilled, baked, and boiled dishes. The wine list consists mostly of Tuscan bottles.

Il Cibreo (Via Andrea del Verrocchio 8r, tel. 05/234-1100, Tues.–Sat. 12:50–2:30 P.M. and 7:30–11:45 P.M., €14–20) doesn't accept reservations, but no one in line seems to care. What they're interested in is the wide range of second courses and whether to order the *polpettine di pollo* (chicken meatballs) or *collo di pollo ripieno* (stuffed chicken neck). The only thing certain is the house red and cheesecake *all'arancio* (orange cheesecake). They also run a trattoria next door that's less expensive than the restaurant.

INTERNATIONAL
Ruth's (Via L.C. Farini 2a, tel. 05/5248-0888, daily 12:30–2:30 P.M. and 7:30–10:30 P.M., closed Fri. evening and Sat. afternoon, €10–12) is the only kosher restaurant in town and has a monopoly on gefilte fish. The kitchen is run by Giancarlo Bloise, who serves a great falafel and prepares classic Mediterranean specials. Tabouleh with vegetable couscous is a local favorite.

Florence's first Japanese restaurant hasn't lost its touch. **Eito's** (Via dei Neri 72r, tel. 05/521-0940, Tues.–Sun. 12:30–3 P.M. and 7–11:30 P.M., €14–18) sushi chefs prepare a good selection of rolls and more ambitious diners can cook their own meals. Choose between a complete skiyaki or shabu-shabu set menu of grilled or boiled meat and vegetables. Service is attentive and the sake can be deceptively strong.

SEAFOOD
Fresh fish is a byword for **Akaia** (Via Ghibellina 5, tel. 05/5263-8244, Mon.–Sat. noon–3 P.M. and 7:30 P.M.–late-night, €10–15). It's brought in every day and steamed, grilled, and baked in ways that manages to preserve all the flavor. There's a beautiful wine cellar and a minimalist decor.

APERITIVO
Rex Café (Via Fiesolana 25r, tel. 05/5248-0331, www.rexcafe.it, daily 5 P.M.–2:30 A.M.) attracts a young crowd eager to get a party started. Drinks are served with snacks brought to your table and the entertainment starts at 10 P.M. Depending on the evening you may stumble upon poetry, monologues, or dance.

CAFÉ
La Via del Tè (Piazza Ghiberti 23r, tel. 05/5234-4967, Mon.–Sat. 9 A.M.–1 P.M. and 4–7:30 P.M., closed Mon. morning) is proof that Italians don't drink just coffee. The two owners are mad about tea and have used their expertise as importers to pass that enthusiasm onto clients. There's a great assortment of rare blends that can be tasted within an original setting.

GELATO
Not everyone likes their gelato creative but if the idea of ice cream with extra virgin olive oil and saffron tempts you, **Boutique del Cioccolato** (Via dei Macci 50, tel. 05/5200-1609) is waiting with a scoop or two.

Gelato at Vivoli (Via Isola delle Stinche 7, tel. 05/529-2334, Tues.–Sun. 8 A.M.–midnight) tastes so good because the family who have run this shop since 1930 enjoy making it so much. All the ingredients are easily pronounced and exist without preservatives.

DELICACIES
On March 19, Florentines celebrate St. Joseph. The traditional sweet for the occasion is *frittelle di riso* (fried rice balls) found in *pasticcerias* all over the city for several weeks. It tastes better than it sounds and can easily become addictive. A fair celebrating St. Joseph is held on the weekend following the celebration in Piazza Santa Croce.

Santo Spirito
TUSCAN
⟨ Trattoria la Casalinga (Via dei Michelozzi 9r, tel. 05/521-8624, Mon.–Sat. noon–2:30 P.M. and 7–9:45 P.M., €12–15) is a must for anyone searching for authentic Florentine flavors. Three generations of cooks have passed through the kitchen yet the dishes remain the same. The *ribollita* is rigorously made the old-fashioned way with black cabbage and inspired Robert Harris to mention it in his book *Hannibal Lecter*.

Olio & Conivivium's (Via S. Spirito 4, tel. 05/5265-8198, Mon.–Sat. 10 A.M.–3 P.M. and 5:30–10:30 P.M., €12–15) convenient hours are useful to early diners who want more out of life than pizza. This gourmet institution inside Palazzo Capponi is a gastronomic atelier in search of atypical Tuscan flavors. Walls covered in wine provide the ambiance within a modern setting.

If you spent all day around the Duomo, it's worth discovering **Le Barrique** (Via el Leone 40r, Tues.–Sun. 7 P.M.–1 A.M., €10–12) and the nearby piazze that become animated at night. Wine from all over the world is served with such novelties as *pasta con zucchine e pecorino toscano*.

Tuesday night is steak night at **Ristorante Munaciello** (Via Maffia 31–33r, tel. 05/528-7198, Tues.–Sun. 7:30–11 P.M., €9–13) and a chance to try a Florentine T-bone cooked on the grill. Neopolitan music accompanies pizza and champagne on Wednesdays, and Thursdays are devoted to an assortment of pancakes. New themes are added regularly according to chef Leonardo Lucarelli's whims.

INTERNATIONAL

Raw fish and raw decor are trademarks of **Momoyama** (Borgo San Frediano 10r, tel. 05/529-1840, Tues.–Sun. 7:30–11 P.M., €12–16). Eric Stedman demonstrates the former along with a crew of chefs preparing imaginative sushi, sashimi, and tempura dishes. Good selection of wines and Japanese beers.

Beccofino (Piazza Scarlatti 1r, tel. 05/529-0076, Tues.–Sun. 7–11:30 P.M., €14–17) combines Italian design with modern cuisine. There's an excellent view of the Arno, and top wines are served by the glass or bottle at the bar.

VEGETARIAN

O!O Bar con Cucina (Piazza Piattellina 7r, tel. 05/521-2917, daily 7 A.M.–1 P.M.) is the kind of place a trendy nutritionist might open. The emphasis is on organic, from early-morning muffins to late-evening Mediterranean platters. Even the fresh air on the terrace seems healthier.

PIZZA

Napo Leone (Piazza del Carmine 24, tel. 05/528-1015, Tues.–Sun. 7–11:30 P.M., €8–12) is a good way to begin a stylish night on the town. The vibe is Paris bistro. Pizzas are thick, and fish and meat dishes are tempting options.

APERITIVO

Chalet Fontana (Via San Leonardo 8r, tel. 05/522-5805) near Piazzale Michelangelo has been delighting locals and visitors alike for decades. The *aperitivo* is accompanied by a well-stocked buffet. A Tuscan menu is available in the restaurant serving immense fish platters and pizza from the wood-burning oven. Live music is performed at the piano bar until late.

CAFÉ

For regulars, **Caffé Notte** (Via delle Caldaie 28r, Tues.–Sun. 7 A.M.–10 P.M.) is more of a club than a café. Card games go on all day here accompanied by the occasional espresso, glass of wine, or simple lunch. A quintessential neighborhood spot.

DELICACIES

The fresh baked smell Paolo conjures up every morning is what makes **Forno Frosecchi** (Via delle Caldaie, tel. 05/521-4747, Tues.–Sat. 6 A.M.–1:30 P.M. and 4:45–7:30 P.M.) so popular. Shelves are full of big Tuscan loaves that can be cut depending on your appetite and are sold by the kilo. September is the time to try *schiacciata* (flatbread with grapes).

INFORMATION AND SERVICES
Tourist Information

Tourism is well organized in Florence and there are information points in each of the city's quarters except Santa Spirito. English-speaking staff provide all-inclusive assistance—from finding accommodation to booking theater tickets.

The **main APT office** is at Via Manzoni 16 (tel. 05/523–320, www.firenzeturismo.it, Mon.–Sun. 9 A.M.–1 P.M.). Other branches include: **Stazione Santa Maria Novella** (Piazza Stazione 4a, tel. 05/521-2245, Mon.–Sat. 8:30 A.M.–7 P.M., Sun. 8:30 A.M.–2 P.M.), **San Giovanni** (Via Cavour 1r, tel. 05/529-0832, Mon.–Sat. 8:30 A.M.–6:30, Sun. 8:30 A.M.–1:30 P.M.), **Santa Croce** (Borgo Santa Croce 29r, tel. 05/5234-0444, Mon.–Sat. 9 A.M.–5 P.M.,

Sun. 9 A.M.–2 P.M.), and **Aeroporto Amerigo Vespucci** (Via del Termine 1, tel. 05/531-5874, daily 8:30 A.M.–8:30 P.M.).

Hospitals, Police, and Emergencies
Ospedale Santa Maria Nuova (Santa Maria Nuova Hospital) in the piazza of the same name can be reached on buses 1, 7, 11, 17, or 23. The hospital is open 24 hours daily. The 118 number is operational 24 hours a day for emergencies or for general health questions call 05/527-581. Bars and cafés that display the Courtesy Point sign allow visitors to use their restroom facilities and will assist anyone in need.

Pharmacies
There are a handful of all-night pharmacies in Florence. Anyone with a headache or searching for a toothbrush past midnight should try **Farmacia Comunale 13** (tel. 05/528-9435) inside Stazione Santa Maria Novella, **All'Insegna del Moro** (tel. 05/521-1343) in Piazza S. Giovanni 20r, or **Di Rifredi** (tel. 05/5422-0422) in Piazza Dalmazia 24r.

Government Offices
The United States and Mexico both have consulates in Florence ready to assist travelers in a jam. The **U.S. office** (Lungarno A. Vespucci 38, tel. 05/526-6951) is open weekdays from 9 A.M.–12:30 P.M. Canadians in trouble should head to the **Canadian Consulate in Rome** (Via Zara 30, tel. 06/854-441, Mon.–Fri. 8:30 A.M.–noon and 2 P.M.–4 P.M.) or the **Canadian Consulate in Milan** (Via Vittor Pisani 19, tel. 02/67581).

Internet and Newspapers
Internet Train (www.internettrain.it) is Florence's most convenient place to check email. There are 10 locations around the city, including Via Porta Rossa 38, Piazza Stazione 14, and Borgo San Jacopo 30r. Services include broadband Internet, CD burning, mobile phone rental, and international phone cards. Students receive a discount. Nearly every piazza has a newspaper kiosk that sells the *In-*

ADDRESSES
In Italy, unlike many countries, street names precede numbers. The address system in Florence, however, is slightly different and distinguishes between residential and commercial properties. Black plates are used for houses and red ones are used for shops and businesses. Most restaurants therefore will have an "r" (*rosso* is red in Italian) and may be a little difficult to find. Via Garibaldi 50r, for instance, is not necessarily next to Via Garibaldi 48 and can be several blocks away. Therefore if you can't find the address you're looking for, don't assume they've gone out of business: Just keep walking and look for the relevant color.

ternational Herald Tribune and day-old issues of *USAToday*.

Lost and Found
Oggetti Trovati (Via Circondaria 17b, tel. 05/5328-3942, Mon.–Fri. 9 A.M.–noon) collects thousands of objects ever year handed in by honest citizens. It's worth checking with them before giving up all hope of finding that lost wallet or good luck charm.

GETTING THERE
By Air
Amerigo Vespucci Airport (tel. 05/530–615, www.aeroporto.firenze.it) is located four kilometers from the center of Florence. There are daily flights from most major Italian cities, including Rome's Fiumicino Airport and Milan's Malpensa Airport. **Ataf/SITA** (tel. 800/424–500, www.ataf.net) shuttle buses depart every 30 minutes from the arrivals terminal 6 A.M.–11:30 P.M. and drop visitors off at the train station. A taxi ride into the center takes 15 minutes and costs €15–20.

The nearest transatlantic airport is **Galileo Galilei** (tel. 05/084-9300, www.pisa-airport .com) in Pisa. Delta now flies to the city three times a week from New York. The **train** (tel. 892–021, www.trenitalia.it) to Florence leaves directly from the airport and covers the 80 kilometers in one hour and 20 minutes. **Terravision bus service** (tel. 06/3212-0011, www.lowcostcoach.com) is also available.

By Car

Florence is conveniently located in the center of Italy and reachable by the A11 and A1 superhighways, as well as the Florence–Siena and Florence–Pisa freeways. From Rome take the A1 and exit at the Florence Sud exit.

If you do arrive by car, keep in mind the historic center of Florence is a ZTL or limited traffic zone and entry is limited. If you are staying in this area contact your hotel in order to be issued a temporary permit.

By Bus

Long-distance buses connect Florence with destinations throughout the region and beyond. It's an inexpensive way of reaching the city. The two main companies are **Lazzi Eurolines** (tel. 055 363041, www.lazzi.it) and **SITA** (tel. 05/547-821, www.sitabus.it), which both use Piazza Santa Maria Novella as a terminus.

By Train

The main train station in Florence is Stazione Santa Maria Novella (SMN). Eurostar service from Rome Termini takes 1.5 hours. Trains are frequent and a second-class tickets costs €33. The journey from Milan takes an hour longer but costs the same.

Stazione SMN (tel. 05/589-2021, daily 4:15 A.M.–1:30 A.M.) is practically in the center of the city and is a major transportation hub. Urban and interurban buses depart regularly from the piazza outside. The second train station is **Florence Campo Marte** (Via Mannelli, daily 6:20 A.M.–9 P.M.) east of the Santa Croce quarter on the 12, 13, and 33 bus lines.

GETTING AROUND
By Bus

ATAF (tel. 800/424–500, www.ataf.net) operates the orange buses that get Florentines around the city. Single tickets cost €1.20 and are valid for 60 minutes after being validated in one of the yellow machines onboard. Between 9 P.M.–6 A.M., tickets may be purchased directly on the bus; otherwise they are available at bars, *tabacchi*, newsstands, or the ATAF office in Piazza Stazione.

Scenic bus lines include the 7 between Stazione SMN, S. Domenico, and Fiesole, and the 12 or 13 from Stazione SMN to Piazzale Michelangelo. There are various taxi options depending on the length of your stay and how often you plan on riding buses. A two-day ticket costs €7.60.

By Taxi

There are taxi stands in every major piazza, and cabs can also be ordered by phone (Radio Taxi, tel. 05/54-390 or 05/54-499). During the day, fares start at €2.64 and increase €0.85 per kilometer. At night the initial charge is €5.70.

By Car, Motorcycle, and Bicycle

Renting a car in Florence is a good idea only if you are planning to leave the city. Most rental companies have multiple locations. **Sixt** (tel. 05/5239-9696, www.sixt.com, Mon.–Fri. 9 A.M.–1 P.M. and 2–6 P.M., Sat. 9 A.M.–1 P.M.) rents compact and larger models with both manual and automatic transmissions. Their main office is five minutes from the Stazione SMN in Via Borgognissanti 153r. **Avis** (tel. 05/531-5588, www.avisautonoleggio.it) and **Europcar** (tel. 055 318609, www.europcar.it) also have locations in the center. Parking (www.firenzeparcheggi.it) costs €1.50 per hour or €15 per day in one of the lots outside the historic center. There are spaces in Stazione SMN and Viale Europa.

Mille e Una Bici is a local initiative to encourage two-wheeled transportation in the city. Bikes can be rented from Stazione SMN weekdays and Saturdays 7:30 A.M.–7 P.M. and on Sundays 9 A.M.–7 P.M. One hour costs €1.50 while a full day is €8. A similar service is operated from Piazza Ghiberti. **Alinari** (Via San Zanobi 38r, tel. 05/528-0500, www.alinarirental.com) rents classic Dutch bikes and Honda SH 125 mopeds for €55 per day. Credit card and ID are required.

FLORENCE AND TUSCANY

© PURESTOCK

If you're tired of sightseeing by foot, several companies offer bus tours.

Tours

Several companies operate sightseeing tours. **Florence Citysightseeing** (tel. 05/529-0451, www.firenze.city-sightseeing.it) runs buses along three different routes. The starting point is Stazione SMN and a complete circuit lasts one hour with numerous stops. A ticket valid 24 hours costs €20 and includes audio commentary.

Florence by Bike (Via San Zanobi 120–122r,

tel. 05/548-8992, www.florencebybike.it) takes riders from Florence into the surrounding countryside. There are half-day trips to Fiesole and full-day options through Chianti.

Horse and buggies line the piazza around the Duomo waiting to pick up fares for a tour of the city. It can be a lovely way to discover Florence as long as five o'clock rush hour is avoided and price is negotiated prior to departure.

Greater Florence

The hills to the north and south of Florence are dotted with medieval villas where the town's elite once retreated during warm summer months. A tour here offers great views of the city as well as walks through some of Italy's most delightful gardens. The ancient and charming town of Fiesole is a pleasant half-day trip that can be enhanced with a stop at Badia Fiesolana.

LA PETRAIA

The **villa** (Castello, Via della Petraia 40, daily 8:15 A.M.–7 P.M., closed second and third Mon., €2) was constructed in the 13th and 14th centuries and changed hands several times before becoming property of the Medicis. Additions to the house and garden were frequent and Ferdinando I hired Bernardo Buontalenti to rebuild it altogether.

The Italian-style garden that surrounds the villa on three sides was laid out to complement the building. It contains a variety of geometric designs around a central fountain. There is also a long rectangular pool on the second terrace where fish were once stocked. The views of the city are magnificent.

Getting There and Around

By car head northeast towards Sesto Fiorentino and follow the signs for the villa or take bus 2 or 28 from the train station. There is a tour of villa and gardens every 45 minutes.

VILLA GAMBERAIA

Villa Gamberaia (Via del Rossellino 72, tel. 05/569-7205, daily, 9 A.M.–7 P.M., €10) is just outside of the little village of Settignano and has attracted sculptors and painters for centuries. The building was greatly damaged during World War II and painstakingly restored. Today the villa is a luxury hotel beyond the budget of most travelers, but the gardens are open to all visitors, not just guests.

Sights

Anyone who has ever planted a bush or seeded a lawn will appreciate the gardens divided into a succession of unique environments. The most interesting part is on the south side of the building that was laid out by two local gardeners who divided the area into four rectangular pools of water, bordered by box hedges and arch-shaped cypress trees. Nearby there is a long lawn adorned with statues and a gate that leads to a smaller garden bordered by hydrangeas. The grotto at the end was built out of sandstone and contains terra-cotta statues. The view from the shaded terrace is worth a long pause.

Getting There and Around

The villa is six kilometers from the center and can be easily reached with the number 6 bus from Stazione SMN or Piazza San Marco. Get off at the end of the line in Settignano and walk the rest of the way.

FIESOLE

Fiesole was founded in the 7th century B.C. by Etruscans, who enjoyed the climate and views much as visitors do today.

Sights

The **Duomo** stands in the center of town in the space once occupied by the Roman Foro. It was completed in 1208 and contains frescoes by Cosimo Rosselli and a triptych above the altar by Bicci di Lorenzo. The bell tower looks more defensive than spiritual and measures nearly 50 meters.

Behind the cathedral are the archaeological remains of the city (Via Florentina 6, daily 9 A.M.–7 P.M.). There is a marvelously preserved amphitheater with seating for 3,000 and thermal baths dating from Adriano's reign. Close examination will shed light on how saunas were heated. Etruscan ruins are also present in the form of an impressive wall and the foundations of a temple excavated in the 19th century.

Entertainment and Events

Estate Fiesolana (Teatro Romano, tel. 05/559-8720, www.comune.fiesole.fi.it) is a theater, music, dance, and film festival that takes place in the town's churches and Roman theater June–September. Check the festival's website for program information.

Accommodations

Florence looks different from above and the view from **Bencista** (Via da Maiano 4, tel. 05/559-163, www.bencista.com, €85–150 s/d) will make you glad you chose to stay in Fiesole. The panorama is only one of the draws of this lovely hotel with a characteristic interior and talented kitchen.

Villa Le Rondini (Via Bologese Vecchia 224, tel. 05/540-0081, www.villalerondini.it, €165–230 s/d) lies on a large estate outside of town. Even the Medicis would be impressed with the pool, sauna, and extensive sporting facilities. Parking is available unless you prefer to arrive by helicopter.

Camping Panoramico Fiesole (Via

Peramonda 1, tel. 05/559-9069, www.florencecamping.com, €10.80 pp) welcomes campers with open arms. Various-sized bungalows are also available if you prefer to sleep on a mattress and the restaurant/bar stays open until late. There's a great view from the swimming pool.

Food

Perseus (Piazza Mino da Fiesole 9r, tel. 05/559–143, Tues.–Sun. 12:30–2:30 P.M. and 7–10:30 P.M., €7–10) is famous for homemade cooking without any pretensions. After sampling the mixed Tuscan antipasto, a plate of fresh pasta is in order. Choose from ravioli, pici, or taglioni. Starting in early spring, brightly colored chairs and tables are set on the sidewalk outside. The *gelateria* next door is an obvious place for dessert.

Anyone who decides to extend an afternoon in Fiesole into an evening affair can settle down at **Blu Bar** (Piazza Mino da Fiesole 39b). The vibrant decor attracts fashionable Florentines.

Getting There and Around

Fiesole is 20 minutes away by car or bus from Stazione SMN on the 7 bus. The area around town is quite steep and cyclists should bring lots of water when pedaling towards the town.

Around Fiesole

Before the Edict of Milan officially authorized Christianity worshippers met in secluded places like **Badia Fiesolana.** The tomb of St. Romulus, a pioneer evangelist, lies nearby and a small chapel was later constructed. An abbey was added in the 11th century and several orders of monks treaded the stone corridors. Much of the renovation of the church was financed by Cosimo il Vecchio, who insisted on a single apse and barrel vaulting. The view from the Badia terrace is a hint of landscapes to come.

PRATO

Prato is an old textile town northwest of Florence where over 100 mills once operated. The center is tranquil and retains much of its medieval past.

Sights

To understand the significance of thread, visit **Museo del Tessuto** (Piazza del Comune, tel. 05/7461-1503, Mon.–Fri. 10 A.M.–6 P.M., Sat. 10 A.M.–2 P.M., Sun. 3–7 P.M., €5). Four exhibitions recount how ancient fibers were produced, and many of the original instruments of the trade are on display.

Piazza del Comune and **Palazzo Pretoria** are the result of a textile trade that once thrived here. The Roman/Gothic style is balanced by the ornate bronze fountain in the center of the piazza.

The **Duomo** (€6) can be deciphered with the help of an audio guide that recounts its construction. There are also descriptions of the many frescoes, including Filippo Lippi's handiwork in the *cappella*. Michelozzo and Donatello both contributed to the 15th-century marble pulpit.

The major annual event is the **Fiera di Santa Maria** on September 8. The town gets into full medieval regalia and there are hundreds of participants in the historic parade.

Accommodations

Located in a stunning historic building, **Villa Rucellai** (Via di Canneto 16, tel. 05/7446-0392, www.villarucellai.it, €80–90 s/d) has a unique view overlooking vineyards and olive trees. Rooms are decorated with style and a good night's sleep is assured.

Flora (Via Cairoli 31, tel. 05/7440-0289, www.hotelflora.info, €90–140 s/d) is well positioned near the center of Prato. Service is considerate and the communal areas and rooms are comfortable.

Food

Cibbé (Piazza Mercatale 49, tel. 05/7460-7509, Mon.–Sat. noon–3 P.M. and 7–10 P.M., €7–10) gets its name from the street game children once played in the piazza. The trattoria is run by the Panerai family and doesn't serve anything fancy. Start with a taste of crostini and *salumi* that includes slices of *mortadella di Prato*. Giuseppina in the kitchen can follow that up with *pappa al pomodoro* (tomato stew) and a *bollito* (beef stew) if you're really hungry. Otherwise save room for her *torta di farro e noce* (grain and nut tart). The wine menu is more than acceptable.

For the fancy stuff, try **Volver** (Via Bovio 2, tel. 05/742-2382, Tues.–Sun. noon–3 P.M. and 7–11 P.M., €12–15). Local ingredients are mixed by an innovative chef who likes updating Tuscan classics. The interior is elegant and the selection of wine by the glass extensive.

To prepare your own snack, start with the breads at **La Bozza di Prato** (Via Matteotti 11). If you've tasted the *sciocco* in Florence see if you can detect the difference with the one made here using natural yeast.

Information and Services

The information office (Via S. Maria delle Carceri 15, tel. 05/742-4112, Mon.–Sat. 9 A.M.–1:30 P.M. and 2:30–7 P.M., Sun 10 A.M.–1 P.M. and 3–6:30 P.M.) provides a map of town and a brochure of local events.

Getting There and Around

Prato is 17 kilometers from Florence and off the A1. There is frequent train service between the two cities along the Florence–Bologna line. CAP and LAZZI buses make the 30-minute journey from Stazione SMN to Piazza Adua.

Chianti

It's hard not to be seduced by Chianti. If the trademark rolling hills don't get you the wine surely will. The region has no clear geographic borders, but is divided into Florentine Chianti in the north and Sienese Chianti in the south. The influence of the two cities can be seen in the architecture as well as on the tables of the region's restaurants. The first mention of wine in the area dates from 1404 and an export business began almost immediately. By the 18th century, cultivation was firmly established and early visitors were taking note.

GREVE

Greve is the first town on the road from Florence to Siena and considered the gateway to Chianti. It's an ancient market town notable for its architecture and gastronomy. **Piazza Matteotti** is triangular and the arcades that run along the sides are filled with shops and restaurants. The statue in the middle is Giovanni da Verrazzano, who was born nearby in Castello di Verrazzano and made several journeys to the New World.

Sights

Santa Croce (Piazza Santa Croce, free admission) lies at the pinnacle of the piazza on the site where a medieval chapel once stood. It is

not as old as it looks and was completed in 1835 by Luigi de Cambray-Digny in a neo-Renaissance style. Inside, the works of art include a triptych of the Madonna and child by Bicci di Lorenzo.

Festivals and Events

Estate di San Francesco is held on the panoramic terrace of the Museo di San Francesco (Via S. Francesco 4, tel. 05/5854-4685). Every Thursday during the summer, concerts, tastings, and theatrical shows take place. Events start at 9:15 P.M. and cost €3.

In the first week of November, Piazza Matteotti is taken over by dozens of local wineries ready to uncork hundreds of their best bottles. During **Chianti d'Autunno** (tel. 05/7774-1392, www.chiantidautunno.it) you can purchase an empty glass and make the rounds from booth to booth sampling as much as you like. The event is held simultaneously in seven other Chianti towns.

Shopping

The market spirit has not faded in Greve and the piazza regularly fills up with farmers and merchants selling locally produced goods. On the last Sunday of each month, **Il Pagliaio** (Piazza Matteotti), or organic market, is the occasion

WINERIES IN CHIANTI COUNTRY

Italy is covered with vineyards and the rising popularity of gastronomic tourism has encouraged each region to create its own *strada dei vini* (wine roads). These are usually well indicated with brown signs that point drivers to hundreds of wineries where locally produced vintages can be tasted and purchased. Besides great bottles of red, the Chianti region offers a succession of charming towns and lovely Tuscan landscape between Florence and Siena. You can start in either city and should take turns being the designated driver. It's best to take the journey at a leisurely pace and spend a night in each town along the way.

GREVE

Many wineries in the area are located in converted castles, and **Castello di Querceto** is full of medieval charm. You can also spend the night here or drive to **Castello di Uzzano** and let your palate compare the Sangiovese, Trebbiano, and Malvasia produced by the two vineyards.

RADDA

The **Consorzio Chianti Classico** was founded in this town in 1924 to promote the area. The tourist office can let you know about the frequent summer and fall tastings held in the central square. If there's nothing scheduled, steer towards the small vineyard of **Podere Terrano** that doubles as an *agriturismo*. If you spend the night, they'll gladly show you around the cellar during the day, otherwise visits should be arranged in advance. You can stop by **Castello d'Albola** any day of the week for a glass of Classico served in a 12th-century farmhouse.

GAIOLE

The most vibrant time in Gaiole is during the *vendemmia* (Sept.) when the grapes are harvested and locals celebrate the year's haul. Rent a bike to get to the vineyards on the back roads and try dinner at **Azienda Agricola Rocca di Castagnoli** which features an outstanding wine list.

MONTERIGGIONI

This small town, with fewer than 200 residents, features wine resort **Castel Pietraio.** The resort is surrounded by olive trees and vineyards that are the perfect backdrop for long post-lunch walks.

---

to sample handmade olive oils and cheeses. Producers are happy to explain the process involved to curious visitors discovering new flavors. Between May and September on the third Thursday of each month is an opportunity to have a late-night snack. **Stelle e Mercanti** (Piazza Matteotti) is a nocturnal market that starts at 6 P.M. and runs until 11 P.M.

Accommodations

Casa Nova (Via di Uzzano 29–30, tel. 05/585-3459, www.casanova-laripintura.it, €75 d) is a typical Tuscan farmhouse a kilometer from Greve. The *agriturismo* is surrounded by a shaded park and breakfast is served on the patio in summertime. Children under eight stay for free and wine produced on the small estate is available at the small store.

Food

Underneath the porticos is a small restaurant where Mirna serves her husband's dishes. 【 **Mangiando** (Piazza Matteotti 80, tel. 05/5854-6372, Tues.–Sun, 12:30–3 P.M. and 7:30–11 P.M., €7–10) doesn't stray very far from tradition and the crostini are a classic Tuscan appetizer. There are half-a-dozen pastas but if you've had your fill of carbohydrates the steaks are an excellent alternative. Chianti is the prevalent wine.

If you prefer making your own panini, **Antica Macelleria Falorni** (Piazza Matteotti 71, tel. 05/585-3029, Mon.–Sat. 8 A.M.–1 P.M. and 3:30 P.M.–7:30 P.M., Sun. 10 A.M.–1 P.M. and 3:30 P.M.–7 P.M.) next door can slice up some *prosciutto crudo, capocollo,* or *soppressata.* For wine, visit **Le Cantine di Greve** (Piazza delle

Cantine 6, tel. 05/5854-6404, daily 10 A.M.–7 P.M.). This super-stocked *enoteca* carries 1,200 types of wines, 150 of which can be sampled. There's also a small museum inside.

Information and Services

The tourist office (Viale Giovanni da Verrazzano 59, tel. 05/5854-6287, Mar.–Oct., Mon.–Sat. 9 A.M.–1 P.M. and 2:30–6:30 P.M.) can help find last-minute accommodations and provides a list of monthly events. Chianti Slow Travel (tel. 05/5854-6299) is a source for gastronomic itineraries and events in the area.

Getting There and Around

Greve is 30 kilometers south of Florence on the SS222. SITA buses from Stazione SMN are available daily and take 45 minutes to reach the town. There's a taxi stand in the central piazza where scooter and car rental are also available.

PANZANO

Panzano is the next town along the SS222 halfway between Florence and Siena. The name sprang from Roman tongues but the town's origins go back to Etruscan times. Ancient walls, gates, and a medieval castle are all well preserved.

Sights

The **castle** is located on the hill that separates Val di Greve from Val di Pesa. It's privately owned but the courtyard and vicinity can be visited. The houses along the way have a medieval character and the road itself has remnants of large paving stones laid down by the Romans. The churches are worth visiting especially in summer when their cool interiors offer respite from the Tuscan heat.

The 13th-century Santa Maria Assunta was given a facelift in the 19th century and contains noteworthy paintings like *Annunciazione,* attributed to Ghirlandio. The parish church of San Leolino is much older. To visit the beautiful cloister and splendid tabernacles inside, just ring the bell.

Entertainment and Events

April 25 is a national holiday when the people of Panzano celebrate the start of the *buona stagione* (good season). There are Renaissance costumes, a medieval market, and many gastronomic stands.

Thank Dario Cecchini for **Festa del Nocciolo** (Hazelnut Festival) which takes place on August 14. He fills long tables placed along the streets with cured meats and other specialties from his butcher shop. There's a jovial mood as locals and visitors rub shoulders the evening before Ferragosto (Aug. 15).

Vino al Vino is a wine festival on the third weekend of September. The main square hosts a large outdoor tasting. Local wines are in the majority and music adds gaiety to the atmosphere. The grape harvest varies from year to year. It's always an interesting time to visit and there are many events organized around this period.

Accommodations

Air conditioning or a view of the surrounding hillside? That's the choice at **Villa Sangiovese** (Piazza G. Bucciarelli 5, tel. 05/585-2461, www.villasangiovese.it, €108–125 s/d), made even more difficult during the hot summer months. Fortunately the shaded courtyard and pool provide some relief at this pleasant, efficiently run hotel decorated with antiques. The restaurant serves regional dishes and is closed on Wednesdays.

Food

Views from **Oltre il Giardino** (Piazza Bucciarelli, tel. 05/585-2828, Tues.–Sun. 1–3 P.M. and 7–10:30 P.M., €8–12) complement the excellent Tuscan dishes. Ingredients are local and the menu varies according to the season. The *fettunta antipasto* (thick slices of toasted country bread rubbed with garlic and topped with extra virgin olive oil and salt) is unheard of outside of Tuscany and the *tagliatelle con piccione* (tagliatelle with pigeon) is equally unique. Chianti Classico Riserva is aging in the cellar.

The local fruit and vegetable market is on Sunday mornings until 1 P.M. in the central piazza. Fruits, vegetables, cheese, and roast chicken can all be purchased.

Getting There and Around

Panzano can be reached by car in under an hour from Florence or Siena on the SS222. SITA bus service also links the town with two cities.

Wine tours can be arranged with Angela (angie@chianti.info, €100 pp) for one or more days. She takes groups across the Chianti countryside by car to vineyards that would be hard to find without a guide. Her knowledge of the area is impeccable but it's her friendliness that is most memorable.

To understand Chianti you need to slow down. Luca Granucci (www.soleombra.com) can help. His trekking company gives all levels of walkers an introduction into the land and culture of the region. Few secrets are unknown by this local who can keep you walking and discovering for an entire week.

RADDA

Radda is in the heart of Chianti Classico and in 1415 it was declared the capital of the Lega del Chianti. It has been greatly influenced from the power struggles between Florence and Siena and finally found peace at the end of the Sienese Republic. Only the partial remains of walls and towers hint of this violent past.

Sights

For over 400 years, **Palazzo del Podestà** was the center of justice in Chianti. The building was enlarged in the 17th century and a second story and prison was added. Some of the 51 coats of arms on the exterior date from the 14th century. Under the loggia is one of the oldest, which belonged to Franceso Ferrucci, the *podestà* (mayor) in 1479.

Propositura di San Niccolò is a church in the heart of Radda and reached by a long flight of steps. The new facade is dominated by a wide arch that protects a fresco built during a restoration project two centuries ago. **Compagnia della Misericordia,** the chapel next door, can also be visited and has been active since it was founded in the 12th century. The simple, sin-

gle nave interior contains an ancient wooden cross preserved by an order of monks.

Accommodations

Hotel Palazzo San Niccolò (Via Rome 16, tel. 05/7773-5666, www.hotelsanniccolo.com, €140 d) is surrounded by history. The recently restored rooms all come with wood-beamed ceilings, terra-cotta floors, and marble bathes. Personalized tours can be organized upon request and guests have access to the Palazzo Leopoldi spa and fitness area.

Borgo di Vescine (tel. 05/7774-1144, www.vescine.it, €170 d) is a tiny 13th-century village three kilometers from Radda that's been converted into a picturesque hotel. The complex includes a wine cellar where Chianti Classico can be sampled, a bar and reading room with an immense fireplace, and a panoramic pool. Excursions on foot or bicycle are plentiful and there is no shortage of neighboring hamlets to explore.

Food

La Cantina di Colle Bereto (Piazza IV Novembre, tel. 05/7773-8276, Tues.–Sun. noon–3 P.M. and 7–11 P.M., €8) is at the entrance of the *borgo.* Olive oil never tasted this good and the modern stone interior makes this a wonderful lunch stop.

Getting There and Around

From the A1 exit at Valdarno and drive along the SS408. Turn right after Badia and follow the signs. From Florence on the SS222 turn left onto the S.P. 2/bis and continue for 10 kilometers until you reach Radda.

Around Radda

Within a short distance of Radda there are a number of interesting half-day excursions. **Castellina** is situated on a hill overlooking three valleys. The fortified walls enclose a small hamlet once defended by the imposing tower in the center. **Castello di Volpaia** lies on some of the most picturesque slopes in Chianti and many of the medieval houses have been converted into *enoteche,* restaurants, and bed-and-breakfasts.

Terre di Siena

SIENA

Siena first rose to prominence under the Lombards. It experienced a population influx during the Middle Ages when wealthy families began building their houses along the Via Francigena on the highest part of town. Prosperity brought about conflict with Florence and the numerous battles that ensued are immortalized in Dante's *Divine Comedy*. Beating the Florentines was one thing but surviving the plague of 1348 was another. The Black Death brought construction to a halt and began a long period of instability, which ended with Siena's submission to its larger neighbor.

Numbers have special relevance in Siena. The nine sections of the Piazza del Campo represent the Council of Nine, which ruled the city in the 13th and 14th centuries. There are 17 *contrade* (parishes) that inspire loyalty from birth and from which contestants are selected during the two annual *palios* (horse races). Then there are the Terzi, the three districts the town has been divided in since its founding. Terzo di Città is where the Duomo and Siena's oldest buildings stand.

Sights

Wherever you enter Siena, you are inevitably drawn to **Piazza del Campo.** The main square has inherited its famous seashell shape from the whims and jerks of medieval urbanization. Fonte Gaie fountain at the northern end is a beautiful replacement to the 15th-century original sculpted by Jacopo della Quercia and kept safe in Santa Maria della Scala.

Palazzo Pubblico (Piazza del Campo, tel. 05/7729-2226, 10 A.M.–6 P.M., €7) is at the bottom of the sloping piazza and was constructed in a Gothic style at the end of the 12th century. The elegant structure has a gentle concave facade, and on the side **Torre del Mangia** rises 88 meters into the sky. All that separates

FLORENCE AND TUSCANY

© ALEXEI J. COHEN

The seashell-shaped Piazza del Campo is where Siena's Palio delle Contrade is held twice a year.

you from a view reminiscent of the frescoes in the rooms below is 300 steps.

The **Duomo** is hard to miss. It's the largest building in town, an immense marble ship moored in the center of everything. It might even have been the biggest church in the world had the plague not brought construction to a halt. The alternating white and black marble is its most striking feature and the large number of columns on the inside creates many unexpected perspectives. The pavement built in the 15th century is unique and made of 56 immense squares featuring mythological and biblical figures. The pulpit carved by Nicola Pisano illustrates the life of Christ in a highly dramatic fashion. Inside the Duomo are the library and **Museo dell'Opera Metropolitana** (tel. 05/7728-3048, www.operaduomo.siena.it, 9 A.M.–7:30 P.M., €6), featuring remains of the unfinished section of the church, painting, and sculpture that once resided in the church.

Ospedale di Santa Maria (Piazza Duomo 2, tel. 05/7722-4828, daily 10:30 A.M.–6:30 P.M., €6) was the first hospital in the city. It was where pilgrims would get their blisters looked at and anyone with a serious disease might find a little relief. It was operational until a few years ago and now houses a museum. Sala del Pellegrinaio was built in the 14th century and the frescos added shortly afterwards illustrate the treatments provided to the sick. Exhibitions are frequent and cover a wide variety of interests.

Since the 1920s, Palazzo Buonsignori has housed the **Pinacoteca Nazionale** (Via San Pietro 29, tel. 05/7728-6143, Tues.–Sat. 9 A.M.–7 P.M., Mon. and Sun. 8:30 A.M.–1 P.M., €6) and a premier collection of Sienese artwork. Most of the paintings date from the 13th–17th centuries and presents a clear picture of how art developed in the city over the years. There is an unrivaled quantity of gold painted canvases, many of which were donated by local churches and convents. Works by Ambrogio and Pietro Lorenzetti, Sassetta, and Beccafumi are all on display. The sculpture room in the second-story loggia has an excellent view of the city.

The **Terza di Camollia** district is in the northern edge of the city; although it was re-

Siena's Duomo is the largest building in town.

built in recent centuries, many of its medieval monuments have been preserved. **Via di Camollia** runs through the center of the neighborhood and is the home of churches San Pietro and Santa Maria, completed in 1484. At the end of the road is Porta Camollia. Anyone who understands Latin will be able to read the inscription welcoming visitors to Siena.

Catherine Benincasa is the patron saint of Italy and Europe. She lived in the area and had her visions inside **Basilica di S. Domenico.** There are several portraits of her within this Gothic church overlooking the Fontebranda Valley. Halfway along the nave on the right side is a chapel dedicated to the saint with a sculpture and frescos by Sodoma recalling her short life. Perhaps it's no coincidence she died at the age of 33.

East of Piazza del Campo is **Terzo di San Martino.** Via di Città is the main thoroughfare flanked by the city's finest palazzi. Palazzo Piccolomini is distinguished by immense blocks of ashlar Rossellino used to bring a little Florentine style to Siena. Almost directly opposite is the slightly curved Palazzo Chigi-Saracini that now houses a music academy. Further down on the right is Loggia dei Mercanti, which marked a transition between Gothic and Renaissance architecture. The loggia was in fact added in the 16th century. The street also passes Piazza Salimbeni, enclosed on three sides by three buildings in three different styles. It's a good test for anyone who gets Gothic, Renaissance, and Baroque confused.

Biagio Bartalini liked plants so much he founded the **Orto Botanico** (Via P. A. Mattioli 4, tel. 05/7729-8871, Mon.–Fri. 8 A.M.–12:30 P.M. and 2:30–5:30 P.M., Sat. 8 A.M.–noon, free) in 1784. The 2.5-acre botanical garden situated in a small valley near Porta Tufi is divided into three sections. The first contains the most local Tuscan species you'll see in one spot. They include herbs, aromatic, and medicinal varieties that were used by Santa Maria della Scala hospital in the 18th century. Aquatic plants, fruit trees, and cacti grow in the other areas and a tepidarium protects vulnerable leaves. The garden is a favorite destination of birds that serenade visitors with song. Serious horticulturists can reserve a tour of the grounds.

Festivals and Events
FESTA DI SAN GIUSEPPE
Lots of saints are celebrated in Siena but it's Festa di San Giuseppe on March 19 that's the most spirited. Via Dupre in the contrade dell'Onde is the center of festivities. There is a great display of arts and crafts along the street lined with stalls selling toys and sweets. Around Piazza del Campo and the church of San Giuseppe the intoxicating smell of *frittelle* (fried rice) is hard to resist and outdoor stands remain open until late.

◖ PALIO DELLE CONTRADE
Twice a year Siena turns back the clock and transforms the Piazza del Campo into a racetrack where thousands cram to watch the Palio delle Contrade. For locals the main event is on July 2, while the second race on August 16 is nicknamed the "*palio* of the tourists." Both

days begin with a parade around the outer perimeter of the piazza, which is covered in sand to prevent horses from slipping. It's best to arrive several hours before the mid-afternoon start. The best places to stand are on the outer edges to the left or right of the fountain from where nearly the entire course can be observed. The race consists of three laps and an anything-goes approach with the winner carried back to his *contrade* for a victory dinner where the horse is the guest of honor.

SETTIMANA MUSICALE SENESE
Settimana Musicale Senese (Accademia Musicale Chigiana, Via di Città 89, tel. 05/772-2091, €14–20) began in 1939 as a week-long event to rediscover the music of Antonio Vivaldi. The composer had fallen out of favor but after several successful editions gained widespread popularity that has yet to wane. Today the festival continues to search for lesser-known composers and introduce them to the public. Italian artists like Scarlatti, Pergolesi, Galuppi, Caldara, and Salieri have been the subject of recent editions and many forgotten operas are performed for the first time in years. Concerts are held at 9:15 P.M. during the second week of July in Teatro dei Rozzi and various churches.

Shopping
Via di Città is the main shopping street in Siena and contains clothing, book, food, and craft shops. Most days it's filled with tourists hunting for souvenirs. Don't let that stop you from taking a look and stopping by some of the more interesting addresses.

Antiques aren't hard to find in Siena. What is hard to find is a selection as vast as **Antichità Monna Agnese** (Via di Città 60, tel. 05/7728-2288). The store is a favorite with collectors who appreciate Italian country furnishings and can date objects down to the decade. Novices who can't distinguish between centuries may still find the collection of antique jewelry interesting. Agnese usually participates in the craft and antique market held on the third Sunday of each month in Piazza Mercato.

Bruna Fontana spends so much time chatting

with clients it's hard to believe she ever has time to finish any of the needlework that fills her small shop. **Siena Ricama** (Via di Città 61, tel. 05/7728-8339, Mon.–Sat. 9 A.M.–1 P.M. and 3 P.M.–6 P.M.) is the place to go for embroidery and you'll find everything from handmade lampshades to handkerchiefs that can be personalized. The designs Bruna creates have a medieval quality and are nearly as interesting as the frescos nearby.

The ceramics of **Ceramiche Artistiche Santa Caterina** (tel. 05/7728-3098, Mon.–Fri. 9 A.M.–11 A.M. and 4:30 P.M.–6:30 P.M.) are produced in Via P.A. Mattioli 12 and displayed in several shops on Via di Città 74–76. Marcello Neri and his wife have been behind the pottery wheel for decades and trained at the most important studios in Tuscany. The Sienese style is recognizable by its exclusive use of black and white, with designs inspired directly from the Duomo. Utilitarian and more fanciful objects line the shelves. It's best to ask before touching anything.

Stained glass may not be high on your souvenir list but the artists at **Vetrate Artistiche Toscane** (Via della Galluzza 5, tel. 05/774-8033, Mon.–Sat. 9 A.M.–1 P.M. and 3 P.M.–6 P.M.) may change your mind. Their secular and religious creations come in every size and shape, and make a nice addition to nearly any wall. The store doubles as a workshop where craftsmen can often be observed. They also run glass blowing apprentice workshops during the summer.

Accommodations

San Francesco (Vicolo degli Orbachi 2, tel. 05/774-6533, www.bb-sanfrancesco. com, €75–100 s/d) is in the *contrada* Bruco, a working-class neighborhood where support for the local *palio* rider is always high. The 16 rooms at the bed-and-breakfast are immaculate and equipped with the essential. There's something homey about the simplicity and the Tuscan greeting that guests receive from owner Massimo Giuliani. He is the best person to ask for shopping, dining, or sightseeing advice. A 30 percent advance deposit may

be required depending on the season. Check with Massimo.

Dante mentions ◖ **Albergo Cannon d'Oro** (Via Montanini 28, tel. 05/774-4321, www. cannondoro.com, €80–99 s/d) in his "Purgatory" poem and it may have something to do with the old set of stairs guests must climb to reach their rooms. If stairs aren't a problem (there are several rooms on the ground floor), this medium-sized hotel at the intersection of a vibrant neighborhood near Piazza Salimbeni is an excellent option. Breakfast is included and the friendly staff can provide assistance 24 hours a day.

The Cicogna family has restored a medieval palazzo and turned it into an ideally located bed-and-breakfast minutes from the Piazza del Campo and Duomo. Each of the five rooms of **Antica Residenza Cicogna** (Via dei Termini 67, tel. 05/7728-5613, www.anticaresidenzacicogna.it, €83–100 s/d) is decorated in a unique style and benefits from high frescoed ceilings. Breakfast is the occasion to taste local biscuits and breads such as *cavallucci, copate,* and *panforte.* Fresh fruit and yogurt are also served.

Antica Torre (Via di Fieravecchia 7, tel. 05/7722-2255, www.anticatorresiena.it, €90–120 s/d) has preserved the marble paving and cast-iron beds that might have greeted medieval travelers. There are two rooms per floor at this small hotel 10 minutes from Piazza del Campo. The two on the last floor provide rooftop views and a glimpse of Tuscan countryside in the distance. Breakfast is an additional €7.

Palazzo Ravizza (Pian dei Mantellini 34, tel. 05/7728-0462, €120–180 s/d) is a vintage palazzo with 30 rooms that haven't lost their Renaissance charm. The hotel dates from the 1920s and has been run by the same family in a peaceful *contrade* within walking distance of everything. Modern comforts have been added without sacrificing the building's character and the shaded garden provides a welcome refuge in summertime. Parking is available and the restaurant is more than adequate.

The parishioners who run **Santuario Santa Caterina** (Via Camporeggio 37, tel. 05/774-4177, €65 d) understand the relation between cleanliness and godliness. Rooms may be stark but they couldn't be any cleaner, and if you don't mind the 11:30 P.M. curfew, this may be the best place to contemplate Siena. Many of the 31 rooms in the sanctuary have views of the Duomo and San Domenico. It goes without saying that there's no TV, and the front desk can be slightly irritable.

Food

Mass tourism may have lowered standards of some Siena restaurants but **Castelvecchio** (Via Castelvecchio 65, tel. 05/774-9586, Mon.–Sat. noon–3:30 P.M. and 7–11 P.M., €7–12) is not one of them. Simone Romi is attentive to the quality of food he serves and the service he provides both locals and visitors. The menu changes everyday and the prix-fixe (€25) is a good option if you want to get a wide sampling of Tuscan flavors. It comes with an antipasto, three different pastas, two seconds, and dessert.

Historic may be a strange way to describe a restaurant but it's the only way to summarize the traditional food and lively atmosphere of **Trattoria Papei** (Piazza Mercato 6, tel. 05/7728-0894, €10–14). The selection of grilled meats will satisfy carnivores and the informality of waiters provides excellent entertainment while waiting for the next carafe of house wine to arrive.

Thanks to the outdoor tables added in the summer the wait at **Osteria la Chiacchera** (Costa di Sant'Antonio 4, tel. 05/7728-0631, daily 12:30–3:30 P.M. and 7–11 P.M., €7.50–9) is considerably reduced. In all other seasons it's wise to make a reservation and assure you get a taste of traditional dishes served in this minuscule restaurant.

Cravings for cheese and cured meats can strike at any moment in Siena and when they do ◖ **Grattacielo** (Via dei Pontani 8, tel. 05/7728-9326, €10) has a cutting board ready. The restaurant also prepares one locally inspired dish each night. But perhaps the best thing about this place is the feeling you get walking in the streets afterwards realizing how little you paid for such good food.

FLORENCE AND TUSCANY

SCHIACCIATA CON L'UVA

Food changes according to the season and when *Schiacciata con l'uva* starts to appear in Tuscan bakeries you know autumn has arrived. This flatbread with grapes goes hand in hand with the harvest and has peasant origins. Grapes are usually sangiovese or canaiolo extras that don't make the Chianti cut. They're large and watery, and when baked turn into jelly. The ingredients are simple and suitable for the strictest vegans. All it takes to make this delicious sweet bread is flour, water, yeast, black grapes, sugar, and olive oil. Some bakers also add a dash of rosemary or fennel seeds. It's best eaten warm and can easily become addictive.

Getting to **Grotta di Santa** (Via della Galluzza 26, tel. 05/57728-2208, Tues.–Sat. and Sun. lunch noon–3 P.M. and 7–11:30 P.M., €8–11) is half the fun. The labyrinth of streets leading to the restaurant are some of the most suggestive in the city. The owner is a former *palio* rider and the tables outside provide a unique environment to have lunch or dinner. The cooking is strictly Sienese and offers a wide choice of seasonal dishes. Wine is mainly from the Rufina and local hillsides.

Hosteria Il Carroccio (Via di Casato di Sotto 32, tel. 05/774-1165, Thurs.–Tues. lunch noon–3:30 P.M. and 7–11 P.M., €7.50–10) remains one of the most affordable options around Piazza del Campo. Service may be a little hurried but it's always efficient. Waiters dispense with menus in the evening and you may have to ask them to repeat themselves a few times. Antipasto includes *salumi* and there is generally some variation of wild boar pasta. Surprisingly good salads are also served. The dozen or so tables on the inside are set within a small room carved out of rock. Nearby on the same street **Cantina in Piazza** sells nearly all of the wines produced in the DOCG (appellation) areas of the province.

Antica Trattoria Botteganova (Via Chiantigiani 29, tel. 05/7728-4230, Mon.–Sat. 12:30–2:30 P.M. and 7:30–10:30 P.M., €10–14) is considered one of the best restaurants in Siena and even though it's outside the city walls on the SS408 in the direction of Montevarchi gourmets won't mind the detour. An elegant, rustic interior and refined table settings complement the elaborate fish and meat dishes chef Michele prepares. The three *degustazione* menus (€37–45) are an introduction to creative Sienese cuisine and should be approached on an empty stomach. Reservations are almost always required on weekends.

There's nothing like a leisurely drink at one of the outdoor tables at the cafés around the Piazza del Campo. The selection process should be made more on your preference for sitting in the sun or the shade as the bars themselves are similar and offer a standard menu priced slightly higher due to the location.

Nannini (Via Banchi di Sopra 22, tel. 05/7723-6009) is the most famous bar in Siena and earned its reputation one espresso at a time. The sweets are especially memorable and gelato fans may add it to their top–10 list.

Since 1943, **Pasticceria Bini** (Via Stalloreggi 91, tel. 05/7728-0207) has baked all of the town's high-octane specialties, from *panforte margherita* to *cannoli alla mandorla*. The selection is best in the morning but mid-afternoon is a quiet time when you can browse the sweets in relative calm.

Japanese tourists love posing in front of **Antica Drogheria Manganelli's** (Via di Città 73, tel. 05/7728-0002) antique storefront. The goods sold here can't be captured on film and should be tasted. Pasta is all handmade by small producers in the area and some of the vinegar is 80 years old. If you'll be exploring smaller villages you may want to put off purchases, as prices are generally higher in the larger towns. If not, shop away.

Information and Services
The Siena **APT office** (tel. 05/7728-0551, www.terresiena.it, daily 9 A.M.–7 P.M.) is located on Piazza del Campo and is extremely well organized. If you've come without a plan, they have countless ideas for spending time in the city and province. Museum tickets are on sale and there are various combination offers.

Getting There and Around
Florence and Siena are linked by a *superstrada*. Journey time is under an hour. Arriving from the south on the A1 exit at Chiusi for a scenic drive along the N146 or take the following exit at Valdichiana if you're in a hurry.

There are regular **SITA** and **Train** (Piazza Gramsci, tel. 05/7720-4246, www.trainspa.it) buses leaving from Florence Piazza Santa Maria Novella. The journey takes 1.5 hours and makes a dozen stops along the way. A one-way ticket to Siena costs €6.50 and may be purchased at the SITA office in the piazza. Siena **buses** (Piazza Gramsci, tel. 05/7728-3203) link the city with Milan and Bologna.

Trains from Florence leave every hour for Siena between 5:32 A.M. and 11:07 P.M. Most departures are 10 minutes past the hour. It's a 90-minute trip that costs €5.70 for a second-class seat. All trains from Rome require a transfer at Grosseto or Chiusi.

The historic center of Siena has been pedestrian-friendly since the 1960s and there is no better way of exploring the narrow streets and alleys than on foot. Public buses run through the modern parts of town and there is extra-urban service to many of the surrounding communities leaving from Piazza Gramsci. A car is useful for reaching San Gimignano or San Galgano and can be rented from **Hertz** (Via Sardegna 37, tel. 05/774-5085, daily 9 A.M.–7 P.M.).

Around Siena
Monteriggioni is what most people imagine when they consider the Middle Ages. This magnificent walled village barely 15 kilometers from Siena has all its bricks in place. The 13th-century defenses were insurance against marauding Florentines and now provide visitors with an instant medieval experience. Two restaurants on the inside serve full meals or just gelato.

Central Tuscany has some of the most beautiful landscapes of the entire region and

Trenonatura (APT Siena, tel. 05/7728-0551, www.terresiena.it) carries visitors on "nature trains" past wonderful scenery. The vintage diesel and steam engines make morning stops in local towns where trekkers and bicyclists can get off and explore the pristine hills around Siena before catching the evening train back to town. Theme outings are also organized around wine and cheese served onboard. Reservations are required and departures are 8:30–10:30 A.M. The price of tickets depends on the itinerary but never exceeds €25.

ⓒ SAN GIMIGNANO

At first glance the San Gimignano skyline could be mistaken for Manhattan. Height once mattered here too and the skyscrapers made of stone reach a dizzying 50 meters. They're the result of competition between patrician families trying to outdo each other back when pilgrims regularly used the Via Francigena and demand for saffron was high. Although only 14 of the 72 towers have survived, the feudal atmosphere has not faded.

Sights

The medieval flashback begins as soon as you step through Porta San Giovanni. The street of the same name leads upwards towards **Piazza della Cisterna,** lined with towers, residences, and warehouses. The piazza gets its name from the well in the center and much of the original brick paving has remained intact. A narrow opening at the northern end of the piazza leads to **Piazza del Duomo.** This was the administrative center with its public buildings and Duomo.

Faith and devotion financed the art inside the **Duomo** or *Collegiata* and transformed the church from a simple chapel to the present building consecrated by Pope Eugenio III in 1148. It has a classic wide staircase leading to an unadorned entrance with a Gothic silhouette. Detail is saved for an interior containing striped marble arches and a ceiling painted in bright, unexpected colors. Frescoes tell the story of the Old and New Testament as interpreted by Bartolo di Fredi. It's generally filled

© ALEXEI J. COHEN

Piazza della Cisterna is named after the well in the center of the square.

FLORENCE AND TUSCANY

with a half-dozen impressed visitors and a couple of locals manning the pews.

Torture was no joke in the Middle Ages and even the toughest knights succumbed under pressure of the rack or Chinese thumbscrews. There was a wide array of machinery for making prisoners talk and many of these macabre devices have been preserved inside **Museo della Tortura** (Via del Castello 1–3, tel. 05/7794-2243, daily 10 A.M.–8 P.M., €8). Two other museums with a more multimedia approach to imprisonment are also located in town for anyone with a fascination with pain.

San Gimignano's second ring of walls was built in the 13th century and is best admired from the outside. A path lined with cedars follows the contours of town and overlooks the Valdelsa. This is a great way to walk off lunch and avoid the crowds that gather in the piazze during the summer. It can be reached from any of the main gateways and is especially scenic around Porta San Jacopo and Porta delle Fonti, named for the well where villagers once washed their clothes.

Entertainment and Events

The first performance inside **Teatro dei Leggieri** (Palazzo dell'Orologio, Piazza del

Duomo, tel. 05/7794-0742) dates from 1537 when an amateur troupe forcefully inaugurated the theater. It seats 100 and is mainly used for chamber music and piano recitals. Concerts are regularly held on New Year's Day, December 26, and during the San Gimignano classic music festival in September and October.

During the first week of August, Piazza della Cisterna becomes the backdrop of nightly opera performances. In previous years *Tosca* and *Madame Butterfly* have been staged in the open air. Tickets cost €15 and are available at the tourist office. The plastic folding chairs are not that comfortable and music can be heard equally well from palazzo steps for free.

La Ferie delle Messi dates from 1258 and is celebrated on the third weekend of June. Groups from all over the region, as well as the Cavalieri di Santa Fina, take to the streets in full medieval garb recreating life as it once was in San Gimignano. There is a lively market where craftspeople use nearly forgotten skills to turn wood, stone, and metal into art. Piazzas are animated by musicians and singers, and above town in Rocco Montestaffoli medieval flavors simmer while the crossbow tournament is staged. Festivities continue the next day when participants parade through the streets and knights from the town's four *contrade* compete for the *Spada d'Oro* (golden shield).

Saffron is known as yellow gold in San Gimignano; it helped make the town wealthy during the Middle Ages when it was exported to eager clients in Northern Europe and Asia. It still holds an important place on people's plates and the **Mostra Mercato dello Zafferano di San Gimignano** at the end of October is the chance to learn more about this versatile spice. A similar event dedicated to the town's olive oil is held during the last week in December.

Giro d'Italia is the most famous bicycle race in Italy but the country organizes hundreds of lesser-known one-day events for amateurs and professionals. The **Gran Fondo** starts and finishes in San Gimignano and to win it takes calves of steel. It's a festive occasion and the young local riders are determined to sweat it out. The race is held on the second week of May in Piazza della Cisterna and culminates with the honoring of the winning cyclist.

Shopping

There must be artists busy at work in the hills around San Gimignano because **Galleria Gagliardi** (Via San Giovanni 57, tel. 05/7794-2196) has no shortage of ceramic sculptures, abstract paintings, bronze, and works in steel, iron, and wood. It's an impressive collection that gets creative juices flowing.

Via San Giovanni has a high concentration of souvenir and specialty shops. A walk down the street should solve any gift-giving dilemmas.

Sports and Recreation

Naturalists can pitch their tents within sight of San Gimignano at **Camping Boschetto di Piemma** (Santa Lucia 38c, tel. 05/7794-0352, www.selvadelletorri.com, May–Sept., €9–20 pp). Bungalows are also available at reasonable prices and facilities include tennis courts, an Olympic-sized swimming pool, and a restaurant you wouldn't expect to find in the woods. A shuttle bus (€.50) makes the six-minute journey to town every hour between 8:50 A.M. and 7:35 P.M. Otherwise, it's a pleasant walk. Ecologists can sleep soundly in the knowledge that water at the campsite is heated using solar energy.

If you're in good health and have always wanted to fly, Walter Bardi (tel. 334/777-9747, www.parlapendio.it) can teach you how. The first introductory **parasailing** lesson is free and provides a fleeting sensation the Wright brothers would have enjoyed. Book one day in advance and make sure to wear the clothing Walter recommends.

Accommodations

It doesn't get much more central than the nine rooms at **Casa dei Potenti** (Piazza delle Erbe, tel. 05/7794-3190, www.casadeipotenti.com, €60–70 s/d). This small hotel has a bohemian feel and breakfast is served in view of the Duomo.

If a steep set of stairs doesn't put you off, the **Palazzo al Torrione** (Via Berignano 76, tel.

05/7794-0480, www.palazzoaltorrione.com, €110 d) offers stunning views of San Gimignano in each of its antique-furnished rooms. There is a strong sense of cozy and the woman who manages the hotel is a gracious host. Pickup and drop-off to private parking is available upon request. If they are full, there may be room at the Al Torrione II next door.

Hotel l'Antico Posto (Via San Matteo 87, tel. 05/7794-2014, www.anticoposto.com, €100–135 s/d) is a bright, airy hotel on the main street that benefits from a rooftop terrace and barman skilled in the art of cocktail-making. The hotel organizes horseback, hot-air balloon, and wine tours that leave an unforgettable impression.

Food

Ninety types of bruschetta might be a new Tuscan record. Each of the grilled bread appetizers at **Antica Taverna** (Vicolo Mainardi 10, tel. 05/7794-3174, €8) is topped with local ingredients and served with a rich green olive oil. It's best to order a few kinds and share dishes tapas-style. Selecting a wine is another enjoyable dilemma.

If you prefer lunch or dinner with a view, look no further than **Le Terrazze** (Via Piandornella 15, tel. 05/7794-0270, €9–12). There are plenty of tables on the terrace, yet it's still wise to make a reservation. The interior has a cellar-like atmosphere that's equally pleasant and provides the same *ribollita* (stew) and bean specialties served with *Vernaccia*. To become instantly acquainted with the wines of the region try one of the four *menu degustazione vini*. Each proposes several glasses of DOC caliber vintages that are perfect with the *pappardelle al cinghiale* (pasta with wild boar).

La Griglia (Via San Matteo 32, tel. 05/7794-0005, €10–13) is located within a medieval tower and is actually two restaurants in one. The Brasserie serves pizza and lighter fare while a large appetite is mandatory at La Griglia. This is the place to try *bistecca alla fiorentina* (Florentine-style steak), wild boar, and porcini mushrooms. During the spring and summer it's possible to dine on the terrace.

The maestro behind the counter at **◖ Gelateria di Piazza** (Piazza della Cisterna 4, tel. 05/7794-2244) is Sergio Dondoli. On a good day he'll have prepared 35 flavors that can't be tasted anywhere else. *Dolceamaro* (sweet and sour) is an award-winner and *cioccolato* (chocolate) remains a well-guarded secret. Flavors vary depending on the season; late summer is time for a sorbetto with Sangiovese grapes that sells out quickly. The steps leading to the old well in the center of the piazza is where gelato enthusiasts generally congregate.

Information and Services

The tourist information office (tel. 05/7794-0008, www.comune.sangimignano. si.it, 9 A.M.–1 P.M. and 3–7 P.M.) is in Piazza del Duomo 1. Sylvia can help find accommodations and restaurants, book bus tickets, and decipher train schedules. She can also provide an updated list of events, Internet access, and a public payphone. The audio guide (€5) takes visitors on three itineraries lasting a total of two hours.

If you get a sudden urge to hit the road there's a **Hertz** (tel. 05/7794-2220) on Via dei Fossi 1. If all you need is a taxi, call **Bruno Bellini** (Via Rome 1, tel. 05/7794-0201 or 348/827-3155).

Viviana Girola (tel. 05/7730-1101) is an authorized tour guide for San Gimignano and Siena. Anyone with an abundance of curiosity will appreciate her explanations, which are comprehensive without being boring.

Getting There and Around

By car from Florence or Siena take the Florence–Siena *superstrada* and exit at Poggibonsi Nord. Follow the road for 11 kilometers until San Gimignano. If you're traveling south on the A1, get off at Florence Certosa or Valdichiana if you're driving north. Once you arrive park in one of the three lots at the entrance to town and forget about your car. Everything in San Gimignano is best reached on foot unless your luggage is extremely heavy, in which case you can drive in to unload.

Trains from Florence to Poggibonsi/San Gimignano are frequent and run between

5:32 A.M. and 12:45 P.M. on weekdays. The journey takes a little over an hour and costs €4.80. Trains from Siena run on the same line and arrive in 30 minutes. The station however is a bit of a misnomer and passengers must complete the voyage by bus or taxi. A bus leaves every hour on weekdays between 6:50 A.M. and 9:15 P.M. from Largo Gramsci in Poggibonsi and reaches San Gimignano in 20 minutes.

AREZZO

If Arezzo looks familiar, it's because you've already seen it on film in *La Vita è Bella* or *The English Patient*. If it doesn't look familiar, prepare to get acquainted with one of the wealthiest towns in Tuscany. Although Arezzo was greatly damaged during World War II, what the bombs missed is a precious reminder of man's other capabilities.

Sights

Whether Arezzo's oddly slanted **Piazza Grande** was the site of a Roman forum is debatable. It is certainly the center of activity and hosts an antiques fair on the first Sunday of the month and the Giostra del Saracino festivities two weekends a year. At all other times, it's a good place to watch locals coming and going and admire the ingenuity of Giorgio Vasari, who designed many of the 16th-century palazzi bordering the square.

The frescoes inside **Basilica di San Francesco** (Piazza San Francesco, tel. 05/7590-0404, daily 8:30 A.M.–6:30 P.M.) were painted by Piero della Francesca between 1452–1466. He seems to have gotten his inspiration directly from heaven. The scenes in **Cappella Maggiore** (Mon.–Fri. 9 A.M.–5:30 P.M., Sat. 9 A.M.–5 P.M., Sun. 1–5 P.M., €6) depict the Legend of the True Cross and are notable for their treatment of light. The lowest section on the right of the altar is particularly impressive. A 15-year restoration has paid off and the colors are some of the most vibrant in Tuscany.

Vasari was a local whose talents with a brush can be seen inside the Duomo and **Casa di Vasari** (Via XX Settembre 55, tel. 05/754-090,

Wed.–Mon.) he built for himself in 1540. His mosaics and a fine collection of majolic pottery are on display at **Museo d'Arte Medioevale e Moderna** (Via di San Lorentino 8, tel. 05/750-9050, Tues.–Fri. 9 A.M.–7 P.M., Sat. and Sun. 9 A.M.–1 P.M., €4).

Entertainment and Events

Giostro del Saracino was a military training drill used until 1810. Now it's Arezzo's big day. Each of the four neighborhoods presents a team of two riders equipped with wooden lances. On the last Sunday of June and the first Sunday of September, they compete to score points by striking a shield placed on a mock Saracen wielding a chain. The game begins in the late afternoon following a historic parade. Spirits throughout are high and crowds cheer their riders passionately.

Arezzo Play Art Festival (www.playar ezzo.it) is a summer-long series of music, theater, literature, and new media. Peter Gabriel, Lou Reed, and multidisciplinary acts from around the world have graced the main stage in Piazza Grande. This is where the slanted piazza starts to make sense. Sight lines are excellent and many performances free.

Improvisation is the only rule during **Festival del Teatro Spontaneo** (Centro di Aggregazione Sociale Fiorentina, Via Vecchia 11). The festival takes place April–May. Check with the APT office for tickets. Eight theater companies flout their spontaneity in Italian and local vernacular at the small theater on Via Vecchia 11. Performances run every Friday throughout June and start at 9:15 P.M. Much of the acting is physical and audience participation encouraged. If you do end up on stage, just keep smiling.

Shopping

The technique of working gold into fine shapes was developed by the Etruscans and has remained alive in Arezzo ever since. Noblewomen and the church kept jewelers busy and helped them prosper. Industrialization hasn't caused any downsizing here and the area remains a vital center of Italian jewelry production. Heavy machinery hasn't eliminated craftsmen, who rely on creativity and quality to survive.

Jewelry stores are spread out all over town and are hard to avoid. Anyone who hasn't bought a necklace or ring in a while will find Arezzo hard to resist. Gold and silver are the primary metals and precious stones are used in original ways. The best jewelers are working jewelers—not just selling bracelets and earrings, but creating them. **Carniani** (Via del Gavardello 62, tel. 05/7538-1847, Tues.–Sun. 9 A.M.–1 P.M. and 3 P.M.–7 P.M.) and **Garzi** (Via del Maspino 30, tel. 05/7598-4341, Tues.–Sun. 9 A.M.–1 P.M. and 3 P.M.–7 P.M.) fall into that category.

Piazza Grande is big and when it fills up with antiques it feels like an endless outdoor living room. Browsing takes on epic proportions and sellers are happy to bend your ear with stories about this candelabra and that oil lamp. The Fiera takes place on the first weekend of every month.

Accommodations

Vogue Hotel Arezzo (Via Guido Monaco 54, tel. 05/752-4361, www.voguehotel.it, €108–138 s/d) is 300 meters from the train station and parking is available for free. The 26 rooms vary in style, but each contains a bathtub. The front desk can change currency and will serve breakfast in your room upon request. The bar is open 24 hours a day.

After buying that jewelry, you're going to need a safe or somewhere to propose. **AC Arezzo** (Via A. Einstein, tel. 05/7538-2287, www.ac-hotels.it, €137–187 s/d) delivers on both counts and does so with style. A night here provides enough fond memories to last a lifetime, and if that sounds like an overstatement just call room service.

One kilometer isn't far to go for a little charm. **Agriturismo la Striscia** (Via dei Cappuccini 3, tel. 05/752-6740 or 340/063-0192, www.lastriscia.com) has four photogenic apartments and landscapes that look like they were painted by Piero della Francesca. The Italian garden has a bohemian atmosphere and guests

lie about on the chaise lounge sipping wine produced by the owner.

Food

The obvious restaurant is **Buca di San Francesco** (Via San Francesco 1, tel. 05/752-3271, Wed.–Sun. 12:30–3 P.M. and 7–10:30 P.M., €7). After all it's next to the church, the medieval atmosphere can't be beat, and no one has ever complained about the food.

Antica Trattoria da Guido (Via Madonna del Prato 85, tel. 05/752-3760, Mon.–Sat. noon–2:30 P.M. and 7–10:30 P.M., €8–13) lies on one of Arezzo's oldest streets. Teresa welcomes guests with a smile and keeps the restaurant animated with her good cheer. The menu is Tuscan with a pinch of Calabrian thrown in as a reminder of the family's origins. All the first courses are based around fresh pasta and the traditional soups are filling. Duck and roast rabbit make excellent seconds for anyone with extra capacity.

Near Piazza Grande, **La Torre di Gnicche** (Piaggia San Martino 8, tel. 05/7535-2035, Thurs.–Tues. noon–3 P.M. and 6 P.M.–1 A.M., €6–10) is a one-room enoteca that spreads to the steps outside in summer. Tuscan finger food and a bottle of wine can be enjoyed until late and heartier appetites can sample the *ribollita* (stew) or *baccalà* (fish). If the desserts don't attract your attention, visit **Cristallo** (Piazza San Jacopo) for a dose of chocolate. **Coffee O'Clock** (Corso Italia 184, tel. 05/7533-3067, daily 7 A.M.–7 P.M.) serves a Dominican blend purchased through fair trade markets. The selection of 30 teas meets English standards.

Information and Services

There are two APT offices. One is in Piazza della Repubblica 28 (tel. 05/7537-7678, daily 10 A.M.–3:30 P.M. and 3–6 P.M., www.apt.arezzo.it) and the other is on Via Ricasoli XX (tel. 05/7537-7829, daily 10 A.M.–6 P.M.). Chiara works in the first and can help find accommodations, book train tickets, or suggest a good restaurant. The visitor's card costs €12 and permits entry into several museums and monuments. The best way to get a virtual taste of town is at the office in Via Ricasoli XX. The 360-degree film projected on five screens lasts 15 minutes and provides an introduction to all the major sights. Projections are shown upon request and cost €2.50.

Getting There and Around

Trains from Florence and Siena are frequent. The journey from the capital takes an hour and costs €5.20. From Siena, it's necessary to transfer at Chiusi and the standard fare is €8.70. **ATAM** (Via Setteponti 66, tel. 05/7538-2651) operates 10 bus lines, most of which stop at the train station. Tickets cost €.90 for 70 minutes of travel. Taxis can be ordered by calling 05/7538-2626 or hailed directly at the station.

CORTONA

One of the oldest hill towns, Cortona also happens to be one of the most captivating. The Middle Ages left a mark and signs of the town's glorious heyday, when it managed to resist the advances of Siena and Arezzo, are evident throughout the maze of enchanting streets. If a lot of it starts to look alike, it's because the same soft bluish-gray stone was used for medieval, Renaissance, and Baroque constructions, making it seem like everything was built at once.

Sights

The farther you climb to the top of Cortona, the more you get to know the town. Porta Montanina is as intimate as it gets, with views revealing rooftops and the entire Valdichiana Valley. Etruscan roots are displayed at **Museo dell'Accademia Etrusca** (Palazzo Casali, Piazza Signorelli 9, tel. 05/7563-0415, Apr.–Oct. Tues.–Sun. 10 A.M.–7 P.M., Nov.–Mar. Tues.–Sun. 10 A.M.–5 P.M., €5) and pride of place goes to a 5th-century bronze chandelier weighing 50 kilograms. Egyptian finds and Tuscan paintings can also be seen.

There are beautiful churches both within and outside the walls that inspired Henry James to wear sunglasses. **San Francesco** contains work by the homegrown artist Pietro di Cortona and on the southern slope the guild of tanners erected **Santa Maria al Calcinaio** (1485–1513) in recognition of the miracles the Virgin was performing at the time. The interior owes a lot to Brunelleschi's ideas about space and took Renaissance interior design to a new level.

Festivals and Events

A festival dedicated to the art of living makes sense in a town like Cortona. **Festival del Sole** (www.festivaldelsole.com) combines music with wellness and wine tastings. Lectures cover topics like sustainable agriculture, Chinese medicine, and the history of Renaissance banquets. Events run throughout the first two weeks of August and tickets may be purchased at the APT office or online.

Giostra dell'Archidado (www.cortonaweb. net) is staged every May with great pageantry. The main event is the crossbow competition but there are also falconry exhibitions and historical recreations of the town's medieval history. Most of the action is centered around Piazza Signorelli and starts in the early evening.

Accommodations

Rugapiana Vacanze (Via Nazionale 63, tel. 05/630-712, www.rugapianavacanze.com, €95 d) is a four-story bed-and-breakfast with double rooms and apartments. Walls reveal original stone construction, and furnishings are all vintage (except for the minibar and satellite TV). Parking is 100 meters from the entrance and half-board is available.

Built on the hill, **Hotel San Luca** (Piazzale Garibaldi 2, tel. 05/7563-0460, €80 d) offers simple bedrooms and magnificent panoramas of the valley from reception. Service is attentive and the hotel's size makes it easy to socialize with other guests.

It's too bad **San Michele** (Via Guelfa 15, tel. 05/7560-4348, www.hotelsanmichele.net, €120–150 s/d) isn't a chain. The hotel is on the doorstep of history, staff is friendly, rooms decorated tastefully, and there's a sense of tranquility everywhere.

◖ **Relais Corte dei Papi** (Via La Dogana 12, tel. 05/7561-4109, www.lacortedeipapi.com, €195 d) is refined from the period furniture to the swimming pool to the wood-beamed restaurant. It would make a good setting for a fairy tale or romantic getaway minutes from Cortona. The limited number of rooms and suites come with every comfort and impeccable service is standard.

Food

The cured meat and cheese platter at **Osteria del Teatro** (Via Maffei 2, tel. 05/7563-0556, Thurs.–Tues. 12:30–3:30 P.M. and 6:30–10:30 P.M., €7.50–10) is further proof that you can't get too much of a good Tuscan antipasto. Traditional bean and mushroom soup is also satisfying and Emiliano Rossi is skilled at suggesting the right wine.

Monumental is the only way to describe the wine menu at **Taverna Pane Vino** (Piazza Signorelli 27, tel. 05/7563-1010, Tues.–Sun. 12:30–3 P.M. and 7–11:30 P.M., €7–10). Debora and Arnalda have been giving their palates a workout for years with special attention to smaller vineyards. Tastings are held in the cellar on Thursdays when it's not too hot and the kitchen delivers simple dishes just the way you imagined them.

Getting There and Around

Say goodbye to those gentle curving roads they use in car commercials and get ready to grip the steering wheel with both hands. Take exit Casello Valdichiana off the A1 and follow the E45 towards Perugia until Cortona San Lorenzo. Otherwise leave the transportation to the **LFI bus drivers** (Arezzo, Via Guido Monaco 37, tel. 05/753-9881, www.lfi.it), who seem at home on the edge of a cliff. There are daily services from Siena and Arezzo. Cortona is also reachable directly by train from Florence, Milan, Rome, and Naples.

Autonoleggio Il Girasole (Via Licio Nencetti 6, Terontola di Cortona, tel. 05/7567-8687, www.autonoleggioilgirasole.it, €35/50 per day) rents mopeds that are easy to handle and will turn novice riders into Valentino Rossi within a curve or two. Bikes, cars, and minibuses are also available.

Around Cortona

Another famous Arezzo native is Saint Elias, who spent most of his days in meditation at the **Convento delle Celle**. It's another steep climb up Mount Sant'Egidio 10 kilometers north of Cortona where monks have been plying their trade since 1211.

MONTEPULCIANO

Some towns are like wine. Montepulciano has been getting better with age since being founded on a high ridge by enterprising Etruscans. The number of noteworthy palazzi are too numerous to count, especially after a glass of the town's acclaimed *vino nobile*. Piazza Grande provides an eyeful of Renaissance architecture.

Sights

Montepulciano was greatly influenced by the Renaissance. After a steep climb up Via Corso, many of the town's finest buildings can be admired in Piazza Grande. Palazzo Communale will look familiar to anyone who has been to Florence. It is a smaller version of Palazzo della Signoria, however here the clock tower cannot be visited. The Duomo is the work of Ippolito Scalza and contains a triptych painting of the Assumption by Taddeo di Bartolo. Further examples of Florentine and Sienese painters are contained in Palazzo Neri Orselli that houses the **Museo Civico** (Via Ricci 10, tel. 05/7871-7300, Tues.–Sun. 10 A.M.–1 P.M. and 3–6 P.M., €4). The two main rooms present 300 years of painting. Tempio di San Biaggio is on the edge of town. It's Antonio da Sangallo's masterpiece built on a Greek cross plan with two bell-towers. The symmetry on the outside is as impressive as the marble altar sculpted by Lisandro Albertini that is still used every Sunday.

Entertainment and Events

Cantiere Internazionale d'Arte di Montepulciano (Palazzo del Capitano, Piazza Grande 7, tel. 05/7875-7089, www.fondazionecantiere.it) was conceived in 1976 as a way for professional musicians, dancers, and actors to interact with students, aficionados, and anyone who enjoys singing in the shower. The goal is to create a collective performance where everyone takes part. Many of the locals participate and the result of this original collaboration is performed throughout July and August. Even passing visitors are encouraged to lend their voices. Events are held in Palazzo Comunale and several other palazzos around town.

The rolling of the casks, or **Bravio delle Botti** as it's called here, is a daylong event on the last Sunday in August. The casks weigh 80 kilograms and are pushed uphill through the streets of Montepulciano by neighborhood teams. The historic parade starts at 4 P.M. and the race itself begins at 7 P.M. from Colonna del Marzocco. The finish line is in Piazza Grande, where the winning team receives the prized banner that has been contested for 600 years.

Accommodations

Elena Trovati knows how to make guests feel at home and her small hotel on the ramparts of town overlooking the lakes of Val di Chiana is a good place to start the day. **Il Borghetto** (Via Borgo Buio 7, tel. 05/7875-7535, €100–115 s/d) is well located for visiting Montepulciano and adjacent parking makes it easy to head off on excursions. Ask for a room with a view.

The pastel-colored rooms of **Il Rondo** (Via di Martiena 9, tel. 05/7871-6899, www.albergoilrondo.com, €95 d) lie 500 kilometers from the entrance to town in a peaceful villa steeped in 18th-century decor. There's plenty of parking out front and wireless Internet available for surfing in the garden.

Fattoria San Martino (Via Martiena 3, San Martino, tel./fax 05/7871-7463, www.fattoriasanmartino.it, €130–160 s/d) takes ecology to the next level. The *bioturismo* on the outskirts of Montepulciano serves an organic breakfast with many ingredients grown on the farm. Water is heated using local wood and the sun, while king-size mattresses have been specially constructed to remove any electromagnetic waves that may be floating around. The chemical-free bio-pond is an innovative compromise between man and nature, and of course the owners encourage use of the bus that stops half a kilometer away.

Food

If you imagined sunsets overlooking the Val d'Orcia with a glass of *vino nobile* in your hands you probably already know about **E Lucevan le Stelle** (Piazza San Francesco 5, tel. 05/7875-8725, €7). The terrace is a pleasant place to relax after a day of Tuscan exploration and the interior is equally intriguing with its oversized doors and archway framing a modern lounge ambiance. Live jazz is often performed.

Situated in the highest part of town, **Le Logge del Vignola** (Via delle Erbe 6, tel. 05/7671-7290, Wed.–Mon. 7–10:30 P.M., €8–12) provides 10 finely set tables within elegant surroundings. Dishes balance a respect for tradition and innovation that the chef expresses primarily in his first courses. The wine does not stray very far from home and different-size carafes are available for anyone intimidated by an entire bottle.

Information and Services

Strada del Vino Nobile (Piazza Grande 7, tel. 05/7871-7484, www.stradavinonobile.it, Mon.–Sat. 10 A.M.–1 P.M. and 3–7 P.M.) is the tourist office in Montepulciano. It provides the usual information and is the place to sign up for a tasting. Organized walking, cycling, and minibus tours leave daily for the wineries and should be booked in advance. There's also a film tour that's especially gratifying for fans of *The English Patient*. All visits leave from Piazza Grande, last several hours, and cost €20–35 per person. Search for *strada vino nobile* on Skype and speak with Bruna or Nick for more information about the town.

Getting There and Around

There are only two Train bus departures from Stazione Santa Maria Novella in Florence and it may be more convenient to take the train to Chiusi followed by an **LFI bus** (tel. 05/7831-1774). There are four daily Train departures from Siena.

PIENZA

It's easy to be proud of your hometown when you're from Florence, Siena, or Pisa. But if you happen to be from Corsignano, there isn't a whole lot to be excited about—or there wasn't until Pope Pius II. In order to provide his birthplace with a sudden dose of prestige, he commissioned Bernardo Rossellino in 1459 to transform a medieval town into an ideal city. The construction that followed was the first based entirely on principles of Renaissance urban planning. Piazza Pio II and Palazzo Piccolomini presented a new way of treating public space that influenced architects for centuries to come. To complete the transformation the town was renamed Pienza.

Sights

Pienza was Rossellino's big break. After studying under Leon Battista Alberti, he was bursting with ideas, and this commission from an enlightened Pope was the opportunity to make a lasting impression. **Piazza Pio II** became the center of this creativity around which all the new structures would be angled.

Palazzo Piccolomini (Corso Rossellino, tel. 05/7728-6300, www.palazzopiccolominipienza.it, Tues.–Sun. 10 A.M.–6:30 P.M., €3) was inspired by Palazzo Rucellai in Florence and cost a small fortune to complete. It is built around an internal courtyard and hanging garden that looks out over the Val d'Orcia. This was Pope Pio's summer residence and he was hosting dinner parties here a mere three years after work had started. Guided tours take visitors through halls that have retained their period furnishings and reveal secret passages that allowed quick getaways.

Next to the Palazzo stands the **Duomo,** constructed at the same time and nearly as fast. The facade is divided into three vertical and horizontal sections aligned with the paving in the piazza. Comparing the medieval church of San Francesco with the Duomo, it becomes clear that times had changed. Inside the Pope requested Gothic based on German models of the time. The *Assunzione* by Vecchietta is the highlight of the interior.

© ALEXEI J. COHEN

Piazza Pio II in Pienza

Palazzo Vescovile, also on the piazza, received a makeover by Rossellino, who enlarged the doors and windows and made them conform to the overall plan of the square. The complex contains the **Museo Diocesano** (tel. 05/7874-9905, Wed.–Mon. 10 A.M.–1 P.M. and 3–6 P.M., €4.10) and several illustrious examples of 13th- and 14th-century religious painting.

Entertainment and Events

Closing time is early in Pienza and ordering an after-dinner cocktail would be impossible if it weren't for **Bar il Casello** (Via del Casello 3, tel. 05/7874-9105, daily 9 A.M.–1 A.M., €5). During the day they serve coffee, tea, and iced drinks that taste better when sipped on one of the chairs outside the bar overlooking the valley.

Pienza is already beautiful, but when the town is covered in flower displays it becomes enchanting. **Mostra-Mercato di Piante e Fiori,** which recreates Renaissance designs with petals on the second weekend in May, is a must for gardeners.

Every August, towns in the region participate

in the **Festival della Val d'Orcia.** Depending on the year, themes may focus on theater, music, or dance. What remains constant are the stunning outdoor backdrops to the events.

Pienza is known as the capital of cacio pecorino cheese. The reputation stems from aromatic grasses in the area, which produce sheep's milk with a particular flavor. **Gioco del Cacio Fuso** occurs on the first Sunday in September and is the opportunity to witness the town celebrate its produce. Craft and culinary stands line the main piazza offering visitors a taste of local ingenuity.

Shopping

Hammer, anvil, and fire. That's all they need at **Biagiotti** (Via I Maggio 1, tel. 05/7874-8478, Mon.–Sat. 9 A.M.–1 P.M. and 3–7 P.M.) to turn out wrought-iron objects of exceptional beauty. There are candelabra, wall-mounted dragons, and beds that recall a medieval past.

Sports and Recreation

Road bike or racing bike is the question at **Cicloposse** (Via I Maggio 27, tel. 05/7874-9983, www.cicloposse.com, Mar.–Oct. daily 8:30 A.M.–1 P.M. and 2:30–8 P.M.). Whichever you choose comes equipped with helmet, lock, handlebar bag, and mileage counter. A full-day costs €20 and anyone who wants to learn more about the scenery can join Marco on one of the day- or week-long cycling tours the company regularly organizes.

Accommodations

Il Chiostro di Pienza (Corso Rossellino 26, tel. 05/7874-8400, www.relaisilchiostrodipienza.com, €150–160 s/d) is a former monastery in the center of town. The monks left a while ago but the large, airy rooms overlooking the valley are still there. Beds are more comfortable now and the outdoor restaurant is a delightful option.

Outside of town off the SS146 is a bed-and-breakfast that feels like an oasis. **La Saracina** (SS146 km 29,700, tel. 05/7874-8022, www.lasaracina.it, €230–270 s/d) is a restored farmhouse in a picturesque landscape away from

anything even remotely stressful. Two rooms and one apartment form the basis of the accommodation that's a favorite with newlyweds. A large swimming pool and a variety of sporting activities help pass the time.

Food

Enoteca Baccus (Corso Rossellino 70, tel. 05/7874-9080, daily 9:30 A.M.–9:30 P.M.) serves Brunello di Montalcino by the glass or bottle accompanied with light snacks. There are six varieties of *bruschette* and *crostini toscani* that are an appetizing interlude to a visit of the town.

Innovation is a dirty word at **Trattoria Latte di Luna** (Via San Carlo 2, tel. 05/7874-8606, Wed.–Mon. 12:30 A.M.–3 P.M. and 7:30–10 P.M., €7–11). Here the two sisters doing the cooking rely on traditional handmade pasta and *ragù* that's been simmering since morning. Tables outside enjoy a little *piazzetta* all to themselves and the wine list includes around 30 local labels.

It's easy to organize a picnic in Tuscany. All the food you need is at shops like **Da Marusco e Maria** (Corso Rossellino 15, tel. 05/7874-8222, daily 9 A.M.–1 P.M. and 3–7 P.M.), which has an extensive variety of pecorino cheeses wrapped in straw and flavored with nuts. Fresh bread is a few doors down and the scenery is everywhere.

Most of the brands inside **La Cornucopia** (Piazza Martiri della Libertà 2, tel. 05/7874-8150, daily 9:30 A.M.–1 P.M. and 2:30–7:30 P.M.) will never be household names. The proprietors of this food emporium scour local farms and vineyards in search of the best products they can find. Standards are high and so is the quality of the wine, oil, and cheeses inside. If you can't decide they are happy to advise wavering palates.

An organic market is held in Piazza Galleti on the first Sunday of every month between March and December.

Information and Services

The **tourist office** (Piazza Pio II, tel. 05/7874-9905, daily 10 A.M.–1 P.M. and

3–7 P.M.) is inside Museo Diocesano. They can provide a map of town and a monthly list of events in the area. They can also arrange tours and recommend accommodations.

Getting There and Around

Pienza is located on the SS146 between San Quiricio d'Orcia and Montepulciano. Drivers can arrive via the Cassia or A1 highway by exiting at Bettolle or Chiusi. The closest train station is Chiusi–Chianciano Terme from where a Train bus (tel. 05/7720-4111) completes the journey.

MONTALCINO

Montalcino, 32 kilometers south of Siena, is a pleasant detour on the way to or from Pienza and Montepulciano if you can handle the curvy roads on the way there. Located in an idyllic Tuscan countryside, the town overlooks the Via Cassia. It was a key trading route and often violently contested during the Middle Ages. The town is one of the highest in the region and thick fortifications are now used for admiring the views rather than keeping anyone out. This is the home of Brunello wine and the grape tradition goes back centuries.

Sights

Most of the timeless streets lead to **Piazza del Popolo,** which contains several interesting buildings. Palazzo dei Priori is notable for its fine loggia. Towering above is the Rocca, built in the 14th century by military architects. From the top on a clear day you can see a patchwork of fields all the way to northern Lazio. The ramparts of the **Fortezza** (Piazzale della Fortezza, tel. 05/7784-9211, daily 9 A.M.–8 P.M., €3.50) can be circumnavigated and the *enoteca* inside is a pleasant place to sample the area's red wines.

Accommodations

Giglio Hotel (Via Soccorso Saloni 5, tel. 05/7784-6577, www.gigliohotel.com, €70–100 s/d) has recreated a bygone atmosphere in 12 rooms with hand-painted ceramics, cast-iron beds, and pastel colored walls. The smell of freshly baked bread is the only alarm you need and is waiting every morning as soon as you can tear yourself from the panorama.

A pool with a view and breakfast served on a magnificent terrace are the main draws of **Hotel dei Capitano** (Via Lapini 6, tel. 05/7784-7227, www.deicapitani.it, €100–115 s/d). The building was once used by Sienese patriots fleeing Florentine armies and is decorated with basic, utilitarian furniture.

Food

Owner and chef Gianluca Dipirro subscribes to a Slow Food philosophy that he puts into practice every day at **Ristorante al Giardino** (Piazza Cavour 1, tel. 05/77-849076, Thurs.–Tues. 12:30–3:30 P.M. and 7–10:30 P.M., €8–10). Pasta is all rigorously made in–house, as is the bread, which has been known to ruin appetites. Desserts are a highlight that can be walked off later.

Alle Logge (Piazza del Popolo, tel. 05/7784-6186) is a sophisticated wine bar where selections by the glass always include a significant Brunello.

Getting There and Around

It's a shame to drive from one town to the next without ever stopping to admire what's in between. The Val d'Orcia is a World Heritage Site for a reason and bicycle may be the best way to approach the valley. **Bike Montalcino** (tel. 347/053-5638, www.bikemontalcino.it) leads guided 25–kilometer itineraries through Brunello vineyards, Crete mountains, and local castles.

Around Montalcino

According to legend, Charlemagne founded the **Abbazia di Sant'Antimo**. The abbey eight kilometers south of Montalcino grew quite wealthy in the 12th century and control of the lands was often disputed with Siena. Onyx and alabaster sculptures on the Romanesque facade are unusual and the interior includes a woman's gallery above the two aisles.

La Versilia and Maremma

PISA

Pisa owes its prosperity to the sea. It served as a naval base for the Romans and rivaled the maritime republics of Genova and Venice in the 12th century. Trade in those days financed the city's monuments and the foundation of a university where Galileo Galilei contemplated gravity.

The city is most famous for its leaning tower. Visitors can opt for the quick tour around the Campo dei Miracoli or spend a full day discovering the overlooked parts of town. Roman remains, Gothic churches, and Renaissance buildings make interesting diversions from the usual trek towards the Duomo.

Sights

There's more to Pisa than most people know. After all, this was one of Keith Haring's favorite cities and the painter left his trademark images on the church of Sant'Antonio (Piazza Vittorio Emanuale). A visit should include a walk along both sides of the Arno and a stroll through all four of the city's central neighborhoods. **Piazza dei Cavalieri** was the historic center of the city and the palazzo of the same name is noteworthy for the facade decorated by Vasari. It still houses the Scuola Normale Superiore founded by Napoleon. The adjacent church of Santo Stefano was built in 1569 and is wrapped in white, green, and pink marble.

There are many leaning towers in Italy, but it's the one in Pisa that gets the most attention. The tower however is only one of four stellar buildings in **Campo dei Miracoli** (Square of Miracles). To get the best view, enter from Porta S. Maria and visit each of the buildings in succession. You won't be alone. Where tourists tread, street vendors naturally follow. Do your best to avoid them, or if you do need a pair of cheap sunglasses make sure to negotiate.

BATTISTERO

The Battistero was started in 1153 and the exterior combines Romanesque on the lower facade with Gothic on the upper windows. The distinct oddly shaped dome ends in a truncated pyramid. There are four portals leading to the majestic interior filled with light and decorated simply with alternating shades of marble. The pulpit is the work of Nicola Pisano. It rests on a single column and is surrounded by five panels recounting the life of Christ.

DUOMO

Booty captured on expeditions to the Middle East paid for the spectacular Duomo. The facade is unique and the four-columned loggias provide a sensation of weightlessness that recalls the Far East. The marble is from local quarries and the bronze doors set a new standard in church entrances.

Inside it's hard not to be impressed. The church stretches 100 meters in length and numerous columns support three naves. Perspective changes with each step and it's worth taking a seat in one of the pews to admire the sculptures. *Pergamo* by Giovanni Pisano is perhaps the most beautiful of these and is stunning in its complexity. Nearby is the so-called Galileo lamp that inspired one of the thinker's many theories.

𝄖 LEANING TOWER OF PISA

To get an idea of just how far the **Torre Pendente** (the leaning tower) is leaning approach from the Duomo. It's only five degrees off center but looks like it could fall any moment. Perhaps that's why visitors haven't been allowed to the top in a decade and engineers have worked overtime to stop the tower's annual two-centimeter progression towards earth. The 670 tons of reinforced concrete seem to have done the trick. Galileo's famous gravitational experiments conducted here could still be a foreshadowing of things to come.

Someone should have known better than build a tower on sandy, silt-ridden soil, but the Torre Pendente got the go ahead in 1173 and started to lean a hundred years later when it was barely halfway done. Strangely that didn't stop

Leaning Tower of Pisa (Torre Pendente)

© ALEXEI J. COHEN

were buried here and the frescoes are particularly realistic. *Il Trionfo della Morte* is a good reminder about the brevity of life.

Most great cathedrals also have great museums. On the ground floor, the **Museo dell'Opera del Duomo** contains Pisan sculpture from the 12th–16th centuries and a Madonna with Child made out of ivory. Upstairs there are paintings, ancient texts, and an Episcopal wardrobe.

MUSEO NAZIONALE DI S. MATTEO
Museo Nazionale di S. Matteo (tel. 05/054-1865, Tues.–Sun. 8:30 A.M.–7 P.M., €4) demonstrates the impact Pisa had on the arts during the Renaissance. Most of the work is religious in nature and the subjects are given a dramatic representation rarely seen up to that point. There are several pieces by members of the Pisano family.

SANTA MARIA DELLA SPINA
Santa Maria della Spina is named after the thorn from Christ's crown that was once preserved here. It is much more intimate than the Duomo and the exterior is a masterpiece of Pisan Gothic architecture pierced by twin rose windows and capped with three delicately sculpted pinnacles. It's hard to tell that the church was entirely rebuilt in 1871 after being severely damaged by flooding.

Entertainment and Events
Piazza Garibaldi is a popular square in the center of the city. Most evenings it's packed with locals preparing for a night on the town or just hanging out on the lungarno walls. There are many bars and restaurants in the area and outdoor tables fill up fast in the summer.

More artistic pursuits take place regularly at **Teatro Verdi** (Via Palestro 40, tel. 05/094-1111, www.teatrodipisa.pi.it). This beautiful theater was built in 1867 and would make a good home for a phantom. If the box seats are sold out you can still get a good view from the balcony. The season includes opera and ballet performances.

June is a lively month in Pisa. On June 16,

the architects or convince them to dig deeper foundations. Instead the tower was completed in 1350 and its gravity-defying angle became an attraction almost immediately. Recent interventions decreased the lean to 38 centimeters, but the tower remains closed for safety's sake. You can admire the relief sculpture near the entrance that celebrates Pisa's naval glory or lie on your back underneath the tower to appreciate the graceful marble arcading that adorns six of the tower's eight stories.

For more leaning towers visit Via San Martino. Many 17th-century noblemen called this street home and earlier residents built their impregnable *case-torri* (tower houses) here.

CAMPOSANTO
Camposanto was designed by one of the architects responsible for the leaning tower, but construction was halted after the battle of Meloria was lost against the Genovese. It was finally completed in the 14th century and consists of a long single-story rectangular structure bordered by an internal portico. Illustrious Pisans

a spectacular street festival, the **Luminara,** takes place. The entire town is lit by candlelight and at 11 P.M. fireworks illuminate the sky. Concerts are organized in nearly every square and a party atmosphere prevails in the streets. The day after is more subdued. It's **San Ranieri Day,** dedicated to Pisa's patron saint.

Il Gioco del Ponte is a modern version of the ritual battles waged between the inhabitants living north (Tramontana) and south (Mezzogiorno) of the river. The event is held on the Ponte di Mezzo and involves two neighborhood teams trying to push a seven-ton metal carriage into the adversaries' territory. It's basically an intense tug-of-war that can last up to 20 strenuous minutes. The event is held on the last Sunday in June and is preceded by a military parade of 16th-century military combatants.

Regata delle Repubbliche Marinare is a three-way rowing event between Pisa, Genova, and Venice. The location varies from year to year and is usually held during early June. Eight-man crews receive considerable support from locals lining the river and bridges.

Classical music in exceptional surroundings is the idea behind the month-long **Festival Anima Mundi.** Starting in mid-September, international orchestras and soloists perform within the Duomo and Camposanto to mesmerized audiences. Seats aren't very comfortable but the melodies are worth the sacrifice.

Shopping

Corso Italia is the busiest street in Pisa and a good place to shop. Many popular brands have stores here. **Borgo Stretto,** on the other side of the river, is the more elegant option. Under the arches you'll find clothing boutiques and a high concentration of jewelers. A Christmas market selling ornaments and Nativity scenes is held in December. Piazza delle Vettovaglie nearby is home to many shops and a vibrant vegetable market that provides a glimpse of Pisan shoppers in action. Mercatino dell'Antiquariato (tel. 05/040-0096) is held on the second weekend of each month except July and August.

Sports and Recreation

Pisa Marathon (www.pisamarathon.it) in mid-May starts in Pontedera and weaves its way through several pretty towns before finishing near the leaning tower. It's a flat course that attracts a lot of first-timers. The entry fee is cheaper the earlier you sign up and there's a five-kilometer fun run for less toned athletes.

A couple of kilometers northeast of Pisa is the spa town of **San Giuliano Terme,** where Shelley once spent his summers in reverie. **Bagni di Pisa** (Largo Shelley 18, tel. 05/0885-0432, www.bagnidipisa.com, Mon.– Sat. 9 A.M.–7 P.M., Sun. 9 A.M.–1 P.M.) offers a wide assortment of treatments, from aqua gym and watsu in the thermal pool to the steam rooms of the hammam and Turkish bath. The vast menu of massages includes Shiatsu, Chinese Tuina, and a titillating four-handed rub. A half-day of pampering is priceless.

The affordable option is a dip in the newly built swimming pool at **Campo Sportivo Comunale** (Via Bonanno 2, tel. 05/029–233), where a pick-up game of basketball is also possible.

Parco di San Rossore (Località Cascine Vecchie, tel. 05/053-9111, www.parks.it/parco.migliarino.san.rossore) lies on the western edge of Pisa and stretches up and down the coast for 20 kilometers. Scenery alternates between grassland, marsh, and elm and alder groves where wild boar roam. The park is divided into several areas, many of which can be visited for free. San Rossore Visitors Center organizes horse-powered tours every day but Monday (9:30 A.M.–1:30 P.M. and 3:30–6:30 P.M.) or you can ride the *trenino* (train) that follows a 30-kilometer circuit. The guestbook includes words of admiration from Tony Blair. A bus leaves regularly to the park from Porto di Livorno.

Accommodations

Hotel Galileo (Via Santa Maria 12, tel. 05/040–621, €60 d) is a good option for anyone who values eating well over sleeping in style. Nine rooms all have their own facilities, modern furniture, and large windows. The

LA VERSILIA AND MAREMMA **167**

location near Piazza del Duomo is unbeatable for the price and the money saved can be spent on dining.

Hotel Terminus & Plaza (Via Cristoforo Colombo 45, tel. 05/050-0303, www.hotel terminusplaza.it, €100 d) provides clean modern rooms within walking distance of the train station. The staff is accommodating and the breakfast buffet covers all the major food groups.

Everyone is in a good mood at **Royal Victoria Hotel** (Via Lungarno Pacinotti 12, tel. 05/094-0111, www.royalvictoria.it, €110–130 s/d) and the feeling is contagious. The comfortable, well-appointed rooms overlook the Arno and a fourth-floor roof terrace provides a nice view of the city. This is where Dickens, Ruskin, Dumas, and Pirandello chose to sleep.

Relais dell'Orologio (Via della Faggiola 12, tel. 05/043–290, www.hotelrelaisorologio.com, €260–380 s/d) is a favorite with honeymooners and travelers looking for an unforgettable night in a 13th-century Pisan palazzo. It's rustic with all the trimmings and has a dining room that makes antique dealers drool with delight. The hotel restaurant gives couples an added reason to hang the Do Not Disturb sign.

Food

Sometimes the best entertainment is watching a professional like Ettore Masi meet, seat, and serve customers on a busy weekday lunch hour. The routine is down pat at ▐ **Osteria dei Cavalieri** (Via San Frediano 16, tel. 05/058-0858, Mon.–Fri. 12:30–2:30 P.M. and 7:30–11 P.M., open Sat. dinner, €8–12), where classic Pisan dishes reach tables in record time. Ask about the fish of the day, or give *ossobuco con fagioli* a try. Porcini mushrooms start showing up on the menu in the fall and the tripe is available year-round for curious stomachs.

If you're wondering where Carlo Silvestrini does his food shopping, all you have to do is look outside his restaurant. The daily fruit and vegetable market held in the piazza is the source of most of the dishes at **Vineria**

di Piazza (Piazza delle Vettovaglie 13, Mon.–Sat. 12:30–2:30 P.M. and 7:30–10:30 P.M., €6–10). It's no wonder the menu varies month by month and everything tastes fresh. The cheese and cured meat plate is a good start to lunch or dinner and can be followed by a savory *pappa al pomodoro* or vegetable lasagna. Save room for the apple pie and dine under the arches in spring and summertime.

La Clessidra (Via Santa Cecilia 34, tel. 05/054-0160, Mon.–Fri. 1–3 P.M. and 7:30–11 P.M., open Sat. dinner, €9–14) is a simple restaurant with a talented chef who prepares Tuscan flavors with a dash of originality. The pleasant dining room is located in one of Pisa's well-heeled neighborhoods, which has been particularly well preserved.

In the heart of the city, **La Mescita** (Via Cavalca 2, tel. 05/054-4294, Tues.–Sun. 1–3 P.M. and 7:30–11:30 P.M., €10–12) offers a menu that combines tradition with innovation. The two dining rooms are warm and welcoming. Waiters have a sixth sense and the colonnades and piazze outside are just the thing for walking off lunch or dinner. Reservations help avoid disappointment.

Before you give up looking for **Artilafo** (Via Volturno 38, Mon.–Sat. 1:30–3 P.M. and 7:30–11:30 P.M., €8–12), remember that some of the best cheeses from around Italy are sliced here and the reputation for creative cuisine gets stronger with every bite.

Any restaurant with the word *"spaghetteria"* in the name deserves attention. The word general signals a place where spaghetti is the main ingredient and the menu contains dozens of sauce variations. That's exactly what you get at **Spaghetteria alle Bandierine** (Via Mercanti 4, tel. 05/050-0000). If you can't decide on one dish, ask for a sampling of several.

Antica Trattoria il Campano (Via Domenica Calvaca, tel. 05/058-0585, €10–12) is a safe haven from the hordes of tourists invading Piazza dei Miracoli. It's a great lunch spot that may not look like much on the outside but serves homemade dishes like *pici* (a type of long pasta) with radicchio and walnut sauce on the inside. There are a couple of outdoor tables for those who can handle the odors coming from the nearby fish market.

To understand Pisan flavors, have a slice of the local pizza cooked in baking tins upside down or a piece of *cecina,* a soft thick omelette made from chickpea flour and eaten with or without peppers and focaccia. There is no shortage of quality pizzerias and singling one out would take the pleasure away from sampling them all.

You may not buy anything at **Falciani** (Piazza delle Vettovaglie 28, tel. 05/054-07089, Tues.–Sun. 12:30 P.M.–3 P.M. and 7:30 P.M.–10:30 P.M.), but if you ever wondered how fresh pasta was made it's worth having a look. All kinds of stuffed *tortelli* and ricotta are prepared and displayed in this small shop that gives the term "fast food" a new meaning.

"Best cappuccino ever" is a claim often made after emptying a foamy cup at **Caffè della Panna** on Via dei Mille. **Caffè dell'Ussero** (Lungarno Pacinotti 27, tel. 05/058-1100, Sun.–Fri. 7 A.M.–9 P.M.) is a favorite with locals who take their espresso black and never tire of gazing at the Arno. The 14th-century redbrick building has been popular with artists and patriots since its founding in 1794. **Bar Settimelli** (Borgo Stretto 34) is a good place to pause and rub shoulders with coffee drinkers of all ages and nationalities. The fact Galileo was born in the palazzo upstairs is an added bonus. **Pasticceria Salza** (Via Borgo Stretto 44, tel. 05/058-0244, Mon.–Sat. 7 A.M.–1 P.M. and 3–6 P.M.) bakes a variety of sweet Piedmont specialties as well as several tasty salty snacks.

Any debate about the best gelato in Pisa generally ends in agreement. The crowd inside **La Bottega del Gelato** (Piazza Garibaldi 11, tel. 05/057-5467, Thurs.–Tues. noon–8:15 P.M.) is another confirmation, but it's only after you taste the coffee or hazelnut flavor that further argument becomes pointless. Fortunately the shop is open late and gelato enthusiasts can lick their cones leisurely.

Information and Services

There are several APT information points in Pisa, one of which is situated in the arrivals hall of the airport. Two others are conveniently located in Piazza Vittorio Emanuele II 16 (tel. 05/092-9777) and Piazza Arcivescovado 8 (tel. 05/056-0464).

If you need an Internet café, there's one in Via della Nunziatina near the Feltrinelli bookshop and two others in Piazza Gambacorti and Piazza la Pera.

Getting There and Around

Reaching Pisa became a lot easier when Delta began operating flights from New York. **Galileo Galilei Airport** (tel. 05/084-9111, www.pisa-airport.com) has been expanding ever since and serves many locations in Italy and Europe. The airport is less than two kilometers from the center, which can be reached by rail or LAM Rossa express bus (€1). Direct connections to Florence by land or rail are frequent.

It's possible to reach Pisa by bus. The city is well connected to Lucca and destinations along the coast. Train, however, is often more convenient. Two important lines run through **Stazione di Pisa Centrale** (tel. 05/892-021, www.trenitalia.com), linking it with Naples, Rome, Genova, and Turin. It can be a slow journey but what you lose in speed you gain in scenery. Pisa San Rossore is a smaller station near Piazza dei Miracoli that connects the city with Lucca and Pistoia.

By car from Rome or Bologna, take the A1 until Florence. Follow the *autostrada* Florence–Mare until the Pisa Nord exit and continue along the SS1 Aurelia south for six kilometers until you reach the city. The Autostrada A12/E80 is an alternative route from Rome.

Street parking inside the historic center is restricted and it's best to leave cars behind. There is no shortage of lots, including two Park and Rides north of the leaning tower where drivers can park for free and either walk or take the Navetta C shuttle bus into town.

Public bus transportation is operated by the CPT (Consorzio Pisano Trasporti, www.cpt.pisa.it) and gets you anywhere you want to go. Tickets can be purchased at any tobacconists, many bars, and newsagents. You can also buy one on board the bus. Once on the bus, validate your ticket by punching it in one of the yellow control boxes. A standard 60-minute tickets costs €0.85 while the daily option is €2.90. It's sometimes worth paying a little more to travel a little farther.

Pisa is immensely walkable but if you feel like pedaling around the flat streets as many of the natives do, rent your wheels from **Eco Voyager** (Via U. Della Faggiola 41, tel. 05/056-1839, www.ecovoyager.it). They have some four-wheeled options that can keep an entire family occupied and they offer guided tours. The city runs a *trenino,* a little train (tel. 05/053-3755), that's actually on wheels and snakes its way past historic monuments. It starts from Piazza Arcivescovado and is a treat for young children or anyone with sore feet. **Il Navicello** (tel. 05/053-0101, www.il-navicello.it, €5 and up) runs cruises along the Arno April–October. The Natura tour heads east all the way to Parco di San Rossore. The tourist office provides a free tour on the second Saturday of each month. To make reservations and get details of the itinerary, call 05/091-0350.

◼ LUCCA

Few Italian towns are as thoroughly well preserved as Lucca. Time ticks differently here and the winding alleys, campaniles, and piazzettas never looked so good. The street pattern is a remnant of Roman engineers who followed in the footsteps of the Ligurian and Etruscan founders. A striving silk trade and shrewd banking led to steady growth during the late Middle Ages and Renaissance. Friction with neighboring towns never extinguished Lucca's independence, of which locals are rightfully proud.

Sights

The **Lucca ramparts** are the symbol of the city and probably had something to do with preserving the beauty inside. They are actually the fourth set of walls and were transformed into a park during the 19th century. A walk around the four-kilometer tree-lined perimeter provides good views of the city and the surrounding countryside. The walls include 10 heart-shaped bulwarks built to resist attacks. The ramparts can be reached at any of the six gates or by way of numerous streets within the town.

Take a good look at **San Michele in Foro** (Piazza San Michele, daily 7:40–midnight and 3–6 P.M.). It may not be as large as the churches in Florence or Pisa, but size doesn't matter when the details are this good. Each column in the triple-tiered facade is different and the inlaid marble fits to perfection. Religious iconography is absent from the exterior, except for a winged figure of Saint Michele above the pediment. The inside is unusually bare, which makes it a good place to sit and think.

On the corner across the street is the house where the great opera conductor Puccini was born. **Casa di Puccini** (Via di Poggio), however, has closed following a legal battle between descendants of the musician and operators of the museum.

Several of the towers that once dotted Lucca's skyline are still standing and if legends are true the devil was once spotted on **Torre delle Ore** (Apr.–Oct., daily 10:30 A.M.–7:30 P.M., € 3.50) in Via Fillungo, the main thoroughfare of the city. Nearby **Torre Guingi** (Via Guingi, daily 9:30 A.M.–7:30 P.M., open until 10 P.M. Jul.–Aug., €5) was built in the 14th century and distinguishes itself with Holm oaks growing on the top. On clear days there are good views of the city and the Apuan Alps.

Piazza del Mercato has a strange shape to it. The reason lies underneath the ground and the Roman amphitheater that once stood here. In the Middle Ages, the stone was used to build houses and in 1830 the Bourbons cleared the central area to preserve the original elliptical form. Remains of the two rows of 54 arches can still be seen.

Museo Nazionale di Villa Guinigi (Via della Quarquonia, tel. 05/834–960, Tues.–Sat. 8:30 A.M.–7:30 P.M., Sun. 8:30 A.M.–1:30 P.M., €4) combines cultural artifacts and artwork. The archeological section on the ground floor contains many fragments from the past and examples of ancient funerary devices. The shield once worn by a medieval Lombard warrior is quite impressive, as are two paintings by Fra'Bartolomo.

Pinacoteca Nazionale di Palazzo Mansi (Via Gallitassi 43, tel. 05/8358-3461, Tues.–Sat. 8:30 A.M.–7 P.M., Sun. 8:30 A.M.–1 P.M., €4) was the home of a 16th-century nobleman and has since been transformed into a museum. The luxurious interior includes a hall of mirrors and Sala dell'Alcova with many intricate tapestries. The museum possesses a variety of artistic movements donated by Leopold II in 1847. Venetian, Lombard, Roman, and Flemish artists are all present. Tuscan paintings include work by Bronzino, Andrea del Sarto, and Pontormo's *Portrait of a Young Man*. A combined ticket to visit both museums costs €6.50.

Gardeners have a choice between the 18th-century formal gardens punctuated by Baroque statues at **Palazzo Pfanner** (Via degli Asili 33, tel. 05/8395-4029, daily 10 A.M.–6 P.M., €3) and the **Orto Botanico** (Botanical Gardens, tel. 05/834-8785, daily 10 A.M.–6 P.M., €3) that contains a variety of rare species. Both are quiet places to take a stroll under shaded paths and are at their loveliest in late spring.

Entertainment and Events

Sagra Musicale Lucchese is a series of concerts throughout May and June performed within the town's churches. Recent editions were dedicated entirely to the organ and newly restored instruments played. The repertoire varies between forgotten classics and new compositions very often sung by local choirs. Tickets generally do not exceed €10 and concerts begin at 9 P.M.

New festivals are inaugurated every year in Tuscany and one interesting addition to Lucca's cultural scene is **Look At** (La Manifattura Tabacchi, tel. 05/8318-05194, free). The weeklong event at the end of May is an opportunity for 10 local video artists to create sight specific installations. An old tobacco factory is just the sort of cavernous building that sets creativity buzzing and inspired a lot of experimentation during the first edition.

Luminara di Santa Croce, on September 13, honors the cross that was supposedly brought back from Palestine by a monk and now rests in the Duomo. The nighttime procession is illuminated by thousands of torches that add a surreal effect to proceedings.

Lucca Comics and Games Festival (Centro Storico, tel. 05/834-8522, www.lucca comicsandgames.com) is for anyone with fond memories of playing Dungeons and Dragons or those who prefer their literature to be illustrated. The 10-day event at the beginning of November is dedicated to fans of Spiderman and Diabolik and if you prefer to dress up as your favorite superhero you won't be alone. For serious comic strip junkies, **Museo Nazionale del Fumetto e dell'Immagine** (Piazza San Romano 4, tel. 05/835-6326, daily 10 A.M.–7 P.M., €4) is a must. The newly founded museum demonstrates the techniques used by Italy's premier illustrators and hands-on exhibits will thrill Disneyphiles whether they speak the language or not.

Shopping

Lucca's shopping district is concentrated along **Via Fullungo**. For original gifts and a pleasant atmosphere, visit one of the town's many markets. Mercato di Corte del Biancone in Piazza San Giusto sells used books, prints, stamps, and general nostalgia weekday mornings and Saturdays. For anything related to food, stop by Mercato del Carmine in the piazza of the same name. Mercato dell'Antiquariato is the second-largest antiques and ethnic market in all of Italy and fills several piazze with furniture and collectibles of every style, period, and type. The popular event is held on the third weekend of every month. On the last weekend of the month Mercato di Arti e Mestieri presents handmade Tuscan arts and crafts in Piazza San Giusto.

Sports and Recreation

Two parks on the immediate outskirts of Lucca enhance the natural beauty that surrounds town.

Parco del Nottolini starts 50 meters from the train station and extends three kilometers towards the Pisani Mountains. You can walk or bike along the 12-meter-high aqueduct, completed in 1851 by local architect Lorenzo Nottolini. The 400 arches carry water from a source at San Quirico di Guamo and if you make it all the way to this small *borgo,* fill up a bottle of water at the fountain.

Northwest of town along the Serchio river is the **Parco Fluviale.** There are several itineraries to choose from, including one by horse that follows forested paths that periodically reveal great views of Lucca and the valleys beyond. The cost for a two-hour trot is €32 and includes explanations of the surroundings. Contact Susanna or Marcella at **Club Ippico Lucchese** (Via della Scogliera 877, tel. 05/8346-7054 or 349/074-5600) to reserve a saddle.

Accommodations

⟨ **Ostello San Frediano** (Via della Cavallerizza 12, tel. 05/8346-9957, www.ostellolucca. it, €19–48 pp/d) challenges many of the stereotypes surrounding hostels. First, it's not just a large dormitory for backpackers and second it's not located outside the center of town. Instead there are rooms of many different sizes, and the location between Piazza San Frediano and Piazza Antifiteatro is enviable. What remains true, however, is affordability. At €9.50, the lunch and dinner served in the large dining room is one of the best deals in Lucca.

Hotel Stipino (Via Romana 95, tel. 05/8349-5077, www.hotelstipino.com, €50–70 s/d) should get an award for most original wallpaper. Even if some of it clashes, this two-star is endearing. More importantly it's an affordable base 400 meters outside the town walls.

It doesn't get much more central than **Piccolo Hotel Puccini** (Via di Poggio 9, tel. 05/835-5421, www.hotelpuccini.com, €60–90 s/d). All of the town's monuments are around one corner or the other of this comfortable hotel. Breakfast is an extra €3.50 that will seem wisely spent.

If you ask for a view at **Hotel Universo** (Piazza del Giglio 1, tel. 05/8349-3678, www.universolucca.com, €120–190 s/d), you'll be asked if you prefer the Duomo, Piazza Napoleone, or Piazza del Giglio. Whatever room you choose,

it's bound to be refined. The standard of service is high and the newly refurbished restaurant offers haute cuisine in a quiet setting.

The entrance is the first clue that **Palazzo Tucci** (Via C. Battisti 13, tel. 05/8349-6078, www.palazzotucci.com, €300 d) is not an average bed-and-breakfast. This historic residence provides an idea of how 19th-century nobles once lived. The high frescoed ceilings and spacious apartments decorated in period furnishings are authentic down to the bedposts. Satellite TV, wireless Internet, and air–conditioning are the only concessions. A stay here does wonders for the ego.

Food

Lunchtime service at **Buatino** (Borgo Giannotti 508, tel. 05/8334-3207, Mon.–Sat. noon–3 P.M. and 7:30–11 P.M., €8–12) can be hectic as everyone's eager to get their forks into the specials. Dinner is more relaxed and the atmosphere often includes live music. The *tagliatelle al piccione* (tagliatelle with pigeon) make a good first course and seconds include *bollito misto in salsa verde* (mixed meat stew with green sauce). The wine menu includes 150 bottles from Tuscany and other regions.

What started out as an inn where weary travelers could rest their horses and feed themselves hasn't changed much. Although the horses are gone, the farro soup at **La Buca di Sant'Antonio** (Via della Cervia 3, tel. 05/835-5881, Tues.–Sat. 12:30–3 P.M. and 7–11:30 P.M., €12–15) is pretty much the same. Puccini and Pound once dined here, so reservations may be a good idea.

Agli Orti di Via Elisa (Via Elisa 17, tel. 05/8349-1241, Thurs.–Tues. 1–3 P.M. and 7–11 P.M., €7–11) is a new restaurant operated with gusto by an energetic young team of entrepreneurs. The two large dining rooms offer traditional gastronomy and wood-oven-baked pizzas during the evening.

For gelato, try **Gelateria Santini** (Piazza Cittadella 1, tel. 05/835-5295, summer daily 9 A.M.–midnight, winter Tues.–Sun. 9 A.M.–9 P.M.). Besides a dozen homemade flavors they also serve *zuccotti* and *semifreddi* desserts.

Information and Services

Lucca goes a long way to welcome visitors and there are three main APT offices as well as several smaller information kiosks around the city. **Centro di Accoglienza Turistica** (Piazzale Verdi, tel. 05/8358-3150, www.luccaturismo.it, daily 9 A.M.–7 P.M.) provides the most complete services. You can deposit bags, find a hotel, rent a bike or audio guide, and purchase tickets to museums. Detailed maps and updated event listings are also available. The offices in Piazza Curtatone (tel. 05/8349-5730, daily 10 A.M.–6 P.M.) near the train station and Porta Elisa (tel. 05/8346-2377, daily 9 A.M.–5 P.M.) provide slightly slimmed-down service.

Currency can be converted at **Punto Money** (Via S.Paolino 105, tel. 05/8358-2823) or at the **APT regional office** (Piazza S. Maria 35, tel. 05/8391-9931)

The local hospital, **Ospedale Campo di Marte** (Via dell'Ospedale, tel. 05/839–701 or 800/869–143), is just outside the walls near Porta San Jacopi. Consultations can be made over the phone, and pharmacists are useful for resolving minor mishaps. If you can't find the right words, just mime the injury or ailment. **Farmacia Comunale** (Piazza Curtatone, tel. 05/8349-1398) is open 24 hours and located in front of the train station. Most *tabacchi* carry stamps, but a stop at the post office can also be an interesting cultural experience. The main office is on Via Vallisneri 2 and there are smaller branches near Piazza Carmine and outside the walls near Piazza del Risorgimento.

Getting There and Around

The nearest airport to Lucca is Galileo Galilei in Pisa. There are trains directly from the airport and Stazione Centrale. Arriving by rail from Florence is also convenient. Lucca is off the A11 highway that connects the A1 near Florence with the A12 near Pisa. Lazzi bus service is available from the train stations of Pisa and Florence.

Railway tickets may be purchased at **Stazione Ferroviaria di Lucca** (tel. 05/834-7013) in Piazza Ricasoli. There's a taxi stand directly outside the station as well as in Piazza Santa Maria, Piazzale Verdi, and Piazza Napoleone. To order a cab, call **Radio Taxi** (tel. 05/8333-3434) or **Taxi Lucca** (tel. 05/8395-5200). Drivers can choose from 10 lots within the walls or park outside in Vialle Europa. Cycling is a great way to explore the city, circle the ramparts, and move out into the countryside. Bikes can be rented at the tourist office in Piazzale Verdi, Cicli Bizzarri (Piazza S. Maria 32, tel. 05/8349-6031), or Crono (Corso Garibaldi, 93, tel. 05/8349-0591), and guided tours of the city can be arranged.

Turisti in Casa is dedicated to anyone discovering Lucca for the first time. These guided walks organized by the tourist board reveal lesser-known aspects of the town. Tours begin at 10 A.M. on Saturdays in Piazza S. Donate. Reservations (tel. 05/8344-2944, accoglienza@consorzioitinera.com) should be made one week in advance. The cost of a memorable two-hour visit is €3.50.

VIAREGGIO

Viareggio was a small fishing village wedged between the pine forests along the Versilia coast until Giuseppe Barellai founded a hotel there in 1861. It didn't take long for word to spread about the beautiful stretch of sand and the resort quickly became a favorite destination for Victorian jet-setters.

Sights

Most of the sights are concentrated along the seafront promenade. There is a succession of Art Nouveau hotels, villas, and cafés built in the 1920s after a fire destroyed the original boardwalk. Puccini was a regular visitor and wrote the majority of his operas nearby in Torre del Lago. **Gran Café** (Viale Margherita 30, tel. 05/8496-2553, daily 7 A.M.–11 P.M.) is the epitome of the retro style and a memorable place to stop for an iced cappuccino. On the other side of Viale Regina Margherita are beach establishments where deck chairs and umbrellas can be rented by the hour.

Entertainment and Events
◖ **VIAREGGIO CARNEVALE**
February 12–March 12, the smell of papier-mâché and glue fills Viareggio in anticipation

of the Viareggio Carnevale. Dozens of floats parade up and down the boardwalk as exuberant onlookers partake in one of the oldest carnivals of Italy (www.viareggio.ilcarnevale.com). Themes generally deal with current events and giant figures of politicians are common. On each Sunday, the first (over 40 tons) and second (over 30 tons) category floats take over the streets. Fat Tuesday is the longest day. Locals sleep in their costumes and meet in Piazza Mazzini to hear the world's largest band, made up of over 1,000 musicians. Not all of them are in tune. Being caught up in the crowd is an exhilarating experience that doesn't end until early the next day.

FESTIVAL PUCCINIANO
Every year Festival Pucciniano (www.puc cinifestival.it) presents four of the composer's operas sung by the world's greatest lyricists. Performances are held nightly mid-June–mid-August in an outdoor theater overlooking a lake where the composer once lived. Tickets start at €31 and may be purchased directly from the box office.

Getting There and Around
By car from Florence follow the A11 until Lucca and the Viareggio extension towards the sea. The train station is on the Turin–Genova–Rome line with local trains arriving hourly from Torre del Lago and Florence. Cycling the length of the boardwalk can be accomplished after a visit to Due Ruote e Dintorni (Via Cavallotti 205, tel. 05/8496-2385), which rents mountain bikes, racing bikes, and cycles for young riders.

ELBA
Elba is the kind of island first-graders draw. It has no recognizable shape and straight lines are rare. Instead, the 147 kilometers of coastline are a continuous series of bays, coves, and beaches. Italy's third-largest island forms part of the Tuscan Archipelago and the largest marine park in Europe. But if 17,000 meters of secluded sands don't get you excited, there is plenty of distinct fauna to admire across the mountainous scrub landscapes of the interior and the unmistakable traces of history within Elba's port towns. The island's strategic location and wealth of minerals have made it particularly prized by one empire after another, not to mention 17th-century pirates and one famous exile.

Sights
Porto Ferraio is the capital and main port of Elba. It is set on a promontory overlooking a wide bay that attracted early Ligurian, Etruscan, and Greek settlers. Cosimo Medici is responsible for the town's present look and even rebaptized the town Cosmopoli. The name didn't stick, but the system of fortifications he started in 1548 to protect the area from intruders did. Today both the imposing **Stella** (overlooking Portoferraio near the lighthouse, Tues.–Sun. 10 A.M.–6 P.M., €2) and **Falcone** (Via Guerrazzi, Tues.–Sun. 10 A.M.–6 P.M., €2) fortresses can be visited and provide excellent views of the bay.

An annual pension of two million francs and a beautiful island would satisfy most people. Napoleon, however, wasn't the average deposed emperor looking for rest and relaxation. Even the title of Regent of Elba could not curb his ambitions, and one February evening in 1815, 10 months after his exile had began, he sailed away. The traces of his time on the island are visible everywhere from the bars and piazze that bear his name to the museums that recall his stay.

Museo Napoleonico di Villa dei Mulini (Piazza Napoleone III, tel. 05/6591-5846, Tues.–Sun. 9 A.M.–7 P.M., €5 or €9 combined ticket with Villa San Martino) was the official residence and headquarters of Napoleon's entourage. Little has changed since his departure and the building's character remains intact. Of particular interest are the study where Napoleon may have planned his escape, portraits of the emperor, and the gardens where he took his daily excercise.

Even if Napoleon only spent one summer on the island he still required a summer residence and he chose **Villa San Martino** (tel.

05/6591-4688, daily 9 A.M.–7 P.M., €5), two kilometers outside of town. Each year the museum presents an exhibition dedicated to one facet of Napoleaon's military career or legacy. The villa gardens are a delightful break from the beach and bus service from town is available on the number 1 line.

Marina di Campo is on the south coast of the island within easy reach of many picturesque beaches. The town has been synonymous with fishing for centuries and remains true to its roots. The oldest part of town is around the Pisan tower, where many fishermen still live and their characteristic houses can be admired.

There is no lack of nightlife during the summer when enthusiastic visitors supply the gyrating bodies in local clubs and discos. Natural pursuits can be had outside of town. The sandy coves of **Ogliera, Giardino,** and **le Tombe** are within walking distance of the center and reached by a small path near the port. Facilities are slim to nonexistent and sun-worshippers should pack everything they need before setting off. **Fetovaia** is a perfect peninsula nine kilometers east along the coast road. It's famous for its fine white sand and clear water but should be avoided in high season, when the bikini count reaches triple digits. For something more intimate, explore the coast near Cavoli where the sea has carved out natural swimming pools in the rock at **Piscine del Seccheto** and **Seccheto. Palombaia** is another tranquil beach. The sand here is darker and the seabed drops off within several meters of shore. **Fonza** is good for anyone who prefers silence. Follow the signs for the aquarium and campground where drivers can park. From the lot, follow the rugged path down to the tiny inlet.

For a view of nearly the entire island and Corsica in the distance, drive to Marciana. The cable car ride up the 1,018 meters of Monte Capanne reveals fabulous scenery in every direction.

Festivals and Events

May is Napoleonic month in Portoferraio and the town organizes a variety of events to celebrate the sovereign's brief visit. There are guided tours of the emporer's old haunts, conferences for Bonaparte scholars, and concerts for everyone else.

The hairpin roads of Elba turn even the most cautious drivers into rally pilots. If you want to see how professionals handle the curves in vintage automobiles, just grab a seat on the side of the road in late September when **Rallye Elba Storico** (www.rallyelbastorico.it) sets out from Marina di Campo and covers just about the entire island over the three-day event.

Sports and Recreation

Elba isn't just a place to lie on the beach. There are dozens of activities for anyone who wants to work up a sweat, and **Genio del Bosco** (Via R. Manganaro 7d, tel. 05/6593-0837, info@geniodelbosco.it) in Porto Ferraio can keep you active for an entire month. Every Tuesday and Friday in summer, its guides set off on a three-hour trek of the coast. Groups usually number around 15 and the cost of an excursion is €20. If that sounds tame and mountain biking seems dull then opt for a sea kayak (www.seakayakitaly.com) and discover the rocky inlets around Capo Bianco. Equestrian tours and diving expeditions are also organized on a weekly basis.

Terme San Giovanni (tel. 05/6591-4680, www.termelbane.com, Apr.–Oct.) doesn't just use any mud in their baths. Here you get covered in a special marine mud renowned for alleviating rheumatism and arthritis pains. There are a dozen thermal treatments, all priced under €30. The spa is located 500 kilometers outside of Portoferraio on the road leading towards Porto Azzurro.

Accommodations

Tourism is Elba's greatest asset, but the influx of summer visitors has an impact on the environment. Local authorities are determined to preserve the island's resources, and **Ecoalberghi** (www.elbaecohotels.it) is one of the initiatives that lets tourists enjoy themselves without damaging the landscape. All of the 26 "biohotels" that belong to the group support sustainable tourism in different ways.

Some use solar panels and low-consumption bulbs, while others are built on the principles of bio-architecture. The hotels vary in size and they are located around the entire island; service is good.

It doesn't get more ecological than camping, and the island has plenty of sites for anyone looking for a place to pitch a tent. Many of the campgrounds are located on or near the sea and most also have bungalows for rent. **Camping Arrighi** (Località Barbarossa, tel. 05/659-5568, www.campingarrighi.it, €10 for a two-person tent) is near Porto Azzurro on a small bay that is especially popular with Danes reacquainting themselves with the sun. There's a restaurant and apartments are also available within walking distance of the beach.

Food
A pink exterior and blue neon sign should usually be avoided when searching for a restaurant. **Stella Marina** (Portoferraio, Via Vittorio Emanuele II, tel. 05/6591-5983, Tues.–Sun. 12:30–3 P.M. and 7–11 P.M., €10–14), however, is the exception to that rule. This institution near the ferry terminal serves good surf-and-turf platters. Sit outside on the terrace if there's room and treat yourself to lobster cooked the Catalan way.

On the road out of Portoferraio towards Bagnaia across the bay, the Olivari family have transformed an old farmhouse into **La Carretta** (Località Magazzini 92, tel. 05/6593-3223, Thurs.–Tues. 7–11 P.M.). The area has deep farming roots and their restaurant serves typical Elban dishes like *spaghetti allo scorfano* (pasta with fish) and *gnocchetti alla gallinella* (mini pasta balls with fish) that can only be found on the island. Good pizza and homemade desserts are also available.

Back when Rio Marina was a mining town, **Da Oreste alle Strega** (Rio Marina, Piazza Vittorio Emanuele 6, tel. 05/6596-2211, Tues.–Sun. 12:30–3 P.M. and 7–10:30 P.M., €8) was where miners ate. The cooking has evolved since then thanks to Claudio, who has perfected his trade in some of Italy's finest restaurants. The old fisherman's dish of *tonnina alla riese* makes a nice antipasto and the *linguine alla bottarga e vongole* (linguine with fish eggs and clams) is the solution for anyone who likes their pasta with a seafood flavor. Bread is made in-house and the two dining rooms are well furnished.

Pasticceria (Via Palestro 11) is the place to try local specialties *schiaccia briaca* (sweet bread with raisins) and *pan del marinaio* (sweet bread with raisins, pine nuts, and candied fruit). Both take longer to pronounce than to eat. Rosemary- and chestnut-flavored honey can be purchased at Apicoltura Ballino Cavo in the nearby town of Montegrosso.

La Botte Gaia (Porto Azzurro, Viale Europa 5–7, tel. 05/659-5607, Tues.–Sun. 12:30–2:30 P.M. and 7–11 P.M., daily in summer, €8–12) is a few meters from the main square in the pedestrian-only zone of Porto Azzurro. The restaurant is housed in a former church that was transformed into a wine warehouse. Local ingredients and the fish of the day are the basis of a menu that includes memorable seafood *ragù* and anchovy pasta. Snacks and glasses of wine are served at the bar and in the garden during the summer.

After climbing Monte Capenne, **Osteria del Noce** (Marciana Alta, Via della Madonna 18, tel. 05/6590-1284, Tues.–Sun. 1–3 P.M. and 7–10:30 P.M., €9–14) is a welcome sight. This little restaurant near the Pisan fortress is almost entirely dedicated to fish, and the tables on the flowered terrace will satisfy both mind and stomach. The fried, grilled, and baked fish dishes are all appetizing.

Information and Services
The **APT office** (Portoferraio, Calata Italia 26, tel. 05/6591-4671, www.aptelba.it, Mon.–Sun. 9 A.M.–7 P.M.) located near the port provides maps of the island and can help find accommodation in a hurry.

Getting There and Around
Toremar (Nuova Stazione Marittima, tel. 05/653-1100, www.traghetti-toremar.com, €10.90) and **Moby** (Piazzale Premuda, tel. 199/303–040, www.moby.it, €14) both run

ferry service between Piombino and Portoferraio on Elba. The ferry terminal can be reached by train or car. In the summer, boats leave every half-hour and make the journey in 50 minutes. Passengers should arrive a half-hour prior to departure. Toremar also operates an express hydrofoil service to Rio Marina and Porto Azzurro. Cars can be taken to the island, but a reservation is required. The earlier you book the less you pay. Two adults with a medium-sized car in August costs €150.

If you arrive without a car, an enjoyable way to see the island is by moped or motorcycle. There are rental companies in each of the ports and Portoferraio has half a dozen agencies. **TWN** (tel. 05/6591-4666) is located 50 meters from the ferry terminal in the small *piazzale*. They also rent bicycles, kayaks, and cars. Renting a 125cc moped for two days costs €80 and requires a deposit. There are three other offices on the island including one in Marina di Campo. Public transportation does exist and ATL runs three interurban routes that connect Portoferraio with Marina di Campo (116), Porto Azzuro and Rio Marina (117), and Bagnaia (118). Single, daily, and weekly ticket options are available.

Around Elba

Parco Nazionale Arcipelago Toscano includes six other islands with interesting geologic origins. **Capraia** is volcanic and surrounded by a crystalline sea. It's much smaller than Elba and has a more remote feel, which explains why a penal colony was once located here. The island is not a bad place to pass the time and human presence dates from antiquity. Wildlife goes much farther back and shearwaters, black-headed gulls, and monk seals use the island as a stopover when migrating between north and south. Tourism is limited and the island attracts visitors who want to reacquaint themselves with nature and enjoy starry nights staring at infinity.

Toremar (www.toremar.it) operates a ferry from Porto Mediceo in Livorno. Frequency depends on the season and daily service is only offered in summer. The journey takes 2.5 hours;

if you're lucky you'll be greeted by dolphins. Although you may bring your car, there's only one small road on the island that connects the port or lower town with the *paese* or upper town. Two wheels are preferable to four and Agenzia Viaggi e Turismo Parco (Capraia, Via Assunzione 42, tel. 05/8690-5071) rents all types of land and sea vehicles. They can also help with accommodations across the island and provide guided tours.

◀ PARCO NATURALE DELLA MAREMMA

Maremma is the area of low coastal plains that stretches from Piombino to northern Lazio. There is a high concentration of charming villages with Etruscan and Roman origins, each with its own culinary tradition and distinct Mediterranean aroma. The regional park founded in 1975 preserves one of Italy's last pristine stretches of coastline. It is home to wild boar, birds of prey, and flamingos that enjoy 10,000 hectares of marshland, dunes, and pine forests. Visitors can choose from a dozen clearly marked paths that crisscross the park.

Sights

Nature is the primary attraction and wet and dry habitats provide a refuge to hundreds of species. The park was recently named one of the top 10 bird-watching spots in Italy and excursions are frequently organized. Groups leave twice a day from the visitors centers and are limited to a maximum of 12 people. To reserve a place, call 05/6440-7098.

The manmade relics of the park include the old Spanish towers, which once guarded the coast from pirates, and **San Rabano** in the center of the park. This decaying Cistercian abbey built in the 12th century lies on a hill overlooking the sea where seven paths converge.

One of the most interesting itineraries is along the Ombrone estuary. This path, which starts at **Marina di Alberese**, is five kilometers long and takes around two hours to complete. It is an entirely flat route along the sea and salt marshes accessible to all.

© PURESTOCK

Agriturismo Il Giardino di Sofia is surrounded by olive groves.

Accommodations

Il Giardino di Sofia (Strada Comunale di Cupi 1, tel. 05/6440-7024, www.ilgiardino-disofia.com, €75 d) is five kilometers from Alberese. The *agriturismo* is almost a park in itself surrounded by sunflowers, olive groves, and vines. There are even some longhorn Maremma cows grazing the fields nearby. The Pucci and Maggi families give their guests a warm welcome and the rustic rooms provide a pleasant place to rest after a day on the trails.

Agriturismo Podere Isonzo (Via Aurelia Antica 91, tel. 338/456-2086, www.podere-isonzo.it, €80 d) is also conveniently located near the park entrance on 45 hectares of land. All types of sports can be played on the lawns around the 18th-century farmhouse, and mountain bikes and tandems are available for free. Rooms are the wood-beamed variety and a chorus of birds is the first thing guests hear in the morning. Horseback and canoeing tours of the Ombrone River are available a short way from the *agriturismo*.

Food

Maremma has traditionally produced average table wines, but since the 1980s effort has been made by growers to favor quality over quantity. The result is labels like Morellino di Scansano, produced near the park from Sangiovese grapes. **Poggio Argentiera** (Banditella di Alberese, tel. 05/6440-5099, www.poggioargentiera.com) is a picturesque estate run by a young couple who enjoy sharing their passion with visitors.

Nadia Svetoni introduces virgin palates to Maremma cooking. Her restaurant, **Il Canto del Gallo** (Grosseto, tel. 05/6441-4589, Mon.–Sat. 12:30–3 P.M. and 7:30–10:30 P.M., €8–11), in the historic center of Grosseto serves *tortelli maremmani* and wild boar prepared in the traditional spicy fashion. All the wines are locally produced and genetic modification is unthinkable.

Information and Services

Ente Parco Regionale della Maremma (Alberese, Via Bersagliere 7–9, tel. 05/6440-7098, www.parco-maremma.it, daily

7:30 A.M.–6 P.M., €3–9) is the main visitor's center. Entry fee depends on which of the eight itineraries you choose. A second center is located in Talamone (Via Nizza 2, tel. 05/6488-7400) and includes a small aquarium. There are three itineraries from this location.

Getting There and Around

By car from either north or south, take the SS1 Via Aurelia road until the Alberese exit and follow the brown signs towards Parco Naturale della Maremma. There are parking lots in Alberese, Marina di Alberese, and Talamone. Anyone arriving by train should get off in Grosseto and take the Rama bus from outside the station to Alberese.

Walking is the preferred means of transportation in the park, but there are several bike rental companies in Alberese and the ride to the beach is quite scenic.

Around Maremma

Saturnia is all about the water. There may be other monuments in this old Etruscan town, but what keeps most people coming back are the springs. They've been enjoyed since antiquity and are legendary for their healing qualities. A dip in one of the pools leaves weary travelers revitalized.

There are several springs in and around town. These natural hot springs are open night and day and are very crowded in the summer. They're at the end of a dirt road two kilometers from town near an old mill. There's a bar in the parking lot. Most bathers opt to soak in one of the naturally formed pools that remains a constant 37.5°C. **Cascata del Mulino** is free, but during the summer it may be hard to find a seat. If you're searching for intimacy, follow the small stream above the twin cascades toward the volcanic source. A late night swim isn't a bad alternative if you value elbow room. Otherwise, visit one of the centers built in the 19th century when the town rediscovered itself. A full day at **Terme di Saturnia** (tel. 05/6460-0111, www.termedisaturnia.it, 9:30 A.M.–7:30 P.M.) costs €22. The variety of treatments at this spa, which doubles as a luxury hotel, is endless and you may be too relaxed to leave.

Hotel Saturnia (Via Mazzini 4, tel. 05/6460-1007, www.hotel-saturnia.it, €55–85 s/d) is two kilometers from the springs, and there are many natural and archeological pursuits nearby if your skin is starting to wrinkle. Rooms are simple and the shaded garden is a nice place to rest before dinner. Breakfast buffet is included.

LIGURIA

Liguria owes its character to its location. Rough Apennine Mountains in the north and the Ligurian Sea to the south border this thin boomerang-shaped region. It is commonly known as the Italian Riviera, a place where former aristocrats came to enjoy the warm sunny climate and where the maritime trade played a decisive role in the region's history.

Given the lack of space, most of the towns are of the small fishing village variety, where the pace of life is decidedly leisurely and beaches plentiful. Cinque Terre offers a good taste of these and walking along the coastal paths provides an endless series of spectacular views interrupted only by pastel-color houses and family-run restaurants that haven't changed their menus in years.

The only city is Genova, which lies in the center of the region and is famous for a certain sailor who mistakenly discovered America. But there's more to Genova, as any visitor who embarks on a walk through the old town or spends an afternoon in the revitalized port soon discovers. Palazzi along Via Balbi and Via Garibaldi are filled with some of the finest collections of paintings and sculptures in northern Italy. The old port is less rough than it once was and the aquarium and other attractions now bring great numbers of visitors to the area.

The two stretches of coast from Genova each have their own unique personality. The western half, known as Riviera di Ponente, extends all the way to the French border and consists of a nearly unbroken beachfront holidaymakers flock to in the summer. On the

HIGHLIGHTS

◖ Porto Antico: This complex of museums, libraries, and exhibition spaces features the largest aquarium in Europe and is one of Genova's most visited areas (page 184).

◖ Portofino: Maupassant didn't exaggerate when he said, "I have never felt as I did when I entered Portofino." This miniature town nestled in a small bay where pine trees grow in the main square is like being on a film set. Everything is in vibrant Technicolor and even the sheets hanging out to dry seem glamorous (page 202).

◖ Cinque Terre: The five isolated, pastel-colored villages built on rocky cliffs north of Portovenere are positioned on one of the most stunning coastlines in the Riviera. The scenic coastal views are best experienced along the Via dell'Amore (Lover's Path), a spectacular stretch between the towns of Manarola and Riomaggiore (page 204).

◖ Grotte di Toirano: Grotte di Toirano (Toirano Caves) is the quickest way to go back in time 100,000 years. Guided tours reveal the prehistoric footprints of cave dwellers and the animal bones they left behind. A second cave in the underground complex is nature's version of a cathedral built from stalactites and stalagmites that have formed over the ages (page 213).

◖ Dolceacqua: Centuries pass, governments change, but places like Dolceacqua remain the same. Its medieval bridge, 12th-century castle, and DOC wine are the ingredients that make up a fairytale setting (page 217).

LOOK FOR ◖ TO FIND RECOMMENDED SIGHTS, ACTIVITIES, DINING, AND LODGING.

and many types of ravioli stuffed with local herbs and spices grown on the hillsides. Fish is plentiful and there are endless variations in how it's prepared; in Portovenere, they prefer to grill, while in San Marino, the fish salad is served cold and washed down with Ligurian Vermentino.

PLANNING YOUR TIME

Liguria's size and shape make it one of the easiest regions to visit. Most towns are located along the long coast and are accessible by car, train, or bus. The SS1 Aurelia road that runs along the shore is the scenic route but is often clogged in the summer, while the A10 and A12 highways are for travelers with less time on their hands. Rail lines skirt the sea and local trains can be a fun way of getting an eyeful.

Genova lies in the middle of the region, and Porto Antico and the medieval streets that Richard Wagner raved about deserve a day or two of exploration. If nothing is pressing, the capital makes a good base from which to go whale watching or discover the hill forts immediately inland. The city is not overrun with visitors and makes a good break for anyone tired of avoiding tour groups in Florence or Rome.

As in any big city you'll need to stay alert when getting on and off the metro and buses, and if you do decide to buy from the numerous street vendors, avoid pulling out large amounts of cash from your wallet or purse. The alleys in the center are too narrow for police cars and bad lighting is an asset to petty criminals. Avoid walking around alone after dark and don't be surprised to see prostitutes waiting for their next customer along Via Maddalena.

The 175 kilometers from Genova to the French border is known as the Riviera di Ponente. Nearly every town from Arenzano to Sanremo has long wide beaches that have been enjoyed since the Victorian era. During the summer, these are covered with Italian families who traditionally take their summer holidays in July and August. Restaurants are filled, bars are packed, and there's a festive feeling in the air as children build sandcastles and everyone else works on their tans.

© LAURIE ELIE

the rocky shores of the Riviera di Levante

other side is the Riviera di Levante, which offers a rocky coastline and where fishing villages like Portofino have become a breeding place for millionaires.

Location is also responsible for the consistently mild climate; winters here are warmer than other regions in the north. Early autumn is the best time to visit, as the sea is still warm enough for a swim and the delicacies produced from the terraced hillsides and gathered in the forests are at their peak. Winter temperatures hover around 7–10°C while summers are not as scorching as they can be farther south, averaging 25–28°C.

There are 17 protected areas in the region, including Parco Naturale di Portofino, where cars are the endangered species and must give way to pedestrians. Here regattas are organized nearly every weekend in the summer and water sports thrive. If you prefer your exercise on land, there's no shortage of trails that can be taken on foot, bike, or horseback.

Any appetite that builds up will be easily satisfied, thanks to local specialties like pesto

LIGURIA

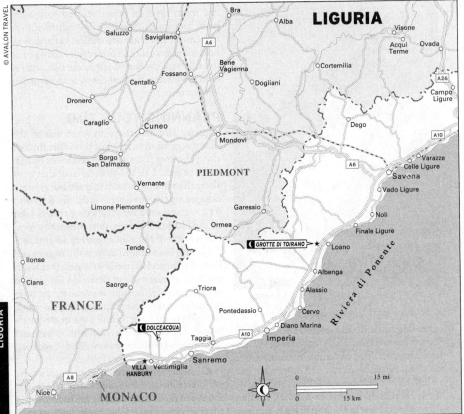

If sand isn't your thing, the old town centers of Albenga and Noli have something for visitors who prefer to stay dry and it's easy to escape summer chaos with a drive inland along panoramic roads to prehistoric caves or earthquake prone villages renovated by artists. A day is all it takes to explore the mountainous interior around Dolceacqua or Grotte di Toirano and gain another perspective on the region.

Riviera di Levante weaves its way from Genova to the Tuscan border and is opposite in character. The coast is wild and rocky and there are few places to lie on a beach. Towns are smaller and some, such as the five known as the Cinque Terre, are best visited on foot by way of the coastal trail that connects them. A leisurely trek requires three days, otherwise Portofino or Portovenere can give you a general idea of what a Ligurian fishing village resembles.

HISTORY

Humans have called Liguria home for a long time and even traces of Neanderthal and Cro-Magnon living have been discovered in the caves of Balzi Rossi. It was the Liguri, however, who first seriously populated the area and those that sided with the Romans during the Punic wars became part of the 10th region known as Liguria that extended all the way to the Po River. Around this time, the Aurelia and Augusta roads were built, which helped

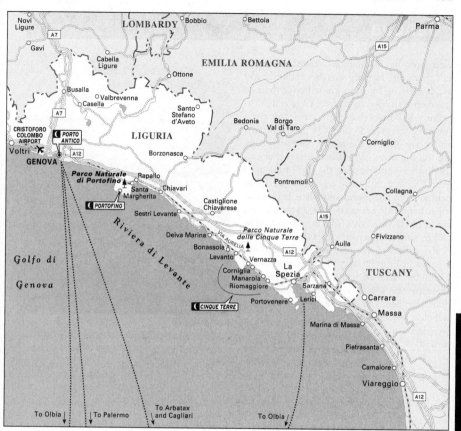

increase commerce and reinforced the unity of the territory. Along the coast, the towns of Albenga, Ventimiglia, and Luni developed into major centers of trade later dominated by the Byzantines, Longobardi, and Franks who filled the vacuum left after the decline of Rome.

Genova began to dominate the area in the 10th century and, once the threat of Saracen pirates was eliminated, the town grew in importance largely due to spice trade with the Middle East. The city's navy played a major role in the first crusade and between the 12th and 14th centuries, Genova was the most powerful marine republic. Commercial and military success gave way to years of internal struggle when Milanese, French, and Spanish rulers alternated control of the city. Andrea Doria's alliance with the Spanish king ushered in a period of relative tranquility but the French Revolution was felt even in Liguria and Napoleon annexed the region in 1805. Foreign interventions helped foster a nationalist movement spread by such patriots as Mazzini and Garibaldi, who departed from Ligurian shores with his band of 1,000 to liberate Sicily. Economic growth followed unification and Genova was part of the trio, along with Torino and Milan, that spread the industrial revolution to Italy and after World War II helped the country make a miraculous economic recovery.

Genova

Geography has no doubt influenced the Genova's character. The city stretches endlessly and locals arriving by train know better than to stand up at the first sight of the 19th- and 20th-century buildings that characterize this steep town constrained on one side by mountains and on the other by the sea. It's not easy getting around the maze of medieval streets that easily disorients travelers but the three funiculars help. This is a city where leaving breadcrumbs behind would be useful and where backtracking is frequently necessary. The sea should be a landmark, but even that fades in and out of view and is more often sensed rather than seen.

Regardless of its great seafaring tradition, Genova tends to be wary of the outside world. Columbus, after all, had to go to Spain to find someone who would back his venture. Trends don't start here and many shops look like they were last decorated in 1950. Even the products on sale are from a different era, inconceivable nowadays, like the man specializing in cork stoppers or the family selling every type of vegetable and fish *sott'olio* (under oil) imaginable.

Porto Antico

Still Genova isn't exactly sitting still, even if there are more 70-year-olds here than anywhere else in Italy. The 500th anniversary of Columbus' discovery in 1992 helped the city rediscover its links with the sea. Porto Antico was redeveloped and attractions like the aquarium have become new symbols of a city full of surprises. The rough side may have disappeared a little but there's still an edginess to Genova that you don't find in most Italian cities.

People work hard in Genova and locals know the value of a euro. They spend their money wisely and offer some of the best bargains in Italy, which has many benefits for travelers. For one thing, meals are quite affordable. This is the hometown of pesto and an infinite variety of fish that most people can't name. The former should be sampled with lasagna or pasta shapes that have never been exported beyond the old port.

If you have the time, ride the bus out to Boccadasse and watch the fishermen in the small

port returning from their morning labors at sea. The docks are alive with activity and the bakery overlooking the small fishing boats is continually pulling pizza Genovese out of the oven. If you only associate pizza with Naples or Rome, then get ready for a new favorite.

SIGHTS

Most of what's worth seeing in Italy's sixth-largest city is concentrated around the Porto Antico and old town. If the weather's good you can walk to the port from Stazione Principe in under 15 minutes and hop on a *battello* (boat) for a tour of harbor. It's all uphill from there, so when the legs start to give take a cab to Villa Garibaldi and relax in one of the rare gardens in the center. For that panoramic picture, ride the Portello or Righi funicular and have your camera ready.

◖ Porto Antico

There is nothing the Genovese are prouder about than their port. From the 13th to the 15th centuries, it was one of the most important in Eu-

one of Renzo Piano's contributions to the waterfront renovation

rope and it remains commercially active. That's not to say it was always a pretty place and when Renzo Piano was awarded the task of renovating the area, things could only get better. The result is a complex of museums, libraries, and exhibition spaces that have turned the Porto Antico into Genova's most-visited area.

Little has changed inside **Palazzo Reale** (Via Balbi 10, tel. 010/271-0272, Tues.–Wed. 9 A.M.–1:30 P.M. and Thurs.–Sun. 9 A.M.–7 P.M.). All the furniture and artwork the Kings of Savoy once enjoyed are exactly where they left them. The Hall of Mirrors was the disco of its day and would impress even Louis XVI. There's no shortage of wall space and the kings broke the monotony with paintings. Parodi and Carlone were favorites and Van Dyke's *Crucification* was given a place of honor. The height of ceilings in palaces like this is always impressive and has a way of making you feel very small. Maybe that's what royalty wanted; in any case, the garden comes as a relief. It slopes gently towards the old port and is designed around a central fountain.

Acquario di Genova (tel. 010/234-5678, www.acquariodigenova.it, €15 or €22 combined museum ticket) is the city's biggest attraction and more than a million visitors discover Europe's largest aquarium every year. There's a lot to see and you can choose from several themed tours besides the basic entrance. You'll need a good half-day to explore the 70 tanks that re-create aquatic habitats from the Great Barrier Reef to the Caribbean Sea.

The aquarium is home to over 6,000 marine animals. All the familiar faces are here, like dolphins, sharks, seals, and penguins, as well as some special guests including a hummingbird-filled forest. The manta ray touching pool is for anyone who prefers the hands-on approach to nature. The rays are friendly, but you should avoid stroking their eyes or gills. Flash photography is not allowed and you're better off buying postcards or posters of your favorite amphibian at the aquarium shop near the exit.

During the summer the aquarium can get crowded and visitors may be issued a 30-minute window of entry to avoid logjams at the shark tank. If time is pressing, skip the 3-D movie in the aquarium theater. The snack bar in the center of the complex, on the other hand, is a nice way to break up a visit and there's an outdoor terrace with excellent views of the harbor. Exotic plants are on display inside the **Biosfera** next to the aquarium and you can get a behind-the-scenes tour that lasts one hour and includes watching dolphins have lunch.

Galata Museo del Mare (Calata De Mari 1, tel. 010/234-5655, www.galatamuseodel mare.it, Tues.–Sun. 10 A.M.–7:30 P.M., €10 or €22 combined aquarium ticket) is housed in a modern glass building five minutes from the aquarium. If you don't feel like walking, a little train shuttles visitors back and forth along the promenade. The four floors recount the history of the port from the Middle Ages until today with models, multimedia films, and interactive exhibitions that keep even small attention spans interested. The big draw is the 17th-century Genovese galleon that's 40 meters long and nine meters high. You can board the ship and get an idea of what travel was like 500 years ago. **Galata Cafè** serves light snacks, and on Wednesdays there's a tempting ethnic buffet 6–10 P.M.

The quickest way to get a panoramic view of the city is by visiting **Il Bigo** (Porto Antico next to the aquarium, Apr.–Oct. daily 10 A.M.–6 P.M., Jul.–Aug. daily 10 A.M.–11 P.M., Nov. Sat.–Sun. 10 A.M.–5 P.M., Dec. 26–31 10 A.M.–5 P.M., €3 or €2 with aquarium ticket). Part crane, part Beaubourg leftover, this elevator provides a 360-degree view of harbor and old town from 40 meters above the aquarium. You also see the highway that runs through the heart of Genova and keeps urban planners awake at night. Panels inside and audio commentary explain the surrounding before setting you back down to earth.

Even if 70-year-olds outnumber toddlers in Genova, you wouldn't know it by stepping inside **La Citta' dei Bambini** (Magazzini del Cotone, tel. 010/247-5702, www.cittadeibambini. net, Oct.–Jun. Tues.–Sun. 10 A.M.–6 P.M., Jul.–Sept. Tues.–Sun. 11:30 A.M.–7:30 P.M., chil-dren €5, adults €7). This vast complex keeps children occupied with hands-on exhibits and displays that form the largest recreational area in Italy. If you ever wondered where the water goes after you flush or how electricity works then this is a good place to brush up on basic science and technology. Everything is presented in a stimulating context where touching is encouraged. It's most appreciated by kids ages 3–14 but good fun for parents or anyone entertaining the idea of parenthood.

On the other side of the overpass (it may soon be replaced by a tunnel) is **Piazza Caricamento.** This was the site of the medieval harbor and later replaced with warehouses where goods were unloaded and taxes paid. Today it links the Porto Antico with the historic center and contains the beautiful **Palazzo San Giorgio,** which marks the beginning of the *centro storico* (old town).

Centro Storico

To understand the historic center of Genova you have to do two things. First take the Portello funicular up to **Castelletto** and get the macro view. From the hillside, however, the rooftops can be deceiving. What looks like one solid mass is actually teeming with narrow alleys and passages known as the *caruggi*. Even locals get lost here and former scouts will need to work very hard to earn their Genova badge.

Strada Nuova (New Street), also called Via Garibaldi, is situated between Piazza Fontane Marose and Piazza della Meridiana. It was first opened in 1550 when the community sold lots to wealthy merchants and within seven years the first palazzi were being built. It quickly became the choicest address in town and where wealthy families wanted to live, and it became an architectural example for all of Europe to follow. Palaces are mostly three or four stories tall and feature beautiful courtyards and loggias overlooking compact gardens. Today many of the palazzi have been converted into museums and are home to important picture galleries such as Palazzo Rosso, Bianco, and Spinola.

Galleria di Palazzo Bianco (Via Garibaldi 11, tel. 010/557-2193, www.stradanuova.it,

Tues.–Sun. 9 A.M.–7 P.M., €7), also known as Palazzo Grimaldi, was built in the 15th century by Luca Grimaldi and completely transformed in 1711 by Maria Durazzo Brignole. The gardens are a luxury in a town as congested as Genova and from the terraces you can appreciate the surrounding neighborhood. Inside the *pinacoteca* (gallery) is a collection of Genovese, Italian, and European paintings from the 16th to the 18th centuries. Rubens hangs next to Van Dyke, Caravaggio's *Ecce Homo*, and works by hometown artist Alessandro Magnasco.

Nearly opposite is **Palazzo Rosso** (Via Garibaldi 18, tel. 010/247-6351, www.museopalazzorosso.it, Tues.–Fri. 9 A.M.–7 P.M., Sat.–Sun. 10 A.M.–7 P.M., €7) and another fine collection of artworks once owned by the Brignole-Sale family. Here, too, there are good views of the street and surroundings from the two terraces.

At the end of the street is Via XXV Aprile, which slopes downward towards **Piazza de Ferrari.** The bronze fountain was constructed in 1936 and is where Genovese football fans meet to celebrate momentous victories. It's also the cultural center of the city, and is flanked by Teatro Carlo Felice and **Palazzo Ducale** (Piazza Matteotti 9, tel. 010/557-4021, www.palazzoducale.genova.it, €7), which hosts blockbuster exhibitions and is the most famous building in Genova. The palace was built in the 13th century and modified many times over the years. Although it looks old, the present facade was only completed in the 19th century. Inside you'll also find an excellent restaurant, library, and shops. Buildings like this can sometimes be intimidating but should be explored even if art isn't your thing. You don't need a ticket to examine the courtyard and check out the view on the top floor.

One block away is the **duomo of San Lorenzo** (Piazza San Lorenzo, Museo del Tesoro di San Lorenzo, tel. 010/265-786, Mon.–Sat. 9 A.M.–noon and 3–8 P.M., €5.50, admission free), which looks like three buildings combined into one. The 9th-century church has been tweaked over the centuries and the Norman portals were perhaps the most

LIGURIA

© LAURIE ELIE

Piazza de Ferrari

spectacular addition. Inside the 14th century naves is a chapel dedicated to St. John the Baptist. The entrance to the treasury is nearby and the underground rooms contain gold and silver ornaments crafted by local artists.

If you backtrack a little you'll come to **Porta Soprano,** which was the eastern gateway when there was still a wall around the city. The flags flying above the two curved towers are not a tribute to England but to St. George, who is quite popular in Genova. This is a good place to take a breather and you can rest in the little garden that contains the remains of a 12th-century cloister.

It's also a good time to ask yourself whether Christopher Columbus (or Colombo as he's known in Italy) was actually Italian. Some Portuguese and Spanish towns are convinced it's a case of mistaken identity, but the DNA evidence has proved inconclusive so far. The ivy-covered house where he might have been born is nearby and may be the only tourist trap in Genova. There's not much to see really except a couple of pretty bare rooms. If you're a fan of the sailor, you're better off going to **Palazzo Tursi** (Via Garibaldi 9, tel. 010/557-2193, Tues.–Fri. 9 A.M.–7 P.M. and Sat.–Sun. 10 A.M.–7 P.M., €7 or €5 with museum card), where three of his letters and part of his ashes are preserved.

ENTERTAINMENT AND EVENTS

Genovese may seem reserved but that doesn't mean they don't like to go out. In the summer, Piazza delle Erbe near Palazzo Ducale is generally where the party starts. There are a half-dozen bars on the piazza and the adjacent streets are packed with locals most nights of the week. Drinking outside has become a necessity since smoking was banned inside bars and restaurants but none seems to care. Culture isn't lacking either and the recently restored **Teatro Carlo Felice** is one of the finest theaters in Italy. Forget that the last director was forced to quit and his choice of conductors was always controversial; the music is excellent and tickets reasonably priced. Entertainment

grows exponentially in the summer, when concerts are staged nearly every evening and blues, rock, and electronica can all be heard.

If you prefer a more underground ambiance, try the winding streets off Via Garibaldi and Maddalena. Porto Antico is fast becoming an evening hot spot and the clubs there tend to be on the slick, designer side.

Nightlife
BARS AND DANCE CLUBS
Le Corbusier (via San Donato 36/38r, tel. 328/696-7446, daily 5:30 P.M.–1 A.M.) started out as a student bar near the architecture school, which explains the name. It's grown over the years and is now a pillar of the scene around Palazzo Ducale. The bartender here has a photographic cocktail memory and can shake up well over 100 concoctions. Vodka connoisseurs will be impressed with the 30 labels behind the bar, extending way beyond Absolut. On weekends, the resident DJ spins lounge tunes and live acts are occasionally invited, but people really come here just to hang out with friends and flirt a little.

The guys who opened **Beautiful Loser** (Vico Dietro il Coro di San Cosimo 6r, tel. 010/254-1254, www.beautifulloser.it, Tues.–Sun. 6 P.M.–1 A.M.) may have some unresolved childhood issues but they know how to run a music bar. The name is actually from a Leonard Cohen book and the space that once belonged to a mechanic took a year of hard work to restore. Graphic designers should be pleased with the red and white tones used sparingly in the cavernous main hall—which leads to three smaller monochrome rooms where you can hypnotize yourself by staring at the walls. Campbell's soup can lamps are a nice touch and a small stage hosts DJs, live bands, and cabaret.

Zerodieci (Piazza Embriaci 1r, www.0dieci. org, Fri.–Sun. 6 P.M.–4 A.M., €6) is a mix of music, art, cinema, and dance in an underground atmosphere that has a speakeasy feel. It's one of those places that requires a membership card that can be acquired instantly at the door. Saturday night is devoted to electronica with international DJs alternating between eurotrash, drum 'n' bass, and minimal. On Sundays, they project the kind of movies that require thinking and downstairs is the technology zone with free wireless Internet where you can download the club's podcast.

Corso Italia becomes the summer headquarters for clubs like **Mako** (Corso Italia 28r, tel. 010/367-652, Fri.–Sun. 9 P.M.–2 A.M.) and **Mucca Bar** (Corso Italia 7, daily 7 P.M.–late-night) that serves cocktails on a terrace overlooking the sea and organizes events, including speed dating evenings where you get 200 seconds to impress an Italian.

LIVE MUSIC

Between September and July, **Teatro Carlo Felice** (Passo Eugenio Montale 4, www.carlofelice.it, box-office Galleria Cardinale Siri 6, tel. 010/589-329, Tues.–Sat. 11 A.M.–6 P.M.) is the home of classical music, opera, and ballet. The theater was badly damaged during World War II and wasn't completely renovated until 1990. Inside, the walls were built to resemble a street scene and contain windows and balconies. It's a very strange effect that occasionally distracts from what's happening on stage. Getting a seat isn't usually a problem and 30 tickets are always sold at half-price one hour before each performance. There are also a limited number of standing-room tickets.

For good live jazz in Genova, check out the **Louisiana Jazz Club** (Via T. Reggio 34r, tel. 010/585-241) on Thursday nights at 9 P.M. and the **Borgoclub** (Via Vernazza 7/9r, tel. 010/376-0090), which has its own big band. They also organize the Spring Jazz Festival in March at the Teatro della Gioventù. Rock, pop, and indie are the realm of **Madeleine Café** (Via della Maddalena 103r, daily 11 P.M.–3 A.M.) and **Senhor do Bonfim** (Porta Anita Garibaldi 25r, tel. 010/372-6312, daily 8 P.M.–late-night) in Nervi.

Festivals and Events

The city that invented pesto has the right to stage the world championships and decide who makes the best sauce. Every year, 100 competi-tors from all over the world with secret recipes turn up at Palazzo Ducale with the intention of winning the **Campionato Mondiale Di Pesto** (tel. 010/247-6926, www.pestochampionship.net). You can judge for yourself how good these chefs are and get some tips on making this unique sauce. There can only be one champion and if two chefs are tied the winner is determined by speed of preparation. During the mid-March event, dozens of restaurants offer a prix-fix pesto menu. You can pick up an updated list at the palazzo.

If you like boats, **Salone Nautico** (Fiera di Genova, tel. 010/53911, www.fiera.ge.it/salone_nautico) can keep you occupied for days. Every year, in early October, the nautical industry turns up to show off the latest creations in a sector that continues to grow worldwide. There are over 2,400 motor and sailing crafts on display both on land and in the 23 piers next to the Fiera. The showstoppers are the 80 maxi-yachts destined for Saudi royalty and Russian nouveau riche. A full tank of gas in one of these costs more than most people earn in an entire year.

Columbus Day in Genova feels different than anywhere else. Here festivities take place outside the explorer's (supposed) house on October 12 and include costumed performances paying tribute to the sailor. There are guided tours and a wreath-laying ceremony.

Every June, Piazza delle Feste underneath Il Bigo in Porto Antico hosts 10 days of multiethnic song, dance, and culture. **SUQ** includes a market with over 50 craftspeople from around the world making unique objects. There are lessons for anyone who wants to improve their rhythm and literary events. Also in June is the **Festival Internazionale di Poesia.** Prestigious locations around the city are handed over to poets and words with an equal focus on experimentation and traditional verse. During the festival, participants can follow the **Percorsi Poetici,** the Poet's Path (tel. 010/541-942), which traces the footsteps of Byron, Nietzsche, Shelley, Flaubert, Twain, Dickens, and other literary greats who were inspired by the city. One night of the festival is reserved for **La Notte della Poesia,** when *palazzi* along Via Garibaldi remain open until sunrise with events celebrating the spoken word. You can even sign up for a workshop if you feel inspired.

Dance, house, and drum 'n' bass fans have had little to get excited about until the **Play Festival** (tel. 010/246-7506, www.arciliguria. it) was launched in Genova a couple of years ago. It's one of the only events dedicated to electronic music in Italy and was an immediate success from the start. The music kicks off on the second to last weekend in June at Parco della Lanterna. It draws youthful crowds who dance 8 P.M.–3 A.M. There are five stages to choose from and DJs in past editions have included Goldie, Alex Gopher, and Spiller. Entry is €13.

There is no shortage of musical events in July. **Goa Boa** (Porto Antico, Arena del Mare, tel. 010/593-650, www.goaboa.net) is the largest music festival in Liguria dedicated to rock and hip-hop. Both Italian and international artists alternate on stage and concerts start at 9 P.M. and cost €10. The **Gezmataz** (www.gezmataz.org) at the end of the month is all about jazz improvisation and is held on the piazza in the Porto Antico. Tickets are €12 and the Saturday show is free.

Saint John the Baptist is honored on June 24 with traditional games and fireworks in the *centro storico.* In the afternoon, you can follow the long procession from the cathedral to the port, where relics of the city's patron saint are aired out and the sea is blessed.

Genova is home to the most famous violinist of all time. In October, **La Paganiniana** celebrates Niccolò Paganini and international heavyweights spend a week at Teatro Carlo Felice paying tribute to the master. Every two years a prestigious violin competition, the **Premio Paganini,** is also held at the Conservatorio (Via Albaro 38, tel. 010/557-4215, www.paganini.comune.genova.it). The actual instrument the virtuoso played is on permanent display in Palazzo Tursi.

Clowns get their chance to shine during **Circumnavigando** (tel. 010/860-0232) in December. The street theater and circus festival concentrates on the art of laughter and artists from all over the world turn the piazze of Genova into an outdoor circus that involves passersby whether they like it or not. A big top is also set up in Porto Antico for traditional acrobatics and bearded women.

Euroflora (www.fiera.ge.it) requires patience. The most important Italian flower show only happens once every five years but when it does expect everyone to show up. The 11-day event is held inside the Fiera and attracts 500,000 flower fanatics. It's an explosion of colors, smells, and form of every flower and plant imaginable. The next edition is scheduled for 2011.

Genova has an old tradition of setting up manger scenes outside many of the city's churches. These are generally displayed throughout December and January and you can spend an afternoon visiting the over 40 different displays. Two of the most intricate scenes are inside the **Convento dei Cappuccini** and **San Giuseppe.** If the elaborate wooden figures catch your attention, an entire collection is on display at the **Museo Luxoro** (Via Mafalda di Savoia 3, tel. 010/322-673, Tues.–Sat. 9 A.M.–1 P.M.) in Nervi. Many of the smaller towns also make a point of setting up mangers that are usually in the main square and involve the participation of the entire population.

The *centro storico* becomes one big stage for New Year's Eve. DJs and bands take over the streets and piazze, while children get their own special party at Palazzo Ducale.

SHOPPING

The main shopping districts in Genova can be found around Piazza De Ferraris. Boutiques and designer clothing stores are located on Via XX Settembre and Via Rome, while Galleria Mazzini is a long, elegant covered passageway built in 1870. To visit the handmade and artisan shops that have resisted the 21st century, take a walk down Via Orefici, which is also home to several fine antique and bargain shoe stores. Sottoripa near the Porto Antico is another of the city's characteristic shopping areas, where spices and dried fruit compete with fried fish shops for the attention of passersby.

Except for the big department stores, most shops are usually closed on Sundays. Some owners also keep the shutters down on Monday mornings and nearly everyone takes a two-hour lunch break in the middle of the day.

Department Stores

La Rinascente (Via E. Vernazza 1, tel. 010/586-995, daily 8:30 A.M.–7:30 P.M.) is the Italian version of a big department store. It's spread out on four floors and usually crowded. Perfume and clothing are on the ground floor. The quality is high as are the prices, except during the sale season (Jan. and June) when you can find some bargains. There's also an interesting ethnic department upstairs.

The new **Coin** (Via XX Settembre 16A, tel. 010/570-5821, daily 9 A.M.–7 P.M.) is worth a look even if you don't like to shop. The interior is one big open space with a central, transparent elevator shaft that takes shoppers up towards a giant skylight. On the second floor there's an extensive kitchenware department with all the gadgets you'll need to make a great pesto. The cafeteria is run by Zeffirino and is a favorite pit stop for Genovese with a need for espresso or salad.

Sporting Goods

If you get the urge to take up sailing, **G. Bollo & C.** (Via F. Turati 50r, tel. 010/247-7618, Mon.–Sat. 9 A.M.–12:30 P.M. and 3:30–7:30 P.M.) can help you look the part. They've got the nautical jackets that keep sailors warm no matter what the weather and gadgets like compasses and waterproof matches you'll need if you end up on a desert island. There are also materials for keeping boats shipshape and books on tying knots.

Camisasca (Piazza Campetto 11r, tel. 010/247-2376, Mon.–Sat. 9:30 A.M.–12:30 P.M. and 3:30–7:30 P.M.) is the largest sports store in the city. They have a complete line of hiking, skiing, and rock climbing gear. The outdoor department also carries tents and camping equipment that could be useful for anyone heading to the Alta Via. Clothing and equipment for more traditional sports

like tennis, golf, and soccer are also available inside this vast store.

Clothing

Genova is a natural town for vintage and **Betty Page** (Via Ravecca 51r, tel. 347/485-7379, Tues.–Sat. 10 A.M.–12:30 P.M. and 3:30–7:30 P.M.) has a roomful of second-hand glamour for sale. The red interior has a fun boudoir feel that encourages browsing through the racks of coats last worn in the 1970s and bathing suits popular during Eisenhower's administration. Dresses, trousers, and shoes with improbable heels are all immaculate and if the style wasn't so retro you might think they were brand new.

Accessories

You'll find **Maiolino** (tel. 010/566-666, Tues.–Sat. 9 A.M.–7:30 P.M.) underneath the arches of Via XX Settembre 260r in a newly restored shop with one window devoted to female footware and the other dedicated to men's shoes. In Italy you don't go into a shoe store without window-shopping first. If there's a pair you like then you enter, wait for a clerk, and point out the model you want to try. It makes everything much easier and saves a lot of time. Here the shoes are generally classic styles in good quality leather that doesn't easily go out of fashion. It's the perfect store for a city that values elegance over extravagance.

Gianni Agnelli (the legendary owner of Fiat) ordered his ties at **Finollo** (Via Rome 38r, tel. 010/562-073, Tues.–Sat. 8:30 A.M.–12:30 P.M. and 3:30–7:30 P.M.) and the Art Nouveau doorway is some indication of the quality that awaits inside. They've been measuring arms, chests, and shoulders for over 100 years and the clerks can size you up in a glance. Be careful, if you do treat yourself to a one of their cashmere sweaters or customized shirts (embroidered with initials), the rest of your closet will never feel the same.

Toys

Centro Gioco Educativo (Corso Buenos Aires 3r, tel. 010/592-691, Tues.–Sat.

9:30 A.M.–12:30 P.M. and 3:30–7:30 P.M., Mon. 3:30–7:30 P.M.) wants to help people raise smarter children. They sell educational toys for toddlers ages two and up. Most of the puzzles, games, and building materials are made of wood and designed to encourage exploration. There are a lot of games based on logic and an entire aisle of teddies in all shapes and sizes. If video games are what you're after, this is the wrong place.

Music
Folk, R&B, northern soul, be-pop, pop, beat, punk, reggae, disco, and elevator music are just a few of the sections at **Modern Groove** (Via Luccoli 77r, Tues.–Fri. 9:30 A.M.–7:30 P.M.). This popular record shop with a colorful 1970s theme is one of the places to look in Genova for rare LPs that could be worth a fortune on eBay. The staff is happy to play the old records on their low-tech hi-fi and if you forget the name of a single all you need to do is hum it for them and they'll find it. There's also a collection of new CDs impossible to find anywhere else by groups who may just be on their way to fame.

Pink Moon (Piazza Ferretto 1r, tel. 010/255-695, Mon.–Sat. 10 A.M.–7 P.M.) is an institution and the friendly staff have been advising Genovese music lovers for years. They could go on all day talking about a Van Halen guitar solo or the merits of Keith Jarrett's trio. The selection of CDs changes nearly daily and you'll hear everything in here. Located in a busy piazza, it's a gold mine of musical culture and the posters are just further proof of how extreme the musical tastes within this shop run.

Books
Libreria di Piazza delle Erbe (Piazza delle Erbe 25r, tel. 010/247-5347, Mon.–Sat. 9 A.M.–12:30 P.M. and 3:30–7:30 P.M.) is the quintessential used bookstore. You'll recognize it from the blue wood on the outside and the dust on the inside. Many of the books are rare Italian titles, although other languages are also well represented. If you tire of your guidebook you can try selling it here for a couple of euros.

Browsing is encouraged but if you're looking for something in particular the owner is happy to search the shelves.

Batman is given a place of honor at **Il Mondo del Fumetto** (Via Montevideo 2r, tel. 010/362-9187, Mon.–Sat. 9:30 A.M.–12:30 P.M. and 3:30–7:30 P.M.), where it's easy to feel 12 years old again. Besides all the usual American comics, they carry a wide range of manga and the local variety known as *fumetti*. If you haven't read *Tex* or *Diabolique,* you've got a lot of catching up to do. There are some great models and gadgets for anyone who likes to see their superheroes on a pencil or keychain.

Libreria Ducale (Palazzo Matteotti 5, Mon.–Sat. 9 A.M.–7:30 P.M.), next to the ticket office in Palazzo Ducale, specializes in art publications, exhibition catalogues, posters, and the kind of design objects usually found in museums. One publisher to look out for is Tormena, which only produces books about Genova and its artists. They also make Genova-themed souvenirs like little sketchpads and unusual postcards that are too cute to send.

Housewares
Walking into **Home Furnishing** (Via Garibaldi) is like walking into someone's house. All the furniture, china, kitchenware, and even the Alvar Aalto vases are displayed in situ. The store itself is located within Palazzo Campanella on the most elegant street in Genova. It's hard not to sit on one of the couches and imagine living under such beautiful frescoes. There are plenty of gift ideas for all budgets, with a tile hotplate or olive spoon stirring set both priced under €10.

SPORTS AND RECREATION
Sailing
Yacht Club Italiano (Porticciolo Duca degli Abruzzi, tel. 010/246-1206, www.yci.it, Mon.–Fri. 9 A.M.–6 P.M. and Sat. 8 A.M.–1 P.M.) is the oldest and most prestigious sailing club in Italy. Their mission nowadays is to introduce the sea to people who don't usually have contact with water. They're based in the Palazzina Genovese near the Porto Antico and the **Scuola di Mare**

GENOVA CRICKET AND ATHLETIC CLUB

You'd think something that gets Italians so excited would be homegrown, but football (soccer) is actually an import. There was a large community of foreigners in Genova after the opening of the Suez Canal, and the English who resided here needed a place to play cricket. A group of 30 gentlemen founded the Genova Cricket and Athletic Club in 1895. Football came later, given that it was generally considered a game for the lower classes and was played by younger members of the club. Two Scottish industrialists donated the field and games were scheduled every Saturday. The sport was much slower than today's high-speed version, and you could seriously hurt your foot kicking the ball if you weren't careful.

Three years later, the man who is considered the founder of Italian football arrived in the city. James Richardson Spensley was a well-educated doctor who cared for English seamen. He was an admirer of the Orient and spoke Sanskrit and Greek, among other languages. In his spare time he worked as a correspondent for the *Daily Mail* and founded the first troop of Italian boy scouts.

Above all, Spensley had a passion for football – a sport he practiced regularly. He began by training a team based on the English model of the game and recruited sailors from the numerous ships that happened to be in the harbor. On April 10, 1897, he was able to pass a motion allowing Italians to become members of the club. Initially only 50 Genovese could join, but after a couple of years that limit was removed and the rest is history – and four World Cups.

runs sailing courses for children and adults with or without experience. Most courses last about a week but there are some single day activities, which must be reserved in advance.

Fishing

If you'd rather someone else do the navigating and just concentrate on fishing, contact **Cooperativa Janua** (Sestri Ponente, Via Eridania 7, tel. 010/645-5365), which takes out small groups for deep sea or coastal expeditions that last a half-day. They'll provide the rods and all the bait you can handle. Most of what is caught is thrown back, but if you want to benefit from your hard work they can recommend a few local restaurants that will grill your fish for you.

Boat Tours

Cooperativa Battellieri del Porto di Genova (tel. 010/265-712, www.battellierigenova.it) organizes one-day excursions across the Ligurian Sea. You can choose from Portofino or a cruise along the Cinque Terre coastline.

The most memorable boat tours are the **whale-watching** trips in the Cetacei Sanctuary led by Worldwide Fund for Nature (WWF) specialists. Boats leave on Wednesday (9 A.M.–7 P.M., €35) and Saturday (10 A.M.–5:30 P.M., €32) from the aquarium. A light jacket, sunglasses, and suntan lotion will come in handy. Advance reservations are necessary and the cooperative also runs tours from Savona and Varazza.

Parks

Parco Urbana delle Mura is slightly outside of Genova towards the mountainous interior. It's where the Genovese escape to on weekends. There are great views of the countryside, historic forts, and footpaths along 17th-century fortifications. The park can be reached by car or public transport using the Zecca–Righi funicular.

Genova-Casella (Piazza Mani, tel. 010/837-321, www.ferroviagenovacasella.it, daily, €2) is a rare example of a small railway line that has survived the onslaught of automobiles. On weekends and especially Sundays the train is crowded with tourists and Genovese families enjoying a day out over steep hills and rolling countryside. The vintage trains make a half-dozen stops and each is worth exploring if you have the time or inclination. It takes an hour to reach Casella, where you can rent a bike; they'll give you a small discount if you show your ticket. There are eight departures from Piazza Mani (take bus 34 from Stazione Principe) between 7:38 A.M. and 7:32 P.M.

ACCOMMODATIONS

Genova has a good selection of hotels in every price range. There are also many cozy bed-and-breakfasts in the heart of the historic center where guests can get real insight on how locals live. If the crowds of the Old Town are unappealing, you can choose to sleep in the quiet suburb of Nervi, only 10 minutes away by train or bus. There are also many *agriturismo* options in the surrounding countryside.

Under €100

A short walk uphill and you've arrived in **La Meridiana** (Via Salita 7a, tel. 010/246-2756, www.bblameridiana.it, €70 d). This bed-and-breakfast is in the heart of Baroque Genova on the last floor of an 18th-century palazzo that Egizia Gasparini has decorated with care. Skylights from which a sea of rooftops can be glimpsed illuminate the three attic rooms. The only drawback is the single bathroom, which makes this property well suited for students, families, and groups of friends.

Hotel Bruxelles Margherita (Via XX Settembre 19/7, 4th fl., tel. 010/589-191, www.hotelbruxellesmargherita.it, €80–95 s/d) is midway down one of Genova's main shopping streets 10 minutes from Brignole train station. The iron beds, upholstered armchairs, and watercolor paintings add personality to a hotel that isn't afraid to be a bit retro. What matters more is tranquility and a pleasant, smiling staff who provide four-star service in two-star surroundings.

Hotel Bonera (Nervi, Via Sarfatti 8, tel. 010/372-6164, www.villabonera.com, €90 d) is a half-kilometer from the Nervi train station but they also provide free parking if you're arriving by car. The villa was built in the 16th century and contains 28 spacious rooms with lovely painted ceilings and views of the garden where breakfast is served in summer. Nearly everything in the restaurant is white, and large windows light up the tables that many guests choose to book for their evening meal.

€100-200

Metropoli (Piazza Fontane Marose, tel. 010/246-888, €112 d) is a comfortable three-star hotel in a stately building that has conserved its original slate staircase among other things. If you're afraid of heights make sure to hold the wooden railing. The 48 rooms were all given a fresh coat of paint in 2004 and the owners chose warm colors rather than the usual white. Soundproofed windows ensure a good night's rest and in the morning you can count on focaccia and warm brioche in the elegant breakfast room.

High-tech meets the 15th century inside **◖ Locanda di Palazzo Cicala** (Piazza S. Lorenzo 16, tel. 010/251-8824, www.palazzocicala.it, €175 d) opposite the duomo. Rooms are minimalist in style and come with Internet, satellite TV, and DVD players. It's like a modern-day monastery where guests can recuperate after a day exploring the backstreets of Genova. There's no restaurant but they do provide a nice outdoor *aperitivo* with views of the city. Rooms 103 and 106 are especially stylish.

Nervi is the place to stay if you suffer from claustrophobia and prefer greenery over cobblestones. **Villa Pagoda** (Nervi, Via Capolungo 15, tel. 010/372-6161, www.villapagoda.it, €180 d) is a 17th-century palazzo done up in an Asian style with period furniture and marble floors. Many rooms have a view of the sea while others look out onto the Parco di Nervi. The hotel is a short distance from the center by bus or train and parking is available.

€200-300

Hotel Savoia (Via Arsenale di Terra 1, tel. 010 261-641, hotelsavoiagenova.it, €180–220 s/d) is in an elegant building overlooking Stazione Principe and within walking distance of the port. The floral patterns on the walls are part of a Liberty theme that runs from the lobby to each of the 44 rooms. You never go thirsty here as the bar downstairs provides complimentary drinks throughout the day. Besides basic doubles with parquet floors and wireless Internet, there are also several large executive suites that come with a whirlpool tub and a small kitchen.

To fully appreciate Genova you should sleep at sea. **Tender To** (tel. 010/247-5012, €240 d) can arrange a night on one of their yachts docked in the Porto Antico. Instead of a room you get a cabin with private bath and breakfast served by uniformed crew. The city looks different from on deck and romance is assured.

Over €300

The biggest Italian hotel chain is **Jolly** (Via Martin Piaggio 11, tel. 010/83161, www.jolly hotels.it, €310 d), and their Genova location is full of four-star perks. The 143 rooms are all equipped with air-conditioning, mini-fridges, and safes. Bathrooms are covered in marble and if you want your shoes shined or need a shirt ironed, hotel reception can be on the case in minutes.

FOOD
Ligurian

The stockfish displayed on the walls is a clue to what the star ingredient is inside **Antico Osteria di Vico Palla** (Vico Palla 15r, tel. 010/246-6575, Tues.–Sun., noon–3 P.M. and 7–11 P.M., €8–12). Here it's boiled with potatoes and cooked *alla Genovese*. Minestrone is served cold during the summer and desserts like the apple pie and tiramisu are all homemade. Thursday–Sunday, reservations are nearly always necessary inside the recently enlarged restaurant near the old port. Service can be on the hurried side.

Sa Pesta (Via dei Giustiniani 16r, tel. 010/246-8336, Mon.–Sat., 12:30–3:30 P.M. and 7–10 P.M., €7–9, cash only) is easy to reach from the aquarium and the streets leading to the trattoria are full of restored palazzi. The greeting may not be particularly warm but the oven with piles of wood nearby welcomes the stomach. Tables are set simply with paper tablecloths and glasses that have been used by generations of diners. The pesto pasta is the classic dish but at lunch there's also a great assortment of fried and stuffed foods. Dinner must be reserved and it's better to practice your Italian before making the phone call.

There's likely to be a line outside **Antica Osteria della Foce** (Via Ruspoli 72r, tel. 010/553-3155, daily noon–2:30 P.M. and 7:30–10 P.M., €7–11). Locals come for the *farinata* (flatbread made with chickpea flour) that's only served at night and the fried foods that are a constant. Pesto and minestrone are prepared the old-fashioned way and served inside or out at this *osteria* near the Fiera di Genova.

The glass that separates the chef from the dining room at **La Buca di San Matteo** (Vico David Chiossone 5r, tel. 010/869-0648, Mon.–Sat. noon–4 P.M. and 7:30 P.M.–11:30 P.M., €13–23) attracts attention. It doesn't take long for Ligurian classics to emerge onto the tables under wood beams and whitewashed ceilings. Waiters are as good as the food they serve and go about their business smoothly. These aren't want-to-be actors, but professionals.

Ombre Rosse (Vico Indoratori 20–24r, tel. 010/275-7608, Mon.–Sat. noon–3 P.M. and 6 P.M.–midnight, €10–15) is located in an 800-year-old house on one of the city's only tree-lined squares. The chef's mantra is *"buono, pulito, e giusto"* (good, clean, and honest) which translates to simple food with first-class ingredients. Diners can choose from soups in winter and summer, vegetable cakes, and *pesce azzurro* (blue fish). There are few tables within the narrow dining rooms, which look as though they've been carved out of rock. Reservations are always necessary on weekends.

A few steps from Piazza Portello and the funicular is a new restaurant with one of the best locations in town. **(Anciôe Belle Donne** (Salita San Girolamo 2r, tel. 010/253-4255, Mon.–Sat. 7:30 P.M.–midnight, €7–10) has inviting red and yellow pastel walls and chairs that don't always match. Claudia and Natalia take the orders and will happily guide you through the 20 or so dishes that have been handed down from generation to generation.

During the summer, they open for lunch and set tables outside in the shaded garden. The bill is always a pleasant surprise.

You don't have to look very far for a restaurant after visiting Palazzo Ducale. **Disopra** (Piazza Matteotti 5, tel. 010/595-9648, www.disopra. it, Mon.–Sun. 12:30–2:30 P.M. and 8 P.M.–midnight, €8–10) is just downstairs and an elegant dining option. There are two medium-sized rooms, each with a particular mood. The one near the entrance is decorated perfectly for Valentine's Day and is quite cheerful, while the striped wallpaper in the internal room gives it a more austere feeling. Two very intimate tables in the niches can instantly spark romance. On weekdays you'll find an extensive buffet option for €12 and on weekends brunch is served until 3 P.M. The evening menu is quite balanced and each course has four meat and fish options.

Seafood

Raffaele Balzano learned his trade working on cruise ships, and along with his Neapolitan wife has maintained a Michelin star for the last 13 years. The focus of **La Bitta nella Pergola** (Via Casaregis 52r, tel. 010/588-543, Tues.–Sat. 12:30–2:30 P.M. and 7–10:30 P.M., €12–20) is fish prepared using both Northern and Southern techniques. In the mahogany-covered dining room that resembles the interior of a boat, dishes have long names like *tartare di pesce con crema di limone* (fish tartar with lemon cream sauce) that thrill the gourmet regulars. Bread, sweets, and pastries are all made in-house at this prestigious address near the Fiera di Genova.

Antica Osteria del Bai (Via Quarto 12, tel. 010/256-425, Tues.–Fri. 12:30–3 P.M. and 7–10:30 P.M., €12–18) serves fish and Ligurian dishes with a big side of history. The 14th-century fortress that houses the restaurant was the site of several battles and Garibaldi refreshed himself here before setting off to Sicily. You can't get any closer to the sea without getting wet. The friendly owners have preserved the original stone walls and set up tables outside during in the summer.

For some reason, artists, writers, and intellectuals have always been attracted to **Da Franca**

BASIL AND PESTO

If the colors in the Italian flag represented food, the green would be basil. In Liguria, it's arguably the most important ingredient and there'd be a culinary crisis without it. You'll find basil in nearly every course and most cooks keep a pot growing in their garden or on their balcony. In the markets it's usually sold with the roots still intact so leaves remain fresh and maximum flavor can be obtained. You can appreciate basil with bruschetta or pizza, but to truly get to terms with this versatile herb you'll need to make pesto.

Every household has a pesto recipe – and the world championships are held in Genoa – but it really comes down to a very simple dish. All it takes is basil, pine nuts, pecorino or Parmesan cheese, and olive oil (preferably Ligurian). Non-traditionalists sometimes add garlic and a dash of lemon. Most people don't have time to use a pestle anymore and prefer to mix all the ingredients and blend them in a food processor. The result can be combined with any pasta, although in Liguria they tend to use short shapes like penne. Once you've seen how easy it is, tomato sauce may have a little competition.

(Vicolo Lepre 8r, tel. 010/247-4473, Tues.–Sun. noon–2:30 P.M. and 7:30 P.M.–11 P.M., €10–14). It could be theory linking brain health to fresh fish consumption, or the medieval interior that just inspires better conversations than a fast-food outlet might. None of this has gone to the head of the owner, who remains firmly grounded and treats all stomachs as though they were created equal. Tables are few so make a reservation if you want to dig your spoon into their *cucchiaio* dessert.

Quick Bites

The tradition in Genova is to have *farinata* wrapped to go and eat it while strolling along Via Roma. The crowd of students, office workers, and old-timers outside **La Farinata**

dei Teatri (Piazza Marsala 5r, Mon.–Fri. noon–2 P.M. and 6–8:30 P.M., €5) may put you off but it's worth getting in line. The small shop (there are only three much-sought-after wooden tables) has an irresistible smell and pretty much resembles the black and white photo Fortunato Bertorelli keeps behind the counter. Service is fast and ovens work overtime to keep customers satisfied.

On the other side of the city near the port, **Gran Ristoro** (Via Sottoripa 27r, tel. 010/247-3127, Mon.–Sat. 7 A.M.–7 P.M., €5) makes Genova's most famous sandwiches. There are hundreds to choose from but mackerel is still number one with the multiethnic clientele who populate this street where spices, dried fruits, and counterfeit CDs are for sale. A little farther down at **Carega** (Via Sottoripa 113r, tel. 010/247-0617, Tues.–Sat. noon–8 P.M., €6), the counter is full with lunchtime crowds eating fried fish and focaccia. Unlike the usual light Genovese dishes, the food here is robust and they go heavy on olive oil.

In 100 years the only thing that's changed at **Ostaia di San Vincenzo** (Via San Vincenzo 64r, tel. 010/565-765, Mon.–Sat. 9 A.M.–2:30 P.M. and 6–9:30 P.M., €5–7) is the name. The family and the Ligorean specialties are the same even if the Calabrian cook occasionally throws in some Southern flavors for nostalgia's sake. The *farinata* and the prices are strong points. Minestrone *alla Genovese* is a very reasonable €5 and even the unfashionable decor starts to grow on you after a while.

Wine Bars

Two architects with a passion for wine opened **l'Antica Cantina i Tre Merli** (Vico Dietro il Coro della Maddalena 26r, tel. 010/247-4095, daily except Sat. lunch and Sun. noon–3 P.M. and 7:30–11 P.M., €7) in a small alley near the Strada Nuova. They managed to preserve the old bar, arcades, and many of the tiles that give the *enoteca* its warm character. There are over 300 bottles to choose from with Piedmont and Tuscany well represented. Cheese and cold-cut platters are a natural with wine and the fondue makes eating fun.

What could be more natural than a book in one hand and a glass of wine in the other? Andrea Bisso and Andrea Campisi couldn't think of anything so they opened **La Nouvelle Vague** (Vico dei Gradi 4r, tel. 010/256-272, Tues.–Sun. 6 P.M.–1 A.M.). The books aren't exactly best sellers, with most titles published by small Italian publishers. Wines may be more familiar and the 600 labels come from all continents. You can drink at one of the square wooden tables or grab a stool at the bar in this cavernous library where a two-for-one happy hour runs 6:30–9 P.M. and browsing goes on until late.

There are awards for mixing a great cocktail and the barmen at **Il Blu di Ravecca** (Via Ravecca 65r, tel. 010/251-1147, Mon.–Sat. 7 A.M.–midnight) have won their fair share. The intimate atmosphere makes it popular with couples and the vast selection of wine can be mind-boggling. The dessert menu is also extensive and may spoil your appetite.

Aperitivo

From the outside **Cdream** (Via XII Ottobre 4, tel. 010/548-3020, Mon.–Sat. 11 A.M.–9 P.M.) looks like an art gallery and isn't the kind of place you enter comfortably in shorts and a t-shirt. It's a concept space where the C stands for the local holiday cruise company. *Aperitivo* is the perfect excuse to lap up the designer technology. Cocktails cost €8 and come with an endless choice of finger foods. On Thursdays starting at 6 P.M. they style things up a notch with tartare and Champagne, where €15 gets you a glass of bubbly and all the raw steak, fish, and vegetables you can digest.

Bakeries

Panerello is the cake most Genovese children eat on their birthdays and is the main reason to go visit the pastry shop of the same name on Via Galata 67 (Mon.–Sat. 7:30 A.M.–7:30 P.M.). They make a mini version of the dessert that locals eat at the bar, which is overcrowded most mornings.

Confetteria Villa di Profumo (Via del Portello 2r, tel. 010/277-0002, daily 7 A.M.–7 P.M., closed Sun. afternoon) looks a lot like it did when it first opened in 1827. The frescoed vaults, vases filled with confectionary, and—most importantly—the brightly colored pastries haven't changed. Only the faces are new and the latest generation of the Profumo family (Maurizio in the kitchen, Marco and Elena at the counter) still packs their sweets in small, blue boxes that make great gifts. They roast the nuts themselves with the praline recipe perfected by grandfather Giuseppe. One taste of the *averosa* or *cobeleti* is enough to see why tradition matters.

Food Shops

What started out as a means for local farmers to promote their produce has grown into an oasis of traditional Ligurian foods. **Tavola de Doge** (Piazza Matteotti 80r, tel. 010/562-880, Tues.–Sun. 9 A.M.–2 P.M. and 3:30–7:30 P.M.) carries all the region's DOC wines and Paolo Antonelli is always on the lookout for new flavors that respect the environment. Even the shop interior is painted green and the shelves are full of pasta, sweets, honey, and different varieties of pesto that just might make it past customs. In the fresh food section are local cheeses *Brigasca* from sheep's milk and *Sant'Alberto* from goat's milk.

The **Torielli** (Via San Bernardo 32r, Mon.–Sat. 9 A.M.–noon and 3:30–7 P.M.) brothers are still behind the counter of their spice, nut, and tea emporium just as they were 50 years ago. The store is entirely covered in white wood and all the jars on the shelves have hand-written labels. It's a joy for eyes and nose. The chocolate is different every day and could be a white version with lemon or a dark cacao with rum. If the place isn't overrun with customers the brothers are big talkers and love to spread their love of food to newcomers to Genova.

Gourmets should explore Via San Vincenzo and Via Colombo, around the Brignole train station, which are lined with bakeries, pastry shops, and specialty stores. **Mercato Orientale** (Via Galata and Via XX Settembre, Mon.–Sat. 7 A.M.–7 P.M.) is a frenetic covered market nearby. If you're after some fresh Ligurian olives, fruits, or just want to smell basil, this is the place to go.

INFORMATION AND SERVICES
Tourist Information

The central tourist office is located in Piazza Matteotti near Palazzo Ducale. **GenovaInforma** (tel. 010/868-7452, daily, 9:30 A.M.–8 P.M.) can provide you with maps and a calendar of events, and can assist with all traveler needs. They also sell a very cost-effective museum card. Other information points are located on Via Sottoripa 5 (Mon.–Fri. 9 A.M.–1 P.M. and 2–6 P.M.), Stazione Principe train station (daily 9 A.M.–1 P.M. and 2:30–6:30 P.M.) and the airport (daily 9 A.M.–1 P.M. and 1:30–5:30 P.M.).

Card Musei di Genova allows entry into over 20 museums including those on the Strada Nuova and Palazzo Ducale. It's the best option for art lovers or rainy days and is valid 48 hours. The basic card costs €16 but for €4 more you can also get unlimited transportation around the city. Cards are available at all participating museums, tourist offices, and online at www.happyticket.it.

Hospitals, Police, and Emergencies

The Guardia Medica or **Medical Guard** (Via Cavalieri 42, tel. 010/782-292) can answer any health questions and indicate the nearest hospital. If you need an ambulance immediately, call 118. There are police stations in Piazza Giuseppe Verdi (tel. 010/562-237) and Piazza Giacinto Rizzolio 19 (tel. 010/648-001). To get officers by your side in a hurry, call 112.

Pharmacies

There are a dozen pharmacies in the historic center, many of which like **Farmacia Cappuccini** (Piazza Del Portello 13r, tel. 010/251-4300) and **Antica Farmacia della Maddalena** (Piazza della Maddalena 16r, tel. 010/247-4242) are located in the larger piazze. All pharmacies display a list outside their door of colleagues open at night. Night pharmacies keep their green-cross sign illuminated and the bell visible. If the shutters are down, just ring.

GETTING THERE AND AROUND

By Air

Cristoforo Colombo Airport (tel. 010 60151, www.airport.genova.it) is six kilometers from the center. Alitalia connects the city to Rome and many European capitals. The closest alternative international airports are in Milan and Nice. **Volabus** (€4) leaves every hour from outside the arrivals terminal and drops passengers off 20 minutes later at Stazione F.S. Principe. The station is the center of transportation in Genova and from there you can catch **AMT** (tel. 010/558-2414, www.amt.genova.it, Mon.–Fri. 8:15 A.M.–4:30 P.M.) buses, the subway, and local trains. The Volabus ticket is good for the entire day on all forms of transport and may be purchased on board, at the train station, or the automated AMT machines around the city. Once you're in the city you can buy single tickets for €1.20 good 90 minutes or a pack of 10 for €11.

By Train

Genova has two main stations. Eurostar and Intercity trains from Rome and Torino stop at both **Porta Principe** and **Brignole.** A night train leaves from Reggio Calabria at the tip of the Italian boot daily at 6:20 P.M. and pulls into Genova the next morning at 8:35 A.M. Unless you have a very good back, it's best to reserve a berth in a sleeping car. The price of the ticket depends on whether you choose a two-, four-, or six-bed compartment.

Local trains are a great way of traveling to Riviera Levante and Ponente, both of which can be reached from either Principe or Brignole.

Funicular Railways

Genova has three funicular railways that run up the steep slopes of the city. **Sant'Anna** connects Piazza Portello with Corso Magenta; the two cars operate daily 7 A.M.–12:30 A.M. An elevator nearby can take you even farther up for a great view of the city. **Zecca-Righi** runs from Largo della Zecca to different neighborhoods along the Righi hill and makes several

stops. At the top you can walk around the old fortifications or stop at one of the restaurants with a view. The third funicular is really a rack railway that links Piazza del Principe to Granarolo. All three cost €1 and tickets may be purchased at the departure stations.

Ferries

Taking a ferry is the scenic way to reach Genova, and in many cases you can take a car although finding parking once you arrive could be a problem. **Tirrenia** (tel. 010/26981), **Moby Lines** (tel. 010/252-755), and **Grimaldi** (tel. 010/55091) boats leave from Stazione Marittima to Sardinia, Corsica, and Spain. There's increased service during the summer and a handful of tour operators connect to Rapallo and Santa Margherita.

Taxis

Taxis are expensive in Genova and cost €3.25 before you've even closed the door. If you're traveling with a dog that's an extra €0.50 and groups of three or more pay an additional €1. Taxis can be ordered by phone 24 hours a day by calling **Radio Taxi** (tel. 010/5966).

Driving

Four different highways converge on Genova. From Rome or Florence, take the A11, or the A10 if arriving from the French border. Travelers coming from Torino or Milan should drive south on the A6 and A7. The main parking garage is in Piazza della Vittoria and a park-and-bus combination allows free use of the AMT system while parked in the garage.

Tours

DAFNE (tel. 348/018-2558) organizes tours around the city with a particular focus on history. The group is given special access to sights such as the Forte Sperone, where Genovese troops kept the Austrians from entering the city at the beginning of the 19th century. A similar visit takes place in Forte Sperone, which is part of the Parco Urbano delle Mura.

To discover lesser-known aspects of the city you can book a visit with **Itinera** (tel.

010/609-1603). They offer seven different themed tours including the lives of Genovese women, gastronomic Genova, and mysterious streets. Groups of 10 usually leave on weekends during the summer at 8:30 P.M.

AROUND GENOVA

Urban sprawl has swallowed many of the towns that were once surrounded by open countryside. **Nervi** has escaped this fate for the moment and makes for a pleasant afternoon if you're using Genova as a base or a good introduction to the Riviera di Levante. The 17 and 517 buses and local train from Brignole let you off near the small harbor where the **Passeggiata Anita Garibaldi** begins. The promenade is a nice place to stroll or ride a bike while enjoying views of Genova and the Portofino promontory. It's full of joggers and families enjoying the sunshine during the summer and there are plenty of bars to stop for a drink. A park borders the sea and is full of sunbathers on weekends and famous for an extensive rose garden and the **Museo Luxoro** (Viale Mafalda Di Savoia, tel. 010/322-673, www.museoluxoro.it, Tues.–Fri. 9 A.M.–1 P.M., Sat. 10 A.M.–1 P.M., €4) which features period furnishings and decorative art.

Riviera di Levante

Riviera di Levante is what many people imagine when they fantasize about Italy. It's got wild coastline, idyllic villages, and heavenly bays. Unless you have your finger over the lens, it's impossible to take a bad picture here.

Large stretches have been turned into natural parks that can only be accessed on foot. Parco Naturale di Portofino and the Cinque Terre are the most famous of these and are home to dozens of endangered plants and animals. Although it's the less populated half of Liguria (the only major town is La Spezia near the Tuscan border), it attracts crowds in search of idyllic resorts like Santa Margherita and Lerici. The remote pine-covered interior is the quickest way to avoid the summer hordes and get an instant middle-of-nowhere feeling.

RAPALLO

Rapallo is an elegant beach town in a splendid position in the Gulf of Tigullio at the base of the Portofino promontory. The promenade **Lungomare Vittorio Veneto** runs along the sea and a long line of palms provides shades for the numerous pedestrians. There are a lot of cafés and restaurants along the promenade where locals spend afternoons exchanging gossip and visitors sample the numerous pizzerias selling focaccia. D. H. Lawrence and Ezra Pound were inspired here and if you ever saw *The Barefoot Contessa* get ready for some déjà vu.

Sights

At the end of the promenade is a small 16th-century castle built on the water. There's a single narrow staircase that leads inside where exhibits are regularly held. On the hill above town sits **Santuario di Montallegro** (Via al Santuario 24, tel. 018/523-9000, Nov.–Mar. daily 8 A.M.–noon and 2:30–5 P.M., Apr.–Oct. daily 7:30 A.M.–noon and 2:30–7 P.M., free admission) and a Byzantine painting some locals believe has the power to heal. If you're suffering from anything it's worth putting the icon to the test.

Not all the buildings are as quaint as those around the port, and much of the 1960–1970s construction is at odds with the natural beauty that surrounds the town. **Santo Stefano,** the 11th-century church that was rebuilt several times over the years, is a consolation and remains the heart of the historical center.

Events

Rapallodanza (www.comune.rapallo.ge.it) is an international dance festival held on alternating Sundays in July and August. A Russian com-

© LAURIE ELIE

Rapallo's palm-lined promenade

pany is almost always invited and choreography fluctuates between classical ballet and modern. Performances start at 9 P.M. in the outdoor theater of Villa Tigullio within Parco Casale.

Sports and Recreation

Rapallo is a base for many of the scuba divers headed for Parco Marino di Portofino, and when someone needs a new mask, a diving watch, or a wetsuit they go to **Maresport** (Corso Italia, tel. 018/550-290, Wed.–Sat. 8:45 A.M.–12:30 P.M. and 3:30–7:30 P.M.). Stefano has contacts with all the scuba clubs in the harbor, many of which advertise their services in his shop. If you need gear or want advice on where to snorkel, this is the place to ask.

Circolo Golf e Tennis Rapallo (Via Mameli 377, tel. 018/526-1777, golf.rapallo@libero.it, closed Wed.) is the only golf course on the Riviera di Levante and one of the oldest in Italy. Woods encircle the 18-hole par 70 course. The seventh hole is within a slice of an old monastery and the Boate River nearby has swallowed more than a few balls since the club opened in

1931. The green fee is €53 on weekdays, and €87 on weekends. Golf carts or caddies are available. Non-golfers can enjoy a drink in the clubhouse or opt for a game of tennis on the clay courts instead.

Accommodations

Stella (Via Aurelia Ponente 6, tel. 018/550-367, hotelstella@tigullio.net, €85 d) is a pink villa in the center of town with views of the sea from the roof terrace. The 27 rooms are simple and furnished with a less-is-more philosophy. Beds are comfortable and all you need if you're planning on getting up early and exploring the area on foot as many of the other guests do. The owners can point you in the right direction whether you want to take a ferry to Portofino or rent a couple of bicycles.

Food

There's a comic book feel inside █ **U Giancu** (Via San Massimo 78, tel. 018/526-0505, Thurs.–Tues. 12:30–3 P.M. and 7–10:30 P.M. €9–11). Walls are covered with colorful characters and the cartoon theme continues on the pages of the menu. Besides a penchant for superheroes, Fausto Oneto is a believer in fresh ingredients and traditional methods of preparation. On a warm summer day, you can taste his classic antipasti in the large garden, followed by a wild herb salad and roasted pork. Mushrooms are a staple May–November and the gelato is churned in-house.

Sotto la Scala (Via Cerisola 7, tel. 018/553-630, Tues.–Sun. 12:30 P.M.–3 P.M. and 7 P.M.–10:30 P.M., €9–12) is near the train station inside an old villa decorated with rustic furnishings and old lamps. The walls are covered with 18th-century silverware the owners have collected over the years. Their passion for food is expressed in a traditional Ligurian cuisine that covers fish and meat. Reservations on weekends are a wise precaution.

Getting There and Around

Rapallo is 20 kilometers from Genova by way of the A12 highway or Aurelia. Trains from the capital take around 50 minutes and cost less than €3. Bus service is available through **ATP** (Piazza delle Nazioni, tel. 018/523-1108, www.tigul liotrasporti.it, daily 7:05 A.M.–7:35 P.M.). Ferry service is available through **Consorzio Servizi Marittimi del Tigullio** (tel. 018/528-4670) and **Consorzio Marittimi Turistico 5 Terre** (tel. 018/773-2987). Both make frequent stops in Rapallo during the summer.

◖ PORTOFINO

Portofino is like an Italian St. Tropez but smaller. Everything here is miniature except the prices in the boutiques and bars lining Via Roma. It's obvious the town is exclusive from the yachts berthed in the small port. Arriving by car is a risky proposition and the parking in Piazza della Libertà is generally full by 9 A.M. during the summer. Fortunately there are other options and the town's pedestrian atmosphere is liberating.

Sights

Portofino is within the Parco Naturale di Portofino that was instituted to protect the great number of fauna and vegetation growing on the promontory. There are several panoramic roads and numerous itineraries to follow on foot but most people start with a visit of town, and **Piazza Martiri** is people-watching central in summer.

Castello San Giorgio (tel. 018/526-9046, daily 10 A.M.–5 P.M., €3.50) is accessed from the steps near the church of the same name by the port. There's a good view of the town and the gulf below. If you prefer nature to glamor, continue along the olive- and pine-covered path towards the **lighthouse**. It's especially beautiful in the early evening before the sunset when the last rays of light illuminate the entire bay. Plan on about an hour to get there and back.

Events

The sailing season opens officially with the **Spring Regattas** held in mid-May. The races are organized by the **Italian Yacht Club** (tel. 010/246-1206, www.yachtclubitaliano.it) and take place off the Portofino peninsula. Participation is high and includes Wally and Swan classes. Regattas can be followed from the port or the coastal trails that run above the rocky shore.

Shopping

Portofino is not the place to find a bargain. All the big designer names have opened stores here, including Armani, Hermes, Dolce & Gabbana, Missoni, and Louis Vuitton. Beautiful salespeople can be a little intimidating but they are always happy to find your size.

Sports and Recreation

Before Portofino became trendy, it was just another undiscovered fishing village where men woke before dawn to cast their nets in the Ligurian Sea. To get an idea of the old way of life and enjoy a half-day reeling in sea bass, contact the **Cooperativa Pescatori** (Camogli, Via della Repubblica 140, tel. 018/577-2600). *Pescaturismo* (fishing holidays) are becoming more frequent along the coast and although the cooperative is based in the nearby town of Camogli, they'll happily pick you up in Portofino and take you where the fish are always biting.

© LAURIE ELIE

yachts in the small harbor in Portofino

Accommodations

Portofino isn't the place to stay if you're counting euros. It's become a regular haunt of celebrities and millionaires and prices have gone up accordingly. **San Giorgio** (Via del Fondaco 11, tel. 018/526-991, www.por tofinohsg.it, €250 d) isn't the most expensive but it's one of the brightest hotels in town. The 18 rooms are all painted in Ligurian pastels and soundproofed to ensure a good night sleep. Room service is available 24 hours a day and the plasma TVs are equipped with satellite channels and Internet. Several suites come with Turkish baths.

The most elegant cocktail in town is served at the **Hotel Splendido** (Via Roma 2, tel. 018/526-7801, www.hotelsplendido. com, €500 and up). The Duke of Windsor was the first person to sign the guest book in 1952 and Bogart, Bacall, and Gable all stayed here. Today the hotel has lost none of its class and the views from the terrace will cure what ails you.

Food

Piazza Martiri is a popular place to stop for a coffee or light snack and the tables on the square are full from breakfast until dinner. A short distance away is a small trattoria that's reasonably priced and has a few outdoor tables that tend to fill up fast. **El Portico** (Via Roma 21, tel. 018/526-9239, Wed.–Mon. noon–2:30 P.M. and 7–10:30 P.M., €10–12) serves traditional Ligurian dishes and their pesto comes in several different varieties. Waiters can be slightly distracted and a menu in English is available if you want to understand all the ingredients. For a view of the bay and a taste of gourmet, try **Puny** (Piazza Martiri 5, tel. 018/526-9037, Fri.–Wed. 12:30–3 P.M. and 7–11:30 P.M., €11–14). Contrary to what the name suggests, their wine list is the longest in town and contains all of the top Ligurian labels.

Information and Services

The **IAT information office** (Via Roma 35, tel. 018/526-9024) has maps of town and trails around the park. Small boats can be rented by the hour or day from **Mussini Giorgio** (Calata Marconi 39, tel. 018/526-9327). Don't worry if you've never held an oar and can't distinguish between bow and stern. These light craft are easy to operate and great for exploring the coast around the peninsula.

Getting There and Around
The beauty of Portofino is a sharp contrast to the chaotic traffic that fills the only road into town during the summer. Driving all the way is a nightmare in high season and it's wiser to leave the car in Santa Margherita and complete the five-kilometer journey by foot along the panoramic path, via the public bus, or better yet by boat.

Servizio Marittimo del Tigullio (tel. 018/528-4670) runs frequent ferry service from Rapallo, Santa Margherita, and San Fruttuoso. A round-trip costs €3–12.50 depending on the season and the port of departure.

Around Portofino
The isolated village of **San Fruttuoso** is on the coast in the center of the park. You can get here by boat from Camogli or Portofino in under a half-hour. Otherwise it's a little over two hours by foot through a wonderfully scenic path from Portofino. If you choose the latter option bring along a picnic, as there are several rest areas where you can stop to eat while enjoying great views of the sea.

The hamlet is famous for **Abbazia di San Fruttuoso** (tel. 018/577-2703, Oct.–Apr. daily 10 A.M.–4 P.M., May–Sept. daily 10 A.M.–6 P.M., €4.50), a beautiful monastery situated among olive trees in a narrow valley directly on the beach that can only be reached by sea or on foot along a dirt path from Portofino (90 minutes). Inside is a 12th-century courtyard and tombs of the wealthy Doria family who financed much of the complex. A small museum recounts the abbey's history and the life of the Benedictine monks who once called it home. The other main attraction is a bronze statue of Christ standing on the seabed with outstretched arms that can be seen at low tide.

The former medieval town of **Santa Margherita** near Portofino seems big in comparison. It has developed into a vibrant resort with stylish hotels and a bustling harbor that still does a brisk trade in fish. Visit **Villa Durazzo** (Piazzale S. Giacomo 3, tel. 018/520-5449), the 16th-century villa above town, for excellent views of the coast.

◖ CINQUE TERRE
The Cinque Terre is one of those magical places that remains in the mind long after you've left the crystal-clear water, terraced vineyards, and olive groves behind. It's an area best covered on foot and hikers will have no shortage of paths to ponder. If you prefer swimming or sailing this is the perfect place to spend several days beach hopping. The five villages that give the area its name are Monterosso, Vernazza, Corniglia, Manarola, and Riomaggiore. Each is more charming than the next and visiting just one would be a shame. All were named world heritage sites by UNESCO and deserve exploration. From Genova, the first town in

the rocky coastline of the Cinque Terre

the quintet is **Monterosso al Mare,** the only one with an ample beach and boardwalk. **Vernazza** is full of steep steps, known as *arpaie* in the local dialect. **Corniglia** is slightly inland surrounded by the terraced vineyards that produce the local dry white wines. **Manarola** and **Riomaggiore** are a patchwork of houses and are the most authentic of the bunch.

The arrival of the 21st century has had little impact on the Cinque Terre. The five isolated villages built on rocky cliffs north of Portovenere are still hard to reach and that's probably why they've conserved many of their traditions and all of their magnificent landscape. It is one of the few places in Italy protected by a national park and marine sanctuary. Sustainability is on many people's lips, and cars are almost entirely off-limits. Although train service connects the towns, walking is the most rewarding means of transportation here. The Apennines that run behind the coast shelter the area from north winds and the Ligurian Sea keeps temperatures mild throughout the year.

If you plan on hiking up or down the Cinque Terre travel light and make as many stops as time allows. If bags are a problem use Corniglia as a base and take day-trips in either direction. There are trails for all levels. **Cinque Terre High Trail** is one of the most challenging and runs slightly inland. It takes about six hours to complete the entire route but you can always decide to cut it short and take one of the many tributary trails that travel down to the villages. The **Blue Trail** is the most famous and links the towns. The 11 kilometers can be covered in five hours and there's a €3 fee to walk this route. If Cinque Terre is the reason you've come to Italy then you won't want to miss the **Sanctuary Trail.** There are sanctuaries in the hills above each town and the 12 kilometer trail that connects them is less trodden than the others. Between the towns of Riomaggiore and Manarola the trail is called the **Via dell'Amore** for reasons that quickly become obvious. It's partially carved out of the rock and takes vertigo-inducing swists and turns along the coast. If you came to Italy for romance, this is the place to get down on one knee or pop any questions you may have. The well-indicated path starts just outside the Riomaggiore train station.

If you're interested in a guided tour of the area, **Cooperativa Arte e Natura** (Via Firenze 27, La Spezia, tel. 018/771-2038) is a good option.

Vernazza

Vernazza is the most fascinating of the villages, with a Gothic church and colorful houses overlooking a small port that remains quite active. This town is near the highest point along the coast and the trail down into town weaves past Mediterranean shrub and ancient fields. It was founded around 1,000 A.D. and has always been closely linked with the sea. The architecture is distinct, and elaborately carved loggias and porticos provide hints of economic prosperity that the other Cinque Terre towns never attained. Arrival here by sea is the best way to admire the pastel houses and cafés that line the port.

Corniglia

It's hard to find Agostino Galletti in a bad mood. Most days he's inside his small traditional *osteria* making diners smile with Ligurian humor and recipes. **A Cantina de Manana** (Via Fieschi 117, tel. 018/782-1166, Wed.–Mon. 12:30–3 P.M. and 7–10:30 P.M., €8–11, cash only) serves anchovies marinated with oil and covered in onions. If you don't like fried or grilled fish, there's still the rabbit or pesto to try. A few local wines are stored in the canteen and the *sciacchetrà* dessert shouldn't be missed.

At number 159 on the same street, **Er Cantu** offers a wide selection of cheeses, pesto, and other local specialties.

Manarola

Fishing is still an important source of livelihood to the residents of this town, who don't generally warm to visitors. Don't take it personally as even people from the next town over are considered strangers. Sunday mass inside the 13th-century church is well attended and Riomaggiore is only 15 minutes away on the Via dell'Amore.

terraced vineyards in Manarola

© LAURIE ELIE

You might not want to stay at ☾ **Ca'd'Andrean** (Via Discovolo 101, tel. 018/792-0040, cadandrean@libero.it, €85 d) if you've come with multiple suitcases. This hotel is on a steep pedestrian street in the high part of town. The 10 large rooms have been refurbished with hints of a farming past that are the definition of rustic. Downstairs a large chimney dominates the sitting room and guests can rest under lemon trees in the garden after a day of hiking. The hotel only accepts cash and the plentiful breakfast is an additional €6. **Marina Piccola** (Via Lo Scalo 16, tel. 018/792-0103, www.hotelmarinapiccola.com, €115 d) is another lodging option in town.

Riomaggiore

If there are more senior citizens in Liguria than anywhere else in Italy it has something to do with villages like Riomaggiore. Just getting to the bakery is a workout and the steep steps are what keep the local doctor's waiting room empty. The old houses are clustered around a narrow valley and layers of black rock typical of the region surround the tiny port.

A good place to begin a visit of the area is **Hotel due Gemelli** (Via. Litoranea 1, tel. 018/792-0678, duegemelli@tin.it, €80), four kilometers east of town. There's no direct access to the sea but the view from each of the 13 rooms is a great way to start the day. The panorama from the terrace where meals are served is equally stunning at this family-run hotel that values simplicity over luxury.

☾ **Ripa del Sole** (Via de Gaspari 282, tel. 018/792-0143, Tues.–Sun. noon–3 P.M. and 7–10:30 P.M., closed Nov., €8–12) is in the high part of town. The restaurant run by a brother-and-sister team is decorated with a fishing theme and the large indoor dining room has wide windows from which to admire the sea. In summer the terrace opens. Don't skip the antipasti that includes dozens of stuffed and fried vegetables. Fish ravioli and seafood risotto are highlights of the first course. The wine list covers many Ligurian whites as well as some DOC-caliber wines from other parts of Italy.

If all you want is a light snack stop in at **Al Bar Amore** in a prime position along the Via dell'Amore. Their white house wine goes perfectly with the anchovies they serve.

Monterosso

Monterosso is the western most town of the Cinque Terre where the Sentiero Azzurro (Blue Trail) is at its most challenging. One of the best beaches in Liguria is near this town's port—it's cozy and small and the crystalline water is mesmerizing. Facilities with umbrellas, pedalboats, and motorboats are open from May to October. The most impressive building is the medieval **Aurora tower** on Cappuccini hill. The **church of San Francesco** contains some notable art, including a painting attributed to Van Dyck.

Information and Services

The main tourist office is **Consorzio Turistico Cinque Terre** (Monterosso al Mare, Piazza Garibaldi 29, www.cinqueterre.it). Each of the towns in the Cinque Terre has a small information office in its rail station. You can pick up maps as well as the **Cinque Terre Card,** valid one (€5), two (€8), three (€10), or seven (€18) days. Among other benefits, the card provides access to all trails, entry to museums such as the aquarium in Monterosso, use of a bicycle for three hours, and discounts at the visitors centers scattered around the coast.

Getting There and Around

By car from Genova, take the A12 and exit at Casello di Carrodano to reach Monterosso. From the south, drive along the Litoranea to reach Riomaggiore and Manarola. The narrow tortuous road that looks like it's poorly maintained on purpose connects the towns but is probably best avoided unless you're training for Paris–Dakar.

Rail is the ideal means of reaching all five towns in the Cinque Terre. Departures from La Spezia, which is on the Genova–Pisa line, are frequent. During spring and summer, there are ferry connections to the towns from La Spezia, Lerici, and Porto Venere. There is also regular rail service between the towns themselves.

PORTOVENERE

Portovenere is in the extreme western edge of the Golfo dei Poeti (Gulf of Poets) and one of Liguria's World Heritage Sites. The center expanded significantly in 1100 when the Genovese captured the area while the castle was a later addition transformed into a prison during the Napoleonic interlude.

Directly in front of the town is the island of Palmaria, a regional park with a white marble quarry and plenty of caves. Trails along the island are immersed in Mediterranean vegetation and if you climb to the top you can see the *isolotti* (small islands) of Tino and Tinetto that are navy property and off-limits to the public.

Sights

The 12th-century church of **San Lorenzo** stands in the upper part of town and contains an intricate marble altar by unknown artists. The sculpture above the door is a reminder of how the saint met his death. A flight of steps leads from the piazza outside the church to the **Castello Doria** (daily 10 A.M.–1 P.M. and 2–5 P.M., €2.10) that was built on pre-existing Roman fortifications. This is the best view of the pastel houses and the entire gulf. Town hall recently had the idea to rent the castle out for weddings and you can get married here for €610. The lower part of town is squeezed into a long promontory. Narrow streets culminate with **San Pietro.** Like many other Italian churches, San Pietro was built in gratitude of something and in this case it was a victory over the Pisans. The builders chose a great spot on a small promontory and laid their stones on top of Paleo-Christian and pagan ruins. The roof was completed in 1277 after 21 years of labor. On the outside of the church horizontal strips of black-and-white marble decorate an austere facade and bells in the campanile tower keep locals on time.

Entertainment and Events

Women take center stage during the month of August for **Teatro Donna** (tel. 018/779-4800), when Piazza San Pietro and Castello Doria become the background for female creativity.

fishing boats along the promenade in Portovenere

© LAURIE ELIE

Events include theater, music, and dance involving artists and companies from around Europe. On the last day of the festival, audiences elect their favorite performer.

Accommodations

Even in Italy, hotels built into the side of castles are rare, but that's only part of **Genio's** (Piazza Bastreri 8, tel. 018/779-0611, €85–105 s/d) attraction. It's also located in the center and priced well below most other hotels in town. The seven rooms are simple and a television is about the only concession to modernity, but they score high on atmosphere.

Albergo Ristorante Paradiso (Via Garibaldi 34–40, tel. 018/779-0612, www.hotel portovenere.it, €115–140 s/d) is a 21-room hotel overlooking the gulf. Breakfast is served on the terrace with views of l'Isola Palmaria until 10 A.M. and at night the restaurant cooks grilled fish and Ligurian classics. You can leave your passport in the room safe and ask the hotel shuttle to drop you off in any of the adjacent towns.

Food

La Pizzaccia (Via Capellini 96–98, tel. 018/779-2722, Fri.–Wed. 9 A.M.–9 P.M., daily in Aug., €5) makes a good *farinata*. They add pepper and rosemary and use an electric oven but the result is still delicious. The dining area is small and slices of vegetable pizza and *focaccine* (small focaccia) with pesto can be wrapped to go. San Pietro and the old *borgo* nearby are wonderful to explore while you chew.

Getting There and Around

By car take the La Spezia–Santo Stefano–Magra exit off the A12 and continue along the Aurelia until you reach Portovenere. The closest train station is La Spezia, from where **ATC** (018/752-2511) buses complete the 10-kilometer journey around the gulf.

There are plenty of boats waiting to take tourists around the island of Palmaria for closer examination of the sea caves, including Grotta Azzura. **Navigazione Golfo dei Poeti** (www. navigazionegolfodeipoeti.it) leaves six times a day 10 A.M.–4:30 P.M. The one-hour cruise costs €10. They also make longer trips to the Cinque Terre and can drop you off on Palmaria if you feel like exploring the island for a couple of hours. **Consorzio Barcaioli** (www.barcaioliportovenere.com) runs excursions up and down the coast and organizes snorkeling and diving trips. They're located to the left of the only dock. If you feel like setting your own course you can rent a boat from **Franco Vigna** (Calata Doria, tel. 338/395-2994) or **Palmaria Noleggio** (Calata Doria, tel. 338/854-8957). Prices are generally posted on the craft.

LERICI

Lerici is one of the last coastal towns before the Tuscan border, across the gulf from Portovenere. What was a fishing village is now a popular resort where D. H. Lawrence and Yeats once tanned themselves. The public beach is walking distance from the imposing castle built to protect the bay.

Sights

Castello Monumentale di Lerici (Piazza San Giorgio, tel. 018/796-9042, Tues.–Sun. 10:30 A.M.–1 P.M. and 2:30–6 P.M., www.castellodilerici.it, €5) sits high above town and is one of the best examples of military architecture in Liguria. It was the site of many skirmishes between Pisan and Genovese sailors, who captured the castle from their rivals in 1256. They added the pentagon-shaped tower and thickened the walls by several feet. A little Gothic chapel has remained where defenders prayed before battle. The castle also contains a small geological museum with prehistoric fossils and often hosts special exhibits. Concerts are occasionally organized in the courtyard that's populated with plastic models of dinosaurs.

Recreation

A short distance from the center is the free beach of **Venere Azzurra** (www.venereazzurra.com), which has received the prestigious *Bandiera Blu* (blue flag) rating since 2000 for the quality of the water and services. There are three restaurants on the beach, aqua gym classes, babysitting, and water skiing. Chairs and umbrellas can be rented and a newspaper kiosk nearby supplies reading materials in English.

Under water between Maramozza and Maralunga are the remains of a Roman ship and its cargo, a popular site for divers. **Oasi Blu** (Cadimare, Via della Marina 32, tel. 018/777-8305) arranges dives there and other points between Lerici and the Cinque Terre. A full-day excursion with lunch onboard their 17-meter boat is €80 on weekdays and €160 on weekends.

Accommodations

Doria Park (Via Doria 2, tel. 018/796-7124, www.doriaparkhotel.com, €75–100 s/d) has won awards for their breakfast buffet, which covers all the food groups and should keep you filled until well past lunch. Rooms vary from standard doubles overlooking the private park surrounding the hotel to suites that come with a rooftop veranda where you can soak in a hot tub while you enjoy the view. Lerici is only two minutes away on foot but many guests prefer to spend their afternoons on one of three terraces.

Food

You can order à la carte or choose from one of three fixed-price menus at **Trattoria San Rocco** (Via Marconi 6, tel. 018/796-7269, Fri.–Wed. noon–3 P.M. and 7–10:30 P.M., €7–9). The €20 option includes three courses of fish, coffee, a carafe of wine, and half-liter of water. The family-run restaurant benefits from a central location and during the summer they set tables up in Piazza Garibaldi.

Information and Services

The IAT office is located on Via Biaggini near the Venere Azzurra beach. From May until September the office is open daily 9 A.M.–noon and 3–6 P.M. They take Sunday afternoons off.

Getting There and Around

From La Spezia train station, you can take the L or S bus that leave every 15 minutes. The

LIGURIA

journey varies depending on the time of departure. The ride to Lerici costs €1.15. You can also arrive to town on the Lazzi (tel. 055/363-0441) bus from destinations in Tuscany, including Viareggio, Lucca, and Florence.

Around Lerici

La Spezia is a mediumsized navy town with a large industrial port that builds yachts, among other things. It's not the kind of place you'd normally want to see but being halfway between Portovenere and Lerici makes it hard to avoid. The one bright spot is **Museo Lia** (tel. 018/773-1100, Tues.–Sun. 10 A.M.–6 P.M., €6), located within a 16th-century convent that contains 1,100 artifacts collected by Amedio Lia and donated to the city. The pieces range in age and are divided into several themes, such as Roman, religious artifacts, paintings, and glass. The first room contains a wooden Madonna and child from the 13th century, a Roman bust that may have been Caligula's sister, and Baroque ivory cups. Lea had an eclectic taste and was as interested in old French crosses as he was Italian painters. You'll leave the museum with a new appreciation of history.

Riviera di Ponente

Riviera di Ponente is virtually a continuous stretch of beach. Some towns like Albenga also have beautiful historic centers full of medieval towers while Sanremo is a favorite with Italian holidaymakers and the site of the country's annual song festival. Inland, a stark contrast to the busy sands, winding roads lead to small villages and mushrooms and olives outnumber tourists. The exceptional year-round sunlight has been a boon for floriculturists who grow plants in the countless gardens and nurseries that line the coast.

SAVONA

The historic center of Savona is concentrated within a rectangle of streets made up of Corso Mazzini and Via Paleocapa in the north and south and Via Manzoni and Gramsci on either end. Inside are a score of Renaissance buildings, a 15th-century Duomo, and the fortress where the patriot Giuseppe Mazzini was imprisoned in 1830. The port is one of the busiest in Italy and ships Fiats around the world.

Sights

Palazzo Ferrero may now be the chamber of commerce, but it was once home to the most important merchants. What's impressive about the inside is the succession of frescoes by Ottavio Semino and his helpers who managed to cover all the ceilings and walls above the central staircase that leads to the second floor and a view of the port.

When the Genovese captured Savona in 1542, they destroyed much of the area around the port and built a fortress to ensure their domination lasted. **Priamar** is not a very friendly-looking building and wasn't meant to be. It's an excellent example of military architecture and contains remnants of pre-existing *palazzi* within the thick defensive walls. Today the complex houses the **Museo Civico Archeologico** (Corso Mazzini, tel. 019/822-708, www.museoarcheosavona.it, Tues.–Sat. 10 A.M.–noon and 3–5 P.M., Sun. 3–5 P.M., €3) with a collection of Roman finds dating from the second Punic War, two art museums, and a youth hostel.

The church of **Nostra Signora di Castello** next to the Duomo contains several fine paintings by Vincenzo Foppa picturing the Madonna surrounded by various saints.

Shopping

Every Monday from morning until evening the central market in Piazza del Popolo is alive with street vendors. There are over 270 stalls selling everything from vegetables and fruit to shoes and household items. Although prices are often listed you can always try bartering

LE BANDIERE BLU

You can tell a good beach in Italy by the flag. *Le Bandiere Blu* (blue flags) are the sign of a clean stretch of sand. They're awarded each year by the Foundation for Environmental Education and you won't find them everywhere. The distinction is difficult to achieve and there are less than 100 in the entire country. It takes serious commitment by communities to respect and care for nature. Beaches are judged on the quality of the water, the overall condition of the coastline, services provided to bathers, and for educational initiatives that help future generations avoid the pollution mistakes of the past. Liguria received 13 blue flags in 2007. The beaches are distributed across all four provinces, with Savona home to over half.

Genova: Chiavari, Lavagna, Moneglia
La Spezia: Lerici
Imperia: Camporosso, Bordighera
Savona: Spotorno, Bergheggi, Savona, Albisola Superiore, Celle Ligure, Varazze

especially towards the end of the day when merchants are eager to get rid of any remaining goods. If you're interested in any of the shoes or clothing, try items on before you buy.

Accommodations

You barely need a map to find **Mare** (Via Nizza 89r, tel. 019/264-065, www.marehotel.it, €150–210 s/d), which is off the highway directly on the sea. The beach out in front of the hotel is a constant temptation and the town is walking distance away if you prefer a little history. Rooms are modern and come in several varieties, with the Presidential suites providing the most comfort at reasonable prices. On the grounds there's a swimming pool and a restaurant that specializes in fish and provides a pleasant ambiance before a midnight stroll along the water.

Food

Fried dough may not sound appetizing, but at **Vino e Farinata** (Via Pia 15r, Tues.–Sat.

noon–2 P.M. and 6–9:30 P.M., €7–10) it's made the classic way with chickpea flour and has been satisfying Ligurian appetites for centuries. The dish is only one of the simple recipes you'll find at this trattoria, which has survived without a telephone and where diners wait to be seated in one of two dining rooms. Daily specials are handwritten on a paper menu with a strong selection of fish and some inland specialties like the minestrone. Dessert options are slim and the wine list could be improved, but the moderate prices and friendly atmosphere should leave you in a forgiving mood.

In the Fornaci neighborhood west of the Letimbro River **L'Arcata dell'Homo** (Via Saredo 100r, tel. 019/801-670, Wed.–Sun. 7–10:30 P.M., €7–9) specializes in white (chickpea) and yellow (fermented) *farinata*. Service is friendly and portions leave little room for seconds. Ligurian classics like stuffed anchovies and *buridda* (fish stew) are also served in this rustic two-room restaurant.

The covered market in Via Giuria is filled with vegetable and fish stalls. In the morning, the *tripperia* stands sell a broth made of tripe and **Il Grigio**, a stand within the market, usually has a stunning display of freshly netted crustaceans.

Getting There and Around

Trains from Genova, Milan, and Rome all make stops in Savona. The station is 800 meters from Piazza Mameli, where a line of taxis is usually waiting. From Genova or Ventimiglia by car take the *casello autostrada di Savona* exit four kilometers from the center.

NOLI

Noli never got the recognition it deserved. It's like a fifth Beatle that was overshadowed by Genova in the 14th century but at one point rivaled the other four maritime republics. The town lies southwest of Savona in a small bay that Greek settlers found appealing when the town was still known as Neapolis.

Sights

The glory days are evident in *borgo medievale*, where buildings like the 14th-century

LIGURIA

Palazzo del Comune and San Pietro hint of an illustrious past. San Paragorio is the most ancient church in town and the crucifix inside is nearly 1,000 years old.

Today fishermen still bring a good haul back to port every morning and the old houses and medieval towers lining the streets provide a strong whiff of seafaring history.

Accommodations
None of the hotels are exceptional in Noli but most are located near the sea. That's the case with **Miramare** (Corso Italia 2, www. hotelmiramarenoli.it, €70–100 s/d) where you can fall asleep listening to the waves in one of their pink or blue rooms. The three-story building with green shutters doesn't show its age and the restaurant on the ground floor has large glass windows where dinners can observe the happenings on the promenade. It actually starts to grow on you but if you prefer accommodations with a small private beach slightly outside of town, then maybe the **Monique** (Lungomare di Noli, tel. 019/748-268, www. monique.it, €75 d) is the answer.

Food
Closing Piazza Milite Ignoto to traffic was one of the best things that ever happened in Noli and did wonders for **Caffè Gino** (Piazza Milite Ignoto 1, tel. 019/748-457, daily 7 A.M.–9 P.M., €5 and up). Tables have replaced cars on the sidewalk and views of the clocktower and flowered balconies are undisturbed by *motorini*. Nearby **Pasticceria-Focacceria Scalvini** (Via Columbo 3, tel. 019/748-201, daily 8 A.M.–1 P.M. and 3 P.M.–7 P.M.) has been turning out bread and pastries for over 200 years. The almond tarts and focaccia make a great takeaway snack.

Getting There and Around
By car exit the A10 at Savona and continue west along the Aurelia until you reach town. The nearest train station is the Spotorno–Noli, from which buses regularly complete the journey into town.

ALBENGA
The plain around Albenga is the most extensive in Liguria but it wasn't always as fertile as it is today. It took centuries for farmers to transport sand from the coast and transform swampland into high-nutrient soil. One of the results of their efforts is a unique violet asparagus that has 40 chromosomes instead of the usual 20. A great number of fruits and vegetables are also grown and should be tasted.

The town has conserved its Roman street plan and has one of the best historic centers on the Riviera di Ponente. It's a necessary stop for anyone tired with the monotony of lying on a beach.

Sights
The medieval heart of Albenga is clustered around the cathedral of **San Michele** and a late Gothic tower built in the 13th century. In the central nave there is a trompe l'oeil that has caused double-takes since it was painted. The **baptistery** nearby is from the 5th century and covered with mosaics representing the 12 apostles similar to those in Ravenna. It's one of the oldest Christian buildings in all of Liguria. Behind the baptistery is a small cobblestone piazza with stone lions that originally stood in Rome and give the piazza its name.

Museo Navale Romano (Palazzo Peloso-Cepolla, tel. 018/251-215, Tues.–Sun. 9:30 A.M.–12:30 P.M. and 3:30–7:30 P.M., €3) shows how the Romans used the seas to spread their influence around the Mediterranean. The star attraction is a 40-meter boat that carried up to 10,000 amphorae (clay vases), which were once a standard unit of trade. Many of these vases are on display, and there's also an extensive collection of black ceramics.

Sports and Recreation
Sightseeing and sweat can be combined during the **Albenga marathon and half-marathon** (tel. 018/255-8444) held in the historic center. The course is 4,210 meters long and you'll need to complete 10 laps to receive a medal. The race is held in mid-June and starts at 6 P.M. from Piazza San Michele.

Autumn and winter are the windiest seasons in the region; waves can reach substantial heights and surfers in wetsuits start paddling out to sea. The beaches around Varazze and Andora are the closest Liguria gets to California and offer especially good conditions for windsurfers and kitesurfers. If you'd like to try a new water sport or keep your surf skills from getting rusty, you can rent long and short boards from **Surfactivity** (Via Nazario Sauro 112, tel. 018/253-426, Tues.–Sat. 9 A.M.–12:30 P.M. and 3:30 P.M.–7:30 P.M.). They'll also give you a meteorological update and let you know where the waves are best on any particular day.

Accommodations

The Zanchi family is proud of their retro decor and laugh at the suggestion of a makeover. You won't find anything modern at **Marisa** (Via Pisa 28, tel. 018/250-241, www.marisahotel. com, €65–85 s/d), only large rooms with wood paneling and Liberty lamps that would make a good setting for an Agatha Christie novel. Downstairs in the lobby guests play chess while they wait for breakfast to be served in the large dining room with dotted ceiling. Half-board is available during the summer and the barman makes a decent Bloody Mary.

Food

Marco and his father may not seem the most gracious hosts but behind the rough exterior the owners of **◖ Hosteria Sutta Ca** (Via Ernesto Rolando Ricci 10, tel. 018/253-198, Mon.–Sat. 12:30–2:30 P.M. and 7–10 P.M., closed Thurs. evening, €7–9) are really quite friendly. The menu is recited orally and lacks *antipasti*. Instead *focaccette* and slices of vegetable cake are immediately brought to your table to help pass the wait. First courses are generous and the pesto dishes (lasagna and *gnochetti*) are popular with local diners. There's also a good selection of vegetable side dishes, but make sure to leave room for the almond and marmalade desserts.

Essaouira Beach (Via Michelangelo Vadino, tel. 081/255-5547, www.essaouira.it,

daily during summer 9 A.M.–late-night, €20) brings a little bit of Morocco to Liguria. During the day it's a great place to enjoy the beach and at night it is a lively restaurant and bar. You enter through a large Arabian-style portal leading to a tented restaurant that lights up with candles as soon as the sun goes down. There's an *aperitivo* every day and on weekends dancing on the tables is encouraged. If fire breathing isn't your thing, there's always a bamboo lounge chair available on the private beach.

Getting There and Around

Aeroporto Internazionale Clemente Panero (Villanova D'albenga, Viale Generale Disegna) is a small regional airport with regular flights from Rome. **Airone** (www.flyairone.it) is the main carrier and a round-trip ticket purchased 21 days in advance on the Internet costs €116.50. Bus service links the airport with Albenga and Alessio. Hertz (tel. 018/264-8242) and Maggiore (018/264-3382) have rental offices within the arrivals terminal.

Around Albenga

◖ GROTTE DI TOIRANO

Italian cavemen and women made their homes in Grotte di Toirano (Toirano, Piazzale delle Grotte, tel. 018/298-062, www.toiranogrotte. it, daily 9:30 A.M.–12:30 P.M. and 2–5 P.M., €9), 10 kilometers north of Albenga. The Neolithic hunters who once lived here left behind footprints, torches, and clay weapons. You can even get an idea of their diets from the animal bones in **Grotta della Basura.** The long series of caves is filled with stalactites and stalagmites and the last section has incredibly smooth walls. Professional tour guides take small groups through the passageways on a journey back in time. There are daily buses from Albenga and Loana.

ALASSIO

For centuries Alassio was an anonymous fishing village dominated by the larger towns along the coast. In the 19th century, the residents recognized the potential of tourism and the

LIGURIA

first hotels were built. Fortunately none of the charm was sacrificed and typical neighborhoods like the **Il Budello** centered around Via XX Settembre were left undisturbed. The small island of Gallinara opposite town has also been preserved and is now part of a regional park and a popular morning or afternoon trip.

Sights

Il Budello is a typical Ligurian *caruggio* (narrow street) that runs parallel to the coast. Along the passageways you'll pass many well-preserved *palazzi*. The intersection where Via Vittorio Veneto and Vico Freghetti meet is the center of the neighborhood and notable for the Napoleonic **Palazzo Scofferi**, which now houses a pharmacy on the ground floor and has especially large windows. At Via XX Settembre 23 is the old **Palazzo Comunale**, which features a rotating series of art exhibits on the first floor. Various events are organized for children in the small adjoining garden equipped with benches that are perfect for taking a five-minute breather. A little farther down stands **Palazzo Bonfante**, built in the 18th century. The family coat of arms is prominently displayed above the white marble entrance. Many of the facades are painted with religious scenarios and niches above the entrances contain sculptures of the Madonna. Il Budello ends in **Piazza Partigiani**, which was created in the 1930s where a monastery once stood.

Alassio's walk-of-fame is called the **Muretto.** Instead of stars, celebrities have marked their passage through town by signing colorful ceramic plaques in a wall near Via XX Settembre.

Accommodations

A view of the sea has a price but €10 seems reasonable enough. Parking, however, is free and a sense of relaxation almost immediate at **Hotel Beau Sejour** (Via Garibaldi 102, tel. 018/264-3075, www.beausejourhotel.it, €135 d). The lobby is decorated simply with white armchairs and antique mirrors where guests peruse a vast collection of books from the library. The fourth-floor terrace is a great

place to spend a couple of hours squinting at the Mediterranean and the barman will deliver drinks to the beach if you prefer spending time on the sand directly in front of the hotel. Rooms are comfortable and remain completely dark even after the sun rises.

Sports and Recreation

In nearly every beach resort along the coast you'll find a sailing school or club where boats can be rented by the hour. There are also week-long sailing camps and competitions organized for experienced skippers. If you ever wanted to learn how to sail, this is the place to learn to tie real knots and come to terms with rigging. **CNAM Circolo Nautico al Mare** (Porticciolo L. Ferrari, tel. 018/264-2516) has patient instructors that take novices on small boats to get acquainted with the wind.

Food

I Mattetti (Viale Hanbury 132, tel. 018/264-6680, Tues.–Sun. noon–2:30 P.M. and 7–10:30 P.M., open daily in summer but only dinner in Aug., €8–10) is a recent addition to Alassio's gastronomic scene, but dishes are more retro than nouveau. Options are written on the board in the front of the *osteria* that's covered with old elementary class photos. The seasons play a big part in what comes out of the kitchen and the chef seems to have a preference for ingredients derived from the earth. His vegetable pie and rabbit cooked Ligurian-style prove that the region isn't only about fish.

Osteria Mezzaluna (Vico Berna 6, tel. 018/264-0387, Tues.–Sun., daily in summer, 12:30–2:30 P.M. and 7:30–10:30 P.M., €7–10) satisfies any cravings for local cheese and cold cuts. Tables and walls are decorated with *maioliche* tiles and live music isn't uncommon. The *bruschette* make a good starter and there are several hot options on the menu.

Via Neghelli is notable for **Pasticceria Briano,** which prepares wonderful pastries and sells traditional desserts such as the chocolate *baci di Alassio* (kisses of Alessio) and *gobeletti* (jelly-filled pastry).

Getting There and Around

From Genova on the A10, take the Albenga exit and follow the signs for eight kilometers until town. If you arrive from the opposite direction, exit at Andora. Stazione Ferroviaria di Alassio is conveniently located in the center of town. The nearest airport is Aeroporto di Villanova d'Albenga.

CERVO

Unlike most villages along the Riviera di Ponente, which are at sea level, Cervo was founded on a small ridge above the coast. The narrow lanes that crisscross the town are a reminder of the early Middle Ages. The castle at the top that once dissuaded enemies from attacking now hosts exhibits about the history and culture of the region. Tourism has replaced coral fishing as the major employer without disturbing the character of this down-to-earth town.

Sights

Baroque made it all the way to Cervo and the best example of the style is the concave facade of **San Giovanni Battista** (Via Due Giugno 13, tel. 018/340-8095, daily 8 A.M.–7:30 P.M., chorus rehearses on Wed. at 3 P.M.), started in 1686. The architects were as concerned about the stairs as anything else, which accentuate the height of the church as well as the thin *campanile.* The bell tower is the tallest building in town and rings out every hour. Inside the church parishioners outnumber tourists drawn to the colorful naves. It's remarkably cool and explains how past generations survived with air-conditioning.

Entertainment

The **International Chamber Music Festival** (tel. 018/344-9111, www.cervo.com) takes places in July and August. It's held outdoors in Piazza San Giovanni (opposite the cathedral) and presents a series of world-class solo artists and chamber orchestras with a few jazz detours. The public knows the music almost as well as the musicians and never fails to applaud at the right moments.

Sports and Recreation

The nearby *circumnaviga* trails are four trails that wind steeply up the green hills immediately outside of town. Villa Colla is at the top and offers a great view of the coast. Trails start near each of the parking lots and are well indicated. Head north on the Red Trail for a workout that takes more than two hours to complete or head east for a leisurely climb toward Parco Comunale Ciapà. You can pick up a map of the trails from any of the newspaper kiosks in town. The shortest route is marked with a "1" circled in red and starts from Piazza Castello. Parts of the path follow the Via Aurelia, once used by the Romans to reach Gaul (modern-day France). The journey lasts about an hour and is doable for any level of hiker. On your way back to town you pass **il Pilone, Marina delle Reti,** and **il Porteghetto** beaches and can rent an umbrella and lounge chair from any of the *stabilimenti.*

Accommodations

Finding a hotel in Cervo is harder than you would think, considering how attractive the town is. **Le Notti Mediterranee** (Via Cavour 9, tel. 348/333-6899, www.lenottimediterra nee.com, €100 d) is a good bed-and-breakfast option in the center near a delightful little piazza. All three rooms have their own baths; **Brezza Mediterranea,** with a seashell theme and balcony, may be the most romantic of the trio. If you wake up before the other guests you can take the two bicycles for a tour of the promenade that straddles the sea.

Food

Don't expect to find a table without reserving in advance at **San Giorgio** (Via Volta 19, tel. 018/577-3411, Wed.–Sun. 12:30–3 P.M. and 7:30–11 P.M., €12–18). Fish is the main attraction and you can choose to eat one of several abundant prix-fixe options on the quiet street outside or inside this well-run restaurant.

Getting There and Around

Cervo is about a 100 kilometers from Genova at the San Bartolomeo al Mare exit. Very few trains stop in Cervo and you may find it easier to get off in Diano Marina and ride the public bus (€1) or taxi three kilometers into town.

TAGGIA

Taggia lies between fruit and olive trees in the valley of Argentina. In the 14th–15th centuries it was an important center of artistic activity and attracted many painters who bridged the gap between Gothic and Renaissance. The walls of the town are still well preserved and surround a wonderful collection of fountains and *palazzi*.

Sights

Ludovico Brea was one of the artists who called Taggia home. He spent most of his days painting inside the **Convento di San Domenico** (Piazza Beato Cristoforo 6, tel. 018/447-6254, daily 9 A.M.–noon and 3:30 P.M.–5 P.M., free admission). It took him years to complete the interior and remarkable expressive works like the *Battesimo di Cristo*. If you've come with a sketchpad, this is the occasion to use it. Across the 16th-century bridge and up the hill you'll come to **Santi Giacomo e Filippo,** which some say was designed by Bernini and others attribute to local architects. Whoever is responsible had a penchant for marble. This Baroque church has a vast, solemn interior containing a mix of architectural styles and some interesting paintings of the saints.

Food

Informality reigns at **Germinal** (Via Gastaldi 15b, tel. 018/441-153, Wed.–Sun 7–11 P.M., open weekend lunches during the summer, €8–11), where marble tables are covered with napkins and the menu isn't above a spelling mistake or two. Enrica and Roberta manage the *osteria* located in the center of town, while Danilo uses his experience as an fisherman to make sure everything that comes out of the kitchen causes immediate salivation. Fried anchovies, fish soup, and *tagliolini* with fish *ragù* are all safe bets. There are a few red wines from Piedmont and a local Vermentino that goes well with everything.

SANREMO

Tourists have loved Sanremo since Russian princesses and English barons made the town their stomping ground in the late 19th century. Some of the elegance has faded but the Casino is still operating and the Pigna neighborhood is a reminder that Sanremo has more to it than meets the eye.

Sights

The **Casino** (Corsodegli Inglesi 18, tel. 018/45951, slot machine room daily 10 A.M.–3 A.M., free admission; European and American game rooms daily 2:30 P.M.–3 A.M., €7.50 Fri.–Sun.; minimum age 18, I.D. required) started with a generous loan from a wealthy banker that allowed the construction of the Liberty-style building bordered by twin spires. The roulette tables started spinning in 1905 and encouraged heads of state, monarchs, and millionaires to try their luck. It's no surprise there's a rather strict dress code and you won't find anyone playing baccarat, roulette, or poker in t-shirts, shorts, and flip-flops. The casino isn't all about gambling, however, and frequently presents art shows and concerts in the theater.

La Pigna is a compact neighborhood on a hill that got its name due to its resemblance of a pinecone. It's full of narrow streets, stairways, covered passageways, and small shops. It is the town's medieval quarter which was built in concentric circles to dissuaded pirates from attacking. The arcaded streets and small piazzas are now only accessible by foot and haven't been spoiled by mass tourism. Start in Piazza Santa Stefano and work your way up to the sanctuary at the top of the hill. Via Palma is the principal street in town and is home to several interesting churches and bell towers.

Events

In Italy, Sanremo is famous for the annual **Festival della Canzone Italiana** (tel. 018/450-7070, www.sanremo.rai.it) held over five days at the end of February. It's a love-or-hate affair where Italian singers present a song especially composed for the event. A celebrity panel and millions of television viewers judge participants. Foreign celebrities make an appearance each year; John Travolta and Penelope Cruz have graced the stage of the Ariston Theater in past years.

Milan-Sanremo (tel. 018/450-2528) is a one-day bicycle race on the second Sunday of June that covers 290 grueling kilometers. It's contested by the world's top riders and usually ends with a final desperate sprint along Via Roma. Spectators pack the street several rows deep near the finish line in the center of town and bands entertain the crowds throughout the afternoon.

Accommodations

The moderate option in Sanremo is **Nyala** (Via Strada Solero 134, tel. 018/466-7668, www. nyalahotel.com, €100 d). It's popular with couples and is located in a residential part of town. Most of the 81 rooms are large. Many guests prefer spending time around the pool, which is surrounded by a tropical garden, rather than head to the beach. The high stakes option is the **Royal** (Corso Imperatrice 80, tel. 018/45391, www.royalhotelsanremo.com, €250 d), which has been open since 1872 and knows how to treat guests. The hotel is opposite the sea but the best view may be from the terrace. Bedrooms are comfortable and decorated in light pastoral colors that are easy on the eye. There's a swimming pool and gym, and leisure activities are organized by the front desk. Room service is available 24 hours a day.

Food

There's a wine for every palate inside **Enoteca Marone** (Via San Francesco 61, tel. 018/450-6916, Mon.–Sun.). The owners are passionate about grapes and choose the 1,200 labels themselves directly from producers. Bottles are elegantly displayed and if you ask for advice be prepared for a thesis. If you want to accompany drink with some traditional Ligurian starters try any of the *antipasta* options.

Getting There and Around

Sanremo is off the A10 and easily reached by car, train, or **Riviera Trasporti** (tel. 018/459-2706, www.rivieratrasporti.it) bus. The euro star service from Genova takes a little less than two hours and costs €13.

Nyala Wonder Travel (Via Solaro 134, tel. 018/466-6986) organizes day trips and longer excursions around the Mediterranean. Their most popular cruise is onboard the *Corsara* for a six-hour adventure in search of sperm whales and dolphins in the marine sanctuary that forms a triangle between Liguria, Corsica, and France. A marine biologist onboard can answer questions about any of the 2,000 species you may come across. In summer, reservations are recommended. If Nyala is full, you can also try **Sanremo Navigazione** (tel. 018/450-5055, www.sanremonavigazione.it), which operates similar whale-watching tours.

Around Sanremo

The earthquake of 1887 changed the village **Bussana Vecchia** (eight kilometers northeast of Sanremo) forever. Castle, churches, and most homes were largely destroyed, leading to a mass exodus of the population. Access to the town was closed and it remained a ghost of its former self for nearly 70 years. A Torinese artist rediscovered Bussana in the 1950s and had the idea of creating an international artistic colony. A sort of constitution was created outlining the rules and soon the town was being renovated by a small, determined group of painters, sculptors, actors, designers, and writers attracted by the bohemian lifestyle of the village. Today the town remains a magnet for creative spirits who live permanently or spend part of the year here. The town now has an *osteria* called **Osteria degli Artisti** (tel. 018/451-0756, hours vary, call ahead), and visitors are welcome to explore the dozens of studios and craft shops in the center. For a list of upcoming exhibitions and events in this artist colony visit www.bussanavecchia.it.

◖ DOLCEACQUA

Dolceacqua ("sweet water") is seven kilometers from the sea. The medieval village is located on both sides of the Nervia River and connected

LIGURIA

by an elegant bridge that could easily be the backdrop for a fairy tale. The town is famous for its DOC wine and *michetta* (bread) dessert, which even has its own popular holiday. The town's center is dominated by **Castello dei Doria** (Téra in the local dialect). To get to the top of the castle you'll need to navigate a romantic maze of narrow sloping lanes. Along the way are small shops and restaurants where you can duck in for a fine meal. A visit here should start with a walk across the gracefully shaped bridged that Monet once raved about.

Sights

The medieval bridge leads to Castello dei Doria (tel. 018/420-6444, Sat.–Sun. 10 A.M.–5 P.M., €3), a 12th-century castle that was once inhabited by the Doria family, who purchased the town in 1250. The castle was renovated in 2007 and is now a museum that exhibits work by local artists and features historical exhibits about the castle and the town.

Sports and Recreation

A marked path connects Dolceacqua with the **Alta Via dei Monti Liguri** (AVML) trail that crosses the entire Ligurian interior. After a few minutes of walking, you'll reach a little 17th-century church at San Bernardo. It's an uphill climb, past olive groves and the Nervia Valley that takes less than an hour to complete. At the top there's a great view of town and the castle.

If you arrived by bus from Sanremo you can walk back along the AVML. The three-hour journey is mostly downhill through Rossese vineyards and past the Terre Bianche rocks formed by millions of years of erosion. The ancient churches of Madonna della Neve and San Giacomo make wonderful rest stops. Vegetation is typical Mediterranean shrub and the trail is walkable year-round.

Accommodations

The Italo-English family that runs **⬤ Casa Villatalla** (Localita Villatalla, tel. 0184-206379, www.villatalla.com, €70–90 s/d) provide five rooms on the hillside overlooking town. Each has its own balcony or terrace and is decorated

A LONG WALK

Alta Via dei Monti Liguri is a hiker's dream. It runs for 440 kilometers from Ventimiglia to La Spezzia with the Alps on one side and the sea on the other. The roads, dirt tracks, and trails are divided into 44 individual sections that can be covered in a day. At the end of each section is a refuge where you can eat and sleep affordably (half-board is usually around €37). Some stretches can also be cycled, but you'd have to be an expert rider to follow the full Alta Via by mountain bike.

More exotic sports like paragliding can be attempted near Colle San Bernardo (trail 6/7). There's a good launch sight here for gliders and events are regularly organized. For information contact the **San Bernardo Hotel** (tel. 018/332-8724). If you come in winter, there's a five-kilometer cross-country ski run near Monti Liguri (trail 4/5). You can rent equipment and spend the night at the **Franco Allavena** refuge (tel. 018/424-1155).

in a friendly country style. The phone isn't missing, it's been left out on purpose—but if you want to make a call you can use the one downstairs in the comfortable living room where guests gather throughout the day. Marina can prepare a picnic lunch if you're heading for the Alta Via or a candlelight dinner with a little notice. The dog is friendly and spends most of his afternoons playing by the pool.

Libro Verde (Via Forno 13, tel. 348/580-2630, www.libroverde.it, €40–60 s/d) is a small bed-and-breakfast in the heart of Dolceacqua. The narrow entrance leads to a barreled ceiling apartment with walls painted with ivy and flowers. The rooms are a bit cramped but intimate, and the one on the second floor has a little terrace overlooking town.

Getting There and Around

By car take the Casello di Bordighera exit off the A10 near the French border. After

Vallecrosia, drive upwards along the Nervia Valley. Dolceacqua is the first town after Camporosso. There are also buses that make the journey to town from outside the train station in Ventimiglia.

Around Dolceacqua

When Sir Thomas Hanbury purchased the Palazzo Orengo in 1867 he had gardening in the back of his mind. Today **Villa Hanbury** (Capo Mortola, località Mortola, tel. 018/422-9507, daily 9 A.M.–6 P.M., €12) on the Mortola promontory continues to benefit from a mild climate that is conducive to the growth of exotic plants, as well as Mediterranean varieties. There are 5,800 species in all that are cared for by world-class botanists from the local university. Visitors can explore several routes, which include the four seasons, an aloe zone, a Japanese garden, and exotic fruits. There is also a long alley dedicated to olives, bamboo, and palms. In 1960, the villa was purchased by the Italian state and opened to the public.

During the summer, guided tours of the gardens are frequent and jazz and classical concerts are held every Thursday. A bar in the villa itself provides refreshments and tables are set up on the delightful terrace.

By car, take the A10 towards France and exit at Ventimiglia or the SS 1 Aurelia towards Francia Ponte San Luigi. Directions to the villa are clearly posted. The closest train station is Ventimiglia. The Autobus Riviera Trasporti (tel. 018/459-2706) in Via Cavour 150 meters from the station leaves every half-hour for the villa.

LIGURIA

PIEDMONT AND AOSTA VALLEY

The landscape of Piedmont and Aosta Valley is dramatically different from anything else in Italy. Here the Alps are a constant background and there are more peaks than people. One-quarter of the population is concentrated in Turin, leaving a lot of unspoiled countryside to explore. The Italian conservation movement began here and Parco Nazionale del Gran Paradiso was the first national park in the country.

The western edge of both regions is bordered by snowcapped mountains that provide a natural border with France. Altitude hasn't prevented cultural exchange and many of the small Alpine villages have been profoundly influenced by the *transalpini* (as the French are known). Language, architecture, and cuisine all have a Gallic touch and for hundreds of

years the Kingdom of Savoy ruled the area. The region's noble origins are evident in castles, sanctuaries, abbeys, and churches that dot the landscape. In between are vine-covered hills that have been a feature of the countryside for centuries and yield some of the most prestigious wines in Italy.

Italy's longest river starts with a trickle 3,841 meters up Monviso. The Po eventually flows through Turin and across the Padana plain that is the source of the country's finest grapes and much of its rice production. Risotto dishes outnumber pasta dishes here.

Piedmont isn't just agriculture though. The region has an industrial tradition that predates anything in Lombardy. Turin is home to Fiat and factories have been churning out cars since the 1900s. It's a contrast to the

HIGHLIGHTS

◖ Cattedrale di San Giovanni and the Holy Shroud: Turin's duomo contains one of the country's most famous relics, the Holy Shroud, which is believed to be the sheet that covered Christ after his crucifixion. It attracts a regular stream of pilgrims and skeptics (page 227).

◖ Mole Antonelliana: The Mole is Torino's most stunning sight. Its long, narrow dome can be seen from every angle of the city, as well as on the Italian two-cent coin. Enjoy remarkable vistas of the Alps from the building's rooftop terrace (page 227).

◖ Museo Egizio: During the 19th century, when mummies were the rage, Italian archeologists combed the deserts in search of ancient Egyptian tombs. What they uncovered is now a world-class collection of Egyptian artifacts (page 228).

◖ Market Day in Cuneo: Nearly every town in Italy has a market, but this one fills up a square the size of a football field with everything from mushrooms to mandolins. The real fun is watching the animated sellers using the oldest marketing method of them all: their loud, melodic voices (page 240).

◖ Palio di Asti: This lively festival and horse race takes place yearly in mid-September and has been held since the 13th century. A colorful parade in Piazza Alfieri with over 1,000 participants in historic Renaissance costume precedes the race (page 245).

◖ Aosta: The town of Aosta has some of the best-preserved Roman ruins in Northern Italy and has long been called the Rome of the North by archeologists. Some must-see sights are the ancient Porta Pretoria, the entrance to the town, and the well-preserved facade of the Roman amphitheater, still a wonderful venue to see a concert (page 249).

◖ Parco Nazionale del Gran Paradiso: Italy's first national park has remained unspoiled and as the name suggests is a paradise for hikers, cross-country skiers, and naturalists. A no-nonsense network of mountain refuges helps visitors get face-to-face with wilderness that covers both regions and extends to the French border (page 254).

◖ La Palud Cableway: Ski lifts and cable cars are a common sight across the region. These are a great form of transportation and none provides more adrenaline than La Palud cableway over the Alps into France. It reaches 3,842 meters and provides an unrivaled view of the Monte Bianco (page 257).

LOOK FOR ◖ TO FIND RECOMMENDED SIGHTS, ACTIVITIES, DINING, AND LODGING.

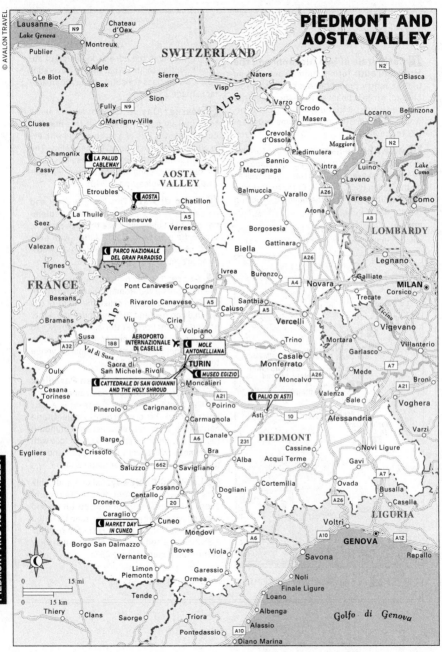

© AVALON TRAVEL

PIEDMONT AND AOSTA VALLEY

traditional costumes worn during Carnevale and slate-covered lodges tucked into the sides of Valle di Susa. That doesn't seem to bother locals, who balance innovation with age-old traditions. They're less likely to be sipping cappuccino than the hot chocolate recipes Piedmontese lips have long preferred.

Ancient festivals include the Palio of Asti and Carnevale of Ivrea, where locals have hurled oranges at each other for hundreds of years. No one needs much encouragement to don brightly colored costumes and partake in processions or plays. Specialties revolve around a few typical products, none of which is more treasured than the truffle. In autumn, specially trained dogs scour the forests searching for this underground delicacy that's used in dozens of recipes.

Asti and Monferrato are the premiere wine-producing areas but the entire region is renown and grape varieties like *barbera* and *dolcetto* have a different flavor depending on the province. Other specialties include *grissini* (breadsticks), invented in the late 17th century for delicate aristocratic stomachs; Vermouth, created in 1786 by Antonio Benedetto Carpano; and Fernet, first distilled in 1865.

Aosta Valley is embedded within the Alps. There are no plains, no hills, only high peaks and narrow valleys with small towns that grow incrementally during the winter season when the skiers arrive. The tallest mountain of all is the Monte Bianco; at 4,807 meters, it towers over everything else in Europe. If you shout here, chances are no one will hear. The Romans colonized the region relatively late and few legionnaires asked to be garrisoned in the remote outposts. Aosta started out as one of these and the largest town has retained an ancient amphitheater and triumphal entrance. Culture, however, isn't the main draw. Italians come to escape the pollution of cities and strap on their skis or hiking boots. Parco Nazionale del Gran Paradiso, which straddles the two regions, is a wilderness of breathtaking mountains and meadows. Resorts like Cogne and Courmayeur are world-class winter destinations with modern lifts and Heidi-like chalets where snow-lovers come to spend their winter holidays.

PLANNING YOUR TIME

Piedmont and Aosta Valley are tucked in the northwest corner of Italy. Their location makes them first or last stops in the country, rather than pit stops between other regions. Turin is in the center and by far the largest city. If you like museums it will take several days to visit them all. The highways from Genoa and Milan make reaching the regional capital convenient, and from there Aosta Valley is under an hour away.

Both regions are for people who prefer mountain landscapes. There's no sea here unless you count glaciers as oceans. Unlike regions with a coastline, this one doesn't have to be avoided in August. In fact, that's one of the best times to come as the valleys are much cooler than destinations farther south and there are few traffic jams 2,000 meters above sea level.

A week exploring a single valley can be more rewarding than trying to see it all. Every day you'll be able to hike different paths and admire verdant green slopes in spring and summer. Temperatures drop significantly during winter and they usually get a white Christmas. Skiing is a big attraction and many Italians choose to spend their *settimana bianca* (weeklong winter holidays) on the trails that recently hosted Olympic downhill racers and in the elegant resorts of Aosta Valley, where warm, cozy chalets with chimneys spouting plumes of drifting smoke over snow-covered countryside are the norm.

HISTORY

Piedmont and Aosta Valley are cold in winter and were the last places a Roman legionnaire wanted to be stationed. That probably explains why they weren't fully colonized until under Augustus and why Paleolithic predecessors spent most of the time in caves near Monfenera. When the empire stuttered, Goth, Ostrogoth, and Lombard tribes eagerly took over. In those days the land was divided in dukedoms and many religious orders founded abbeys like the Abbazia di Novalesa in the quest for converts. Carlo Magno (Charles the Great) defeated the Lombards in 773 and he used the Via

Francigena to surprise his enemy. The road later served as a vital pilgrim route and increased cultural exchange dramatically.

After the decline of the Franks and the development of a mercantile class in the Middle Ages, cities like Turin, Novara, and Asti began to rule themselves autonomously. This period of independence was short-lived as outside threats from Federico Barbarossa forced towns to unite in the Lega Lombarda. Around this time the Savoys began their rise to power and by the treaty of Cateau-Cambrèsis in 1559 they ruled most of modern-day Piedmont and Aosta Valley.

Italy owes a small debt to Piedmont and the country might not exist if it weren't for the region. This is where the Risorgimento movement started and the idea of a united Italy was hatched. Patriotic thinkers like Garibaldi, Cavour, and Mazzini met to discus their vision in Turin and after three wars they eventually achieved their goal in 1861.

Turin

For most Italians Turin is Fiat and football. The city however is more than heavy industry and a crowded trophy cabinet. This is where Italy was born and the Risorgimento movement turned a dream into reality. It was even briefly the capital of the country, and that sense of grandeur is still evident along the tree-lined avenues and wide piazze surrounded with Baroque, though generally underrated by tour operators.

Even the Romans didn't give that much importance to Turin, and it wasn't until the 16th century when the Savoys moved their headquarters here that the city took off. The building spree they initiated still marks the city and royal architects did not skimp on

the Mole Antonelliana with the Alps in the background

© ALESSIA RAMACCIA

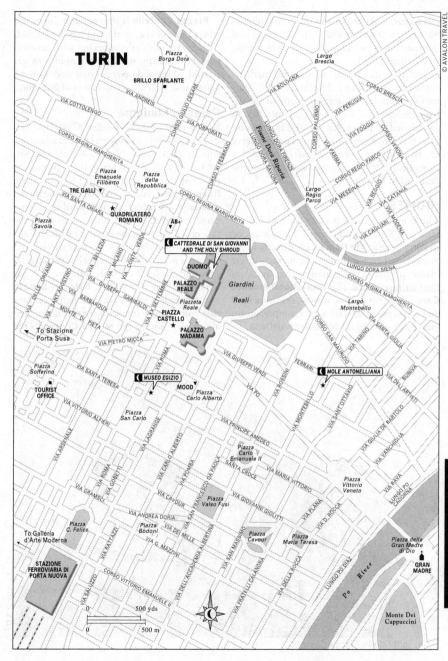

TURIN

PIEDMONT AND AOSTA VALLEY

extravagance. After Italian unification, motors became more important than monarchs and industrial heavyweights like Fiat changed the way Italians travel.

Today the city is full of museums, markets, and a vibrant art scene. The recent 2006 Winter Olympics has spruced up many of the dilapidated parts of town and given new life to abandoned factories. Eating well is a passion here and movements like Slow Food preserve the art of dining. But if all you're interested is chocolate, then this may become your favorite destination in Italy.

SIGHTS

The center of Turin is compact and has retained its Roman grid pattern. From Stazione di Porta Nuova, **Via Roma** leads directly to the aristocratic heart of the city. Along the way are piazze, porticos, and museums that make for fascinating detours. The **Touristic+Piemonte Card** is vital for anyone who wants to see it all and if you prefer to start with a comprehensive view head straight for **Mole Antonelliana.**

Piazza Castello is the center of Turin and where most of the royal buildings are located. These were once all connected with internal passages making it easier for nobles to get around. Many wide avenues now lead from the piazza and Via Po is a succession of Baroque.

Palazzo Madama

Palazzo Madama (Piazza Castello, tel. 011/443-3501, www.palazzomadamatorino.it, Tues.–Sun. 10 A.M.–6 P.M. and Sat. 10 A.M.–8 P.M., €7.50) lies in the center of the piazza on top of Roman ruins. The towers date from the 10th century and the building served primarily defensive functions until the Savoys came to power. Filippo Juvarra was given the task of redecorating the exterior by Maria Cristina (for which the palace was later named) and there is a noticeable difference between the facade and the back of the building, which has a more somber appearance. **Sala del Senato** is the grandest room, with immense ceilings that hosted the first meeting of the Italian Senate. It now houses the **Museo Civico d'Arte**

Palazzo Reale in Piazza Castello

Antica and 10 centuries of art and jewelry. Antonello da Messina's famous portrait hangs in the Torre dei Tesori. Don't miss enjoying a coffee or *tramezzini* (triangle-shaped white bread) sandwich inside the elegantly decorated **Caffè Madama** on the ground floor.

Palazzo Reale

When the Savoys moved from Chambéry to Turin in 1563, Palazzo Reale (Piazza Castello, tel. 011/436-1455, Tues.–Sun. 8:30 A.M.–7:30 P.M., €6.50) became the royal residence. Carlo Morello was responsible for the Baroque exterior and redecoration of the interior was always a work in progress. The Throne and Audience rooms haven't changed much and are filled with tapestries and ornaments. This is where people came to bow and ask for favors. After the unification of Italy and the transfer of the capital to Florence (and eventually Rome), the palace lost its importance. It's hard to imagine living in a place where you could run the 100-yard dash in the corridor. Behind the palace is a delightful garden laid out by the same gardener responsible for Versailles. Most visitors don't bother to take a stroll but it's a pleasant place to rest and admire the many sculptures.

◖ Cattedrale di San Giovanni and the Holy Shroud

Dedicated to San Giovanni, the Duomo is the only Renaissance church in the city and was built next to the royal palace. The red brick of the campanile and stairs is a marked contrast to the white marble of the church, which has a simple facade and consists of three naves. The interior is less minimalist and there are plenty of statues and paintings to admire. What attracts the most attention is the Holy Shroud. Even if carbon dating has proved it wasn't the sheet used to wrap Jesus after the crucifixion, it still draws a crowd. The relic is preserved inside a silver box in the **Cappella della Sacra Sindone** and is rarely opened. The last time the cloth was made visible was in 2000. However, a fire has closed the chapel for restoration. A photograph of the shroud is on display in the opposite chapel. Visitors can see a replica and an exhibition about the Holy Shroud's legendary past at **Museo della Sindone** (Via San Domenico 28, tel. 011/436-5832, daily 9 A.M.– noon and 3–7 P.M., €5.50).

Via Po

The most architecturally homogenous street in Turin is Via Po and kings once used the porticoes on the left side to reach the river. They're continuous, unlike the ones on the right, which were for common folks. Today the choice is up to you and both lead to Piazza Vittorio Veneto. There's a good view of the Turin hills from the square that ends with a bridge built by Napoleon. The **Gran Madre** church on the other side is just average by Italian standards but it does lead to **Monte dei Cappuccini.** Be prepared for a 284-meter climb to a hill overlooking the city. At the top is **Museo Nazionale della Montagna** (Via G. Giardino 39, tel. 011/660-4104, Tues.–Sun. 9 A.M.–7 P.M., €1), a reference point for anyone interested in mountains. There's a good view of the Po and the entire city from the museum restaurant that recreates a chalet-like atmosphere.

◖ Mole Antonelliana

Mole Antonelliana (Via Montebello 20, tel. 011/817-2080, Tues.–Sun. 10 A.M.–8 P.M., €4) is the tallest building in Turin and the city's most stunning sight. The structure was originally meant to be a synagogue, but funding problems led to it being completed by the city in 1878. You can get one of the best views from the panoramic terrace and a close-up of the Alps. It has a place of honor on the two-cent coin and today houses the **Museo Nazionale del Cinema** (tel. 011/813-8560, www.museocinema.it, Tues.–Fri. and Sun. 9 A.M.–8 P.M., Sat. 9 A.M.–11 P.M., €5.20). The exhibits are laid out on six floors and cover the history of film as well as the filmmaking process. There's a great bit dedicated to the Lumiere brothers, who loved to terrorize audiences still unfamiliar with the new art form. In the main hall under the dome, lounge chairs are spread out where visitors can watch classic

© ALESSIA RAMACCIA

Turin's iconic Mole Antonelliana

films projected on giant screens. The Ciak (Action) Bar is a multimedia cafeteria with monitors embedded in the tables.

◖ Museo Egizio

Turin may not seem like the obvious choice for a world-class collection of Egyptian artifacts, but the only way to see more ancient relics would require a trip to Cairo. Museo Egizio (Via Accademia delle Scienze 6, tel. 011/561-7776, www.museoegizio.it, Tues.–Sun. 8:30 A.M.–7:30 P.M., €6.50 or €8 combo) was Carlo Felice's idea. Most of the pieces were purchased from Ernesto Schiaparelli, who made a name for himself among archeologists during his many expeditions. The museum covers three floors and includes humble items like a pair of sandals and everyday cooking utensils to Nefertari's tomb, and a hall dedicated to monumental statues of pharoses, including Ramses II, who ruled when Turin was still a forest. The paintings in room five show sacrificial ceremonies and the making of beer. There are 30,000 objects in all and

the audio guide is a good investment unless you're an Egyptologist. **Galleria Sabauda** (tel. 011/547-440, Mon., Fri–Sun. 8:30 A.M.–2 P.M., Wed. 2–7:30 P.M., Thurs. 10 A.M.–7:30 P.M., €4 or €8 combo) is housed in the same building and a combined ticket makes it worth having a look. The gallery contains artwork collected by the Savoys over many years and reflects their changing tastes. Prince Eugenio was particularly fond of Dutch painters; Memling, Rembrandt, and Brueghel were his favorites.

Galleria d'Arte Moderna

Contemporary art isn't lacking in Turin and Galleria d'Arte Moderna (Via Magenta 31, tel. 011/442-9628, www.gamtorino.it, Tues.–Sun. 10 A.M.–6 P.M., €7.50) possesses mostly Italian works from the 18th century to the present. There's only room for a small part of the 20,000 photographs, paintings, and installations, and there's talk of eventually moving the museum into a bigger space. Futurist painters are well represented and international canvases include Chagall, Klee, and Ernst.

Fondazione Sandretto and Fondazione Merz

For more contemporary sculpture, photography, and events, there's the Fondazione Sandretto (Via Modane 16, tel. 011/379-7600, www.fondsrr.org, Tues.–Sun. noon–8 P.M., Thurs. noon–11 P.M., €5). The building is an ex-factory with loft-like spaces and a constantly changing number of exhibits. **Fondazione Merz** (Via Limone 24, tel. 011/1971-9437, www.fondazionemerz.org, Mon.–Sun. 11 A.M.–7 P.M., €5) has been called the mini-Tate Modern and since 2005 has displayed the works of the self-taught artist Mario Merz.

ENTERTAINMENT AND EVENTS
Nightlife

The last few years has seen a migration of bars and nightclubs towards the **Quadrilatero Romano** neighborhood and along the Po. There have been many new openings, with a tendency towards clubs that combine food, music, and design. During the summer, thousands of the city's night crawlers frequent these zones and give Turin a lively feeling well after dark.

DANCE CLUBS

The Beach (Arcata 18 Murazzi del Po, tel. 011/888-777, daily in summer 11 A.M.–4 A.M.) is directly on the embankment of the Po and every evening has a different musical theme, although the overall tendency is towards electronic music. Wednesdays and Sundays during the summer are peak *aperitivo* times. Happy hour starts at 7 P.M. and comes with a counter full of finger food. There are rows of tables along the river and crowds mingle outside and inside this spacious air-conditioned club. Thursdays and Saturdays are the big dance nights with house DJ Gigi Marshall spinning requests until dawn.

All Turin clubbers have stepped inside **Supermarket** (Viale Madonna di Campagna 1, tel. 011/259-450, Wed.–Sun. 10 P.M.–5 A.M.) at least once and often make it a regular stop. It's not just for dancing but often hosts concerts with guests like Servant and Hooverphonic. There are two floors, each with a bar and video projectors. The large dance floor is downstairs and gets most crowded on Saturday nights.

AB+ (Piazza Cesare Augusto 1, tel. 011/070-2032, Tues.–Sat. 7:30 P.M.–3 A.M.) is situated in the Quadrilatero Romano overlooking the Porte Palatine and archeological park. It's an excellent spot for an *aperitivo* or nightcap. Besides the prime position and high-tech touches like the 15-meter-wide video installation the club has a knack for putting on good music. Jazz and indie bands from around the world regularly perform throughout the year and all concerts are free. The party continues on the terrace with DJs who favor soul, house, hip-hop, bossa nova, and electronica.

Many clubs are just outside the historic center and require a short bus or taxi ride. That's the case with **Spazio 211** (Via Cigna 211, tel. 011/1970-5919, Tues.–Sun. 9 P.M.–3 A.M.), set within a small park. It's a multifunctional space that has become a destination for the Turin alternative and underground crowd. There are

several environments where you can have a drink, watch concerts, or dance to house, reggae, and acid jazz. The focal point of the club is the central courtyard, decorated with contemporary art installations. In the summer they throw their own music and vegan festival. If you've never heard of Motorpsycho or Radio Dept, this is a chance to widen your musical horizons.

LIVE MUSIC

Zoo Bar (Corso Casale 127, tel. 011/819-4347, Fri.–Sat. 11 P.M.–4 A.M., no cover) keeps the sidewalks along Corso Casale busy until late. This club has been all about live music since it opened in 1993. Upstairs is a big industrial space that is reminiscent of a New York loft with designer furniture. Downstairs is given over to rock and the long bar space is covered with vinyl records and guitars. Independent bands get the most spotlight and Smash, UK Subs, and other Brit pop groups make regular appearances.

The music at **Brillo Sparlante** (Via Borgo Dora 14, tel. 347/418-2824, Tues.–Sun. 7 P.M.–3 A.M., no cover) never prevents conversation. It does encourage drinking in a bistro-style club with Philippe Starck chairs and original artwork on the ceilings and walls. The cocktail of choice is the Cuba libre, which the barmen prepare with panache. The staff smiles a lot and there's a relaxed and friendly feel about the place that makes meeting people easy. It's also very close to the center and is a convenient after-dinner destination.

WINE BARS

Marco Peyron and his sister Federica have given new life to the historic **Antica Enoteca del Borgo** (Via Monferrato 4, tel.011/819-0461, daily 9 A.M.–9 P.M., closed Mon. and Sun. morning). It's not far from Gran Madre church and Monte dei Cappuccini could be insurmountable if you stop here first. Hospitality and service are unmatched and it's clear these guys are passionate about wine. The cellar covers most of the region's DOC areas and there are many good bottles from Alba. The list also includes many Tuscan and French names with a particularly good selection of Champagne. The place gets very animated for the *aperitivo* that starts in the early evening.

Aperitivo starts at 6 P.M. at **Tre Galli** (Via Sant'Agostino 25, tel. 011/521-6027, Mon.–Sat. 5 P.M.–late-night) and there are usually people waiting for the minute hand to signal the start of happy hour. This *vineria* also prepares food but the real star is the wine. Tastings are organized weekly and if you do get hungry a *salumi* and cheese plate will keep your stomach satisfied.

Vinicola al Sorij (Via Pescatore 10c, tel. 011/835-667, Mon.–Sat. 6 P.M.–late-night) is a popular wine bar behind Piazza Vittorio with a solid kitchen and an extensive selection of regional, national, and international labels. After a few glasses it's difficult to resist staying for dinner and if you do make sure to sample the risotto.

A good cocktail is a natural match for a good book and that's the whole concept behind **Mood** (Via Cesare Battisti 3, tel. 011/566-0809, Tues.–Sat. 10 A.M.–9 P.M., café opens at 8 A.M.). The location is one of the nicest in Turin and there's no lack of conversation starters on the shelves. They even let you take books outside and do a little open-air reading at this highly original café-bookstore hybrid.

Performing Arts

Aperitivo is a ritual in Turin and a good way to start an evening. Local cocktails use Vermouth, invented here in 1786, and are generally served with *tartines* and salted snacks. Choosing a drink is the easy part. The selection of classic, pop, and jazz concerts ranks with the best in Italy. **Auditorium Giovanni Agnelli** (Via Nizza 262, tel. 011/667-7415) and **Conservatorio Giuseppe Verdi** (Piazza Bodoni, tel. 011/817-8958) both have their own symphonies and last-minute tickets are available on the day of performances from the box office or tourist office in Piazza Solferino. **Teatro Regio** (Piazza Castello 215, tel. 011/881-5241) has the most ornate interior and a busy calendar of concerts, operas, and ballets performed by international companies.

Festivals and Events

Cacao has been popular in Turin since it was first imported from the New World. The city excelled in finding delicious uses for the ingredient and **Cioccolatò** is a month-long festival chocolate lovers won't want to miss. Resolutions are forgotten at the end of February when gastronomic tents are set up all over the city. Getting a fix of dark, milk, or white is easy, although you'll have to wait in front of the most popular stands. True fanatics can pick up a Chocopass at the tourist office.

The **Fiera del Libro** (Lingotto, tel. 011/518-4268, www.fieralibro.it) has a different theme each year. The 2007 fair was dedicated to adventure and books about travel, science, and exploration. The fair attracts hundreds of publishers and thousands of bookworms who come to meet bestselling writers like Paulo Coelho. During the event in early May, Turismo Torino (tel. 011/535-181) organizes tours around the city's literary hot spots.

Movies arrived in the late 19th century in Turin and many production houses opened during the early days of cinema. Until Cinecittà Studios was founded in Rome, this was the movie capital of Italy and the **Torino Film Festival** (www.torinofilmfest.org) reinforces the city's links with cinema each November. The festival is the second-most important after Venice and features a retrospective of famous actors and directors along with world premieres often projected in the Museo del Cinema. It's much more laid-back than Cannes and tickets are easy to come by.

Turin has an active art season but the date most artists circle in their diaries is the second weekend of November. **Artissima** (Fiera di Torino, tel. 011/442-9518, www.artissima.it, Fri.–Sun. 11 A.M.–8 P.M.) is a three-day event exhibiting contemporary art from around the world. There are several sections, including Present Future for up-and-coming painters, sculptors, and some people who defy category, and New Entries, which spotlights galleries. A lot of curators show up and there is a business side to the event that is interesting to observe.

Each year Turin gets a little brighter around

Christmas time. Starting in November, the neon begins to appear and artists reinvent the city. Vias Garibaldi, Rome, and Po are completely covered in lights. **Luci d'Artista,** a cultural event that is held every winter, features light installations on the streets of Turin created by invited artists. Tours of the works are organized on Saturdays by the tourist office (tel. 800/015-475). The event transforms piazze and palaces and some illuminations like Mario Merz's work on the Mole have become permanent fixtures.

SHOPPING

Shopping in Turin is unique. It's done under 18 kilometers of porticos that keep shoppers dry whatever the season. Underneath the arcades of **Via Roma** are brand-name designers as well as historic stores that have been outfitting locals for centuries. Piazza San Carlo, with its twin churches, divides the street and you can always find a café table from which to contemplate your next purchase.

For something a little trendier, visit the boutiques along the completely pedestrian-friendly **Via Garibaldi.** Side streets like Via Consolata and Bellezia lead to the **Quadrilatero** neighborhood, where hammering can still be heard and handmade goods are the norm. On the other side of Piazza Castello, **Via Po** is home to the city's oldest jeweler and workshops where craftspeople continue to make and repair furniture the old-fashioned way. There's also a high concentration of contemporary art galleries with moderate price tags.

Stores in Turin are generally closed Monday mornings and Sundays. Hours are 10 A.M.–1 P.M. and 3:30–7:30 P.M. with some centrally located shops open nonstop.

Clothing

It's almost worth seeing **San Carlo-Palazzo Villa** (Piazza San Carlo 169, tel. 011/511-4111, www.sancarlo1973.it, Mon. 3:30–7:30 P.M., Tues.–Sat. 10:30 A.M.–7:30 P.M.) for the interior alone. This lifestyle store covers 5,000 square meters of an 18th-century palazzo. There's a beautiful internal courtyard that

might distract you from the designer clothes, cosmetics, music, and food creatively displayed in different corners of the store.

Sticky Fingers (Via delle Orfane 24d, tel. 011/521-7320, www.sticky-fingers.it, Tues.–Sat. 9 A.M.–1 P.M. and 3–7 P.M.) is one of the most sought-out stores in the city for vintage fans who can find threads dating all the way back to the 1930s. Although clothes take up the most room in this mecca of long-gone-out-of-style fashions, accessories and furniture are also available.

Women looking to upgrade their closets generally leave **Liù** (Via Barbaroux 12, tel. 011/517-2258, Tues.–Sat. 11 A.M.–7 P.M.) carrying a shopping bag. This boutique, decorated like Liberace's home, sells dresses, shoes, and accessories for every occasion. There's also some vintage clothing and the owner serves tea and biscuits to customers.

Accessories

Ocularium (Via Fratelli Calandra 1bis, tel. 011/882-574, Mon.–Sat.) is more of a living room than a traditional eyeglass store. The eclectic owner goes out of his way to find styles that are way beyond common. They carry Zenka, Face à face, and Iyoko. Originality has a price and most of the trendy eyewear is over €100.

It's hard not to notice the black and gold entrance of **Musy** (Via Po 1, tel. 011/812-5582, Mon.–Sat.) at the beginning of Via Po. This is where the Savoys shopped for their jewelry and they've been in business since 1707. It doesn't cost anything to look at the rings, bracelets, and necklaces, all of which are one of a kind. Stick around until closing and you'll understand how they keep their diamonds safe.

Books

Browsing the shelves of **Druetto** (Via Roma 227, tel. 011/561-9166, Tues.–Sat. 9 A.M.–7:30 P.M., Mon. 3–7:30 P.M.) is enjoyable whether you read Italian or not. It's one of the largest bookstores in the city and has managed to survive the onslaught of chain stores with a mixture of tradition and modernity.

The classic interior doesn't hurt and if you want to improve your Italian the salespeople can pick out a book that's suitable for your level. **Tastebook** (Corso Vittorio Emanuele II 58, tel. 011/540-385, www.tastebook.it, Mon. afternoon–Sat.) is a more innovative approach to literature where readers can sample wonderful desserts along with interesting titles published in-house.

Markets

Piazze have a practical purpose in Turin and many fill up regularly with markets. **Mercato di Porta Palazzo** (Piazza della Repubblica, Mon.–Fri. 8:30 A.M.–1:30 P.M., Sat. 8:30 A.M.–6:30 P.M.) is the most characteristic and largest outdoor market in Europe. It's where locals come for low-priced vegetables and fruits, and Chinese spices compete with Moroccan hairdressers and Indian DVDs. On Saturdays and the second Sunday of every month the **Balôn** and **Gran Balôn** are held in Piazza Borgo Dora, just as they have been since 1856. Colorful stalls sell antiques, carpets, jewelry, and old postcards of the city. Borgo Dora was spruced up prior to the Olympics and **Cortile del Maglio** (Piazza Borgo Dora) is now home to dozens of antique and craft shops. For rare books and engravings browse the porticos around Piazza Carlo Felice on the first Sunday of each month except August. Well-ripened Piedmont cheeses and other natural food products with genuine flavors can be sampled in Piazza Palazzo di Città on the first Sunday and fourth Saturday of the month.

SPORTS AND RECREATION

Turin has two football clubs but it's the black and white of **Juventus** that's by far the most popular in the city and country. *La vecchia signora* (old lady) as they're called, have won more league titles than any other Italian team and despite a recent match-fixing scandal have managed to remain competitive. The club has long been owned by the influential Agnelli family, who take a personal interest in the game and have attracted stars like Platini and Zidane in the past. Juventus and Torino FC play in Stadio delle Alpi and Stadio Olimpico. During the winter you'll want to wear a hat and should have no problem finding a ticket at **Juventus Football Club Store** (Via Garibaldi 4b, tel. 011/433-8709, Tues.–Sat. 10 A.M.–7:30 P.M. and Mon. 3–7:30 P.M.) or **Torino Football Club Store** (Piazza Castello 10, tel. 011/542-348, Tues. 10 A.M.–12:30 P.M. and 3–7:30 P.M., Sat. 10 A.M.–7:30 P.M.).

The **Torino Marathon** (www.turinmarathon.it) is held every April and is one of the most prestigious races in Italy. The course is particularly fast and the race is preceded by a five-kilometer fun run through the center of the city.

Rowing is a popular pastime along the Po and many clubs line the river. **La Reale Società Canottieri Cerea** (www.canottaggiopiemonte.it) organizes competitions, including the Silver Skiff regatta that is a timed endurance event covering 11 kilometers from Turin to Moncalieri and back again. For something less competitive you can rent a skiff or canoe from **ES.PA Sport Canoa e Rafting** (Corso Matteotti 10, tel. 011/561-7484, Tues.–Sun. 9 A.M.–1 P.M. and 2:30–7 P.M.) for a couple of hours and give your arms a good workout.

The XX Winter Olympic Games in 2006 did wonders for the city's sporting infrastructure. Although the flame went out a while ago, the spirit lives on and many of the sights where gold medals were won can be visited on the **Torino Passione Olimpica** tour (leaves from the main tourist office in Piazza Solferino, tel. 011/535-181). Otherwise skating and ice hockey events are frequently held in the Palavela, l'Oval Lingotto, and Palasport Olimpico.

Le Corbusier once said Turin was the city with most the beautiful natural surroundings, and 17 square kilometers of park also make it one of the greenest in Italy. **Parco del Valentino** (Corso Massimo D'Azeglio) on the Po is popular with residents and contains a castle, a botanic park with 4,000 species, and remnants of the Universal Exposition held in 1884. The **medieval village** (tel. 011/443-1701, www.borgomedioevaletorino.it, daily 9 A.M.–7 P.M.) within the park, created for the Esposizione

© ALESSIA RAMACCIA

The 2006 Winter Olympics helped transform the city.

Generale Italiana Artistica e Industriale in 1884, is located on Viale Virgilio. You can eat along the river near the **Borgo Medievale** (tel. 011/669-9372), where hydroplanes once took off for Venice and Trieste. **L'Idrovolante** (Viale Virgilio 105, tel. 011/668-7602, Tues.–Sun. lunch and dinner) is especially romantic at night when the candles get lit.

Giardini Reali is another central park with well-manicured lawns and sculptures galore in the center of the city. A little farther away is **Parco della Pellerina,** an ideal place for an early morning jog or bike ride. Contemporary art and music fill the park in summer during the **Traffic Free Festival** (www.trafficfestival.com), a series of concerts and DJ sets that has included groups like Daft Punk and the Artic Monkeys in past editions. Another former royal park near where three rivers meet is **Parco della Colletta.** Every year from June until November **Parco Michelotti** hosts Experimenta, an interactive exposition that focuses on science and technology that's illustrated in a spectacular and fun fashion.

ACCOMMODATIONS
Under €100
A few steps from the Po, **Alpi Resort** (Via Bonafous 5, tel. 011/812-9677, www.hotel alpiresort.it, €80–90 s/d) is a comfortable, medium sized, three-star hotel. Each of the 29 rooms is equipped with a power shower, Internet, and minibar. Breakfast buffet is included and car rentals can be arranged at the front desk.

Fans of the Olympics can absorb a little of the competitive spirit at **Art Hotel Olympic** (Via Verolengo 19, tel. 011/39997, www.artho telolympic.it, €80 d). The complex was built specifically for the games and served as the media headquarters before being converted into a hotel. This isn't the center of the city but it's only a 10-minute bus ride to the Mole. There are two major shopping malls and Eataly should solve any dining dilemmas. The 147 modern rooms are spread out on eight floors.

Train stations can be on the seedy side in Italy's big cities, but that's not the case with Porta Nuova. **Hotel Genio** (Corso Vittorio Emanuele

PIEDMONT AND AOSTA VALLEY

II 47, tel. 011/650-5771, www.bwsitemanager. co.uk, €95 d) is right next door and travelers can drop their bags off before starting down Via Roma towards the monuments. Staff at this Best Western chain are perennially smiling, and rooms, although generic, are comfortable and spacious.

€100-200

If you want to sleep with the ghosts of Verdi, Mozart, and Napoleon III, then the only choice is **Hotel Dogana Vecchia** (Via Corte d'Appello 4, tel. 011/436-7272, www.hotel doganavecchia.com, €110 d). During Turin's brief stint as the Italian capital, it was also popular with bureaucrats and foreign emissaries. Nowadays its proximity to the Quadrilatero Romano makes it a good choice for anyone who wants to walk to the major sights. Drivers can leave cars in the hotel parking and enjoy a proper breakfast in the morning.

From the outside, **Hotel Santo Stefano** (Via Porta Palatina, 19, tel. 011/522-3311, www.nh-hotels.com, €140 d) looks like a postmodern medieval tower equipped with LED lights and plated glass. It's popular with business travelers and those who appreciate design. Service is professional and efficient. Breakfast varies everyday and the beds are some of the most comfortable in Italy. Suites are spacious and decked out with oak floors, metallic furniture, and flat-screen TVs. There's a hammam on-site that should be reserved in advance and a great view from the top.

If you book a room at (**Hotel Boston** (Via Massena 70, tel. 011/500-359, www.hotelbos tontorino.it, €110–140 s/d), you could sleep with Andy Warhol. Robert Frenci has decorated all 87 rooms with his personal art collection. The Diabolique, Crocodile, and Red rooms are especially creative. They all come with postmodern and ethnic furnishings that can be disorienting at first. The restaurant serves Piedmontese classics along with an endless selection of wines.

A stay at **Town House 70** (Via XX Settembre 70, tel. 011/1970-0003, www.townhouse. it, €159 d) is full of perks. Upon arrival guests receive fresh fruit and a bottle of wine. Don't worry about keeping your voice down, as all rooms are soundproofed. The large double and junior suites are decorated in natural-colored furniture. Ask at the front desk about the Magic Turin tour that's included with the price of a room.

Villa Sassi (Strada al Traforo di Pino 47, tel. 011/898-0556, www.villasassi.com, €180–220, s/d, closed Aug.) lies on a hill overlooking Turin. The 16th-century villa is surrounded by a large park near the Basilica di Superga. You'll need a car to get here but once you do you may not want to leave the aristocratic atmosphere and 16 rooms decorated with thick Persian carpets and four-poster beds. Most guests are the jacket-and-tie variety and many choose to dine in the restaurant rather than travel the six kilometers into town.

FOOD
Piedmontese

The ancient clocks, mismatched frames, and other oddities decorating **Trattoria Valenzia** look as though they came from the **Balôn** market nearby and hint of another century. This is very old-school Turin, where the owner is likely to pick up his guitar while you chew and strum songs that haven't been heard in a while. *Bollito* (bolied) or *brasato* (braised) make for good encores to the antipasto. Coffee drinkers should not hesitate to order an espresso. It's a secret recipe everyone would love to know.

If the *osteria* is a new concept to you, then **Antiche Sere** (Via Cenischia 9, tel. 011/385-4347, Mon.–Sat. 7–11 P.M., €8–12, cash only) is vital for your gastronomic education. It's located in the working-class neighborhood of *borgo* San Paolo, where gourmet has yet to make inroads and sizable portions are standard. The vivacious Antonella greets diners, most of whom she knows by name, while her brother sweats it out behind the ovens. All dishes originated in their hometown outside of Turin and even the wine hasn't traveled very far. The stuffed vegetables are a reliable starter, but the real stomach pleasers are the *gnocchi con ragù* and rabbit cooked in white wine.

Checkered tablecloths can sometimes be misleading but at **Dai Saletta** (Via Belfiore 37, tel. 011/668-7867, Mon.–Sat. noon–3 P.M. and 7:30–10:30 P.M., closed Aug., €9–13) the authenticity of the two small dining rooms is equaled by the authenticity of the food. Dishes represent both mountain and urban traditions and if you don't see *tagliolini alla langarola* (local pasta) on the menu it's a sad day for stomachs. Nitpickers might complain about the temperature of the red wine in summer but everyone else is usually too distracted with the food to notice.

Two minutes from the Gran Madre church on the other side of the Po lies █ **Imbianchini e Decoratori** (Via Lanfranchi 28, tel. 011/819-0672, Thurs.–Tues. noon–3 P.M. and 7–11:30 P.M., €8 lunch/€22 dinner). This former cooperative has a large garden that is full of locals at night and is often the scene of some musical or literary event. The best bet on the dinner menu is the €22 prix fixe that changes every day and includes three *antipasti,* two pasta dishes, a second, and dessert. The house red deserves respect but refined drinkers will also find some higher pedigree bottles on the wine list.

L'Oca Fola (Via Drovetti 6g, tel. 011/433-7422, Mon.–Sat. 7–11 P.M., €8–12) is behind Turin's Stazione Porta Susa, and many of the diners in this simple *trattoria* have just stepped off a train. Bottles line the walls and geese decorate the tablecloths and plates. The menu depends on what Claudio bought at the market that day and a selection of five *antipasti* is served even before you've sat down. In winter the rice and bean soup will banish any chills and refreshing chicken salad is often featured in the warmer months. Chocolate cake is the finale year-round. Nearby in Piazza Statuto 13, you can taste Turin's famous breadsticks at *Guala* along with a crunchy version of focaccia.

International

Almost directly in front of Mole Antonelliana on a quiet pedestrian street, **Sotto la Mole** (Via Montebello 9, tel. 011/817-9398, Thurs.–Tues.

7–10:30 P.M., €9–15) is nearly as memorable as the Museo del Cinema. Simone attends to the kitchen while his wife Anna Rosa delivers carefully prepared dishes that vary according to the season. Cheese enthusiasts should appreciate the assortment of *tome* (a type of cheese) made from both cow's and sheep's milk. Desserts are good but if you feel like stretching your legs, **Florio** (tel. 011/817-0612, Tues.–Sun. 8 A.M.–1 P.M.) around the corner at Via Po 8 serves first-rate gelato and hot chocolate.

Three is the magic number at **Vitel Etonné** (Via San Francesco da Paola 4, tel. 011/812-4621, www.leviteletonne.com, Tues.–Fri. 5 P.M.–1 A.M., Sat. 10:30 A.M.–1 A.M., Sun. 10:30 A.M.–3:30 P.M., €10–14). Every day this *osteria*/wine bar proposes three new *antipasti,* first, and second courses. And every day diners leave smiling. Service is informal and it's a great place to start an evening. The *vitel tonné* is the drink of choice among regulars.

Cafés

If you like hot chocolate, you'll love Turin. *Bicerin* is served in all the historic cafés and consists of coffee and chocolate topped with cream and served in a glass. It's pretty much the local drink and has seduced everyone from Dumas to Nietzsche. You can try it at **Caffè Platti** (Corso Vittorio Emanuele 72, tel. 011/506-9056, Tues.–Sun. morning) while waiting for a train. They've been in business since 1875 and the Liberty-style interior is original. The barman adds Cointreau to the hot chocolate and serves *torta platti* (house tart) with fruit. **Caffè San Carlo** (Piazza San Carlo 156, tel. 011/532-586, daily) is legendary and sitting in the outdoor tables has become a major pastime ever since the piazza was made pedestrian-only. At lunch there's a buffet with daily specials and an à la carte menu in the evening. Brigitte Bardot and Jimmy Stewart preferred the chandeliers and fireplace inside **Caffè Torino** (Piazza San Carlo 204, tel. 011/545-118, daily 7:30 A.M.–1 A.M.) next door. Artists and aristocrats once frequented the marble tables of **Caffè Mulassano** (Piazza Castello 15, tel. 011/547-990, daily 7 A.M.–7 P.M.), famous notwithstanding its modest size. Locals keep coming for the appetizing *tramezzini* (sandwiches) and the history.

Specialties

From Aztec chocolate to Indian bread by way of sushi and Scottish biscuits, **Emporio Sicomoro** (Via Stampatori 6b, tel. 011/1950-3061, Mon.–Sat.) stocks half the world's flavors. It's a cult location for local chefs who can spend hours browsing the shelves of this culinary boutique. **Enoteca Parola** (Corso Vittorio Emanuele II 76, tel. 011/544-939, Mon.–Sat.) has sold Italian and foreign wine since 1890. The shelves go all the way to the ceilings and the selection of Champagne and Vermouth is nearly complete.

Anyone on a chocolate pilgrimage may find it difficult to leave **Guido Gobino** (Via Cagliari 15b, tel. 011/247-6245, www.guidogobino.it, Mon.–Sat. morning). Cacao takes on new forms here and even the packaging hasn't been left to chance. Once the pastry chefs to the kings, **Rivetti** (Via Monferrato 5, tel. 011/819-5264, Tues.–Sat.), next to the Gran Madre, now serves the masses elaborate bonbons made from rice flour and cacao that taste out of the ordinary.

Eataly (Via Nizza 230, tel. 011/1950-6821, www.eatalytorino.it, shops daily 10 A.M.–10:30 P.M., restaurants noon–3 P.M. and 7–10:15 P.M.) is the first gastronomic supercenter in Italy. It was inspired by the Slow Food movement and is housed on three floors of an 18th-century factory that once produced Vermouth. Every flavor can be found here. There's a market, eight restaurants, a cellar with 40,000 bottles, and a bakery museum. Tastings are regularly organized and chefs demonstrate their skills daily. It's an absolute must for gourmets.

INFORMATION AND SERVICES

Turin's three Information Points are at **Atrium Torino** (Piazza Solferino, daily 9 A.M.–7 P.M.), **Stazione Ferroviaria di Porta Nuova** (daily 9:30 A.M.–7 P.M.), and **Aeroporto Internazionale di Caselle** (daily 8 A.M.–11 P.M.). The city also runs a **call center** (tel. 011/535-181, www.turismotorino.org, daily 9:30 A.M.–9:30 P.M.).

At these information points, you can pick up information on museums and historic cafés, book hotel rooms, and purchase the Torino+Piemonte Card. Ask for the monthly events calendar and a map with suggested itineraries. The main office is the Atrium inside two modern glass and steel pavilions built during the Olympics. One is dedicated to upcoming events and the other, **Torino Olimpiadi Forever,** preserves memories of the 2006 games.

Torino+Piemonte Card is vital for anyone planning to stay in the area for several days. It provides entry into 150 museums, monuments, and historic residences. The card also includes transportation on city buses, **TurismoBus,** and certain boat tours as well as car rental, skiing, and theater discounts in Turin and around the region. It can be purchased online or any Information Point for visits of two (€18), three (€20), five (€30), or seven (€35) days.

If all you're interested in is chocolate, grab the **ChocoPass** (€10 or €15), which lets you sample the labors of Turin's best chocolate makers. It comes with either 10 or 15 visits, over one or two days, to the city's best cafés and pastry shops, and includes a map.

GETTING THERE
By Air

Aeroporto Internazionale di Caselle (Strada San Maurizio 12, tel. 011/567-6361, www.aeroportoditorino.it) is 11 kilometers north of the center and can be reached by train, bus, or taxi in 30 minutes. It won the Best Airport Award in 2007, which means luggage is rarely lost and gates are well indicated. **Sadem** (www.sadem.it, daily 5:15 A.M.–10:45 P.M., €5) buses leave every half-hour from the arrivals hall and drop passengers off at the Porta Nuova train station. Holders of the Torino+Piemonte Card receive a 25 percent discount. The **GTT Trenibus** (www.gtt.to.it) train connects the airport with the Dora and Madonna di Campagna stations. Bus 11 completes the journey to

Stazione Porta Nuova. It costs €3 or is free with the Torino+Piemonte Card. Taxis are parked outside the arrivals hall and an average journey into town costs €30–40. If you prefer someone holding a sign with your name on it, **CTA** (tel. 011/996-3090, www.ctataxi.it) provides personalized service 24 hours a day. Otherwise there's **Pronto Taxi** (tel. 011/5737) and **Radio Taxi** (tel. 011/5730).

By Car

Turin is easily reached by car and five highways connect the city with Northern Italy. From Milan or Venice, take the A4. From Genova, use the A6 or A21; if coming from France or Northern Europe, follow the A32 or A5. All the highways end in the ring road that forms a half-crescent around the city. There are parking lots near both train stations and Piazza Vittorio Veneto. The historic center is a ZTL (limited traffic zone) and off-limits 7:30 A.M.–10:30 P.M. unless you have a permit.

By Train

The big commotion is recent years has been the construction of the TAV high-speed train line between Lyon, France, and Turin. Nearly everyone has an opinion on the project that would require tunneling through a good portion of the Alps. But even without this line, Turin is well connected to Milan and Rome. There are four train stations and most mainline trains pull into Porta Nuova (Corso Vittorio Emanuele II 53, tel. 848/888-088) and Porta Susa (Piazza XXVIII Dicembre 8). There's also daily international service to Paris with Artesia (www.artesia.eu) and Barcelona with Elipsos (www.elipsos.com). The bus terminal (tel. 011/433-8100) is in Corso Vittorio Emanuele 131.

GETTING AROUND

Gruppo Torinese Trasporti (GTT) operates trams, buses, and the driverless subway that consists of a single line for the time being. Most transportation runs 5 A.M.–1 A.M. Tickets are available in *tabaccherie,* newsstands, and anywhere you see a GTT sign posted. You can also buy them at most parking meters, although these are only valid for 80 minutes from the moment purchased. All other tickets cost €0.90, are good 70 minutes, and need to be validated when boarding any mass transit vehicle. An all-day pass is €3 and a pack of 15 tickets is €12.50. There are other formulas for families and shoppers. Itineraries can be calculated at www.5t.torino.it.

The city has 70 kilometers of bicycle paths and several pedestrian streets that make two-wheeled transport a good way of getting around. The Information Points provide route maps and from May until September bicycles can be rented in all the parks. At Parco del Valentino (Corso Massimo d'Azeglio) and Piazza Vittorio Veneto you'll get 50 percent off if you have the Torino+Piemonte Card. **Amici della Bicicletta** (Via San Domenico 28, tel. 011/561-3059) and **Bici & Dintorni** (Via Adorno 35b, tel. 011/888-981, www.biciedintorni.org) also provide rentals.

The Po is navigated by the **Valentino** and **Valentina** (GTT, tel. 800/019-152) boats that make five stops along the river. The most convenient landing is at Borgo Medioevale in Parco del Valentino. It's a relaxing ride past majestic bridges and parkland that's free for Torino+Piemonte Card holders, who can stay on as long as they like.

TurismoBus (€6 or free with Torino+Piemonte Card) leaves every hour from the tourist office in Piazza Solferino 10 A.M.–6 P.M. It makes 15 stops around the city and visitors can get on and off whenever they please. The tour is narrated in several languages and tickets may be purchased onboard. There are also a dozen themed walking tours (cinema, food, Baroque, etc., €6.50) that depart every Saturday at 6 P.M. from the same location.

If you want to get 15 meters under Turin and visit the galleries built by Emanuele Filiberto, an old air shelter, and other subterranean curiosities contact **Somewhere Tour Operator and Events** (Via Nizza 32, tel. 011/668-0580, www.somewhere.it). Groups leave Wednesdays and Fridays at 8:30 P.M. from Piazza Vittorio 5.

AROUND TURIN

Basilica di Superga is a short drive east of the city. It stands on a hill 670 meters up and looks quite imposing from the winding road that leads to the top. Vittorio Amedeo had it built in 1717 to commemorate surviving a Franco-Spanish siege. He's buried here and you can visit the royal tombs inside. The facade is monumental and the eight columns look as big as the ones used in the Pantheon in Rome.

If you don't want to drive up the hill, you can take the streetcar from **Stazione Sassi** (Piazza Modena, tel. 800/019-152, Mon.–Fri. 9 A.M.–noon and Sat.–Sun. 9 A.M.–8 P.M.,

€3.20) that departs every hour on the hour and reaches the basilica in 18 minutes. During the summer, the wait can be long. There's a great view of Turin, the Po plain, and the Alps in the distance. Souvenirs are priced to sell and it's not worth waiting to see if you find something cheaper in the city. You won't. For more spiritual pursuits, there are small praying rooms with statues of saints and candles worshippers have lit. If you want to extend the visit, just pick one of the trails that start near the church and enjoy a hike through oak and chestnut forests. The area around the basilica is now a park.

Alpi Cozie

Alpi Cozie lies in the center of the western Alps and are visible from Turin. The range contains several important valleys that run from east to west and link Italy to France. Valle di Susa is the widest valley, where abbeys built remarkably high up the hillsides once hosted a steady stream of pilgrims headed for Rome. Today traffic is less spiritual and the A32 highway regularly jams. There are good secondary roads throughout the area that offer better scenery. If winding curves aren't your thing, stick to the foothills and market towns such as Saluzzo and Cuneo where you can admire the peaks at the edge of the Padana Plain.

SALUZZO

It's no accident Saluzzo is known as "the Florence of Piedmont." It was an influential place in the 12th century and many of the new ideas from Tuscany were incorporated in the buildings and fortifications around this fascinating town. Try to arrive on a Wednesday or a Saturday, when the market is in full swing, or in May, when the antiques fair fills the main piazza.

Sights

The town was founded on the crest of a hill and **Porta di Santa Maria** (1379) leads to the medieval Piazzetta di San Giovanni. **Torre Civica** (Via

San Giovanni, tel. 335/126-9142, summer Thurs.–Sun. 9:30 A.M.–12:30 P.M. and 2:30–6:30 P.M., Oct.–Feb. Sat. and Sun. 9:30 A.M.–12:30 P.M. and 2:30–6:30 P.M., €1.30), the tower that dwarfs everything else in Saluzzo, and **San Giovanni** dominate the square much as they did in the 14th century. If you're up to it, you can climb to the loggia of the tower for a panoramic view of the town and the Alps with the Padan Plain in the distance. Inside the San Giovanni church is a wonderfully engraved wooden choir.

Salita al Castello is a busy street that leads to a castle commissioned by Tommaso I in 1270. The walls were torn down several times and the most recent additions were added in the 19th century. It was the home of a Marquise and later donated to the town. **Museo Civico** (Via San Giovanni 5, tel. 017/541-455, Apr.–Sept. Thurs.–Sun. 10 A.M.–1 P.M. and 2–6 P.M., Oct.–Mar. 10 A.M.–1 P.M. and 2–5 P.M., Tues. and Wed. at 11 A.M. and 4 P.M., €4) contains many works once hanging in the royal residence of Casa Cavassa. Highlights include *La Madonna della Misericordia* by Hans Clemer and *l'Adorazione dei Magi* by Jacopino Longo.

Entertainment and Events

Held throughout the month of May, **Mostra Nazionale di Antiquariato** (tel. 017/543-527, www.fondazioneamletobertoni.it) is one of the most prestigious antiques fairs in Italy. Not just anyone can set up a stand here and most of the merchants selling 18th–20th century furnishings also have their own shops in the region. It's better to ask before touching and if you want the long explanation about the origin of anything you'll usually get it.

Shopping

If you miss the fair, you can always drop into **Capelotti Michele** (Corso Piemonte 38, tel. 017/543-362, Mon.–Sat. 9 A.M.–1 P.M. and 3–7 P.M.), which specializes in 17th- and 18th-century antiques. Everything in the small store is very high quality and the Meissen and Sèvres porcelain has survived hundreds of years without a single chip. Besides selling antiques, **Casa d'Arte Amleto Bertoni** (Via Griselda 22, tel. 017/545-541, Mon.–Sat. 9 A.M.–1 P.M. and 3:30–7 P.M.) restores picture frames and broken chairs in its workshop. They also use pieces of old wood to make antique look-alikes that have fooled some experts.

Accommodations

The 34 ultramodern, air-conditioned rooms and bright colors of **Hotel Griselda** (Corso XXVII Aprile 13, tel. 017/547-484, www.hotelgriselda.it, €85 d) are a different world from the cobblestones outside. The second floor is for smokers. There's parking for hotel guests and you won't need a car as long as you stick to the center.

Elegance is overflowing at **Poggio Radicati** (Via San Bernardino 19, tel.017/524-8292, www.poggioradicati.com, €135 d). This small *relais* (a fusion of a hotel and a bed-and-breakfast) offers panoramic views over the city and several of the nine rooms have their own private gardens. None of the furniture is the same and if your feet hurt, a couple of minutes in the hydro massage will have you feeling better in no time.

Food

L'Ostu dij Baloss (Via Gualtieri 38, tel. 017/524-8618, Tues.–Sat. noon–3 P.M. and 7:30–11 P.M., €8–12) means "rogue" in the Piedmontese dialect, but that's not what comes to mind inside this stylish restaurant. Well-manicured round tables fill several rooms that are decorated with rustic flair. The menu includes classics like *tortino cipolle con tartufo nero* (onion pie with black truffles) and a selection of cheeses that could be an entire course. The chocolate desserts should not be missed.

Next to the house of Silvio Pellico is **La Gargotta del Pellico** (Piazza dei Mondagli 5, tel. 017/546-833, Wed.–Mon. 12:30–3:30 P.M. and 7:30–10:30 P.M., closed Tues. and Wed. lunch, €10–15), an intimate locale where the courtesy is palpable. It's just the place to sample artichokes with chickpea cream or veal stewed in Barolo wine. If time is pressing and pizza or salad will do **Le Quattro Stagioni d'Italia** (Via Volta 21, tel. 017/547-470, Thurs.–Tues. 12:30–3:30 P.M. and 7–11 P.M.) is a reliable option with a fixed price buffet at lunch (€10.50) and dinner (€17.50).

For a cocktail or coffee, grab a seat at the outdoor tables at **Caffè della Castiglia** (Piazzetta dei Mondaglia, tel. 017/521-7484, Tues.–Sun. 8 P.M.–1 A.M.) in Piazzetta dei Mondagli. **I Formaggi di Franco Parola** (Piazza XX Settembre 6, tel. 017/524-8262, Tues.–Sat. 8 A.M.–noon and 4–7:30 P.M.) is stocked with dozens of Alpine cheeses, such as Raschera di Alpeggio and Serass, that have a pleasant herb flavor.

Information and Services

The IAT office (Piazza Mondagli 5, tel. 017/546-710, www.comune.saluzzo.cn.it, Tues.–Sun. 9 A.M.–noon and 2:30–5 P.M.) provides maps and a list of certified tour guides that take visitors on one-hour itineraries around the medieval, Renaissance, and Baroque monuments of town.

Getting There and Around

The fastest way from Turin to reach Saluzzo by car is along the A6 highway. Exit at Marene and continue on the SS 662 for 20 kilometers. The slower, more scenic route is the SS 20, which you can pick up directly from the Turin ring road. The town is off the main train line and requires a transfer at Savigliano. The journey takes 1.5 hours and costs €4.40, unless you want to spend an extra two euros on a first-class ticket. Trains leave every hour from Torino Porta Nuova.

ATI buses (Via Circonvallazione 19, tel. 017/547-8811, www.atibus.it) depart from Corso Marconi in Turin and make a dozen stops on their way to town. A ticket is €3.90 and bicycles can be transported for an additional €7. In Saluzzo bus tickets can be purchased at Cartoleria Jolly (Piazza Cavour 4) and Edicola Parisa e Pignatta (Corso Rome 51).

Around Saluzzo

Overlooking the Monviso Mountains near the town of Manta is the luxurious **Castello della Manta** (Manta, Via al Castello, tel. 017/587-822, www.comunemanta.it, Tues.– Sun. 10 A.M.–6 P.M., €5 including an audio guide). It isn't much from the outside but you'll get a neck ache looking at the amazingly detailed frescoes on the inside. The property belonged to an aristocratic family and was purchased by the Italian state in 1948. What they got were rooms like Sala Baronale, with a Gothic version of a comic strip recounting the adventures of various knights. Ceilings in the hallway and bedrooms are all painted and recount legends and myths in stunning Technicolor.

CUNEO

Cuneo lies on a triangular strip of land between the Gesso and Stura di Demonte Rivers. The waterways facilitated trade and Piazza Galimberti has been hosting a market for hundreds of years. The Savoys rebuilt much of the town in the 18th century, which explains the wide avenues absent from other towns in the area. Mountains fill the horizon and many travelers spend their nights here while exploring the Valle Stura during the day.

Sights
DUOMO
The heart of Cuneo runs along Via Roma, where an old chapel stood even before the city was founded in 1198. The duomo, as locals

call the building that looks more like a courthouse than a church, was ransacked several times by enemies before receiving a complete restoration in the 17th century. The inside is designed along Greek lines and contains a baptistery font near the fancy altar.

TORRE CIVICA
Overlooking Piazza Audifreddi, Torre Civica (Via Roma, tel. 017/163-4175, €2.10 or €3.65 with museum entry) is the tallest structure in town. It was built after a peace accord was finally reached with the rival town of Mondovi in 1317. Ironically it was later used to spot Middle Age enemies and survived nine sieges. It was also instrumental in the resistance movement during World War II. You can ride the elevator to the top for a good view of the Langhe province and Monte Rosa.

MUSEO CIVICO
The 14th-century convent of San Francesco now houses Museo Civico (Via Santa Maria 10, tel. 017/163-4175, Tues.–Sat. 8:30 A.M.–1 P.M. and 2:30–5:30 P.M., Sun. 3–7 P.M., €2.60 or €3.65 with Torre Civica) and a collection of everyday peasant objects behind glass recounting Alpine living. There's typical furniture, tools, and even 1930s-era dolls.

◖ MARKET DAY
Everyone in Piedmont knows that Tuesday is market day in Cuneo, as it has been for hundreds of years. People get up earlier than usual and the sounds of merchants setting up their goods can be heard in Piazza Galimberti starting at 5 A.M. The colorful stalls fill every inch of the vast, animated square and offer everything from World War I medals of honor to the handcrafted iron objects the town is famous for. Food stalls are generally on the outside near the arcades and sell gorgonzola, toma, and robiola cheeses produced in the region. Hundreds of shoppers create quite a bustle and it can take hours to see everything. If you're traveling in a group, there's chance you'll get separated. The statue in the center of the piazza is a convenient rendezvous point or place

to observe the good-humored banter between clients and stall owners.

Entertainment and Events

Writers get a lot of respect in Cuneo and every year in mid-November the city invites contemporary authors to read their work during **Scrittorincittà** (tel. 017/165-236, www.scrittorincitta.it). It's not all in Italian and the readings are accompanied with expositions and concerts throughout town.

Residents wake up a little earlier on Tuesdays and the monumental train station is busier than usual. There are different accents and languages in the air and people come from as far away as Nice to fill up their shopping bags with gastronomic goodies. Piazza Galimberti becomes a patchwork of umbrellas from dawn until dusk and the cafés under the arcades that surround the square are ideally positioned for watching the drama as buyers and sellers negotiate prices.

The grey- and white-faced **Teatro Toselli** (Via del Teatro Toselli 9, tel. 017/144-4276) is a long way from La Scala. The theater was actually once a church and is now operated by the town that presents two seasons of theater and music performances. Tickets start from €10 and can be purchased directly from the box office one hour before the curtain rises.

Sports and Recreation

Parco Fluviale Gesso e Stura (along Stura and Gresso Rivers, entrances on Viale degli Angeli and Via Basse S. Anna, tel. 017/144-4501, www.parcofluviale.cuneo.it) is the newest park in the region, with 100 kilometers of cycling and hiking trails where small mammals run wild. The park officers organize bird-watching courses during the mating season and provide binoculars if you've left yours at home.

Accommodations

Palazzo Lovero (Via Roma 37, tel. 017/169-0420, www.palazzolovera.com, €130 d) is one of the oldest palazzi in the historic center along the main street. There are 46 spacious rooms and

even in high season you may feel like you've got the hotel to yourself. Giorgio and his wife Stefania also operate a restaurant and provide one-day cooking courses for anyone who wants to take home more than a gigabyte of photos.

Food

You'll need a little luck to find a table at **Osteria della Chiocciola** (Via Fossano 1, tel. 017/166-277, Mon.–Sat. 12:15–2:30 P.M. and 8–10 P.M., €7–10). Cuneesi (as locals are called) love the food and the reasonable prices. The menu all depends on the season. In summer, porcini and potato pie make an appearance, along with fried zucchini flowers and *ramassin* (plum typical of the region). Marc Lanteri combines a French touch with Piedmont simplicity inside **Delle Antiche Contrade** (Via Savigliano 11, tel. 017/148-0488, Tues.–Fri. 12:30–2:30 P.M. and 7–11 P.M., Mon. 7–11 P.M., €9–13), where dining proceeds at a leisurely pace and the cheese cart is always ready to roll. Make sure to try the chestnut flavored desserts.

Hemingway was a big fan of the rum cocktails mixed at **Caffè Pasticceria Arione** (Piazza Galimberti 14, tel. 017/169-2539, daily 9 A.M.–6 P.M.) since 1923, but if you want something more refreshing ask for a *glacé*. Tables inside are surrounded by red, leatherbound chairs where tea and beer drinkers are equally at home. After picking up some salami (lanzardo is the local favorite) from **Salumeria Ariano** (Via Pascal 2, tel. 017/169-3522, daily 7 A.M.–noon and 2:30–7 P.M., closed Mon. morning) you can choose from dozens of types of breads inside **Panetteria Rossi** (Corso Nizza 41, tel. 017/166-621, daily 8 A.M.–1 P.M. and 4–7 P.M.). Salted, unsalted, white, dark, thin, long, it's all here. They even sell loaves more often found in Tuscany or Aosta Valley.

Getting There and Around

From Turin drive south on the A6 until Fossano and follow the state road for 25 kilometers until Cuneo. Trains leave every hour from Turin and cover the 50 kilometers in 80 minutes. A one-way ticket costs €5.30.

Langhe

The rolling hills of the Langhe are where Piedmont gets its reputation for wine. It's here in the towns of Bra, Alba, and Asti that *barolo* and *spumante* are produced. The countryside is especially verdant in spring and the area's forests are renown for the truffles locals unearth with the help of trusted sniffer dogs. Well-traveled stomachs claim this is the best place to eat in Italy. One taste of the *fonduta al tartufo bianco* (white truffle fondue) is all the convincing a palate needs.

ALBA

Alba is a city of towers. Locals say there were 100 at one time but now only about 20 remain. They date from the Middle Ages when the biggest threat was Asti just down the road and a tower was the best means to dissuade an enemy. From the top, a sea of vineyards emerges beyond the rooftops. The hexagonal shape you may notice if flying overhead is a remnant of Roman walls, a little of which can still be seen.

Sights

The main entrance to the city is through Porta di S. Martino which leads to Via Vittorio Emanuele II, also known as Via Maestro. It's the main commercial thoroughfare and remains busy throughout the day. At number 13 is **casa-forte Riva,** one of the tallest towers that rise starkly above the town, however it is not open to the public. At the end of the street is the **Cattedrale di San Lorenzo** in Piazza Risorgimento. It's pink and has a sedate Baroque interior. The rose window in the center is at its best around midday under a strong light. The cathedral is open to the public and it is free to enter.

The city fell into the hands of the Savoys in 1631 and once the plague had passed there was a general rebirth—symbolized by the renovation of **Palazzo Comunale** (tel. 017/329-2454, Tues.–Sat. 8:15 A.M.–12:15 P.M., free admission) in 2005, which was built next to the cathedral on Roman ruins. It includes arcades, a common feature of many Piedmont towns, and many spectacular frescoes on the inside.

Entertainment and Events

They've been digging up white truffles around Alba for centuries, but the **Fiera del Tartufo Bianco** (Piazza Medford 3, tel. 017/336-1051, www.fieradeltartufo.org) isn't just about an underground delicacy. The month-long festival in October is the occasion to race donkeys, dress in medieval costume, witness falconry displays, and peruse the daily market. Gerard Depardieu comes nearly every year and never goes home empty handed. A truffle auction is also held in **Castello di Grinzane Cavour** (tel. 017/326-2159, usually second Sunday of November starting at 8:30 A.M., €3) outside of town. It gets pretty heated with telephone bidders from as far away as Tokyo raising prices into quadruple digits.

Sports and Recreation

Hot air balloons lift off every morning into the skies above Alba. The route depends on the wind, but chances are you'll see at least one castle and a whole lot of rows of white and red grape vines. **Fly in Balloons** (Santa Vittoria d'Alba, tel. 335/584-4664, www.flyin balloons.com) provides transportation to the launch site, breakfast, training by licensed pilots, and a one-hour flight. From Monday to Thursday the cost is €180 and on weekends it goes up to €220. The basket can hold up to four passengers.

If you prefer to keep your feet on the ground and want to take in a little countryside, try walking the path that leads to the village of Barbaresco. From Piazza Monsignor Grassi, leave the city on the asphalt road, go 200 meters, and take the first left after the railroad crossing. It's all hills, vineyards, and river after that. The nine-kilometer hike is suitable for all levels and follows a well-marked trail.

Accommodations

◖ **Villa la Favorita** (Località Altavilla 12bis, tel. 338/471-5005, www.villalafavorita.it, €115 d) rests on a hillside less than two kilometers from Alba. The farmhouse is set on a large estate covered in vineyards and fruit trees. Grapes are used to produce Nebbiolo d'Alba, which the owner will encourage you to taste for free. Four rooms are decorated with furniture that's been handed down several generations and modern conveniences include air-conditioning and satellite TV. None of the guests miss the plentiful breakfast and homemade jams served in the garden.

For something closer to town, there's the modern **Castelli** (Corso Torino 14, tel. 017/336-1978, www.hotelicastelli.com, €95 d) with a panoramic terrace or **Hotel Savona** (Via Roma 1, tel. 017/344-0440, www.hotel savona.com, €100 d), which can't be beat when it comes to location.

Food

Eating is a pleasure in Alba and *Tajarin all'albese* (white truffle dish with chicken liver and onion) is one of the must-taste pasta dishes invented here. The handmade *tagliolini* is seasoned with fresh butter and *tartufo* (truffle). *Carne all'albese* is thinly sliced raw beef flavored with oil, lemon, and *parmigiano.*

◖ **Piazza Duomo Ristorante e Piola** (Piazza Risorgimento 4, tel. 017/344-2800, www. piazzaduomoalba.com, Tues.–Sat. noon–3 P.M. and 7–11 P.M., €8–20) provides two dining options in one 16th-century location. The restaurant upstairs features the creativity of Enrico Crippa in a refined dining room where British and American accents can be heard marveling after every chew. Service matches the quality of the food, while downstairs things are more laid back. Piola recreates a typical Piedmontese *osteria* with standard dishes served in a rustic atmosphere. Underneath the arcades **l'Antico Caffè Calissano** (Piazza del Duomo, tel. 017/344-2101, daily 7 A.M.–7 P.M.) is where artists and intellectuals once met and the best place to sip a coffee or Vermouth and observe life in a medieval town.

Via Vittorio Emanuele is lined with stores selling locally made pasta and cheeses. Il **Piacere del Gusto,** at number 23, combines wines with books written by authors from the region. If you miss the truffle auction, head to **Tartufi Morra** (Piazza Pertinace 3, tel. 017/364-271, www.tartufimorra. com, Oct.–Dec. daily 9 A.M.–12:30 P.M. and 3:30–7:30 P.M.). They've been around since 1930 and are open every day during truffle season only.

Information and Services

The tourist office (tel. 017/335-833, www. langheroero.it, Mon.–Sat. 9 A.M.–12:30 P.M. and 2:30–6:30 P.M.) is located in Piazza Risorgimento 2. They can provide you with information about local wineries or find you a guide if you'd like to get to know the town better.

You can tell a town is wealthy when it has its own bank. Branches of Banca d'Alba operate in Corso Italia 4, Via Vittorio Emanuele 32, and Corso Langhe 102. There are four pharmacies around town and the one near the Duomo in Piazza Risorgimento 5 (tel. 017/344-0024) stays open late. Travelers can access the Internet at the tourist office, public library (Cortile della Maddalena, Via V. Emanuele 19, tel. 017/329-0092), or Mail Boxes (Piazza Cristo Re 2, tel. 017/336-4678).

Getting There and Around

From Turin, there are several ways of reaching Alba by car. The fastest is on the A6 south until Carmagnola, after which you'll need to keep eyes peeled for signs and take a series of smaller roads. If maps aren't your thing, the A21 to Asti Est then south on the SS231 may be the safer option. Trains leave every hour from Porta Nuova and require a transfer at Cavallermaggiore. A one-way tickets costs €4.80.

It only takes a morning to see Alba and once you've gotten your fill of the arcades it's nice to hop on a bike and pedal your way to the next town. Mountain and racing bikes can be rented from **Cicli Gagliardini** (Via Ospedale 7, tel. 017/344-0726) or **Motocicli De Stefanis** (Via S. Margherita, 2, tel. 017/344-0462).

Around Alba

Alba is in the center of the Langhe and Roero valley and any road you chose leads to antiquity, castles, and good food. If you have the time drive along **La Strada Romantica di Langhe e Roero** (tel. 017/336-4030, www. turismoinlanga.it), which covers 11 towns—including **Nieve,** which could easily become your favorite *borgo* in Italy. In Barolo, stop by **Marchesi di Barolo** (Via Roma 1, tel. 017/564-491, daily 10:30 A.M.–5:30 P.M.) to sample local wines and come to grips with this famous grape.

For four days in mid-May, the residents of **Bra** only have one thing on their minds. Cheese (www.cheese.slowfood.it) brings every type of *formaggi* to this little town and none of it comes plastic-wrapped. To accompany the endless varieties, local beer brewers set their taps up in Piazza della Birra. Restaurants offer special menus but you could easily fill yourself on the samples offered at the colorful stalls lining the streets of the small town.

ASTI

Asti is synonymous with the *spumante* (sparkling wine) that gives Champagne a run for its money—and the Moscato grape is the secret. The town of 74,000 is in the center of Italy's most prestigious wine region. It's a laid-back city (except during the Palio di Asti in September), with a well-preserved medieval core, graceful churches, and rolling green countryside all around.

Sights and Events
PIAZZA ALFIERI AND PIAZZA SAN SECONDA

Asti's main square is actually more of a triangle. The proud-looking statue in the middle of Piazza Alfieri is the poet Vittorio Alfieri, who has remained popular except with schoolchildren forced to read his tragic novels. This is where the Palio di Asti is held every September and locals sit chatting under oak trees the rest of the time. Nearby Piazza San Seconda has a more typical shape and is the real center of medieval Asti.

Torre Troyana in Piazza Medici

Bricks have a unique color here and if you've been paying attention to rooftops you'll notice these have a slightly different hue about them. The **Duomo** is a case in point. It dates from the 15th century and is a textbook definition of Gothic. Even subsequent alterations haven't managed to reduce the austerity. The *campanile* (1266) next to the church is the first of many towers that intensify Asti's skyline. **Torre Troyana** (Piazza Medici 6, tel. 014/139-9489, Apr.–Oct. Sat.–Sun. 10 A.M.–1 P.M. and 4–7 P.M., €2) is the best preserved and one of the symbols of the city (you'll see it on an infinite number of postcards). It's also the only one open to the public and the view from 44 meters up gives you a chance to examine the layout of the city.

SANT'ANASTASIO

You can take the back streets or Corso Vittorio Alfieri to reach Sant'Anastasio. What's really interesting here is underground in the crypt, where Roman and medieval foundations were discovered after renovations. Part of the church is now an archeological museum (Corso Alfieri 365a, tel. 014/437-454, Tues.–Sun. 10 A.M.–1 P.M. and 4–8 P.M., €2.50) containing antique crypts and ancient tombs, as well as the remains of preexisting buildings. For an extra €0.50, you can buy a combined ticket and visit **San Pietro in Consavia** (Corso Alfieri 2, tel. 014/353-072, Tues.–Sun. 10 A.M.–1 P.M. and 3–6 P.M.) on the other side of town. The complex was built to host pilgrims heading to and from Rome. A cloister in the center is built with the same typical red bricks of the towers, and there's a museum full of fossils discovered in the Andona Valley.

PALIO DI ASTI

This historic festival and horse race (tel. 014/139-9399, www.palio.asti.it) was first held in 1275 while the town was laying siege to their eternal rivals of Alba nearby. Today it's held on the third Sunday in September. On that Sunday morning, there's a long parade with 800 costumed participants dressed in the colors of their *rione* (neighborhood). It leaves from Piazza della Cattedrale and winds through the streets to **Campo del Palio** (horse race track). The race starts in the afternoon and 21 competitors riding bareback attempt to make the last cut. The final is three laps around the Piazza Alfieri for a total of 1,300 meters. Falls are frequent but even riderless horses can win the race. The triumphant neighborhood celebrates its victory until late that evening. The top prize is a *palio* (banner) and the rider who comes in last receives an anchovy and keeps a low profile for weeks afterwards. The race coincides with a wine festival and there are lots of opportunities to sample the latest vintages from outdoor kiosks. Sidewalks around the piazza are packed but stands are set up and it's a good idea to show up early for the event.

Accommodations

Priore Hotel (Corso Galileo Ferrari 58, tel. 014/159-3688, www.hotelpriore.it, €85 d) is close to the railway station and a few minutes by foot from Piazza Alfieri. The ancient exterior is a contrast to the 25 rooms equipped with 21st-century comforts. A buffet breakfast is included and the receptionist doubles as a tour guide. If you prefer rooms decorated with country furniture, the recently restructured **Palio** (Via Cavour 106, tel. 014/134-371, www.hotelpalio.com, €90 d) may be more to your liking. The mini-suites have whirlpool tubs and panoramic terraces. The owners operate the Falcon Vecchio restaurant nearby, which serves traditional Piedmontese fare.

Hotel Aleramo (Via E. Filiberto 13, tel. 014/159-566, www.hotel.aleramo.it, €140 d) was named after the legendary Marquis of Monferrato, a 10th-century nobleman known for his love of luxury. The hotel might not quite meet his standards, but it is conveniently located near the train station and historic center of Asti. Business travelers and tourists pass each other in the hallways on their way to rooms awash in minimalist style. The price includes a breakfast buffet in the large dining room downstairs, which is served until 10 A.M. on weekends.

Food

Da Aldo di Castiglione (Via Gioberti 8, tel. 014/135-4905, Fri.–Wed. 12–3 P.M. and 7–10:30 P.M., €8–10) is a reliable address to taste Piedmontese specialties in the center of town. Aldo and his daughter run the kitchen while Franca recites the menu. If your Italian is rusty, have a look at the list posted outside before entering. You can count on Franca to make a good choice on a wine selection that won't set you back more than €10. Classic starters include *carne cruda* (thin strips of raw beef marinated in lemon and olive oil), *mousse di robiola* (cheese mousse), and *insalata russa* (vegetable salad). Leave it to Aldo to make a great risotto and roasted duck.

Piedmont meets Liguria in the kitchen of **Osteria del Diavolo** (Piazza San Martino 6, tel. 014/130-221, Wed.–Sun. 7–11 P.M., €8–12). During the summer, the little square outside the restaurant fills up with tables. Inside, three small air-conditioned rooms are usually packed and Fabrizio Barberis is busy serving *capon magro* (type of bird similar to a turkey) and *tajarin* (white truffle dish). Cheese is taken very seriously here and comes directly from local producers. Many of the desserts use hazelnuts and the apple pie is as good as anything grandma makes.

Besides making an excellent espresso, **Caffè Torrefazione Ponchione** (Corso Alfieri 151, tel. 014/159-2469, daily 9 A.M.–7 P.M.) sells local wines at honest prices. In a Liberty-style shop a little farther down the street, you'll find handmade pastries and chocolate. **Pasticceria Giordanino** (Corso Alfieri 254) even bakes a tart in honor of the *palio*. You can smell **Fucci Formaggi** (Piazza Statuto 9, tel. 014/155-6343, Mon.–Sat. 8 A.M.–12:15 P.M. and 3:30–7:30 P.M.) from a distance and the cheeses inside could inspire you to have a picnic right there on the spot.

Information and Services

The tourist office in Piazza Alfieri (tel. 014/530-357, www.astiturismo.it) is open daily. The city is just big enough to require a map and it's useful to stop in and get an updated list of activities.

Getting There and Around

Asti is 50 kilometers east of Turin, directly off the A21 highway. There are two exits and the SS10 runs parallel to the highway if you have time to spare. Asti is on a main train line; depending on what service you catch from Torino Porta Nuova, the journey takes 30 minutes to an hour.

Around Asti

Legend has it the **Abbazia di Vezzolano** (northeast of Asti on the SS458, Str. dell'Abbazia, tel. 011/992-0607, Tues.–Sun. 9 A.M.–12:30 P.M. and 2–6:30 P.M., admission free) was founded by Carlo Magno, and the first document that mentions the abbey was written 1,000 years ago. It doesn't look that old and will probably outlast some skyscrapers. The entrance is unadorned except for alternating shades of brick. Color was saved for inside and a delightful series of frescoes that run down the central nave. Inside the abbey there's a permanent exhibition about Romanesque architecture in the province. If the abbey door is closed during working hours ring the doorbell on the side of the church. If you have time, there is another abbey nearby in Mongiglietto that is worth a visit.

Val di Susa

The Val di Susa begins just west of Turin. Some of the earliest settlements in Italy can be found here and it was a vital passage towards Gaul for the Romans. In the Middle Ages, the Via Francigena that runs through the valley was a busy pilgrim route. The abbeys underneath snowcapped mountains are remnants of those long journeys and inspired Umberto Eco to write *In the Name of the Rose*. Sport has revitalized the area and many world-class skiing events are held here annually. Unique products include *Vino del Ghiaccio* (ice wine) that is harvested in January and *Reblochon*, a red-crusted cheese aged in mountain caves.

SACRA DI SAN MICHELE

Back in the Middle Ages when a nobleman wanted to be forgiven for his sins, he offered to build something for the pope. Hughes de Montboissier must have had a lot of skeletons in his closet. Besides building this impressive monastery 962 meters above the valley, he also was the guiding force behind Mont-Saint-Michel in France.

Sights

Sacra di San Michele (tel. 011/939-130, www.sacradisanmichele.com, Tues.–Sun. 9:30 A.M.–12:30 P.M. and 2:30–6 P.M., €4) is a steep climb and most of the 140 Benedictine

Susa lies near the France border.

monks who lived and prayed here rarely left the compound. After the metal gates go up the **Scalone dei Morti,** which is named the staircase of death because it was once lined with the bodies of dead monks. The main chapel was started in the 12th century and marks a transformation from Romanesque to Gothic style.

The abbey declined after the abbot was excommunicated in 1380, and was abandoned entirely for over 200 years. Carlo Albert was behind its rebirth and invited the Rosmini order to occupy the building. They've been there ever since and now gladly provide tours of their extraordinary home.

Getting There and Around
By car from Turin, take the A32 west towards Frejus and exit at Avigliana Est. From there it's 12 kilometers and the abbey is clearly indicated off the SP188. The nearest train station is Sant'Ambrogio and it's a one-hour walk through pine forests to the abbey.

SUSA
Susa lies at the juncture of two roads leading to France and gained the nickname *la porta d'Italia* (doorway to Italy) when Latin was still a spoken language. The strategic position hasn't always been beneficial and the town was sacked several times since its founding by Celtic tribes. Monte Rocciamelone rises 3,538 meters and is the main attraction for skiers, who regularly descend upon the town in wintertime.

Sights
If you see the town's coat of arms, you'll understand what's missing from two cylindrical towers of **Porta Savoia.** The entrance is still impressive though and was built at the same time as the walls that once encircled Susa. Next door is the cathedral consecrated in 1027 and given a Gothic makeover in the 14th century. On the south side is a Romanesque *campanile,* which unfortunately is closed to the public.

The oldest monument in town is the **Arco di Augusto,** erected in 8 B.C. to commemorate

© ALESSIA RAMACCI

The Arco di Augusto commemorates the
Gaulish-Roman alliance.

a deal between the Roman emperor and local
warlord. It's where bulls were sacrificed. Other
ancient remnants include an aqueduct, bath,
and arena where La Castagna d'Oro folk festival is held every autumn.

Sports and Recreation

Susa-Moncensisio (tel. 012/262-2386) is the
oldest automobile race in the world. The first
edition was held in 1902 along the same four
kilometers of road that is used today in late
May. Drivers wear helmets now and spectators
are advised not to stand in the curves.

The only red and white fir trees growing in
Piedmont are in the **Parco Naturale del Gran
Bosco** (tel. 012/285-4720). The 2,000 hectares
of mountainous terrain was once where the military got their wood and many of the beams inside the Superga in Turin came from this forest.
You can walk the old military road up to the
Lago Ghiacciaia up to the Testa dell'Assietta
plain where locals celebrate the battle of Cati-
nat every July 19. It's a four hour walk from the
valley west of Susa and if you'd like something a

little less challenging you can follow the Sentieri
dei Franchi that Carlo Magno took on his way
to defeat the Lombards.

Accommodations

Susa e Stazione (Corso Stati Uniti 4, tel.
012/262-2226, www.hotelsusa.it, €80 d) has
been providing travelers with a place to rest
since 1906. The rooms have been upgraded
considerably since then and a lot of cyclists
use it as a base while exploring the mountain
roads leading to France. Parking is available
right outside the hotel and it's just a short walk
from the train station.

Back in the 1970s, **Hotel Napoleon** (Via
Mazzini 44, tel. 012/262-2855, www.hotel
napoleon.it, €85 d) was modern. Nowadays it's
just kitschy and comfortable. If you don't judge
a hotel by the furniture, then you'll thank the
Vanara family on the way out. The center of
Susa can be reached in minutes and guests have
access to a gym, sauna, and lounge.

Food

Steaks cooked to order are the main attraction at **Meana** (Piazza IV Novembre 2, tel.
012/232-359, Thurs.–Tues. 12:30 P.M.–3 P.M.
and 7:30–11 P.M., €8–11). Meat is the main attraction in the two dining rooms and if you've
never tasted bison this is your chance. Don't
leave without a small glass of their after-dinner
liqueur, which the owner generously offers to
his regular clients.

◖ Antica Trattoria la Stellina (Via Gia-
glione 3, tel. 012/262-9289, www.anticatratto
rialastellina.it, Tues.–Sun. 12:15 P.M.–2:45 P.M.
and 7:30–11 P.M., €9–12) is just outside of
town in a 17th-century farmhouse where the
Longhino family have being serving *cucina po-
vera* (poor food) for years. Poor in this case is
a good thing and consists of wonderful soups
and broths with simple everyday ingredients
like bread, beef, and porcini mushrooms.

They make their own focaccia in Susa
using a special wood oven found only in the
valley. You can try a slice at **Favro** (Corso
Stati Uniti 118, tel. 012/262-2498, daily
8 A.M.–1 P.M. and 3–7 P.M.). Local bakers in-

vented *pan della Marchesa* in honor of Marquis of Susa, which is sweet and made daily at **Pasticceria Pietrini** (Piazza Bartolomei 10, tel. 012/262-2303, daily 8:30 A.M.–1 P.M. and 3:30–7:30 P.M., closed July).

Getting There and Around

Three roads lead to Susa. You can take the SS24 or the SS25, but the A32 highway is the fastest way and can be picked up off the Turin ring road. Trains depart frequently and the journey takes an hour. Make sure to take one that doesn't require a transfer at Bussole. The station is just outside of town and local buses and taxis complete the journey to town. GTT buses leave from Corso Turati 19.

Around Susa

Eight kilometers northeast of Susa lies the **Abbazia di Novalesa** (tel. 012/265-3210, Mon.–Fri. 9 A.M.–noon and 3:30–5:30 P.M., Sat. and Sun. 9–11:30 A.M.). From Susa take the road heading toward Moncenisio. At Novalesa there are signs that will lead you to the abbey. The abbey's central cloister and four chapels were built to host pilgrims in A.D. 726. The frescoes inside Cappella di S. Eldorado recount the story of the saint and the mountain air has helped retain the vivid colors. To help them last even longer the chapel is closed whenever it rains or snows. The abbey has been active since its founding, and today the Benedictine monks dedicate themselves to restoring ancient manuscripts. There aren't many places to eat along the way, so bring a snack if you think you'll get hungry. Accommodations are available in the monastery for anyone who wants to recharge their spiritual batteries. In July and August there are guided tours offered Monday–Friday at 10:30 A.M. and 4:30 P.M.

Aosta Valley

Italy's smallest and least populated region is also one of its most independent. It is officially bilingual (Italian and French) and proud of its cross-cultural past and breathtaking views. The region is home to over 130 castles and the oldest national park in Italy, where winter sports thrive. Ecotourism plays an important role in the region's economy and many people make a living with the skill of their hands.

AOSTA

Aosta, the largest town in the region, is situated on a plain where the Dora Baltea and Buthier Rivers meet. The Romans conquered the area in 25 B.C. from Salassian Gauls and built their trademark forum, amphitheater, and arches, which still stand in the center. The old town is essentially a large rectangle surrounded by travertine walls with towers at each corner in various states of decay. Of the four original entrances only Porta Praetoria is fit to receive an emperor—or the tourists surprised to find such well-preserved antiquity. There's a reason Aosta

is called "the Rome of the north," even if the scale of the monuments is much smaller.

Medieval Aosta saw the addition of towers used by the Challant family and dukes of Aosta to control access into the valley. Proximity to France and Switzerland makes the town a natural crossroads for tourists heading towards more remote corners of the region.

Sights

The town offers prehistoric, Roman, and medieval remains inside the old defensive walls. Most of the center has been pedestrianized and can be covered on foot or bicycle in under an hour. The Sant'Orso complex is just east of the Arch of Augustus, and the spectacular cable car up the mountain to Pila leaves from behind the train station.

If you want to enter the city as the Romans did, you'll have to pass through the **Arch of Augustus,** built to honor the emperor and now the center of a large roundabout. It's much simpler than any of the arches in Rome

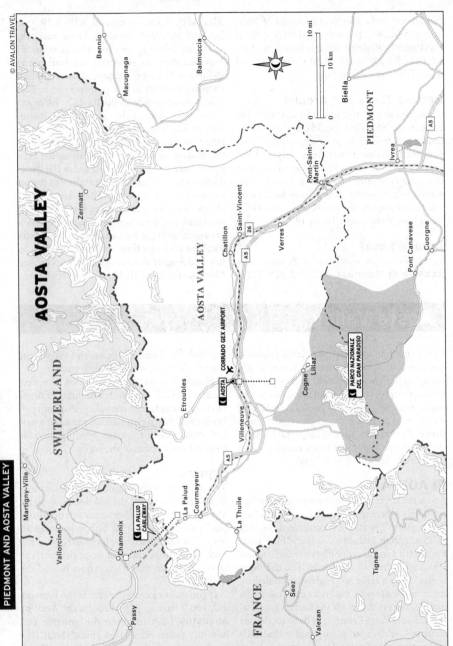

PIEDMONT AND AOSTA VALLEY

© ALESSIA RAMACCIA

Aosta Valley surrounded by the Alps

and dark local stone is used rather than travertine. The only blemish is the roof that was added in the 18th century. **Porta Praetoria** is over three meters thick and you can still see slabs of the marble along the top that once covered the entire structure. The central arch was used for animals and carts entering town, while the smaller entrances on the sides were for pedestrians.

The **Roman theater** (Via Baillage, daily 9 A.M.–7 P.M., free admission) nearby is in equally good condition. Its facade stands 22 meters high. It's believed the theater was actually enclosed and could accommodate up to 3,000 spectators. The stage and semi-circular seating are still used today for concerts and are a wonderful place to rest. To visit the **amphitheater** (Via dell'Anfiteatro, tel. 016/526-2149, daily by appointment only), you'll need to enter the monastery of Santa Catarina; during the off-season, it's safer to phone ahead. The entire Roman population could fit in this arena, which has preserved eight arches and where medieval duels were

fought. **Museo Archeologico** (Piazza Pietro Leonardo Roncas 12, tel. 016/531-572, daily 9 A.M.–7 P.M., free) contains many coins, sculptures, and funeral objects uncovered in the town. The northern wall is currently being excavated and they are still making discoveries.

The most peaceful spot in Aosta is the **Sant'Orso monastery** (Via Sant'Orso, tel. 016/526-2026, daily 9 A.M.–noon and 3–5:30 P.M., €4) just ten minutes by foot from the center of town. The Gothic buildings have simple facades, are covered in dark slate, and are arranged in a medieval cluster. Frescoes inside date from the 11th century and recount the life of the apostles. Saint Orso is buried in the crypt below where the first Christians in the valley once prayed.

Entertainment and Events

One thousand years ago, people still believed in miracles, and when a Scottish monk crossed the Alps and arrived in town a new holiday was added to the calendar. The monk's name was Sant'Orso and his festival is one of the oldest in Italy. Today **Fiera di Sant'Orso,** on the last two days of January, is a chance to see local craftsmen at work and to buy a pair of wooden sabots. The streets get so crowded that the mayor had to institute a one-way rule for pedestrian traffic. Just follow everyone else and when you get cold grab a cup of *vin brulè* (warm wine), which you'll find sold on every corner.

Expo Vallée (call the ATP office at tel. 016/533-352 for details) in July and **Fiore d'Ete** (tel. 016/523-6627) on the Saturday before Ferragosto weren't created to charm tourists. Rather, they're a way for dispersed mountain populations to exchange news and do some trading. The reunion of artisans is also a chance to purchase traditional food and craft items. **Ferragosto** originated with the Romans and was originally a month long celebration of the emperor Augustus. Today it takes place on August 15 and is dedicated to the Virgin Mary. Most Italians will take this day off from work and high-season peaks during the days leading up to this popular holiday.

You never know what to expect at the **Festival dell'Improvvisazione** in the second half of August. Concerts are held in the Roman theater and generally kick off at 9:30 P.M. Most of the improvisation has jazz undertones and musicians encourage audiences to participate with their hands, feet, or whatever else inspires them.

Silent movies get their due during **Festival Strade del Cinema** (10/e loc. Borgnalle, tel. 016/506-0106, www.stradedelcinema.it). It's perhaps the only chance to see original Charlie Chaplin and Harold Lloyd films accompanied by orchestras playing original scores; more recent avant-garde silent films are also projected. The action starts at 9:30 P.M. throughout August in the Roman theater.

Shopping

A pocketknife always comes in useful in the mountains and carving wood is one of the region's great traditions. Walnut is used for furniture and figurines, while maple is favored for kitchen utensils and traditional drinking cups. You'll find both at **K100** (Via de Tillier 21, tel. 016/531-884, Mon. 3–7 P.M. Tues.–Sat. 9 A.M.–1 P.M. and 3–7 P.M.). The owner does the sculpting himself and can carve roosters and miniature cows practically blindfolded. **Giorgio Jaccod** (Via M. Solarolo 5, tel. 016/544-585) uses rock instead of wood, and **Rene Monjoje** (Via S. Anselmo 44, tel. 016/532-343) creates ceramic statues, vases, and ornaments in his workshop, which has a strong smell of clay.

Sports and Recreation

The nearest ski resort is **Pila,** 18 kilometers above town. Take the underpass at the train station and walk left until you reach the cable car (daily 8 A.M.–12:15 P.M. and 2–6 P.M., €5 round-trip) that carries passengers over 1,000 meters up the mountain. There are 70 kilometers of *piste* (tracks), with 8 blue, 52 red, and 10 black. Eleven lifts connect different parts of the mountain—from baby Pila, for beginners, to Couis, 2,705 meters above sea level. Most rental shops provide maps and snowboarders can reach the snow park equipped with quarter- and half-pipes via the Chamolé lift.

The **Consorzio Turistico l'Espace de Pila** (Fraz. Pila 40, tel. 016/552-1055) organizes rafting excursions during the summer and day trips to Giardino del Gran Paradiso, a botanical garden in the Parco del Gran Paradiso.

Accommodations

Nabuisson (Via E. Aubert 50, tel. 016/536-3006, www.bedbreakfastaosta.it, €65) is a two-room bed-and-breakfast 10 minutes from the train station down a lovely cobblestoned street. Each room has its own separate entrances and a private bath. Dark wood and wide floorboards predominate. Breakfast is served in bed and the owner is happy to answer any questions about town.

Campeggio Milleluci (Loc. Porossan-Roppoz, 15, tel. 016/544-274, €8 per person) is one kilometer from the historic center on a hillside from which many excursions are possible. The grounds are covered with pines and in the center is a hotel (€80 d) where a more traditional stay is possible and breakfast is served to campers.

Food

◖ Trattoria degli Artisti (Via Maillet 5–7, tel. 016/540-960, Tues.–Sat. 12:30–3:30 P.M. and 7–10:30 P.M., €9–11) is on a narrow side street off Via Aubert in the center of Aosta. The artists in the name refer to paintings and sculptures that complement the mountain furnishings. Apart from a couple dishes imported from other regions the menu mainly features food from the Aosta Valley). First and second courses are robust and substantial in every season so make sure you arrive with an appetite. *Antipasto del camino* is a classic mixed plate of cured meat, and the *polenta grassa* (polenta with fontina cheese and butter) is great when temperatures drop outside. Set within the old Roman walls **Vecchia Aosta** (Piazza Port Pretoria 4c, tel. 016/536-1186, Thurs.–Tues. noon–3 P.M. and 7–10:30 P.M., €9–11) serves regional dishes like risotto and terrine. During the summer, you can eat outside and choose from the fixed-price menu that offers a mix of specialties.

To buy locally produced fontina and other goat's and cow's milk cheeses, head to **L'Angolo del Formaggio** on Via Trottechien 13. **Le Grand Paradis** (Via Sant'Anselmo 121) is the place to taste local vintages while sampling a range of salami.

Information and Services

Tourism is very well organized in Aosta and there are two offices in town that can help maximize your visit. The **Piazza Chanoux 2** location (tel. 016/523-6627, www.regione.vda. it/turismo) provides maps and brochures about the city, while the office in **Piazza Narbonne 3** (tel. 016/533-3521, www.aiataosta.com) covers the entire region. Aosta Valley is also the only region to have a tourist point in Rome (Via Sistina 9, tel. 06/474-4104), so you can pick up a bag full of hotel, transportation, and skiing information before you arrive.

Every day during the summer, free guided walks are organized around the historic cen-

ter. Tours leave at 10 A.M. from Piazza Arco d'Augusto and reservations can be made by calling tel. 333/808-8036

Aosta Bike Tour is a recent initiative meant to help visitors get the most out of their stay. Yellow bicycles are provided for free and come with a handheld GPS upon request that leads to 30 of the town's sights. At each stop, there's a multimedia explanation (currently only available in Italian and French). Keys for the bikes are provided by the **Ufficio Informazioni Turistiche** (tel. 016/523-5343) in Piazza Arco d'Augusto daily 8:30 A.M.–6:30 P.M. Just leave an ID and start pedaling.

Getting There and Around

Aosta is in the center of the region and it's possible to reach all the resorts quickly by car, train, and an efficient bus service. **L'Aeroporto Corrado Gex** (www.avda-aosta.it) is two kilometers east of town off the A5 at the Aosta Est exit. The main airline is **Air Vallee** (tel. 016/530-3303, www.airvallee.com), which connects Aosta with Rome daily. There's only one rail line, which runs parallel to the A5 highway and connects Turin, Milan, and Genova with Aosta. **Savda** (tel. 016/526-2027) buses leave from Stazione Autolinee across from the train station and connect many of the smaller towns with Aosta.

Around Aosta

Castello de Fénis (Fénis, tel. 016/576-4263, Mar.–Aug. 9 A.M.–7:30 P.M., Oct.–Feb. 10 A.M.–noon and 1:30–4:30 P.M.), 12 kilometers east of Aosta, looks like a castle you might have imagined as a child. The central mass of square towers is ringed by two sets of walls. The strategy was to let the enemy over the first and attack once they were trapped in the middle. The interior is less grim and consists of an elegant courtyard and frescoed central dining room painted by Giacomo Jaquerio, the official painter of the Savoia court. On the first Sunday of August there's a historical reenactment with knights, squires, and maidens who parade from the castle to the medieval market of Tzanti.

Five minutes from the castle, Luigina Voyat

ins **Le Bonheur** (Località Chez Croiset 53a, tel. 016/576-4117), an *agriturismo* with 10 rooms where half-board is €45 a night. You can make reservations for lunch or dinner for a fixed price (€25, excluding wine). The meal includes five types of antipasto, two first courses, a farm-raised second course, and dessert. It's also possible to work off the meal with a horseback ride through the *valclavalite* (valley near Aosta) afterwards.

PARCO NAZIONALE DEL GRAN PARADISO

Gran Paradiso is the oldest national park in Italy. It was founded in 1922 and before that the vast area served as a royal hunting reserve for the kings of Savoy. Mountains vary from modest peaks of 800 meters to the Gran Paradiso in the center of the park, which is a shade over 4,000 meters. Vegetation consists of alpine prairies, glaciers (many of which are rapidly melting), and forests of red and white fir. Ibex live above the treeline and have recovered from near extinction during the 19th century. Off-season is the opportunity to see chamois, marmots, eagles, and foxes. In June and September, the valleys are still quiet and nature is at its fullest. If you can only get away in winter, February and March are the sunniest months.

The park can be reached from either Piedmont or Aosta Valley. Cogne is the main resort from which to explore the park. Lillaz is farther down the Val di Cogne and is literally the end of the road. Alpinists have always preferred Valnontey for its glacier views and vicinity to dozens of trails.

Sights

Whatever season you arrive there's likely to be snow not far from **Cogne.** The town sits in a wide meadow surrounded by V-shaped mountains. It's a good base, although it tends to be a little crowded during the winter. As one of the main information centers, there's no shortage of activities.

Further down the Cogne Valley is the village of **Lillaz,** where the asphalt ends and dirt

an Alpine plant growing in the Parco Nazionale del Gran Paradiso

© ALESSIA RAMACCIA

roads begin. Most people don't make it this far, which leaves the rustic village unaffected by mass tourism. To the east of town is the long cascade that transforms into a full-blown waterfall in spring. **Valnontey** is popular, especially for serious hikers who use it as a base camp for reaching the Gran Paradiso. You don't have to climb 4,061 meters to spot ibex that graze in groups along the mountainside. Footpaths start from directly on the edge of town and yellow signposts indicate the distance between villages and refuges where hikers can spend the night.

Giardino Botanico Paradisia (Valnontey, tel. 016/574-040, Jun.–Set. daily) was founded in 1955, and today 1,500 plant species grow with little interference from humans. The garden's main point of interest is the Gran Piano di Noasca, which is one of the least-known areas and an ideal destination for whoever wants to observe herds of chamois and ibexes grazing in natural surroundings.

Entertainment and Events

You'll need to wake up early if you want to catch the beginning of **Carnevale** (tel. 016/574-040) in Cogne. The festival takes place in February and starts at dawn with the arrival of a wagon loaded with a barrel of wine. It stops in the main square where it's promptly distributed. Traditional folk dancing starts soon after the first cups have been drained, accompanied by a local band that includes tambourines, which are a favorite instrument in the area and played in a unique fashion.

Sports and Recreation

Step outside of Cogne and you're in the countryside. There are trails leading in every direction and an enclosed cable car at the edge of town that takes hikers and skiers up 1,000 meters to Montzeuc at the **Cogne ski resort** (Funivie Gran Paradiso, Via Laydetré 29, tel. 016/574-008). Downhill skiing is relatively limited compared to other resorts, and most trails are for cross-country skiers. There are a number of rental shops in Piazza Chanoux, such as **Desaymonte** (tel. 016/574-441, daily

8 A.M.–8 P.M.), and once you've strapped your skis on you can choose to head towards Lillaz, Valnontey, or Epinel, no more than five kilometers away. If snow isn't your thing, there's also an outdoor ice rink and a very challenging climbing wall in town.

Much of the area in the park is nearly virgin and it doesn't take long to lose all trace of man. During the summer, **Guide Alpine Cogne** (Piazza Chanoux 1, tel. 016/574-835, www. guidealpinecogne.it, daily 9 A.M. to 12.30 P.M.) organizes canyoning, climbing, and trekking excursions (both day trips and multiday adventures). The longer excursions require roughing it out in a tent or bivouac, where you can experience absolute silence. In the winter they take groups off-track and heli-skiing.

Accommodations

Hotels in Cogne are comfortable and the steady demand keeps prices fairly high. **Du Grand Paradis** (Via Grappein 45, tel. 016/574-070, www.cognevacanze.com, €140 d) is one of the simpler options. Service is welcoming and rooms are fairly bare. There is a nice garden and solarium where guests can lie out and order drinks ordered from the bar. Breakfast is included and parking is right outside.

Mountain air comes with every comfort inside **Bellevue** (rue Grand Paradis 22, tel. 016/574-825, www.hotel.bellevue.it, €250 d). The charm starts from the communal hall decorated with a collection of traditional tools, like a butter churner and an old-fashioned iron. The 30 rooms all have their own personality and the *romantica* and *panoramica* are especially prized by honeymooners. Singles are only available in low season. The swimming pool is indoors next to a sauna and Turkish bath. You can take cooking lessons, but it may be more rewarding to eat in the cheese bar or brasserie, where all the waiters are dressed in typical mountain costumes.

If budget is a concern you may want to stay in some of the smaller hotels of Valnontey such as **La Barme** (tel. 016/574-9177, www.hotelbarme. com, €90 d), which is situated inside a traditional wooden chalet that's covered in flowers during the summer. The restaurant serves typical mountain dishes and a small beauty center is available for guests to relax. Hikers can also use the remote refuges and bivouacs that dot the entire park. These are used to reach the remote areas and offer basic service. It's good way to meet nature lovers and get close to mountain lakes beyond the roads that run through the main valleys. **Rifugio Vittorio Sella** (Parco Nazionale Gran Paradiso Conca di Lauson, tel. 016/590-8769, www.rifugio sella.com, Mar.–Sept., €38 s with breakfast) is 2.5 hours from Valnontey near Lake Lauson. There are 161 beds during the summer and 13 during the winter.

Situated in the nearby village of Valnontey, **Camping lo Stambecco** (tel. 016/574-152, www.campinglostambecco.com, €6) has terraced sites partly surrounded by pine woods. The campground is run by a friendly family and is an ideal starting point for exploring the park. There are two sets of showers on the grounds and barbecuing is permitted. Coin-operated washing machines are available and a bus stop at the entrance to the site can drop you off in Cogne, Lillaz, or Epinel during the summer months.

Food

After a day on the slopes exploring the park, it's a pleasure to enter **La Brasserie du Bon Bec** (Rue Bourgeois 72, tel. 016/574-9288, Tues.–Sun. noon–3 P.M. and 7:30–10:30 P.M., €7–10). This is chalet-style decoration without too much excess or unnecessary folklore. It's also a rare example in Italy of a restaurant with a children's menu. The dishes are as scenic as the mountains outside and the *braserade* (cold cuts, *reblochon* cheese, potatoes, and crepes) or *pierrade* (mixed meat platter) are quite filling. The owner also runs the **Bar à Fromage** (tel. 016/574-9696, Wed.–Mon.) in Rue du Grand Paradis, which leaves you smelling like cheese.

Les Pertzes (Via Grappein 93, summer daily noon–11:30 P.M., €8–11) is a distinctive chalet near the Piazza del Mercato. What makes it special is flexibility and quality. You can come here mid-afternoon or late night when most restaurants are closed to enjoy

cheese or *salumi*-based snacks served with roasted chestnuts. Emanuele will happily take you down to the cellar to choose a good bottle that can be sipped by the fireplace.

To try the local sweet bread, visit **Gerard** (Via Bourgeois 49) or **Perret** (Via Bourgeois 57). **La Cave de Cogne** (Via Bourgeois 50, tel. 016/574-498) has a good selection of wine and locally distilled spirits.

Information and Services

AIAT Cogne Gran Paradiso (Rue Bourgeois 34, tel. 016/574-040, www.cogne.org) provides daily weather conditions and if you're planning on setting out alone in the winter it's best to check in here first. Hikers go missing every year and straying from the beaten path can be dangerous unless you're an experienced alpinist. The **Soccorso Alpino Valdostano** (Grand Chemin 34, Saint-Christopher, tel. 016/523-0253), the Alpine rescue squad, are on alert 24 hours a day and are where St. Bernards get their reputation.

Getting There and Around

To arrive by car, exit the A5 highway at Aosta Ovest near the town of Aymavilles and continue south along the state road for 12 kilometers until you reach Cogne. The closest train station is in Aosta. **Savda** (www.savda. it) buses from the Autostazione in Via Carrel depart seven times daily 8:05 A.M.–7:45 P.M. There's a ticket office in the bus station and the journey takes 50 minutes.

COURMAYEUR

Courmayeur (Coor-MY-er). The name says it all. This Alpine town 1,224 meters above sea level has a reputation for winter sports and *après*-ski nightlife. Everywhere you look there are mountains and none is more impressive than the Monte Bianco, which towers above everything else. Most people come to ski and there are *piste* (tracks) for every level and interest. Snowboarders, down-hillers, and cross-country types will all find their trails on the 20 lifts that criss-cross the mountains above town. It's even possible to ride a cable car over to France.

cable cars on the way up Monte Bianco

© ALESSIA RAMACCIA

Sights
◖ LA PALUD CABLEWAY

Sure, €87 may sound a little steep for a cable car ride, but La Palud Cableway (Funivie Monte Bianco S.P.A.–Frazione La Palud 22, Courmayeur, tel. 016/589-925, www.montebianco.com/prezzi.asp, year-round 8:30 A.M.–12:40 P.M. and 2–4 P.M., departures every 20 min.) is one of the highest in the world and a chance to see three countries in a single hour. The full trip to Chamonix, France, takes 90 minutes and requires seven cable transfers. Monte Bianco is on the left and gets closer every meter. On your right are the Swiss Alps and a view over Glacier du Geant and dozens of Alpine lakes. Cars are enclosed and hold up to 10 passengers comfortably. If you've seen the movie *Where Eagles Dare*, you'll have a better idea of what to expect. The return journey from France is by bus through the Monte Bianco tunnel, but you can also stop on the Italian side and stay in the **Rifugio Torino** (tel. 016/584-6484, www.rifugiotorino.it, Jan.–Oct., €40 pp) and wake up 3,329 meters high. The cableway and ticket office are four kilometers away in the village of La Palud.

Entertainment and Events

Beuffons (clowns) are the main attraction of Courmayeur's **Carnevale** in early February. They dress in colorful military-style costumes and are responsible for keeping the crowds on their toes. Don't be surprised if you get surrounded and playfully harassed. Their belts are lined with bells that ring every evening until Mardi Gras.

Detectives take center stage during **Courmayeur Noir in Festival** (www.noirfest.com, first week of Dec.). New films, literature, and comics are presented to a public that prefers a good thriller to a love story any day. Each year, writers of nail-biters like Jeffrey Deaver and Ed McBain are invited to share their secrets.

Sports and Recreation
SKIING

The **Peindeint lift** (tel. 016/584-6658, www.courmayeur-montblance.com) takes skiers up the mountain and a network of 36 kilometers of trails suitable for all levels. A full-day pass in peak season is €40. Non-skiers can enjoy the

© ALESSIA RAMACCIA

Val Ferret

view from the enclosed cabins that have been transporting people across the Alps since the 1950s. An €18 round-trip ticket takes you 800 meters in 12 minutes on two incredible rides with Monte Bianco visible the whole time.

Cross-country skiers can cover snow-covered landscapes from November until the end of May in Planpincieux. Trails leave directly from the town and wind their way through Alpine forests of the **Val Ferret.** Itineraries vary 3–20 kilometers and the snow along the way is well packed. Equipment can be rented in Planpincieux at **Bonora** (Loc. Planpincieux Val Ferret, tel. 016/589-376) or **Club des Sports** (tel. 016/589-570). A ski school, **Scuola di Sci e Snowboard Monte Bianco** (Strada Regionale 51, tel. 016/584-2477, Mon.–Sat. 9 A.M.–noon and 2:30–6 P.M.), operates during the high season. Visitors can check out www.skisnowboardeurope.com for more information on skiing in this area.

As the air gets thinner and altitudes reach quadruple digits, guides become a necessity. **Società Guide Alpine Courmayeur** (Strada Villair 2, tel. 016/584-2064, www.guidecour

mayeur.com) has been showing people the beauty of the Monte Bianco since 1850, and offers mountaineering, climbing, and skiing excursions year-round. They organize day-long bike tours (€50) in spring and summer and six-day ascents (€750) that take you to the most impressive peaks of the western Alps. Your fitness level dictates what is most suitable, but not everything requires a great amount of expertise. Many of the guides are following in the footsteps of their fathers and grandfathers, and their passion is contagious.

ADVENTURE SPORTS

If Tarzan is your role model, **Parco Avventura Monte Bianco** (Strada del Piccolo San Bernardo, tel. 335/591-8089, www.parcoavventuramontblanc.com, Jun.–Sept., daily 10 A.M.–5 P.M., €21) is the place to spend the day swinging, sliding, and climbing. The park is divided into five parts with varying levels of difficulty. Each area is suspended above the forest and requires participants to move from tree to tree using rope bridges and Boy Scout technology.

THERMAL BATHS

The waters of Pré-Saint-Didier have been famous since antiquity, and a spa was built here in 1834. The thermal baths were one of the main attractions, and the old splendor of the building has been preserved during a recent restructuring of **Terme Pré-Saint-Didier** (Allée des Thermes Pré-Saint-Didier, tel. 016/586-7272, www.termedipre.it, Mon.–Thurs. 10 A.M.–9 P.M., Fri.–Sat. 10 A.M.–11 P.M., Sun. 8:30 A.M.–9 P.M., €32 weekdays, €38 weekends). Entry includes a towel, flip flops, and a light lunch. There are dozens of sauna rooms, Turkish baths, and outdoor pools. Soaking in 37°C water with a view of Monte Bianco could become a habit.

Accommodations

Camosci (Via Entrèves 7, tel. 016/584-2338, €80 d) is a family-run two-star hotel close to the center. Rooms were recently painted and most have a view of Monte Bianco. A restaurant on the ground floor prepares *valdostana* specialties, and if you crave fondue you won't have to go very far. Four rooms come with their own small kitchen and there's also one suite.

Auberge da la Maison (Via Passerin d'Entreves, tel. 016/586-9811, www.aubergemaison.it, €190 d) is a charming hotel in the hamlet of Entreves. Imagine a handful of houses around an old palace that was once the residence of the nobles who ruled Courmayeur. Monte Bianco is practically in the front yard and it's an ideal base for winter and summer excursions. The chalet interior is as welcoming as the front desk and covered with wood-carved details. Each of the 33 rooms has its own stove, old prints of mountain landscapes, and view. The hotel also rents three apartments perfect for groups of four.

Camping Aiguille Noire (La Zerotta Val Veny, tel. 016/586-9041, www.aiguillenoire.com, €5) is six kilometers from Courmayeur, surrounded by woodlands at the foot of the Monte Bianco near a cold mountain stream. Outdoor enthusiasts can explore the area on foot, bike, or along well-marked footpaths that criss-cross the countryside. This is also a good base camp for anyone with ambitions of a high-altitude climb; guides can be hired directly from the camp office. In the summer, bus service links the site with Courmayeur. A bar, restaurant, and mini-market are all on-site.

Food

There may be three dining rooms inside **Le Vieux Pommier** (Piazzale Monte Bianco 25, tel. 016/584-2281, Tues.–Sun. 12:30–3:30 P.M. and 7–11 P.M., €9–13) but that still doesn't make it very intimate. This is mountain dining with large tables, an efficient kitchen, and fast, friendly service. It's easy to make friends here, especially in the largest room, where the *antipasto* and dessert tables attract a lot of attention. The onion soup and polenta are the fastest ways to warm up when temperatures drop. The family also has five rooms for rent. **Pierre Alexis 1877** (Via Marconi 50a, tel. 016/586-9095, daily lunch and dinner, €13–18) is a slightly more elegant dining option with whiter-than-snow table clothes and more silverware than most restaurants set on a table. The valley cuisine features a wonderful pistachio ravioli dish and deer steak flavored with rosemary.

Caffè della Posta (Via Roma 51, tel. 016/584-2272, daily 8:30 A.M.–1 A.M.) is a historic meeting place. Tables and chairs are all antique and arranged around a 14th-century fireplace. In the morning, the croissants are served warm and at lunch locals enjoy panini and wine.

Marcello Panizzi (Via Circonvallazione 41, tel. 016/584-3041, Wed.–Mon.) produces fresh and aged *tome* cheese from locals cow's and goat's milk that's also used to make wonderful yogurts.

Information and Services

AIAT Monte Bianco (Piazzale Monte Bianco 13, tel. 016/584-2060, www.aiat-montebianco.com) provides detailed maps of the slopes. If you plan on staying for several days or skiing your way across the region, it may be useful to buy the **Skipass Valle d'Aosta** (tel. 016/523-8871, www.skivalle.it). The pass is

..epted in all resorts and available for 3–14 day periods. Local hotels distribute the Mont Blanc Card free of charge; it provides access to the town's tennis, squash, ice rink, and climbing wall inside the Forum Sports Center. The card also gets you discounts when renting mountain bikes or buying cable car tickets.

Getting There and Around

Courmayeur and the Valle del Monte Bianco can be reached with the SS 26 and recently extended A5. Much the highway is through tunnels and the maximum speed in 100 kph. From France or Swizerland, take the Mont Blanc or Gran San Bernardo tunnels. In summer, the Gran San Bernardo and Piccolo San Bernardo passes are also open. The town is 37 kilometers from Aosta and 784 from Rome. Prè S. Didier is the closest train station and Savda buses make daily connections 6:30 A.M.–8:35 P.M.

Around Courmayeur

If you've made it to Courmayeur and a long drive through the Mont Blanc tunnel to the beautiful French town of Chamonix isn't on the cards, you can choose to stay in Italy and drive along the **Val Veny** or **Val Ferret** valleys. Both roads are ultra scenic and will easily distract drivers. They aren't very crowded and at the end of each are refuges (Elisabetta and Elena) where you can explore some of the most remote areas in Europe.

MILAN, LOMBARDY, AND THE LAKES

Milan isn't famous for being the most beautiful city in Italy and it might not even make the top 100 list, but it is Italy's financial and fashion capital, which means there's lots of money and lots of things to spend it on. People work long hours and a surplus of jobs has attracted generations of Southern Italians. Nowadays they've been replaced with a new wave of international faces that provide a cosmopolitan feel and more dining options than anywhere else in Italy.

Milan is fast paced by Italian standards and locals keep their heads down until *aperitivo,* when they play as hard as they work. This is as modern as it gets. The tallest skyscraper on the peninsula is Gio Ponti's Pirelli tower, but that's set to change in 2016 when Hadid and Libeskind are scheduled to transform Milan's cityscape. For now things are still fairly grey and the attraction remains the interior design of the super boutiques lining the Quadrilatero—and unrivaled works of art collected by the city's powerful families.

The Milanese know their city can't compete aesthetically with Florence or Rome. It may rain a lot but the lakes are just under an hour away, the mountains only a little farther, and the sea is always an option. Lombardy provides plenty of alternatives. Italy's most populated and productive region extends from the Swiss border and the Italian version of the Great Lakes down to the flat plains of the River Po, where industry and large-scale agriculture thrive. Wealthy towns line lower Lombardy, and dynasties in Bergamo, Cremona, and Mantova have left behind an inheritance of exceptional palazzi and churches.

© ALESSIA RAMACCIA

HIGHLIGHTS

◖ Piazza del Duomo: Milan starts in Piazza del Duomo and a walk down the porticoed buildings surrounding the square is the quickest way to get a feel for the city. In the center of it all is the impressive, newly restored Duomo (page 265).

◖ La Scala: If you have some opera on your iPod, La Scala is the place to hit play. The five-tier, red velvet interior is a delight for the eyes, but the true experience can only be

AUSTRIA

SWITZ.

Alps

Isola Bella

Lake Como

Trento

Lake Maggiore

Castello Sforzesco

La Scala

Milan

Piazza del Duomo

Lake Garda

Santa Maria delle Grazie

Pavia

Certosa di Pavia

Piacenza

Po River

Alessandria

Genova

Golf di Genova

0   30 mi

0   30 km

heard in this mythic theater where the spirit of artists Toscanini, Callas, and Pavarotti live on (page 268).

◖ Castello Sforzesco: Castello Sforzesco dominates Milan's Sempione neighborhood and the courtyards inside provide a welcome respite from city traffic. The interior of the castle has been converted into one of the city's finest museums, where Renaissance paintings and one of Michelangelo's last sculptures are on display (page 269).

◖ Santa Maria delle Grazie: Santa Maria delle Grazie is a beautiful 15th-century convent with a cloister designed by Bramante. What makes it unforgettable though is Leonardo da Vinci's world-famous painting *The Last Supper* in the refectory (page 270).

◖ Certosa di Pavia: The Visconti family burial shrine is stunning in every detail, from its elaborate marble floors to the intricately sculpted facade (page 290).

◖ Isola Bella: All three Borromean Islands are worth visiting, but Isola Bella is the grandest of the three, where 17th-century luxury has been perfectly preserved in a palazzo and garden with a 360-degree view of Lago Maggiore (page 299).

◖ Lake Como: Italy's most famous lake is surrounded by mountains and sumptuous villas where the rich and famous have retreated for centuries. Resort towns along the shore are each more enchanting than the next and the efficient ferry service is an ideal way to see them all. Otherwise the road around the lake is one endless scenic route (page 301).

LOOK FOR ◖ TO FIND RECOMMENDED SIGHTS, ACTIVITIES, DINING, AND LODGING.

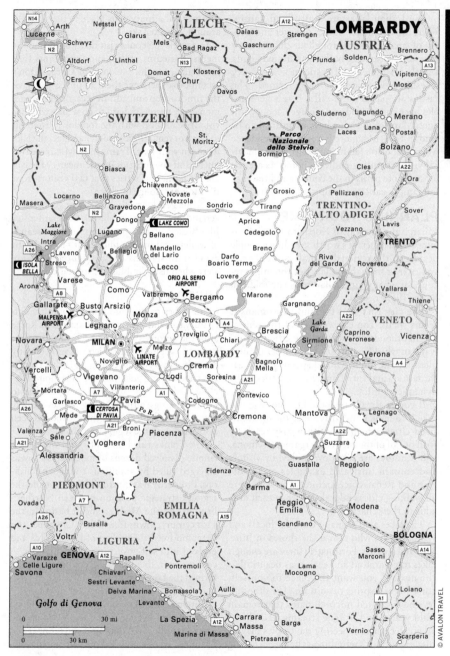

© AVALON TRAVEL

The Italian lakes are a gift from nature. There are five major bodies of water and dozens of smaller lakes throughout the northern valleys. The Romans built ports around Garda and there's a medieval castle in nearly every lakeside town. Como is more refined. The castles are palaces and villas here where nobles once entertained and George Clooney still does. Many of the lakes have islands; on an island in Lake Maggiore is a gem of a residence where Napoleon fell in love. Beyond the magical vistas spanning endless kilometers are the most remote parks in the country and traces of humanity's earliest attempts at art.

PLANNING YOUR TIME

Milan is the gateway to Northern Italy, and as long as you're here it's worth spending a couple of days in the regional capital. Not only can you recover from the jet lag, but you might reconsider what your Sicilian seatmate told you on the flight over.

The city isn't that big and to Romans it seems small. You can visit all of the central neighborhoods on foot and the efficient subway can whisk you to *The Last Supper* in minutes flat. The fun in Milan happens at night, as the fashion and entertainment industries fuel a dynamic nightlife.

If you've already seen the Duomo, you can take a tour of Lombardy's elegant medium-sized cities, which are within easy reach by road or rail of the capital. Bergamo, Cremona, and Mantova are often overlooked by visitors and contain unrivaled examples of Middle Age and Renaissance architecture. These are all walking cities and a sleepover in each only adds to their charm.

The lakes are the major draw for locals and visitors alike, who crowd the shores in June, July, and August. Fortunately there are enough lakes to go around and each is as beautiful as the next. If you want the place to yourself, come in early spring or autumn. The deep valleys have created microclimates that remain mild year-round. Alpine streams feed all the lakes, so bathers expecting the tropics may be disappointed. It's refreshing at best even during summer but a marvelous place to fish, paddle around, or water-ski.

In a week you could visit many of the monuments, museums, villas, and restaurants that line Lake Maggiore, Como, or Garda. Don't attempt to experience them all unless you have the time to stop and admire a castle here and a monastery there. It's hard to go wrong whether you drive around with the top down listening to Bach or rent a 150cc scooter and feel the lake winds in your hair. Trains from Milan are frequent and the most dramatic means of travel are the numerous ferries that taxi visitors from port to port along the shore.

Crime gets lower the closer you get to Switzerland, but Milan and larger Lombard cities like Brescia attract petty criminals in search of wallets and mobile phones. It's advisable to avoid train stations late at night and to stay alert when using public transportation.

HISTORY

Celtic tribes moved into Lombardy in the 5th century B.C. and were easily conquered by Rome after the Second Punic War. The area became part of Cisalpine Gaul, which was subsequently ransacked by Vandals, Goths, and other Northern tribes taking advantage of the empire's decline. During A.D. 568–774, it was home to Lombard kings; although they were eventually defeated by Charlemagne, their name has been associated with the region ever since.

The Franks ruled until 887 and when their empire dissolved dozens of independent towns emerged ruled by ambitious counts and bishops. Prosperity was due to the Po River and the region's strategic position between Northern Europe and the Mediterranean basin. In the 11th century, towns like Milan, Cremona, and Bergamo freed themselves of feudal lords and evolved into self-governing municipalities. A century later, these thriving commercial cities formed the Lombard League and defeated Frederick Barbarossa, who threatened autonomy.

Internal conflicts, however, eventually led to the rise of overlords like the Visconti and Sforza families in Milan and the Gonzaga in Mantova, who established miniature dynasties.

Milan conquered most of its neighbors in the 14th century and became the most powerful city in the region. Nevertheless little could be done about Swiss (they weren't always neutral) and Venetian incursions in the early 16th century, and after French invasions Spanish Hapsburg troops entered the city. Mantova resisted foreign domination until 1713, when the Austrian Hapsburgs annexed the entire region. Napoleon briefly interrupted Vienna's rule but after Waterloo the territory was restored and Austria founded the Lombardo-Venetian kingdom. After two unsuccessful attempts, a Franco-Piemonte army finally defeated the Austrians and their Croatian conscripts in 1859 and Lombardy joined a unified Italy.

Milan

Milan, in the middle yet on the right—in geography and politics. Economically advanced with perpetual clouds according to anyone south of Florence. The Milanese may have a little chip on their shoulders and it's not all to do with the weather. They've drunk two black espressos by 10 A.M. and are nearly out of cigarettes by dinner. They respect more rules than average and ignore others (but who doesn't?).

Nightlife and shopping are consolations for a grey sky and like residents of any second city, the Milanese think that they are the best. Occasionally they are when AC Milan hoists another Champion's League trophy and Silvio adds a dozen implants for the occasion. It's a fast-paced city where even the nuns are in a hurry to visit the largest Gothic cathedral in the world and pine under *Il Cenacolo* (*The Last Supper*).

Outside on the streets, high heels move at frenetic pace. No one wants to be late for *aperitivo* or the latest Armani sample sale. This is the land of see-and-be-seen where television starlets play a game of merry-go-round with VIPs on their way to leather-clad locales even Bruce Willis can't always access. No one said a vacation here would be easy, but if you've chosen to stay in Milan for a few days you're in for a ride.

SIGHTS

The Duomo is the traditional place to start your exploration of Milan. It's the geographical core, if not the spiritual one, that lies somewhere between the San Siro *football* stadium and the Quadrilatero, where fashion lives and trends are born. In between are Brera, Magenta, and Sempione. Not exactly beautiful neighborhoods, but gritty in a pleasant way with the charms of a city looking ahead rather than behind.

Rush hour in Milan is one of the worst in Italy. It's wise to stay in bed until 9:30 A.M. and avoid traveling 5:30–7:30 P.M. to avoid paralysis. Also be aware of pickpockets, especially around the stations and on subways and buses. They're often children working for adults. Keep wallets in front pockets and backpacks tightly zipped.

◖ Piazza del Duomo

If Milan had a downtown this would be it. The area around Piazza del Duomo is congested most of the day with shoppers, office workers, and tourists looking for the Duomo. Two subway lines intersect here and above ground the avenues and streets lead to Milan's other neighborhoods. Scaffolding is a common sight and luxury brands are revitalizing the Galleria and streets around the impressive church. At night the curtain goes up at La Scala and the barman at the only seven-star hotel in town gets ready for another long shift.

DUOMO

On a beautiful, sunny day, the duomo (Piazza del Duomo, tel. 028/646-3456, www.duomo milano.it, daily 7 A.M.–7 P.M., free admission) may hypnotize you with its 100 thin, Gaudi-like spires about to take off into the sky. It's

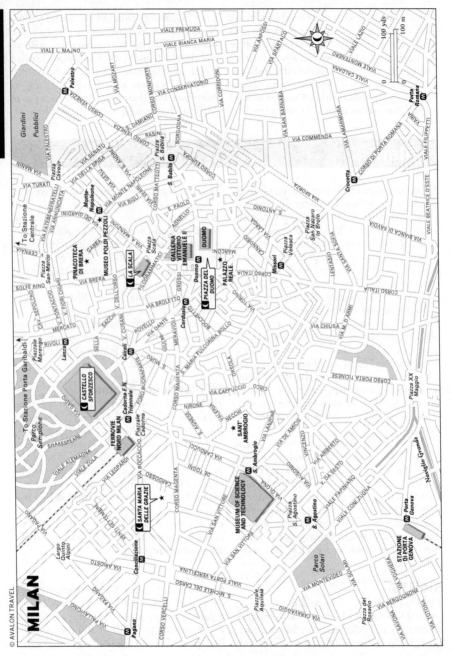

MILAN AND LOMBARDY

© ALESSIA RAMACCIA

a lesser-known side of Milan's Duomo

the kind of church Godzilla wouldn't want to step on. Gian Galeazzo Visconti commissioned it in 1386 and it wasn't completed until the 1800s, which is late by modern Milanese standards. The piazza around it is less grand and the church looks slightly cramped. Outside, pigeons brush against pilgrims on their way to the gloomy interior and a collection of Christian icons and relics. The confession boxes do a swift business while tourists light candles and marvel at the coolness.

The roof is open to the public and provides a nice view. Take the elevator (€6) unless you consider yourself fit enough for the stairs (€4). On the Saturday closest to September 14, the archbishop removes a nail of Christ's cross from its resting place behind the altar.

PALAZZO REALE
Bordering the Duomo on the southern edge of the piazza is the oddly shaped Palazzo Reale (Piazza del Duomo 12, tel. 02/860-165, Tues.–Sun. 9:30 A.M.–5:30 P.M., free). This was the seat of government and the walls were meant

to reflect power. After it was partially demolished to make room for the Duomo, Francesco Sforza looked after the renovations in 1452. It was later used by Spaniards and has been modified significantly over the centuries. Today it houses the Tourist Office and is worth a stop to see **Sala delle Cariatidi** on the second floor, which was once a theater.

GALLERIA VITTORIO EMANUELE II
On the other side of the piazza is Galleria Vittorio Emanuele II (tel. 02/7252-4301), a beacon for shoppers since Giuseppe Mengoni won the competition to build it in 1863. This proto-shopping center was completed quickly and has remained a good place to find shoes. Even if footware isn't your thing, the two long promenades covered with a Belle Epoque iron and glass roof make for an elegant stroll. Keep an eye out for mosaics on the floors. The bull near the center is where Milanese get their good luck. There are plenty of cafés around the Galleria, although prices tend to be unfashionably high.

PINACOTECA AMBROSIANA

The oldest museum in Milan, Pinacoteca Ambrosiana (Piazza Pio XI 2, tel. 02/806-921, www.ambrosiana.it, Tues.–Sun. 10 A.M.–5:30 P.M., €8), houses paintings donated by Cardinal Borromeo in 1618. Masterpieces include Leonardo's da Vinci's *Portrait of a Musician* and Caravaggio's *Fruit Basket*. Lines are shorter than outside the Duomo and the 23 rooms are often nearly deserted except for scholars in the library examining Leonardo's incredible sketches and drawings.

LA SCALA

La Scala (Via Filodrammatici 2, tel. 02/7200-3744, www.teatroallascala.org) opera house opened in 1778 and audiences have been hoping for encores ever since. The stage is one of the largest in Europe and acoustics within the horseshoe-shaped theater are perfect. On days when no performances are held you can visit the adjacent **Museo Teatrale** (€5) which contains costumes and sets from past productions. The museum also provides a look inside at the four tiers of velvet-clad boxes and two balconies under an impressive chandelier.

The best way to experience Italy's most famous theater, however, is by attending a performance. Artistic directors change but the program remains dedicated to classics and a season usually includes some Rossini, Verdi, or Puccini. Performances sell out quickly and it's best to reserve before your arrival by phone or over the Internet, although a block of standing-room-only tickets are put on sale a half-hour before every show. Prices range from €10 in the upper decks to €170 if you want to feel the wind from the conductor's baton. Tickets can be purchased at the central box office in the Galleria off Piazza Duomo (daily noon–6 P.M., closed Aug.) or at the evening box office at the theater. This is La Scala, so proper attire is required, which means a tie and jacket for men. If you left your blazer at home, you can contact Francine Garino (02/8879-2090, garino@fondazionelascala.it) for guided tours which cost around €30.

Montenapoleone

This neighborhood is also known as the Quadrilatero (www.viamontenapoleone.org), and is made up of the streets between Via Montenapoleone and Via delle Spiga. Versace, Dolce & Gabbana, Prada, and Gucci have turned the area into a paradise for shoppers. During the day, heiresses and sheiks are common sights browsing the glamorous storefronts, while models parade by on their way to the next photo shoot. At night, the sidewalks are deserted.

MUSEO POLDI PEZZOLI

Shopping isn't the only attraction. Museo Poldi Pezzoli (Via Manzoni 12, tel. 02/794-889, www.museopoldipezzoli.it, Tues.–Sun. 10 A.M.–6 P.M., €8), near the Montenapoleone subway stop, was one of the first museums in the city and contains the personal collection of the wealthy Poldi family. Their taste can be hit and miss and if armor or tapestry isn't your thing, head straight to the second floor. The Golden Room contains an early Botticelli and Pollaiolo's stunning *Portrait of a Woman*. From here there's also a good view of the gardens outside. The other highlight is the Jewelry Room, which has an extensive collection of diamond-encrusted watches, miniature goblets, fine porcelain, and crucifixes. Don't look for a café, since there isn't one.

MUSEO BAGATTI VALSECCHI

Not far away from Museo Poldi Pezzoli, Museo Bagatti Valsecchi (Via Santo Spirito 10, tel. 02/7600-6132, www.museobagattivalsecchi. org, Tues.–Sun. 1–5:45 P.M., €6, €3 on Wed.) is a house-museum where you can get an idea of how 19th-century Milanese bourgeoisie once lived. It wasn't a bad life and the elaborate furniture and finely decorated rooms demonstrate that luxury has always been in style.

VILLA BELGIOJOSO BONAPARTE

If you continue north along Via Manzoni, you'll reach the public gardens that are a nice way to escape the heat in summer. There's a small lake in the center where people feed the ducks. On the edge of the park are the Museo del Cinema, Natural History Museum, and Planetarium. Villa Belgiojoso Bonaparte (Via Palestro 16, tel. 02/7600-2819, www.villabel giojosobonaparte.it, daily 9 A.M.–1 P.M. and 2–5:30 P.M.) borders the park, and it's free to visit this grand neoclassical 19th-century villa where Napoleon briefly lived. It now houses an art gallery and on summer evenings regularly hosts classical music concerts in the extensive gardens.

Brera

Brera is where Milan *really* begins. The rest is just wrapping. It's populated with creatives at all hours and is the center of a vibrant art scene. Small galleries with big prices line Via Brera and Via Fiori Chiara behind La Scala. Good *pasticcerie* and *trattorie* are on every corner and this is where natives come for their *aperitivo*. At night the streets fill up with fortune-tellers, rose peddlers, and vendors of fake designer bags hoping to make a euro.

PINACOTECA DI BRERA

Pinacoteca di Brera (Via Brera 28, tel. 02/722-631, www.brera.beniculturali.it, Tues.–Sun. 8:30 A.M.–7:15 P.M., €5) is Milan's most important art gallery. Housed in a 17th-century palazzo, it was restored a decade ago and now offers white-walled tranquility under high vaulted ceilings. Chairs are spread out throughout the gallery, making it easy to rest a few moments and observe Tiziano and Caravaggio. Paintings span seven centuries and Room 24 is the home of Raphael's *Marriage of the Virgin*.

SAN SIMPLICIANO

Some of the city's only Roman ruins can be seen within San Simpliciano (Piazza San Simpliciano 7, tel. 02/869-0683). Lower walls date from the 4th century, when Christianity was just gaining popularity in the area. Later interventions enlarged the church and added the current triple nave layout. Many concerts are held inside and the acoustics are excellent, although the pews can get uncomfortable after an hour.

Sempione

If you take the shuttle train from Malpensa airport you arrive in Sempione. Next to the station is Castello Sforzesco, a symbol of Milanese power, and behind that the park where the Torre Branca rises 108 meters into the Milanese skyline. The area is a center for Italian design and many ingenious objects are created here.

◀ CASTELLO SFORZESCO

Castello Sforzesco (Piazza Castello, tel. 02/8846-3703, www.milanocastello.it, Tues.–Sun. 9 A.M.–5:30 P.M., €3 or €7 combo ticket), a square-shaped fortress guarded by four imposing towers, has had many occupants since it was first conceived in 1386 by Gian Galeazzo Visconti. During the Renaissance, Bramante and Leonardo da Vinci were commissioned to renovate the fortress. Military goals were replaced with cultural pursuits in 1893, and the castle now shows off a fine collection of furniture and other treasures in the Sala Castellana and Sala del Tesoro. With a guide you can also explore the network of passages below the castle and walk along the battlements. Tours last over two hours and begin every Sunday at 3 P.M.

PARCO SEMPIONE

Behind the castle is Milan's biggest park. Parco Sempione occupies the old parade ground and was completed in 1890 in an English style. It was the site of the 1906 World's Fair and one pavilion was later transformed into an **Aquarium** (Via Gadio 2, tel. 02/8846-5750, www.aqua riocivico.mi.it, Tues.–Sun. 9 A.M.–1 P.M. and 2–5:30 P.M., free) with a spectacular transparent bridge for viewing the fish, and vice versa. The hard-to-miss **Torre Branca** (Viale Luigi Camoens, tel. 02/331-4120, Apr.–Oct., open Wed. and weekends) is next to the **Triennale di Milano** (tel. 02/724-341), where exhibitions are held. It is vaguely reminiscent of the Eiffel Tower and provides an excellent view of the city. From the top you may be able to spot the fountain designed by De Chirico. There are a great variety of trees in the park with oak, cedars, pines, and beech all providing shade on hot summer days.

Magenta

This might be Milan's chicest area and having *The Last Supper* in the neighborhood hasn't hurt the value of property. It's largely residential, with many restaurants and boutiques. Corso Magenta is the main thoroughfare and nearby you can discover why Leonardo da Vinci was a genius.

◖ SANTA MARIA DELLE GRAZIE

Don't expect to just walk in the Santa Maria delle Grazie convent (Piazza Santa Maria delle Grazie 2, tel. 02/8942-1146, www.cenacolovinciano. org, Tues.–Sun. 8:15 A.M.–6:45 P.M., €6.50) and see *The Last Supper*. You need a reservation for this famous painting and it's wise to book a few weeks before your arrival. Even if your name is on the list, you only get 15 minutes with Jesus and the apostles. No more than 25 visitors at one time can enter the room inside the convent in order to keep the temperature down.

It took Leonardo da Vinci four years to complete the painting commissioned by Ludovico Sforza. He used a dry technique that allowed greater flexibility and special color effects. The portrayal was innovative and for the first time apostles were featured in a single plane beside Jesus. If you step back from the larger-than-life figures, the symmetry of the painting becomes more evident and there's a subtle 3-D effect.

Fifteen minutes may seem like a long time with one painting, but as you'll learn from the audio guide there's a lot of history behind it—for instance, the time that monks cut a doorway through the wall and permanently damaged the savior's feet, or when Napoleon's troops used the room as a stable. There's no chance of that now and the 21-year restoration has gotten the painting back in top shape. After seeing the remarkable work you can reflect on the achievement in the cloisters, which are often overlooked.

MUSEUM OF SCIENCE AND TECHNOLOGY

The Museum of Science and Technology (Via S. Vittore 21, tel. 02/485-551, www.museosci enza.org, Tues.–Fri. 9:30 A.M.–5 P.M. and Sat.–Sun. 9:30 A.M.–6:30 P.M., €8) may seem like an odd chaser to *The Last Supper*, but they've also recreated 30 of Leonardo da Vinci's inventions, in addition to being home to dozens of interactive libraries. It turns out that his helicopter really could fly and that the catapults he designed were some of the most lethal weapons of the time. Outside you can also look through the periscope and explore the narrow metallic corridors of Italy's first submarine.

SANT'AMBROGIO

Sant'Ambrogio (Piazza Sant'Ambrogio 15, tel. 02/8645-0895, http://santambrogio-basilica.it, Mon.–Fri. 7 A.M.–noon and 2:30–7 P.M., Sat.–Sun. 7 A.M.–1 P.M. and 3–6 P.M.) is dedicated to Milan's patron saint and is the best-looking Romanesque church in the city. Bramante was responsible for the 15th-century renovations but the mosaics and golden altar are much older. The remains of Sant'Ambrogio are kept in the crypt along with other early Christian remains. His feast day on December 7 is a standing-room-only affair when locals come to pay tribute to the "reluctant bishop" who became governor of the city by popular demand.

ENTERTAINMENT AND EVENTS

Milan is home to world-class opera and classical music events that multiply exponentially during the summer. There's also a surplus of bars serving *aperitivi* and discos for dancing until dawn. Nightlife is concentrated around the cobblestone streets of Brera and along the Naviglio canal southwest of the Duomo. Both neighborhoods are lined with jazz clubs, bars, and cafés.

If you prefer a less random approach, the *Corriere della Sera* newspaper comes with an entertainment supplement every Wednesday, as does the *La Repubblica* on Thursday. Otherwise you can buy *Milan,* which is the most complete events guide to the city.

Nightlife

LIVE MUSIC

Named after the legendary record label, the **Blue Note** (Via Borsieri 37, tel. 899/700-022,

Mon.–Sat. 2 P.M.–midnight and Sun. 7–11 P.M., €15–35) is a temple of jazz. It's open seven days a week and there are generally two sets per night. The stage is visible from all corners of this intimate club where it's possible to dine prior to each performance. Prices are high but the music helps digestion.

Scimmie (Via A. Sforza 49, tel. 02/8940-2874, Thurs.–Tues. 8 P.M.–2 A.M., €8 cover includes one drink) presents an eclectic range of music. You can listen to live blues, soul, or rock while eating a good pizza and nursing a pint of Italian lager. Of course there's no rule against dancing and the three zones of this versatile club fill up with people of all ages who appreciate a good beat. Jazz has a special place in the owner's heart and the big screen behind the bar shows Serie A football games on weekend afternoons.

Cascina Monluè (Via Monluè 70, www. eastiswest.org and www.monlue2007.it, doors open at 7 P.M., concerts start at 9 P.M., €5) and **Bernareggio** (Via Prinetti 29) are geared towards world music and admission is usually free. Concerts start at 9 P.M. Big international headliners play the **Datch Forum** (Via G. Di-Vittorio 6, tel. 199/128-800 or 02/4885-7220, www.forumnet.it, check website for showtimes) in nearby Assago. It's where the **Festival LatinoAmericano** (www.latinoamericando.it) is staged every August and a chance to catch Cuban salsa, and Paraguan folk bands bring Latin spirit to the city. **Idroscalo** (Segrate, Via Rivoltana 64, tel. 02/7020-0902) is a park just west of the center where open-air performances are staged and the annual summer concert series brings the likes of The White Stripes, Chemical Brothers, and Gods of Metal to town.

Tickets to events can be purchased directly at box offices before each performance and at **Ricordi** (Galleria Vittorio Emanuele, tel. 02/869-0683) and **Feltrinelli Libri e Musica** (Piazza Piemonte 2, tel. 02/433-541).

NIGHTCLUBS AND DISCOS

Designers are no longer restricted just to clothes. In Milan all the big names have branched out into hotels, restaurants, spas, and the most obvious extension: nightclubs. **Gold** (Via Carlo Poerio 2a, tel. 02/757-7771, daily 8 A.M.–1 A.M.) is the Dolce & Gabbana contribution to the trend and one of the gaudiest. As the name suggest it's all about the carats here, which makes it a regular stomping ground for Paolo Maldini, Kylie Minogue, and the Hilton sisters. The restaurant on the first floor prepares super-refined plates of Mediterranean-inspired dishes, and many of the ingredients are for sale. The ultra–health conscious will want to keep the menu as a souvenir.

Alcatraz (Via Valtellina 21, tel. 02/6901-6352, Fri.–Sat. 11 P.M.–4 A.M., €6 women, €10 men) was once a warehouse and now it's the biggest discotheque in the city. The vast space is divided into three low-lit rooms and there's little chance of bumping into someone unless you want to. On Friday, the main room plays retro dance hits from the 1970s. Saturday is slightly less commercial and there's a rock edge in the Extreme lounge led by DJ Gaucho. Live concerts are frequent.

Farenight (Via Giuseppe Ferrari 10, tel. 02/3651-4435, Thurs.–Sun. 8 P.M.–3 A.M.) is part of a new generation of Milan clubs that combines dining, dancing, and design. You can have a drink at the elegant bar, enjoy a creative meal, or listen to carefully selected music. Decoration is inspired from the four elements and each occupies a separate zone. Head for the earth tones and low couches in the chillout area if you want to relax or the waterfall if you want to eat. Friday is dedicated to funk and house hits, and Sunday the Shanghai band plays live during *aperitivo*.

There's ostentation to spare at **Just Cavalli Café** (Via L. Camoens, tel. 02/311-817, daily 8:30 P.M.–3 A.M.) inside Parco Sempione. Zebra prints and techno keep models occupied and for €10 you can sip on a glamorous cocktail and enjoy the garden during the summer. The kitchen is open until 1 A.M.

The beverages are what count at **Nottingham Forest** (Viale Piave 1, tel. 02/798-311, Tues.–Sun. 6 P.M.–2 A.M., €6). The cocktails are some of the best in town and, regardless of the name, the island decor is inspired from a club in Antigua. Dario Comini is the barman with a long pedigree of mixing drinks and if you're tired of Sex on the Beach try his sake-based concoction with a pearl in the bottom.

Hollywood (Corso Como 15, tel. 02/659-8996, www.discotecahollywood.it, Tues.–Sun. 11 P.M.–4:30 A.M.) is one of the most famous discos in Italy and being famous usually gets you through the doors quickly. If you haven't signed a multi-million contract to play for AC Milan or wrapped up shooting your last film, kindly let the models, designers, actors, and politicians pass. If you aren't discouraged and your heels are high enough, getting in is a breeze. Couples generally have a better chance of entering (especially on Tuesday nights) and if you've come from a D&G shopping spree there should be no problem brushing against VIPs until dawn. If it's dancing on tables and funk, house, or techno you prefer, **Plastic** (Viale Umbria 120, tel. 02/733-996, www.thisisplastic.com, Thurs.–Sun. 11 A.M.–late-night, Fri. €20 cover, Sat. €25 cover) is the

place to load up on rum and tequila and groove the night away. Sweat is always guaranteed.

WINE BARS
Gusto Arte Vino (Via Accademia 56, tel. 02/2890-1370, daily 5:30 P.M. until late) mixes contemporary art, food, and wine in a refined atmosphere where you can alternate sipping red, white, or rosé with admiring canvases by Milan's most promising painters. Argentinean, Chilean, and Australian wines are not excluded from a wine list that's regularly updated by a sommelier who will happily advise. Hot and cold snacks are prepared quickly and the cheese plates are served with a side of honey.

Oil gets as much attention as wine at **Oil Bar Café** (Via Zuccoli 6, tel. 02/6698-3712, daily noon–3 P.M. and 6:30 P.M.–1 A.M., closed Sat.–Sun. lunch, €8–13), located inside an old tram garage that seats 200. Waiters enjoy their jobs and the dedication shows. There are over 1,000 types of olives and once you've tasted the hand-pressed single varieties on the menu your palate will be able to distinguish virgin from

Milan's wine bars offer an array of excellent vintages.

the stuff Mrs. Brady used. Don't be surprised to see people sniffing and holding oil up to the light. That's how to tell a good batch.

Rustic can be elegant and **Barabba** (Via Belfiore 15, tel. 02/462-021, Mon.–Fri. noon–3:30 P.M. and 7–11:30 P.M., Sat. dinner only) is a case in point. The wooden tables are all made to measure and topped with Murano shaded lamps that provide this wine bar and restaurant with a pleasant glow that gets more comforting after every glass. The kitchen is strictly Mediterranean and the dining room fills up with families and friends.

C Moscatelli (Corso Garibaldi 93, tel. 02/655-4602, Mon.–Sat. 7:30 A.M.–midnight) is one of the oldest *vinerie* in the city and nearly every Brera resident can point the way. The interior harks of old Milan and the dusty bottles lining the walls invite drinkers to sample some well-aged wines. They aren't stuck in the past however and the 6 P.M. happy hour features a rich buffet of tempting *salumi, focacce,* and *bruschette* snacks.

Oysters and wine seemed like an obvious combination to Francesco Zanoletti, who opened **Ostriche & Vino** (Via Col di Lana 5, tel. 02/5810-0259, Mon.–Sat. 7 P.M.–12:30 A.M., closed Sun.) several years ago. The modern interior has a bistro style and colors that recall the sea. The oysters are delivered fresh from France and cost €1.50–2.50 each, depending on the variety. For €10 you can order a kilo of mussels (which translates into about 80 shells). The seafood can be accompanied by dry or slightly sweet Italian whites that dominate the wine list.

The Arts
PERFORMING ARTS
L'Auditorium di Milano (Largo Gustav Mahler, tel. 02/8338-9201) is the city's newest concert hall and home of Milan's symphony orchestra. They have a preference for the classics here and anything composed in the late 19th century and early 20th century. Mahler is a favorite and Shostakovich is often on the program.

It's hard to compete with La Scala but **Sala Verdi** (Via Conservatorio 12, tel.

02/7600-5500) is a close second. The centrally located concert hall presents symphonic music every Tuesday night and holds 1,600 comfortably. Many of the musicians from the house orchestra have attended the conservatory that forms part of the complex.

It took decades to restore **Teatro dal Verme** (Via S. Giovanni sul Muro 2, tel. 02/87-905) but it was worth the wait. It's a wonderful place to hear symphonies the way Bach, Beethoven, and Bernstein intended.

Many churches devote one day per week to music and the acoustics of **Chiesa di San Maurizio** (Via Luini 2, tel. 02/7600-5500) and **San Simpliciano** (Piazza San Simpliciano 7, tel. 02/862-274) are perfect for listening to Baroque. Both periodically present organ concerts that are often free.

CINEMA
Anteo Spazio Cinema (Via Milazzo 9, tel. 02/659-7732), **Arcobaleno Film Center** (Viale Tunisia 11, tel. 02/2940-6054), and **Mexico** (Via Savona 57, tel. 02/4895-1802) project movies in their original languages. If you always fantasized about George Clooney speaking Italian you can catch him and other Hollywood bilinguals at **Cinema Brera** (Corso Garibaldi 99, tel. 02/2900-1890) or **Cavour** (Piazza Cavour 3, tel. 02/659-5779). Most movie theaters have reduced prices during the summer and tickets on Wednesdays are €5. Otherwise expect to pay around €7 for a show.

GALLERIES
The area around Corso Como has experienced a rush of gallery openings in recent years and Via Pietro Maroncelli is home to a fair share selling everything from traditional artwork to vintage glass. **Galleria MK** (Via Pietro Maroncelli 2, tel. 02/655-1035) deals in lamps that look like sculptures and are instant collectables. The shelves of the **Tingo Design Gallery** (Via Alessandro Volta 18, tel. 02/2901-7239, www. tingo.it) display more conversation pieces than you'll ever have time to discuss. Does the name Ugo La Pietro ring a bell? This is the place to find his glass and ceramic pieces.

Galleria Blu (Via Senato 18, tel. 02/7602-2404, www.galleriablu.com, Mon.–Sat. 10 A.M.–12:30 P.M. and 3:30–7 P.M.) organizes group shows of recognized artists, many of whom are already hanging in museums. Up-and-comers are likely to be found at **Ciocca Arte Contemporanea** (Via Lecco 15, tel. 02/2953-0826, Mon.–Fri. 2–7:30 P.M.), which generally presents one-artist shows. A number of galleries specialize in photography and the **Nepente Art Gallery** (Via Volta 15, tel. 02/2900-8422, Tues.–Sat. 3–7:30 P.M.) presents reportage while **Cargo High Tech** (Via Meucci 39, tel. 02/272-2131, Tues.–Sun. 10:30 A.M.–8 P.M.) and **Carla Sozzani** (Corso Como 10, tel. 02/653-531, Tues.–Sun. 10:30 A.M.–7:30 P.M.) deal in black and white, abstract, and landscapes.

Festivals and Events

The ancient basilica of S. Eustorgio contains a large sarcophagus with the relics of the Magi kings inside. It was recently returned to Milan from Cologne, where Federico Barbarossa had taken it after he sacked the city in 1162. The tradition of airing out the remains goes back to the 13th century, and on the morning of the **Epiphany** (Jan. 6), a procession in medieval costume accompanied by camels and an elephant departs from the Duomo and winds its way slowly back to the basilica.

Triennale di Milano (Viale Alemagno 6, tel. 02/724-341, www.triennale.it, Tues.–Sun. 10:30 A.M.–8:30 P.M., €8) in Parco Sempione is a major staging point for one-off design exhibitions and annual events like the **Festa per L'architettura,** which highlights new trends in architecture every August. There's also a permanent collection of Italian graphic and urban design. The bookstore has a great collection of design books that are hard to find anywhere else.

Massimiliano Fuksas' **Fiera Milano** (Rho Fiera MM1, tel. 02/49971, www.nuovosistema fieramilano.it) trade fair is a 40-minute subway ride from the center. It's the most modern building in town and locals call it *la vela* because of its resemblance to a sail. For aspir-

Fiera Milano is the most modern building in the city.

© ALESSIA RAMACCIA

ing architects it's a sight in itself and for everyone else there are events held every week. The **Salone del Mobile** furniture show in April/May is one of the most notable—even those not obsessed with coffee tables might be inspired to redecorate their homes.

Oh Bej, Oh Bej on December 7 and 8 is named after the words stall owners use to catch the attention of passersby. The fair celebrates the city's patron saint near Basilica di Sant'Ambrogio with hundreds of market stands selling flowers, sweets, and *panettone* specialties that Milanese can't do without in the run-up to Christmas. It's a colorful couple of days and one of the most popular festivals in the city.

No one leaves the **Artigiano in Fiera** (Craftsmen's Expo) empty-handed. This is the largest craft event in the world, held every December in the Fiera Milano. It's attended by skilled woodworkers, weavers, and jewelers from 90 countries. If you're looking for a stocking stuffer, you'll find it here.

Milan runs on the fashion calendar. February/March and September/October are the trendiest months, when designers show off their newest lines and models, media, and VIPs are a dime a dozen. Parties, concerts, and cultural events are frequent and you could be rubbing up next to Naomi Campbell if you aren't careful. Getting a ticket to **fashion week** in Milan is difficult if you are not an editor at *Vogue,* but there are many peripheral events organized by fashion houses that are open to the general public. Check out www.cameramoda.it to find out about the various events.

SHOPPING

Shopping is one of Milan's main attractions and there are infinite places to start admiring windows or giving credit cards a workout. The Quadrilatero is crammed with brands and the pedestrianized Via della Spiga is a good place to decide whether you prefer Gucci, Prada, Armani, Dolce & Gabbana, Versace, or Gianfranco Ferré.

There are more affordable options along Corso Vittorio Emanuele and Corso Buenos

Galleria Vittorio Emanuele II, a beacon for shoppers

© ALESSIA RAMACCIA

Aires, which runs all the way to Piazzale Loreto. You'll find popular chains like H&M, Zara, Max Mara, and Benetton. For more original boutiques and one-of-a-kind clothing and crafts, try Brera and Via Solferino. The streets off the canal in Navigli sell second-hand clothing and eccentric housewares. The market on the canal is the most eclectic in the city.

Most shops are open from Monday afternoon to Saturday and the elegantly dressed clerks take a break between 1 P.M. and 3:30 P.M. Stores in the center tend to skip the lunchtime pause and most close around 7:30 P.M. On Sundays the area around the Duomo remains active.

Piazza del Duomo
ANTIQUES

Enrico Cortona has a reputation for selling antique prints and paintings of all genres. He's on a first-name basis with museum curators from around the world and his dusty **Antiquariato** (Corso Monforte 38, tel. 02/784-617) is like a little corner of the 16th century.

MUSIC

Italian pop gets a bad rap but you can use the listening booths in the basement of **Ricordi Mediastore** (Galleria Vittorio Emanuele, tel. 02/8646-0272) to judge for yourself. Start with Elisa, Ligabue, or Vasco Rossi, who sells out at San Siro every couple of years. The classical collection on the ground floor is also well stocked and if you need a book for the long train ride ahead, visit **FNAC** or **Feltrinelli** in Piazza Duomo.

CLOTHING

Irene Hong (Via San Maurilio 20, tel. 02/7200-4586) may not have the most recognizable name on the block, but her women's line is just as beautiful as anyone else's. Recent collections have been inspired by nature and she tends to use a lot of colorful fabrics with interesting prints. The clothes are as seductive as is the little store, which is far less intimidating than the average Milan boutique.

The **Fendi** (Via Sant' Andrea 16, tel. 02/7602-1617) sisters are legendary in the design world and have built a fashion empire around their signature look. You can smell the leather as soon as you enter their store, which is less interested with being trendy than concerned with being classic. The clothes certainly look as though they'd make good hand-me-downs to future generations.

SHOES AND ACCESSORIES

There are six **Prada** stores in Milan, but the one in Galleria Vittorio Emanuele II is where Mario Prada started out with modest expectations in 1913. Very little has changed inside this chandelier-lit boutique with black and white checkered floors and brass furnishings. The leather goods are kept inside glass cases and once you've held a real Prada bag, the fake versions just won't do.

Borsalino, also in the Galleria, is where anyone who cherishes headgear comes for a hat. To keep your ears warm in winter, try on one of the traditional models lined with hare fur.

HOME

Danese (Piazza San Nazarro 15, tel. 02/5830-4150, www.danesemilano.com) sells retro furniture and design objects that are getting harder and harder to find. Many of the lamps and dishes were last used in the 1950s but collectors are starting to take notice and an Enzo Mari bowl or Bruno Munari desk set can easily get into triple digits. Stock changes periodically and much of it is difficult to find anywhere else.

DEPARTMENT STORES

Rinascente (Piazza del Duomo, tel. 02/88-521, www.rinascente.it, Mon.–Sat. 9 A.M.–10 P.M.) provides an instant shopping fix. Milan's largest store is spread out on multiple floors dedicated to men, women, and children. It's all here from perfume to mobiles. When you need a break, the terrace bar on the last floor has one of the best views of the Duomo. There's a smaller branch in Viale Certosa 29.

Montenapoleone

ANTIQUES

Behind Piazza San Babila and surrounded by beautiful *palazzi,* **Antica Fonte** (Via San Damiano 5, tel. 02/7600-0236) is an elegant store specializing in furniture. The antiques here look as though they were never used and the cherry desks and walnut dressers all have intricate inlaid woodwork. Francesco Piva can tell you the story behind each piece and is especially attached to his Louis XVI armchairs.

SPECIALTY

White Star Adventure (Piazza Meda, tel. 02/8905-1500, www.wsadventure.com, Mon. noon–9 P.M., Tues.–Fri. 10 A.M.–9 P.M., Sun. 2–7 P.M.) makes traveling easy. The three floors are packed with maps, guides, backpacks, and safari clothing. There's a specialized travel agency that can help you reach uncommon destinations and that holds regular seminars about adventure travel. A second store recently opened in Piazza Belgiojoso.

BOOKSTORES

Milan's largest bookstore covers six floors and contains over 150,000 titles. **Hoepli** (Via Hoepli 5, tel. 02/864-871) has an extensive collection of foreign books including the latest best-sellers in English. They're also very strong in fashion and design. If you forgot your map of Lombardy at home, this is where to pick one up.

CLOTHING

Armani ventured beyond clothing a long time ago and at his store on Via Manzoni 31 (tel. 02/7231-8600) you'll find his name on everything from lamps to chocolate. The three floors of this ultra-modern fashion warehouse contain the latest prêt-à-porter fresh from the runways, as well as Emporio Armani, Armani Jeans, and Armani Casa. Shoppers with a taste for sushi can stop by Nobu and head downstairs to the designer's cocktail bar, **Armani Privé** (Tues.–Sat. 11:30 P.M.–2 A.M.), to put his clothes to good use.

SHOES AND ACCESSORIES

Once you've slipped on a pair of shoes from **Sergio Rossi** (Via della Spiga 5, tel. 02/7639-0927), there's no going back to anything else. The store carries men's shoes, and offers a wide selection of styles and leather. Custom-made shoes are also available; they'll be on your feet in one month and the extra cost will feel well spent.

Tino Cosma (Piazza Conciliazione 5, tel. 02/4800-9900) learned to make ties from his father Vittorio and opened his own shop two decades ago. These aren't the banal kind, but hand-stitched cravats that shirts dream about. Every man should own at least one of these silk neckpieces that can be made to measure and monogrammed while you wait.

HOME

Fashion gets a lot of attention in Milan but the city is also at the forefront of furniture and product design. If the paper clip ever needed a makeover, this is where it would come. **Alessi** (Corso Matteotti 9, tel. 02/795-726) has been transforming everyday objects into art for years. Their bottle opener is a classic and many of the company's kitchen utensils are too affordable not

to buy. This store has a complete selection of the items they produce in their nearby headquarters on Lake Orta.

Nearby **Dadriade** (Via Manzoni 30, tel. 02/7602-3098) sells Philippe Starck accessories, coat hangers that glow in the dark, and clocks that talk. The bookshelves and kitchens may be too big to bring home but it doesn't hurt to discover how people will be cooking in the future.

OUTLETS

Everyone likes a bargain and the Milanese are no different. Fortunately, you don't have to drive long distances to save money in Milan. Many designer outlets are near the center, including **Diffusione Max Mara** (Galleria San Carlo, tel. 02/7600-0829), **Bruno Magli** (Via Manzoni 14, tel. 02/781-264), and **Etro** (Via Spatacos, tel. 02/5502-0218). All three sell clothing from old collections at reduced prices. **Valextra** (Via Cerva 11, tel. 02/7600-3459) is good if you want to replace a suitcase and **Bassetti** (Via C. Botta 7a, tel. 02/5518-3191) has linens covered.

Brera

ANTIQUES

Antichita' Baroni (Via Madonnina 17, tel. 02/804-504, Tues.–Sun. 10 A.M.–1 P.M. and 3–7:30 P.M.) is more a showroom than a store and has a vast assortment of objects from the old to the very old. There's an extensive collection of 18th-century mirrors and the ceiling is covered with oil, gas, and early electric lamps. The lacquered neoclassical furniture is also worth considering and items can be shipped anywhere.

STATIONERY

Rigadritto (Via Brera 6, tel. 02/8058-2936) is the best card store in the city and their selection of handmade papers and envelopes could encourage even the most fanatical emailer to take up letter writing. There's an extensive collection of colorful erasers, rulers that transform into pens, and mouse pads that double as sketchpads.

BOOKSTORES

The shelves of **L'archivolto** (Via Marsala, tel. 02/2901-0444) are covered with books about architecture, town planning, landscaping, design, and the decorative arts. It's usually full of students and scholars browsing one of the best collections in the city. There's a rare book section and a small underground gallery with regular installations. The store has also begun publishing its own titles.

Sailors or anyone with an interest in the sea should head to **La Libreria del Mare** (Via Broletto 28, tel. 02/8646-4426), which carries construction manuals, nautical maps, illustrated books, and magazines on the subject.

CLOTHING

Clothes are just one of the reasons to visit **10 Corso Como** (Corso Como 10, tel. 02/2900-2674). Others include home, beauty, bags, and the bar. There are also books and music on the second floor of this vast store that includes a small bed-and-breakfast (www.3rooms-10corsocomo.com, €310 d) shopaholics dream about.

Even footballers have their own line of clothing in Milan. **Sweet Years** is the brainchild of Paoli Maldini and Bobo Vieri, who opened their flagship store in Via Arco 1 and sell casual sportswear to young trendsetters.

SHOES AND ACCESSORIES

Unlike many of the stores dedicated to a single brand, **Antonia** (Via Ponte Vetero 1, tel. 02/869-0216) isn't afraid to mix Chloé bags with Marc Jacobs shoes. The white interior feels like a museum where accessories are displayed like artwork.

Francescatrezzi (Corso Garibaldi 44, tel. 02/8691-5103) sells handbags and shoes and can even deck out dogs with colorful leashes or travel beds.

It's hard to pass the windows of **Spelta** (Via Pontaccio 2, tel. 02/805-2592) without taking a look. They're filled with rows of colorful hand-stitched shoes, and choosing a model is the easy part. Each comes in countless shades and fabrics, which leads many shoppers to buy several pairs.

HOME

Eclecta (Corso Garibaldi 3, tel. 02/876-194) is true to its name and this original gallery can cure any home of the Ikea blues. There's an extensive selection of ethnic furniture and design objects for study, office, and kitchen. They also produce a small line of hand-painted clothing, jewelry, and accessories.

MARKETS

Mercato d'Antiquariato (tel. 02/794-593) features 70 stalls along Via Fiori Chiara every Sunday morning. Tables are filled with antique watches, jewelry, Sheffield porcelain, ceramics, and glassware that attracts collectors from across the city. The market makes for a pleasant walk along one of the city's most elegant streets.

Magenta

WATCHES

It's all about minutes and seconds at **Era l'Ora** (Corso Magenta 22, tel. 02/8645-0965), which deals exclusively in watches. They come in all sizes and prices. There are gold pocket watches and Omega wristwatches from the 1950s and you'll also find trendier, digital models and prestigious brands like Rolex, Jaeger, and Constantin. If it's stopped ticking, they'll fix it.

MUSIC

In the age of MP3, stores like **Buscemi** (Corso Magenta 27, tel. 02/805-6410) are in danger of extinction. For the time being, there are enough rock, jazz, and classical fans in Milan who enjoy listening to music on vinyl, CD, or even cassette. Prices are honest and many hard-to-find records can be dug up here.

BOOKSTORES

The interior of **Feltrinelli Libri e Musica** (Piazza Piemonte 2, tel. 02/433-541) was designed by Miguel Sal and could be the set for a *Star Wars* sequel. Photographs of famous writers line the walls and there's a café and box office selling concert tickets. It's a long walk down Via Magenta or a quick subway ride to the Wagner station. If you're searching for books in English, you're better off heading to **Feltrinelli International** (Piazza Cavour 1, tel. 02/659-5644, Mon.–Sat. 9 A.M.–7:30 P.M., Sun. 10 A.M.–1:30 P.M. and 3:30–7 P.M.).

CLOTHING

Looking good is what **Bardelli** (Via G. Pascoli 7, tel. 02/902-5181) is all about. The two floors of this men's and women's store feel like one big closet, where even impatient shoppers can find the shirts, sweaters, or shoes they've been searching for. Quality is as high as the prices but these outfits will last a lifetime.

SHOES AND ACCESSORIES

Mephisto (Via Dante 15, tel. 02/809-978) gives feet something to smile about. The practical line of shoes features non-slip soles and patented inserts that prevent sweat and gently massage the toes. Heels are designed to absorb body weight but most importantly these shoes look good and come in a range of classic, sport, and sandal styles.

HOME

After years of globe-trotting, Orsetta Mantovani returned home with a whole lot of decorating ideas in her head. Her store, **Orsetta Mantovani** (Corso Magenta 66), has an eclectic selection of housewares for bedroom, bath, and kitchen that can add originality to any home. She also custom-makes clothing and displays the work of local artisans.

Naviglio
MARKETS

The two biggest flea markets in Milan are in the Naviglio neighborhood, which is also a good place to find a lot of the city's edgier stores. Every Saturday morning, Viale d'Annunzio fills with Indian, South American, and African vendors selling clothes, old furniture, scented candles, pirated DVDs, and comics. It's always possible to find a bargain at **Fiera di Senigallia** among the noise and color of the stalls while Senegalese musicians pound away on their drums, which provide a steady beat for browsing.

Nearby along the Naviglio canal, an **antiques market** (tel. 02/8940-9971) is held on the last Sunday of every month except July. On a sunny day, it's a great way to spend a morning shopping for clocks, porcelain, dolls, walking sticks, old radios, and countless other collectables sold by 400 dealers who line both sides of the canal. It's also the site of an annual flower festival in April and an art fair in May. During the summer, much of the area is converted for pedestrian use, and 20,000 bulbs light up the waterway during the Christmas season.

SPORTS AND RECREATION
Soccer

AC Milan are the New York Yankees of Italian football. The team is loved by half the city and loathed by the other half, who resent their disconcerting habit of winning. There are Brazilian stars, hardcore fans, and a tradition that dates back to 1899 by way of Van Basten, Gullit, and Rijkard. **Inter Milan** are the crosstown rivals who are more like the Mets and regularly cause their supporters heartache. Both squads play in the **San Siro** stadium and twice a year face off against each other in a sold-out derby. Stadium tours leave from the **museum** (Via Piccolomini 5, Gate 21, tel. 02/404-2432, www.sansirotour.com, daily 10 A.M.–6 P.M., €7 museum or €12.50 with tour), which is dedicated to both of the teams, and help visitors relive some of the legendary games played here.

Basketball

Italian basketball has taken sponsorship to an entirely new level. In addition to the stadiums, the teams themselves are sponsored and their uniforms are covered with corporate logos. **Armani Jeans** (tel. 02/7000-1615) is the official name of Milan's team and they regularly vie for the top spot in the league. The squad contains the usual ex-NBA journeymen, a couple of mammoth Lithuanians, and some local talent. They play 20 minutes southwest of the center in the **Assago Datch Forum** (Oct.–Apr., tickets €14–48) and average about 10,000 fans per home game.

Gyms and Spas

Getting a good workout in the city isn't as hard as it used to be. Most joggers head for the paths around Parco Sempione, although marathon-level runners may need to complete many laps before breaking a sweat. If it's dumbbells you're looking for, try **Downtown** (Piazza Diaz 6, tel. 02/863-1181) or **Caroli Health Club** (Via Senato 11, tel. 02/7602-8517). Both are open daily and provide moderate rates for one-time visitors.

Day spas are increasingly turning up around the city and like many things it's the designers who have imported the trend first. **Bulgari Spa** (Via Privata Fratelli Gabba 7b, tel. 02/8058-05200, daily) relaxes the eyes as well as the body. Guests can enjoy a Turkish bath and a dip in the gold mosaic pool followed by one of a dozen treatments. The hot stone therapy will leave you nearly unconscious. For a hammam that can remove all the air pollution from your pores, visit **Habits Culti** (Via Angelo Mauri 5, tel. 02/4851-7588) in Magenta. Prepare to be rubbed, peeled, and massaged in a succession of hot and cold environments that would have impressed even the Romans. A restaurant next to the spa prepares light snacks and healthy drinks.

ACCOMMODATIONS

Hotels open as often as new stores in Milan and range from the tacky but affordable to €13,000 a night presidential suites. In between there's a lot of hardwood flooring, attention to design, and sophisticated service. Location is less important than in Rome because neighborhoods are close together and it's easy to sleep in Brera and shop in Montenapoleone or dine near the Duomo and hit the sack in Naviglio.

Piazza del Duomo
UNDER €100
Milan Duomo (Via Torino 46, tel. 347/779-6170, €90–100, s/d) is a small bed-and-breakfast on the fourth floor of an 18th-century palazzo three minutes from the Duomo. Small is not an understatement. There is only one double room with private bath and

a separate entrance. The three windows look out onto a courtyard and let in a lot of light. Breakfast is served in your room whenever you're ready for a strong coffee and *cornetti*.

Vecchia Milan (Via Borromei 4, tel. 02/875-042, www.hotelvecchiamilano.it, €90 d) may evoke memories of dorm living, except here the rooms are spotless and you can bounce a euro off the tightly made beds. About the only luxury is the hairdryer but considering the central location and the price it's not such a bad deal.

Rooms may be small and the air-conditioning powerless against the heat outside, but no one complains about the service at **Hotel London** (Via Rovello 3, tel. 02/7202-0166, €100 d). The family-run hotel sees many repeat guests, who appreciate the hotel's central location on a quiet street between the Duomo and Castello Sforzesco. A continental breakfast is served downstairs in the wood-paneled dining area.

€100-200
Fresh flowers are the first indication **Locanda alle Meraviglie** (Via San Tomaso 8, tel. 02/805-1023, www.allemeraviglie.it, €165 d) is not just a place to sleep. Each of the six rooms is simply decorated and benefits from high ceilings and thick mattresses. The public rooms are quite nice, but breakfast is a bit pricey and you're better off searching for a *pasticceria* in the streets nearby.

€200-300
Hotel de la Ville (Via Ulrico Hoepli 6, tel. 02/879-1311, www.delavillemilano.com, €229 d) is a classic four-star with aspirations for a fifth. It's spread out on six floors in the heart of Milan and all 109 rooms are carpeted. Bathrooms are covered in Italian marble and they have some nice complimentary creams that make nice souvenirs. Breakfast features an extensive buffet and the T-Club on the roof has a small pool with views of the Duomo.

OVER €300
The unadorned concrete walls at **Straf** (Via San Raffaele 3, tel. 02/805-081, www.straf.it, €310 d) are a nod to Le Corbusier and provide rooms

with a rawness designers that love to wake up in. Vincenzo de Cotiis also used brass, iron, stone, and glass to give all 64 rooms a touch of Zen. The Well-Being rooms on the sixth floor come with Japanese auto-massage beds, while the bar downstairs is more like a hip art gallery and serves an à la carte menu all day long.

Montenapoleone
UNDER €100
Book early if you want to stay in one of the three rooms at **Foresteria Monforte** (Piazza del Tricolore 2, tel. 02/7631-8516, www.foresteria monforte.it, €100 d). The style is contemporary and the service is do-it-yourself. It's really just a side job for the owners, who run the pharmacy downstairs. Each room is equipped with LCD TVs, lightning-fast Internet, and air-conditioning. Guests are free to use the kitchen and it's a short walk to the shops or S. Babila subway.

€100-200
Downtown Genius (Via Porlezza 4, tel. 02/7209-4644, www.hotelgenius.it, €170 d) is a mid-sized hotel with professional staff and an opulent breakfast that's within walking distance from the Duomo. Let them know what newspaper you prefer and they'll slip it under your door in the morning. The bar service is available 24 hours a day and all rooms come with private bath, air-conditioning, and pay TV. One of the four floors of the hotel is reserved for non-smokers.

  Grand Hotel Visconti (Viale Isonzo 14, tel. 02/540-341, www.grandviscontipalace.com, €175 d), on the doorstep of the Duomo, is more a resort than hotel. It's hard to believe the building was once a mill, as it now caters to travelers accustomed to getting what they want. All the public areas are furnished to the nines and the hotel includes a pool with a garden view, beauty center, and elegant restaurant. There are 162 classic doubles and 10 super suites.

€200-300
Tucked away in an 18th-century palazzo in the historic center of the city, the **Gran Duca di York** (Via Monet 1, tel. 02/874-863, www.

ducadiyork.com, €225 d) is a sure bet if you're looking to spark a little romance. Ask for the courtyard rooms on the third floor, which are quieter and have been redecorated in pastel yellows and blues.

  You can get a cozy bed-and-breakfast feel at **Townhouse 31** (Via Goldoni 31, tel. 02/701-5600, www.townhouse.it, €250 d) that's a far cry from the generic reception offered at bigger hotels. The 17 rooms are done up in ethnic themes and several have terraces. There's a tented bar popular with the *aperitivi* set, but for dining you'll need to head out into the city. A second Townhouse was opened in Piazza Gerusaleme 12 (tel. 02/8907-8511); it attracts a younger crowd that downs vodka cocktails in the Nordic-style ice bar.

OVER €300
The Gray (Via San Raffaele 6, tel. 02/720-8951, www.hotelthegray.com, €340 d) has all the five-star comforts within a very selective setting. Unlike at the larger luxury hotels, you won't be bumping into many millionaires. There are only 21 rooms, including two duplex suites and two rooms equipped with their own sauna and private gym. After working up a sweat you can reserve a table at Le Noir restaurant, where everything is rigorously painted black.

Brera
UNDER €100
Hotel Star (Via Dei Bossi 5, tel. 02/801-501, www.hotelstar.it, €60 d) is a 30-room hotel with services usually found at larger properties, such as various breakfast options and complimentary daily newspapers. It's five minutes from the center and the owners have been welcoming guests for decades. Smokers are the only people they frown upon and the breakfast buffet ends at 9:30 A.M. on the dot.

€100-200
Jolly Hotel Touring (Via Tarchetti 2, tel. 02/63351, www.jollyhotels.com, €109 d) is convenient for anyone arriving by car and is just 200 meters from the nearest subway stop

(Repubblica). All the rooms have been given a makeover and most bathrooms come with tubs.

€200-300

Staff seem to be standing at attention throughout **Hotel Cavour** (Via Fatebenefratelli 21, www.hotelcavour.it, tel. 02/620-001, €220 d) ready to serve. With comfortable and modern rooms, a reliable restaurant, and minibars, there's not much missing. The location is excellent for exploring the Brera art scene.

Hotels aren't for everyone, which is how **Glamour Apartments** (Via Privata Passarella 4, www.glamourapartments.hotelsinmilan.it, €220 d) came to be. Its rooms are located in historic *palazzi* and feel more like staying at a friend's house than at a crowded hotel. Although there's no front desk and room service is non-existent, you get more space and feel like a native. All rooms must be reserved online.

The bed-and-breakfast **10 Corso Como** (Corso Como 10, tel. 02/2900-2674, www.3rooms-10corsocomo.com, €310 d) is just three suites, done up with loads of mosaics and comfortable 1970s furnishings of the Eero Saarinen, Isamo Noguchi, and Eames variety. The ambience is much more apartment-like and each suite has a private entrance overlooking a cozy tea garden where "slow breakfast" is served. Shopping, nightlife, and art are just around the corner.

OVER €300

Bulgari (Via Privata Fratelli Gabba 7b, tel. 02/805-8051, www.bulgarihotels.com, €550 d) isn't just about jewelry anymore. They made the transition to hotels and sleeping in Milan hasn't been the same since. Half of the 58 rooms overlook a garden and are decked out in oak, bronze, and black marble. The hotel's luxurious spa is one of the best in the city and the Turkish bath is free for guests recovering from a day of heavy-duty shopping. Even if the rooms are out of your budget it's worth stopping by for Sunday brunch or *aperitivo,* served daily from 6:30–9 P.M. on the terrace outside.

Sempione
UNDER €100

The **Lancaster** (Via A. Sangiorgio 16, tel. 02/344-705 www.hotellancaster.it, €99 d) is within a 19th-century Liberty building on a quiet residential street near Corso Sempione and the park. Service is friendly and there's a snack bar downstairs that stays open until late. The rooms themselves are on the kitschy side, with unusual paintings and functional furnishings. Still it's clean and for Milan it's reasonably priced.

€100-200

Hotels are on nearly every corner these days, but the **Enterprise** (Corso Sempione 91, tel. 02/318-181, www.enterprisehotel.com, €200 d) was one of the first to include good design as standard. Some of the trendiest bars are minutes from the industrial interior, where you can spend an entertaining evening.

€200-300

There's been a boom in boutique hotels in Milan and **Town House 12** (Piazza Gerusalemme 12, tel. 02/8907-8511, www.townhouse.it/th12/it/, €250) is one of the most gracious. Everything has been studied here from the color of the corridors to the placement of toothbrush holders. The moment you enter it's hard not to relax, so leaving might be traumatic. They serve great vodka cocktails at the bar, which fills up for an intimate *aperitivo.*

The paint always smells fresh at **L'Hotel Nasco** (Corso Sempione 69, tel. 02/31951, www.hotelnascomilano.it, €275 d), which opened in 2001 and hit the ground running. Interiors are large and the windows let in a lot of light. Guests are a mix of tourists and business travelers who take advantage of the free shuttle to the Fiera Milan. No one complains about the buffet. The internal garage is convenient for drivers and there's an Internet point in the lobby.

Magenta
UNDER €100

If you can get past the name, **King Mokinba** (Corso Magenta 19, www.mokinba.it, €85 d) provides all the comforts you could ask for, as well as old-fashioned furniture. Air-conditioning, hairdryer, satellite TV, minibar, and radio are all included. Breakfast is substantial even by U.S. standards, and there's a parking garage 50 meters away. Staff can help you understand how the subway works and sell you tickets. Lunch and dinner are not served but there are plenty of restaurants nearby. The yellow bikes are free.

€100-200

Antica Locanda Leonardo (Corso Magenta 78, tel. 02/4801-4197, www.anticalocandaleonardo. com, €150 d) is situated within a noble palazzo on one of Milan's most prestigious streets. The Frefel family are old hands at hospitality and can tell what you need before you do. Atmosphere is elegant and furniture is a delightful mix of antique and modern. Choose between a sweet or savory start to your day in the breakfast room, which doubles as the bar every evening. Guests can enjoy the garden in the summer and have access to free parking.

During the Middle Ages, (**Hotel Palazzo delle Stelline** (Corso Magenta, 61, tel. 02/481-8431, www.hotelpalazzostelline.it, €175 d) was a boardinghouse for beggars and orphans. It's been renovated since then and the stench of the plague is a distant memory. Now this three-star hotel offers a historic night's sleep under vaulted ceilings and stone arches. The cloister may be the most peaceful spot in Milan to rest and admire the beautiful magnolia that perfumes the entire hotel.

€200-300

Ariston (Largo Carrobbio 2, tel. 02/7200-0556, www.aristonhotel.com, €250 d) is the only choice for Al Gore and anyone who cares about the environment. It's the first eco-hotel in the city and all the fittings, mattresses, paints, and pillows are natural and non-toxic. Oxygen is purified and each room provides an air quality analysis that allows guests to breathe easier. Breakfast is strictly organic, recycling is mandatory, and bicycles are provided free of charge.

Naviglio and Tortona
UNDER €100

BBHotels operates several characteristic bed-and-breakfasts around the city but the one near Milan's canals is the nicest. **B&B Navigli** (Via Gentilino 7, tel. 02/8738-1614, www.bbhotels. it, €90 d) is located within a tranquil courtyard and the nightlife on the adjacent streets is great for anyone who prefers late nights.

€100-200

The factories in this neighborhood have been replaced by restaurants, bars, and sleek hotels like (**Nhow** (Via Tortona 35, tel. 02/489-8861, www.nh-hotels.com, €150 d), located inside the former GE building. Rooms have novel layouts and are decorated in a sort of post-1970s style with special attention to lighting that's far from mundane. There are 249 standard and junior suites, along with a terrace and spa where many guests end their day.

FOOD

Breakfast in Milan is usually a cappuccino and a *cornetto* eaten quickly standing at a bar. Things get more intricate at lunch, when all types of *panini, tramezzini,* and *focaccie* start to appear at the many cafés and *pasticcerie.* What Milan does best, however, is dinner and the variety of restaurants is enormous and constantly changing.

If the idea of eating sushi, crepes, or even tacos is off-putting, you can stick with the local specialties. *Nervetti* (strips of beef or veal served with onions, peppers, and beans) is a traditional *antipasto* that tastes better than it sounds. Rice is a mainstay of the first courses and *risotto alla Milanese* is the classic flavored with beef broth and saffron. Anyone who makes it to the seconds can try *cassoeula,* made from the parts of a pig that wouldn't be appetizing if they weren't boiled and mixed with cabbage and green vegetables. The trademark dish is *cotoletta,* veal cutlet that's breaded and usually served alone with a slice of lemon. If you want a side of roasted potatoes or sautéed spinach, they should be ordered separately. Finding a local wine to match a meal is no problem and the variation from province to province and even from town to town can be enormous. The Lambrusco grapes grown near Mantova are generally a safe bet.

Restaurants start to get busy at 8 P.M. and many are closed on Sunday or Monday and remain shut throughout August. Reservations are a good idea if you want to guarantee a table.

Piazza del Duomo
MILANESE

Trattoria Milanese (Via Santa Marta 11, tel. 02/8645-1991, Wed.–Mon. noon–3 P.M. and 7–11 P.M., closed Aug., €10–14) isn't the easiest restaurant to find and locals like it that way. All you'll get here are the classics and if you want to fit in just order the risotto or *cotolette alla Milanese* (Milanese-style steak). It gets crowded at lunch with white-collar workers from the financial district.

The best time to eat at **Hostaria Borromei** (Via Borromei 4, tel. 02/8645-3760, Mon.–Fri. noon–2:30 P.M. and 7:30–11 P.M., €8–12) is summer, when tables are set out in the vine-covered courtyard and the hearty pasta dishes are served nearly as fast as you order them. Dessert is the highlight of this family-run *osteria,* and you shouldn't leave without sampling a pear or orange tart, made in-house every day.

PIZZA
The owners of **Agnello** (Via Agnello 8, tel. 02/805-3373, €7–12) don't follow fashion or worry about being trendy. What matters here is the pizza, which has been prepared the same way for years and never disappoints the locals who fill the informal room. They also serve traditional fried starters and there's always fresh fruit for dessert.

CAFÉS
Gucci Caffè (tel. 02/859-7991, Mon.–Sat. 10 A.M.–7 P.M. and Sun. 2–9 P.M., €6) inside Galleria Vittorio Emanuele is less expensive than it looks and coffee comes with specially designed chocolates stamped with the store's logo.

Pasticceria Marchesi (Via Santa Maria alla Porta 11a, tel. 02/876-730, Tues.–Sat. 7:30 A.M.–8 P.M., Sun. 3–8 P.M.) is an old-fash-

ioned café that gets crowded at lunchtime with office workers stuffing themselves with panini. If you're not assertive, you'll never get served or taste any of the homemade cakes baked on the premises.

DELICACIES
Princi (Via Speronari 6, www.princi.it, Mon.–Sat. 7 A.M.–9 P.M.) is synonymous with bread but it isn't an old-fashioned bakery. The look of the place is as important as the organic flour and the sleek interior could be mistaken for a hip bar—except here you can see a wood-burning oven and can graze over a long glass counter offering every possible bun imaginable.

Montenapoleone
MILANESE
The charm of **Da Oscar** (Via Palazzi 4, tel. 02/2951-8806, €10–14) is the owner and namesake of the restaurant, who skipped finishing school and treats customers as though he were doing them a favor. Once you you've tasted the calamari or *pasta alla oscar* (simple tomato-based pasta dish), you won't mind the insults—which only locals can understand anyways.

If you only have one meal in Milan, have it at **⟨ Bagutta** (Via Bagutta 14, tel. 02/7600-2767, Mon.–Sat. noon–2:30 P.M. and 7–11:30 P.M., €10–13). The entrance may not look like much, but that's not how to judge a restaurant. This place is so historic that it has its own museum with a collection of menus dating back 70 years. The interior is a maze of darkly lit rooms covered in photographs of the writers, artists, intellectuals, and regular Giuseppes who have turned the restaurant into an institution. When the landlord threatened to evict the owner 15 years ago, there was a popular outcry in the neighborhood and a law was passed so that places like this would never close. The crew of lifetime waiters dress in white shirts, black vests, and ties. They'll bring you a menu printed that day with just about everything you've ever wanted to eat and then some. Although the restaurant is big enough to have a coatroom, it's wise to reserve a table especially if you want to eat in the garden.

VEGETARIAN

Pietro Leeman might have been a poet if he wasn't such a good chef. He uses the menu at **Joia** (Via Castaldi 18, tel. 02/2952-2124) to express some of his literary aspirations. All the dishes have original names and it's best to consult the elegantly dressed waiters if in doubt. The soups are especially good and presentation is everything inside the modern, Japanese-style interior. Lunch is the more affordable option and comes as a €25 prix-fixe or €15 *assaggini* (tasting) option.

PIZZA

Paper Moon (Via Bagutta 1, tel. 02/7602-2297) lies between via Montenapoleone and via della Spiga and has gained cult status among pizza lovers—and you'll also find a good breaded steak and an extensive wine list. It's not very big, so if you're tired of people-watching this is the place to do some people-bumping. The walls are the domain of famous diners.

JAPANESE

Nobu (Armani Via Manzoni 31, tel. 02/6231-2645, www.giorgioarmani.it, €30), Nobuyuki Matsuhisa's famed Japanese restaurant is located inside the Armani clothing store and is as elegant as the clothes. The space is spread out on two floors and you can watch the chefs in action at the bar. Diners can select from a wide range of sushi, tempura, and kuskiyaki. There are four Bento box options with different meat, fish, and vegetable combinations. Much of the menu is also infused with South American flavors.

CAFÉS

They've been serving cappuccinos at **Biffi** (Corso Magenta 87, tel. 02/4800-6702) since 1847. The old wooden bar and chandeliers haven't changed and still attract a steady stream of notable Milanese names eager for a plate of *pasticcini*. **Cova** (Via Montenapoleone 8, tel. 02/7600-0578) is even older and it's a great place to pause in between bouts shopping and watch a succession of fashionable locals down their coffees in under a minute.

DELICACIES

Garbagnati (Via Victor Hugo 3, tel. 02/860-905) bakes fresh bread every morning in dozens of intriguing shapes. They use a variety of flours and prepare a great, yeast-free flatbread similar to matzah. They also make Austrian-influenced strudel and Sacher tortes. At Christmastime, this is the place to sample *panettone*.

Brera
MILANESE

The husband and wife team who run **Arturosa la Latteria** (Via San Marco 24, tel. 02/659-7653, Mon.–Fri. noon–2:30 P.M. and 7–11 P.M., €8–12) are on a quest to preserve Italian flavors of the past. If you want to know what the 1960s tasted like in Milan (and parts of Tuscany), this is the place to take your tongue on a gastronomic flashback. It's not that big and it's popular with journalists who come for the *antipasto* and the chocolate mousse.

Milan is a long way from Campania, but you can still count on **Obikà** (Via Mercato 28, tel. 02/8645-0568, www.obika.it, daily noon–3:30 P.M. and 6–11:30 P.M., €8–12) to serve fresh *bufala* cheese in their *mozzarella* bar. Try all four varieties shipped daily at this metallic-themed restaurant that's also great for *aperitivo*.

To see the city while eating, the **ATMosfera** (tel. 800/808-181, Tues.–Sun., €50) dinner tram is the only choice. It leaves at 8 P.M. from Piazza Castello and provides a four-course fish- or meat-based fixed-price meal. The romantic journey lasts 2.5 hours and includes coffee, dessert, and wine. It's best to arrive 10 minutes early so as not to miss the departure.

TUSCAN

Torre di Pisa (Via Fiori Chiari 21, tel. 02/874-877, Tues.–Sun. noon–3 P.M. and 7–10:30 P.M., €8–12) prepares substantial Tuscan fare in four brightly lit rooms decorated with plates and a ceramic leaning tower that recalls the owner's origins. The open kitchen can be observed from some of the tables and watching the chefs wield their knives is reassuring. Waiters are friendly and will gladly help deconstruct the menu. The house specialty is osso buco, a tender cut of veal shank stewed on the bone.

SEAFOOD

Fish and crustaceans are all you'll find at **Tintero** (Via Quintino Sella 2, tel. 02/3655-7743, Mon.–Fri. noon–3 P.M. and 7:30 P.M.–12:30 A.M., Sat.–Sun. 7:30 P.M.–12:30 A.M., €10–15 or €35 prix fixe). Diners can choose to eat at the long elegant counter, which can be entertaining, or at a table in the large dining room filled with couples and groups of friends. Spaghetti with clams is one of the house specialties and shrimp and fried mussels are also very good. There's no end to the white wine on offer.

Magenta
MILANESE

Boccondivino (Via Carducci 17, tel. 02/866-040, €9–14) is perfect for anyone who can't decide and waiters show up with cured meats before you've sat down. They'll also roll the cheese cart your way and be disappointed if you don't try the locally produced *toma* or *taleggio*. A sommelier is on hand to advise drinkers and the separate room for smokers keeps Marlboro men dry.

Listen to Elena, she won't steer you wrong and has been advising hungry stomachs for years. **Brisa** (Via Brisa 15, tel. 02/8645-0521, €8–13) is a lively place, with the occasional VIP face and an excellent chef. Sit in the garden if you can and enjoy *cannelloni* stuffed with *ricotta* and asparagus. Desserts are freshly made and change according to the season.

INTERNATIONAL

Noon Cafè & Restaurant (Via Boccaccio 4, tel. 02/4802-4607, www.noonmilano.com, daily 7:30 A.M.–2 P.M. and 6 P.M.–2 A.M., closed Sun. lunch and Mon. morning, €8–15) is a big hit at any hour. They serve brioche and muffins in the morning, which can be nibbled on the orange, brown, and beige chairs of the main eating room. Christian Deventi pre-

pares pizza and finger food at lunch and his colleague Pasquale lets ethnic influences infiltrate the evening menu. The three floors fill up quickly at *aperitivo*. The entirely white lounge bar can be disconcerting after a while.

There's a waiting list to eat at **Zero Contemporary Food** (Corso Magenta 87, tel. 02/4547-4733, Tues.–Sun. 7–11:30 P.M., €15–20) on weekends but you can usually find a table at lunch inside this mecca of Japanese gastronomy. The chefs prepare sushi rolls and sashimi inside a glass cube in the center of the dining room. Takeaway is available at the counter near the entrance.

Parco Sushi (tel. 02/7200-3520, www.parcosushi.it, Mon.–Sat. 12:30–2:30 P.M. and 6:30 P.M.–12:30 A.M., Sun. 6:30–11:30 P.M., €10–14) has five branches in the city; the one on Corso Magenta 14 serves great salmon rolls imported fresh everyday.

DELICACIES

Chococult (Via Buonarroti 7, tel. 02/4802-7319, www.chococult.it, daily 7:30 A.M.–2 A.M.) is the home of chocolate and a delight for all the senses. The three floors overlooking Piazza Wagner provide unlimited cacao stimulation, from the gelato to solid versions flavored with green tea, wasabi, and balsamic vinegar. Try the tasters' platter of five different varieties, or spend a winter afternoon enjoying the *Etoile* coffee and cocoa drink in one of the beanbags observing fellow addicts.

INFORMATION AND SERVICES
Tourist Information

The central **IAT tourist office** (tel. 02/7352-4350, www.milanoinfotourist.com, Mon.–Sat. 8:45 A.M.–1 P.M. and 2–6 P.M., Sun. 9 A.M.–1 P.M. and 2–5 P.M.) is on Via Marconi 1 off Piazza Duomo. They provide a useful map that lists 54 of the main sights in Milan. There are also brochures for each neighborhood and a monthly events guide in Italian and English. You can also pick up the Castelli Pass and other combination offers that provide discounts to castles and villas throughout the region. There is a secondary office inside **Stazione Centrale** (tel. 02/7252-4360, Mon.–Sat. 9 A.M.–6 P.M., Sun. 9 A.M.–1 P.M. and 2–5 P.M.).

Hospitals, Police, and Emergencies

The closest hospital to the center is **Ospedale Maggiore** (Piazza Ospedale Maggiore 3, tel. 02/6444-2381) at the Crocetta stop of the MM3 (yellow) subway line. If a toothache is ruining your holiday, call the emergency dentist hotline anytime at 02/865-460. Ambulances are 118, police 113, and if you need the fire brigade call 115.

Pharmacies

There's a 24-hour pharmacy (tel. 02/669-0935) inside the departures hall at Stazione Centrale or call Pronto Farmacia on 800/801-185 to find a closer one. Most pharmacies don't close for lunch and are recognizable by their green neon crosses.

Banks and Currency Exchange

Banks are open 8:30 A.M.–1:30 P.M. and 3–4 P.M. with slight variations. Most financial institutions are closed on weekends, but ATMs are common. **Banca Ponti** (Piazza Duomo 19, tel. 02/722-771, Mon.–Fri. 8:30 A.M.–4:15 P.M., Sat.–Sun. 9:10 A.M.–12:45 P.M.) is the most convenient place to change money. Contact American Express (tel. 800/864-046) or Visa (tel. 800/821-001) if cards have been stolen or you need to increase your line of credit.

Government Offices

The U.S. consulate (tel. 02/290-351, www.milan.usconsulate.gov) is located on Via Principe Amedeo 2 and operates weekday mornings. Canadians should head to Via V. Pisani 19 (tel. 02/67581, www.canada.it).

Newspapers and Internet

Milan is the most Anglo of Italian cities and the continuous stream of business travelers make finding English-language newspapers a breeze. Most kiosks in the center carry *USA Today* and the *International Herald Tribune*, along with

LIFEGATE

Turn the FM dial to 105.1 in Milan and you may notice something strange. Not only is the music selection perfect for driving, but there are some unique ads. What you will hear on Lifegate radio are ecological initiatives and ways listeners can reduce their carbon footprint from switching energy companies to buying sustainably produced jeans.

Lifegate isn't just a radio station. In fact, when Marco Roveda and his wife had their environmental epiphany in the 1970s, all they were interested in was raising the biological standards of food on Italian tables. They did that and a lot more. In 15 years, Italy went from cultivating 5,000 hectares of naturally grown produce to a million (an area the size of Le Marche), becoming the world leader in the sector.

The Rovedas didn't stop there and after selling their biological enterprise they founded Lifegate. The mission is to spread the eco-cultural word, raise people's awareness about environmental issues that threaten the future, and promote a form of bio-capitalism that balances profit, respect for nature, and social equality. It's not easy teaching old dogs new tricks, but communication is at the heart of their strategy. The radio station, Internet portal, and magazine all aim to help draw attention to environmental issues without boring listeners. They also assist companies attempting to raise their ethical standards and encourage consumers to recognize the part they can play in influencing corporate behavior.

The *impatto zero* (zero impact) slogan isn't just talk. In Milan, Lifegate has opened a cafe that puts the organization's philosophy into practice. Don't expect any chemicals or genetically modified ingredients here. They also run a holistic clinic where anyone can find harmony through traditional remedies and modern science. Like all environmental entrepreneurs, they are confident they can make a difference and for anyone who hates listening to radio advertising they already have.

French, Spanish, and German dailies. There are Internet points at the **Fnac Cafè** (Via Torino) and **Grazia** in Piazza Lima and Duca d'Aosta 14 near the central train station.

Lost and Found

Lost items are kept for an entire year at the **Ufficio Oggetti Rinvenuti** (Via Friuli 30, tel. 02/8845-3900, Mon.–Fri. 8:30 A.M.–4 P.M.) before going to auction. It's best to call first and bring along an ID. There's usually a small fee to pay and you will be required to describe the object in detail. If you lost something on a train, try the **Ufficio Ferrovie dello Stato** (Stazione Centrale, tel. 02/6371-2212, daily, 7 A.M.–1 P.M. and 2–8 P.M.).

GETTING THERE
By Air

Milan has two airports. **Malpensa** (tel. 02/7485-2200, www.sea-aeroportimilano.it) serves intercontinental destinations and is 40 minutes north of the center. The Malpensa Express (www.ferrovienord.it, €11) connects the airport with Cadorna station and operates daily 4:20 A.M.–11:30 P.M. You can also opt for the Malpensa Shuttle (tel. 02/3391-0794) that runs 24 hours a day. It's half the price of the train but often takes twice as long, especially during rush hour. A taxi can be astronomical unless it's split a couple of ways.

Linate (tel. 02/7485-2200) is the second airport and serves domestic and European destinations. It's closer to the center and bus 73 (€1) outside the arrivals hall drops travelers off at Piazza San Babila in under 30 minutes. A taxi to the center is around €30.

By Train

Milan is a main hub of the Italian rail network and trains from Rome and all points south pull into **Stazione Centrale** (tel. 892-021). The station also serves European destinations and travelers can reach the center using one of two subway lines located in the piazza outside the station.

Ferrovie Nord Milan (tel. 199/151-152) leaves from Cadorna near Castello Sforzesco. It operates regional service across Northern Lombardy and is used by commuters and anyone heading for the lakes.

By Car

Five highways lead to Milan's ring road (Tangenziale Est and Tangenziale Ovest), one of the busiest strips of asphalt in the country. The A1 connects the city with Bologna, Florence, and Rome. It's a toll road and the fee is based on distance traveled. The A4 east leads to Venice and Verona while if you take it west you can be in Torino in just over an hour. The A7 connects with Liguria and the A8 and A9 head north towards the lakes and Switzerland.

By Bus

There are a half-dozen bus companies serving national and international destinations. There is no central bus station and most tickets can be purchased on board or in advance over the Internet. **Eurolines** (tel. 05/535-7110, www.eurolines.com) travels to many European cities from Piazza Freud, while **SILA** (tel. 02/8954-6132, www.sila.it) departs daily for Pavia and regional destinations from Famagosta.

GETTING AROUND
By Bus, Tram, and Subway

Public transportation runs 6 A.M.–midnight and includes bus, tram, and subway. A ticket costs €1 and is good for 75 minutes. Tickets can be purchased anywhere you see the ATM sign, which usually means newsstands and *tabacchi*. You can also purchase 24-hour passes (€3) and 48-hour passes (€5.50), which allow unlimited transportation. The old orange trams are a good way to see the city but if you're in a hurry the MM1 (red), MM2 (green), and MM3 (yellow) subway lines are fast and efficient.

By Taxi

Taxis are white in Milan and generally parked at stands in the larger piazze. At night it might be easier to order one by calling Radio Taxi (tel. 02/8585 or 02/4040) but keep in mind the meter starts once the car has been ordered. Tipping is not expected, although rounding up is common.

By Car

Parking is restricted in the city center. Yellow lines are for residents and blue lines are for everyone else. Don't forget to buy a ticket at one of the parking meters. An hour costs €1.20 during the day; if you return and your vehicle is missing, call 02/772-7232 to see if it's been towed.

Tours

Milan is one of the rare Italian cities not located on the sea or the banks of a river. This transportation dilemma was solved by digging the canals that once circled the city. Most have been covered over, but the two that are left can be circumnavi-gated. **Naviglio Lombardi** (tel. 02/6702-0288, www.naviglilombardi.it, May.–Oct., Fri.–Sun. 10 A.M.–7:30 P.M., €10–15) leaves every hour from the Darsena dock near Porta Genova subway station on the MM2 (green) line. They offer pleasant 1–3-hour tours on barges that journey outside the city past villas, churches, and open countryside. Tickets can be purchased in advance or just prior to boarding.

Sightseeing Milan (Foro Bonaparte 76, tel. 02/867-131, www.city-sightseeing.it, €20) double-decker bus tours leave from Piazza Castello. There are two itineraries that last 90 minutes and leave every half-hour daily 9:30 A.M.–6:45 P.M.

Eastern and Southern Lombardy

Lower Lombardy starts where the Brianza hills end and the Alps give way to fertile plains that have been cultivated for centuries. Rice is the cash crop around here and the paddies form a symmetrical horizon of well-irrigated fields. Flat expanse of farmland are punctuated by windbreaks of poplar trees that are Lombardy's equivalent of Tuscany's cypress.

The farther east you travel, the more evident is the Venetian influence on architecture, food, and language. The maritime republic controlled the eastern parts of Lombardy in the 15th–18th centuries and cities like Mantova and Cremona evolved independently of Milan.

PAVIA

Before the rise of Milan, Pavia was the Lombard capital and it was here that emperors Carlo Magno and Barbarossa chose to be crowned. The city's golden age lasted for centuries and a walk around the center alternates Roman ruins with Middle Age piazze and Renaissance cathedrals. Although some monuments were destroyed during World War II (such as the beautiful covered bridge over the Ticino River), even experts could be fooled into thinking the current structure is an original.

Sights

All roads seem to converge on **Piazza della Vittoria** in the center of town. There are several ancient buildings around the square, including the town hall and recently restored Duomo. Leonardo da Vinci and Bramante worked on the church, which was begun in 1488 and not completed until the 19th century. If the dome looks newer than the intricate facade, it's because it was the last part of the structure added. A tower once stood to the right of the church. It collapsed in 1989 and, unlike the bridge, was never rebuilt, though there has been talk of reconstruction.

Although not as ancient as Bologna's university, the school here is over 700 years old and still turns out graduates in various disciplines. The alchemy major unfortunately is no longer offered. Most of the university buildings are adjacent to **Strada Nuova,** lined with neoclassical courtyards that bashful tourists often miss. At the end of the street is **Castello Visconteo,** which once defended the city and now serves as the **Museo Civico** (Piazza Castello, tel. 03/823-3853, www.museicivici.pavia. it, July–Aug. Tues.–Sun. 10 A.M.–6 P.M., Dec.–Jan. Tues.–Sun. 9 A.M.–1:30 P.M., €6). Located on three floors, there's something for everyone in this museum, including photography, modern sculpture, archaeological exhibits, and an entire wing dedicated to the Renaissance. Exhibitions are also regularly organized here.

Anyone familiar with Dante's *Paradiso* will recognize **San Pietro in Ciel d'Oro**. The red-brick church shows clear signs of reconstructive surgery since being founded in the 7th century. Carvings along the Romanesque portal are especially intricate and the piazza itself is one of the quietest places in town. The gold has disappeared from the ceiling on the inside but there is a shrine to St. Augustine and the philosopher Boethius is buried in the crypt.

Accommodations

Aurora (Viale Vittorio Emanuele II 25, tel. 03/822-3664, www.hotel-aurora.eu, €78 d) is near the train station and a short distance from the pedestrianized center of town. All rooms are equipped with air-conditioning and Internet access is available downstairs. The bar stays open until midnight and breakfast is served in the small dining room. It may not be the most glamorous hotel, but it's definitely functional.

Hotel Moderno (Viale V. Emanuele 41, tel. 03/8230-3401, www.hotelmoderno.it, €150 d) is also conveniently located close to the center and the price includes an extensive breakfast buffet and entry to the beauty center, which has a swimming pool, whirlpool tub, and Turkish bath. Rooms are modern, as the name suggests, without being generic.

Food

A restored barn is now the home of **Osteria del Naviglio** (Via Alzaia 39b, tel. 03/8246-0392, Tues.–Sun. noon–3 P.M. and 7:30–11 P.M., closed Sat.–Sun. lunch, €9–15), which serves some of the best contemporary dishes in the province. The chef has no qualms about using saffron or garlic in unexpected ways. The interior of the elegant restaurant is air-conditioned but if you can withstand the heat, dining at the tables on the narrow street makes for a pleasant lunch or dinner. The wine menu is exceptional and it's hard to find more local vintages in a single cellar. If you prefer sleek dining,

there's **San Michele** (Viale San Michele 4, tel. 03/822-0716, Tues.–Sun. €7–11 P.M., €10–15), where tradition is frowned upon and fantasy is the mantra inside the kitchen.

Getting There and Around

Pavia is 45 kilometers south of Milan. By car take the A7 towards Genova and exit at Bereguardo-Pavia Nord and continue on the A53 until Pavia-Via Riviera. Without traffic it's a 40-minute drive. There's daily train service from Stazione Centrale every 30 minutes. Tickets cost €2.95.

Around Pavia
◖ CERTOSA DI PAVIA

Five kilometers outside the city stands the magnificent Certosa di Pavia or Pavia Charterhouse (Certosa, Viale Monumento, Apr.–Sept. Tues.–Sun. 9–11:30 A.M. and 2:30–6 P.M., Oct.–Mar. Tues.–Sun. 9–11:30 A.M. and 2:30–4:30 P.M., mass held at 9:30 A.M., 11 A.M., and 4:30 A.M.) that Gian Galeazzo Visconti, the Duke of Milan, commissioned in 1396. Like most noblemen, he wasn't excited at the thought of being buried in just any church, and as his family gained power and wealth he hired Venetian architects to build a lasting memorial. The facade is indeed quite lavish and every square centimeter is covered with sculptures and inlaid marble. A loggia runs across the center and the top, which was never completed. On the right side are the lodgings where visiting family members would come to visit the dead. The interior recalls the Duomo in Milan and the stained glass windows let in tinted rays of light. Even when there are tour groups admiring the paintings by Perugino and Bergognone in the side chapels, the church still looks empty. The tombs themselves are near the altar but not all of them are occupied. The stone couple lying on a bed of marble are actually resting in Milan. Carthusian monks occupied the cloisters that were added later and spent their time studying and meditating in the 24 cells.

Nearby, **Locanda Vecchia Pavia al Mulino** (Via al Monumento 5, tel. 03/8292-5894,

Tues.–Sun. noon–3:30 P.M. and 7–10:30 P.M., closed Wed. lunch, €12–17) prepares dishes nearly as elaborate as Certosa di Pavia. It's all very light and the fixed-price menu provides a nice sample of regional specialties. In summer, a lovely terrace holds a dozen tables where diners receive immediate attention from the aristocratic waiters. Prices may be above average but this is a treat for your taste buds.

CREMONA

Cremona is a small provincial city in the middle of the Po Valley where people actually say good morning to each other. It's famed for violins and its main piazza, where the medieval Torrazzo bell tower rises above the elegant facade of the duomo. It was the home of Antonio Stradivari, whose violins are still played and are now worth millions. Hundreds of artisans continue to make string instruments and this is the only place in Italy to take lute lessons. The gastronomic traditions are related to oil, cheese, and mustard.

Sights

Cremona's **Duomo** is a good place to start a visit. It's the tallest medieval tower in Italy and linked to the church by an elegant arched loggia. If the thought of 487 steps doesn't put you off, you can climb to the top of Torrazzo for a panoramic view of the city and Po River. The main feature of the Romanesque Duomo is the rose window in the center, under which statues of the Virgin and various saints are housed. The outdoor pulpit is where passing preachers would inspire local Christians. Inside, 16th-century frescoes line chapels that are also decorated with fine tapestries.

The octagonal **Battistero** flanks the church. Builders seem to have run out of marble during its construction. Several sides are covered in brick and the entrance is guarded by a pair of ferocious-looking lions. When it's open, you can see the font carved from a single block of marble that's still used to baptize newborns.

Opposite the Duomo is **Palazzo del Comune,** which dates from the 13th century and contains several violins by the legendary

craftsman who changed the way music sounded. To learn more about how the instrument was made and the techniques Stradivari used during his long career, visit **Museo Stradivariano** (Via Ugolani Dati 4, tel. 03/7240-7770, Tues.–Sun. 9 A.M.–6 P.M., €7). The museum displays drawings, blueprints, models, and several violins created by the master.

To admire Caravaggio and Magnasco head to the **Pinacoteca del Museo Civico** (Via Ugolani Dati 4, tel. 03/7246-1885, Tues.–Sun. 9 A.M.–6 P.M., €7) within Palazzo Affaiti. The 16th-century building also houses a collection of wood carvings, ceramics, and archeological treasures.

Entertainment and Events

August 24 is all about San Bartolomeo. He's the patron saint and the reason bands play in Piazza del Duomo. Traditional local specialties are prepared for free and the day usually ends with fireworks. **Sagra degli Gnocchi** is held on the same day in Piazza Leonardo da Vinci. Gnocchi are the most fun you can have with potatoes and are usually covered with a hearty *ragù* sauce.

Cremona is home to *torrone* (nougat), which was invented here in 1441 for the wedding of Francesco Sforza and is a traditional Christmas dessert. **Festa del Torrone** (tel. 03/7280-0243, www.festadeltorronecremona.it) celebrates this delicacy on the third weekend of November in Piazza del Duomo. Chefs gather in the square to mix honey, nuts, and sugar into one very long example of the sweet, which is offered to the public for free. If you miss the event, stop by the **Sperlari** (Via Solferino 25, tel. 03/722-2346 or 800/782-9008) factory for a guided tour.

On the third Sunday of every month, except July and August, the historic center is transformed into an outdoor antiques market. In mid-May, look out for the classic cars that fill up the piazze for the annual **Mille Miglia.**

Accommodations

Hotel Astoria (Via Bordigallo 19, tel. 03/7246-1616, €70 d) is a mid-size three-star hotel conveniently located near all the city's monuments. Some of the furniture isn't exactly

© ALESSIA RAMACCIA

Cremona's Duomo and Battistero

trendy, but the beds are comfortable and service is prompt. If elegance matters more than price, try the **Impero** (Piazza della Pace 21, tel. 03/7241-3013, www.hotelimpero.cr.it, €110 d), also well positioned in the historic center. All 53 rooms come with air-conditioning, minibar, and satellite TV.

Fifty meters from the tallest medieval bell tower in Europe, **Delle Arti** (Via Bonomelli 8, tel. 03/722-3131, www.dellearti.com, €190 d) provides 33 rooms with an edge. Floor-to-ceiling windows let a lot of light into the high-tech interiors. There are regular expositions in the dining hall and experimental videos are projected on the exterior of the hotel. Breakfast is a traditional cappuccino and brioche.

Food
Hosteria 700 (Piazza Gallina 1, tel. 03/723-6175, Wed.–Sun. noon–3 P.M. and 7–11 P.M., Mon. noon–3 P.M., closed Tues.,

€9–13) is in the center of town in a palazzo that hasn't lost its charm. The yellow, white, and red rooms are decorated with frescoes by local artists, under which gourmets regularly gather. Risotto is the main attraction and on the second Thursday of each month you'll find 20 varieties waiting to be sampled. Cheeses are also first-rate and there are 150 bottles of wine to select from.

Claudio Nevi chooses the vegetables himself and won't even look at a carrot if it's been genetically modified. He organizes frequent gastronomic events inside **❲ La Sosta** (Via Sicardo 9, tel. 03/7245-6656, Tues.–Sun. lunch 12:30–3 P.M. and 7:30–11 P.M., €10–14) and has perfected a *fettuccine al ragù bianco di coniglio* (fettuccine pasta with white rabbit *ragù*) regulars rave about. The cheese platter is served with mustard and marmalade, and desserts include *sorbetti, gelati,* and *panna cotta.*

Everyone receives a smile upon entering

the family-run **Porta Mosa** (Via Santa Maria in Betlem 11, tel. 03/7241-1803, Mon.–Sat. noon–3 P.M. and 7–10:30 P.M., closed Aug., €9–13) and the limited number of tables means Roberto Bona can spend more time chatting and advising guests about the day's menu. One regular offering is tagliatelle covered in a light porcini sauce. Wines are numerous and supplied by the family wine shop.

Sperlari on Via Solferino 25 provides some of the town's best dessert in an 18th-century atmosphere. Dozens of different salamis are hanging from the ceiling of **Saronni** (Corso Mazzini 38) and if you're looking for a bottle of red to accompany a picnic there are 3,500 labels waiting at **Catullo** (Via S. Maria in Betlem 28, tel. 03/723-2077) opposite **Ristorante Osteria Porta Mosa** (Via S. Maria in Betlem 11, tel. 03/7241-1803).

Information and Services
The IAT office (Piazza del Comune 5, tel. 03/722-3233, Mon.–Sat. 9 A.M.–12:30 and 3–6 P.M., Sun. 9 A.M.–12:30 P.M.) is the best source for information about the city and province. They sell combo tickets to Cremona's museums for €10 and **Associazione Guide Turistiche Cremona** (tel. 03/723-7970) starts its tours outside the office on Mondays, Wednesdays, and Fridays at 3:30 and 5:30 P.M.

Getting There and Around
Cremona is 85 kilometers southeast of Milan off the A1. There are frequent daily trains from Milan Centrale that take 60–90 minutes depending on the service. A second-class ticket costs €5.40 and the view is better from the left side of the train facing backwards. Local buses cost €1 and the daily pass is €2.50 and available at the station and many *tabacchi*. There are taxi stands at Piazza Rome (tel. 03/722-1300) and Piazzale Stazione (tel. 03/722-6740).

Europcar on Via Brescia 84 (tel. 03/7243-1158) has good prices on compacts or if you prefer a mountain or city bike by the hour or day head to **Mata** (Via S. Tommaso 9, tel. 03/7245-7483).

MANTOVA
Mantova almost feels like a city near the sea. It lies on a promontory along the Mincio River at a point where the waters widen and form three small lakes: Superiore, Mezzo, and Inferiore. It gets humid in summer, which may explain why the town isn't overrun with tourists. The Roman poet Virgil was born here and the austere architecture was fit for the Gonzaga dukes who controlled the city during the Renaissance.

Sights
Piazza Sordello is the largest square—actually more of a cobblestoned rectangle. The Duomo on the southern end is a little deceiving. The stark facade was completed in the 18th century while the frescoes on the inside by Guilio Romano are 300 years older.

The Gonzaga clan lived on the opposite end in **Palazzo Ducale** (tel. 03/7635-2100, Tues.–Sun. 8:45 A.M.–7:15 P.M., €6.50). The family extended their home over the years, which is full internal passageways, courtyards, and a perfectly geometric garden. The complex also includes Castello San Giorgio and a basilica. Before Versailles came along, it was Europe's biggest palace. The 500 rooms may take a while to visit. They're filled with artwork that culminates in portraits and frescoes by Mantegna. He was a master of perspective and the ceiling inside **Camera degli Sposi** will probably look vaguely familiar. The walls show members of the family and everyone seems to be looking in a different direction. Although it may be tempting to take a picture or shoot a movie, they prefer if you buy postcards from the museum shop. Cell phones are also frowned upon.

One palace is never enough. On the other side of town Federico Gonzaga built **Palazzo Tè** (Viale Te 19, tel. 03/7636-9198, www.cen tropalazzote.it) in the 16th century as a residence from where he could go horseback riding and entertain. Trompe l'oeil was a favorite technique of the time and the painted giants of **Sala dei Giganti** look as though they're tearing down the place. Federico's love of riding and astrology is evident everywhere. The second

Piazza Erbe in Mantova

floor of the palace is home to Museo Civico and a collection of medals, coins, and measurement tools used before the metric system was invented. Most interesting of all, however, are the Mesopotamian relics a local architect brought back from Baghdad.

If you have time, stop by **Piazza Erbe,** home to **Basilica di Sant'Andrea** and an interesting row of arcaded shops. The building with the clock tower and Roman numerals is the former courthouse.

Virgil isn't the only famous Mantovano, and if you're a motor-racing fan you may have heard of **Museo Tazio Nuvolari** (Piazza Broletto 9, Apr.–Oct., daily 10 A.M.–1 P.M. and 3:30–6:30 P.M., €3). Even if you haven't heard of the museum dedicated to the driver who won 109 races in his career, it is a nice break from the palaces. It takes less than 10 minutes to visit the five rooms full of trophies, models, photographs, and other memorabilia. The small store is an opportunity to buy an original gift.

Entertainment and Events

For five days during the third week of May, the **Mantova Musica Festival** (tel. 02/2040-4727, www.mantovamusicafestival.it) stages more than 70 concerts of every genre. Piazzas are turned over to musicians who perform night and day in front of avid audiences. Piazza Erbe is usually reserved for the big names and opening and closing of the festival.

Accommodations

Mantova is the kind of town where bed-and-breakfasts flourish. Staying in one can make a visit memorable. **Armellino** (Via Cavour 67, tel./fax 03/7622-1672, €80 d) has a view of the Basilica di Sant'Andrea from its garden and four rooms that have conserved their original 17th-century fittings. The yellow one has hardwood floors, two tin beds, and hand-painted ceilings. Antonella prepares breakfast in the bright kitchen with her husband Massimo, who is full of suggestions on what to see and do. The only drawback is that guests must share the two bathrooms.

Casa San Domenico (Vicolo Scala 8, tel./fax 03/7632-0942, €150 d) is an elegant bed-and-breakfast a few steps from the river. Donata and Alberto serve fresh fruit and drinks to their guests upon arrival. The four rooms pair antiques with modern design, and each is soundproofed and comes with plasma TV, stereo, and a luxurious bathroom. Breakfast is served in bed and the suites have their own relaxing sitting area.

Near Casa del Mantegna, **◖ Palazzo Costa** (Via Fratelli Grioli 46, tel./fax 03/7636-2357, €75 d) provides three rooms on the top floor of a Renaissance-era building. Each is named after the frescoes on the ceilings and comes with rooftop views of the city. Beds are the large wooden kind and are fit for a prince. Internet, minibar, and air-conditioning are part of the deal. Gregorio is a friendly host and there's private parking around the corner.

Food

The menu at **Osteria dell'Oca** (Via Trieste 37, tel. 03/7632-7171, Wed.–Mon. 12–3 P.M. and 7:15–10:45 P.M., €8–11) isn't divided in the traditional first course, second course manner but by flavor. Nadia who runs the dining room can help translate *bigoli* (long pasta with Venetian origin) or *trippa* (tripe) for curious diners. Coffee is served in wooden cups.

Underneath the cupola of Sant'Andrea in the old backstreets of Mantova an eclectic chef prepares variations on traditional dishes. Worn tables and peasant furniture provide the decor at **Il Portichetto** (Via Portichetto 14, tel. 03/7636-0747, Tues.–Sun. noon–3 P.M. and 7:30–11 P.M., €10–14) and the artwork on the walls is for sale. Fixed price menus vary €22–28 and often feature freshly caught river fish. The *crème caramel* is a happy ending to any meal.

Due Cavallini (Via Salnitro 5, tel. 03/7632-2084, Wed.–Mon. noon–3 P.M. and 7–10:30 P.M., €8–12) has been serving working-class dishes to working-class people since 1939. The factories have closed but this trattoria with a dark wood interior hasn't changed. *Salumi* is a must and if you haven't tried polenta yet this is the place to initiate your palate. During the summer, tables are set up in the courtyard under the shade of an arbor.

Clos Wine Bar (Corte dei Sogliari 3, tel. 03/7636-9972, Tues.–Sun. 11 A.M.–11 P.M.) is a good place for an afternoon *aperitivo* or after-dinner glass of wine. To understand what makes Mantovese pasta different from other towns in Italy, visit **Freddi** in Piazza Cavalotti 7 or **Truzzi** in Via XX Settembre 4.

Information and Services

The **tourist office** (tel. 03/7643-2432, daily 9:30 A.M.–5:30 P.M.) is located in Piazza Sordello 23. You can mail letters or change currency at the **central post office** (tel. 03/7631-7723, Mon.–Fri. 8:30 A.M.–1:30 P.M. and 2:30–5:30 P.M., Sat. 8:30–1 P.M.) in Piazza Martiri di Belfiore 15. For tickets to concerts and local events, visit **Best Music** (Corso Libertà 3, tel. 03/7622-2294, Mon.–Fri. 9 A.M.–1 P.M. and 2–7 P.M.).

Getting There and Around

By car, Mantova can be reached via the A4 (after Brescia, drive south on the N236) or from Cremona along the N10. The train journey is over two hours and usually requires a transfer at Cremona or Verona, depending on the train you catch. Tickets are €8.55. **APM** (www.apam.it) buses connect Mantova with Brescia, Parma, Modena, and Cremona. They also operate the local bus service, although the center of town is small enough to navigate on foot.

There are taxi stands in Piazza Sordello (tel. 03/7632-4408) and Piazza D. Leoni (tel. 03/7632-5351) near the train station. Cars can be rented from **Avis** on Via Acerbi 28 (tel. 03/7622-2111) or **Hertz** in Via Bettinelli (tel. 03/7622-4607). This is a great town for pedaling and bikes are available from **Mantua Bike** (Viale Piave 22b, tel. 03/7622-0909, daily). It's €1.60 per hour or €8 for the day.

There are several companies that tour the lakes and Mincio River Valley. **Barcaioli del Mincio** (tel. 03/7634-9292, www.fiumemincio.it) leaves from the Mulini bridge near the train station and the town of Grazia eight kilometers west of Mantova. A 90-minute journey on one of their open boats is €8. Canoeing and kayaking are also quite popular and single or double crafts can be rented in the little port of **Grazia** (tel. 340/499-5854).

Around Mantova

Sabbioneta, southwest of Mantova on the N420, is another of the Renaissance experiments in urban planning. This ideal city was devised by Vespasiano Gonzaga Colonna, who envisioned a hexagonal outer wall interlaced with streets leading to public buildings built to the measure of man. It works and it's hard to find an odd angle or take a bad photo. A tour leaves from the information office in Piazza d'Armi and takes in the old theater and Palazzo del Giardino. Try to make it to town on Wednesday, when a colorful market is held in the main square.

BERGAMO

Bergamo lies at the foot of the Orobian Alps on the northern edge of the Padana plain. The city of 115,000 has Celtic origins and the name literally means "house on the hill." It's divided in a low *(bassa)* and high *(alta)* part surrounded by medieval walls and intersected by narrow streets that join the two areas. Most of the monuments are concentrated in **Bergamo Alta** around Piazza Vecchia and Piazza del Duomo, which is studded with 13th- and 14th-century *palazzi* built by the Venetians when they ruled the town.

Bergamo Bassa is a modern residential and commercial area planned by the Austrians in 1837. Viale Vittorio Emanuele II is the main street that's lined with shops and leads to the railway station. Although it's not as pretty, architects in the early 20th century did their best to build low, unobtrusive buildings that don't disturb the views and the **Sentierone** walk up the hill.

Sights

Piazza Vecchia is the masterpiece of the city and the buildings lining the square form one of the most architecturally harmonious spaces in the region. **Torre del Comune** is the tallest of these and its bell rings out every night at 10 P.M. That was the curfew in the 12th century, but is now ignored by the teenagers and young couples who sit on the **Palazzo della Ragione** steps planning their evenings.

The lions nearby are a symbol of the Venetians, who controlled the city for 400 years. The arcades of the law courts lead to the adjacent Piazza del Duomo with a neoclassical church and a chapel that has a threedimensional facade Q-bert would love. **Cappella Colleoni** was built in 1476 and the city's leading politicians were buried inside. Next door are the baptistery and **Santa Maria Maggiore**

Basilica, which presents a severe front and an ornate Baroque interior some might consider over the top.

At the end of the Via della Noca stairway that links Bergamo Alta with Bergamo Bassa is Piazza Carrara and the neoclassical **Galleria dell'Accademia Carrara** (Piazza Giacomo Carrara 82, tel. 03/539-9640, Tues.–Sun. 10 A.M.–1 P.M. and 2:30–5:30 P.M., €2.60). The museum was founded in 1796 as an art school and picture gallery and contains 2,000 Italian and European paintings dating from the 14th to the 19th century. Works by Botticelli, Titian, Raphael, and Perugino all hang here, along with expatriates like Dürer and Velazquez. Opposite is **Galleria d'Arte Moderna e Contemporanea** (Via San Tomaso 82, tel. 03/539-9528, www.gamec.it, hours vary, €8 exhibitions, €2.60 permanent collection), which houses contemporary art in all its forms and regularly stages exhibitions.

Entertainment and Events

Festival Danza Estate (CSC Anymore, Via D. Luigi Palazzolo 23c, tel. 03/522-4700, www. cscanymore.it, Mon.–Fri. 9:30 A.M.–12:30 P.M. and 2:30–6 P.M.) has been attracting international dance companies to Bergamo for over 20 years. Locals seem to have a little jump in their step throughout the event, which takes place for three weeks in June and July in the former Sant'Agostino church in Piazzale della Fara (it's best to arrive on foot). Every edition has a different theme, but tango and modern dance tend to predominate. All tickets are €12 and can be purchased on the night of the performance or from the CSC box office.

The 17th-century theater **Teatro Donizetti** (Piazza Cavour Camillo Benso14, tel. 03/5416-0611, www.teatrodonizetti.it, €12–28) features Tolstoy, Broch, and Pirandello. The Festival Bergamo Jazz also takes place in this venue. Tours of the theater can be booked in advance.

Shopping

Lombardy looks out for its most historic stores and if you see *negozio storico* (historic shop)

© ALESSIA RAMACCIA

one of the grand entrances to Bergamo's historic center

on a window it's because they've left shoppers satisfied for over 50 years. There are a number in Bergamo and if you're after jewelry or a new silver set check out **Riva** (Via G. Paglia 7b, tel. 03/524-9071, www.rivagioielli.it, Tues.–Sun. 9:30 A.M.–12:30 P.M. and 3:30–7:30 P.M.), around since 1928. **Ottica Isnenghi** (Piazza Matteotti 21, tel. 03/524-9611) has been selling eyewear even longer, although the frames are up-to-date.

Accommodations

Reaching Città Alta on foot can be a problem if you've got lots of luggage in tow and it may be worth taking a €10 taxi ride to **San Lorenzo** (Piazza Mascheroni 9a, tel. 03/523-7383, www. hotelsanlorenzobg.it, €125 d). The hotel is in a quiet spot and allows guest to immerse themselves in a medieval environment. Rooms are comfortable and falling asleep is easy. It's getting up that's a problem.

Mercure Bergamo Palazzo Dolci (Viale Papa Giovanni XXIII, www.mercure.com, €150 d) has all the comforts of a major hotel chain and the personality of an independent. The four-star accommodation is near Teatro Donizetti in Città Bassa, 200 meters from the train station and close to the shuttle bus that runs every 30 minutes to Bergamo airport. The 88 rooms have been recently modernized without destroying the charm of the 19th-century palazzo. Breakfast, lunch, and dinner are served in the elegant dining room on the ground floor and front desk staff can arrange guided tours of the city.

Food

Osteria di Via Solata (Via Solata 8, tel. 03/527-1993, Wed.–Mon. noon–2:30 P.M. and 7–11 P.M., €10–16) is on the hill in Bergamo Alta. They take food seriously here and the chefs wear white hats. The pastel colors inside the restaurant are a prelude to delicate flavors as pleasing to the eye as to the stomach. This isn't the place to come to feel stuffed but where you will experience new flavors based on risotto, meat, and vegetables.

The menu changes everyday at **Antica Trattoria Sant'Anna** (Via S. Anna, 21, tel. 03/557-4341, www.anticatrattoriasantanna. it, €8–12). Enrico makes everything from the bread to the desserts himself and his partner Luca is responsible for entertaining the guests in this family restaurant just outside of the city. In April and May, the veranda is opened and it's possible to walk off a meal through the woods of the Canto Mountains nearby. *Cannelloncini* and *gnocchetti* pastas are excellent and wild boar with polenta leaves little room for anything else.

The Naples pair who opened **Ristorante Pizzeria Vesuvio** (Via Borgo S. Caterina 96, tel. 03/521-9101) in 1953 never forgot their origins. The pizza still comes out of the wood oven thick and if you order pineapple toppings they'll have a good laugh.

Information and Services

There's a tourist office on Piazzale Marconi (tel. 03/521-0204, daily 9 A.M.–12:30 P.M. and 2–5:30 P.M.) outside the train station and one up the hill in Bergamo Alta in Via Gombino 13 (tel. 03/524-2226, daily 9 A.M.–12:30 P.M. and 2–5:30 P.M.). Both offer pretty much the same information, although the one near the station is usually more crowded and they tend to run out of maps and brochures more often.

If you want an inside look at the city, the members of the **Bergamo Tourist Guide Association** (Via Borgo Canale 5, tel. 03/526-2565, www.guideagiatbg.it) can show you around the hidden parts of town. **Elena Miano** (tel./fax 03/522-6225, elena.miano@ alice.it) is a native with a knack at recounting thousands of years of history without causing a single yawn. She speaks English and French, and her rates vary according to the season.

Getting There and Around

Orio al Serio Airport is three kilometers outside of Bergamo and the 3C shuttle bus runs to the city center every 30 minutes. You can also catch a bus from the arrivals hall directly to Milan or Brescia. The airport is a hub for low-cost airlines such as Ryanair, which offers flights to destinations across Europe.

Bergamo is a 30-minute journey from Milan by train and connections to Cremona, Como, and Venice are frequent. The station is located in Bergamo Bassa walking distance from all the sights. By car, Bergamo is 50 kilometers from Milan and a short drive along the A4 highway.

The Lakes

When the glaciers melted during the last ice age they left behind a half-dozen oddly shaped lakes, which have attracted humans ever since fishing became a viable option. The most renowned of these and the one most popular with Milanese weekenders is **Lake Como**. It was famous before George Clooney and his *Ocean* cronies moved in and is ringed by idyllic, graffiti-free towns that may make you think you've entered Switzerland by mistake. **Lake Maggiore** is actually shared by both countries and is dotted with many pretty islands where royalty and the financially endowed have spent their free time for centuries. All the lakes are served by efficient ferry service and the farther north you travel the quieter things get until all you hear is the flapping of golden eagles over the Alps.

LAKE MAGGIORE

Lake Maggiore is the second-largest Italian lake and lies on the northern border between Lombardy and Piedmont. It flows all the way into Switzerland, with the Alps forming a spectacular backdrop. The Lombards have held sway over both sides of the lake and the western shore from **Arona** to **Stresa** is still a favorite weekend getaway for Milanese families. Carlo Borromeo chose the tiny **Isola Bella** to build a palace for his wife that is hard to match for splendor.

Sights

Arona is a natural place to begin touring the area and contains many artistic and historic monuments. In the center you can visit the church **Chiesa dei Santi Martiri** with a Baroque facade and neo-Gothic interior. Nearby are the remains of the old port once used by Roman sailors. In the characteristic Piazza of San Graziano lies the former Benedectine abbey and the **Museo Archeologico** (Piazza Cittadella 9, tel. 03/224-8294, Tues.–Fri. 9 A.M.–12:30 P.M. and 2:30–6 P.M., Sat.–Sun. 9 A.M.–7 P.M., free), where a covered market stood.

La Statua del San Carlone (on the hill behind Arona, tel. 03/2224-9669, Apr.–Sept. daily 9 A.M.–12:30 P.M. and 2–6:30 P.M., Oct.–Mar. Sat.–Sun. 9 A.M.–12:30 and 2–4:30 P.M.) is a 35-meter-tall bronze statue on a hill behind town. It's possible to enter the statue (much the same way the Statue of Liberty can be visited) and observe the lake from its eyes.

Islands
BORROMEAN ISLANDS

Ten kilometers north is the elegant resort of **Stresa.** It's the best place to reach the Borromean Islands and admire a score of five-star hotels that line the shore. Even if you can't afford to stay here, taking a stroll through the gardens is free. When you get tired of azaleas head for the yellow cable car (www.stresa-mottarone.it) that links the town with Monte Mottarone. It's a 20-minute ride with one stop where you can stretch your legs and visit gardens at the **Giardino Botanico Alpinia** (Piazzale Lido 8, tel. 03/233-0295, www.giardinoalpinia.it, €2).

◀ ISOLA BELLA

Isola Bella (tel. 03/233-0556, www.borromeoturismo.it) is the grandest of three small islands off the shore of Stresa. You could walk from end to end in five minutes but a visit usually lasts much longer. Carlo Borromeo began transforming the island in 1632 and the enormous **palazzo** (Mar.–Oct. daily 9 A.M.–5:30 P.M., €11 or €16 combined with Isola Madre) he started was completed by his

son. It's synonymous with Baroque and was the backdrop for some of the greatest parties ever thrown. Today the ground floor and *piano nobile* are open to the public. Gold and silk abound and the sense of luxury extends from doorknobs to ceiling moldings. **Sala da Ballo** and **Salone delle Feste** are half a football field in length and where hundreds of guests could be entertained.

The Italian gardens behind the palazzo make up the rest of the island and are the work of Carlo IV, viceroy of Naples. They extend over 10 terraces that provide wonderful views of the lake. This is where Napoleon and Josephine liked to meet, and visitors can lose themselves among the many nooks. Along the alleys and gravel paths are rare roses, exotic species, and hundreds of types of plants and flowers. Serious botanists can join one of the tours in summer or just enjoy a peaceful stroll near the water the rest of the year. For more details about the island, stop by the **APT office** in Stresa (Via Principe Tomaso 70, tel. 03/233-0160).

Entertainment and Events

Settimane Musicali (tel. 03/233-1095, www.settimanemusicali.net) is the classical music event of the summer and has been held in Stresa and Isola Bella for the last 40 years. Orchestras, soloists, and conductors turn up from around the world to play a series of outdoor concerts throughout August and September, many of which are free.

Sports and Recreation

There are three challenging golf courses bordering the lake and each one is open to non-members who like to putt with a panorama. **Golf Club Des Iles Borromees** (Motta Rossa, tel. 03/2392-9285, www.golfdesilesborromees.it, €43 Mon.–Fri., €65 Sat. and Sun.) is 600 meters above Stresa. It's a highly varied course and none of the fairways are flat. If your driving isn't up to par, you may be better off at **Golf Club Alpino di Stresa** (Vezzo, Viale Golf Panorama 48, tel. 03/232-0642, www.golfalpino.it, €33 Mon.–Fri., €50 Sat. and Sun.), where the first Italian Open was held in 1925 and the clubhouse restaurant looks out on the last hole. There's also a nine-hole course at **Golf Club Arona** (Arona, Via Prè, www.golfapino.it, €25 Mon.–Fri., €30 Sat. and Sun.); tee times can be booked by calling 800/333-444.

If you prefer horseback riding, lakeside **Club Ippico Ticino** (Castelletto Ticino, Via Glisente 29, tel. 03/3192-0187, Tues.–Sun., prices vary per itinerary) near the Lagoni park can saddle you up with some very tame mares. They also run tours and let experienced riders hit the trails unaccompanied.

Accommodations

Hotel Antares (Arona, Via A. Gramsci 9, tel. 03/2224-3438, www.antaresona.com, €85 d) may not be as lavish as the villas with private beaches on the lake, but this small bed-and-breakfast is near the train station and two minutes from the shore. Rooms are decorated without great fanfare and you are unlikely to hear anything but silence in the morning. A gym and spa are accessible to all guests and parking is available out front. If you can't do without a view, **Il Giardino di Alice** (Arona, Via Motto Mirabello 51, tel. 03/225-7212, www.ilgiardinodialice.com, €100 d) will provide an eyeful. This historic chalet sits on a hill surrounded by a grove of chestnut trees.

Isola dei Pescatori is one of the most romantic spots in the lake, where you can spend the night at **Albergo Belvedere** (tel. 03/233-2292, www.belvedere-isolapescatori.it, €100 d). Its eight delightful rooms are each equipped with a balcony or terrace to admire the bell tower of San Vittore and the lake all around.

If money isn't an issue, then **Grand Hotels Iles Borromees** (Stresa, Corso Umberto I 67, tel. 03/2393-8938, www.borromees.it, €260 d) is the place to experience the five-star treatment. This impeccable 19th-century hotel was built in 1861 and still exudes class from the high chandeliered ceilings to the uniformed bus boys manning the doors. It isn't stuffy though and the beautiful garden, heated outdoor swimming pool, and tennis courts aren't

just for show. Look out for millionaires landing in the heliport outside.

Twenty kilometers from the Swiss border on the western shore of the lake, **☑ Cannero** (Cannero Riviera, tel. 03/2378-8046, www.hotelcannero.com, €115 d) is a 50-room hotel in a sleepy town that doesn't really wake up until the height of summer. All the rooms are large and a couple have balconies with direct access to the garden. Junior suites come with Hermès toiletries and bathrobes you can wear out to the pool. The restaurant offers a good four-course fixed-price option for €22 and breakfast can be brought to your room upon request. Maria and her son set out the welcome mat every day and you'd be hard pressed to find a friendlier reception. They offer loads of advice and the ferry landing is just minutes away.

Food

Ristorante del Barcaiolo (Arona, Piazza del Popolo 23, tel. 03/2224-3388, Fri.–Tues., Fri.–Tues. 12:30–3 P.M. and 7:30–10:30 P.M., Thurs. 7:30–10:30 P.M., €12–15) serves local specialties within a 13th-century palazzo in the center of town. During the summer, tables are set up outside under the arcades. If all you want is a snack, order the cheese plate and a carafe of the house wine.

For fish, go next door to Hosteria al Vecchio Portico. Loretta and her husband have been running **Vecchia Arona** (Arona, Lungolago Marconi 17, tel. 03/2224-2469, Sat.–Thurs. noon–3 P.M. and 7:30–11 P.M., €10–15) for over 30 years. The menu is handwritten and the fish and meat dishes change daily. Decoration hasn't been updated in a while and entering this cozy restaurant is like stepping into the past. Afterwards enjoy a walk along the lake.

Information and Services

Every medium-sized town on the lake has an IAT tourist office. In Arona, it's located in Piazzale Duca di Aosta, and in Stresa it's in Piazza Marconi 16. Both provide maps and can be very helpful explaining the numerous ferry options that exist.

Getting There and Around

By car, Arona is under an hour from Milan on the A8 highway. The town is one of the first exits and a single lane road circumnavigates the entire lake. There are frequent trains (www.trenitalia.it) from Milan Stazione Centrale to many lakeside towns. A ticket to Stresa is €4.40.

Lago Maggiore Express (Arona, Via F. Baracca 1, tel. 03/2223-3200, www.lagomaggioreexpress.com) operates trains and boats around the lake. The journey between Arona and Stresa is 15 minutes by rail and one hour by water. There are several ticketing options including a daily excursion (€28) that leaves Arona by boat at 10:30 A.M. for Locarno, Switzerland, and returns in the evening by train. It's a great way to cover a lot of territory in a limited time. Lunch is served onboard.

From Stresa ferries run every 30 minutes (Apr. 1–Sept. 23) to the Borromean Islands (Isola Madre, Isola Pescatori, Isola Bella) and the €11.50 excursion ticket allows visitors to explore each at a leisurely pace.

◖ LAKE COMO

Lake Como is surrounded by high mountains, gentle hills, and small villages on rocky slopes overlooking the lake. It's 46 kilometers long and from above looks like a dancer in mid-leap. At the foot of the left "leg" is **Como,** an elegant town less than an hour from Milan. The natural beauty has attracted nobles for centuries; the luxurious villas along the shores have manicured gardens that benefit from an unusually mild climate. Tropical plants as well as laurels and olive trees are common. The winds have names here and are reliable enough to allow sailing, windsurfing, and hang-gliding. Canoeing, waterskiing, golfing, horseback riding, and cycling are also widely practiced. The farther north you travel, the more peaceful things become.

Sights

Como is a pretty town at the southwestern tip of the lake surrounded by hills. Piazza Cavour is where most of the action takes place. If you're after churches, the two most interesting examples are **Basilica di Sant'Abbondio** (Via Regina Teodolinda 35, tel. 03/126-9563, admission free) and the **Duomo,** which is topped with a Baroque dome completed in the 18th century. The Basilica di Sant'Abbondio is a good example of the Romanesque Lombard style. Built in the 11th century it features dark marble that marks the perimeter of a Paleo-Christian church that lies underneath the church. There are also five cavernous naves divided by rows of impressive columns. More recent examples of innovative architecture can be seen behind the cathedral, where Italy's leading proponent of Rationalism built the **Casa del Fascio** in the 1930s. The building that now houses the customs service is in perfect proportion down to the railing.

Among the famous natives are Plinius, who witnessed and wrote about the eruption of Mount Vesuvius, and the scientist Alessandro Volta. The energizer bunny has Volta to thank. He invented the battery in the 18th century and volt has been a unit of electricity ever since. Look out for both names on street signs, storefronts, and cafés.

Bellagio, a small town northeast of Como, is in a splendid position in the center of the lake. The narrow streets lead to exclusive shopping and an elegant promenade full of cafés with wonderful views. **Villa Melzi** (Lungolario Marconi Bellagio, tel. 02/8699-8647, Mar.–Oct., €5) has preserved its period furnishings, 19th-century frescoes, and lavish garden. Heads of state, however, prefer the more secluded **Villa Serbolini,** built in the 18th century. It's now the property of the Rockefellers.

Shopping

For centuries Como has been a center of silk production, evident from the great number of shops selling cloth and the monthly fairs held in the area. **La Tessitura** (Viale Roosevelt 2a, tel. 03/132-1666, daily 10 A.M.–8 P.M.) is the most colorful store in Como. They sell silk and other fabrics inside a wonderfully renovated 19th-century factory. There's also the **Loom Cafè,** a fun place for a drink, brunch, or just to listen to music on the brightly colored plastic chairs.

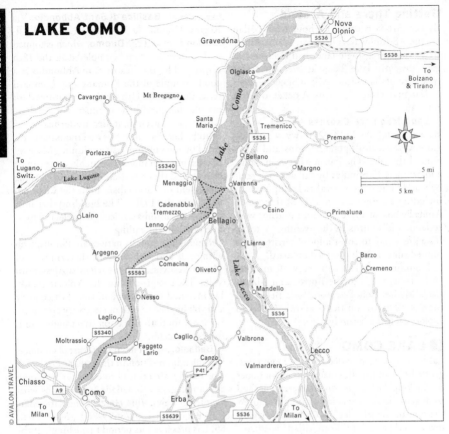

© AVALON TRAVEL

Accommodations

Just up the hill above the port from where the ferries regularly depart, **Hotel Quarcino** (Como, Salita Quarcino 4, tel. 03/130-3934, www.hotel-quarcino.it, €55–80, s/d) provides 13 comfortable rooms. A garden surrounds the 1920s-era building and guarantees tranquility within this no-frills two-star hotel. For the frills, just walk over to the cable car five minutes away and take the ride up to Brunate.

Hotel Metropole Suisse (Como, Piazza Cavour 19, tel. 03/126-9444, www.hotel metropolesuisse.com, €150–210, s/d) overlooks the lake, as well as the cafés and shops lining the port. It's an institution that has been welcoming international guests since 1892. Rooms are large and accessible to all.

Before cars took over, travelers would rest their horses at **Hotel Ristorante Posta** (Piazza S. Rocco 5, Skype hotelposta, www.hotel-posta. it, €145 d) and grab a bite to eat before galloping around the lake. Three centuries of hospitality adds up to something special and the Taroni family, who have run the hotel since the 1970s, are careful to combine modern amenities with enduring style. There's a magnificent panorama from the restaurant that's a short distance from Como on the western shore town of Moltrasio where Winston Churchill spent a couple of summers getting his feet wet.

La Pergola (Piazza del Porto 4, tel. 03/195-0263, www.lapergolabellagio.it, €120 d) lies in the small fishing village of Pescallo 10 minutes from Bellagio by foot. The 16th-century building once served as a convent; a recent restoration has returned the frescoes and patrician staircase to their former glory. Guest rooms have low, stone arched ceilings typical of the region and the restaurant serves lake fish and polenta on a terrace close to the water's edge. This is a great point of departure for treks up the Triangolo hills behind Bellagio. Motorboats can be rented nearby.

Food

Cantinainfrasca (Como, Via XX Settembre 10, tel. 03/134-2251, Tues.–Sun. noon–3 P.M. and 7:15–11:15 P.M., €9–12) is an authentic *osteria* where waiters fly by with plates of delicious-smelling pasta in their hands. If you can't make sense of the chalkboard menu, just order what the guy at the next table is having. It's all very simple and the cheese and *salumi* platters with a carafe of house red make for a satisfying lunch.

The three-kilometer drive to **Crotto la Sorgente** (Lora, Via P. Castelli 5, tel. 03/445-5270, www.crottolasorgente.it, Thurs.–Tues. noon–3:30 P.M., closed Sept., €8–12) will seem less of a hassle once you start eating. Anna and her brother are the guardians of some of the oldest recipes on the lake and their passion for cooking is edible. Both of the dining rooms are pleasant, but the one with worn wooden tables underneath vaulted brick ceilings may have a slight edge. When the weather is good, you can eat outside and taste their classic saffron risotto with sausages or the onion soup in wintertime. The cold cuts are produced locally from chestnut-fed swine.

Most of the grand hotels that line the lake have their own restaurants. Dining at a hotel restaurant can be a good way of experiencing the style of the Belle Epoque without spending a fortune on a room. **La Terraza** (Tremezzo, Via Regina 8, tel. 03/444-2491, www.grand hoteltremezzo.com, €15–25) at the Tremezzo Palace provides an instant lesson in the *art de vivre*. The chef prepares a wide array of local and international dishes with great zest. It's almost a shame to stick a fork into the spinach and cheese soufflé or Torta Valentina, named after the owner's daughter. If all you crave is a cocktail, try the intimate piano bar or outdoor beach bar with a view of Bellagio.

Getting There and Around

Como can be reached by way of the A9 highway from Milan. From there you can drive along the shore towards Bellagio on the N583 or on the western edge via the N340. Roads are windy and get crowded during the summer and on weekends, when the Milanese descend on the lake.

Both Como and Lecco on the eastern "leg" can be reached by train. To fully enjoy the lake, it's best to hop on one of the Navigazione Laghi ferries that connect dozens of towns along the shore. Faster hydrofoil service is available if you're in a hurry and cars can be transported between Bellagio, Giante, and Varenna in the middle of the lake. A round-trip ticket between Como and Bellagio is €15.60 and makes stops at Villa Melzi and Villa Serbelloni.

LAKE GARDA

Lake Garda, or Lago di Garda, is the largest Italian lake bordered by Trentino and Veneto. The farther north you go, the more dramatic the scenery becomes and the snowcapped mountains can be admired from 45 kilometers of beaches. The shore is also home to over a dozen medieval towns, historical villas, and ancient castles (a fine example is preserved at Sirmione). Much of the land around the lake is used for grazing and covered in vineyards that produce world-renowned wines like Bardolino and Custoza.

The lake is dotted with sailboats and motorboats in summer and locals with rod and reel are a frequent sight. Ecological tourism thrives in the area and hikers are especially spoiled for choice. If it's an old-fashioned roller coaster you're after, you can find that too and give the Italian version of an amusement park a test at Gardaland.

Sights

The west side of the lake is known as Riviera dei Limoni and has fascinated poets from Goethe to Joyce. Like everyone else, they were captivated by the gentle hills that progressively give way to harsher terrain. **Sirmione** lies in the south on a thin peninsula four kilometers into the lake and provides an enchanting view of both shores. **Rocca Scaligera** castle (Piazza Castello, tel. 03/091-6468, Oct.–Mar. daily 9 A.M.–1 P.M., Apr.–Sept. daily 9 A.M.–6 P.M.) dominates town and was built in 1250 by a Veronese lord to guard the lake. After crossing the drawbridge, narrow lanes lead to Roman ruins at the tip of the peninsula. The small archeological park is lined with olives and cypress trees that surround one of the best-preserved imperial age villas in Northern Italy.

The town of **Desenzano** was also occupied by the Romans and served as an important port. Most of the streets in the center are pedestrian-only and lead to the medieval castle built in the 10th century to keep barbarians at bay. The town of **Salò** was where Mussolini gave his last orders in 1943. Today pastel-colored houses line the lakeside promenade of this popular resort. The Gothic **Duomo** dates from the 15th century and contains many works of art. If you can take your eyes off the wonderful bay, the interior of **Palazzo della Magnifica Patria** (Via Lungolago Zanardelli 53, tel. 03/652-0366) is also worth a visit.

The destination of choice for 19th-century aristocrats and magnates was **Gardone Riviera.** It's full of Art Nouveau villas, hotels, and cafés where society life still thrives. The town is split into lower and upper parts, both of which contain an amazing selection of citrus and palm trees that grow to incredible heights in the mild climate. The poet Gabriele D'Annunzio built his residence here; it's now open to the public and provides a glimpse into his eclectic life. The ferry from nearby **Maderno** carries cars during the summer and is a quick way to reach the other side of the lake.

Riva del Garda is the northernmost town on the lake and was once protected by the imposing **Rocca Scaligeri** fortress (tel. 03/091-6468, Mar.–Oct. 14 daily 8:30 A.M.–7 P.M., Oct.

Lake Garda, Italy's largest lake

15–Feb. daily 8:30 A.M.–5 P.M., €5), built in 1124. There are many hotels and restaurants to choose from and the waters offshore are popular with wind-surfers who come for the consistently strong winds. After a day in the water, locals and visitors tend to gather in the historic central piazza with unique combination of Lombard- and Venetian-style buildings.

Sports and Recreation

Nearly every town on the lake has a port where sailboats and motorboats can be rented. Gargano is a favorite with sailors and the site of regattas nearly every weekend in the summer. **Centomiglia** (tel. 03/657-1433) in September is the most famous and attracts thousand of onlookers to both shores.

For four days at the end of April, Riva del Garda becomes a pedaling paradise. During **Bike Festival** (Palazzo dei Congressi, tel. 04/6456-0113), you can watch BMX acrobats perform death-defying stunts, test the latest gear, and participate in one of the numerous competitions. There are obstacle courses, night races, and a bike marathon of more than 80 kilometers (riders can chose appropriate levels of difficulty). During the event, rental points are opened around the lake and guided excursions are organized.

Cascate del Varone (Via Cascate 12, tel. 04/6452-1421, www.cascata-varone.com, daily 9 A.M.–6 P.M., €5) is an impressive 90-meter waterfall three kilometers north of Riva. There's a lower and upper observation point, both of which are reached by way of a lovely botanic garden.

The **Lake Garda Marathon** (tel. 03/6595-4781, www.lakegardamarathon.com) on the third Sunday in September starts in Limone and finishes 42 kilometers later in Malceseni. Almost the entire course is run along the lake and the scenery should provide all the encouragement needed to complete the race.

Gardaland (Castelnuovo del Garda, tel. 04/5644-9777, www.gardaland.it, €28 daypass) is near the southwestern lake town of Peschiera and is the largest amusement park in Italy with four theme villages and 23 attractions. Roller coasters don't need translation and Magic Mountain is one long 85-kph scream.

Tamer rides include a panoramic tour, Colorado rapids, and an African safari. There's also an aquatic theater where dolphins get up to their usual tricks and leave audiences soaked. Few people come to Italy to risk vomiting on the Top Spin or Moonraker, but it's hard to resist not experiencing this Italian take on Disneyland. The park is easily reached by car and there's a shuttle every 30 minutes from the Peschiera train station two kilometers away.

Accommodations

Built around the early 1900s **⟨ Hotel Laurin** (Salò, Viale Landi 9, tel. 03/652-2022, www.laurinsalo.com, €150 d) started out as a private residence for the Simonini family and briefly housed the foreign ministry of a forgotten republic. It became a hotel in the 1970s thanks to the Rossi family, who preserved many of the details that make the villa one of the best examples of Art Nouveau in Northern Italy. Frescoes are signed by Bertolotti and Landi, and delicate cast-iron sculptures punctuate much of the elegant interior. There are three room types: *piccola e carina* (small and cute), cheek to cheek, and traditional (which comes with a view).

In Gardone Sopra near Gabriele D'Annunzio's villa, **Locanda agli Angeli** (Piazzetta Garibaldi 2, tel. 03/652-0832, €90 d) provides lake views from a tranquil corner of town. The Pellegrini family have run this historic inn since the 1970s when they transformed an *osteria* into nine attractive rooms. They also added a pool and opened a *trattoria* that serves seasonal dishes. It's a good place to try *bagòss* (mountain cheese) or *tortino di caprino* (savory pie made with goat milk).

Brione (Riva del Garda, Viale Rovereto 75, tel. 04/6455-2484, www.hotelbrione.it, €85) is a moment away from the beach and port with enchanting views of the Dolomites in the distance. The family who runs the hotel is big on relaxation and will encourage you to take a dip in the pool or lay out in the garden. Surfers and cyclists can leave gear near the lobby and enjoy a cone in the *gelateria* with a great view of the lake. **Mirage** (Riva del Garda, Viale Rovereto 97/99, tel. 04/6455-2671,

€70 d) is not an illusion. Rooms are beautiful in a minimalist way and every window comes with a stunning view. It's a lively hotel with a restaurant and lounge bar where local musicians perform every weekend. Bikes are free, as is access to the sauna and Turkish bath.

Food

La Contrada (Via Bagatta 12, tel. 03/0914-2514, Thurs.–Tues. noon–2:30 P.M. and 7–10:30 P.M., €9–13) is on a quiet street with porticos in the high part of Desenzano. Marta runs the small restaurant, which doesn't feel cramped because she keeps tables far apart. The menu promotes local specialties like the ravioli stuffed with lake fish and oven-roasted quail. A good selection of wines is busy maturing in wooden casks in the cellar. To get an idea of what exactly can be caught in the lake, visit **Cavallaio** in Via Castello and if you do plan on doing some fishing don't be afraid to ask for some suggestions on what bait to use.

€ **Osteria di Mezzo** (Salò, Via di Mezzo 10, tel. 03/6529-0966, Wed.–Mon. 12:30 P.M.–3 P.M. and 7:30–11 P.M., €8–12) is just out of reach of the main tourist flow and more authentic than any of the restaurants on the promenade. The Vanni family restaurant remains open from noon till night, which is unusual in Italy, and you can stop by for a meal or just a light snack. Most of the fish Dory grills in the kitchen were swimming in the lake that morning. The cheese and cold cut plate is a good option and almond tart is prepared without butter or flour. Gino will be happy to write down the recipe. If chocolate is on your mind, head to **Pasticceria Vassalli** (tel. 03/652-0752, Wed.–Mon. 8:30 A.M.–8:30 P.M.) around the corner at Via San Carlo 86.

Grappa comes in every flavor imaginable at **Enoteca Lega Antianalcolica** (Riva del Garda, Via Santa Maria 23, tel. 04/6452-2163). The blueberry and apple are especially potent and regarded as the perfect post-dinner drinks. After a few rounds, you may discover that your Italian is better than you thought.

Getting There and Around

The N572, N45b, N249, and N11 are different numbers for the same single-lane road that circles the lake. Most of the drive is along the shore but occasionally there are deviations inland, like near Tignale and Tremisone, where it runs through the Brasa ravine and later rises up to provide one of the best views of the lake.

Navigazione Lago di Garda (Desenzano, Piazza Matteotti, tel. 03/0914-9511, www.navigazionelaghi.it) operates ferries on the lake and Desenzano and Riva del Garda are the main terminals. Tickets, however, can be purchased directly at any port and you can choose from single trips (Desenzano to Sirmione is €4) or day passes for the southern (€16.80), northern (€14.80), or the entire (€24.60) lake. It's a great way to avoid traffic and see a lot of different towns. Boats operate 8 A.M.–8 P.M. and cars may be transported between Maderno and Torri in the middle of the lake and from Limone to Malcesine farther north where a cable car climbs 1,745 meters to the top of Monte Baldo and a spectacular view of Garda.

TRENTINO-ALTO ADIGE

Trentino-Alto Adige may be one region on the map, but it's formed by two distinct provinces. Trentino in the south is home to the regional capital, where it's more common to hear Italian or Ladino, while Alto Adige has been influenced by its geographic and cultural proximity to Austria. German is spoken and locals will tell you that the name of the province is Südtirol.

Both provinces share the Dolomite Mountains, which form a continuous backdrop. There are 80 peaks over 3,000 meters and ancient glaciers have left behind broad tree-lined valleys that attract skiers in winter and hikers the rest of the year. Towns have been constrained by nature to remain small and have an Alpine charm that's in complete contrast to other areas of Italy. Architecture is heavily influenced by climate and Austrian building techniques. The chalet is king and interiors are carved entirely of wood.

The region's position on the frontier between Northern and Southern Europe has influenced local customs since before the Romans founded many of the towns. The Neolithic man discovered near Bolzano is evidence of prehistoric traffic that continues up to the present day and hasn't always been peaceful. Hundreds of castles line the valleys, and given the display of weapons at Castel Coira, there must have been bloodshed. More modern fortifications overlooking Val Sugana recall how bitterly the region was contested during World War I.

Today residents prefer to be known for their hospitality and intensely flavorful mountain cooking. The 80,000 milking cows are the

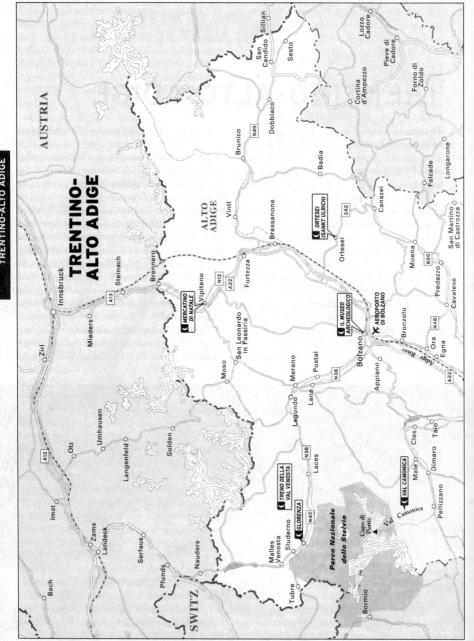

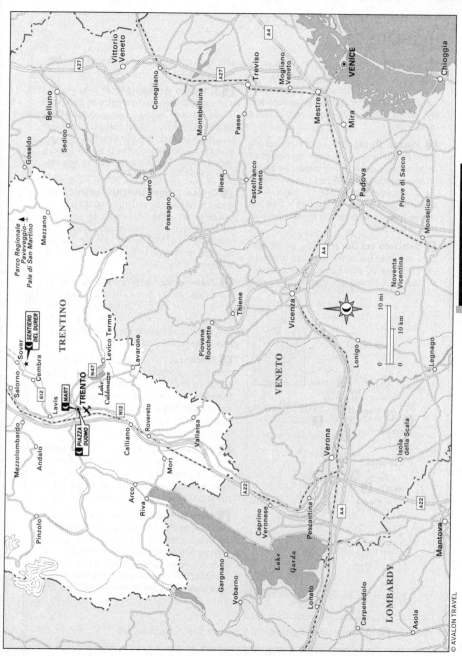

© AVALON TRAVEL

HIGHLIGHTS

◖ MART: Contemporary art fans will not want to miss this world-class museum. You can spend an entire afternoon exploring the permanent collection focused on Italian Futurism and artists like Balla, Depero, and Severini (page 312).

◖ Piazza Duomo: Trento's main square pulsates with locals and is the equivalent of an immense outdoor living room. The piazza is lined on all sides by elegant frescoed buildings and the Baroque fountain in the center is where couples gather. The action is best observed from a café table underneath the porticos (page 314).

◖ Sentiero del Durer: Hiking on the Sentiero del Durer trail is the best way to experience the Piramidi di Segonzano, a rare series of pillar rock formations that dot the valley

and reach as high as 30 meters above the forest (page 319).

◖ Il Museo Archeologico: Time stands still inside Museo Archeologico in Bolzano, where artifacts from all ages provide a history lesson you won't want to miss. The crowd pleaser is Iceman, a 5,000-year-old hunter found buried in the snow, the center of a fascinating exhibit recounting the life and times of prehistoric humans (page 325).

◖ Ortisei (Sankt Ulrich): A white Christmas is never an issue in Ortisei and the trails of this ski resort in the Dolomites cater to all levels of downhill and cross-country skiers. The vast network of lifts makes each run unique so skiers never have to slalom down the same trail twice (page 328).

◖ Treno della Val Venosta: Alto Adige is too beautiful for drivers to stay focused on watching the road. Between Merano and Malles you can leave the car behind and hop a train that chugs along one of the most pristine valleys in the region (page 331).

◖ Glorenza: The city of Glorenza may only have 800 inhabitants, but it has been recognized as a city since the Middle Ages. The walls that have protected the central market for centuries could still withstand a barbarian invasion. A visit here isn't complete without a walk along the ramparts (page 332).

◖ Val Camonica: This glacier-formed valley features more than 180,000 Neolithic engravings. The best-preserved images are concentrated around Capo di Ponte in the Parco Nazionale delle Incisioni Rupestri (page 334).

◖ Mercatino di Natale: Christmas is the best time to visit Alto-Adige. It's very easy to get into the holiday spirit here, especially at Vipiteno's Mercatino di Natale. Enjoy a slice of *zelten*, a traditional holiday fruit cake, while shopping the well-stocked stalls that should have something for everyone on your list (page 337).

AUSTRIA
Innsbruck
Alps
Vipiteno
Mercatino di Natale
Malles
Ortisei (Sankt Urlich)
Treno della Val Venosta
Ortisei
Glorenza
Bolzano
Il Museo Archeologico
Val Camonica
Trento
Sentiero del Durer
MART
Piazza Duomo
Treviso
Lake Garda
Vicenza
Padova
Verona
Venice
Gulf of Venice
0   30 mi
0   30 km

LOOK FOR ◖ TO FIND RECOMMENDED SIGHTS, ACTIVITIES, DINING, AND LODGING.

source of an infinite number of soft cheeses best accompanied with over 70 types of breads. The Adige Valley is apple territory and even has a DOC status similar to the hearty wines on the sun-drenched slopes surrounding Cembra. *Speck* is the region's answer to prosciutto and takes 25 weeks of smoking, drying, and aging before it's ready to be savored along with recipes like *zuppe di vino* (wine soup) that sound odd until tasted.

PLANNING YOUR TIME

Seasons have a significant effect on the region. In winter the snow is never in doubt and the mountains attract thousands of skiers. Tourism is well organized in both provinces and in nearly every town there are APT offices that help visitors discover natural, sporting, and cultural highlights.

The principal artery is the A22 Autostrada del Brennero that runs up the center of the region through both provinces. The largest towns are located along this route, which remains busy year-round. It's often more gratifying to take a slow drive in the valleys that radiate from the Adige River. Roads get smaller and train service is limited but buses connect destinations that aren't served by rail.

The ideal way to visit the region is by foot or bicycle. There are over 600 kilometers of bicycle paths and 380 cableways that allow visitors to get vertical in a hurry. The many historical and Alpine trails are a delight for hikers, and mountain refuges provide a way of exploring the region without the necessity to backtrack. Alto-Adige has been especially active in getting tourists to abandon their cars. Mobil Card (www.mobilcard. info) is one of the flexible transportation initiatives that allows travel by rail, bus, or cable car.

HISTORY

The first permanent settlers in Trentino-Alto Adige were the Reti, who had little chance of resisting the Romans and Augusto who conquered the Dolomites. The decline of the Empire was an opportunity for the Longobards to move in. During the Middle Ages, the region was dominated by the principality of Trento until 1363, when it fell into the hands of Austrian kings. It remained a part of the Austro-Hungarian Empire for centuries (with a brief intermission accorded to Napoleon) and only joined Italy at the end of World War I. Despite fascist attempts to Italianize the province, German culture has survived and today many inhabitants are bilingual.

Trentino

With barely half a million residents, Trentino provides the elbow room that's missing in other parts of Italy. It's a land of gentle rolling hills, vast expanses of grazing meadows dotted with crystal clear lakes, and majestic peaks that are never out of sight. There is no end to the old villages, delightful churches, and fascinating castles. Spa towns retain the elegance of the Belle Epoque, when European aristocracy came to treat their ailments and breathe in the pure air.

ROVERETO

Rovereto's importance is related to geography and its position at the entrance to the Adige Valley. From here, all movement up and down

the region could be controlled—which explains the Roman settlement and the Middle Age castle built to oversee traffic. During World War I, it was the site of heavy fighting and is now home to a war museum that tells the story of many conflicts fought in the region. The town is also famous for a *sagre* devoted to wine and several theater and dance festivals.

Sights
CASTLE AND MUSEO STORICO ITALIANO DELLA GUERRA
The octagonal castle (Via Castelbarco 7, tel. 0464/438-100, Tues.–Sun. 10 A.M.–6 P.M., €5.50) overlooking Rovereto was started in the

13th century, and Venetians later added the tower and turrets that protected the city until the Hapsburgs were forced to leave after World War I. Since then it has housed **Museo Storico Italiano della Guerra,** a war musuem where decommissioned cannons, mortars, and rifles along with uniforms and a room dedicated entirely to Napoleon's armies do less harm than they did in the past. The highlight is a Nieport 10 biplane that last saw service in 1918.

OSSARIO DI CASTEL DANTE

Next to the castle, a steep stairway leads to Ossario di Castel Dante (Via Castel Dante, tel. 04/6443-0363, Apr.–Oct. Mon.–Sat. 9 A.M.–6 P.M., Nov.–Mar. Mon.–Sat. 8 A.M.–2 P.M.), a military memorial containing the remains of 20,000 Italians and Austrians who died during the firstWorld War. It's worth climbing the steps for the marvelous view of the valley and the battlefield trenches that have been preserved as a vivid reminder for future generations. The bell that rings each day at sunset is the Campana dei Caduti, four kilometers away. It's cast from melted-down World War II artillery and commemorates the dead of all wars. Below the castle lies the ancient *borgo* and Via della Terra, from which the remains of the double walls that once ringed the city are still visible. **San Marco,** back in town in the piazza of the same name, is the best-preserved church, and the original 14th-century building was significantly enlarged two centuries later.

◼ MART

The exterior of MART (Corso Bettini 43, tel. 0464/438-887, Tues.–Sun. 10 A.M.–6 P.M. and until 10 P.M. on Fri., €5) is hardly noticeable and blends perfectly into the medieval townscape. It's only once you step inside that it becomes clear there's some serious architecture going on here. Many visitors come just to see the building. It was designed by Mario Botta in 2002, and contains a wide array of modern and contemporary art. The bulk of the permanent collection is focused on Italian Futurism and artists like Balla, Depero, and Severini. There are spaces dedicated to

Pop Art and regular exhibits that attract art pilgrims from around the world.

Festivals and Events

Every September, contemporary dance companies from all over the world participate in the **Oriente Occidente Festival** (www.orienteoccidente.it) staged within the MART and Teatro la Cartiera. There are also free outdoor performances in the town's piazze.

Accommodations

Nearly everything is red inside the **Leon d'Oro** (Via Tacchi 2, tel. 0464/437-333, www.hotelleondoro.it, €90 d) from the carpets to the bed covers to the curtains. The 53 rooms vary in typology: silver comes with an all-you-can-drink minibar, while leon d'oro includes free parking, pay per view, and the newspaper of your choice delivered to you door (they may have trouble locating a copy of the *Pittsburgh Post-Gazette*).

Hotel Rovereto (Corso Rosmini 82d, tel. 0464/435-222, www.hotelrovereto.it, €125 d) is situated between the train station and the historic center. Each of the 49 rooms in the 19th-century building is spacious and individually decorated. The **Novecento** restaurant on the ground floor has the longest wine list in town and a delightful terrace for summertime dining.

On the outskirts of Rovereto driving north along the N12 is a peaceful bed-and-breakfast built in an Alpine style. **Sant'Ilario** (Viale Trento 68, tel. 0464/411-950, www.hotelsantilario.it, €105 d) is surrounded by a pleasant garden where guests can enjoy a dip in the pool and views of the countryside.

Food

Pettirosso (Corso Bettini 24, tel. 0464/422-463, daily noon–3 P.M. and 7:30–11 P.M., €9–14) is a convenient stop before or after a visit to MART. The ground floor of Paolo Torboli's *osteria* serves snacks and wine by the glass while upstairs you can taste local specialties like *tonco de pontesèl* and *canderli,* which are a cross between gnocchi and meatballs, made from *speck* ham, bread, and flour and cooked in a broth. They also serve fish from the nearby lakes and desserts made from Marzemino wine.

The old silk mill on Via Tartarotti was converted into a restaurant, and many of the spinning machines and wooden beams were left intact. **Antico Filatoio** (Via Tartarotti 12, tel. 0464/437-283, Wed.–Mon. noon–3 P.M. and 7–11 P.M., €8–12) is one of the most characteristic places to eat in town. They serve *carne salada* along with fresh fish imported daily from the Adriatic.

Enoteca Stappomatto (Corso Bettini 56a, tel. 0464/432-551, Tues.–Fri. 9 A.M.–8 P.M., Sat. 10 A.M.–3 P.M., 5–8:30 P.M., Sun. 11 A.M.–3:30 P.M.), also near MART, has more bottles than you can count. Most are produced within 100 kilometers of this impressive shop. In Via Fontana, **Exquisita** (Via Fratelli Fontana 10, tel. 0464/420-757, May–Aug. daily 9 A.M.–7 P.M., closed Sun.) sells both wine and chocolate. It's a combination that could easily become addictive. For coffee, *gelato,* pastries, or a quick snack **Bar Meeting** (Via Fiume 2, tel. 04/6443-0363) prepares a wide assortment of delicacies.

Getting There and Around

Rovereto is on the southern edge of Trentino near the Veneto border. It's directly off the A22 highway and easily reached from the north or south by rail and bus. The APT office in Piazza Rosmini can provide local bus tickets and a map for navigating the winding streets of the center.

Around Rovereto

Eramo di San Colombano (L'Eremo di San Colombano, tel. 0464/424-615, Apr.–Sept. Sun. 2:30–6:30 P.M., admission free) is located three kilometers outside of town on a cliff where hermits found peace from the outside world. They hand-carved the 120 steps up the hillside, which intimidate anyone who has over-indulged in strudel and provide a challenge for everyone else. An inscription at the top dates the first human presence to A.D. 735. Inside the chapel are several 15th-century frescoes, and there's a saint struggling against a

dragon within the grotto. An evocative midnight mass on December 24 begins at 10 P.M.

CASTELLO DI SABBIONARA D'AVIO

The Adige Valley has been a gateway between northern and southern Europe for thousands of years and dozens of castles were built along the valley to defend the interests of local lords. Castello di Sabbionara d'Avio lies near the Veneto border and was built in the 11th century. From its towers, there are unobstructed views, and inside many frescoes depict ancient battle scenes.

Sights

The castle (Sabbionara, tel. 0464/684-453, Mar.–Sept. Tues.–Sun. 10 A.M.–5 P.M., €3.50) lies on a hillside and the perimeter wall has remained intact. Inside, a gravel path lined with cypress trees leads upwards towards **La Casa delle Guardie** (guard house), decorated with a cycle of frescoes depicting knights in blue helmets marching into battle. The keep dominates the fortress and there is an excellent view from the single tower. On the last floor is the **Stanza dell'Amore,** named for the couple locked in a kiss, and other romantically themed frescoes.

Accommodations

There are no accommodations in the immediate vicinity of the castle but many *agriturismi* nearby are perfect bases for exploring the lower Adige Valley, Mount Lessino, and even the northern tip of Lago di Garda. Many, like █ **Al Picchio** (Sdruzzinà 20, tel. 0464/672-825, www.agrituralpicchio.it, €30 pp or €40 with half-board), are working farms and if you arrive in late August or September you can join them in the apple or grape harvest. There are eight large rooms decorated in dark wood and no TV—except in the communal lounge where guests compare travel notes before dinner in the stone-vaulted living room. Reserve one of their bikes if you'd like to hit the open country or stick to the cycle path that's less than two kilometers away.

Food

Castellum Ava (tel. 0464/684-299, €4) is the castle restaurant. It recreates a medieval environment, except the part about eating with your hands. It's only open for lunch. If all you want is a slice of pizza or some outdoor dining, there are several options in Sabbionara and Avio.

Getting There and Around

From north or south take the Ala-Avio exit off the A22 and follow the signs for the castle. The parking is 450 meters from the gate. The nearest train station is in Avio. There are frequent departures from Trento that make the journey in 30 minutes.

TRENTO

Trento is the largest city and the capital of the region. It's an attractive town that was heavily influenced by Renaissance trends and has several fine Romanesque-era churches. The Counter-Reformation met here during the Council of Trent (1545–1563) when it was decided that

bishops needed to reside in the city they represented and indulgences could no longer be exchanged for cash. After Napoleon's defeat in 1814, the city was turned over to the Austrians and only became part of Italy after intense fighting during World War I.

Sights
◖ PIAZZA DUOMO

The majestic Duomo (tel. 0461/980-132, daily 6:30 A.M.–noon and 2–6 P.M., admission free) was begun in the 12th century in a Romanesque Lombard style. On the northern facade is a window decorated with *Fortune*, shown predicting the destiny of humanity. On the inside the impressive staircase is original and leads to the bell tower that is closed to the public. It took three centuries to complete the church, which has a remarkably uniform appearance considering the time lapse and generations of laborers who worked on the building. Underneath the altar, remains of a previous basilica were uncovered and the foundations of this earlier structure can be visited (€1).

© ALESSIA RAMACCIA

The Piazza Duomo was once the site of the Roman forum.

The piazza outside the duomo was the site of the old Roman forum and a fountain of Neptune holding a trident recalls the town's original name of Tridentum. Many relics as well as tapestries and sculpted wooden panels are displayed in the **Museo Diocesano** (Piazza Duomo 18, tel. 0461/234-419, Wed.–Mon. 9:30 A.M.–12:30 P.M. and 2:30–5:30 P.M., €4) inside **Palazzo Pretorio,** where paintings illustrate the heated proceedings during the Council of Trent.

CASTELLO DEL BUONCONSIGLIO

Castello del Buonconsiglio (Via Bernardo Clesio 5, tel. 0461/233-770, www.buonconsiglio.it, Tues.–Sun. 9:30 A.M.–5 P.M., €6) formed part of the town's defensive system and was enlarged several times after it was founded in the 13th century. The prince-bishops who ruled over the town lived in the **Magno Palazzo** section of the castle and the sumptuous frescoes hint of a luxurious lifestyle. Many of the rooms now form part of the Museo Provinciale, which houses ceramics and carvings as well as Roman and Etruscan remains.

Entertainment and Events

Given the mountain location, it's no surprise that the **TrentoFilmFestival** (tel. 0461/986-120, www.trentofestival.it) highlights nature's special effects rather than the manmade kind. For the past 50 years, this festival has projected documentaries on the environment, exploration, and wilderness adventure. Nearly 300 films are projected for a week at the end of April and there's little chance of being trampled by paparazzi, although you might run into some penguins.

Trento Estate (tel. 0461/213-834) provides a full schedule of theater and music performances throughout the summer. Many concerts are held in the Centro Santa Chiara (www.centrosantachiara.it) cultural center and most are free. The Orchestra Haydn performs in local parks and an outdoor cinema is set up in the Centro Civico Matterello. Itinerary Folk is a festival within the festival that highlights local and international groups.

In June, locals celebrate their patron saint during **Feste Vigiliane** (tel. 0461/216-000,

TRENTINO-ALTO ADIGE

© ALESSIA RAMACCIA

Castello del Buonconsiglio was part of Trento's defense system during the Middle Ages.

www.festevigiliane.it) with a series of medieval parades and traditional dances reminiscent of square dancing.

Sports and Recreation

Trento is a bicycle-friendly city and many citizens use two wheels to get around. The APT office rents bicycles in four locations, including the tourist office on Via Mancini. Holders of the Trento Card can use the service for free 9 A.M.–6 P.M. on weekdays. A **bicycle route** also connects Trento with Bolzano in the north and Verona in the south. It's mostly flat and runs along the Adige River past many points of natural and historic beauty.

Parco di Gocciadoro southwest of the center is the largest city park and can easily be reached on foot or by means of the 1, 2, or 7 bus. It's a good place for a morning jog or long walk over the gentle hills and along the stream that cuts the park in half. There are several playgrounds, outdoor exercise equipment, and open fields where anyone who wants to join a game of pick-up *calcio* is always welcome.

Accommodations

The Tabarelli family have run **Hotel Venice** (Piazza Duomo 45, tel. 0461/234-114, www.hotelveneziatn.it, €50–70 s/d) since 1930 and not even a direct hit in World War II could put them out of business. Rooms are simple but many look out onto the fountain of Piazza Duomo and all the city's monuments are just a moment away. There are two separate entrances and the front desk is open 24 hours a day.

Hotel America (Via Torre Verde 50, tel. 0461/983-010, www.hotelamerica.it, €100 d) is situated at the beginning of the pedestrianized city center a short way from the train station and the duomo. Wood fixtures and light colors are the leitmotif of the 67 rooms, many of which offer views of the castle and mountains beyond. The price includes a buffet breakfast and there's a decent restaurant if you prefer to eat in.

◖ Accademia (Vicolo Colico 4, tel. 0461/233-600, www.accademiahotel.it, €100–150 s/d) is a comfortable hotel with a wonderful courtyard where breakfast is served under an oak tree and guests dine by candlelight. The 40 rooms have modern furnishings and the two suites on the top floor have a nice view of the duomo. All rooms come with air-conditioning, minibar, and satellite TV.

The youth hostel **Ostello Gioventù Europa** (Via Torre Vanga 11, tel. 0461/263-484, www.gayaproject.org/ostello/ostello_ita.html, €25pp) is adjacent to the train station and bus depot. There is no age limit and what counts is a youthful spirit and getting along with owner's dog. Rooms vary in size, and all come with private bathrooms. International travelers gather for pizza on the ground floor, admire the view from the terrace, and catch up with laundry in the basement.

Food

Scrigno del Duomo (Piazza Duomo 29, tel. 0461/220-030, daily, noon–3:30 P.M. and 7 P.M.–midnight, €9–15) provides two atmospheres in a single restaurant. The ground floor courtyard functions as an *osteria* and wine bar where locals gather after work to taste regional vintages and enjoy Alpine cooking. The restaurant in the rear is decorated with paintings and sculptures created nearby and run by impeccable waiters. There aren't many tables but during the summer roast rabbit, *strangolapreti* pasta, and strudel can be enjoyed outside.

Fabrizio Pedrolli's love of wine eventually led him to open **◖ Il Libertino** (Piazza Piedicastello 4, tel. 0461/260-085, Tues.–Sun. 12:30–3 P.M. and 7:30–11 P.M., €8–12). There are two small dining rooms and a minuscule wine bar inside this vaguely Art Nouveau–styled *osteria*. Cured meats and cheeses are present in great abundance on a menu that changes weekly. The *tortel de patata* (potato pie) is filling and polenta is served when temperatures start to drop. The wine list is extensive and most of the labels can be sampled by the glass.

Dinner and a movie is the idea behind **Astra** (Corso Buonarroti 16, tel. 0461/829-002, daily 7–11:30 P.M., closed Aug., €8–10). The small cineplex and *osteria* is run by the Artuso family, who project high-caliber films in the recently renovated theater. Anna handles the cooking and soups are one of her strong points. She also makes good lasagna and there are many vegetarian options on the menu. Occasionally she'll prepare the same dishes you'll see on the screen afterwards and every Thursday is theme night, usually dedicated to mushrooms, asparagus, or other seasonal vegetables.

Trattoria al Volt (Via Santa Croce 16, tel. 0461/983-7776, daily 12–3 P.M. and 7:30 P.M.–midnight, closed Thurs. and Sun. lunch) is where traditionalists go for food that has remained the same for generations. Those in search of a gastronomic experience in a centuries-old *osteria* should reserve a table at **Le Due Spade** (Via Don Rizzi, tel. 0461/234-343, Mon. evening–Sat., €12–20).

In Via Brennero near the Astra cinema, **La Sgeva** (Via Brennero 20, tel. 0461/829-672) is an ideal spot for sipping Trentino vintages and smooth grappa until late. **Antichi Sapori Trentini** (Via Belenzani 56, tel. 04/6126-0535, Tues.–Sun. 9:30 A.M.–3 P.M. and 5–11 P.M.) has a vast selection of cured meats and cheeses. The clerks are happy to let you sample items and will gladly assist in picnic preparation. A few doors down the same street is **Casa del Cioccolato** (Via Belenzani 21), where chocolate lives in many shapes and flavors.

Information and Services

The **APT office** (Via Mancini 2, tel. 0461/216-000, www.apttrento.it, daily 9 A.M.–10 P.M.) is a useful stop if you plan to remain in the city more than 24 hours. It's where you can pick up the **Trento Card** that provides free access to museums, the botanic garden, public buses, the cable car, and bicycles. The card comes with a visitor's kit in English and is available for 24-hour (€10) and 48-hour (€15) periods.

Guided tours leave every Saturday at 10 A.M. for Castello del Buonconsiglio and at 3 P.M. for the historic center. Groups depart from the APT office and cost €3 unless you have the Trento Card. Visits at other times can be arranged through the **Associazione Guide Turistiche** (Via Maccani 207, tel. 0461/434-217, Mon.–Fri. 8:30 A.M.–12:30 P.M.).

There are many Internet points around town and prices vary from free to €5 per hour. **Call Me** (Via Belenzani 58, tel. 0461/983-302, daily 9 A.M.–9 P.M.) charges €1 every 15 minutes with a 15-minute minimum. **Internet Arena** (Via XXIV Maggio 2, Mon.–Sat. 10 A.M.–2 A.M. and Sun. 4 P.M.–2 A.M.) works out to €3 per hour. The **public library** (Via Roma 55, tel. 0461/884-368) offers free Internet for one hour but reservations must be made in advance to guarantee a computer.

For medical emergencies, call the Guardia Medica (Via Malta 4, tel. 0461/915-809) 24 hours a day or head directly to Ospedale S. Chiara (Largo Medaglie d'Oro 9, tel. 0461/903-111). Pharmacies can help relieve minor pains or replace a misplaced toothbrush. They nearly all have green neon signs and use a ticketed number system similar to deli counters to avoid any confusion about who was first in line. **Grandi** (Largo N. Sauro 30, tel. 0461/239-805) and **Dall'Armi** (Piazza Duomo 10, tel. 0461/236-139) are the biggest and both post a list of other pharmacies in neighborhood when they are closed.

Getting There and Around

Trento is directly off the A22 and a main stop for trains and buses from Rome and Milan. Getting around the city by foot or bus is simple and there is a free shuttle between the Zuffo (near the highway exit) and Monte Baldo (near the stadium) parking lots. The cable car near San Lorenzo bridge takes riders up 600 meters to Sardagna for an unmissable look at the valley. Public transportation tickets are available at the train station and many *tabacchi*. Visitors can buy 70 (€.90) or 120 (€1.20) minutes of travel. A day pass is €2.30 and a family pass for two adults and up to four children under 18 is €4.60. Cars can be rented from **Europcar** (tel. 0461/260-359) on Via Torre Vanga 8.

LEVICO TERME

Levico Terme is an 18th-century town that has lost none of its elegance. Houses are built in Alpine style with long, low angled roofs for keeping the snow off the streets. In summer balconies are filled with flowers and many visitors come to heal aches and pains in the mineral rich **thermal baths.** A small lake with a public beach and beautiful public garden make for a pleasant half-day of cycling or strolling before moving farther along the **Val Sugana** in the footsteps of pre-historic hunters. Many battles have been fought in the valley, from Napoleon's rout of Austrian troops in 1796 to the siege of World War I fortresses that still show signs of carnage.

Sights

Lago di Levico, or Lake Levico, is the smaller sibling of Lake Caldonazzo. It's lined with beech trees that turn beautiful colors in autumn. The water is some of the cleanest in Italy and although it can be quite frigid families enjoy the public beach throughout the summer. Trout, black bass, carp, and perch can be caught, and canoes and windsurfing equipment rented from along the shore near town. If your digital camera needs recharging, make sure it's fully powered before arrival.

Once you've tasted polenta, you'll want to know how it's made. Fortunately the only museum in the world dedicated to the local specialty is in Levico Terme. **Museo della Polenta** (Piazza Venice, tel. 0461/701-831, open only upon request) contains 500 pieces of equipment, much of them patented, used to turn flour into a finger-licking recipe. Entrance is free but requires a reservation. One of the curators will gladly show you around.

Via Claudia Augusta was the old Roman road that ran through the valley connecting Trento with Feltre. There are still traces of the Empire including stone markers used to indicate distance and tombs such as the one in front of the **Parco delle Terme** on the eastern edge of town. Military cemeteries are not an unusual sight in the region and demonstrate how fiercely the area was contested during World War I. **Forte Vezzena** and **Forte Verle** were part of a string of forts that made up the Austrian line of defense and were heavily bombarded throughout the war. Both have commanding views and unless you are in Olympic form it's best to drive up the mountain on the

steep, scenic road from Asiago through the Val d'Assa. Park at Albergo Nuova Vezzena, where the footpath to both forts starts. It's about a five-hour hike roundtrip and requires a good pair of hiking boots.

Sports and Recreation

Arsenic-laced water may not sound like the kind you'd want to soak in, but since it began bubbling to the surface in the 16th century the spas in town have cured aches and pains as well as helped stressed modern city dwellers relax. **Terme di Levico** (Viale Vittorio Emanuele 1, tel. 0461/706-077, Mon.–Sat. 6:30 A.M.–12:30 P.M., www.termedilevico.it) is the main bathing complex, open April–November. Treatments vary from a basic session in the mineral-rich pools (€19) to a sedative mud bath (€30) guaranteed to reduce anxiety.

At the end of the 19th century, the renowned German gardener Georg Ziehl designed Parco delle Terme and planted trees from nearly every continent. There are South American magnolias, giant sequoias, Lebanese cedars, and Himalayan pines all living in tranquil harmony. The Austrian Princess Sissi spent her summers here walking along the same wide lanes used by locals today. It's a great spot for picnic and easily reached from the center of town.

The **cycling path** that starts near the Caldonazzo Lake stretches 60 kilometers along the Valsugana Valley all the way to Veneto. Most hotels rent bikes and a map of all the possible itineraries is available from the APT office in Levico.

Accommodations

Many of the hotels in town are equipped with facilities for enjoying the natural springs. The **Imperial** (Via di Silva Domini 1, tel. 0461/706-104, www.imperialhotel.it, €150 d) is as refined now as it was when the Habsburgs spent their summers here. Service is fit for a noble and there are three restaurants to choose from. Guests can also enjoy the pool, work out in the gym, or relax in the thermal spa. The 37 room **Ambassador** (Viale Vittorio Emanuele 14, tel. 800/501-662, www.eden-hotel.it,

€80–120 s/d) may have one less star but the historic palazzo and welcoming atmosphere make for a pleasant stay. There's a pool, a spa, and a restaurant that serves good fish dishes.

Food
The secret to the pasta dish *strangolapreti* served at **(** **Boivin** (Via Garibaldi 9, tel. 0461/701-670, Tues.–Sun. 7–10:30 P.M. and for lunch on Sun., €10–12) is the sweet onions and vanilla that have been added—a method used for generations. It's hard to find more typical cooking and Carla Bosco still uses the same mountain herbs she picks every spring that give her dishes a unique flavor. The gnocchi and chestnut soup are wonderful but be sure to leave room for the honey-drenched strudel.

Information and Services
Valsugana has its own tourist office (Villa Sissi, tel. 0461/706-101, www.valsugana.info), which promotes all the towns in the valley and provides information on the many sporting activities available to visitors. The **Medico Turistico** (tel. 0461/706-271) is dedicated to tourists and can make hotel calls depending on the nature of the injury. There are two pharmacies in the center and if one isn't open the other will be.

Getting There and Around
Levico Terme is 20 kilometers east of Trento off the N47, which narrows from a two lane freeway into a one lane road after Pergine. Local trains depart every hour from Trento and complete the journey in around 40 minutes. It's a scenic ride and there's a nice view of Lake Caldonazzo if you sit on the left.

Around Levico Terme
On the other side of the Brenta River is a quiet little valley. A couple of local artists had the idea of creating a sculpture park that was in harmony with the natural beauty of the surroundings. They invited dozens of artists to participate in **Artenatura** (Borgo Valsugana, tel. 0461/751-251, Jun.–Oct. daily 10 A.M.–6 P.M., May and Nov. Sat. and Sun. only, €3, www.artesella.it) and the result is a three-kilometer art walk between the villages of Sella and Malga Costa. All 39 of the works use organic materials and many have a primitive, *Planet of the Apes* feel.

CEMBRA
The road to Cembra, known as the *strada del vino,* winds its way through endless hillside vineyards where the famous Müller Thurgau grapes are grown. The town is the center of production and home to several canteens where the latest vintage can be sampled. Geologists will enjoy the effects erosion has had over millions of years in Segonzano a few kilometers away.

Sights
SAN PIETRO
The church of San Pietro in the center of town is the principal monument. It's characterized by an impressive Gothic portal and a rose window that reveals its true colors on the inside. The frescoes that line the walls date from the 15th century and the bell tower with a pyramid-like roof was the last addition to the building.

PALAZZO BARBI
Palazzo Barbi was once home to the wealthiest family in town. Today it's where you'll find the tourist office and several well-preserved rooms. **Sala degli Stemmi** contains the coat of arms of all 11 communities located in the valley and a characteristic vaulting covered in frescoes by Egidio Petri di Segonzano.

(SENTIERO DEL DURER
The German artist Albert Durer traveled extensively in Italy and Sentiero del Durer is the trail he took during a visit to the valley in 1492. It's worth following in his footsteps to see the old bridge over the Avisio River, the castle, and especially the **Piramidi di Segonzano,** which fascinated Durer so much that he dedicated a series of watercolors to the rare rock formations. Some of the pillars tower 30 meters above the forest and look nearly manmade. It's a steep climb along a clearly marked path with information panels along the way, but if time is short you can drive there on the SS 612.

Entertainment and Events

Every year during the first week of July in Palazzo Barbi, the best local bottles of Müller Thurgau are compared and contrasted with over 100 wineries from Germany, Austria, and Switzerland. Visitors to **Mostra di Cembra** (tel. 0461/680-117, www.mullerthurgau-mostra.it) are provided with a glass and encouraged by sommeliers on each stand to taste the difference geography can have on the flavor of the same grape variety.

Sports and Recreation

Bocce is very popular in Northern Italy and Trentino has fielded its fair share of world champions. Most small towns have their own special facilities and the **bocciodromo** (tel. 0461/683-475, summer daily 1:30–10 P.M., admission free) in Cembra is on Viale IV Novembre. If you aren't traveling with a set of bocce balls, you can borrow them or just watch the old-timers getting serious during the frequent summer tournaments.

Accommodations

Agriturismo Maso Val Fraja (Via Val Fraja, tel. 0461/680-096, €50 d) is surrounded by vines a short distance from town. Instead of stars, *agriturismi* are rated by daisies, and this one was awarded four. The five rooms have traditional interiors with quilts knit by the owner's grandmother. Breakfast is a sweet or savory affair with *salumi*, cheese, marmalade, and cakes all made in-house.

Anyone who can survive without a private bathroom will enjoy 🌑 **Albergo Rifugio Lago Santo** (tel. 0461/683-066, €50 d). This refuge, near the lake and surrounded by woods, epitomizes peace and quiet. The spartan rooms are balanced by the extraordinary panorama outside. There are plenty of clearly marked trails to choose from and the restaurant prepares typical regional dishes at night.

Food

The cured meats and cheeses are displayed on a 10-meter-long counter at **Macelleria Zanotelli** (Via IV Novembre 48, tel. 0461/683-012,

7:30 A.M.–noon and 3:30–7 P.M., closed all day Mon. and Wed. mornings), well-stocked since 1949. You'll find *speck* ham, *carne salada*, and smoked hams all produced within a short radius of town. **Cantina Valle di Cembra** (Via IV Novembre 78, tel. 0461/680-010, Mon.–Sat.) sells all the local wines, including a DOC Müller Thurgau grown at 900 meters of altitude. Pinot Nero and Chardonnay enthusiasts will also find something to uncork here.

Information and Services

The **IAT office** in Piazza Toniolli 2 (tel. 0461/683-110, www.aptpinecembra.it, Tues.–Fri. 9 A.M.–noon and 3–5 P.M., Sun. 9 A.M.–noon) is a good place to find brochures and maps of the Cembra Valley. They can also find you a hotel that fits your budget. **Pharmacy Cembra** (Viale IV Novembre 44, tel. 0461/683-021) is open 8:30 A.M.–noon and 3:30–7 P.M. every day except Wednesday. Dr. Martini can help diagnose whatever is troubling you.

Getting There and Around

From Trento head north on the N12 and turn right at Lavis onto the N612. This road is initially very steep and drivers who aren't accustomed to mountain curves should take it slow. There are no trains to the valley; however, Atesina buses leave daily from the bus station in Trento adjacent to the railway.

Around Cembra

If there's time for a detour take the small steep road that leads to **Lago Santo** five kilometers north of town. The red pines, beech, and fir turn Vermont-like colors in autumn. The lake is 1,200 meters above sea level and was formed by glaciers. In summer it's dotted with fishermen and the **Happy Ranch Saloon** stables (tel. 0461/683-518) take visitors on horseback excursions through the woods. The saloon transforms into a popular disco pub on Friday and Saturday nights. Curlers turn up every weekend in winter to sweep the ice and practice one of the area's favorite sports. Beginners can learn the fundamentals from Adolfo Mosaner (tel. 338/742-4853) who runs the local club.

CAVALESE

Cavalese is the largest town in the Val di Fiemme. Traces of a Bronze Age settlement were discovered near this natural plain on the Avisio River that's surrounded by forests and pastures. During the summer, fields turn into a rainbow of color as wildflowers bloom and grazing cows enjoy a little variety in their diets. Most people come for the excellent sporting facilities that can be enjoyed year-round.

Sights

Palazzo della Magnifica Comunità (Piazza C.Battisti, tel. 0462/241-111) was started in the 13th century and completed 200 years later in Renaissance style by bishop Bernardo Clesio. It was used as a noble residence and administrative nerve center of the valley, which had a tradition of autonomy. The facade is covered in frescoes that sleet and rain have smudged over the years. You can still see the coat of arms of the different communities and fragments of religious portrayals. The palazzo is currently being restored and is scheduled to reopen in 2008. A new museum has been added dedicated to the school of painting that developed in the valley in the 16th–19th centuries.

Entertainment and Events

Marcialonga (www.marcialonga.it) is a 70-kilometer cross-country race that finishes in Cavalese. It's held on the last Sunday in January, and anyone can enter. There's a big party afterwards in the pubs and bars to celebrate the winner of this exhausting competition. After a day of skiing, there's nothing like a night listening to jazz played beside a roaring fireplace. That's the idea of **Fiemme Ski Jazz** (www.fiemmeskijazz.com) in mid-March, when intimate concerts are held in the mountain refuges and pubs around town. Tickets are €10 and can be purchased at the APT office on Via Bronzetti 60.

Shopping

Wood is carved for decorative as well as practical purposes throughout the region. You'll find toys, pipes, cups, bottle tops, and figurines that make original souvenirs. **Artigianato**

Fiemmese (Via Chiesa 40, tel. 0462/231-353) is a cooperative of craftsmen with a wide range of styles. **Il Picchio** (Piazza Rizzoli, tel. 0462/232-030, closed Thurs. and Sun.) is also worth a look just to watch the chisels being wielded with great skill in the workshop. A large market is held on the last Tuesday of every month except July in Piazza Fiera and Viale Libertà. Fruits and vegetables go on sale every Tuesday and Friday in the same piazza. The area is famous for apples and the Golden Delicious here have a different flavor than the ones grown in North America or China.

Sports and Recreation

Cavalese is rock climbing country and climbers practice in a gym on Via Dolomiti at the entrance to town on the SS48. There are 12 options on the training wall, which is 20 meters high and caters to levels 6a–7c. Giancarlo Alessandrini and Ivo Cristel are local alpine guides who work there and can set you up with all the equipment you need if you decide to tackle something steeper.

Ski Service di Gilberto Vanzo (Via Cascata 7, tel. 0462/231-760) and **Sport Cermis** (Piazzale Funivie, tel. 0462/231-002) rent snowboards, cross-country, and downhill skis. The cableway to the slopes is on the edge of town and there are five ski resorts in the valley accessible with a single skipass (www.dolomitisuperski.com) that costs €31 during the peak winter season. Runs range from slopes suitable for debutantes to Olympic-caliber *piste* with 28 degree angles that would give Bode Miller goosebumps.

Many lifts keep running after the snow has melted and the Fiemme Mountain Pass (www.valdifiemme.info, €9.90) is the quickest way to **Alpe Cermis** (2,229 meters).

Palazzo del Ghiaccio (Via Cermis, tel. 0462/231-252, 3–5 P.M. and 9–11 P.M., €4) is the local covered ice rink, open throughout the year morning, noon, and night. Skates are available at the rink and instructors are on hand for anyone who wants to perfect their triple lutz. Hockey, ice dancing, broomball, and curling events are frequently staged.

Accommodations

Rooms at **La Stua** (Piazza Dante, tel. 0462/340-235, www.hotelstua.com, €70 d) were decorated by Giuseppe Nones and most have changed little since 1774. They are entirely covered in wood, a practice known as stube, and many face south in order to maximize the rays of sunlight during the long winters. It's particularly suited to motorcyclists, who can eliminate any aches and pains in the Turkish bath.

If you arrive on Valentine's Day, **《 Hotel Garni Laurino** (Via Antoniazzi 14, tel. 0462/340-151, www.hotelgarnilaurino.it, €70–100 s/d) is a must. The half-dozen rooms are decorated with natural wood and the owners have turned bioarchitecture into their mantra. The Romantica room has a lovely four-poster bed, minibar, and full bath that should satisfy romantics. Breakfast is served in the garden during the summer and the tables are covered with organic products and homemade sweets you'll want the recipes for.

Hotel Excelsior (Piazza Cesare Battisti 11, tel. 0462/340-403, www.excelsiorcavalese.com, €110) was once the 15th-century home of a noble Austrian family who liked their ceilings high and their rooms large. Furnishings are very elegant, except for some of the wall-to-wall carpets—which serve a practical purpose in winter. Many guests spend evenings in the lovely frescoed *birreria* (you don't need to be a hotel guest to drink here) where you can sit on one of the barstools and order a cold beer fresh from the taps.

Food

El Molin (Piazza Cesare Battisti 11, tel. 0462/340-074, Wed.–Mon., closed May and Nov., €11–16) seats about 20 inside an old mill where diners can expect refined rather than hearty. There's a great selection of cheeses and this is the place to sample *speck* ham. Upstairs is a small wine bar with Müller Thurgau, Teroldego, and hundreds of other local labels lining the walls. Loris Welponer puts a twist on tradition at **Al Cantuccio** (Via Unterperger 14, tel. 0462/235-040, Tues.–Sun., €10–12) and his dishes are likely to surprise the palate.

To purchase typical valley sweets, marmalade, honey, and grappa, stop by **Le Cose Buone da Paola** (Piazza Scopoli 12, tel. 0462/340-266, daily in summer). Or if liquor is what you're after, visit **Paolazzi Distillati** (Via dei Rododendri 2, tel. 0462/230-344, closed Thurs. and Sun.), where it's been distilled for generations.

Getting There and Around

Cavalese is in the next valley over from Cembra on the N612. If you're traveling southbound on the A22 exit at Egna-Ora and proceed along the N48, which skirts the Corno Park and offers one panorama after another. There is no train service in the valley, but you can ride the rails to Egna-Ora and catch a bus from there that departs hourly.

There are a series of cable cars and ski lifts (tel. 0462/340-490) that start on the southern edge of town and carry visitors 2,000 meters up to Lake Lagorai. Facilities are open July–September 8:30 A.M.–12:30 P.M. and 2–6 P.M. A round-trip costs €12.50 for the full journey.

SAN MARTINO DI CASTROZZA

According to legend, San Martino di Castrozza was founded by eight Camaldolese monks in around 1000. According to historians, it was first inhabited in 1027 on orders from the bishop of Feltre. Neither date really matters since Austrian troops burned the town at the outbreak of World War I leaving **Chiesa di San Martino** as the only historic sight. The church once sheltered travelers crossing the Rolle Pass every spring on their way through the valley and has a nice Romanesque *campanile* (bell tower). Much of the original complex was damaged by retreating Austrian troops during World War I.

Sights

The real draw here is nature, and the town has attracted tourists since the 18th century. There are many hotels and restaurants ideally located for visiting **Parco Regionale Pavéveggio-Pale di San Martino.** Here walkers and skiers can ride the cableways up into the Southern Dolomites.

During the spring and summer, woods that were once chopped to make Venetian boats are covered with Alpine flowers and nesting birds.

Entertainment and Events

I Suoni delle Dolomiti (www.isuonidelledolomiti.it) takes music to the mountains. Every summer, a series of concerts is organized in different outdoor settings. Individual events are usually scheduled in the early afternoon, when musicians and audience meet for the hike up. Some of the most suggestive performances start at sunrise when instead of a curtain it's the first rays of sunlight that are the cue to strike up the trumpet, horn, or violin. The list of names from past editions is impressive and finding a seat is never a problem.

Sports and Recreation

The folks at **Guide Alpine** (Via Passo Rolle 165, tel. 0439/768-867, www.sanmartino.com) have been guiding visitors around the mountains since the first Germans and English showed up in the 19th century in search of vertical thrills. Today they take groups on multiple-day excursions, bring skiers to virgin slopes, and give free climbing courses to all levels. Rates are reasonable considering how well they know the area, and instruction can be arranged to suit any interest.

Accommodations

There are dozens of refuges and bivouacs scattered on the mountainside that provide basic lodging to hikers. Most are open June–September, when hikers take the lifts up and hike from one to the next along the well-indicated paths. A full list is available at the APT office.

Rifugio Pedrotti (Altopiano delle Pale, tel. 0439/68-308, €35 pp) is one of the main staging points for hikers, and is easily reached from the Rosetta cableway. From here, the Fradusta glacier and the highest peaks in the park can be reached in 20 minutes. The lodge has a bar and restaurant serving typical food and 80 beds that are best reserved in advance in order to avoid a night on the rocks.

Information and Services

There are several **visitors centers** (tel. 0439/768-867, daily 9 A.M.–12:30 P.M. and 3:30–7 P.M.) for the park. The one in San Martino is located on Via Passo Rolle 165. Outside the office is a small garden with many examples of the local flora.

Getting There and Around

The quickest way by road from Trento is the SS47 along the Valsugana and then the N50 that becomes progressively steeper after Passo Rolle. The last 10 kilometers can take 40 minutes and 180-degree curves up the mountain are frequent. The town can also be reached by rail from Borgo Valsugana or Feltre on the Padova-Calalzo line, from where buses depart regularly for town.

Alto Adige

Alto Adige, or Alto Adige/Südtirol as it's officially known, has been heavily influenced by centuries of Austrian rule. Except for large towns like Bolzano, which lies in the center of the region, German is spoken more commonly than Italian and street signs are written in both languages.

The province is even less populated than Trentino, and 20 percent of the territory is protected parkland that is intersected by hundreds of beautiful trails. The first ski lift in the world was built in Bolzano in 1908 and the province now counts 380 cable cars that ferry visitors up and down the mountains.

Inhabitants of the narrow valleys have adapted what little fertile land was available and managed to thrive over the centuries.

Unlike Trentino, where farms were divided and subdivided over generations, in Alto Adige the firstborn got the land—which meant that wealth remained intact. Agriculture based on grapes, fruit, and chestnuts still prospers today. More apples are grown here than anywhere else in Europe, and all 12 varieties can be found in the markets that are held in every village square. Pinot and Chardonnay are the varieties to taste, along with Traminer and the after-dinner grappa made from a mix of grapes. There are wine and cheese trails where the gastronomically inclined can hop from cantina to cantina sampling local vintages and discovering the process behind the product.

Snow is present nearly six months out of the year and in some places like Val Senales it never melts. Beginning in early December, winter sports enthusiasts can find well-packed trails and some of the best ski resorts in the world. **Dolomiti Superski** (www.dolomitisuperski.com) has 1,000 kilometers of trails ideal for snowboarders, sledders, and cross-country types. An electronic ski pass provides access to this group of 12 ski resorts straddling eastern Alto Adige and western Veneto starting in December until the snow runs out. Three days of skiing in high season (Dec. 23–Jan. 5 and Feb. 2–Mar. 24) is €119 for adults and €83 for children and young adults under 16.

BOLZANO (BOZEN)

Bolzano regularly tops the charts of Italy's most livable cities and if there are more people smiling here it's because things work better. Being in the center of the Dolomites also helps and a mild climate with more sunlight than you'd expect in a city surrounded by 1,000-meter peaks is the clincher.

The capital of the Alto Adige province is an officially bilingual city with a strong Austrian identity visible everywhere—from the street signs to the strudel. There were strong efforts to Italianize the population after World War I, but locals have managed to preserve their roots and balance the two cultures.

Vineyards and castles are a common sight near the town of Bolzano.

© ALESSIA RAMACCIA

Sights
PIAZZA WALTHER

Piazza Walther is in the medieval center flanked by a 15th-century Gothic Duomo. The dark stone contrasts with a light mosaic roof and gold-topped spire that looks incredibly light. Unlike many church doors the entrance is bare of saints and instead shows workers harvesting grapes. The piazza gets its name from the 13th-century poet Walther von der Vogelweide, whose statue lies in the center of the square.

◖ IL MUSEO ARCHEOLOGICO

Il Museo Archeologico (Via Museo 43, tel. 0471/320-100, www.iceman.it, Tues.–Sun. 10 A.M.–6 P.M., €8) is arranged chronologically from the Paleolithic rock tools used 17,000 years ago to models of Middle Age villages. The *Mona Lisa* of the museum is the Iron Age hunter, dubbed Iceman, who died over 5,000 years ago in a snow drift near Senales. He was found by accident in 1991 and made headlines around the world. After archeologists poked at him for several years, he and his possessions were transferred to the museum. His body now lies in a refrigerated case on the ground floor next to panels describing how he was found and the scientific techniques used to unlock his secrets. According to research, he was 46 years old when he died, had a preference for leather hides, and was probably killed by rival hunters. A model recreates what he may have looked like and interactive videos describe life at the time he made his last journey. The €2 audio guide is available in English and worth the expense.

MUSEION

Contemporary and modern art have been the realm of Museion (Via Dante, tel. 0471/977-116, www.museion.it, €3.50) since 1987, and in spring 2008 the foundation moved into a new site worthy of the international collection on display. The new facility is a concave, glass-fronted building with a spacious interior that hosts themed exhibitions, events, a cafeteria, and the mandatory museum shop. The nearby *casa atelier* is a workshop for resident artists that can also be visited.

Entertainment and Events

Festa degli Schützen is the day all archers of Bolzano dream about. The arrows fly on the last Sunday in May in a contest that dates from the Middle Ages. It's also an occasion to watch locals parade by in traditional costumes and see folk dancers high-step it while the communal band plays. Also in May is **Festa dello Speck** (tel. 0471/300-381, www.speckfest.it), when local producers bring their finest smoked hams to town and prove once and for all that all *speck* doesn't taste the same.

Summer is devoted to music and dance. In June, every street, piazza, theater, and pub is a potential stage for the musicians that descend upon the town during **Jazzfestival** (tel. 0471/927-777, www.jazzfestivalbz.com). Concerts are free and several big names usually headline the event. For two weeks in July, dancers and choreographers animate **Bolzano Dance** (tel. 0471/304-130, www.bolzano-danza.it), which also organizes workshops, classes, and seminars for anyone interested in what happens behind the curtain.

There's never any danger of not having a white Christmas in Bolzano, and each year streets are brightly lit and traditional carols provide a continuous soundtrack that gets even humbugs into the holiday mood. Piazza Walther is the center of festivities and home to a **Christmas market** that begins in late November and runs until just before the big day. The 80 booths sell handmade ornaments, wooden sculptures, glass, ceramics, and traditional sweets. Revelers stay warm with tea and *vin brulé.*

On New Year's Eve, Associazione Laeuferclub Bozen (Portici 46/II, tel. 0471/979-901) organizes the **Boclassic** run through the town. Streets can be slippery but there's a good deal of camaraderie, similar to a polar bear club outing.

Nearly every town in Alto Adige has a band, and some have two. You'll hear them tuning

Bolzano's Christmas market

their instruments on Saturday afternoons in the church or community hall as they prepare to animate another festival or holiday. Each band is made up of a minimum of 20 instruments (horns are very popular) and distinctive costumes. **Stadt Kapelle Bozen** (info@stadt kapellebozen.it) are the local Bolzen group. They wear red and green lederhosen and have a wide repertoire of folk tunes they regularly play indoors and out.

Shopping

Bolzano has been a crossroads for merchandise transiting between Northern and Southern Europe for 1,000 years. There's still a strong culture of trade and many shops selling traditional crafts in the center. Via dei Portici and Via Museo are well stocked with one-of-a-kind shops, and if you can't find a souvenir here you won't find one anywhere. The former culminates in Piazza Erbe and a daily fruit and vegetable market where locals love to exchange small talk. There are dozens of weekly and monthly markets in the piazze

around town and artisans display their work on the first weekend of every month in Piazza del Grano and throughout December in Piazza della Mostra. If you prefer boutique over rustic, browse the exclusive shops on Via delle Mostre or the modern porticoes of Corso Libertà on the other side of the Talvera bridge.

Accommodations

Stadt Hotel Città (Piazza Walther 21, tel. 0471/975-221, www.hotelcitta.info, €90–125 s/d) is hard to beat for location. The grand four-story building overlooks Piazza Walther in the heart of Bolzano. There's a pleasant café under the arcades on the ground floor that serves double cappuccinos. Rooms are a mix of modern and Central European decor. Some are equipped with waterbeds. The fitness center is free for guests.

The Bergers treat guests like family and if you ask for directions there's a good chance they'll show you the way. **Hotel Post Gries** (Corso Libertà 117, tel. 0471/279-000, www.hotel-post-gries.com, €79–100 s/d) is modern in a sort of

Howard Johnson way. It can come as a relief after nights of wondering if the shower will work. The breakfast buffet is served inside or out and always includes an excellent strudel.

Franz Staffler was tired of the usual kitschy hotels with wood interiors that make tourists gasp. He had something more modern in mind, and the interior of the 🏝 **Hotel Greif** (Piazza Walther, tel. 0471/318-000, www. greif.it, €170 d) is a clear sign that design has arrived in Bolzano. The 33 rooms are decorated with Iranian carpets, African baskets, and furniture fresh from the factory. Best of all are the paintings, sculptures, and photographs that give the hotel an art gallery–like quality. Before heading out on the town, stop by the Grifoncino lounge, which might start a trend in mountain minimalism.

Food

🏝 **Cavallino Bianco** (Via Bottai 6, tel. 0471/973-267, Mon.–Sat. noon–3 P.M. and 7–11 P.M., €8–11) is an authentic *gasthaus* (guesthouse) with centuries worth of cooking behind it. Locals in traditional dress or workers with blue overalls crowd into this *osteria* moments from Piazza Walther. The three big rooms are never empty and the buzz of conversation begins around midday. Dinners eat elbow to elbow on long wooden tables and most opt for the *gulasch,* Wiener schnitzel, or the *salsicce di casa* (house sausage). Portions are generous and the restaurant is usually less animated at night.

Bozner was the first beer made in Bolzano. It's brewed at **Hopfen & Co** (Piazza delle Erbe 17, tel. 0471/300-788, Mon.–Sat. 11:30 A.M.–3:30 P.M. and 7 P.M.–midnight, €7–10), which occupies three floors overlooking the historic piazza. The ground floor is divided into two dining rooms that are especially welcoming in winter. The menu presents many roast dishes, along with *weisswurst* served with a sweet mustard and *bretzel,* a very distant cousin of the New York pretzel. The upstairs rooms are more modern, tables are arranged intimately, and service is slower.

Along Corso Libertà, **Avalon** prepares delicious gelato without the use of preservatives.

Paolo Coletto only uses seasonal fruits from the Venosta Valley and the strawberry, apricot, and wild berry flavors all deserve space on a cone. A **market** is held every morning in Piazza delle Erbe; locals come here to buy fresh fruit, vegetables, cheeses, and cured meats like the *speck* ham that makes a great panini.

Information and Services

The **APT office** (Piazza Walther 8, tel. 0471/307-000) publishes a guide for walkers who want to explore the woods, high plains, or mountains around town. It costs €2 and is available in English.

Getting There and Around

Bolzano is immediately off the A22 and can be easily reached from Milan via the A4 or Rome with the A1 until Modena. There's a direct train from Milan every morning at 7:05 A.M. Otherwise it's necessary to transfer in Verona for a total travel time of around 3.5 hours. The Eurostar train from Rome leaves at 9 A.M. and pulls into Bolzano at 4:08 P.M.

Aeroporto di Bolzano (tel. 0471/255-255) is a small regional airport south of the city where propellers outnumber jet engines. Air Alps in collaboration with **Alitalia** (tel. 06/2222) operates four flights a day from Rome. A round-trip ticket averages around €130, with some fluctuation depending on the season.

Around Bolzano

There are three cableways that leave from Bolzano and take passengers 1,000 meters up to the high plains above the city and unparalleled views of the Dolomites. Each makes for a half- or full-day excursion along the many trails above town, or simply a quick panoramic round-trip. **Colle** is the oldest cableway in the world; anyone with a fear of heights should rest assured the infrastructure has been modernized since the original lift opened. You can visit one of the original cars near the ticket office. **Renon** is the longest and it stops at the town of the same name five kilometers up to a pristine Alpine lake. **San Genesio** drops travelers near a small mountain village with several lodges perfect for anyone who wants to spend the night a kilometer above sea level.

Strada delle Dolomiti is a panoramic 100-kilometer Alpine road that starts in Bolzano and winds its way up to the Passo di Costalunga in the Val di Fassa. Drivers may need oxygen as some stretches are over 2,000 meters above sea level. The road passes the region's only surviving glacier near Mount Marmoralda, and if you continue east, it eventually enters Veneto and reaches the world-famous resort of Cortina.

◖ ORTISEI (SANKT ULRICH)

Ortisei and the Gardena Valley are a mecca for winter sports and a regular stop on the World Cup downhill circuit. There are 275 kilometers of trails with 84 lifts and a ski pass that allows skiers to test all the moguls. The resort is also home to some of the best craftsmen in the region and many fine examples of woodcarving can be seen inside the local museum and church of St. Ulrich. The center is off-limits to cars, so once you've parked it's better to travel by cable car.

Sights

Woodworking started as a hobby in the valley and still keeps locals busy during long winters. The tradition in Ortisei and Val Gardena goes back centuries and developed into an industry as objects were exported across Europe. A visit to **Museo Ladino** (Piazza Sant'Antonio, tel. 0471/797-554, mid-March–Oct. Tues.–Sun. 10 A.M.–6 P.M., Sept.–mid-March Wed.–Fri. 2–6 P.M., €6) can illuminate this ancient tradition. There's a large collection of sculpted nativity scene figures as well as non-religious animals that took months to whittle. To see live woodcarving and a gallery full of handiwork, stop by **Unika Galaria** (Typakcenter, Via Arnaria 9, tel. 339/179-2227, daily 10 A.M.–noon and 2–7 P.M., admission free).

Sports

Swimming pools might seem out of place in the Alps, but there are several large aqua complexes in Alto Adige. **Mar Dolomit** (Promeneda 2, tel. 0471/797-131, www.mardolomit.com, daily 9:30 A.M.–8 P.M., €8.50/€16.50 sauna) is open

rugged Dolomite peaks near Ortisei

© ALESSIA RAMACCIA

year-round and provides visitors with swimming and sauna options in a family-friendly facility, including an outdoor pool with a long water slide. An on-site restaurant allows you to splash around all day long.

There are a half-dozen shops that rent snowboards and skis. Most also sell passes to the nearby resorts. If you need equipment, try **Olympic Seceda** (Strasse Val d'Anna 2, tel. 0471/786-242) or **Carlo's** (Strasse Rezia 71b, tel. 0471/798-225). The trails around Ortisei are rather limited, so experienced skiers are better off riding the cable car up to **Alpe di Siusi,** where the real fun starts. The majority of runs are blue (medium level) and the season lasts December–April. Unless you like waiting in lines, avoid mid-February and the week around Easter, when Italians hit the slopes en masse.

First-time cross-country skiers can test the one-kilometer-long Minert trail or the scenic Pinei, a short distance from town on the road to Castelrotto. Seasoned athletes can follow the 60 kilometers of woodland trails above town. A half-day ski pass in high season is €29, a full day is €39; if you plan on remaining on the slopes for over a week, it's worth getting the **my dolomiti skicard** (www.dolomitisuperski.com). Sledding is also very popular and **Rasciesa,** on the edge of Ortisei, is a six-kilometer run open day and night. Sleds are available at **Panoramalift Rasciesa** (Via Resciesa, tel. 0471/796-174, www.resciesa .com, winter daily 9 A.M.–4:30 P.M., summer daily 8 A.M.–5:30 P.M.).

Accommodations

Mark Hofer transformed the family bed-and-breakfast into a small hotel that he runs with great enthusiasm. **Garden** (Via J. Skasa 68, tel. 0471/796-021, www.gardenhotels.it, €90 d) overlooks town and most guests set out from the chalet-style lodge early to explore the trails along the Gardena Valley. They make a point of returning in time for dinner, especially the hard-to-resist dessert buffet. Winter evenings are spent around the fireplace sipping mountain grappa.

Hell may not sound like a place you'd want to spend a holiday, but you might change your mind after a few days at █ **Hotel Hell** (Via Promeneda 3, tel. 0471/796-785, www.hotel-hell.it, €110 d). This year-round accommodation on the outskirts of town has a variety of room types, ranging from a comfortable standard to an immense duplex apartment. All are soundproofed and most come with terraces overlooking the pool. During the winter, you can practically ski back to the hotel and a restaurant with a menu that changes weekly.

Food

Anna Stuben (Strasse Vidalong 3, tel. 0471/793-615, Tues.–Sun 7–9 P.M., €14–20) is a gourmet restaurant, which means they bring out dishes covered with metallic domes and when these are removed it's hard not to gasp or at least take a photograph. Armin Mairhofer is the maestro here; he is as concerned with preservation and flavor combinations as with the ingredients he shops for himself in local markets. The dining room puts stomachs at ease and has a way of cheering up even the grumpiest guests. Everything is made of wood in this *stuben* (traditional Alpine room), from the floors to the ceilings to the cabinets and solid chairs. The restaurant is on the ground floor of the Hotel Gardena Grödnerhof, with a good view of the Gardena Valley.

Choosing between Tyrolean classics or pizza isn't easy at **Terrazza** (Strasse Sneton 9, tel. 0471/796-366, daily 7:30 A.M.–10:30 P.M., €8–12). A daily menu provides another economic option that fills dinners up with polenta and lots of different sausages. The restaurant gets crowded at lunch, but there's usually no problem finding a seat at one of the checker-clothed tables.

Getting There and Around

Ortisei is 30 minutes northeast of Bolzano. Exit the A22 at Chiusa-Val Gardena and continue along the N242d for 15 kilometers. **SIT** (Bolzano, Via Crispi 10, tel. 0471/415-480, www. sii.bz.it) buses depart frequently from the Bolzano and Bressanone train stations and make numerous stops along the Gardena Valley.

MERANO (MERAN)

Merano was a Roman frontier town and home to an important marketplace during the Middle Ages. It didn't expand beyond the medieval walls until the 18th and 19th centuries, when the Art Nouveau craze left a mark on many of the palazzi around town. Except for the small, dense historic center that induces claustrophobia, the rest of Merano is very green and spread out in a haphazard way along the Passirio River, which provides a nice walk towards the old Roman bridge and tree-lined boulevards of the new town.

Sights

The Gothic duomo, built between 1367 and 1495, has a plain facade with a single rose window and what looks like a football goalpost above the doorway. Many architects worked on the building, which explains the lack of symmetry. Inside are two ornate wooden altars and stained glass recounting scenes from the New Testament. Statues of the apostles were carved by an Austrian artist back when the town was under Vienna's influence.

The duomo is near the **Steinach** neighborhood, which has retained traditional houses with exposed wood beams on the exterior. **Via dei Portici** is the most characteristic street that runs from the church to Piazza del Grano. Both sides of the street are a succession of arches and colorfully painted houses with occasional murals.

Entertainment and Events

On Easter Monday, the clip-clop of horse and carriage can be heard on the cobblestoned streets of Merano. Riders wear colorful folk outfits (as do the horses) on the way to the Maia Bassa track, where **Corse degli Avelignese** (tel. 0473/272-000) races are held in the afternoon. Many of the horses also pull wagonloads of tourists around the countryside in their spare time.

Ippodromo Merano Maia (via Scuderie 37, tel. 0473/446-222) holds many races during the year, but the Kentucky Derby of Alto Adige is the **Gran Premio Merano,** which has been held each September since 1935. The track can be reached on the 11 or 12 bus.

Sports and Recreation

Merano Thermal Baths (Piazza Terme 9, tel. 0473/252-000, daily 9 A.M.–10 P.M., €9.50 for 2 hrs., €10.50 for 3 hrs., €14 day pass) is the most relaxing place in town. It's also a great example of glass and steel architecture where hikers can recover in the pool and sauna zones. There's a restaurant with a low-cal menu and a hotel attached to the complex for anyone who wants to prolong the feeling of tranquility.

On the right bank of the river **Passer Promenade** offers a pleasant stroll under palm trees and a series of "living" sculptures. Dozens of cafés and *gelaterias* line the way making it a popular weekend destination.

Accommodations

Sittnerhoff (Via Verdi 60, tel. 0473/221-631, info@bauernhofurlaub.it, open Mar.–Nov., €30pp) is a beautiful rural residence with flowers overflowing from the windows and a mural on the facade. It's a 10-minute walk to the nearest café in Merano or the Parco Naturale Gruppo di Tessa. There are three doubles all decorated with simple country beds. If you haven't played ping-pong in a while, this is the place to reacquaint yourself with a paddle. The pool has a marvelous view of the mountains.

If the Addams Family were on holiday in Alto Adige, they'd feel at home at **Castello Labers** (Via Steinach 25, tel. 0473/448-553, €110 d). The spacious medium-size hotel is full of nooks and crannies that haven't been overly refurbished or gentrified. It still smells like a castle and the antique furnishings and solid oak beds suit the rooms perfectly. There are wonderful views of vineyards and Merano in the distance.

Food

Named after the Austrian princess, **Sissi** (Via Galilei 44, tel. 0473/446-282, Tues.–Sun. 12–3 P.M. and 7–10:30 P.M., €10–13) serves a seasonal menu that combines traditional and contemporary dishes based on the area's local cured meats and cheeses. Dining is inside an elegant 19th-century building where waiters look after diners with great attention.

Artemis (Via Giuseppe Verdi 72, tel. 0473/446-282, closed Jan.–Mar., daily noon–3 P.M. and 7–11 P.M., €11–15) is close to the center and a good place to have Sunday brunch. On weekends, a small ensemble plays classical music and if you arrive early there's a good chance of getting a table outside.

Getting There and Around

Merano is 28 kilometers north of Bolzano. Drivers can choose from the N38 freeway, which runs west of the Adige River, or the slower local road on the other side, which passes through a half-dozen small communities. Most trains from Bolzano leave at 5 and 35 minutes past the hour. Journey time is around 30 minutes.

◖ TRENO DELLA VAL VENOSTA

If heading towards Malles Venosta, consider the Treno della Val Venosta (tel. 0473/201-500, www.fer roviavalvenosta.it) that skirts Parco di Stelvio and follows the old Imperial Roman road. It's a beautiful ride and bicycles can be taken onboard or rented at most stations along the way. If time is tight, take the four-hour round trip (€10) or the two-hour-plus round-trip (€6.50), but for €14 you can get a bike and helmet in Merano, hop on one of the dedicated bike trains that depart every two hours, and get off whenever the scenery inspires you to start pedaling. From Merano, colorful state-of-the-art trains head east towards the Swiss border and Parco di Stelvio. Treno della Val Venosta passes 60 kilometers of the most remote landscape in the region with four stops along the way. It's wise to pack a picnic lunch.

Around Merano

Merano's mild, near-Mediteranean climate and rich vegetation has been recommended by doctors since the 19th century as a cure for all sorts of illnesses. The most famous patient was Elisabetta d'Austria (aka Princess Sissi), who spent two long stints in **Castel Trauttmansdorf** (Via San Valentino 51, tel. 0473/235-730,

Mar.–Nov., daily 9 A.M.–6 P.M., until 9 P.M. in summer, www.giardinidisissi.it, €9.80). The botanic gardens around the castle are home to 5,400 plants and the garden paths lead to a splendid panoramic platform. Guided visits cost €4.50 and last 90 minutes; otherwise, there's an audio guide (€2.50) available in English from the ticket office.

MALLES VENOSTA (MALS IM VINSCHGAU)

Malles Venosta is a frontier town close to the Austrian and Swiss borders. It was a customs point where traders in the Middle Ages were required to declare goods they imported into the region. There are several Gothic churches that can be spotted from a distance, but the eye tends to be distracted by jagged peaks that rise in every direction.

Two kilometers south of Malles is the medieval gem of **Glorenza,** surrounded by perfectly preserved walls and **Castel Coira,** which gets military historians into a fluster.

Sights

San Benedetto (Via San Benedetto 31, Jul.–Aug. Fri. 3 P.M.) is the oldest of the Gothic churches and is also the simplest. The 9th-century building is made of local stone quarried in the surrounding hills and the frescoes inside recount the religious trials and tribulations of its patron. In June, September, and October, visits must be arranged one day in advance with the tourist office (Via San Benedetto 1, tel. 0473/831-190).

Sports and Recreation

Nordic walking started in Scandinavia in the 1990s and quickly spread throughout Europe, including the Alps. Ski poles are all it takes to enjoy this sport, which could also be described as mountain speed walking. There are many trails in the Venosta Valley and a new 7.8-kilometer course was opened in 2007 on the road towards Glorenza. If you'd like to spend a couple days walking from village to village, **Alta Venosta Vacanza** (tel. 0473/831-190) can help plan an itinerary.

Twelve kilometers north of Malles are the lakes of Muta and Resia, where the Adige River starts. The N40 road to the lakes is steep and scenic with several spots where drivers can pull over to admire the view. At San Valentino on the northern tip of Lago di Muta, there's a cable car (tel. 0473/634-603, year-round) that takes riders up to an elevation of 2,149 meters. The ride lasts under 10 minutes but there are hours worth of trails to follow before returning to the valley.

Accommodations

Garberhof (Via Nazionale 25, tel. 0473/831-399, €140 d) is a typical Swiss-style chalet with 29 modern rooms overlooking the valley. The hotel is on the edge of town and has several terraces where guests can take the sun in any season and catch up on their reading. The pool is open June–early September, and the restaurant is a reliable option after a day navigating the winding roads in the area.

Food

Pobitzer Klaus runs the kitchen at **Garberhof** (Via Nazionale 25, tel. 0473/831-399) and combines international flavors with German and Italian specialties. The interior is on the romantic side, and waiters light candles as soon as diners sit down. There's a buffet with plenty of fresh salads and vegetable dishes, meats are grilled during the summer, and typical Tirolese plates featuring *wurstel* and sauerkraut are available all year long.

Vegetarians can stop pulling their hair out. **Greif** (Via Generale Verdross 40a, tel. 0473/831-429, Mon.–Sat. noon–3 P.M. and 7–11 P.M., €8–12) has a complete menu of local vegetables that the able chef transforms into Tyrolean specialties. In the summer, there is seating along the shaded narrow street and a selection of white wine that should satisfy most amateur sommeliers.

Getting There and Around

Malles is easily reached by car from Bolzano along the N38, which takes a sharp left after Merano and runs parallel to the Adige River all the way to Malles. Train service is also available from Trento, Bolzano, and Merano.

◖ GLORENZA

Small, even by medieval standards, Glorenza—just south of Malles, on the edge of Parco Nazionale Dello Stelvio—gained city status in 1304 due to the important market held on Piazza Città. Little has changed since then and the 15th century walls that form a trapezoid around the narrow porticoed streets look as good as new. There are towers on each of the corners and three entrance gates that lead to the central piazza where a weekly market is still held and many of the 800 inhabitants buy their fruit.

Porto Sluderno is the most convenient entrance and the town can be visited alone or with a guide who divulges the secrets of the best-preserved ramparts in the region. The walk takes two hours and begins at the Associazione Turistica Glorenza in Piazza Municipio (tel. 0473/835–224).

Castel Coira (Sluderno, tel. 0473/615-241, www.castelcoira.com) has the largest private weapons collection in the world with enough shields, swords, and rifles to equip a small army. The castle lies on the outskirts of town and you'll need an hour to see it all.

Accommodations

◖ **Gruner Baum** (Piazza Città 7, tel. 0473/831-206, www.gasthofgruenerbaum.it, €150 d), the 15th-century palazzo that dominates Piazza Città, has been a hotel since 1730, but has received a makeover since then and now combines modern interiors with antique furnishings. All 10 rooms have dark wooden floors, white walls, and comfy beds. There's a lot of attention to lighting and in the hallway you'll find the town's oldest bicycle. Meals are served on the ground floor dining room or on the terrace overlooking Parco dello Stelvio. Half-board is available at a reasonable cost.

Post (Via Flora 15, tel. 0473/831-208, www.hotelpostglorenza.com, €44 pp includes breakfast) is a three-star hotel in the center of town with a mix of modern and traditional rooms. There is an abundance of wood furniture and

© ALESSIA RAMACCIA

Parco Nazionale dello Stelvio is home to ibexes and chamois.

many of the beds are elaborately carved. Half and complete board are available, and meals are served in one of three cheerful dining rooms where tables are decorated with flowers during the spring and summer. There's an ample garden with a small playground for kids and plenty of Alpine atmosphere to breathe in.

Food
Restaurants in Glorenza serve mostly Tirolese dishes, and *speck* (ham) figures heavily. **Ristorante Stambecco** (Via Flora 9, tel. 0473/831-495, Tues.–Sun. 12:30–3 P.M. and 7–10:30 P.M., €9–12) is one of the friendliest places in town. Don't be put off if waiters start describing the specials in German. They can quickly switch to Italian or English and are happy to describe the difference between one *wurstel* and the next. In winter a lot of soups are served, and the main dishes generally involve roasted pork or lamb. Travelers fond of meat and potatoes won't be disappointed. **Ristorante Pizzeria Renate** (Via Flora 39, tel. 0473/831-198) is the fast-food option, with great pizza that proves a good pie can be baked well above sea level.

Information and Services
Associazione Turistica Glorenza (Piazza Municipio 1, tel. 0473/831-097) can help sort out accommodations and provide a map of town and the many hiking options outside the town walls.

Getting There and Around
Glorenza is five kilometers south of Malles. **SII buses** (tel. 800/846-047, www.sii.bz.it) leave from the train stations in Merano or Malles. The journey from Malles takes about 15 minutes.

PARCO NAZIONALE DELLO STELVIO
Italy's largest national park lies on the border between Lombardy and Trentino-Alto Adige. It's in the northeast corner of the region and deserted compared to the densely populated towns and cities along the Po River. The Dolomite Mountains dominate the area, and although the glaciers recede a little more every year, there are endless trails for hikers to admire Alpine lakes, peaks that reach nearly 4,000 meters, and eagles that accompany visitors from above.

Information and Services

On the Lombard side, the park is best entered from Bormio or Potedilegno. The former is more accustomed to receiving visitors and slightly larger. There's also a thermal bath in the center and two cable cars near the river that carry people up the mountain. The only Internet point is **Valtline** (Bormio, Via Roma 87, tel. 03/4290-2424, www.stelviopark.it). Banca Intesa is on the same street and provides ATM and exchange services. If you're planning a picnic, stop by **Pozzi La Sceleira,** also on Via Rome where most of the town's businesses are concentrated.

Consorzio del Parco Nazionale dello Stelvio (Bormio, Via Roma 26, tel. 03/4291-0100) provides updated weather conditions (essential in winter) and detailed maps, and can arrange for guided tours of the park's valleys, lakes, and mountaintops. A similar office in Potedilegno is located on Piazzale Europa (tel. 03/6490-0721).

Mountain bikes can be rented from **Alta Valtellina** (Bormio, Via Monte Braulio 34, tel. 335/710-8156, www.mtb.stelvio.net). Between June and September, they also run a school and offer 17 itineraries across all types of terrain and altitudes.

Getting There and Around

Bormio is 200 kilometers from Milan and the journey by car takes around three hours. Drive towards Lecco on the SS36 until Colico then take the SS38 straight into town. During the summer, **Perego** (tel. 03/4270-1200, www.busperego.com) buses (€16) leave from the Lampugnano subway stop (MM1) in Milan at 7:15 A.M. on weekends. If getting up that early isn't appealing, take the train to Tirano and the Perego shuttle (€3.50) the rest of the way. It runs daily and leaves 10 minutes after the train arrives.

Around Stelvio

◀ VAL CAMONICA

Val Camonica (Camonica Valley) is a glacier-formed valley south of Stelvio that features over 180,000 Neolithic engravings both outdoors and within the numerous caves. Neolithic drawings continue to be discovered and many of the best-preserved images are concentrated around **Capo di Ponte** in the **Parco Nazionale delle Incisioni Rupestri** (Nadro di Ceto, Via Piana 29, tel. 03/6443-3465, www.arterupestre.it, Tues.–Sun. 9 A.M.–6 P.M.). You'll find the Naquane rock here covered with hundreds of figures and primal hunting scenes. There are four possible itineraries and guides can be hired from **Museo Nazionale della Valcamonica** (Via Roma 23, tel. 03/6434-4301, Tues.–Fri. 8:30 A.M.–2 P.M., €3). If you bring along paper and pencil, this is a great place to make rock rubbings. **Centro Camuno** (Via Mancini 7, tel. 03/644-2091, Tues.–Sun. 9 A.M.–6 P.M., www.ccsp.it) nearby studies the prehistoric settlements that once dotted the valley and periodically exhibits its finds.

BRESSANONE (BRIXEN)

In the Middle Ages, Bressanone was the religious and political capital of a vast area and the town's location at the point where the Isarco and Rienza Rivers converge was a major factor in its development. The bishop of Sabiona moved his headquarters here in the 10th century and the subsequent building boom resulted in a half-dozen churches and palazzi. On the other side of the Isarco is the Stufles neighborhood that was outside the ancient walls, where medieval craftsmen went about their trades and traditional wood-carving shops still operate.

Sights

Porta Torre Croce leads into the medieval core of town. Here narrow alleys are clustered around the duomo and **Palazzo Vescovile,** which was once the bishop's residence. The palazzo now houses **Museo Diocesano** (Piazza Palazzo Vescovile 2, tel. 0472/830-505, Tues.–Sun. 10 A.M.–5 P.M., €4) and a collection of rare Middle Ages relics, as well as **Collezione di Presepi,** which displays the handiwork of local artists.

Many houses are painted in pastel colors and arcades along Via Portici Maggiori protect locals during the harsh winters. The facade of the duomo is squeezed between two twin bell towers. Inside there's the 15th-century **Krenzgang** (tel. 04/7283-6401) in which the vaulted ceilings are covered with frescoes.

Entertainment and Events

MERCATO DEL PANE E DELLO STRUDEL

On the last weekend of September Piazza Duomo becomes the gastronomic capital of Alto Adige. Mercato del Pane e dello Strudel (11 A.M.–7 P.M.) is a chance to watch bakers prepare 70 different types of loaves (*Schuttelbrot* and *paarl* are two of the most popular flat breads) and decide whether you prefer raisins or pine nuts in your strudel. The piazza is covered with stands selling *speck,* cheese, and many local desserts. Event info available from the APT office (Bahnhofstraße, tel. 0472/836-401, www.brixen.org).

Accommodations

Although the **Dominik** (Via Terzo di Sotto 13, tel. 0472/830-144, www.hoteldominik.com, €110 d) is relatively new as far as buildings go all the furniture inside is antique and provides this luxury chain with a pleasant rustic atmosphere that's popular with romantics. The 36 rooms look out on a small garden and guests who want to stretch their legs after a meal in the hotel restaurant can take a walk on the banks of the Rienza or in the nearby park.

Food

If you've already tasted the standard yellow polenta, then you may want to try the black version served at **Fink** (Via Portici Minori 4, tel. 0472/834-883, Thurs.–Tues. noon–2:30 P.M. and 7–10:30 P.M., €8–11). It's popular with locals, who dine outside or in the neatly arranged interior decorated with Alpine furniture. The wine list is extensive and they serve a notable array of dumplings stuffed with a variety of meat and vegetarian fillings. **Oste Scuro** (Vicolo Duomo 3, tel. 0472/835-343, Tues.–Sun. 12:30–3 P.M. and 7–11 P.M., €9–12) is a few steps from the duomo in one of the oldest buildings in the center. Nevertheless the chef isn't a slave to tradition and enjoys revitalizing traditional recipes.

Getting There and Around

Bressanone is 30 kilometers northeast of Bolzano on the A22 or N12. The town is on the region's main train line and there are frequent departures from Trento and Bolzano.

From the train station, Viale Stazione leads directly to the historic center five minutes away by foot. Taxis waiting outside the station can get you there faster or to any of the hotels on the outskirts of town.

BRUNICO (BRUNECK)

Halfway along the Rienza Valley lies the fortified town of Brunico. The castle at the highest point of the historic center was founded by Bishop Bruno in the 13th century. The town's origins go back to the Romans, who built an ancient rest area along a road that connected the Danube with the Adriatic. Today the walls serve only to impress tourists, who play a major role in the local economy.

Sights

Via Pacher is the natural entrance to the old town and the Gothic church of Salvatore built along the city walls in 1412 and later enlarged to its present proportions. **Via Centrale** is the most characteristic street, with a series of highly ornamental palazzi. Many have family coats of arms above the front doors and **Palazzo Sternabach** (Via Ragen) is a good example of local architectural preferences.

The closer you get to the **castle** (Vicolo Castello, tel. 04/7455-5722, Mon.–Sat. 10 A.M.–1 P.M. and 4–7 P.M.), the steeper things get. The imposing medieval fortress was erected on Roman foundations in the 13th century and has commanding view of the river below. It was expanded many times over the years and recently given a modern restoration treatment.

Museo Etnografico (Via Duca Diet 24, tel. 0474/552-087, Apr.–Oct., Tues.–Sun. 9:30 A.M.–5:30 P.M., Sun. 2–6 P.M., €5) in the outlying village of Teodone (less than 10 kilometers northeast) is a folklore museum that preserves local costumes and gives visitors a chance to experience life as it was like back in the 16th century. The highlight is the restored farmhouse and barn, but there's also a very nice restaurant in the museum.

Accommodations

If you prefer your furniture made out of plastic, you'll be disappointed by **Andreas Hofer** (Via Campo Tures 1, tel. 0474/551-469, www.andreashofer.it, €115 d). Everything here is wood and the beds have traditional headboards found only in the province. The pool is set in a small garden and the family that operates the hotel also serves classic sausage and sauerkraut platters in the restaurant.

Food

Oberraut (Ameten, Via Ameto 1, tel. 0474/559-977, summer daily noon–3 P.M. and 7–11 P.M., fall, winter, and spring Tues.–Sun. noon–3 P.M. and 7–10 P.M., €9–11) is a typical Tyrolean restaurant with hand-carved wooden chairs and a fireplace that sees a lot of action during the winter when the smell of *canederli* fills the dining room. In autumn, the owner regularly reconnoiters the hills for mushrooms. If the menu leaves you undecided, try the fixed-price option, which provides a sample of everything. Desserts are not lacking.

Getting There and Around

By car, from Trento or Bolzano, follow the A22 until the Bressanone/Val Pusteria exit and continue along the N49 for 25 kilometers. Train passengers must transfer at Fortezza for the local service to Brunico. The **cableway and skilifts** (Brunico, Michael Pacher Str. 11a, tel. 0474 555447, 8:30 A.M.–4:30 P.M., www.kronplatz.com) in nearby Plan de Corones are open all summer and a round trip costs €11.

Around Brunico

Twenty kilometers east of Brunico is Dobbiaco, famous for the Dolomiti Balloon Festival (tel. 0474/972-458, www.balloon festival.it) held in the second week of January. Balloonists from around the continent come to fly over the Dolomites and give anyone with enough nerve the thrill of a lifetime. Flights last half-a-day and should be reserved in advance. The basket holds five, including the pilot and enough ballast to make it over the highest peaks. If you do decide to brave the skies make sure to dress for sub-degree temperatures in the atmosphere above Dobbiaco.

Throughout July, the town presents dozens of orchestras and ensembles interested in a single composer. Gustav Mahler was Dobbiaco's most famous guest and **Settimane Musicali Gustav Mahler** (tel. 0474/976-151, www.gustav-mahler.it) celebrates his stay in the area and his music.

VIPITENO

This northern town 14 kilometers from the Austrian border has a strong Tyrolean flavor and has benefited from its mineral-rich waters for centuries. It's divided into an old and new town—a bit of a misnomer considering Città Nuova was begun in 1443 after a fire ravaged the city.

Sights

Before rushing into the *centro storico*, it's worth stopping by the **Ospedale Civico,** on the street of the same name, that was founded by Teutonic Knights in 1241. There are two churches in the immediate vicinity with highly elaborate frescoes.

Via Città Nuova is the main artery through town and is porticoed most of the way. In the courtyard of **Palazzo Comunale** are reminders of the town's Roman past, including a sculpture of the Goddess Mitra from the 3rd century A.D. Any nobles and bishops who happened to be passing through town would lodge at the **Casa dei Principi.** The nearby **Torre Città** in Piazza Città marks the division between the old and new town and was restored after the fire of 1867. The Santo Spirito church, also on the piazza, was a stopping point for ancient pilgrims and lies next to the **Museo Multscher** (Via Commenda 9, tel. 0472/765-325, Tues.–Sat. 9:30 A.M.–12:30 P.M. and 2–6 P.M., €2.50), where Hans Multscher's ornate wooden altar is kept.

Festivals and Events
ⓒ MERCATINO DI NATALE

Christmas is a great time to visit Alto Adige. Nearly every town puts up a tree and organizes a Christmas market. In Vipiteno lights get strung up on the edges of the clock tower in Piazza Città where the **Mercatino di Natale** (tel. 0471/999-999) could teach Santa's workshop a thing or two about toys. The stalls appear after advent and outdoor tables with portable heaters are set up for enjoying the festivities at night. *Vin brulé* is the prefered way of keeping warm and best accompanied by a slice of *zelten,* a traditional holiday fruit cake. Don't worry about the masked devils walking the streets on December 6th. Those are the *Krampus* who carry whips and are the evil ying of Saint Nikolaus' good yang. If you're interested in doing some Christmas market hopping make sure to also visit Bolzano, Merano, Brunico, and Bressanone.

Sports and Recreation

Many of the region's rivers are navigable by raft and after the snow melts in spring, rapids can be quite challenging. **Rafting Sterzing** (Zona Sportiva di Sterzing, tel. 0472/765-660, www.raftingsterzing.it) in Vipiteno offers 10 itineraries along the Isarco River and adjacent valleys. An easy ride down the 12 kilometers to Le Cave lasts three hours and costs €36 per person. Wetsuits, life preservers, helmets, and instructions on how to avoid the rocks are provided by Robert Schifferle and his certified guides.

Accommodations

Hotel Schwarzer (Piazza Città 1, tel. 0472/764-064, www.schwarzeradler.it, €100 d) is pleasantly located in the central piazza and all 35 rooms have good views of the historic center. There's an indoor pool and sauna facility that's convenient for eliminating after-ski aches. The hotel restaurant is as good as any in town and the terrace provides excellent views of the surrounding mountains.

Food

The large restaurant at **Hotel Schwarzer Adler** (Piazza Città 1, tel. 0472/764-064, www.schwarzeradler.it, Tues–Sun. 7–11 p.m., €100 d) doesn't stray far from tradition, and there are fixed-price three- (€29) and four-course (€39) options that provide a solid introduction to the region's culinary delights. The interior is cozy, and all four rooms have an Alpine feel that is soothing. The wine list is quite extensive, and dessert includes freshly made strudel.

Located on Vipiteno's main street, **Kleine Flamme** (Città Nuova 31, tel. 0472/766-065, Tues.–Sun. noon–3 p.m. and 7–11 p.m., €10–14) provides distinctive local cuisine within an elegant 16th-century building. Some people come just for the wine list and the impeccable service.

Getting There and Around

Vipiteno is the last town off the A22 conveniently reached by rail or road. Be careful, however, not to catch one of the slow trains that stops in Brenner or Fortezza. The direct journey from Bolzano should last under an hour.

Around Vipiteno

If you've made it to Vipiteno, it's just another 15 kilometers by car to Austria and the Brenner Pass, which links Northern and Southern Europe. Besides the chance to set your foot down in another country, you'll be following in the footsteps of Romans who passed through on their way to conquer the Danube and German and Austro-Hungarian forces who traveled south in their long occupation of Trentino-Alto Adige.

VENICE, VENETO, AND FRIULI-VENEZIA GIULIA

Like the waters of the Adriatic, the regions of Veneto and Friuli-Venezia Giulia have been influenced by the tides of history. Both regions were vital frontier areas for the Romans, who founded the cities of Vicenza, Padua, Verona, and Treviso along an extensive road network. Later the Republic of Venice created a naval empire, allowing it to amass wealth that can be seen in the architecture and artworks of the region's towns and cathedrals. Here natural and manmade beauty compete for the traveler's attention.

La Serenissima (Her Most Serene) is the Italian name synonymous with Venice. Sensual, elegant, exotic, and fragile, Venice's orientation toward the East gives it a quality unlike other major Italian cities and unlike any other city in the world. The sea, the lagoon, and the canals have a peculiar quality, luminosity, and mystery that have attracted a variety of artists over the years. Almost any visitor would concur that Venice is the world's most romantic city, with enough of a thread of melancholy to keep it real. Leave plenty of time to navigate this radiant city, whether it's a sail around the lagoon, a *vaporetto* ride, a ferry to the Lido, or a glide through the canals at midnight on a gondola.

Move outside of Venice and you arrive in cities with ancient underpinnings, such as Padova and Verona, which trace their roots back even before the Romans arrived. The Veneto region is as varied as Venice is extravagant. Travel to Belluno and Cortina and you can see the very mountains that Titian had in view while creating his masterpieces, stroll along the river

© JUDY EDELHOFF

HIGHLIGHTS

⟪ Grand Canal: Venice's main waterway features one ornate palazzo after another. Although you can see parts of the canal from the Ponte degli Scalzi or Rialto Bridge, the only way to see all of this incredible stretch of Venetian history is on board a *vaporetto* (page 348).

⟪ San Marco: It may be a magnet for tourists and pigeons but Venice's San Marco neighborhood, with Piazza San Marco as its center, took Napoleon's breath away for a reason. The Basilica San Marco and Palazzo Doge that line the piazza were built to stun and the Gothic architecture that once housed the city's rulers remains impressive inside and out (page 349).

⟪ Dorsoduro: The Dorsoduro is a bustling neighborhood in Venice where university students and old-time residents rub shoulders in the Campo Santa Margherita. The canals that run through the area are bordered by impressive palazzi like the Ca' Rezzonico (page 358).

⟪ Carnevale Venezia: Carnevale Venezia is Venice's main street party. Bring your own costume or buy or rent one at a Venice costume shop and join in the festivities (page 366).

⟪ Torcello: When Venetians want to get away from it all they head to Torcello. The small island in the northern corner of the lagoon houses the area's oldest cathedral and the throne where Attila the Hun held court (page 390).

⟪ Cappella degli Scrovegni: Giotto's style of painting in Padova's Scrovegni Chapel, which he completed in 1305, led the world in a new artistic direction. His vivid figures express emotion in various ways, from Christ's physical rage in *Expulsion of the Merchants* to grief in *Lament over the Dead Christ* (page 396).

⟪ Teatro Olimpico: Architect Andrea Palladio created an astonishing number of villas, churches, bridges, and theaters that still influence contemporary architects. Teatro Olimpico stands out for its enchanting 16th-century stage decorations still in use today (page 402).

⟪ Anfiteatro Arena: The world's third-largest amphitheater, once the stage for mock battles, gladiator contests, public executions, fairs, and bullfights, now hosts a prestigious opera and concert season. Take a tour or catch an evening performance (page 407).

⟪ Trieste: The city of Trieste, one of Northern Italy's best kept secrets, features a first-rate aquarium and city center. The city has lots of character with hints of Austrian, Slovenian, and Italian culture in the architecture and food (page 415).

VENICE

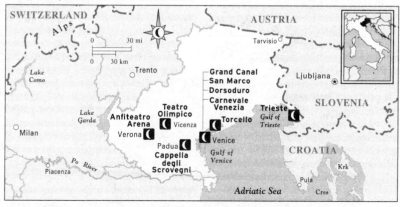

LOOK FOR ⟪ TO FIND RECOMMENDED SIGHTS, ACTIVITIES, DINING, AND LODGING.

VENICE

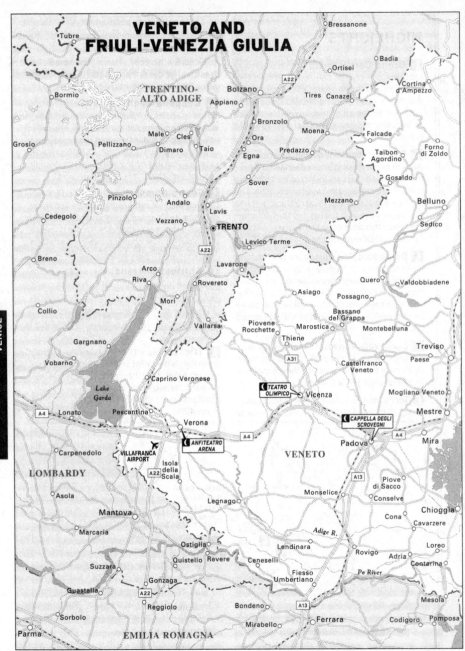

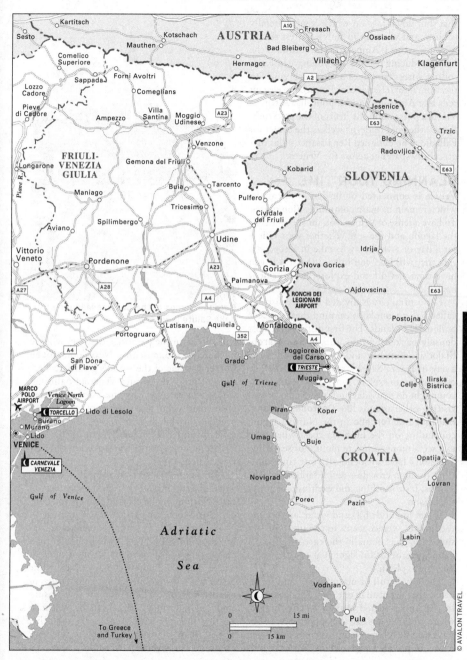

© AVALON TRAVEL

that shot down logs on which Venice literally is built, and wind up in Italy's hottest ski resort at Cortina d'Ampezzo. Travel toward the wine-producing regions and you have hillsides rolling with grapevines and superb wines to try, from light, effervescent Prosecco to elegant reds like Amarone and Valpolicella. A trip to Vicenza puts you in the heart of the gold rush, that is, the gold trade, as well as the center for Palladio, who designed Renaissance villas that gracefully span out across the Veneto.

PLANNING YOUR TIME

Venice is connected by bridges and canals, which remain its main communication routes. To have a sense of Venice, you must experience the lagoon and the sea. Whether your visit is for a day or a week, try to take in a *vaporetto* ride that will lead you toward the sea. If you have time, get off and explore; if not, ride it back.

The central city is divided into six districts called *sestiere,* but keep in mind that Venice is built on 117 islands. The first district and most densely packed with visitors is **San Marco.** Major sights are here and you could while away a day in Piazza San Marco. Pick at least one other *sestiere* to explore, too. If you have a week, you might do two a day and spend a day or two visiting other islands like **Certosa, Murano, Burano,** and **Torcello** in the North Lagoon, concluding on the **Lido** sea coast where you can see a more complete picture of seafaring. You don't have to spend all your time shuffling through crowds—rent a sailboat or take lessons. It's a soothing and exciting way to see the lagoon.

When high tide hits and water laps up into the squares, Venice seems to rise up from—or sink into, as is actually the case—the sea, a hauntingly beautiful sight that testifies to its precarious plight.

The city is full of masterpieces and fortunately they're not all in one spot. Spend an hour in the under-visited **Museo Archeologico,** where great masters had the opportunity to observe and sketch much of this collection when it was in private hands. Many of the figures

© PURESTOCK

Baroque domes of the Basilica Madonna della Salute in Venice

will appear in the paintings that you will see in churches and museums. Next door, **Museo Correr** has one of the world's greatest collections of pre-17th-century Venetian painting, where you can see why these painters were great colorists but also masters of form. Don't overlook the churches, interesting not only historically and architecturally, but for the rare chance to enjoy art in the space for which it was created.

Plan on at least one great meal in Venice, where the star is bounty from the sea. Lagoon crabs, shrimp, mollusks, and fish are in abundance and some are particular to this area.

Try Prosecco, a sparkling Veneto wine was invented in the 19th century to be lighter than champagne and come to market more quickly. There is also an endless choice of local white Soave and red wines including Valpolicella, or relative newcomers like Amarone that was introduced in the mid-20th century by winemakers that tinkered with Valpolicella and other grapes. Many wines are impossible to find back home or even in other parts of Italy, so ask for suggestions at the better restaurants and *enoteche*, where they will gladly guide you to new taste sensations.

Venice still produces some of the crafts that it has traded in for centuries, like textiles, gold, and glass. Disappearing are the lace makers, but a few are left stitching intricate designs.

For all its richness and glory, Venice is a great equalizer of class when it comes to street life. Traditionally the poor lived in the same block as the wealthy and were not segregated in different neighborhoods. Even the wealthiest Venetian that wants to conduct business or pay a call must walk and use the same street as mere mortals. There are no limousines in the center. Venetians mingle and see one another every day, several times, on the streets. The count, CEO, or socialite knows the trash collector, mailman, baker, and others by name. They'll have a coffee at the bar together, where even the humblest can offer his neighbor a few minutes of banter before they are on their parallel ways.

About three-fourths of the residents seem to be over 75, which leaves little future for the few young that remain unless they enter the tourism industry in some way. The late 20th century brought about soaring prices and an exodus of Venetians from the city, who can no longer afford it or find fewer services for residents in a city that caters so well to tourists.

All that wine and gold that arrive in Venice from the Veneto makes an interesting entrance for the visitor, too. Although Verona has its own airport, the closest airport for most international flights is in Milan. Either way, Verona makes an ideal start. It offers a bit of everything, from ancient Rome with its Arena, to the medieval world of Romeo and Juliet, and a modern business center that attracts major trade shows from Italy's most important wine expo to furniture, horse, and boat shows. A short hop northeast to Vicenza offers the Renaissance elegance of Palladio's architecture, from the good life in the country villas to theater and church design. Their harmonious proportions seem to transmit a sense of well-being and tranquility. The area is full of villas that date from the 16th–19th centuries, where you can visit or even stay or dine, a wonderful way to prolong and savor the experience. From Vicenza you can swoop north to enjoy Bassano del Grappa and Marostica, easily done in the same day. Then head further north to Belluno and Cortina d'Ampezzo. Or from Vicenza you can head south first toward Padova, a town with its own medieval and Renaissance charms, as well as the towns in the Eugenée Hills with their thermal waters and spas. From Belluno or Padova you can head to Treviso, for a canal town that's lovely but very much oriented toward 21st-century life rather than the tourism on which Venice thrives. If you have difficulty finding a room in Venice or find it too steep for your budget, Vicenza, Padova, Treviso, and smaller towns scattered among them make for a delightful base and are an easy hop on the train for day trips to Venice. You'll return to a lovely setting that offers a welcome break from the throngs of San Marco in Venice.

Venice is an ideal departure point to head for Friuli Venezia Giulia. Here you'll find influences evident from the ancient Romans to the Austro-Hungarian Empire that dominated Venice, too. Breezy light sea ports and towns lead into hills and Alps, where the strong influence of Middle European culture is present, evident in folk traditions and food from Austria, Hungary, and Slovenia. You can drive or take the train directly to Trieste, then meander back down through Udine, Aquileia, Grado, and other points. Or make your stops on the way to Trieste, then hop a boat to points in Slovenia or Greece. Or from Trieste take a northerly route west skirting the Alps for mountain scenery across Friuli to Cortina d'Ampezzo and come down through Belluno, which lets you do both regions without backtracking.

HISTORY

Built on wooden pilings by early refugees fleeing barbarian attacks in the early Middle Ages, the city was settled almost 1,000 years later than Rome or Florence, where trade with Etruscans and Greeks was already well established.

Early Venice in Torcello dates to the 5th century, when Attila the Hun invaded and plundered the Veneto from the north. Mass migration from the mainland to the lagoon islands intensified as the Longobards swept through the following century. The first doge was elected in 697, although the first to be documented was Doge Orso Ipato in 726. In 774, Venice requested Charlemagne's assistance to push the Longobards out of the region. Venetian merchants stole the body of St. Mark from Alexandria, Egypt, in 828 and four years later the first Basilica San Marco was completed.

The First Crusade for the Holy Land in 1095 departed with ships and supplies from Venice. In the year 1000, having rid the Adriatic Sea of pirates, Doge Pietro Orseolo celebrated the occasion with the first Marriage of Venice to the Sea, an annual ritual that continues to the present. The *sestieri,* the six districts of Venice, were established in 1171 and the Rialto Bridge went up two years later. In 1204, having defeated Constantinople, Venice brought back booty that included the four golden bronze horses once poised atop San Marco. By the end of the century, Marco Polo set forth from Venice on his famous journey to China. Fifty years after his journey, the bubonic plague wiped out half the population and would decimate the city again in the 16th and 17th centuries. In 1380, Venice rebounded to become the Mediterranean maritime superpower when it defeated Genova in the Battle of Chioggia. The 15th century brought two of Venice's greatest artists, Giovanni Bellini and Titian, into the world. That artistic genius was followed in the next century by Vicenza architect Andrea Palladio and painters Tintoretto and Veronese. It's also the century in which the Jews were rounded up and confined to the Venetian Ghetto.

The Republic came to an end in 1797 when Napoleon invaded the Veneto and the last Doge abdicated. By 1815, the Austrians had driven the French out of Venice, just in time for Lord Byron to swim up the Grand Canal in 1818, a new twist on the Grand Tour. A more efficient way of entering the city was established in 1846 when the first train line linked the city to the mainland. Death in Venice became the rage, not only did Thomas Mann write about it, but in the 19th century composer Richard Wagner and poet Robert Browning made their final exits here. The first art Biennale was established in 1895 and the first Venice Film Festival opened in 1932, although the stars had to fly in elsewhere because the airport wasn't opened until 1960.

Having been abandoned after the decadent 1700s, Carnevale was revived in the 1970s. Not long after, Venetians began a slow exodus caused by a high cost of living with the tourist invasion. Fewer opportunities in services and employment outside the tourism sector has left a population little more than 50,000, of which more than two-thirds are over 70. Venetians, when you see them, are indeed an endangered species.

Venice

Made up of more than 100 islands, Venice, like the love goddess Venus, seems to rise up from the sea. Historically, its role as a seafaring town and trade center brought openness perhaps unequaled by other Italian cities. Its trade with Asia opened it to new ideas, goods, and lifestyles that came in and out of the port, as well as by land routes. The heady aroma of exotic spices and perfumes mingled with the sea air and added a sensual component unrivaled by other Italian city. That East-meets-West atmosphere is evident in many ways from grand architectural expressions to textile design and spices used in favorite dishes.

Hospitality is nothing new to Venice, where doges had to entertain visiting ambassadors and dignitaries and foreign merchants needed a base from which to conduct business. Even when at war with the Ottoman Empire, the Turks continued trade in their section of town.

Venetian women, who participated freely in the antics of Carnevale, made a startling impression on other European visitors. Carnevale attracts visitors even today for the beauty of the costumes, although now it is an event staged more for tourists than as the spontaneous celebration that was once its trademark. Even so, it still offers the allure of changing one's identity and of an all-out celebration before continuing on about the daily business of life, even if one doesn't follow with the traditional Lenten period of abstinence and sacrifice. If the Carnevale crush is not for you, Venice is not at a loss for pageantry. Throughout the year you can find festivals that celebrate the mystical marriage of the doge with the sea, or others that celebrate the city's gratitude for good health and deliverance from the plague. Regattas are great fun and often very decorative. Most of them have some theatrical aspect, from costumes to decorated boats to fireworks, as well as solemn religious processions.

The Grand Canal that curves right through the center of the city not only is a major communication route, it's Venice's prime real estate. For centuries Venetian socialites have whiled away entire cocktail parties or lute recitals sizing up whose residence faces the Grand Canal and how much of it.

Venice's signature blown glass, textiles, velvets, silks, sculptures, and Renaissance paintings reflect back the light, textures, and colors that make this city so radiant. And the goldsmiths of the Veneto still turn out more gold than any other market, working it into magnificent jewelry and decorative objects.

Journeying around Venice is part of the fun, whether it's the heady experience of zipping around in a water taxi or gliding on a gondola or simply strolling into a back alley with beautiful lighting where water threatens to lap over the sidewalk, it adds up to moments to be savored.

More than ever before, Venice makes it easy for the visitor to discover some of its mysteries. A series of English-language walking tours, some newly introduced in 2007, from the sacred to profane can show you how to visually "read" the

religious symbols in St. Mark's or can elaborate on the world of an 18th-century courtesan.

Venice awakens your senses with sights, sounds, smells, and tastes—not so exotic that you feel disoriented but different enough to become completely enchanted.

SIGHTS

St. Mark's Square is one of the world's most beautiful squares and is justifiably famous. The museums are also first-rate here, like Museo Correr, Palazzo Doge, Museo Archeologico, Peggy Guggenheim, and Accademia museums. Be sure not to miss the details of the palaces and the rooms as you walk through. If you haven't had time to read up on history and art before you arrive, take advantage of some of the museum, church, and walking tours. They will help you understand much more about the intricate workings of government and society that make history come alive. A guided tour through the Doge's Palace, for example, will lead you into the world of political intrigue, a balance as delicate as the natural habitat of the Venice Lagoon, while another shows you secret passages. They will explain and show details that you may not even notice otherwise that brings life into the beautiful forms you see. A tour through St. Mark's Basilica explains imagery that perhaps any illiterate medieval Venetian understood, but that might be lost on a 21st-century visitor who steps in from a different religious and social context. A full immersion even for just an hour or two will enrich your experience considerably. As you learn about symbols here, you'll enjoy looking for clues in art that you see in other churches and in other cities.

The churches in Venice are splendid temples of architecture, revered holy places that along with the spiritual offer their own earthly masterpieces. Santa Maria del Giglio is home to the only Rubens painting in Venice, with a luminous fleshy and fashionably Renaissance Madonna with her exuberant child. On the Giudecca, Santissimo Redentore, the Renaissance church designed by Andrea Palladio, remains very much a vital part of Venetian life.

VENICE

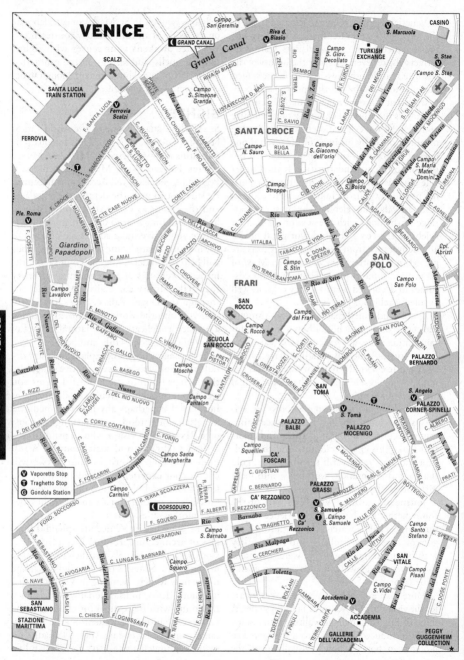

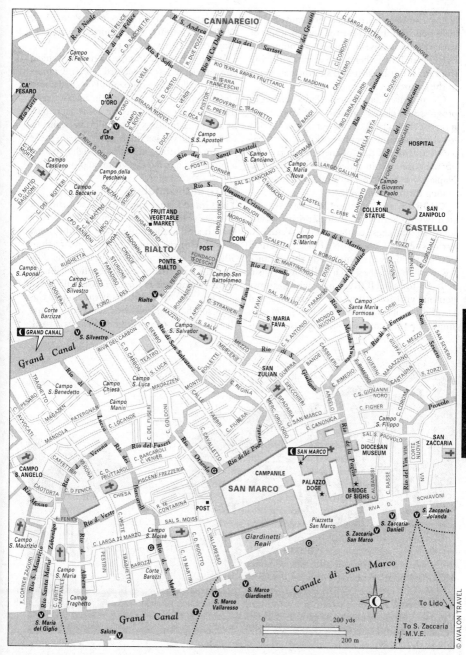

VENICE

Many churches have excellent acoustics, an ideal opportunity to hear the compositions of native Antonio Vivaldi and other composers. Both he and his father could earn their living from the art of music thanks to the patronage of the Church.

On any given day you can find a concert in progress in a church, an option if Venice's famous opera house has sold out or is a bit rich for your budget. Opera lovers know that Venice's La Fenice is part of the famous triad of opera houses that includes those of Milan and Naples, the three most prestigious in Italy and among the top worldwide.

CHORUS, the Venetian Churches Association (www.chorusvenezia.org), organizes visits to 16 churches scattered across Venice in various *sestieri*. They also offer a combined pass that will save you money on the entrance fee to all 16 churches, each well worth a visit. It is €8 for a CHORUS pass which allows you one visit to each of the 16 churches and is valid for one year. Without the pass, each single entrance costs €2.50. The pass is available at the CHORUS office (San Polo 2986, tel. 041/275-0462, www.chorusvenezia.org, Mon.–Sat., 10 A.M.–4:45 P.M.).

When you're plannning your time in Venice, remember the less frequented *sestieri*: Cannaregio, Castello, Dorsoduro, San Polo, and Santa Croce. Try to spend some time in at least one of these. Not only will you get out of the main tourist crush, each has its own important sights to see and when you get further off the main paths you can get a better sense of each neighborhood's identity and its unique rhythms and traits.

◖ Grand Canal

The Grand Canal moves like a serpent in a reverse "s" to form what even a 15th-century French ambassador called "the world's finest street" with the "finest houses." More than 500 years later, you are likely to agree. The Grand Canal is not a neighborhood, but it spans five of Venice's *sestieri*. (Castello is the odd one out) If you begin at the Grand Canal's southern end where it spills into Canal di San Marco, to your right on the east bank

the Grand Canal

© PURESTOCK

you'll have palaces like Palazzo Gritti, Palazzo Barbaro, Palazzo Macenigo, Palazzo Fortuny, Palazzo Grimani, and Palazzo Forsetti Loredan. Just after you go under the Rialto Bridge is Fondaca dei Tedeschi, former German warehouses and now a post office, all still within the *sestiere* of San Marco. As you continue north, the palaces of Cannaregio will appear, like the once-gilded Ca' d'Oro, the Casino, Palazzo Gritti, and the train station at Fondazione Santa Lucia. As you begin along on the west bank to your left the Dorsoduro *sestiere* shows off Basilica Madonna della Saluta, the Peggy Guggenheim Collection, Palazzo Barbarigo, the Gallerie dell'Accademia as you pass under the Ponte Accademia, and Ca' Foscari. You'll then pass the *sestieri* of San Polo and Santa Croce, where you'll see Ca' Pesaro and Piazzale Roma. When you pick up a map, make sure it's detailed like the Hello Venezia map that clearly shows these palaces. Some are now museums or hotels, while others are private residences.

The best way to explore the Grand Canal is on a **vaporetto** (water bus). Calling it a water bus, though, robs it of its allure. Mass transportation it is, but Line 1 glides from one end of the Grand Canal to the other past historic palaces. The real joy is using *vaporetti* to island hop for a grand tour of the Venice North Lagoon (Line 41 or 42) to Certosa, Murano, stopping for lunch in Burano or Torcello, then on to a view of the sea and dinner at the Lido.

San Marco

Venice's most famous district and one of its smallest, San Marco is where most visitors begin. Venice's main square, **Piazza San Marco,** is elegant, grand, lively, and exotic with its elaborate basilica, soaring bell tower the Campanile, Doge's Palace, Correr Museo, and arcade with lovely cafes and shops. The Piazzetta leads from St. Mark's Church to the canal. The island across from the Piazzetta, **San Giorgio Maggiore,** belongs to this *sestiere,* too. During the warmer months, the live music from two cafe orchestras in Piazza San Marco is cherished as much by residents as by tourists. In this grand, expansive, outdoor marble salon, you're likely to sense that for centuries other footsteps have brought intrigue, merriment, flirtation, and debate to this most glorious of meeting places. Even Venetians can be spotted here, taking their late afternoon *aperitivo* in a cafe or exchanging greetings in their sing-songy, clipped dialect with its slight lisp. The sense of East-meets-West is immediate here, with the church itself a blend of Byzantine and Western styles. The oldest part of the *sestiere* of San Marco is between Piazza San Marco and the Rialto; the area along the Grand Canal was built later. It's crowded, so be sure to move on and explore other parts of this *sestiere* and beyond.

PALAZZO DOGE

Palazzo Doge (Piazza San Marco 1, tel. 041/520-9070, www.museiciviciveneziani.it, Apr.–Oct. Tues.–Sun. 9 A.M.–7 P.M., Nov.–Mar. Tues.–Sun. 9 A.M.–5 P.M., closed Dec. 25 and Jan. 1, €12 or €18 Museum Pass good for 6 months and many more museums) is the doge's residence and the seat of Venetian government. The Venetian government, a superpower in its heyday, functioned with intricate checks and balances of power. Tour through their council chambers, delicately decorated residential apartments, and prison cells that were connected with the Bridge of Sighs. The world's largest oil painting, by Tintoretto, is here, as are works by Titian, Veronese, Vittoria, and Tiepolo. Note the anonymous suggestion box in the upper level. Book an English-language tour for a good background; a Secret Passages Tour is given three times in the morning.

BASILICA SAN MARCO

Built by an unknown architect to replace an earlier church, **St. Mark's Basilica** (Piazza San Marco, tel. 041/522-5205) was designed to enshrine the body of St. Mark and to reflect the ever-increasing power of the Venetian Republic. So rich in detail and crowned with five huge domes, it's almost impossible to fathom in one visit. Look for the four horses above the facade (replicas of the original bronzes are now

VENICE

THE WORLD'S LARGEST PAINTING

Imagine that you had the power and funds to commission the largest canvas painting in the world. In 1582, Venice held a competition for exactly that – to paint **Paradise in the Great Council Chamber of the Doge's Palace** (Piazza San Marco, tel. 041/520-9070, www.museicivicive neziani.it). That magnificent room in the Doge's Palace was the epicenter of political power in the Venetian Republic. The doge and his counselors occupied a dais along the eastern wall, above which was a massive fresco of *The Coronation of the Virgin*, known as *Il Paradiso*, painted in about 1365 by the most famous local artist of the day, Guariento. The painting deteriorated, then was irreparably damaged by fire in 1577, and a decade later was covered by Tintoretto's huge canvas painting, *Paradiso*, which remains to this day.

Why was a religious subject chosen – first in the 14th and again in the 16th centuries – for the chamber that housed the highest authority of secular government within the Republic of Venice? And why did the government give the commission to Tintoretto? Competition was fierce. Prestigious artists like Paolo Veronese, Francesco Bassano, Jacopo Palma the Younger, and the final – but not the first – winner Tintoretto competed; perhaps also competing was "foreigner" Federico Zuccari, an unsuccessful candidate for an earlier competition for San Rocco School. Initially the commission was awarded to two artists: Paolo Veronese and Francesco Bassano. However, perhaps due to their differences the work was still incomplete in 1588 when Veronese died suddenly. The commission was then awarded to Tintoretto, who painted this work 1588-1592, assisted by his son Domenico. Palma the Younger (1548-1628), who had submitted one of the most innovative compositions, was appointed to paint a *Last Judgment* in the Sala dello Scrutinio, the room that led to the Great Council Chamber.

inside the church museum), the elaborately carved doorways (the central one shows the Labors of the Months), the early 15th-century gilded St. Mark and angels atop the central arch, and elaborate 17th-century mosaics that show scenes from the life of St. Mark. Inside a masterpiece of the goldsmith's art is the 10th-century Pala D'Oro, made of 250 panels each adorned with gems and enamel. Much of the church reflects the influence of Byzantium in details like the mosaics in the enormous central Ascension Dome and the icon of 11th-century Archangel Michael in the Treasury. A free tour in English offered by the Patriarch's Office (tel. 0441/241-3817, by reservation) will explain the Biblical significance of the mosaics.

TORRE DELL'OROLOGIO

The clock face on Torre dell'Orologio (Piazza San Marco, tel. 041/520-9070, €12 includes admission at Correr and Archaeological Museums and Marciana Library) has beautiful gold stars and signs of the zodiac in relief on a blue background. It faces the sea, and once provided useful information for ships and merchants. The Clock Tower (1496–1499) reopened in 2007 for public visits, which let you see the complex clockwork and walk out onto the upper terrace for a splendid view of Piazza San Marco and much of the city.

MUSEO CORRER

The Picture Gallery of Museo Correr (Piazza San Marco 52, te. 041/520-9070, Apr.–Oct. Tues.–Sun. 9 A.M.–7 P.M., Nov.–Mar. Tues.–Sun. 9 A.M.–5 P.M., closed Dec. 25 and Jan. 1) has one of the world's best collections of Venetian Renaissance paintings, and includes great masters like Lorenzo Veneziano, the Bellini family, Carpaccio, Lorenzo Lotto, and Antonello da Messina. The neoclassical rooms beautifully display the early 19th-century sculpture of Antonio Canova, an artist that was also a skilled diplomat and managed to bring back to Italy some of the art treasures carted off to France by Napoleon. The museum hosts excellent temporary shows like the 2007 John Singer Sargent and Venice exhibit. Inquire about free guided tours of the

© PURESTOCK

Piazza San Marco

Biblioteca Nazioanle Marciana (www.marci
ana.venezia.sbn.it), which you enter through the
Correr Museum. All the museums in Piazza San
Marco offer a single ticket of €12 which is valid
for admission to Palazzo Doge, Museo Archeologico, Museo Correr, and the monumental
rooms of the Biblioteca Nazionale Marciana.
Special exhibits may require a separate ticket,
which costs less if purchased at the same time
you purchase the museum ticket.

MUSEO ARCHEOLOGICO
One of Venice's most unjustly overlooked
museums is Museo Archeologico (Piazza
San Marco 52, tel. 041/520-9070, Apr.–Oct.
Tues.–Sun. 9 A.M.–7 P.M., Nov.–Mar. Tues.–
Sun. 9 A.M.–5 P.M., closed Dec. 25 and Jan. 1).
Renaissance artists could sketch classical works
from ancient Greece or Rome bequeathed by
16th-century curators of the Statue Collection,
Domenico and Giovanni Grimani. Often these
figures were later depicted in their own paint-
ings. Egyptian works were added from the
Correr collection.

BIBLIOTECA NAZIONALE MARCIANA
The library overlooking St. Mark's Square,
Biblioteca Nazionale Marciana (San Marco
52, entrance at Museo Correr, Tues.–Sun.
9 A.M.–5 P.M.), is decorated with 16th-century
paintings, some with Venetian sea battles or
maritime traffic jams, and has some rare and
beautiful maps and globes.

PALAZZO FORTUNY
The Gothic Palazzo Fortuny (Campo San
Beneto, tel. 041/520-9070, hours and admission vary according to current exhibitions) once
belonged to the Pesaro family and opens only
when a special exhibition is on. The former
palace residence and atelier of Mariano Fortuny shows the owner's flair for textile design,
photography, painting, and stage design.

PALAZZO GRASSI
Facing the Grand Canal, Palazzo Grassi
(Campo San Samuele, tel. 041/523-1680, www.
palazzograssi.it, hours and admission vary)
was built in the 1730s and now is also used for

temporary exhibitions. The 1496 **Clock Tower** shows the signs of the zodiac and the phases of the moon and sun on its face, but is most famous for the **Two Moors** that strike its bell.

The bell tower, **Campanile** (Piazza San Marco, tel. 041/296-0630, daily 9 A.M.–3:45 P.M., closed Jan., €6), was completed in 1912 to replace the previous tower. It was first used as a lighthouse in 1173, later served as a medieval torture chamber, was restored after a 16th-century earthquake, and suddenly collapsed in 1902, killing the custodian's cat.

PIAZZETTA DEI LEONCINI

Next to the clock tower, Piazzetta dei Leoncini takes its name for the two porphyry lions in the square, symbols of St. Mark, of Venice, and of power. The church here, now deconsecrated, was once dedicated to San Basso and the Palazzo Patriarchale with a 19th-century neoclassical facade. The Patriarch of Venice transferred here in 1807 from San Pietro di Castello when San Marco became the cathedral of Venice. Near the square's center is an ancient well.

Castello

Castello is the largest of Venice's six *sestieri* districts and was probably once the site of a fort. Here vestiges still remain of Venetian daily life, with laundry strung across side streets off the wide **Viale Garibaldi.** The only noise is the squeaking of a clothesline being pulled, a man carting home his groceries on a wooden wagon, an old opera disc playing an aria, water lapping against the side of a palazzo, and the occasional loud blast of a fog horn at sea. These are sounds that you can't hear and sights you won't see unless you leave the crowds of San Marco behind. This is the Venice that makes your heart ache at the thought of leaving, with quiet canals and expanses of green in the Public Gardens. (Venetian supremacy was linked to its sea power, which depended heavily on its ability to build and repair galleys.)

NAVAL MUSEUM

The **Arsenale's** earlier use probably was to store arms, weapons, and rigging. By the 14th century, teams of carpenters, sawyers, caulkers and their apprentices worked to get ships afloat. Today the Italian navy still occupies part of this area. For most visitors, however, Arsenale is synonymous with Venice Biennale, the major world art exposition that takes place here every odd year. The Naval Museum (Ex Granai della Repubblica, Castello 2148, Arsenale, tel. 041/520-0276, www.marna.difesa.it, Mon.–Fri. 8:45 A.M.–1:30 P.M., Sat. 8:45 A.M.–1 P.M., closed holidays, €1.55) covers the history of the navies of Venice and later Italy, with navigational instruments, model ships and fortresses, and relics of a decorated galley.

SAN PIETRO DI CASTELLO

San Pietro di Castello (Campo San Pietro, open mornings and late afternoons, closed midday, admission free) is early Christian Venice on its own little island. This was the original cathedral of Venice, dating back over 1,000 years. Built in the 9th century, San Pietro became the cathedral of the Venetians with its own bishop in the 15th century, power that passed to St. Mark's Basilica in 1807. Old-timers are likely to be chatting on benches in Campo San Pietro, while other residents pass by walking dogs. Inside the marble throne is said to be the Chair of St. Peter, used by the apostle in the Orient, which ironically has verses from the Koran on its back. There are paintings by Paolo Veronese and Luca Giordano among others.

To reach San Pietro di Castello from Arsenale, walk east across Calle Largo San Pietro, the bridge that spans Canale di San Pietro, to reach San Pietro Island.

ISLAND OF SANT'ELENA

Southeast of the Arsenale and across the bridge from the Public Gardens is the Island of Sant'Elena, with a 12th-century church and convent dedicated to St. Helen. The island is home also to the **Naval College** and the soccer stadium, **Campo Sportivo Gianluigi Penzo** (Fondamenta Sant'Elena). You'll find breathing room in Castello and the green shade of **Giardini Pubblici,** the public gardens that Napoleon had created by draining marshland.

CAMPO SAN MARTINO

At the southwest corner of the Arsenale is Campo San Martino. The Church of St. Martin was founded in the 7th century by refugees from the Veneto mainland and dedicated to the first non-martyr saint in Christianity. At age 15, St. Martin (316–397) joined the Roman army, the period of the famous episode of Martin sharing his cloak with a poor man, a story that you can see in a 15th-century bas-relief in the Oratory of the School of St. Martin and also painted in 8th-century frescoes. Martin was known as Apostle of the Gauls for his evangelizing work with pagans in the countryside and miracles that accompanied him. Inside just above the entrance to the church is a mammoth organ, enlarged and modernized in 1799. Just below it is a striking vividly colored Last Supper painted in 1549 by Gerolamo da Santa Croce. The present church, redesigned in 1546 by Jacopo Sansovino, has an unusual floor plan in the shape of a square with two chapels on each corner.

CAMPO SAN FRANCESCO DELLA VIGNA

On Castello's northern side near Fondamenta Nuova is San Francesco della Vigna. One of several churches dedicated to St. Francis (1182–1226), San Francesco della Vigna is also dedicated to the vineyard that was given to the Franciscans in 1253, less than 30 years after the saint's death; it became the site of their monastery and church. Rebuilt by Jacopo Sansovino in 1534 in the form of a Latin cross, the harmonious Renaissance facade (1562–1572) was designed by Andrea Palladio. Inside is Veronese's 1562 altar piece, Sacra Conversazione (the Holy Conversation). San Francesco's cloisters remain firmly in 14th-century medieval Gothic style.

CAMPO SAN ZANIPOLO

On Castello's northwest end near Fondamenta dei Mendicanti is Campo Santi Giovanni e Paolo, more easily said in Venetian dialect as Campo San Zanipolo. This square, once known as the "square of the marvels," is where the June Regata dei Santi Giovanni e Paolo concludes

with ceremonies and awards after the winner arrives at the Mendicanti Bridge, named for a church and hospital once dedicated to lepers. Begun by Dominican friars in the late 13th century and completed in the 15th century, Chiesa Santi Giovanni e Paolo and Chiesa dei Frari remain two grand examples of Venetian Gothic architecture. Both are final resting places of doges, of whom at least 25 are buried here. The interior has five apses and notable art that includes Giovanni Bellini's polyptych (a multi-paneled painting), Lorenzo Lotto's *The Almsgiving of St. Anthony,* paintings by Vernonese, and a window made by Murano glassblowers.

CAMPO SANTA MARIA FORMOSA

South of the Rio di Santa Maria narrow canal is Campo Santa Maria Formosa. Reconstructed in 1492 from an 11th-century building, it has three busts of Admiral Cappello, conqueror of the Turks, on its facade. Inside the gray and white interior takes the form of a Latin cross. Especially noteworthy are paintings by Barolomeo Vivarini, Palma the Elder, and Gimabattista Tiepolo. Outside the bell tower has 17th-century reliefs that even include a masklike grimacing face, influenced by ancient images as well as Venice's rage for the theater in that century. From the rear of the church, the bridge leads to **Palazzo Grimani,** where visiting artists would have been able to sketch ancient Greek and Roman sculpture, donated to the city of Venice and now in the National Archeological Museum. If what you've really been longing for is to be whisked into the private world of a noble's palace with period furniture, **Palazzo Querini-Stampalia** (Santa Maria Formosa, Castello 5252) grants your wish. Your host is absent—Count Giovanni donated the palace, furniture, art, and documents to Venice in 1868—but along with his art collection he left a splendid library to be used in his apartments and the Foundation Querini-Stampalia (www.querinistampalia.it) to run it.

CHIESA SAN GIORGIO DEGLI SCHIAVONI

Near Ponte dei Greci is Chiesa San Giorgio degli Schiavoni. San Giorgio has a fresco cycle of paintings dedicated to Saints George, Tryphon, and Jerome. Famous for slaying the dragon in Libya, where he saved the king's daughter, George is portrayed in one scene in knight's armor charging on his gray stallion as he lances the beast. St. Tryphon liberated an emperor's daughter from the devil. Jerome was a scholar famous for translating the Bible into Latin for early Christians and for his trials in the desert. Not surprisingly, Jerome is patron saint of librarians, archivists, writers, editors, and translators. In one famous episode, Jerome extricates a thorn from a lion's paw. The nearby school Istituto Ellenico has **Museo Dipinti Sacri Bizantini** (tel. 041/522-6581, 9 a.m.–5 p.m., €4) a collection of Byzantine icons from Greece, Crete, and the Veneto that date from the 14th–18th centuries. Greeks, present in Venice from the 11th century, significantly increased in numbers during the Renaissance and in the 16th century were given permission to practice their own Orthodox rites.

SANT'APOLLONIA CLOISTER

Across the canal from the Doge's Palace and north of the Bridge of Sighs, the patron saint of linen weavers had a church and school for weavers dedicated to her. Sant'Apollonia Cloister (Ponte della Canonica, Castello 4312, www.museodiocesanovenezia.it) now has a collection of religious objects from abolished churches, a beautiful Romanesque cloister, and occasional temporary exhibits, such as religious engravings by Dürer.

CAMPO SAN ZACCARIA

Campo San Zaccaria is a tranquil break from nearby Riva degli Schiavoni crowds. When Benedictine nuns occupied the convent, they closed off the entire square at night. Founded in the 9th century, the Chiesa San Zaccaria has a 10th-century Romanesque crypt, while the ground floor reflects its Venetian Gothic transformation in the 15th century. Note the brilliant colors in Giovanni Bellini's 1505 *The Holy Conversation* and the altarpieces by Antonio Vivarini and brother-in-law Giovanni

d'Alemagna. The nuns hailed from super-rich families that ensured they lived well while there and then left plenty of money to the church when they died. They lived as freely as other members of their class, entertaining the elite with balls, masquerades, and performances in the 18th century. Even Casanova himself is said to have enjoyed their company. In the 21st century, the convent is considerably less lively—now it's a *carabinieri* (police) station and there are no nuns to arrest for disturbing the peace. Two hotels on the square would have made great observation posts, and now are handy for modern Casanovas or more demure guests that arrive at the San Zaccaria *vaporetto* stop.

RIVA DEGLI SCHIAVONI

Unless it's too crowded with tourists to move, at the southeast corner of the Doge's Palace along Canale di San Marco, Riva degli Schiavoni makes for a lovely walk, day or night, to see activity on the canal or the movement of boats and ships. It's also ideal for a sunny coffee or lunch. The Schiavoni or Dalmatians were the first people conquered by the Venetians in what now is mostly Croatia. The *riva* leads into the southern end of the Castello district toward the Arsenale.

Cannaregio

Cannaregio's name either comes from **Canal Regio,** the most famous canal after the Grand Canal, or from a bed of *canneti* (reeds) that once grew in this marshy land. Cannaregio is Venice's second-largest *sestiere* and is the first seen by visitors who arrive by train. The Grand Canal flows along its southern boundary, where the 19th-century arrival of the railroad transformed this manufacturing district into a residential area. About a third of Venice lives here. One of the *sestiere*'s most famous 13th-century residents was Marco Polo. The famous "golden house," Ca d'Oro, was built here, while gold flows out of the pockets of gamblers at the nearby Casino. The world's first Ghetto, home of Venice's Jewish community, once thrived here, as did a Merchant's School. The Canale delle Fondamenta

Nuove flows along the northern side, which is a handy point for catching the *vaporetto* to Isola di San Michele with its cemetery, and then beyond to Murano, Burano, Torcello, and Isola di Certosa. A boat ride on Canal Grande that begins at the Santa Lucia train stop shows Cannaregio on your left. You'll pass Church of the Scalzi (Church of the Barefoot, a reference to the Carmelites), and where the last Doge of Venice is buried. The next church, **San Geremia,** has a painting by Palma the Younger that shows Madonna assisting at the coronation of Venice. San Marcuola was founded around 1000, is dedicated to Saints Ermagora and Fortunato, and has Tintoretto's painting *La Cena* (1547). The Ca' Vendramin Calergi palace now is home to the Casino. The once gilded Ca' d'Oro now is a museum.

CA' D'ORO

Ca' d'Oro (Cannaregio 3932, tel. 041/522-4064, www.cadoro.org), built 1422–1440, was once lavishly gilded and is one of the city's finest examples of Venetian Gothic architecture. The museum Galleria Franchetti is worth a visit with paintings by Mantegna, Giorgione, Titian, Guardi, as well as by Dutch and Flemish artists. But don't forget to look at details of the building while you're inside, starting with the courtyard where you'll begin. Upstairs, you can step onto some of the balconies, beautiful not only for the view of the Grand Canal and cityscape, but also for the lovely interplay of light on the exquisitely carved stone.

SANTI APOSTOLI

Santi Apostoli, a church dedicated to the Holy Apostles, probably dates to the 9th century. It has one of Venice's tallest bell towers and paintings by Veronese and Tiepolo. Your canal tour of Cannaregio ends here on the Grand Canal just before you reach Fondaco dei Tedeschi and the Rialto Bridge.

SANTA MARIA DEI MIRACOLI

Near the Rialto is Santa Maria dei Miracoli, built 1481-1489, a Renaissance masterpiece with an unusual rounded pediment on the upper level and a facade beautifully decorated with colorful marble inlays. Its shape suggests a jewel box and indeed it was designed to hold a treasure, the 1409 painting by Nicolò di Pietro of Madonna and Child that is above the altar and is credited with performing miracles.

TEATRO MALIBRAN

Teatro Malibran dates to 1678, but this theater is a contender as the possible original location of the house of Marco Polo (1259–1323), who wrote *Il Milione* about his voyage to the Far East and his years in the court of the Grand Mogul.

SAN GIOVANNI CRISOSTOMO

San Giovanni Crisostomo (Salizzada San Giovanni Crisostomo) was originally built in 1080 on the opposite side of the street and rebuilt here 1497–1504. The square outside has a 15th-century well with four lion heads and fruit festoons. The church interior in the shape of a Greek cross is one of the best examples of Venetian Renaissance. The church's masterpiece, painted by Giovanni Bellini in 1513 during his final years, shows brilliant colors and fine use of space in his painting of Saints Christopher, Jerome, and Augustine.

ANCIENT SYNAGOGUE AND MUSEUM OF THE JEWISH COMMUNITY OF VENICE

The Ancient Synagogue and Museum of the Jewish Community of Venice (Cannaregio 2902, tel. 041/715-359, www.museoebraico.it, Sun.–Fri. 10 A.M.–6 P.M., closed Jewish holidays, entrance and guided tour €8.50) rests on the site of two synagogues founded during the Renaissance. This was the same period in which William Shakespeare wrote *The Merchant of Venice,* which addresses the uncomfortable ambiguity of Jews in Venetian society. In the 14th and 15th centuries, Jews were allowed to remain in Venice a maximum of 15 days. When Venice suffered a major military defeat in 1509, Venetians became more pragmatic about the presence of Jews when funds of Jewish bankers and merchants came to the Republic's assistance. A 1516 proposal moved Jews into the Ghetto Nuovo ("ghetto" derives from "geto," or "foundry" near where Jews were located). Jews were protected from hostile residents, but also were monitored and had a curfew imposed to prevent their mingling with Christians. The Venetian Council tolerated the presence of Jewish moneylenders because the government heavily taxed them and controlled their operations. During the French occupation, the gates to the Ghetto were destroyed in 1797, when the distinction between Jews and other citizens was abolished until it was renewed under Fascism in the 20th century. On the opposite side of the square, a plaque is dedicated to Venetian Jews deported to Nazi concentration camps on December 5, 1943, and August 17, 1944. Next to it are a booth with armed security guards and a Jewish retirement home. Part of Luchino Visconti's film *Senso* is set in the Ghetto.

SANTA MARIA ASSUNTA

The Jesuit priests, once educators of Italy's power elite, have their church in Venice. Santa Maria Assunta (Campo Gesuiti, admission free) contains tall corkscrew columns that spiral toward the cupola above the altar and puffs of clouds, and a representation of St. Michael, who looks more like Mars outfitted for war, as he stomps on the devil. Right of the altar, figures writhe from a serpent attack. Tintoretto's Virgin soars upward. Titian painted the first chapel on the left. Particularly beautiful are the figures and lighting in Titian's dramatic *Martyrdom of St. Lawrence* (1558–1559), in a left side altar. Angels are plentiful, painted on the ceiling, as well as Archangels at the pilasters in the transept and in the sanctuary. Two churches in Venice are sometimes called Santa Maria Assunta. Santa Maria Assunta, also called Chiesa dei Jesuiti, is framed by Rio di Santa Caterina on the south, Rio dei Jesuiti on the east, and Fondamenta Nuove to the north. (The other Santa Maria Assunta, also known as Santa Maria Glorioso dei Frari, is in San Polo.)

SCUOLA NUOVA DI SANTA MARIA VALVERDE DELLA MISERICORDIA

A few blocks west of Santa Maria Assunta, the wide Canale della Misericordia frames the east side of one of Venice's six great schools, Scuola Nuova di Santa Maria Valverde della Misericordia (Campo di Abbazia). It was built by the Brotherhood of Misericordia (1534–1583), then sold to the silk-weaver's guild and now houses the City Archives.

MADONNA DELL'ORTO

Tintoretto is buried in Madonna dell'Orto (Campo Madonna dell'Orto, Mon.–Sat. 10 A.M.–5 P.M., closed Sun., Dec 25., Jan. 1, and Easter, €2.50 OR CHORUS pass), and his *The Universal Judgment* is also here. Its Matteo Ponzone's panels show St. Jerome holding a model of the church in his hands. Works by Titian and Bellini hang here, too. The floor with marble laid in diamond patterns creates a 3-D effect, much like the mosaics popular in ancient Roman villas.

SANT'ALVISE

Sant'Alvise (Campo Sant'Alvise, Mon.–Sat. 10 A.M.–5 P.M., closed Sun., Dec 25., Jan. 1, and Easter, €2.50 or CHORUS pass) is 14th-century Gothic in style and has a wide simple facade. Inside above the entrance note the 15th-century wood choir to separate the nuns. Christ with the Crown of Thorns and the Flagellation are early works by Giambattista Tiepolo, who a few years later painted Descent from Calvary in the Presbytery.

SAN GIOBBE

Toward the west end of the *sestiere* across the Canale di Cannaregio, Ponte Tre Archi links to San Giobbe (Campo San Giobbe, Mon.–Sat. 10 A.M.–5 P.M., closed Sun., Dec 25., Jan. 1, and Easter, €2.50 or CHORUS pass). The rectangular facade of San Giobbe is rather sparse on the upper half, but inside the third chapel on the left, the Martini Chapel, shines from the multi-hued glazed terra-cotta with fruit festoons and medallions of Christ and the Evangelists from the workshop of Luca della Robbia. Doge Cristoforo Moro and his wife are buried here. Behind them is a carved wood altar that dates to 1500. In the sacristy to the right of the nave and cupola is a triptych painted by Antonio Vivarini with Giovanni d'Alemagna (1440–1450) that has the Annunciation in the middle with Saints Michael and Anthony on either side.

OTHER SIGHTS

Bridges don't go up every day in Venice, but in August 2007 a bridge designed by Spanish architect Calatrava was constructed in pieces in a Marghera foundry at a cost of €10 million and installed to connect Piazzale Roma in Santa Croce with the train station in Cannaregio. The bridge had been in planning for more than 11 years; it must pass at least a year of testing before anyone can walk across it.

From the Fondamenta Nuove, you can catch the *vaporetto* to **Isola San Michele** (7 A.M.–4 P.M.), where legend says San Romualdo (c. 956–1027), the founder of the Camadolese order, once lived. The church dedicated to warrior Archangel St. Michael dates back well before 1212. Its bell tower is ornately decorated in Venetian Renaissance style. From here you can find some of the island's permanent residents, as the entire island is a cemetery, officially Greek-Orthodox. Igor Stravinsky, who composed *The Rites of Spring,* is buried here, as is Sergei Diaghilev, who choreographed a ballet to that piece that created a scandal when Nijinksy danced it. Poet Ezra Pound is here, too. From here you can return the way you came or continue on the same *vaporetto* line to Murano and Burano.

San Polo

San Polo, Venice's smallest district, was a hubbub of trade in the Middle Ages. Polo, Venetian dialect for Paolo or Paul, is the saint that gives this *sestiere* its name. Everything from fish and produce to luxury products like spices and fine textiles were dealt by a melting pot of traders. That intense trade launched legal, banking, insurance, and other businesses, and also boosted the world's oldest profession.

In the 16th century, prostitutes made up more than 10 percent of the population, and many dwelled close to the Rialto. The most successful courtesans lived in prime real estate furnished as sumptuously as they dressed. Well-rounded individuals, they were good musicians, often quite savvy about politics, and well acquainted with patrician families. Rio Terà de le Carampane was a prime center since 1400.

The **Ponte Rialto,** the first bridge to span the Grand Canal, links San Polo to San Marco. The original in wood dated to 1172; this design, by the aptly named Antonio Da Ponte, was completed in 1591 and restored in 1977.

Trading still goes on today well past dusk in the luxury and souvenir shops favored by visitors. "Casa e bottega," or "house and workshop," have been defining features of San Polo for centuries, where even today some craftsmen live above their workshops, which also are stores. The Ponte Rialto in San Polo leads directly to the goldsmiths' street, Ruga degli Oresi (Venetian dialect for *orefici* or goldsmiths). Immediately to the right of the bridge is Palazzo dei Camerlenghi, where the Republic's finances were collected, with the ground floor reserved for the jail cells of tax evaders. This was the commercial heart of Venice, their Wall Street where merchants established their contracts. Since the 12th century, Banco Giro here permitted the circulation of credit, located in the *sottoportego* or underpass. The city's three biggest markets—L'Erbaria, la Pescaria, and la Beccaria—were here. Farther up along the Grand Canal near Santa Croce was the Riva dell'Ogio, Venetian dialect for "oil" used for food, cooking, and lighting. Not surprisingly, Calle dei Boteri, the street of the coopers who made barrels for oil, leads up to it. At its opposite end, the Campo de le Becarie is where *becheri* (butchers) sold meat. Venice in 1500 was world famous for its soap, and more than 25 soap-makers worked on or around Calle dei Saoneri. Local legend says that the street Ramo del Forner pays homage to a young *forner* (Venetian dialect for baker) that was erroneously executed for homicide. Jacopo Sansovino was the architect for Fabbriche Nuove, the headquarters for the magistrates in charge of commerce.

Carlo Goldoni, Venice's most famous playwright, was born in San Polo in 1707, probably in the 15th-century palazzo that is now **Museo del Teatro,** a museum of Goldoni and theater memorabilia.

SAN GIACOMO

San Giacomo, nicknamed San Giacometto for its diminutive size, is a contender for Venice's oldest church. The outer wall had a panel inscribed urging merchants to be honest, fair, and not to cheat on weights or measures. The "Gobbo" or "hunchback" sculpture perhaps bears the burden of taxation. In the square in front near the pink granite podium, Pietra del Bando, decrees of the Republic were read.

CAMPO SAN POLO

Campo San Polo became one of Venice's largest squares in 1750 when the San Antonio canal was filled in. Venetians used this square for races, bullfights, and masked parties during Carnevale. Chiesa di San Polo (Camp San Polo) has been here much longer—probably founded by Doge Pietro Gradonico in 737, and was significantly modified in the 14th and 15th centuries. The bell tower, in its present form with cone-shaped cuspids and two lions at its base, dates to 1362. Inside the church has paintings by Tintoretto, Palma the Younger, and Gian Domenico Tiepolo. In September, during the Venice Film Festival, this square becomes an open-air cinema that shows films the evening after their Lido previews.

SANTA MARIA GLORIOSA DEI FRARI

Venice's largest church, Santa Maria Gloriosa dei Frari (Campo dei Frari, Mon.–Sat. 9 A.M.–6 P.M., Sun. 1–6 P.M., closed Dec. 25, Jan. 1, and Easter, €2.50 or CHORUS pass), was built in 1231. After the Franciscans' 1225 arrival, Doge Tiepolo gave them this land to construct the church. Here you can compare works of major Venetian artists including Titian, the Vivarinis, and Bellini. When you enter, stand so that you can see both Titian's enormous tomb on the right and his *Annunciation* that hangs over the main altar, you'll see how the tomb (at three o'clock) mirrors the composition of Titian's painting (at noon). The 15th-century wood choir in the center is a masterpiece with some 50 panels carved that show Venice street scenes and interiors, a document in *intarsio* (inlaid wood) of daily life back then.

Bellini's triptych, signed and dated 1488, has figures that look like they are ready to step out of the panels. In the sacrament chapel, a 14th-century knight in armor makes his final rest. Look at the brilliant colors by Vivarini in three chapels, some with the artist's signature tacked on as a "note." The Vivarini family of artists had their workshops in Murano. Across from Titian's tomb is the enormous pyramid tomb of artist Antonio Canova, where the Lion of Venice itself and an angel mourn.

Canova, a famous sculptor, also was a skilled negotiator and diplomat; he convinced the French to give back some of the art treasures that Napoleon looted, although many remain today in the Louvre. A 1669 funerary monument has four enormous black Moors that strain to prop up Giovanni Pesaro, an interesting social comment.

Dorsoduro

Dorsoduro's name, "spine," probably refers to its high and narrow position. The *sestiere* is bordered by the Grand Canal to its north and the Giudecca Canal to its south. The eastern point, Punta della Dogana, in the San Marco Bacino, was the 17th-century customs area for Venice, and was once lined with warehouses.

The action in this *sestiere* centers around the expansive **Campo Santa Margherita,** a student hangout near the Carmini Monastery, which is picturesque with buildings that date to the 1300s. Lively throughout the day and well into the evening, it's also near the university auditorium. The **Basilica Madonna della Salute** and Accademia are in this *sestiere,* as are former 18th- and 19th-century factories on the southeast end that form part of Venice's university.

From San Marco there are two ways to cross Grand Canal to Dorsoduro. The closest to Piazza San Marco is the gondola ferryboat stop **Santa Maria del Giglio** near **Hotel Gritti** where a rowboat (€0.50) stops very close. The other way from San Marco is via Ponte Accademia. Otherwise, the *sestieri* of San Polo and Santa Croce link to Dorsoduro.

Fondamenta Zattere, on the Giudecca Canal along Dorsoduro's southern bank, faces the Island of the Giudecca. The island is administered by Dorsoduro.

A ride along the Grand Canal provides a nice overview of Dorsoduro's northeast side. From Dorsoduro facing south, there is a marvelous vista of Madonna della Salute. Along the Grand Canal are the large Palazzo Genovese, the Peggy Guggenheim Collection, Palazzo Barbarigo, and Palazzo Loredan. Ponte Accademia connects San Marco to the Accademia galleries. Ca' Rezzonico, a 1667 noble palace, now has Museo del Settecento Veneziano, with paintings and furnishings for a full immersion into the 1700s. Down a side canal behind Ca' Rezzonico near Campo San Barnaba is Ponte dei Pugni ("Bridge of Punches," known as such because rival factions in Venice, the Castellani and the Nicolotti, frequently came to blows here). Ca' Foscari, the university buildings, and Palazzo Balbi are on the Grand Canal where Dorsoduro leads toward San Polo.

Dorsoduro's south side can be seen by boat too, also offering a view of the Giudecca. The ferry from Tronchetto offers a high perch from which to view it all. Dorsoduro has the port where large commercial ships and passenger liners dock near Banchina del Porto Commerciale and the Maritime Station at Fondamente Zattere Ponte Lungo, a reminder of Venice's continued importance as a port city. The Fondamenta Zattere ai Gesuiti is home to **Santa Maria della Visitazione.** The church's ceiling was painted by Tiepolo, who put Dominican friars up there after they took the church from the Jesuits. The Casa degli Incurabili was for people with chronic diseases, as well as for orphans.

On the Giudecca's west end is Mulino Stucky, a renovated redbrick mill converted to residences and a hotel that opened in 2007. Also visible from the canal are the churches Sant'Eufemia, Palladio's splendid **Il Redentore,** and the Zitelle. The eastern tip of the Giudecca reaches toward the next island, Isola San Giorgio, where the church of **San Giorgio Maggiore** faces Dorsoduro. Not quite as wild and overgrown as when Michelangelo visited in 1529, the Giudecca still offers tranquility.

As you walk around Dorsoduro, a few off-beat street names to look for are Rio del Malconton, named for the ne'er-do-wells that made it likely that one would be robbed there. The passageway, Sottoportego del Casin dei Nobili, was a house of "gentlewomen" frequented only by nobles, evidence that their trade was easily spread out around town. On the other hand, Rio de le Romite, in dialect referred to female Augustinian hermits that were very pious and often of high social rank.

Near Dorsoduro is **Campo San Rocco,** where a church was dedicated to the saint that is supposed to protect the population from the plague. Its school, **Scuola Grande di San Rocco,** is famous for the series of paintings by Tintoretto that adorn the rooms.

BASILICA MADONNA DELLA SALUTE

Basilica of the Madonna della Salute (Campo della Salute, daily 9 A.M.–noon and 3–6:30 P.M., free admission) is on Dorsoduro's eastern tip. This is the church that in 1630 the Senate chose to build as thanks for *salute* (health), for being delivered from the plague. Baldassare Longhena, who is also the architect for Ca' Rezzonico and Ca' Pesaro, was inspired particularly by the works of architect Andrea Palladio for this Baroque architectural masterpiece. The floor plan is octagonal, and there is an exuberant display of statues and ornaments. The spiral-shaped volutes in the mid section—called *orecchioni* (big ears) by the Venetians—serve as buttresses to the dome that crowns the central space of the church. A smaller dome rests above the choir. The church has two bell towers. For the November 21 Festival of the Salute, worshippers walk across a temporary wooden bridge and gondoliers have their oars blessed by a priest on the steps of the basilica.

FONDAMENTA ZATTERE

If you want a stroll along southern Dorsoduro, cross the bridge and walk south past the Ex Ospizio along Fondamenta Zattere. Today the Zattere makes for a nice sunny stroll, but its name refers to the huge tree trunks that came barreling down the river from the northern Veneto latched together in rafts, a dangerous trade that made merchants like Vecellio (the Renaissance painter Titian's family) wealthy. This trade continued well into the 19th century. The 1516 pier is where timber was unloaded from the northern Veneto forests of Cadoro.

The **Ospedale degli Incurabili** was built by the Venetian Republic in the 16th century for those with incurable and contagious diseases, as well as for orphans. After the Zattere *traghetto* stop, turn right onto the west (left) bank of the canal to **Campo San Trovaso.** Next to the 16th-century **San Trovaso** church built on a plan by Palladio, the **Squero** was constructed in the 17th century to build gondolas, which it still does today and is one of the last remaining in Venice. Its wooden design is very much like the houses farther north in the Veneto along the Cadore River from where many of the carpenters came, some from near Titian's home in Pieve di Cador.

GALLERIE DELL'ACCADEMIA

One of Venice's most prized art museums, the original function of the Gallerie dell'Accademia (Campo della Carità, tel. 041/522-2247, www .gallerieaccademia.org, Mon. 8:15 A.M.–2 P.M., Tues.–Sun. 8:15 A.M.–7:15 P.M., €6.50) was to instruct art students and to house the Venetian Republic's artistic heritage. The Renaissance period of the 15th and 16th centuries is well represented here by Giovanni Bellini, Carpaccio, Giorgione, Titian, Tintoretto, Lorenzo Lotto, Veronese, and Bassano. Many other artists may be less familiar to you, but they also show remarkable skill. Drawings by Leonardo da Vinci and Canaletto are here, too, and later painters like Tiepolo are also present.

PEGGY GUGGENHEIM COLLECTION

One of the 20th century's most savvy American art collectors made Venice her base in this 1749 palace. Peggy Guggenheim bought this property in 1949 and she remained here until her death in 1979. The Peggy Guggenheim Collection (Dorsoduro 704, tel. 041/240-5411, www.gugenheim-venice.it, Wed.–Mon. 10 A.M.–6 P.M., Vaporetto 1 or 82, Accademia stop) is a must for modern art, with a focus on

20th-century avant-garde and Surrealists, as well as special temporary exhibits. The gallery restaurant is also a good spot for lunch on the Grand Canal.

CA' REZZONICO AND THE MUSEUM OF 18TH-CENTURY VENETIAN ART

Located right on the canal, the Ca' Rezzonico (Fondamente Rezzonico 3136, tel. 041/241-0100, www.museiciviciveneziani.it, Wed.–Mon. 10 A.M.–5 P.M., €6.50) houses the Museum of 18th-Century Venetian Art, featuring a superb collection of objects and paintings. You'll see an antique gondola before you ascend that majestic staircase to reach the *piano nobile* (noble floor). With its frescoed walls with trompe l'oeil architectural perspectives, this grand ballroom today is occasionally used for concerts (check with the museum or tourist office). You'll see gorgeous inlaid wood furniture, large statues of Moors made of ebony, vases from China, and Delft from Holland. Other rooms bring the 1700s to life with more furniture and frescoes. Some rooms are decorated in color themes, like the Yellow or Green Rooms. Poet Robert Browning, a guest in Saletta Browning, died here in 1889, and the room has memorabilia of the poet where your English-language skills will come in handy. Other rooms are dedicated to ceramics or tapestry. In the Throne Room, Tiepolo painted the *Allegory of Merit* on the ceiling. A portico faces the Canal and another series of rooms continues, then on the second floor. If you like decorative arts of this period, plan to savor the experience and linger. Many furniture collections over time become dispersed, so here is your chance to see what was the rage in the 1700s for palace decor.

PALAZZO ZENOBIO

On Rio dei Carmine, the 17th-century Palazzo Zenobio (Fondamenta del Soccorso 2596, tel. 041/522-8770), the Armenian College, has a splendid grand ballroom with 17th-century frescoes by Dorigny. Check events listings in the newspapers or with the tourist office for occasional concerts in this memorable setting.

SAN SEBASTIANO

San Sebastiano (Campo San Sebastiano, tel. 041/275-0462, Mon.–Sat. 10 A.M.–5 P.M.) has beautiful paintings by Paolo Veronese—who chose to be buried here—that depict scenes from the life of St. Sebastian, before Emperor Diocletian ordered him shot full of arrows. In recent centuries, the martyred saint has unofficially been adopted as the patron saint of gay people.

Giudecca

The island of Giudecca faces from the south bank of the canal. Its name might derive from *giudei,* Jews who lived here in medieval times, but more likely derives from *guidicati,* naughty aristocrats who were banished here. Converted from a patch of thorny brambles to a manufacturing center, its skyline still reflects a hodgepodge of high towers, chimneys, cranes, and old warehouses. In recent decades, this old neighborhood of laborers and fisherman has been converted to more tony residences and luxury hotels. On the eastern tip, **Cipriani** was the pioneer, and on the western tip, Hilton opened the converted 1895 Stucky flourmill as a modern hotel in 2007. The **Redentore** and **Zitelle** churches form its most famous silhouettes, which you can see along the bank as your boat makes its way along toward the Grand Canal and San Marco. Il Redentore was begun by Andrea Palladio to express Venice's gratitude for having been delivered from the plague. The Festa del Redentore in July remains one of Venice's most popular and authentic annual celebrations during the year. The church was designed by Palladio, but was completed by Antonio da Ponte in 1592 after Palladio's death in 1580. Although the church has paintings by Bassano and Tintoretto, it's its use of space that makes a visit here so pleasing. Palladio also designed the nearby Church of the Zitelle to house spinsters that were taken in as "honest" girls to make highly prized famous Venetian lace.

Along the Fondamenta delle Convertite, an oratory from the 16th century housed women who repented their sins and decided to become nuns.

Santa Croce

Santa Croce is the *sestiere* that you enter when you arrive by car or bus in Piazzale Roma. Ironically, the church that gives the *sestiere* of Santa Croce its name was torn down in the 19th century. Santa Croce has some of the most magnificent palaces on the Grand Canal, as well as the western section that became more modernized in the 19th century. Narrow, densely packed streets and intimate squares lead you into a less touristy Venice.

The former monastery next to San Nicola Tolentino now is the university architecture school. San Giacomo dell'Orio has undergone modifications over the centuries, but still shows traces of its Byzantine origins that date to the 9th century.

CA' PESARO

Venice's most important Baroque palace, Ca' Pesaro (Santa Croce 2070, tel. 041/520-9070, www.museiciviciveneziani.it, Nov.–Mar. Tues.–Sun. 9 A.M.–5 P.M., Apr.–Oct. Tues.–Sun. 9 A.M.–6 P.M., €5.50) was created by unifying three existing palaces in the 17th century. Now its first two floors are dedicated to **Galleria Internazionale d'Arte Moderna,** a museum of important 19th- and 20th-century art founded during the Venice Biennale of 1897. Fine works by Klimt, Chagall, Kandinsky, Klee, Matisse, and Moore are displayed. The third floor is home to **Museo Orientale,** Italy's most important museum dedicated to East Asian art. The collection includes paintings, sculpture, lacquer, ivory, arms, and costumes. China and Japan are well represented, as are other Asian countries.

FONDACO DEI TURCHI

The Turks' Warehouse, Fondaco (or Fontego) dei Turchi on the Grand Canal, was a 1621 initiative of the Seigneury that rented space to Turkish merchants, who continued trade even during times of war. However, it also let officials keep an eye on their movements, and required the Turks to check their money and weapons upon arrival, and permitted no Christian women or boys to enter the area, which also had a Turkish bath house. The Turks remained until 1838. Now the Fondaco is dedicated to other denizens in Venice's **Museum of Natural History** (Santa Croce 1730, tel. 041/520-9070, www.museicivicivenezieni. it, Tues.–Fri. 9 A.M.–12:30 P.M., Sat.–Sun. 9 A.M.–3:30 P.M., closed Dec. 25, Jan 1, and May 1). Discover the Venice Lagoon and its fauna here, including *Ouranosaurus nigeriensis,* one of the rarest and most interesting dinosaur finds. On the ground floor aquarium you can see the biodiversity of the *tegnue,* the shelf of seabed rocks off the Venetian coast. Other rooms have pre-Roman finds that date back to the Iron Age.

MUSEO DI PALAZZO MOCENIGO

If you're wondering what it would be like to step into a furnished 18th-century patrician palace, visit Museo di Palazzo Mocenigo (Santa Croce 1992, tel. 041/520-9070, www.mu seicivicivenezieni.it, Nov.–Mar. Wed.–Mon. 10 A.M.–5 P.M., Apr.–Oct. 10 A.M.–6 P.M., closed Dec. 25, Jan. 1, and May 1). Its original collection of 18th century Venetian paintings by Tiepolo, Canaletto, the Guardi, Longhi, and Rosalba Carriera was enhanced by the acquisition of more than 300 other works that include paintings by Vivarini and Tintoretto. The **Study Center for the History of Textiles and Costume** is also housed here.

The Lido and the Southern Lagoon

The Lido gracefully stretches across the Lagoon on its east side and embraces the sea on the west side. From Porto di Lido at Canale di San Nicolo to Porto di Malamocco it extends 12 kilometers.

The Lido's original beach bums, who launched its popularity in the 19th century, were Romantic poets like Byron and Shelley. It wasn't long after that the world's largest beach resort went up. The Lido has a stylish, laid-back informality about it. Except for July and August, when the bathing beauties arrive, or during the Venice Film Festival in September, look for hotel bargains here. The Lido could be just the antidote for tired feet after sightseeing. It's possible to swim in the sea here, with waves that break against the east coast of the Lido, go for a ride on a bicycle (easily rented at Gran Viale and Via Zara), or play a round of golf at the course near the fort at Alberoni. The Lido's wide promenades also make for good shopping.

The first beach platforms went up in 1857, followed in 1888 by the first wooden *capanne* (the family beach spot to change, lunch, and play). Not long after, the luxury hotels followed. Try to stop in for a drink at Hotel Des Bains or Grand Hotel Excelsior to enjoy their posh turn-of-the-century atmosphere, which in the early 20th century made the Lido one of the world's most prized, large, and luxurious beach resorts.

Stroll along the Lungomare Marconi and the beach to see the Adriatic Sea, so important in the rise and wealth of Venice. Play golf or go horseback riding here, with a view of Venice not far away and behind the city the mountains of the pre-Alps.

Sunbathers will enjoy the beach's yellowish sand that owes its unique hue to the Piave River. The river brings sand from the Dolomite Mountains that is full of quartz and magnetic iron. The water here remains quite shallow for some distance, which makes this a tranquil spot for swimmers of all levels. Stroll along the beach to pick your favorite *stabilimento* (concession) to rent a beach umbrella and *lettino* (lounge chair).

If you want to explore the **Southern Lagoon** by land, you can do it by bus or on a bike, if you wish. Depart from the Lido, take the ferry at Alberoni and continue south to **Chioggia,** the ancient port town that later led to river routes to Padova. Pellestrina had to fend off invasions from Hungary in 965, but today is better know for its fisherman that provide much of the catch for Venice, as well as for its orchards, gardens, and vineyards. The **Isola di San Lazzaro degli Armeni** still has an important collection of Eastern art and documents, with Armenian monastery, cloister, and library to visit. Two other Southern Lagoon islands have undergone major changes. **Isola di San Servolo,** once home of Venice's insane asylum now is used for conferences and special events. **Isola di Poveglia,** site of a geriatric hospital, has a project planned for a multipurpose student center.

ANCIENT JEWISH CEMETERY
There are guided tours of the **Ancient Jewish Cemetery** (tel. 041/715-359, Apr.–Oct., €8.50) on the Lido on Sundays at 2:30 P.M. Many tombstones date to the 16th and 17th centuries.

CHURCH OF SANTA MARIA ELISABETTA
Much of the Lido architecture dates to the late 19th or early 20th century. However, it has two 16th-century churches: the Church of Santa Maria Elisabetta and the Church of San Nicolò di Lido. The Church of Santa Maria Elisabetta (Piazzale Santa Maria Elisabetta) leads to Gran Viale di Santa Maria Elisabetta, a wide boulevard lined with shops, villas, gardens, hotels, and bed-and-breakfasts.

CHURCH OF SAN NICOLÒ DI LIDO
On the Lagoon side of the Lido, the Church of San Nicolò di Lido (Piazzale San Nicolò) was founded in 1044 and then restyled in 1624 by Benedictines. The patron saint of Russia, the Mediterranean, sailors, and navigators, Nicholas was famous for his generosity (thus the gift-giving tradition and St. Nick) and is credited with various miracles. The Baroque church's interior is dedicated to the saint. The 1625 choir in the apse has scenes from his life carved in wood. Its convent, once a haven for monks, has been transformed to a planetarium, the **Planetario di Venezia** (Lido di Venezia, Lungomare d'Annunzio, tel. 041/731-518, www.astrovenezia.it, Oct. 1–May 31 Sun. at 4 P.M., closed holidays and summer, admission free).

MALAMOCCO
Situated between the Lagoon and the sea, the town of Malamocco is in the southern part of the Lido. According to legend, the town was founded by Padovans fleeing the 6th-century Longobard invasion. In 742, the doge made Malamocco the government seat for the Lagoon islands, which in 811 was transferred near the Rialto. Now it's considerably more tranquil with villas and orchards. The 15th-century Gothic Church of the Assumption has a bell tower that was modeled after St. Mark's campanile.

ALBERONE
Near the Lido's southern tip, the town of Alberone (tall trees) was named for the trees that adorned the ancient fort. Once used to defend the port, now golfers can defend their titles at its golf course, **Circolo Golf Venezia** (Zona Alberoni, tel. 041/731-333, www.circologolfvenezia.it).

ISOLA DI SAN LAZZARO DEGLI ARMENI
The Isola di San Lazzaro degli Armeni was named for Lazarus, the patron saint of lepers, where a leper asylum was established in 1182. The convent that the Armenians constructed in 1740 still has an important collection of Eastern art and documents. Known for their hospitality, the priests welcome visitors to their monastery, cloister, print shop, and library. Rare illuminated manuscripts, an 8th-century document regarding rituals, and a 13th-century history of Alexander the Great are among its treasures. A room dedicated to Lord Byron features mementoes and rare books. Byron was a frequent 19th-century guest in the convent and stayed in an adjacent room.

PELLESTRINA
Pellestrina had to fend off invasions from Hungary in 965, but today is better know for its anglers that provide much of the catch for Venice, as well as for its orchards, gardens, and vineyards. Its shoreline stretches for about three kilometers and is still a center for lacemakers that use the *tombolo* (bobbin) method. Along the littoral that separates the Lagoon from the sea, you can see defensive sea walls. In the town's center, the multi-sided Church of Santa Maria in Vito was reconstructed in 1723 to reflect Palladian proportions, which were still the rage two centuries after Palladio made his architectural mark in Venice.

CHIOGGIA
Chioggia, the ancient port town that later led to river routes to Padova, is situated in the southernmost part of the Lagoon about four kilometers from the Brenta Canal entrance. It

is composed of two main islands, Tòmbola and Sottomarina, that are linked by a bridge that spans Isola di Unione and Isola dei Cantieri. Already settled in Roman times, it is a precursor to Venice and in the 9th century was proclaimed Venice's "second city." As the southern access in the Lagoon to Venice, it was often the site of major naval battles. The most famous of the battles was the defeat of Venezia at the hands of Genova in 1379.

Chioggia remains a seafaring city. About five times the population of Pellestrina, it's one of Italy's most important fishing ports. The old part of town is the most picturesque. The easternmost island of Chioggia, **Isola dei Saloni,** is known for its fruit and vegetable market, *mercato orto-frutticola* that supplies produce to much of Venice and the Lagoon islands.

Chioggia claims female painter Rosalba Carriera (1675-1757) as its own, whose paintings are displayed in Ca' Rezzonico in Dorsoduro as well as in Venetian churches.

On Tòmbola, **Chiesa dei Filippini** (Canale della Vena) is named after the followers of Filippo da Neri who dedicated his life to the poor and disenfranchised. Constructed in 1772 by the Manin family, this church belonged to the last Doge of Venice. **Biblioteca Comunale** (Corso del Popolo) began in 1537 as Church Monte di Pietà.

San Giacomo's (Corso del Popolo) facade remained unfinished even after its 1788 renovation. Inside a 15th-century painting (*Madonna della Navicella*) is much venerated by locals for its subject, the miraculous appearance of the Madonna on the Sottomarina Lido. Also on the Corso, the exterior of 18th-century **Palazzo Morari** is admired for its architectural embellishments that include corner balconies. The small 1454 church **San Francesco** (Corso del Popolo), also called Delle Muneghette, faces the house that was once the residence of painter Rosalba Carriera and lawyer/playwright Carlo Goldoni.

The Gothic **Church of San Martino** (Campo San Martino) was built in 1392 to replace three churches destroyed by the Genovese during the war. Inside, the 1349 multi-paneled painting attributed to Paolo Veneziano shows his fine use of color.

The **Duomo** (Campo San Martino) dates back to the 11th century and is dedicated to the town's patron saints, Felice and Fortunato. (Their names, "Happy" and "Lucky," are ironic because they both were tortured in a variety of ways before they were beheaded.) In 1110, it was granted status as a cathedral with bishop's seat, then rebuilt in 1623 after a fire destroyed the earlier version. The sacristy has another version of the miraculous appearance of the *Madonna della Navicella*. This 1593 version by Andrea Vicentino is displayed alongside other paintings that relate to that episode. The 1751-1753 oval paintings in the Sacrament Chapel are by another local painter, Michele Schiavon, also called Il Chioggiotto.

The neighborhood near the cathedral (the area around Piazza Vescovile and Canale Perotolo) has been chosen by landscape painters for centuries. **Porta Garibaldi,** built in 1520, leads to **Ponte Lungo,** the "long bridge" built in 1758 and modified in 1872 that joins Chioggia to the west and the *terraferma* (expression that Venetians use to indicate land that pertains to the mainland).

From Calle San Giacomo, two bridges across Canale San Domenico and Canale Lusenzo lead to Chioggia's eastern island, **Sottomarina.** Sottomarina mainly catered to beach tourism in the 1960s, with beach facilities created to lure residents from nearby Veneto and Lombardia regions. As industry increased in southern coastal cities on the mainland, its allure has declined.

ENTERTAINMENT AND EVENTS

Venice is lively with events and festivals, including Cinema on the Lido in September and the Biennale, which runs June–November in odd years. Religious festivals are a major aspect, too, from Carnevale to various feast days. Count on colorful celebrations. As for nightlife, keep in mind that restaurants tend to close earlier than in Southern Italy—sometimes as early as 10 P.M.—while the discos and the casino stay open late. Since most workers cannot afford to live in Venice, closing times are sometimes dictated by transportation schedules to Mestre or other outlying towns. Campo life on city squares can run quite late in the summer. When opera and theater season are in full swing, look for places that cater to the post-theater crowds.

Nightlife
LIVE MUSIC
The **Venice Jazz Project** (www.venicejazz project.com) has cut some CDs and play frequently in the area.

Centrale Restaurant Lounge (San Marco Piscina Frezzaria 1659, tel. 041/296-0664, www.centrale-lounge.com, Wed.–Mon. 6:30 P.M.–2 A.M., €70) has a chill-out music lounge and serves dinner until late.

A sophisticated crowd swings at the swank **Hotel Gritti Palace** (Campo Santa Maria del Giglio, tel. 041/794-611), which occasionally throws jazz evenings.

Dinner and a classical concert at **Hotel Luna Baglioni** (Calle Vallaresso San Marco 1243, tel. 041/528-9840, €35 concert only, €120 with dinner) is a lavish affair in a historic hotel that once lodged the Knights Templar.

BARS
Bacaro Jazz Ristorante & Cocktail Bar (S. Marco 5546, tel. 041/528-5249, www.bacaro jazz.com) features jazz with international and Italian cuisine. Happy hour runs 4–6 P.M. and doors don't close until 2:30 A.M. It's one of the few places where you can eat after midnight.

If you're homesick for a sports game on a jumbo screen with a lively bar crowd, **Planet Venezia** (Calle Cassalleria 5281, tel. 041/522-0808) attracts a young crowd for televised international events and offers a bargain meal for €13.50 for three courses. Beer and pizza is their mainstay.

WINE BARS
Between Piazza San Marco and Ponte Rialto, **Le Bistrot de Venise** (Calle dei Fabbri, tel. 041/523-6651, www.bistrotdevenise.com) is open

until 1 A.M. Earlier in the evening, cocktail hour draws a sophisticated, arty, literary clientele.

Baccaro Lounge Bar (San Marco 1345, tel. 041/296-0687) is open to 2 A.M. and also serves food quite late.

Once the orchestras stop playing in Piazza San Marco, younger revelers are likely to turn up the volume in **Aurora Caffè Cocktail Bar** (Piazza San Marco 48–50, tel. 041/528-6405, Wed.–Sun. 8 P.M.–2 A.M.). The bar has inside seating and tables are set outside, weather permitting.

Tiny wine bar **Al Timon** (Fondamenta dei Ormesini, Canareggio 2745, tel. 346/320-9978, Thurs.–Tues. lunch and dinner) has four or five rough wooden tables inside and a few outside on the canal. Daily wines on the blackboard reflect the owner's knowledgeable, eclectic palate and are reasonably priced by the glass or bottle. A few hot Venetian dishes, salads, or salami and meat platters are happily digested.

CASINO
The site of Casanova's elegant romantic exploits, **Casino di Venezia** (Cannaregio 2040, tel. 041/529-7111, www.casinovenezia.it, daily 2:45 P.M.–2:30 A.M.) has been luring in gamblers to make their fortunes or squander their inheritance since 1638. The world's oldest casino has French games and slot machines. There is a dress code here. They require a jacket, but if you don't have one, they can loan you one inside. Casual attire is permitted at their other location near the airport, which has American-style games.

Performing Arts and Cinema
Along with Milan and Naples, Venice has Italy's most prestigious opera house, **La Fenice** (Campo San Fantin 1965, San Marco, www. hellovenezia.com). The opera, concert, and ballet season begins at the end of September and runs through spring.

Complete operas in costume are staged at the **Scuola Grande dei Carmini** (www. prgroup.it) and at **Scuola Grande S. Giovanni Evangelista** (www.operahouse.it). Both offer lower prices (€35) in historic settings.

Churches, schools, and palaces are the backdrop for concerts by **I Musici Veneziani** (www. musiciveneziani.com), who perform in period clothing. **San Moisè** (Campo San Moisè) periodically presents free organ symphonies in their **Vespri D'Organo** series. Check the newspaper for specific performance times.

When you're fed up with Vivaldi, head for the experimental series of rare and researched music at the **Giorgio Cini Foundation Institute** (www.cini.it). There's a free around-the-world series on Saturdays at 5:30 P.M.

Carnival the Show: Celebrating the Story of Venice is a music and multimedia presentation about the history of Venice. The evening at **Teatro San Gallo** (Campo San Gallo, www. teatrosangallo.com, €79) opens with drinks and buffet finger food.

Teatro Goldoni (San Marco 4650/b, tel. 041/240-2011, www.teatrostabileveneto.it) has its own resident company, Teatro Stabile del Veneto. It is Venice's most famous theater for drama, and stages mostly classical plays, plus occasional ballets and concerts.

Catch a film in **Palazzo del Cinema** (tel.041/526-0188), which becomes star central during the Venice Film Festival.

Festivals and Events

Current information for all of Venice's festivals and events can be found at www.comune. venezia.it.

CARNEVALE VENEZIA

Once a religious festivity, February's Carnevale (various neighborhoods, www.carnevale. venezia.it, begins two Fri. before Tues. before Ash Wednesday) has become Venice's main street party and since the 1980s has become big business.

Carnevale began in the 11th century as Venice's spontaneous February celebration before the arrival of Lent and its required period of abstinence. By its 18th-century peak, beautiful, sophisticated, outlandish, and amusing characters all joined in to let loose. Celebrants changed or disguised their identities behind masks and costumes that eliminated social class distinctions.

masked revelers on their way to Carnevale Venezia

© JUDY EDELHOFF

VENICE

Its later decadence brought about its 19th-century decline until it was revived in the 1970s. The streets are choked with spectators hoping to glimpse a carefully orchestrated costume parade. Where are the Venetians? Either out of town or at private parties in palaces from which they will whoosh in and out. You can enjoy it most if you dress up, too. Bring your own costume, the more lavish the better, or buy or rent one at shops that have costumes worthy of a Hollywood blockbuster. The traditional masks are made of papiermâché masks and often reflect characters from Renaissance *commedia dell'arte* theater.

VENICE FILM FESTIVAL

The Venice Film Festival or **Mostra Internazionale d'Arte Cinematografica** (Palazzo del Cinema, Piazzale del Casinò, tel. 041/521-8711, www.labiennale.org) is one of the city's main annual events and attracts an international star-studded line-up in September while films are being screened and judged. Most action takes place on the Lido, although star sightings can occur anywhere in the city.

FESTIVAL GALUPPI

Historic palaces, theaters, and churches are the settings for 18th-century concerts in September and October sponsored by Festival Galuppi (www.festivalgaluppi.it).

FESTA DEL REDENTORE

The Giudecca's big bash and one of Venice's festivals that still remains authentic is Festa del Redentore (Feast of the Redeemer), which takes place the third Sunday in July. Venice celebrates its deliverance from the plague of 1576. Boats form a bridge across the Giudecca Canal so that worshippers can walk across them to attend Mass in Palladio's Redentore Church. The night before, a grand fireworks display attracts crowds along the Zattere and in boats to see them reflected on the water.

SU E ZO PER I PONTI

The second Sunday in March brings Su e Zo Per i Ponti ("Up and Down the Bridges"), when racers trample up and down city streets and bridges.

FESTA DI SAN MARCO

The Patron Saint of Venice, St. Mark, is celebrated on April 25 with Festa di San Marco. Gondolas race between Sant'Elena and Punta della Dogana, locals dine on *risi e bisi,* and men give roses to their wives and/or sweethearts.

FESTA DELLA SPARESEA

Cavillino, the source of produce for Venice, throws Festa della Sparesea, a May 1 festival for new asparagus which includes a regatta.

LA SENS AND VOGALONGA

Begun by Doge Orseolo in 1000, La Sens is the ritual marriage of Venice with the sea. Absent a doge, a local official flings a ring and laurel crown into the sea on the Sunday after Ascension Day. A week later is Vogalonga (the Long Row) a 32-kilometer race from Piazza San Marco to Burano and back.

BIENNALE

In odd-numbered years like 2009 and 2011, the Biennale becomes the world's largest contemporary art exhibition, The bash occurs June–November in various locations in Venice; its major center is at the Arsenale.

REGATA STORICA AND REGATA DEI SANTI GIOVANNI E PAOLO

The Grand Canal is the setting for the Regata Storica the first Sunday in September, with gondoliers and rowers that race in costume and vintage boats rowed in procession.

The June Regata dei Santi Giovanni e Paolo is a race designed to encourage passion for single-oar rowing among the young—all competitors are under 25. The race begins in Murano, heads to the Fondamenta Nuove, and concludes at the Ponte Mendicanti near Campo Santi Giovanni e Paolo.

FESTA DEL MOSTO

Isola Sant'Erasmo, Venice's garden island, puts on Festa del Mosto the first weekend in October, when grape crushers go barefootin' to make wine. The island also boasts a new resort hotel, where the whole island practically becomes your base.

VENICE

VENICE MARATHON

Venice Marathon (www.venicemarathon.it) is one of Italy's most important track-and-field events of the year. It is held in October and begins in Stra on the Brenta Canal and ends in Venice.

SHOPPING

Venice rose in power with trade and plenty still goes on. Textiles are among Italy's most beautiful and luxurious, fine fabrics for interior decorating or for clothing. In fact, Venice can be the place for a total fashion makeover- it has good men's shops for a traditional or sleek look and elegant women's apparel. Eager to please price-conscious tourists, some merchants offer hybrid designs that use less precious fabrics or even imports from China. If you are looking for a Venice souvenir or craft, chances are that if it's a great bargain, it was not made anywhere in the area or even on the continent. Venice is the place for quality, where bargains are few and far between. Lace, for centuries a specialty, has fallen on hard times—partly due to fashion and partly due to the maintenance required to keep it looking good. Many lace makers have abandoned the business. The best lace is likely to be antique and pricey, but a few stalwarts remain that make fine lace. Glassblowers moved to Murano in medieval times, but some have showrooms in the center. They can make anything from fine beads for necklaces and earrings to grand sculpture and chandeliers. Leather goods can be very nice here. Look for crafts, from small items like jewelry and handmade paper to large items such as gondolas or other wooden boats and yachts. Venice has been indulging whims and fantasies for a millennium. Spices no longer are exotic to Americans accustomed to multi-ethnic cuisines. There still is plenty of exotic fantasy though, including Carnevale masks (traditionally papier-mâché), and accessories from hats to costumes to let your fantasy side cut loose. Even if you only wear it once, you have a great wall decoration. Shops fan out in all directions from San Marco in a density that makes it easy to compare price and quality—just don't forget where you saw a favorite object, as it's easy to get confused if you've been winding around the city without memorizing landmarks.

Please note that Venice shops are generally open 9 A.M. or 10 A.M. to 1 P.M. and 3 P.M. or 4 P.M. to 7 P.M. Some shops have "nonstop" hours and do not close at lunch. These hours may extend during peak season or may be reduced during lulls. Most shops are closed on Sundays and on Mondays some stores are only open in the afternoon.

San Marco
ARTS AND CRAFTS

Papier-mâché masks start from €18 for the long noses, traditional Commedia dell'Arte characters, and the Venetian Joker and Moon masks at **Veniceland** (San Marco 617, tel. 041/528-9568, daily 11:30 A.M.–6:30 P.M.). They don't mind if you try them on but will start to get annoyed if you try to take photos.

In front of the post office, **La Carta** (San Marco 5547/a, tel. 041/520-2325) sells handmade paper specializing in marbleized sheets and their own calendars and agendas. If you forgot your diary at home, this is the perfect place to buy a new one and start jotting down your impressions of Venice. There's also a decent selection of pens and pencils.

Upscale art gallery **Contini Galleria d'Arte** (San Marco 2765/2769, Calle dello Spezier, Campo Santo Stefano, tel. 041/520-4942 or 041/520-4942, www.continiarte.com) represents prestigious artists here and at their two galleries in chic Cortina d'Ampezzo. The pristine interior is often filled with one-man shows that vary between portrait, abstract, and landscape.

ANTIQUES

Near Campo San Bartolomeo, **Le Gioie di Bortolo** (San Bortolomio 5536, tel. 041/522-6436, Mon.–Sat. 10 A.M.–12:30 P.M. and 4–7 P.M.) has antique jewelry from the 1800s–1950s and will redesign your old pieces. It's mostly under lock and key so if you are interested in seeing if the ring fits just ask the owner, who enjoys practicing his English.

CLOTHING

If your budget can handle it, Giorgio Armani, Emilio Pucci, Roberto Cavalli, Valentino, and Missoni all have stores here. Gentlemen ready for an extreme makeover can head straight to **Ermenegildo Zegna** (Bocca di Piazza San Marco 1241, www.zegna.com). **Buosi** (San Bortolomio 5382, tel. 041/520-8567) men's shop near the Rialto Bridge has kept Venetian men looking good since 1897. They make shirts, jackets, trousers, and suits to measure and have a selection of ready-to-wear all made in Italy, including some classy ties that have Father's Day written all over them.

If Venice has put you in a romantic mood, luxury lingerie is waiting at **Jade Martine** (San Marco 1645, Frezzeria, tel. 041/521-2892, daily 10 A.M.–6:30 P.M.). The small shop carries many different lines that vary from French maid to less than skimpy. Less is more, especially when it comes to price.

COSTUMES

Historically accurate costumes, papier-mâché masks, tuxedos, wigs, capes, hats, and shoes will transform you completely at **Atelier Flavia** (Santa Marina, Corte Spechiera 6010, tel. 041/528-7429, www.veniceatelier.com, by appointment only). It's the ideal place to come during Carnevale if you're after that *Eyes Wide Shut* look. Costumes can be rented or purchased.

ACCESSORIES AND SHOES

Trevisan (San Marco 349, tel. 041/523-2688, Tues.–Sun. 9 A.M.–1 P.M. and 3–7 P.M.) once specialized in Burano lace, but as demand for lace dropped they turned to Italian leather, silk ties, and scarves in velvet, silk-cashmere, and rayon-wool blends at moderate prices (€18–25).

Forgot your walking shoes or tired of teetering around the canals on heels? **Calzature Bonato's** (Calle delle Bande 5277, tel. 041/520-3702) small, utilitarian shop has a selection of unglamorous but comfortable walking shoes at very reasonable prices. Their Berkemann orthopedic line promises to "re-educate" tired feet.

Break your eyeglasses? **Ottica Mantovani** (San Maraco 4860, tel. 041/522-3427), in business since 1871, claims to have prescription glasses ready in 30 minutes.

Hatmaker **Modisteria Giuliana Longo** (Campo San Salvador Calle del Lovo 4813, tel. 041/522-6454) manages to pile herself, an assistant, and an amusing selection of hats into this tiny shop that dates from 1901. She will custom make you the classic three-corner Carnevale hat for €35.

HOME

Damask, silk, and velvet fabrics for home decorating as well as bedcovers are at **Ca'Nova** (San Marco 4601, tel. 041/520-3834). They will make drapes, covers, or other items to order and then ship them to you in about a month.

Fortuny lamps are at **Venetia Studium** (San Marco 2425, 723, or 4753 near Teatro Goldoni). They also have Venetian textiles, including silk velvet scarves and stoles that range €78–105.

Il Prato (Calle delle Ostreghe 2456/9, tel. 041/523-1148) doesn't encourage casual browsers, but if you have a serious interest in good design papers, glass, or plates, stop in at this elegant store next to Hotel Gritti.

Castello and Cannaregio
ANTIQUES

You'll find antique lace, purses, pillows, ceramics, and furniture at **Antichità al Ghetto** (Cannaregio 1133/1134, tel. 041/524-4592). The shop was opened in 2006 by Elisabetta and Giuliano, who also collects locks (a passion he explains as "a Freudian thing"). The friendly couple is knowledgeable about the goods they sell and will happily explain the production process of any item.

BOOKSTORES

Libreria Editrice Filippi (Castello 5284) is dedicated to books on Venice, most of which are in Italian. Postcard reproductions of old Venice in black and white make for interesting souvenirs and provide a stark contrast with the present.

ACCESSORIES

The best shop to buy the ultimate power tie is in Castello right on the square at **Campo Bandiera e Moro** (tel. 041/528-4686). Bill Clinton wore a Pierangelo Masciadri tie from this shop when he was elected President, which also appears in his photo on the *Time* magazine cover. In the 2004 debate against Kerry, President Bush wore Masciadri's Roman Mosaics tie. He makes lovely scarves, too, including some that pick up details from Andrea Mantegna paintings and others with Greek mythological themes.

GIFT AND HOME

Elegant divans, pillows, and textiles for the home are at **TSL** (Cannaregio 1318, tel. 041/718-524, www.tslgroup.it). They also have a few scarves and shawls.

Bookbinder **G. L. Pitacco** (Castello Ruga Giuffa 4758, Mon.–Sat. 9 A.M.–12:30 P.M. and 3–8 P.M.) specializes in fine bindings, traditional or modern. Some diaries, photo albums, and address books are in stock, otherwise you can have them bind or repair your own. They hand-make sheets of marbleized paper, which can also be found at **Domino** (Castello 4685, S. Zaccaria, tel. 041/523-0090), another place to find leather-bound books.

ARTS AND CRAFTS

Find watercolors of Venice scenes by a thirty-something artist at **Itaca Art Studio** (in two locations, Calle delle Bande 5267/a, Castello, tel. 041/520-3207 and San Lio 5765, Castello, tel. 041/241-2403). They're available as original paintings or inexpensive prints for €5–3,000. Many are already framed and ready to ship via FedEx anywhere in the world.

San Polo and Dorsoduro

COSTUMES

Period costumes for rent (€160 and up) or sale (€1,500 and up) can be found at **Atelier Pietro Longhi** (San Polo 2671, tel. 041/714-478). They can also make you an original costume to measure from paintings, photos, comic books, or an off-the-wall idea.

Depending on the season, it usually takes about a week before you'll be able to go out trick or treating.

HOME

Textiles, trim, pillows, bedcovers, brocades, velvets, scarves, and ties are available at **Colorcasa** (S. Polo 1989–1991, tel. 041/523-6071, www.colorcasavenezia.it).

ACCOMMODATIONS

Hoteliers consistently remark that Venice no longer has a "low" season. Visitors come in great numbers year-round. Rooms can be hard to find and discounts are less frequent. Book far in advance for February when Carnevale is in full swing and in September during the Venice Film Festival. From June–November in odd-numbered years contemporary art lovers arrive in droves for the Venice Biennale.

For more economical rates, July and especially August are a bit more reasonable because Italians traditionally head for the sea (although in summer months, rooms are hard to come by in the Lido). November–mid-December and after the January 6 holiday can also be good for price breaks. A big celebration, convention, or trade show will spike prices, but generally for just a few days.

Americans usually complain that even luxury rooms in Venice are small. Many of these hotels are in ancient palaces that must secure permission before they can bang a nail or knock down a wall. Changes often are not practical in narrow buildings designed 500 years ago for different lifestyles. Some properties do not have elevators, so ask when you book if there are any stairs that need climbing. If space is important, ask to see the room layout. Expect to pay accordingly for a large room.

If you have difficulty with prices or availability, bedroom communities like Mestre and Marghera are easy commutes. Cities farther away, like Padova, Vicenza, Treviso, or a tiny town in wine country, can all work easily by train. After you see the Venice crowds it may be a bonus rather than last resort to sleep outside of the city.

San Marco
€100–200

The friendly owner at [C] **Ai Do Mori** (Calle Larga San Marco 658, tel. 041/520-4817, www. hotelaidomori.com, 11 rooms, €60–140 d, no elevator) has luminous rooms (no. 11 has a terrace) with lovely textiles. Most come with a view of the San Marco bell tower. Prices are very reasonable but you'll need to book way in advance.

Palazzo del Giglio (Campo Santa Maria del Giglio 2462, tel. 041/271-9111, www.hotelgiglio .com, 24 rooms, €100–225 d) offers good rates at a top location and has several furnished apartments where guests can get a glimpse of what it might be like to live full-time in Venice.

Next to Palazzo Contarini Fasa, the legendary home of Shakespeare's tragic Desdemona, a young couple have put stylish East Asian touches into **Hotel Flora** (Calle dei Bergamaschi 2283/a, tel. 041/520-5844, www.hotel flora.it, €140–190 d). Period furniture from the end of the 17th century, or in 16th-century Venetian style, adds elegance, as do damask tapestries and golden cornices.

Operated by the same family for two generations, **Hotel Do Pozzi** (Via XXII Marzo, 2373 San Marco, tel. 041/520-7855, www.ho teldopozzi.it, €130–280 d) also runs two other hotels and the Raffaele Restaurant. It's a convenient boat stop to Santa Maria del Giglio on Line 1. In warm weather, breakfast is served outside in the little piazza.

Room prices range widely depending on your view at **Hotel Violino d'Oro** (San Marco 2091, tel. 041/277-0841, www.violinodoro. com, 26 rooms, €60–400 d). If you come during the low season, ask for a room with the lovely view of Campiello or San Marco Canal. You can sometimes find a real bargain in this hotel, which is classically furnished in tones of gold, ivory, blue, and green.

€200–300

Run by the same family since the 1920s, **Hotel Concordia** (Calle Larga San Marco 367, tel. 041/520-6866, www.hotelconcordia.com, 56 rooms, €185–440 d) is a 17th century Venetian home with a new white marble lobby. Guest rooms are done in Venetian style, and several have views of St. Mark's. The La Piazzetta restaurant on the ground floor serves local specialties and offers particularly good service.

Facing the Grand Canal, **Hotel Metropole** (Riva Schiavone 4149, tel. 041/520-5044, www. hotelmetropole.com, 70 rooms, €210–500 d) has rooms decorated in different styles with the owner's fondness for antique travel trunks and clocks in evidence. The lobby has exotic perfume wafting through it. Check for lower rates January, July, August, and November.

Hotel La Fenice Et Des Artistes (S. Marco 1936, tel. 041/523-2333, www.fenicehotels. com, €150–280 d) attracts a clientele of opera goers and art fans.

A 15th-century monastery watchtower in a sunny, cheery square was successfully transformed into **Santo Stefano** (Campo Santo Stefano 2957, tel. 041/520-0166, www.hotelsan tostefanovenezia.com, 11 rooms, €120–320 d). Halls are decorated with Carrara marble and ceiling frescoes, while rooms are equipped with gilded mirrors, Barovier & Toso Murano glass lamps, whirlpool tubs, and other fine touches.

If you time your visit right, rates can be very low at the centrally located **Casanova** (San Marco 1284, tel. 041/520-6413, www.hotelcasa nova.it, 47 rooms, €60–256 d). Rooms have more simple lines similar to the Deco of the 1930s, ideal if you prefer clean lines to opulence.

Private boat access, a wood-paneled bar and lounge, original Palladian floor, antique stone fireplace, wood-paneled breakfast room with silk wall coverings, and windows that overlook a canal are how to enjoy the public spaces in **Palazzo Sant'Angelo sul Canal Grande** (San Marco 3878/b, tel. 041/241-1452, www.palaz zosantangelo.com, 14 rooms, €200–660 d). Guest rooms have silk wall coverings with color schemes in gold and red and marble baths, and if a gondola doesn't go fast enough, there's a *vaporetto* stop next to the entrance.

OVER €300

Venice's oldest hotel is located northwest of St. Mark's Square. In the days of the

Templars, the Locanda della Luna (The Moon Tavern) offered travelers a comfortable shelter. Some 800 years later, **Luna Hotel Baglioni** (San Marco 1243, tel. 041/528-9840, €406–771 d) is a classy hotel of refined elegance. Ristorante Canova downstairs has a polished ambience and has won awards for its cuisine.

A French fashion titan converted a 1500 palace to **Palazzino Grassi Hotel & Residence** (San Marco 3246/a, tel. 041/528-4644, www.palazzinagrassi.it, 28 rooms, €180–700 d) in 2006, with some refinements in 2007. Colors are neutral, with doors and windows that offer views of the Grand Canal (its main entrance and pier are here), the lagoon, or a small piazza. The attic suite, its crown jewel, has a chaise lounge to languidly enjoy the view of Venice.

Residence Bauer Casa Nova (BauerVenezia, San Marco 1459, tel. 041/520-7022, www.bauervenezia.com, 19 rooms, €350–715 d) has luxury apartment suites and 10 double rooms across from its 🅲 **Bauer Il Palazzo Hotel** (191 rooms, €360–1,350 d), with a Grand Canal entrance. It always has been and always will be one of Venice's top hotels. Many rooms are very spacious and each has a distinct color scheme. The bar has a rounded Deco look to it, while the gourmet De Pisis Restaurant terrace has a fab view of the Grand Canal.

This former home of a 14th century Venetian admiral exudes elegance with its fine writing desks, large mirrors, fireplace, carved wooden staircase with lattice panels, stained glass, secluded courtyard, well appointed restaurant, and summer breakfast on the rooftop sun terrace. **Hotel Saturnia & International** (Via XXII Marzo 2398, tel. 041/520-8377, www.hotelsaturnia.it, 89 rooms, €197–492 d) has been meticulously run by the same family since 1908 and service is snappy. Every room has antiques and Art Deco furniture.

Castello and Cannaregio
UNDER €100
Istituto San Giuseppe (Castello 5402, tel. 041/522-5352, sangiuseppe.venezia@virgilio.it, €70–76 d) may offer a good deal but it certainly isn't for night owls. This comfortable religious house with 14 rooms has an early curfew in the evening and if you're not back by 10 P.M. you'll have a lot of explaining to do to the monks.

An easy walk from the train station (left down Lista di Spagna), **Hotel Arcadia** (Rio Terà San Leonardo, Cannaregio 1333/d, tel. 041/717-355, www.hotelaracadia.net, €70–120 d) is situated next to Venice's Casino in a 17th-century *palazzo*. Its nice sitting area has a huge chandelier and doubles as the morning breakfast room. Rooms are basic with some nice antique touches that make this good value in a convenient transportation hub.

€100–200
Step inside **Hotel la Residenza** (Campo Bandiera e Moro, Castello 3608, tel. 041/528-5315, www.venicelaresidenza.com, €80–180 d) and it still has the air of a private residence expecting the arrival of guests, with lovely rooms and a gracious salon for breakfast. From the square outside, you can see Palazzo Badoer's magnificent 15th-century Gothic facade, which has central window joints decorated with 10th-century Byzantine sculpture.

A rare collection of original prints and art copies of master works hang in **Hotel Giorgione** (SS. Apostoli 4587, Calle Larga dei Proverbi 4587, tel. 041/522-5810, www.hotelgiorgione.com, 76 rooms, €100–400 d), the only residence in Venice that belongs to the exclusive Abitare la Storia, a group of prestigious hotels in Italian historic centers and the countryside.

Along the Riva degli Schiavoni in 1569, sculptor Alessandro Vittorio, Jacopo Sansovino's apprentice, bought his own rooms in this *palazzo* for his studio. Now **Hotel Bisanzio** (Riva degli Schiavoni, Calle della Pietà, Castello 3651, tel. 041/520-3100, www.bisanzio.com, 46 rooms, €100–390 d) is part of the Best Western chain and offers rooms furnished in simple lines with neutral tones that leave Venetian opulence to the others. Breakfast is in a sunny dining room or on the terrace. Most rooms face the central courtyard and are very quiet.

On Canal Grande in Lista di Spagna, just before Strada Nova is **Hotel Continental** (Lista di Spagna, Cannaregio 166, tel. 041/715-122, www.hotelcontinentalvenice.com, €155 d). It has one of Venice's lower rates and is conveniently located between the train station and the Rialto. Rooms are comfortable, not opulent.

Take your first two lefts as you exit the train station and step into the former Monastery of Barefoot Carmelite Friars at **C Hotel Abbazia** (Calle Priuli dei Cavaletti, Cannaregio 68, tel. 041/717-333, www.abbaziahotel.com, €90–250 d). You'll sing with joy when you see this tranquil oasis. Comfortable sitting areas and an enchanting courtyard garden are perfect for tea, writing, or getting re-aquainted with your sketchpad. A recent restoration preserved the charm of the ancient abbey that blends hospitality with tradition. Rooms, some with courtyard views, are attractively furnished in various color schemes without being fussy.

Founded by father and son gondoliers who switched from water to land, **C Ca'Gottardi** (Cannaregio 2283, tel. 041/275-9333, www.cagottardi.com, 14 rooms, €130–200 d) exudes elegance with its traditional textiles, hand-painted wood ceiling beams, grand high windows in the lobby breakfast area, and Murano chandeliers juxtaposed with interesting contemporary art and terrazzo floors. Each room has its own color scheme like gold, burgundy, or terra-cotta with gold accents. It's conveniently located between the Ca'd'Oro and the Venice Casino.

Locanda del Ghetto (Campo del Ghetto Novo, Cannaregio 2892/2893, tel. 041/275-9292, www.locandadelghetto.net, €100–185 d) started out as a 15th-century *palazzo,* was later converted to a synagogue, and seems to have found its true calling today as a lovely guesthouse. Rooms have views of the Campo or canal.

The Orsoni family villa in Cannaregio opened five rooms in 2005 to launch **Domus Orsoni Hotel** (Cannaregio 1045, tel. 041/275-9538, www.domusorsoni.it, €97–290). Run by Lucio Orsoni, it's decorated with mosaic tiles, a family specialty for over 100 years in places like Sacre Coeur in Paris and Gaudi's Sagra Familia church in Barcelona. They also offer mosaic classes and private tours of the Basilica with a mosaic restorer, Giovanni Cucco.

A short hop to Campo Santa Maria Formosa takes you to **Hotel al Piave** (Ruga Giuffa 4838/40, Campo Santa Maria Formosa, Castello. tel. 041/528-5174, www.hotelalpiave.com, €110–165 d). Rooms have pale neutral walls, terrazzo floors, brocade bedcovers and drapes.

The lobby of **Hotel Belle Epoque** (Cannaregio 127/128, tel. 041/244-0004, www. hotelbelleepoque.it, €130–250 d) shines as if it's been completely lacquered, an effect accentuated by the mirrors and chandeliers. The guest rooms in shades of red or green are decidedly calmer.

€200-300

A fourth room overlooking the Grand Canal and new elevator will be christened in 2008 at **Hotel Paganelli** (Riva degli Schiavoni 4182, tel. 041/522-4324, www.hotelpaganelli.com, €220). The hotel has 15 rooms plus 7 in annex around the corner that faces the Benedictine abbey, along with updated furnishings. This is just the spot if you have a lot of luggage or this is your first time in Venice and want to find your hotel easily. It's directly in front of the Zaccaria *vaporetto* stop.

Around the corner in Campo San Zaccaria overlooking the Benedictine abbey where nuns once threw lavish parties is the 1875 **Hotel Villa Igea** (Campo San Zaccaria, Castello 4684, tel. 041/241-0956, www.hotelvillaigea. it, 30 rooms, €152–232 d). The morning sun and pastel decor (renovated in 2005) with gold, green, or blue color schemes make for rooms with plenty of light. Breakfast is hearty and generous.

Hotel Amadeus (Lista di Spagna, Cannaregio 227, tel. 041/220-6000, www.hotelamadeusvenice.it, 63 rooms, €165–355 d) has a bar and Japanese restaurant, TV room, delightful garden, and common areas decorated with Murano mirrors and glass, precious marbles, and

VENICE

elegant fabrics where guests relax and exchange gondolier stories. Rooms are in Venetian style with a modern flair and typically vibrant color schemes.

A 16th-century noble palace is the setting for **Casa Verardo** (Castello 4765, tel. 041/528-6138, www.casaverardo.it, €180–360), run by Daniela and Francesco in a small hotel with only nine rooms, ideally located on the "noble" floor of the palazzo. The breakfast buffet is on the terrace in summer.

Liassidi Palace (Ponte dei Greci 3405, castello, tel. 041/520-5658, www.liassidipalacehotel.com, €190–490) is a 15th-century palazzo near the Byzantine museum. It has its own dock on the canal should you wish to arrive by water taxi. The mirror-adorned lobby has lovely crimson and gold antique furniture with Murano chandeliers. Some rooms have high ceilings and chandeliers, others have cozy wood-beam ceilings. Bedrooms have neutral color schemes, some with splashy red accents and pretty mosaic tile baths.

OVER €300

Maria Callas created a scandal in 1957 by canceling her performance in Edinburgh to attend a party for the Danieli hotel family. Founded in 1822 and favored by artists and writers like Dickens, Proust, Wagner, and Balzac, **Hotel Danieli** (Castello 4196, tel. 041/522-6480, www.hoteldanielivenice.com, 233 rooms, €1650–1,400 d) occupies a *palazzo* that went up in the early 1400s and was home to four Doges. It has a grand marble staircase and the crowning glory is the Doge's Suite, with gloriously golden ceiling frescoes painted by a pupil of Tiepolo. The decorator added the perfect sense of drama to the guest rooms, as if you've just stepped into a Hollywood set, but fortunately you are in the real Venice.

San Polo and Dorsoduro
UNDER €100

When the university is not in session, rooms are sometimes available to visitors on the Giudecca at **Residenza Universitaria** (www.esuvenezia.it, €45–70 d). This is dorm-style accommodation that may or may not bring back fond memories of higher education. Most rooms come with private bath. Another low-budget option with shared bath and breakfast is **Ostello Venezia** (Fondamenta delle Zitelle 86, tel. 041/523-8211, www.ostellionlin.org, 20 rooms, €24 pp). This popular hostel is full of young international travelers and friendship blossoms here daily. It's on the Giudecca and easily reached by *vaporetto*.

€100–200

In Vittore Carpaccio's 1494 painting that now hangs in the Accademia, you can see the sign for **Locanda Sturion** (San Polo 679, Calle Sturion, tel. 041/523-6243, www.locandasturion.com, 11 rooms, €60–320 d). Used by the Doges in the 12th century to house foreign merchants who came to sell their wares at the Rialto market, the decor is now 18th century, an ambience picked up in the furnishings and brocades. Some rooms face the Grand Canal. Guests receive a discount at the Le Bistro de Venise, a wine bar that makes an ideal spot for dinner and are encouraged to browse the small library.

At the foot of the Calcina Bridge on the sunny Zattere promenade lies **La Calcina** (Zattere, Dorsoduro 780, tel. 041/520-6466, www.lacalcina.com, 29 rooms, €138–201 d). "The Lime House" faces the Giudecca Canal, which you can enjoy from the roof terrace. Prices vary according to the view and rooms have recycled Art Deco furniture from an earlier inn. La Piscina Café (Tues.–Sun.) serves all day inside and out in warm months.

The art is good, the decor is shabby genteel, and that seems to suit guests like Ezra Pound, Modigliani, President Carter, Robert De Niro, Brad Pitt, Mick Jagger, and David Bowie at **Locanda Montin** (Fondamenta delle Romite, Dorsoduro 1147, tel. 041/522-7151, www.locandamontin.com, 12 rooms, €185 d). It also attracts students and professors from the neighboring Cà Foscari University, who appreciate its courtyard garden, restaurant, and bar. Rooms, some with a view of the quiet canal, are all blissfully lacking TVs and air-conditioning.

Mini apartments with a kitchen are ideal for

those that don't want to eat all their meals out or for adventurous cooks ready to experiment with the local fish and vegetable markets. As its name implies, the Art Nouveau **Residenza Grandi Vedute** (Giudecca 812/814, tel. 041/723-050 or 041/241-1450, 8 apartments, €75–225) has great views of some 40 bell towers.

Next door, in the same converted Stucky Mill factory complex, is the new **Hilton Molino Stucky** (Giudecca 753, tel. 041/272-3311, www.hilton.com/venice, €190 d). It has all the conveniences of a Hilton including the possibility of using your traveler's points. There are great panoramic views at the Skyline Rooftop Bar and a free shuttle service to San Marco and Zattere.

€200-300

The 17th-century Villa Maravege, nicknamed "Villa of Wonders," once served as the Russian Embassy and is now **Pensione Accademia** (Dorsoduro 1058, tel. 041/521-0188, www.pensioneaccademia.it, 27 rooms, €114–285 d). The prestigious Grand Canal location has two large gardens, rooms in Venetian style with antiques, and the Accademia Galleries nearby.

Lively, quirky elegance is yours at **Ca' Pisani Hotel** (Dorsodoro 979/a, tel. 041/240-1411, www.capisanihotel.it, 29 rooms, €192–480 d). Designers had an Art Deco ball here stylishly putting in clever details and commissioning individual works that enhance original 1930s and 1940s pieces in each room. La Revista, the restaurant with wine and cheese bar, keeps the energy flowing with hardwood floors accented with black and purple tables and splashy art.

Near Santa Maria della Salute, **Ca' Maria Adele 1** and **2** (Dorsoduro 111-114 and 112, tel. 041/520-3078, www.camariaadele.it, €60–800 d) offers a great variety of different styles and prices. Offerings include deluxe rooms with brocades in colors that remind you that gold is neutral in Venice, as well as five theme rooms—like the Doge's Room, perfect for those that can never have too much red, Marco Polo's Oriental Room, and other bold schemes full of drama.

OVER €300

Built by Giuseppe Cipriani, the founder of Harry's Bar who pioneered development of the Giudecca for tourism, **Hotel Cipriani** (Giudecca 10, tel. 041/520-7744, www.hotelcipriani.com, €570–1,400 d) is now owned by Orient Express. Rooms are very lavish and you can pamper yourself at the La Prairie Casanova Beauty & Wellness Center. The outdoor Olympic-size heated pool with filtered salt water is in a great location near the water— one good push and it looks like a boat could flop in, too. Chef Renato has been turning out Venetian specialties since 1990.

Santa Croce and the Lido

Lido prices zoom up in summer when Venetians seek to escape the heat and in September during the Venice Film Festival. The rest of the year it can offer some real bargains. Frequent *vaporetto* service connects you quickly to the center. A stay here gives you a good sense of the sea and the lagoon, intrinsic to understanding Venice but sometimes never seen by visitors. It's a treat to see the comings and goings on water, from small fishing boats to major cruise liners.

Don't worry about being stranded on the Lido, it has excellent boat service with full-service ticket windows (near the Esso gas station). Public transportation runs about every 20 minutes, 24 hours a day. If you plan to use it a lot, buy the more-economical 24- or 36-hour ACTV passes, also good for the island's bus transportation.

€100-200

The main part of **Villa Mabapa** (Riviera S.Nicolò 16, www.villamabapa.it, €125–341 d) dates back to the 1930s. Villa Morea and Casa Pradel complete the scenario, all connected by a covered gallery near a wide, relaxing garden. You can opt for half or full board, which comes in handy if you just want to kick back, watch the sunset, and have dinner on the island.

In the heart of the Lido, **Atlanta Augustus** (Via Lepanto 15, www.hotelatlantaaugustus.com, €140 d) is an Art Nouveau villa close to the sea that dates to the early 1900s. Some suites overlook the canal and have a balcony or small terrace. Each room is decorated in a different style. Rates fluctuate from as low as €40 to over €400.

At **Hotel Buon Pesce** (Riviera San Nicolò 50, tel. 041/526-8599, www.hotelbuonpesce. com, €70–350 d) on the eastern tip of the Lido, you are well positioned to see ships as they turn into and out of the lagoon into the Adriatic Sea. Popular for its reasonable rates, **Villa Tiziana** (Via A. Gritti 3, www.hotelvillatiziana.net, €40–340 d), has only 12 rooms and fills up quickly. It's across the canal behind the Lido Casino.

€200-300

Hotel Des Bains (Lungomare Marconi 17, tel. 041/526-0113, www.starwooditaly.com, €65–600 d) is a must for anyone on a literary tour of the city. It's where Thomas Mann wrote *Death in Venice* and Luchino Visconti shot the film. The hotel is in a beautiful Belle Epoque property with a swimming pool that faces the Adriatic Sea. Some rooms look onto the sea, while others face the garden side. Sheraton Starwood manages the hotel, which often closes in winter months.

OVER €300

Westin Excelsior (Lungomare Marconi 41, tel. 041/526-0201, www.starwooditaly.com, €250–885 d) is movie-star central during the Venice Film Festival in September, when A-list celebrities are bumper-to-bumper in the sleek lounge. In 1907 it opened as the world's largest luxury resort, with Moorish style down to the beach cabanas. The interior is designed for creatures of comfort and the staff make satisfaction a priority.

Camping

Campsites are popular with Northern Europeans on a budget. **Camping al Boschetto** (Via delle Batterie 18, tel. 041/966-145, www.alboschetto.it, €8.50 per person or €19–80 for a bungalow) is close to the sea and has a full range of activities. If you aren't packing a tent

you can rent rustic bungalows on the grounds amidst the trailer park.

FOOD

The glorious bounty of the lagoon and the sea are the highlight of Venetian cuisine. *Baccalà* (cod) that has been salted and cured is a Venetian tradition, as are other humble dishes like liver and onions. Meat and game are a stronger tradition in the region, but are easy to find in Venice, so keep in mind that generally meat and vegetable dishes are available too, even where fish or seafood is indicated as a house specialty. There are a variety of Veneto wines and good restaurateurs are delighted to suggest wine pairings with your meal.

If you're accustomed to the later dining hours in Southern Italy, remember that in the north meals begin at 7:30 P.M. and thus kitchens close earlier. These hours can catch some visitors by surprise. Some kitchens may close as early as 9:30 P.M. or 10 P.M., so phone ahead to make reservations and confirm serving hours.

Many of Venice's touristy restaurants dole out frozen and microwaved dishes that provide no sense of the uniqueness of Venetian cuisine or how flavorful it can be. Look at the market prices for fish. If your menu offers a "bargain," it probably came out of a freezer and from someplace else. Fish is labor intensive and must be delivered and consumed quickly—it's not cheap. Some fish or meat dishes are sold by the *"etto"* or 100 grams. A portion of fish is likely to be at least 300 grams, so multiply by three or more if you want to calculate the price of the fish.

Grand Canal
REGIONAL

Some locals dine daily on the Grand Canal, others frequent eateries there once every 10 years. They all count on ◖ **Harry's Bar** (Sestiere San Marco 1323, tel. 041/528-5777, daily 10:30 A.M.–11 P.M., €87) to deliver their favorite drinks or dishes exactly as they remember them. Harry's delivers and hums with success. The atmosphere is cozy and unpretentious while the food is reliable and consistent from one day or one decade to the next. Everyone complains

© PURESTOCK

canal-side dining

about the prices but no one complains about the food or service. The spinach and cheese ravioli are light as a feather, the *tagliolini* covered with ham and cheese is a meal of comfort food, and the Sunday special of *ossobuco* and *risotto alla Milanese* is delicious. And of course Arrigo (Harry) is still at the helm of the food empire his father and British business partner Harry began. You can also stop at the bar that's been a celebrity watering hole for over half a century. There is no sign, just the name etched on the glass window panels near the gondola station.

San Marco
REGIONAL

The owner of **⟨ Le Bistrot de Venise** (Calle dei Fabbri, tel. 041/523-6651, www.bistrot devenise.com, daily noon–3 P.M. and 7 P.M.– midnight, €65–85) usually has 50 luscious wines available by the glass and many more Italian and international labels by the bottle. The cuisine specialty is Venetian, contemporary and historic. The Sample Historic Venetian Cuisine Menu takes dinners back to 14th- and 15th-century Venetian recipes, adjusted to modern palates, like *Scampi in Saor* (€20), battered fried shrimp with sweet-and-sour sauce. There's also an 18th-century Carlo Goldoni menu and modern cuisine. Locals come for literary events and other happenings. Outside seating is near the canal. Inside the bar is ideal for trying those wines and mingling and it's open late. Service is attentive.

The atmosphere and cuisine of the famous Orient Express train that once connected Paris and Istanbul is served at **Trattoria do Forni** (468/457 Calle Specchieri, tel. 041/523-2148, www.doforni.it, daily noon–3 P.M. and 7 P.M.– midnight, €65–85).

INTERNATIONAL

The nonstop lunch and late evening dining mean that you can get a hot meal at **Ristorante al Colombo** (San Marco 4619, tel. 041/522-2627, daily noon–midnight) at off hours, late afternoon or late evening. Near the Teatro Goldoni, it also attracts Italian actors and theatergoers for its outside seating. Here retro cuisine like crepes Suzette never left the menu and waiters love to put on the flame show.

SOUTHERN ITALIAN

If you want to break away from Venetian food for Southern flavors, only Neapolitan cuisine will do and that's all they serve at **Acqua Pazza** (San Marco 3808/10, Campo Sant'Angelo, tel. 041/277-0688, daily noon–3 P.M. and 7 P.M.–midnight, €65–85) in generous portions.

PIZZA

Pizzeria Marciana (Calle Larga San Marco 3671b, tel. 041/520-6524, Tues.–Sun. 11 A.M.–9:30 P.M.) just behind the basilica is where you can sit down and get a quality pizza at a good price, most under €10. An important bonus is that they stay open in between lunch and dinner hours, when most places close. Quality pizza by the slice with many toppings to choose from is available from **Sansovino** (San Marco 2628, near Campo San Maurizio, Tues.–Sun. 11 A.M.–9 P.M., €2.50).

CAFÉS

Venice's most beautiful cafe is right on St. Mark's Square. **Caffè Florian** (Piazza San Marco, tel. 041/520-5641, www.caffeflorian. com, daily 10 A.M.–11 P.M., Nov.–Feb. closed Wed., €10–13) has been luring visitors since 1720. Its various theme rooms are beautifully frescoed, adorned with antique mirrors, cushy red seats, and small marble or wood tables. This is not a place to dine, but to snack. Have a dainty sandwich with Prosecco or champagne, a cappuccino, or one of their good homemade pastries or gelatos. Outside an orchestra plays in warmer months and some couples dance. A simple snack is likely to run €25. If the orchestra is playing, there's a cover charge but you can linger inside or out for hours.

A well-kept secret is the upstairs cafe in the corridor of **Museo Correr** (Piazza San Marco, daily 9 A.M.–4 P.M.), open during museum hours. Some tables have a view of Piazza San Marco, an ideal perch for a cappuccino, light lunch, or glass of wine. The museum entrance and meal tab combined will cost less than the same in the square, plus you get to see the art.

For breakfast rolls, a light lunch, or a snack, you can sit down at **Bar Lucano** (San Marco 480 at Campo della Guerra, tel. 041/528-5294) where they serve adequate fare at economical prices.

The small **Teamo Café and Wine Bar** (San Marco 3795, lunch only), which opened only in 2007, serves wine by the glass and a selection of appetizing sandwiches and salads in an atmosphere that is both modern and historic.

Every pastry is displayed like a jewel at **Le Café** (Campo Santo Stefano 2797, tel. 041/523-7201, www.lecafevenezia.com, Wed.–Mon. 8:30 A.M.–9 P.M.), an ideal spot for coffee, tea, and pastry, or a Prosecco with some little salty snacks or delectable little panini.

An artistic and mouthwatering display of perfect pastries is at **Andrea Zanin** (San Marco 4589, tel. 041/522-4803, Mon.–Sat. 7:30 A.M.–8 P.M. and Sun. 9:30 A.M.–6:30 P.M.). Especially good are the little cakes and pastries, but it's a good stop for breakfast rolls, too.

GELATO

Gelaterie are all over Venice and easy to spot. Trickier is to find a good one where you can also sit down. The fanciest and priciest is **Caffè Florian** (Piazza San Marco, tel. 041/520-5641, www.caffeflorian.com, daily 10 A.M.–11 P.M., Nov.–Feb. closed Wed., €10–12). Especially good are the hazelnut, pistachio, and vanilla flavors made on the premises.

Castello and Cannaregio
VENETIAN

In recent years, quality has slipped a bit at **Aciugheta** (Campo SS Filippo e Giacomo, Castello 4357, tel. 041/522-4292, lunch and dinner, €12–14), but the *pranzo di operaio* ("worker's meal," a daily luncheon special that is under €10) is a break from the fray and opportunity to hear real Venetian accents. Fried fish is reasonably good.

REGIONAL

Despite its name and some fine meat options like Chianina steak, ◖ **Fiaschetteria Toscana** (S. Giovanni Grisostomo, Cannaregio 5719, tel. 041/528-5281, Wed.–Mon., €12–18) is a bastion of superb Venetian fish and seafood. If it's in season, try the fried *moeche* (soft-shelled spidery lagoon crab). Film director Ang Lee dined here in 2006 and 2007 when he was in town for the Venice Film Festival. And don't miss the desserts or wines, as the chef is a master at preparing and selecting both.

Lucia selects great wines for **Corte Sconta** (Castello 3886 Calle del Pestrin, tel. 041/522-7024, Tues.–Sat., lunch and dinner, €50 for 3 courses), so let her expertly pair them to your dishes. Nephew Marco adds the perfect touch of ginger to clams sautéed in a white wine broth, and knows to leave the red giant crab simple to savor its delicate flavor. Don't miss the Venetian artichoke bottoms if they are in season. Creative desserts go from light and fruity to decadent. Reserve a table in the courtyard in warm months.

Creative cuisine that avoids eccentricity is Chef Agostino's mantra at **L'Osteria di Santa Marina** (Campo Santa Marina 5911 Castello, tel. 041/528-5239), which attracts an international clientele as well as Venetians. The raw fish is a good starter. Look for unusual pairings like grilled tiny *calamaretti* on a bed of lime mashed potatoes or red mullet with foie gras, which the sommelier can enhance with wines by the glass or bottle. Desserts are heavenly. Even the coffee is especially good. Service is attentive and you can dine outside in the square or indoors.

Regional cuisine is a specialty at **Alle Testiere** (Castello 5801, S. Lio Calle del Mondo Novo, tel. 041/522-7220, www.osterialletestiere.it, Tues.–Sat. lunch and dinner, €45 for 3 courses).

At the intersection of the Grand Canal and a smaller canal Rio di Ca' di Dio near Hotel Gabriele is cozy **Ristorante Carpaccio** (Castello Riva Schiavoni 4088-4089, tel. 041/528-9615, www.ristorantecarpaccio.com) with a few outdoor tables wedged in at the base of the pedestrian bridge under the bustle of a nonstop parade of people and water taxis. The raw and fried fish are tasty, as are the *tagliolini* with lagoon scallops. Wines are good, the fig and ricotta tarts are excellent, and service is friendly.

Al Covo (Castello 3968, Campiello della Pescheria, tel. 041/522-3812, www.ristorantealcovo.com, Fri.–Tues., €60 for 3 courses) specializes in local and regional cuisine. Chef Cesare Ben's seafood dishes and the reasonably priced wines are the highlights. His wife, Diane, prepares the desserts.

Former market fishmonger Loris brings his expert knowledge to **Al Fontego del Pescatore** (Cannaregio 3726, Calle Priuli, tel. 041/520-0538, Tues.–Sun., €43 for 3 courses). Count on excellent raw fish for starters and fried squid. Fresh vegetables grown on the Island of St. Erasmus served tempura-style are delicious. A lovely garden in front is ideal for outdoor dining, while inside jazz recordings accompanies the food.

The Ghetto's main kosher restaurant, **Gam-Gam** (Sottoportico di Ghetto Vecchio, Cannaregio 1122, tel. 041/715-284, Sun.–Thurs. noon–10 P.M., €12–14) has traditional international specialties from around the Mediterranean and beyond including falafel, kebabs, couscous, fried artichokes, and latkes.

Il Nuovo Galeon (Castello 1308, Via Garibaldi, tel. 041/520-4656, Wed.–Mon., €45 for 3 courses) is on a broad avenue and specializes in seafood.

Wines are the forte of **Vini da Gigio** (Cannaregio 3628-near Ca' d'Oro, tel. 041/528-5140, www.vinidagigio.com, Wed.–Sun., €43 for 3 courses), but don't miss the tasty pumpkin and shrimp risotto. Grilled vegetables are especially good here. Laura's desserts are excellent and her *pannacotta* with berries may be the best in town. The cozy atmosphere has wood beam ceilings, iron wall lamps, small prints, and wine bottles everywhere.

QUICK BITES

Good breads, rolls, pastries, and variations on pizza (this is not a pizzeria) are at **Panificio Milani** (Castello 4745, tel. 041/523-6605), perfect for a picnic or a snack. **L'Angolo della Pizza di Bacco** (Cannaregio 1588–1589, tel. 041/717-453, daily) sells a good assortment of pizza by the slice.

VENICE

VENICE

café nightlife in Piazza San Marco

© PURESTOCK

CAFÉS

Camillo Marchi's **Caffè Costarica** (Cannaregio 1337, tel. 041/716-371, Mon.–Sat. 8 A.M.–6:30 P.M.) mixes its own special blend of roasted coffee beans that are worth bringing home. Fortunately, the store also serves one of Venice's best cups of espresso or cappuccino, which is why the locals pile in.

DESSERTS

A tasty, dense *torta di pistacchio* (pistachio cake) at **Bar Pasticceria Pitteri** (Cannaregio 3843, tel. 041/522-2687) in an individual portion is enough to fuel you for hours. In the Ghetto near Tam-Tam a pastry shop under the arch sells Jewish specialties. Thre is no name or address posted on the storefront, but you can easily see the arch from the square.

San Polo and Dorsoduro
VENETIAN

Traditional Venetian fish and seafood dishes are the specialty at **Ai Gondolieri** (Dorsoduro 366, San Vio, tel. 041/528-6396, www.aigondolieri.com, Wed.–Mon., 3-course meal averages €55).

Count on **Antiche Campane** (S. Polo 1911, Rio tera delle Carampane, tel. 041/524-015, www.antichecampane.com, Tues.–Sat., €45 for 3-course meal) for a good variety of traditional Venetian and seafood meals.

REGIONAL

Da Ignazio (S. Polo 2749, Calle dei Saoneri, tel. 041/523-4852, Sun.–Fri. lunch and dinner) has keeps regulars contented with Venetian and regional specialties. A typical three-course meal runs €45 and generally last about 90 minutes from the first bread stick to final sip of coffee.

Osteria da Fiore (San Polo Calle del Scaleter 2202, tel. 041/721-308, Tues.–Sat., €90) remains one of Venice's most "in" restaurants and keeps locals as wells as tourists coming in for the varied seafood and fish dishes, as well as an extensive wine selection.

DELICACIES

A small but good cheese shop, **Latteria Ronchi** (San Polo 1053, tel. 041/523-0589) sells select local and Italian cheeses. Anyone with an aversion to fermentation should enter at their own risk. Everyone else can ask for a sample slice before buying.

Santa Croce and the Lido
VENETIAN

The *fritolin* (shops for fried local fish) are fast disappearing but **Vecio Fritolin** (Santa Croce 2262, Calle della Regina, tel. 041/522-2881, Tues.–Sun. lunch, €9–13) near the Rialto is the local favorite. They still serve fish to-go wrapped in paper, the traditional and economical way.

On the Lido, **Al Vecio Cantier** (Alberoni Lido, Via della Droma 76, tel. 041/526-8130, Tues.–Sun.) is an old-style *trattoria,* where Chef Dario superbly prepares all manner of fish from the sea and lagoon. **Trattoria La Battigia** (Via Nicosia 10 Ve Lido, tel. 041/276-0599, Thurs.–Tues.) near the Lido's marina is another favorite with locals for its fish dishes.

A favorite of area winemakers and perfect with Prosecco is the Lido's **La Favorita** (Via Francesco Duodo 33, tel. 041/526-1626, Tues. dinner–Sun.) where *scampi in saor* (shrimp with a sweet and pungent sauce) is a must.

Giudecca **Harry's Dolci** (Giudecca 773, tel. 041/522-4844) began as a tearoom but then added Harry's great cocktails and some of the dishes.

INFORMATION AND SERVICES
Tourist Information

A good map of Venice and the islands is essential. The tourist offices (Terre di Venezia, www.turismovenezia.it) sell them and they're also available from most newspaper kiosks around the train station. Be sure that your map shows the location of the islands in relation to St. Mark's so you can easily plot your transportation routes.

Tourist information offices are at the S. Lucia Train Station, St. Mark's Square 71f (near the Museo Correr), Piazzale Roma, and the arrivals terminal at Marco Polo Airport. They are not self-serve, but you wait in line to speak to an assistant at the desk, who will provide you with the material you need or will make reservations for tours and events. For city events and other visitor needs, call **HelloVenezia** (tel. 041/2424, www.hellovenezia.com) or the **APT** (tel. 041/529-8711).

Venice Card (www.venicecard.it) offers combined discounts for transportation, sights, and services. Check with the tourist office for updated offers or HelloVenezia.

St. Mark's Square, Venice, and other Veneto cities are designated open-air museums. They value the tourist income but want to preserve their dignity. Fed up with tourists and locals that turn historic centers into picnic areas, strict codes have been enacted that if enforced might drain your wallet. Even a local Verona resident in 2007 was fined €50 on the spot as her four-year-old son prepared to sink his teeth into a kebab near the Arena. Italians traditionally confine eating to homes, hotels, bars, or restaurants. Avoid street munching and certainly don't plan to dine on public transportation. Communities now fine citizens or visitors that do not conduct themselves as deemed appropriate, including public intoxication or disruptive behavior. Keep in mind that shorts are not allowed in many churches and that walking in bare feet or exposing one's torso is only done during Carnevale.

Government Offices

Lost or stolen passports should be reported to the U.S. Consulate in Milan (tel. 02/290-351, Mon.–Fri. 9:30 A.M.–12:30 P.M.). They can also help out with any diplomatic problems you may encounter.

Hospitals, Police, and Emergencies

For medical emergencies call the 118 hotline or the Guardia Medica Turistica (Ca' Savio, tel. 041/530-0874) that is dedicated entirely to diagnosing the ailments of visitors. If you can walk to the hospital try Ospedale Fatebenefratalli

VENICE

(Cannaregio 3458, tel. 041/783-111) or Ospedale Civile (tel. 041/5290-4111). City police can be reached on 041/274-7070.

Glasses broken or lost? **Ottica Mantovani** (San Marco 4860, tel. 041/522-3427) claims to replace them in 30 minutes. Worried about drifting away in *acqua alta*? **Centro Maree** (tel. 041/241-1996) provides daily tide information. Siren blasts warn of particularly high water when boots should be worn.

Banks and Currency Exchange

American Express (tel. 0411/520-0844) and major banks with *bancomat* (cash withdrawal machines) are directly off St. Mark's Square on Salizzada San Moisè. There's usually a long line around lunchtime so if you need euros it's best to stop by early or late in the day.

Internet

Venetian Navigator (www.venetiannavigator.com) is an Internet and calling point with several locations around the city, including Calle Casselleria 5300 near San Marco and Calle Stagneri 5239 near Rialto Bridge. **E Copie da Toni** in Castello 5265 (S. Lio Calle delle Bande, www.ecopiedatoni.dyndns.org) has Internet, international calling, copy, scanning, and fax services.

Lost and Found

There's an airport lost and found (tel. 041/260-6436) in the arrivals terminal and another one in town at the **Vigili Urbani** (Piazzale Roma, tel. 041/522-4576). Found items that aren't retrieved are eventually sold at auction.

GETTING THERE

Pack light. Many hotels, even in upper categories, do not offer porter service. If your bag is over the limit, you will pay for that whenever transportation is involved. If your car is parked in a secure place with no visible luggage, consider bringing just an overnight bag with only the essentials for your stay. A handbag may be more practical than luggage on wheels, which can be hard to navigate through crowds and carry up steps.

Air

Many travelers to Venice arrive at Milan's Malpensa Airport because there are more flights and route competition that may result in better fares. If you are planning the Rome–Florence–Venice triad, you can start north and move south or vice-versa.

Delta (www.delta.com) and Alitalia (www.altialia.it) have flights from New York to **Marco Polo Airport** (www.veniceairport.it). Discount airfares to Venice are likely to be from other European destinations like London. **Alpi Eagles** (www.alpieagles.com) has budget fares within Italy and some international destinations.

Alilaguna (www.actv.it) connects the airport to the historic center, Murano, Fonte Nove, and the port. If possible avoid water taxis, as the cost will be high.

Car

Cars cannot enter Venice. Generally the closer you park to the city, the more expensive the parking rates. The closest parking areas are at **Piazzale Roma** and at **Tronchetto Isle.** Other parking is at Fusina, Marghera, Tessera Treport, and Punta Sabbioni. See locations and compare rates at: www.asmvenezia.it, www.garagesan marco.it, www.veniceparking.it, www.marco polo2002.com, and www.garagestazione.it.

If you plan to rent a car and travel in the Veneto or elsewhere, it may be more economical to pick it up after your Venice visit rather than pay for parking on the days that it just sits. Rental agencies in Venice and the Veneto include Avis, Hertz, Europcar, and Maggiore, with locations at airports and major train stations.

Car ferry from Tronchetto to Lido is by **ACTV** (www.actv.it). Vehicles are divided into 10 categories, to which a different rate is applied based on the route involved. Vehicle fares do not include the fee for the driver, except for anyone traveling by bicycle (€6.50) or moped (€7) up to 50 cc.

Bus

The bus terminal is near the Grand Canal at Piazzale Roma (at *vaporetto* stop Piazzale Roma).

ACTV connects to different destinations in Venice and SITA travels into the Veneto.

Train

The **Santa Lucia station** (tel. 84/888-8088, www.trenitalia.com) is conveniently located right at edge of the Grand Canal (at *vaporetto* stop Ferrovia).

If you want to try the refurbished **Orient Express** (www.orientexpress.com), trains depart from Venice on Wednesdays with stops in Innsbruck and Paris before arriving in London.

Boat

Cruise ships, ferries, hydrofoils, and mega-yachts arrive at **Venezia Terminal Passeggeri** (Marittima, Fabbricato 248, www.vtp.it). Venice connects directly to Istria and Lussino by the Adriatic Sea's fastest catamarans or by ferry served by Venezia Lines (www.venezialines.com).

GETTING AROUND

Venice has one of the world's most complex, fascinating, efficient, and fun transportation systems. Unless you get out and explore the lagoon and various islands, you won't really understand how beautiful and varied is La Serenissima. A ride in a *vaporetto* may be just the down time that you need.

Get a good map of Venice that shows the historic center and the lagoon area. The historic center is divided into six neighborhoods, *sestiere*. Don't miss excursions to other islands, a ride that is shorter than from Central Park to Greenwich Village. Think of the water as a means to speed up communication, not as an impediment.

Piazza San Marco, St. Mark's Square, is the most famous and streets near it the most congested. See it, savor it from a cafe, visit the Basilica, its museums, climb the campanile, and then move on.

Everyone gets lost in Venice. That's part of the fun. You may feel like a rat trying to get through a maze, but one wrong turn may lead to another that will show you a Venice that

tourists don't often see. Get lost and love it. Use your map to get to appointments. Here are a few terms to help you find your way. *Calle* is street, *rio* is canal, *campo* is square, *fondamenta* is a street that runs along a canal, *salizzada* is a main street. Bridges are a means of transport, so do not block them. Take your photos quickly from the edge and move on.

Venice Card offers some savings that might encourage you to visit other sights. If you use a water taxi or gondola, always determine the fare before you board.

Venice is subject to frequent flooding, especially in fall and winter months. A warning siren announces exceptionally high tides. Many areas will put down wooden walkways. Tall rain boots are handy to get around other areas but makeshift plastic bags around your feet and ankles will also do.

If you have too much baggage or need assistance finding your way, you can hire a porter from *stazione portabagagli* at Ferrovia, Accademia, Piazzale Roma, San Geremia, or San Marco (5 stand locations). Fares from those points into Venice City are regulated: €18 for 1 item; €24 for 2 items; €30 for 3–4 items; each additional item is €6. Fees are higher for islands, Giudecca, Lido, Sant'Elena (€14.40–48). These fares were valid in 2007, but may increase. Any other porterage points are unregulated and should be negotiated in advance.

The city has accessible routes for visitors with disabilities. Check with HelloVenezia or **Informahandicap** (tel. 041/274-8144, www.comune.venezia.it/informahandicap) for barrier-free itineraries, tactile maps, and routes.

As anywhere else in Italy, beware of occasional transportation strikes, almost always announced days or weeks in advance. Your hotel or daily newspaper should be able to give you an update on union sentiment.

Air

If the *vaporettos* are too crowded for your taste, you can always book a helicopter tour of the lagoon with **Heliair Venice** (Lido Airport, tel. 041/525-0125, €55) that lasts 40 minutes and is a favorite for marriage proposals.

Bus

ATVO (tel. 041/520-5530, www.atvo.it) operates on the Lido, Pellestrina, and other *terra ferma* locations.

Taxi

Taxi Acquei, the boat taxi service, is pricey but convenient, with stands on the major (San Marco and Rialto) and smaller canals as well as the Lido, airport, train, and Piazzale Roma parking areas. Rates, established by Regional decree, were last changed in June 2003. The fares: €8.70 base fare before departure; €1.30 every 60 seconds (travel and waiting); €6 call charge; €5.50 surcharge for night (10 p.m.–7 a.m.) service; €1.50 for each parcel over 50cm; €5.90 holiday surcharge (not to be added to the nightly rate); €1.60 for each person exceeding four passengers.

    Taxi Terrestri, land taxis, are available at Piazzale Roma and the Lido.

Boat

When or where else has mass transportation been so romantic? **ACTV** (Isola Nova del Tronchetto 32, Hellovenezia, tel. 041/2424 or 041/272-2111, www.actv.it) provides various options for getting around by boat.

    Vaporetti are slow, make all the Grand Canal stops, and also serve other locations. *Motoscafi* are lower in the water, slightly faster, and make fewer stops. *Motonave* are larger and make longer crossings like the Lido or Punto Sabbioni. The ferry carries cars and trucks.

    Ordinary fare is €6 and allows travel on all services (except for those to Alilaguna, Clodia, and Fusina) for one hour from the time of stamping. Transfers are allowed in the same direction, but the ticket does not include the return journey. You are allowed to take one piece of luggage of up to 150cm (the sum of its three dimensions).

    Water service tickets are sold at the HelloVenezia offices and authorized resellers. Tickets may also be purchased with no penalty from the *marinaio* (sailor/attendant) on the platform before boarding.

    Travel Cards are the most economical solution to get around Venice and its surroundings. ACTV offers unlimited waterborne

© JUDY EDELHOFF

Vaporetti are the best way to discover Venice.

services (except Alilaguna, Clodia, Fusina) and on land within the municipality (comune) of Venice, Lido, and Mestre. Transport of one luggage item is allowed. Tickets are available from HelloVenezia and authorized resellers in 12-hour (€13), 24-hour (€15), 36-hour (€20), 48-hour (€25), and 72-hour (€30) travelcards.

For an additional fee, you can transport a bicycle on lines 13, N, Pellestrina–Chioggia and the ferry boat. Before you board a boat, take off your backpack. Do not wear it on board for safety.

Often you can arrive at your destination within Venice faster on foot, but a canal ride makes for a leisurely panorama of palaces. If you manage to find a seat, it's a rest from shuffling through the throngs flocking to San Marco.

You could see the entire lagoon in a full day by *vaporetto,* if you don't want to linger over a languid lunch or at other stops. Buy a 24-hour pass and you'll be more likely to put it to use; it's only €3 more than the price of two one-hour tickets.

Gondola rates are set by the City of Venice and the last fare change was June 2006. A gondola seats up to six passengers. The fares are: €80 for the first 40 minutes; €40 for each additional 20 minutes; personalized and standard night tours (7 P.M.–8 A.M.) cost €100 the first 40 minutes and €50 each additional 20 minutes. If you want a singer, negotiate that price separately.

The *ferro* is the ornate metal work on the prow of the boat that gives the illusion that the gondola slices through air. Once called "the dolphin," its shape evolved over time. The present form dates from the 18th century. The upper part suggests the Doge's cap worn by the leader of the Republic. The six metal teeth underneath represent the *sestiere,* Venice's six districts. The seventh tooth points away and represents the **Guidecca,** which is part of the Dorsoduro *sestiere* but is geographically opposed to the others.

Tours

There is no shortage of land or sea tours in Venice. Good walking tours are offered by the **City Museums** (www.museicivicineziani

an off-duty gondola

© PURESTOCK

.it, €12–15) by appointment. You can climb up the clock tower in San Marco, meander through secret passages at the Doge's Palace, or other interesting spots. Tours are booked at the tourist information offices or at the site and it's best to make reservations a day or two in advance.

Tours of **San Servolo island** (www.sanservolo.provincia.venezia.it) and the **Insane Asylum Museum** (tel. 041/524-0119) are also available. Lodging (tel. 041/276-5001) on the island is available only if you are participating in a conference or study program.

Serenissima Motoscafi depart daily from Ponte della Paglia in front of Hotel Danieli near Palazzo Ducale (Castello 4545, tel. 041/520-4640, www.serenissimamotoscafi.it, 2:30 P.M. and in summer also 9:30 A.M.) for boat tours of Murano with stops in a glass factory (45 min.), Burano (35 min.), and Torcello (35 min.), which leaves no time for lunch or lingering but gives a quick overview.

The Patriarch of St. Mark's offers tours in English to explain the Biblical significance of the Basilica's mosaics (tel. 041/241-3817, www.basilicasanmarco.it, admission free, by reservation). **CHORUS,** the Venetian Churches Association (www.chorusvenezia. org) organizes visits of other important Venetian churches with works by Veronese, Bellini, Titian, Tintoretto, and Tiepolo. Buy the pass and you can do a self-guided audio tour in each church on the circuit.

A 45-minute audio guide tour of the **La Fenice Opera House** (www.hellovenezia.it, €7) goes through the Foyer, Great Hall, Royal Box, and Appolonian Hall. Tours of **San Giorgio Maggiore** (www.cini.it, €12, 1 hour) explain the workings of this former Benedictine monastery. You can also see the inside of a typical Venetian palace on Saturday tours of Richard Wagner's apartment at **Ca'Vendramin**

Calergi (San Marcuola, tel. 338/416-4174, must book by Fri.).

Places described in the novel *Sherlock Holmes in Venice* begin in Campo San Stae (Vaporetto Line 1 from San Polo, Trattoria Antica Sacrestia, tel. 041/523-0749, Sun 11 A.M.). There's also an all-day canal cruise along the **Riviera del Brenta** from Venice to Padova that passes some 50 Veneto villas as you glide by on a canal boat. On the way you will stop to visit several palaces, have lunch, and return by bus. Depart on **Il Burchiello** (Pontile della Pietà, Riva degli Schiavoni, tel. 049/820-6910, www.ilburchiello.it, Mar.– Oct., Tues., Thurs., Sat.). Or reverse the trip on alternate days and depart from Padova. Inquire about bringing luggage if you do not want to make the return trip.

Vicinity of Venice

CERTOSA

Certosa has become a haven for sailors and designers, for workshops and classes as well as chartering a boat for a few hours or days. Until fairly recently, Certosa remained one of Venice's neglected islands.

On a clear day from the marina you can see the beginning of the Dolomites as well as silhouettes of Venetian domes. Certosa's beauty, seclusion, and good facilities lured the top-secret Venice Film Festival committee to meet here in September 2007.

Monks arrived on the island of Certosa in 1086, which was the domain of friars in their *certosa* (charterhouse) from 1432–1806. Austrians took over in 1866 and built warehouses to store their weapons and gunpowder. The island was relegated to storage until 1968, then abandoned for a few decades. A new plan was developed, and construction began in 2005 to once again make this a living island for Venetians and visitors. The result a few years later is a small marina, a *cantiere* (shop) for building and restoring traditional wooden boats that demonstrates Venice can thrive without becoming a theme park.

In the few short months since facilities opened in 2007, the island now attracts yacht designers, sailors, and first-time visitors who prefer a base away from the tourist crush of San Marco. Inquire about stopping by to see boat builders in action, repairing historic boats, or handcrafting new wooden yachts.

Recreation

Boat builders hand-craft wooden boats in the *cantiere* and sailors dock their craft in the harbor. You can take sailing courses from basic to specialized at **Race & C.** (tel. 393/969-0870, www.raceandc.com).

Sailboats can be rented for cruising the lagoon or sailing all the way to Croatia. Catamaran and single-hull options are available by the day or week, with or without crew from **Vento di Venezia** (www.ventodivenezia.it).

Designers find creative inspiration on Certosa to pursue yacht, fashion, and film projects at **Istituto Europeo di Design** (www.ied.it). Many courses are conducted in English and vary in length from weekend workshops to a few weeks or a year.

Accommodations

An enterprising young team runs everything from boat-building and a sailing school to boat rentals at the friendly **《 Vento di Venezia Certosa Hotel** (Isola della Certosa, tel. 041/520-8588, www.ventodivenezia.it, €150 d). Rooms are spacious with hardwood floors, modern furniture, writing desks, and plenty of good lighting. The informal atmosphere is the perfect place for mingling with creative souls involved in all sorts of design projects. The hotel has a free night boat service so you can return easily after you dine or disco out.

Getting There and Around

Vaporetto 41 and 42 depart from St. Mark's, Zaccaria, and other locations for a 5–10 minute ride. When boarding, ask the crew to stop at Certosa, as the island is by-request only. To depart the island, at the dock push the button that lights the signal in the direction you want to go.

MURANO

Murano is a play in one act. The star is glass and the action is shopping. Shoppers will find an endless number of stores to peruse at quality levels that vary widely. An hour visit is plenty of time if shopping is not your goal.

In ancient times, the Altinati took refuge in Murano when the Huns invaded. Murano is first mentioned in a document that dates to 840. In 1292, Venice moved glassmakers to the island to reduce the danger of fire and ambient smoke in the city center.

In the years 1441–1450, important Venetian Renaissance painters Antonio Vivarini and his brother-in-law Giovanni d'Alemagna chose Murano for their *bottega* (studio). Vivarini's brother Bartolomeo and son Alvise also worked here. Their paintings are in churches and museums throughout the Veneto and Italy.

Sights

Begin at the Faro stop by the Murano lighthouse. Glassmakers need iron tools that stand up to the heat, so you will see *"ferro"* signs where blacksmiths work. Some local glass studios are open to the public and you can observe the furnaces from a safe distance. A demonstration is fun to watch, after there will be pressure to buy, but no obligation.

Walk along Bressagio and take a sharp right on Calle Briati to see the original Murano school, established in 1862. **Scuola del Vetro Abate Zanetti** (Calle Briati 8/b, www.abatezanetti.it) is now defunct but evolved into a learning center in this industrial building. Courses and workshops at all levels teach glass techniques like blowing, lamp work, gold leaf decoration, jewelry beading, enameling, and design in a friendly atmosphere. You might plan your Italy trip to fit in a weekend workshop and try your own hand at glassmaking.

The two main churches and the glass museum round out a typical visit to Murano. The first mention of the **Basilica di Santa Maria e Donato** dates to 999, but it probably replaced a church dedicated to Mary in the 7th century. As you walk inside this Italic-Byzantine church, look down at the 1140 floor with its geometric tiles and fanciful creatures, peacocks, an eagle, and two roosters carrying a hare on a stick. The eye-popper in the apse is the 12th-century Byzantine mosaic of Mary as she elegantly stands in blue surrounded by gold mosaics. The Romanic-Gothic **San Pietro Martire** inside has clear Murano chandeliers.

A brief survey of glass from ancient Roman to recent decades can be found displayed on two floors at the glass museum, **Museo del Vetro** (Fondamenta Giustinian 8, tel. 041/520-9070, Thurs.–Tues. 10 A.M.–5 P.M., €5.50 or €18 with a museum pass). This is a handy benchmark before going off to purchase contemporary glass. The small museum shop has books on glass and some glass objects.

Shopping

Prized Murano glass ranges from public sculpture and chandeliers fit for a palace to small ornaments, jewelry, and paperweights with prices that range accordingly. Inexpensive souvenirs may not be Italian, so examine them carefully. If in doubt, look for the names of established glassmakers.

Some visitors complain about brusque treatment in shops. Like central Venice, the sheer volume of visitors has left artisans weary of explaining their craft. Unless you are a serious buyer, some shops may treat you with indifference. Shops that give demonstrations may be especially pushy to buy.

Shops are generally open from 9 A.M. or 10 A.M.–1 P.M. and 3:30–7 P.M. Many shops are closed on Sundays.

Good traditional designs are at **Vetreria Seguso Viro Fermei** (Fondamenta Vetrai 143, tel. 041/739-423). Jewelry designer and glassmaker **Davide Penso** (Fondamenta Riva Longa 48, tel. 041/527-4634, www.davidepenso.com), teaches pearlizing and jewelry-making at the glass school. His shop has lovely pieces, but the staff could be more welcoming.

Many other glassmakers also have studios in town. **Vivarini Murano** (F.ta Serenella 56, tel. 041/736-977) has been in operation since 1967 and **Ferro & Lazzarini** (Fondamenta Navagero 75, tel. 041/739-299, www.ferrolazzarini.it) are twice as old. **Ars Cenedese Murano** (Fondamenta Venier 48) create works in antique and modern style.

Wooden boats are built and sold at **Cantiere Serenella** (Sacca Serenall, tel. 041/739-792, www.cantiereserenella.com). If that's a heftier purchase than you have in mind, you can get a ride in one if you book their limousine service (fax 041/522-6973, limousine@cantiereserenella.com). They frequently do airport transfers.

Food

Dining is better in Burano or Torcello, so have your main meal there or back in the center. If you visit on Monday when many bars are closed, **Bar Gelateria al Ponte** (Riva Longa 1/c, tel. 041/736-278) will be open. Stop by in the morning when the local ladies are likely to be holding court at the tables.

Getting There and Around

Murano can easily be combined for a morning or full day of island-hopping that includes its rhyming neighbor Burano. The 41 and 42 *vaporetti* go there with convenient boarding points around Venice. Get off at the Faro stop. Faro is Italian for "lighthouse" and the lighthouse is visible from the boat.

Some hotels offer a free Venice–Murano shuttle with the idea that you will buy, but you may not be master of your own time. If you want to visit other islands, the 24-hour ACTV (€6) ticket gives you a full day of sightseeing to island-hop at your own pace.

Around Murano

The *vaporetto* stop before Murano is **San Michele,** the cemetery island that will be of particular interest to poets, dancers, and musicians, or anyone looking for a tranquil, quiet spot. The Greek Orthodox **Cimitero di San Michele** (daily 7:30 A.M.–4 P.M.) is the final resting spot of Ezra Pound, Diaghilev, and Stravinsky. If interested, hop off; if not, keep on sailing.

BURANO

Locals attribute the vivid colors of Burano's houses to medieval times, when homes were whitewashed with lime to disinfect the premises after a plague victim had died there. Then color was added, partly for sheer fantasy and partly to erase the depressing whiteness of death. The colors reflect in the canals and make for a pleasant stroll.

Burano's claim to fame was once its lace-makers, women who often worked in teams, with each adding her own specialized stitches. The final product may have taken days or weeks to finish, depending on its size or intricacy. The art is dying out. There is no way that local lacemakers today are furnishing all the Burano shops. Buyer beware. The goods you purchase in Burano may be made in China or elsewhere. Asking is no guarantee, it's up to the customer to recognize handmade from mass-produced.

The restaurants here are better than those in Murano, so plan to do your eating here. A lunch *al fresco* or dinner timed to enjoy a spectacular sunset will revive you.

Sights

The best sight in Burano is the multicolored town itself. Small canals run through it and mirror the colors. Boats occasionally putter through to load and unload cargo that would be an ordinary sight anywhere else. Here it's an extraordinary scene that gives *On the Waterfront* new meaning.

Have a look at the vanishing art of lace-making at **Museo di Merletti** (Piazza Galuppi 187, Nov.–Mar. Wed.–Mon. 10 A.M.–4 P.M., Apr.–Oct. Wed.–Mon. 10 A.M.–5 P.M., closed Dec. 1, Jan. 1, and May 1, €4). There are around 200 works here that document Venetian lace-making during the 16th–20th centuries. The museum also houses the archives of the the Andriana Marcello Lace School founded in 1872. Changing lifestyles have significantly diminished the demand for lace. It takes hours to properly clean and iron a lace tablecloth and few 21st-century households have servants dedicated to such tasks. Still lace-makers remain. Train your eyes first at the lace museum to recognize quality and local stitches that are far more intricate than the machine made variety. Then go out and have a look at the shops. Real Burano lace has become very expensive, especially the antique lace.

© PURESTOCK

a feline resident of Burano perched on an iron overhang

Shopping

Two shops where you will find things done the old-fashioned way are **Martina Burano Home Collection** (Via San Mauro 307, tel. 041/735-523, closed Jan. 7–31), which specializes in luxury linens for the home, and **Tagliapietra Anna Maria** (San Mauro 305, tel. 041/735-301). Authenticity comes with a price tag, but start here if you want a piece of cloth that doesn't go out of style, has unique texture, and will no doubt become a family heirloom.

Food

Burano has two excellent merits-the-trip restaurants and several casual trattorias that are perfect for lunch. Otherwise, catch the late afternoon *traghetto* when most tourists are gone and watch the sunset over dinner.

Romano at ◖ **Trattoria da Romano** (Via Galuppi 221, tel. 041/730-030, www.daromano.it, closed Tues.) welcomes artists, who sometimes paid with their works that hang on the walls. Romano passed the traditon on to his son and the food is still good. Fish is the specialty. Try any of their risottos, especially *gobius* (Goby fish), or the *brodetto* seafood soup. There are plenty of wines, some 55 from Venice and Friuli alone. Enjoy the view on the main drag, where regular diners often outnumber the tourists that have included Henri Matisse, Katherine Hepburn, Keith Richard, Ezra Pound, Michelangelo Antonioni, Charlie Chaplin, Fellini, Armani, and others dropping by for the food and the ambience. The owner of Harry's Bar in Venice wrote, "here I feel like a human being."

Trattoria al Gatto Nero (Fondamenta Giudecca 88, tel. 041/730-120, www.gattonero.com) is a newer rival and is the darling of the Venetian smart set, who love its seafood and good wine list.

You can get snacks from a *forno* or *pasticceria* like **Giorgio Garbo Panificio Pasticceria** (Via San Mauro 336) or **Biscottificio Palmisano Carmelina** (Via V. Galuppi 355), which bakes its goods in Jesolo and boats them in.

VENICE

The vivid colors of Burano's houses are reflected in the water of the narrow canals.

© PURESTOCK

Getting There and Around

From the lighthouse stop in Murano take the *vaporetto* and get off at Mazzorbo, between Murano and Burano. It's a five-minute stroll on this tourist-free island and you can cross the footbridge to Burano. Otherwise, if your feet are complaining, wait for the Burano stop.

◖ TORCELLO

Although it might be an exaggeration to say that Torcello is to Venice what the Palatine is to Rome, Torcello more or less is where Venice began. Its inhabitants fled Barbarian invaders and settled here in the 5th–7th centuries.

The island is tiny, but was a rest stop for Attila the Hun as he swept through in 452 before dying a year later up north on his wedding night.

Today this island north of Venice has a pleasant overgrown wildness to it and is free of kitschy souvenir shops. Ancient ruins are still being excavated and Torcello is ideal for nature walks, a good lunch, and a climb up the medieval bell tower for a commanding view of the lagoon and

sea. Next to it is an early Christian church that reached its 1,000th anniversary in 2008 and has enchanting carved figures and vivid mosaics.

All the major sights and restaurants are along the canal path that leads to the *vaporetto* stop.

Sights

The Veneto-Byzantine-style **Basilica di Santa Maria Assunta** (Mar.–Oct. daily 10:30 A.M.–6 P.M., Nov.–Feb. daily 10 A.M.–5 P.M., €3) dates from 1008 and used remnants from an earlier church. The *iconostasis,* a screen of carved marble panels of peacocks, lions, and foliage, closes the nave at one end. The Domesday Mosaics vibrantly portray the *Last Judgment.* The 12th–13th century Madonna in the apse very much resembles Murano's. Here, too, she stands regally in blue, but holds the infant Christ. The **Campanile** (Mar.–Oct. daily 10:30 A.M.–5:30 P.M., Nov.–Feb. daily 10 A.M.–4:30 P.M., €3) next door was reopened in 2007, and athletically inclined visitors can climb the stairs to the top for a panoramic view of the lagoon and islands.

Archeological digs are still in progress on Torcello and many of the relics discovered are on display inside **Museo Provinciale** (Mar.–Oct. Tues.–Sun. 10:30 A.M.–5:30 P.M., Nov.–Feb. Tues.–Sun. 10 A.M.–5 P.M., €3). There is an abundance of Greek and Roman antiquities, Etruscan and Paleo-Veneto finds from the estuary, ancient documents, and church treasures. The marble seat is said to have served as Attila's throne in A.D. 452 during a visit to Italy when Huns still outnumbered tourists.

A graceful portico frames the entrance to the octagonal **Santa Fosca.** Its low dome tops a simple interior built in the 10th–12th centuries.

Accommodations

Founded in 1935 by Giuseppe Cipriani, who was also behind Harry's Bar, **Locanda Cipriani** (Piazza S. Fosca 29, tel. 041/730-150, www.lo candacipriani.com, €200–360 d) has six light, comfortable rooms in pastel colors with a period look, and no TV but a library with books. It's a two-story rustic yellow house with dark shutters that is peaceful enough to have hosted Ernest Hemingway, Charlie Chaplin, Paul Newman, and the Royal Family of England. This is one sure escape from the tourist invasion of St. Mark's, barbarian or otherwise.

Food

If you stay for dinner, **Locanda Cipriani** is the spot to enjoy a cozy, rustic atmosphere. In winter, the *fogher* (country fireplace) blazes in the bar. There are more options for lunch, including **Ristorante Villa '600** (Fdm. Borgognoni 12, tel. 041/527-2254, Thurs.–Tues.

lunch only). Young, gracious Pierluigi runs this tranquil restaurant in a restored 17th-century country house. Vegetables come to your plate from the villa's garden and fresh fish is brought in daily from Burano. Meat and game are featured during the cooler months.

Slightly right of Attila the Hun's throne, depending on your perspective, is **Ristorante al Trono di Attila** (Via Borgognoni 7/a, tel. 041/730-094, www.altronodiattila.it), where you can wake up with a cappuccino, sit down for lunch, or grab a snack under the wood-beamed ceiling or next to the canal.

Getting There and Around

The *vaporetto* ride from Venice is about half an hour to Burano. From there, a boat departs directly for Torcello. Don't bother looking for a number. When the captain yells "Torcello," just jump on aboard.

Around Torcello

Once the site of a charity hospital, a medieval rest stop for pilgrims en route to the Holy Land, magazine for gunpowder, and a lunatic asylum (briefly in the 19th century), **San Clemente** has found its true calling as an oasis of tranquility.

The island now aims to soothe visitors with secluded luxury. The buzz is on about the new **San Clemente Palace Hotel & Resort** (Isola di San Clemente 1, tel. 041/244-5001, www. sanclemente.thi.it) for the stylish renovation in a space once occupied by an ancient Camaldolese monastery. The **Ristorante Ca' dei Frati** inside offers a sweeping view of the lagoon. The swimming pool is large.

VENICE

Veneto

There are a variety of ways to experience the Veneto. Skiing buffs will enjoy the elegance and challenge of Cortina d'Ampezzo, also ideal for hikes when the snow is gone. Clothes horses also like it because fashions appear here first. Linger a bit on the road south and you can follow the Cadore River, once the transport system for Venice's vital logging trade and on-location for the background of Titian paintings. Padova is the major financial center, but also a treasure trove of art with Giotto's masterpiece, the Scrovegni Chapel. As you wind your way around Padova, Verona, and Vicenza, you'll see the strong influence of Renaissance architect Andrea Palladio, whose villas set a standard for others that followed in the 17th and 18th centuries. You can visit some historic villas, see others from the outside, and even stay in some. Verona is often a hit-and-flee town, with visitors coming in to see Juliet's balcony and perhaps its ancient Roman amphitheater, but the entire city is charming so don't be too quick to leave. Vicenza is the center of goldsmiths, where more gold is traded and bought than in any other Italian city; it also has some of Palladio's major masterpieces, like the **Teatro Olimpico.** Marostica, with its giant chess board played with human pieces, merits a visit, game or not, as does lovely Bassano del Grappa. Wine is a major product here, so whether you are a novice or connoisseur, you'll enjoy the beauty of the vineyards and tastings, along the wine roads, from Prosecco near Valdobbiadene to Amarone, a 20th-century creation by Valpolicella winemakers. The Venetian dialect has a pleasant sing-songy lilt that will charm you. Despite its northern location, some climate zones can be surprisingly mild. If you want to heat up a bit more, head for a good thermal soak in one of the spa towns.

Vicenza, Verona, the Brenta Canal, and the Veneto countryside serve as the backdrop for magnificent Renaissance villas built not merely as summer pleasure palaces, but as sophisticated agricultural enterprises that further enriched the ruling class with the production of silk, grain, wine, olive oil, and other commodities. Today they still inspire architects, just as Palladio's Villa Rotonda inspired Thomas Jefferson in his design for Monticello and the University of Virginia. A few Veneto villas now accept paying guests, so a lucky few can get a taste of this genteel, country living.

BELLUNO

Belluno was originally settled in the 5th century B.C. by Venetici and Celts, who were eventually replaced by Romans in the 2nd century B.C. But it's really the Renaissance and artists like Titian that have a grip on the city today. The painter (a hometown celebrity) was born in and spent his waning years "putting his house in order" on Pieve di Cador. Look carefully at some of his portraits and religious paintings and you'll see those Bellunesi Dolomites in the background of many including his last paintings.

Sights

Belluno makes for a lovely half-day stroll with its medieval residences, markets, nice quality shops, and at least two or three restaurants that merit a stop. Local hotels are not glamorous but are eminently comfortable and make for a good base. In winter, skiers looking for affordable rates snatch them up quickly. Winter is the season when the town really hops, but year-round the fresh air and mountain scenery make this a worthwhile detour for art and ambience lovers.

Shopping

Cashmere sweaters and knitwear have been woven since 1985 by **A.M.D.** (Piazza Mazzini 16, tel. 043/729-4709) for the likes of Krizia and Armani. Their factory showroom (Via Ubaldo Bracalenti 46, tel. 043/796-7582, www.amdmoda.com) is open nearby in Limana. Both feature classic and updated designs in a wide spectrum of colors and patterns. Classic sweaters lure traditionalists, while other styles are more current. All are comfortable, warm, and under €100 for men and women.

Pellicceria Silvana & Gino (Piazza Mazzini 15, tel. 043/794-0466) will help you restore your old coat or recycle your fur as a luxury throw with cashmere. They design stoles, collars, and hats, along with jackets and coats.

Accommodations

The building dates to 1843, but **Cappello e Cadore Hotel** (Via Ricci 8, tel. 043/794-0246, albergo.cappello.bl@libero.it, 32 rooms, €50–100 d) is decidedly 21st-century rustic-modern with simple pine wood furniture. Some rooms have whirlpool baths and a view of the Dolomite Mountains. It's a five-minute walk from the train station and in the heart of Belluno's historic center.

Food

Count on Giovanni to help you to pair superb wines with the daily fare at **Enoteca Mazzini** (Piazza Mazzini 6, tel. 043/794-8313, Thurs.–Tues. lunch and dinner). If you come at lunchtime, his father Mario presides over tables and supplies the local color. Look for traditional dishes on the menu like *baccalà* (cod), sausage in tomato sauce with polenta, porcini mushroom lasagna, as well as for the innovative dish of the day.

For pure medieval tavern atmosphere, stop by **Ristorante Taverna** (Via Cipro 7, tel. 043/725-192, €8–16) near Teatro Comunale. The starters include an assortment of vegetable and cheese strudels and local cured meats and salamis. Good hearty soups like pureed beans with barley keep diners warm during the winter. Firsts and seconds include homemade pastas and grilled meats.

Forno i Ragazzi del 99 (Piazza Duomo 28) can satisfy a grumbling stomach in seconds. Their local version of *grissini* (long pizza-like strips) and *torta sabbiosa* (sandy cake) make great snacks. They are closed mid-afternoon.

Getting There and Around

Belluno is 67 kilometers from Padova and 61 kilometers from Vicenza. From Venice (82 km) or Treviso (37 km), take Autostrada A27 and exit Belluno. Continue farther up the road and you're in Cortina d'Ampezzo. The Padova–Calalzo train (www.trenitalia.com) is slow but takes you through a lovely winding route that is about 2.25 hours from Padova to Belluno. You can also take the Venezia–Belluno train that stops in Treviso and Conegliano on the way to Belluno.

CORTINA D'AMPEZZO

Italy's most in-vogue ski destination has been a resort since the 1800s when northern Europeans came for mountain climbing. The big push as a ski capital came in the 1930s. Cortina D'Ampezzo's fame was secured as site of the 1956 Winter Olympics, after which *La Dolce Vita* film crowds settled down for a couple of decades and kept the spotlight shining on the magnificent Dolomites. Those 1960s photos of Bridget Bardot learning to ice skate or Marcello Mastroianni on the slopes were all snapped here.

Jet set or not, the town boasts one of the largest mountain valleys in the Alps, plenty of challenging variety in the ski runs, and great food on the mountain slopes as well as in the town center.

Like Aspen, Cortina is an epicenter for fashionistas. Here, in part, it's because the latest styles arrive in Cortina and Milan stores before their Roman or Venetian rivals can get their paws on them.

Cortina is for the glam set. No surprise that prices can be high. But there are surprising bargains in peak ski season if you avoid the traditional Italian surge for the December 8 holiday, the period from just before Christmas to January 6, and during February's Settimana Bianca (White Week) when schools are off for the ski holiday.

Sights

Famous mountain climber Reinhold Messner has established a chain of five **mountain museums** (www.monterite.it) including the world's highest museum. **Museo delle Nuvole** (tel. 0435 890 996) has a population of yaks, the long-haired bovines from Tibet prized for their wood, milk, and meat. Visit the website or call for directions and hours.

Accommodations

Look for bargains in mid-January and March, when you can enjoy Italian glamour and snow for less. Keep in mind that prices fluctuate wildly depending on whether your vacation coincides with Christmas or February ski weeks. Many hotels require a weekly stay during those peak times but are very flexible at other times.

The glory is in the details at (**Hotel Ambra** (Via XXIX Maggio 28, tel. 043/686-7344, www.hotelambracortina.it, €130–220 d), from its bright yellow facade with contemporary frescoes to the interior with its cozy sitting room and bar, and art exhibits on each floor that change every few months. Rooms have lovely textiles on beds and drapes, and tasteful paintings. The abundance of pine closets, cupboards, and drawers is for neatly stowing ski gear or fashion props for weekly stays. Breakfast is generous, with fresh fruit and substantial options that keep mountain trekkers going. The staff is especially friendly, well informed, and attentive. They have no restaurant, but if you arrive after-hours don't be surprised if they magically produce an attractive fruit and cheese plate, Prosecco, or hot drinks. Ask about their intriguing upscale excursions for individuals or a small group. Some rooms have flower-filled wooden balconies or mountain views, but all have charm and you're right in the center.

Food

Restaurants in and around Cortina are uniformly high quality. Look for Italian cuisine with bits of Austro-Hungarian influence. Dolomite Mountain cheeses are superb and are sometimes hard to find elsewhere. Malga Misurina, northeast of Cortona in Auronozo di Cadore, makes excellent *malga* (from cows that graze on mountain flowers and herbs, sharpness depends on aging), ricotta cheeses, and butter. Malga Ciauta in Vodo di Cadore also makes excellent *malga* and ricotta cheeses, as well as

spersala and *zigar* (cone-shaped cheese, light consistency, tangy, with a hint of salt, pepper, and chives). The whole Dolomite region is dotted with dairy farms, so stop at a good cheese shop, an *enoteca* that serves cheese platters and have a glass of wine, or see how cheeses are creatively used in local cuisine. Game and wild fowl are in abundant supply during hunting season. Mountain trout caught here are tastier than their farm-raised cousins.

Just a few kilometers south of Cortina (a 10-minute drive) in Vodo di Cadore the friendly Gregori family has turned an ancient tavern into restaurant **Al Capriolo** (Via Nazionale 108, tel. 043/548-9207, www.al capriolo.it, Wed.–Mon. lunch and dinner, €55–65). The decor varies from a hunting theme to a cozy cantina with wines imaginatively selected by Massimiliano. Try Bellenda's bubbly Prosecco, a red Colli Orientali del Friuli by Moschione Davide made with Refosco and Schioppettino grapes and a hefty Amarone della Valpolicella by Viviani here. Dishes range from delicate tartare and mousse of mountain trout to hefty mountain fare. The *vellutata* made from seasonal ingredients is likely to feature local mountain cheese. Venison or lamb chops are perfectly prepared here. Don't miss the superb homemade gelato or strudel. (Bus 30 from Cortina stops in front of the restaurant on request. You can also ask about hotel shuttle service during peak season.)

Try Chef Graziano Prest's modern creative cuisine near Corso Italia at **Tivoli Ristorante** (Loc. Lacedel 34, tel. 043/686-6400, Tues.–Sun., €60), with a terrace view of the Dolomites. In 2005, the Melon family took over Ristorante Al Camineto, now called **Meloncino al Camineto** (Località Rumerlo 1, tel. 043/644-32, Wed.–Mon., €60), which features a cozy fireplace and specialties that include local cuisine like *stinco* (braised veal). The *stufe* (hearth stoves) of Majolica tiles will be blazing in winter at **Baita Fraina** (Loc. Fraina 2, tel. 043/626-34, Tues.–Sun., www. baitafraina.it, €38), where Alex cooks while brother Adolfo and wife Anna cater to diners.

They have over 500 wines and spirits to choose from. Jerry's legendary **Enoteca Cortina** (Via del Mercato 5, tel. 043/686-2040, www. enotecacortina.it, €15) keeps even finicky gourmets and restaurateurs delighted with excellent wine selections, a convivial atmosphere, and light snacks. **Pontejèl Ristorante** (Largo delle Poste 11, tel. 043/625-25, Thurs.–Tues., €35) is a cozy, casual, and welcoming place in the center to dine on regional specialties without breaking the bank (plus they have a handful of rooms upstairs at reasonable weekly rates).

Dining in a *rifugio* (alpine hut) can be surprisingly elegant. You get to know the mountains and dine in style in a rarified atmosphere. On Monte Nuvolau, at 2,575 meters, is **Rifugio Nuvolau** (tel. 043/686-2085, open only in summer). A favorite of gourmets, **Rifugio Averau** (tel. 043/646-60), at 2,416 meters, will also cater meals for sleigh rides in winter and jeep rides in summer. Call ahead to see when both of these restaurants are open.

Information and Services

If you want to get around on foot with a **mountain guide** (tel. 043/686-8505 or 047/184-7037), history buffs can hike the Great War trails to important World War I sites. For information on trails, chair lifts, ski facilities, and the mountaineering school contact **Tourist Office Cortina** (Piazzetta San Francesco 8, tel. 043/632-31, www.apt-dolomiti-cortina.it).

Getting There and Around

Cortina is 170 kilometers north of Venice, 69 kilometers north of Belluno, and 132 kilometers north of Treviso. From Venice, take the A27 north, which becomes a two-lane road most of the way to Cortina. Bus service links Cortina d'Ampezzo with Padova, Treviso, Venice Piazzale Rome, or the Marco Polo Airport on **ATVO** (tel. 043/686-7921, www.atvo.it). By train from Verona, Padova, Venezia, Treviso or Belluno get off at the Calalzo Station and transfer to Bus 30, which will be about an hour ride to Cortina.

PADOVA

According to legend, the Greek hero Antenor founded Padova, but its origins can be dated to 3,000 years ago in the Paleoveneti Age. By the 4th century B.C., Padova already was an important trade center situated on the banks of the Brenta River. Allied with the Romans against the Gauls, Patavium became a Roman *municipium* with thriving agriculture and horse-trading, as well as river commerce. It's easy to see how Padova got a jump-start to become today's economic capital of the Veneto region. Not that all was easy sailing: the Longobards destroyed Padova in 602, then the Ungarns took their turn in 899. After the year 1000, the town began to rebound under Emperors Henry III and IV. Major development under the Seignuery of the Carrara family (1338–1405) put Padova at the height of its military and economic might. The famous University of Padova (1222) was Italy's second to be founded. Nine years later, St. Anthony died here and construction immediately began on the St. Anthony Basilica. Giotto turned the Western world toward 3-D, thanks to major artistic innovations in his 1304 cycle of frescoes in the Scrovegni Chapel. Poets Dante and Petrarch spent time here. In the 15th century, geniuses like Donatello and Mantegna left their own artistic imprints. Mantegna began his career in Padova and left enigmatic paintings that graced Renaissance courts further afield, like Urbino's in Le Marche. The Renaissance brought 16th-century rule under the Serenissima Republic of Venice and scientific innovators like Galileo Galilei, who was a professor at the university. Its medical school became famous for the Anatomy Theater, which offered a rare opportunity to observe dissections. After four centuries of domination by Venice, Napoleon took his turn, then Austria, and in 1866 Padova became part of the Kingdom of Italy. The two World Wars of the 20th century brought severe destruction, from which Padova rebounded as economic leader.

Padova also is the name of its own province. The Euganean Hills to the southwest are fertile with vineyards and bubbling with thermal waters, along with plenty of castles, villas, monasteries, and sanctuaries. The northern province has villas, too, and splendid walled medieval towns. The southeast is where to find roots still grounded in traditional cultural and rural ways.

Sights

Sights are easily reached on foot or by bicycle. The Padova Card will help you save money on entry fees. As with many cities, most museums are closed on Mondays. The most popular sight, the Scrovegni Chapel, can be seen only by reservation by timed visits with limited visitors permitted to enter, so you are wise to reserve well before your arrival to Padova. Early risers might want to begin with a visit to St. Anthony's Basilica, as it opens hours before the other sites, then move on to watch the morning markets as they open.

No visit to Padova would be complete without seeing the cycle of frescoes painted by Giotto in the Scrovegni Chapel. Get a feel for how civic, commercial, and social life has been so intricately intertwined in Padova by visiting Palazzo della Ragione. Its market stalls remain a busy hubbub of meat, produce, and soft goods—set under the arcades of the palace dedicated to meting out justice—that spill into the two major squares.

PALAZZO DELLA RAGIONE

Register your sale, pay your fine, try your case—while the going gets tough, the tough go shopping under Palazzo della Ragione (tel. 0419/820-5006, Tues.–Sun. 9 A.M.–6 P.M.), which the locals refer to as their "grand salon" now that the courts have moved elsewhere and the halls are used for special events. Built between 1218–1219 over Roman-era ruins, this was the symbol of communal power through its courts of justice, but also center of community life abuzz below in the markets. After a 1420 fire destroyed previous decorations, Pietro d'Abano painted an enormous fresco cycle of the zodiac and its astrological influence on man and events, as well as some religious images. The symbolism, complex and mysterious to modern man, now is explained through interactive points in the hall or through audio guides that were installed in late 2007. The hall also boasts a giant wooden horse attributed to Donatello (1466) and a contemporary version of Foucault's Pendulum.

As you wind your way under the arcade beneath Palazzo della Ragione, you can step out into either **Piazza delle Erbe** or **Piazza dei Frutti**, both busy scenes of a daily market that gets going at about 8 A.M. and continues until 1 P.M. or so, and on Saturdays even later.

PIAZZA DEI SIGNORI AND PIAZZA CAPITANIATO

Gracious buildings frame Piazza dei Signori, especially Palazzo del Capitano (1599–1605) on the west side with its Torre dell'Orologio that has an astronomical clock that originated in 1344.

Pass under the Clock Arch to Piazza Capitaniato, where the Arts Faculty inside has the **Sala dei Giganti** with 16th-century frescoes of giants.

◖ CAPPELLA DEGLI SCROVEGNI

The ancient Roman amphitheater is adjacent to Cappella degli Scrovegni (Piazza Eremetani, tel. 049/201-0020, www.cappelladeglis crovegni.it, by reservation only, admission €12 also includes entrance to the Eremitani Museum and Palazzo Zuckerman), which houses one of the great masterpieces of art, Giotto's cycle of frescoes painted during 1303–1305. Built by banker Enrico Scrovegni, this barrel-vaulted room has the world's most complete fresco cycle by Giotto (1266-1337). Giotto's groundbreaking series of paintings broke away from his predecessors and launched "a brave new style" in art that brought humans into the third dimension from the flatter forms of medieval painting. Giotto's vivid blue backgrounds are radiant with predominantly pink, orange, gold, and red tones. The use of architectural elements shows Giotto's interest in executing perspective to create a natural pictorial space, a decisive departure from the Byzantine style. The center panel that frames the altar on

© JUDY EDELHOFF

Prato della Valle in Padova

each side has the **Coretti,** two panels that create the illusion of a room that extends beyond the Gothic arches he painted.

EREMITANI MUSEUM
Early archeological finds from Paleovenetian, Roman, Etruscan, and early Christian periods are in one section of the Eremitani Museum (Piazza Eremetani, tel. 049/820-4551, Tues.–Sun. 9 A.M.–7 P.M., admission €10), while another has works by Bellini and Vivarini's exquisite *Portrait of Man with Hat.* Don't miss the **Angel Room,** with its militant angel warriors by Guariento and Giotto's Crucifix. The **Ovetari Chapel** has fragments of young Andrea Mantegna's fresco cycle, recently partially restored to repair damange from being bombed in World War II.

PALAZZO ZUCKERMANN
Inside Palazzo Zuckermann (Corso Garibaldi 33, tel.049/820-4513, Tues.–Sun. 10 A.M.–7 P.M., admission free) is architect Daniel Libeskind's **Memory and Light** memorial dedicated to the victims of the September 11, 2001, attack on the Twin Towers in New York. The palace is also home to the **Museum of Applied and Decorative Arts** (Corso Garibaldi 33, tel.049/820-4513, Tues.–Sun. 10 A.M.–7 P.M., admission free).

BASILICA DI SANT'ANTONIO
Next to Musei Civici degli Eremitani, Basilica di Sant'Antonio (Piazza del Santo, tel. 049/878-9722, daily 6:30 A.M.–7 P.M.) is called "Basilica of the Saint" by locals, as if anyone should wonder "which saint?" Anthony of Padua, who died in Padua 1231 but was not born here, is so intertwined with the town that it's just implied. The Romanesque Gothic exterior has Eastern influence in its eight domes and spires. Donatello's bronze bas-reliefs (1444–1448) for the main altar are here, with panels that tell stories of Anthony's life (like the Miracle of the Donkey). The church is rich with colorful frescoes by Altichiero and Giusto de'Menabuoi—be sure to see the scene of the saint as he gestures toward the city of Padova.

Anthony's body is also here, which makes the church an important stop for pilgrims.

On the same square, pop in to nearby **Oratorio di San Giorgio,** St. George Oratory (daily 9 A.M.–12:30 P.M. and 2:30–5 P.M.), to see three 1511 frescoes painted by Titian.

CATTEDRALE

Michelangelo was one of the designers of the Cattedrale, also called Duomo (Piazza Duomo), built in the 16th–18th centuries. Note especially the round *Paradise* painted 1375–1378 by Florentine Giusto de' Menabuoi in the dome, with a whole cast of saints and others lucky enough to get in. His frescoes of St. John the Baptist and Stories of Mary are also vibrant with color and interesting architectural settings, rather like those you walk through in town. The **Baptistery** (tel. 049/656-914, daily 10 A.M.–6 P.M., admission €2.50) next door, named for St. John, dates from the 12th century.

OTHER SIGHTS

Along **Via Cesarotti,** you'll pass the 16th-century **Loggia** and **Cornaro Odeon,** prime Renaissance architecture in Padova.

Palazzo del Bo (Via VIII Febbraio) is the municipal government complex erected in 1542–1601. The **1222 University of Padova** (tel. 049/827-3044) has a Renaissance courtyard, **Cortile Antico.** Inside **Room of 40** you'll see Galileo's chair—he taught here 1592–1610. The **Anatomy Theater,** famous for its dissections, dates from 1594.

Founded in 1545 by the Faculty of Medicine, the Botanical Garden, **Orto Botanico** (Via dell'Orto Botanico, tel. 049/827-2119, winter Mon.–Sat. 9 A.M.–1 P.M., summer daily 9 A.M.–1 P.M. and 3–6 P.M.), has an important collection of rare plants as well as a library and the University's botany collection.

Have a look at the town walls and their gates, as well as the canals and rivers as you walk through town.

Entertainment and Events

Padova's **Teatro Verdi** (Via dei Livello 32, tel. 049/877-7011, tickets tel. 049/877-70213)

hosts an opera season that gets underway in September and runs through December. Look for performances and other special events.

Check newspaper listings for **Prato della Valle,** once a Roman theater, now a spot for fairs and other events. Its present look dates to 1775, when a Venetian decided to reclaim the swampy land and divided the elliptical island into four quadrants separated by boulevards with connecting bridges and 78 statues. Palazzo Angeli houses **Museum of the Magic Lantern and Pre-Cinema** (Palazzo Angeli Prato della Valle, tel. 049/876-3838, Sept. 15–June 14 10 A.M.–4 P.M., June 15–Sept. 14 4–8 P.M.), also a site of interesting programs and exhibits. Historic re-enactments, jousting, parades, and other events are more frequent in summer and early fall.

Antiques are big business in Padova, where shops as well as fairs throughout the province display and sell their wares. Look for Antiquari in newspapers or inquire at the tourist office.

The annual **Strapadovavia,** a walk of 2, 6, 11, or 18 kilometers takes place in September to benefit cystic fibrosis.

Shopping

Padova's open-air markets sell everything from food to clothes and accessories. The central markets are at **Piazza delle Erbe** and **Piazza dei Frutti,** but check around for other markets. Via Dante is lined with nice shops. Look for women's shoes, at which Padovan shoemakers are so skilled that Louis Vuitton has some of their top-quality women's footwear made here. Leather goods in general are very nice.

A tiny store with everything shoved in that you might need, like a rain poncho in a pinch, is at **Pelletterie Bassan** (Via Dante 4). Massimo Guerra is the goldsmith at **Alterego Gioielli** (Piazza dei Signori 26) with angular, tubular, modern designs.

Accommodations

Summer is low season in Padova, so if you are traveling then look for good discounts in many hotels or inquire at the tourist office.

Hotel Plaza (Corso Milano 40, tel.

049/656-822, www.plazapadova.it, €125 d) won't win awards for its decorating scheme, which is impersonal but functional. It has a good central location, conveniences that satisfy its business clientele, a gym on the third floor with good hours, and a breakfast buffet with some wonderful local baked goods. Its convenient parking garage, about €15 per day, is in the back and moves cars around on a conveyor belt.

The elevator is so tiny at **Albergo Verdi** (Via Dondi dall'Orologio 7, tel. 049/836-4163, www.albergoverdipadova.it, €100 d) that you might have to send your luggage upstairs first, but it was remodeled in 2006 to offer more comforts and modern design, which, along with its friendly staff, attract theater performers from Teatro Verdi a few steps away and university professors.

In the historic center, **Majestic Toscanelli** (Via dell'Arco 2, tel.049/663-244, www.toscanelli.com, €120–200 s/d) dates to the 18th century with rooms mostly in pastel colors.

Food

The interior is modern at **Ristorante Enoteca Patanegra** (Via Beato Pellegrino 119, tel. 049/872-4744, €11–15) and its young Calabrese chef prepares innovative cuisine that uses top-flight ingredients without going over the top, a hit with locals although a bit pricey. For appetizers try crostini with duck breast, cheese, and wild herbs or the local Patanegra Bellott prosciutto, aged 36 months. Risotto is a specialty, along with meat like their *filetto di manzo in salsa Rossini* (beef filet in their special sauce).

A cozy, homey simple place surrounded by books to buy or magazines to read, **Osteria Re Porco Wine Bar and Library** (Via S. Pietro 47, tel. 049/876-1289, Tues.–Sun., €9–11) has limited choices, but the menu changes daily and everything is made fresh. Prices are economical and service is doting.

A sophisticated setting for superb but pricey cuisine is **Al Cicheto** (Via dei Savonarola 59, tel. 049/871-9794, Mon.–Sat. 8–11 P.M., €8–12). It features excellent dishes from the Veneto,

and is a favorite with locals. The portions are generous and prices reasonable at **Da Mario & Mercedes** (Via S. Giovanni da Verdara 13, tel. 049/871-9731, Thurs.–Tues., €9–11), specialists in traditional Padovan cuisine.

A Padovan who wants to entertain guests or clients in style is likely to go to **Il Tinello** (Via Ognissanti 29, tel. 049/807-1456, Mon.–Sat. noon–3 P.M. and 7:30–11 P.M., €10–14), where Carla and Rodolfo have dished out traditional Padovan cuisine as well as creative dishes since 1989 in the University neighborhood. They always feature fresh, seasonal ingredients and have over 200 wines. Their garden with 40 seats is open year-round.

Near Teatro Verdi, Mario di Natale's **Antico Brolo** (Corso Milano 22, tel. 049/664-555, www.anticobrololo.it, Tues.–Sun. noon–2 P.M. and 7–11:30 P.M., closed Mon. lunch, €11–15) attracts business clientele and well-heeled tourists for their polished service and pricey cuisine that is traditional Veneto with some new twists. They also run the more economically priced pizzeria **Al Teatro at Teatro Verdi** (tel. 049/654-465, daily 7 P.M.–midnight, pizzas €4.50 and up) located in the downstairs tavern.

A Sardinian restaurant popular with locals for its friendly atmosphere and economical prices is **La Piccola Trattoria** (Via R. Da Piazzola 21, tel. 049/656-163, www.piccolatrattoria.it, Mon.–Sat., noon–2:15 P.M. and 8–10:30 P.M., €8–12), which specializes in fish but also serves good meat dishes like steak seasoned with mirto and potatoes on the side (€14).

Neoclassic **Caffè Pedrocchi** (Via VIII Febraio 15, tel. 049/878-1231, daily 9 A.M.–9 P.M.) with its ornate Gothic wing has been a meeting spot since 1831 and was the scene of a student uprising in 1848. Don't miss its special house coffee, a creamy concoction with a hint of mint. Locals come here for coffee and tea, to read the paper, and to socialize. The famous Anatomy Theater is next door and upstairs is the **Museum of the Risorgimento and Contemporary Age** (tel. 049/878-1231, 9:30 A.M.–12:30 P.M. and 3:30–6 P.M., closed Mon. and holidays, €4 or free with Padova card).

A casual, modern coffee bar with a few tiny tables, **Bottega del Caffè** (Via Dante 2, Mon.–Sat. 8 A.M.–6 P.M.) is favored by local merchants and residents. They roast their own coffee beans, which they also sell by the bag. There's also a refreshing *centrifuga* (fresh-squeezed fruit and/or vegetable juice). If you'll be in town awhile, ask for the "tessura," which gets you a free cup after the first 10.

Colli Euganei Rosso is the local red made from Cabernet Franc, Cabernet Sauvignon, Merlot, Raboso, and Barbera grapes. The Novello is ready November 1; Rosso d'annata four months after harvest; and Rosso Riserva after two years. The white Colli Euganei Bianco mixes seven grape varieties and also comes in a sparkling version *(spumante brut).*

Information and Services

Check with the APT (tourist office) at the train station, Galleria Pedrochi, or Piazza del Santo for combined discounts with **Padova Card** (tel. 049/876-7911, www.turismopadova.it, €14). It's valid for 48 hours, which not only gets you reduced rates on museums and other sights, but free parking in specified lots and other benefits. Banks are open weekdays 8:30 A.M.–1:15 P.M.

Getting There and Around

Trains connect Padova directly to Venice and Verona or from Rome or Milan take the Venice line. If you have a bike, see about bringing it on the train (www.trenitalia.com). Otherwise consider using the Brenta Canal to get to Venice, if you want a leisurely cruise past villas.

You can rent a bicycle at the train station (tel. 348/701-6373); it's a fun way to see the (flat) city center. A car is handy for country excursions, and Avis, Hertz, Europcar, and Maggiore have offices by the train station on Piazzale Stazione. If you are staying in the city center, check the Padova Card parking garages, where parking is free, or garage at the train station (Piazzale Stazione, 6 A.M.–1 A.M.). APS and SITA are the bus lines. For an overview by bus, **City Sightseeing Padova** (www.padova.city-sightseeing.it) offers two bus tours, Line A tours the city and B goes to the ther-

mal towns. You can also go medieval with a horse-drawn tour; carriages depart from Piazza del Santo (tel. 348/775-9203, Thurs.–Sun. 10 A.M.–1 P.M. and 2:30–6 P.M.) or arrange for the carriage to meet you at the station when you arrive.

Around Padova

Padova is surrounded by geothermal as well as artistic phenomena. Hotel rates are much cheaper in nearby spa towns like **Terme Euganée** and **Abano Terme** than in the center of Padova, and using these towns as your base can help revive both body and spirit. The Terme Euganee spa basin has more than 100 hotels, most with indoor and outdoor pools and spa therapies. Look for good deals on half- or full board, an option many Italians choose. Have a good soak in a thermal pool, massages, and a mud wrap—great to remove the paint splatters of an artist's palette or to revive weary travel legs.

Thermal waters are the main draw of the town of Abano Terme, but it also has a duomo dedicated to St. Lawrence, an art musuem, monastery, International Hamlet Mask Museum, and historic villas if you want to while away part of a day exploring the town.

Bathers are likely to be chattering away in French, Italian, German, Russian, and English in the nicely landscaped thermal pool at **Abano Grand Hotel** (Abano Terme, Via V. Flacco 1, tel. 049/824-8100 or toll-free 800/881-18811, www.gbhotels.it). Its plush rooms are large as Vegas, thermal treatments range €12–70, and beauty treatments include olive oil, grapes, or chocolate (on you, not in you—save that for the restaurant).

Abano Terme has its own opera season in **Teatro Parco Magnolia** and hosts galas periodically.

The tourist office in Via P. d'Abano 18 (tel. 049/866-9053, daily 9 A.M.–12 P.M. and 3–6 P.M., www.turismopadova.it) can provide a full schedule as well as a map of town. There is direct bus service every 20 minutes to **Stazione Terme Euganée** from Padova train station. By car, take the Autostrada to SS250.

Monselice, a nearby town with a spectacular castle, offers dancing in the piazza under the tower in nice weather.

You can take the **Burchiello** canal boat on a day trip from Padova to Venice, where you will leisurely pass Veneto villas, visit four or five, and have lunch along the way. Delta Tour (www.deltatour.it) operates year-round.

VICENZA

Vicenza is famous for Renaissance architect Andrea Palladio. His villas for centuries inspired others architects from Thomas Jefferson's design of Monticello to present-day Hollywood retreats. The villas are more than expressions of beauty. They were major power centers and successful commercial enterprises where mulberry trees were cultivated for silk production and vineyards produced wine. They are scattered throughout the Veneto and there are 16 in the province of Vicenza alone. Built primarily for merchant families whose wealth skyrocketed as trade with the Orient increased, the Palladian villas were declared treasures by UNESCO.

Other Palladio architectural masterpieces, like his Olympic Theater in Vicenza's center and his bridge in nearby Bassano del Grappa, show further range of his genius. Palladio events hit a new peak with the 500th anniversary of his birth in September 2008, with exhibits and villa openings that will continue into the years ahead.

Despite periodic Italian protests in 2006 and 2007 demanding the closure of a large U.S. military base in the outskirts of Vicenza at Ederle, the American presence is still strong and contributes greatly to the local economy. Thus, transactions in English are generally easy and events are sometimes held in English language.

Sights

Card Musei (€8) includes access to both the Teatro Olimpico and Pinacoteca di Palazzo Chiericati.

VILLA ROTUNDA

The most celebrated of Andrea Palladio's Renaissance buildings, Villa Rotunda (www.

palladio.vicenza.com, inside building Mar. 15–Oct. 15 Wed. 10 A.M.–noon, garden Mar. 15–Oct. 15 Tues.–Thurs. 10 A.M.–2 P.M. and 3–6 P.M., €10 building, €5 garden) is still privately owned and open to visitors only part of the year. Located in the outskirts of Vicenza, its perfection of proportion inspired Jefferson and many others with its round central salon covered by a cupola and its four sides with pronaos that each have six ionic columns. Stucco and statues embellish the exterior. The interior has frescoes that were painted by Giandomenico Tiepolo.

PALAZZO CHIERICATI AND MUSEO CIVICO PINACOTECA

Palladio has a number of works in the center of Vicenza. He began Palazzo Chiericati (Piazza Matteotti 37/39, tel. 044/432-348, www.comune.vicenza.it) in 1551 and it wasn't completed until the following century. Since 1885 it has hosted the Museo Civico Pinacoteca (tel. 044/432-1348, Sept.–June Tues.–Sun. 9 A.M.–5 P.M., July–Aug. Tues.–Sun. 9 A.M.–7 P.M.). The museum has paintings and sculptures from the medieval period through the 18th century with the majority of works from 16th-century Veneto artists, including Paolo Veronese, Lorenzo Lotto, Jacopo Tintoretto, Jacopo Sansovino, Jacopo Bassano, Antony Van Dyck, Jan Bruegel, and Giambattista Tiepolo. A section in the museum is also dedicated to engravings and sketches by various artists, such as Palladio. Another section has coins and statuary.

PALAZZO DELLA RAGIONE AND CASA PIGAFETTA

Palazzo della Ragione has colonnades designed by Andrea Palladio in 1549. Palladio's first public commission shored up the palace that had begun to subside. Near it is the narrow 12th-century tower.

Look at the fanciful designs on the facade of the 1481 Casa Pigafetta, built for the owner who had sailed with Ferdinand Magellan 1519–1522 and was one of the few survivors of the round-the-world voyage.

VENICE

Palazzo della Ragione was Andrea Palladio's first public commission.

❰ TEATRO OLIMPICO

Verona's Arena and other ancient Greek and Roman theaters inspired Vicenza's Teatro Olimpico (Contrà San Pietro 67, tel. 044/430-2425, www.olimpico.vicenzia.it), which Andrea Palladio began in 1579, and his pupil Vincenzo Scamozzi completed in 1585. The details continued down to stage sets that are still used today, as well as courtyard sculptures, costumes, and the Odeon frescoes of the gods of Mount Olympus, for which the theater takes its name.

Sports and Recreation

Experienced motorcyclists love the six-day excursion on Ducati S4Rs or S2R 1000 motorcycles with **Dynamic Ducati Driving** (Via S. Agostino 34, tel. 348/704-0827, www.jpbari.com, Apr.–Sept., €4,000). Tour on Monsters through Vicenza, Lake Garda, the Dolomite Mountains, Marostica, Bassano, and other breathtaking spots with roads specifically selected for the challenge and beauty. The package includes the Ducati motorcycle of your choice, guide, transport vehicle, accommodations, breakfast, gourmet dinners, and airport shuttle from Venice or Treviso.

The nearby Berici Hills are yours to race through in early October on a mountainbike at the annual **La Via dei Berici** (www.bericamtb.it, €20). The race began with 200 participants in 1994 to benefit the ill and those with disabilities, and now attracts about 2,000 riders. **Il Corto** is the short 21-kilometer route, **Il Lungo** is 37 kilometers on more difficult hilly terrain, and in 2007 the 57-kilometer Marathon was inaugurated on very challenging roads. If you don't bring your own bike, several of the pre-registration sites are bike shops where you can buy or rent a bike.

Sunny winters and good soil drainage keep golfers swinging towards the 18 holes at **Golf Club Colli Berici** (Strada Monti Comunali, tel. 044/460-1780, open year-round). The front nine overlook the Po Valley and offer magnificent views of the Lessini and Piccole Dolomiti Mountains while the back nine extend into a forest of oaks, hornbeams, and chestnut trees.

Shopping

All that glitters in Vicenza probably is gold. More of that precious metal is bought, sold, traded, and crafted here than in any other Italian city. It's a world leader, with some 1,200 goldsmiths, 13,000 employed in the gold business in the Veneto, and almost €5 billion in annual sales. There's no lack of jewelry right in the center and security all over the place. Main and side streets are crammed with shops.

Before you redo your bathroom, patio, or line your swimming pool, have a look at **Bisazza Mosaics** (36075 Alte, Vicenza, tel.044/470-7511, www.bisazza.it) manufactured in Alte. If you always wanted to be the first person to tile your car you're too late, and the evidence is parked here.

One of the region's largest wineries, **Casa Vinicola Zonin** (Via Borgolecco 9, tel. 044/464-0111, www.zonin.it) is five kilometers from the A4 Montebello exit. They offer tours and tastings, and will ship bottles to any address in the world.

Accommodations

In Vicenza's historic center **Hotel Campo Marzio** (Viale Roma 21, tel. 044/454-5700, www.hotelcampomarzio.com, €95–245 d) has 22 standard and 13 superior rooms. The superior rooms are recently renovated and more elegantly furnished (one has a hot tub and the others have showers with hydromassage). Downstairs there's a bar, restaurant, and handy private parking near some of Palladio's architectural masterpieces. **Hotel Castello** (Contra' Piazza del Castello 24, tel. 044/432-3585, www.hotelcastelloitaly.it, 18 rooms, €150 d) is in the heart of the historic center and has been a guesthouse since the mid-1800s.

In Arcugnano close to Vicenza's Fiera, a 19th-century family bakery was transformed into **Residence Nogarazza and Trattoria** (Via S. Agostino 34, tel. 044/428-8900, www.nogarazza.com, €160 d). Suites have a living room with kitchen range and refrigerator, and the bedrooms are large and comfortable. Only four kilometers from the Vicenza A4 exit Ovest, this is a good base to zip around the area to visit Palladian villas, tour wineries, shop for ceramics in Nove, play golf, visit art cities like Padova and Venice, or taste grappa in Bassano. Paolo arranges for train trasfers and presides over the restaurant that attracts a faithful local clientele.

Also in Arcugnano, **Hotel Villa Michelangelo** (Via Sacco 35, tel. 044/455-0300, www.hotel villamichelangelo.com, 52 rooms, €200) is inside a converted 18th-century monastery. They added a swimming pool and an elegant restaurant the monks could have never imagined. Guests who fancy a round of golf can play for free at the local course.

Next to a Palladian-style villa in its own historic complex, **Villa Pasini Bed & Breakfast** (Via Roma 4, tel. 044/427-0054, www.villa pasini.com, €120 d) has tastefully furnished bright, spacious rooms. An unusual plus is architect and designer Aldo Cibic, whose studio is on the premises and suffuses the atmosphere with creative energy. His American wife Cynthia worked for years in the fashion industry and adds her flair to their home. Bus 17 stops across the street.

Food

Nogarazza and Trattoria (Via S. Agostino 34, tel. 044/428-8900, www.noga razza.com, Mon.–Sat. noon–2:30 P.M. and 8–10:30 P.M., €8-12) offers tasty pastas, grilled meats and regional *baccalà* (cod) with polenta and must-taste desserts like the homemade cheesecake and whipped cream creations. Lorenzo bakes superb fresh breads every morning at this family *trattoria*.

If you want to stick with a Renaissance theme, dine in the nearby town of Caldogno in an old mill. The owners of **Molin Veccio** (Via Gironi 56, tel. 044/458-5168, Wed.–Mon. noon–3 P.M. and 7–11 P.M., €30–40) have researched the 16th-century cuisine that periodically appears on the menu.

Getting There and Around

From Verona or Padova, take Autostrada A4 to the Vicenza exit. Vicenza has frequent service on Eurostar and local train lines.

Around Vicenza

Recoaro Terme's thermal waters have attracted visitors for centuries. The town, northwest of Vicenza and west of Marostica and Bassano, is a good base to explore Vicenza and beyond. From Vicenza, take SS248 north to Marostica or from Bassano del Grappa take the same road south. By car exit the A4 at Montecchio Maggiore. **Terme di Recoaro** (Località Fonti Centrali, tel. 044/575-016) has mud, baths, inhalation, and massage therapies. By the 1700s it had a hydrotherapy center and in the 1800s hotels followed. Water comes from the Amara, Lelia, Lorgna, Lora, and Nuova springs that combine with water from other springs in the treatment center. The area has a view of the Piccolo Dolomiti mountain chain.

Hotel Trettenero (Via Vittorio Emanuele, 16/e, tel. 044/578-0380, www.hoteltrettenero. it, 53 rooms, €250 d) has a Belle Epoque atmosphere and gardens with stately trees. The more moderately priced **Hotel al Castello** (Via G. Zanella 13, tel. 044/578-0300, €150 d) is a short walk from *centro storico* and central fountains. Both hotels have restaurants and accept pets.

The **IAT tourist office** (Via Roma 25, tel. 044/575-070) has information on booking spas, alpine sports, hotels, and other facilities.

BASSANO DEL GRAPPA

Bassano del Grappa's scenic setting is along the Brenta River gorge spanned by a wooden bridge designed by Andrea Palladio. The view of forested Mount Grappa makes a beautiful backdrop and looks serene now, but it's been the site of bloody combat. The town once was more famous for fine engravers and for its ceramics, but now is known for grappa. Distilleries are clustered outside of town, but the center has plenty of *grapperie* to sample the potent brew made from distilled grape leftovers. Museums here are quite specialized, and include Grapperia Poli, which explains the grappa process, Palazzo Sturm with its important collection of prints and ceramics, the Alpine Soldier Museum, and the Car Museum with vintage automobiles. Dining here is good and prices are excellent. The atmosphere is lovely enough to make as a base to explore the Veneto, which you just might want to do lodged in a historic 18th-century villa on the edge of town. Despite its pre-alpine location in the province of Vicenza, the climate is surprisingly mild, as evidenced by the olive trees. The town has good grappa bars.

Sights

One of Italy's best collections of prints and engravings opened in 2007 in **Palazzo Sturm** at **Museo Remonidini** (Via Schiavonetti 7, tel. 042/452-4933, www.comune.bassano. vi.it, Tues.–Sat. 9 A.M.–1 P.M. and 3–6 P.M., Sun. and holidays 10:30 A.M.–1 P.M. and 3–6 P.M., €4, €5 includes access to Museo Civico). Among the masters are Rembrandt, Dürer, Mantegna, and Canova, who was born in nearby Passignano. Be sure to open up the doors in the cabinet room to see the exquisite prints. Another section is dedicated to ceramics. Don't miss the frescoes of the *Giants* and of *Venus Giving Arms to Aeneas,* then step onto the terrace that affords a grand view of the Palladian Bridge, Brenta River, and Mount Grappa. This is the landscape that Jacopo dal Ponte (a.k.a. Jacopo da Bassano) preferred to paint even though he had spent time in Venice. Jacopo often hiked in the hills and mountains in the area and it's the **Museo Civico** (Via Museo 12, tel. 042/452-3336 or 042/452-2235, www.comune.bassano.vi.it, Tues.–Sat. 9 A.M.–1 P.M. and 3–6 P.M., Sun. and holidays 10:30 A.M.–1 P.M. and 3–6 P.M., €4, €5 includes access to Museo Remonidini) that has the largest collection of his paintings, although his works adorn many churches especially in the Veneto and Venice. Antonio Canova's self portrait in sculpture is here, and it's larger than life-size. There's an interesting subject by Antonio Zona (1814–1892), *Titian Encounters Young Veronese on the Ponte della Paglia,* a mythical or actual meeting between the two great painters.

Mount Grappa, just a few kilometers from town, is a massif situated between the Brenta and Piave rivers. Its peak reaches 1775 meters and the area above 1,700 meters is now a sacred zone and houses the museum **Sacrario Militare di Cima e Museo** (tel. 042/354-4840, Sept.–May daily 8 A.M.–noon and 1:30–5 P.M., June–Aug. daily 8 A.M.–noon and 1:30–6 P.M., admission free). This national military memorial is dedicated to the 12,615 Italian soldiers who lost their lives in war, of whom more than 10,000 remain unknown. The road that leads here, Cadorna Highway, begins at Roman d'Esselino and its tunnel, Galleria Vittorio Emanuele, penetrates 1.5 kilometers of the mountain. The tomb of General Giardino and the 1901 chapel of Our Lady of Mount Grappa are on the peak.

Festivals and Events

In summer, Bassano has an active performance season with the **Veneto Jazz Festival** (www.operaestaste.it). Opera is featured, and classical concerts feature the Fenice Opera Orchestra or soloists. Dance showcases national companies or touring troops like the New York City Ballet.

The town of Bassano was awarded a gold medal for valor by the Prime Minister in 1946 for its bravery in World War II and its 31 partisans that were hung in town—some from trees that overlook the Brenta Valley—on September 26, 1944. The city commemorates the massacre on Mount Grappa on September 20–23 every year.

Shopping

Shops here are generally open 9 A.M.–1 P.M. and reopen at 3 or 4 P.M. Most shops are closed on Sundays.

Bottega del Porcino (Via Menarola 17/21) has local dried beans and polenta. As for crafts, the wooden walking cane with a grappa flask holder and bell might come in quite handy.

There are over 400 ceramic workshops, so find a style that you like. **Christian Parise** (Salita Ferracina 4, tel. 042/422-8359) does nice handpainted ceramics and you can see him at work. **Galleria d'Arte** (Piazzotto Montevecchio 22, tel. 042/422-0272) has lovely silver objects, paintings, and prints. Also in the same square, **Il Sagittario** (tel. 042/452-5022) has a nice collection of pens and other writing supplies. If the sight of the mountains has you in the mood for a mountaineer look, head to **Petri** (Via Ferracina 30, tel. 042/452-7838) for Tyrolean fashions. Near the **Grapperia Drogheria Menon** (Piazzotto Montevecchio 3, tel. 042/452-2302), an eccentric and friendly shop, has excellent teas (not so easy in most Italian stores), candies, ginseng and other energizers, spices, paint, detergent, and local Marostica cherries—an odd assortment.

Accommodations

In an 18th-century villa **Hotel Villa Ca' Sette** (Via Cunizza da Romano 4, tel. 042/4338-3350, www.ca-sete.it, €170 d) is imaginatively furnished with contemporary designs and is just one kilometer from Bassano's historic center. Its restaurant is handy in case you just want to kick back in the villa.

Hotel Villa Palma (Via Chemin Palma 30, tel. 042/457-7407, www.villapalma.it, €125 d) is a restored 18th-century villa with an elegant setting in Mussolente, five kilometers from Bassano.

Food

White asparagus is the food specialty of Bassano and a must in April and May. It was first bred in the 19th century, and has a fat stalk without stringy fibers that has a delicate taste. It's often served with hardboiled eggs. Grappa is in great evidence, but so are beer and wine.

Under the arcade at **((Garibaldi Trattoria Birreria** (Via Lazzaro Bonamigo 37, tel. 042/523-796, Wed.–Mon., €8–11), don't miss grandpa's great *strudel primo* (tri-colored fresh pasta with spinach, semolina, and tomatoes rich with butter and Grana, a hard sharp cheese somewhat like Parmigiano). This friendly spot opens early for coffee and serves lunch to 2 P.M., then reopens at 6 P.M. and serves to midnight or later. The menu is full of options that will please vegetarians, or go for the organic couscous with chicken or hearty sausage and polenta. Almost everything on the menu is priced under €10, which makes this a great value with plenty of good beer and wine on hand. A bit more upscale is the historic **Birreria Ottone 1870** (Via Matteotti 48–50, tel. 042/453-3306, Wed.–Mon. lunch, €10–14), run by two sisters.

Grapperia Nardini (tel. 042/422-7741, Mon.–Thurs. 8 A.M.–8:30 P.M., Fri.–Sun. 8 A.M.–9 P.M.) is the most historic *grapperia*, dating from 1779. It boasts a breathtaking location on the **Ponte Vecchio** and the original copper distilling equipment is still in working order. Just on the opposite side of the Palladian bridge is **Taverna al Ponte** (Via Angarano 2 at Ponte Vecchio, tel. 042/450-3662, Tues.–Sun. 9 A.M.–2 A.M.), which also houses the **Alpine Troops Museum** (tel. 042/450-3662, 8:30 A.M.–8 P.M., admission free), where downstairs you can see memorabilia and upstairs grab a cappuccino or something stronger at more reasonable prices (shots of *grappa* here cost €2–6). If all you want is a light snack, try **Bottega del Pane** on Piazza Libertà. On Piazza Garibaldi across from the entrance to Museo Civico is **Caffé Danieli,** a pretty bar with outside seating that serves gelato. **Trattoria el Piron** (Via Z. Bricito 12, tel. 042/452-5306, Fri.–Wed.) is popular with locals and serves pastas and appetizers ranging €6–8 and main dishes €7–12.

Getting There

From Vicenza the trip to Bassano is about 39 kilometers, which takes about 50 minutes by car (via SS53 to Cittadella, then SS47 to Bassano del Grappa). From Padova, Bassano is almost directly north. Directly from Venice, the drive is about 81 kilometers and just under two hours. Take the A4/E70 toward Milano A13, then Exit Padova Ovest. From Padova, take SP47 past San Giorgio in Bosco, then SS47 past Rosà. Bassano is about 30 minutes southwest of Valdobbiadene in Prosecco country. Marostica is about a 10-minute drive southwest of Bassano del Grappa, clearly marked. By train (www.trenitalia.com) from Venice, the trip is under two hours and costs about €4.25; from Vicenza, the trip requires a change of trains.

MAROSTICA

If you arrive in Marostica in September of 2008 or 2010 (or any even year), you have the chance to see a game of chess played with giant human pieces. Each knight is mounted on a real horse, the king moves one square at a time, and the queen can be devastating. Players have limited time in this popular tournament that lasts two hours: speed chess for the masters keeps the crowd from toppling like pawns. The tradition is thanks to Taddeo Parisio, Lord of Marostica, whose daughter Lionora in 1454 had two suitors vying for her hand. Her noble father forbade the two to duel and instead had them slug it out over a game of chess, with the winner to wed Lionora and the "loser" to wed Lionora's younger sister Oldrada, presumably a win-win situation. Bleachers help Kasparov types get an overview of the board, which is on the main city square in front of the lower castle. There is also a procession. Then wander off to see the upper castle and have a tasty meal up there or back in town. Visit Marostica even if you can't make the chess game. Nothing beats a chance to stand in the queen's square and contemplate your next move. Marostica is a fun half-day visit with a stroll through town,

intrigue on the main square, two castles, and a good meal where you can dine like a king on a pawn's wages.

Food

Move diagonally like a bishop from the square to **Osteria Madonneta** (Via Vajenti 21, tel. 042/475-859, Fri.–Wed. 9 a.m.–midnight, €20–25) in an informal, cozy atmosphere to revive you with good down-home cooking. The small coffee bar is open in the morning, when locals are likely to be reading the paper.

Getting There and Around

From Vicenza, take SS248 north to Marostica (from Bassano del Grappa, take the same road south).

VERONA

Verona is a sophisticated, lovely town that most visitors under-budget for time. They plan an hour or so to see Juliet's house, but depart wishing they had spent the day here. It makes a good base, and at least one night is what you need to savor its delightful atmosphere and take in the sights.

Verona has the best Roman remains in Northern Italy, with sections of Imperial era bridges, a theater, and an amphitheater almost as large as Rome's Colosseum. Today often called *l'Arena,* the amphitheater is the summer setting for prestigious opera and concert performances. These ruins also attracted Renaissance artists like Andrea Mantegna, whose interest in ancient Rome was heightened here and became an element in his paintings. Mantegna had his workshop here and some of Europe's most talented artists honed their skills in the city. A few works remain but most eventually found homes in the world's prestigious museums. Today, like Padova and Treviso, Verona is a city of antique dealers and art restorers, where you are likely to catch a glimpse of an artisan restoring paintings, a wood intarsio (inlaid wood) table, or a 17th-century bookcase. Some of the back streets are hazy with sawdust and the sound of pounding resonates from workshops all day long.

The Middle Ages brought the rise of artisans and merchants, with families forming alliances and vying for power, dramatic material for Renaissance writers like William Shakespeare who used local rival families in his tragic play. Luigi da Porto of Vicenza wrote the story of *Romeo and Juliet,* which Shakespeare turned into a play toward the end of the 16th century.

Sights
◖ ANFITEATRO ARENA
The world's third-largest amphitheater after Rome's Colosseum and Capua's near Naples, Anfiteatro Arena (tel. 045/800-0361) in Piazza Bra was once the stage for mock battles and gladiator contests, public executions, fairs, and bullfights. Today, opera, theater, and classical concerts flourish here, in part thanks to the Arena Conservationists, a group that has maintained the amphitheater since the 16th century. The amphitheater is a good reference point, where ancient Romans were entertained 2,000 years ago, visiting Renaissance artists would have been busy sketching, and the ill-fated medieval lovers must have rendezvoused. It's open year-round and tours are offered daily. In the summer, the prestigious opera and concert season is in full swing and catching an evening performance is mandatory.

MUSEO DI CASTELVECCHIO
From Piazza Bra, follow Via Roma to see Verona's art treasures in Museo di Castelvecchio (Corso Castelvecchio 2, tel. 045/594-734, Tues.–Sun. 8:30 A.M.–7:30 P.M., Mon. 1:30–7:30 P.M., €3.10) across the Adige River in a fortified castle connected by the 14th-century Saliegero Bridge.

CASA DI GIULIETTA
William Shakespeare immortalized the medieval intrigues of the Capulets and Montagues, known locally as Capuleti and Montecchi. The latter owned Casa di Giulietta (Via Capello 23, tel. 045/803-4303, Tues.–Sun. 8:30 A.M.–7:30 P.M., Mon. 1:30–7:30 P.M., €3.10), a 13th-century house with a balcony for Juliet to pine away her

Verona's Anfiteatro Arena and Piazza Bra

© JUDY EDELHOFF

evenings. Most visitors don't enter the house, but are content to step into the small courtyard for their photo op under the balcony (where chewing gum has been plastered onto romantic messages on one wall). There's a small souvenir shop that sells postcards and Romeo and Juliet branded gifts.

TOMBA DI GIULIETTA
If you are ready for the final act, skip the magic potions and take a brisk 10-minute walk to Juliet's tomb near the Adige River, flanked on one side by Via Shakespeare. Admission into the cemetery and Tomba di Giulietta (Via del Pontiere 35, tel. 045/800-0361, Tues.–Sun. 8:30 A.M.–7:30 P.M., Mon. 1:30–7:30 P.M., €2.60) includes a visit to the Fresco Museum, which displays Renaissance Veronese frescoes that have been detached from various sites.

GIARDINO GIUSTI
The 16th-century Giusti Palace and Gardens at Giardino Giusti (Via Giardino Giusti 2, tel. 045/803-4029, Apr.–Sept. daily 9 A.M.–8 P.M., Oct.–Mar. daily 9 A.M.–7 P.M., €5) have attracted visitors from kings and princes to composers and musicians of Mozart's caliber. The Renaissance gardens were designed by Agostino Giusti, a knight of the Venetian Republic, in 1580. The palace is located at a lower point than usual. The garden swoops up toward the wilder upper woods and links to a

VENICE

series of stone terraces to a belvedere with a city view. The highlights here are the avenue lined with cypresses, hidden fountains, a grotto, and a spiral staircase.

OTHER SIGHTS
Famous for its panel painted by Renaissance artist Andrea Mantegna, the church of **San Zeno Maggiore** (Piazza San Zeno near Porta San Zeno, one of the city's ancient entrances, Nov.–Feb. Tues.–Sat. 10 A.M.–4 P.M., Sun. and public holidays 1–5 P.M., Mar.–Oct. Tues.–Sat. 10 A.M.–6 P.M., Sun. and public holidays 1–5 P.M., admission free) has a splendid marble clad interior. **Palazzo della Gran Guardia** near Piazza Bra reopened in 2006 after years of restoration. It periodically hosts special exhibits and events.

Entertainment and Events
Arena di Verona (Via Dietro Anfiteatro 6/b, tel. 045/800-5151, www.arena.it) attracts international stars who perform *Carmen, Aida, Tosca,* and other favorites in the magical setting of Verona's ancient Roman amphitheater. Some operas are staged by film directors like Franco Zeffirelli and are nearly always sold out. Tickets should be purchased in advance, although last minute travelers will usually find a scalper selling cheap seats at moderate prices. Always negotiate. The venue marks its 86th season in 2008.

Shopping
Verona is a good shopping town, as quality is relatively high for clothes and other goods. **Via Mazzini** and streets that lead to Piazza Erbe are good bets. Locals pile in late afternoon for their pre-dinner *passeggiata* (Italian promenade).

Local products include great red wines like Valpolicella and Amarone, its more intense, elaborate younger relative, first bottled in 1940; both are from the plains and hills leading toward the Monti Lessini. Bardolino, another red from the Verona area, is celebrated in its *novello* phase, just a few months after grape harvest. Custoza wine also comes from the area. Soave, a medieval town south of Verona, gives its name to the local white wine from grapes grown in the Mezzane, Illasi, and Alpone Valleys. There are half a dozen wine shops where all the local vintages can be purchased.

Accommodations
Two major factors affect price and availability of rooms in Verona: trade fairs at the Fiera and the summer opera season. At those times, rooms are hard to come by (even in the outskirts) and prices often rise accordingly.

A central location, large doses of elegance, tasteful furnishings, grand public areas, and helpful staff make **Due Torri Hotel Baglioni** (Piazza S. Anastasia 4, tel. 045/595-044, www.baglionihotels.com, €250 d) an unforgettable stay in Verona's historic center.

Upscale, traditional **Hotel Colomba D'Oro** (Via C. Cattaneo 10, tel. 045/595-300, €275) has a lovely lobby and cocktail bar, and its attractive sitting area is perfect for conversation or a good read. The breakfast area has stone walls and mosaics.

Near Piazza Bra, **Hotel Bologna** (Piazzetta Scalette Rubiani 3, tel. 045/800-6830, www.hotelbologna.vr.it, €200 d) is cute on the outside and convenient on the inside, even if the pink tablecloths in the dining room seem a bit excessive. Breakfast is bountiful and the buffet is well stocked even if you arrive late.

The economical **Hotel Torcolo** (Vicolo Listone 3, tel. 045/800-7512, www.hoteltorcolo.it, €135 d) has a small lobby, but rooms are large and nicely furnished. **Hotel Verona** (Corso Porta Nuova, 47/49, tel. 045/595-944, www.hotelverona.it €120 d) is centrally located near Porta Nuova. Comfortable and modern rooms have Wi-Fi, fluffy pillows, and well-stocked mini-bar. The staff is especially nice.

Food
Informal and cozy **Trattoria i Masenini** (Via Roma 34, tel. 045/806-5169, Mon.–Sat. 12:40–2 P.M. and 7:40–10 P.M.) is a favorite with museum officials. Start with a local platter of cured meats or other antipasto. For pasta, try the tortelli. Steak with Amarone red wine sauce is a good main dish.

VENICE

Picnic basket fixings are waiting at **De Rossi il Fornaio** (Corso Porta Borsari 3, tel. 045/800-2489, Mon.–Sat. 9 A.M.–7:30 P.M.). The walnut bread is especially tasty and goes well with any cheese.

A small fruit and vegetable market is set up daily in **Piazza Erbe,** Verona's beautiful medieval square where major shopping streets converge.

Information and Services

Verona Card is a combined museum ticket good for one day or three and includes public transportation. It's available at churches, museums, *tabacchi,* as well as the tourist offices (www.tourism.verona.it) in Piazza Bra and the train station.

Getting There and Around

Verona's Villafranca Airport has some European flights, but most overseas visitors fly into Milan or Venice. **AMT** (www.amt.it) buses are for city routes, while **APTV** (www.apt.vr.it) goes farther out into the province. The train station is near Porta Nova and Corso Porta Nova leads straight to Piazza Bra. Verona is on major Eurostar high-speed train routes as well as local lines (www.trenitalia.com).

Around Verona

Marble is big business in Verona, which has over 500 local companies. The largest concentration is in **Valpolicella** near **Sant'Ambrogio** and **Dolcé.** Companies tend to specialize either in quarrying or in cutting. In November, **Bardolino Novello** celebrates the release of the "new wine" with tastings in various towns around Verona.

Consistently rated as one of Italy's top 10 hotels, ◖ **Villa del Quar** (Pedemonte, Via Quar 12, tel. 045/680-0681, www.hotelvilladelquar.it, 18 rooms, 10 suites, €255) is a Renaissance villa hidden amidst Valpolicella vineyards northwest of Verona. Its atmosphere and service merit the splurge at this dream destination. The helicopter pad near the parking area is convenient for top executives and celebrities, but most guests arrive by car. Bedrooms

with wood floors and ceilings are beautifully furnished with antiques, oriental rugs, prints and engravings, gold brocade drapes, and fine linens. The lobby and sitting areas are comfortable and classically decorated with gold; it's plush but not ostentatious. The tea room, library, sun room, outdoor pool, garden gazebo with bar, dining rooms, and lobby are designed for elegant comfort and good conversation. Its ◖ **Ristorante Arquade** has won awards for its chef and wine cellar, two more reasons why you might not want to leave the premises. Book well in advance.

TREVISO

Trevigiani, the inhabitants of Treviso, are happy that their lovely city remains somewhat of a secret. Close to Venice, yet much less expensive, this picturesque medieval town has its own network of canals. Known in the Middle Ages as the capital of the "Marca gioisa et amorosa" ("the joyous and amorous land"), Treviso is just that. Its houses are even frescoed on the exterior, the **Sile River** flows past, and the city layout tseems designed for the comfort and convenience of its residents. **Calmaggiore** (literally, "main street") is the center of action, and has been since ancient Romans called it "Callis maior."

Emperor Claudius considered the area so important that he had the **Via Claudia Augusta** road built to improve north–south access in the first century A.D. The area had been inhabited since the 14th century B.C. (a millennium before the Romans), when it developed on an island in the Sile River. Its importance early on was due to its direct connection to the Adriatic Sea, making it a vital transportation and trade stop. **Piazza dei Signori** is the town's outdoor drawing room, where locals meet and *ciacolare* ("chat" in local dialect). The morning fish market is just behind the **Duomo.**

Treviso was a fortified town but the 16th-century walls you see were erected by order of the Venetian Serenissima Republic. Their military function has been transformed to a promenade for walking or jogging, with three particularly striking gates, **San Tommaso,**

Santi Quarante, and **Altinia.** The Univerisity of Treviso dates to 1263, added most of its academies in the 18th century, and now is a branch of the Universities of Padova and Venezia. The Latin Quarter is the town's newest, especially popular with young Trevigiani.

Sights
Piazza dei Signori certainly makes for a great place to *ciacolare.* The Palazzo della Prefettura dates to 1874–1844, while the **Torre Civica** (City Tower) rings loudly with the **Campanòn** (Big Bell). Palazzo dei Trecento was restored after it was bombed on April 7, 1944. The 1491 Palazzo del Podestà is in Renaissance Lombard style with 20th-century modifications. Follow the portico-lined Calmaggiore from Piazza dei Signori to the Duomo. The Romanesque **Loggia dei Cavalieri** adorned with baroque frescoes is at the crossroads of the ancient Roman *cardo* and *decumano,* the two principal streets in any Roman town.

A stone marker on the south side of the Baptistery next to the **Duomo** indicates the spot's importance as a major ancient Roman intersection, while the north facade has a Roman funerary *stele* inserted into the wall. The cathedral has seven domes (five are above the axis of the nave inside) and is dedicated to St. Peter. The Romanesque crypt below probably was completed in 1030, while the part above was erected shortly thereafter with modifications over the centuries. The light-filled Duomo sports excellent acoustics. Most famous for Titian's *Annunciation,* don't miss Il Pordenone's fresco, *Adoration of the Magi.*

The Black Death halted construction on **San Nicolò** (8 A.M.–5:30 P.M., admission free) in 1348–1350, when Europe was struck by the Great Plague. The Dominicans then called in Tommaso da Modena to paint frescoes on the walls of Sala del Capitolo of their convent. The portraits of the priests that gaze down at visitors are especially interesting and may be the first representation in art of a person wearing spectacles. Lorenzo Lotto also painted frescoes here. If you want to see more of Tommaso da Modena's frescoes, stop in the

CARLO SCARPA

A great admirer of Frank Lloyd Wright, Venetian architect Carlo Scarpa (1906-1978) visited the United States in 1967 specifically to see Wright's buildings. Most of Scarpa's constructions are in Venice, the Veneto, and Friuli. In Udine, **Casa Veritti** (1955-1961) was part of his "American" series influenced greatly by Wright. In the province of Treviso, Scarpa broke away from the use of traditional contrasting exhibit colors to show opaque white sculpture against various shades of white in the **Gipsoteca Canoviana** in Possagno (1955-1957), which features a collection of the works of sculptor Antonio Canova. One of Scarpa's works in Venice is a courthouse where he later spent time for a dispute over an *abusivo* structure, a work constructed without a permit (in this case, a lowered ceiling). Also in Venice, Frank Lloyd Wright's proposal for **Fondazione Masieri** was rejected for the Grand Canal structure; however, later the contract was awarded to Scarpa and completed posthumously (1968-1978). **Casa Ottolenghi** in Bardolino (1974-1978) features a "natural" terrace. On June 2, 2006, the **Carlo Scarpa Center** (tel. 02/4335-3522, www.carloscarpa.it) opened in Treviso, and it now contains over 30,000 drawings and designs.

simpler church of **St. Francis,** where he and assistants painted the left aisle.

The 14th-century church dedicated to St. Catherine and its monastery now form **Museo Civico** (Borgo Cavour 24, tel. 042/265-8442, www.comune.treviso.it, 9 A.M.–12:30 P.M. and 2:30–6 P.M., €3). The city museum has an archeology section with findings from 2000 B.C. up to the early Middle Ages. Tommaso da Modena, who by now seems like the town's favorite artist, painted a beautiful fresco cycle of the life of St. Ursula. The legendary early Christian teacher of 11,000 virgin martyrs, Ursula—according to one version—and her

the Sile River in Treviso

students were killed by Huns as the British princess returned from a pilgrimage to Rome. Artists to look for here are Lotto, Bellini, Titian, and Tiepolo.

Shopping

The *pescheria* (fish market) dates back to 1856 during the Hapsburg heyday, when the Austrians connected isles of the **Cagnan Grande** canal behind the Duomo. Come for the colorful fruit and vegetable displays, the small shops, and informal *osterias*. The main shopping street is Calmaggiore. Casual fashion buyers might be interested to know that Benetton originated here.

Accommodations

Boscolo Hotel Maggior Consiglio (Via Terraglio 140, tel. 042/240-9409, www.boscolohotels.com, €110–209 d) has full business services and a restaurant, as well as a swimming pool to soothe you after a day of sightseeing. Pets are permitted.

Set amidst a garden and surrounded by trees, **Hotel al Giardino** (Via S. Antonio 300a, tel. 042/240-6406, www.hotelalgiardino.it, €85–106 d) offers a tranquil setting with good services convenient to the center.

If you are looking for a simple budget room in the center, try **Locanda al Gambero** (Via Roma 64, tel. 042/282-1346, www.locandaalgambero.it) or **La Quinta** (Piazza della Conciliazione 5, Spercenigo, tel. 042/289-3388); both offer comfortable rooms for under €80.

To try apartment living and do your own cooking, contact **Palazzo Brando Apartments** (Via Manzato 2, tel. 042/240-6642, www.palazzobrando.it, €50–110).

Food

Treviso may be best known for its *radicchio rosso* or *radicchio di Treviso,* which has curved elongated leaves loosely gathered at the base rather than the tightly wrapped ball of regular radicchio. Its pleasantly bitter flavor when raw becomes delicate when cooked in a good risotto, pasta, or grilled as a *contorno* (side dish). If you want to use a bit of local dialect at the bar, have *un'ombra di vino,* glass of wine with *cicchetti,* local appetizers, or creamy local cheese, Casatella Trevigiana. As for wine, you are right near Prosecco territory.

Getting There and Around

Treviso is a short distance to the west of Venice. It has its own airport, A. Canova,

VENICE

although for the best airfares check Venice, Ancona, and Milan. By train, take the Venice–Udine or Bolzano lines, or connect directly from Vicenza. By car, take Autostrada A27 and exit at Treviso Nord or Sud; from the A4, exit at Cessalto. Tourist information (www.marcatreviso.it) is at Piazzetta Monte di Pietà (Via S. Andrea 3, tel. 042/254-7632), Museo Civico, and at the airport.

Around Treviso

A drive to **Maser,** northwest of Treviso on the way to Possignano, will put you into the heart of Treviso's villa territory, with villas that date to Renaissance times and others that followed with variations on the villa theme up to contemporary times. Pick up information at the Treviso tourist office.

Villa Barbaro is one of Andrea Palladio's masterpieces with interiors painted by Paolo Veronese. The villa's **Tempietto,** another Palladian church dedicated to The Redeemer, is both villa chapel and parish church for the town of Maser. **Ca'Pesaro,** a Dominican Renaissance house, is also here, as is 16th-century **Villa Pellizzari,** which has a stucco interior and Venetian floors. **Villa Sernagiotto** is an 18th-century villa with Palladian stone floors.

All it takes is a look at a few Veneto villas and your urge likely will be to play country squire and lounge in one yourself. Get your map of the Province of Treviso and head for some of these beauties.

Near the Sile River in **Casale sul Sile, B&B Relais Villa Canossa** (Via Cave 21, tel. 042/282-2759, www.relaisvillacanossa.it, €100–170 d) has just three rooms available. The splendid entrance lures you right up to the door.

Tiny bubbles are close at hand amidst beautiful rolling Prosecco vineyards. **Strada di Prosecco** leads past many small wineries, plus there are four or five major Prosecco makers.

Bisol (Bisol Desiderio & figli, Santo Stefano di Valdobbiadene, Follino, tel. 042/390-0138, www.bisol.it) is an *agriturismo* in a beautiful location amidst Prosecco vineyards that consistently wins high praise and makes a good range of Proseccos. Each one has its own distinct personality that depends in part on which hills the grapes are grown and their particular soils.

The beautifully furnished rooms and rolling hills at ((**Relais Duca di Dolle** (Via Piai Oriental 5, Rolle, 0438/975-809, www.bisol.it, €120 d) provide a sense of the rhythm of the land and comfortable surroundings to experience an evening of joyful silence and a dramatic sunset that shifts colors across the hills. The pool is surrounded by grape vines and is good for sunning in warm weather. Breakfast is served here, and nearby restaurants offer tasty cuisine at good value.

Move from Luigi Cosmo's effervescent bubbles at **Bellenda Winery** to the adjacent bed-and-breakfast **Alice Relais nelle Vigne** (Via Giardino 90, tel. 043/856-1173, www.alice-relais.com, €110–135) that features warmly decorated rooms. There are lots of thoughtful extras here, such as Prosecco happy hour, great breakfasts, and in-room teapots.

Hotel dei Chiostri (Piazza IV Novembre 3, Follina, tel. 043/897-0001, www.hoteldeichiostri.com, €130–155 d) is a converted Renaissance abbey with furnishings in an eclectic mix of stylish modern and antique in the heart of Prosecco country. Nearby historic **Villa Abbazia** (Via Martiri della Libertà 9, tel. 043/897-1277, www.hotelabbazia.it, €200–255 d) has antique surroundings from the doorknobs to the candelabra. The cafe/bar is especially pretty, as is the patio that's perfect for drinks or tea.

Neither Lino nor his most famous guest is with us anymore, but every year for a month or two Marcello Mastroianni holed up right here in a room at ((**Locanda da Lino** (Via Brandolini 31, Solighetto, tel. 043/882-150, www.locandadalino.it, €95 d) to get away, read scripts, and prepare for roles. In town, Marcello could play cards with the locals undisturbed. Marcello's daughter, who knew of his affection for Lino's place, designed furniture for the room that he always took. That room with the furniture is still here, and the cooking at Da Lino is still wonderful. Other rooms are available, too, though they come with contemporary furniture. The owners are happy to shuttle you to the train station if you decide you'd like to make

PROSECCO

Prosecco has become Italy's most famous sparkling wine. Developed in Conegliano laboratories at the end of the 19th century as an alternative to the more costly Champagne method, Prosecco is fermented and bottled usually within a matter of months. (Champagne, exclusive to its own region in France, needs to be pampered and wooed for 3-5 years.) Prosecco is made from the Prosecco grape, which as a D.O.C. wine (Denomination of Controlled Origin) must be grown in the hilly zone between Conegliano and Valdobbiadene in one of the 15 communities proscribed by law, and the wine must be bottled within the Province of Treviso. Alcohol content is regulated at 11.5 percent. In 2007, some 126 wineries were bubbling with Prosecco, which requires special wine bottles that won't explode under pressure. The Consortium for the Protection of D.O.C. Prosecco ensures observance of the regulations and winemaking standards from the vineyard to the bottle.

Prosecco grapes can be transformed into sparkling, semi-sparkling, or still versions of the wine. A more limited version with a higher sugar content, Cartizze, must be made from grapes grown in a more rigidly restricted area. Many winemakers make all three. Italians consume it year-round as an *aperitivo*, especially in late afternoon to "close" the day. Foreign sales zoom up as the Christmas and New Year holidays approach. In Italy, however, Prosecco consumption is fairly steady throughout the year, with a spike in warm weather when some of the robust red wines are put on hold until heartier cuisine returns with cooler weather. Serve it in a chalice, or tulip-shaped glass if you want the bubbles to linger. However, at tastings you may be offered a wider-mouthed glass so that you can better smell its bouquet.

Many wineries are small operations, so almost all require an appointment. Some are not set up to receive casual visitors and prefer to greet the public with their effervescent liquid during **Vino in Villa** tastings during the third week of May or during **Primavera di Prosecco** festivals that take place March-June and also feature local tradition and folklore. If you want to find a particular winery, pick up a Prosecco map at a tourist office in the Province of Treviso or at many hotels. A phone call will determine if the winery has visiting hours, or they can recommend a local *enoteca* or restaurant that offers a good selection.

A few wineries also run bed-and-breakfasts where you can sample their various wines in comfort and style. Two excellent winemakers run especially nice *agriturismi*. Bisol, toward the western end of Prosecco territory, has its **winery in Santo Stefano** and lodgings in the town of Rolle with rooms and apartments (ask especially for the upstairs suite in the Casa Rossa) at **Relais Duca di Dolle,** which has a swimming pool. East toward Vittorio Veneto in Carpesica, the **Bellenda Winery** (www.bellenda.it) has bed-and-breakfast **Alice Relais nelle Vigne** with cheery rooms that all face south, a delicious breakfast with home-baked treats, lovely cocktail hour that features one of their Proseccos, a backyard whirlpool tub, and rooms year-round.

The Prosecco method is relatively new, but in ancient times Romans had already discovered that the Dolomites shelter the area from northern winds and the nearby Adriatic Sea keeps the climate milder. As the wealthy Venetian merchant class looked to expand their enterprises into the countryside, the Renaissance villa-building boom began. Andrea Palladio was the most sought-after architect. Others followed and graced the Veneto with their villas. Some owners now rent out rooms, either from their main villa or the *barchessa,* an adjoining wing that once served as workshops or storage for their agribusiness affairs. Film actor Marcello Mastroianni appreciated the low-key discretion of the Veneto's small towns. He would stay for a month or two in a simple motel, play cards and chat with the locals, and move about unobserved – or at least not hassled – a routine he followed until his death.

this your base while you explore other spots in the Veneto—it's even an easy hop to Venice.

Antica Osteria di Via Brandolini (Via Brandolini 35, Solighetto, tel. 043/882-590) has a fireplace, fresh flowers attractively arranged, and friendly service. The main course specialty is grilled meat, but vegetarians will be happy too. The antipasto is an excellent beginning, with a wide variety of vegetables as well as cheeses and excellent prosciutto and salami.

ASIAGO

One of the first democratic governments was in place 1310–1807 in Asiago. Today Asiago is known for its cheese, honey, and distilled herbs. Skiing is popular in Asiago year-round, and there's even grass skiing in the summer. Asiago claims to have the best linked cross-country ski tracks in the world, as well as plenty of downhill skiing. Step fanatics can head for Cala del Sasso, one of the world's longest flights of steps (4,444 of them), made of limestone in 1388–1392. If you're looking for something more extreme, you can try bungee jumping, free climbing, paragliding, and more at the Alto Piano, where there is an Extreme Sport Center. The Italian Astrophysics Observatory is here, but with any luck you'll be on the right end of the telescope observing other objects in space.

Entertainment and Events

August is the month for Asiago's cheese fair, **Mostra Prodotti Latte-Caseari** and a chance to sample many of the town's best milk products.

La Grande Rogazion is a local procession that takes place the first day of the Quaresima (40 days of fasting from Ash Wednesday to Holy Saturday). If you want to try star-gazing beyond the Venice Film Festival, try **Osservatorio Astrofisico dell'Università di Padova** (Via Osservatorio Astrofisico, tel. 042/460-0034).

Sports and Recreation

Asiago is proud of its 18-hole, par-70 golf course at **Circolo Golf Asiago** (Via Meltar, tel. 042/446-2721, daily May–Oct.), which welcomes players of all handicaps.

Atopiano di Asiago (Via Stazione 5, 042/446-2661) has information on ski packages in 22 ski areas, 70 centers, and 200 kilometers of downhill slopes; also check here for hiking or golf. **Associazione Jonas** (tel. 044/430-3001, www.jonas.it) offers ski packages (from €260 per person) that include lodging, a ski pass, a ski class, and a snow card.

Shopping

Cheese is the main attraction here. A consortium sells local products at **Consorzio fra i Caseifici dell'altopiano di Asiago** (Via Baracca 14, tel. 042/464-844) or try **Latteria San Rocco Morar.** Also look out for honey and jams made from wild forest berries.

Accommodations

Linta Park (Via Linta 6, tel. 042/446-2753, www.lintaparkhotel.com, €71–151 d) has a covered pool, tennis courts, and garden, and it's accessible to travelers with disabilities.

Golfers might want to hole up right at **Golf Hotel Villa Bonomo** (Via Pennar 43, tel. 042/446-0408, www.hotelvillabonomo.it, €60–150 d), which has an 18-hole golf course and restaurant, but only 11 rooms; book well ahead.

Food

Cuisine of the Veneto is a specialty and in cooler weather you can look forward to wild fowl and forest mushrooms at **Casa Rossa** (tel.02/446-2017, tel. 042/446-2017, Fri.–Wed., €30–40). Pasta is freshly prepared here, as are the wild berry tarts. This restaurant is located near many local ski slopes.

The specialty cake is *torta Ortigara* at pastry shop **Pasticceria Carli** (Piazza Mazzini 2, tel. 042/446-2143), with other temptations to satisfy your sweet tooth.

Getting There and Around

From Vicenza, it's 50 kilometers. Take A31, exit Piovene Rocchette, then SS 249 north. The closest train stop is Vicenza. Frequent bus service runs from Vicenza as well as Padua (64 km), Bassano del Grappa, and Thiene.

Friuli-Venezia Giulia

Friuli-Venezia Giulia is overshadowed by the glamour of its neighbor to the southwest, Venice. That works to the traveler's advantage. This region has some similarities, like the lagoon area of Grado, villas built in Palladian style, and even some public buildings designed by Palladio himself. Here though, even the casual visitor will be aware of the strong influence of Austrian and Slovenian culture.

Signs of the two World Wars are very present. Friuli saw some of the bloodiest and most intense fighting. Trenches are still visible and the collective memory remains scarred. For centuries, invaders have come and left their mark: Romans from the south, Attila the Hun and Lombard dukes from the north. Even in the 20th century, Austria had control over much of the region. It's left a rich and varied heritage that comes out in local dialects, dress, architectural styles, religions, and food. The Friuli of today, even with its industrial focus on new technology and shipping, remains primarily agricultural.

Outdoor enthusiasts will find plenty, from beaches near the city to thermal parks, sailing, and many other water sports. The region also has the world's largest cave open to the public. Mountains offer skiing, and when snow falls on the golf resorts, they convert fairways to cross-country trails. One of the most beautiful sailing regattas offers a spectacle of thousands of boats launched at once.

The regional capital, **Trieste,** is bursting with arts activity while it also maintains its lead as an Adriatic Sea port and as shipbuilder of cruise ships. It's also a city of grand cafes, which were a magnet for temporary residents like James Joyce.

A delightful example of how a city can expand and develop in an aesthetically pleasing way is evident in **Gorizia.** Its pastel buildings and gardens provide a sense of well-being. But in the second half of the 20th century, the Iron Curtain went down here, right through the center of town, dividing main squares between

Italy and then Yugoslavia—a reminder of the ethnic sensibilities the town still must juggle to live in harmony with great diversity.

Aquileia offers ancient Roman ruins to explore with some of the most intricate and sophisticated mosaics with marine and plant life—and some of the most beautifully sculpted portraits—that you'll find anywhere.

Then you enter the early medieval world of the Lombard dukes and their headquarters in **Cividale del Friuli.** The rich colors and bold patterns are preserved in mosaics, jewelry, ivory, and gold.

Due south is **Grado,** where you can pretend that you are in a mini-Venice. Explore the town, and its ancient sights, and move about the various islands to see how they link together, all at prices that won't break the bank. **Palmanova** is a wonderful star-shaped town, so if someone says he wants a piece of the pie, he could be referring to the shape of his neighborhood that joins with another five slices to form a grand square in the center.

(TRIESTE

Turn-of-the-century cafes in Trieste with their Belle-Epoque atmosphere offer one thing that the great cafes of Paris and Vienna can't: the sea. Situated on the Gulf of Trieste, its luminous light streets and squares make a fetching contrast with the blue sea in this city that is the region's capital. While the cafe society discusses politics, ponders their literary masterpieces, or shows off the latest fashions, sailors are in paradise here, with one of Europe's most important annual races.

Trieste, the largest seaport on the Adriatic, is a major commercial shipping point and passenger liners and ferries depart for destinations like Greece and Slovenia daily. Antiquities buffs will find plenty of Roman ruins to track down, as well as the traces of political exiles who sought refuge here. James Joyce, a resident for several years, found literary inspiration.

Celts and Illyrians were among the earliest

© JUDY EDELHOFF

Palazzo del Comune, Trieste's city hall

VENICE

residents before the Romans swept in to establish the trading area of Tergeste. Links with Rome may be ancient, but Trieste did not join Italy at its unification in the 19th century, but was united with the Kingdom of Italy in 1919. In the Middle Ages, Trieste was under the control of the Patriarch of Austria, then in 1202 under Venice, rebelled in 1382 and placed itself under the protection of Austria, often playing the role of mediator between the two rivals in the following century. (Even today, Trieste moves more goods from Austria and the former Yugoslavia than from Italy.) Charles VI brought prosperity to Trieste when he declared it a free port in 1719 and set the headquarters here for the French Trading Company. Many of Trieste's fine palaces were erected during the rest of that century and the next. At the beginning of the 20th century, the town was known for its literary circles, dominated in part by local novelist Italo Svevo, who frequently set his stories in Trieste.

The rest of the arts thrive, too. Theater and music are in full swing on the city's numerous stages—nothing new to this town, which also boasts an ancient Roman theater. Throughout the region June–September ancient and classical court music is featured in **Musica Cortese.** In May, wineries throughout the region throw open their doors for **Cantine Aperte.** If Carnevale in Venice is not in your budget or you don't like crowds, consider one of Friuli's cities or small towns, where everyone gets into the act in February.

Sights

Spend an hour or so at the top of Colle di San Giusto, the Hill of St. Justus, where the Roman city began. Museum hounds could spend a couple of weeks here, Trieste has more than 15 that form its network of history and art museums, **Civici Musei di Storia ed Arte** (www.triestecultura.it). If you don't have that much time, pick up your city map at the tourist office and head for your area of interest, whether it be ancient Greek or Roman artifacts, railroads, theater, Oriental or modern art, military, Jewish heritage (the community dates back to the 13th century), postal, or the sea. That doesn't include other sights like the aquarium, botanical gardens, and theaters. Or the summer beach scene and thermal pools. The port and ships that move through are always engaging, but never more stunning than in October when thousands of sailboats set off to race in the **Barcolana.**

Probably built over a former temple, **Basilica di San Giusto** (Piazza Cattedrale), also referred to as the Duomo or Cattedrale, dates originally to the 5th century. Major modifications in the 14th century joined two early basilicas together, which is why the church has two thrones rather than just one. The most striking feature inside are the 12th-century mosaics that show the Virgin Mary enthroned between two Archangels, Michael the warrior and Gabriel, who will announce her future as the mother of Jesus, and the 12 Apostles. The frescoes of the life of San Giusto were painted just after the turn of the first millennium. Back outside is the campanile, bell tower, with fragments of Roman columns embedded in the

© JUDY EDELHOFF

The Basilica di San Giusto is two 5th-century churches in one medieval church.

lower level. Climb to the top and you have a great view of Trieste and the sea.

Before you head down to the harbor, have a look at **Castello di San Giusto,** built by the Venetians in 1368, now home to an interesting collection of weapons and armor. It makes it easy to see why Archangel Michael has such a cult following throughout Italy (a street and more than one church named after him here, too). The 19th-century prints will put you in the mood for the cafes that you can visit later, some of which have changed little.

Less than five minutes down the street, **Orto Lapidario and Museo Civico Ed Storia d'Arte** (Via della Cattedrale 15) is a history and art museum that has an interesting archeological collection highlighting trade with the ancient Greek world. On your way down to the seafront, you might want to veer off on **Via del Teatro Romano** to have a look at the ancient Roman theater.

The story of the sea and ships is at **Museo del Mare** (Via Campo Marzio 5, tel. 040/304-885), which has enough exhibits to keep armchair navigators enthralled. It's on the seafront near the railroad station and the seawater thermal pool.

The town's major attraction, however, is several blocks north along the seafront, where sea creatures are in movement at **Aquario Marino e Pescheria Centrale** (Molo Pescheria 2, tel. 040/306-201), ideal for a family outing.

If what you crave are more recent trends in art, head one block up from the aquarium on Via San Giorgio to **Galleria d'Arte Moderna** (Via Diaz 27, tel. 040/675-4158).

North along the seafront past Molo Bersaglieri is **Piazza dell'Unità d'Italia,** one of Italy's largest squares. The piazza is graced with early 20th-century architecture in **Palazzo del Governo** (the government palace), **Palazzo del Comune** (city hall), and **Palazzo del Lloyd** (the former headquarters of Lloyd Trieste and now the regional government seat of Friuli Venezia Giulia).

North of the city, Villa Opicina has lovely views, and makes for a nice getaway outside of town. The funicular **Opicina** takes you to the Altipiano Carsico. Look toward the sea and down below is the lighthouse that also serves as a World War I memorial to fallen soldiers, **Faro Vittoria.** Turn the opposite way and you can see Slovenia in the distance.

Entertainment and Events

Since 1985, the Latin American Film Festival, **Festival del Cinema Latino Americano Trieste** (www.cinelatinotrieste.org), has been spicing things up here. In 2007, over 150 feature films, documentaries, and shorts were shown. Chilean director Miguel Littin presided over the jury during the November event. The science fiction film festival, **Festival Internazionale della Fantascienza** (www.scienceplusfiction.org), in October will let you decide which is stranger, real life or fantasy.

Throughout the region on St. Nicholas Feast Day, December 8, parades are held and **Fiera di San Nicolò** is its Christmas fair.

May is the month that has a week-long celebration dedicated to sports and culture in **La Bavisela.** Trieste's antiquarian fair, **Mercato d'Antiquario,** takes place in October.

Accommodations

Elegant with fine furniture and attentive service, right on Trieste's grand square is the **Grand Hotel Duchi d'Aosta** (Piazza dell'Unità d'Italia 2, tel. 040/760-0011, €230–379 s/d) which provides guests with swimming and water sports activities. **Harry's Grill** inside the hotel offers a panoramic sea view.

Hotel Abbazia (Via della Geppa 20, tel. 040/369-464, www.hoelabbaziatrieste.it, €128 d) is centrally located and frequented mostly by businessmen, but is a handy base for tourists.

If you'd like a stay on the coast with a view of the Miramare Castle, try **Riviera & Maximilian's** (Strada Costiera 22, tel. 040/224-4551, €100–240 s/d), which has traditional decor in a 1898 building. The new wing offers rooms with balconies. A scenic elevator takes you down to two beaches, one with a swimming pool. The hotel has a boat, too, so inquire about booking a trip. The restaurant specializes in fish and overlooks the sea.

Food

The cuisine of Trieste reflects the influences of Hungary, Greece, Germany, and Slavic countries. *Rebechin* are the snacks, like tapas, that you can eat in a bar. Fish is the preferred main course, with *sardoni* being the most popular, served fried, breaded, or *in savor* (fried and marinated with onion and vinegar), but many varieties of fish and shellfish are available. *Osmizze* are rural Slovenian houses that open for short periods to serve homemade wine, salami, and cheese, something you'll see only on a country excursion. *Jota* is a soup with a base of beans, potatoes, and sauerkraut. Sweets also reflect international influences and the krapfen (cream or jam-filled doughnut) and strudel are musts.

When it comes to wine, even in the Veneto when a host wants to impress a guest he'll pull out a bottle from Friuli—known for its lively, intense whites and reds with decisive flavors.

Be sure to enjoy the ambience of the historic cafes, a tradition since the 1700s, when they became a center for literary, political, and arts circles. **Caffè Tommaseo** (Piazza Tommaseo 4/c, tel. 040/362-666, daily 8 A.M.–midnight) opened in 1825 during the Hapsburg era, and it's still reflected in the decor. **Caffè degli Specchi** (Piazza dell'Unità d'Italia 7, tel. 040/365-777, daily 7:30 A.M.–11 P.M., €8–25) and **Stella Polare** (Via Dante 14, Piazza Sant'Antonio, tel. 030/632-742, Mon.–Sat. 7 A.M.–9 P.M.) were favorites of James Joyce. Near Corso Italia is **Antico Caffè Torinese** (Corso Italia 2, tel. 040/632-689) which dates from 1919 and sells *boiseries* in the shape of ships. Around the corner from the Synagogue, **Caffè San Marco** (Via Cesare Battisti 18, tel. 040/363-538), with its high ceilings and spacious rooms dating from the Belle Epoque, still attracts literary and intellectual clientele.

Fish is the specialty at family-run **Ai Fiori** (Piazza Hortis 7, tel. 040/300-633, info@aifiori.com, Tues.–Sat., €35–50), which uses local produce in creative ways.

Since 1897, pork, fresh or cured, has been king at ⓒ **Buffet da Pepi** (Via della Cassa di Risparmio 3, tel. 040/366-858, Mon.–

Sat., €12). It's served with *kren* (freshly grated horseradish) in sandwiches or on platters. The mixed platter (€10) has ham, ribs, sausages, *testina* (head), *zampone* (foot), *cotechino,* and other specialties that are best washed down with a beer. If you just want a simple pork meat sandwich ask for *porcino.* And if you eat your sandwich standing up, it only costs €2.50. Similar types of *trattoria-buffets* are **Buffet da Mario** (Via Torreianca 41, tel. 040/639-324, Mon.–Fri., €10), **Buffet da Siora Roa** (Piazza Hortis 3, tel. 040/301-460, Mon.–Fri., €10), and the decidedly more upscale and pricier **Buffet Birreria Rudy** (Via Valdirivo 32, tel. 040/639-428, Mon.–Sat. 9 A.M.–midnight, €13–15), where you can skip the wine and focus on Bavarian beers. Near the station is buffet **Re di Coppe** (Via Geppa 11 tel. 040/370-330, Mon.–Fri., €9). Most buffets open at 8 or 9 A.M. and keep serving anywhere from 8 P.M. to midnight.

Near Cattedrale San Giusto, try **Antipastoteca di Mare** (Via della Fornace 1, tel. 040/309-606, Tues.–Sun. lunch and dinner, €15–20), which as its name suggests specializes in fish and seafood *antipasti,* appetizers ideal for grazing or a meal.

For a quick take-away meal, a good assortment of vegetable or meat *torte* are baked at **Pastificio Mariabologna** (Via Battisti 7) and for breads try **Panificio Jerian** (Via Combi 29). **Salumeria Gastronomia Villanovich** (Via delle Torri 1) sells a wide selection of salamis and cheeses. **Prosciutteria al Porton** (Largo Santorio 1) specializes in ham, wine, snacks, and hot dishes.

Granmalabar (Piazza San Giovanni 6) has a good selection of coffees and excellent wines by the glass. Local, national, and international wines are offered at **Enoteca Bere Bene** ("drink well") at Viale Ippodromo 2–3. **Enoteca Nanut a Ponterosso** (Via Genova 10E, tel. 040/360-642) has wines by the glass plus daily specials and occasional tastings guided by a sommelier.

Traditional sweets like *presnitz* are at **Pasticceria Bomboniera** (Via XX Ottobre 3, tel. 040/632-752) or try **Penso** (via Diaz 11).

James Joyce was a regular patron at **Pasticceria Caffè Pirona** (Largo Barriera Vecchia 12, tel. 040/636-046, Tues.–Sun. 7:30 A.M.–8 P.M.).

If you take the funicular up to Opicina, try **Antica Trattoria Valeria** (Strada per Vienna 52, tel. 40/211-204, Wed.–Mon., €9–12), founded in 1904. Now Milli and her son David dish out local specialties. If you like it up here, they have rooms to rent, too.

Viale XX Settembre, originally Viale dell'Acquedotto when it was built in the early 19th century, is a good place for a summer stroll, with outside tables placed under a row of trees that extends for over a kilometers.

Information and Services

The **APT office** (Via San Nicolò 20, tel. 040/679-6111, www.triestetourism.it) and its satellite location in Piazza dell'Unità d'Italia 4/b are well furnished with maps and tourist information. They can also help find you an accommodation and provide an updated list of local events.

Getting There and Around

The closest airport is Gorizia's Ronchi dei Legionari (www.aeroporto.fvg.it), which can be reached by buses leave regularly from Piazza Libertà. Options by sea can easily connect you to Greece on Anek Lines, Turkey on Samer (www.samer.com), Albania (www.agemar.it), or Slovenia, and Croatia. Complete information on shipping and passenger lines is available at the port (www.informare.it). By car from Venice or Treviso, take the A4 Autostrada, exit for the center at Trieste-Sistiana, then take either the coastal road, Costiera SS14, or SS202 Grande Viabilità all the way into town. Trains arrive at **Stazione Trieste Centrale** (Piazza della Libertà 8, www.trenitalia.com), which is also where the **Autolinee** (tel. 040/425-020) buses to other destinations in Italy, Slovenia, and Croatia depart. Rental cars options include Avis and Hertz (both at Molo Bersalieri 3), Maggiore (Piazza Libertà 8), and Europcar (airport).

Trieste Trasporti (Via d'Alviano 15, www .treistetrasporti.it) buses serve the city and

VENICE

outlying areas, with many that depart from Piazza Goldoni. The city connects with Altipiano Carsico and Opicina (tel. 800/016-675) byway of a historic funicular train built in 1902 that was one of the world's first. Departures are every 20 minutes in Piazza Oberdan.

Special-interest tours satisfy various interests. Early 20th-century literature fans can follow in the footsteps of Rilke, Svevo, and Joyce, who worked on *The Dubliners* in Trieste (his sister Eileen was married in Cattedrale San Giusto). A Grotte tour takes you through a network of caves that begins near Aurisina. There's a military history path along important sites during World Wars I and II. A Jewish history tour begins in the 13th century, when Jews are first documented in Trieste, to 1684–1758 when they were confined to living in the Ghetto, to the Trieste Synagogue, the persecution of 1938–1945, Jewish Museum, and Cemetery, and even to a kosher olive oil company. You can book tours or get information to guide yourself from the tourist office.

Around Trieste

The 1995 entry in the *Guinness Book of World Records* for largest cavern in the world was **Grotte Gigante** (Borgo Grotta Gigante, tel. 040/327-312). It's spectacularly decorated with natural phenomena, and has impressive dimensions. Located north of Opicina on the way to Sgonico, it's well worth a detour. The skeleton of a prehistoric bear-like mammal, *Ursus spelaeus*, was found here—the largest inhabitant thus far discovered. As the Italian Alpine Club continues to explore it, new sections gradually open to the public, all spectacularly illuminated.

AQUILEIA

Pre-Roman settlements in the Aquileia area date to the 9th century B.C. According to legend, when the town boundaries were being ploughed by the Romans in 181 B.C., an eagle *(aquila)* soared above, which explains the name. Augustus used this as his base in his military campaign against the Germanic tribes. Excavations have uncovered ruins behind the Basilica that include the Via Sacra (Sacred Way)

that led to the port, as well as houses and the forum. Alaric's Visigoths attacked in 401 and 408. Attila's Huns laid siege to and torched the town in 452, before the Ostrogoths took a try at it in 489.

Sights

Even if mosaics were its only treasures, this would still be one of Northern Italy's most intriguing archeological sites. The 11th-century **Basilica** (Piazza Capitolo, tel. 043/191-067, www.aquilea.net, daily 8:30 A.M.–12:30 P.M. and 2:30–5:30 P.M., admission free), built over a 4th-century building, was a power center in the years 554–1751, an important patriarchate that was ruled by bishops. The mosaic floors were laid in 313. The northern hall was dedicated to liturgy and the southern hall to educate people not yet baptized. The Jonah panels are a riot of action, from Jonah being swallowed by a sea monster, then vomited out amidst a sea of cavorting fish, then resting under an arbor of squash vines, while angels fish from a row boat. Symbols in the church are somewhat puzzling, as not all seem to be Christian in origin. Some seem to be zodiac signs, while others are animals, plants, men, and geometric forms. The 9th-century crypt has Romanesque frescoes.

The adjoining monastery **Museo Nazionale Paleocristiano di Monastero** (Loc. Monastero, tel. 043/191-131, daily 8:30 A.M.–1:45 P.M., admission free) in the former Benedictine abbey lets you view the floor mosaics from two large balconies above, while other sections have fragments of a bird in a cage, a peacock, and bas-reliefs with interesting subjects. From the north aisle of the church, you can reach Cripta degli Scavi, which has a 4th-century mosaic floor.

Findings from local digs are in **Museo Archeologico Nazionale** (Via Roma 1, tel. 043/191-016, Mon. 8:30 A.M.–2 P.M., Tues.–Sun. 8:30 A.M.–7:30 P.M.), which has three floors of treasures. The lower part of a Roman ship found in Monfalcone is here, which you can compare to a Roman bas-relief of a cargo ship. Don't miss the mosaics showing the fish in the sea, with accurate detail. It shows an

© JUDY EDELHOFF

Roman ruins surrounding Aquileia

ivy branch or grape vine bound with a ribbon tied into a bow full of graceful form and effective perspective. The ground floor has a series of marble busts with expressive faces, among which are portraits of young Augustus and Tiberius. The first floor has some of the most beautiful Roman glass objects that you'll see anywhere, with many in vivid jewel colors and a terra-cotta oil lamp with gladiators portrayed. The same floor has a gem room, where you can see how skilled the Romans were at carving gems for a cameo effect. The third floor has rooms with military paraphernalia and works carved in amber, the fossil resin from the Baltic thought to have special virtues. Aquileia was renowned for crafting amber into rings, pendants, spindles, and amulets. There are other fashion accessories, a beautiful bronze head of a wind deity, and a good coin collection.

From the basilica, step outside onto Via Gemina and turn left after you cross the river onto **Via Sacra,** where the Roman river port once was abuzz with food, spice, wood, marble and gem merchants heading off to Danube

markets. Part of the Istria stone docks are visible, which had a double loading wharf, ramps, warehouses, and city gates. Near it along Via Giulia Augusta lies the Roman Forum—center of business, politics, and justice. As you turn left on that road onto Strada Comunale, you can see traces of the ancient Roman road where it has wheel ruts grooved in from carts steadily rolling through laden with goods.

There is still plenty to visit, including the Cossar excavations that turned up some of the most beautiful mosaics, including a trompe l'oeil unswept floor. The cemetery is along Via Annia, and has sophisticated 1st-century A.D. monumental tombs.

Accommodations and Food

In the center near the basilica and archeological museum, **Patriarchi** (Via Giulia Augusta 12, tel. 043/191-9595, www.hotelpatriarchi. it, €74–96 s/d) has a small garden, restaurant, and comfortable rooms. Also in the center are **Aquila Nera** (Piazza Garibaldi 5, tel. 043/191-045, €80–90 d) and **Alla Basilica** (Viale della Stazione 2, tel. 043/191-7449, €65–75). Both hotels offer board at lunch or dinner for about €13–15. **Ca' Ospitale** (Via Beligna 107, tel. 043/191-7423, www.caospitale.com, €54-76, high season July 1–August 31) is an *agriturismo* on the outskirts of the area and offers a swimming pool, garden, and country setting.

Outside the center in a rustic atmosphere **La Colombara** (Via Zilli 2, tel. 043/191-513, Tues.–Sun., €19–45) specializes in fish and offers outside dining in the summer.

Getting There and Around

By car take the A4 from Venezia or Trieste, exit at Palmanova, Grado is 28 kilometers to the south on SS 352. The closest train station is Cervignao del Friuli or Udine. Azienda Provinciale Trasporti (tel. 0481/593-511, www.aptgorizia.it) links Trieste with Grado by boat, with three daily departures from each city.

The tourist office, APT for Aquileia is in Grado (www.gradoturismo.it), although the bus terminal and the Pro Loco office (Piazza

VENICE

Capitolo 4, www.aquileiaturismo.info) might have some information.

Around Aquileia

Continue north of Aquileia on the SS 352 and you'll soon arrive at **Palmanova,** one of Europe's few towns laid out in a star shape. The large hexagonal main square is right in the center of the star, with roads that run to the star shaped city walls. Book a helicopter ride so that you can see it from above, the best way to see how precise the town planning was.

If you can't resist sleeping in a star-shaped city, a room at **Hotel Commercio** (Borgo Cividale 15, tel. 43/292-8200, www.alber gocommerciozarra.it, €56) fortunately has normally shaped beds and a restaurant on the premises.

If you are still in an ancient Roman mood, you can follow traces of the ancient Via Julia Augusta north, a route that on the SS352, SS-52bis, and B110 takes you through Udine, Tricesimo (Ad Tricesimum, Gemona del Friuli, Tomezzo, Zugio (Iulium Carnicum), Passo di Monte Croce Carnico, and then into Austria.

GRADO

Grado is situated on an island across the Grado Lagoon from the mainland south of Aquileia. Like Venice, its light shifts and changes throughout the day. Grado first developed as an ancient Roman maritime suburb of Aquileia, then became a refuge in 452 when Attila destroyed Aquileia. Now it offers pleasant sightseeing, life on a lagoon, and since 1892 a full range of thermal baths treatments. There's also a good collection of sacred art and ancient Roman objects, an odd coupling in Museum of Sacred Art and Underwater Archeology. The latter has the hull and cargo of a Roman ship from the 2nd century A.D.

Sights

Bishops built churches, the most important of which is the **Basilica of St. Eufemia** (Campo Patriarca Elia 1, tel. 043/180-146), also called the Duomo. This was for more than eight centuries the cathedral of the Patriachate, who,

along with the cult of St. Mark the Evangelist, moved to Venice in 1451. Inside are elegant colonnades and beautiful floor mosaics. Two Roman sarcophagi and altars date to the 2nd and 3rd centuries A.D. The octagonal baptistery dates to the 6th century, while the medieval bell tower near the basilica entrance is crowned with the Anzolo, a 1462 angel-shaped weather vane.

Recreation

Le Terme (Parco Termale Acquatico, tel. 043/189-9111, www.gradoit.it), Grado's thermal baths, have a whole center dedicated to aesthetic and rehabilitative treatments. You can get sand baths, massages, cave therapy, and other treatments based on the high level of iodine and salt in the water and sand. The Thermal Water Park has submerged seats in the pool so you can imbibe while remaining in the water. The indoor seawater pool is open year-round and the beach in summer expands your options.

Festivals and Events

In 2003, **Laguna Movies** (tel. 040/762-667) was launched in Grado and the lagoon and has become an annual July/August event that projects films in pubic squares and places that could be mistake for movie sets. A parallel kiddie event, **Lagunacartoon,** also swings into action at the same time.

Accommodations

Grado has a good range of hotels due in part to the thermal waters, which attract Italians who usually come for two-week stints. After a morning or afternoon trek through Roman archeological ruins, have a swim in the pool at **Grand Hotel Fonzari** (Piazza Biagio Marin 6, Grado, tel. 043/187-7753, €140–240, all suites), which has a lovely view of the town, *campanile,* the sea, and even the archeological site.

Hotel Abbazia (Via Colombo 12, tel. 043/180-038, www.hotel-abbazia.com, €88–145 s/d) is built to resemble an abbey. Most rooms have their own balconies, and there's a restaurant and indoor pool. **Metropole** (Piazzetta San Marco 15, tel. 043/187-6207, www.gradohotel. com, €94–140 s/d) is a grand dame of a yellow palace situated on the waterfront. Some rooms have a water view. **Antica Villa Bernt** (Via Colombo 5, tel. 043/182-516, www.hotelbernt.it, €80–165 s/d) has comfortable rooms and a bit of a garden in back. **Villa Reale Pensione** (Via Colombo 11, tel. 043/180-015, www.hotelvillareale.com, 135–175 d) rises up with Art Nouveau decorations and arched windows, and has its own restaurant.

Food

Two brothers run **All'Androna** (Calle Porta Piccola, tel. 043/180-950, Wed.–Mon., €40–55), a refined restaurant that specializes in fish and seafood. In the summer there are tables outdoors too.

In Grado's historic center, **De Toni** (Piazza Duca d'Aosta 37, tel.043/180-104, Feb.–Dec. Thurs.–Tues., €33–50) specializes in fish and homestyle cooking. Near the Duomo, **Al Canevon** (Calle Corbatto 11, tel. 043/181-662, Thurs.–Tues., €35–45) also specializes in fish.

North of town (about 10 km) winemakers run **Alla Buona Vite** (Località Boscat, tel.043/188-090, Mar.–Dec. Fri.–Wed., €30–45).

Fish reigns in Grado, so carnivores should head to Giuliano's busy **Wine Bar** (Piazza Duca D'Aosta 7, www.beligna.it, Wed.–Mon. 10 A.M.–11 P.M., €8–15) where there's no fish in sight, only meat. He serves hot meals at lunch and dinner. If you arrive in between lunch and dinner, try a salami-and-cheese platter. He raises pigs and makes his own salami.

Information and Services

Tourist information for Aquileia and Grado is available at the office on Viale Dante 72 (tel. 043/189-9278, www.gradoturismo.it).

The tourist office, also called **APT**, for Aquileia (Via Giulia Augusta, tel. 043/191-9491, www.turismo.fvg.it) is next to the bus terminal. The Pro Loco also has a tourist office (Piazza Capitolo 4, www.aquileiaturismo.info).

Getting There and Around

SS 352 connects Aquileia to Grado, 10 kilometers to the south.

Two bus lines serve Aquileia from here. You can choose either **APT** (tel. 048/159-3511) or **SAF** (800/915-303, www.saf.ud.it).

GORIZIA

Gorizia is called Italy's Garden City, but it is also Italy's divided city. At the end of World War II, Gorizia remained Italian, but it was forced to divide the province and border with then-Yugoslavia (now Slovenia) by running a wall right through the city itself. The last bricks of the Iron Curtain came down here in 2004, where they divided Piazza Transalpina.

The name Gorizia, probably from Slovenian *gorica* for "little mountain," first appeared in a 1001 document. The heart of the city is the castle, beautifully set on a hilltop accessed by a steep 16th-century road and surrounded by lush green slopes.

The architecture in the town below works in harmony with the natural surroundings to create a gracious city that reflects central European influences in its cafes, street layout, cupolas, and building silhouettes. The medieval district was either a melting pot or cauldron, depending on how well the delicate balance of Latin, Slavic, and German nationalities and ethnic groups mixed. Narrow streets of the old center lead to elegant 20th-century villas. Like many towns in the northeast, it has a small Jewish ghetto.

The surrounding Collio countryside west of Gorizia is known for its wine, especially white. Cherries make a a showy display when they blossom in spring in the area of Dolegna, Monte Quarin, and Sa Floriano, where winemakers Castello Formentini have set up a **Wine Museum** (Piazza Libertà 3, tel. 048/188-4034, www.castelloformentini.it).

Sights

The castle above affords a lovely view of the town and countryside. Inside in the Sala dei Cavalieri are reproductions of arms and armor used in the 13th–16th centuries.

Down in town, stroll along Corso Verdi and

WINERIES NEAR GORIZIA

Capriva del Friuli, about 12 kilometers west of Gorizia, is a good base for many wineries in the area.

Castello di Spessa (Via Spessa 1, tel. 048/180-8124, www.paliwines.com), a castle rebuilt in 1881, has a winery with five guest rooms, bicycles, and an 18-hole golf course nearby. The winery makes good whites and reds that include Collio Segè Sauvignon Cru and Collio Conte di Spessa made from Merlot, Cabernet Sauvignon, and a touch of Cabernet Franc.

It's also near two other excellent wineries including **Villa Russiz** (Via Ruzziz 6, tel. 048/180-047, www.villarussiz.it) that made a velvety, spicy 2004 Collio Merlot called Graf De La Tour and also produces good whites that include Sauvignon Tocai Friulano.

Known for its whites, winery **Mario Schiopetto** (Via Palazzo Arcivescovile 1, tel. 048/180-8073, www.schiopetto.it) makes a Tocai Friulano, a Pinot Bianco, and a Blumen.

Cormóns, a few kilometers to the west of Capriva, has two special wineries. Historic winery **Livio Felluga** (Via Risorgimento 1, Brazzano di Cormóns, tel. 048/160-052, www.liviofelluga.it) makes excellent Picolit, Sossó (Refosco dal Peduncolo Rosso with Merlot and Pignolo), and Vertigo. Look for the distinctive Felluga label that has an antique map background. This winery is consistently among Italy's best. **Ferlat Silvano** (Via Savaian, Cormóns, tel. 048/161-367) is a small winery that turns out a good red (Venezia Giulia Grame made from Malvasia Istriana grapes).

The towns of **Dolegna del Collio, Prepotto,** and **Spessa** are all clustered near each other northwest of Gorizia near the border of Slovenia. Dolegna del Collio makes an excellent base for a visit to the **Venica & Venica** (Località Ceró 8, tel. 048/160-177, www.venica.it) winery. Don't miss their light, flowery, and fruity Collio Bianco Ronco delle Cime made from Tocai Friulano grapes. Not only does Giorgio makes excellent white wines with very decisive flavors, they also run an *agriturismo* with six rooms and two apartments (Apr.–Oct.).

Prepotto is in the province of Udine, but is only minutes from Dolegna, about two kilometers to the north. Woman-owned **Vigna**

Petrussa (Via Albana 47, Prepotto, tel. 043/271-3021, www.vignapetrussa.it) turns out excellent wines. Don't miss Hilde's Colli Orientali del Friuli Schioppettino, a full bodied red wine, or her velvety and fruity Friuli Venezia Giulia Richenza made from four varieties of white grapes. An 18th-century villa is the splendid setting of **Grillo Iole** (Via Albana 60, Prepotto, tel. 043/271-3201, www.vinigrillo.it). The winery is also woman-owned and has four guest rooms. Anna Muzzolini runs the winery, which is especially noted for its whites that include Tocai and Sauvignon. In this area *agriturismo* **Tinello di Sant'Urbano** (Prepotto, tel. 043/271-3080) has guest rooms too.

South of the city of Gorizia there are a number of noteworthy wineries. In **Lucinico,** near the southwest edge of the city, the prestigious Tuscan winery **Conti Attems** (Vial Giulio Cesare 36/A, Lucinico, tel. 048/139-3619, www.attems.it) makes a good Sauvignon.

West of Lucinico in the small town of **San Lorenzo Isontino, Lis Neris** (Via Gavinana 5, tel. 048/180-9592, www.lisneris.it) turns out excellent white wines that include Pinot Grigio and a good red Merlot.

Farra d'Isonzo is the hometown of quality winemaker **Silvio Jermann** (Via Monte Fortino 21, tel. 048/188-8080, www.jermann.it). Jermann's famous for his white wines, but he also makes knockout red Venezia Giulia Pignacolusse made from Pignolo grapes. **Casa Zuliani** (Via Gradisca 23, tel. 048/188-8506), a much smaller winery, is also in this town.

A few kilometers west of Farra is **Gradisca d'Isonzo,** home of winery **Marco Felluga** (Via Gorizia 121, tel. 048/196-0270, www.marcofelluga.it), where Roberto and Raffaela make an interesting selection of whites and reds. Make sure to try their Collio Rosso, an intriguing blend.

Tenuta di Blasig (Via Roma 63, Ronchi dei Legionari, tel. 048/147-5480, www.tenutadiblasig.it), in the south of Gorizia near the airport, is a woman-owned winery that makes a good white (Malvasia) and red (Venezia Giulia Gli Affreschi). If you want to stay in the area, try **Doge Inn** (tel. 048/177-6286, www.dogeinn.it).

Corso Italia to see gracious villas and gardens that exude 18th-century atmosphere that, along with its mild climate, has casued Gorizia to be dubbed "the Austrian Nice"—an Austrian-style French Riviera with arcaded streets and pastel houses. The same architect that designed City Hall also built the 18th-century Palazzo Attems-Petzenstein. In **Piazza Transalpina,** you can walk across with one foot in Italy and the other in Slovenia. A round plaque marks the spot where the Iron Curtain divided the two in 1947–2004, years after the Berlin Wall came down.

The city's most important churches are the Baroque **Sant'Ignazio** on Piazza della Vittoria with its elaborate facade and onion dome, and the Cathedral.

Entertainment and Events

In July, the **Premio Sergio Amidei** (www.turismo.fvg.it) film festival highlights about 10 films and hands out awards for the best screenplays. Directors like Ettore Scola recently participated in this event, which has been going since 1971.

August features international folklore at **Festival Mondiale del Folclore,** with additional programs in Aviano and Tarcento. Musicians set up in the piazzas around town and the notes resonate through town for several weeks. Many bands are accompanied by dancers in colorful costumes.

Accommodations

The perfect way to enjoy Gorizia is to stay where King Charles V of France stayed with his entourage, **C Grand Hotel Entourage** (Piazza Sant'Antonio 2, tel. 048/144-0235, www.entoruagegorizia.com, €125–150 s/d), thus the name. The courtyard has an ancient well and comfortable rooms are furnished in elegant 19th-century style. The bar is open 24 hours, and with **Il Bearnese** restaurant and *enoteca* **Il Vinattier di Chamboard** on the premises, you might need an entourage to pry you away.

Food

In Gorizia near the market, customers used to pile into bars or wine shops before 10 A.M.

ready for their first substantial snack of the day—having been up since before dawn. This old tradition is making a comeback, and you may notice many *osteria* or *trattorie* already are open by 8 or 9 A.M., to brace you until lunchtime. The restaurants in this area feature an interesting mix of Italian, German, Austrian, Hungarian, and Slovenian cuisine.

Traditional Gorizia specialties have been served at **Alla Luna** (Via Oberdan 13, tel. 048/153-0374, Tues.–Sun. lunch) since 1876. The *osteria* takes its name from merchants who traveled by the full moon. A substantial meal rooted in Italian and Slovenia cooking is likely to cost under €20.

Set two kilometers outside the center next to a stream used to raise trout, **Al Ponte del Calvario da Mirko** (Località Vallone delle Acque 2, tel.048/153-4428, Wed.–Sun.) serves river shrimp and a plethora of meat dishes. In nice weather, there is outside dining by the stream.

The simple atmosphere remains at **Vito Primozic** (Via XX Settembre 134, tel. 048/182-117, Sat.–Thurs.), a tradition since 1922 when they began serving hearty local dishes to peasants that descended from the hills on market days.

Salami or cheese platters are the specialty, at **Al Tajeto** (Piazza De Amicis 7, tel. 347/981-1947, Mon.–Sat. lunch), though they also serve a few traditional steaming dishes in winter and newer, lighter dishes in the summer. It opens early so you don't have to wait until noon to start grazing.

Look for plates with creative twists as well as traditional favorites at **Rosen Bar** (Via Duca d'Aosta 96, tel. 048/152-2700, Tues.–Sat., €10–12). Their wines reflect the mix of Gorizia residents, Italian, Friulani, and Slovenian.

A late 19th-century *locanda* with rooms transformed in the early 20th century into an *osteria;* at **Vecia Gorizia** (Via San Giovanni 14, tel. 048/132-424, Mon.–Fri., €9–13) dishes are still traditional and are served with house wine or beer. Specialties include gnocchi, goulash, *spätzli,* polenta, and *cevapcici* (ground veal and pork with onions, garlic, and spices).

Information and Services

Tourist information for Gorizia is available at Via Roma 5 (tel. 048/138-6222, or 048/138-6225).

Around Gorizia

Monfalcone is a major ship-building center with a medieval fortress, La Rocca. It houses the **Museo Paleontologico** (Via Valentinis 86, tel. 048/192-172, Sat.–Sun. 10 A.M.–noon and 4–7 P.M.) which takes visitors 500 million years into the past. The Grand War Park nearby has preserved World War I trenches and fortifications that date back to 1915–1918.

CIVIDALE DEL FRIULI

Although the Romans founded Forum Julil, Cividale in 50 B.C., there is evidence that the Celts probably were in the area first. Today a visit to Cividale del Friuli is a step into the medieval world of the Longobardi (Lombards), who made the town their capital for over 200 years.

Cividale del Friuli tourist information is on Corso Paolino l'Aquileia 10 (tel. 043/273-1461).

Sights

Ponte del Diabolo, the 1442 Devil's Bridge, spans 50 meters across the steep ravine and 22 meters above the Natisone River. It rests on two arcades on a boulder that legend says was thrown there by the devil. **Tempietto Longobardo** (Piazetta San Biagio, tel. 043/270-0867, Mon.–Fri. 9:30 A.M.–12:30 P.M. and 3–6:30 P.M., Sat.–Sun. 9:30 A.M.–1 P.M. and 3–7:30 P.M., €2.50), the Lombard Chapel, on the north bank is a rare 8th-century church, decorated a century later with imaginative reliefs in stucco and magnificent frescoes. The finely carved 15th-century wood stalls are a good example of medieval craftsmanship. **Museo Archeologico Nazionale** (Piazza Duomo 13, tel. 043/270-0700, Mon. 9 A.M.–1 P.M., Tues.–Sun. 8:30 A.M.–7 P.M., €2) is housed in a Renaissance palace designed by Andrea Palladio, **Palazzo dei Provveditori Veneti** (Piazza Duomo 13, tel. 043/270-0700, archeologico-

civdale@libero.it, Tues.–Sun. 8:30 A.M.–7 P.M., Mon. 9 A.M.–2 P.M.,€2) and has intriguing artifacts from Roman and Lombard times like weapons, carved ivory, and jewelry. The **Duomo,** also of early origin, was rebuilt in the 15th century, but its **Museo Cristiano** (Piazza del Duomo, tel. 043/270-1211, Mon.–Fri. 9:30 A.M.–noon and 3–7 P.M., Sat.–Sun. 3–7 P.M., free admission) has sculpture from the earlier church that dates to the mid-8th century. Lombard designs generally were not as finely rendered as those made during Rome's golden age, but nevertheless can be elegant in their simplicity or even with touches of whimsy.

Entertainment and Events

On January 6, **Cividale Messa dello Spadone** (the Mass of the Broadsword) takes place in the Duomo and commemorates the 1366 entry of the Patriarch Marquado di Randeck.

In July, Cividale hosts **Mittelfest: Festival del Teatro della Mitteleuropa,** a Central European theater festival, and the **Cronoscalata Cividale-Castelmonte,** a timed uphill race. In August, the town celebrates the Palio of San Donato, and in November comes the fair of St. Martin.

Accommodations

An early 19th-century castle, **Locanda al Castello** (Via del Castello 12, tel. 043/273-3242, www.alcastello.net, €110 d) has tastefully furnished rooms. The castle's garden has an outdoor pool and the restaurant serves dinner.

Spessa at Rosa Rubini (Via Privata Rubini 3, Spessa, tel. 043/271-6141, Mar.–Nov.) is a country house annexed to a 17th-century Veneto villa with an outdoor pool, hot tub, and bikes to rent.

If partying is not your plan, maybe you would enjoy a spiritual retreat in the imposing sanctuary of Casteldemonte, with Cappuccino monks and a simple private room with bath, mini-fridge, and phone. If so, you can sleep in the 1480 house constructed by the Confraternity of Santa Maria just eight kilometers from Cividale. **Casa del Pellegrino** "Pilgrim's House" (Santuario Castelmonte,

tel. 043/273-094, info@santurariocastelmonte.
it) also has a simple restaurant, **Al Piazzale**
(tel.043/273-1161, www.mangancastelmonte.
it) with a terrace view. An elevator from the
parking lot below, which has ample space for
the busloads of pilgrims that arrive, allows for
wheelchair access.

Food and Wine

In Cividale del Friuli's historic center, the fare
is traditional plus some innovative dishes using
local ingredients at **Ai Tre Re** (Via Stretta San
Valentino 29, tel. 043/270-0416, Wed.–Mon.,
€10–12). The chef makes liberal use of wild
herbs, stuffed in local cheese or with *lardo,* or
rice. Most main dishes are meat, but the Friday special is still fish. *Gubana* is the traditional dessert.

Cividale del Friuli is in the Colli Orientali
del Friuli winemaking region. They count at
least 15 important D.O.C. varieties of white
wines and 13 red varieties. Following in the
footsteps of the ancient Etruscans and Romans, **Giovanni Crosato** (Via Castelmonte 1,
tel.043/273-0292, www.vinicrosato.it) decided
instead of using oak barrels to age his Venezia
Giulia Rosso d'Argilla, that he would use terra
cotta *amphorae* (urns). The amphorae imported
from Siena are quite a sight in Giovanni's wine
cellar. The red wine is made with Merlot and
Refosco dal Peduncolo Rosso grapes. His Venezia Giulia Don Giovanni are also made with
those grapes, as well as Cabernet Franc and
Schippettino grapes. The *pignolo* grape is put
to elegant use by **Moschioni** (Via Doria 30, tel.
043/273-0210), a great winery to visit to get to
know wine made from this grape.

Getting There

From Trieste, Cividale Friuli is 73 kilometers,
a drive that will take just over an hour. Take
SS58/E61 to SS202, then the Autostrada A4/
E70. Exit Villesse Gorizia. Take RA 17 and
SS252 to Gradisca D'Isonzo, then SS352,
SS305, SS56, SS356. Bus service on SAF
(www.saf.ud.it) requires a change in Udine, as
do the trains (www.trenitalia.com) that have
service at least every two hours, if not hourly.

UDINE

A 1st century B.C. Roman castrum on a hilltop
evolved into Udine. In the mid-5th century,
one legend says that Attila the Hun's soldiers
brought back soil from where the castle now
stands in their helmets so their commander
could see the sight of Aquileia burning in the
distance. From 568–776, the Lombards ruled
their Duchy from nearby Cividale. In 1420,
Udine became the capital of the Patria di Friuli (Friuli Homeland) and part of the Venetian Republic, and the Venetian governor took
up residence in the Castello. When Venice fell
in 1797, Napoleon's troops occupied Udine,
which the next year was annexed to the Hapsburg Empire. The French and Austrians continued their tug of war with Udine until it
joined the Kingdom of Italy in 1866. During
World War II, Udine suffered great loss of life
and received the gold medal for military valor
in 1947.

Sights

The heart of Udine is in **Piazza della Libertà**,
framed by Renaissance monuments that include Loggia di Lionello (1448), the Loggia
di San Giovanni (1533), and the Clock Tower
(1527) that surround a 1542 fountain. From
the square, there's also a view of the castle.

Andrea Palladio, famous for his villas as well
as his public buildings, created **Arco Bollani**
(1556–1570), the triumphal arch that leads to
the castle on the hill and Palazzo Antonini.

Now home to the **Civic Museums**,
Udine's **Castello** (Piazzale del Castello, tel.
043/227-1591, www.comune.udine.it, Tues.–
Sat. 9:30 A.M.–12:30 P.M. and 3–6 P.M., Sun.
9:30 A.M.–12:30 P.M., €3.20) houses the Archeological Museum with artifacts from the
Bronze Age to the Renaissance; Numismatic
Collection (coins); Gallery of Ancient Art,
which includes works by Caravaggio and
Tiepolo; Collection of Drawings and Prints;
and the Museum of Photography, which emphasizes the art form's earlier years.

Painter Giambattista Tiepolo was busy in
town in the years 1726–1759, when he painted
frescoes in **Palazzo Patriarcale** (Piazza

VENICE

Patriaracato 1, tel. 043/224-003), now home to **Museo Diocesano.** Walk up the Grand Staircase, which he painted in 1726, to see his 1729 frescoes in the Red Room and others he painted in the Guest's Gallery. Tiepolo's singing angels (ca. 1725) protrude from the **Santissimo Chapel** inside the **Duomo** (Piazza del Duomo, tel. 043/250-6830, www.spaziocultura.it) and his 1759 frescoes decorate the Oratorio della Purità.

Entertainment and Events

Carnevale comes in February, but so does the St. Valentine Fair. Beer drinkers get their turn to celebrate in May at Friuli d'Or, which features boutique beers from small breweries throughout the region.

June brings **Udine Jazz** and the **International Guitar Festival,** which continue on into July.

International performing artists arrive in Tarvisio's Piazza Unità d'Italia and at **Villa Manin Passariano** in Codroipo for the **No Borders Music Festival** in July, which recently featured Björk and other international performers.

Udine showcases wines from Friuli in **Friuli D.O.C.,** held in October, the same month that dancers dip and glide in the **Tango Festival.**

Christmas markets spring up in town and throughout the region in December.

Dates for annual events will vary from year to year. For current information contact the tourist office (Piazza Primo Maggio 7, tel. 0432/295-972 or 0432/299-774).

Accommodations

The historic **Ambassador Palace** (Via Carducci 46, tel. 043/250-3777, www.ambassador palacehotel.it, €90–148 s/d) has been carefully restored. It has a spacious restaurant and guest rooms to fit different budgets.

A refined Art Nouveau villa with swimming pool, **Clocchiatti** (Via Cividale 29, tel. 043/250-5047, www.hotelclocchiatti.it, €85–240 s/d) has elegantly furnished rooms in a more intimate setting that lets you live the good life in Udine.

Là di Moret (Viale Tricesimo 276, tel. 043/254-5096, www.ladimoret.it, €100–160 s/d) is a Best Western Hotel with a pool and sauna.

Food

Al Vecchio Stallo (Via Viola 7, tel. 043/221-296, Thurs.–Tues., €9–11) is a former postal station with a 1950s look that prepares traditional *osteria* food. They serve *tajut* (appetizers) at the bar before dinner, then move on to classic local dishes like gnocchi, *stinco di maiale,* and strudel. Finish with a shot of grappa for dessert.

Try the mixed fried vegetables at tiny **Al Ristorantino** (Via Vertaldia 25, tel. 043/250-4545, Mon.–Fri. noon–3 P.M. and 7–10 P.M., Sat. 7–10 P.M., €30), which is also a good spot to warm up with soups like onion, *orzo* (barley), or asparagus. If you liked the light touch with the fried vegetables, you might want to conclude with *frittele di mele* (apple fritters served with cinnamon and ice cream).

For local sweets like biscuits and chestnut cake, stop by **Il Laboratorio del Dolce di Danilo D'Olivo** (Vicolo Sottomonte 2).

Information and Services

The Udine tourist office is at Piazza Primo Maggio 7 (tel. 0432/295-972 or 299-774, daily 9 A.M.–6 P.M.).

Getting There and Around

From Venice or Trieste, take the A4 to the A23 and exit at Udine. The train station is on Viale Europa Unita near Via Roma (www.trenitalia. com) where taxis are usually waiting. The bus terminal is across the street toward the right on Viale Leopardi.

Around Udine

When cinemas began to close around Italy in the 1970s, a collector began assembling equipment from them to create **Piccolo Museo Storico delle Macchine per la Fotografia e la Cinematografia** (Fraz. Pieria, tel. 043/369-208, by appointment only) in **Pieri.** One of the donors was Dante Spinotti, the virtuoso cinematographer for *L.A. Confidential* and *Heat,* who is a Friuli native and resides in Val Degano.

On October 17, 1797, Napoleon signed the Treaty of Campoformido with Austria at **Villa Manin** in **Codroipo**. Construction on the villa began in the mid-1600s, a design very much influenced by Andrea Palladio's villas. Two side *barchesse* (storage wings) were added toward the end of the century. In the early 1700s, the horseshoe-shaped exedra was added; it leads from the wings to the two entrance towers. Inside the villa has wide, gracious halls and the central entrance is three stories high. The eastern hall is decorated with frescoes of the *Triumph of Spring* (1708) and other mythological or allegorical themes. There is also a section with weapons and carriage. The rear entrance opens to vast French gardens. Some rooms have period furniture.

Today the **Villa Manin Centre for Contemporary Art** (Piazza Manin 10, tel. 043/282-1211, www.villamanincontemporanea.it, Tues.–Sun., hours vary per exhibit, €2) has established a national reputation as a source of some of Italy's most interesting contemporary art exhibits. A 2008 exhibit, Hard Rock Waltzer, was a play on words that linked the lightness of Austrian dance to the concrete weight of stone sculpture in a show of 14 contemporary Austrian artists.

Codroipo's **Archeological Museum** (Via Santa Maria Maggiore, tel. 0432/820-174, Tues. and Sun. 9:30 A.M.–12:30 P.M.) is in a 19th-century prison, where you can look at artifacts from the Bronze Age to the Renaissance. Almost every month the town celebrates a saint's feast day with a fair or other celebrations.

Tourist information for many of these sights is at Villa Manin (tel. 0432/900-908).

Buttrio, about 10 kilometers southeast of Udine off SS305 has two stellar wineries. For more than 500 years the family at **Conte d'Attimis-Maniago** (Via Sottomonte 21, tel.043/267-4027, www.contedattimismaniago.it) has been working the land in Buttrio. Their Colli Orientali del Friuli Tazzelenghe, made of Tazzelenghe grapes, is an excellent red wine that has hints of plum, berries, and tobacco. Their white Picolit has a flavor with hints of honey and flowers. They produce more than 400,000 bottles of wine annually and also have a wine museum along with their historic cellars.

Girolamo Dorigo (Via del Pozzo 5, tel. 043/267-4268, www.montsclapade.com), founded in 1967, makes an excllent red. Their signature Colli Orientali del Friuli Montsclapade combines Cabernet Sauvignon and Merlot grapes. They also turn out other fine reds (a Merlot and a Refosco) and whites that include a Ribolla Gialla and a Chardonnay. For dessert, try the sweet *passito* wine made from Picolit grapes.

East of Udine in **Spessa di Cividale, Rodaro Paolo** (Via Cormons 60, tel. 043/271-6066) has a large winery. For reds, try Schiopettino 2005 (very smooth with a hint of blackberries), the 2003 Refosco (hints of wild cherries and plums), or the white Picolit. You can stay nearby at **Villa Rubini** (tel. 043/271-6141, www.villarubini.net).

North of Cividale del Friuli in **Togliano di Torreano, Volpe Pasini** (Via Cividale 16, tel. 043/271-5151, www.volpepasini.it) turns out an especially good Merlot, plus some crisp whites. They also run an *agriturismo*.

VENICE

EMILIA ROMAGNA

Emilia Romagna is truly a hidden gem. Still relatively untouched by the mass tourism that draws art lovers to Tuscany and nature lovers to Umbria, this central Italian region has both artistic and physical beauty in abundance, and beckons quietly with much of the best of what Italy is all about. This is the region that gave birth to famed neo-realist film director Federico Fellini, and noble burial to the father of Italian poetry, Dante Alighieri. Renowned for good food and food sensibility, it is home to the EU's authority on food safety. It is also one of Italy's wealthiest regions, with extensive livestock and dairy farming in the Po Valley as well as a large food industry (Barilla pasta is based here). Both Lamborghini and Ferrari cars are made in Emilia Romagna.

The region's wealth becomes self-evident in the capital city of Bologna. In the Santo Stefano area of the city's vast historical center, nearly every other palazzo was formerly a noble's residence, many of them still housing prestigious art works. Stop at the Casa Berti, and you might be lucky enough to meet one of the elderly residents who will usher you inside to see *la scala* (the staircase), to the right of a sweet little courtyard, silent except for violin music trailing down from above. The marble staircase has a stunning statue of Greek gods entitled *Giunone, Venere, Amore,* and *Minerva* (representing Power, Love, and Science), and leads up to a former lodge replete with 18th-century frescos.

Bologna also boasts Europe's oldest university, with museums dedicated to archeology and anatomy. Tasteful boutiques and good places to eat and drink line the city's porticos.

© ALESSIA RAMACCIA

HIGHLIGHTS

◖ Piazza Maggiore: Spend a few moments just taking in the stately beauty of Bologna's central piazza – well kept, lively but not rowdy, noble but not pretentious: a paradigm for the city's own spirit (page 438).

◖ Bologna's Arcades: Take shelter from rain, snow, and sun, and enjoy your proper Italian *passeggiata* (stroll) under these elegant arches, called *porticos* in Italian. Built in the Middle Ages, they span some 38 kilometers inside the city's historical center (page 438).

◖ Abbazia di Pomposa: This Benedictine monastery outside of Ferrara, one of Italy's most important for its bell tower and Romanesque period architecture (c. 800-1000), also housed the monk who invented modern musical notation, Guido D'Arezzo (page 461).

◖ Ravenna: The main attractions in this artistic capital are the early Christian and Byzantine mosaics. Visit Basilica di San Vitale or Mausoleo di Galla Placidia to view these stunning and intricate works, some with pieces of gold, illustrating Byzantine interpretations of the most common biblical scenes imprinted in the imagination (page 463).

◖ Rimini: This beach town features 15 kilometers of sandy beach – said to be Europe's longest. Bring your dancing shoes, too, because Rimini has some of Italy's best nightclubs, a nice ending to a lazy day at the beach (page 466).

◖ Po Delta: Nature lovers can take a river tour on the Po Delta followed by a trip to Po River Delta Regional Park, which has more than 350 species of birds (page 469).

LOOK FOR ◖ TO FIND RECOMMENDED SIGHTS, ACTIVITIES, DINING, AND LODGING.

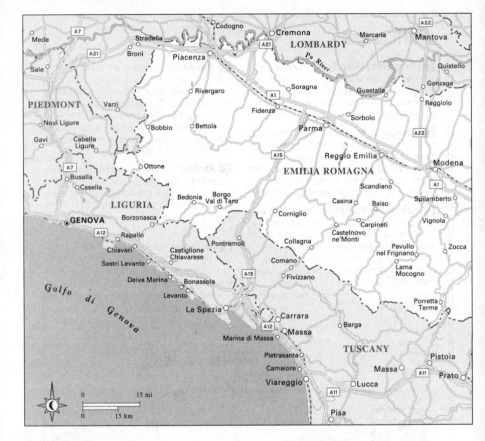

If Bologna is a great college town, it's the region's smaller cities—Ferrara, Ravenna, and Modena—that showcase why small and medium-sized towns are largely considered the best places to live throughout Italy. The main mode of transportation in these towns, Ferrara especially, is not the car, nor even the eponymous Italian scooter. It's the bicycle! And not even the modern-day mountain bike, but bikes with 20 or 30 years on them with a basket in the front (convenient for running errands) and a baby seat in the back for carrying tots.

These cities' historical centers are well preserved and elegant, and treasure troves

of art. People flock to Ravenna to see the 5th-century Byzantine mosaics—UNESCO World Heritage sites—or to pay homage to Dante's tombstone.

Parma, another medium-sized city, is synonymous with good food and music, and it enjoys Italy's highest standard of living. Since 2004 it has been the headquarters of the EU food safety authority, EFSA. For centuries it has groomed Italy's severest opera public. Well-bred Italians know that Milan's La Scala is not the real heart of the Italian opera scene. If La Scala, with its fur coat VIP crowd, is about opera-goers, Parma is about the opera itself. The public

at the Teatro Regio di Parma comes to listen and show their approval or disapproval, namely by booing or applauding until red in the palms.

Emilia Romagna is also about enjoying the proverbial good life and Italians' generosity oozes out of this bountiful territory. The food is consistently top-quality here and the people make it taste even better. They won't let you rush a meal and you won't want to, whether it be a wholesome plate of *tortellini con brodo* (tortellini in broth) in the wintertime, or a light *hostaria* meal of thinly sliced meats (like mortadella and *coppa di Parma*) and parmesan cheese accompanied by a glass of Lambrusco. Come to Emilia and you've entered the gateway to Italy's real *dolce vita*.

PLANNING YOUR TIME

One week is plenty of time to see much of the region's riches, and if you can squeeze in two weekends, by all means do so, since many of the destinations make for lovely weekend retreats. Take one weekend to visit the Po River Delta, Ferrara, and Ravenna; if beaches are your fancy, save the other weekend to languish in the sun at Rimini's fantastic beachfront. The cities are best lived during the week, so you can experience the moderate-paced bustle of life.

© ALESSIA RAMACCIA

Piazza Maggiore is Bologna's emblematic main square and site of the tourist office.

(Note: The afternoon siesta is still practiced in these parts—enjoy!)

The region has a temperate rather than Mediterranean climate. Bologna's snow-topped roofs in the winter are a pretty sight to behold, and the porticos built during the Middle Ages in many of the cities provide a gentle shelter from temperatures that drop but never so alarmingly as to make a *passeggiata* (stroll) unpleasant. Summers can be humid because much of the region is landlocked, but beaches in nearby Liguria and Rimini provide easily accessible respite. July and August are actually considered low season for tourism here, so you will get cheaper hotel rates if you brave the summertime heat. High season is April–June and September and October.

The most pleasant time to visit the region is early autumn during the grape harvest; this is also the season when porcini mushrooms, truffles, and chestnuts are ripe for the picking, with food festivals throughout the region where you can savor the goods. September and October are usually still warm enough to go to the beach, but it is also the rainy season, so bring an umbrella. If you're a literature buff, September is when Ravenna holds readings and celebrations to commemorate poet Dante Alighieri, who died here on September 13, 1321.

You can't go wrong in the spring anywhere in Italy, and Emilia Romagna is no exception. You'll find flowers in bloom, festive towns celebrating their medieval roots, and delights like the asparagus festival—in honor of the celebrated vegetable of the Po River Delta—during the first week of May in Meésola, 50 kilometers east of Ferrara.

Renting a car will make your life easier but the regional trains (and buses) are frequent and generally run on time. If you are really feeling inspired, rent a bike for a week. The bike is the most popular and convenient mode of transportation in many of Emilia Romagna's cities, and much of the countryside is flat enough for pleasant countryside journeys.

HISTORY

In prehistoric times (roughly 10,000 years ago), Emilia Romagna was one vast forest. Following deforestation, various settlements have been traced to the area, from the Neolithic period through the Bronze Age. In the 9th century B.C., the Villanova farming and shepherding culture emerged, civilizing the area and effectively ending its prehistoric age. The Etruscans founded the city that would become Bologna, calling it Felsina in 534 B.C. They also established trade with the East through the Port of Spina (whose beach is today praised for environmental soundness). The Celtic Boi tribe ran the Etruscans out of the area in the 4th century B.C.

Two centuries later, the Romans defeated the Celts, constructing the Via Emilia to link Rome to its newfound colonies Rimini, Ravenna, and Piacenza.

The Byzantines, or the Greek-speaking "Romani," moved into the area in the 5th century, making Ravenna the capital of the Eastern Roman Empire. The city had its heyday, with the creation of enduring riches like the mosaics in the basilicas of San Vitale and Sant'Apollinare. The roots of the region's name had also been laid, with Emilia referring to the Roman road, and Romagna in reference to the Eastern Roman Empire. (It wasn't until 1947, with the drawing up of the region's constitution, that the region officially become known as Emilia Romagna.)

Later on during the Middle Ages, the cathedrals in Modena and Parma were built, and Bologna became an important city. It gave rise to Europe's first university in the 11th century, and its wool industry gained notoriety. In the mid-13th century, Bologna instated the Paradise Law, which abolished serfdom and freed slaves using public money. Its San Petronio Basilica was built at that time.

The Renaissance period was the dawn of an even more intense flowering of Emilia Romagna's artistic culture and wealth, with two main aristocratic noble families as the leading protagonists. The Farnese family controlled Parma and Piacenza, with the D'Este family

the back streets of Parma

© ALESSIA RAMACCIA

in possession of Ferrara and Modena. Ferrara became the paradigm of Renaissance urban planning, while the newly constructed Palazzo Ducale in Modena was also a showcase of period architectural splendor.

Ferrara also gave birth to two of Italy's greatest poetic masterpieces—Torquato Tasso's *Gerusalemme Liberata* (Jerusalem Liberated) and Ludovico Ariosto's *Orlando Furioso*.

Meanwhile, Bologna kept apace with its progressive reputation: Under the noble Bentivoglio family's rule, women could earn university degrees, and excelled in some professions.

The free-minded city met the rule of Pope Julius II in 1506, initiating a course of papal rule in the whole region that would last until Napoleon came to town in 1797. Many of

EMILIA ROMAGNA

Bologna's churches were constructed during the rule of Pope Julius II (and 96 convents, more than any other city in Italy).

Napoleon ruled much of Emilia Romagna until the Vienna Congress in 1815 restored papal rule to Bologna and Ferrara, leaving Parma in the hands of Marie Louise of Austria (Napoleon's second wife), and Modena and Reggio Emilia under the rule of the archduke Francis of Austria, an heir to the Este family.

Various insurrections against these rulers would play out in the region until Italy became a united country in 1861, incorporating Emilia Romagna rather pacifically.

But the peoples' taste for solidarity and the vindication of their rights was firmly grounded, and Italy's Socialist Party was founded in Reggio Emilia in 1896. One of its principal adherents was Benito Mussolini, later to become Italy's Fascist dictator, who was a native of Predappio, a small town in the southwest part of the region.

During World War II, Bologna and surrounding areas became strong footholds of the resistance movement. One of the worst civilian massacres of the war took place in the hills outside of Bologna at Marzabotto, when the German SS, in reprisal of partisan operations, killed an estimated 770 people.

Bologna remained Communist, giving rise

rooftops of Reggio Emilia

© ALESSIA RAMACCIA

to its "red" reputation, following the war. The city was dealt a radical rebuttal in 1980, when far-right terrorist groups bombed the main train station, killing 85 people.

Emilia Romagna continues to be a stronghold of center-left politics, and in the last national elections, in April 2006, 60 percent of its votes went to current Prime Minister Romano Prodi, a native of the region.

Bologna

Bologna, Emilia Romagna's capital city with a population of nearly 375,000, has three nicknames: *La Dotta* (the learned), *La Grassa* (the fat), and *La Rossa* (the red).

Bologna is a learned city because it is home to the world's oldest university, the University of Bologna, founded in 1088 as a law school to gather the masters of the day in rhetoric, grammar, and logic. Today it has 23 faculties, with medicine and law as the most reputable and at least one rock star faculty member: Umberto Eco, best known for his novel *The Name of The*

Rose, who is a professor of semiotics (the study of signs and symbols).

The city is relaxed about its scholarly reputation, though, and that makes for a collegial atmosphere that is neither nerdy nor pretentious. A tradition unique to the *Alma Mater Studiorum* (hence Alma Mater—mother of studies) is that graduates are crowned with a laurel wreath like that which Dante Alighieri wore (the medieval poet also studied here). It's a great place to meet students from all over Europe at the many bars and cafes along Via Zamboni and

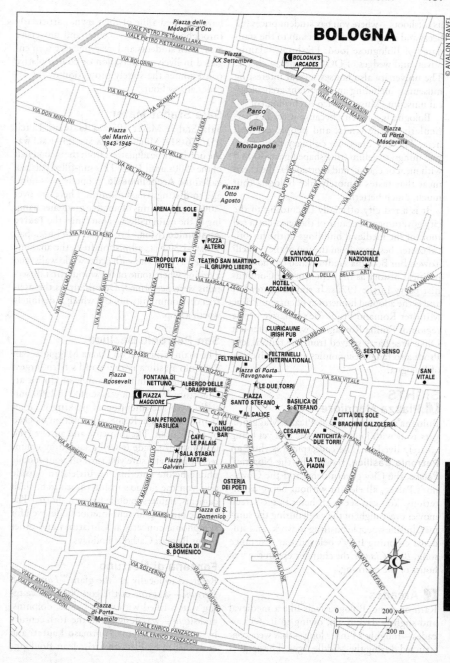

© AVALON TRAVEL

BOLOGNA

Piazza delle
Medaglie d'Oro
VIALE PIETRO PIETRAMELLARA
VIALE PIETRO PIETRAMELLARA
VIA BOLDRINI
Piazza
XX Settembre
(BOLOGNA'S
ARCADES

VIA MILAZZO
VIA GRAMSCI
VIA GALLIERA
VIALE ANGELO MASINI
VIALE ANGELO MASINI

VIA DON MINZONI
Piazza
dei Martiri
1943-1945
VIA DEI MILLE
VIA GALLIERA
Parco
della
Montagnola
VIA CAPO DI LUCCA
Piazza
di Porta
Mascarella
VIA MASCARELLA

VIA DEL PORTO
Piazza
Otto
Agosto
VIA DEL BORGO DI SAN PIETRO
VIA IRNERIO

ARENA DEL SOLE
VIA RIVA DI RENO
PIZZA
ALTERO
VIA DELL'INDIPENDENZA
VIA DELLA MOLINE
CANTINA
BENTIVOGLIO
PINACOTECA
NAZIONALE
VIA ZAMBONI

VIA GUGLIELMO MARCONI
METROPOLITAN
HOTEL
TEATRO SAN MARTINO-
IL GRUPPO LIBERO
VIA DELLA BELLE ARTI

VIA NAZARIO SAURO
VIA GALLIERA
VIA MARSALA ZEGLIO
HOTEL
ACCADEMIA
VIA MARSALA

VIA OBERDAN
VIA DELL'INDIPENDENZA
CLURICAUNE
IRISH PUB
VIA ZAMBONI
SESTO SENSO

VIA UGO BASSI
FELTRINELLI
FELTRINELLI
INTERNATIONAL
VIA PETRONI
SAN
VITALE

VIA RIZZOLI
Piazza di Porta
Ravegnana
VIA SAN VITALE

Piazza
Roosevelt
FONTANA DI
NETTUNO
ALBERGO DELLE
DRAPPERIE
LE DUE TORRI

PIAZZA
MAGGIORE
PIAZZA
SANTO STEFANO
BASILICA DI
S. STEFANO
CITTÀ DEL SOLE
BRACHINI CALZOLERIA

VIA S. MARGHERITA
SAN PETRONIO
BASILICA
VIA CLAVATURE
AL CALICE
STRADA MAGGIORE

VIA BARBERIA
CAFÉ
LE PALAIS
NU
LOUNGE
BAR
VIA CASTIGLIONE
CESARINA
ANTICHITÀ
DUE TORRI

VIA MASSIMO D'AZEGLIO
SALA STABAT
MATAR
Piazza
Galvani
VIA FARINI
VIA SANTO STEFANO
LA TUA
PIADIN

VIA URBANA
OSTERIA
DEI POETI
VIA DEI POETI
VIA GUERRAZZI

VIA MARSILI
Piazza di S.
Domenico
VIA CASTIGLIONE
VIA SANTO STEFANO

BASILICA DI
S. DOMENICO

VIALE ANTONIO ALDINI
VIALE ANTONIO ALDINI
VIA SOLFERINO
VIALE XII GIUGNO

Piazza
di Porta
S. Mamolo
VIALE ENRICO PANZACCHI
VIALE ENRICO PANZACCHI

0   200 yds
0   200 m

EMILIA ROMAGNA

its offshoots—where you pay student prices (€2 beers and sangria) with buffets up to the standards of Bolognese food: Fresh-cut salamis, olives, and wedges of DOC parmesan cheese. The university also houses several interesting museums, including an important archeological museum (Museo Civico Archeologico).

Bologna is a fat city because it cradles particularly fertile lands, and people eat well here. The city draws its culinary fame from two things: tortellini (ring shaped pasta stuffed with meat or cheese) and mortadella, the cured meat that tastes remotely like bologna (but much, much better).

It is a red city officially (according to the city government) because of the terra-cotta red roofs of the medieval buildings in the historical center, best seen from the top of the Asinelli Tower. But Bologna's redness also connotes its political history as the center of the Communist party in the 1970s. It stayed center-left and is the adopted hometown of current Prime Minister Romano Prodi (he's a native of the region of Emilia Romagna), whose center-left Olive Tree party strayed from the radical left. Prodi also taught economics at the University of Bologna.

SIGHTS
◖ Piazza Maggiore
Bologna's central piazza, Piazza Maggiore, gets away with looking majestic and yet being entirely lived in. The centerpiece is the **San Petronio Basilica,** flanked by the Notaries' Palace, the City government, and the Governor's Palace, all elegant without being ostentatious. You can see it all here: Large-screen movies every night of the week during the summer, businesspeople bustling to work, and students crooning Italy's beloved war resistance song, *Bella Ciao* on the church steps in the wee hours of the morning.

◖ Arcades
Rain or shine, Bologna feels like a medieval and slightly dark town, owing to its 654 arcades—roughly 24 miles long—that were constructed during the Middle Ages. The arcades

have spawned a life of their own, particularly throughout the historic center and university area, with students and everyone else seen engaged in lively conversation or contemplative pause under the stately protection of the arcades at any hour.

Sala Stabat Mater
Sala Stabat Mater (Piazza Galvani 1, tel. 051/276-811, Mon.–Sat. 9 A.M.–1:30 P.M.) was the university headquarters from the second half of the 1500s until 1803. This sun-filled palazzo, called the **Archiginnasio,** properly pays homage to distinguished alumni. There are over 7,000 coats-of-arms of notable graduates hanging in the main hallway. Don't miss the **Teatro Anatomico** (Mon.–Fri. 9 A.M.–6:45 P.M., Sat. 9 A.M.–1:30 P.M., admission free), the anatomy theater, a tiny room with cedar wood walls, and a ceiling where some of the world's first dissections were performed. Downstairs is the user-friendly community library, which is definitely worth a stop.

San Petronio Basilica
The main attraction on Piazza Maggiore, San Petronio Basilica is the world's fifth-largest church and a stunning example of Gothic architecture. Work on it was started in 1390, initially with the intention of making it larger than St. Peter's in Rome, an ambition blocked by the Vatican. The immense and austere (and unfinished) facade is well guarded by volunteers who make sure you turn off your mobile phone before entering. (A little sign outside tells you the no-no's inside the church: flash cameras, lighters, mobile phones, shorts.) The simple but magnificent interior bodes well for symphonic concerts at Christmas and other major Roman Catholic holidays.

Fontana di Nettuno
Referred to locally as "the giant," *Fontana di Nettuno*—a statue of the god Neptune calming waters filled with water babies, dolphins, and sirens—was designed in the 16th century by a Sicilian sculptor Tommaso Laureti and embellished by Flemish artist Jean Boulogne

(also known as Giambologna). Pope IV asked for changes to the original design, but some erotic mermaids were untouched.

Le Due Torri

Le Due Torri (twin towers) are definitely fraternal rather than identical. The **Garisenda Tower** leans more and is about half as tall as the **Asinelli Tower.** They are named for the families believed to be responsible for their construction in 1109–1119. Climb to the top of the Asinelli Tower (97.2 meters, or 498 steps) for the best view of the city. It's open every day 9 A.M.–6 P.M. (until 5 P.M. during the winter). Last entrance is at 5:40 P.M. and 4:40 P.M., respectively, and a ticket costs €3.

Piazza Santo Stefano

Also known as Seven Churches Square in the center of Bologna, the Piazza Santo Stefano indeed counts seven chapels, along with a Benedictine cloister, said to have been built by Bishop Petronius in the 5th century, who also happens to be the city's patron saint. Enjoy an ice cream from **Gianni's** ice cream shop (Via Santo Stefano 14a), which has flavors like Dante's Inferno, or check out the **Circolo degli Artisti** underground artists' cove (Via Santo Stefano 16b). The churches can be visited daily 9 A.M.–noon and 3:30–6:30 P.M.

Pinacoteca Nazionale

Take a peek inside the city's national art gallery, the Pinacoteca Nazionale (Via delle Belle Arti 56, Tues.–Sun. 9 A.M.–7 P.M., €4) formerly Bologna's Fine Arts College. The gallery houses paintings that date from the 14th–18th centuries, with works by Raffaello, Giotto, and the local master of the high Baroque style, Guido Reni.

Madonna di Luca

It is a hike up to the Madonna di Luca sanctuary—three kilometers and 666 arches to be exact—but it's a welcome respite from this pleasantly social city that no less begs an occasional solitary time-out. **The Guardian of Bologna,** as the sanctuary is also referred to, dates back to the 8th century, when the daugh-

Bologna's twin towers (Le Due Torri)

© ALESSIA RAMACCIA

ter of a wealthy family established a convent, monastery, and church on her family's land. Start walking at the **Porta di Saragozza,** built in the 17th century, until you reach the church. Open daily March–Sept. 7 A.M.–12:30 P.M. and 2:30 P.M.–7 P.M., Oct.–Feb. 2:30 P.M.–5 P.M.

Museo Civico Nazionale

Save a few hours to visit Bologna's archeological museum, Museo Civico Nazionale (Sat.–Mon. 10 A.M.–6:30 P.M. and Tues.–Fri. 9 A.M.–3 P.M., €4 or €2 for people over age 60, and teens ages 15–18), with its vast collection of archeological ruins from the Etruscan, Greek, and Roman civilizations. Also on display are ancient Egyptian artifacts from local artists' collections, and Italy's most important coin collection with coins from ancient Rome, Greece, and the Byzantine Empire. It's located in a beautiful 15th-century palazzo next to Piazza Maggiore.

ENTERTAINMENT AND EVENTS

Bologna is a college town par excellence with a nightlife to match. You can find discos with

EMILIA ROMAGNA

Abbazia di Santo Stefano in Piazza Santo Stefano

every genre of music, and pubs and wine bars for every taste. The city attracts many internationally renowned artists, and dance troupes like Momix are regulars at the city's largest theater, the **Teatro delle Celebrazioni.** On Thursday night, Erasmus students flood the bars and pubs since it's their night to drink cheaply at locales throughout the city: Check out the **Cluricaune Irish pub** (tel. 051/263-419, Mon.–Fri. noon–2 a.m. and Sat.–Sun. 3 p.m.–2:30 a.m.) at Via Zamboni 18b to meet twenty-somethings from all over Europe!

You can also easily just wander in the center, making your way to Piazza Maggiore, where there will invariably be an open-air Chaplin or Neo-realist flick showing, or an orchestra concert.

Nightlife
LIVE MUSIC
With internationally renowned DJs like Tony Humphries and Frankie Knuckles in charge of the tunes, you won't get bored at the **Matis**

Dinner Club (Via Rotta 10, tel. 051/619-9418, Tues., Fri., and Sat. 10 p.m.–4 a.m., no cover) and you can satisfy your craving for sushi or Indian if you're all pasta-ed out.

Bologna's best-known venue for live jazz (and a great place to drink a glass of wine and get a bite to eat) is the **Cantina Bentivoglio** (Via Mascarella 4b, tel. 051/265-416, www. cantinabentivoglio.it, daily 8 p.m.–2 a.m., no cover), in the heart of the students' district. It has pleasant outdoor seating in the summer.

Bologna's oldest *osteria,* the **Osteria dei Poeti** (Via dei Poeti 1B, tel. 051/236-166, Tues.–Sun. 12:30–2:30 p.m. and 7:30 p.m.–1 a.m., no cover), features live jazz and folk music in a medieval palazzo, with brick-vaulted ceilings, stone walls, and ancient wine barrels.

NIGHTCLUBS AND DISCOS
Only in Bologna, a city that deftly mixes the progressive with the trendy, could you find an R&B haven inside a medieval palazzo. And with a name like **Soda Pops** (Via Castel Tialto 6, tel. 051/272-079, daily 10 p.m.–3 a.m., no

© ALESSIA RAMACCIA

EMILIA ROMAGNA

SAGRE FESTIVALS

People come to Emilia Romagna at least in part to eat *parmigiano Reggiano, prosciutto di Parma*, mortadella, *tortellini al brodo*, and an endless list of delicacies. Although you can taste these regional foods pretty much wherever you go here, attending food festivals, called *sagre*, where food is the main focus, brings out the real flavor – and the fun.

Going to a *sagra* is also the best chance to get a taste of Italian country life, since most of them are held in small towns. Getting there can be tricky if you are without a car, but invariably some train or bus could get you there (though they often run less frequently on weekends).

The festivities usually take place in the town's main square, with local bands providing the entertainment. When people are done eating, they sometimes dance, and you will likely get pulled onto the dance floor too, such is the spontaneous nature of these feasts!

Many of the *sagre* last all weekend, beginning Friday night and ending Sunday at lunch. Midday is when most of the locals seem to gather, and you often see whole families with grandma and grandpa at the helm and a score of kids running around. Italian piazza life is known to bring together many generations, and these are good occasions to savor this sweetness.

The various *sagre* can be very different from each other, so come without expectations and with a hearty sense of adventure. You might take a few wrong turns in the countryside, but when you see cars parked in a long queue leading to the town, you know you're in the right place.

Prepare to wait in a food line that might wrap around town, but the wait is usually well worth it: Homemade pasta, grilled meat or sausage, and local wine are standard fare, which are embellished depending on the *sagra*. At the *sagra del tartufo* (truffles), your pasta, probably fettuccine, will come with *tartufo* sauce.

Simplicity is the order of the day, which is a celebrated feature of Italian food: Go elsewhere to satisfy cravings for fancy food; here you just eat well. For dessert, try the dried cookies dipped in sweet wine, or a piece of *crostata* (tart with marmalade or chocolate).

Emilia Romagna has over 400 *sagre* throughout the year. Don't miss the asparagus festival the first week of May in Mesola. The asparagus is the most celebrated vegetable of the Po Delta, and they serve it here in fried rice balls or with pumpkin risotto.

Other notable festivals include the *sagra del tortellino* in Malalbergo outside of Bologna the first week of June, serving tortellini in several different ways – with truffles, butter and sage, or *alla boscaiola* (woodman's pasta with sausage and mixed mushrooms). You can eat on the lawn of the Castello Giovanina at Cento's *sagre del bue* (oxen) in mid-August.

Come to Emilia Romagna with an appetite, and take your palate into account when planning your travel itinerary. For a complete list of *sagre* in Italy, visit www.prodottitipici.com/sagre_eventi.

---

cover), you know you're in for a good time. Don't miss Friday house night.

Indulge your sixth sense at **Sesto Senso** (Via Petroni 9c, tel. 051/223-476, Mon.–Fri. noon–11 P.M. and Sat. 6–11 P.M., no cover), a trendy artists' colony locale with something for everyone: video art, figurative art, indie sounds and all types of dance music. It's an easy five-minute walk from the city's towers.

Go ahead and feel cool at the **Nu Lounge Bar** (Via de'Musei, tel. 051/222-532, Mon.–Sat. noon–4 P.M. and 8:30 P.M.–1 A.M., Sun.

8 P.M.–midnight, no cover), along with fashionable thirty-somethings (and above). Great dry martinis and green olives.

WINE BARS

At **Al Calice** (Via Calvature 13a, tel. 051/264-506, Mon.–Sat. 7 A.M.–2 A.M.), they've been perfecting the *aperitivo* experience since opening in 1939 as the local watering hole in the Piazza Maggiore neighborhood. You can't go wrong with cocktails and wine, and for snacks, they've got everything from peanuts and cashews to duck and caviar.

Café Le Palais (Via de'Musei 4, tel. 051/648-6963) is an intriguing place to come for a glass of wine (over 35 labels) and a light meal. You can also hop across the street to the accompanying clothing store (Inde Le Palais), the city's first "concept store" selling a bit of everything, hand-selected, including John Galliano couture evening gowns. Wonderfully fun for window shopping and browsing, too!

Theater
Arena del Sole (Via Indipendenza 44, tel. 0512/910-910, Mon. 3:30–7 P.M., Tues.–Sat. 11 A.M.–7 P.M.) is a convent-turned-theater. It dates back to the beginning of the 1800s and is the city's oldest theater and arguably its most celebrated.

The year 1968—the heyday of student protests and experimentation with the unconventional at large—was when **Teatro San Martino–II Gruppo Libero** (Via Oberdan 25, tel. 051/224-671, Mon.–Fri. 9 A.M.–2 P.M. and 3–5 P.M.) began showing experimental theater productions. Today it also stages contemporary dance and musical productions.

If you're in the mood to see *Evita, Jesus Christ Superstar,* Momix dance performances, or Italian television comedy programs (the tasteful ones), enjoy an evening at the **Teatro delle Celebrazioni** (Via Saragozza 234, Mon.–Sat. 2:30–6:30 P.M.), the city's largest theater, close to the city center.

Festivals and Events
Bologna has hosted the world's largest **Children's Book Fair** (www.bookfair.bolognafiere.it) for the past 45 years, drawing publishers, literary agents, illustrators, and lovers of kids' books every late March and early April.

Every December, car makers and car aficionados come to the city for the **International Motor Show** (www.motorshow.it), featuring car races and test drives of the latest from Ferrari to Mazda and Mitsubishi.

The patron saint's day, **San Petronio,** falls on the first weekend of October—get a free mortadella sandwich at Piazza Maggiore and enjoy concerts and fireworks.

SHOPPING
Shopping in Bologna can be both a sophisticated and fun experience. Tasteful boutiques line the streets, with up-to-date department stores like H&M and Zara never far from view. If Milan is the country's fashion authority, and Rome caters to both fashionistas and the masses, Bologna is the city where real people can shop. That doesn't just mean clothes. Bologna's art galleries, shoe stores, and salami shops all bespeak of the city's true sense of taste. For clothing, the **Galleria Cavour** at Piazza Cavour has many high-end Italian name brand stores like Bulgari and Gucci.

Other main shopping streets include Via Ugo Bassi, Via Rizzoli, and Via dell'Indipendenza (in these three streets you can find just about everything, from Zara to Gucci). For more local boutique color, head to Via Farini, and duck your head in the art galleries and finer clothing shops. If walking in seems too intimidating, window-shopping under the shaded porticos can be equally as fun!

Don't miss the flea and antique market on Friday and Saturday at the **Parco della Montagnola.** It's fun to poke through the odds and ends, and you might even walk away lucky, with that pair of shoes you saw sitting in a store window for twice the price.

Antiques
If you're into old tomes and love browsing, stop at **Libreria Nanni** (Via dei Musei 8, tel. 051/221-841, Mon.–Sat. 8:30 A.M.–1 P.M. and 3–7:30 P.M.), the city's bookstore specializing in antique books, located in the city's traditional book vending spot.

Antichità due Torri (Strada Maggiore 17, tel. 051/236-448, Mon.–Sat. 9 A.M.–1 P.M. and 3–7 P.M.) offers a wide selection of antiquities in the 19th-century English style, such as ceramics and porcelain and glass objects, along with furniture.

Specialty
If you swear by homeopathic cures, pick up some herb-based medicines and natural cosmetics at the **Antica Erboristeria Provenzale**

(Via Pescherie Vecchie 3, tel. 051/223-957, Mon.–Sat. 9 A.M.–1 P.M. and 3:30–7:30 P.M.), a reference point for healthy-minded locals since 1947.

Le Due Torri (Via della Grada 9, tel. 051/522-433, Tues.–Sat. 9 A.M.–1 P.M. and 3–7 P.M.) was created for chess aficionados. It has everything from chessboards to computerized chess sets (come see for yourself), and many books on the game.

You'll find "ecological" furs and large women's sizes at **Camilla Forest** (Via di Corticella 98, tel. 051/368-974, Mon.–Sat. 9 A.M.–1 P.M. and 3–7 P.M.).

Bookstores

Locals call this **Feltrinelli** (Piazza Ravegnana 1, tel. 051/266-891, Mon.–Sat. 9 A.M.–8 P.M., Sun. 10 A.M.–1:30 P.M. and 3–7:30 P.M.) the best bookstore in the region, which says a lot for a chain bookstore in a very bookish town. It's conveniently located near the Due Torri. Nearby is **Feltrinelli International** (Via Zamboni 7b, tel. 051/268-070, Mon.–Sat. 9 A.M.–7:30 P.M.), with a vast selection of English and foreign-language books and travel guides.

Clothing

Working Overtime (Via San Felice 37, tel. 051/221-846) is a clever misnomer for this free and frilly vintage clothing, handmade by local designer Giovanna Guglielmi.

Shoes and Accessories

Be prepared to pay a pretty penny for gorgeous hand-stitched dress shoes (€4,000) at **Branchini Calzoleria** (Strada Maggiore 19, tel. 051/648-6642). Where Made in Italy gets serious.

Coccinelle (Via Ugo Bassi 7, tel. 051/270-548, Tues.–Sun. 9 A.M.–1 P.M. and 3–7 P.M.) purses and wallets are arguably less expensive than Fendi and Furla, but just as fashionable.

Children

Stylish kids' clothing at unusually reasonable prices are on the racks at **SanPol** (Via Massarenti 25, tel. 051/614-2055, Mon.–Sat. 9 A.M.–1 P.M. and 3–7 P.M.). You'll find Geox, Balducci, and Starry.

Città del Sole (Strada Maggiore 17, tel. 051/266-432, Mon.–Sat. 9 A.M.–7:30 P.M.) sells toys galore at their centrally located store with all types of action figures, games, and books for kids of all ages.

Home

Spazio Minghetti (Piazza Minghetti 3, tel. 051/265-670, Tues.–Sat. 10 A.M.–7 P.M.) sells Fendi furniture with lots of *swists* (personality). They carry animal skin sofas and rugs, and there's a garden out back.

For rugs, fine Italian couch and bed covers, and curtains, stop in at **Decor House** (Strada Maggiore 5b, tel. 051/235-456, Mon.–Sat. 9:30 A.M.–1 P.M. and 3:30–7:30 P.M.) near the Due Torri.

Markets

The huge city market at **Piazza VIII Agosto,** between the train station and the center, has everything from clothes and shoes to books, household items, and food. It's open every morning except Sundays.

For fresh fruits and vegetables, meats, and other foods, go to the open-air market along **Via Oberdan** near **Piazza Maggiore**.

The city's famed **antiques market** is held every second weekend of the month in Piazza Santo Stefano. The vendors take a break in July and August.

SPORTS AND RECREATION
Parks

Parco Montagnola (Piazza VIII Agosto, entrances at Via Indipendenza, Via del Pallone, Via Irnerio, daily Apr.–Sept. 7 A.M.–midnight and Oct.–Mar. 7 A.M.–7 P.M.) is centrally located and worth a stroll if you want a bit of respite from the (pleasant) noise of this lively town. It's small, so it's better for people-watching and relaxing than serious running, but no one will raise an eyebrow if you are in the mood to take a few laps. The park was in fact built for more sedate purposes.

During the 17th century, air ballooning took place here, followed by the construction of the lovely gardens and water fountain that are still standing.

Giardini Margherita (entrance Viale Gozzadini, daily 6 A.M.–midnight) is a bit far afield from the city center but is a great place to jog or walk off some pasta. There's a little lake filled with goldfish and turtles. The chalet inside the park sells coffee and ice cream during the day and turns into a club at night.

Bologna's **botanical garden** (Via Irnerio 42, tel. 05/135-1280, Mon.–Sat. 8:30 A.M.–12:30 P.M.) contains one of Europe's largest herbariums, with thousands of dried plant specimens. The greenhouses contain over 5,000 types of vegetation, including many tropical and exotic plants. At its founding in the mid-16th century, the Orto dei Semplici, as it was known, cultivated simple medicinal herbs.

Basketball

This is perhaps the only town in Italy where basketball matters more than soccer. The city boasts two of the strongest teams in Italy, which recruit some of the best players in the world. **Virtus Pallacanestro Bologna** (www.virtus.it) has won eight Italian Cups and one Euroleague championship, while **Fortitudo** (www.fortitudo.it) has won one Italian Cup. Locals divide their passions between the two. Look out for the annual local derby, when the two teams meet in a highly contested game. You can buy tickets directly at the arenas where games are played. Virtus Arena is to the southwest of the city, in an area called Casalecchio di Reno. Fortitudo play in the center of the city, at the Paladozza Land Rover Arena. The season runs October–May.

Other Spectator Sports

Going to a soccer game could seem anti-climactic given all the fuss about the city's legendary basketball teams, but consider going to a match for the sheer ease of getting there. Games are played at the centrally located **Stadio Renato Dallara,** and you can buy tickets at the box office in Piazza della Pace in front of the *stadio,* or at any San Paolo bank branch.

The **Bologna White Sox** are one of six Italian teams supported by the Italian Association for the Blind. Games are played with a ball that makes different noises as it moves through the air, and two non-blind helpers standing behind second and third bases provide a little guidance. Home runs are rare but it's still inspiring to watch these sluggers at Stadio Lioni in the Casteldebole area in the western edge of the city play June–October.

ACCOMMODATIONS
Under €100

For a flashback to student days, check in at **Hotel Accademia** (Via delle Belle Arti 6, tel. 051/232-318, www.hotelaccademia.it, €60 d). It's spartan, clean, very friendly, and located in the heart of the university district.

A traditional guesthouse since the 1800s, the **Albergo delle Drapperie** (Via delle Drapperie 5, tel. 051/223-955, www.albergodrapperie.com, €92 d) has perfected the art of the bed-and-breakfast. The half-dozen rooms are located in the historic district just 100 meters from Piazza Maggiore.

Get a glimpse of the Emilian countryside without straying too far from the city (just a half-kilometer) at the **San Vitale** (Via San Vitale 94, tel. 051/225-966, €75 d). Rooms are bright and clean, and the hostel provides free Internet access.

€100-200

If you want avant garde in the heart of the city, try the **Metropolitan Hotel** (Via dell'Orso 6, tel. 051/229-393, www.hotelmetropolitan.com, €110–160 s/d). There are pleasant gardens and Eastern statues in the lobby. If you want to splurge, stay in the Olive Court rooms on the second floor and enjoy your own terrace and garden.

Get thee to a nunnery in style and stay at this former convent and church; in the gardens the nuns grew silk worms, hence the name, **Convento dei Fiori di Seta** (Via Orfeo 34/4, tel. 051/272-039, www.silkflowersnun

nery.com, €150–180 s/d), or convent of the silk flowers. An unforgettably lovely experience where none of the six rooms are standard.

€200-300

Treat yourself to luxury at Bologna's only five-star hotel. The recently restored **G.H. Baglioni** (Via dell'Indipendenza 8, tel. 051/225-445, www.baglionihotels.com, €270–520 s/d) is centrally located and has a great in-house restaurant, **I Carracci**, that never closes.

With tower rooms and original wood beamed ceilings from the 12th century, staying at the **Albergo dei Commercianti** (Via de'Pignattari 11, tel. 051/233-052, €210 d) is indeed a privileged experience. Marvel at the Carrara marble desks, custom built according to a 15th-century design.

Over €300

Corona d'Oro 1890 (Via Oberdan 12, tel. 051/236-456, €350 d) was home to the noble Azzoguidi family in the 15th century. It still has some of their original furnishings, and Gothic vault windows. It also boasts an abbundant English breakfast buffet.

FOOD

Bologna, with its colder climes, does not follow the Mediterranean diet, and coming here in the winter is the best time to get a taste of why the city is known for its food. The country embraced Bologna's staple dish, tortellini with broth, as a Christmas Eve dinner tradition. The ring-shaped pasta comes stuffed with meat, ricotta cheese, or pumpkin.

Bolognese

Try tortellini with broth in the elegant Santo Stefano neighborhood at **Cesarina** (Via Santo Stefano 19/b, tel. 051/232-037, closed Mon. and Tues. at lunch, €10), a legendary restaurant in a 14th-century palazzo beneath the arcades in the city center. Also worth trying are the lasagna, ravioli, and gnocchi, followed by oven-roasted rabbit or goat seasoned with truffles and herbs. Come in the heart of winter and try *zampone*, pork sausage meat that has

been stuffed back inside a *zampa* (pig's foot). It's considered a delicacy, and Italians all over the country eat it on New Year's Eve, with lentils, as a traditional pagan plea for good luck and money in the coming year.

Known as the temple of tagliatelle, **Antica Trattoria della Gigina** (Via Stendhal 1/b, tel. 051/322-132, daily 12:30–3 P.M. and 7–11 P.M., €8) has developed a solid reputation over 50 years for some of the best handmade pasta in the city: lasagna, *tortelli*, and tortellini served with classic Bolognese meat sauce (which the rest of world calls *ragù*), or butter and sage. Try the *zuppa inglese* to finish it off. It's close to the town racetrack just outside of the city center.

If you like meat, **Da Bertino** (Via Lame 55, tel. 051/522-230, closed Sun. and Mon. at lunch, €10) is for you. Brave travelers should try the *bollito*, boiled parts of animals most people have never tasted, like beef tongue and veal brisket. More traditional dishes such as roast lamb and pork whet carnivorous appetites while cold meats like mortadella and prosciutto serve as tasty appetizers. Fresh pasta is also made here.

Quick Bites

The city has a couple of late-night lifesavers including **Pizza Altero** (tel. 051/234-758, Sun.–Fri. 8 P.M.–1 A.M. and Sat. 8 P.M.–2 A.M.) on Via dell'Indipendenza 33c, where you can get fluffy squares of *pizza margherita* (that's just tomato sauce and mozzarella cheese) for €1. Add a drink for another euro and you've got the perfect midnight snack.

Another good place is **Pizza Leggera** (Via Pietra Mellara 61), which means "light pizza." A misnomer, perhaps in jest, because these pizzas are anything but light. It serves whole pizzas rolled into wraps, both tomato and mozzarella varieties, or with added vegetables. There are also sweet pizzas, filled with chocolate or cream, all for under €3. Wash away the guilt with a low-cal soda.

Join the students for a quick bite at **La tua Piadina** (Via Borgonuovo 17, tel. 051/270-959), dedicated to making the perfect *piadina,* a grease-free, flatbread sandwich filled with soft cheeses and veggies.

International

If you're sick of pasta, **Ristorante Adal** (Via Giorgio Vasari 7, tel. 051/374-991, Tues.–Sun.) has good, reasonably priced Eritrean food, often accompanied by live music and dance.

For great Indian food and a lovely ambience, try **Taj Mahal** (Via San Felice 92d, tel. 051/524-894, daily 7–11:30 P.M., €8), reputably one of Italy's best Indian restaurants.

Cafés

Look no further for an espresso than **Bar Giuseppe** (Piazza Maggiore 1, tel. 051/264-444), said to be the city's best—and come back later for a gelato. For a reliable coffee and *cornetto,* come to the centrally located **Pasticceria Impero** (Via Indipendenza 39, tel. 051/232-337, daily 7:30 A.M.–8:30 P.M.).

Bar Piccolo (Piazza Verdi 4, tel. 051/220-004) is a cheap student hang-out in the heart of the university. It also serves cocktails in the early evening, and stays open until 2 am on weekends.

Gelato

Watch award-winning ice-cream being churned at **La Sorbetteria Castiglione** (Via Castiglione 44, tel. 051/233-257, Tues.–Sun. 8:30 A.M.–midnight). Undoubtedly the best ice cream for kilometers around.

The organic food craze has even reached gelato, and **Gelatauro** (Via San Vitale 98, tel. 051/230-049, daily 8 A.M.–11 P.M.) has organic orange ice-cream, along with flavors like jasmine and bergamot.

Legendary kiosk **Agnese delle Cocomere** (Piazza Trento and Trieste, tel. 338/209-1560, daily 1 P.M.–3 A.M., closed winter) owes its name to the slices of watermelon it serves (*cocomero* is watermelon in Italian). But it also makes homemade fresh fruit flavored ice cream, fruit shakes, and cocktails.

Expect great ice-cream sandwiches (with brioche or cookies) at **Gelateria delle Moline** (tel. 051/248-470, daily 10 A.M.–11 P.M.), a students' hang-out on Via delle Moline 13d.

Delicacies

Try a cognac-filled chocolate at **Roccati** (Via Clavature 17a, tel. 051/261-964), a historic chocolate shop that made *gianduja* chocolate for the princes of Savoy.

One of the most reputable wine vendors in Italy, **Enoteca Italiana** (Via Marsala 2b, tel. 051/227-132, Tues.–Sat.) sells the finest labels from around the country. Come at lunchtime, and enjoy a glass of your favorite wine with a freshly made panini.

INFORMATION AND SERVICES
Tourist Information

The main tourist office is in Piazza Maggiore 1, and is open daily 9 A.M.–8 P.M. (tel. 051/239-660). There are also offices at the train station (tel. 051/246-541) and airport (051/647-2036), both open 9 A.M.–7 P.M.

Hospitals, Police, and Emergencies

In case of a medical emergency, call 118, or go to the hospital emergency room (Pronto Soccorso). The city's main hospital is the **Ospedale San Orsola Generale** (Via Massarenti 9, tel. 051/636-311). Take bus 14 from Via Rizzoli.

Pharmacies

The **Farmacia Comunale** (tel. 051/239-690) at Piazza Maggiore is open 24 hours and can fill any prescription or advise you regarding minor medical ailments.

Banks and Currency Exchange

Conveniently located in the center is **Unicredit** (Via Irnerio 14, Mon.–Fri. 8:30 A.M.–1:30 P.M. and 2:30–4:00 P.M.), a branch of Italy's largest bank.

For a local bank, go to the **Fondazione Cassa di Risparmio** (Via Castiglione 8, tel. 051/230-727, Mon.–Fri. 8:30 A.M.–1:30 P.M. and 2:30–4 P.M.), the city's bank, founded in 1837.

Newspapers, Radio, and Internet

You can pick up copies of international newspapers at kiosks near the train station

view of Bologna from the Asinelli Tower

© ALESSIA RAMACCIA

and along Via dell'Indipendenza. There are a couple of handy Internet cafes in the center, including **Easy Internet** at Via Rizzoli 9 (daily 9 A.M.–11 P.M.) and **Happynet** on Via Oberdan 17b (tel. 051/1998-4179, Mon.–Fri. 9 A.M.–11 P.M., Sat–Sun. 10 A.M.–11 P.M.).

Lost and Found
Although no formal lost and found exists in Bologna, people are generally honest and not known to be swindlers. Nonetheless, the main police station (Questura) at Piazza Galileo 7 (tel. 051/6401-1111) is the best place to report theft or search for a lost wallet.

GETTING THERE
Air
Guglielmo Marconi international airport (tel. 051/647-9615, www.bologna-airport. it) is seven kilometers northwest of the city, at Borgo Panigale. There are Aerobuses every half hour to the city that stop at Via Ugo Bassi, Via dell'Indipendenza, and at the main train station. One-way tickets cost €4.50.

Car
To get to Bologna from Milan or Rome, take the **Autostrada del Sole** (Highway of the Sun), otherwise known as the A1. It takes about 2.5 hours from Milan, and 3.5 hours from Rome.

Train
Trains between Rome and Bologna run frequently, sometimes as often as three times every hour. A one-way second-class ticket on the Eurostar costs €42, with a traveling time of 2 hours and 45 minutes. The slower IC train takes about 4 hours and a one-way second-class ticket costs €34. For more detailed information, check out www.trenitalia.it.

GETTING AROUND
Buses
Although Bologna is pleasant to get around on foot, most buses stop at the centrally located landmarks of Piazza Nettuno or Piazza Maggiore. Tickets are available at newspaper stands and *tabacchi* shops. One ticket costs €1, and is good for one hour; for €3 you can get a ticket

EMILIA ROMAGNA

good for 24 hours; a booklet of eight tickets (a city pass) costs €6.50. Validate your ticket as soon as you get on board. You can be fined €100 for not having a ticket or having one that hasn't been validated.

Taxi

To get a taxi, flag one down New York style or go to the larger piazze, where a row of cabs are generally waiting. Otherwise you can also call 051/372-727 or 051/534-141 and be picked up.

Car, Motorcycle, Bicycle

You can rent a car in Bologna through Avis (Via Pietramellara 27d, tel. 051/255-024) or Hertz (Via G. Amendola 16, tel. 051/254-830, or at the airport). Bikes and scooters can be rented from **Senzauto** (tel. 051/251-401, www. senzauto.com) near the train station.

Tours

To visit the city's main monuments and museums, you can purchase the **Carta Bologna dei Musei** museum card. A one-day ticket costs €6, and a three-day ticket is €8.

Walking tours (tel. 051/296-0005, www. guidebologna.com) of the city meet outside the main tourist office at 10:30 A.M. on Wednesday, Saturday, and Sunday. Art-focused tours (tel. 051/275-0254) meet outside the main tourist office at 3 P.M. on Saturday and Sunday.

For a two-hour bike tour of the city's main highlights, contact **Prima Classe** (tel. 347/894-4094, €18). Bike rental is included and the same company organizes walking tours that start in front of Neptune's Fountain at 11 A.M. on Monday and Friday, and 4 P.M. on Tuesday and Thursday.

Po River Valley

The Po River Valley, also known as the Po Valley, runs along Italy's longest river, which starts at the Pian del Re on the French border and ends up near Venice before emptying out into the Adriatic Sea.

The main attraction here is the Po River Delta, a stunning landscape containing numerous wetlands where rice and sugar beet were once cultivated. Today it's home to large freshwater and saltwater basins, and many tributaries. Carps, eels, and royal perches are just a few of the indigenous fish found in abundance here.

The marshes are also on the migratory bird route from northern Europe and count over three hundred different species of birds, so come with open eyes and ears and a good pair of binoculars.

PIACENZA

This pleasurable city might make you feel as if you are in a bit of a time warp: The absence of tourists and tourist-friendly signposts is a refreshing glimmer of real life. The presence of a McDonald's is always the exception and it's

here as well, right next to the station. But even the McDonald's seems anchored in the past, if only for the legendary Ronald McDonald statue sitting out front! The **Borgo Fax** mall next door is a user-friendly and air-conditioned (and nearly empty) emergency shopping point, replete with perfume stores and eateries.

Moving quickly beyond this 1980s aside, introduce yourself to the city through the **Giardini Margherita** across from the train station. This lovely green oasis provides just enough of a pause before you venture towards the center of town through **Via Roma,** a narrow street with lovely horizons lined with Renaissance-style aristocratic *palazzi*-turned-lawyers' and architects' offices. Take a left at Via Cavour and you're almost at **Piazza dei Cavalli,** named for the two bronze statues of the Farnese dukes that flank the piazza, seemingly standing guard.

Sights

The central piazza is majestic yet understated. The few main attractions around **Piazza dei**

Cavalli speak for themselves: **Palazzo Gotico,** a 13th-century red brick palazzo with arches, is now home to the city government. Take a peek at the nice war memorial monument for fallen Italian soldiers in Italy's scuffles with its African colonies. Across the way is the Gothic-style **San Francesco** church (tel. 052/332-1988, daily 8 A.M.–noon and 3–6:30 P.M.), characteristically austere but equally inviting. You can also conveniently hop on a city bus in this piazza as most of them pass through here. The **tourist office** (tel. 0523/329-324, Apr.–Sept., Tues.–Sun. 9 A.M.–1 P.M. and 5 P.M.–8 P.M., closed Sun. Oct.–Mar.) is also located in the piazza.

Sprouting like a sunflower at the end of Via XX Settembre is the **Duomo** (Piazza Duomo, tel. 052/333-5154, daily 7:30 A.M.–noon and 4–7 P.M.), built 1122–1233 in two styles, Gothic and Romanesque. Gaze up at the peculiar facade of the **Palazzo Vescovile** next to the church. Enjoy a gelato or cappuccino at one of the cafes in this peaceful piazza.

Ready your sights for Italy's oldest octagonal tower, of the **Basilica di Sant'Antonio** (tel. 052/332-0653, Mon.–Sat. 8:30 A.M.–noon and 4–7 P.M. and Sun. 8 A.M.–noon and 8–9:30 P.M.), an 11th-century Gothic church that was built on the site of the town's first Paleochristian basilica, built between 350–375.

Italians' obsession with zodiacal signs was once sacred. Come and find how your month was illustrated in the 12th century on the mosaic floors of the church of **San Savino** (Via Alberoni 35, tel. 052/331-8165, daily 8 A.M.–noon and 4 P.M.–6 P.M.), named for Piacenza's second bishop.

Shopping

Need a pair (or more) of basic meant-to-be-worn Italian leather shoes? Pass by **Pirola** (Via Cavour 35, tel. 052/332-4293, daily 9 A.M.–12:30 P.M. and 4–7:30 P.M.) on your way to Piazza dei Cavalli. Slip on one of their classic black or brown numbers and your feet will start to understand what it means to be Italian.

Move right along and get your wedding dress next door at **Parisina** (Via Cavour 33,

tel. 052/332-5215, Mon.–Sat. 9 A.M.–noon and 3:30–7 P.M.). This is the place to knock 'em dead.

If you're heading to the mountains and need gear or clothing (that will easily pass as stylish street wear), check out **L'Altro Sport** (Via Felice Frasi 25c, tel. 052/338-5827, 9 A.M.–1 P.M. and 3:30–7:30 P.M., closed Thurs. and Sun.) in the city center. Italian trademark **Napapijri** backpacks come in every shade imaginable.

Accommodations

With its long-standing tradition of trusted hospitality since 1932, **C Hotel Nazionale** (Via Genova 35, tel. 052/371-2000, www.hotelnazionale.it, €120 d) won't disappoint, and it's only a 15-minute walk from Piazza dei Cavalli. Ask for a top-floor room with terrace at no additional charge.

If you can bear with a splash of comehither modernity, the **Grande Albergo Rome** (Via Cittadella 14, tel. 052/332-3201, www.grandealbergoroma.it, €175 d) provides a comfortable stay, with a sauna and gym, a seventh-story breakfast terrace, and an excellent restaurant.

Food

Eat in noble style at the **Antica Osteria del Teatro** (Via Verdi 16, tel. 052/332-3777, Tues.–Sat. noon–3 P.M. and 7–10:30 P.M., closed Aug., €20), the city's most reputable dining room, located in a medieval palazzo near Piazza dei Cavalli. This small restaurant offers a refined and creative menu, with exceptional desserts.

For a quick bite to tide you over, **Gusta** (Via Alberoni 20, tel. 052/332-2523, Mon.–Sat. 10:30 A.M.–2 P.M. and 6–11 P.M., €1.50–2.50) serves pizza of all types. Try the summer pizza with fresh tomatoes, mozzarella and *rucola* (arugula). They also serve *piadine* and pastas. Service is quick, but it's a sit-down locale.

Don't leave town without trying the local specialty of *pisarei e faso* (a curly pasta with red beans and sage). It's on the menu at **Santa**

EMILIA ROMAGNA

PROPERTY HUNTING

Romanticizing about a dream home in Italy? You could have the Tuscan sun (and Chianti), the Umbrian hillsides, or Sardinian beaches. So why consider buying a home in Italy's less glamorous breadbasket, Emilia Romagna? Apart from the food, of course.

Much like its undiscovered tourism potential, Emilia Romagna's property is largely untapped by foreigners seeking more popular destinations for their Italian holidays.

Certainly, Lord Byron and Oscar Wilde waxed poetic about Ravenna, where Dante Alighieri before them had blessed this, his noble refuge. But mainstream Italophiles have traditionally overlooked this subtly seductive region.

Foreigners in the last three or four years, however, have gradually started buying property in the countryside of Emilia Romagna, having discovered that it is actually a wise investment – and one that beats buying in the vicinity.

Emilia Romagna has one of Italy's most thriving, productive, and lively economies, which is not tourism-dependent; its property market is not intrinsically linked to the demand for holiday homes. With the region's long-standing economic soundness ensuring market stability, you too could consider making a long-term investment in a lifelong second home.

Renovating a farmhouse provides the perfect opportunity, and there are even some grants provided by various communities to fix up abandoned country dwellings, called *rustico* (rustic). These stone or wood dwellings usually have several rooms and are multi-leveled.

Expect to pay between €60,000–80,000, whereas a fully renovated farmhouse costs around €350,000.

As an agricultural region, farmhouses abound everywhere, but try the area of Lama Mocogno on the Tuscan Emilian Apennines if you fancy being near hiking trails and ski resorts.

People in Emilia Romagna are generally friendly without being invasive, so you can settle here as anonymously as you wish, or integrate without too much frustration. Soon you'll be on a first-name basis with your local butcher and postman, provided you stick to the smaller towns and countryside, which is recommended: Save Bologna for day or weekend trips, since housing both inside the city and in its periphery is just as expensive as Rome or Milan.

If you don't want to bother with restoring, and can't afford that re-made farmhouse, look into buying a newer property with modern amenities. There are one-, two-, and three-bedroom apartments (some with swimming pools) at the Val di Taro near Parma, a convenient one-hour drive from the airport and five kilometers from the village of Albareto. Prices for these new apartments start at €70,000.

For listings see www.homesinitaly.co.uk or keep tabs on property throughout Emilia Romagna at www.keyitaly.com. You'll get guidance on traversing Italy's tricky property rules and regulations (and renting your house out to tourists when you are not there – a lucrative endeavor) from www.realpointitaly.com.

Teresa (Corso Vittorio Emanuele II 169 b/c, €6–9). This homely restaurant is a cheap and tasty eatery that doubles as a bar with cappuccino, *cornetti,* and sweets.

Information and Services

The tourist office (Piazzetta dei Mercanti 10, tel. 052/332-9324) is just off Piazza dei Cavalli and provides several color brochures about the city's monuments and monthly events.

Getting There and Around

The closest airports to Piacenza are Milan Linate, Bergamo Orio al Serio, and Brescia Montichiari. By car, the town is easily reached by the A1 from either Northern or Southern Italy. Most intercity (IC) trains stop at Piacenza. The city is best explored on foot, but if you're short on time you can catch local buses at the train station as well as Piazza dei Cavalli.

FIDENZA

If you have a bit of time on your way to or from Parma, make a stop in Fidenza, a town of about 25,000 people whose main attraction is its duomo, one of the best-preserved Romanesque cathedrals in Northern Italy.

Sights

The lions are ready to greet you when you come to **Cattedrale di San Donnino** (Piazza Duomo 16, tel. 052/451-4883, daily 8 A.M.–noon and 3–7 P.M.). You can't miss these marble statues, attributed to Benedetto Antelami, who sculpted similar lions for Parma's cathedral. Antelami, a leading Romanesque school sculptor, also did the statues of David and Ezekiel above the lions. Inside you'll see Antelami's bas-reliefs of Christ's infancy and the life of Saint Donnino, who was killed here in 293 B.C. and whose remains are in the church's crypt. The present church was built between 1202–1268. The church was an obligatory stop for pilgrims, mainly coming from France, heading to Rome on the Via Francigena.

The cathedral museum, **Museo Diocesano** (tel. 052/451-4883, Tues.–Sun 10 A.M.–12:30 P.M. and 2:30–5:30 P.M.), contains Antelami's statue *Madonna in Trono col Bambino* and a baptismal fountain from the 7th century. The entrance is on Via Don Minzoni.

Entertainment and Events

Every year between September and November, this little town comes alive with exhibits, food festivals, concerts, and Shakespeare productions during the **Gran Fiera di Borgo S. Donnino** (tel. 052/451-7214, www.comune. fidenza.pr.it), named for the original name of Fidenza, and inspired by the saint (Donnino) who generated a cult following here. The festival's grand finale is a re-visitation of part of the pilgrims' path to Rome, followed by chestnuts and chocolate for everyone in Fidenza's **Piazza Garibaldi.**

For a more intensive pilgrimage experience, take 10 days to walk the original route to Rome on Via Francigena, starting in Fidenza, and arriving in Lucca, in Tuscany. You can hire a guide to walk with you the entire route or choose to do just one weekend or one day's worth of hiking. In keeping with the Middle Ages–inspired tour, modern-day amenities are kept to a minimum, with hostels and convents providing accommodation. The 10-day package (including breakfast) costs €450. For information, visit www.turismobenesser.it or contact the European Institute of Cultural Routes (www.culture-routes.lu).

Shopping

Just outside of Fidenza on the way to Parma is one of Italy's best outlet malls. **Fidenza Village** (Via San Michele Campagna, tel. 052/433-551, www.fidenzavillage.com, daily 10 A.M.–8 P.M.) has over 60 stores carrying brand names like Versace and Trussardi discounted up to 70 percent.

Accommodations

A simple and pleasant hotel, the **Astoria** (Via Gandolfi 5, tel. 052/452-4314, www.hotelas toriafidenza.it, €75 d) is perfect for an overnight stay (breakfast included) and has a nice in-house restaurant that serves both pizza and regional pastas.

Food

If you're ready to take a break from a day of shopping, **Barlumeria** (Via San Michele Campagna, tel. 052/420-1533, daily until 8 P.M., €8) is a nice restaurant at your feet (it's inside the mall). There are homemade salamis and *parmigiano* to start, followed by hand-cut pasta, big salads, and gorgonzola cheese for dessert. The kitchen closes at 3 P.M. but after that you can enjoy sandwiches and salads.

Getting There and Around

Fidenza is small enough to get around on foot. There are a couple of trains every hour from Parma and Fidenza, and the journey takes about 10 minutes. You can head straight to **Casa Cremonini** (Piazza Duomo 16, tel. 052/383-377) for tourist information.

PARMA

Dedicate at least one day to Parma, an elegant city in Emilia known for its prosciutto ham, *parmigiano reggiano* cheese, and opera. Walking the streets of Parma's historical center in the early evening is a reminder that good taste and simplicity go hand in hand. There is nothing ostentatious about Parma. Its monuments, clothing and food shops, and restaurants exude elegance and comfort. This is a city that respects its past without unduly dwelling on it.

The city's sensibility to the finer things in life extends to everything. A good example is Acqua di Parma perfume, in its trademark bright yellow box on display in many perfume store windows. It gained notoriety as the brand of choice amongst Ava Gardner and Humphrey Bogart in the 1950s. French writer Stendhal featured the city during Napoleonic rule in the early 19th century in his masterpieces *The Charterhouse of Parma.*

Start strolling on **Strada Garibaldi**—where you'll end up in front of the legendary **Teatro Regio** opera house—taking side turns to visit the Cathedral and its famous Baptistery.

Sights

Austere but elegant, Parma's **duomo** (Piazza del Duomo, tel. 052/123-5886, daily 9 A.M.–12:30 P.M. and 3–7 P.M.) is one of Italy's greatest works of Romanesque-style architecture from the 12th century. In the southern transept of the church is the highly moving sculpture *Descent from the Cross,* completed by Benedetto Antelami in 1178. Look up at delightful cherubs in frescoes by Antonio Allegri da Correggio, a local late Renaissance period painter.

Next to the duomo is the impressive **Baptistery** (Piazza del Duomo, tel. 052/123-5886, daily 9 A.M.–12:30 P.M. and 3–6:30 P.M., €4), commissioned by the city government at the end of the 12th century and today considered one of the most important medieval monuments in Europe. Of octagonal shape in pink marble, the church was designed by Benedetto Antelami, and contains many of his most intriguing and intense sculptures, including the *Adoration of the Magi, The Last Judgment,* and *Flight into Egypt.*

It was at the **Teatro Regio** that famed opera composer Giuseppe Verdi, who came from the nearby countryside, received his first acclaim for *Il Trovatore, La Traviata,* and *Rigoletto.* One of the world's best-known opera theaters, Parma's Teatro Regio has been hosting highbrow audiences (seating more than 1,400) since 1829. You can book a half-hour tour Tuesday–Saturday 10:30 A.M.–noon.

Considered Parma's cultural center for good reason, **Teatro Farnese** (tel. 052/123-3309, Tues.–Sun. 8:30 A.M.–2 P.M., €6) is an immense Renaissance complex built for the noble Farnese family that ruled Parma (and Piacenza) in the years 1545–1731. It houses an archeological museum, library, and art gallery that contains Leonardo da Vinci's *Head of a Child.* Enter the theater and you realize that the noblemen of the day really got all the perks. In fact it was built expressly for the visit of Tuscan aristocrat Cosimo de' Medici. Today it stands as the prototype of the modern playhouse, as well as a gem of post-war reconstruction after being bombed in World War II.

The Renaissance church of **San Giovanni Evangelista** (Piazzale San Giovanni, tel. 052/123-5311, church open Fri.–Sun. 9 A.M.–noon and 3–6 P.M.) was built for the Benedictine order and contains works of art by local artists of the day, including Correggio and Parmigianino (the nickname for Girolamo Francesco Maria Mazzola). The intriguing monk's pharmacy (Borgo Pipa, tel. 052/150-8532, Tues.–Sun. 8:30 A.M.–1:45 P.M.) next door pre-dates the church. It was opened in 1201 and monks made and sold medicine from their quarters until 1766. Come and see how they relieved medieval ailments.

Parco Ducale (April 1–Oct. 31 6 A.M.–midnight, Nov. 1–March 31 7 A.M.–8 P.M.) is a royal respite from Parma's beautiful buildings and artworks. The Duke of Parma in the 16th century put together vegetable gardens, rosemary and myrtle hedges, and fruit trees, thus creating a park for the ruling Farnese family.

RUNNING WITH VERDI

Runners: leave your iPods at home – Giuseppe Verdi is here to encourage you as you run through his native land, with his most well-known arias performed in the towns along the way, including Verdi's own village of **Ròncole.**

If you love running, or even like it well enough to use as an excuse to travel cheaply and eat well, take a runner's holiday at the **Maratone delle Terre Verdiane,** also known as the **Verdi Marathon.** (No, you do not have to do the entire marathon to participate – options include the 31k, a half-marathon, or the 10k fun run.) Running tourism in Italy is still largely undiscovered by tourists, but it's growing in popularity; try it while it's still a niche, local, inexpensive, and totally exploratory experience.

Running instead of walking gives you a more intense experience of places you are seeing for the first time. It's just you and the road out there, without distractions. The friendly camaraderie and light competitiveness of your fellow runners adds to the experience.

Plus, your well-earned runner's high is rewarded with a beautiful place to explore after the race, and good eating. You'll pass by the modest and moving house where Verdi was born in the village of Ròncole. After the race, you can backtrack to visit his home, **La Casa Natale di Giuseppe Verdi** (daily 9:30 A.M.-12:30 P.M. and 2:30-7 P.M., €4). Note: Don't arrive at the last minute, as the curators anxiously watch the clock. A €8 ticket allows you to visit Busseto's **Teatro G. Verdi,** which opened its doors in 1868 to the tunes of *Rigoletto,* and the **Casa Barezzi,** where Verdi lived and composed his greatest works.

One of the perks of this race is the food:

the standard pasta party the night before the race includes the region's best ingredients in an ample buffet fit for a king: *parmigiano Reggiano,* mortadella, *prosciutto,* pasta, cakes, and Lambrusco wine. Don't be afraid to elbow your way through the hungry lines if necessary.

Ditto after the race with an equally rich feast – just don't overdo it at the pit stops along the road, replete with fruit, hot and cold tea, cookies, and chunks of *parmigiano Reggiano.*

Races end in different places, but buses bring you back to the starting line in **Salsomaggiore,** where thermal baths provide the perfect post-race therapy. In the heart of town is the **Terme di Salsomaggiore.** Depending on how hard you've run, you may be barely able to walk when you go inside, but your body will thank you when you walk out. Ease into a proper pampering: First a doctor chats with you about your needs and desires, and recommends a regime of massages, baths, and hot/cold treatments. Gentle assistants wrap you in heated towels as you get out of the tubs. Call 052/458-2723 for an appointment.

To register for the Verdi Marathon, log onto www.verdimarathon.com. The race organizers can suggest hotels that offer reduced rates to runners. There are several races held in Emilia Romagna throughout the year, with most during the fall and winter. Check out the complete list of Italian races at www.podisti.net/calendario. There's no need to present qualifying times to participate, but you do need to bring a doctor's certificate or evidence of membership in a running club.

Their demise left the park abandoned. Later on, Napoleon's wife cleaned it up, recreating English-style gardens. Stop at the **Palazzo Ducale** (Mon.–Sat. 9 A.M.–noon, €3), where you can visit a few rooms with original Renaissance period frescoes painted by regional artists. Today it's the headquarters of the European Food and Safety Commission, as well as the local police.

At the southeast corner of the park is **La Casa Natale di Arturo Toscanini** (Borgo Tanzi 13, tel. 052/103-1170, Tues.–Sun. 9 A.M.–1 P.M. and 2–6 P.M.), the birthplace of the famed Italian conductor, where some of his personal objects and writings are on display.

Want to see what was fit for a princess on her wedding? On display at the **Museo Glauco Lombardi** (Palazzo di Riserva, Strada

Garibaldi 15, tel. 052/123-3727, www.museo lombardi.it, Mon.–Fri. 9:30 A.M.–3 P.M., Sat.–Sun. 9 A.M.–6 P.M., Jul.–Aug. 9 A.M.–1:30 P.M., €4) are the jewels and wedding dress of Napoleon's second wife, Marie Louise of Austria, along with the *corbeille de mariage,* an ornate statue that was her wedding present from the emperor. These objects are part of the collection of the late local archivist and historian Professor Glauco Lombardi.

To see the real *parmigiano* cheese in the makings (800 years of noble tradition), go for a two-hour tour of **Consorzio del Parmigiano Reggiano** (Strada dei Mercati 9/a, tel. 052/129-2700, www.parmigiano-reggiano.it) first thing in the morning, 8:30–10:30 A.M., in the wonderfully smelling factory just outside of the city center.

Shopping

Don't leave town without some *salumi,* prosciutto, and *parmigiano reggiano* cheese in your suitcase! And a couple of bottles of Lambrusco wine if there's room. You can get it all at **Salumeria Verdi** (Via Garibaldi 69a, tel. 052/120-8100, Mon.–Sat. 8 A.M.–1:15 P.M. and 4–7:45 P.M.). Ask the friendly staff for tips in picking out items for yourself and gifts for food obsessed friends.

Accommodations

The friendly and reasonably priced **《 Albergo Brenta** (Via G. Borghesi 12, tel. 052/120-8093, www.hotelbrenta.it, €75–85 s/d) offers thematic guided tours of the city to discover the best of its artwork, culture, and food. Book ahead or on the spot with the courteous staff. Conveniently located near the train station. Breakfast is an extra €5.

Simple, straight-forward lodging near the central Piazza Garibaldi, **Hotel Button** (Borgo Salina 7, tel. 0521/208-039, €85–95 s/d) is a nice place to collect your bearings at the end of a long day. It boasts well-priced large rooms and a well-stocked bar that's open 24 hours a day.

Hotel Torino (Via Mazza 7, tel. 052/128-1046, www.hotel-torino.it, €89–130 s/d) offers simple and convenient accommodation for opera aficionados, with the Teatro Regio just around the corner. Ask for one of the four top-floor rooms with a view. Closed for one week during Christmas, fDec. 22–28.

Palace Hotel Maria Luigia (Viale Mentana 140, tel. 052/128-1032, www.palacemarialuigia.com, €150–242 s/d) is arguably Parma's most stylish and comfortable hotel in the center, with cozy two-level junior suites, and an ambience that uplifts and enhances your visit of this elegant city.

Comfort and convenience are in order at **Du Parc** (Viale Piacenza 12/c, tel. 052/129-2929, www.starhotels.com), a modern hotel near the Parco Ducale and a short walk to the center. It only has double rooms and suites. They start at €110 in low season (Nov.–Feb. and Jul.–Aug.) and at €130 the rest of the year. Visiting VIPs generally check into the presidential apartment on the last floor.

If you want the seclusion and prestige of staying at a villa, **Hotel Verdi** (Via Pasini 18, tel. 052/129-3539, www.hotelverdi.it, €110–150 s/d), across from the Parco Ducale, is for you. The Santa Croce restaurant next door adds a nice touch.

For a hands-on experience in regional cooking and serious relaxation in the countryside, book a weekend at the **Azienda Agricola Ciato,** just south of Parma (Strada Pilastro 8, località Panocchia, tel. 052/163-5281, www.ciato.it, €50–70 s/d). Targeted to those seeking "intelligent vacations," here you can learn how to make your own pasta, whip up tomato sauce, and top it off with a scenic bike ride. There is one apartment with two rooms and optional use of the kitchen. Breakfast is included in the price, but you will need to book ahead if you want to eat lunch or dinner (€20–25).

Food

That Parma became Europe's food authority in 2004 is no coincidence (though certainly it was helped by then Prime Minister Silvio Berlusconi's intrepid insistence on Italy's superior food IQ). The food here really is top notch, starting with the city's trademark *parmigiano* cheese and prosciutto ham. Keep in mind that

© ALESSIA RAMACCIA

Parma's cobblestone streets

many restaurants are closed the entire month of July, considered low season for tourism in the city.

La Greppia (Strada Garibaldi 39, tel. 052/123-3686, Wed.–Sun. noon–3:30 P.M. and 7–11 P.M., closed July, €10–15) features reliable fare so you can afford to be adventurous. Go for the salad on a bed of *rucola* with balsamic vinegar, followed by *tortelli d'erbetta alla parmigiana* (tortelli with herbs and grated cheese) or *pappardelle alla Greppia* (house pasta dish). If you still have room for a second course, try chicken with chestnuts.

Simple but elegant is the trademark of **Angiol d'Or** (Vicolo Scutellari 1, tel. 052/128-2632, Wed.–Mon. 12:30–3 P.M. and 7–10:30 P.M., €9–12) near the cathedral. This small restaurant boasts of great second courses like *stracotto con polenta* (stewed beef with polenta) or *straccetti di manzo saltati nel Lambrusco* (thin strips of beef cooked in red wine), all accompanied by an extensive wine list.

For a stylish setting and original dishes, you can't go wrong at **Parizzi** (Via Repub-

blica 71, tel. 052/128-5952, Tues.–Sun. noon–3 P.M. and 7:30–11 P.M., €11–15) Try the *risotto con cotechino* (a rich pork sausage from Modena) and truffles or a Cornish hen with dried fruit. Top it off with the triple mousse chocolate dessert.

◖ Bottiglia Azzurra (Borgo Felino 63, tel. 052/128-5842, Mon.–Sat. noon–2 P.M. and 6:30–10:30 P.M., €8–10) is an exquisite hole-in-the-wall type restaurant that feels more like a wine cellar with wood tables and racks of bottles running the gamut from famous labels to new releases, called *vini novelli*. Drink to live jazz and enjoy the full range of local dishes.

Frequented by travelers and local jetsetters alike, **Trattoria Corrieri** (Via Conservatorio 1, tel. 052/123-4426, daily lunch and dinner, €8–10) brings out the goods quickly and amply (come here on an empty stomach). Order with confidence (it's all good), but do start with the *torta fritta*, a kind of fried pizza bread served warm with a side of prosciutto di Parma.

A family-run business with mom in the kitchen, **Cocchi** (Via Gramsci 16, tel. 052/198-1990, Sun.–Fri. noon–3 P.M. and 7–10 P.M., €10–12) stands for classic good cooking. There's something for everyone including various homemade pastas, *bomba di riso al forno* (baked rice ball with pigeon meat), liver pâté, and roasted duck. For dessert (catch your breath), dive your fork into *salame al cioccolato* (chocolate parfait) or an almond-based *semifreddo croccante* (ice-cream cake).

For a down-to-earth meal with prices to match, **Le Sorelle Picchi** (Via Farini 27, tel. 052/123-3528, Mon.–Sat. noon–3 P.M., €12) hits the spot. Start with an appetizer of salami and prosciutto, followed by homemade pasta of tagliatelle with mushrooms or *ragù* sauce, pasta, and beans. Roasted veal, pork, or beef are the main seconds. *Zabaione* with warm chocolate and *zuppa inglese* never disappoint for dessert.

The Three Little Pigs, or **◖ Le tre Porcelline** (Borgo del Correggio 60/a, tel. 052/123-6138, Wed.–Mon. noon–3 P.M. and 7:30–11 P.M., €10) is the perfect name for this restaurant. Owners Filippo and Marco chose it

EMILIA ROMAGNA

to make you feel at home while easing you into gluttony. Try one of their pork-themed appetizers (various salamis or prosciutto). You won't want to limit yourself to just one pasta from the eclectic selection, including gnocchi with gorgonzola cheese and walnuts, or tagliatelle with bacon and zucchini.

Information and Services

The main tourist office in Parma is at Via Melloni 1a (tel. 052/121-8889, www.turismo.co mune.parma.it, Mon.–Sat. 9 A.M.–7 P.M., Sun. 9 A.M.–1 P.M.). Along with maps, they provide free Internet access. There's also an information office at the train station, open 8:30 A.M.– noon and 2:45–5:45 P.M.

You can pick up an international newspaper at the station's newsstand, open 5:20 A.M.–8 P.M.

In case of an emergency, call 118. The city's main hospital is the **Ospedale Maggiore** (tel. 052/170-2111) at Via Gramsci 14, west of the center and reachable by buses 3, 4, 5, 9 and 10.

Main pharmacies include **Allegri Chemist Shop** at Via della Repubblica 70b (tel. 052/123-0162l) and **Amadasi** at Via D'Azeglio 72b (tel. 052/120-7055).

The lost and found service is reachable at 052/121-8738.

There are several banks. Two centrally located ones include **Banca Carisbo** at Via Dante 3 (tel. 052/122-8317) and **Banca Commerciale Italiana** at Piazza Garibaldi 3a (tel. 800/020-202). Banks are open 8 A.M.–1 P.M. and 3 P.M.–4 P.M.

Internet access costs €2 for every half-hour and €4 for every hour at the **Libreria Fiaccadori** (Strada al Duomo 8a, tel. 052/128-2445, Mon.–Sat. 9 A.M.–7:30 P.M., Sun. 10 A.M.–1 P.M. and 3:30–7:30 P.M.).

Getting There and Around

Giuseppe Verdi (Via dell'Aeroporto 44a, tel. 052/195-1511, www.aeroportoparma.it) is Parma's aptly named airport. The main airlines with services to the city include Alitalia, Ryanair, Cimber Air, and Bellair, which have regular flights from Milan and Rome.

There are several car rental services at the airport, including **Avis** (tel. 052/129-1238), **Sixth** (tel. 052/194-2235), **Hertz** (tel. 052/194-2063), and **Europcar** (tel. 052/194-2561). Bus 6 runs between the airport and train station at half past every hour.

If you come to Parma by car, take the A1 highway from Milan in the north and Bologna in the south.

There are several trains each day to Parma from both Milan and Bologna.

The main bus terminal in Parma, for buses both within the city and to surrounding areas, is at Piazza Ghiaia 41a, and is open Mon.–Sat. 7:45 A.M.–7:10 P.M.

There are two taxi services. Call 0521/771-077 or 0521/252-562.

You can also rent bikes and scooters at the **train station** (tel. 052/178-2687, Mon.– Sat. 5:30 A.M.–10:30 P.M.). There are other bike rental places throughout the city, such as **Puntobici** (Viale Paolo Toschi 2a, tel. 052/128-1979, www.parmapuntobici.it). They'll rent you tandem and electric bikes, too!

MODENA

"We have work, services, a good pub scene, great theater, and the place to come for an *osteria*," said a Sicilian man, speaking about Modena, his adopted northern home. "Expensive, yes, but a very livable place." The city's wealth goes way back to when it was ruled by the noble Estes family from the late 13th century until the Italian unification in 1861. They were arts patrons during Italy's brilliant Renaissance period and created a legacy of artistic patronage that hasn't diminished with time. It's no wonder Modena gave birth to beloved tenor Luciano Pavarotti in 1935. Today the city boasts high-end car manufacturers Ferrari, Maserati, and Lamborghini, not to mention the much-sought-after balsamic vinegar.

Even for passersby, this refined but robust town will leave its mark on your travels. People jog here, and the bike lanes, well respected, are wide enough for Smart cars to use. To reach the historical center, follow the Corso Vittorio

Emanuele until it ends or take a detour through the **Giardini Pubblici** (public gardens) past the military academy.

Sights

The unassuming **Piazza Grande** sneaks up on you, then seizes your attention with two monuments that are protected by UNESCO. The **duomo** (Corso Duomo 3, tel. 059/216-078, daily 7 A.M.–12:30 P.M. and 3:30–7 P.M.), or cathedral, considered one of Italy's most important legacies from the Romanesque period, was started in 1099 and is notable for the bas-relief figures on the front of the church: these book-of-Genesis depictions, like *The Creation* and *The Temptation of Adam and Eve,* were done by Guglielmo da Modena in the 12th century. Visit the **museum** (Via Lanfranco 6, Tues.–Sun. 9:30 A.M.–12:30 P.M. and 3:30–6:30 P.M., €3) at the north side of the cathedral. For €1 extra you can take an audio tour of both the museum and church.

UNESCO also placed the church's campanile, the **Ghirlandina,** under protection. The 13th-century 87-meter tower was built with marble from the old Roman city. You can climb to the top (€1) on Sunday 9:30 A.M.–12:30 P.M. and 3 P.M.–7 P.M. It's closed in August and on major holidays but open on January 31, the day of patron saint San Gimignano.

Royalty in no small measure, the **Palazzo Ducale,** built in 1634, is stunningly grandiose and elegant. It was the seat of the Estes family court until their rule came to an end with Italy's unification in the middle of the 1800s. Today it is home to officers in training as the seat of Italy's military academy. West Pointers drop to your knees, these guys—and gals—look elegantly official when they parade out front. You can take a guided tour of the military museum, which recounts the academy's history, on Sunday 10–11 A.M., year-round except in August. For further information, call 059/206-660.

Get a combined ticket for €6 to visit the cathedral museum and the **Palazzo dei Musei,** which includes the **Galleria Estense,** the Estes family's collection of artwork, including works by El Greco and Velázquez. It also holds the **Biblioteca Estense;** with over 4,000 manuscripts and letters belonging to the Estes family, it is one of Italy's most extensive and important collections.

Take a peek inside the **Chiesa del Voto** (Via Emilia, tel. 059/203-2660, Tues.–Sun. 10 A.M.–noon and 4–6 P.M.), a severe-looking church that was built as a public offering to celebrate the end of the plague in 1630. A canvas painting inside called *La Pala della Peste* (Altarpiece of the Plague), by Ludovico Lana from the 17th century, tells the story of the church's peculiar construction—see for yourself! About 50 meters up the street is the **Chiesa di San Giovanni Battista,** built 1723–1730. Inside the extraordinarily moving life-sized terra-cotta sculpture *Lamentation over the Dead Christ* by Guido Mazzoni.

Ferrari fans are truly at home in Modena. Just south in Maranello, **Galleria Ferrari** (Via Dino Ferrari 43, daily 9 A.M.–6 P.M., €12) displays the world's largest collection of Ferrari cars and an array of red memorabilia like baseball hats and mugs. This is where the latest Formula 1 models are tested and Michael Schumacher became a legend.

Festivals and Events

Find the festival that suits your fancy in Modena: The city shows off everything from cars and balsamic vinegar to philosophy.

Enjoy the show as local carmakers Ferrari and Maserati show off their cars' legendary style at the **Terra di Moto** (www.modena-terradimotori.com), held the first or second week of April or the second and fourth week of May.

Come and taste for yourself what all the fuss is about the city's claim to culinary fame: balsamic vinegar. At the **Gusto Balsamico** (www.gustobalsamico.it), dab it on fresh strawberries or put a drop on a hunk of *parmigiano reggiano* cheese at this three-day festival at the beginning of October.

Romp and play as a local Renaissance-period citizen would have during the **Serate Estensi**

EMILIA ROMAGNA

(Via Galaverna 8, tel. 059/203-2707, www.co mune.modena.it/seratestensi) summertime festival. These splendid evenings in late June and early July include banquets, balls, and costume parties.

Philosophy can be fun if you give it a chance. **Festival di Filosofia** (www.festivalfilosofia.it) features three days of debates, lectures, exhibits, and dinners with some of the world's most renowned thinkers like Marc Augé on cultural memory. The event is held in mid-September and may help answer those big questions that keep you up at night.

Shopping

Everything looks a touch prettier in Modena than elsewhere. Chain stores like **Alta Moda** (Corso Canalgrande 63, tel. 059/219-286) beckon from under the porticos in the city center. Other delightful stores around the corner on Via Emilia include **Marisa Haute Couture** at number 72 (tel. 059/236-055) and **Divina** at number 74 (tel. 059/220-085). There's also a properly placed **La Perla** lingerie store on the Piazza Duomo.

If you want to shop on the heels of locals, head to Canal Chiaro—at number 17 is **Popoli** (tel. 059/222-309), specializing in funky and brightly colored housewares. Keep walking until you reach number 59, **Nuvolari** (tel. 059/219-697), which is named after the racecar driver who won countless races with the locally manufactured Maserati. This boutique specializes in cool clothing like Denny Rose—at a discount.

For a change of pace, ready yourself for some serious food shopping up the street, at number 139, home of the **Salumeria Gastronomia Fini** (tel. 059/223-320) that has been selling artesian cheese and salami for over a century. Don't leave without your requisite bottle of balsamic vinegar.

Accommodations

For privacy look no further than the **Hotel Cervetta** (tel. 059/238-447, www.hotel cervetta5.com, €60–85 s/d) at Via Cervetta 5, a side street near the duomo. It's clean, com-

fortable, and convenient at €85. If you don't feel like lugging your suitcases far from the train station, **Hotel Milan** (Corso Vittorio Emanuele 68, tel. 059/223-011, www.mod enahotel.it, €90 d) is a convenient and inexpensive choice on the main drag to the center of town.

Hotel Centrale (Via Rismondo 55, tel. 059/218-808, www.hotelcentrale.com, €175 d) is a recently restored palazzo from the beginning of the 1900s offering modern conveniences (air-conditioning, bar service, satellite television) in the heart of the city. Breakfast is included and bathrooms have recently been refitted with marble tiling.

A Renaissance convent turned 18th-century noble residence became the present **Canalgrande** (Corso Canalgrande 6, tel. 059/217-160, www.canalgrandehotel.it, €175–250 s/d) hotel in the 1970s. Antique paintings and furniture mix with modern conveniences like wireless Internet access. There's also an excellent in-house restaurant called **La Secchia Rapita** where local specialties are served by friendly waiters.

Food

Locals swear by the quality of **Trattoria La Bianca** (Via Spaccini 24, tel. 059/311-524, Mon.–Fri. 12:30–3 P.M. and 7–10:30 P.M., plus Sat. dinner, €10–15). Start with the *ciccioli*, fried pizza bread filled with slabs of prosciutto and salami and berry marmalade, a sweet and sour paradise for your palate.

(Zelmira (Via San Giacomo 27, tel. 059/222-351, Fri.–Wed. noon–3 P.M. and 7:30–11 P.M., €9–12) was born in obscure circumstances—or, rather, inside a former church at the turn of the last century. It's since become pagan—to our palate's delight! A good start to the fantasy-filled menu is the *sformatino di parmigiano*, a baked quiche-type treat made with potatoes, leeks, parmigiano cheese, and balsamic vinegar.

This Michelin-rated restaurant wears its name well. **La Francescana** (Via Stella 22, tel. 059/210-118, Tues.–Sun. 12:30–2 P.M. and 8 P.M.–10 P.M., Sat. dinner only, €25) serves tiny gourmet-style portions of refined food like risotto with asparagus or *cotechino* (pork sausage) with *Lambrusco* (wine) sorbet. Desserts are so pretty you will want to take a picture before you eat them! Relish the ambience too, with works of art hanging on the walls and the restored medieval church of San Francesco next door.

For traditional Modena cooking, the **Taverna dei Servi** (Via dei Servi 37, tel. 059/217-134, Wed.–Mon. noon–2:30 P.M. and 7–10:45 P.M., €8–13) serves homemade pasta, an ample selection of second courses like *zampone* (leg of the pig), and Cornish hen. The house specialty *Torta Barozzi* is mandatory for dessert.

K2 Gelateria (Corso Canalgrande 67, tel. 059/219-181, Thurs.–Tues. 9 A.M.–midnight) makes ice-cream cones that look like works of art. Gelato is wrapped one around the other to resemble the petals of a flower. For a more gluttonous treat, get an ice-cream sandwich with dollops of whip cream (focaccia is what it's called—like the pizza bread, except sweet). Top flavors include After Eight and pistachio. Red grapefruit is a dream.

Information and Services

Turn left exiting the train station and a block away you'll find bright yellow bikes in front of the domed temple for war victims. To rent the bikes, go to the city's tourism office (Via Scudari 10, tel. 059/220-022, Mon. 2:30–6:30 P.M., Tues.–Fri., 9 A.M.–1 P.M. and 2:30–6:30 P.M.). A €20 security deposit gets you unlimited use of the bike and your money back when you're done.

The main tourist office is at Piazza Grande 14 (tel. 059/206-660, www.turismo.modena.comune.it, Mon. 3–6 P.M., Tues.–Sat. 9:30 A.M.–2:30 P.M. and 3–6 P.M. and Sun. 9 A.M.–12:30 P.M.).

Policlinico di Modena (tel. 059/375-050) hospital has a night watch, Monday–Friday 8 P.M.–8 A.M. and weekends 10 P.M.–8 A.M.

The 24-hour pharmacy is **Farmacia Comunale di Pozzo** (Via Emilia Est 416, tel. 059/360-091).

Getting There and Around

There are trains to Modena from Bologna every half-hour. It's a 20-minute ride and costs €2.50. Modena has two train stations, **Piazza Dante** is the main one, while **Piazza Manzoni** serves local destinations. You can take a shower at the main train station for €0.50.

If you come by car, take the A1 and exit at Modena. Bologna's airport is only 36 kilometers from Modena. You can take trolleybus 7 from the main station to the museums and Via Emilia or a bus on Via Molza for Maranello.

FERRARA

Ferrara is a reminder that some cities really do live in function of the finer things in life. It's a beautiful place and you should come here to feel entranced but not intimidated by its splendor. Good looks don't always come by accident and great minds worked hard to make this city spectacular. Ferrara was the humanists' ideal city during the Renaissance, paving the way for modern urban planning; it was also home to two of Italy's best poets, Torquato Tasso and Ludovico Ariosto. In 1995, UNESCO's World Heritage Committee put the city on its Heritage Protection list. A couple of days are all you need to relish a short and sweet visit to Ferrara. Rent a bike and follow your own fancy, but enjoy pedaling along the city's majestic curves with everyone else.

Sights

A stunning white building, the **Palazzo del Diamante** was named for its diamond-like studded facade, made with peculiar white diamond-shaped stones. This was the noble Estes family's grandest palazzo in the 15th century. Walk inside and visit the city's art gallery, the **Pinacoteca Nazionale** (Corso Ercole I d'Este 21, tel. 053/220-5844, Tues.–Wed. and Fri.–Sat. 9 A.M.–2 P.M., Thurs. 9 A.M.–7 P.M., Sun. 9 A.M.–1 P.M., €4), which has a permanent collection of paintings from the Bolognese and Ferrarese schools, and also hosts special exhibits.

Castello Estense (Viale Cavour, tel. 053/229-9233, Tues.–Sun. 9:30 A.M.–5:30 P.M.,

€6) in the center of town looks so unconsciously perfect (there is even a shallow body of water that could be a moat) that it seems like a play castle. Quite the contrary, it was built to defend the Estes family from rebels angry about tax increases at the end of the 14th century. Tragedy also graced these seemingly invincible walls when one of the Estes discovered that his wife and son were lovers. You can visit the underground prison where he tortured them before having them beheaded. Today the government occupies most of the castle, but you can visit a few rooms replete with original frescoes.

When aesthetical perfection and substance meet, you know you've got quality art, and Ferrara's **duomo** (Piazza della Cattedrale, tel. 053/220-7449, Mon.–Sat. 7:30 A.M.– noon and 3–6:30 P.M., Sun. and holidays, 7:30 A.M.–12:30 P.M. and 3:30–7:30 P.M.) provides a stunning example. Its three-tiered marble facade attracts and holds the gaze. Step inside to see Sebastiano Filippi's fresco *The Last Judgment,* said to have inspired Michelangelo's version in the Sistine Chapel. Along the church's right-hand side are the 15th-century artisans' shops known as the *Loggia dei Merciai,* re-creating the lovely little village this was during the Renaissance.

Ferrara is home to one of Italy's most important Jewish communities, dating back to the end of the 2nd century. Visit the synagogue (tel. 053/221-0228) at Via Mazzini 95 and museum next door, which features objects from the community that recount its importance in attracting Jewish immigrants from Italy and all over Europe. Guided tours start at 10 A.M., 11 A.M., and noon Sunday–Thursday.

The Estes family came to the **Palazzo Schifanoia** (Via Scandiana 23, tel. 053/224-4949, Tues.–Sun. 9 A.M.–6 P.M., €3) to escape boredom. Literally that's what its peculiar name means in Italian. Think long indulgent banquets and other happy affairs. The main attraction today is, appropriately, the fresco called the *Salone of the Months,* Cosimo Tura's pagan cycle of the months as allegorical pageant with Olympian gods.

Museo Giovanni Boldini (Corso Porta Mare 5/9, tel. 053/224-4949, Tues.–Sun. 9 A.M.–1 P.M. and 3–6 P.M., €5) displays the lovely paintings by 19th-century painter Giovanni Boldini, a native of Ferrara but an émigré to Paris. His work's keen sensibility of women may remind you of Edgar Degas, who was in fact a close friend of Boldini's. Two of Degas' portraits are in the collection. In the same **Palazzo Massari** location is the modern and contemporary art museum featuring works by Filippo De Pisi, another local, 20th-century painter.

Chiesa di San Cristoforo (Piazza Borso 50, tel. 053/220-5619, guided visits upon request) is slightly off the traditional tourist track, but as long as you're on your bike, or even footing around town and ready for a peaceful interlude, half an hour is all it takes to visit this church and the **Certosa** monastery next door. Biagio Rossetti, the same architect credited with creating much of Renaissance Ferrara, designed the building.

Entertainment and Events

The world's oldest *palio* (horse race) took place in Ferrara in 1279, and every year the city celebrates the **Palio of San Giorgio,** the city's patron saint, with a race on the last Sunday of May. Festivities start at the beginning of the month. For information and tickets online, go to www.paliodiferrara.it.

Ferrara Buskers (www.ferrarabuskers.com) brings together buskers, or street musicians, from all over the world and livens up the town for one week, usually towards the end of August. This non-competitive event attracts actors, clowns, jugglers, and musicians who are accompanied by happy audiences packed inside Ferrara's gentle streets.

Ferrara's annual **hot air balloon festival** (www.ferrarafestival.it) at the end of September is one of Europe's largest. For 10 days, over 40 balloon companies from all over the world fly the skies overhead the Parco Urbano Bassani. Go up in one and enjoy an aerial view of this medieval town.

Accommodations

Conveniently located across from the train station, **De la Ville Jolly** (Piazzale Stazione 11, tel. 053/277-2635, €70–95 s/d) offers no-frills comfort and amenities at a reasonable price. It also proves its mettle as a four-star hotel with an ample continental buffet breakfast at its otherwise decent in-house restaurant.

Stay where Italian composer Giuseppe Verdi stayed at the **(Hotel Europa** (Corso Giovecca 49, tel. 053/220-5456, www.hoteleuropa ferrara.com, €100–145 s/d), with the room's original 19th-century furniture and precious ceramic tile floor. But you won't go without modern conveniences like wireless Internet, minibar, and a lovely dining room.

If staying at a place with only four rooms doesn't just say homey, then the homemade cakes and jams at **Locanda Borgonuovo** (Via Cairoli 29, tel. 053/221-1100, www.borgon uovo.com, €95) will. Enjoy the shaded patio and free usage of bicycles.

A wonderful place to rest your head in the center of town, the elegantly furnished rooms at the **Locanda Modigliani** (Corso Giovecca 124, tel. 053/220-3042, www.locandamo digliani.it, €100 d) successfully take you far from home and into fantasyland. Reproductions by the artist for whom it is named hang over every bed.

Rooms at **Annunziata** (Piazza della Repubblica 5, tel. 053/220-1111, www.annunziata. it, €200–225 s/d) come with a view of Estense Castle. It has a tasteful ambience with antique furniture and modern art. Help yourself to a bike for exploring the city.

Food

Another Ferrarese institution where you can rub elbows with the ghosts of the past, **Al Brindisi** (Via Adelardi 11, tel. 053/220-9142, Tues.–Sun. 9 A.M.–1 A.M., €8) claims to have fed both Renaissance painter Titian and real Renaissance man Benvenuto Cellini. Opened in 1435, it's had plenty of time to hone the marriage of good regional cooking and fine wine. Place your trust in their menu.

Quel Fantastico Giovedi (Via Castelnuovo 9, tel. 053/276-0570, Fri.–Tues. noon–2:30 P.M. and 7–10:30 P.M., closed Aug., €10) is a renowned restaurant serving an eclectic menu

with items like duck liver scallops (but also any run-of-the-mill reliable pasta you might fancy). Good desserts can be enjoyed with live jazz music in the background.

Divine Providence seems to have spoken at this simple and elegant eatery. **La Provvidenza** (Corso Ercole d'Este 92–94, tel. 053/220-5187, Tues.–Sun. noon–3 P.M. and 7–10:30 P.M., €8) is just around the corner from the Certosa Monastery. Try fresh pasta with porcini mushrooms and truffles or pasta stuffed with pumpkin.

La Ripa (Via Ripagrande 21/a, tel. 053/276-5310, Wed.–Mon. 12:30–3 P.M. and 7–11 P.M., €8) serves traditional Ferrarese cuisine in a characteristically elegant Ferrarese building from the 15th century. Try pasta stuffed with pumpkin and *scaloppa alla estense* (veal steak). Top it off with pineapple mousse for dessert.

Information and Services

The main tourism office (Viale Cavour inside Castello Estense, tel. 053/220-9370, Mon.–Sat. 9 A.M.–1 P.M. and 2–6 P.M., Sun. 9:30 A.M.–1 P.M. and 2–5 P.M.) gives out a free guide called *Seven Bicycle Routes in the Province of Ferrara*. Start with the nine-kilometer path along the city's ancient city walls and pack a picnic if you plan on journeying any farther afield. For updated event information, visit www.ferrarainfo.com or www.estense.com.

Getting There and Around

The closest airport is in Bologna, about 45 kilometers away. If you are coming by car, take the A13 and the Ferrara North or the Ferrara South exits.

Around Ferrara
(ABBAZIA DI POMPOSA

The Benedictine monastery of Abbazia di Pomposa near Ferrara is one of the most important Romanesque buildings in Northern Italy dating from the middle of the 9th century. It houses a basilica, towering campanile, refectory, and dormitory that has been converted into a museum with displays of fine sculpture

EMILIA ROMAGNA

and paintings collected by the monastery over the centuries. Inside these walls the Italian composer Guido d'Arezzo devised the musical notes musicians still use today. The summer music festival **Musica Pomposa,** held June–September, celebrates classical and other genres with world-class performers from Italy and beyond. You can visit the museum next door to the monastery from 10 A.M.–12:30 P.M. and 2:30–5 P.M. in winter (closed Mon.), and 9 A.M.–1 P.M. and 2–7 P.M. in summer.

FAENZA

Faenza owes its name (originally Faïence) and notoriety to the earthenware pottery that potters have been making here since the second half of the 16th century. Visiting this town of roughly 50,000 people makes a nice day or half-day trip from nearby Ravenna, and is reachable by train.

Sights

Learn about the centuries-old tradition of ceramic-making at the **Museo Internazionale delle Ceramiche** (Via Campidori 2, tel. 054/669-7311, Tues.–Sat. 9 A.M.–7 P.M., Sun. 9:30 A.M.–1 P.M. and 3–7 P.M., €6). Pots, plates, and fine tableware from all over Italy, the Middle East, Far East, and North Africa are on display, along with modern works of art by Chagall, Matisse, and Picasso.

Piazza del Popolo, one of Italy's longest piazze lined with graceful arcades is home to two majestic palazzos: the **Palazzo del Podestà,** formerly the magistrate, and the **Palazzo del Municipio,** now the city government. The piazza runs into the **Piazza della Libertà,** which has an austere medieval cathedral **(Cattedrale di San Pietro Apostolo)** open every day 7 A.M.–noon and 4–6:30 P.M. Take note of the bronze, Baroque-style lions out front.

Entertainment and Events

Get ready for some medieval-style entertainment at the **Palio del Niballo** (www.racine.ra.it/niballo), held during the month of June. The noble Manfredi family started this competition between horsemen of the city's five neighborhoods in the Middle Ages and it's been luring onlookers ever since.

Pick up locally made ceramics and support the local ceramicists' guild during **Estate Ceramica** (Summer Ceramics). This popular summer-long event runs from June to the end of October and is held at the Exhibition Center in Corso Mazzini 92 (daily 10 A.M.–7 P.M., admission free). Forget mass production, these craftsmen shape their ceramics and other wares the old-fashioned way, using a lathe. At the **Mondial torninati,** held the first weekend in July, lathe experts descend on Faenza for a friendly competition amongst themselves.

Sports and Recreation

The annual 100-kilometer running race from Florence to Faenza gathers a couple thousand hard-core runners the last weekend of May. To beat the heat, you run through the night, starting in Florence at 3 P.M. on Saturday, and arriving in Faenza the following day, passing through at least a half-dozen pretty villages along the way. To register, go to www.100km. dinamica.it.

Accommodations

For a super quaint bed-amd-breakfast, rest your head at the **Locanda Paradiso** (Via Gallo Marcucci 48, tel. 054/623-400, www.locanda paradiso.it, €70 d). The 12 rooms are near the center of town and the Bucci Park, perfect for an early morning jog. They provide bikes, and you can bring your dog.

◖ **Vittoria** (Corso Garibaldi 23, tel. 054/621-508, www.hotel-vittoria.com €86 d) opened its doors in 1861, the same year that Italy became a united nation. The hotel has a strong sense of history in every room with lovely frescoed ceilings. There are gorgeous sitting rooms, an in-house restaurant, and even a gym with a swimming pool.

Food

In terms of ambience, you have the best of both worlds at **San Biagio Vecchio** (Via Salita di Oriolo 13, tel. 054/664-2057, Thurs.–Tues. 12:30–3 P.M. and 7:30–10:30 P.M., €8–10).

The interior feels like a quaint mountain chalet and has a fireplace, and you have a beautiful view of the whole of Romagna and the sea. The eclectic menu is built on the basics. The full meal option *(degustazione)* includes two appetizers, first and second courses, and a dessert, and is a good bargain (€25).

At **Marianaza** (Via Torricelli 21, tel. 054/668-1461, Thurs.–Tues. 12:30–2:30 P.M. and 7:30–10 P.M., €8), a matriarchal restaurant if there ever was one, the women run the kitchen and everything else—just like the wives of farmers who turned the region into a rich agricultural region. You could order the *piadine* for starters, followed by pasta (tagliatelle or tortelloni). Or you could skip all that and go straight to the heart of the matter: grilled meats, stuffed rabbit, or cod fish baked with leeks. There's mascarpone for dessert.

Getting There and Around

Fauna is a 30-minute train ride from Ravenna, and there are one or two trains every hour. The tourist office is in Piazza del Popolo 1 (tel. 054/625-231). It's a pleasant city to visit on bike or on foot.

The Adriatic Coast

The strip of Romagna along the Adriatic Coast has some of Italy's most sprawling sandy beaches. Rimini Riviera claims the country's longest coastline, at about 40 kilometers, so if you want a beach holiday, this is a good place to take it. And since the Romagnoli in these parts have been hosting tourists since before the country was unified in the mid-1800s, they've perfected lots of fun activities for visitors. You can enjoy modern-day water sports, thermal baths, discotheques, and of course, the great food for which the whole region is known. The best time to visit is late spring or summer.

◖ RAVENNA

Ravenna is to Emilia Romagna what Florence is to Tuscany. It's the undisputed capital of artistic wealth. Ravenna has the advantage of being lesser known than its Tuscan counterpart, and is relatively free of long lines of tourists to its main attraction—the early Christian and Byzantine mosaics. Tourists to Ravenna are a self-selective bunch. After all, it's not everyone who will queue to pay homage to Italy's father of poetry, Dante Alighieri, whose tomb lies in the center of town. But whether you consider yourself a highbrow tourist or more run of the mill, Ravenna should be on your agenda. All it takes is one morning or afternoon (though indulging yourself with one whole day here will only enrich) to absorb the city's subtle but powerful splendor.

Ravenna is near the Po River Delta, and not far from Ferrara, so you can easily spend a day or half-day listening to the call of birds at the Po River Delta park in between visits to these two artistic gems of cities.

Sights

Basilica di San Vitale (Via San Vitale, daily 9 A.M.–7 P.M., admission free) is one of Ravenna's eight monuments on UNESCO's World Heritage list. The octagonal church, begun in A.D. 527, has the largest and best-preserved Byzantine mosaics outside of Constantinople. Feast your eyes on the glory and pomp of the Byzantine world with these images of Emperor Justinian and Empress Theodora. There are also striking images of the Old Testament.

Don't miss Ravenna's oldest mosaics, housed in the **Mausoleo di Galla Placidia** (Via San Vitale, daily 9 A.M.–7 P.M.), built by and for Emperor Teodorico's daughter Galla Placidia. The powerful images, particularly *The Good Shepherd,* are bar none owing to the piercing blue and yellow colors in which they were done.

Take some time to visit the nearby **Museo Nazionale** (Via San Vitale, tel. 054/434-424, Tues.–Sun. 8:30 A.M.–7:30 P.M., €4), which

EMILIA ROMAGNA

monks started in the 18th century to keep tabs on their precious collections of prehistoric, Roman, Christian, and Byzantine artifacts.

You will feel the silence of reverence as you approach **Dante's tomb**, in part because a city ordinance calls for silence in this "Dante zone," in part because Italians have deep respect for their glorious man of letters, Dante Alighieri. Ravenna was the last place that Dante lived, and he died here in 1321. Ravenna was his most beloved city of exile (from his native Florence), and the city where he wrote the final verses of *Il Paradiso,* part of his masterpiece trilogy *The Divine Comedy.* A votive lamp filled with oil from Florence hangs above his tombstone. Pass by to pay your respects any time (8:30 A.M.–6 P.M. you can go inside the temple where the tomb rests). However, dusk or thereafter provides a particularly moving atmosphere.

The austere-looking **Chiesa di San Francesco** (daily 7:30 A.M.–noon and 3–7 P.M.), near Dante's tomb, is where the poet's funeral was believed to have taken place. Hold your breath before you visit the stunning 10th-century mosaics beneath the flooded crypt. As long as you are communing with literary ghosts, have a look at Lord Byron's house nearby.

Just behind the city's cathedral (also worth a quick visit, though this 1733 construction inevitably pales in comparison to all the town's pearls) is the **Museo Arcivescovile** (Piazza Arcivescovado, tel. 054/433-696, daily 9 A.M.–7 P.M., €3), housing objects from the city's first cathedral, the Ursiana, along with statues of the city's Byzantine emperors and other period objects.

Look up and envision the baptism of Christ surrounded by the 12 apostles (in mosaic form) in the dome of the **Battistero Neoniano** (Via Battistero, tel. 054/421-9938, daily 9 A.M.–7 P.M., €7.50). This structure likely began as a Roman bathhouse and was converted to a baptistery in the 5th century.

A bit outside town is **Sant'Apollinaire in Classe** (Via Romea Sud, tel. 054/447-3569, Mon.–Sat. 8:30 A.M.–7:30 P.M., Sun. 1–7:30 P.M., €2), a stunning 6th-century basilica built on the burial site of Ravenna's patron saint, Sant'Apollinare, responsible for converting the city to Christianity in the 2nd century. Take bus 4 to reach the church.

Accommodations

Dog lovers look no further. Come and pet the eight beautiful greyhound dogs at the **Palazzo Manzoni** (Via Ponte della Vecchia 23, tel. 054/455-4634, www.palazzomanzoni.it, €100 d) just outside of Ravenna (your own favorite companion will also feel right at home in the 20,000-square-meter fenced-in meadow). Staying at this 15th-century landowner's mansion will make you feel like you've gotten lost in the Secret Garden for a few days. Kick back, take one of the owner's bikes for a ride in the countryside or in town, and enjoy the homemade regional cooking.

If color-coordinated rooms are your fancy, consider **Mclub** (Piazza Baracca 26, tel. 054/437-538, www.m-club.it, €70–120 d). There are five rooms in five different colors in a recently restructured 15th-century palazzo. Count yourself lucky to get one of them, as you'll be surrounded by luxury for an evening (at least)! Located in the historical center near the mosaics. Price depends on the color of the room.

With tastefully decorated rooms featuring hardwood floors and canopy beds, **Hotel Diana** (Via Girolamo Rossi 47, tel. 054/439-164, www.hoteldiana.ra.it, €68–110 s/d) offers a comfortable respite not far from the main sights. There are four types of rooms, ranging from standard to executive (the difference is mainly in size). The hotel has parking next door for €10 a night, free on Sundays.

Food

Ravenna's most reputable restaurant, **Ca' De Ven** (Via Corrado Ricci 24, tel. 054/430-163, Tues.–Sun. 12:30–3 P.M. and 7:15–10:45 P.M., €8–12), is well deserving of its reputation. Even the basic *pasta e fagioli* (with beans) is done exceptionally well, not to mention the *cappelletti* and *tortelloni.* Try *ravioli con marmalade* for dessert.

The family-run **Antica Trattoria al Gallo** (Via Maggiore 87, tel. 054/421-3775, www.anticatrattoriadelgallo.191.it, Wed.–Sat. 12:30–3 P.M. and 7:30–11 P.M., Sun. 12:30–3 P.M., €7–11) has been doing pasta right for nearly a century. The largely vegetarian menu owes nothing to trends; they have simply stuck to Italy's best products all these years, so fresh tomato sauces feature widely.

Hats off to the world's best *brioche* (Italian-style croissant), in a cozy bar located just before the entrance to the historical center of town, appropriately called **C Dolci Fantasie** (Via Cesarea 3, tel. 338/503-9553, Thurs.–Tues.). You can choose between cream, ricotta cheese, marmalade, or chocolate versions. Even the *tramezzino* (the standard white bread sandwich) is delectable.

Information and Services
The main tourism office is at Via Salara 8 (tel. 054/435-755). The lost and found service operates from the city government headquarters at an office called **Servizio Economato** (Via Malfalda di Savoia 14, tel. 054/448-2152). The main police station is at Via Rocca Brancaleone 1 (tel. 054/448-2999).

The main hospital is **Ospedale Santa Maria delle Croci** (Via Randi 5, tel. 054/428-5111). There are several pharmacies in Ravenna called Farmacie comunali, and they take turns staying open 24 hours. There's one near the train station at Piazza Farini 6 (tel. 0544/212-835).

Getting There And Around
Trains run every hour from Bologna at eight minutes past the hour. The train station is at Piazza Farini Carlo Luigi 13. The main taxi stands are also at the train station, or you can call 054/433-888 to order a cab.

If you come by car, take the A14 from the north or the A14 or A1 from the south.

Ravenna has several car rental services. Two main ones are **Avis** (Via Candiano 12, tel. 054/459-1545) and **Europcar** (Via dell'Abate 21, tel. 054/461-675).

You can also rent a yellow bike at the tourism office, 8:30 A.M.–6:30 P.M.

CERVIA
This small seaside hamlet, a 20-minute train ride from Ravenna, is famous for its salt. It became a salt pond in the Middle Ages, and then languished into a marsh until Pope Innocent XII ordered new storage containers for the salt soon after the town became part of the Papal States. Today the salt museum is the biggest attraction.

Sights
Museo della Civiltà Salinara (Via N. Sauro, tel. 054/497-7592, €4) will teach you everything you ever wanted to know about salt—from how it was cultivated, the wars it sparked, and the trade that once thrived in Emilia Romagna. The museum closes at 6:30 P.M., but opening hours vary considerably from month to month so it may be worth calling in advance. Be sure to walk along the row of salt workers' homes in the town center.

Entertainment and Events
In homage to the sea and the fruits of the sea (like octopus, sea bass, and other seafood specialties)—and of course to the salt that gave Cervia its well-being and fame—locals gather for the **Sposalizio del Mare** (Circonvallazione Sacchetti 99, tel. 054/491-5211, www.comunecervia.it/turismo), one of Italy's most important sea celebrations. Follow devout Catholics to the port and onto boats, one of which is steered by a bishop who says mass and blesses the holiness of the sea. People have been practicing this rite since 1445. The Sposalizio usually takes place at the end of May.

Sports and Recreation
Deep in the heart of a pine forest is the perfect spot for some spa therapy at the **Terme di Cervia** (Via Forlanini 16, tel. 054/499-0111, Mon.–Sat. 7:30 A.M.–noon and 4–5:30 P.M.). Choose from a variety of mud, steam, and massage therapies that open up the pores and regenerate the skin.

Aquaria Park (Via dei Cosmonauti 23, tel. 054/499-0111, June–Sept.) in the Pinarella di Cervia is the place to entertain kids for an afternoon. It has a picnic area with a playground and a lake where you can go paddle boating. It also has its own nightclub.

Accommodations

If you are lucky enough to be at the **Jazz Country Club B&B** (Via Valle Felici 12, tel. 054/498-6123, www.jazzcountryclub.it, €60) on the third Friday of the month, you'll get serenaded by a jazz trio along with having a good night's sleep. During the day, ride one of the bikes to the sea or simply relax on the veranda.

For a great bargain that is a little more mainstream, stay at the **Antares Hotel** (Viale Italia 282, tel. 054/498-7414, www.antareshotel.it, €47–68 pp). Here you've got the lush surroundings of both the forest and the sea, enjoyed from the balcony in your room, plus a pool and a playground for the kids. The price includes all meals, plus access to the beach (and beach umbrella).

A luxurious hotel with its very own beauty farm, the **Hotel Aurelia** (Viale 2 Giugno 34, tel. 054/497-5451, www.selecthotels.it/hotel_aurelia, €71–145 s/d) also benefits from a private beach and is a few minutes' walk from the center of town. As if all that wasn't enough, it even has a lovely pool for beach-weary travelers. It's worth paying a little more for a room with a seaside view.

Food

A seafood lover's delight, the **Locanda dei Salinari** (Via XX Settembre 67, tel. 054/497-1133, daily noon–3 P.M. and 7–11 P.M., €10) has an eclectic menu that includes grilled octopus with baby tomatoes, and *branzino affumicato in casa servito con pan brioche* (smoked sea bass served with Italian sweet, soft bread called *pan brioche*).

The menu at **Al Teatro** (Via Circonvallazione Socchetti 32, tel. 054/471-639, www.ristorantealteatro.it, Tues.–Sun., €10) matches the ambience in tastefulness. Expect fresh fish, homemade bread, and fine wines. There are no meat dishes.

Getting There and Around

Trains run every hour between Cervia and Ravenna (it's the Cervia–Milan route). The trip takes 20 minutes. The tourism office is at Viale dei Milli 65 (tel. 054/497-4400).

◖ RIMINI

You meant to come to the Italian Riviera, but it looks rather like the Atlantic City boardwalk here. Don't worry, the beach is arguably more beautiful, and Italy's big beach party town (and Europe's longest stretch of sand, at 15 kilometers), is more than the beloved *mare* with all of the glitz that surrounds it. Like all Italian towns, Rimini is not bereft of its *centro storico,* with a castle, ancient Roman ruins, and a temple housing the tomb of the mistress of Italian Renaissance prince par excellence Sigismondo Malatesta. So wake up, beach bums, and journey inland!

Sights

The **Tempio Malatestiano** (Via IV Novembre 35, Mon.–Sat. 8 A.M.–12:30 P.M. and 3:30–6:30 P.M., Sun. 9 A.M.–1 P.M. and 3:30–7:30 P.M.) is a burial chapel for Sigismondo Malatesta and his mistress Isotta degli Atti. Note the fresco of Sigismondo kneeling before his patron saint, Sigismondo. The Malatesta family, who ruled Rimini during the Middle Ages, is best known for another secret love affair. Gianciotto killed his wife Francesca da Polenta, and his brother Paolo, for adultery, an episode that Dante immortalized in the *Inferno* of the *Divine Comedy*. The unfinished facade on the front of the church was a work in progress by Renaissance architect Leon Battista Alberti.

Sigismondo Malatesta had **Castel Sigismondo** (Piazza Malatesta, tel. 054/129-192, Tues.–Fri. 8:30 A.M.–12:30 P.M. and Sat.–Sun. 5–7 P.M.) built in 1438 in the southwestern corner of town. The feckless leader was condemned to hell by Pope Pius II for sins including adultery, rape, and murder.

Take a walking tour of Rimini's Roman remains (the city was an important Roman colony called Ariminum), starting at the **Arco di Augusto** (Arch of Augustus), built in 27 B.C. at the southeastern end of Corso d'Agosto. Moving along in time you'll find the **Ponte di**

© ALESSIA RAMACCIA

Ponte di Tiberio leading to Rimini

Tiberio (Tiberius' Bridge), built in the 1st century A.D., at the west end of Corso d'Agosto. At the corner of Viale Rome and Via Bastioni Orientali are remains of a Roman amphitheater, with a former Roman forum beneath Piazza Tre Martiri.

Nightlife

Cure your craving for Guinness at one of Italy's best Irish pubs, the **Barge Pub** (Viale Tintori 13, tel. 054/170-9845, Tues.–Sun. 11 A.M.–1 A.M.), which also serves Kilkenny and Harp beer, along with homemade Irish food and live music.

For a relaxing beachside cafe, visit the **Sari Café** (Lungomare Spadazzi 142, tel. 054/137-7171, Apr.–Sept.), and bask in sunsets until late September. Its patch of beachfront is run by the Ricci family, who have been in business for 60 years and know the art of relaxing by the sea.

Mingle with the locals at **L'Ombelico del Mondo** (Piazzale Kennedy 11, tel. 054/121-105, daily open 24 hours), an informal but very chic

cocktail bar in the center of Rimini where the *mare* (sea) is never out of sight.

Il Caffé delle Rose (Viale Vespucci 1, tel. 054/123-038, Tues.–Sun. 9 A.M.–1 A.M.) captures local film director Federico Fellini's idea of *la dolce vita* better than any other place in town. Enjoy live jazz music and regional snacks like *piadine* and salamis until late.

Discoteca Byblos (Via Pozzo Castello 24, tel. 054/169-0252, daily 9 P.M.–2:30 A.M.), is an old villa turned nighttime retreat with two floors of dancing, a pool, and a bar.

Sports and Recreation

Since the end of the 19th century, people have been coming to the coast here for sports and recreation, from beach volleyball to the all-night discos. The **Blue Beach Center** (Zona Pascoli along *lungomare*, tel. 0541/382-456) is the heart of it all, with canoes, pedal boats, surfing, motorboats, sailboats, and banana boats. Come for a day (or two) of fun.

If you've never seen dolphins outside of Florida, here's your chance. See them perform

EMILIA ROMAGNA

EMILIA ROMAGNA

THE EMILIA ROMAGNA DIFFERENCE

Watch some Fellini films (obligatory is his autobiographical *Amarcord*), and ready yourself for good times in Emilia Romagna, where the men are said to be as ornery as the women are boisterous. The people here are known for being unabashed in their moves and yet irreproachable. Life is live theater – just as it was for Federico Fellini, a frontiersman of neorealism during Italy's golden era of cinema, who turned real life into art, using non-professional actors to capture daily life in post-war Italy.

Fellini himself was from Rimini, and several of the movement's star directors like Michelangelo Antonioni and Cesare Zavattini also hailed from Emilia Romagna. These guys were masters at tapping into the heart and soul of the real Italy because they were surrounded by it.

Although Italy's post-war economic well-being would start to morph (and arguably corrupt) the Italian soul in certain parts of the country, in Emilia Romagna, ironically Italy's wealthiest region, the soul may have duly turned a shade staid, but it basically stayed intact.

Walk into a bar, and it's likely that the waiter will pick up on your accent and ask you where you're from, and also if you like his city. People everywhere dispense good advice just as they serve you their gold-standard Lambrusco wine: with know-how and pleasure.

And some things appear to have truly stayed the same since Fellini's 1953 *I Vitelloni* (The Young Bulls), the story of four rabble-rousing fellas out to make sense of life and have a good time. Women, take note: It's been observed that the guys here do like to flirt. They seem to have radar for attractive foreign females, whom they chase without the vulgar come-ons you might get elsewhere in Italy.

But take the ego boost in kind. Remember that life is generally playful in these parts, and look around and you'll soon discover the local women are truly fine (try to decode and steal their secrets). And they're not roosting at home either, where stereotypes have always said the men want them.

You see beautiful women who are mothers and professionals dressed to perfection, strolling confidently with their adorably dressed children. You meet grandmotherly types on trains and buses, or kneeling in church. They wear lively but not gaudy jewelry, thick wire-framed glasses, and maybe the latest Armani diamond-studded t-shirts. And they are all smiles: You wonder nearly out loud how they get away with such style, sweetness, and strength at the same time. Their fortitude and aplomb come with a history. Women in this region fought alongside men in the partisan movement during World War II, and they were the first women to study at university in Italy, at the University of Bologna.

Observe their moves while people-watching in Bologna's Piazza Maggiore or walking the streets of Emilia Romagna's fun-loving and graceful towns. Your privileged gaze is privy to lessons that Miss Manners' charm school don't impart.

Some people say there's a notable difference between the people of Emilia, the inland part of the region, and the people of Romagna, the coastal region. The former are known to be serious, hard-working, precise – traits associated with Northern Italians; while the latter look like Fellini's characters: outgoing, funny, and full of fantasy.

Whatever the distinction might be, the people here are unlikely to change soon. Italians' love of tradition and reticence to change (hence their ubiquitous attachment to their hometowns) is well rooted in Emilia Romagna. Here that means being groomed to be charming and friendly, so if you meet a nice *pizzaiolo*, rest assured he will likely still be there come the next decade, ready to greet you again.

live at the **Delfinario** (Via Lungomare Tintori 2, tel. 054/150-298, www.delfinariorimini.it, €11), which also has a sea gallery showcasing the whole underwater universe. It's open June–September with several shows everyday, usually starting at 4:45, 6, and 9 P.M.

Fiabilandia (Via Cardano 15, tel. 054/137-2064, www.fiabilandia.net/, two-day passes cost €18) is a child's dream park come true. It's a man-made island of pure fun, with water slides, theme rides, and even a disco just for the kids.

Accommodations

Well placed on the boardwalk, with fabulous views of the sea, the **Hotel Kyriad Vienna** (Viale Regina Elena 11, tel.0541/391-744, www.ciminohotels.it, €45–102 pp) is an excellent choice for a sea-going holiday. Guests have access to the hotel's private beach and a rather garish-looking in-house restaurant that changes the menu daily and serves the freshest catch of the day.

Staying at the **Grand Hotel di Rimini** (Parco Federico Fellini 1, tel. 0541/560-00, www.grandhotelrimini.com, €150–300) is a privileged experience, one that seems unchanged from its inauguration in 1908. Film director Federico Fellini immortalized his hometown's hotel when as a boy he described the elegant institution as "a fable of riches, luxury and oriental splendor."

To get away from the beach-seeking throng, head to the hillside. **Agriturismo Case Mori** (Via Monte L'Abbate 9, località San Martino Monte L'Abbate, tel. 054/173-1262, www.casemori.it, €70–90) is near a refreshing little lake as well as a forest if you fancy a hike. Meals are served on request and consist of typical regional food made with fresh farm products.

Food

At least once during your trip you should treat your palate really, really well. The **Acero Rossi** (Viale Tiberio 11, tel. 054/153-577, www.acerorosso.it, Tues.–Sun. noon–3 P.M. and 7:30–11 P.M., €9–13), an unpretentious but refined eatery in the old part of town, responds to the task with a menu that is nuanced and creative, and deeply satisfying. Try tortellini stuffed with seafood.

Fish lovers, the *grigliata mista* (grilled fish) is great at **Picnic** (Via Tempio Malatestiano 3, tel. 054/121-916, €10). It's appropriately named, as they have a bit of everything, including pizza. Start with some simple and very fresh *spaghetti allo scoglio* (spaghetti with seafood). Come with good company because service is slow.

If you're tired of fish and craving grilled meat and good pasta, the **Osteria Tiresia** (Via XX Settembre 41, tel. 054/178-1896, Tues.–Sun. 12:30–3:30 P.M. and 7–10:30 P.M., €8–10) will treat you well. It has a lovely rustic ambience with a piano that regularly gets played at lunch and dinner.

Information and Services

The main tourism office is located at Piazza Malatesta 28 (tel. 054/171-6371, daily 8:30 A.M.–7 P.M.). There are a few other tourist offices throughout the city, including one at the main train station, at Piazzale Cesare Battisti (tel. 054/151-331).

For emergencies, call 113. The main police station is at Corso d'Augusto 192. The **Infermi Hospital** is at Via Settembrini 2. For emergencies, call 054/170-5111.

Getting There and Around

Rimini has its own airport, the **Rimini-San Marino International Airport** (www.rimini-airport.com). For information and booking, call 054/171-5711. There are daily flights from Rome and Milan, as well as European cities. You can take the train directly from Rome or Bologna, or arrive by car on the A14 from Milan or Bari, and get off at Rimini Sud.

Rimini is easy to reach by train and the station is at the northern edge of the small historic quarter. It's a very walkable city, and walking in any direction, you're bound to hit the beach.

◖ PO DELTA

The Po Delta is a vast plain covered by wetlands and reedy marshes, a stunningly romantic landscape, particularly on misty days that

EMILIA ROMAGNA

typify the climate. Apart from visiting the natural park, with more than 350 different species of birds, you can visit the Great Woods of Mesola, an untouched nature reserve with the same flora and fauna that existed when the woods were the hunting grounds for the noble Renaissance Este family. One of Italy's most important monasteries is also located in the delta, at Pomposa, a Benedictine monastery built between the 6th and 7th centuries.

Sights

The **Po River Delta Regional Park** (tel. 053/331-4003, www.parcodeltapo.it) covers 700 square meters and has been protected as a UNESCO World Heritage Site since 1995. You can spend one or two intense days exploring its mysterious and enriching landscape, which is filled with rare species, from orchids to whitewater lilies, and many species of birds.

Within the park is the **Eco-Long Grass Folk Museum** (Bioregione Valle del Lamone Villanova di Bagnacavallo, tel. 0545/471-22), a one-of-a-kind museum featuring over 2,000 objects made out of the same long grass that grows in the Po River Delta. Watch weavers craft mats, brooms, shoes, and hats from the grass.

Accommodations

Youth Hostel Antico Convento di San Francesco (Via Cadorna 10, tel. 054/560-622, www.ostellosanfrancesco.com, €30) is located in a former 13th-century Franciscan convent and has 19 large rooms with single or bunk beds, with communal television and breakfast rooms. Ideal for singles and families alike. You don't have to be a "youth" to stay here.

Conveniently located in the heart of the delta, the **USPA** (Piazza della Libertà 9, tel.

0533/999-817, €85 d) is an ideal place to stay for exploring the Po Delta for a few days. An in-house restaurant serves delicious seafood specialties.

Food

With an eclectic menu replete with both meat and fish courses, the **Due Leoni** (located in the village of Ariano Polesine, tel. 042/637-2129, www.ristorantedueleoni.it, €10) is a tasty aside during your park tour. It also doubles as a small hotel. Top off a meal with the fig gelato.

In the midst of the park, **Locanda del Bosco** (Via Forconcelli 2, tel. 053/379-5546, www.locandadelbosco.it, €10) treats hikers to local cooking in an old farmhouse villa near the Great Woods of Mesola.

Information and Services

The park is divided into six stations: Volano, Mesola, Goro; Comacchio; Valli of Comacchio; San Vitale Pinewood and Piallasse of Ravenna; Classe Pinewood and Cervia Salines; and Campotto di Argenta, where you can begin your visit by bike or boat.

The main **park office** is in Comacchio (Province of Ferrara, tel. 053/331-4003, www.ildeltadelpo.it) at Via Cavour 11. Ask about their unmissable motorboat tours through the delta.

Getting There and Around

To get to the park by car from the A13 highway, take the Ferrara/Comacchio/Lidi motorway. From the A14 take the Ravenna exit and follow the signs for the park.

By train, you can stop at stations in Ferrara, Ostellato, Codigoro, Argenta, Alfonsine, Ravenna or Cervia.

LE MARCHE

Dolce, the Italian word that means both gentle and sweet, best describes the landscape and people of one of Italy's least-visited regions. The soft rolling hills and the often-reserved nature of the inhabitants invites comparison with the Iowa landscapes that Grant Wood painted. Green takes on another hue in Le Marche, where its color is more emerald than Tuscany's and brighter than the deep greens of neighboring Umbria. Le Marche firmly remains the land of small family industry and farms. Shoemakers still cut leather and hammer shoes in their homes or in small workshops. Here even a person from the next town over is a stranger.

Marchigiani exude neither the spirited, dark wit of Neapolitans nor the bravado of Romans. "Better a dead person in the house than a Marchigiano at the door," is the old Italian saying that refers to their role as tax collectors for the pope. No wonder few Italians visit the region. That specter has been replaced by a region that has now set out the welcome mat. Residents are eager to assist visitors and make time for conversation. They like to share the beauty of their territory and their fine crafts. They will pause to give you exacting directions or even walk or drive you to the sight you seek. That's just part of Le Marche.

Castles, fortresses, lovely hilltop towns, wineries, the sea, fine paintings, architecture that reflects the measure of the land, medieval monasteries, and the Sibylline Mountains round out the picture. Le Marche's hills are dotted with silvery olive trees, lined with vineyards, and covered with amber grain that in early spring

HIGHLIGHTS

Urbino: Birthplace of artistic genius Raffaelo, Urbino was abuzz as an intellectual think-tank and magnet for Renaissance artists that aspired toward The Ideal City. Renaissance palaces now house a city lively with university students and arts programs (page 478).

Urbania: Regal Urbania is known for its ceramics and language schools, and also features a palatial hunting lodge set in a wooded landscape. It's easy to integrate into town life here if you want to go beyond the scope of a casual tourist (page 482).

Fano: The town of Fano features significant ancient archeological artifacts from Picene to Roman times, as well as an advantageous location on the Adriatic Sea. Enjoy exploring the artistic treasures that inspired Robert Browning, watch contemporary gladiators compete in a chariot race during the Fano dei Cesari festival,

or just relax under an umbrella and lounge chair by the shoreline (page 485).

Pesaro: As the birthplace of composer Gioachino Rossini, the city of Pesaro is a pilgrimage for opera buffs. Fans journey here for the Rossini Festival in July and August and to visit Rossini's birthplace, now a museum and art gallery. Pesaro is also the best place to buy Italian ceramics. Check out the Museo delle Ceramiche to see superb Renaissance plates (page 488).

Senigallia: The sandy beach scene attracts Northern Europeans to this town, but Italian food connoisseurs head to Senigallia for one of Italy's best seafood meals at Uliassi restaurant. This is the kind of cuisine foodies will travel hundreds of kilometers to savor (page 491).

Conero Peninsula: Even seasoned travelers spoiled by the beauty of the Caribbean or Hawaii will succumb to the charms of Parco Conero, which is also an important winemaking area. Sip your Rosso Conero or Lacrima di Morro d'Alba while you stay in a Napoleonic fort at the edge of the sea or perched in a hilltop medieval town with a panoramic view of pristine water and forests that reach the rugged coastline (page 498).

Urbisaglia: The Roman amphitheater in Urbisaglia's valley and a hillside theater are part of Le Marche's most important ancient ruins. Once a contemporary of Pompeii, this town still puts on impressive shows, including a delightful annual Roman banquet where the townsfolk outfit you in period garb (page 511).

Ascoli Piceno: Elegant Ascoli Piceno, the region's southern star on the border of Abruzzo, is paved with luminous stone that in Piazza del Popolo forms a grand outdoor drawing room. Ascoli's ancient towers rival those in San Gimignano, and its medieval pageant is one of Italy's best (page 521).

SAN MARINO

Adriatic Sea

Pesaro
Fano
Urbino
Urbania
Senigallia
Ancona
Conero Peninsula
Fabriano
Perugia
Urbisaglia
Ascoli Piceno
Apennine
Spoleto
L'Aquila
Mountains

0   30 mi
0   30 km

LOOK FOR **(** TO FIND RECOMMENDED SIGHTS, ACTIVITIES, DINING, AND LODGING.

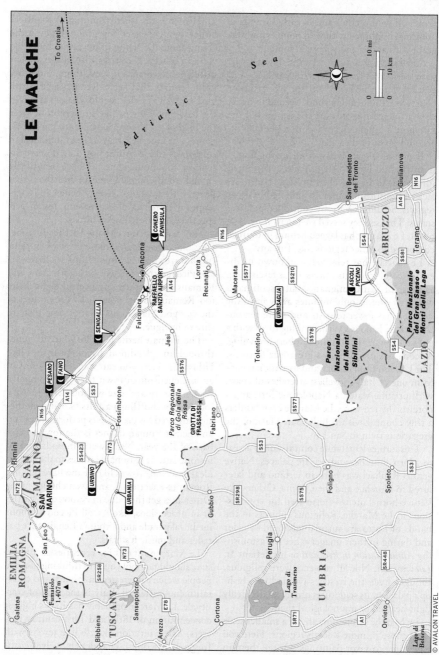

LE MARCHE

© AVALON TRAVEL

shows off wild orchids and in early summer is drenched bright red with wild poppies and fragrant with acacia and yellow broom.

Small theaters enliven even the tiniest towns with performances. Le Marche's palaces and castles were the backdrop for Renaissance courts in Urbino and beyond. Second to none, they attracted not only artistic genius but the foremost mathematicians, philosophers, writers, and poets of their day.

Economic power is dispersed among family industry and farms. All this has contributed somewhat to Le Marche's mystery and to its lack of significant tourism compared to other regions. So did its Vatican-controlled political status. That secrecy served well in its time. As a result, Le Marche has lagged behind in tourism compared to other regions like Tuscany.

Le Marche has relatively unknown medieval Ascoli Piceno: its towers are as fascinating as those of San Gimignano, but Ascoli has a warmer luster, is only minutes away from the sea, and has fewer tourists and more reasonable prices. Fano is a yacht-making town with a guardian angel that inspired Robert Browning. Ancona has one of Italy's great jazz festivals. The Conero Promontory and its national park form one of Italy's loveliest stretches of coast, with pristine water, a Napoleonic fort, and a noteworthy red wine. Le Marche even borders a tiny country within Italy, San Marino, the gregarious twin to San Leo.

This former Papal state commissioned artists to adorn churches and private palaces. Native genius Raphael was born in Urbino and later lured to Florence and then Rome. Others like Venice-born Lorenzo Lotto vied for commissions in Le Marche. Religious subjects in the hands of Lotto are surprisingly bold in color and daring in their imagery: See his astonishing *Annunciation in Recanati* or his defiant *St. Lucy* in Jesi. Not all subjects were religious, though. Even the frescoes painted in a bishop's palace or its sculptures often had decidedly light-hearted or mythological themes.

Le Marche's museums are on a smaller scale than those in more-known regions. Here you have time to savor paintings. Or see them in situ, like in Fano, where paintings by Raphael's father, by his master Perugino, and even the young apprentice hang in the same church, so you can observe the styles that link as well as differentiate them. Or see Urbino and other noble courts that were Renaissance think tanks as well as residences for the top artists of the day. Small towns like Fossombrone were the birthplace of noteworthy Baroque artists: names like Guerrieri may be less familiar than celebrities like Bernini, but they deserve attention, too. Some churches have beautifully carved wood choirs by master craftsmen that portray Renaissance street scenes and cityscapes with remarkable precision, use of perspective, and sometimes whimsy.

You can also travel back further in time. City and archaeological museums have intriguing bronzes and ceramics from ancient warrior Picenes, their Greek trading partners, and Romans that set their engineering sights here, too. Roman frescoes or miniature sculptures of the war god Mars in his "Napoleonic" hat are sure to intrigue.

The Roman heritage of Le Marche comes through in splendid archaeological sites like Urbisaglia. Here you can wander the ruins of an ancient Roman town that was Pompeii's contemporary and size without 21st-century tour groups shuffling past. Its two ancient theaters are used for prestigious performances and an ancient Roman dinner is the town's main bash of the year. Nearby accommodations in historic sites at reasonable prices make this an ideal base, too. Towns liked Fano have popular Roman re-enactments and even chariot races. Other ages get their due in Napoleonic battles or in processions, like Ascoli Piceno's famous medieval parade and Urbino's Renaissance parades and music festivals.

Le Marche's status for centuries as a Papal state should not fool you into thinking that the people weren't interested in fantasy and entertainment—after all, Italy is the land of Carnevale. Le Marche probably has Italy's highest concentration of 18th- and 19th-century theaters. Their interiors dazzle like jewels with frescoes, balconies, chandeliers, velvet cush-

© JUDY EDELHOFF

Macerata

ioned seats, tassels, fringe, and stucco. Attend a performance to enhance the pleasure, but don't miss at least a peek.

The region is also full of mystery and surprises. Legends are everywhere: the Sibyls and their prophecies in the mountains named for them; the devil that butted his horn to form holes in Tolentino's bridge; the infant in Urbisaglia that preferred to be nursed by a she-goat instead of a human; the alchemy of Cagliostro that landed him in San Leo's prison; and the Holy Family's house that became airborne in the Holy Land, transported by angels that set it down in Loreto.

Performing arts are alive and well here, even in the smallest town. Music in all forms is first-rate. Jazz swings in Ancona and in small-town venues. Or see opera in Pesaro, Rossini's town. Don't miss outdoor performances in Urbisaglia's ancient Roman theater or amphitheater. Or opera in Macerata's prestigious Sferisterio outdoor arena. World-class performers and directors work their magic in opera, jazz, classical music, and theater.

Demanding gourmets will be delighted in this land of star chefs. Italians from other regions admit that some of Italy's best cooks hail from Le Marche. Much of the cuisine is grounded in tradition, but master chefs bring food to new heights like Senigallia's two sublime fish restaurants that create the latest trends. On the coast, tradition reigns alongside innovation. The seafood stew, *brodetto,* varies from town to town but almost always calls for 13 types of fish, shellfish, and crustaceans. Simple cuisine like fried food requires a deft touch, at which towns like Ascoli excel. In less than an hour you can be in the mountains in the midst of the terrain of wild boar, mushrooms, and truffles.

Le Marche is the Italy everyone is nostalgic for: small *trattorie,* superb fresh ingredients, simple decor, and reasonable prices. A meal in a rural home here can easily beat most gourmet restaurants abroad. Even the family pig eats pasta and table scraps for dinner. Marchegiana steaks, Ascolani olives, and local produce are Italy's best. And prices won't break the bank, even for the superb wines. Festivals, especially frequent in summer, usually feature food and drink. Mix in with the locals. Watch that reserve slip away as the excellent local wine and conversation flow.

As for recreation, on the coast the beach scene is at its peak in August and offers a complete range of water sports. Those that prefer sardine-like mobs head for Civitanova, while the unspoiled rugged Conero coastline offers stunning natural beauty and plenty of hiking in the hills. Mountain sports include winter skiing. Neither has the chic patina of some Tuscan beaches or Cortina resorts, so expect a more laid-back atmosphere and lower prices. There are densely wooded forests and some of Europe's most spectacular caves to explore.

If you prefer nature a bit cushier, head for the yachts in Fano. If you want to relax or get massaged into shape, the hills and mountains are dotted with small spas fed by various types of mineral springs that gush nearby, some already well tested by ancient Roman or medieval travelers. Bear in mind that most spas are reasonably priced because they have not yet been gussied up.

Dress in Le Marche is informal. Power suits are still essential for a presentation to buyers from Milan, at trade fairs, and special occasions. But in the vineyard, shoe factory, or on the farm, the reigning style is practical. People are aware of the trends, though—after all they are making shoes and clothes for fashion houses around the world. This is a place for leisure, so measure your pace accordingly and you'll cherish your visit.

PLANNING YOUR TIME

Le Marche is the only region in Italy that refers to itself in the plural (The Marches), as if to hint that its treasures are not centralized. Indeed, as you drive through the region they are dispersed. Le Marche has no blockbuster city like Florence or Rome, no one showstopper like Assisi in Umbria that draws art crowds as well as religious pilgrims. If you're exhausted from intense cultural marathons in Italy's major art capitals, Le Marche offers the right antidote.

Its lovely cities and towns have no shortage of masterpieces that unfold before you along with the rolling landscape.

Low-cost air service to Ancona makes Le Marche fly-into instead of fly-over land. Raffaello Sanzio Airport, also called Ancona-Falconara, sees few American tourists but the British have been wise to it for some time. Ryanair offers direct flights daily from London Stansted and other European cities. A car is by far the best way to see the small towns of Le Marche. Begin in Ancona, a city that is much less intimidating for a first-time visitor to navigate than driving in Rome or Milan. Avis, Europe Car, Hertz, and Maggiore Budget have offices at the airport.

If you want to move around Italy without a car from Ancona, it's easy by train. The Ancona–Rome line is east–west, while the Milano–Lecce line covers north–south points. Both are served by the speedier Eurostar. If you want to move around mostly within Le Marche, note that many towns are not served by train and that bus connections will require a bit more planning. Ancona's main bus terminal is at Piazza Cavour. If you don't speak any Italian, it's usually better to ask for bus route information in a major city like Ancona where more English-speaking staff is likely to be present. Inquire about bus company names, too. Unlike the national train system, inter-city bus travel is not dominated by a single company.

Ancient Greeks, Romans, and others shuttled around the Adriatic and Eastern Mediterranean by ship and you can do the same. From luxury Mediterranean cruise to inexpensive overnight ferries, you can shove off from the Port of Ancona (tel. 071/207-891, www.autoritaportuale. ancona.it) to Greece, Croatia, Turkey, Cyprus, or Israel, to name a few. If you've purchased a car abroad or have a long-term rental, keep in mind that you can roll right onto some ferries with it; ships often arrive at port in early morning hours when you can drive off at your next destination before rush-hour traffic begins. Sea options work equally well for pre-planners or free spirits that decide it just might be fun to do lunch in Dubrovnik today.

HISTORY

Two major influences in the formation of Le Marche are everpresent: the ancient Picenes that were later subjugated by the Romans, and the Catholic Church that dominated the region in later centuries. The origin of the Picenes is unclear, but they most likely came from across the Adriatic. Their range extended throughout Le Marche and down into Abruzzo. They had early links with the Etruscans in the 7th and 6th centuries B.C. as well as the ancient Greeks. The Picene confederation formed an alliance with Rome in 299 B.C. and unsuccessfully rebelled 30 years later. That act resulted in the forced transfer of many Picenes to the Gulf of Salerno, south of Naples. Picenes used war chariots and buried their dead, often with amber beads, which suggest a strong Eastern influence.

Christianity initially took hold from the East through Ancona, with additional maritime ports like Pesaro, Fano, and Senigallia coming under Byzantine influence. Known as "Marca," or "border territory," in the 10th century, Pepin the Short and Charlemagne gave this region to the Popes. In the 13th–15th

centuries, various noble families dominated and their territory expanded from the major towns. Into the spotlight stepped families like the Montefeltro in Urbino, who rose to power 1155–1508 and were later overthrown by the Della Rovere clan. The Malatestas ruled Pesaro up to 1445 and the Sforza family were also active movers and shakers. The widespread power of local dynasties eventually fell under Papal rule with a brief interruption of the status quo during Napoleon's Italian campaign.

Communities developed small cottage industries alongside traditional agricultural enterprises that had been going since 1000. Tenant farming and the lack of trade opportunity kept towns self-sufficient and isolated. The unification of Italy at the end of the 19th century brought little rapid change. Today the area still excels at industries like shoe, clothing, furniture, and even accordion manufacturing. Le Marche remains hampered by lack of major communication routes (its only *autostrada* is on the coast) and earthquakes in the last decade haven't helped things. For visitors, this means pleasant secondary roads to explore and a great way to discover of Le Marche.

Pesaro-Urbino and Northern Le Marche

Urbino is the undisputed star in Le Marche's crown, but the province of Pesaro-Urbino is full of delightful jewels to keep a traveler enchanted. Urbino is Raffaello's birthplace and was home to one of the Renaissance's most brilliant courts. Like most of Pesaro-Urbino's northern interior, Urbino is set against a backdrop of dense forest, mountains, gushing springs, and rivers that provide a scenic, winding entry into neighboring Tuscany, Umbria, and Emilia Romagna. This Renaissance town built by Duke Federico da Montefeltro quickly rivaled that of Florence, Venice, and Rome for its cultural and scientific riches and lively intellectual court.

San Marino, the flashier medieval twin city to Urbino, also happens to be a country, tiny as

it is, within Italy. It lures sightseers giddy with the novelty of visiting this foreign turf, who also find it's great for shopping.

Urbania's Renaissance leisure palace, designed by the same architect that helped the Duke Federico da Montefeltro create a world-class city in Urbino, has a bright feel to it and now hosts an intriguing ceramics collection. Urbania's northern interior forests are perfect for hikers, its monasteries offer remote retreats, and the rivers are great for rafting and fishing. Gourmets appreciate that both white and black truffles, which are perfect with Le Marche's excellent wines, can be sniffed out in late fall and winter,

On the coast, the city of Pesaro, Giocchino Rossini's hometown, lures opera buffs. Known today for its furniture makers and agriculture, Pesaro has a ceramics tradition that dates back to the 16th century. Pesaro also has charming Art Nouveau villas near the beach and is close to Renaissance palaces in the surrounding towns.

The city of Fano has a more lighthearted atmosphere than the other cities in the region. They say all roads lead to Rome, and the Via Flaminia that begins in Rome's Piazza Venezia ends right here in Fano on the coast. This road makes for a lovely approach to hill towns like Fossombrone, from where you could dart up to Urbino, then back to continue toward Urbania and then eventually into Tuscany.

◖ URBINO

Duke Federico of Montefeltro was a politician, a patron of the arts, and a mathematician, and he had the determination to build an ideal city. He created a network of castles and forts in the land where Urbino sits aloft in the northern hills of Le Marche, isolated and majestic. The Duke's court was a genius magnet. In his time (1442–1482), it attracted artists and mathematicians like Piero della Francesa and architects like Leon Battista Alberti and Luciano Laurana that would leave their pleasing sense of proportion, perspective, color, and geometry as an imprint on this city—as did poets, diplomats, and writers. The buildings, the art, and treatises they left provided a sense of aesthetics that permeated down to the cobblestones.

Today, students at the university outnumber the townsfolk by more than two to one and help mold the contemporary personality of the town. The 15th-century castles and palaces catch the sound and reverberate lively youth and contemporary trends. Urbino also has tourism, but its remote location results in a flow rather than a logjam. Visitors seek the town's splendors, which come with a Renaissance patina. It's hard to grasp in a single day, because life at court itself was not a day trip, it took time. The journey to Urbino was long, and upon arrival immersion was full.

You may only have a day to dedicate to Urbino, but once you immerse yourself in it,

the house where Raffaello was born in Urbino

you can admire its past splendors. Observe a bit more and today's Urbino will come through, too. Urbino could be a one-act Renaissance industry, but even when it stays in theme it offers quality period music, skilled instrument makers, and a bookbinder that does students' theses but also keeps up the finer art of the trade. What you are not likely to see right away is that rather than being overshadowed by the Renaissance, intellectual and artistic exchange continues to flourish. As godfather to the late Francesco Amatori's children, Michelangelo received much appreciated "care packages" of *caciotta d'Urbino* cheese from his widow, mentioned in their letters between 1557 and 1561. Later he even bought farmland in Le Marche near Casteldurante to be sure that his cravings for the cheese would continue to be satisfied and future supplies expedited.

Urbino takes on another air in the summer when the students are gone. There are workshops for musicians, artists, writers, and those who wish to improve their Italian language skills through one of the university programs.

Immerse yourself in Urbino and you might come closer to the ideal that the powerful Duke sought to create.

Sights

Galleria Nazionale delle Marche (Palazzo Ducale, tel. 0722/322-625, Mon. 8:30 A.M.–2 P.M., Tues.–Sun. 8:30 A.M.–7:15 P.M., €8), Urbino's art museum, is within the Ducal Palace, as are museums of archaeology, ceramics, and an underground section (not all are always open, ask at tourist office). Highlights include the *Mute Woman* by Raffaello, incredible 16th-century *intarsio* (inlaid wood) doors and panels that adorn the palazzo. There's also a painting of *An Ideal City*, and Piero della Francesca's enigmatic *Flagellation of Christ.*

To see where Raffaello was born, visit **Casa Natale di Raffaello** (Via Raffaello 57, tel. 0722/320-105, daily 9 A.M.–1 P.M. and 3–7 P.M., €3). The house is furnished as it would have been in the artist's time and contains one fresco by Raffaello and several paintings by his father.

Fortezza Albornoz (daily 9 A.M.–6 P.M., admission free) is in Parco della Resistenza, a hilltop city park with a panoramic view of Urbino and the countryside, ideal for a picnic.

Biglietto Unico, a discount ticket with admission to a number of sights, costs €10 and must be purchased at the information center (Mon.–Sat. 9 A.M.–6 P.M. and Sun 9 A.M.–1 P.M.) outside the city walls at Borgo Mercatale. Sights include the **Oratorio San Giovanni** (Via Barocci 31, tel. 0722/320-936, Mon.–Sat. 10 A.M.–12:30 P.M., 3–5:30 P.M., Sun. 10 A.M.–12:30 P.M.), a late 14th-century church dedicated to John the Baptist, with a 1416 fresco cycle that is considered Italy's best expression of the International Gothic style of painting. Next door is **Oratorio San Giuseppe** (tel. 0722/320-936, Mon.–Sat. 10 A.M.–12:30 P.M. and 3–5:30 P.M., Sun. 10 A.M.–12:30 P.M.) was built in the 16th century by the Confraternity of St. Joseph, a reminder of Joseph's cult following that recognizes his sainthood and role in the Holy Family. A small chapel has a Nativity scene

constructed in stucco. Next to the Duomo, **Museo Diocesano Albani** (Piazza Pascoli 1, tel. 0722/2892, 9 A.M.–noon and 2–6 P.M.) features 14th-century frescoes removed from another church (San Domenico), precious silver, gold, and bronze objects, illuminated hymnals, and majolica ceramics from Casteldurante (Urbania). **Le Grotte del Duomo** houses the cathedral's crypt, with a 16th-century Pietà sculpted by Giovanni dell'Opera (check inside the Duomo for visiting times).

Entertainment and Events

Held annually in July, **Urbino Musica Antica** revives Renaissance arts patronage of Federico da Montefeltro in his court through Renaissance and Baroque music. The main program is performed outdoors in Palazzo Ducale's courtyard. Dusk Harmonies 7–8 P.M. complement the main programs with a series of period concerts, choral music, and dance in squares and other scenic points in Urbino. Ticket information can be obtained at the tourist office (tel. 0722/2631). Information on workshops and featured musicians is available from **Fondazione Italiana per la Musica Antica** (www.fima-online.org).

Contemporary art shows are held three times a year during Easter, September and the *Belle Arti* season. **Aquilone Annual Kite Festival** takes place each September. The event continues a 500-year-old tradition of kites that fly sporting only traditional Renaissance forms and shapes. Contact the tourist information center (tel. 0722/2613) for specific locations and times.

Italian language instruction is available in July through the University of Urbino (www.uniurb.it). The University has Italy's oldest journalism school founded in 1949 and gives an annual award to an American journalist (usually in May).

Accommodations

San Giovanni (Via Barocci 13, tel. 0722/2827, €58) takes a while to grow on you. It has industrial carpeting in public areas, a 1 A.M. curfew, no elevator (pack light), no breakfast (coffee bars nearby), no room TVs (ground floor has small TV room and lobby has TV), and doesn't accept credit cards. But the rooms are clean and the Cecconi family is friendly. Room 24 has views of the Duomo and 26 looks onto rooftops and a country panorama. It attracts a steady clientele of young Italians. There's a pizzeria and restaurant on the premises.

Just inside Urbino's city walls, Count Marcucci Pinoli converted his grandfather's villa into **Hotel Bonconte** (Via delle Mura 28, tel. 0722/463, www.viphotels.it, €50–79 s/d). Breakfast is served in a private garden in warm weather and some bedrooms have a countryside view.

Albergo San Domenico (Piazza Rinascimento 3, tel. 0722/-626, www.viphotels.it, €81–112 s/d) has modern, elegant rooms in the former Dominican monastery that faces Palazzo Ducale. Staff are attentive, the breakfast lavish, and second-floor rooms have lots of extras like massage chairs. Private parking is available.

Hotel Raffaello (Vicolino S. Margherita 40, tel. 0722/4784, www.albergoraffaello. com, €90–115) was Urbino's first seminary, now it has a marble interior updated in 1995. The third floor has pretty cityscape and countryside views; there are also some views on the second floor. It's located a few doors away from where Raphael's mother was born and on the street above Raphael's house.

Ca Andreana (Via Padana 119, tel./fax 0722/327-845, €47.50) is an *agriturismo* about four kilometers northwest of Urbino in Località Gadana (past the hospital). Its restaurant specializes in truffles, which are best ordered in fall or winter when the real thing is in season.

Food

Il Cortegiano (Via Puccinotti 13, tel. 0722/320-307, €8–10) is directly across from Palazzo Ducale. There's casual dining and snacks in the bar and outside on the square, as well as excellent cuisine with formal service in the back room, a good wine list, and an adjacent garden patio. Breakfast and lunch only. The bar is open daily 7 A.M.–7 P.M.

La Trattoria del Leone (Via Cesare Battisti 5, tel. 0722/329-894, daily 7–10:30 P.M., €7–9), a few steps from Piazza della Repubblica, has excellent ravioli and other pastas, rooster stew, plus plenty of choices for vegetarians.

Getting There and Around

By car from Ancona, take the A14 towards Bologna and exit at Castello Fani. Proceed along the SS3 Flaminia. After Fossombrone, take the SS423 all the way to Urbino. The closest train station is in Fasano from where Soget (tel. 0721/549-620) buses depart regularly 6:45 A.M.–11:30 P.M. and complete the journey in under an hour.

FOSSIMBRONE

Step into Fossombrone and you're sure to notice the refreshing scent of pines in the air. The town is surrounded by forested hills that are ideal for hiking excursions. This delicious atmosphere must have been a draw for country residents from the time it was a former Roman colony through the lords of Urbino. Remains of former Roman baths are on the way to Pesaro and probably were the perfect antidote for weary travelers.

An exploration of town begins on **Corso Garibaldi**, lined with Renaissance and Baroque palaces and churches. **Corte Rossa** was the 16th-century residence of the dukes of Urbino and the Palazzo Ducale. Like Ancona, Fossombrone had its own Pentagon in the Rocca Malatestiana, a five-sided fortress for defense. If your plan is to head for the forests, Fossombrone makes a good stop to replenish supplies or tend to needs like camera equipment and repairs.

If you were smitten with Piero della Francesca's paintings in Urbino, this is a good stop on your way to crossing the mountains that separate Le Marche from the **Casentino** in Tuscany. Della Francesca was born in San Sepulcro and painted masterful frescoes in Arezzo. Meanwhile, Fossimbrone hometown artist Francesco Guerrieri merits a gander. His work is visible throughout Le Marche as well as Rome, but his painting in **San Filippo** is especially vibrant. The town also has a small art and archaeological museum. Gourmets will want to keep in mind the bounties of the forest, including truffles that are at their peak in winter months.

Sights

As you walk Corso Garibaldi, pop into the **Church of San Filippo** (Corso Garibaldi, 9 A.M.–12 P.M.). Guerrieri painted an intriguing judgment of souls, with Christ above, the scales being tipped toward saint or sinner, and angels aloft in position. The main altar is stucco central. The church has an intriguing meridian in the floor—just the place to consult the sun's movements along the zodiac signs. The wood choir is beautifully executed and a Caravaggesque painting adorns one wall. St. Cecilia, patron saint of music, is above the organ pipes.

The first floor of **La Corte Alta** (tel. 0721/716-324, summer Tues.–Sun. 10:30 A.M.–12:30 P.M. and 4–7 P.M., €3) is the home of **Museo Archeologica Vernarecci,** while the throne room contains the **Pinacoteca Civica,** an art gallery. The former has several fine Roman-era sculptures that suffered the indignation of having their noses removed. When families or emperors fell out of favor this was a popular method of extracting revenge and ridiculing adversaries. For an extra €2, you can also visit **Casa-museo Cesarini** (Via Pergamino 23, tel. 0721/714-650, same hours as Corta Alta, €3). The house-museum, on the edge of town, was owned by an avid collector of sculpture and paintings. Little has changed inside and the 19th-century furnishings are nearly as interesting as the art.

Festivals and Events

Trionfo del Carnevale is on the second Sunday in May and is a historical pageant to celebrate Cardinal Della Rovere's return in 1559. The White Truffle Market is the first Sunday in March. As part of the event, restaurants compete to find the best combination between *bianchetto* truffles and Bianchello, the dry white wine produced in the surrounding hillsides. It's generally a win-win situation for diners who

help judge the various creations. Many of the other towns in the area also celebrate truffles and many events are held in autumn. If you develop a taste for this delicacy, check with the tourist office to see what's scheduled.

Sports and Recreation

FOCA Canoe Club in Val Metauro (Via Metauro 1, tel. 0721/714-893) organizes excursions to **Marmite di Gigante,** two kilometers from Fossimbrone. You can get a good view of the miniature canyon by crossing the Diocleziano bridge. Cliff divers would probably be tempted to take the plunge here, but it's safer to follow the path that follows the narrow chasm. Some of the grottoes below are four meters in diameter. The Furlo Valley nearby offers delta plane adventures and hang-gliding.

Accommodations

There are three hotels in Fossimbrone that stand out not only for their comfortable rooms but also for their restaurants, where you can enjoy a complete meal for under €20. **Mancinelli** (Corso Garibaldi 160, tel. 0721/716-550, €50 d) and **Albergo da Marco** (Via Giganti 20, tel. 0721/714-917, €60 d) are small two-star hotels with clean rooms and well-ironed sheets that are tightly tucked. They may not be beautiful, but they're meticulous and would certainly earn praise from a marine sergeant. **Da Marco** (Gola del Furlo, tel. 0721/726-129, €55) is slightly outside of town surrounded by forested hills on all sides. The swimming pool is rarely crowded and the front desk can lend you a couple of rackets if you fancy a game of tennis.

Food

La Taverna del Falco Ristorante & Pizzeria (Via Vichi 6, tel. 0721/715-396, Mon.–Fri. dinner, Sun. lunch, €7–10) just off Piazza del Mercato is downstairs in a medieval cantina with high vaulted ceilings. The friendly staff serves regional specialties for lunch and dinner at reasonable prices. Mushrooms and *tartufi* (truffles) infiltrate many of the dishes.

Da Gigi (Piazza Petrucci 18, tel. 0721/714-990, closed Mon. and Tues. evening,

€8–10) is a modest trattoria specializing in grilled meats. The smell hits you as soon as you enter the door and vegetarians would be advised to steer clear.

Anyone with a cholesterol problem can sample the barley bread that's supposed to do wonders for clogged arteries. **Eridi Archilei** (Viale Martiri della Resistenza 31) bakes it fresh every morning along with other flavored loaves in all shapes and sizes. Don't feel obliged to buy an entire loaf. Just ask for the amount you need and they'll cut off a portion. **Pasticceria Rinci** (Via Roma 34, tel. 0721/714-858, Tues.–Sun. 6 A.M.–1 P.M. and 4–7 P.M.) near the Duomo has a good selection to satisfy a sweet tooth, including continental specialties like their beignet with *crème chantilly*.

Information and Services
The **Pro Loco tourist office** (tel. 0721/716-324) is in Piazza Dante. They provide a monthly schedule of events and a list of registered tour guides.

Getting There
To get to Fossimbrone from Pesaro drive west toward Urbino. Fossimbrone is a short drive south on SS423. From Fano drive west on Via Flamina (SS3) or if you don't have a lot of time take the smaller highway SP73.

◖ URBANIA
Urbania offers theater, mummies, ceramics, and a palatial hunting lodge all set in a wooded landscape. The Montefeltro family selected this location for their hunting lodge, which is hardly a modest affair. Unlike the interior, with its rolling hills, Urbania is flat like the coastal towns. The Metauro River flows through town and continues into the truffle territory of Acqualagna and Sant'Angelo in Vado. Thanks to clay from the river, the town has been known for its ceramics since the 13th century, when at one time there were at least 32 workshops. Majolica was especially popular. Known then as Castel delle Ripe and then Castel Durante, the town's present name dates to 1636 and derives from Pope Urban VIII.

The town is still known for its ceramics and Museo Civico has an interesting collection, including some charming modern folk art. There are also ceramics workshops that vary in length from a half day to several weeks. The town has several Italian language schools. One group of residents that won't be saying much are the mummies that are preserved in the church, **La Chiesa dei Morti**. Thanks to a fluke of nature, some dozen bodies remained naturally mummified. For more lively entertainment, don't miss the town theater, **Teatro Bramante,** a gem built on three levels but with only 350 seats.

Sights
Museo Civico (Corso Vittorio Emanuele 23, tel. 0722/317-175, Tues.–Sun. 10 A.M.–12 P.M. and 3–6 P.M., €4) has a ceramics display of interest both for its older pieces that date from the Renaissance as well as its more contemporary collection. The modest but intriguing 19th- and 20th-century folk art was donated by a collector who managed to transport all of the pieces to Urbania by train—no small feat considering both their size and fragility. If the museum is closed, inquire with the librarians at the adjacent *biblioteca,* which was founded by Federico da Montefeltro. They will be pleased to open the museum just for you. The collection is housed in the Ducal Palace.

Chiesa dei Morti (Via Ugolini, call Giovanni Maestrini at tel. 349/819-5469 for guided tours, Tues.–Sun., donations accepted) is better known in town as the church of the mummies. In the 17th century, a rare phenomenon occurred: Bacteria attacked corpses in a way that caused them to preserve much of their skin and body tissue. One mummy is of a 19th-century physician who experimented with formulas to see if he could preserve himself, too. It wasn't a bad attempt, but he's not quite on par with his other companions.

Accommodations
Hotel Bramante (Via Roma 92, 0722/319-562, €50) is close to the theater and is where the entertainers generally stay. **Il Mulino** (tel.

0722/310-326, €70 d) is an *agriturismo* two kilometers outside of Urbania and provides simple country accommodations in a few rooms, as well as home-style cooking.

The swimming pool at **Orsaiola** (Via Orsaiola 36, tel. 0722/318-888, www.agriturismorsaiola.it, €50 d) offers a rolling view of emerald hills from a restored country house that dates to about 1900. The fireplace in the dining room doubles for grilling lamb, wild boar, or goat. Rooms are simply furnished. Color reigns at the pink country house, **La Rosa Tea** (Località Santa Ceclia 18, tel. 335/547-9606, www.agritursimolarosatea.it, €85–95), where each of the seven rooms is furnished in a different color scheme—from lilac to cobalt—with early 20th-century furniture. In summer, the aqua pool offers a view of the valley and Apennines; or enjoy the fireplace inside in cool weather. Ask about their language, cooking, or ceramics courses too.

Food
Osteria da Doddo (Via delle Cererie 4, tel. 0722/319-411, lunch and dinner Sun.–Fri., €12–25) offers excellent traditional local cuisine and a warm family welcome. Whatever they suggest is sure to please. The interesting wine list features good local wines plus some national and foreign labels. **Ristorante dal Pigattin** (tel. 0722/317-587) is frequented by theater staff and entertainers. **Pasticceria del Teatro** (Piazza San Cristofero 4, tel. 0722/318-738) next to the theater serves pastries, ice cream, and local gossip. It's a favorite *aperitivo* spot for the locals.

Getting There and Around
From Ancona take the A14 north 85 km until Pesaro and then the SS423 past Urbino until you reach town. There are frequent buses linking Urbino with Urbaina, just don't let the similarity of the names confuse you.

SAN LEO
San Leo is a curious and delightful blend of natural beauty, medieval Romanesque churches, 18th-century alchemy, and a population that has decided that it really isn't at all part of Le Marche. The lovely mountaintop town has its own magic. Pagan in origin, the mountain was renamed in 1000 for Leo, the spiritual friend of Marino who made his home on Mount Titano. Often paired as a destination with mountaintop nation and city San Marino to the east, the two make a pleasant contrast. San Marino is the well-oiled tourist and financial center, while San Leo offers a laid-back small-town atmosphere. Its visitors often arrive on bike and hit local hiking trails. The town is small but restaurants and shops offer good quality.

As you approach San Leo, you'll spot a mountain in the distance with ruins that spiral around the rock and resemble images of Dante's Inferno. Dante, in fact, was a visitor to San Leo in 1306. Perhaps atop San Leo, he too appreciated its breezy, light atmosphere. Today that's a good fit with the unpretentious accommodations that offer wonderful views. Its excellent local restaurants feature bounty from the valleys and forests. As for the locals, chat a bit and you will quickly discover that they don't think of themselves as Marchigiani. Never mind official map boundaries, citizens of San Leo think that they are part of Emilia Romagna, the region to Le Marche's north.

Near San Leo's main town square are two Romanesque churches, **La Pieve** and **Il Duomo**, made of local golden-hued bricks. They add their own air of early medieval mystery. Both churches are constructed as living rock, where the rock foundation rises into blocks that form the church. This technique is used both inside and out. Neither church has a typical front entrance: Each is entered from the side.

Sights
Museo della Fortezza (Via Leopardi, tel. 0541/916-302, www.museialtavalmarecchia.it, Apr.–Sept. daily 9 A.M.–7 P.M., Oct.–Mar. daily 9 A.M.–12:45 P.M. and 2:30–7 P.M., €8) is the fort museum. As you enter the fortress conveys a sense of how impregnable it was. The first rooms and main tower have interesting exhibits of arms and armor and a section

PRISON, PRISONER, AND LEGEND

The medieval fort dominating San Leo's skyline is a masterwork of military architecture and was used as a high-security prison for almost 400 years. The fortress was under control of the lords of Montefeltro in the 11th century and St. Francis visited in the 13th. It fell under the control of the Malatesta family and through the next century with ownership alternating frequently. In 1502, while his father was pope, Cesare Borgia managed to grab hold of it for a year. It passed back into the hands of Montefeltro, then Della Rovere families. In 1531, when it fell under control of the Papal States, the fort became a prison – its function through the early 20th century.

The dynamic Count Cagliostro was imprisoned here in the 18th century for founding a Lodge of Freemasons dedicated to Egyptian rites and for practicing alchemy. He was silenced for good when he died inside. The Church destroyed his numerous books on magic and alchemy. Born in 1743 in Palermo as Giuseppe Balsamo, in his early twenties charismatic Cagliostro and his wife fascinated even Casanova upon their first meeting in 1769. Cagliostro's prison cell is visible. Its isolation, heavy wooden door backed with stone, and observation window show how great the fear was that he might either charm his fellow inmates or the guards into liberating him. Upon his death on August 26, 1795, due to poor health, Cagliostro was buried in an unmarked grave outside the walls. Remaining prisoners were liberated in 1797 by a Polish general. Local legends vary. One says that upon liberation, the prisoners' first act was to locate Cagliostro's body. Others say ex-guards or soldiers found it and used his skull as a drinking cup.

upstairs has antique guns. Several rooms are dedicated to magic, medicine, and alchemy. An 18th-century recipe used scorpion oil to treat rheumatism, a St. Benedict medal kept witches away, coral protected infants from "negative energy"; tobacco was an 18th-century cure for fever, syphilis, and epilepsy. Other rooms have various torture devices.

The description of a Renaissance chastity belt notes that its primary function was to protect women during journeys or enemy invasions, rather than to prevent wayward females from straying: often husbands were away at war for several years, so such a heavy, cumbersome device was highly impractical to wear for very long. The barrel punishment for drunkards wasn't so comfy either. All exhibit captions and books in the shop are in Italian.

Named for the 3rd–4th century Dalmatian saint, **La Pieve** is the oldest church in San Leo and is a splendid example of organic architecture. The Romanesque exterior is a metaphor for a ship (a symbol of the Church), on a bed of rocks, a solid foundation. Inside, notice how the walls rise up from rocks and boulders on the floor instead of from straight edges. The *ciborio* (canopied altar) dates from 882.

Construction of the **Duomo** began in the 9th century. Most of what is visible today was completed in 1173. Instead of a soaring cathedral, the interior seems like rock that evolves into a building. San Leo's remains are in the crypt.

On May 8, 1318, St. Francis of Assisi met with Count Orlando Cattani from Chiusi on the second floor of **Oratory of St. Francis** in Palazzo Nardini. The count signed an agreement that gave his land on Mt. Verna to St. Francis. La Verna, over the mountain range in the Casentino area of Tuscany, is where Francis received the stigmata.

Festivals and Events

In late May, Pietracuta di San Leo has a cherry festival. A medieval festival takes place in mid-June. The end of August is dedicated to an alchemy festival.

Shopping

Mercatino della Fortezza is the town market for antiques and collectibles held on Sundays

9 A.M.–6 P.M. April–June and again September–December near the fortress. Homemade liqueurs are available at a small bar and shop just off the main square near Piazza Dante.

Accommodations

Service is friendly at **(Albergo Castello** (Piazza Dante 11–12, tel. 0541/916-214, albergo-castello@libero.it, €55–75 s/d) and has been since they opened in 1955. Rooms in the small hotel are light, furnished in Ikea style, and rates are reasonable. Some have marvelous views of the valley and nearby mountain ranges. Breakfast is likely to feature some home-baked breads and cakes. The restaurant downstairs also serves lunch and dinner, with pleasant outside seating in Piazza Dante.

Osteria Belvedere Ristorante Bar (Via Oselli 19, tel. 0541/916-361, www.belvederesanleo.com, €70 d) has a few rooms above the restaurant. Room 3 has a view of the sea and castle.

Food

Ristorante Bettolino (Via Montefeltro 4, tel. 0541/916-265, €4–10) has simple decor with excellent food. All the pastas and *piedina* (flatbread sandwiches with a variety of fillings) are prepared in-house, beef and lamb are flavorful, and there are many vegetarian options. Excellent value with a good selection of inexpensive dishes.

Bottega di Mario (Via Montefeltro, tel. 0541/916-251) has tasty sheep's milk cheeses that are wrapped and aged in *foglie di noce* (nut leaves), which imparts a unique flavor. The longer the cheese is aged, the more bite it has. It's also a good spot to pick up local wine, wild cherry jam, and honey. The town *forno* (bakery) is excellent for breads and biscotti.

Getting There and Around

San Leo makes a good visit paired with San Marino—two contemporary saints and twin cities. The most direct approach is from Pesaro via A14 Autostrada north, then take 72 west toward San Marino, and then 258 toward San Leo. For information, contact **Pro Loco** (Piazza Dante 14, tel. 0541/916-231) or

Ufficio Turismo (Piazza Dante, Palazzo Mediceo, tel/fax 0541/916-306).

Many Italian day-trippers visit during the weekend, especially Sunday. Weekend drivers should arrive early or you may find that you have to park well down the side of the mountain and enter on foot.

(FANO

After crossing the Rubicon in 49 B.C., Julius Caesar occupied Pesaro, Ancona, and Fano. Fano's advantageous location on the Adriatic Sea and its position on the ancient consular road, Via Flaminia, assured the town's continued importance. You can still see the **Arch of Augustus,** but the Visigoths cut down its ancient splendor in 558 in their desperate fight against Byzantine general Belisarius.

In the Middle Ages, the area was a center of conflict between warring nations and even families. The town coat-of-arms sports rival family colors in red and white and its motto warned *ex concordia felicitas* (happiness does not evolve from disharmony).

It's here that poet Robert Browning found his Guardian Angel, yachts roll through the streets at night, the Roman goddess Fortune holds court, and the reigning *brodetto* champ camps.

The town of Fano offers a bit of everything for the visitor. The sea attracts swimmers in the summer and boating year-round. It has significant ancient archeological artifacts from Picene to Roman times, with particularly striking mosaics. Fano's artistic treasures inspired poet Robert Browning, and can be found in churches as well as in the art museum. Its festivals include Fano dei Cesari, which originated during Roman times, as well as its own Carnevale. The town is very flat, so it's easy to explore on bike. Bike rentals are available at various beach locations.

Sights

Museo Civico e Pinacoteca (Piazza XX Settembre, tel. 021/828-362, Tues.–Sat. 9:30 A.M.–12:30 P.M. and 4–7 P.M., Sun. 9:30 A.M.–1 P.M.) houses *The Guardian Angel*.

The 1641 painting by Guercino (Giovanni Francesco Barbieri) inspired Robert Browning to write his poem in eight stanzas, *A Picture at Fano*, in his 1848 visit with wife Elizabeth Barrett.

Back then the painting still hung in the church of Sant'Agostino, for which it was painted, but due to poor conditions was moved to the art museum. A 1912 visit for the centenary of Browning's birth prompted a Yale University English professor to hold annual seminars in Fano on the poet's May 7 birthday. He also founded the Fano Club. To become a member, one had to visit Fano, see the painting, and mail a postcard of the image postmarked from Fano back to the United States. The Yale Fano Club eventually disappeared after Phelps' death, but a Texan who participated in a 1930 seminar with Phelps founded another club that is still active. Instead of mailing the postcard to Yale, it must be sent to Armstrong Browning Library in Waco, Texas.

The art museum also has an ancient Roman mosaic (2nd century A.D.) of a deity riding a leopard, a Roman coin collection, a 1593 statue of the goddess Fortuna that originally was in Piazza XX Settembre (replaced by a copy), and a painting of St. Helen by Raphael's father, Giovanni Santi. *Penitent Magdalene* is by Fossombrone artist Giovanni Francesco Guerrieri.

Santa Maria Nuova (Via De Tonsis, tel. 0721/803-534, 9 A.M.–noon, admission free) is a must for Raphael fans. *The Visitation* by Raphael's father and teacher, Giovanni Santi, is here. Raphael's next master, Perugino, painted the *Annunciation* as well as *Madonna in Throne with Infant and Saints* (1497). The *predella* (horizontal panel of paintings) under it is probably the work of the young Raphael. Note also the beautifully hand-carved wood choir behind the main altar.

The church of **San Agostino** (Via Vitruvio, daily 9 A.M.–noon, admission free) is said to have been built from the Roman Temple of Fortuna. Under the same church is a Roman arch that was designed by superstar Roman architect Vetruvius.

Teatro della Fortuna di Fano (Piazza XX Settembre, tel. 0721/800-750), built 1845–1863, is resplendent in red, ivory, and gold. It has 650 seats and three tiers; winged chimeras separate boxes in the first tier, while the top tier has a row of mythological sculptures above it. The performance season runs October–April, but look for special events at other times.

If you choose to stay in Fano, keep your eyes and ears open after dark. Fano is famous for its yacht-building. When these beauties are finished, they roll through Fano's streets at night from the factories to the port.

Head toward the coast for **Museo di Biologia Marina** (Viale Adriatico 1n, tel. 0721/802-689, Sat. 3–6 P.M. and Sun. 9 A.M.–noon, admission free). The explanations are in Italian, but it's a chance to see local sea life.

Festivals and Events

Fano's **Carnevale** is less famous than that of Venice, but has been going on since 1347 and has its own peculiar rituals and a bonfire on Fat Tuesday. Look for giant papiermâché figures and other creations that get carried on floats.

In the summer, Fano hosts one of Italy's best-orchestrated Roman historic parades in costume set circa 2,000 years ago. **Fano dei Cesari** even has *biga* (chariot) races and a chance to recreate a *Ben-Hur* scenario. It's usually in July, as is Fano's **International Jazz by the Sea.** In August, Fano hosts a festival of organ concerts. October is the month for **Fano Film Festival,** which projects short and medium-length films.

Shopping

Fano's center has shops that range from fine quality contemporary furniture at **Poltrona Frau** (made in Le Marche), antique shops, and goldsmiths. Several of the clothing stores carry a nautical take on sportswear, ideal for the yacht set or classy casual dress. **Baracchino** (Via Montevecchio 94, €10–40) is priced economically while **Leda** (Via La Malfa 20) is pricier. The ultimate toy is a yacht, and several companies manufacture them here if you're in the market for something extravagant.

Sports and Recreation

The beach scene in Fano is divided into two distinct areas: the **Lido** to the north is narrow and sandy, whereas **Sassonia** to the south is long, pebbly, and has a fishing village with pastel-colored buildings. Pilots can check Fano's three flying clubs. **Mondo Blu Club Subacqueo** (Via L. Ghiberti 7, tel. 0721/801-714) has scuba equipment and organizes outings. Check with the tourist office, too, for fishing, horseback riding, and golf. Windsurfers can rent boards at **Circolo Sportivo Windsurfing** (Via Pizzetti 8, 0721/808-652) or **Circolo Windsurfing Ponte Sasso** (Via Cappellini).

The city of Fano is flat and ideal for renting bikes. Consider rolling further afield, as the tourist office (IAT, tel. 0721/803-534) has a map of 11 bicycle routes. Ask for the *Marcabella natura vestitats di storia* itinerary that comes in both Italian and English. Two of the routes are easy—one along the sea, one on gentle hills—while the others offer more challenging terrain.

Accommodations

Built within the walls of an abbey dating to about the year 1000, **[C** **Castello di Monterado** (Monterado, Piazza Roma 19, tel. 071/795-8395, www.castellodimonterado.it, €190–230 d) is about 20 minutes from Fano. It's adorned with enchanting mythical frescoes and superbly furnished with family antiques. The ancient monastery passed through the hands of the Duchy of Urbino and the Della Rovere family. In the 18th century, architect Luigi Vanvitelli expanded it. Rooms are adorned with 19th-century frescoes painted by Corrado Corradi. Castle views span the Cesano Valley between the Apennines and the Adriatic Sea. Napoleon's nephew, Prince Maximilian de Beauharnais, spent his honeymoon here with his bride, the daughter of Czar Alexander of Russia. Four guest suites are named for their frescoes. Pallas Athena imparts wisdom over

the bed while the adjoining lounge has Eros and Psyche. The Bridal Suite with Apollo and Venus and Mars on the ceilings has a private terrace. The Aphrodite suite even has frescoes in the bathroom. Cherubs cavort in the Amorini bedroom, while the lounge has walls frescoed with Roman landscapes and windows overlooking Italian gardens. Breakfast is in the sunny east dining room. The doorbell is by the iron gate.

Theater performers in Fano tend to stay at **Hotel-Ristorante Augustus** (Via Puccini 2, tel. 0721/809-781, www.hotelaugustus.it, €70–95 s/d) or **Hotel-Ristorante del la Ville** (Viale Cairoli 1, tel. 0721/838-000, www.hoteldelavillefano.com, €65–72), which has a garden, provides quiet rooms, and accepts pets.

Food

Fano is famous for its *brodetto alla fanese,* the fish stew made with tomatoes and spiked with a splash of vinegar. It's also where men frequently ask for "a little brunette" after lunch or dinner. *La moretta,* the brunette, was born in the port area and "she" is coffee with sugar, anise liqueur, rum, brandy, and lemon zest. This is how the fishermen warm up, but it works quite well for landlubbers, too.

Casa Nolfi Ristorante (Via Gasparoli 59, tel. 0721/827-066, www.casanolfi.it, Mon.–Sat. dinner 7:30–11:30 P.M., lunch in fall/winter, €35–50) is known for Gabriele's *brodetto alla fanese.* He has won "best *brodetto*" awards for his recipe and the champ also has a good wine list. It's open in evenings only during summer, when dining expands to the square outside.

The aptly named Dionisia runs a wine bar, **Il Bottigliere** (Via Bonaccorsi 12–14, tel. 0721/822-989) that is staffed entirely by women and has casual dining. Theater performers often dine at **La Perla** (Viale Adriatico 60, tel. 0721/825-631).

Getting There and Around

Fano is 60 kilometers from Ancona directly off the A14 highway. The train station is in the center of town and there are frequent departures from Ancona. The journey time varies but regional service takes 35 minutes and costs €2.95.

There are taxis and buses waiting outside the station. Cars can be rented from **Europcar** in Via Toniolo 1 (tel. 0721/854-708) or at **Hertz** (tel. 0721/881-786) next door.

Fano tourist information is at **IAT** (Via Battisti 10, tel. 0721/803-534, Mon., Wed., and Fri. 9 A.M.–1 P.M., and Tues. and Thurs. 3–6 P.M.).

█ PESARO

Pesaro is the northernmost port city in Le Marche before you cross into Emilia Romagna and the mass beach scene of Rimini. The city has ancient Picene and Roman roots. Its grand Renaissance boom came during the reign of the Delle Rovere family. It's known for its ceramics, but before you scour the town for your own check out **Museo delle Ceramiche,** to see superb Renaissance plates and the later Pesaro Rose pattern that graced Victorian tables.

As birthplace of composer Gioacchino Rossini, Pesaro is as much of a pilgrimage for opera buffs as Loreto is for devout Catholics. Opera fans flock here for the **Rossini Festival** in July and August. Year-round they visit Rossini's birthplace, now a museum and art gallery. **Teatro Rossini** opened in 1818 and is an architectural delight.

SAN MARINO

San Marino's festive air in part comes from the quaint idea of visiting a nation within a nation. Encircled by Le Marche and Emilia Romagna in Italy, the Republic of San Marino, its capital city of San Marino, and small towns are well equipped to handle the mass tourism that ascends upon this mountaintop fairy-tale-in-progress. Italians come for the modest shopping discounts as much as for the breathtaking views. Gourmets enjoy its restaurants, which on the whole have reasonable prices and excellent quality.

St. Marino selected his refuge here on Mount Titan in A.D. 301. Marino later sent his associate priest, Leo, off to his own mountaintop hermitage. The republic now is dotted with castles and forts. Its rulers, the Captains Regents, can be traced back by name to 1244. They still rule, but today's San Marino lacks no modern conveniences, which makes a visit here pleasurable.

The surrounding towns and countryside allow for pleasant outings, whether you prefer vigorous hiking, river sports, or a leisurely meal in the country. The Marano River and its lake offer fishing near the town of **Faetano. Acquariva** is the town from which forest hiking excursions depart for Monte Cerreto. **Serravalle** was cited as early as 962 in a document that pertains to King Otto. Hike to the top of Mount Domignano and you have a point to admire both the Adriatic Sea and Mount Titan.

FESTIVALS AND EVENTS

When San Marino celebrates, count on fancy uniforms, lots of pomp, and occasional fireworks. The **Investiture Ceremonies** on April 1 and October 1 celebrate the Captains Regents, the two heads of state that will reign over the republic for the next six months. Formal protocol is observed, followed by a period costume parade through crowded streets. The foundation of the Republic is observed on September 3, the feast day of St. Marinus (Marino). Antique cars pass through as part of the **Mille Miglia,** the legendary 1,000-mile car race; they make a stop in Piazza Libertà to be admired. Medieval Days take place in May and Christmas markets are held from December through January 6. New Year's Eve offers music in the piazza plus fireworks.

SHOPPING

Although the currency used in San Marino is the euro, they mint their own coins and issue stamps that are highly prized by collectors. Expect to find all of the top Italian and some foreign designers here, plus plenty of crafts and budget souvenirs. **Borgo Maggiore** has a

Sights

As you walk around Pesaro, look out for its charming Art Nouveau villas. An excellent example is the pistachio-colored Art Nouveau villa in the circle near Pesaro's tourist office. You won't see the interior because it's in private hands. But a few steps away is a villa that was converted into the luxurious Hotel Vittoria. You can wander the beach, then head back into town for a look at the archeological museum, the cathedral with its medieval mosaics, and the fort. If you want to get out on the sea, this is an easy area to hook up with water sports. If you prefer to just lounge around, walk along the beach and stake your claim in one of the 80 *stabilimenti* (beach clubs) that have umbrel-

las or chairs for rent and often serve reasonably priced food for lunch.

Picenes steal the show at **Museo Archeologico Oliveriano** (Via Mazza 97, tel. 0721/333-44, Oct.–Apr. Tues.–Sun. 9 A.M.– 1 P.M., May–Sept. Mon.–Sat. 9 A.M.–7 P.M. and Sun. 9 A.M.–1 P.M.), with a rich collection of works from 8th–5th centuries B.C. A late 18th-century library is housed in another section with some 5,000 volumes dating to the 16th century.

The art gallery in **Musei Civici** (Piazza Toschi Mosca 29, tel. 0721/333-44, Oct.–Apr. Tues.–Sun. 9 A.M.–1 P.M., May–Sept. Mon.– Sat. 9 A.M.–7 P.M. and Sun. 9 A.M.–1 P.M.) includes paintings by Guido Reni, Giovanni

market every Thursday morning. San Marino also has its own wine consortium.

ACCOMMODATIONS

Hotel Cesare (Salita alla Rocca 7, tel. 0549/992-355, www.hotelcesare.com, €80–120 s/d) is known for the unusual configurations of its rooms. Each has its own unique color scheme and philosophy that reads like a horoscope. The terrace restaurant serves regional specialties.

Hotel Titano (Contrada del Collegio 31, tel. 0549/991-006, www.hoteltitano.com, €90–130 s/d), in the historic center, dates from 1894. It's traditional in style and tastefully decorated. Terrazza Ristorante on the premises has a panoramic view, as do many of the 48 rooms.

FOOD

The mountain forests offer specialties like mushrooms of many varieties, truffles, and wild game. Local chefs are experts at selecting quality meat as well as fish from the sea. If snacking is your plan, try the *piadina*, a flat sandwich bread that is somewhere between a tortilla and pita, filled with all kinds of cold-cuts that can make a good picnic or perfect budget lunch.

La Taverna di Righi (Piazza Libertà 19, tel.

0549/991-257, closed Sun. evening, €8-12) expertly manages that tricky balance of pleasing everyone. They serve simple salads and sandwiches that satisfy tourists, but better yet is the gourmet menu. Their superb chef works wonders with seasonal bounty from fava beans and artichokes to wild game, meat, and fresh-from-the-sea crustaceans and fish. The wine list is extensive and well selected; if you want to go local, try white Caldese or red Brugneto or San Marino Tessano.

Pane e Tulipani (Via Brandolina 69, tel. 0549/902-769, Tues.-Sun., €8) is known by locals for its superb selection of wines as well as creative comfort food. **Cantina di Bacco** (Contrada Santa Croce 19, tel. 0549/992-840) has a casual atmosphere and quality food that attracts plenty of local clientele.

GETTING THERE AND AROUND

The roads to San Marino are well marked. Summertime traffic is especially heavy, so if you are headed toward Pesaro, Urbino, or San Leo, consider taking the road that goes through Fiorentino to avoid the main routes. Parking is plentiful and probably easiest in garages below town; their elevators make the ascent toward the center easier than trying to find street parking.

Bellini, and other artists from Venetian, Tuscan, and Bolognese schools, but the show stealers in the Musei Civici are the ceramics rooms at Museo delle Ceramiche. Colorful Renaissance ceramic plates, bowls, goblets, and other objects showcase splendid mythological and religious scenes—some sacred and others quite profane. Here you can see some of Raphael's influence on design, as well as the later Pesaro Rose pattern that no upstanding home wanted to be without in the 19th century.

Don't miss the choir stalls of inlaid wood carved with magnificent scenes of Pesaro that date from the late 15th–early 16th centuries in the presbytery of **Sant'Agostino** (Corso XI Settembre, daily, 9 A.M.–noon). On the facade, the church shows its Venetian influence in the Gothic portal, lions, and statues that adorn it.

Ancient Roman foundations are under the Romanesque-Gothic **Cattedrale** (Via Rossini, daily 9 A.M.–noon, admission free), including some ancient Roman floor mosaics.

Opera pilgrims can't miss the birthplace of Gioacchino Antonio Rossini, who made his stage entrance at **Casa Rossini** (Via Rossini 34, tel. 0721/387-357, Oct.–Apr. Tues.–Sun. 9 A.M.–1 P.M., May–Sept. Mon.–Sat. 9 A.M.–7 P.M. and Sun. 9 A.M.–1 P.M.) in 1792. Rossini's operas include *Tancredi* and *The Barber of Seville* as well as 20 operas from 1815–1823, including *Otello*. Not only does this Pesaro house have plenty of memorabilia, it has the Rossini home's original furnishings.

Festivals and Events

Rossini Opera Festival (Teatro Rossini, Via Rossini 24, tel. 0721/38001, www.rossinioperafestival.it) is held every August and celebrates its hometown musical hero. Each year several of the composer's works are staged and many are given a contemporary setting. In addition to the Bologna orchestra and the Prague choruses, many international musicians participate in the annual event. Most performances are in the Teatro Rossini, but other venues are occasionally used.

Mostra Internazionale del Nuovo Cinema

features films that don't get wide public distribution. The festival is held in June and October. The historical re-enactment of the marriage of Camilla d'Aragona takes place in July in the Novilara Castle.

Shopping

Pesaro's market is the third Sunday of each month. An antiquarian market is held late January and early February. The area is known for ceramics.

Sports and Recreation

Piscina Berti (Parco Della Pace, Via Redipuglia 32, tel. 0721/405-029, Mon.–Thur. 8:30 A.M.–10:30 P.M., Fri. 8:30 A.M.–9 P.M., Sat. 8:30 A.M.–6 P.M., Sun. 9 A.M.–1 P.M., €5), a community swimming pool, will do for those that dislike sand or salt water. For hiking or bicycle excursions and rental information, contact **Club Alpino Italiano** (Via Baracca 77, tel. 0721/390-792). **Fishing Club Insomnia** (Via Lucio Accio 1, tel. 072/123-342) is one of several clubs that organize fishing excursions. The tourist office has information on horseback riding. A handful of scuba outfitters are in town, including **Centro Sub Pesaro** (Via della Sanità 24, tel. 072/125-520), and waterskiing is possible with **Air Fly Club** (Via Cecchi 92, tel. 072/125-727). If you want a quick game of golf **Club Vallugola** (Via S. Barolo, tel. 072/120-8354) has an odd 3-hole par-29 course and a driving range.

Accommodations

◖ **Hotel Vittoria** (Piazzale della Libertà 2, tel. 07/213-4343, www.viphotels.it, €84–113 s/d) is a lovely Art Nouveau villa that makes a perfect base for opera fans (splurge on the Peter Ustinov suite). It's just steps from the sea but the atmosphere has the formality of an early 20th-century home rather than a beach hotel.

Food

A cozy atmosphere in an ancient palazzo in Pesaro's center makes **Lo Scudiero** (Via Baldassini 2, tel. 07/216-4107, www.ristorante

loscudiero.it, Mon.–Sat., €60) an ideal setting. Choose from meat or fish entrees with new twists on traditional recipes.

Seven km outside the city center is a fish and seafood extravaganza at **Da Gennaro** (Via Santa Marina Alta 30, Santa Marina Alta, tel. 0721/273-21, Tues.–Sat. lunch and dinner, €30–35), where the menu changes daily depending on what the fishermen haul in.

The two Andreas at the helm of **La Canonica** (Via Borgata 20, Casteldimezzo, tel. 07/212-09017, Tues.–Sun. dinner only, €30–35) make this restaurant a draw in Casteldimezzo, a small hilltop hamlet 12 kilo-

meters from Pesaro's center. The menu excels at both surf and turf prepared in creative ways, like lamb fricassee or fish sausage. Have a go at some of the wines by the glass, or opt to have three perfect wines selected for you (€9–10).

Getting There and Around

Pesaro is on the SS16, which runs along the Adriatic coast. Drivers can also arrive by way of the SS3 Flaminia and A14 highway. The town is on the Adriatic train line and the station is in the center a short distance from the sea. Tourist information is available at **APT** (Viale Trieste 164, tel.07/216-9341).

Province of Ancona

If you want solitude you can find it in this region in the hillside forests or out on the sea, but you can also count on architectural stunners like the Napoleonic fort that is now a hotel, the gemlike theater in Sirolo, and the well-kept little medieval towns. The cuisine is also superb in this region, with an emphasis on fish and seafood. Non-fish lovers can delight in the bounty of mushrooms, wild boar, and other game here.

The Conero Peninsula, south of Ancona, has spectacular coastlines and forests and has managed to retain a sense of wild beauty that seems improbable in a coastline that is so developed just a few kilometers in either direction. The Conero crowds come in summer, but late spring is also a great time to visit. During that time of the year the air is perfumed with acacias, broom, and other heady scents and the vivid colors of the spring blooms can be experienced in relative solitude.

◖ SENIGALLIA

North of Ancona, Le Marche's capital, Senigallia is Della Rovere family territory. The reason most visitors come here is for the long, sandy strip of beach. Perhaps it's really the town's two star chefs that have put Senigallia on the map,

though. Gourmets come from across Italy to dine in the town's two superb restaurants, a short distance from each other on the same beach strip.

Sights

You can visit the Renaissance Della Rovere family fort, **Rocca Roveresca** (Piazza del Duca, tel. 071/63-258, daily 8:30 A.M.–7:30 P.M., €2), and see some of their art collection. The fort was built in 1480 by Giovanni Della Rovere, and the architect may have been influenced by Luciano Laurana, who designed the ducal palace in Urbino in the form of a square anchored by four cylindrical towers. A permanent exhibit highlights the Della Rovere family and also includes undergound passageways and patrol walks.

Accommodations

Right on Senigallia's beach, **Duchi della Rovere** (Via Corridoni 3, tel. 071/792-7623, €65–239) has in-room DVD and CD players, plus a breakfast extravaganza with about 70 tempting options. The hotel caters to business clientele and is equipped with a pool and garden. Look for reduced rates on the weekends outside the summer months. Parking is very handy.

Food

A meal at **◖ Uliassi** (Banchina di Levante 6, tel. 071/65-463, Tues.–Sun. lunch and dinner, €15–20), one of Italy's best seafood restaurants, is a destination in itself. As a bonus, the Adriatic Sea is your view, a spectacle in fair or stormy weather. Sit outdoors on the veranda overlooking the coast or in the bright airy interior that provides the perfect set for Uliassi's culinary show. Begin with Champagne and delights like raw fish, a fried shrimp cutlet, and a burst of passion fruit sorbet. Raw *riccione* in coconut sauce with lime zest was inspired by chef Mauro Uliassi's Polynesian travels, another garnished with wild fennel, guanciale, and olive paste. Crusty light breads made of grano, cuttlefish ink, or onion focaccia are superb. In spring, try dishes like shrimp, asparagus, and strawberry arranged on a clear tomato *gelatina*. Red *triglia* (mullet) is enriched with melon and foie gras. Rigatoni is mixed with wild pigeon and a cheese sauce. Non-fish dishes are few, but include treats like breasts of allodole (small birds) in a balsamic vinegar sauce or wild pigeon nesting with spinach, onion marmalade, and apples in a brown sauce. Red wines can accompany fish: Try Strologo's Traiano with raw fish and Mario Lucchetti's Lacrima di Morro D'Alba with some of the other dishes. Desserts are light and zesty, like ginger ice cream topped with tiny cubes of candied ginger resting in a pool of lemon tea with mint, or heavenly pistachio ice cream. Digest all this with Varnelli's liqueur from Macerata. A major feast here is not cheap, but the value is excellent. Tasting menus come in various price ranges and the à la carte choices are extensive.

In the township of Marzocco along the coastal road, Senigallia's other star chef, Cedrone, runs **Madonnina al Pescatore** (Lungomare Italia 11, tel. 071/698-267, Tues.–Sun. lunch and dinner, €14–19). It's perhaps even more boldly creative with food combinations, so count on flair and flavors that pop. Situated across the road from the sea, the restaurant offers a serene, modern atmosphere.

If both these restaurants are too steep for your budget, try **Il Clandestino,** also Cedrone's, south of Ancona.

Getting There and Around

By car, take the A14 *autostrada* to the Senigallia exit; head for "Centro" and the beach. Flaminia SS 3 is slower but scenic, otherwise take the SS 76 to the coast and head north past Le Marche's hills and wineries. The town is well served by trains (www.trenitalia.com) that rumble up and down the coast. From the railroad station, it's a 5–10-minute walk north to Uliassi. For bus connections, see companies in the *Macerata* section. Pick up a map at the tourist office in Piazzale Morani 2 (tel. 071/792-2725).

ANCONA

The bay north of Le Marche's rocky promontory has been a hub of shipping activity since the 4th century B.C. when Picenes traded with Greeks from Syracuse. The Picenes had settled in the area as far back as the 10th century B.C. with remains of Villanovan dwellings excavated on Ancona's Cappuccini Hill. The Sicilian Greeks elbowed out the pointy-helmeted Picenes, pushing them further into the hills.

Ancona takes its name from the Greek *ankòn* for its elbow-shaped harbor, rather than their adroit military maneuver. The city's fortune remained closely linked to trade. The city developed on the Guasco hill with its acropolis and a temple visible from the sea, probably dedicated to the goddess Venus Euplea, protector of sailors. One of the early commodities traded was *purpura*, a substance extracted from mollusks to make prestigious purple dyes generally reserved for royalty or high officials. The Romans founded several colonies in the area and the remaining Picenes were Romanized: either absorbed into Roman culture or eliminated, especially after the Battle of Sentium (295 B.C.).

Ancona retained its Greek name but the names of new Roman colonies are still reflected in Latin names today, like Senigallia (Sena Gallica). Trade with the Orient, especially Alexandria in Egypt, during the Illyrian Wars brought further prosperity to Ancona. Roman rule became official after Caesar's soldiers occupied the area and made Ancona first a town council, then a colony, and finally granted residents Roman citizenship. Saracens ransacked and destroyed Ancona in 839, but by the end of the 10th century the city had rebounded and trade flourished with the Orient. In the Middle Ages, Ancona suffered several invasions, especially from the north, but there was also a construction boom in church building.

Many Crusade ships departed from Ancona, as did vessels seeking to halt the Turks' expansion of the Ottoman Empire. Medieval shipping merchants had transactions with the East as well as with Venice and rival Ragusa in Sicily. Already decimated by an economic crisis in the 17th century, the city was further devastated by a 1690 earthquake. By the early 1700s, there were no ships in the port, as they'd been seduced by duty-free trade in rival Venice. In 1732, Pope Clement XII commissioned architect Vanvitelli to build the Lazzaretto fortress, which was the beginning of the port's revival.

The 19th century began with rule by Napoleon, returned to Papal hands, and then became part of Italy when the country was unified. The 20th century was not kind to Ancona, which was bombed by the Austrians in World War I; in World War II, over 180 bombings destroyed entire neighborhoods. Severe earthquakes in 1930 and 1972 further devastated the city, as did a 1982 landslide.

Ancona still shows some of its scars from the last earthquake, which makes its present boom seem almost miraculous. The port is thriving. As Le Marche's capital, Ancona has the worldliness and sophistication of a trading center that looks inward on a region that for centuries was a Papal State ruled by the Vatican. It's easy to see that deft power maneuvers in that realm would require subtlety rather than flamboyance, which explains in part the reserve of a Marchigiano in contrast to the bravado of a Roman or colorful drama of a Neapolitan. The population is little over 100,000, which gives Ancona the benefits of a small-town lifestyle with less traffic and noise, while it weighs in with the cultural programs and commerce of a major city. Most of the historical monuments are on Ancona's four main hills: **Guasco, Cappuccini, Cardeto,** and

Astagno. The city's oldest quarter is near the port and sites like the **San Ciriaco Duomo** are linked by narrow, winding streets. Graced by the light from the sea and local pale-colored stone churches, palaces, and squares, the effect is one of cheer rather than gloom and intrigue. The 18th-century part of Ancona has wider, straighter streets, and more trees and gardens. The port dominates as Ancona's ancient and modern commercial center. That *ankòn* elbow shape, incidentally, means that it's possible to see both a sunrise and a sunset over the sea in Ancona if you position yourself properly. The university adds a young buzz to the city and the arts scene is lively with a prestigious theater, **Teatro delle Muse** that also puts on Ancona's famous annual jazz bash every summer.

Sights

Some 1,000 years after the Greeks arrived, the Senate of the Elders decided that 14th-century Ancona needed a place befitting the goods that arrived from overseas that were displayed, bartered, and traded. Those men in tights did their negotiating and trading inside **Loggia dei Mercanti** (Via della Loggia). The Venetian Gothic facade mostly completed by 1459 shows a knight charging on his horse, the symbol of Ancona, while the four statues symbolize Christian merchant virtues of hope, strength, justice, and clarity. The masks on the Via della Loggia facade were added after a 1556 fire did more than warm up the theater for Carnevale. True to its origins, the Merchants' Loggia presently is owned by the Chamber of Commerce and is rarely open to tourists.

Emperor Trajan (A.D. 53–117), a successful military leader as well as engineer of civic works, greatly modified the port in Ostia and built one of the earliest shopping malls, Trajan's Markets. Trajan chose Ancona as his Roman base to begin his triumphant military campaign against Dacia (now Romania). In Ancona, Trajan fortified the port by enlarging the harbor and extending the north pier. Superstar architect Apollodoro of Damascus completed **Arco di Traiano** (Trajan's Arch, located on the waterfront, tel. 071/33249, daily year-round, admission free) in A.D. 115, which originally had more bronze ornamentation on the marble and local limestone. Access to Trajan's Arch was once much simpler. In 2007, port security became stricter and visitors may need to present a passport or other identification. Check with the tourist office for current procedures.

The city is best seen on foot and the tourist office has maps to plot your own route. Go up to the **San Ciriaco Duomo** (Piazzale Del Duomo, tel. 071/52688, daily 8 A.M.–12 P.M. and 3–6 P.M., admission free) for the view outside as well as its medieval interior. Since ancient times when a Greek temple stood here, this holy spot has been a reference point for sailors. Take time to look at the architectural detail on the churches and palaces.

Santa Maria in Piazza (Via della Loggia, tel. 071/52688, admission free), known in earlier times as Santa Maria del Mercato for its market location, once was the church of bakers and masons. Its 1210 facade has intricate figures and plants carved on the bas-reliefs and portal. **SS Sacramento** (daily 9 A.M.–12 P.M., admission free) between Piazza della Repubblica and Piazza Kennedy has a bell tower with a spiral staircase. Modifications completed in 1776 were inspired by Borromini's St. Ivo in Rome. Inside there are Roman ruins on the lower level.

The face of the clock on the **Torre Civica** (City Tower) next to **Palazzo del Governo** has its frame and numbers made of red Verona marble instead of the usual black. Walk up **Via Pizzecolli** to the late Renaissance palace, **Palazzo Bosdari** (tel. 0712/225-041, Mon. 9 A.M.–1 P.M., Tues.–Fri. 9 A.M.–7 P.M., Sat. 8:30 A.M.–6:30 P.M.), the present home of the **Pinacoteca** (City Art Museum) and **Modern Art Museum.** The staircase outside the church of **San Francesco alle Salle** on its square near Via Pizzecolli leads to one of Lorenzo Lotto's later paintings.

Piazza Stracca was once called Piazza della Farina or Flour Square for the trading of grains and food that took place here. **Tredici Cannelle** fountain was built in 1560 and has 13 water spouts coming out of the mouths of bronze satyrs and fauns. Browse morning markets between Piazza Roma and Corso Mazzini, stroll the Passetto, sip an *aperitivo* in Piazza del Plebescito, and catch the sunset at Campo Ebrei. The Jewish synagogue (Via Astagno 10) may have once had a Turkish Mosque in the same building, both frequented by important traders in the city. **Campo degli Ebrei** on the Cappuccini Hill facing the sea is the site of some of Europe's oldest Jewish graves, dating to the mid-16th century. Study, restoration, and cataloging are underway for some 1,058 tombs.

Entertainment and Events
NIGHTLIFE
In a way, nightlife really gets primed in Italy with the *aperitivo* (the drink before dinner). Piazza del Plebescito has two bars, **Plaza Café** (Piazza Del Plebiscito 3, tel. 071/202-415) and **Nu 54** (Tues.–Fri. 11 A.M.–4 P.M. and 6 P.M.–2 A.M., Sat.–Sun. 6 P.M.–2 A.M.). Via degli Orefici has **London** and Via della Beccheria has **Gnao Gatti Osteria** (tel. 0712/072-076). Corso Mazzini is lined with bars and pubs, **Enopolis Winebar** (tel. 0712/071-505) is at No. 7, and **Classic Cafe** (tel. 0712/03000) cocktail bar is at No. 19. The Passetto area has two cocktail bars, **Old Fashioned** (tel. 071/358-0312) and **L'Acensore** (The Elevator, tel. 071/358-0388, concerts start at 10:30 P.M.). **Barfly** in the Baraccola neighborhood has occasional live concerts and a dance floor.

PERFORMING ARTS
Teatro delle Muse (Via della Loggia, box office tel. 0731/525-25, www.teatrodellemuse. org) is Ancona's most prestigious theater. Most popular are the plays scheduled by **Teatro Stabile Marche**—all performed in Italian, followed by opera, jazz, concerts, symphony, and ballet (in that order). The symphony program is performed by the Philharmonic Orchestra Marchigiana and composed of local musicians. Jazz year-round mixes international stars with emerging national talent. Concerts, opera, and ballet feature international performers and companies: most offer classic rep-

ertoire. Upstairs the Sala Principale has 1,159 seats. Downstairs the intimate Ridotto has 180 lemon-colored seats and acoustics that musicians like so much that many decide to record here. If the seats seem particularly comfortable and plush in both, it's because they were renovated by Poltrona Frau, a company based in Le Marche that makes some of the world's most sought-after and pricey sofas. **Teatro Sperimentale** (Piazza della Repubblica, tel. 071/502-1611) in a nearby building seats 427. The box office bookshop and bar make for good mingling.

Teatro Stabile Marche (Via della Loggia, box office tel. 0731/525-25, www.stabilemarche.it) programs plays for the Teatro dell Muse and as a resident theater company performs one or two of the season's 10 or so plays. The other Muse performances feature Italian regional companies that perform primarily Italian, Neapolitan (playwright Edoardo De Filippo is almost de rigueur in a theater season and sometimes is performed in dialect), and international classics in translation. In turn, the company of actors travels around Italy with its productions and performs on regional stages.

FESTIVALS

Ancona Jazz (www.anconajazz.com) summer festival offers one of Italy's most prestigious summer jazz programs. The event usually lasts for two weeks during mid-July with concerts in Teatro delle Muse in two lovely halls—one grand, the other intimate. Music spills out into other theaters and venues like piazzas, clubs, a winery on the Conero, and in 2007 for the first time in Parco Cardeto. If you're an aspiring jazz musician, consider applying in May or June for the workshops (in 2007, American jazz drummer Matt Wilson led a workshop for drummers).

Shopping

Piazza Roma is the central focus for shopping in Ancona, with the main streets being Corso Mazzini to Corso Garibaldi and Corso Stamira. A book market and half-price book sale takes place daily on Via XXV Aprile 28h (tel.

071/548-10). **Acme** (Via San Martino 6, tel. 071/207-5365) has comics, illustrations, and videos. **Sonnino** (Piazza Cavour) sells used books. **Feltrinelli** (Corso Garibaldi, 35, tel. 071/207-3943) has a small selection of books in English. Shops are generally open on Monday 4–7 P.M., Tuesday through Friday 9 A.M.–1 P.M. and 4–7 P.M., and Saturday 9 A.M.–1 P.M.

Sports and Recreation

Parco Cardeto is the newest park in town and still in a phase of transition. Near the central shopping district, the city purchased it from the military and only recently opened it to the public. In 2007, it became a venue for Ancona Jazz. The great urban outdoors with Roman ruins including Temple of Venus makes for an interesting stroll.

Ancona Sotteranea (tel. 071/222-5064) organizes tours of Underground Ancona with speleologist guides. Tours are periodically put in limbo so even if you book in advance confirm that they are running.

The Passetto (Viale della Vittoria) in its heyday could have been a Busby Berkeley entrance to the shore. Descend the monumental staircase (there is also an elevator behind the gardens that operates 8 A.M.–9 P.M.) to the beach and head northwest toward the grottoes—some are natural, while others were carved out by fishermen. In the distance is a natural rock formation nicknamed **La Seggiola del Papa** (the Pope's Seat).

You can try your luck at bingo at **Bingo Five** (Via della Ricostruzione 1, tel. 0712/800-014) and **La Nuova Fortuna** (Strada Pontelulngo 159/B, tel. 0712/861-470) in Baraccola. Just make sure to review your Italian numbers before playing. For a souvenir that won't wear off, visit the tattoo parlors across from the port.

Accommodations

Hotel Roma & Pace (Via G. Leopardi 1, tel. 071/202-007 or 071/207-3743, www.hotelromaepace.it, €95 d) is sought after by theater performers and others who yearn for its pleasantly old-fashioned lobby and bar with Art Deco furniture and fine wood details.

HISTORIC THEATERS

One of Le Marche's best-kept secrets is its extraordinary network of town theaters. Perhaps nowhere else in Italy is there such a concentrated abundance of architectural gems that date mostly from the mid-1700s to the late 1800s. The interiors offer frescoes of mythological creatures on the ceiling, painted curtains, curvaceous balconies, gilt trim, plush seats, lobbies for gossip, and chandeliers that dazzle. Add to that some coffee and wine bars and what you have is merely icing on the string of bonbons in Le Marche.

Performing arts were in the fabric of small-town life in Italy throughout the centuries and theaters aren't new to the region. Romans built extravagant theaters and amphitheaters 2,000 years ago in Urbisaglia and Ancona. But the 18th and 19th centuries brought an almost giddy abundance of theaters with elaborate designs to even some of the smallest towns in Le Marche. Famous architects of the time created interiors that are breathtaking to behold. Some are diminutive in size, but no ornamentation was spared. Perhaps it's their smaller scale that so accentuates their splendor. Some theaters were paid for by a grand benefactor, others by local nobility that either converted their private theaters or pooled their resources for common amusement. Others, like the one in Sirolo, were chosen by the townsfolk – who chose a theater rather than a road when put to the vote on public works projects.

Le Marche's theaters are exceptional creations that for the most part have been lovingly restored to their original splendor. They are easy to find, but to experience the full effect you must see the interior – often a complete contrast to a modest or austere exterior. The best way see these is to attend a performance; like U.S. theaters, most are kept locked except during a show. You may even have the good fortune to wander by during rehearsals or other programs. Otherwise to have a peek at the interior, some persistence may be necessary.

The first option is to attend a performance, which may be a happy coincidence in your travels but may be difficult to plan. Some town theaters do not publicize or even schedule performances far in advance. Others permit several groups to independently schedule their own theater programs, but information may not be centralized. The best point of contact is the town or provincial tourist office. If unable to obtain advance information, stop in when you arrive. As you travel, look for theater posters affixed around town. Stroll by the theater to look for listings or see if the box office is open. (If all attempts are

---

In a restored palazzo with 40 rooms, **Grand Hotel Palace** (Lungomare Vanvitelli 24, tel. 071/201-813, €110 d) is practically across from the Port of Ancona. It's only one kilometer from the train station, Fiera, and historic Vanvitelli fort for exhibits. There's a parking garage that is especially handy for reaching the historic center. There's no restaurant on the premises, but the front desk provides special discount cards to neighborhood restaurants and there's an on-site bar.

Food

Specialties in Ancona include the *stoccafisso* (cod with tomato, potato, olives, anchovy, and herbs), *brodetto* (fish stew usually prepared with

13 varieties of fish and shellfish), *coniglio in porchetta* (rabbit with wild fennel), and *crescia* (a thin pizza-like bread). The best white wine probably is Verdicchio dei Castelli di Jesi, while red wine lovers will want to go for the Rosso Conero and Lacrima di Moro d'Alba.

Near the port, Piazza della Repubblica and Teatro le Muse, **(La Cantineta Bar Trattoria** (Via Gramsci 1c, tel. 071/201-107, www.cantineta.it, Mon.–Tues. 7–10:30 P.M., €8–10) is a popular, noisy, welcoming trattoria that specializes in fish. Specialties are Ancona-style *stoccafisso* and excellent fried fish like sardines. Homemade *tagliolini allo scoglio* (pasta with mixed seafood) can be found throughout Italy, but here the seafood is fresh and local.

thwarted, at worst you will have seen another lovely small town in Le Marche.)

Performance options vary. Concerts (concerti) are ideal if you don't understand Italian. The quality of classical or jazz is often superb. But even plays, if you know the work already – say a play by Shakespeare or Tennessee Williams – are enjoyable for the staging and the atmosphere. The performance may be secondary anyway if your goal is to see the architecture. It's also your own performance debut into the local culture and a glimpse at the social life. Mingle with the locals during intermission. The theater has its own coffee bar or one is probably within steps of the theater. So few Americans visit Le Marche compared to other regions of Italy that often curiosity pushes the usual Marchegiano reserve away, in turn replaced by enthusiasm to share the region's treasures.

HISTORIC THEATERS IN LE MARCHE

Province of Pesaro-Urbino
Cagli: Comunale
Fano: Della Fortuna
Pesaro: Gioachino Rossini
Urbania: Bramante
Urbino: Sanzio

Province of Ancona
Ancona: Le Muse
Fabriano: Gentile da Fabriano
Jesi: Giovan Battista Pergolesi
Osimo: La Nuova Fenice
Sirolo: Cortesi

Province of Macerata
Caldarola: Comunale
Camerino: Filippo Marchetti
Corridonia: Giovanni Battista Velluti
Macerata: Lauro Rossi
Mogliano: Apollo
Montecosaro: Comunale
Montefano: Rondinella
Pollenza: Comunale
Recanati: Giuseppe Persiani
S. Severino Marche: Feronia
Sarnano: Della Vittoria
Tolentino: Nicola Vaccai
Urbisaglia: Ancient Roman amphitheater and theater

Province of Ascoli Picino
Amandola: La Fenice
Ascoli Piceno: Ventidio Basso
Ascoli Piceno: Dei Filarmonici
Fermo: Dell'Aquila

The house red wine is Rosso Conero. Pasta plus a fish course runs €18–20.

La Moretta (Piazza del Plebescito 52, tel. 071/202-317, www.trattoriamoretta.com, €20–35) was founded in 1897 and is run by the fourth generation. It offers two attractive seating options: a table outside to savor scenic Piazza del Plebescito (a.k.a. Piazza del Papa) and watch the action, or the cozy dining room inside. Traditional Anconan food is on the menu. Its popularity with locals makes it wise to book ahead.

Osteria Strabacco (Via Oberdan 2, tel. 071/567-48) is populated by a hip crowd enjoying traditional food and drinks at economical prices. Look for special events, too, like Ancona Jazz aperitivo evenings in July.

For sweets, try **Pasticceria Patrignani** (tel. 071/202-040) on Via del Gallo between Corso Mazzini and Corso Garibaldi; **Saracinelli** (tel. 071/202-096), known for its coffee, on the Corso Vecchio; **Foligni** (tel. 071/202-728) on Via Marsala; or **Pasticceria Moldavia** (Viale della Vittoria toward Passetto, tel. 071/31787). Gelato is popular with locals at **Yo Yo at the Port, Cremeria Rosa** (tel. 071/203-408) near Tredici Cannelle Fountain, and **La Gelateria Martini** (tel. 071/205-246) on Piazza Pertini.

Historic bars include **Giuliana** (corner of Piazza Repubblica and Corso Garibaldi) and **Caffè Torino. La Tazza d'Oro** (Corso Giuseppe Garibaldi 134, tel. 071/203-368), like Rome's, vies for the best cup of espresso or cappuccino.

Information and Services

Hospital Ospedale Umberto Primo (Piazza Cappelli near Piazza Cavour) has an emergency room *(pronto soccorso)* and ambulance service (tel. 118). First aid service for tourists is sometimes open at the Passetto in the morning (9 A.M.–1 P.M.) as well as the airport and train stations. The number for the police is tel. 113. Money exchange is possible at the port in the Marittima train station, as well as at other banks around town. The central post office is at Marittima train station in Largo XXIV Maggio (look for the 1926 Fascist-era architecture). The city **APT office** is at Via Torresi Mario 48 (tel. 071/898-377). Information about the province is available at Via Thaon de Revel 4 (tel. 071/33249).

Getting There and Around

The Ancona airport offers hourly bus shuttles (buy ticket at newsstand) to downtown Ancona. The Castelferreti train station in front of the airport connects to Ancona's central station, while Stazione Marittima is close to the port and nearer the historic sites. A walk from the central train station to the historic district takes about 30 minutes. Taxis stands are outside. City buses (Line 1 or 1/4) depart about every seven minutes.

Conerobus (main office Corso Mazzini near Piazza Cavour, tel. 071/283-7411 or 800/218-820, www.conerobus.it) run the buses around town. Number 11 goes up and down Ancona's hills in the historic district, but does not run regularly. Bus stops are in Piazza Roma and Piazza della Repubblica in front of the theater. Number 93 goes to Poggio in the Conero area and in summer 94 goes to Portonovo (stops at central train station or Via Vecchini at Piazza Cavour). B and C go to Palombina, with the only sandy beach (the others are pebbles or rocks). Purchase tickets at *tabacchi* and newsstands.

Bus connections between Ancona and Macerata are on **SASP** (tel. 0733/663-137), and the **Roma-Marche** (tel. 0733/818-638) line serves points between Rome. Taxis are by the central train station (tel. 071/43321), Piazza Roma (tel. 071/202-895), and in Piazza della Repubblica (071/204-200). Ancona's port (www.autorita portuale.ancona.it) has 25 or so maritime agencies; some are freight and others are passenger ships. The tourist office has a complete list.

Around Ancona

Morro d'Alba is the territory for one of Italy's most intriguing red wines, Lacrima Morro d'Alba, made from the grape named for the area and the phenomenon of "tears" that form as it matures. Its unusual aroma has strong floral scents of roses and violets that might seem distracting, yet in the mouth it's fresh and pleasant. Surprisingly versatile, Lacrima Morro d'Alba pairs well with poultry, game, meat, and even fish. Production is limited, so the wine may be hard to find outside of Le Marche.

Wine maestro Piergiovanni at **Luigi Giusti** (Via Castellano 97, Montignano, tel. 071/918-031, www.lacrimagiusti.it) tends his Lacrima di Morro D'Alba vineyards in the nearby town of Montignano, and in an 18th-century cellar in the *centro storico* of Castelferretti recently restored by Piergiovanni Giusti. Two winemakers are right in the town of Morro D'Alba: **Stefano Mancinelli** (Via Roma 62, Morro d'Alba, tel. 0731/63021, www.mancinelli-wine.com) and **Mario Lucchetti** (Via Santa Maria del Fiore 17, Morro d'Alba, tel. 0731/63314, www.lucchettiwines.com), which features a tasting room overlooking the vineyards in Morro d'Alba. All three make excellent wines. On the way from Ancona toward the Falconara airport, take the exit toward Chiaravalle and follow directions for Morro d'Alba.

◖ CONERO PENINSULA

With the natural rugged beauty of the sea and forests, the superb dining and locally made wine, plus interesting jazz concerts and other events, the Conero Peninsula a must-see stop for any trip.

Play a word association game with Conero and a wine aficionado will shout *Rosso*. That is

© JUDY EDELHOFF

cliffs on the Conero Peninsula

if he or she has ever heard of it. Actually the wine Rosso Conero is probably as little known as is the **Conero Promontory** south of Ancona with its spectacular coastline, forest, and sea. Anconans are wise to the fact that they have easy access to natural beauty that resembles a mini Big Sur or the cliffs of the Irish coast. Just pick your favorite rocky, dramatic seashore anywhere in the world and the Conero Promontory probably matches it for beauty. The sea is pristine and ever changing.

The Conero isn't Newport or Palm Beach, so shopping is not the highlight (although wine lovers will enjoy shopping around for Rosso Conero). The wineries are small and each has its individual personality. Rosso Conero red wine is the star, but winemakers are likely to be experimenting with other grapes, too. Just ask a friendly sommelier or make a visit to a winery.

Sights

Just south of Ancona is **Portonovo.** The former Napoleonic fort with rounded bastions was built about 1810 using stones from an an-cient monastery. It was to be part of Napoleon's network to control the Adriatic and Mediterranean and to thwart foreign trading ships from calling on British ports. The French chose Portonovo as the site for this fort to defend Ancona from the south and to prevent British access to fresh spring water near the fort. The Portonovo fort, painstakingly restored from its dilapidated condition in the 1960s, is now the luxurious Fortino Napoleonico hotel with modern comforts. There is access to nearby beaches, but parking is limited.

Events

In mid-May, French and Italians seek to repel the British attack on Calcagno Bay in a historical re-enactment held at **Fortino Napoleonico** in Portonovo. An encampment and military exercises are followed by a military parade of soldiers and cavalry in beautiful early 19th-century uniforms. They even set up tents and camp near the old fort. After they have faced off in battle, don't be surprised to see French and English soldiers dining outside together chatting in Italian.

Sports and Recreation

Conerobike (Via Peschiera 30a, tel. 071/933-2270, www.conerobike.com) has information on bicycle rentals, guided tours, repair shops, and good detailed maps of the area. Hotel Emilia and some of the others can arrange boat excursions.

Accommodations

Fortino Napoleonico (Via Poggio 166, tel. 071/801-450, www.hotelfortino.it, €240 d) is easily the area's most historic and romantic hotel, set in a Napoleonic stone fort that dates from the early 1800s. The sea practically laps up to the door. Rooms are furnished with Empire touches with lovely textiles and face inward toward a courtyard. One stunning suite has its own terrace with sea view. Management is very present, so service is attentive and no detail is overlooked. The circular former commander's center in the courtyard is the restaurant.

Hotel Emilia (Collina di Portonovo, tel. 071/801-145, www.hotelemilia.com, €230 d), set on the hill above the sea, is an example of 1960s architecture that translates well into the 21st century. The exterior and rooms are very white and uncluttered. Lovely antique accents and kilim rugs add warmth and splashes of color. The lobby has a video library for guests. Terraces and balconies are angled so that each is very private. The garden has a swimming pool and the beach is a lovely walk downhill.

Rocco in Campagna (Via Cave 13, tel. 071/933-0558, www.locandarocco.it, €160 d) is run by the same owner as the Locanda Rocco hotel in town. Here the setting is the hills of Parco del Conero in the middle of the country, with a profusion of wild pink roses and a pool that offers a view of the sea down below. The town of Sirolo is only 1.5 kilometers away. Breakfast is served outside in good weather or in a light-filled dining room in cooler weather.

Food and Wine

The former commander's center inside the Napoleonic fortress has been transformed into **Il Fortino** (Via Poggio 166, tel. 071/801-450, www.hotelfortino.it, dinner daily, €35–60), a cozy and rustic restaurant with excellent food and service. Breakfast includes wonderful homemade breads and pastries. Locals come here, too, when they want to treat themselves to lunch and dinner. The upstairs terrace has a sweeping view of cliffs, sea, and forests the inner courtyard is chirping-bird tranquil; and either is ideal for drinks. The polished service contents powerbrokers, is discreet enough for honeymooners, and pampers down-home locals on their special night out.

La Torre Ristorante (Numana, Via La Torre 1, tel. 071/933-0747) has elegant dining with a lovely view of the harbor with pristine white boats that shine from below even at night. The kitchen has some creative dishes but what particularly shines is the traditional cuisine, like simple but flavorful linguine *con astice* (fresh lobster with pasta).

Silvano Strologo Winery (Camerino, Via Osimana 89, tel. 071/731-104, s.strologo@libero.it) has some of the best Rosso Conero you're likely to find anywhere, so give Julius, Traiano, or Decebalo a try. If you want something lighter, Silvano introduced a good rosè, so look for the label with the pink rose on it—a play on *rosato* for the color. Phone ahead and be prepared to use your Italian, but if it's not open, the local gas station usually has a few bottles to sell. Other good wines to seek out are Moroder, Umani, Ronchi, and Leopardi. Some wineries can be visited by appointment; check with the tourist office.

Locals rave about **Il Clandestino** (Contrada Portonovo, Località Poggio, tel. 071/801-422), Cedrone's more casual and economical fish stand on the beach south of Ancona. The restaurant specializes in Mediterranean raw, marinated, and smoked fish.

Getting There and Around

To get to Portonovo from Ancona, head south and follow signs for Parco Conero or Riviera del Conero and Portonovo. Roads in the area are well marked and maintained. Hotel Fortino arranges transfers for guests from the airport in Ancona-Falconara or the train station in Ancona. Summer visitors might want to use the Conero Bus (see *Ancona*), as parking on the promontory is extremely limited.

Around the Conero Peninsula

Sirolo is situated on the Conero coast south of Portonovo and north of Numana. The town is worth a stroll for its bright atmosphere, which is in part due to the use of the local creamy-pink Conero stone that is no longer quarried. In 1872, the mayor gave the citizens a choice between a new road with beach access or a public theater; they voted for the latter. **Teatro Cortese** opened in 1875 and is one of Le Marche's stunning theaters. Its horseshoe-shaped interior has 220 plush red seats with two rows of boxes and the walls are decorated in a red and cream color scheme. The ceiling is painted with decorative frescoes and a chandelier. Contact the tourist information office (IAT, Piazza Vittorio Veneto, tel. 071/933-0611) for visiting hours and performance times.

Hotel Locanda Rocco (Via Torrione 1, tel. 071/933-0558, www.locandarocco.com, €160 d) is an ideal spot for those looking to be guided by a hip, young owner. There's also a superb intimate gourmet restaurant in cream tones with a purple floor. This is the sort of place that winemakers like to take clients to because they can depend on the food to show off their wines. **Country House L'Antico Mulino** (Via Molini II 7, tel. 071/933-0265, €110 d) is made of the lovely local whitish stone and was renovated in 2004. Each of the eight rooms has a different color scheme, wrought-iron beds, oak-beam ceilings, and some antique accents.

LORETO

Loreto is to Le Marche what Assisi is to Umbria: a major religious pilgrimage site that has a very central focus. According to some estimates, Loreto is second only to Lourdes in France in terms of the numbers of pilgrims seeking healing that it attracts. Documented as such since about 1294, the town is focused on one main figure, the Virgin Mary, and on one main object, **Santa Casa** (the Holy House). As a subject for painting and sculp-

ture, the Madonna of Loreto has been portrayed widely, perhaps most notoriously in Caravaggio's *Madonna di Loreto,* a painting that hangs in Rome. The house, according to tradition, is where Jesus, Joseph, and Mary lived. According to legend, the house was miraculously transported from Palestine in the air on the backs of angels. At first, the house stopped in Istria, but that site was not satisfactory. The house became airborne once again and came to rest in Loreto.

Pilgrims arrived soon after and the ritual of arriving on foot remains a strong tradition to this day. One annual pilgrimage route of about 30 kilometers goes from Macerata to Loreto; another leaves from the Conero area. Visitors arrive using all means of transportation, including many busloads. The impressive influx of visitors in the Middle Ages attracted merchants ready to meet the demands of the faithful for lodging, food, crafts, souvenirs, transportation, and other needs. Almost immediately as you enter the town, you sense an operational precision. Today's innkeepers and shopkeepers are nonplussed by the daily need to tend to thousands, which has also brought the area a certain prosperity that is evident as you walk toward **Piazza della Madonna,** the center of action.

Sights

The **Holy House** now sits inside **Basilica of Loreto** (Piazza della Madonna, tel. 071/974-7198, admission free) under the dome. The house is surrounded by a marble screen designed by Bramante in 1509. The floor around it has depressions formed from the faithful that encircled the house on their knees. Inside the small house, people pray or walk through to touch parts of it. The church is rich with art from different periods, but of particular note is the **Sacristy of St. John Evangelist,** which was decorated in 1479 by Luca Signorelli and his workshop, with particular figures attributed to Signorelli himself: the Doctors of the Church, Saints Ambrose, Matthew, and the angel above Jerome. Note, too, the beautiful inlaid woodwork in some of the chapels.

Pinacoteca della Santa Casa (daily Tues.–Sun.) museum is in the Apostolic Palace (Basilica della Santa Casa, tel. 071/974-7198) adjacent to the Basilica. The collection houses important paintings by Lorenzo Lotto (1480–1557), a native of Venice who had a number of major commissions throughout Le Marche. His paintings are interesting for his use of color, humanity, and for his close association with Loreto. *Saints Christopher, Rocco, and Sebastian* (1532–1535) shows a giant Christopher amidst the other two, perhaps because such strength was needed to ferry the infant Christ across the water. Other museum highlights include the tapestry collection of Belgian works woven to designs by Raphael, the furniture collection, and the ceramics collection of Majolica pharmacy jars.

Shopping

Loreto attracts thousands of religious pilgrims, so religious objects can be found in almost every shop in all price ranges, including the museum shop at Pinacoteca della Santa Casa. **Paolo Cupido** (tel. 071/980-228, Apr.–Sept. 6:15 A.M.–12:30 P.M. and 2:30–8 P.M.; Oct.–Mar. 6:45 A.M.–12:30 P.M. and 2:30–7 P.M.) makes lovely mirror and glass objects.

Accommodations

Lodging in Loreto accommodates the large numbers of pilgrims that arrive so is likely to be fairly basic, but it's also reasonably priced. The most expensive rooms are under €120 and budget rooms are as low as €20, with most falling somewhere in the middle. Given the mass tourism, for most the city is a day trip. Unless Loreto is of special importance, it's probably more pleasant to stay in Recanati, the Conero, or Urbisaglia, where for similar rates accommodations and dining may be better quality and more personal. For those requiring a stay in town, the **Pellegrino e Pace** (Piazza della Madonna 51, tel. 071/977-106, www.pelligrinoepace.it, €63–76 d), near the sanctuary, has 28 rooms, some with a view of the sea in the distance.

Food

Game, fresh pasta, and house innovations are the specialties at **Andreina** (Via Vuffolareccia 14, tel. 071/970-124, www.ristoanteandreina. it, Wed.–Mon. lunch and dinner, €40–45).

Information

The tourist office, **Pro Loco** (Corso Boccolini, tel. 071/977-748, www.prolocoloreto. com) has information on lodging, dining, and sightseeing, as well as suggestions for visitors with disabilities.

Getting There and Around

Loreto is easy to reach by car. From Ancona, take *autostrada* A14 south for about 20 km to the Loreto exit. As you travel around Italy, if you read church bulletins or notices, you'll see frequent postings for bus trips to Loreto. As a major pilgrim site, Loreto is well connected by bus from most major Italian cities and many provincial towns.

JESI

Jesi is one of the seven towns in Le Marche that permanently display Lorenzo Lotto's paintings. Lorenzo Lotto would have several important commissions in Jesi, a lively, breezy lovely hill town that one visitor observed is "big enough to have a Max Mara shop in it." Its Pinacoteca Civica Comunale is home to several Lotto works, but it's Lucy, patron saint of Syracuse, that steals the show in the art museum. Be sure to stop in **Piazza Federico II,** which is where Emperor Frederick II was born in a tent pitched in this square during his mother's journey.

Sights

The main attractions in the town art museum are the paintings of Lorenzo Lotto, many of which are found at **Pinacoteca Comunale di Jesi** (Palazzo Pianetti, Via XV Settembre 10, tel. 0731/538-342, www.lorenzo-lotto.it, winter Tues.–Sat. 10 A.M.–1 P.M. and 4–7 P.M., Sun. 10 A.M.–1 P.M. and 5–8 P.M., summer Tues.–Sat. 10 A.M.–8 P.M., €5.50). In Lotto's 1532 painting of *St. Lucy,* he gives the young woman great majesty, dignity, and beauty in her dramatic moment of defiance. After her mother's miraculous cure in Catania at St. Agatha's shrine, Lucy distributed most of her riches to the poor. Her enraged, greedy fiancé denounced her to the Governor of Sicily, who at this moment condemns the Christian woman to a life of prostitution. In the lower left, note the handsome woman of color in a deeper yellow dress as she kneels to support the toddler that reaches out toward Lucy. Note also the panel underneath with the internal mechanism of a clock, the courtroom scene, and statue of Roman god Saturn (the Saturnalia, a Roman agricultural festival, was held in December, too). Lotto's final payment for this painting commissioned for the hospital in Jesi was less than half what was due to him from the Friars of St. Lucy. It wasn't until nine years later that Lotto received the money.

Lucy is the most striking of Lotto's paintings in Jesi but others are interesting, too. His 1512 *Deposition* has vibrant clothing colors and a distant landscape that could be Le Marche. Lotto's 1526 *Annunciation* in two panels is full of movement: The athletic angel alights in a balletic leap and startled Mary falls to her knees. *Madonna of the Roses*, Lotto's 1526 work in two panels, shows brilliant color and humanity. In the lower panel, rose petals have been strewn below Mary, who holds her lively infant as he energetically reaches out toward Joseph. Visitors can buy a multiple ticket for €7.80 good at four museums with Lotto exhibitions: Jesi Art Gallery, Ancona Art Gallery, Villa Colloredo Museum in Recanati, and Holy House Art Gallery in Loreto.

Along Via Pergolesi (ex Via degli Orefici, or Street of the Goldsmiths) are the **Domus Verronum Portal** and **Piazza Colocci,** where **Palazzo della Signoria** was built in 1486. It served as City Hall until 1585, then became Palace of the Governors when it came under pontifical rule. Inside the courtyard are the initials of Andrea Contucci, the Tuscan architect better known as Andrea Sansovino, who is credited with the first row of loggias in the inner courtyard. The tower and door were later additions. Now the palace is home of the public library, the

historical archives, and the city museum with Roman statues, ceramics, and mosaics.

Some might credit Apollo, who's up on the ceiling vault in *The Story of Apollo* frescoes, while others would claim it's the curved shape of the hall that makes for fine acoustics in **Teatro Pergolesi** (Piazza della Repubblica, 9, box office tel. 0731/206-888, www. fondazionepergolesispontini.com, Tues.–Sun. 9:30 A.M.–12:30 P.M. and 5–7:30 P.M.). The theater opened in 1798 for Carnevale. Prince Beauharnais donated the clock on the facade in 1839 as thanks for his enjoyable visit to Jesi. Inside the 1850 stage screen tells the story of the entrance of Frederick II into Jesi (although he was born in Jesi, the emperor never returned in 1220, as the legend would have it). In 1953, Renata Scotto gave her first performance of *Madam Butterfly* here. Franco Zeffirelli directed opera and ballerina Carla Fracci danced here. Pergolesi puts on plays, opera, children's programs, and festivals. **Festival Pergolesi Spontini** celebrated its 40th season in 2007. Aspiring divas can apply to audition for the festival.

Outside Jesi's town walls is **Chiesa San Marco** (Costa San Marco 11, tel. 0731/4804), which was probably dedicated to St. Francis and built over the remains an earlier Benedictine church. In the second half of the 13th century, Franciscan friars modified it to its present appearance. Of special interest inside are the detailed, vivid 14th-century frescos of Giotto's school attributed to Giovanni and Giuliano from Rimini.

Accommodations

Set just outside of Jesi's center in its own park with swimming pool, **Hotel Federico II** (Via Ancona 100, tel. 0731/211-079, www.hotelf ederico2.it, €130 d) is in a modern building that has a view of the surrounding hills. It has a fitness room, sauna, and restaurant.

Food

The regional government promotes its own wines in several *enoteche.* In **Enoteca of Le Marche Jesi** (Via F. Conti 5, tel. 0731/213-386) you can taste Jesi's prized white wine, Verdicchio di Jesi, or any number of wines that are produced throughout Le Marche. They serve local specialties, too, like salami and sausage platters or the local lasagna, *vincis grassi.*

An Argentinian runs the wine and coffee bar **Piazza F2** (Piazza Federico II 2 a/b, tel. 0731/215-683, Tues.–Sun. 7 A.M.–10 P.M.) so it's no surprise that although he stocks Italian wines, he sells more from Argentina. If you're craving a snack, try the tapas.

Information
The tourist office in Jesi is located at Piazza della Repubblica (tel. 0731/538-420, Apr.–Sept. daily 10 A.M.–6 P.M.).

Getting There
From Ancona, the easiest way to connect to Jesi is off the A14 *autostrada* heading west.

FRASASSI
Inside the Frasassi caves you can literally disappear off the face of the earth into a magical world of mineral formations that have eroded, dripped, or otherwise formed this subterranean fantasy. That effect is further enhanced by dramatic lighting. **Frasassi National Park** is Le Marche's largest protected wildlife area and the "wild" is here in abundance. Boars, foxes, golden eagles, peregrine falcons, wolves, badgers, hares, porcupines, and other animals inhabit the area. The woods vary by the climatic zones and are home to hop hornbeam, durmast oak, and beech. The caves were originally carved out by the Sentino River, which, along with the Esino, offers opportunities for exploration by canoe or trail. All that sulfurous-chlorinated-sodium mineral water that cleared out the caves is used at the **San Vittore Spa** for clearing out respiratory systems or for mud therapy to soothe aching joints.

Sights
Grotte di Frasassi (Consorzio Frasassi, Genga, tel. 0732/90090, www.frasassi.com) are caves discovered in 1971 by a group of speleologists with the Italian Alpine Club (CAI). After ex-

ploration, Cesarini of Senigallia added dramatic lighting, and the caves were opened to public. It's a subterranean world of stalactites and stalagmites that have dripped into all kinds of shapes. At 13 kilometers long, it is considered to be one of Italy's most important caverns. The Sentino River's bicarbonate water met with sulfurous mineral water from underground to erode and create this underground world.

The entrance is at the **Ancona Abyss,** the largest cave in Europe and tall enough to fit a cathedral inside. Only drops of water interrupt the silence. Further along are the formations imaginatively called Giant, Niagara, Dead Tree, Crystallized Lake, Room 200, Witches Castle, Sword of Damocles, Obelisk, Grand Canyon, Organ Pipes, Candle Room, White Room, Bear Room, Room of Infinity, and Angel Hair. All visits are guided. The regular visit takes about one hour. You can also reserve a guide for a longer speleological visit of two or three hours. Be sure to come with a jacket or sweater as the temperature is a constant 14°C. On busy days, especially Sundays and holidays, the wait to enter can be several hours or more. Binoculars are handy if you want to see something up close that is off limits (use them later for bird-watching in the park or to see detail in churches).

Tours of the caves leave daily at 9:30 A.M., 11 A.M., 12:30 P.M., 3 P.M., 4:30 P.M., and 6 P.M., March through October; every 10 minutes from 8 A.M. to 6:30 P.M. in August; and at 11 A.M. and 3 P.M. November through February. The caves are closed most of January. Admission is €15; guided tours are €35 for 3 hours and €45 for 4 hours.

The caves are the main draw, so the other sights play second fiddle. The area is scattered with small towns that merit a stop to explore the main squares and churches, and to check the pulse of small-town life.

Sports and Recreation
Apart from the caves, the **Gola della Rossa** and **Frasassi Regional Park** (Parco Gola della Rossa e di Frasassi, Serra San Quirico, tel. 0731/86122, www.parcogolarossa.it) form

the region's largest protected habitat. The area has hiking trails of varying difficulty and the Sentino River is popular for canoeing or rafting. The Esino and Sentino both have clear water that makes for attractive hiking on nearby paths. In winter the area has skiing. Perhaps the caves will inspire you to take speleology lessons. Check with the park office for further information on lessons, rentals, and other activities.

Stabilimento Termale San Vittore (Via S. Vittore Terme 8, tel. 0732/90444, www.termesanvittore.it, May–Nov.), with its sulfurous-chlorinated-sodium mineral water, specializes in respiratory cures, mud treatments for joints, and even hearing disorders. The water is channeled directly from a nearby spring. Some treatments may require medical permission, but a staff physician is present on the premises so you can book a visit there first; it even has a pediatrics department. If all you want is to be pampered, book a massage or cosmetic treatment. The Roman Bridge with pointed arches and a Gothic tower is nearby.

Accommodations
Terme San Vittore Hotel (Via S. Vittore Terme 8, tel. 0732/90012, www.termesan

vittore.it, €55–80 s/d) is annexed to the spa but guests don't need to have treatments. Its thermal pool is open in summer, plus there is a park and playground for children.

Getting There and Around
The easiest approach to Frasassi is on highway SS76, exit Genga/Grotta di Frasassi/Serra San Quirico. Smaller roads connect to Frasassi from Cingoli and Jesi. Follow signs for *biglietteria* (ticket office). By train (www.trenitalia.com), take the Rome–Ancona line and get off at Stazione Genga–San Vittore Terme.

Around Frasassi
Take a detour on SS 76 west toward Umbria and the town of Fabriano. There you can visit the **Museum of Paper** (Largo Fratelli Spacca 2, Fabriano, tel. 0732/709-297), beautiful **Teatro Gentile** theater (Piazzetta del Podesta, Fabriano, tel. 0732/3644, box-office Thurs.–Fri. 4–7 P.M., Sat. 10 A.M.–1 P.M. and 4–9 P.M. when performances are scheduled), and **Pinacoteca** (Via del Poio 18, Fabriano, tel. 0732/709-255) with local artists minus Gentile da Fabriano, whose works were carted off by Napoleon's troops.

Province of Macerata and Monti Sibillini

Macerata is both a province and a city within Le Marche. The city has the lively air of a university town. The arts get a boost in the summertime when Sferisterio draws world-class opera, theater, and concert performers. Northwest of Macerata is Cingoli, the balcony of Macerata, with its sweeping views and some charming accommodations and restaurants.

Northeast of Macerata toward the coast is Recanati, with its "hills of infinity," home once to poet Giacomo Leopardi and to one of Renaissance artist Lorenzo Lotto's most extraordinary paintings.

Southeast of Macerata is Urbisaglia, a medieval hilltop overlooking the extraordinary

ruins of the ancient Roman town of Urbs Salvia. Urbisaglia celebrates its heritage with an ancient Roman banquet every August, with theater performances and concerts in its ancient theater and amphitheater.

West of Urbisaglia, Tolentino has the Basilica of San Nicola, with an extraordinary series of painted frescoes that not only celebrate the life of St. Nicholas, but provide insight into the colorful world of custom and fashion of the Middle Ages. The Abbey of Chiaravalle di Fiastra continues the medieval theme, but it wonderfully combines ancient facilities and traditions with a friendly atmosphere in the hotel, restaurants, bars, tourist center, and an ancient abbey with monks still in residence. The abbey's grounds are a wildlife sanctuary and its lawn provides a picnic setting where residents socialize practically every holiday.

The drive southwest from Tolentino or Urbisaglia leads toward the Monti Sibillini, the mountains full of legends—from mystical Sibyls to the lake that Pontius Pilate plunged his chariot into (the unofficial reason the lake turns bright red during certain months). Enchanting towns close to the Parco Sibillini entrance include San Ginesio, Sarnano, Caldarola, and Camerino, and make for good stops along the way. Most have stunning churches or delightful theaters regally awaiting performances. The mountains offer plenty of skiing and hiking, including "sleeper" ski resorts challenging enough to have some fun and blessedly devoid of crowds.

Cross over the mountains and head west to find yourself in Umbria in Castellucia, which is famous for its lentils that bloom in late spring and early summer, then head down into Norcia. The legendary Sibyls attracted a boom in tourism in the late Middle Ages and early Renaissance, when even mathemetician-architect Leon Battista Alberti and Michelangelo followed these legends for inspiration. Michelangelo even painted the Sibyls on Rome's Sistine Chapel.

Whether you stumble onto the Sibyls or merely hike the mountain trails, you are sure to become enchanted with Province of Macerata.

RECANATI

Set amidst rolling emerald hills and a patchwork of olive trees and agricultural crops, Recanati is just a few kilometers to the east of Porto Recanati, near where Romans founded the town of Potentia in 184 B.C. Frederick II established Porto Recanati as a place where he could fish. Further inland, Recanati developed and today attracts art, poetry, and opera buffs, as well as those who simply wish to kick back and admire the landscape. Renaissance painter Lorenzo Lotto is the big draw in the art museum, while Giacomo Leopardi's family pal-

ace is a museum dedicated to the 19th-century poet, and there's also a museum dedicated to the opera star who sang 12 consecutive seasons at the Met in New York.

Sights

Museo Villa Colleredo Pinacoteca Comunale
(Via Gregorio XII, tel. 071/757-0410, www. spaziocultura.org, Jul.–Aug. Tues.–Sun. 9 A.M.–1 P.M. and 3–8 P.M., Sept.–Jun. Tues.–Sun. 9 A.M.–noon and 3–7 P.M.) has some extraordinary Lorenzo Lotto paintings, particularly his *Annunciation,* almost shocking for the very human reaction of Mary to the Angel, that is splendidly athletic as a ballet dancer. Ask here about a map for all seven Lorenzo Lotto towns and combined ticket for museums (churches are free). The interior of **Teatro Giuseppe Persiani** (Corso Cavour, tel. 071/757-9445, www.teatrop ersiani.com, box office Tues.–Sat. 11 A.M.–1 P.M. and 4–8 P.M., performances €10–30) is an architectural gem.

Casa Leopardi, birthplace of Giacomo Leopardi, is a pilgrimage site for fans of this beloved Italian poet who wrote about the "hill of infinity" that so well describes the splendid vistas from Recanati and the landscape of Le Marche. That wasn't enough to keep Leopardi here, though. The poet had a love-hate relationship with Le Marche, left for good, and died in Naples.

Nightlife

The number-one disco in Le Marche, **Babaloo** (Potenza Picena, Contrada Terranova, tel. 073/388-1145, www.babaloodisco. it, summer Wed.–Sun.) is open in summer only; it has dance pads that bounce up and down. **Discoteca Green Leaves** (Via Salvo D'Acquisto 1, tel. 071/979-8145, www.green leavesdisco.com, Fri.–Sun. 9 P.M.–2:30 A.M., €15) has been going since the 1970s.

Accommodations

Gallery Hotel Recanati (Via Falleroni 85, tel. 071/981-914, www.ghr.it, €79 d) is just steps from the art museum and is set on an ancient palazzo. The modern interior has spacious guestrooms, some with marvelous hillside vistas.

ON THE ROAD WITH LORENZO LOTTO

Lorenzo Lotto left behind some extraordinary paintings, as well as some mysteries in Le Marche. Born in Venice around 1480, Lotto abandoned the very city that nurtured other artists like Titian. Instead Lotto turned to the provinces. Lotto's first stop in Le Marche was Recanati, where he arrived in 1506.

By that year, fellow artist Raphael had left Le Marche and his hometown of Urbino to seek masters and commissions in Umbria, Florence, and Rome. Lotto, too, arrived in Rome and even worked for a time with Raphael in the Vatican apartments. But Lotto was not to remain long. His volatile personality made it hard for him to woo patrons, win commissions, and maintain friendships. He also had legal problems. Throughout his restless life, Lotto sometimes made Le Marche his base.

In his life on the move, however, Lotto left behind a brilliant trail of color and sometimes astonishing drama. Recanati, Lotto's first stop in Le Marche, is a good base and an excellent point to begin. His astonishing *Annunciation*, painted 1527-1529, now hangs in **Museo Villa Colleredo Pinacoteca Comunale.** The angel's hair and garments are blown back from the force of his ballet landing: He has just dropped into Mary's room to announce (thus "Annunciation") that she is to bear the son of God, who gestures toward the empty canopied bed from the clouds above. A cat, back arched, scampers away from the angel. The heavenly angel casts an earthly shadow. Mary crouches and flees toward the viewer. Her vivid red, coral, and blue garments blow back as she rushes forward. But you can't embrace her or change the course of history.

Le Marche has seven towns with paintings by Lorenzo Lotto, and each merits a visit. The bonus is the humanity and variety that Lorenzo Lotto, shows in his paintings. Jesi's **Pinacoteca Comunale** has another *Annunciation,* painted a year earlier: It is vivid, too, in color but with more restraint in its action. It also has Lotto's stunning painting of *St. Lucy,* shown as a young woman unafraid of death as she points heavenward. Lucy had donated most of her fortune to the poor, an act that defied the wishes of her greedy fiancé and of the authorities.

In the town of Monte San Giusto, Lotto's painting of *The Crucifixion* (1529-1534) is magnificent for its large scale as you step into the small church of Santa Maria in Telusiano. In Cingoli, the town called "Le Marche's Balcony," Lotto's painting hangs in the church of San Domenico; he painted 15 circular scenes with the *Mysteries of the Rosary* above his 1539 *Madonna.*

Ancona's **Pinacoteca** has Lotto's *Madonna and Child with Saints* (also 1539), which shows his gift for psychological nuance in his use of light and shadow. *The Assumption of the Virgin* (1548) is a later painting that is much less vivid; it is symbolic of the triumph of Christianity over paganism as Mary rises toward heaven above ancient monuments. This painting in the church of **Arcipertale di Santa Maria** is in Mogliano, a town famous for its hat-makers.

Loreto, where Lotto retreated to the monastery and spent his final disillusioned years, has several paintings. The unfinished *Presentation at the Temple* (c. 1555) was probably Lotto's last painting; the elderly figure with the white beard may be a self-portrait. Lorenzo Lotto died around 1557. There is no grave and no record of his death.

A combined ticket for Lorenzo Lotto exhibitions (www.lorenzolotto.it) allows entry to four museums for €7.80: Jesi's Pinacoteca Civica, the Pinacoteca in Ancona, Museo Villa Collerado Pinacoteca Communale in Recanati, and Loreto's Pinacoteca della Santa Casa. The churches are free.

Information and Services

Recanati's tourist office (Piazza G. Leopardi 31, tel. 071/981-471) has brief hours. Villa Colleredo has good town information, and its hours make this a better resource.

Getting There and Around

By road, exit the A14 *autostrada* near Porto Recanati, then head a few kilometers west on SS 77 to Recanati. From here it's an easy jaunt to meander on to Monefano, Macerata,

Urbisaglia, and Pollenza, or to head back to the coast for a visit to the pilgrimage town of Loreto. See *Macerata* for information on bus lines.

MACERATA

Macerata displays its 17th-century charms with the exuberant air of a university town. Situated atop a hill with the Potenza River Valley to the north and the Chienti River Valley to the south, its center affords lovely views of the surrounding hills. Only in recent decades has the agricultural economy shifted more toward trade and manufacturing. Macerata's main cultural draw is in the summer when the opera season is in full swing and the town becomes cosmopolitan with international visitors vying for tickets to the Sferisterio, Macerata's outdoor theater. The town also has museums and churches to explore. Don't miss the interior of 18th-century Teatro Lauro Rossi, a gem of a theater that makes any event special.

Sights

Cattedrale di Macerata is dedicated to Macerata's patron saint, Giuliano, born in the 9th century. A previous church was dedicated to him on this site, then reconstructed in 1771–1790. As a knight, he made his pilgrimage from Belgium to Le Marche, where he ferried passengers across the Pollenza River. He appears as a knight in Pagani's 16th-century painting and in a charming sculpture astride his horse surrounded by creatures of the forest. Nuzi da Fabriano's 1369 triptych in the sacristy is brilliantly gold with beautiful details in the textiles of the figures.

Giorgio di Chirico's *Disquieting Muse* (1950) is one of the better known paintings in **Museo Palazzo Ricci** (Galleria Palazzo Ricci, Via D. Ricci 1, tel. 0733/232-802 daily 10 A.M.–1 P.M. and 4–8 P.M., admission free), which has works of art that reflect major trends in the 20th century. Ivo Pannaggi's geometric prisms set his *Train in Motion* (1922). Lucio Fontana's monochromatic *Spatial Conception* is an exploration in texture, form, and the color green.

The 478-seat **Teatro Lauro Rossi** (Piazza della Libertà 21, tel. 0733/256-306, www.

comune.macerata.it) built in 1774 is one of Le Marche's ornately decorated architectural masterpieces and hosts performances year-round. The bell-shaped interior has three levels of seats. Check with the theater or tourist office about a visit, even if you don't plan to catch a performance.

Entertainment and Events

A magnet for opera buffs, **Sferisterio** (Piazza N. Sauro, box office Piazza Mazzini 10, tel. 0733/230-735 or 800/907-080, www.sferisterio.it, €15–150) attracts a full house in its 3,500 seats for the quality of its opera productions and for its acoustics. It's remarkable that the acoustics are so excellent, given that the structure was not originally designed for opera, but was instead built to host sporting events. Its back wall was installed for the ball games and pens where bulls once waited to meet matadors. Inaugurated in 1829 for sports fans, it wasn't until a century later that the first opera, *Aida,* was staged. In recent years, Sferisterio has hosted Luciano Pavarotti, Placido Domingo, Marilyn Horn, José Carreras, and other opera stars. Jazz was introduced in Sferisterio after World War I. Miles Davis, Don Cherry, Chet Baker, Stan Getz, Dizzy Gillespie, B. B. King, Ray Charles, and Sarah Vaughn all performed here. The opera season begins in late July and concludes in early August. **Musicultura** is a festival of musicians, poets, and writers held in June. Teatro Lauro Rossi hosts performances year-round and delivers a fantasy setting as only old-fashioned theaters do; even if you don't understand the language, go for the whole scene.

Cinema Multiplex 2000 (Via Velluti, tel. 0733/288-114, www.multiplex2000.it) is outside the center in Piediripa. The owner put headsets in one theater so students could improve their foreign language skills, and it offers a rare chance to watch a film in its original language.

Other evening denizens can head for spots like **Discoteca** (Vicolo Coltelli Paolo 13, www.metropolino.com/macerata, daily), **Discoteca Number One** (Vicolo Coltelli 13, www.metropolino.com/macerata, daily), and **Il Pozzo** (Via Costa 5, tel. 0733/232-360, www. ilpozzo.com, closed Tues.) where DJs play a mix of disco and lounge until the early hours. Macerata is a sleepy city and 2 A.M. is very late around here.

Shopping

Ginesi and Varagona weave textiles at **La Tela** (Vicolo Vecchio 6, tel. 0733/232-527) on a variety of looms right on the premises. Some of their traditional patterns date back to the 1300s but they have plenty of modern designs, all made of natural fabrics and using traditional equipment. Prices range from €10 for small towels to €2,000 for a hand-loomed bedcover. If you'd like to learn or advance your weaving skills, ask them about lessons. The locally made liqueur, Varnelli (Distilleria Varnelli, Pievebovigliana, Muccia, tel. 0733/647-000), is anise-based; unlike Ascoli's, it's not sweet, which makes it surprisingly versatile. Try it with a splash of water and ice with appetizers, an artichoke dish, or even a *porchetta panino*. It's just the thing on a hot summer day. A splash of Varnelli to "correct" an espresso is the way to warm up. Or sip a shot glass after a meal and savor the flavor.

Accommodations

Don't be put off by **Hotel I Colli's** (Via Roma 149, tel. 0733/367-063, www.hotelicolli.it, €80–130 s/d) bland modern exterior. Inside it has pleasantly contemporary rooms with hardwood floors, efficient service, and friendly staff that attract business travelers year-round and opera-goers in summer. It has a convenient location at the edge of the town and is walking distance to the sights in the center. There's a fitness center and free parking.

Food

Osteria dei Pigliapochi (Vicolo della Rota 8, tel. 073/326-4393, closed Sat. and Sun. lunch, €15–25) serves traditional dishes at reasonable prices in the *centro storico*. For cheap eats, university students frequent two cafeteria-style establishments, handy for those with limited Italian who want to point and eat: **Il Ghiottone Ristorante Self Service** (Via Gramsci Antonio 30, tel. 0733/234-219) and **Self Service Break** (Piazza Garibaldi Giuseppe 9). (Keep in mind that Italians use the word "self-service" to mean "cafeteria," while *caffetteria* is an espresso-maker.)

Bar Gelateria Il Ghiotto Mariotto (Piazza Mazzini 46–48) is a favorite with kids likely to be packed in here as soon as school lets out. **Da Nino Pasticceria** near Hotel Colli below the historic center is not historic, but it's where the locals head for morning coffee and sweets.

Getting There and Around

Trains (Piazza della Croce Rossa, 1, www.tren italia.com) are practical for longer hops. The local bus companies **Contram** (Piazza XXV Aprile 1) and **APM** (Viale Don Bosco 34) move around small towns, as well as further afield. When school is not is session (i.e., summer, Sundays, holidays), service is often reduced. Keep in mind as you travel that Macerata is both the name of the city and also the name of its province in Le Marche. Towns in the province of Macerata often have an **(MC)** that follows the town name, i.e., Montefano (MC).

Around Macerata

Some of the best places to eat, sleep, and shop are not in the larger towns but in smaller hamlets like **Cingoli,** a place that Rip Van Winkle would immediately recognize even if he had dozed off for a few hundred years.

The bounty at ◖ **Natura e Profumi** (Cingoli, Via Duomo 17, tel. 0733/610-269, www. naturaeprofumi.it) comes in part from Maria's lawn, sure to be knee-high with weeds that might have produced the day's pesto for the pasta. This herb lady cooks up a savory storm in her modest country house. Lunch is the best time to observe the birds and the bees over Le Marche's green hills from her living and dining room. Homemade pasta, rabbit *in porchetta* with wild fennel, vegetables, and sauces are all excellent. If you have specific food preferences, let her know when you reserve. Don't miss dessert. She selects excellent Rosso Conero or other local wines. A meal without wine is about

ITALY'S SHOEMAKERS

Marchigiani (MAR-key-johnny), as Le Marche residents are known, are eager to promote the "Made in Italy" quality admired by the rest of the world for design, craftsmanship, food, and wine. Its inhabitants are industrious but they see the threat of competition looming ever closer. Watch closely at what happens in the shoe industry. Underneath homes on the ground floor, often someone is cutting leather, stitching soles, crafting shoe uppers, making heels, or working on some other part of the shoe. Smaller workshops look like a scene from *The Shoemaker and the Elves*. Along with the craftsmanship comes a lot of transport, mostly in short hops. The previous expert in the shoe chain delivers to the next or picks up pieces to continue where another left off – rarely does one shoemaker make the entire shoe from beginning to end. This industriousness and hopping around is like observing bees, with the shoemakers pollinating the landscape with shoe parts.

The town **Civitanova Marche,** near Macerate, is a mecca for shoes. Well-known shoemaker **Cesare Paciotti** has a shop in this town. Paciotti's shoes range from practical to glam. (See the *Around Macerata* section for more information on Paciotti's shop.)

Lucina Calzature, a shoe store in Urbisaglia, turns out finely crafted leather sandals and shoes that are meticulous and comfortable copies of ancient Roman styles. (See *Shopping* in the *Urbisaglia* section for more information on Lucina Calzature.)

and Sat. 6–10 P.M., Sun. from noon, Tues.–Thurs. by reservation only, €30–40). Downstairs his descendants run this restaurant with two great dining options. The fine dining room has especially good pumpkin soup, gnocchi with *funghi* porcini or truffles, and roast veal *en croute*. There's also a casual pizzeria (€6–15) and very inexpensive wine tavern.

In the midst of green, tree-covered hills and Verdicchio (white wine grape) vineyards is the 11th-century abbey **Badia Benedettina di San Vittore** (San Vittore di Cingoli, tel. 0733/617-114, www.villadellarovere.com). The medieval *borgo* of San Vittore di Cingoli makes a convenient point to head for the Frassassi Caves or for the sea. Your room will be a former monk's cell.

To look like Queen Elizabeth, Casanova, Eleanor of Aquitaine, or a flapper, head to **Arianna** (Corridonia, Via dell'Artigianato 11, tel. 0733/283-067, www.ariannacostumi.com, rentals run €50–500, Tues.–Sun.). Elvia's son does the historical research while she and her seamstresses sew costumes for theater, opera, historical processions, Carnevale, and even your wedding dress, if you choose. Finds in the vintage clothing section range from elegant 17th-century items to kitschy RAI TV sequin dresses circa the 1980s. Buy or rent costumes and clothing for men and women. She has a great hat selection, too. Seamstresses are in the next room cutting, sewing, and dying exquisite fabrics with a wall full of trim and accessories.

A detour to **Montefano,** from where you can see the Monti Sibillini, gives you an excuse to see the town theater, **La Rondinella** (Montefano, Piazza Braccaccini, tel. 346/966-0805, tickets at Mediateca UBU di Montefano, Via della Vittoria 10, daily 6–8 P.M., €10). It was redesigned in 1887 by Virginio Tombolini, director of La Fenice opera house, who wished to re-create the Venetian theater in miniature here. La Rondinella Theater re-opened in 2004 after 20 years of restoration.

If only a historical address will do, stay in Montefano, a medieval *borgo*. Marchesa Rangoni Machiavelli's (yes, that Machiavelli)

€20. Dining is by reservation only, and you'll need to phone several days in advance. If you wish that you had a favorite cousin to visit in Le Marche, this is as close as it gets.

Pious VIII was born upstairs in **La Cantina del Palazzo Vineria** (Cingoli, Via Benedetto da Cingoli/I Ponti 30, tel. 0733/602-531, Fri.

palace, **Hotel Palazzo Carradori** (Via della Vittoria 7, tel. 0733/850-339, www.palazzo carradori.com, €180 d), has eight rooms plus a suite with a wrought-iron *baldachin* bed. The breakfast room has a huge fireplace. Three brothers run the place; one is the chef for the grand dining room.

Civitanova Marche is a mecca for shoes. The town is short on charm and is best for a shopping hit-and-flee. **Cesare Paciotti** (Zona Industrial B, tel. 0733/79061, www .cesare-paciotti.com, daily 10 A.M.12:30 P.M. and 3:30–7:30 P.M.) was launched into the fashion stratosphere by Gianni Versace. Paciotti's shoes range from styles naughty enough to wear with Versace, practical enough for work, glam enough for an evening out. His 4US line is sporty but too sleek to be mistaken for chunky jogging shoes. Prices, about 30 percent lower than retail, generally range €140–300 (higher for winter shoes and boots); €50–150 for tops and pants. He also sells a line of sportswear, purses, belts, and kids shoes. Enter the gate between 1A/1 and 3; the Paciotti plaque is a small sign on the left side of a tan brick building marked "Paris." Italians regularly comb through the racks.

C URBISAGLIA

Set on a hilltop that supports the medieval fortress La Rocca, Urbisaglia's real heyday was in ancient Roman times when the town of **Urbs Salvia** was situated down below in the valley. A contemporary of Pompeii in the first century and similar in size with 21,000 inhabitants, Urbs Salvia's importance was due partly to its strategic location near the ancient consular roads that led toward Rome, the Flaminia and the Salaria. However, its valley location was too vulnerable, as Alaric aptly demonstrated by clobbering the town in 408–409 A.D.

Locals then began to settle Urbisaglia on top of the hill. During the Gothic War (535–552), Belisarius swept up from Sicily with his troops in 538, causing more mayhem. When the nearby Cistercian abbey **Santa Maria di Chiaravalle di Fiastra** was founded in the 12th century, the area began to revive. Dante even mentions

the town in Canto XVI of *Paradiso*. Urbisaglia never matched ancient Urbs Salvia for size or splendor, and for a grim period in World War II it had an internment camp. At least present inhabitants in this quiet town can claim a peaceful existence. Though the town is now only about a tenth of its Roman size, townsfolk still know how to throw a bash in summer when the two Roman theaters are enlivened with concerts, plays, and even a Roman banquet.

Sights

Named for Salus, goddess of healing and cohort of the god of medicine, Aeschlypius, the town of Urbs Salvia now is Le Marche's most important ancient Roman archeological site. **Parco Archeologico Urbs Salvia** (Pro Loco Tourist Office, Via Sacrario 9, tel. 0733/506-566, www. urbisaglia.com) is just off the SS77 down the road from the medieval abbey **Chiaravalle di Fiastra.** Below the present town of Urbisaglia, its hillside theater was one of the largest in the Roman Empire and perhaps is the only to still have remains of frescoes painted in the Pompeii style. In summer, both the hillside theater and the amphitheater down in the valley below host concerts and prestigious dramatic performances. The amphitheater also is the site of an annual Roman banquet in August: It's ideal for mingling with the locals, parading around in togas, and dining on ancient recipes.

Abbazia di Fiastra (sometimes written *abbazia* or *abbadia*, tel. 0733/202-942, daily, closes midday) is the abbey founded in 1142 by Cistercian monks. The eight monks that live in relative seclusion permit you to visit the cloisters, the church, and part of the monastery, including their winemaking area.

Take a stroll uphill to present-day Urbisaglia inside the town walls to see **La Rocca,** the medieval fortress last modified in 1507. Elderly men sit and gossip under its corner towers shaped like badminton birdies. From above on a clear day it affords a view of the sea and the Sibylline Mountains. The nearby church dedicated to St. Lawrence was completed in 1800 and was based on the round design of an early medieval church in Rome, Santo Stefano in Rotunda.

INFANT AND THE GOAT

General Belisarius was accompanied by his secretary Procopius, who wrote an official account of the Gothic War and recorded a curious sight in Urbisaglia in 538: a goat nursing a motherless infant. Women that had not been carted off or killed during the siege returned and found the abandoned infant. Some tried to nurse him but he refused human milk and cried until the goat returned, nursed him, and fiercely protected him from any intruders, including Procopius himself when he tried to approach the infant. The story of infant Egisto (little goat) still circulates among local townsfolk. In addition to his official writings, Procopius went on to pen *The Secret History*, which recounted scenes of his commander and Emperor Justinian that depicted the early medieval elite to be as kinky as their Roman predecessors.

Entertainment and Events

Check your 21st-century clothes at the door. Urbisaglia's annual **Cena Romana,** the town's ancient Roman banquet, is held in the 1st-century amphitheater on the first or second Saturday of August. When night falls, torches and candles light up. The dress code is decidedly 1st century and the locals will happily loan you a costume from head garland to toga and sandals. Hide those wristwatches, purses, and cell phones, or you'll look like a B-movie actor. The banquet is held August 9–15. Festivities start at 7:30 P.M. and cost €35, including costume rental, a meal with wine, and Roman entertainment

Teatro Antico, the ancient Roman hillside theater, is one of the settings for a series of June jazz concerts in the province of Macerata that culminate in a prize sponsored in memory of Italian saxophonist Massimo Urbani. Previous winners include Max D'Avola, who began his career playing classical flute before he made the switch to jazz. The ancient Roman theater of Urbs Salvia is the setting for classical Greek and Roman plays, often with internationally known directors like Peter Stein.

Unlike Ascoli's elegant Palio (competition to win the banner), which has been fine-tuned with meticulous medieval costumes and pageantry, this Palio is conducted on donkeys—a marked contrast to Ascoli's. The Pro Loco tourist office is the best resource for purchasing tickets and getting information.

Tickets for both are available at Pro Loco Tourist Office (Via Sacrario 9, tel. 0733/506-566, www.urbisaglia.com, daily 10 A.M.–1 P.M. and 3–7 P.M.).

Shopping

Most of the women in the modern, pebbly gray building are busy working on shoe uppers for shoemaker Anna Piergiacomi. But **Lucina Calzature** (Loc. Montedoro, tel. 0733/506-931, www.lucinacalzature.it, Mon.–Thurs. 9 A.M.–5 P.M., Fri. 9 A.M.–1 P.M., other times by appointment but always best to phone) also turns out finely crafted leather sandals and shoes that are meticulous and comfortable copies of ancient Roman styles. They pair surprisingly well with modern garb. Perhaps the most famous—or infamous—are *caligae* worn by Emperor Caius Caesar Germanicus, better known as Caligula. The emperor's nickname, "Little Boots," came from his fetish for soldier's footwear, which he fancied and wore from boyhood until his final days. The moniker has stuck through 2,000 years of history. The shop also makes classy elegant suede travel slippers that will comfort a weary traveler or make a great gift. Prices at Lucina Calzatura are reduced almost by half of their catalogue. To get there, travel on SS78 towards Urbs Salvia from the Abbazia di Filastra, turn left at the non-working traffic light (km 6 marker), take the first right, and then the first left. In 2007, they branched out with ancient Greek designs as well as some contemporary styles.

Gocce Imperiali, a strong liqueur concocted two centuries ago by Fra Eutimio, is still made by the Liquoreria dell'Abbazia di Casamari and sold at the **Abbadia di Fiastra** shop (across from the church, tel. 0733/202-942, hours vary). The bright yellow liquid claims to aid digestion, clear respiratory passages, and save travelers from *l'imbarazzo di stomaco* (stomach embarrassment) in moving vehicles. Or simply "correct" your espresso with it. Other liqueurs, herbal products, and local food specialties are also available.

Sports and Recreation

On Italian holidays, locals from surrounding towns outnumber Urbisaglia's 2,800 inhabitants when the abbey grounds become one huge picnic patchwork of those that prefer the communal crowd scene to a simple family affair. The grounds are set on the edge of a nature preserve (near the intersection of SS 77 and SS 78) ideal for running, hiking, or bicycling without worries about traffic on the narrow roads in the area.

Accommodations

(Hotel la Foresteria (Abbazia di Fiastra 11, tel. 0733/201-125, www.laforesteria. it) opened in 2004. The stone outbuilding is near the medieval Abbey di Fiastra and on the edge of a nature preserve, and makes an ideal base of operation to explore the province of Macerata and the region. Basic but comfortable rooms have wood beam ceilings and terra-cotta floors, and many also have a courtyard view. Each room has a DVD player; rent DVDs in multiple languages at the front desk or bring your own, great for rainy days or for down time from sightseeing. An overnight stay in a double room with no board is €75; a three-day stay with half-board is €75 per day per person with breakfast plus lunch or dinner.

Locanda le Logge (Corso Giannelli 34, tel. 0733/506-788, www.locandealelogge.it, €80 d) opened in the historic center in 2004. It has three tastefully furnished rooms with wrought-iron beds and walnut furniture: Sogno has a *baldachin* bed and Cielo has a skylight and sitting room. The hotel has an inviting cozy restaurant open lunch and dinner (lunch is about €15, seats 60, and is closed on Wed.) with select

wines from the region and French champagnes. The bubbly is a hit with British guests that find it more reasonably priced than back home.

If you are on a tight budget and don't mind spartan rooms on par with a college dorm, continue on SS 78 past Urbs Salvia toward Loro Piceno. **Le Grazie** (Via Grazie Fiastra, Loro Piceno, tel. 0733/509-660, €47 d) has low rates favored by a working-class clientele that often stay several weeks and seek an inexpensive, clean place. Usually they opt for full- or half-board, as the restaurant food is great although the ambience is institutional. The hill views are better than those from the industrial side of the building.

Food

(Ristorante da Rosa (Abbazia di Fiastra, tel. 0733/203-552, morning coffee, lunch daily, dinner only on weekends, closed Thurs.) is just to the left of the church in the Fiastra Abbey. The coffee bar in front has saloon-style swinging doors. Saunter through them into a cozy room with a courtyard view and a dozen tables. Pasta is homemade and the gnocchi are especially good. It's priced right, with pastas €4–5 and meat dishes €4–6. The wine list changes periodically, so ask about good local reds like Rosso Piceno, Rosso Conero, and Lacrima di Morro d'Alba, or whites like Verdicchio.

Ristorante la Foresteria (Abbazia di Fiastra 11, tel. 0733/201-125, www.laforesteria.it, €5–7) has a coffee bar with outside seating and simple fare like breakfast rolls and sandwiches. The reasonably priced cafeteria pulls in locals at lunchtime. At lunch and dinner, the restaurant specialties are well prepared and highlight local fare like olive *ascolane,* good pasta, grilled meat, and house Rosso Piceno red wine that's cheaper than water. The fluorescent lights don't jibe with the architecture of the historic stone building, though.

Ristorante le Grazie (Via Grazie Fiastra, Loro Piceno, tel. 0733/509-660, lunch and dinner) off SS 78 between Urbs Salvia and Sarnano is favored by a working-class clientele that don't mind the lackluster decor that recalls a high school cafeteria. Here tables are always laid with linens, though. Regulars come for the ample portions of good traditional local specialties at good value. The pastas are all homemade and the fried food is perfectly executed, from appetizers to vegetables and meats—especially good is the lamb. There are no written menus, but generally a first and second course with house wine and coffee is €15 on Friday and €20 on Saturday; their Sunday extravaganza adds abundant antipasti, salad, fruit, and dessert for €30.

Da Oriana Rosticceria (Corso Gianelli 68, tel. 0733/405-506, Tues.–Sun. 8 A.M.–1:30 P.M. and 4–9 P.M., €3–8) prepares roast chicken (duck and goose by special order) plus various types of lasagna, chicken *galatine,* and meatballs that are good for a quick hot takeaway meal. **Antichi Sapori** (S.P. 78 Zona Artigianale Passo Colmurano, tel. 0733/506-779, €3–8) is past the Urbs Salvia archeological site going toward Sarnano. Locals consider this valley *rosticceria* to be the best, but it's convenient only if you come by car or bike. There's a great selection of pastas, meats, and plenty of vegetarian options at reasonable prices.

Properzi (Corso Giammelli 7, tel. 0733/506-691), on the hilltop in Urbisaglia's historic center, sells excellent sausages, salamis, and other quality meats that pair well with fresh bread and a bottle of wine to make an ideal picnic on the abbey grounds or near the ancient Roman theater. An *etto* (one-tenth of a kilogram, plenty for one person) costs €1–2, so try several cold cuts like *ciauscolo,* the soft spreadable pork salami unique to Le Marche, as well as a version with pork liver. *Lonza* and *lardellata* are local cured pork and salami that were traditionally eaten at breakfast so peasants would have energy to work in the farm fields. The colorful *galatine* is made from chicken, turkey, and pork ground and mixed with vegetables, ideal for a sandwich, an appetizer, or even as a main meat course. Interesting dried pasta makes great inexpensive gifts to take back home and can be transported easily. On Fridays their bread is even better than in the town bakery next to San Lorenzo church, **Forno Tomassini** (Via Roma 9, tel. 0733/50543), which bakes breads and *crostate* tarts.

If you're heading toward the Sibylline Mountains, right on the main route in the town of Sarnano is **Bar Torrefazione** (Via Don Minzoni 119, tel. 0733/657-260), which might just have the best cappuccino en route. The Mariani brothers select their own coffee beans for their secret mix and roast them on the premises. The place is open seven days a week and is always busy with locals and passersby.

Getting There and Around

From Macerata, travel south on SS 78 toward Urbisaglia; as you approach Sarnano the Sibylline Mountains appear directly ahead of you. **SASP** (tel. 0733/663-137) buses connect the town with Ancona and Macerata, while **Roma-Marche** (tel. 0733/818-638) serves points between Rome. The train station is eight kilometers from the center.

TOLENTINO

When Augustinian friar Nicholas arrived on the scene in the 13th century, Tolentino was a thriving commercial center for textiles and leather tanning. The city kept trade moving as a central postal stop in Le Marche between Ancona and Foligno. Now Tolentino's main feature is Nicholas himself. Born in Sant'Angelo near Fermo, Nicholas (1246–1305) is the patron saint of souls in Purgatory and is associated with bread and feeding the sick.

He would have known the church that is now dedicated to him, but he would not recognize it today in its form as a grand basilica. The most stunning addition was the chapel inside dedicated to him, the Cappellone, painted less than a century after his death by a Riminese painter who was a follower of Giotto. Nicholas has the monumental complex with basilica, but Catervo is the patron saint of Tolentino. Catervo has a cathedral dedicated to him that was reconstructed in the 19th century; inside is a 4th-century sarcophagus with the remains of Catervo and his wife.

Although Tolentino has the old Roman consular road, Via Flaminia, running through it, in the Middle Ages it was the Cistercian monks that cleared this unhealthy malaria-ridden area

© JUDY EDELHOFF

rolling hills near Tolentino

and brought about a development boom. In the 18th century, Napoleon Bonaparte cut a swath through Tolentino and in the 1797 Treaty of Tolentino forced the pope to surrender land and money. You can see a palace with period furnishings that mark Napoleon's visit.

Stroll through this pleasant, medieval town to admire its architecture, browse in shops, and have coffee with the locals. If your time is limited, don't miss the Cappellone and the theater, two very different artistic and architectural gems but both central in the fabric of town life here. Shoppers will be interested to know that the area has some outlets, several close to the medieval Castello della Rancia. You might want to check out the spa town of Santa Lucia if you need to recharge or get realigned; its specialty is sports medicine.

Sights

Basilica di San Nicola (Piazza San Nicola, tel. 0733/976-311, www.sannicoladatolentino.it, daily 9:30 A.M.–noon and 3–8 P.M.) was built up and around an existing church to honor the medieval Nicholas. He was named after the Bishop of Myra (Bari's patron saint and the St. Nick that became Santa Claus), to whom his parents had prayed in hopes of conceiving a child. Most of his years were spent in Tolentino, where he is credited with having performed some miracles. The lower row of the Cappellone's frescoes shows the *Life and Miracles* of St. Nicholas, which is intended to mirror the upper level *Scenes from the Life of Christ* to show that in his own life Nicholas closely followed that of Christ. What the painter also shows in remarkably vivid colors is a wonderful window on medieval life. The clothing, costumes, dining, and drinking—including a woman with wine pouring into her mouth—all have Biblical references. Step into this room for full immersion in quotidian medieval life.

Ponte del Diabolo (Bridge of the Devil, on Via del Ponte) was built in 1268 to a design by Master Bentivegna. According to local legend, the builder was having difficulty in completing his work on time. He made a pact with the Devil and it was completed that night; in exchange the Devil would have the first soul that crossed the bridge in the morning. Nicholas got wind of the scheme and arranged for the first soul to be a dog. In a fit of pique, the Devil butted the bridge with his horns and the two holes punched in the side are traces that remain today of his temper tantrum. The medieval bridge has five arches below and is spanned by a protective tower.

Visible from SS77 is a 12th-century edifice that was converted in 1357 to **Castello della Rancia** (Contrada Rancia, tel. 0733/973-349, Tues.–Sun. 10 A.M.–12:30 P.M. and 3–6:30 P.M., €6). The castle has been a site of many battles, the best known being the 1815 Battle of Tolentino when the Austrian army crushed Joachim Murat's forces. In 1882, a small archeological museum was added. There you can see what the area's earlier inhabitants, the Picenes, were up to before the Romans knocked them out of the game. It also hosts special events.

As you walk through town, other sights to note include **Palazzo Sangallo** (Piazza della Libertà, tel. 0733/969-797, Tues.–Sun. 10 A.M.–1 P.M. and 3–6 P.M.). The palace begun in 1540 by architect Antonio da Sangallo the Younger was finally completed in 1932. The second floor has the **Museum of Caricature and Humor in Art** plus temporary exhibits. If you're in the mood for 18th-century decor, head to the **Palazzo Bezzi-Parisani** (Via Della Pace 20, tel. 0733/969-797). It's where Napoleon Bonaparte signed the 1797 Treaty of Tolentino and has period furnishings and documents.

Entertainment and Events

Every odd year, Tolentino puts on its **International Biennial of Art Humor** (tel. 733/901-365, www.biennaleumorismo.org), which means mostly caricature but can be any work of art on paper. Entries are due in April and the event runs July–October. The topic for 2007 was "What Happened to the Macho," which carried a €5,000 first prize plus a one-man show of up to 30 works. The next contest will be in 2009.

St. Nicholas' Feast Day, September 10, is observed with a procession and ceremonies that go on for a week. Other celebrations include **Festa del Pane,** a celebration of bread to recall the bread that Nicholas distributed to the poor. Catervo's feast day is October 17.

Built with funds from local noble families, **Teatro Nicola Vaccai** was completed in 1795. Its foyer is decorated with mythological creatures and leads to a splendid circular theater with a decorated ceiling that has an umbrella effect, modeled after architect Vanvitelli's ceiling in Caserta's grand palace.

Recreation

Terme di Santa Lucia (Contrada Santa Lucia 8, tel. 0733/968-227, daily, closed midday) has three types of mineral waters: the Santa Lucia spring has a mineral bicarbonate taken as a drinking cure; Rofanello produces sulfurous waters for respiratory cures; and the sodium chloride-bromide-iodide waters are for other treatments. The ancient baths have disappeared, so the atmosphere will be clinical rather than hedonistic. Specialties include sports medicine, rehabilitation, physiotherapy, treatments for deafness, and a spa beauty center, plus a pediatrics section for children. The spa is three kilometers from Tolentino and you can book a massage or simply get beautiful. The season is April–December for the spa, the rest is open year-round.

Shopping

Tombolini has a classically stylish shop in Rome near the Pantheon, but in Tolentino's outskirts **Area T Tombolini** (Contrada Rancia 8, tel. 0733/961-735, www.tombolini.it, Oct.–Dec. Mon. 4–8 P.M., Tues.–Fri. 9:30 A.M.–1 P.M. and 3:30–8 P.M., Sat. 10 A.M.–8:30 P.M., Sun. 4–8 P.M.) has a spacious, nicely illuminated store that offers classic men and women's fashions, most from their own line, priced 30 percent or so lower. Men's fashions are on the ground floor, the basement has colorful linens and towels, and women's clothes are upstairs. Suits are their strong point, but they also carry classy sportswear and a few evening pieces. If you want to move on to other quality outlets, pick up a brochure here.

A few buildings past Area T Tombolini, turn right onto the dirt road between Pollenza and Tolentino and you'll reach the **Il Pollenza Winery** (Via Casone 4, tel. 0733/961-989, www.ilpollenza.it). The winery opened in 2001 and its wines made on the premises have an international style. Despite the grand entrance with flags flying it has a wine for every budget. Their signature wine is full-bodied red Il Pollenza made from Cabernet Sauvignon, Cabernet Franc, Merlot, and a hint of Petite Verdot. The 2003 vintage (€37) will be hitting its prime in 2009: it's velvety, persistent, and full of body. Their first Pinot Nero (Pinot Noir) was made in 2003 and merits attention, too. Or think sweet and go for the gold dessert wine, **Pious IX** 2003 (€21), with its pleasing hint of apricots and guava. If this sounds too fancy, enjoy the sight of the vineyards and do what the locals do: buy *vino sfuso*. This wine is sold in bulk, so bring an empty bottle or buy one at the shop; for about €2, you'll be off with a mild, but pleasant white or red priced right for an everyday lunch or dinner wine. The shop often runs free tastings.

Food

Tucked off on a side street in the historic center, **Osteria S. Nicola** (Via Flaminia 6, tel. 0733/967-448, www.osteriasanicola.it, lunch and dinner Wed.–Mon., €12–25) caters to locals that range from winemakers to bankers. This is a place that you're welcome to go simple and order a big salad as an alternative to a five-course extravaganza. It's also a good place to try local wines that you won't find easily elsewhere, like Il Pollenza from the next town over.

When the Area T Tombolini store closes at lunch and dinner, **AreaCafé** (Contrada Rancia 8, tel. 0733/971-1891, €8–20) inside opens its cool blue and white modern space. The menu features lighter interpretations of traditional local dishes made with organic products. Fish is featured on Friday; specials include free dessert with dinner on Thursday and Friday. It attracts some Brits and a fashionable local clientele looking for newer, trendy cuisine.

Information and Services

Piazza della Libertà has the best concentration of services. Here you'll find the **I.A.T. office** (tel. 0733/972-937), which has a good town map and historical information. The square also has a pharmacy and an Internet point. Post offices are in **Galleria Europa** (Via F. Tambroni) and on Viale G. Brodolini.

Getting There and Around

From Urbisaglia, take SS 78 north, turn left at the sign marked Tolentino to take the short cut or take it all the way to the exit onto SS 77, the four-lane highway that leads to Tolentino.

PARCO NAZIONALE DEI MONTI SIBILLINI

The park of Monti Sibillini is probably as full of legends as it is of spectacular mountain scenery. After all, its name means Mountains of the Sibyls, variously defined as prophetesses, witches, magic women, and priestesses of Apollo. This area rises out of the central provinces of Macerata and Ascoli Piceno and shares the mountain range with Abruzzo to the southwest and Umbria just above it. There are also stories that the locals tell about four Sibyls on four mountains. From the 14th to the 16th centuries, legends circulated throughout Europe about the presence of the Apennine Sibyl on Montemonaco, with intense searches for her grotto or cave. Even today, locals say that in the mountains at the bottom of Lago de Pilota is the final resting place of Pontius Pilate; when he fled Rome, his chariot and the horses galloped full force into the lake with him, never to be seen again. Another version says buffaloes pulled Pilate's corpse there. The lake takes on a red or coral hue from a rare organism that gives off a peculiar tint in the fresh water, but is attributed to Pilate's presence. Other names suggest more legends and mystery. If you go to Ambro, you can hike to Gola dell'Infernaccio (the Throat to Hell). At the church of Sant'Angelo in Montespino, a crypt was built by monks over a pagan temple and a giant *rospo* (toad) is said to live in the crypt. Whether you find any mysteries or not,

THE SIBYLS OF MONTI SIBILLINI IN LE MARCHE

Since ancient times that pre-date the Romans, the Sibyls have been famous for prophesies, magic, and their allure. Sometimes witches, often ambiguous, and gifted with prophecy, they captured the imagination not only of locals but well beyond as their fame spread, first in the pagan world and then in Christian lands.

In the early Middle Ages, the tradition of the Cuman Sibyl was closely linked to the Apennine Sibyl. By the Middle Ages, the Sibyls shed some of their pagan past to become Biblical prophetesses that foretold of the Redeemer. The "Il Guerrin Meschino," who Andrea da Barberino Guerrino called "Il Meschino," is described both as prophetess and seductress. In searching for his parents, Il Meschino heard of a Sibyl hidden in a cave in Le Marche's Apennine Mountains. According to the tale, Guerrino was able to get past the guards posted at the cave's entrance. He faced a series of trials and finally reached a metal door that led to the throne of the Sibyl. Enchanting maidens led him to the queen, who was a spectacular beauty. However, she never responded to his questions because she failed to seduce him.

Another adventurer, Antoine De La Sale, claimed to have reached her cave but did not enter, and tells the tale in "Le Paradis de la Reine Sibille," a work that he dedicated to Agnes of Bourbon. Locals told him of a German knight and his attendant that reached the cave and then so thoroughly enjoyed this land of enchantment that they indulged in every imaginable pleasure and finally after 330 days emerged from the cave. They repented and went to Rome to ask the Pope's pardon. The Pope was so impressed with the degree of their sins that he kicked both out without the pardon. The two returned to the cave and never surfaced again. This knight's fame lives on *Tannhäuser*, the opera created by Richard Wagner.

Another tale tells of five youths that descended three miles into Montemonaco and found "fearful storms." A priest, Antonio Fumato, traveled with two knights and reported terrible winds until they reached the metal door, then inside found a long bridge above a torrential river where the knights went ahead but never returned. Even the name, Mount Monk, probably was selected as a reminder of the Benedictine monks that colonized the mountain in the Middle Ages – and to loosen the tenacious grip that the Sibyl held on the fascination of the populace.

The great Renaissance humanist, scientist, and architect Leon Battista Alberti found time – when not designing Santa Maria Novella in Florence or writing mathematical treatises – to write stories of enchantment that he had heard from his father in his "Descrittione di tutta Italia." Sibyls appear in Greek and Roman myths and they were depicted in ancient times as well as in sacred Christian art. In the sanctuary at Ambro, Martino Bonfini painted 12 Sibyls above the main altar next to Old Testament prophets, and in Rome, Michelangelo painted four Sibyls among his figures in the Sistine Chapel.

---

you will certainly find beautiful landscapes and plenty of good trails to hike. You can seek out descriptive spots like Peak of the Redeemer, Holy Valley, Hell's Throat, Devil's Cave, and Bad Pass if you wish. Legends go back thousands of years, but the Parco Nazionale dei Monti Sibillini was created in 1993.

Much of the region's water comes from rivers that have their source in the Umbria–Marche Apennine Mountains. Almost all flow northeast toward the Adriatic Sea, with the exception of the Nera River that begins on Mount Porche and flows in the opposite direction to the Tyrrenean Sea via the Tiber River.

Wildflowers are at their peak here in spring. Some, like gentian, are used for various tonics, amari, and liqueurs. One tradition that goes back centuries takes place the night of June 24, when herbs are gathered to prepare "water of John the Baptist." Essential to the recipe is Madonna's herb (also called santamaria, St. Peter's herb, and envy herb), which is combined with lavender, citronella, wheat grain, rose petals, and leaves from oak, walnut, and laurel trees.

Family members wash their faces with this ablution to keep envy and illness away. Other flowers famous for their blossoms are the lentils that bloom in Colfiorito on the border with Umbria. This is also the area where Hannibal came after winning the battle of Trasimeno in Umbria in 217 B.C. Here on the shores of Lago Plestino, he encountered the last line of defense composed of 5,000 Roman soldiers. Legend says that Hannibal was so impressed with their courage that after defeating them he hid some of his own armor here as tribute to them.

Sports and Recreation

Visso has the park headquarters (www.sibilliniturismo.it, tel. 073/796-8026), with major park offices also in **San Ginesio** (Via Piave 14), **Amandola** (tel. 073/684-8598), **Sarnano** (tel. 073/365-7144), and **Fiastra** (tel. 073/752-598). Other offices open seasonally for skiing or hiking.

Rock climbers and alpine skiers head for Monte Vettore, Pizzo del Diavolo, Monte Bricco, Monte Bove, Cima del Redentore, Monte Argentella, Palazzo Borghese, Monte Porche, Cima Vallelunga, Monte Sibilla, Monte Zampa, Cima Cannfusto, Monte Priora, Forca della Cervara, Pizzo Berro, Pizzo Tre Vescovi, Monte Castel Manardo, Monte Rotondo, Monte Pietralata, Monte delle Rose, Poggio di Croce.

Ski slopes that are outfitted with lifts and trails are at **Monte Prata, Frontignano, Pintura di Bolognola** and **Sassotetto.** Ice skaters head for the town of **Ussita** in the foothills of **Mt. Bove.** Spelunkers explore caves, with some that aim for the Sibyl's cave. Mountain bikers make use of the roads and various paths.

In warmer months, the **Chienti and Tenna Rivers** are spots for rafting. A golf course is at **Riserva Naturale dell'Abbadia di Fiastra,** which also has a tourist office.

Thermal waters sprout up from these mountains that are credited with curing various ailments from digestive to kidney, circulation, and gynecological, while some are used to enrich the diets of children. Terme di San Giacomo is near Sarnano, Terme di Santa Lucia is near Tolentino, and Terme di Villa Saline is near Penna San Giovanni.

Getting There and Around

About 38 towns make up the Comunità Monatane (the Mountain Towns) surrounding Parco Nazionale dei Monti Sibillini. Of these the best facilities are in Urbisaglia, just off SS77, which leads into the northwestern section of the mountains. From the A14 *autostrada* near Civitanova Marche, take the exit for SS77 that leads toward Macerata and continue west.

One approach into the mountains is to begin in southern Macerata and wind your way south through delightful small towns to seek out the unknown Sibyl yourself on her mountain. Abbadia di Fiastra, near Tolentino and Urbisaglia on SP 78, makes a good base for accommodations. From there you can easily make stops in the towns of Sarnano, Amandola, Abbazia di San Ruffino, Comunanza, Montefortino, Ambro, Monte Monaco and conclude on Monte Sibilla, the Sibyl's Mountain. A second option is to follow water routes and canyons, beginning in the southeastern edge of Macerata. Start in Visso, the park headquarters, near Route 209 and wind your way southeast to Castelsantangelo sul Nera, then north again to Ussita, north to Fiastra, southeast to Acquacanina, farther southeast to Bolognola, to Sarnano, and back to base in Tolentino or Urbisaglia.

AMBRO

Near Montefortino, Ambro has a sanctuary dedicated to the Madonna that was founded in the year 1000 after the Virgin Mary bestowed the power of speech to a girl that was mute from birth. A later church was built between 1601 and 1640 to accommodate the number of pilgrims dedicated to the cult of Mary, which in Le Marche were second in number only to those traveling to Loreto. Inside the church of Madonna dell'Ambro in the chapel behind the main altar, Martino Bonfini painted 12 Sibyls next to the prophets of the Old Testament. From here it's an easy hike of an hour to Gola dell'Infernaccio. The hike follows an easy trail that skirts the Ambro

LE MARCHE

River, and the "throat" is a gorge created between the rocks. If you continue uphill another three hours, you will reach the entrance to another lovely gorge. Beyond this is a monk's church and sanctuary where an elderly hermit lives in seclusion but does receive visitors.

Festivals and Events

This is Italy, so a lot of events focus on food, like a "*sagra*" where some local produce or meat or other product is featured. But if what you want is to be on the move, Caldarola hosts the **Giro cicloturistico** "Gran Fondo dei Sibillini," a cycle tour, in July. Fiastra organizes **Triathlon dei Monti Sibillini** on the first Sunday in July. As for the offbeat, Montefortino hosts Carnevale in mid-August. On October 31, Sarnano celebrates **Stregoni e Mazzamurelli,** a nod to witches and magic that is synchronized with the American celebration of Halloween.

Accommodations

Fabio's rustic hotel, **Da Peppinè** (Loc. Ambro, tel. 0736/859-171, €60 d, closed winter except holidays) has a sign up in the lobby that reads "we are confused, but we're nice." Both are apt descriptions. The rooms are basic and the setting is just below the Madonna del Ambro church. There's a rustic, lively restaurant and bar on the ground floor.

Food

For lunch by a babbling brook near the Le Marche–Abruzzo divide, head to **Osteria del Nonno** (located on the left side of the square facing the church, tel. 333/791-9961, open daily in summer, €5–15). Paola Pieroni's shack is just to the left of the medieval church Madonna del Ambro. Worth a try is the delicious *girella*, a spiral lasagna filled with spinach and tangy sheep's milk ricotta cheese. Paola serves assorted grilled meats but the local lamb is the best. Order the house wine, a simple red table variety from the other side of the mountain. It's open from Easter to December.

Getting There and Around

One approach into the mountains is to begin in southern Macerata and wind your way south through delightful small towns to seek out the unknown Sibyl yourself on her mountain. Depart from Tolentino or Urbisaglia on SP 78 and make stops in the towns of Sarnano, Amandola, Abbazia di San Ruffino, Comunanza, Montefortino, Ambro, Monte Monaco and conclude on Monte Sibilla, the Sibyl's Mountain. A second option is to follow water routes and canyons, beginning in the southeastern edge of Macerata. Start in Visso near Route 209 and wind your way southeast to Castel Sant'Angelo sul Nera.

Province of Ascoli Piceno

The Province of Ascoli Piceno was chosen by the Picenes for its strategic position, but the medieval period and the feudal estates have most left their imprint upon the region. To the south, Ascoli Piceno shares its border with Abruzzo, home to the national park Parco Nazionale del Gran Sasso e Monti della Laga. From Ascoli you can follow SS4, the ancient Roman consular road Via Salaria. At the southern end of Ascoli Piceno and the northern tip of the Gran Sasso national park is Aquasante Terme, known for its mineral waters. The western edge of the province leads toward Monti Sibillini, entered at Arquata del Tronto.

From Arquata, head west across the mountains and enter the region of Lazio on the other side, where the Via Salaria leads to Rome. Or head north from Arquata along the western Ascoli Piceno and following the edge of Parco Nazionale dei Monti Sibillini where you'll wind up at Sarnano, a great place to take a lovely walk through a medieval town. From Sarnano, enter the Monti Sibillini toward Sassotetto–Maddalene where ski lifts can place you at elevations of 1,624–1,680 meters for summer hiking or winter skiing.

The eastern side of the province ends at the Adriatic Sea, with towns like Porto d'Ascoli at the southern end. Head north pass coastal towns like San Benedetto del Tronto, Grottammare, and Cupra Maritima.

The city of Ascoli Piceno is unquestionably the star of Ascoli, and it is just as striking for its medieval beauty as its more famous northern neighbor (Urbino in Le Marche) is for its Renaissance beauty.

C ASCOLI PICENO

Ascoli Piceno has ancient Picene and Roman underpinnings, but the medieval towers and their luminous stones with their vertical light and elegant air will charm you immediately. Many of the buildings and even some streets and squares are paved with local travertine. In contrast to the cool, grayish-white travertine of Rome's monuments and churches, Ascoli's travertine has a golden hue that gives the whole town a warmth and splendor like no other. Local builders have been using it for over 2,000 years, so it's hard to imagine that the Dark Ages ever arrived here. If you've been to the Tuscan city of medieval towers, San Gimignano, you can't help but notice some similarities. Ascoli Piceno has an edge because it's more luminous, near the sea, and has fewer tourists.

The city has its roots as far back as an Iron Age settlement in the 9th century B.C., when the Picenes occupied the middle coast of the Adriatic Sea. The Romans put an end to that after a siege in 89 A.D. The only remnants of the Picenes are walls built near a Roman arch and artifacts in the archeological museum. The most obvious imprint of the Romans is the **Via Salaria.** The ancient consular road was a major transport route for salt ("*sale*" or "*salaria*" refers to salt), between the Adriatic Sea and the center of Rome. The museum has Roman artifacts, too, but other Roman monuments are still standing. As you stroll through town you can cross a bridge built by Augustus and ruins of a Roman theater.

The Longobards would have their turn later

at ruling Ascoli. After a siege in 587, Ascoli Piceno came under the rule of the Duchy of Spoleto based in Umbria. The gold jewelry and other artifacts from their occupation show a brightness and peculiar whimsy that has its own appeal, even if their artisans lacked the elegant refinement of Romans at their peak under Augustus.

In the Middle Ages, more than 200 towers soared up in the luminous travertine, built by wealthy patricians as both status symbols and for defensive purposes. King Frederick II, who was born farther north in Jesi, wasn't keen on this power concentration and ordered the destruction of some 90 towers. The city still has traces of about 50; some towers are fully intact, while others have been incorporated into buildings and two have been converted into bell towers. Once you begin a walk through town to admire them, note that the word *via,* the Italian word for street, often is replaced with *rua,* your first word in local dialect.

This is definitely a town to savor details. Look up under the awnings of medieval roofs and under some you will see a triangular or geometric pattern unique to Ascoli Piceno. Locals weren't content to leave bare beams and terra-cotta for passersby to see. They cast special tiles with an enamel glaze to insert under the roof awnings. Ascoli Piceno is also a town of messages. More than 100 inscriptions and mottoes in Latin are inscribed on the architraves above doorways. Some are religious, but others are cultural or impart folk wisdom.

Piazza Arringo is an ideal place to begin your visit. Then move on to the beautiful Piazza del Popolo, where you can pause for a cappuccino or *aperitivo* in its historic Art Nouveau cafe.

Sights

Piazza Arringo was named for public assemblies that took place in the square where citizens would often harangue *(arringo)* the speakers. **Cathedral of St. Emidio** anchors it on one end, and to its left is the evocative octagonal baptistery dedicated to St. John. Also here is the **Arengo Palace** (Pinacoteca Civica, Piazza dell'Arengo, tel. 0736/298-213) that serves as city hall as well as the municipal art museum. You can pay a call on the Picenes at the **Museo Archeologico** (Palazzo Panichi, tel. 0736/253-562, Apr.–Sept. 8:30 A.M.–7:30 P.M. and Oct.–Mar. 9 A.M.–1 P.M. and 3–6 P.M., €2).

St. Emidio, a native of Germany, was the first Bishop of Ascoli and was martyred in 303. Along with the Virgin Mary, Emidio is Ascoli's patron saint. Emidio is invoked as a protector against earthquakes and his feast day is August 5. Inside **Sant'Emidio Cathedral**, a five-paneled painting on wood by Carlo Crivelli (1473) is even more beautiful than his works in the art museum; central is *Madonna with Infant* surrounded by saints, all in a magnificent wood frame.

The star of **Pinacoteca Civica** (Palazzo Arengo, Piazza Arringo, tel. 0736/298-213, €5), Ascoli's municipal art museum, is Carlo Crivelli (c. 1434–1495), who was born in Venice but died in Ascoli Piceno. The museum has several of Crivelli's works, some with fascinating details like the center panel of his triptych with its big apple on the floor. These are a good prelude to Crivelli's even more magnificent painted panels in Sant'Emidio. A 1265 mantel has some remarkable embroidery on it, a wonderful medieval fantasy with precious gold thread.

Pietro Alemanno's 1474 painting of *The Annunciation* has a detail of Ascoli Piceno in it; the Northern-born artist became a citizen of Ascoli in 1485. His triptych nearby features St. Nicholas on the right holding three golden balls that symbolize the three sisters whom Nicholas saved from a life of prostitution: Nicholas of Tolentino was named for him. The salon has beautiful ebony and ivory furniture in it; note the craftsmanship in the chairs and table. Window treatments in the palace are beautiful too, with fine plush fabrics, lace, and tassels. The modern 19th–20th century room has a poignant selection of art: *Mater Derelicta* is a homeless mother who rests a foot on her suitcase with a child sprawled asleep on her lap; *Refuse of the Sea* shows a drowned man washed ashore with his lantern while his faithful dog mourns nearby.

Piazza del Popolo took its shape in the early 1500s. The Loggia dei Mercanti erected in 1513 offered elegant arched porticos where artisans and merchants could sell their wares. **Palazzo dei Capitani,** constructed in the 13th century served as the seat of government from 1400–1564 and still has its original tower.

St. Francis is important throughout Italy. The church dedicated to him in Piazza del Popolo has special significance because Ascoli is the hometown of the first Franciscan pope, Nicholas IV.

Ascoli Piceno is perfect for wandering around, even without a map, from square to square and tower to tower. Look for the **Twin Towers** (Torre Gemelli), two towers separated by a narrow building on Via delle Torre. **Ercolani Tower** is on Via dei Soderini. This is a town where the squares, especially Piazza Arringo, become like outdoor salons where residents slowly saunter through, stop to chat, gossip, or share an espresso spiked with the local anise-flavored liqueur. Adjust your pace to theirs and you'll savor the delights of the city.

Entertainment and Events

Joust of the Quintana is a tournament that pits six historical neighborhoods of the town against one another. Jousters contend for the Palio, a banner that brings prestige to the bearers. This is considered the best medieval pageant in Le Marche and features a court of 1,500 in medieval costumes that are meticulously made. The event is worth it for the costumes alone. There is a night-time exhibition in July, but the main event is the first Sunday of August.

Piazza del Popolo doubles as salon and ballroom for residents and visitors celebrating **Carnevale** in February. Everyone dons costumes ranging from Commedia dell'Arte to the more bizarre and unusual.

Teatro Ventidio Basso (1846) (Via del Teatro 4, tel. 0736/24459, www.teatroventidiobasso.it) is one of Le Marche's historic architectural gems, where you may be fortunate enough to catch a performance. Also historic are the **Filarmonici Theater** (1832) and **S. Francesco di Paolo Auditorium** (1848).

© JUDY EDELHOFF

Palazzo dei Capitani in Ascoli Piceno

Shopping and Recreation

Ceramics are traditional crafts in Ascoli Piceno and are available in both old and new designs. Most shops are along Corso V. Emanuele and Corso Mazzini.

Caffè Meletti (Piazza del Popolo 20, tel. 0736/259-626) sells bottles of their famous anise-flavored liqueur. It makes a nice summer drink with ice and a splash of water or adds an extra boost to a cup of coffee on a chilly day.

Associazione Agriturist Marche (tel. 071/201-763, info@agriturist.marche.it) offers a three-day weekend package that includes horseback riding excursions and a room in an *agriturismo*, a country house or farm for €142 per person.

Accommodations

A stay at the seaside can be great to recharge. But along Le Marche's coast, the train sometimes runs very close to the sea. That's great for passengers, but not so pleasant if you discover later that your hotel room is near the train tracks. The sudden noise and vibrations could be a jarring jolt at any hour. An easy solution is to stay up in the hillside towns. By car, access to the sea takes only minutes or makes for a pleasant walk, you have a great view, you have small-town life in the piazza rather than the transient aspect of some sea locales, and the noise is down below you.

One of Le Marche's best wineries, **◖ Oasi degli Angeli** (Contrada da Sant'Egidio 50, tel. 0735/778-569, www.kurni.it) is a hillside retreat in the province of Ascoli in Cupra Marittima. Their rooms are tastefully furnished and the country setting is admist vineyards. Their winery turns out one of Italy's best wines, Kurni, a full-bodied red that's won numerous awards for the 2004 vintage. Their small restaurant (30 seats) generally is open only for dinner on Friday and Saturday and for lunch on Sunday.

Palazzo Guiderocchi (Via Cesare Battisti 3, tel. 0736/244-011, www.palazzogiderocchi. com, €399) is the town's most elegant, traditional, historic hotel and is managed with attention to details.

The 13th-century palace of the noble Saladini family, 🍂 **Residenza Cento Torri** (Via C. Mazzoni 6, tel. 0736/255-123, www.cento torri.com, 13 rooms, €140 d) exudes charm. It opened as a hotel in fall 2007 in Ascoli Piceno's historic center. Guest rooms have innovative floor plans, classy textiles, and antique furniture. The sunny winter courtyard garden makes an ideal spot for conversation or drinks. The health club has a gym, massage rooms, beauty treatments and hairdresser, Turkish bath, and sauna and showers scented with fragrance or citrus.

The drab cement building and unkempt grounds on the outskirts of Ascoli's center won't lure you into **Hotel Marche** (Via Kennedy 34, tel. 0736/45575, €67), which is run by a hotel school that is not terribly energetic. But the front desk staff is nice, rooms are clean, parking is free, the rates are low, and there's a pizzeria nearby. If you want a historic building with its own tower at rock-bottom rate, try the **Ostello dei Longobardi** youth hostel in Palazzetto Longobardo (Via Soderini 26, tel. 0736/261-862, €18).

Signora Caucci runs a bed-and-breakfast in her historic home (Via XX Settembre 13, tel. 0736/258-533, www.dimorantica.alter vista.org, €100 d).

Food

Ascoli Piceno has various culinary specialties, but don't leave before you've tasted *olive Ascolane*, the famous fried stuffed olives. They make a perfect snack or *antipasto* before a meal. *Olive Ascolane* are on menus throughout Le Marche and even in other parts of Italy, but here, especially in the small trattorias, you'll find *olive Ascolane* freshly made. You can also find fried vegetables as light as tempura. Lamb, chicken, fish, and seafood are all cooked to perfection, so if you usually shy away from fried food because it can be heavy or greasy, try it here.

In the spring, Ascoli puts on a festival dedicated to fried food, **Fritto Misto all' Ascolana** (www.fritomistoallitaliana.it), where temporary stands are set up in piazzas and monastery cloisters. Chefs from across Italy and some foreign cooks compete to see who can come up with the best assortment of fried food. There's also a special tasting to see which wines and beers pair best with particular fried foods.

La Locandiera (Via C. Goldoni 2, tel. 0736/262-509) is the spot to begin with famous *olive Ascolane*. The pasta is homemade and fried specialties like the succulent lamb have a light touch. If you prefer not to have fried food, they have plenty of other dishes, too, from *antipasto* to dessert. **Gallo d'Oro** (Corso V. Emanuele 54, tel. 0736/253-520) is one of Ascoli's historic restaurants where locals come for traditional Ascolani food.

Everyone eventually meets at the tables outside or in the Art Deco interior of **Caffè Meletti** (Piazza del Popolo 20, tel. 0736/259 626), which specializes in its own sweet anise-flavored liqueur with its slight hint of liquorice. Drink it straight, with water, or in a *cafè corretto*, an espresso with a shot of liqueur to "correct" the coffee. Sit outside in the piazza or inside with the Art Nouveau details. Local wines made by **Velenosi Ascoli Piceno** (www.velenosivini.com) are top quality and well worth seeking out.

Information and Services

The **visitors center** (Piazza Arringo, tel. 0736/298-204) and **IAT Regional Tourist Office** (Piazza del Popolo, tel. 0736/253-045) have excellent town maps, as well as information about the Quintana and other events.

Getting There and Around

If you are in no hurry and have time for the slow lane, you can take the Via Salaria (SS 4) straight from Rome. Otherwise, drive along the A25 towards L'Aquila and connect to the A14 north. Exit at Porto d'Ascoli, then take Via Salaria SS4 west to Ascoli Piceno. By bus, there are major connections from Pescara on Abruzzo's coastal route or from Ancona.

GROTTAMARE

Grottamare is the hometown of Felice Peretti (1521–1590), who became Pope Sixtus V, the pope that commissioned the Sistine Chapel in Rome. It's divided into an upper and lower town. Lodging and dining in the small medieval town atop the hill, **Grottamare Alta,** will be more tranquil. Alta is only a few minutes by car to the sea.

Accommodations

Casa Pazzi is the most stylish hotel here. If you prefer to economize, try the town's bed-and-breakfasts or you can even room above a wine bar. The seashore has hotels, but most are utilitarian rather than attractive. Also, the train tracks run right near the beach, so even if your hotel faces the sea be sure the opposite side is not near the tracks.

The owner of **Casa Pazzi** (Grottammare, Via Sotto Le Mura 5, tel. 0735/736617, www.casapazzi.com, €150 d) is an interior decorator so the independent room and four apartments have nice textiles and tiled baths with lovely views of the sea down below, and terraces or even a little private garden. The flowers in bloom provide a lovely scent. If you leave the drapes open, you can catch sunrise over the Adriatic or even an occasional evening firework display for some celebration. Breakfast is on the communal terrace or in your room—or you might be invited to join the owner in his residence. Ask for the electric pot if you wish to make your own coffee or tea.

Food

Osteria dell'Arancio (Piazza Peretti, tel. 0735/631-059) is set on a lovely small square toward the top of the town. Begin with a glass of Champagne or Prosecco and let your waiter suggest the specials of the day or evening, including fresh fish caught down below or meat procured from the nearby hills. The wine list has some excellent choices and an expert sommelier to guide you, so this is the place to splurge on both food and drink. The menu offers both traditional and trendy gourmet, but the atmosphere is unpretentious. On weekends, fashionable Milanese and Italians from farther afield come to dine. The owner also has a restaurant on Kings Road in London.

Locals consider **Gelateria Cristal** (Corso Mazzini 49, tel. 0735/633-462, Tues.–Sun.) to be the best ice cream around, with flavors that Italians remember from childhood. It has a small cafeteria and wine bar.

Winemaker Simone Cantucci experiments with different varieties of grapes at his winery, **Tenuta Rio Maggio** Contrada Vallone, 41, tel. 0734/889-587, www.riomaggio.it). One of his most successful wines is Pinot Nero. If you wondered what the fuss was about for Pinot Noir in the film *Sideways,* here is your chance to try the Italian version at prices that won't gouge your pocketbook.

UMBRIA

You can tell an Umbrian town by the steepness of the climb. The walls are in good condition and the gates date from Etruscan or Roman times. There's usually a stunning piazza and the wide steps of a palazzo on which to enjoy a gelato before having a look inside the duomo. Until April, the weather is cold and the wind blowing down narrow streets is best confronted with a hat and scarf. Summer is mild compared to other parts of the peninsula and Umbrian hills are a cool alternative to baking on overcrowded beaches. Although it's true you won't find any of the patented Italian crowd pleasers here (no leaning towers or cities covered in ash), what you do discover is nearly as satisfying.

You don't need a sign to know you're entering Umbria, something just feels different. The colors are greener than they are in the south,

the mountains are less imposing than they are in the north, and the sea is missing altogether. Perhaps it is that lack of an outlet that has had the most impact on the region's character. Umbria is a place where people talk less and say more with the words they do use.

It's also the home of saints like San Francesco and San Benedetto, who turned their backs on the material preoccupations of the medieval church and focused their energy on peace and goodwill. Assisi is in many ways the spiritual capital of Christianity, lined with churches, monasteries, and convents still active today.

Baroque and ornate styles, however, never overshadowed the Romanesque evident in nearly every piazza in Umbria. Fortunately the region's centrality did not lead to unwanted

© ALESSIA RAMACCIA

HIGHLIGHTS

◖ **Umbria Jazz:** Umbria isn't the obvious choice for a jazz festival, but three decades after its creation, Umbria Jazz has gained a reputation for unforgettable live performances by the world's best musicians (page 533).

◖ **Gubbio Cableway:** The best six minutes in Umbria are spent on a cableway to the top

of Monte Ingino. It's advisable to keep your eyes on the stunning scenery and avoid looking down (page 538).

◖ **Basilica di San Francesco:** The enormous frescoes Giotto painted along the walls of the Basilica di San Francesco are a visual testament to the saint's life and more enlightening than any biography (page 542).

◖ **Bevagna:** Most people don't make it to this charming village, but it is well worth the trip, especially during Il Mercato delle Gaite, when the town undergoes a dramatic transformation to recreate the spirit of the Middle Ages (page 547).

◖ **Orvieto Underground:** There's just as much to see below the surface of Orvieto as there is above. Take an underground tour of hidden caves, passageways, and cisterns (page 548).

◖ **Cascate delle Marmore:** Created by the Romans in 271 B.C. to prevent flooding, at 165 meters Cascate delle Marmore is the tallest artificial waterfall in Europe (page 557).

◖ **Castelluccio di Norcia:** In the town of Castelluccio di Norcia, you can experience the beauty of the Monti Sibillini from above. The registered flying school stationed there offers parasailing or hang-gliding opportunities in the summer (page 560).

LOOK FOR ◖ TO FIND RECOMMENDED SIGHTS, ACTIVITIES, DINING, AND LODGING.

UMBRIA

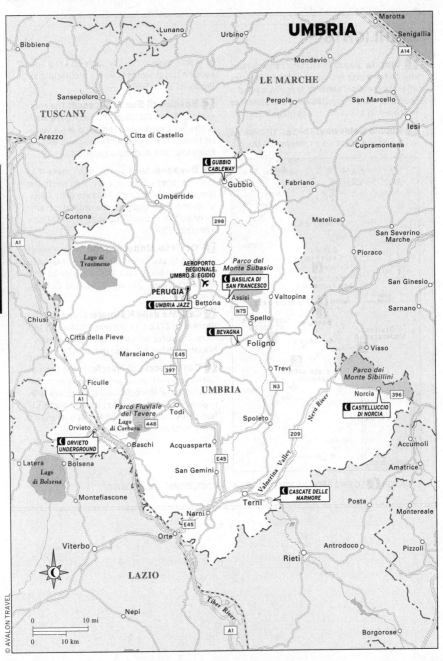

© AVALON TRAVEL

growth. With the exception of Perugia, urban sprawl is limited and destinations like Gubbio and Todi are pristine time capsules from the Middle Ages. A Renaissance man returning to Spoleto after a 500-year nap in the mountains above town would feel little culture shock. Only the clothing has changed, but even fashion turns back time during the many costumed festivals and events reenacting age-old rituals.

Umbria has recognized the importance of the landscape, the products it yields, and the attraction these have for visitors. It's no coincidence that markets selling local delicacies and specialty stores outnumber fast-food outlets; sustainable tourism has become the regional mantra. Environment matters here and Umbrians are determined to preserve it.

Although Umbria is made up of a northern and southern province, there is no natural dividing line between the two. The difference is in the higher density of population in the north and a tradition of ceramic and oil production centered around the towns of Deruta and Spello. Northern Umbria is also earthquake territory and over 80 percent of the area is prone to regular seismic activities. The most recent quakes occurred in 1984, 1997, and 1998, when large parts of Assisi were destroyed. The Lago di Trasimeno near Perugia constitutes the only major lake and is the fourth largest in Italy.

Southern Umbria has a desolate and wild landscape. The region's only national park, Parco Nazionale Monti Sibillini, is located in the southwestern corner of the region on the border with Le Marche. Mountains reach 2,476 meters in height and it's not uncommon to see wild boar and other small mammals a short distance outside of towns. They provide a convenient source of meat that has helped make famous the cold cuts and truffles also found in the area. The high, rugged terrain near Norcia should be seen after the snow has melted and the mountain valleys begin to take on the colors of spring. This is the natural home of free climbing and rafting down the Nera and other local rivers. The hill towns of Orvieto, Todi, and Spoleto are nearly on the same latitude and located within 40 kilometers of each other.

PLANNING YOUR TIME

Henry James advised not to hurry, to walk everywhere, and to observe everything when in Umbria. That may not always be possible, but the region's compact size and infrastructure offer slow travelers a head start. Perugia's position in the center makes it a good jumping-off point as most sights are within a 90-minute drive. It's also one of the most vibrant towns in Umbria and can balance days spent climbing to the top of idyllic hilltop villages with nights animated by a youthful university population. Northern and southern Umbria can be reached quickly via the E45 highway that splits the region in half. Other major roads fan out from Perugia and bus companies link the capital with all the major towns. The most pleasant journeys however are on foot, bicycle, or horseback along Umbria's back ways and through the region's parks, where views get better over every hill.

A tour of Umbria requires two or three days. The general rule is half a day per hilltop town. That gives you enough time to reconnoiter the side streets, look inside the duomo, visit a museum, and, most importantly, spend a leisurely lunch or dinner tasting local ingredients. Umbria's proximity to Rome and Florence also makes it a viable one- or two-day excursion if time is short. It's better, however, to spend more time exploring a single town like Gubbio than to dash through half a dozen towns.

HISTORY

Umbria's history stretches back 3,000 years. The first settlers, who founded small, fortified villages in 1000 B.C., were known as the Umbri. Except for the Eugobine Tablets in Gubbio, there is little trace of this forgotten people. They were slowly overshadowed by Etruscans, who infringed upon their territory from the west, and eventually conquered by Romans at the Battle of Sentino in 295 B.C. The Romans built the Via Flaminia and other roads, which brought increased trade and helped towns prosper. During this period, new walls were built around Spoleto, Assisi, and Spello. It is said the legionnaires recruited from this area were among the most reliable in the Empire. Yet even they could not prevent the fall of Rome.

Barbarians and wars between Byzantines and Visigoths meant Umbria wasn't a very safe place for many centuries. Nevertheless Christianity flourished in this hostile environment and some of Italy's oldest places of worship, such as the Tempietto del Clitunno near Spoleto, were built. It wasn't until the Lombards (or long beards) founded a dukedom in southern Umbria that a degree of stability returned.

The conditions, which produced a renaissance in other parts of the peninsula, eventually spread to Umbria, whose towns began to expand again. The most obvious expression of this recovery was a building boom that resulted in hundreds of new churches, palazzos, and piazze. Romanesque was in full swing during the 12th and 13th centuries and an era of independence began, exemplified by civic buildings in nearly every major town. After 1540, however, the Vatican clamped down on the region and it wasn't until the reunification of Italy that Umbria regained control of its destiny. Industrialization followed and the modern borders of the region were established in 1927.

Perugia

A good rule when visiting any hilltop town is to walk to the top. In Perugia, that means arriving in Piazza IV Novembre. This is where the Romans built their Foro, where medieval stonemasons reached perfection, and where modern citizens take their after-dinner strolls.

Perugia has an Etruscan and Roman past that is less visible than in many cities in Tuscany or Lazio. It's the Middle Ages that left the greatest mark on the city and remains evident to this day. After a period of relative independence when local families vied for control of the town and business flourished, Pope Paul III forcefully intervened in 1540. For three centuries, the Vatican taxed and governed the city and the population took special joy in destroying the Papal fortress of Rocca Paulina after Italy's reunification in 1861.

Perugia is divided into five *rione* (neighborhoods), each with its own color, symbol, and gateway. The color of Sant'Angelo is red and the coat of arms contains the sword and wings representing the warrior angel. There is a high concentration of convents and monasteries here and the road leaving the gate leads to Gubbio. All of the *rione* border Piazza IV Novembre and have a unique character.

SIGHTS
Piazza IV Novembre
Piazza IV Novembre ranks among the most magnificent piazze in Italy and contains three of Perugia's architectural treasures. **Fontana Maggiore** is the centerpiece and remarkable both in size and decoration. The fountain was built between 1275–1278 and was recently restored. It is reminiscent of a wedding cake with two marble pools stacked on top of each other. Each of these is made up of 24 panels recounting the history of the city and its tradesmen. The third tier is smaller and made of bronze. Water flows from a vase held by three nymphs.

It took several centuries to complete the **Cattedrale di San Lorenzo** (daily 7 A.M.–6 P.M., admission free), which was built on the ruins of a Romanesque church. The cathedral presents an unembellished side on Piazza IV Novembre and a more ornate entrance around the corner in Piazza Dante. Inside, large Gothic windows light a floor paved in colored marble and a wooden apse that contains several paintings. The **Museo Capitolare** (Mon.–Fri. 10 A.M.–12:30 P.M. and 4–6 P.M., €5) within the church contains further Renaissance works by Signorelli and Caporali.

© ALESSIA RAMACCIA

medieval Perugia

The **Palazzo dei Priori** (daily 8:30 A.M.–7 P.M., €6.50) was built between 1293–1444 and represents the secular interests of the city. It was here that lawyers met, money was exchanged, merchants traded, and the town's affairs were conducted. The city council still gathers here today. It's no surprise the building is imposing both inside and out. The staircase near the fountain leads to the **Sala dei Notari** (daily 9 A.M.–1 P.M. and 3–7 P.M., admission free), a vast rectangular room covered in paintings recounting the Old Testament. The griffin, which symbolizes the city, is a favorite leitmotif. Other rooms worth visiting are the Sala di Udienza covered in wood paneling and the frescoed ceiling of the Collegio del Cambio, where Renaissance bankers once set their interest rates.

On the third floor of the palazzo is the **Galleria Nazionale dell'Umbria** (Corso Vannucci 19, tel. 075/574-1410 or 075/572-1009,

UMBRIA

www.gallerianazionaleumbria.it, Tues.–Sun. 8:30 A.M.–7:30 P.M., €6.50). If you're only going to visit one art museum in Umbria this is a good choice as it covers the region's artistic development from the 13th to the 18th centuries with particular attention to paintings by Arnolfo di Cambio, Benozzo Gozzoli, and Pietro Vannucci, better known as il Perugino, the man Raffaello called *maestro*.

Behind Palazzo dei Priori is the Santa Susanna quarter and the Via dei Priori that leads to the Porta Trasimeno.

San Bernardino

Nearby in Piazza San Francesco is the Renaissance gem of San Bernardino (tel. 075/573-3957, daily 8:30 A.M.–12:30 P.M. and 3–5:30 P.M.), which could easily win the title of most beautiful church in Perugia. The outside is decorated in pink and blue sculpture celebrating a popular priest who often preached on the site. The architect Agostino di Ducchio opted for simplicity on the inside, which includes a Roman sarcophagus now used as a high altar.

Pozzo Etrusco

Getting water to the top of Perugia has been a problem from the beginning and one the Etruscans solved by building a well in the third century A.D. Pozzo Etrusco (Piazza Dante 1, tel. 075/573-3669, Wed.–Mon. 11 A.M.–1:30 P.M. and 2:30–5 P.M., €2.50) is an engineering marvel constructed from square blocks of travertine stone that would present a challenge to modern builders. If you don't suffer from claustrophobia, the depths of the well can be visited by way of a spiral staircase that requires good quadriceps on the return journey. The ticket includes entry to Cappella di San Severo and Porta Sant'Angelo.

Museo Archeologico Nazionale

Located next to the former convent of San Domenico, the Museo Archeologico Nazionale (Piazza Bruno 10, tel. 075/572-7141, www.archeopg.arti.beniculturali.it, daily 8:30 A.M.–7:30 P.M., €4) displays Umbrian,

the old Etruscan entrance to Perugia

Etruscan, and Roman finds from the area. Many of the objects have been recovered from tombs, including one of the longest Etruscan inscriptions in existence. Scholars are still unsure of the meaning. If the museum whets your appetite, the **Necropolis del Palazzone** (Ponte San Giovanni, Via Assisana 53, tel. 075/539-3329, daily 9 A.M.–1 P.M. and 3:30–6:30 P.M., €3) is a short distance outside the city and contains several spectacular tombs dating from the 2nd century B.C.

ENTERTAINMENT AND EVENTS
Nightlife

There's something for everyone in Perugia. A substantial university population keeps pubs and discos busy until late. Thursday is a big dance night for many clubs who hand out fliers in Piazza IV Novembre to promote special events. Although the murder of an English exchange student in 2007 has put a damper on some of the nightlife rowdiness, it's still possible to have a good time here. The jazz festival during the summer attracts thousands of music lovers from around the world. Many of these events are free and organized around the city's many delightful *piazze*.

BARS AND DISCOS

A lively student population keeps pubs and disco bars busy until late and finding a place to drink until 2 A.M. is no problem. **Blitz** (Corso Vannucci 99, tel. 075/572-8778, Wed.–Mon. 8 A.M.–2:30 A.M.) may not look like much but in the summer this small bar on the main drag is where evenings start for Perugia's party people. Drinks are cheap, which is one reason it's popular, and crowds loiter on the street outside catching up on the day's events. **Kandinsky** (Via E. dal Pozzo 22, tel. 075/572-8130, daily 9 P.M.–2 A.M.) is an icon of Perugian nightlife and a good place to observe locals letting their hair down. For an Irish pub with an Italian twist, **Bratislava** (Via Fiorenzuola 12, tel. 075/573-2487, Tues.–Sun. 8:30 P.M.–2 A.M.) remains the destination of choice. Beer connoisseurs will appreciate the selection on tap. Anyone looking to dance will find the DJs at **Velvet** (Viale Rome 20, tel. 075/572-1321, www.velvetfashioncafe.com, Thurs.–Sun. 8 P.M.–2:30 A.M.) more than accommodating. They actually take requests if there's anything you've been dying to hear. On Friday the Velvet entrance fee is €15 and on Sunday it is €20, but these prices include food and drink. Women can get in free before 12:30 A.M.

LIVE MUSIC

Opus Jazz Club (Via Cesare Battisti 19, tel. 075/573-4428, www.opusjazzclub.com, Mon.–Sat. 8:30 A.M.–2 P.M. and 5 P.M.–2 A.M., €5–10 cover Sat. and Sun.) keeps the city under the bebop sway even after the jazz festival has ended. Nightly live performances feature local artists and international acts. Good acoustics and reasonable drink prices make the Opus a good place to spend the evening. Another jazz venue is the **Bottega del Vino** (Via del Sole 1, tel. 075/571-6181, Mon.–Sat. 7 P.M.–1 A.M.). The music is enhanced by a vast selection of cured meats, cheeses, and local wines.

Loop Café (Via della Viola 19, tel.

328/021-2336, daily 7 P.M.–1 A.M.) proves that dive bars exist beyond Newark. It's the kind of place you might find Ethan Hawke drinking if he only had 24 hours in Perugia. The music comes from a small room upstairs where rock, Brazilian, folk, and indie musicians make regular appearances on the small stage.

Classical and chamber music is performed in **Palazzo dei Priori** (tel. 075/572-2271). The interior of the Sala dei Notari takes on a new dimension when combined with Mozart, Beethoven, and Schubert.

Festivals and Events
FESTA DI SAN COSTANZO
The party is always a little bigger when the patron saint is concerned, and Perugians take special pleasure in celebrating the Festa di San Costanzo (Chiesa Parrocchiale di S. Costanzo, tel. 075/31-041) every January 29. The martyr is remembered with a mix of traditional, artistic, and religious displays.

ARCHEOFESTIVAL
Archeofestival (tel. 075/599-0196, www.archeofestival.com) in mid-May is dedicated to revealing the archeological treasures of Perugia and the entire region. Many sights that are generally closed to the public are opened on this occasion and a variety of events and tours are offered to put history into context.

◉ UMBRIA JAZZ
Dizzy Gillespie, Miles Davis, and Sarah Vaughn. Since 1973 the biggest names in jazz have spent July in Perugia. For 10 days, Umbria Jazz (Piazza IV Novembre, tel. 075/573-2432, www.umbriajazz.com) transforms the city into New Orleans on a hill. The big names perform every night at 9 P.M. in Piazza IV Novembre while up-and-comers are given free reign over the town's spectacular backdrop. Booking a hotel during this period makes finding a needle in a haystack look easy.

EUROCHOCOLATE
Perugia and chocolate go way back and that relationship is celebrated every October.

Eurochocalate (Piazza IV Novembre, tel. 075/502-5880, www.eurochocolate.com) is the largest festival dedicated to cacao in the world, when nearly a million visitors with a craving for milk, dark, or white chocolate descend on the city. It's a chance to taste local and international creations or earn a doctorate in chocolate if you're looking for a career you can eat. On the last day there is a chocolate free-for-all.

SAGRA MUSICALE UMBRA
Sagra Musicale Umbra (various locations, tel. 075/572-2271, www.perugiamusicaclassica.com) is one of the oldest music festivals in Italy. Since 1937, classical and choral groups from throughout the world have demonstrated their talents for two weeks in September. Opening night is in Basilica di San Pietro.

SHOPPING
Perugia excels on the craft front and many workshops preserve the traditions of woodworking, ceramics, and textiles. The styles and patterns produced by local artisans are unique, and items such as the Perugine tablecloth can only be found here. Via dei Priori has a high concentration of boutiques and will satisfy anyone hunting for a souvenir.

There is no shortage of gift ideas at **La Bottega dei Sogni** (Corso Cavour 11, tel. 075/572-0262, Tues.–Sun. 9 A.M.–1 P.M. and 3–7 P.M.). The cloth is made from natural fibers on antique looms that turn out an assortment of tablecloths, napkins, and handkerchiefs.

If you like the idea of a medieval tablecloth, then **Giuditta Brozzetti** (Via Tiberio Berardi 5/6, tel. 075/40-236, www.brozzetti.com, Mon.–Fri. 9 A.M.–12:30 P.M. and 2:30–7 P.M.) can transform your dining room into a manor hall. The patterns produced at the weaving studio are all based on ancient designs and created on period machinery within a 13th-century church. You may not want to serve red wine when using these. Cushions and table runners are also available. Anyone with an interest in traditional hand weaving and embroidery techniques can sign up for one of the weekly courses.

Maybe it's the sunflowers, olive trees, and rolling countryside that adorn the plates that give **Il Pozzo delle Ceramiche** (Via dei Priori 70, tel. 075/573-0252, www.ilpozzodelleceramiche. it, Tues.–Sat. 10 A.M.–1 P.M. and 4–7:30 P.M., Mon. 4–7:30 P.M.) a sense of serenity. All the designs are original and have a practical function, from the lamp bases to coffee cups handpainted in bright vibrant colors.

Everything at **Mastri Cartai Editori** (Via dei Priori 77, tel. 075/572-5549, www.mastricartai.com, Mon.–Sat. 10 A.M.–1 P.M. and 3–7 P.M.) is made of paper. The problem is where to begin. It's all colorful and extremely touchable. Many of the ingeniously made objects—including the pop-ups, lampshades, and bags—have already found their way to trendy museum stores around the world.

A weekly market is held on Saturday morning in Piazza Umbria Jazz. **Umbria Terraviva** (tel. 075/835-5062) sells organic products and displays the work of traditional craftspeople on the first Sunday of each month in Piazza Piccinino. **Mercato dell'Antiquariato e del Collezionismo** (Rocca Paolina, tel. 075/500-5110) takes place on the last weekend of each month and features a mix of antiques and collectibles.

SPORTS AND RECREATION

Volleyball is the third or fourth most popular sport in Italy, but in Perugia it's number one. Sirio Perugia is the town's professional women's team. They've won a cabinet full of trophies and were crowned European Champions in 2006. Games attract sellout crowds to the **Palasport di Perugia** (Pian di Massiano, tel. 075/505-4931, www.pallavoloperugia.com) and tickets are a steal at €10. Take the 13D bus from Stazione Fontivegge or a taxi.

Club Alpino Italiano (Via della Gabbia 9, tel. 075/573-0334, www.caiperugia.it, Tues. and Fri. 6:30–8 P.M.) organizes half-day walks in the surrounding countryside each weekend. During the winter months they also organize cross-country ski excursions throughout the region and beyond. Check their website for upcoming events.

Golf Club Perugia (S. Sabina, Ellera Umbra, tel. 075/517-2204, www.golfclubperugia.it) can help traveling golfers keep their swing from getting rusty. The 18-hole 72-par course lies a short cab ride from the center of town. The longest hole is only 440 meters, but the real challenge is staying out of the sand traps. The green fee is €50 and clubs and carts can all be rented on the spot. The clubhouse is a former lime kiln that's been converted into a bar and restaurant.

ACCOMMODATIONS

Rosalba (Via del Circo 7, tel. 075/572-8275, www.hotelrosalba.com, €50–70 s/d) is a small hotel with large beds overlooking a pleasant square. Staff are welcoming and the price of a room includes breakfast and parking.

Three generations of the Casciarri family make the **Primavera Mini Hotel** (Via Vincioli 8, tel./fax 075/572-1657, primaveraminihotel.it, €48–75 s/d) a friendly and memorable place to stay. Each of the eight rooms on the second floor offers views of the Santa Susanna quarter.

Hotel Fortuna (Via Bonazzi 19, tel. 075/572-2845, www.umbriahotels.com, €88–128 s/d) is the kind of hotel you look forward to seeing after a day meandering the streets of Perugia. Rooms are comfortable and the roof terrace looks out over the town and surrounding countryside. Parking is available nearby.

If rustic is not your favorite adjective and the charm of wood beams is wearing thin, the **Sangallo Palace** (Via Masi 9, tel. 075/573-0202, www.sangallo.it, €132–178 s/d) will not disappoint. Four stars includes pool and fitness area, restaurant, and large carpeted rooms minutes from Piazza IV Novembre.

San Lorenzo della Rabatta (Località Cenerente, tel. 075/690–764, www.sanlorenzodellarabatta.com, €55 pp) is an *agriturismo* nine kilometers from the center of Perugia. It is an oasis of calm among gentle Umbrian hills and an ideal base for exploring the region. The medieval village has been faithfully transformed into seven apartments of various dimensions that are hard to leave.

FOOD

Early spring is when the wild asparagus begins to appear in the forests throughout Umbria and on the tables of its restaurants. **Civico 25** (Via della Viola 25, tel. 075/571-6376, Mon.–Sat. noon–2 P.M. and 7–10 P.M., €8–12) uses the vegetable in a variety of homemade sauces. The wine list here is longer than most novels and comes hardbound. Sagrantino, a DOC grape only grown in Umbria, is a good choice.

€ Enone (Corso Cavour 61, tel. 075/572-1950, Wed.–Mon. 7 P.M.–1 A.M., €10–13) gets progressively more animated as the hours pass. Diners have a choice between Umbrian and international food that includes sushi. It's a good place to sit around drinking wine and work on improving international relations.

Eating at **Dal Mi Cocco** (Corso Garibaldi 12, tel. 075/573-2511, Tues.–Sun. 12:30–3 P.M. and 7–10:30 P.M., €13, cash only) is like eating at a friend's house—except the friend lives in a renovated stable and has learned to cook Umbrian dishes. Guests are greeted with a glass of Vin Santo and choose from a fixed list of local favorites served with bread baked on the premises.

Emilio dreamt about turning the family deli into a restaurant. Fortunately that dream came true and **Trattoria del Borgo** (Via della Sposa 23, tel. 075/572-0390, Mon.–Sat., €18–22) now serves *strangozzi* (long pasta similar to spaghetti), *ciauscolo* (salami), and other Umbrian classics in an environment that makes digesting easy.

Caffè di Perugia (Via Mazzini 10, tel. 075/573-1863, www.caffediperugia.it, Wed.–Mon. 8 A.M.–11 P.M., €15–18) is an institution. The reputation is based on good cooking and an interior that hasn't lost its luster after decades of dining. Its prices are slightly higher than some of the newer restaurants in the area. There is a smoking room.

You can tell the **Mediterranea** (Via Marconi 11, tel. 075/572-4021, €7–11) makes good pizza the moment you enter the restaurant. Logs are stacked high to fuel the wood-burning oven and the Neapolitans who run the place are delighted you came. Choosing a pie isn't easy and it's hard to resist staring at what everyone else is eating. *Primavera* and *Quattro Stagioni* do not disappoint.

A region like Umbria may seem like a challenge to vegetarians but options do exist. **Ferrari** (Via Scura 1, tel. 075/572-2966, Tues.–Sat. 12:30–3 P.M. and 7–11 P.M., €8–12) creates a number of grilled vegetable plates and there is always pizza to fall back on. The *aperitivo* here is one of the best in the city and is accompanied by an excellent soundtrack.

Enoteca Provinciale di Perugia (Via Ulisse Rocchi 18, tel. 075/572-4824, Wed.–Mon. noon–4 P.M. and 6 P.M.–midnight, €4–6) is not an equal opportunity wine bar. The only labels you'll find here were bottled in the region and taste better with the local oils and bruschetta also on the menu.

India may seem a long way from Umbria, but **Karma** (Via M. Angeloni 73, tel. 075/505-6614, Tues.–Sun. noon–3:30 P.M. and 7–11:30 P.M., €8–10) closes the geographical divide. The tandoor oven works overtime here producing a variety of naan breads and all the coconut-based specialties that are missing from Italian menus.

There are two reasons to visit **Cioccolateria Augusta Perugia** (Via Pinturicchio 2, tel. 075/573-4577, Mon.–Sat. 10 A.M.–8 P.M.). The first is that the walk through the Porta Sole quarter and Arco Etrusco is one of the most suggestive in the entire city. The second is chocolate. This isn't the mass-produced kind; it's grade-A, artisan, and high in cacao content—and it blows supermarket candy bars away.

Perugina, a locally produced brand of chocolate, is as renowned in Italy as Hershey's is in the United States. Here the "kiss" is called a *baci* and comes wrapped with a romantic quote some men save in their wallets. The **Negozio Perugina** store (Corso Vannucci 101, tel. 075/573-6677, www.perugina. it, daily 10 A.M.–9 P.M., closed Mon. morning) celebrates the company's 100-year history with all the cavity-inducing products that have made it famous. The Perugina museum and chocolate school (San Sisto, Viale San Sisto, tel. 075/527-6796, Mon.–Fri. 9 A.M.–1 P.M. and 2–5:30 P.M., admission free) are located outside of town and are a must for chocoholics.

Also on Corso Vannucci is the oldest *pasticceria* in town. **Pasticceria Sandri** (Corso Vannucci 32, tel. 075/572-4112, Tues.–Sun. 8 A.M.–10 P.M.) was founded in 1860 and is a popular local meeting point. Nothing much has changed on the inside, which conserves a 19th-century feel. If you're daunted by the vast assortment go with the house specialty *cioccolatini*.

INFORMATION AND SERVICES

A map and guide containing descriptions of the town's monuments are available from the **IAT office** (Piazza Matteotti 18, tel. 075/573-6458, www.perugia.umbria2000.it, Mon.–Sat. 8:30 A.M.–1:30 P.M. and 3:30–6:30 P.M., Sun. 9 A.M.–1 P.M.). The map contains five itineraries that begin and end in Piazza IV Novembre. There is also an Infoturist Point (tel. 075/573-2933) in Piazza Partigiani where guides (www.guideumbria.com) to the city regularly depart. Anyone who prefers random exploration can learn about the city through the 128 plaques scattered around the center.

Perugia CittàMuseo Card (www.sistemamuseo.it) provides reduced entry to a dozen museums and architectural sights. Type A (€7) is valid one day and can be used in four museums. Type B (€12) is good for three days and allows access to all museums. The card is sold at the Galleria Nazionale dell'Umbria and participating museums.

Viva Perugia (€0.80) is a monthly events guide sold at newsstands. It includes cultural and dining information, a map, train schedules, and useful numbers. Pick up a copy if you plan on remaining in the city for several days.

There's always at least one pharmacy open in Perugia, and Tarpani (Piazza Matteotti 28, tel. 075/572-0925) has been dispensing relief since before anyone can remember. If it's closed you'll find information on the nearest open pharmacy posted in the window.

The **central post office** (Piazza Matteotti 1, tel. 075/573-6977, Mon.–Sat. 8 A.M.–6:30 P.M.) is on the other side of the street. Mid-morning and early afternoon are the best times for avoiding a line.

GETTING THERE

Aeroporto Regionale Umbro S. Egidio (tel. 075/592–141, www.airport.umbria.it) is a small regional airport 10 kilometers outside of Perugia. Flight options are limited, however there are two daily flights from Milan. All the major car rental companies have offices in the arrivals terminal including **Maggiore** (tel. 075/500-7499) and **Avis** (tel. 075/692-9346). A shuttle bus (€2.58) operates daily 5:50 A.M.–10:40 P.M. and stops at Stazione Fontivegge and Piazza Italia.

Perugia is easy to reach by car via the A1 highway. From the north exit at Val di Chiana and follow the signs toward the city. If you don't see the Lago di Trasimeno within 15 minutes you're heading the wrong way. From the south exit at Orte direction Terni. Within 20 kilometers you'll see signs for the E45 towards Perugia. This section of highway is under renovation and detours are posted in yellow. Umbrian police have a reputation for being ticket-happy; it's advisable to stay within posted speed limits. There is parking near both train stations and Piazza Partigiani (SIPA, tel. 075/573-2506, www.sipaonline.it), from which the city is easily accessible.

There are five daily **SULGA** (Piazza Partigiani, tel. 075/500-9641) bus departures to Perugia from Rome Stazione Tiburtina 7:15 A.M.–5:30 P.M. on weekdays and two on weekends. The journey takes two hours and 15 minutes. Tickets may be purchased onboard and cost €15 for a one-way journey and €23 for a round-trip. There is also one bus a day to and from Florence, Milan, and Naples.

Perugia has two train stations and twice as many ways of arriving from Rome. On weekdays, **Ferrovia Centrale Umbra** (Largo delle Alpi 8, tel. 075/557-5401, www.fcu.it) runs a daily service leaving Termini at 12:30 P.M. and arriving in Perugia Stazione S. Anna at 3 P.M. Tickets cost €10.15 and the return journey leaves at 7:30 A.M.

Other options require a transfer at Foligno or Terontola and arrive at Stazione Fontivegge (Piazza Vittorio Veneto, tel. 075/500-1288, www.trenitalia.it) three kilometers from the center. The first train leaves Termini at 7 A.M. Tickets cost €11.70 and the journey lasts a little over two hours. *Viva Perugia* contains a full time schedule of bus and train departures.

GETTING AROUND

Perugia was one of the first cities in Italy to banish cars from its city center and benefits from an innovative transport system that includes underground parking, escalators, and light rail. The **Minimetro,** which began operating in 2008, was designed by Jean Nouvel and is a cross between a roller coaster and monorail. It's a must for anyone who appreciates public transportation and is the fastest way of getting to the center from Stazione Fontivegge. Escalators are the modern solution for making it quickly to the top of a hilltop town. The longest connects Piazza Partigiani and the bus terminal with Piazza Italia and operates 6:15 A.M.–1:45 P.M.

APM Bus and Minimetro tickets cost €1 for 70 minutes of travel or a Card Turistico can be purchased for €3.60, allowing unlimited travel for 24 hours. Remember to validate your ticket upon boarding the bus or Minimetro. Tickets can be purchased at Minimetro stations, newsstands, and the IAT office.

There is a taxi stand at the Stazione Fontivegge and Piazza IV Novembre. Cars can also be ordered 24 hours a day from **Servizio Radio Taxi** (tel. 075/500-4888).

Three bus companies serve destinations around the region. **APM** (tel. 800/512–141, www.apmperugia.it) travels to Todi and Assisi. **SSIT** (tel. 075/573-1707, www.spoletina.com) connects Spoleto, Norcia, and Deruta. **ATC** (tel. 07/4449-2711, www.atcterni.it) makes regular stops at Narni and Orvieto. They all terminate at Piazza Partigiani.

AROUND PERUGIA

The best thing about **Deruta** is the pottery. It's one of the oldest centers of ceramics in Umbria, where pottery wheels have been spinning for over a thousand years. The characteristics of the town's production are a white base decorated in distinct orange, blue, and yellow patterns. A good place to observe the versatility and evolution of this art form is the **Museo Regionale della Ceramica** (Largo San Francesco, tel. 075/971-1000, daily 10 A.M.–1 P.M. and 3:30–6 P.M., €3). The museum is housed in a former convent and contains hundreds of pieces from Greek *hydria* vases once used to hold water to 19th-century medicine jars.

Outside there is no shortage of studios in which to observe artisans at work and make a purchase or two. **Mario Sambuco and C.** (Via della Tecnica, tel. 075/971-1625) and **La Gioconda** (Via G. Li Causi 8, tel. 075/971-0080) both have a wide selection of bowls, plates, and vases on display. Via Tiberina is lined with shops, some of which sell their pieces at discounted prices.

Deruta lies 12 kilometers south of Perugia. Take the Deruta Nord exit off E45 and follow the signs towards the town center. There is a parking lot near Porta Sant'Angelo.

UMBRIA

Gubbio

If all hilltop towns are starting to look alike you need to look again. The differences are in the color of the stone, the shape of rooftop tiles, and what's being served in the local trattoria. Gubbio lies on Mount Ingino and was built from the gray limestone quarried nearby. It gives the town an impression of uniformity. The center, which preserves its medieval heritage more than any other in Umbria, is a collection of terra-cotta tiled houses and winding streets from which glimpses of the surrounding Apennine countryside are visible.

SIGHTS

As you see the sights of Gubbio make sure to pay attention to its city walls, which are in remarkable shape. Six of the original gates are still intact. Several of these, such as **Porta di Sant'Agostino** and **Porta di San Pietro,** have retained their coats of arms and embellishments, which symbolize the neighborhoods they once protected.

Palazzo dei Consoli

It's easy to spot the Palazzo dei Consoli (Piazza Grande, tel. 075/927-4298), which dominates the town. The civic palace is entered on a suspended staircase that leads to the great hall studded with Roman and medieval relics. The **Sala dell'Arengo** (daily 10 A.M.–1 P.M. and 2–5 P.M.) houses the **Museo Civico.** The Eugubine Tablets are on display here, giving visitors a chance to brush up on their ancient Umbrian, a language never completely deciphered. A smaller art gallery (daily 10 A.M.–1 P.M. and 2–5 P.M.) is housed on the second floor.

Chiesa di San Giovanni

Piazza di San Givanni is a long rectangular stretch of paving that leads to Chiesa di San Giovanni. It was built in the 12th century and served as a model for later churches built in the town. The simple facade of the church is in stark contrast to the bell tower that looms above. Several Gothic frescoes are still visible around the single nave.

Palazzo del Bargello

Palazzo del Bargello (Largo del Bargello) lacks the splendor of some of the town's taller buildings, but in this corner of Gubbio you get an idea of what 14th-century housing was like. It's said that the magistrate responsible for the city police once lived here. In front there is a fountain known as the Fontana dei Matti. Anyone who runs around it three times receives the honorary title of madman of Gubbio.

◖ Gubbio Cableway

Although it might look a little rickety, Gubbio's cableway (Via S. Girolamo, tel. 075/927-3881) is the best way of getting to the top of Monte Ingino. It takes about six minutes to climb the 900 meters, and the view along the way is what postcard photographers dream about. At the top the little church of S. Ubaldo is expecting you; anyone wise enough to have packed a picnic has the entire valley to themselves. During the summer the cableway runs 8:30 A.M.–7:30 P.M. Off-season hours vary and generally involve a lunch break.

ENTERTAINMENT AND EVENTS

Imagine the running of the bulls without bulls and you get an idea of the **Festa dei Ceri** (www.festadeiceri.it). It's crazy, it's crowded, and if you're not from Gubbio it may not make much sense. Just remember that lifting heavy objects is a common part of many Italian festivals. In Gubbio the object is called a Ceri and has been lifted since 1160. It consists of three prism-shaped wooden poles weighing 400 kilograms and each topped with a saint. On May 15, three teams of 10 set off from a packed Piazza Grande to see which is the most versatile before returning the loads back inside the basilica for safekeeping.

The **Palio della Balestra** is a crossbow

UMBRIA

© ALESSIA RAMACCIA

Teatro Romano, the 1st-century amphitheater outside of Gubbio

competition between Gubbio and the Tuscan town of San Selpocro. The event is held on the last Sunday in May and consists in skilled bowmen trying to hit wooden targets. The winning team is presented with a standard made by local artists. A second tournament is held on August 14 between representatives of the four different neighborhoods of the town.

Throughout the summer, the **Spettacoli Classici** (tel. 075/922-0693) at the Teatro Romano puts on a program of classical concerts. The open-air performances within the Roman theater are a marvelous way to spend an evening under the stars.

Mostra Mercato del Tartufo Bianco e dei Prodotti Agroalimentari, a celebration of the white truffle, lasts four days at the end of October. The Umbrian variety is especially prized and harder to find than the black version. Bargaining can be fierce and buyers and sellers put on their best poker faces. The stalls filling the center of town are also devoted to locally produced specialties and handicrafts.

SHOPPING

Gubbio put itself on the ceramics map back in the 14th century when Giorgio Andreoli incorporated an Arabic technique that added luster to his creations and which is still used today by the artisans at **Ceramiche Rampini** (Via Leonardo da Vinci 92, tel. 075/927-2963, daily 10 A.M.–1 P.M. and 3–7 P.M.).

The Middle Ages weren't just made of stone; they also relied on iron pounded into every shape imaginable for practical and decorative purposes. That knowledge has never been lost and can be seen inside the **Artigianato Ferro Artistico** (Via U. Baldassini 22, tel. 075/927-3079), where ironworkers hammer out intricate designs every day.

Lisart Antichità (Via Baldassini 80, tel. 075/927-4368, Tues.–Sun. 9:30 A.M.–1 P.M. and 3–7 P.M.) sells charm by the boatload and will ship it anywhere that needs a little piece of Gubbio. The shop is filled with antiques, lampshades, crystal, and tableware that will make a lasting impression on any home.

SPORTS AND RECREATION

One of the town's many hiking trails begins at Santa Maria della Vittorina on Via Nino Bixio just outside the city walls. Have a look inside this remarkably simple church that has a great fresco of Saint Francesco preaching to the birds. The walk itself is on pebbled and dirt paths through beautiful pine scenery.

For something a little more intense, **Club Alpino Gubbio** (Piazza S.Pietro 1, www.caigubbio.it) organizes three-day excursions along the Sentiero Francescano. Days start early and there's a good probability of blisters. The cost of €80 covers two nights of room and board, guided tours of the sights passed along the way, and travel to the starting point. Contact Luigino (tel. 338/387-5867) to see when the next journey is planned. They also run a mountain climbing school.

ACCOMMODATIONS

Hotel Consoli (Via dei Consoli, tel. 075/922-0639, www.urbaniweb.com, €92 d) offers eight rooms and one suite within a 13th-century palazzo. The restaurant serves traditional dishes that rely on local ingredients for flavor.

Authentic frescoes and vaulted ceilings are all standard at the **Relais Ducale** (Via Galeotti 19, tel. 07/922-0157, www.mencarelligroup.com, 125–225 s/d). This elegant hotel is run by the Mencarelli Group, which operates two other hotels in the city and has a reputation for quality and service. The Taverna del Lupo restaurant is located downstairs.

For a relaxing stay in a 9th-century castle 14 kilometers from Gubbio, **⟨ Castello di Petroia** (Scritto, tel. 075/924-1079, www.petroia.it, €164 d) is the only option. Each of the rooms is decorated differently and three of them are located in the old tower. Half-board is available for an additional €32, and the swimming pool looks out over a succession of small valleys.

FOOD

La Fornace di Mastrogiorgio (Via Mastro Giorgio 2, tel. 075/922-1836, Wed.–Mon., €12–15) is an institution that provides a warm welcome and simple authentic recipes that have

TRUFFLE HUNTING

In Umbria, finding a truffle is nearly as good as striking oil or gold. That may seem odd considering it's a fungus, but once tasted the *tartufo* quickly gains the respect it has had since antiquity. There are several varieties, but black and white truffles are what most excite diners. The merits of each can be argued endlessly and the only way to resolve a debate like this is to taste both. Generally, truffles are lightly grated over plain pasta, but creative chefs in the region are forever experimenting with new means of exploiting the strong flavor.

Truffle hunting requires patience and a good companion. Traditionally female pigs have been used to discover the delicacy, but a dog with a good nose also works. Early autumn is the best time to find both varieties in the Umbrian forests, especially the area around **Gubbio**. An easier method is to visit one of the many stores selling both the pure, unadulturated version and the many products derived from truffles. The truffle market held in Gubbio each year is serious business; international buyers and local sellers meet to exchange the goods. Prices for a large specimen weighing 100 grams or more can easily reach triple digits. Once purchased, the prized truffle is shipped express to the finest restaurants in New York, Paris, and Tokyo.

been passed down through the generations. The house specialty is *bavarese di pecorino* (vegetables with a goat cheese sauce).

The base ingredients at **La Lanterna** (Via Gioia 23, Fri.–Wed., €8–10) are white truffles and mushrooms. During spring and summer, tables are set outside along the characteristic side street.

Fifteen kilometers may seem like a long way to go for flour, water, and salt but no one has ever complained after making the journey to **Il Panaro** (Cima di Mengara, tel. 075/92-0035,

Wed.–Mon. 12:30 P.M.–3 P.M. and 7–10:30 P.M., €10–14). After all, those are the three main ingredients to flat bread, or what they call *crescia sul panaro* around Gubbio. It's served with *salumi, lonza,* and *prosciutto crudo* cold cuts, but you can always opt for the tagliatelle or barley soup. Nearby the **Distilleria Morelli** (Via Da Vinci 70, tel./fax 075/927-3304) produces a good Amaro liquor that is drunk after dinner to facilitate digestion.

Usually the urge for truffle hits about a week after you leave Umbria. You'll be glad to have stopped at **La Buca del Tartufo** (Via XX Settembre 33, tel. 075/927-1446, Apr.–Sept. daily 8:30 A.M.–7:30 P.M., Oct.–Mar. daily 8:30 A.M.–12:30 P.M.) and stocked up on all the region has to offer. There are sausages, sauces, cheese, and, of course, the one and only *tartufi di Gubbio* (local truffles).

The smell inside █ **Gubbio Salumi** (Via Cavour 6, tel. 075/927-3850, www.gubbiosalumi. it, daily except Thurs. morning) is the result of 150 years of cured meat production. Unless you're a vegetarian, this is heaven. The pork and beef sausages are salted, spiced, marinated, and set out to dry until they are perfect. Point to whatever looks appetizing or go with the *capocollo, lonza,* and prosciutto specialties.

Prodotti Tipici Locali (Via della Repubblica 19, tel. 075/927-3792, daily 10 A.M.–1 P.M. and 3:30–7:30 P.M.) means typical local products and that's exactly what you'll find here. The selection of oil, pasta, wine, pâté, and honey will satisfy even the fussiest gourmets.

INFORMATION AND SERVICES

The **IAT office** (Piazza della Repubblica 15, tel. 075/075/922-0693, www.bellaumbria.net, Mon.–Fri. 9 A.M.–2 P.M. and 3:30–6:30 P.M., Sat.–Sun 9:30 A.M.–12:30 P.M. and 3:30–6:30 P.M.) offers an audio guide (€3) with English commentary explaining Gubbio's monuments and the town's hidden treasures.

GETTING THERE AND AROUND

From Perugia, take the N298 all the way to Gubbio. Much of the 39-kilometer journey is scenic and the hamlets along the way make excellent cappuccino stops. **APM** (tel. 075/50-6781, www. apmperugia.it) buses travel to Gubbio several times a day and a ticket costs €4.30. The nearest train station is in Fossato di Vico, 18 kilometers away. Taxis can be found in Piazza 40 Martiri or by calling 075/927-3800.

AROUND GUBBIO

The **Teatro Romano,** built in the 1st century A.D., is a short distance outside the city walls near the Porta Ortacci. Unlike the example in Ostia Antica it has not been restored, yet enough arches and stage remain to get an idea of what Roman theatergoers once experienced. In July and August the Gubbio Summer Festival (Piazza Oderisi 5, tel. 075/922-0693, admission free) is held here featuring guest conductors from around Italy.

Assisi

Assisi stands out from a distance. The town lies on the slope of Monte Subasio and was the home of San Francesco who is buried in the Basilica. The center is protected by medieval walls and eight fortified gates that have resisted the test of time. The Porta Nuova leads to the main square and a warren of streets with views over the plain below.

If you like churches you've come to the right place. Assisi has two basilicas, a cathedral, and nine houses of worship that vary in size and construction, but the Basilica di San Francesco is the most famous.

As one of the most important artistic and religious centers in Italy Assisi attracts a crowd. Over six million pilgrims visit the town every year, giving rise to stores selling postcards and the Tau cross that was used by

San Francesco to sign his letters. It is possible to find peace from the rush of Corso Mazzini by climbing the steep streets behind Piazza del Comune towards the Rocca Maggiore castle that looms above the town.

SIGHTS
◖ Basilica di San Francesco

Basilica di San Francesco (tel. 075/819-9001, www.sanfrancescoassisi.org, Basilica Inferiore daily 6 A.M.–6 P.M., admission free; Basilica Superiore daily 8:30 A.M.–6 P.M., admission free) consists of two churches built on top of each other. The lower church was begun in 1228 several years after the saint's death. It has a more intimate feel and was intended for the growing number of pilgrims who venerated San Francesco. The upper church dates from 1230 and has a grander style. Both attracted the finest artists of the time who frescoed nearly every centimeter of the interior. The crypt that houses the saint's body was dug in 1818 and is below the lower church.

Giotto nearly single-handedly invented a new perspective. His paintings gave depth to landscapes and figures that had previously appeared flat. The series of 28 frescoes inside the upper church were painted over five years starting in 1290 and illustrate the life of San Francesco. The most dramatic panel shows San Francesco renouncing his father's wealth and stripping himself before God. Giotto's cycle starts on the far right side of the church near the choir. The first painting depicts the future saint in his youth. A man spreads a cloth over the ground where he will step foretelling his destiny of purity. The lower church contains biblically themed frescoes by Lorenzetti and Martini. Two booths outside the Basilica provide free audio guides to the entire complex.

Piazza del Comune

Piazza del Comune is located on the spot of the old Roman Foro. The most obvious reminder of this is the Tempio di Minerva, whose fluted columns are nearly completely intact and form an interesting contrast with the medieval

Basilica di San Francesco

© ALESSIA RAMACCIA

palazzo del Popolo nearby. The inside is lavishly decorated in gold-leafed sculptures.

Basilica di Santa Chiara

Basilica di Santa Chiara was constructed out of a pink stone dug from nearby mountains. Its 12th and 14th century frescoes are particularly well preserved and depict the saint who founded the Clarissa order of nuns. In the chapel on the right along the single nave is the cross on which San Francesco vowed to reform the church.

FESTIVALS AND EVENTS

Calendimaggio (Piazza del Comune 11, tel. 075/816-868, www.calendimaggiodiassisi.it) is a celebration of spring lasting three days and beginning on the first Thursday in May. The event's medieval origins are clear from the costumes, dances, and games in which the high and low parts of town compete. The event begins with a parade and ends with the crowning of the *palio* heroes who relish their victory until the early hours of Sunday morning.

Riti della Settimana Santa (APT office, Piazza del Comune 28, tel. 075/812-534) takes place during the week prior to Easter Sunday. On Thursday the ceremony of the Deposition is reenacted and the statue of Christ is transferred to the Basilica di San Francesco. The next day a solemn procession lit by torches parades the statue through the streets accompanied by a single drummer.

Palio di S. Rufino (APT office, Piazza del Comune 28, tel. 075/812-534) is organized on the last weekend of August. The event starts with a parade through the streets of the center and culminates in a crossbow competition between the three neighborhoods that make up Assisi.

SPORTS AND RECREATION

San Francesco walked everywhere. He traveled frequently throughout the surrounding countryside and onto the Monte Subasio, 1,292 meters above town. The **Montagna di Assisi Association** proposes itineraries that vary 12–36 kilometers in length. Each excursion takes walkers to abbeys, hermitages, and villages where San Francesco once paused.

The guide inside the IAT office sheds light onto each landmark.

Those who prefer a two-wheeled approach can rent bicycles from **Angelucci Andrea** (Via BecCheti 31, tel./fax 075/804-2550, www.angeluccicicli.it) near Santa Maria degli Angeli.

There are two campsites near town. **Fontemaggio** (Via Santuario delle Carceri 24, tel. 075/81-3636, www.fontemaggio.it, €6/pp) is adjacent to Monte Subasio and well positioned for hiking. They claim to be one of the first campsites in Italy and have added an immaculately clean hotel and youth hostel over the years. A huge fireplace where meats are grilled is the main attraction of the restaurant, which serves typical Umbrian dishes on red-checkered tablecloths.

In addition to being a spot to pitch your tent, **Camping Village Assisi** (S. Giovanni in Campiglione 110, tel. 075/81-2335, www.campingassisi.it, €8 pp) has bungalows and mobile homes to rent. There are tennis courts, an outdoor swimming pool, and a restaurant on the grounds.

SHOPPING

Woodworking is a tradition practiced throughout Italy. In Umbria it evolved from a necessity to create practical things into a desire to create objects of beauty. **Immagini d'Arte** (Via Fontebella 8, tel. 075/813-756) illustrates the transformation and just how close craftsmanship can get to art.

Studio Incisione Legno (Via Giotto 8a, tel. 075/812-648, daily) only uses wood from olive trees to create kitchen utensils and souvenirs that feel different to the touch. They also produce detailed nativity characters in a variety of sizes and poses.

Anyone with a passion for hardbound books will enjoy browsing though **Tipografia Zubboli** (Piazza del Comune 5, tel. 075/812-381, daily 9:30 A.M.–8 P.M.), where the paper as well as the marbleized covers are handmade.

ACCOMMODATIONS

Don't be fooled by the website. What **La Fortezza** (Piazza del Comune, tel.

075/81-2418, www.lafortezzahotel.com, €52 d) lacks in new media skills, they make up for in friendly service. Each of the seven rooms comes equipped with wrought-iron beds, parquet floors, and a view. It's a little like staying at an aunt's house, but after dining on the immense portions in the restaurant downstairs you won't regret the choice.

The atmosphere inside **Fontebella** (Via Fontebella 25, tel. 075/81-2883, www.fontebella. com, €90 d) is from another century. Which one exactly is a mystery. The centrally located hotel has great views of the town and a garden. Breakfast is served outside on the terrace, weather permitting, and the hotel restaurant has a notable list of Umbrian wines.

Umbra (Via degli Archi 6, tel. 075/81-2240, www.hotelumbra.it, €105 d) is a tranquil hotel on a picturesque side street moments from the main square. Its garden is delightful and during the summer breakfast is served under the olive vines. The restaurant prepares Umbrian country fare within an elegant atmosphere.

Hotel Windsor Savoia (Viale Marconi 1, tel. 075/81-2210, www.hotelwindsorsavoia.it, €78–115 s/d) has been open since 1908 and its location 100 meters from the Basilica di San Francesco makes it an excellent place to start the day. Located on a relatively quiet street the rooms would seem luxurious to a saint and provide a uniquely Italian experience.

Assisi's monasteries and convents have been welcoming pilgrims and travelers for centuries and there is no shortage of beds within their walls. ◖ **Monastero Giuseppe** (Via S. Apolinaire 1, tel. 075/81-2332, www.msgiuseppe. it, €55 d) provides guests with an idea of what monks do for a living. It's a busy day that starts early and is more than just marathon prayer sessions. The extensive grounds of the monastery overlooking the valley are ideal for contemplation.

FOOD

Every time the bell rings at the ◖ **Trattoria Pallotta** (Vicolo della Volta Pinta, tel. 075/81-2307, www.pallottaassisi.it, Wed.–Mon. noon–2:30 P.M. and 7–10 P.M., €8–12)

something good exits from the kitchen. There are three tasting menus for those who can't decide and many vegetarian options. Visitors are greeted with a smile as soon as they enter and are given a choice of tables in one of two pleasantly decorated rooms. The family also runs a small hotel nearby.

A medieval atmosphere in the center of Assisi is only half the attraction of the **Buca di San Francesco** (Via E. Brizi 1, tel. 075/81-2204, Tues.–Sun. noon–3 P.M. and 7–10:30 P.M., €10–14). The other half is the food, which excels from the appetizers to desserts. *Fantasia di bruschette* is a good way to start and will arrive on your table within minutes. Trust Giovanni Betti to make the right wine selection to accompany your food.

What started out as a hobby for four friends has become **La Piazzetta dell'Erba** (Via San Gabriele dell'Addolorato 15b, tel. 075/81-5352, Tues.–Sun. 12:30–2:30 P.M. and 7–10:30 P.M., €12–15). Their reinterpretation of Umbrian classics includes a salad of pecorino, pear, nuts, and honey.

Once you've tasted Assisi's culinary delights, it's hard to go home empty-handed. **Il Cortile di Casa Mia** (Via San Paolo 7, tel. 075/815-5321, daily 10:30 A.M.–7 P.M.) has everything you need for recreating those flavors, from the truffle sauces to the *strangozzi* pasta and dried lentils. Everything is attractively packaged and can be shipped anywhere.

INFORMATION AND SERVICES

The **IAT office** (Piazza del Commune, tel. 075/812–534, www.assisi.umbria2000.it, Mon.–Sat. 8 A.M.–2 P.M. and 3–6 P.M., Sun. 10 A.M.–1 P.M.)' provides guides, maps, and assistance finding accommodations. There are other information points at the Basilica di San Francesco and Santa Maria degli Angeli. Guided tours can be arranged through the **Associazione Guide Turistiche dell'Umbria** (Via Dono Doni 18b, tel. 075/815–228, www .assoguide.it).

There are six banks in Assisi, including a Unicredit in Piazza del Comune and a Banca

Populare di Spoleto in Piazza Santa Chiara. Rail and bus tickets may be purchased at **Stoppini Travel** (Corso Mazzini 31, tel. 075/812–597). Post offices can be found in Piazza San Pietro and Largo Properizio 4.

GETTING THERE AND AROUND

Assisi is 20 kilometers from Perugia just off the N75. There is a short way and many long ways of reaching town by car. The Santa Maria degli Angeli exit is the fastest route, although traffic can back up near the train crossing. Other approaches to town lead to winding panoramic routes that transform small distances into epic journeys of unforgettable landscapes. There are several parking areas outside the city walls, several of which are set up to accommodate campers. The lot in Piazza Unità d'Italia is the closest to the Basilica but very often filled.

The nearest train station to Assisi is six kilometers away in Santa Maria degli Angeli. Travelers can complete the journey by bus or take a taxi from the *piazzale* outside the station. The journey costs €10. **APM buses** (tel. 800/512–141, www.apmperugia.it) connect Perugia and surrounding towns with Assisi. All journeys start and terminate in Piazza Matteotti. A minibus service operates within the town and connects the principal monuments and piazze. It runs every 30 minutes and tickets may be purchased at newsstands or *tabacchi*.

Taxi stands are located in Piazza Unità d'Italia and Piazza del Comune or may be ordered 24 hours a day from **Radio Taxi Assisi** (tel. 075/813–100, www.radiotaxiassisi.it). Car rentals with a driver are available by calling **Gino Costantini** (Via delle Acquedotti 8, tel./fax 075/816–356).

AROUND ASSISI

Eremo delle Carceri is situated four kilometers from Assisi up a small road on the Monte Subasio. It is one of the most revered Franciscan sights that the saint and his followers used as a retreat for reflection and prayer. A small monastery was added to the original chapel in 1400, which remains an oasis of calm and tranquility. To reach the complex, leave Assisi from the Porta Cappuccinni and continue uphill. Although it's accessible by car, walking is far more rewarding.

Spello

Spello's 8,307 inhabitants live on a spur of Monte Subasio between Assisi and Foligno. There's a lot to look at for such a small town, including some of the best Roman ruins in the area. If you like olives, try to make it here at the end of November, or you can purchase one of the endless varieties of pecorino cheese available on the shops lining Via Cavour.

SIGHTS

Roman heritage becomes evident upon entry into Spello. Both **Porta Venere** and **Torri di Properzio** date from Augusto's reign and testify to the importance the town once had in the area.

The Middle Ages and Renaissance were also fruitful periods for Spello. Construction of **Santa Maria Maggiore** began in 1285 but the structure standing today is most notable for an addition undertaken in 1644, when the original building was substantially elongated. The inside contains a number of artworks, including the Cappella Baglioni frescoed by Pinturicchio in 1501, which depicts scenes from the New Testament.

Palazzo dei Canonici contains the Pinacoteca Civica (Piazza Matteotti 10, tel. 07/4230-1497, Tues.–Sun. 10:30 A.M.–12:30 P.M. and 3:30–5:30 P.M., €2.50) and a wealth of 13th–18th century artwork. The churches of San Andrea and San Lorenzo are both rich in frescoes. The marble tabernacle in the latter is one of a kind.

UMBRIA

ENTERTAINMENT AND EVENTS

Teatro Subasio (Via Giulia 12, tel. 07/4230-1689) presents a steady program of classical and jazz concerts. The theater has the velvet red curtain, box seats, and all the trimmings you wouldn't expect in a town like Spello. Ticket prices range €10–25 and sight lines are excellent.

At two kilometers long, the **Corpus Domini con Infiorata** (June 9 and 10) is one of the most spectacular processions in Italy. The streets are covered in flower petals depicting religious and everyday events. There is great energy during the preparation the night before and locals who live along the street invite strangers onto their balconies to get a better view of the floral compositions. It's wise to show up early before everything has been trampled.

Incontro per le Strade is a two–month long festival of performing arts throughout August and September. Check with the Info Point to find out details of specific events.

Festa dell'Olivo e Sagra della Bruschetta during the last weekend of November is a chance to taste all the area's DOC olive oils. The season's harvest is brought into town on tractors decorated especially for the occasion.

SHOPPING

The rhythmic sound of metal on metal followed by a pause, then more hammering until the shape is just right. It can't be easy living above **Artigianfer** (Via Gigliara 13, tel. 074/265-1387), but fortunately no one has complained. The result is an arsenal of medieval weapons that are likely to end up wielded in one of the local *palios*.

ACCOMMODATIONS

If you can judge a hotel by the palazzo, then **Hotel del Teatro** (Via Giulia 24, tel. 07/4230-1140, www.hoteldelteatro.it, €65–110 s/d) makes a good first impression. The 17th-century courtyard reinforces that feeling and the 11 rooms within deliver everything you might expect in size, furnishings, and comfort.

a narrow street in Spello

© ALESSIA RAMACCIA

Having a fabulous restaurant in your hotel means you may never need to leave **La Bastiglia** (Via Salnitraria 15, tel. 07/4265-1277, www.la bastiglia.com, €85–130 s/d). This former mill at the entrance to Spello also benefits from a good location. The views from the terrace are difficult to top. Some rooms have their own entrances that look out onto a delightful garden.

There's no better way to get that Renaissance feeling than waking up in **Hotel Palazzo Bocci** (Via Cavour 17, tel. 07/4230-1021, www.palaz zobocci.com, €100–160 s/d). Days begin with breakfast in the arched dining room or carefully tended garden and discussion of the morning's itinerary is given increased significance when conducted within the reading room.

FOOD

La Cantina (Via Cavour 2, tel. 07/4265-1775, Mon.–Sat. 12:30–3 P.M. and 7:30–11 P.M., €12–16) offers traditional cuisine with a touch of fantasy. The chef has a fondness for mushrooms, which can be found in many of his recipes.

Around the corner from Santa Maria Maggiore, **Pinturicchio** (Largo Mazzini 8, tel. 07/4230-1003, www.ristoranteilpinturicchio.it, Tues.–Sun. noon–2:30 P.M. and 7–10:30 P.M., €15–16) is a dream come true for cheese lovers. The fondue with truffle is the kind of dish you eat once and will never forget. The lentil soup and grilled lamb are both good options.

INFORMATION AND SERVICES

An **Info Point** (tel. 07/4230-1497) is near Porta Consolare. They sell the Spello Card for €7, which allows access to six of the town's museums and monuments.

GETTING THERE AND AROUND

Spello is 31 kilometers from Perugia just south of Assisi directly off the N75. From Rome take the A1 until Orte and continue along the N20,4 which becomes the N4 after Terni and the N75 after Foligno. The Spello exit is the second one after Foligno.

The journey by train from Perugia takes 30 minutes and costs €3.55 for a first-class ticket and €2.30 for a second-class ticket. Trains leave every hour seven days a week 5:55 A.M.–10:21 P.M. From Rome Tiburtina station, the journey is a little over two hours depending on which train you catch. Service runs 6 A.M.–8:14 P.M. and may require a transfer at Orte or Foligno.

AROUND SPELLO
◖ Bevagna

Although founded by the Romans, it's the Middle Ages that left the greatest mark on the town of Bevagna. This little town has barely 2,000 inhabitants and has retained medieval entrances and parts of the original ring wall. In the center is Piazza Silvestri and many good examples of Romanesque architecture, including the churches of San Silvestro and San Michele.

The best thing about Bevagna though is that most people don't make it here. Being 10 kilometers off the N75 means that most travelers opt for the more convenient options. That's their loss. Bevagna is the beginning of deep Umbria and if you stumble on it in mid-June during **Il Mercato delle Gaite** you may think you've gone back in time. Nearly everyone in town participates in this medieval reconstruction that goes on for 10 days and reenacts daily life as it was in 1250. It's actually a competition between the four neighborhoods of Bevagna, judged by university professors who assign points based on authenticity of dress, behavior, and crossbow skills.

Orivieto

Orvieto lies on a 300-meter high plateau that must have been an obvious choice for the Etruscans who founded the city. Even the steep natural defenses, however, could not hold off the Romans who sacked the place in 265 B.C. and deported everyone. It wasn't until the Middle Ages that the town was repopulated and took on the characteristics seen today. The center is dominated by the cathedral that has made the town a regular stop for travelers since the days of the grand tour.

SIGHTS
Duomo

The Duomo (Piazza del Duomo, 7:30 A.M.–12:45 P.M. and 2:30–5:15 P.M.) is one of the greatest churches built during the Middle Ages. It was commissioned by Pope Niccolo IV in 1290 and the final stone wasn't laid until four centuries later. It was worth the wait, and the mosaics that cover the facade are perhaps the most remarkable thing about the duomo. Three adjacent buildings form the complex of the Palazzi Papali, within which the Museo dell'Opera del Duomo and the Museo Archeologico Nazionale (Piazza del Duomo, tel. 07/6334-1039, daily 8:30 A.M.–7:30 P.M., €3) are housed.

Palazzo del Popolo

The Palazzo del Popolo, which gets its light brownish color from the tufa and basalt stone used, was first mentioned in texts in the 12th century. It is relatively compact in size and has been converted into a cultural center. The Sala dei Quattrocento is decorated with frescos commissioned by the officials who once resided in the palazzo.

Pozzo di San Patrizio

Pozzo di San Patrizio (Viale Sangallo, tel. 07/6334-3768, daily 10 A.M.–6:45 P.M., €4.50) is one of the most unusual sights of Orvieto. It's located near the end of Corso Cavour in a panoramic spot along the town's gardens. *Pozzo* means "well" and this one is a cylindrical masterpiece built with two intertwining staircases that prevent underground traffic jams. Guided audio tours detailing the construction methods used are available. A good workout is assured.

◖ Orvieto Underground

The Pozzo di San Patrizio isn't the only hole in Orvieto. Hundreds of caves were dug into the soft tufa stone over the centuries. New discoveries are still being made, like the ceramic furnace that was recently uncovered in 2006. Orvieto Underground (tel. 07/6334-4891, www.orvietounderground.it, daily 11 A.M.–12:15 P.M. and 4–5:15 P.M., €5.50) gives geologists and lovers of the macabre an unforgettable tour through the hidden parts of the town. Tours are available daily from Piazza Duomo.

ENTERTAINMENT AND EVENTS

Most film festivals don't need a red carpet. That's especially true for the **Orvieto Corto Festival** (tel. 07/6334-0177, www.orvietocortofest.it), which is dedicated to short movies, documentaries, animation, and videos. If you don't like one of the dozens of films shown nightly on the last weekend of May, chances are it will end soon.

Festa del Corpus Domini (tel. 07/6334-0535) is a suggestive festival held in June on the day of the Corpus Domini. Fifty citizens dressed in medieval costume depart from Chiesa di San Giovanni and arrive at the duomo to assist with the ceremony. Afterwards the procession heads towards the Piazza del Popolo, where flag wavers display their talents and medieval dances and songs are performed.

Anyone with a little imagination turns up at the beginning of September for the **Festival del Teatro di Strada** (tel. 07/6330-6404). This festival honoring street performers attracts clowns of all temperaments, musicians, fire blowers, acrobats, tightrope walkers, and other acts that fill the city with energy and enthusiasm.

Gourmets wait all year for **Orvieto con Gusto** (tel. 07/6334-4644), a four-day event in October held throughout the old town. Each day is dedicated to a different edible theme and the event always ends with a Mercantino dei Sapori, where the flavors that have been tasted can be purchased and brought home.

Music doesn't stop just because the temperature drops. **Umbria Jazz Winter** (Teatro Mancinelli, tel. 07/6334-4664) keeps toes tapping in the center of Orvieto with five days of international performances at the end of December. The first notes are blown at the break of dawn and concerts continue throughout the day. The jazz lunch and dinner performances are especially well attended and booking early is advisable.

SHOPPING

Michele Golia is a third-generation artist who likes to get his hands dirty. His studio and **Storie di Terra** (Via dei Magoni 14, tel. 07/6339-3351, www.tiberiarte.it) gallery display the vases he and his grandfather produced as well as a collection of fine sculpture accumulated over years of travel.

Since 1990, Alberto Bellini has been turning terra-cotta into art. **La Corte dei Miracoli** (Piazza dei Ranieri 13, tel. 349/315-6502, daily 10 A.M.–1 P.M. and 3–7 P.M.) features household objects inspired from the past. Medieval symbols and motifs appear on everything.

SPORTS AND RECREATION

Bikes can be rented from **Natura e Avventura** (Piazza del Popolo 17, tel. 07/6334-2484), which also provides guided trekking tours of the area. They will find a trail that suits your ability and interests.

If getting around on horseback sounds more appealing, **Il Poggia** (Via le Grete, 12, tel. 07/6330-2163) stables can saddle you up on one of their horses for a trot through the woods near Orvieto.

ACCOMMODATIONS

◖ **Sant'Anna Bed and Breakfast** (Via Magalotti 7, tel. 339/209-0013, €50–75 s/d) is in the medieval heart of Orvieto a short walk away from Piazza della Repubblica. Each of the three rooms has its own bathroom with shower and tub. Furniture matches the character of the 15th-century palazzo. The common area is a quiet place to study maps under authentic frescoes that stare back at guests. A short way from the bed-and-breakfast is a bus stop that connects with the train station.

Most of Orvieto's hotels have interiors that went out of style in the 1970s. **Albergo Filippeschi** (Via Filippeschi 19, tel. 07/6334-3275, www.albergofilippeschi.it, €60–90 s/d) is one of the rare exceptions and provides reliable three-star service for visitors who prefer comfort to charm.

Il Poggio d'Orvieto (Via delle Crete, 12 La Svolta, tel. 07/6330-2163, www.poggio diorvieto.it, €60–70 s/d) is a couple of kilometers outside of town and ideally located for exploring the Tevere Valley. Rooms are on two floors within a converted farmhouse that has preserved stone and beams nearly as beautiful as the scenery. Activities are all based around nature and enjoying the local landscape.

FOOD

If you've never eaten inside a cave, **Le Grotte del Funaro** (Via Ripa Serancia 41, tel. 07/633-43276, www.grottedelfunaro.it, Tues.–Sun. noon–3 P.M. and 7 P.M.–midnight, €10–15) is the place to try underground dining. Alfredo and Sandra have turned a former Etruscan cistern into a cozy nook that scores high on ambiance. The wine is always at the right temperature and the buffet table is difficult to resist.

Situated on a picturesque street near Palazzo Comunale, **Trattoria la Palomba** (Via C. Manente, tel. 07/6334-3395, Thurs.–Tues. 12:30–2:30 P.M. and 7:30–10:30 P.M., €8–10) has been satisfying diners for over a century. Tried and true recipes are combined with more recognizable flavors and given wonderful names like *Tagliatelle alla Don Marcello* and *Piccione alla Leccarda*. You can ask the waiter for a translation, but instinct never fails in a place like this.

One look at the menu at **Ristorante Zeppelin** (Via Garibaldi 28, tel. 07/6334-1447, www.ris torantezeppelin.it, daily 12:30–2:30 P.M. and 7:30–10:30 P.M., €7–9) and it's clear this restaurant is unlike any other in Orvieto. Dishes are not merely listed but described in detail. Chef Lorenzo Polegri is all about the process and coming up with original flavors based on the feedback he gets from diners. The gnocchi in lamb and green pepper sauce is just one of the many culinary discoveries he has made. Curious palates can sign up to one of his cooking classes.

Caffé Bar Montanucci (Corso Cavour 21, tel. 07/6334-1261, daily 6:30 A.M.–midnight) is the oldest cafeteria in Orvieto and they have the old-timers to prove it. Everything is welcoming, down to the cobblestone floor. Depending on the time of day, you can sit down with a cappuccino and one of the homemade pastries or conduct a tasting of Orvieto reds from the vast selection of bottles behind the bar.

The tradition of pastry making is safe in the hands of Maurizio, whose reputation grows with every batch of *bigné*, cannoli, and pie he pulls out of the oven. **Pasticceria Adriano** (Via della Pace 26, tel. 07/6334-2527,

UMBRIA

Wed.–Mon. 6 A.M.–1:30 P.M. and 4–8 P.M.) is therefore a mandatory stop in Orvieto and the owner's recent experiments with chocolate rank him among Italy's best pastry chefs. Get there early if you want to taste something warm and freshly baked.

INFORMATION AND SERVICES

The IAT office (tel. 07/6334-1772, www.orvi eto.umbria2000.it, Mon.–Fri. 8 A.M.–1:50 P.M. and 4–7 P.M., Sat.–Sun. 10 A.M.–1 P.M. and 3–6 P.M.) is located in Piazza Duomo 24. If you plan to visit several museums, the **Carta Orvieto Unica** on sale here and at the train station could save you a few euros. The full price is €12.50 (students and seniors receive a discount) and allows access to all of Orvieto's museums as well as transportation onboard the town's buses and steep funicular railway.

Elisabetta Martelli (Via Panaro 3, tel. 07/6334-4906 or 340/850-6183, lisamart@ mclink.it) and **Maddalena Ceino** (Via della Svolta, tel. 07/6339-0021 or 347/103-4242) are registered guides and longtime residents of Orvieto who provide tours at reasonable rates.

Banks are easy to find in Orvieto. There are two branches on Via Garibaldi, one in Piazza del Popolo, and another in Piazza della Reppublica, all equipped with ATMs. The main post office is located at Largo Maurizio Ravelli 3 and currency can be changed there if necessary.

The **Farmacia Bonifazi** (Corso Cavour 89, tel. 07/6334-4100, Mon.–Sat. 8 A.M.–1 P.M. and 4:30–7:30 P.M.) operates traditional hilltop hours; a sign in their front window indicates the nearest open pharmacy should they be closed. For emergencies, contact the **hospital** (Via Sette Martiri 7, tel. 07/633-071) or call an ambulance on 118.

GETTING THERE AND AROUND

By car from Perugia drive south on the E45 towards Terni and exit onto the N448 just before Todi. Stay on this road until you reach Orvieto. The town is also easily accessible from northern or southern Italy and within two hours of Rome just off the A1.

There is one ATC bus (tel. 07/4449-2711, www.atcterni.it) between Perugia and Orvieto each day during the week that makes the journey in an hour.

The journey by train can take 1.5–2.5 hours depending on which of the 12 daily trains you catch from Perugia. Tickets cost €7.70. There is a train every hour from Rome Termini 6 A.M.–10 P.M. The ride is a little over an hour and costs €9.

From the train station in Orvieto you can either walk to the top of town or ride the funicular railway (7:20 A.M.–8:30 P.M.) from Piazza della Stazione to Piazza Cahen. From there Corso Cavour leads to the center of Orvieto and the main sights, which can be reached on foot or with the local linea A and B bus lines. Tickets for buses and the funicular railway are €1.

AROUND ORVIETO

On the doorstep of Orvieto lies the **abbey of La Badia** (La Badia, tel. 076/330-1959, www .labadiahotel.it), which dates from the 4th century. The small complex of ancient buildings is immersed in woods and has been converted into a restaurant and hotel. It's a good place to decide whether you prefer the full-bodied Orvieto red or the light and sharp taste of the white. The abbey tower, courtyard, and the ruins of the church, which is now open-air, are worth a look.

Todi

Todi is perhaps the most rewarding climb in Umbria. The ring of ancient Etruscan, Roman, and medieval walls are the sign you're getting closer to one of the best-preserved piazze in the region. The cathedral and public buildings surrounding the Piazza del Popolo are a perfect expression of Middle Age and Renaissance harmony and the ideal place to catch your breath. The narrow streets leading off the piazza tempt travelers with an array of shops and views onto the plains below the town.

SIGHTS

Piazza del Popolo is surrounded by buildings that demonstrate the state of the Middle Age mind. **Palazzo dei Priori** was begun in 1134 and is the former town hall whose windows received a makeover during the Renaissance. The tower is not square but actually a trapezoid, which may or may not have been intentional. The bronze eagle on the facade is the symbol of the town.

Palazzo del Capitano was built around the same period. It rests on a solid portico. The three sets of windows on the second floor are meant to impress while the third floor has a simpler design.

Palazzo del Popolo dates from 1213 and is one of the oldest civic buildings in Italy. It houses the **Pinacoteca** and **Museo Etrusco** (tel. 075/894-4148, 10:30 A.M.–1 P.M. and 2:30–6:30 P.M., €3.50). The piazza itself is the site of the old Roman Foro, of which traces are evident just a few feet underground. The most impressive remains are the Cisterne Romane (Via del Monte, tel. 075/894-4148, Nov.–Mar. daily 10:30 A.M.–1 P.M. and 2:30–5 P.M., Apr.–Oct. Tues.–Sun. 10:30 A.M.–1 P.M. and 2:30–6:30 P.M., €2), which are 80 meters long and eight meters high.

San Fortunato (Via San Fortunato) borrows elements of Gothic and Renaissance architecture. The central portal is especially noteworthy for its array of sculptures. The church is also the resting place of Jacopone da Todi, a Franciscan

© ALESSIA RAMACCIA

UMBRIA

Piazza del Popolo

monk and poet who wasn't afraid to occasionally taunt the Pope with his verse. On the inside is a beautiful fresco by Ferrau Fenzoni that has something of Michelangelo about it and surrounds the stained-glass rose window that was added to the church in 1500, along with the two other windows above the doors.

Tempio di Santa Maria lies on the edge of town and was completed after 100 years of labor in 1607. Many of the most renowned architects of the time worked on the project and Bramante is said to have created the original designs. It is unique in its Greek cross layout and polygonal chapels.

SPORTS AND RECREATION

Mountain bikes can be rented from **Ciclotrekking** (Via Monte Nibbio, tel. 07/6330-1649) and **A.S. Ciclo e Trekking** (Via dei Tigli 29, tel. 338/404-8730), which also organizes guided excursions around Todi.

ENTERTAINMENT AND EVENTS

Antiques fairs don't always live up to their billing, but **Rassegna Antiquaria d'Italia** (www.eptaeventi.it), held inside Palazzo del Vignola, is a must for collectors—as well as for some of the most prestigious dealers in the country, who save their best objects for this annual one-week reunion in mid-April.

Gran Premio Italiano Mongolfieristico is a hot-air balloon competition in mid-July featuring 50 teams from across Europe and North America. Each day features several flights above the town and the event culminates with all the balloons in the air.

The combination of art, music, prose, and dance makes **Todi Arte Festival** (www.todiartefestival.it) one of the most ambitious events in the region. The two-week event in July is held in local monasteries, theaters, and the open air of Piazza del Popolo.

SHOPPING

Tessitura Pardi (Piazza del Duomo 16, tel. 075/894-3785, daily) is synonymous with cloth and Italian style. The choice is between cotton or linen sheets, tablecloths, curtains, and nearly everything else that can be spun. Everything is made of high-quality natural fibers.

The second Sunday of each month, 40 stalls filled with antiques (tel. 348/330-7007) occupy the Piazza del Popolo from early morning to late afternoon. If you play your cards right and remember to mention your Italian origins, you could come away with a future family heirloom.

ACCOMMODATIONS

Bed and Breakfast San Lorenzo (Via San Lorenzo 3, tel. 075/894-4555, www.bandbsanlorenzo.com, closed Jan., €110–150 s/d) specializes in tranquility. There is no need for a Do Not Disturb sign on any of the six rooms. Ask for a room with a view and you get an entire valley.

The history of Orvieto continues inside **Hotel Fonte Cesia** (Via Lorenzo Leonj 3, tel. 075/894-3737, www.fontecesia.it, €116–164

s/d), but this 16th-century palazzo is equipped with Internet and Wi-Fi. The staff will happily organize a wedding if the need strikes.

The monks who once lived in **Casale delle Lucrezie** (Due Santi, tel. 075/898-7488, www.casaledellelucrezie.com, €60–80 s/d) two kilometers outside of Todi kept things in good condition, and the 12th-century farmhouse barely shows a wrinkle. All rooms are decorated in period furnishings and there are several apartments with kitchens for up to six people. For anyone who prefers to get a taste of local flavors, Lucretia offers lunch and dinner in a stone-clad dining room. Mountain bikes are provided free of charge.

FOOD

The trick to getting a table with a view at **Umbria** (Via San Bonaventura 13, tel. 075/894-2737, Wed.–Mon. 12:30–2:30 P.M. and 7:30–10:30 P.M., €14–16) is to show up a little earlier than the Italians do. At 12:30 P.M., the terrace is still empty and on a clear summer day you can see for kilometers. The house specialties are grilled meats and *palombe alla todina* (pigeon stew), but the offer changes regularly. Most of the wines are from the region and the house bottle is above average.

A menu that changes every day is a good sign. They have no choice at **Antica Hosteria de la Valle** (Via Ciuffelli 19, tel. 075/894-4848, Tues.–Sun. noon–3 P.M. and 7:30–11 P.M., €12–14). What they serve depends on what's available at the market that morning, which ultimately depends on the season.

Just up the road is **Pane e Vino** (Via Ciuffelli 33, tel. 075/894-5448, Thurs.–Tues. 12:30–3 P.M. and 7–10:30 P.M., €10–15). It's a traditional *osteria* that's rough around the edges and serves big portions in simple surroundings.

There are more elegant dining options within the **Bramante** (Via Orvietana 48, tel. 075/894-8381, daily 1–2:30 P.M. and 9–10:30 P.M., reservations required, €18–22) and Fonte Cesia hotels if the urge for something gourmet strikes.

Caseificio Montecristo (Pian di Porto, Via

Campette 144, tel. 075/898-7309, www.forma ggimontecristo.it, Fri.–Wed. 9 A.M.–1 P.M. and 3:30–7:30 P.M.) is a must for anyone planning a picnic. There are over 60 cheeses and a good nose will be able to distinguish them all. Everything is produced the old-fashioned way from the cows and goats you may have spotted on your way into town. No artificial flavors or colors here: just *ricotte, caciotte,* and *pecorino* that never have and never will be plastic-wrapped. It's worth the short drive.

INFORMATION AND SERVICES

The Todi **IAT office** (Piazza del Popolo 34, tel. 075/894-5416, www.todi.umbria2000.it, Mon.–Sat. 9:30–1 P.M. and 3–6 P.M., Sun. 10 A.M.–1 P.M.) is under the last arch below the Palazzo del Capitano next to the two ladies selling *porchetta* panini out of a truck on Saturday mornings. The shelves are full of maps and information on events and accommodations.

GETTING THERE AND AROUND

Todi is 45 kilometers south of Perugia directly off the E45 highway. Exit at the Orvieto–Todi ramp and proceed along the N448. From Rome travel north up the A1 until Orte. Head towards Terni and take the E45 towards Perugia. Exits for the city are clearly indicated. Parking is available at several locations along the Circonvallazione Est. A funicular lift, located near the Porta Orvietana, takes the effort out of reaching the heights of Todi.

CLP (tel. 081/531-1707, www.clpbus.it) bus service leaves Perugia Piazza Partigiani daily at 2:30 P.M. and arrives in Todi Bivio Cappuccini at 3:10 P.M. Tickets must be purchased in advance.

Trains from Perugia's Ponte San Giovanni station are frequent and run daily 6 A.M.–9 P.M. to Todi Ponte Rio station. The journey time is around one hour. Passengers from Rome must change at Terni. The earliest train departs at 6 A.M. and the last leaves Termini at 10 P.M. Expect a two-hour trip. There is one direct train on weekdays that leaves Termini at 12:30 P.M. and arrives in Todi at 2:19 P.M. There are taxi stands at Piazza Garibaldi and Piazza Jacopone.

AROUND TODI

Todi is located within the **Parco Fluviale del Tevere** (Civitella del Lago, tel. 07/4495-0732, www.parks.it/parco.fluviale.tevere), which consists of nearly 8,000 hectares of parkland. It's a WWF oasis used by 130 species of migrating birds. Most of these can be seen around the marshes of Alviano (www.oasidialviano.it) and bird-watchers can observe the proceedings from the numerous paths or specially constructed bird-watching stations. The **Agriturismo Fattoria di Vibio** (Località Buchella, Doglio Montecastello di Vibio 9, tel. 075/874-9607 or 347/780-8733, www.fattoriadivibio.com) proposes three equestrian itineraries from one (€30) to four (€100) hours in length.

Centro Canoistico Escursionistico/ Montemarte (Pontecuti, tel. 340/395-9854, www.digilander.libero.it) organizes canoe trips from Pontecue, where a circa 1944 U.S. Army pontoon bridge still gets people across the Tevere to the Lago di Corbara. They also run caving excursions that depart from Titignano at 9 A.M. and last 5–6 hours (€15).

If you're traveling towards Perugia or have a couple of hours to kill before returning to Rome, the N397 road towards Marsciano is a pleasant change from the E45. Here you'll get a glimpse of typical Umbrian landscapes, fortified castles, and active monasteries.

Spoleto

There's no right or wrong way of visiting Spoleto. It's all worth seeing. Put your guide aside, tuck the map in your back pocket, and let yourself be guided by your senses. Here the remains of a Roman theater, there the symmetry of the duomo, and everywhere a maze of narrow streets leading to piazze made for people-watching. Observe the medieval patterns of the cobblestones and the ceramic designs of Roman floors, cross the Ponte delle Torre that blends into the landscape—and if the need for solitude strikes, set out in the footsteps of hermits who devoted their lives to meditation in the nearby hills. There'll be music playing by the time you get back.

SIGHTS

Climbing up Via Sappi, the **Duomo** appears suddenly on your left. From here you are standing nearly above the church and must walk the long shallow steps down towards the piazza.

On Sunday the bells call a faithful crowd of parishioners who turn up in small groups. They pass a man with a cup and unchanging expression drawn on his face. Inside the church is relatively low-key. There is no abundance of frescoes and the rose windows are not stained. The prize possessions include a Bernini sculpture of Urbano VIII.

Basilica San Salvatore was one of the first Christian churches built in Italy in the 4th century by Middle Eastern monks. It was revamped in the 9th century and distinguishes itself with a plethora of objects recycled from Roman buildings.

Bungee jumpers and anyone looking to overcome their fear of heights will appreciate **Ponte delle Torri** on the outskirts of Spoleto. It was built in the 13th century over an old Roman aqueduct and stands 80 meters high. The bridge was closed in 2007 for structural observation, but it can also be appreciated from

Spoleto's 12th-century Duomo

© ALESSIA RAMACCIA

the Via del Ponte. Even if you can't cross the bridge, it is still worth seeing.

FESTIVALS AND EVENTS

Back in 1958, the idea of setting up a festival dedicated to cultural exchange between Italy and the United States seemed revolutionary. **Festival dei Due Mondi** (www.spoletofestival. it) hasn't lost that sense of innovation and there is very little artistic territory it hasn't covered. Young talents are given ample space to experiment and headliners can be admired within an unforgettable backdrop. Performances run in June and July and many events are free.

Corsa dei Vaporetti (www.comune.spo leto.pg.it) is a go-kart race around Spoleto that might bring back childhood memories. These go-karts, however, are aerodynamic racers that resemble bobsleds and consist of a driver and pusher. The race, a one-day event in early May, begins in Piazza della Libertà and ends in Piazza Garibaldi.

Onions may seem like a strange thing to celebrate but that hasn't stopped **Fiera di Loreto** from taking place for the last 400 years on September 8 and 9. The center of festivities is around Porta San Matteo, where farmers set up stalls selling every type of onion imaginable. Back in 1598 Clemente VIII assured himself a supply of onions by granting immunity to the entire town, which always managed to lift spirits.

SHOPPING

Choose from objects of art, antiques, paintings, or prints at **Palatium Antichità** (Via A. Saffi 11, tel. 07/434-7759, www.palatium.it, daily 10:30 A.M.–1 P.M. and 4:30–7 P.M.). There's an old well inside the shop around which everything is exposed.

Cloth is holy inside **Arcarosa Mastro Raphael** (Via dei Duchi 5, tel. 07/434-4467, www.mastroraphael.com, Tues.–Sun. 10 A.M.–1 P.M. and 4–7 P.M.). This famous brand was established in the 1930s in Spoleto and has become a household name for anyone who cares about quality sheets. If the prices are too high here, ask about the nearby outlet, which often has sales of up to 30 percent off.

Bric-a-brac lovers set their alarms a little earlier on the second Sunday of each month. They don't want to miss **Mercatino delle Briciole** (Centro Storico, tel. 07/43-2181, 8 A.M.–6 P.M.) held throughout the old town. Objects vary in quality and most of the fun consists in browsing the extraordinary array of junk and trying to spot the treasure.

SPORTS AND RECREATION

Southeast of Spoleto are the Spoletina and Martani Mountains, which invite walkers of all levels to stretch their legs. Paths begin just outside of town over the Ponte delle Torri, where hikers have a choice between high road and higher road. The Monteluco path rises to 780 meters and runs through the hamlet of the same name. When you get there you may want to stop at **Enoteca L'Alchimista** (Piazza del Comune 14, tel. 07/4237-8558, www.lal chimista.net, €7–10, daily in summer, Wed.–Mon. winter) for a bottle of rosso di Montefalco and *pasta al tartufo.*

The path continues towards Le Aie before making a scenic return towards Spoleto and passing the 12th-century frescoed churches of San Giuliano and San Pietro. The entire journey at a leisurely pace lasts 2.5 hours. The more challenging road reaches a height of 950 meters and ends in the *borgo* of Cese. Bus service from Ceselli back to Spoleto is frequent during the summer. Check with the tourist office in Piazza Libertà for details and a map with other itineraries in the area.

Agriturismo Rivoli (Uncinano, tel. 07/4326-8106, agririvoli@libero.it, €15/per hour) offers horseback riding near the summit of the Monte Spoletine six kilometers from Spoleto. Gualtiero Rivoli knows the 7,000 hectares of terrain intimately and can find a trail to suit any interest. Room and board is also available.

ACCOMMODATIONS

Ostello Villa Redenta (Via di Villa Redenta 1, tel. 07/4322-4936, www.villaredenta.com, €35–60 s/d) may be the best deal in Spoleto. The 16 rooms in the converted palazzo lack

UMBRIA

any thrills, but the extensive gardens where Pope Leone XII once wandered make a stay here all the more memorable.

Wallace describes his ◖ **Art House** (Torre dell'Olio, Via Cecili 26, tel. 07/4322-4187 or 340/7975-0824, www.arthousespoleto.com, €103–130 s/d) as a bed-and-breakfast with added stimuli. What he is referring to is a contagious love for the arts and Umbria. This Scottish expat also makes a good cup of coffee, over which he happily suggests itineraries through town or day trips in the surrounding area. Besides a warm welcome, you get modern rooms within one of Spoleto's last remaining towers, which looks out onto rooftops and the countryside beyond.

San Luca (Via Interna delle Mura 21, tel. 07/4322-3399, www.hotelsanluca.com, €95–190 s/d) is a four-star hotel with three-star prices. That doesn't mean anything is missing. You still get impeccable service 24 hours a day with babysitter, bicycle, and guided tours optional. Room 204, with a writing desk at the window and balcony, is a good number to remember.

Michael Jordan would have trouble touching the ceilings of the **Cavaliere Palace Hotel** (Corso Garibaldi 49, tel. 07/4322-0350, www.cavalierehotels.com, €250 d). Once he stopped trying, he could lie down on one of the big beds and stare up at the 17th-century frescoes. Not everyone feels comfortable with this kind of luxury.

FOOD

Ask one of the locals sitting around Piazza della Libertà where to eat and there's a good chance the name ◖ **Apollinare** (Via S. Agata, tel. 07/4322-3256, www.ristoranteapollinare.it, Wed.–Mon. noon–2:30 P.M. and 7–10:30 P.M., daily in summer, €15–19) will be mentioned. It's a short walk from the Roman theater down a narrow pedestrian street that would look good on a postcard. The stone-walled interior and beamed ceiling are more elegant than rustic, which could easily describe the food, which is prepared with attention to tradition without fear of innovation. The Sagrantino red from Montefalco is a good introduction to Umbrian

a quiet Sunday in Spoleto

© ALESSIA RAMACCIA

wines, and the chef seems remarkably open to sharing his secrets.

Il Tempio del Gusto (Via Arco di Drusi 11, tel. 07/434-7121, www.iltempiodelgusto.com, Fri.–Wed. noon–3 P.M. and 7–11 P.M., €13–15) is located near the Arco di Druso. It's run by a husband-and-wife team who have dedicated themselves to food. The result is candlelight dining that whets the appetite from the first glance of a menu that uses traditional ingredients to defy culinary conventions. A glance at the cellar is equally impressive.

Trattoria del Quarto (Via Carlo Cattaneo 1, tel. 07/4322-1107, daily 12:30–2:30 P.M. and 7–10:30 P.M., €20) has several multi-course tasting menus that give diners a chance to experience many of the flavors of Umbria. Specialties include *strangozzi alla spoletina* (long pasta with tomato sauce) and *tartufi* (truffles).

INFORMATION AND SERVICES

The Spoleto **IAT office** (Piazza della Libertà 7, tel. 07/4323-8911, www.spoleto.um

bria2000.it, Mon.–Sat. 10 A.M.–1 P.M. and 3:30–6:30 P.M., Sun. 10 A.M.–1 P.M.) provides maps, event information, and more.

GETTING THERE AND AROUND

From Perugia by car, travel south on the N75 past Foligno until you reach Spoleto. The journey takes less than an hour. From Rome, exit the A1 at Orte and drive along the N204 towards Terni. The road eventually turns into the N3 and Spoleto is clearly indicated.

SSIT (tel. 07/4321-2208, www.spoletina.com) regional bus service makes several stops around town, including Piazza della Libertà (Edicola Conti). It serves many of the minor towns in the area as well as Spello, Assisi, and Perugia. Journeys by bus are generally slower but slightly less expensive than by train. If you plan to make extensive use of buses, the CityCard is a useful option as it can save you 10–20 percent depending on what time of day you travel.

The train station is located in Piazza Polvani at the end of Viale Trento e Trieste about one kilometer from the entrance to the old town. There are departures every hour from Perugia and the journey time varies depending on the type of train you take. A second-class ticket costs €9. The trip from Rome Termini takes a half-hour longer and costs €11.

There are taxi stands at the train station (tel. 07/4322-0489) as well as Piazza della Libertà (tel. 07/434-4548) and Piazza Garibaldi (tel. 07/434-9990). A car and driver may be hired for an hour or an entire day from **Astra** (Via Flaminia 101, tel. 07/4322-2132).

AROUND SPOLETO

"If you haven't seen the **Fonti del Clitunno,**" Pliny the Younger once advised a friend, "go and see it." In Roman times, this natural spring (Via Flaminia 7, tel. 07/4352-1141, www.fontidelclitunno.com, summer 8 A.M.–7 P.M., winter 10 A.M.–1 P.M. and 2–4:30 P.M., €2) 13 kilometers north of Spoleto was considered sacred and animals destined for sacrifice were cleaned and prepared here. Time hasn't altered the tranquility or the great number of plant and animal species that reside in the area. There is a pleasant restaurant and bar also onsite and olive oil from the trees grown nearby hillside is for sale. Less than a kilometer away is the **Tempietto di Clitunno.** It is one of the oldest places of Christian worship in Umbria and consists of a small column and sculpture dating from the 5th century.

On the first Sunday of each month, 240 antique dealers set up their stalls in the region's largest market, the **Mercato dell'Antiquariato, dell'usato e del collezionismo** (Clitunno, tel. 07/4327-1920).

UMBRIA

Valnerina

Valnerina is a long valley in southeastern Umbria that runs along the Nera river between Spoleto and Terni. The prime interest is the scenery, which consists of tree-lined slopes and occasional secluded hamlets. It's best appreciated by car on the N209 panoramic route.

SIGHTS
San Pietro in Valle

San Pietro in Valle (Ferentillo, tel. 07/4478-0129, www.sanpietroinvalle.com) is just off the main road surrounded by for-

est. It is one of the few remaining traces of the Lombards, who built the monastery in the 8th century A.D. The carvings both inside and outside the chapel are especially notable. San Pietro is now a charming hotel and restaurant and the ideal place to stop for lunch or spend the night.

Cascate delle Marmore

Cascate delle Marmore (Marmore, tel. 07/446-2982, www.cascatamarmore.it, €4) was created by the Romans in 271 B.C. in order to prevent flooding. At 165 meters, it is the highest artificial waterfall in Europe and consists of three cascades. Entry into the park varies according to the season, but it is open daily 10 A.M.–10 P.M. during the summer. The water is now used to produce hydroelectric power and is released periodically.

SPORTS AND RECREATION

Centro Canoa e Rafting Le Marmore (Via Carlo Neri, tel. 330/753–420, www.rafting marmore.com) provides gear for all types of outdoor sports but it's getting wet they prefer. The waterfall is the perfect place for rafting, and riding the rapids of the Nera River is unforgettable. There are courses for both experts and beginners and a single run costs €30. Full-day options are also available, but require booking several days in advance.

For a canyoning experience, **Precipizi Relativi** (tel. 07/4442-8563 or 328/276-8966 www.precipizirelativi.it, €30) operates tours in the Forra di Roccagelli near Chiesa dell'Eremita off the N209. The two-hour hike through narrow gorges and canyons culminates with three breathtaking cascades. Anyone in decent shape can survive this wilderness adventure. Call Stefano Zavka to reserve a place.

ACCOMMODATIONS

La Porta della Valnerina (Vocabolo Centrale di Cervara 13, tel. 347/760-9678, www. laportadellavalnerina.com, €30 pp) is a typical Umbrian farmhouse walking distance from the waterfall. The three rooms are large and the relaxed environment is the perfect place to relax after a day outdoors.

FOOD

Bosco della Marmore (Marmore, Via della Cascata 35, tel. 07/446-7229, Fri.–Wed. noon–3 P.M. and 7–11 P.M., daily in summer, €7–10) is an outdoor trattoria a short way from the waterfall. Tables are spread out in the shade and there's a festive feel in the air. The food is simple and portions generous.

INFORMATION AND SERVICES

There are four Info Points near Cascate delle Marmore (Piazzale Vasi, Belvedere Inferiore, Parco dei Campacci and Belvedere Superiore, tel. 07/446-2982) from which tickets may be purchased and maps of the area are available.

GETTING THERE AND AROUND

Car is the most convenient means of seeing the Valnerina. From Perugia, drive south on the N75 and N3. The exit for the N209 is 10 kilometers before Spoleto. The road is windy and is best enjoyed at slow speed. Italians have a tendency to tailgate but don't let that disturb the marvelous scenery.

Norcia

Norcia is remote even by Umbrian standards. It lies within the Monti Sibillini National Park on the border with Le Marche and is a center for outdoor activities. It's also the birthplace of San Benedetto and there are several active monasteries in the area. Norcia is also renown for its culinary contributions, many of which are based on truffles and the cured hams now synonymous with the town.

SIGHTS

The medieval nucleus of the town is centered around **Piazza San Benedetto.** A statue of the saint was erected in 1860 and stands in the center. Behind is the basilica that also bears his name. According to legend, it was built over his house in the 12th century and the portico and bell tower were added later. The facade is Gothic with a single rose window surrounded by four statuettes that seem somewhat out of place. The crypt contains several noteworthy frescoes.

Palazzo Comunale was built around the same time as the basilica and consists of a double loggia that got a facelift in the 19th century. The bell tower mirrors the basilica and can be visited.

Across the way is **Castellina,** built as a residence for Pope Giulio III, who must have had a few enemies judging by the thickness of the walls. Today it houses the **Museo Civico** (tel. 07/4381-7030, €3).

The city walls date from the 13th century and are nearly completely intact. They include eight gates, of which Porta Ascolana and Porta Romana are in the best condition. Walking through these gives you an impression of what ancient travelers must have felt when entering town.

ENTERTAINMENT AND EVENTS

Mostra Mercato del Tartufo Nero e dei Prodotti Tipici is held during the last weekend of February and the first weekend of March. It is a chance to celebrate the black truffle, which lies buried beneath much of the countryside and is a vital ingredient to many of the area's specialties. Many of these can be tasted during the festival, which includes other typical products as well as folkdancing and musical demonstrations. For more information about the festival visit the AIT tourist office (Piazza Garibaldi 1, tel. 074/371-147).

SHOPPING

Turning pork into every variety of cold cut is second nature to the inhabitants of Norcia, whose town has become famous for cured meats. It's a long process that takes two years from slaughter in early autumn to the final salting, washing, and aging. **Norcineria Ansuino** (Via Anicia 105, tel. 07/4381-6809, Wed.–Mon. 8 A.M.–1 P.M. and 3–6 P.M.) is the place to taste the difference. This is a long way from Oscar Meyer, and the three generations behind the counter will be happy to educate your palate.

SPORTS AND RECREATION

La Mulattiera (www.lamulattiera.it) is a collective of outdoor enthusiasts based near Norcia who offer a variety of activities. All guides are officially recognized and cater to every level of skill and interest. One of their programs includes an overnight trek through the Monti Sibillini National Park accompanied by mules. If you'd rather explore the interior, go caving, or kayak on a mountain lake, they can arrange that as well. For the latest information, contact Roberto Canali on 339/451-3189 or info@lamulattiera.it

ACCOMMODATIONS

La Sibilla di Norcia (Via XX Settembre 8, tel. 07/4382-8452, www.lasibilladinorcia.com, €40–60 s/d) is a quiet bed-and-breakfast near the center of town with three rooms ideal for getting a good night's rest. Breakfast is served in the bright dining room and consists of a selection of homemade breads and cakes.

It doesn't take long to see Norcia and once you have you'll be glad to be in an *agriturismo* like **Il Casale degli Amici** (Vocabolo Cappuccini 157, tel. 07/4381-6811, www.ilcasaledegli amici.it, €40–80 s/d). You could easily spend a week here trying a new sport every day. Horseback riding, rafting, and hang-gliding activities are all based in the area and Norcia is only two kilometers away when you need a dose of culture or truffles. The Casale restaurant serves local meats and cheeses on the terrace or in the stone-vaulted dining room. The *tagliatelle all'uovo* (egg pasta) followed by the grilled meat plate should satisfy any hunger.

FOOD

Beccofino (Piazza San Benedetto 12, tel. 07/4381-6086, Thurs.–Tues., €10–14) is the first restaurant many people see in Norcia and the only one you'll wish were a franchise. This is the place to try an *antipasto* of Norcia hams and truffles. The first course is a toss-up between *strangozzi* and risotto—a win-win situation for stomachs. End the meal with a couple scoops of *gelato di ricotta*.

UMBRIA

INFORMATION AND SERVICES

The **tourist office** (Via Solferino 22, tel./ fax 07/4382-8173, www.comune.norcia.pg.it, Mon.–Sat. 8:30 A.M.–1 P.M. and 3:30–6 P.M.) can help find accommodations and provide a map of town. The same address is also the home of Casa del Parco di Norcia (tel. 07/4381-7090), which organizes excursions of the park and can suggest the best seasonal routes.

There are four banks in town, including a Banca di Umbria on Corso Sertorio 36. The post office is on the same street at number 63. **Farmacia Rossi** (Viale Giovanni XXIII, 07/ 4381-6271) is one of two pharmacies in Norcia.

GETTING THERE AND AROUND

If your rental car has GPS, now is the time to use it. Or else your co-pilot should be ready to do some serious map reading. From Perugia, head towards Spoleto. Before reaching town take a left onto the N209. After the long tunnel head north and drive 20 kilometers until you see signs for the N396. Norcia is at the end of this scenic, winding road. From Rome, drive to Spoleto on the N204 and follow the same directions as above.

Buses from Rome Tiburtina leave every day at 7:30 A.M. and on weekdays there is a second departure at 3:30 P.M. The entire trip takes nearly three hours.

The nearest train station is in Spoleto. **SSIT Buses** (tel. 07/4321-2201) complete the 50-minute trip to Norcia five times a day 5:10 A.M.–8 P.M.

AROUND NORCIA
Abbazia di Sant'Eutizio

Fifteen kilometers north of Norcia is Abbazia di Sant'Eutizio (Piedivalle, tel. 07/439-9659), founded in the 5th century by Syrian hermits. It is one of the oldest abbeys in Italy and initiated the Western monastic movement. San Benedetto was a regular visitor. Mystic is the norm here.

◖ Castelluccio di Norcia

Castelluccio di Norcia is the last town in Umbria before Le Marche. It sits on a small hill overlooking the Piano Grande plain, which has become a spiritual home to the region's hanggliding and parasailing enthusiasts. **Prodelta** (Via Monte Veletta 8, tel. 07/4382-1156, www. prodelta.it, Mon.–Sat. 9 A.M.–1 P.M. and 3:30–7:30 P.M.) has its summer headquarters here and runs a registered flying school. Once you get up in one of their Bolero or Icaro2000 gliders, it'll be hard to come back down to earth. Rentals start at €45 per day or €17 per flight. Novices can choose between a one-day class (€100) or a week-long immersion (€450). Transportation to the area's best launching sites is provided.

ABRUZZO AND MOLISE

Medieval towns, gourmet meals, ancient ruins, superb wines, monasteries, abbeys, sanctuaries, parks, tracks from former cattle drives, rare spindly fishing wharves, and master craftsmen are all waiting for visitors in Abruzzo and Molise.

Both regions have roots steeped in ancient tradition. Abruzzo is home to a million-year-old "elephant," and Europe's oldest man (700,000 years old and counting) resides in Molise. They share a rich culture inherited from Italics, Oscans, Greeks, but most of all Samnites and Romans. The Italian expression for present-day Abruzzesi, inhabitants of Abruzzo, is *forte e gentile* ("strong and kind"). Centuries of hardscrabble existence have toughened them to caprices of nature and hardship, but left plenty of humanity. That description ap-

plies also to inhabitants of Molise, which until recently was part of Abruzzo.

For more than 2,500 years, the transhumance was a biannual event. Shepherds drove their flocks across the vast cattle tracks toward Puglia and back, a journey that took them south toward the coast and kept them away from home for six or seven months a year. Husband and wife even spoke different dialects—he the sing-songy coastal dialect and she the clipped mountain dialect. Only the 20th century broke those ways, when emigration, falling wool prices, other transportation options, and more land development brought that tradition to a halt. You still see signs of the vast cattle tracks throughout both Abruzzo and Molise.

Abruzzo attracts more tourists than Molise

HIGHLIGHTS

◖ **Fontana delle Novantanove Cannelle:** The spirit of Abruzzo's most gracious city is captured in Fontana delle Novantanove Cannelle, the Fountain of 99 Spouts. The number 99 assumes mythic proportions in this town and recalls an old alliance of medieval nobles who united for the good of all (page 570).

◖ **Santa Maria di Collemaggio:** This mystical church's simple Romanesque architecture constructed in muted rose and ivory stone epitomizes medieval architecture in Abruzzo (page 570).

◖ **Parco Nazionale del Gran Sasso e Monti della Laga:** Abruzzo's winter playground and Italy's oldest ski resort, Gran Sasso massif has Central Italy's highest mountain and a festive atmosphere in any season. Italians come here seeking sport, leisure, and a magnificent view (page 573).

◖ **Sulmona:** This lively town is the birthplace of the poet Ovid, the ancient Roman author of numerous Latin works, including *Metamorphoses*. Its Piazza Garibaldi is one of Abruzzo's most lovely squares (page 577).

◖ **Teatro Sannito:** Even if you have seen a dozen ancient theaters in Greece and Italy, you will marvel at the superb design and architecture of Teatro Sannito, the work of ancient Samnites. Make sure to catch a classical play during the summer performance season (page 593).

◖ **Saepinum:** Italy's best example of a provincial Roman town features overgrown Roman ruins, rustic medieval houses still inhabited by present-day farmers, cows and sheep grazing around Roman walls, and idyllic settings to enjoy a picnic (page 596).

LOOK FOR ◖ TO FIND RECOMMENDED SIGHTS, ACTIVITIES, DINING, AND LODGING.

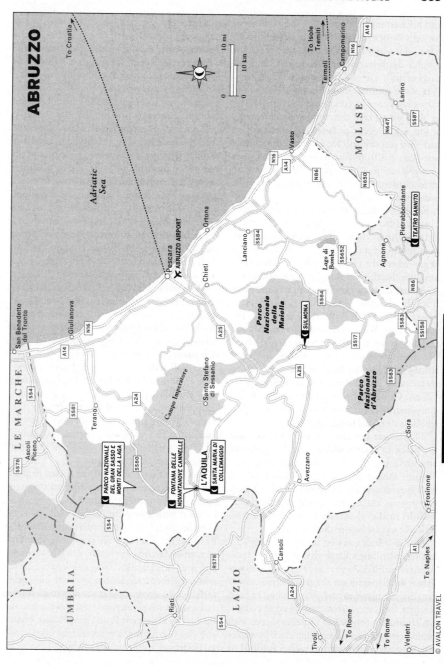

ABRUZZO

To Croatia

Adriatic Sea

To Isole Tremiti

10 mi

10 km

MOLISE

Campomarino

N16

A14

Larino

N647

SS87

Termoli

Vasto

N16

A14

N86

N650

Pescara

✈ ABRUZZO AIRPORT

Ortona

Lanciano

SS84

Chieti

Lago di Bomba

SS652

Agnone

Pietrabbondante

◖ TEATRO SANNITO

N86

San Benedetto
del Tronto

Giulianova

N16

Parco
Nazionale
della Maiella

SS84

◖ SULMONA

SS17

SS83

LE MARCHE

Ascoli
Piceno

SS4

A14

SS81

A24

A25

SS80

◖ PARCO NAZIONALE
DEL GRAN SASSO E
MONTI DELLA LAGA

Teramo

Campo Imperatore

Santo Stefano
di Sessanio

A25

Parco
Nazionale
d'Abruzzo

SS83

SS158

◖ FONTANA DELLE
NOVANTANOVE CANNELLE

◖ SANTA MARIA DI
COLLEMAGGIO

L'AQUILA

Avezzano

Sora

UMBRIA

Rieti

RS78

SS4

Carsoli

A24

LAZIO

Frosinone

A1

Tivoli

To Rome

To Rome

To Naples

Velletri

© AVALON TRAVEL

ABRUZZO AND MOLISE

and has better tourist facilities and accommodations. Both offer outstanding scenery, food, wine, and a rewarding visit. Many traditions that are disappearing or already gone in other parts of Italy are still firmly entrenched here. Part of the reason is infrastructure. Most of the highways were not completed until the 1970s or '80s, which kept the regions in relative isolation until recent decades. In Termoli and San Vito you can still see *trabucco*, the spindly wooden piers from which fishermen cast their nets and scoop up their catch. Bronze bells are molded and cast in Agnone much as they have been for the last 700 years.

Roughly a third of Abruzzo's land is dedicated to national parks. Its mountains are more dramatic than those of surrounding regions, making it Central Italy's favored ski destination—where the focus is on fun and not fashion. Ideal for those looking for active vacations, it also makes for a great place to unwind away from the crowds.

Art buffs will find plenty to admire in the small towns. You can discover artists that you may not know, like the 19th-century Michetti or contemporary artists whose works are beautifully displayed in local exhibits or even in restaurants like L'Angolino di Filippo near Chieti. Collectors will appreciate the skilled craftsmen that turn out fine wares in copper, wood, leather, ceramics, and gold.

This is not the spot for blockbusters, but the place to start noticing detail in patterns and vivid use of color. The stark simplicity of some medieval buildings is often matched with large doses of mystery and wonder. Nearly every town has a great square, like Sulmona, with its medieval aqueduct, or L'Aquila, with its lively square before the Duomo.

Molise is Italy's newest region and only Italian schoolchildren know that it split off from Abruzzo in 1963. As in many regions, the newer urban development on the periphery of towns ranges from bland to unsightly. It's best to head straight for the *centro storico* (historic center), which usually consists of a medieval core with some Renaissance and Baroque added by nobles who had their architectural wishes fulfilled or repaired damage caused by frequent earthquakes that periodically rattle the area.

Even if you've been around the block of antiquities in Greece and Italy, you will find ruins here unlike any others. Nothing resembles the sophisticated theater seating of the Samnites or a rustic ramble through the ruins of Altilia, once ancient Saepinum.

Both regions are pillars of Italian gastronomy, with dishes that range from excellent seafood along the coast to flavorful meats and game from inland hills and mountains. Savory cheese from milk of cows, sheep, and goats is exquisite and you can find it fresh or in its more piquant aged versions. Fruit and vegetables are plentiful and the area around L'Aquila is famous for its saffron. Whether you are looking to have a vigorous holiday, to relax, or to indulge in sensory pleasures, they are all here and at very reasonable prices.

Molise is one of the least known and least visited regions in Italy. Italians have a hard time finding it on a map but it is worth locating this south-of-mid-boot region with 40 kilometers of Adriatic coast and a tough mountain interior that turns cold and grey in winter.

Termoli is on the shore exactly midway between the nearby regions of Puglia (south) and Abruzzo (north). The regional capital, Campobasso, lies inland at the foot of the Sannio Mountains, which run north–south. Molise has two provinces. Isernia is the capital of the smaller and less populated one that borders Lazio and Campania.

Molise is nearly as far off the beaten path as possible in Italy. Nothing is filtered through rose-colored tourist glasses here, and if you want to travel with a smile in August while Italians clog the roads leading toward Sardinia and Sicily this is the place to avoid the queue. If you're accustomed to five-star hotels, you'll have to adjust your expectations. Luxury is a luxury here and most accommodations are bare but comfortable. An *agriturismo* is the way to go if you can spare a couple of days, and there is one in Busso, five kilometers from Campobasso, where you can play bocce, rent mountain bikes, and go horseback riding or trout fishing.

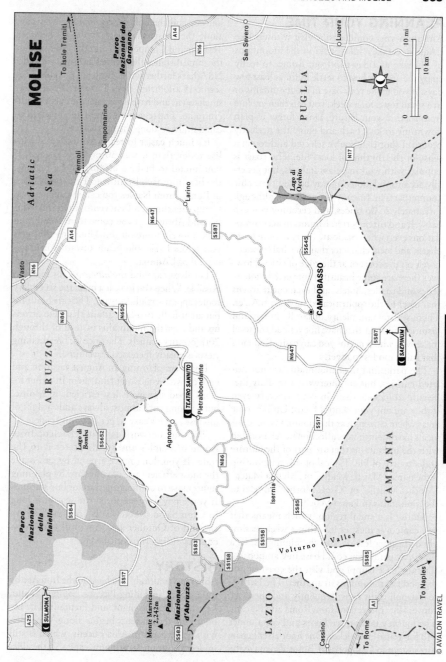

ABRUZZO AND MOLISE

© AVALON TRAVEL

PLANNING YOUR TIME

Although you could easily visit a town like L'Aquila or take a hike or ski in the mountains of Abruzzo as a day-trip from Rome, to really enjoy the area it's best to settle in for at least few days. If you make your base in the mountains or in a small town for a week, you can then explore from there at your leisure. Don't forget to plan downtime to kick back and enjoy the perfectly beautiful spot that you've selected and to get a sense of the rhythm of local life. The coast is popular with working-class Italians, but generally accommodations lag way behind their chic counterparts in Tuscany or Sardinia—although fortunately so do prices, and certainly you can eat well and often better. Mountain accommodations even when rustic are likely to have more charm and local character than the drab modern hotels on the coast or at the edge of cities. However there are some beautiful converted monasteries and castles, hotels, and even entire towns that cater to the sophisticated, upscale traveler. There still remain plenty of family hotels and historic buildings that have not yet had the total makeover, which means you can easily find rates that suit a modest budget.

The parks and their mountains are not isolated entities, but are interwoven in daily life; be sure to include them in your itinerary even if they are not your central focus. Unlike some areas where citizens fear the mountains, here the locals have an intimate, affectionate relationship with the mountains that are part of the culture and a source of life. Typical of this relationship is the name "Majella Madre" or "Magna Mater," "Mother Majella" or "Great Mother," to refer to the mountains in Parco Majella.

Molise is a small region, which means that you can cover most of it within a week or simply dedicate a few days to the highlights. In a three-day jaunt, you could base in Campobasso (literally base camp) and visit the coast in one day and the mountains in another. The Isernia-to-Termoli train runs frequently and there are convenient connections from Roma and Pescara. The journey takes three hours and costs under €10 for a first-class ticket. One hour after departure it stops in Campobasso. Buses also make the journey and the only *superstrada* highway runs along the coast. There are two roads between Termoli and Campobasso and the N647 covers the same distance three times as fast as the older N87 that's farther south. Both are categorized as scenic 15 kilometers from Termoli. If you prefer small towns and have time, take the curvy southern route. The region's second-largest lake is located midway along the northern one.

It's much easier to reach Abruzzo and Molise today than it was 30 or 40 years ago. If you intend to make a beeline to the regions, the best approach by air is to Pescara, Naples, or Rome. From Naples you can meander across Campania through Benevento, then into Molise and Abruzzo. If you come from Rome, you have a lovely route on the Tiburtina that gets you across Lazio and heads toward Abruzzo's capital of L'Aquila.

Locals zip around the *autostrada* as much as possible. When you look at a map, the secondary routes appear straightforward. They are beautiful but are usually two-lane affairs that take drivers up and over the mountains instead of through 20th-century tunnels. The price for breathtaking views is greatly increased travel time.

If you are planning an August vacation and hate crowds, you won't find them in either region. Road signage is less efficient in Molise, but a wrong turn almost always adds a sight of interest and it's easy to get back on track.

The bus network is quite efficient from Rome or Naples and locals prefer it to the train. If you don't move around by car, make the most efficient use of your time by planning sights close to connecting train or bus stations. If you enjoy winter sports, the season is long in Gran Sasso, where roads are closed off by the end of October and downhill and cross-country skiing runs until May.

HISTORY

Abruzzo was already inhabited in the Iron Age by Italic tribes, including Picenes, Sabines, Aequi, Vestini, Marsi, Paeligni, and Frentani. The big boom for the ancients begins along Via Valeri with settlements in Alba Fucens, which is still under excavation, Corfinium, capital of the allies

HERCULES

The cult of Hercules was one of the oldest and most widespread in ancient Samnite, Greek, and Roman cultures. Sacred sites were usually located near a spring and often near cattle pastures and markets. As a god, Hercules was revered by shepherds, soldiers, and merchants. He was protector of springs and healthy waters. The Sanctuary of Curino Hercules, located on the outskirts of Sulmona, dates from the 5th-4th centuries B.C. and took its final form around the 1st century B.C. Since this is one of the major sites dedicated to Hercules, there may also have been an oracle here. During 20th-century excavations, a large bronze *Hercules at Rest* from the school of Lysippus was found, along with many other artifacts, now in Chieti's archeological museum. Most archeological museums in Abruzzo and Molise – and other parts of Italy – have objects that show Hercules on small bronze votives, or depicted on black or red figure vases, mosaics, and even major sculptures.

Christianity didn't edge out pagan gods overnight. Belief was strong and was reinforced with pagan rituals, often tied to the change of season, harvest, weather, and other events – major or minor – in life. Sometimes edicts were sent to parish priests to go into the communities to stamp out pagan practices. Temples fallen into disuse were knocked down, especially by the powerful Benedictine order, to obliterate all visible traces. Parts were recycled into the churches as supporting columns or building blocks for the facade. Archangel Michael is often seen as a composite of Mars, god of war, Hercules, Jove, and even healing gods like Aeschylus. He replaced Northern gods like Odin and others dear to warrior Lombards, some of whom converted to Christianity after they grabbed land and settled in. The cult of Archangel Michael, along with that of the Virgin Mary, remains very strong in Abruzzo and Molise. Many churches are named after him. Often San Michele Archangelo is carved onto the facade or is shown stamping out the Devil or brandishing his armor in paintings. Ovid, a native of Sulmona in Abruzzo – where there was a major sanctuary dedicated to Hercules – was author of the *Metamorphoses*. He wrote about the exploits of the hero, as well as the other gods in the Roman pantheon who eventually were replaced by Christian saints.

that against Roma, and near the coast in Chieti and Pescara. Romans moved in around 200 B.C., suppressed the Samnites, and issued coins that used the word "Italia" for the first time.

During the early part of the Roman Empire, Ovid was born in Sulmona and Tiberius first saw light in Isernia. The Middle Ages brought a succession of power struggles between barbarians, Turks, the Duchy of Spoleto Swabians, Normans, and the Kingdom of Two Sicilies. In 1294, a hermit from Molise was elected pope, installed in L'Aquila, and months later created a scandal by resigning. By the 1400s, L'Aquila was the second power center after Naples under Charles of Anjou, the same century in which its university was created.

In 1503, Abruzzo along with the Kingdom of Napoli fell under Spanish control. Towns like L'Aquila and Lanciano fared poorly, while others managed to gain a toehold through Church connections.

Artisans became major players in the medieval community, a tradition that has remained strong in Abruzzo and Molise despite difficult times. Ceramics from the town of Castelli became the rage in the 17th and 18th centuries. Today you still find craftsmen making bells in bronze, pots in copper, gold jewelry, lace, and many other objects.

Those traditions have remained in part because the Apennine Mountains isolated the regions from metropolitan centers like Rome and Naples to the west. In 1863, the coastal railway connected Ancona to Foggia and added the Pescara–Sulmona line. But the *autostrada* highway system was not in place until the 1970s and '80s. The Gran Sasso National Laboratory for geophysical research opened in 1987, when the highway tunnels under the mountains were finally completed.

A new value was placed on parkland. The Parco Nazionale d'Abruzzo was established in 1934, and in 2002 added "Lazio and Molise" to its name. Two other national parks were created in the 1990s, Gran Sasso and Maiella, plus a regional park in the Sirente-Velino.

The entire region of Abruzzo has less than 1.5 million residents. The post–World War II economy and its geographic isolation led to a large emigration out of the region and even out of the country to seek employment. The area has always had periodic devastating earthquakes after which it must rebuild, an additional financial burden. Land development and falling prices dealt a final blow to the Transhumance, the twice-yearly livestock migration that kept shepherds moving across Abruzzo, Molise, and Puglia. Animal paths that had been used since pre-Roman times fell into disuse. Now some tracts are being converted for recreational use.

The change in technology, in transportation and in the information highway, have opened up the regions. Tourism is moving, but it's not rushing. You can still enjoy fewer crowds and better prices in Abruzzo and in Molise. Some traditions remain strong. Modern conveniences have been added, but a journey here is still one discovery after another.

Molise is Italy's newest region, created in 1963 after a divorce with Abruzzo. Its roots go back thousands of years as a single. Europe's old-est man was discovered here. The ancient Samnite civilization, which extended into parts of Abruzzo and Campania had its earliest and most important sites in this sparsely populated region where elbowroom has never been a problem.

Hannibal gave the Samnites a good whack in 217 B.C. when he swept through, but it was the Romans that eventually absorbed them into the Republic. Barbarians followed. Longobards and Normans were dominating influences as fortifications developed into a network of castles and monasteries in the Middle Ages. Catholic traditions that began as a veneer over paganism are strong and can be witnessed during festivals and everyday life.

Lack of significant resources have led to waves of immigration that only ceased in the 1970s. Today's population in fact is 100,000 less than it was in 1900. Only the three main towns have a density greater than 200 people per square kilometer. If you ask Robert De Niro where his ancestors emigrated from, Molise is his answer.

Molise remains a realm of small industry and business, largely dedicated to farming. The Transhumance, or great cattle drive, shaped vast secondary routes through Abruzzo, Molise, and Puglia. Imprints of those tracks remain and are ideal for hikers, cyclists, and anyone capable of mounting a horse. A sojourn in Molise offers great natural beauty in its mountains and coastal areas, superb cuisine, and picturesque roads to meander.

L'Aquila and Vicinity

Choose a base in or near the elegant city of L'Aquila to explore this area. Although gourmands, hikers, and skiers might prefer a base like Camarda, a small town between L'Aquila and Gran Sasso with a stylish hotel, a restaurant that's worth a detour, and easy access to the city and mountains. North of L'Aquila you can tour north into Parco Nazionale to Gran Sasso and Campo Imperatore, two circular tours that are each about 100 kilometers. Keep in mind the road to the latter closes October–May and you can only reach Campo Imperatore via the air tram. If you want to do serious skiing or hiking, you might prefer to be right on top at Campo Imperatore, while the pampered set may prefer the upscale medieval mountain village atmosphere of Santo Stefano. East of L'Aquila is the saffron area of the Navelli Plateau and the town of Capestrano (paired with California's San Juan Capistrano), a tour of about 40 kilometers, or a pleasant base where several family-friendly bed-and-breakfasts warmly welcome travelers of all ages with plenty of activities. To the south lies the Aterno Valley, whose Aterno River links L'Aquila with the Subequana and Peligna Valleys. Also in the south is the town of Secinaro, which has not only ruins of a pagan temple, but also the Silente Crater, which was formed from a 4th-century A.D. meteor impact but was discovered only in 2001. The Rocche Plateau, a tour of about 38 kilometers from L'Aquila to Ovindoli, takes you to Ocre with a Castello and your possible base in the rooms of the evocative 13th-century Santo Spirito Monastery—isolated, majestic as the mountains in which it's immersed, and mysterious.

L'AQUILA

L'Aquila presents an enticing silhouette from the highway as drivers whiz past the Aterno River Valley. The capital of Abruzzo, as well as its own province, is also the most distinguished city. Its architectural variety matches the majestic setting of the Gran Sasso massif that is a dominating presence. L'Aquila has the energetic buzz of a major university town and a lively arts scene, from music to theater and exhibits.

Begun by Holy Roman Emperor and King of Sicily, Frederick II, it was completed by one of his sons in 1254 and destroyed by another in 1259. Charles of Anjou rebuilt the town and finished the walls in 1316. In 1442, it became the second-most important city in the Kingdom of Napoli. Even today some Abruzzi dialects sound more like that of Naples than they do of Lazio or Le Marche.

The rise of the city increased as satellite villages and their lords formed an alliance to increase their wealth and power. According to tradition, there were once 99 lords, castles, churches, and piazze in town, and the number has taken on mythic proportions. It explains the famous fountain of the 99 spouts.

Time, however, did not stop in the Middle Ages. L'Aquila's decline began under 16th-century Spanish occupation that drained the city of its resources. A succession of rulers, wars, and earthquakes resulted in a tapestry of Renaissance, Baroque, end even some Fascist architecture. L'Aquila's variety makes for a pleasant visit.

Sights

The elegant city of L'Aquila could be broken up into two walking tours to do the northern part, visiting the Castello, various churches, and a stroll to window shop or sip a cappuccino on Corso Vittorio Emanuele. From the south at Porta Bazzano head toward Piazza San Giusta, Corso Federico II, through various squares toward Porta Rivera and the Fontana delle 99 Cannelle, then toward Piazza Duomo and San Flaviano to finish by Basilica di Collemaggio.

CASTELLO CINQUECENTESCO

The Renaissance castle in L'Aquila, Castello Cinquecentesco, houses the **Museo Nazionale D'Abruzzo** (tel. 0862/33-474, www.muvi. org/museonazionaledabruzzo, Tues.–Sun. 9 A.M.–8 P.M., €4), which appeals to any age and interest. The castle itself had the double function of defending the Kingdom of Napoli and of controlling the population. In 1528, the population of L'Aquila rebelled against the Spaniards. By 1534, work began on the fortress one of Italy's most important works of military architecture.

The square fortress has walls 10 meters thick and a wide moat. On the ground floor is **Archidiskodon Meridionalis Vestinues.** The almost-complete skeleton of this prehistoric elephant is about one million years old and seems to be more closely related to the mammoths of the Americas than modern pachyderms. Discovered in 1954 in Scoppio, he was restored 1987–1991 to adjust his posture and other bits. An average man is about knee-high to this elephant, a disproportion that makes for a memorable photograph.

The opposite side of the courtyard has a bar. The lower floors, once used to make olive oil or keep prisoners, now host temporary exhibits. The first floor, remodeled in 2006, displays medieval sculpture. Figures that express wonder and awe were painted in vibrant colors, some with exotic Eastern influences.

Paintings like Iacobello's panel of blond St.

ABRUZZO AND MOLISE

George resplendent in gold armor as he stomps on the dragon make you wonder who came up with the term "Dark Ages."

Coin collectors will enjoy the collection of Roman currency stamped with images of Mercury (think of the old U.S. dime), Julius Caesar, Janus, Augustus, Nero, and company. Other coins date to medieval and more recent periods. Paintings by Matteo Preti and Jusepe De Ribera recall the moody chiaroscuro of Caravaggio. Don't miss the section on ladies' fans that range from finely painted works of art to whimsy and even vaguely burlesque; they are charming in their details and must have an impressive number of flirting years behind them.

◖ FONTANA DELLE NOVANTANOVE CANNELLE

The magic number in L'Aquila is 99. Just to be sure you can count the spouts on Porta Rivera's Fontana delle Novantanove Cannelle. Each of the fountain's gushers has its own unique human or animal face sculpted by Tancredi da Pentima to represent the local lords and their manors. The neighborhood around the fountain is called **Rivera** because of the abundance of water. This unique fountain was a gift to the citizens of the city and a reminder that it takes a unified community to flourish and maintain peace.

The original spigots date from 1272 and were expanded throughout the ages. The wall behind the fountain, built in the 15th century, is of the same rosy pink and ivory stone of the nearby Collemaggio.

◖ SANTA MARIA DI COLLEMAGGIO

A long green leads to the church of Santa Maria di Collemaggio. Here on August 29, 1294, Pietro del Morrone was elected by the conclave, crowned, and installed as Pope Celestine V. When he was called here from his hermitage at Sant'Onofrio above Sulmona, the church was only partly completed. Months later, Celestine resigned as pope. This act, the only of its kind in the history of the Church, occurred during Dante's lifetime (1265–1321). When he wrote his *Divine Comedy,* Dante put Celestine V in Hell for his "refusal."

a medieval square and fountain in L'Aquila

The facade is a beautiful geometric pattern of rosy pink and ivory stone. Its central portal has intricately carved figures that adorn ribbed arches. There's a grand rose window best viewed in mid-afternoon when the sun streams through. The two doors on either side are surrounded by smaller arches and above each are smaller rose windows. The interior of the church has been restored to its medieval simplicity and the marble flooring recalls the colors and patterns of the exterior.

MUSEUMS

L'Aquila also has a **Museum of Speleology** (Via Svolte della Misericordia 2, tel. 0862/86-436, by appointment), **Museum of Natural and Human Sciences** (Convento di San Giuliano, tel. 0862/86-142, Tues.–Sun. 10 A.M.–1 P.M. and 3–6 P.M.), and **Experimental Museum of Contemporary Art** (Via Paganica 17, tel. 086/241-0505, Sat.–Sun. 5:30–8:30 P.M.). **La Lanterna Magica** (Parco di Collemaggio, tel. 0862/487-11, www.istitutocinematografico.it) is a cinematographic institute that puts on a steady stream of programs. The University, the Academy of Fine Arts, and the Music Conservatory are other sources of exhibits.

Entertainment and Events

Year-round L'Aquila is lively with a film festival, plays, classical concerts, and religious processions. The most important religious event is dedicated to the solemn ritual of plenary indulgence instituted by Celestine V, called **Perdonanza** (www.perdonanza-celestiniana.it) and has taken place annually for over 700 years on August 28 and 29. Until 1294, only Crusaders to the Holy Land or to St. Francis' tomb in **Porzincuola** had the right to such a favor. Perdonanza allows the poor and disenfranchised to be received annually on August 29. A historic procession goes through town with participants in medieval garb. The four town quarters vie in various competitions. Events get underway a few days before with a string of concerts and artists who open their studios to visitors.

Pietre Che Cantano International Music Festival (tel. 0862/751-345, www.pietrechecantano.it) takes place late July–late August. "Stones that Sing" are at various historic villas and monasteries throughout the Aterno Valley as well as L'Aquila's castle.

Insomniacs will enjoy the city's version of "white night" that consists of all-night concerts and events. **Magie Notturne** begins at 9 P.M. on the Saturday before Perdonanza and runs until dawn.

Accommodations

On a side street off Piazza del Duomo, **Hotel Duomo** (Via Dragonetti, tel. 0862/410-769, www.hotel-duomo.it, €95 d) dates to the 18th century and is very central. Drivers can park in the garage. If you suffer from heat don't bother looking for the air-conditioning; there is none.

A private home was converted to **San Michele** (Via Dei Giardini 6, 0862/420-260, €95 d). It has 32 rooms and a small communal sitting room for guests. **Hotel Sole** (Largo Silvestro dell'Aquila 4, tel. 0862/225-51, www.solehotel.eu, €135–155) dates to the 18th century and is also in the historic center.

Grand Hotel del Parco (Corso Federico II 74, tel. 0862/413-249, www.grandhotel.it, €130 d) is a modern 36-room hotel with parking near all the major sights. Breakfast is included and is served in a bright dining room where guests tend to linger before exploring the town.

Food

The patina of generations of good dining is evident as soon as you walk into **Ristorante Ernesto ai Benefattori del Grillo** (Piazza Palazzo 22, tel. 0862/210-94, €7.50–10). The name may be a mouthful but is certainly worth repeating. The *antipasti* are likely to catch your eye as soon as you walk in, to be followed with specialties like homemade pastas and meat dishes made with locally raised ingredients.

A short way from Santa Maria Collemaggio, Gregorio and Rosalba dedicate themselves to local cuisine inside **La Conca alla Vecchia Posta** (Via Caldora 12, tel. 0862/405-211, Tues.–Sun. noon–3 P.M. and 7–11 P.M., €8–11). Starters included grilled seasonal vegetables, *mortadella di Campotosto,* and a bean salad that tastes better than it sounds. The gnocchi are a reliable first along with the *chitarrine* pasta covered in a savory tomato sauce flavored with mountain herbs. If you want to eat like a shepherd, try the *surgitti* that hits the spot after leading sheep hundreds of kilometers to winter pastures. The crepes with hazelnut cream are good way to end a meal.

Information and Services

L'Aquila has good tourist information in English. Stop by the **Welcome Point** (Piazza Duomo, tel. 0862/230-21, www.centrostorico.laquila.it) booth for maps and brochures. On Saturdays at 4 P.M. they offer a two-hour walk, **Tour of Mysteries.** Book in advance to be sure to get an English-speaking guide.

Getting There and Around

L'Aquila is an easy two-hour drive from Rome on the A24 *autostrada.* If you are up for an extended journey through Tuscany, Umbria, Abruzzo, Molise, and Campania, you might

ABRUZZO AND MOLISE

want to consider following **Via degli Abruzzi,** which connects Firenze to Naples by way of Perugia, L'Aquila, Sulmona, Isernia, and Capua. Once you arrive at the edge of town, park in one of the designated areas and walk to the center on foot. Pick up a map at the tourist booth in Piazza Duomo and plan your route from there.

ARPA (Via Caldora, tel. 147/865-414) buses connect the city with Rome, Naples, Pescara, and Chieti. One-way tickets do not exceed €20 and may be purchased on board. Trains from Rome can be excrutiatingly long and may require a transfer in Terni or Sulmona. Three hours is considered fast and journeys can be significantly slower if you depart at night. The nearest intercontinental airports are Roma Fiumicino and **Aeroporto d'Abruzzo** (www.abruzzo-airport.it) in Pescara which serves Italy and Europe, and recently began flying to New York and Toronto.

Around L'Aquila
If you choose to head 15 kilometers south of L'Aquila, **Ocre** is right at the northern tip of **Parco Regionale Sirente Velino** and so is the stunningly beautiful ◖ **Monastero-Fortezza di Santo Spirito** (Via Santo Spirito S.N., Ocre, tel. 0862/196-5538, www.monasterosantospirito.it, €45 pp–50 pp), open year-round. The decor of this imposing 13th-century Cistercian monastery is neither too rustic nor too fancy, in harmony with the medieval stone buildings. Restaurant tables are decorated with white tablecloths and iron candleholders, and you can enjoy a delightful dinner for approximately €30. The 12 bedrooms are located in the east and west wings. You have a few perks that perhaps the monks did not, like a sauna, Internet connection, and TV. You can contemplate mountain hikes in the regional park or simply savor the spectacular scenery from the side of the mountain as you overlook valley views and ponder symbols that the Knights Templar etched in the walls.

From Sirente Velino Regional Park, if you want to head west toward Rome, exit the southern end of the park at Celano, which takes you past Avezzano and Tagliacozzo, or

exit the western end near Santa Maria in Valle. From these two, you can make a stop in Carole near the border of Lazio.

CAMARDA
Camarda is a short drive on the SS17 bis northwest of L'Aquila and makes a good base for excursions to Gran Sasso. There is a town atop the hill to explore, but the fine accommodations and restaurants are the main reasons to stay here. From Camarda the drive is just a few minutes to Fonte Cerreto, the base station for the Funivia del Gran Sasso, the cable car that makes a spectacular ride to Campo Imperiale.

Accommodations and Food
◖ **Elodia Relais** (Via Valle Perchiana, tel. 0862/606-830, www.elodia.it, €110–130 s/d) is a modern building with nine rooms that are sunny, large, and appointed with contemporary art and warm colors that lift the spirits. Everything is done with style here. The limited number of rooms makes for a quiet, peaceful sojourn. They're nicely decorated with modern fittings that make guests feel pampered in a Zen-meets-Italy way.

From the serene neutral color scheme to the attentive, professional service, a meal at ◖ **Elodia Restaurant** (Camarada SS 17bis 37, tel. 0862/606-219, Tues.–Sun. noon–2:30 P.M. and 7–10 P.M., €15) offers superb cuisine with inventive flavor combinations using fresh, local ingredients. If you've been longing for a stylish evening out with excellent service and food that teases and pleases the palate, this is the spot. Table settings are lovely with Venetian glassware. There is no separate vegetarian menu but Nadia and Wilma know how to highlight local vegetables in an inventive way. A basket of warm breads arrives immediately at your table along with saffron or wild fennel sticks. Try the *orzo* (barley) spaghetti, tinged purple with red wine sauce, cheese, and radicchio. The *agnello in crosta* is particularly good lamb, but you can also choose from pork, pigeon, wild boar, a plate of cheeses, or good local beef. Let

Antonello guide you with the wines, like red Cerasuolo or Montepulciano d'Abruzzo.

◖ PARCO NAZIONALE DEL GRAN SASSO E MONTI DELLA LAGA

The approach to Gran Sasso is delightful from every direction. In the summer you can drive up to **Campo Imperatore** or take the aerial tram year-round. From the coast, the most direct route is the *autostrada* toward Termoli. Those are the main approaches, but the 17bis/c winds through the park at a slower pace toward the southern part, while SS 80 is the main road toward the north. However, from around the perimeter of the park there are many approaches.

You may want to check with the park about hiking or horseback options, in which case a car may be unnecessary. Your hotel can often hook you up with a local guide, but if you want an English-speaking guide it is always best to request a few days ahead. By far the swankest place to stay is the medieval *albergo diffuso*

in Santo Stefano, but you can choose a whole range from lean-tos to shepherd's huts, hostels, hotels, bed-and-breakfasts, and *agriturismi*. If you have special interests like bird-watching, wolf studies, or bear spotting, be sure to indicate that when you contact the park information service. Italians like to count on a good meal, so as long as there are people there usually is at least a bar if not a restaurant that is handy until you get into the backwoods.

Sights

The approach to **Gran Sasso** offers breathtaking scenery. From the valley below, the drive up takes less than an hour, or a 10-minute cable car ride (€10 round-trip) to Campo Imperatore. When roads are closed October–May, the cable car is the only way to the top. The area is a year-round playground, popular with skiers during winter, and with daytrippers, campers, and hikers in summer. The atmosphere here is festive. Gran Sasso is less fashionable—and less expensive—than the Alps, but the snow arrives early, stays late, and

ABRUZZO AND MOLISE

© ALESSIA RAMACCIA

Campo Imperatore, Italy's highest mountain range south of the Alps

they make none of the artificial kind. If you come here on a hot summer day, plan to bring a light sweater or jacket. Even if the temperature is sweltering in the valley, the breeze at the top can turn suddenly chilly. Cars and campers can park here. Idle visitors sun themselves while the more energetic climb to the top of the peaks, and children run freely in the vast meadows.

Sports and Recreation

Complete summer and winter sports are available. Skiing in the Gran Sasso is less challenging than in the Alps, but is popular for its natural snow, long ski season, and its easy proximity to Rome. Campotosto has canoeing and windsurfing. Visit the Caldernone Glacier. The more intrepid may go for free climbing or frozen waterfall climbing. Monti della Laga has waterfalls at Morricana, Volpara and Barche. There is also an Apennine wolf study area. Special guides are available. For information on horseback riding and trekking, contact the **Gran Sasso Tourist Centre** (tel. 0862/605-21, www.gransassolagapark.it).

Accommodations

The Deco look of **Hotel Campo Imperatore** (Gran Sasso d'Italia, loc. Campo Imperatore, tel. 0862/400-000, www.ho telcampoimperatore.com, restaurant open noon–12:30 P.M. and 7–9:30 P.M., €120 d) would make a good fit in Miami Beach, but here it attracts skiers in winter. Don't worry if you have no equipment, everything you need for a week or weekend of skiing can be rented right here. Guests in winter arrive on the aerial lift from the base and then ski right to the lower level, where the hotel also has a small pool and exercise room.

During World War II, Mussolini was imprisoned here for several days until German paratroopers rescued him. Guests can visit the suite where he stayed for free or pay €250 to spend the night with Il Duce's ghost.

Next to the hotel is a stone building, **Ostello di Campo Imperatore** (Loc. Campo Imperatore, tel. 0862/400-011, daily noon–2 P.M.

and 7–9 P.M., €10–15), that serves as a budget-priced hostel and has its own restaurant. Guests here tend to rise early and set off on long mountain treks.

A medieval Franciscan convent in Barisciano, **Convento di San Colombo** had fallen into disrepair and in the 1990s the town received funding from the Parco del Gran Sasso Monti della Laga to restore and open **Centro Turistico San Colombo** (Via Provinciale km. 4,200, tel. 086/289-9017, www.sancolom botur.com, €72–92 d). For another €21 per person, you can have full board added, which is tempting considering their homemade soups and pastas that highlight lentils, chickpeas, saffron (grown by the manager), spelt, Pecorino cheese, truffles, wines from Abruzzo and beyond, and even liqueurs made from gentian, china, and walnuts. Singles pay only half the double price for rooms and rates for children are discounted. The tourist center in the hotel makes it handy to plan horseback riding, skiing, hiking, and visits to historic towns and archeological sites.

Food

In the summer the mountaintop is an ideal picnic spot, so buy fixings before you set out. At the base near the lift, vendors grill meat and there are a few small taverns. On top at Campo Imperatore you have plenty of options. This is not Cortina or St. Moritz, so prices are reasonable.

Hotel Campo Imperatore (Gran Sasso d'Italia, loc. Campo Imperatore, tel. 0862/400-000, www.hotelcampoimperatore. com) has a formal dining room on the first floor in white tones with windows that face out toward the mountaintop. Downstairs, its round 1930s bar is wood-paneled and rustic, as befits a ski resort. An adjacent room offers an appetizing buffet service, with local specialties. In nice weather a grill is set up outside. Next door at budget-minded **Ostello di Campo Imperatore** there is a bar and cafeteria.

Getting There and Around

Highway connections are good to Gran Sasso.

From Pescara, take the A25; from Rome, the A24 and A25. **ARPA** (www.arpaonline.it) buses serve the area, as do trains on the Roma–Pescara line and L'Aquila–Sulmona line.

Around Gran Sasso

The village of **Santo Stefano di Sessanio** was constructed between the 11th and 12th centuries. In more glorious days, the town changed hands through various powerful families, including the Medicis. The village was abandoned after World War II, but a Milanese investor restored it and infused the ruins with new life. Now the village has eight restaurants and 250 sleeping accommodations in medieval dwellings. Artisans moved in to work in studios. The village hosts an ensemble-in-residence and attracts artists from the worlds of film, theater, and visual arts.

Top on the list of lodgings in Abruzzo has to be **Sextantio Albergo Diffuso** (Palazzo delle Logge, Santo Stefano di Sessanio, tel. 082/899-192, www.sextantio.it, €200 d), where accommodations are in tune with the history of the buildings and in harmony with nature's scenery. The hotel isn't a single building but a series of dwellings that maintain their medieval charm unspoiled by kitsch art or dorm-style furniture. It's carefully decorated with appropriate crafts and fabrics that complement the natural stone interiors. Similar care is taken with the quality of food ingredients and preparations. Their motto could be "It takes a village to pamper a hotel guest."

Rocca Calascio was also abandoned after World War II and is now being renovated by the owner of Sextantio. Its *rocca* (fortress) is the highest in Italy and dates to 1000 and has four round towers that were added in the 15th century. This hamlet served as the set for *Ladyhawke,* filmed in the 1980s.

CAROLE

Via Tiburtina was one of the old consular roads that led to ancient Rome and is still in use today. Carole lies along the way near the Lazio border and makes a good stop by train or car on your way to or from Abruzzo's capital. For

© ALESSIA RAMACCIA

the recently restored town of Santo Stefano di Sessanio

ABRUZZO AND MOLISE

centuries Romans have headed to the hills around the town to avoid summer heat and modern-day visitors still find comfort in the high altitudes (1,000 meters). The journey from Rome is brief enough to just unwind next to the train station with a gourmet meal and superb wine. Or if you prefer to linger, try one of the *agriturismi* where life moves at a snail's pace.

Sights

As an ancient gateway town from Roma to Abruzzo, Carole had strategic importance. Emperor Nerva placed a 43rd milestone on Via Valeria in 97 A.D. Bits and pieces of that Roman history remain. Its medieval historic center, first mentioned in documents of 866, was partially destroyed in World War II. The town makes for a pleasant and leisurely stroll rather than for art trawling. Look for remains of Roman walls built of tufa and later reinforced with limestone. About two kilometers northeast are ruins of an ancient Roman aqueduct.

Accommodations

Stay overnight at *agriturismo* **Azienda Agrituristica Setteponti** (Via Tiburtina Valeria, km. 74.2, tel. 863/997-415, www.agriturismosetteponti.it, €60 d) and you have the pleasure of watching Vittoria and her daughter Paola as they make homemade pasta or bread along with the daily specials. They tend cows that supply milk for the ricotta and procure pecorino sheep's cheese from the neighboring shepherds. The six rooms are sometimes booked for weeks at a time by business travelers

who have grown addicted to Vittoria's cooking. The dining room is plainly furnished, as are the guest rooms with small showers.

Food

Situated next to the train station, **◖ L'Angolo d'Abruzzo** (Piazza Aldo Moro 8, tel. 0863/997-429, Thurs.–Tues. 12:30–2 P.M. and 7:30–10 P.M., €7–12) offers delicious cuisine and lovely service. A wide range of appetizers is available. Especially good are fried sheep's cheese and pumpkin flowers, each in a crisp light batter. The *baccalà* with wild greens and pink peppercorns and tripe in tomato sauce are also excellent. The menu is full of appetizing local cheeses and cured meats all worth sampling. Pastas like homemade *pappardelle* are doused with truffles or wild mushrooms when they are in season in late fall and winter. There are decadent desserts, but don't miss the homemade biscuits served with cherry wine.

Getting There and Around

If you arrive from Rome or Lazio and have time, consider taking the two-lane Via Tiburtina that follows much the same course that the ancient Romans constructed. It's likely to double travel time, but provides a modern immersion into the ancient transportation system and vast network of roads Roman engineers planned. Otherwise take the A24 *autostrada* that connects Rome to L'Aquila. The train (www.trenitalia.it) from L'Aquila runs on a scenic mountain track and takes two hours. Tickets cost €7.70 and passengers must transfer at Sulmona.

Sulmona and Vicinity

Sulmona is a town where you could easily glimpse the highlights in half a day, but it's so pleasant that you'll want to linger to enjoy its medieval aqueduct set on an angle, architecture, shops, social life in the town squares, and noteworthy archeological sites that include a major sanctuary dedicated to Hercules, Santuario Ercole Curino. This makes a nice base,

especially if you want to flex some muscle yourself. There is plenty of hiking, particularly to the hermitage of Sant'Onofrio in Morrone. Here the hermit received word that he was elected pope by the conclave in L'Aquila, and then within months Celestine V became the only pope in history to resign. From Sulmona a 36-kilometer tour southwest toward the Sagittario and Scanno Valleys takes you to see the village of Anversa at the mouth of Sagittario Gorges for the panorama and to meander through churches, and to the town of Cocullo, famous since pre-Roman times for its snake-charming tradition that residents still show off in its annual May snake procession. A tour of some 100 kilometers will take you toward the mountains, Montagne della Maiella, via Pacentro perched on Mount Morrone, a picture-perfect silhouette with its square and cylindrical castle towers rising above medieval village roofs.

You can also cover 119 kilometers by train from Sulmona in Abruzzo to Carpinone in Molise on the park railway that runs through the Apennines from Sulmona to Carpinone, about 10 kilometers east of Isernia, which connects leisurely to other train lines—ideal for the train buff who will be pleased to know this line was saved from near-extinction in the 1980s.

⟨ SULMONA

According to legend, Solimo Frigio, the companion of Aeneas, founded Sulmona. Located in the Peligna Valley between two national parks, the city of some 25,000 is surrounded by mountains. It's a breezy, lively town that buzzes with the energy of social life, from children playing in piazze, to adults paying social calls, and all generations chatting in cafes.

The town's claim to fame is as the birthplace of the poet Ovid, ancient Roman author of numerous Latin works including the divinely entertaining *Metamorphoses* that recounts the lives of the gods and goddesses. Born in 43 B.C., Publius Ovidius Naso was a favorite of Augustus until the Emperor sent Ovid into political banishment and ultimately to his death.

Sights

Begin your visit in **Piazza Garibaldi,** one of Abruzzo's most intriguing and lovely squares. The slanted 1256 aqueduct, built by King Manfred with its 1474 Fontana del Vecchio sculpted from Maiella stone, dramatically frames one side of the piazza

(sometimes called Piazza Maggiore, its former name). Locals pause in the cafes that line the square or peruse the wares in the morning market. The church rises vertically off to one angle.

Of the ancient Roman town gates, **Porta Napoli** at the end of Corso Ovidio is the best preserved. Originally built to quarantine, **Palazzo dell'Annunziata** has detailed Gothic architecture with bas-reliefs sculpted on the facade.

Candy-making machines that date 1783–1930 are in **Museo dell'Arte e della Tecnologia Confettiera** at the Pelino Confetti Factory (Via Stazione Introdacqua 55, tel. 0864/210-047, Mon.–Sat. 8:30 A.M.–12:30 P.M. and 3–7 P.M.).

The cult of Hercules was one of the oldest and widespread in ancient Samnite, Greek, and Roman cultures. Sanctuaries and temples were usually located near a spring and often near cattle pastures or markets. The strongman was revered by shepherds, soldiers, and merchants. He was protector of springs and healthy waters. **Sanctuary of Curino Hercules** is located on the outskirts of town and dates from the 5th–4th centuries B.C. It was a major site dedicated to the god and an oracle may have once predicted the future for anxious pilgrims. During 20th-century excavations, a large bronze *Hercules at Rest* from the school of Lysippus was found along with other artifacts, now in Chieti's archeological museum. The sanctuary is five kilometers west of the center off SS 17.

Near Hercules is the **Morronese Abbey** (Morrone, tel. 086/425-1255, summer Sun. only, by request) that has frescoes in the Caldora Chapel. A half-hour hike above it on the side of the mountain is the **Sant'Onofrio** hermitage, from where the solitary monk was called to L'Aquila to become Pope Celestine V, the only pope in history who quit his job.

Entertainment and Events

The piazze are lively in the summer with music and other performances in the squares.

A bronze statue of Ovid near the town high

school is a reminder that literary events are popular in Sulmona. Students from across Europe compete in Latin compositions and translations. Other events that award literature and screenwriting achievements in past years have recognized Susan Sontag and Martin Scorsese.

The **Fleeing Madonna** ritual is held on Easter morning in Piazza Garibaldi with a procession in which the Virgin Mary escapes. Jousting tournaments take place in late July and early August. **Giostro Cavalleresca d'Europa** in Piazza Maggiore pits a local jouster against a European opponent.

The **Italian Film Festival** (www.sulmonacinema.it) takes place in November. October–April is the active season in town theaters for concerts and plays. Vocal and piano competitions are held in October.

Shopping

Toasted almonds with a crunchy colorful sugar coating are the bonbons for which Sulmona is famous. Try the assortment at **Confetteria Giorgi** (Corso Ovidio 227, tel. 0864/527-11, Tues.–Fri.), **Confetti e Torrone William di Carlo**, and **Confetti Ovidio.**

Goldsmith **Davide di Ruscio** makes lovely jewelry, with particularly nice filigree work that has a modern edge.

If you're inspired to pop the question or are after some extra karats, **Mauro Pacella** has attractive ring designs for under €300. Shop hours generally are 9 or 10 A.M.–1 P.M. and 3:30 or 4 P.M.–7 P.M.

Accommodations

Hotel Meeting (SS 17 km. 95,500, tel. 0864/251-696, www.hotelsantacroce.com, €65–90 s/d) is a two-story motel that offers individual entrances, 78 large quiet rooms, and a swimming pool that the owners have adorned with cast marble statues of Hercules and Aphrodite, in homage to the archeological site on the slopes above town. Locals frequent the restaurant, which was the Santacroce family's main business before they opened two hotels (the second is in the center). This is a good

comfortable base of operation. Domenico and his wife are friendly, gracious hosts.

Food

Sulmona is the spot to try the local agricultural star, *l'aglio rosso di Sulmona* (Sulmona red garlic). Also look for local chefs that use saffron from Navelli.

The atmosphere is simple, but keep an eye on Domenico's menu for interesting theme nights and special menus at **Restaurant Meeting Santacroce** (SS 17 at 95.5 km, tel. 0864/251-696, www.hotelsantacroce.com, daily 12:30–2:30 P.M. and 7:30–10 P.M., €10–30) on the outskirts of Sulmona. He frequently participates in national food competitions, so expect traditional as well as innovative dishes. Night owls will appreciate its 24-hour bar.

The waiters may not have graduated from finishing school but the food is too good to pass up at **Clemente** (Vico Quercia 5, tel. 0864/522-84, Fri.–Wed. 12:30–3 P.M. and 7–11 P.M., €9–12). Don't wait for a menu, as everything on offer is hand-written and can be lost in translation if your Italian is rusty. In the autumn you'll probably see *fettuccine di castagne con funghi di bosco* or polenta when temperatures start to drop. In Piazza Plebiscito 7, the *enogastronomia* shop (9 A.M.–1 P.M. and 4–7 P.M.) sells the A-to-Z of the region's cheeses, cold cuts, wines, and liquors.

Getting There and Around

Sulmona is in the Peligna Valley between two national parks, Parco Nazionale della Maiella and Parco Nazionale D'Abruzzo, Lazio e Molise. Convenient to reach since ancient times, it's on the crossroad of Via Tiburtina and the SS1. The ancient Via Degli Abruzzi went from L'Aquila to Roccaraso, Molise, Campania and finally Naples. The faster route is the A25 *autostrada,* exit Sulmona. Sulmona is served by train (www.trenitalia.it) and the regional bus line **ARPA** (tel. 199/166-592, www.arpaonline.it). Taxis are at the **train station** (tel. 0864/317-46) and tourist information is available from the **IAT office** in Corso Ovidio 208 (tel. 0864/532-76).

SCANNO

From Sulmona you can continue south between two national parks to **Lago di Scanno,** fed by the **Tasso River** and formed by Abruzzo's largest natural basin. The lake is popular for windsurfing, canoes, and pedal boats. There are many sporting facilities as well as restaurants, hotels, and campgrounds. In winter, skiers head for the trails of Mount Totonfo. For an impressive view of the lake from above, take the road toward Frattura.

The town of Scanno has a population just over 2,000, but is lively with cultural events including an annual literary award, Premio Scanno, and several celebrations to Saints Anthony, John the Baptist, and Martin that involve great bonfires. Some women still wear traditional dress with dark skirts, ruffled blouses, colored bodices with silver buttons, and hats known as *cappellitto*. You can continue south skirting the eastern edge of Parco Nazionale d'Abruzzo toward Molise from here. At Alfedena you can choose either to enter the national park or to continue south toward Molise.

PACENTRO

If you head to the park from Sulmona, you'll pass through **Pacentro,** which developed around 11th-century **Castello Caldora.** One of the town's more popular events is the barefoot gypsy race, **Corsa degli Zingari,** when contestants run down and back up the hill on the first Sunday in September. Visitors are welcome to participate but it's a lot harder than it looks and many contestants drop out midway through the race.

 Caldora (Piazza Umberto I 13, tel. 0864/411-39, Wed.–Sun. 12:30–2:30 P.M. and 7:30–10 P.M., closed Mon., Tues., holidays, €35) is worth making a detour. The main dining room is ringed with late 19th- and early 20th-century photographs of writer D'Annunzio's lovers, a decidedly confident and even flamboyant group of women. The terrace has stone walls, a view of the mountains, and a fountain that flows with spring water that arrives on your table in a pitcher. Food is excellent, beginning with mountain specialties of fresh ricotta, aged pecorino cheese, and cured meats. Seconds include local fresh vegetables, wild greens, and meat specialties. They have a good selection of wines. The waiters all serve with flair.

GUARDIAGRELE

Guardiagrele first developed in ancient times on lower ground and then moved up to the top of the hill for protection from barbarian invasions. The first written documentation dates from the 12th century, when the town was already ringing with blacksmiths and bell makers. Even today you'll see goldsmiths and the town coppersmith, a tradition that's been going strong since Nicola di Andrea Gallucci, a.k.a. Nicola da Guardiagrele, worked here. Guardiagrele is at the foot of the eastern slopes of the Maiella massif on northeastern boundary of Parco Nazionale della Maiella.

Sights

Abruzzo was once the ancient territory of Samnites and later Romans. The small **Museo Archeologico Guardiagrele** (tel. 0871/800-460, open daily in August, by appointment other months, tel. 333/758-6860) displays some items found nearby, including relics from burial tombs uncovered in the vicinity.

 Santa Maria Maggiore, founded around 430 A.D. on the remains of an ancient temple, is the town's symbol. The relief on the lunette is attributed to goldsmith Nicola da Guardiagrele. The museum in the crypt houses his silver-gilded processional cross (1431). **San Rocco** has an elaborately carved wooden Baroque confessional and pulpit.

If you've heard about the traditional dress customs, in the Comune (Town Hall), check out **Museo del Costume e delle Tradizioni Guardiesi.**

Shopping

Villa Maiella's master chef Peppino custom orders his copper pots from coppersmith **Adriano Ferri** (Porta S. Giovanni 4, tel. 0871/800-405, www.artigianoabruzzese.it, by appointment only). His wares range from decorative to functional and are displayed in his shop just inside the Guardiagrele's ancient town gate, **Arco Porto della Fiera. Costel Capuzzi** hammers out attractive wrought-iron crafts, from smaller decorative objects to bed frames.

Every August for almost three weeks at **Mostra dell'Artigianato Artistico Abruzzese** (www.artigianoabruzzese.it, by appointment only), Guardiagrele showcases the talents of Abruzzese craftsmen who work in copper, gold, ceramics, wood, lace, wrought iron, hemp, textiles, and other media—usually exhibited in **Palazzo dell'Artigianato** (Via Roma 28).

A short hop down the road in **San Martino sulla Marrucina** is the Masciarelli winery, **Azienda Agricola Masciarelli** (tel. 0871/852-41, www.masciarelli.it, by appointment only) that produces excellent Montepulciano D'Abruzzo, along with other reds and some whites. Masciarelli is one of the biggest exporters to the United States and the winery design is interesting to see.

Sports and Recreation

Strike off on your own or hire a hiking guide from the Alpine Club of Italy **CAI Guardiagrele** (tel. 30/748-736). Keep the forest rangers' **Corpo Forestale dello Stato** (tel. 1515) number handy. Guardiagrele pine, fir, and chestnut forests have the San Giovanni waterfall and fauna such as the squirrel, fox, wild boar, birds of prey, and lynx. **Fara San Martino** is the territory of royal eagles, chamois, wolves, hares, viper, and the endangered Marsican bear. **Montepiano Plain** is good for mountain biking and horseback excursions. In winter, skiers head for nearby ski resorts **Passolanciano and Maielletta,** west of town on the N614.

Accommodations

Book ahead for a room at **(Villa Maiella** (Località Guardiagrele, tel. 0871/809-319, www.villamaiella.it, €99 d). The restaurant attracts gourmets from across Italy, which is why the 14 rooms are frequently booked. The modern building is a convenient base of operation to visit sights in the mountains or seashore. Rooms are large and have nice textiles on the beds and hanging from the windows. Mountain ricotta cheese and honey with local bread, fresh orange juice, and coffee gets you off to a great start in the morning.

Food

After his stint at Venice's Cipriani, Peppino Tinari upscaled the cuisine and transformed his parents' simple 1960s trattoria into Abruzzo's best restaurant. He and co-chef wife Angela attract diners from all over Italy to **(Villa Maiella Ristorante** (Località Guardiagrele, tel. 0871/809-319, www.villamaiella.it, Tues.–Sun. 12:30–3 P.M. and 7:30–10 P.M., €10–14 pastas, €35–40 meal). For appetizers, try *sformato di formaggio* (a mini-soufflé made from local mountain cheese), the *coniglio farcito* (rabbit rolled with pecorino and liver with curly endive salad), and the *pallotto cacio e uova* (a mouthwatering humble Abruzzese tradition of bread, cheese, and egg lightly fried). Homemade *chitarrina al pomodoro* is pasta made with wild herbs from the Maiella mountains. Try one of his dishes that highlight saffron grown in Abruzzo, like lamb *stinco* in saffron sauce or the lamb *filetto* with a tasty crust served with potatoes *al coppo*. An intuitive sommelier matches the wine to your tastes. You might want to try Mascerelli's wine from down the street or select from within or outside the region. Desserts to sink into include a gooey chocolate soufflé, a fruit tart, and Angela's heavenly saffron ice cream that's not to be missed.

Getting There and Around

The Maielleta mountain area is easily reached from the Adriatic coast in about a half-hour. Exit the A14 *autostrada* at Ortona to SS 81 or take a more winding route from exits Pescara Sud or Val di Sangro.

Around Guardiagrele

Just a short hop from the Masciarelli Winery is the completely enchanting Castello di Semivicoli and its 18th-century **(Palazzo**

SAFFRON

Saffron has been around for millennia. "Saffron-robed and rosy-fingered," the Roman goddess, Aurora, appears as Dawn to usher in the day. She was perhaps called "rosy" due to pinching the precious crocus stigma, which became the world's most expensive spice, worth far more than its weight in gold.

In Italy, saffron is cultivated in various regions, but the most prized comes from Abruzzo in Navelli and nearby towns. During the Middle Ages, merchants in L'Aquila and elsewhere became wealthy trading saffron, which was used as a medicine, spice, and for dying clothes. The *crocus attivus* flower that produces saffron resembles the purple crocus that blooms in spring in eastern North America. However, the saffron crocus blooms in fall and produces the stigma, the female part of the flower with the prized three red threads that rise up from a single stem.

The saffron crocus is fragile and easily threatened by enemies like fungus (which can attack bulbs), frost, and wild boars (who find it tasty). The purple and white flower caps are carefully picked by hand early in the morning while the bloom is still closed, then placed gently into a basket. The stigma is carefully removed, preferably leaving the three threads attached. Placed in a shallow pan, they are quickly shaken and toasted over a fire that dries them to preserve taste and color. The dried saffron is bottled in glass vials that should be stored away from humidity and light.

Nothing substitutes for saffron's distinctive taste. Chefs note that the threads are far superior to the powdered version. Restaurants in Abruzzo such as Villa Maiella offer a superb range of saffron dishes, from appetizer to ravioli, lamb, bread, and even ice cream. A few saffron threads slipped into fish dishes or bread dough make a remarkable difference. And of course, it's essential in that Milan classic, *risotto Milanese*.

Pericone (Via San Nicola, Casacanditella, tel. 0871/852-41, www.masciarelli.it, €130-200). Winemaker Giovanni Masciarelli put his zest for perfection into restoring these stone buildings with his talented wife Marina. He insisted that every detail in the restoration of the palazzo employed the use of original materials all crafted with traditional quality from window fittings to floors. The swimming pool set amidst the vineyard is a blissful conclusion or beginning to your day. Bicycles are available to explore the country roads, and there's a fitness center to complete your workout, as well as an *enoteca* for chilling out with a great glass of wine. The panoramic top-floor apartment, generally rented by the week, is a worthwhile splurge. Final touches will be in place for its August 2008 opening.

Fara San Martino on the Verde River is renowned for its pasta industry and produces some of Italy's best commercial pasta. The most famous got its boost in 1887 when Filippo De Cecco invented the automatic pasta-drying machine. Arguably Italy's best commercial pasta is made by Giuseppe Cocco with machinery from the 1950s. The lesser-known Verde brand is considered superior pasta, too. The quality is attributed to the excellent water from the Maiella Mountains, the local semolina wheat, and the use of bronze draw-plates in the production process. The pasta factories are all situated one next to the other.

If you'd like accommodations near the natural mineral springs at **Caramanico Terme** at the base of Monte Morone, try **Locanda del Barone** (loc. San Vittorino, tel. 085/925-84, www.locandadelbarone.it, €70 d), which has a good restaurant on the premises.

Roccascalegna is situated between the Maiella Mountains and the Adriatic Sea. The castle (City Hall, tel. 0872/987-111) clings to a rocky outcrop and you can tour most of its rooms. One wing frequently hosts temporary exhibits. The medieval town makes for a lovely stroll, too. **Il Caminetto Ristorante Pizzeria** (Via Collegrande 3, tel. 0872/987-154, Wed.–Sun.) at the edge of town near the pines is a cozy place to come for homemade pasta and grilled meat.

From Guardiagrele head south on SS81 and take a right south on the secondary road toward Altino.

PARCO NAZIONALE DELLA MAIELLA

The National Park of the Maiella was established in 1991. The highest peak in the **Maiella Massif** is Mount Amaro (2,795 meters). The mountain range, which is geologically related to Gran Sasso, has rounded mountains, so snow sticks longer than on more vertical, sheer peaks. Towns like **Guardiagrele** at the foot of its eastern slope make an excellent base of operation for hiking, bicycling, exploring caves, or even trips to the seashore. It's also a gourmet's paradise with some of Abruzzo's top restaurants. Tradition is valued here. You can chart your own course to seek out master craftsmen that turn out superb products in copper, gold, wood, ceramics, and textiles. The voyage is part of the pleasure. SS 17 across the high plains has a top-of-the worldness about it. Among the mountaintops, space is vast and drenched in light. Many places are open year-round ideal for hikers or hibernators that want to move by foot, sled, or ski. Bring hiking shoes or boots and snow or rain gear if you visit in winter.

Getting There and Around

From Sulmona, head east toward Pacentro, which is just inside he western edge of Parco Nazionale della Maiella. Continue east and you'll hook up with the road that bisects the national park from north to south. Head south and you'll reach Campo di Giove, which has Abruzzo's highest ski lift and cableways. Campo di Giove is a town whose altitude in meters (1,000) is greater than its numbers in population. As its name, Jove's Field, suggests, this town dates back to Roman times. Now it's appreciated for its ski lifts (tel. 086/440-8440) that lead up to 1,650 meters at Guado di Coccia and its ski runs, and in summer to a network of hiking trails toward the Maiella massif. From here to reach

Guardiagrele on the northeastern edge of the park is a windy, scenic, and very slow road. From Sulmona locals generally skirt the park, head north to pick up the Autostrada east, then just before Chieti head south to Guardiagrele. Whether you choose the mountain passes or the route in the foothills depends on how much time you have, what parts of the park you wish to see, and what activities most interest you.

PALENA

Palena sits on the southeastern edge of Parco Nazionale della Maiella. Its accommodations include rooms in a former monastery complex adjacent to the Marsican Bear Museum. If you want to head into Molise, it's a good spot, or from here head northeast toward Casoli and then destinations on the Southern Abruzzo coast like Vasto.

Palena's 20th-century claim to fame is as the birthplace of singer Perry Como's parents. The main draws however, are the natural beauty, an offbeat Marsican Bear Museum, its gem of a theater, and a small museum with a collection of prehistoric fossils.

Sights

A converted monastery now houses the **Marsicano Bear Museum** (Vico II Gradoni 2, tel. 339/862-9165). The first room is darkened so you acclimate to forest sounds. All information is in Italian, but some visuals explain the bear's world without text, including a wall mural with little doors and drawers that open to show signs of the bear's presence.

Some 12–17 million years ago, there was a major climate change in Abruzzo and fossils of fish and shark-like creatures suggest the region once lay under the sea. The paleontology museum, **Museo Geopaleontologico Alto Aventino** (Via Passo Moreno, tel. 0871/930-028, www.prologus.it, Tues.–Sun. 9 A.M.–12:30 P.M. and 3–8 P.M.) is housed in Palena's 11th-century castle. It was once the stomping ground for elephants or mastodons, so perhaps some will be unearthed as fossil excavations continue.

MARSICANO BROWN BEAR

Travelers rarely catch a glimpse of the endangered Marsicano brown bear, estimated to number only about 60 in the entire region of Abruzzo. The Marsicano's natural habitat ranges through Abruzzo and into part of Le Marche. One look at its face and you'll see how much it resembles the grizzly. The Marsicano is a close relative, in fact, although it is only about half the grizzly's size. Standing on his hindquarters, the Marsicano is no taller than an average person. Fish are not abundant in the mountains of Abruzzo, so without access to the fat and protein consumed by the grizzly, the Marsicano does not grow as large. The Marsicano needs to consume 20,000 calories a day. It must cover great distances outside of inhabited areas in the search for food. Apples are a favorite food in the Marsicano's diet, but the 30 kilograms of apples it needs to keep going are hard to come by. A bear will make an occasional raid on beehives for prized honey or take an occasional whack at sheep if it is hungry and has the chance.

Local folks know about the bear's hardships, so some plant a special garden with the bear's favorite plants and trees. *Cultivi a perdere* (throwaway crops) are intended exclusively for the bear's use. The bear garden is surrounded by a fence mounted with a ladder – an upside-down "V" with bars that only bears know how to climb and descend. Thus other foragers are kept out and with any luck, sheep are not disturbed.

Since odds are that you will not see any bears while visiting Abruzzo, the **Marsicano Bear Museum** is the best place to learn about this rare and elusive traveler. The museum occupies part of a converted monastery that also has 18th-century frescoes in the cloister. Enter the first room: It's darkened, so you must rely on your ears. Clever in design, sounds are not amplified to compete with ambient museum noise. Rather you must remain still and train your ears to listen for animal noises. The calls of animals like owls or wolves are faint, just as they would be from a distance. Two floors of bear exhibits and local natural history are here to explore. All information is in Italian, but some rooms, like "Mondo del Orso Marsicano," work well even without reading the information. The "Bear's World" wall mural shows how to look for signs of bears in the forest. Little doors and drawers open and show signs of a den, footprints, food consumption (and yup, the digestive waste product), scratches on tree trunks, animal carcasses, raided beehives, and other ways to tell if a bear has been in the area.

Try to catch a concert or other performance at **Teatro Aventino** (Piazzetta dei Capitoli, tel. 333/433-8507), a 99-seat gem of a theater near Chiesa di San Francesco.

Accommodations

The hunter-owner of **Park Hotel Maiella** (Corso da Colleveduta, tel. 0872/918-734, €100 d) bags wild boar and hare and opens the dining room on weekends. Rooms are simple and modern with vistas of the foothills and mountains.

Food

In the same monastery complex as the Marsican Bear Museum, **Casa dell'Orso** (Loc. Sant'Antonio, tel. 0872/919-009, 12:30–3 P.M. and 7–9:30 P.M.,) serves hearty lunch and dinner at reasonable prices. Upstairs are simple clean rooms (winter €62 d) convenient for families.

La Pineta (Rione Pineta 22, tel. 0872/918-135, €12–25) has a good salami and cheese platter, homemade pastas, grilled meats, and a small fireplace.

Getting There and Around

From Guardiagrele, follow SS81 south, take a right turn onto the road for Casoli and continue to approach the mountain range closer south to Palena. Trains from L'Aquila leave three times a day and the two-hour journey requires a transfer in Sulmona. For information on transportation or other services visit the **APT tourist office** (Via Gradoni 2, tel. 087/291-8951).

PARCO NAZIONALE D'ABRUZZO, LAZIO E MOLISE

Parco Nazionale d'Abruzzo, Lazio e Molise (www.pna.it) was created in the 1920s to protect the ecological balance in the Apennines and joined in 2002 by provinces in Molise and Lazio. The Marsican brown bear, the Italian wolf, and the chamois are a little less endangered now. The area also has lynx, deer, wild boar, foxes, and numerous small mammals. Most regal of the birds of prey is the golden eagle, joined by peregrine falcons, buzzards, griffon vultures, hawks, owls, jays, herons, finches, woodpeckers, and many other species. About 80 percent of the flora in Europe is found in the parks of Abruzzo. Wild orchids include the rare lady's slipper, iris, narcissus, and gentian that cover the slopes in spring. Charming medieval villages, some restored others more rustic, are perched in advantageous positions. The highest mountain peaks are Mount Petroso (2,247 meters) and Mount Marsicano (2,242 meters).

Most travelers approach the park from Sulmona in Abruzzo, as the A25 passes by the northern end of the park in Abruzzo.

Accommodations and Food

Right in the heart of the National Park of Abruzzo, Lazio, and Molise is **Pescasseroli.** A good stopping point for the night is **Villa Mon Repos** (Via S. Lucia 2, tel. 086/391-2858, €150), an Art Nouveau gem. Explore the nearby old town, then relax outside on the rolling lawn with its century-old trees, gazebo, and solarium. The restaurant features creative twists on traditional and regional dishes.

Information and Services

A full range of summer and winter sports is available. Park headquarters are in Pescasseroli (tel. 0863/910-461). The wolf sanctuary is in Civitella Alfedena; contact **Agenzia Wolf** (tel. 0864/890-360) for a guided visit.

Getting There and Around

Highway connections are good to the park. From Pescara, take the A25 to SS84 and 487. From Rome use the A25, or from Naples the A1 and SS17. **ARPA** (www.arpaon line.it) buses serve the area from Sulmona, Pescara, and Chieti. Train routes are on the Roma–Pescara line and Carpinone–Sulmona line. SS83 bisects the park from the north through Pescasseroli, then begins to head east toward Alfedena and then into Molise. From the southeast entrance you could head east into Molise toward Carovilli and Agnone, farther south to Isernia and Campo Basso. Or head northeast and explore Parco Nazionale della Majella.

You can enter the park from Lazio via Frosinone, from the north near Piscina, or from the east at Alfedena. Sulmona is in an advantageous position near one regional and two national parks. You can make a circular route that returns to your starting point, or bisect the park and continue on your way to other sights in Abruzzo or Molise.

Pescara and the Northern Abruzzo Coast

Pescara, Abruzzo's most densely populated city, has yet to turn 100 years old. It's one of Abruzzo's main business centers and transportation hubs and has grown helter-skelter. The modern architecture lures few visitors and you can find better beaches south of the city. The city is bisected east–west by the Fiume Pescara and Porto Canale, the river that flows into the canal that empties into the Adriatic Sea with the maritime station and tourist port, Marina di Pescara, on its south bank. The part south of the canal was ancient Pescara, which you'll have to track down now in museums, as now the modern jumble is dedicated to business. The train station is north of Porto Canale, where on the coast Castellammare Adriatico caters more to the seaside tourist, the best place to walk on the promenade by the sea and get a gelato. Once you leave the sea, toward the mountains the province of Pescara has abbeys and castles to explore.

PESCARA

Pescara caters to the business traveler of decades ago. Rooms are functional and devoid of regional charm, but they sometimes come with a view of the sea. Nevertheless, it is possible to eat well here, which is what you may want to do before moving on. Abruzzo's main airport is just outside of town, as are efficient bus and train connections, which makes Pescara a good point of entry into Italy.

The best time to show up is during one of the festivals, like **Pescara Jazz** or for the procession at sea for **Festa di Sant'Andrea,** both in July.

Sights

It's best to head for a nice meal near the tourist **port** or move farther south along the coast to visit the **Michetti Museum** (Francavilla al Mare, Piazza San Domenico 1, tel. 085/491-2347, Tues.–Fri. 10 A.M.–1 P.M. and 4–7 P.M., Sat.–Sun. 4–7 P.M., €6), which is more stunning than museums in Pescara.

Fans of D'Annunzio will want to stop by **Museo Casa Natale di Gabriele D'Annunzio** (Corso Manthone' 101, tel. 0856/0391, Tues.–Sat. 9 A.M.–2 P.M., closed holidays). Some rooms in the author's birthplace are still furnished as they were when the writer grew up here.

If you're looking to book a yacht or just want to admire a few, head over to **Marina di Pescara Yacht Port** (Lungomare Papa Giovanni XXIII, tel. 0854/54681).

Accommodations

Esplanade (Piazza Maggio 46, tel. 0852/921-41, www.esplanae.net, €100 d) has a private beach and is in an early 20th-century building equipped with 150 rooms and a pleasant roof-top restaurant. Expect modern rather than cozy, and professional service that rarely strays from formalities.

Food

Facing palm trees near the tourist port, **Caffe le Paillotte** (Lido delle Sirene, tel. 085/61809, closed Mon. lunch and Sun., €22) is a tradition in Pescara for a special meal. Fresh fish and seafood from the Adriatic are featured, with *brodetto* on Wednesday evenings. If your budget is tight, try their more casual **Il Granchio Royal** (Lido delle Sirene, tel. 085/61809, closed Mon. lunch and Sun., €5–9 pizza, €15–20 meal), which serves seafood and pizza.

Getting There and Around

Liberi or **Pescara Airport** (www.abruzzo-airport.it) is Abruzzo's international airport. Airlines serving the region include **Ryanair** (www.ryanair.com), **Air One** (www.flyairone.it), **Air Vallee** (www.airvalle.it), and **Brussels Airlines** (www.brusselsairlines.com). If you are interested in ferries to Croatia or Greece, check with the **Marina** (www.marinape.com) for destinations and schedules. Bus service with **ARPA** (www.arpaonline.it) has good regional connections. By car take the A25 from Rome or the coastal A14 highway. Pescara has two train stations, with the major station being Pescara Centrale (www.trenitalia.com).

Abruzzo Promozione **Turismo Regionale** (Piazza Sirena, tel. 085/817-169) has maps and many useful brochures that have been published in English. Some are specialized for sports, crafts, food, or the arts.

Around Pescara

The former convent converted to studio by painter Francesco Paolo Michetti (1852–1921) in **Francavilla al Mare** is now the **Michetti Museum** (Francavilla al Mare, Piazza San Domenico 1, tel. 085/491-2347, Tues.–Fri. 10 A.M.–1 P.M. and 4–7 P.M., Sat.–Sun. 4–7 P.M., €6). This native of Abruzzo never traveled far, yet his use of paint and light recall the 19th-century Orientalists who went to exotic lands for inspiration. His subjects came from the world around him, an Abruzzo of exoticism and mystery. His *Procession of the Snakes* is a ritual that still takes place in **Cocullo** the first Thursday in May in honor of St. Dominic. The museum faces the sea and in summer offers a series of concerts. Throughout the year it hosts exhibits and other programs.

Only 12 kilometers north of Pescara on the coast in Silvi Marina is inviting **Mion Hotel** (Via Garibaldi 22, tel.085/935-0864, www.mionhotel.com, €165) with a swimming pool, whirlpool tub, garden of palm trees, and Sanio Restaurant overlooking the patio. Bedrooms have terrazzo floors and some feature antiques. Owned for generations by ancient Venetian family Mion, its handy location is less than a kilometer from SS Adriatica 16.

From Silvi Marina, **Città Sant'Angelo** is situated about six kilometers to the west, a medieval town probably settled in the site of ancient Vestino and Roman towns. The church dedicated to Abruzzo's cult favorite, St. Michael Archangel, was founded before the year 1000 and is the town's most important monument. Look at the facade before you enter, which has a 7th–8th century stone pulpit and a 1326 portal with pointed arch, simple geometric patterns, and a lone stone sculpture that rests above the door.

If you prefer a base inland, about 24 kilometers from Pescara in Loreto Aprutino is **Castello Chioda** (Via degli Aquino 12, tel. 085/829-0690, www.castellochiolahotel.com, €135–180 d). This castle at the top of an ancient medieval borgo dates to at least 864. Now an elegant hotel, it has 30 rooms and two suites, a dining room, pool, and other amenities that might have appealed to Longobard lords.

Loreto Aprutino is also a good base to head north for a side trip to **Atri** to see Abruzzi's version of the Badlands. Either get a good map and take the winding interior roads to Atri or go to the coastal *autostrada* and follow SS16 west toward Atri. South of the town is **Riserva Naturale Guidata Calanchi di Atri** (tel. 085/878-0088), where badlands were created by soil erosion caused by meteor showers. The vaguely lunar barren landscape recalls the Badlands of the Dakotas. The cliffs and trenches have their own unique flora and fauna. Check with **WWF** (www.wwf.it) about night tours in the summer.

CHIETI

About half the size in population as Pescara, Chieti is the capital of its own province. Its center commands views of the Gran Sasso peaks to the north and the Maiella Mountains to the south.

Originally an ancient Marrucini capital, it became an important Roman town and there's an impressive theater, of which ruins are still visible.

Chieti suffered Barbarian invasions in 401 A.D. and was burned by the Franks in 801. The Aragonese rulers chose it as their regional capital and under Spanish domination (1504–1707) it was given an important role. Later it became part of the Kingdom of Napoli.

Sights

Chieti's busiest street is **Corso Marrucino,** which is lined with shops and cafes. The **Cathedral** is a few blocks off the Corso.

Chieti's historic early 19th-century theater, **Teatro Marrucino,** is on Largo G. Valignani.

Near Largo Trento down Via Zecca are the remains of the Roman Theater that was partially built into the hillside. Back toward the Corso, remains of Roman temples constructed during Emperor Nero's reign are on the other side of Via Spaventa.

Near the Villa Comunale garden is the **Museo Archeologico Nazionale d'Abruzzo** (Villa Comunale 2, tel. 0871/331-68, daily 9 A.M.–7:30 P.M.), which houses some of Abruzzo's most interesting artifacts. The bronze statue of Hercules found in Sulmona is here, as is a colossal sitting Hercules. The 6th-century B.C. statue of a Picene warrior from Capestrano is extremely rare. Important statues from Alba Fucens are prominently displayed. Other artifacts include ancient Italic, Etruscan, and Roman objects. The numismatic collection has 1,000 coins that range from the 4th century B.C. to the 19th century A.D.

Shopping

Goldsmith **Giuseppe Paludi** (Via Porta Pescara 4, tel. 0871/348-156) creates, repairs, and personalizes jewelry. His elegant disc-link bracelets and earrings in silver are reasonably priced.

Leonardo Casa del Cuoio (Via Arniense 46, tel. 320/945-0620) makes handcrafted leather belts, many for less than €25, as well as more elaborate items.

Accommodations and Food

A former 17th-century convent is the setting for **Venturini** (Via de Lollis 10, tel. 0871/330-663, Wed.–Mon.), which features traditional cuisine.

The **Grande Albergo Abruzzo** (Via A. Herio 20, tel.087/141-940, www.albergoabruzzo.it, €90–105 d) is an efficient hotel with quiet rooms and restaurant Akileas.

Around Chieti

Vasto is a popular working-class beach destination that offers the basics at reasonable prices. Everyone comes for its famous *brodetto* (the local fish stew). The recipe is quite different than that in Le Marche, with abundant use of bell peppers spiced with a bit of hot pepper.

A good place to sample the dish is at **Da Nicola Ristorante** (Via Barbaraossa 15, tel. 0873/602-27, Tues.–Sun. 1–3 P.M. and 8–11 P.M., €13 pasta, €13–24 *brodetto*), located in Vasto's historic center above the sea. The *brodetto* here is made with six or seven types of fish, bell pepper, tomato, and garlic. They also serve delicious seafood pasta. Reservations are advised.

Civitella Casanova is on every Italian gourmet's "in" list of towns. **⊂ Ristorante la Bandiera** (Contrada Pastini 4, tel. 085/845-219, www.labandiera.it, Thurs.–Tues., closed Sun. dinner and Wed. lunch, €8–12), in a cozy country house, has superb regional cooking well worth the 30-minute drive from Pescara toward the eastern perimeter of Parco Gran Sasso. Marcello prepares dishes with the bounty of the mountains. Begin with antipasto of *insalatina di gallina* (his special chicken salad) or *uovo croccante* (crunchy egg), or with a plate of mixed vegetables innovatively prepared. For pasta, try the wide *pappardelle* noodles with duck and scallions in a clear sauce or filet with tomatoes. Tasty main courses are *gallo nostrano* (leg of lamb) or lamb liver with *guanciale*. The country atmosphere is brightened by the painting collection. If you decide to linger, they have three rooms to rent (€90 d). From Pescara, take SS 81; from Chieti, drive on SS 602 west toward Gran Sasso.

LANCIANO

According to legend, Lanciano was founded in 1181 B.C. by Solimus, a refugee from Troy who arrived with Aeneas. Between the Maiella and the Adriatic Sea, in ancient times the town was settled by the Frentani, Italic people that eventually allied with Roma against the Samnites and then remained under Roman rule.

Sacked by Goths, destroyed by Lombards, conquered by Byzantines and later Franks, in 981 Lanciano became part of the Duchy of Benevento. In 1060, it became part of the Kingdom of Sicily.

By the 14th century, Lanciano was Abruzzo's largest town, flourishing with merchants and artisans in ceramics, silk, gold, wood, and iron. Under Spanish rule, interest shifted to the New World and Lanciano's fortunes declined. By the 17th century, it had become the possession of a baron.

Today it has a population of about 35,000 spread out between the lower modern section and the old center on four hills. Trade fairs are still important.

Sights

The heart of Lanciano is **Piazza Plebiscito,** where the **Cathedral of Santa Maria del Ponte** stands near the San Francesco bell tower decorated with Maiolica tiles.

The Romanesque church of **San Biagio** and its bell tower that dates to 1059 or earlier stands near the 11th-century **Porta San Biagio,** the last remaining ancient town gate.

Two imposing medieval towers, **Torri Montanara,** on Viale Spaventa are set into Aragonese walls and are the town's last remaining fortifications. **Santa Maria Maggiore,** built to recall the soaring French cathedrals, lies over the site of a temple to Apollo.

The Eucharist Miracle that occurred in San Francesco still attracts pilgrims to that church. In 1700, the host and wine turned to flesh and blood during Holy Communion, thus affirming the faith of a doubting monk. Relics of the chalice and host are on display.

Entertainment and Events

Religious events include the **Dead Christ Procession** on Good Friday. On September 8, **Il Dono alla Madonna del Ponte,** the procession of the Gift to the Madonna at the Bridge is held at the cathedral near a Roman bridge built on a precipice after a statue of the Madonna was found there. The statue is in a niche inside the cathedral.

A traditional procession is held on December 23 to exchange Christmas greetings.

Accommodations and Food

An in-town hotel with swimming pool, **Anxanum** (Via San Francesco d'Assisi, 8/10, tel. 087/271-5142, €90 d) has a bar but no restaurant (breakfast costs extra).

Traditional cuisine in a comfortable atmosphere is at **Corona di Ferro** (Corso Roma 28, tel. 0872/713-029, Tues.–Sat. 12:30–3 P.M. and 7:30–10:30 P.M., Sun. 12:30 P.M.–3 P.M., €8).

Getting There and Around

The A14 *autostrada* connects Lanciano with Pescara. For exploring the Maiella, Lanciano connects with Guardiagrele and other points.

Around Lanciano

Medieval castle **Castello di Sette** (Loc. Castello did Sette 2066030, tel. 087/257-8635, www.castellodisepte.it, €100 d), a few kilometers southeast of Lanciano in Mezzagrogna is now a national monument and a hotel. Also called Septa, the hotel offers plenty of conveniences, including a bar, restaurant, an outdoor pool, and a reading room.

In the beach town of Marina di San Vito Chietino, **(L'Angolino di Filippo** (Via Sangritana 1, tel. 0872/616-32, Tues.–Sun. noon–3 P.M. and 7–10:30 P.M., €9–15) offers some of the best fish and refined dining in Abruzzo. Try the raw tuna with pistachios, the fresh anchovies with balsamic vinegar, or an assortment of *antipasto crudo.* Or for cooked antipasto, try the bluefish poached with carrots and wild fennel, *seppia* (cuttlefish) in its own ink with potatoes, or *pescatrice* (an Adriatic fish). *Cocco rigatoni* with a mix of shrimp and crustaceans is also very good. As a main dish, the mixed seafood in tomato sauce is superb. For dessert you can go for decadent and creamy crepes with wild berries, or try the fresh lemon sorbet spiked with the potent herbal liqueur Centoerba. The place has the professional flair that comes with generations of experience. Fresh flowers are on the tables, jazz wafts through the air, and the whimsical lively art of Vittorio Bruni adds exuberance to the atmosphere. Bruni's mobiles, collages, and painting are formed from found objects along the beach. Some works are on permanent display, others are featured in biennial rotating exhibits. As for wine, who said that you have to drink white wine with fish? The owner drinks red Montepulciano. Sommelier Massimo will find just the right red, white, or bubbly.

If you want to precede dinner with a fishing excursion, outing in a boat, or scuba diving, **Progetto Mare** (Via Nazionale Adriatica 21, tel. 0872/618-665, www.progettomare.it) is in town right near the shore.

Insernia and Vicinity

Isernia is an easy entry point into Molise from Rome (174 km) via Frosinone, from Majella National Park in Abruzzo, or from Naples (110 km), Caserta, or Benevento in Campania. All have good roads with lovely views.

ISERNIA

Isernia stems from the word *"aeser,"* which signifies water and is an apt name. Tributaries from the **Volturno River** feed the land around town and the old **Roman aqueduct** still works. It's a long thin town located on the crest of a gentle hill overlooking two valleys. Maps may call the streams that run to the north and south Carpino and Sordo, but locals know them as **Gianocanense** and **Giovinale.**

For a period in the 18th century, Isernia was the most populated town in the region at a buzzing 5,000. A contingent of these natives managed to prevent French troops from marching on Naples in 1799, and 60 years later their descendents resisted the Piemontese drive to unify Italy. In 1805, there was a devastating earthquake that required many years to repair. Vatican aficionados may have heard of Pope Celestino V who was born here and is the natural patron saint.

Sights

Archeologists have dug inside the **Cattedrale** (Piazza Andrea d'Isernia, tel. 0865/3992, daily) and revealed the foundations of a temple dedicated to the goddesses Giove, Giunone and Minerva. It was built by Italics several centuries before the birth of Christ. Subsequent settlers recycled the ancient stones to build a church and pieces of the altar and columns are visible throughout the building. After the earthquake of 1805 and the collapse of the cu-

pola it was given the neoclassical treatment visible today. The interior is usually empty except during the Sunday service when locals dressed in black occupy the pews.

La Fraterna fountain dates from around the 12th century and was erected in honor of Celestino V, who founded the Frataria benevolent society. The fountain consists of six arches and columns, some of which may have been commandeered from Pontius Pilate's tomb. **Hermitage of Saints Cosma and Damiano** was built in the 16th century over the remains of a temple to Priapus, the overly endowed god of fertility—among other things.

Homo Aeserniensis, Europe's earliest man who dates back 700,000 years and was found in the nearby La Pineta area, is the most famous artifact in **Museo di Santa Maria delle Monache.** The former convent of Benedictine nuns hosts his remains in the **Museo Paleolitico** (Area di Scavo, La Pineta, tel. 0865/413-526). It's a modern, well-illuminated museum with wonderful displays of ancient Samnite and Roman relics from Aesernia, the precursor to Isernia.

Entertainment and Events

In June, Isernia hosts **Festa di Sant'Antonio,** dedicated to St. Anthony, and **Fiera di San Pietro delle Cipolle** (St. Peter of the Onion), a tradition mentioned in 13th-century documents.

Accommodations

Hotels in Isernia for the most part are modern, either because they rose up in parts of town that had been bombed in 1943 or because they serve the needs of business travelers, who generally seek modern conveniences over historic ambience. If you want a *residence d'epoca,* take your cue from Venus and head for nearby Venafro. If you ask residents there if their town name is a contraction of Venus and Aphrodite, they'll just give you a puzzled look or deny it. Nevertheless, you'll find a better love nest in Venafro than in Isernia.

Near Piazzeta del Cristo in Venafro's historic center is **Dimora del Prete** (Via Cristo 49, tel. 0865/900-159, www.dimoradelprete.it), which has guest rooms with frescoes and one with a fireplace. Signora del Prete's family makes their own olive oil and red wine and raises their own animals, so dinner here (€30) is a treat, but for guests only. The older part of the palazzo is from the 17th-century, but is built is over an ancient Roman road with medieval walls as the base.

A modern box design that won't win any architectural awards, **Grand Hotel Europa** (Via S.S 17, 140, tel. 0865/2126, www.grandhotel-europa.it, €110 d) is popular with business travelers. It has a pool open in the summer, Wi-Fi in the guest rooms, and a restaurant that's open seven days a week.

Food

Local foods to look for are *maccheroni all chitarra* (guitar string pasta), Carpino eels, Volturnian river trout, *crostata di gamberi* (Cavaliere crayfish pie), *abbuoto* (grapes), and *pezzata* (breed of cattle).

Part of a former 15th-century church near the Cattedrale is the setting for **Ristorante L'Affresco** (Corso Marcelli 233, 0865/413-836, Wed.–Mon. lunch and dinner, €12–25), with its 30 seats overlooked by frescoes of the Annunciation and St. Gregory. The specialties are pasta and grilled meat.

Take a cue from Bacchus and head for **Grapes** (Corso Marcelli 317, tel. 086/541-5648, Tues.–Sun. lunch and dinner). Ask about local wines from the major wine areas near Pozzilli, Monteroduni, and Pesche. Or let them steer you around Molise and the rest of Italy. For about €20 you can have a good glass of wine, a *primo* of pasta, and grilled meat.

The chef at **Mele Blu** (Via Leonardo da Vinci 10, Venafro, tel. 0865/904-337, Tues.–

Sun. dinner, Wed., Thurs., Sun. lunch) uses all local, traditional ingredients for new creations like black *riso venere* or couscous with duck.

Getting There and Around

Isernia is landlocked in the center of a succession of rolling hills. It can be reached by car, rail, or bus. From Campobasso, the journey is 30 minutes along the N647, which meets the N47 at Bojano, 29 kilometers south of town. From Rome, take the A1 south until Cassino and the N6/85 the rest of the way. Regional train number 2349 leaves from Roma Termini at 9:15 A.M. and arrives two hours later without need for a transfer at Caserta or Cassino. A second-class ticket costs a little over €10. The station is near the center of town and within walking distance of the historic center. To visit some of the ancient remains, a car is useful, but transport can be arranged through the tourist office in Via Farinacci 9 (tel. 086/539-92).

ALBANIAN AND CROATIAN VILLAGES

Present-day Italy copes with a large number of Albanian immigrants, mostly illegal, that arrive annually. There was a much earlier wave of immigration from Albania to Southern Italy in the late 1400s, with towns that developed, prospered, and have even maintained their 15th-century Albanian dialect in written and spoken form. Molise has five such towns that have bilingual street signs and active community efforts to perpetuate both Albanian and Molisan dialects. Likewise there are three towns with early Croatian roots. Periodic festivals celebrate their dual heritage with ethnic food, parades, and theatrical performances in medieval Albanian or Croatian. Pick up a map and visit them. Holidays like Christmas and Easter bring forth baked goods and other specialties.

VOLTURNO VALLEY

The Volturno Valley runs north–south along the western edge of Molise near the Lazio border. There are several minuscule medieval *borgos* perched on the hillsides that are still protected by ancient ramparts and impressive fortresses. It's a short drive from Isernia and the entire valley can be seen in a morning or afternoon.

Sights

At the northern tip of the valley is **Abbey San Vincenzo al Volturno** (tours Athena Org., tel. 0865/951-006). The abbey was founded in 703 by three noblemen from Benevento and is spectacularly positioned in a thick mountain forest. Inside the crypt there's a rare cycle of 9th-century frescoes. The abbot, Epifanio, a former director of the abbey, is depicted with a square halo that signifies he was still alive at the time the frescoes were painted.

As you travel along routes SS 158 and SS 85, you'll find the area dotted with castles and medieval *borghi* that make for pleasant diversions, as well as some offbeat detours.

The town of **Scapoli** is home to **Museo della Zampogna** (Piazza Martiri di Scapoli, tel. 0865/954-143, summer daily 10:30 A.M.–12:30 P.M. and 4:30–6:30 P.M., winter 10 A.M.–noon and 4–6 P.M., admission free) named for the traditional local bagpipe made of cherry or olive wood and goat leather, and displays bagpipes collected from around the world.

In case you are in the market to buy, the bagpipe makers are centered around the hamlet of **Fontecostanza** and produce about 100 per year.

At the southern tip of the valley in **Venafro, Castello Pandone** (tel. 0874/77-281) is best known for its horse-crazy Count Francesco Pandone, who bred and kept some 300 horses and had his favorites immortalized in life-size wall paintings in the castle. Venafro, as the name suggests, is home to the love goddess, Venus. She probably once adorned a patrician Roman villa and now rests in the town's archeological museum. Venafro also has an ancient Roman amphitheater.

Recreation

I Cavalieri del Tratturo (Corso da Foresta, tel. 0865/772-01, cavalierideltratturo@tin.it) organizes horseback rides along the ancient Transhumance.

Entertainment and Events

On the last Sunday of Carnevale, **L'Uomo Cervo** (the Deer Man ceremony) takes place. Locals wear antlers on their heads and perform ancient dances rooted in Apennine culture and pagan rituals.

Scalpoli hosts the **International Festival and Market of the Zampogna** in July, sure to produce a lot of wailing pipes. In November, Colli al Volturno presents the Upper Valley's biggest livestock festival.

Acquaviva di Isernia, on the road between Isernia and the Volturno Valley, in January hosts the **Festa del Fuoco,** a festival of fire. A gigantic bonfire of juniper branches burns through the night on the eve of the festival that honors its patron St. Anastasio.

Getting There and Around

A car or motorcycle is necessary for visiting the valley, which is often covered in snow during winter. The roads around Scapoli are particularly scenic and bicycles can be rented from many of *agriturismi*. From Isernia, it's a short drive on the N85 or the much narrower N627.

AGNONE

The tradition of working bronze goes back almost 3,000 years and they still produce church bells the old-fashioned way in Agnone. Hefty ringers are fired and cast in the **Marinelli Foundry** and are destined to mark the hours in church towers around the world. Plan to begin your walk through town just before noon and you'll hear the octaves of all 14 churches in marvelous harmony. All the bells were molded in the foundry operated by the same family for 700 years. As you stroll through town, some of the church facades have retained their medieval style, although the interiors were often altered to reflect Baroque taste of the 17th and

18th centuries. The bells in San Francesco, the church dedicated to St. Francis in 1343, reverberate every hour.

Sights

The oldest bell in **Museo Marinelli** (Via F. D'Onofrio 14, tel. 0865/78-235, www.campanemarinelli.com, Mon.–Sat. noon–4 P.M.) dates to the year 1000 and may have been cast here, although medieval documents that might have helped verify its origin were burned during the German occupation in World War II. In Rome, Marinelli gave the bells a new ring at Trinità dei Monti atop the Spanish Steps (2006), cast new bells for Richard Meier's Tor Tre Teste modern church (2002), replaced St. Paul's bombed bells, and in 2000 made a Jubilee Year bell for the Vatican garden. Marinelli bells ring in the Tower of Pisa, too. A bell recently dedicated in Monogah, West Virginia, commemorates the 100th anniversary of the tragic coalmine disaster of December 6, 1907, in which 87 miners from Molise died. Each bell has its own sound, which the company can tune according to size and dimension. Even so, the company has a full-time maestro whose job is to make sure that when the bell is cast, the proper note issues forth. The museum itself serves as archive and study area for the craft. Marinelli has reproduced a bronze Oscan tablet that dates to the 3rd century B.C.

The 12th-century church of St. Mark Evangelist on Via San Marco has Romanesque portal and a bell tower with one of Marinelli's bells.

Entertainment and Events

On Christmas night, *'ndocce,* fir-wood torch lights, are carried in a procession through Agnone's streets in **La 'ndocciata.** Other towns host bonfires during the winter season, a holdover from pagan rituals. Easter and Holy Week feature a living **Way of the Cross** procession.

Shopping

Most shops are along **Corso Vittorio Emanuele,** including two copper shops—although most objects are no longer produced by local coppersmiths. Some jewelry shops have designs made by the resident *orafo* (goldsmith). A small shop at **Museo Marinelli** offers reasonably priced bells and other bronze objects. Clothing, shoe, camera, cheese, and butcher shops line the street, as do banks, bookstores, and newsstands.

Accommodations

Despite the center's charm, town hotels lack pizzazz. However, the center does have some mini-apartments available. The countryside is so lovely that you may want to try an *agriturismo* outside of town.

Albergo Diffuso San Pietro (Viale Marconi 18, €70 d) are five mini-apartments in the historic center of Agnone furnished with some antiques.

The sterile utilitarian-kitsch decor of **Hotel Sammartino** (Largo Pietro Micca 44, tel. 0865/775-77, www.ristorantelabotte.net, €70 d) is significantly improved if you can get a room with a view (either 205's valley view or 208's cityscape) and it's very central.

Families enjoy **Staffoli Horses Azienda Agrituristica Selvaggi** (S.P. Montesangrina km. 1, Località Staffoli, tel. 0865/771-77, €37–52 pp) as do guests who like to ride horseback Western saddle, but gourmets should plan on some meals out.

Food

The literary set is drawn to **Bar Caffé Letterario** (Piazza Plebiscito 8, tel. 338/268-4626, dail, 7 A.M.–late), with outside tables across from a lovely fountain. The inside seating generally has Italian newspapers to read. They host occasional book launches and readings. This is the spot for cappuccino, herbal tea, wine, or cocktails.

Gelato is homemade at **Pasticceria 2000** (Corso V. Emanuele 199, tel. 0865/775-79) and the pistachio is particularly good. This is also a coffee bar and pastry shop.

A 10-minute drive to the town of **Carovilli** gets you to the area's best food at **Da Adriano** (Via Napoli, tel. 0865/838-688,

Wed.–Sun. lunch and dinner, Mon. lunch only, €25) where extrovert Adriano presides over the dining room. In the kitchen his lovely wife prepares excellent appetizers including lightly battered fried bread, vegetable variations with eggplant, zucchini, pumpkin, or whatever is in season. Pasta variations like cheese-filled crepes and fettuccine made with dried porcini mushrooms are her own creation. Grilled lamb chops are succulent. Her ricotta cheese pie with fig sauce is dreamy and light. If it's winter, do ask for truffles—the area is known for them. Ask Adriano for Molise's full-bodied red wine, Tintilia, made from local grapes and rarely found in wine shops outside the region.

Melt-in-your-mouth mozzarella, the best for miles, is made in Carovilli at **Caseificio S. Stefano** (Via Roma, tel. 0865/838-032).

Getting There and Around

Whether you come from the coast along the zigzagging N86 or from Campobasso and Isernia via the N651, the drive is lovely.

Bus connections to Agnone are good, with routes originating in Rome, Naples, Pescara, Campobasso, and smaller towns in the area.

There is no train service in the immediate vicinity.

PIETRABBONDANTE

Even on the hottest summer day, this magic spot almost 1,000 meters high has a constant breeze. **Teatro Sannito** is one of the highlights of a visit to Molise and one of Italy's most fascinating archeological sites.

The mountain above it and those nearby make for pleasant hikes with a few surprises, like a meadow atop **Mount Saraceno** that is used for impromptu soccer games. The flora includes a lovely blue flower that looks delicate but is tough and spiny to protect it from strong winds and temperature fluctuations.

In between the mountaintop and the Samnite theater, the small town of Pietrabbondante (abundant stone) is lively with children giggling, old men playing cards, and both sexes gossiping.

Sights
◖ TEATRO SANNITO

Even if you have seen a dozen ancient theaters in Greece and Italy, nothing quite prepares you for the remarkable ingenuity of Teatro Sannito set on a plateau above the Trigno Valley. Skilled warriors, the Samnites also had a strong aesthetic sense demonstrated through their architecture and artifacts. They deserve equal billing for their superb design, especially the ergonomic seats, each carved from a single block (look underneath, too), that were the Poltrona Frau of the 3rd century B.C. Be sure to sit down and enjoy the ideal slant of the seat backs, with a hump that perfectly supports the lower back. You'll forget that you're sitting on stone. The acoustics are superb, too. Stand in the stage area, face the audience with the mountain perfectly centered before you and perform your own sound test. Or better yet, catch a classical play during the July–August performance season. The spectators' vista beyond the stage is of distant mountains and forests. The two arches were rebuilt in 2002. The site also has other Samnite monuments including two temples, shops, and an arcade.

OTHER SIGHTS

A walk through the town of Pietrabbondate is a must. The main drag is Corso Sannitico, but the town is tiny so be sure to walk around it. Some medieval homes rest on bits of boulder. If you were to go inside, you would see the other side of that rock right in the living rooms, a "living rock" effect that pre-dates American architect Frank Lloyd Wright by several hundred years. Go to the church and walk up above it to the cross (wear good walking shoes as the stones are slippery) and you'll have a magnificent panorama of the surrounding forests and mountains. At the base of the town from the square with the bronze Samnite warrior statue, in the opposite direction you can drive or walk up the mountainside of Saraceno with its commanding view, lovely meadows, and woods.

Accommodations

Hotels are scarce in Pietrabbondante and the best bet if you decide to stay the night is an *agriturismo*. **Rural Arco** (tel. 0874/782-061, www.ruralarco.com, €80 d) near Zecca has reasonable rates and red, metal bunk beds reminiscent of childhood sleepover parties. Skiing, fishing, and horseback riding facilities are all 10 minutes away.

Food

Down the hill before you reach Teatro Sannito, gregarious Dino hosts and Angelo cooks at **La Taverna dei Sanniti** (Corso da S. Andrea, tel. 0865/769-007, tavernasanniti@tiscali.it, daily during summer 12:30–2:30 P.M. and 7:30–10 P.M., €15–25 meal, €4–8 pizzas). Locals come here in the evening for bargain (€3–6) pizzas from the wood-burning oven. At lunch or dinner, they serve excellent antipasto, pasta (try the *tacconelle del Sannio* with wine-marinated wild boar sauce or in winter with truffles or porcini mushrooms), and hearty meats. Dino

loves this territory and can help book a local guide to escort you to the Samnite ruins or into the mountains.

Bar Di Pinto (Corso Sannitico 13, Fri.–Wed. 6:30 A.M.–midnight) has an informal, cozy *Twin Peaks* sort of ambience. Drop in for coffee, an *aperitivo*, or the latest gossip. On nice days, old men play cards at the tables outside and won't mind if you watch.

Getting There and Around

To explore the area at leisure, car is the best way, as the town itself has no lodgings. It's 22 slow kilometers from Agnone over narrow roads that offer great views of the patchwork farmland. Without wheels you'll have to carefully plan how to depart and return on a town served by a single bus line. Pietrabbondante is easily covered on foot in less than 15 minutes and Mount Saraceno offers many hiking options on the edge of town.

Campobasso and Saepinum

CAMPOBASSO

Campobasso is the capital and largest city of Molise. The term "city" is nearly an overstatement, as there are barely 50,000 inhabitants and the pace of life is refreshingly slow. The center of the medieval town lies in the shadows of Castello Monforte. The honeycomb of steep, narrow streets keeps locals fit and helps build strong calves. The houses in these parts are all made out of stone and built around internal courtyards. Don't hesitate to take a peek and observe the family insignia carved into the arched doorways of the oldest residences.

The 18th-century building spree saw new neighborhoods erected according to urbanist principles of the time, which put a premium on nature. There are many green areas and streets lined with elegant cedar and gingko trees. The town is twinned with Ottawa, Canada, and the actor Sergio Castellito (*Don't Move*), was born here in 1953.

Sights

The aviation meteorological office, a World War I Memorial, and temporary exhibitions are located in **Castello Monforte** (Colina Monforte, tel. 0874/415-662, daily). Originally constructed as a Longobard fort, in Norman times it evolved into a castle, and was completely rebuilt in 1458 after the 1456 earthquake.

After the 1805 earthquake, the architect assigned to rebuild **Cattedrale Santa Maria Maggiore** (Viale della Rimembranza, 9 A.M.–noon and 4–6 P.M.) killed himself when his design error resulted in bad proportions in the 1812–1819 renovations. Eventually another architect finished the project in 1859.

The 12th-century church, **San Giorgio,** is dedicated to St. George, who miraculously saved the city from a dragon, and has a simple stone facade with three naves inside. **San Bartolomeo** was built around the same time and consecrated to St. Bartholomew, who was flayed alive. The

© JUDY EDELHOFF

an old watchtower in Campobasso

bell tower was reconstructed 70 years after the original was destroyed in the 1805 earthquake.

Open since 1881, **Museo Sannitico** (Via Chiarizia 12, tel. 0874/412265, Tues.–Sun. 9 A.M.–1 P.M. and 3–7 P.M., admission free) once had 2,000 objects in it. It's now down to 500, with the rest simply noted as "lost." The Samnite civilization is revealed through various facets. Female and male accessories feature bronze belts, helmets, and jewelry. Household utensils include vases, oil lamps, keys, knives, weights, and ceramics. Military gear and funerary objects cover later periods, too. Of particular interest is a tomb with a Longobard knight found buried with his horse at the Necropolis at Campochiaro. An amusing 2007 exhibit, *Eros: The 1,000 Faces of Love,* featured many objects from the permanent collection.

Shopping

Across from the Cattedrale, **Antica Cappelleria** features hats as well as nice scarves, men's shirts, and ties. The town has a long tradition of producing sharp objects and many shop windows are filled with scissor and knife displays. Local products are quite good and relatively cheap compared to other regions.

Entertainment and Events

On Corpus Christi Day, the **Procession of the Mysteries** (www.imisteri.it, May or June) features colorfully decorated carts that are rigged to give the illusion that children are miraculously suspended in mid-air.

Accommodations

Hotel San Giorgio (Via Insorti D'Ungheria, tel. 0874/493-620, www.hotelsangiorgio.org, €85–130 s/d) is in the historic center but if you want to stay outside of town and mix a morning in town with an afternoon in nature head to Giovanni Di Niro's *agriturismo* (Contrada Perito, tel. 0874/447-210, gdiniro@interfree. it, €30 pp) a short drive from Campobasso. The small farmhouse is located on six hectares of hillside within sight of town. It's a nice bike ride and the owner has a couple he rents out cheaply. He can also arrange guided tours or show you how he produces the salami, wine, and cheese produced off the land. Breakfast is €3 extra and half-board for €38 comes with hearty evening meals served in the ground-floor tavern. One whiff of the grilled meats will set your saliva on overdrive.

Food

Campobasso's best restaurant (and some say Molise's best) is (**Da Tonino** (Via Trentino Alto Adige 69, tel. 0874/487-500, Tues.–Sat. noon–3 P.M. and 7–11 P.M., €8–11), known region-wide for its meat dishes.

Plan your visit to Campobasso on a weekday or you'll miss out on Concetta's excellent cooking at (**Trattoria Zia Concetta la Grotta** (Via Larino 7, tel. 0874/311-378, 12:30–2:30 P.M. and 7:30–10 P.M., €15–25). Gracious son Fabio, who knows his wines, calls it home-style cooking, but that doesn't begin to describe how mamma gets those fresh flavors to pop. A delight for carnivores or vegetarians, try her stuffed peppers or eggplant lightly wrapped around smoked provolone. Pastas all

ABRUZZO AND MOLISE

are homemade. Ask for *spigatelli*, a wild green less bitter than chicory. Move on to lamb, sausage, or steak.

A historic bar ruined by 2007 renovation in laminate and metal, **Bar Lupacchioli** (Piazza G. Pepe 27, €3–5) is still popular with locals and a handy stopping point down the hill from the archeological museum, for a panini, coffee, or prosecco.

On the square near Via Romagnoli, **Caffè Brisotti** (Corso Vittorio Emanuele 35, tel. 0874/941-07, Mon.–Sat 6:30 A.M.–midnight) offers pastries, snacks, and light lunches. Local cheeses and *bufala* mozzarella can be purchased from the **De Nigris** shop on Via Elena 5. For wine visit **Enoteca Grassi** (Via IV Novembre 89), which carries regional and national bottles as well as locally distilled spirits.

Getting There and Around

From Isernia, drive south on the N17 until the second exit for the N647 (if you accidentally take the first you'll still make it to town). It's a two-hour journey east on the N647 towards the coast and Termoli.

Campobasso also has good bus and train service from Naples, Rome, Pescara, and many points within Molise. Taxi stands are at the train station (tel. 0874/311-587) or Piazza Prefettura. Newspapers publish daily bus and train schedules, *Nuovo Molise* being a better read than *Primo Piano*.

Around Campobasso

A lovely outing from Campobasso for lunch or dinner is a 20-minute drive to **Oratino**. The medieval town is constructed and paved with a light stone and is laid out in an unusual circular pattern. **Ristorante Olmicello** (Via Regina Margherita 48, tel. 0874/382-85, Wed.–Mon. 12:30–2:30 P.M., €15–25) is set in an ancient olive oil mill and offers fine dining. Try the excellent homemade pasta with fresh summer vegetables, hearty wild boar sauce, or many other variations. Ravioli is light and flavorful. Main course specialties are grilled meats.

Southeast of Campobasso in **Ferrazzano** are the remains of a medieval castle, but the town's latest claim to fame touted by locals is that Robert De Niro's ancestors emigrated from here.

Between Campobasso and Isernia, the town of **Frosolone** is the center of cutlers that make knives, scissors, and various blades. Most now are manufactured in factories but a few artisans remain. Frosolone is also home to **Museo Civico delle Forbici e dei Coltelli** (Civic Museum of Scissors and Knives; Frosolone, Via Sant'Antonion).

Tours to the nearby caves are offered by **Gruppo Frosolone Speleo** (tel. 0874/890-734).

◖ SAEPINUM

If you've ever imagined visiting Italy when cows and sheep grazed carefree throughout the Roman Forum and medieval houses were propped against Roman walls, this is your spot. Saepinum was built as a Roman *municipium* in the 1st century B.C. over the remains of a Samnite settlement that dated to the 4th century B.C. As you walk down the main Roman drags of ancient Saepinum, the Decumanus or Cardine, don't be surprised if a renegade calf comes charging out of nowhere, or a woman curses as she tosses hay to her animals with a pitchfork, or the smell of wild mint refreshes as you admire the ruins of the **Temple of Jove Maximus** or the **Basilica.** Come in late summer and you can pluck wild apples or pears from the trees for a snack and see grapes growing on the vines. Prepare your picnic basket en route and you have an idyllic setting worthy of *Tom Jones* or *Cavallieria Rusticana*.

The steadily depopulating town of Sepino lies three kilometers away and is a pleasant stop for lunch or a drink after a summer excursion around the ruins.

Sights

Allow an hour or two to wander through Saepinum's combined time warp of Roman ruins with rustic medieval houses that are still inhabited. Residents cling to old ways and cultivate terrain in small plots. As you leave the local highway, park by the tavern and enter the ancient gate, **Porta Tammaro.** (You can also enter by the three other original gates, Porta Bojano, Terravecchia, or Benevento.) You can see remains of thermal baths, the Forum with its Basilica built during Augustus' reign, the slaughterhouse, residences, fountains, and part of a recently uncovered theater, still surrounded by rustic dwellings of present-day farmers.

Accommodations

If you're more set on Breugel-does-Molise than on glamour where you can dine and sleep in that slightly ramshackle air of the ruins, try **Convivium** (Corsa da Altilia 3, tel. 0874/790-114, www.conviviummolise.it, €40 d, restaurant closed Mon., lunch and dinner by reservation). The grounds are a bit unkempt, rooms are spartan, and the most updated facilities are bikes and a soccer field. But at budget rates you have a friendly host and can play rustic to your heart's content at the edge of ancient Saepinum.

Food

Signora Cristina's simple **Trattoria** (Porta Tammaro, tel. 338/338-5482, lunch only,

€8–15) in Altilia is just to the left before you enter the Roman gate at Porta Tammaro. She specializes in pasta and grilled meats.

Rustics drop in on the opposite side of the site, **Taberna Pytissatoria** (Corso da Altilia 31 A, Thurs.–Tues. 8 A.M.–1 P.M. and 3–9 P.M., €8–12) for a coffee or a late afternoon drink. The only food is likely to be panini and it's closed at lunch.

Getting There and Around

The best way to explore ancient Altilia at your own pace is to arrive by car. As you drive on SS 17/87 near the 111-kilometer marker, watch carefully for the small yellow signs with black lettering that indicate a site of historic interest. If you are zipping along, it's easy to miss and you have little warning of its approach. The small dirt roads behind the site have little traffic and are ideal for bike riding. Despite cows and sheep that may run amok, don't ride your bike inside the historic site but park it outside one of the entrance gates.

Termoli and Vicinity

Molise didn't luck out when it came to kilometers of coast, but what it did get is very clean and sparsely populated. The 30 kilometers of road from the Abruzzo border to the coastal town of Termoli follows the shoreline and is quite scenic. During the summer, many locals park along the dunes and lay their towels on the sandy beaches. There are more organized bathing options south of Termoli in the little resort of **Lido di Campomarino,** where deck chairs and umbrellas can be rented and the main occupation is swimming in the Caribbean-caliber waters.

The Greeks founded Termoli on a small promontory overlooking the Adriatic but traces of prehistoric living have also been discovered in the area. A wall that runs to the edge of the sea and has protected inhabitants for centuries surrounds the historic center. It's where most of

the locals walk off their meals and gregarious old-timers nearly always occupy the benches along the ramparts. On a clear day, you can see the three small Tremiti islands northeast of town. There are frequent ferry departures for the archipelago from the port that is still very active with fishermen. Termoli is one of the rare Molisan towns that is steadily growing and the newer parts of town are located inland and along the southern coast.

SIGHTS AND EVENTS

Near **Castello Svevo,** the Swabian castle built by Frederick II, is the small port, where fishermen haul in their catch and several boats offer daily sea excursions to the **Tremiti Islands** (depart 9 A.M., return late afternoon, under €15). There's a lively fish market (Mon.–Sat.) in the mornings.

Along the coast, a short walk on the shore north of the castle, is a *trabucco,* one of the few remaining traditional spindly wooden wharfs from which nets are intricately rigged and cast directly from the dock for fishing. Almost extinct now on the Adriatic Coast, the *trabucco* catch is better in cool weather but year-round the fishermen haul in their catch straight from their nets at the end of the dock.

In August, Termoli celebrates its patron saint, Basso, with sea celebrations that include night fireworks as a reminder of the invasion by the Turks.

ACCOMMODATIONS

The nicest rooms at reasonable rates are just eight kilometers from Termoli's center in **Guiglionese.** On Route 483 between the 23- and 24-kilometer markers is **(Hotel Le Villette** (Corso da Malecoste 7, tel. 0875/680-655, www.ribomolise.it, €80 d). Opened in December 2006, the single-story motel rooms face east toward the sea in the distance below the hill. The easy style (good for guests with disabilities, too) has spacious rooms furnished with lovely bedspreads in Milanese fabrics, bleached oak furniture with a handy writing desk, wood-beam ceilings, and temperature climate-controls. The real draw is the cuisine in its two superb restaurants, **(Ristorante Ribo** and **Enoteca Terramia.** The new (2006) modern casual wine bar features meat, vegetarian dishes, and salami-cheese platters. Easy parking and access to local roads makes this a good base.

FOOD

Chef Bobo's seafood lunches and dinners at **(Ribo** (Corso da Malecoste 7, tel. 0875/680-655, €12 pasta, special *degustazione* menus €45 fish or €35 meat) are reason enough to make Termoli a destination or to come to Molise. Bobo makes the rounds every morning to pick out the best and freshest seafood, vegetables, and fruit. He makes everything—from his own superb breads and pasta to the des-

serts and *nocino* liqueur made from walnuts—while his wife Rita runs the place. Fish reigns and if you like it raw, this is the place; there are also many cooked variations in pasta and as main courses. Meat lovers can order good steaks, lamb, or pork. Attentive service and the nicely appointed dining room enhance the sublime food.

Enoteca Terramia (Corso da Malecoste 7, tel. 0875/680-655, www.ribomolise.it, dinner only, €15–25), which opened in 2006, is a modern, casual wine bar featuring meat and vegetarian dishes, salami and cheese platters, a fireplace, and a piano that is periodically played. Easy parking and access to local roads makes the restaurant's motel a good base.

GETTING THERE AND AROUND

Termoli has direct bus connections on **Cerella Bus** (tel. 0874/461-171) to Naples (3.5 hours) and Rome (3 hours, 20 minutes). **Sati Bus** (tel. 0874/605-220, www.soc-sati.com) connects Termoli to Pescara. Trains from Campobasso and Isernia stop near the center of town, which can also be reached on the N647. Drivers should look of the one of several lots located near the station indicated with a blue "P" sign. One hour of parking costs €1 and is free on Sundays.

AROUND TERMOLI

South of Termoli, **Campomarino** has beach clubs for passing a day at the beach. The town's best restaurant is **Nonna Rosa** (Via Biferno 41, tel. 0875/539-948), with fresh fish and seafood specialties.

The town of **Larino** has an ancient Roman amphitheater that dates to A.D. 80 that held some 10,000 spectators, about 20 percent of Rome's Colosseum. Above the train station, **Area Archeologica di Larino** (SS 87 near the 197-kilometer marker, tel. 0874/822-787, admission free) is open by request, generally 9 A.M.–1 P.M. There are also remains of Roman residences that date from the 3rd and 2nd centuries B.C.

NAPLES AND CAMPANIA

The energy of Naples is palpable, more like that of New York than any other Italian city. Its streets may be crisscrossed with clotheslines strung with laundry, but Naples is still a major metropolis and the largest city in Southern Italy. Summer heightens the theater of life here, when three million Neapolitans seem to simultaneously live outdoors.

Naples is wealthy in artistic creativity. Artisans and manufacturers have been major players on the world stage since the Etruscans. Even the black market economy, where those skills have periodically been employed in major counterfeiting operations, is an ancient tradition. Upon arrival by train, the city exudes a certain lawlessness. Modern Naples remains choked by political corruption and organized crime that deprive its citizens of basic services. Garbage can go uncollected for weeks, a scandal that repeatedly plagues the city in neighborhoods that are less dependent on tourism and leads to improvised bonfires. Despite these obstacles, artistic life flourishes, perhaps propelled by the same fatalistic energy that life next to an active volcano like Vesuvius generates.

The region of Campania possesses incredible variety. Getting out of Naples is easy and generally great fun. Emperors did it for centuries. Nearby Capua was home to the world's largest amphitheater until the Colosseum was built in Rome. Today trains, buses, and boats take you easily and efficiently to some of the world's most spectacular scenery. Hillsides have been blasted apart by volcanoes, still very active in the region. Caserta has its royal palace and

© ALESSIA RAMACCIA

HIGHLIGHTS

Museo Archeologico: The Museo Archeologico in Naples is one of the world's best archeological museums, featuring one of the most comprehensive collections of Greco-Roman artifacts in the world. Spend an afternoon exploring the vast collection of gems, mosaics, frescoes, and ancient Egyptian artifacts (page 607).

Mount Vesuvius: Vesuvius, a mountain within a mountain, has generated fear and awe since Naples was settled. The volcano's most famous eruption in A.D. 79 covered Pompeii and nearby towns with ashes and debris. Creator and destroyer, its fertile slopes are ideal for grapes and other crops. This ominous, ever-present phenomenon has left an imprint on inhabitants below, who live as if there's no tomorrow (page 626).

Pompeii: Pompeii, the site of the remains of a port city in ancient Rome, is one of Italy's most visited attractions. The site is vast, but make sure to save some time to view the beautiful frescoes in the Villa dei Misteri (page 627).

Benevento: Land of legends and ancient battles, Benevento is Campania's hidden gem. The breezy hill town has a magnificent triumphal Arch of Trajan, theaters in ruin, and seven modern ones. Its forests and mountainsides are stitched with vineyards, a reminder that this is the heart of Campania winemaking country (page 633).

Reggia di Caserta: Designed to match the glory of Versailles, Caserta's royal palace is a regal sight. Its lavishly decorated interior is fit for a king. The expanse of gardens enchants visitors with grand paths to the dramatic waterfall that cascades into pools and finely manicured grounds ruled by mythical gods and goddesses (page 635).

Grotta Azzurra: Although it seems to be illuminated by its own light source, the intensely bright Grotta Azzurra of Capri is a dazzling phenomenon of refracted light. The entrance to the cave is tricky, so part of the fun is flattening out on a rowboat in order to enter the grotto (page 645).

Ravello: Ravello's location on the Amalfi Coast provides both seclusion and spectacular views. The picturesque town has Moorish influences, charming cobblestone streets, and an exciting performing arts scene. The Ravello Festival, its summer music festival, is not to be missed if you're in town (page 652).

Paestum: The ancient Magna Grecia town of Paestum dedicated to Poseidon, god of the sea, is a reminder that some of the best Greek ruins are in Italy. Three temples impress with their size and near-perfect condition. They offer intimacy, too, with curious wall paintings that show divers in fine Olympic form (page 657).

LOOK FOR **(** TO FIND RECOMMENDED SIGHTS, ACTIVITIES, DINING, AND LODGING.

© ALESSIA RAMACCIA

Pompeii's forum

gardens designed to match Versailles in glory and size. Palace architect Vanvitelli took good note of the ancients. His soaring triple-tiered aqueduct still powers the Reggia gardens' gushing waterfall. It spans roads that lead to enchanting small towns, wineries, forests, and fresh mozzarella. Benevento, its dark green forested hills full of mysteries and legends, has Roman ruins that include Emperor Trajan's triumphal arch and ancient and contemporary theaters; after Naples, it is the region's most important center for contemporary art. The ruins of Pompeii open an eerie window on everyday Roman life more completely and dramatically than any other site in the world. Yet, it's only one of many archeological parks in Campania that reveal ancient temples, villas, mosaics, wall paintings, and other treasures. Recreation abounds for hiking, sailing, swimming, and just about any other sport. You may also find prices in most of Campania more reasonable than in wealthier regions to the north.

The islands and Campania's dramatic coast have attracted the rich and famous for centuries. Capri was Emperor Tiberius' island playground long before the Hollywood jet set, European intellectuals, and writers like Graham Greene arrived. Ischia and Procida have clung to their low-key island ways. Russian bal-

let legend Rudolph Nureyev, the dancer of the 20th century, managed to buy his own island here. Ravello was author Gore Vidal's beloved base for decades. The breathtaking views along the Amalfi Coast are famous.

A carefree and happy-go-lucky attitude reigns in Campania, so jump in and enjoy it. The right attitude allows you to escape intact and enjoy the mirth while you're here.

PLANNING YOUR TIME

The first thing to keep in mind is not to skip over Naples. Tour groups ignore it as they pile in to Pompeii, Capri, and the Amalfi Coast, preferring to avoid chaos. The city's treasures are rich and it makes an attractive base for exploring the famous islands nearby. Transportation is easy and a joy in itself to discover. Capri is a natural day-trip and even half a day will give you an idea of how idyllic life can be. If island prices are too steep, stay in Naples, where you can enjoy greater style and luxury for less money. Ferry across during the day and return to the city for some nightlife.

Caserta's palace could be toured in less than two hours, but why rush through its enchanting garden? Vesuvius is the site of a regional park and makes a good excursion for a half-day, where you can walk on the rim of the volcano's crater.

NAPLES AND CAMPANIA

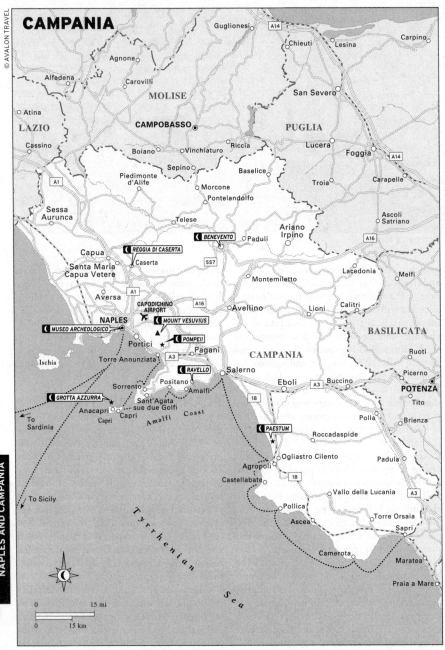

SPARTACUS

Spartacus launched the Gladiatorial War against Rome (73-71 B.C.) from Capua. A Thracian seized by the Romans and pressed into military service, he considered himself a slave of the Romans and deserted. Captured, he was sold into slavery and put into Capua's famous gladiator training school, populated by criminals and slaves. He broke out and escaped with dozens of gladiators to the slopes of Vesuvius. This was no rag-tag group. Spartacus set in motion a revolt that quickly recruited a mass of gladiators, slaves, and bandits that formed an army of 90,000 and for three years ruled most of Southern Italy. Spartacus cut a broad swath to the north, even threatening Rome itself. In the south, Crassus with his eight Legions was unable to defeat the charismatic leader and demanded that the Senate order Pompey to move in from Spain with his troops to help defeat Spartacus. Surrounded, Spartacus first killed his horse then declared, "There will be other Roman victors, but I will not flee in defeat." Downed by a wound to his leg, he continued to fight on his knees until dead and wounded bodies fell upon him. His own corpse was never found. On his way back to Spain, Pompey picked off survivors and chopped them to pieces but could not prevent Spartacus from being remembered as a competent and humane leader.

Spartacus is also the title of an early Stanley Kubrick film in which actor Kirk Douglas brilliantly played the title role. Khachaturian composed a symphony, to which a ballet was choreographed. It remains one of the Bolshoi Ballet's core works and features one of the most magnificently powerful male ensemble pieces of any ballet.

It's set in a park, which can provide days of hiking and the opportunity to spot rare species of flora and fauna. A tour of ancient Pompeii takes a minimum of two or three hours, but that only allows for a quick glance of many sights. Decide what activities and areas you would like to emphasize—whether art, nature, architecture, shopping, sports, or people-watching—but allow enough time to savor the experience once you're there. With a little extra time, you could take sailing, dance, or cooking classes.

HISTORY

Even before the Greeks arrived, Oscans, Samnites, and Etruscans were roaming the territory and setting up major trading centers. The Greeks founded **Neapolis** (New City), where the Siren Parthenope landed after she was rejected by Odysseus. Greeks first settled around Cumae, then Romans invaded and used its deep harbor for trading, military maneuvers, and as a playground of its rich and famous. The Byzantine era re-linked Naples with the East. Later Goths, Saracens, Longobards, and Normans swept through. In the 10th century, the Normans ruled. The French Angevins and Spanish Aragonese established dynasties that made Naples a major center of power and patron of the arts. Bourbon rule began in 1734 under Charles III. Some locals blame events soon after the unification of Italy in 1860 for Naples' demise. In 1861, King Vittorio Emanuele was installed and dealt a crippling blow to the city when the treasury was moved to Turin. Despite plagues, volcano eruptions, overpopulation, congestion, invasions, political corruption, and organized crime, Naples still moves at an energetic beat and creativity flows in abundance.

Naples

Travelers on the Grand Tour turned Naples into a must-see destination. During the 18th and 19th centuries it was more popular than Rome, Florence, and even Venice. The city was a magnet for the artistic, sophisticated, worldly, or just curious traveler. Naples still has more castles, museums, restaurants, churches, and shops than you can fit into a month. Once a recreation ground for emperors and headquarters for sovereigns, the original city by the bay has provided diversions to visitors for a few thousand years.

No city in Italy, or perhaps the world, is considered more musical than Naples, where song bursts forth now and then in the streets. San Carlo reigns supreme for opera. Naples' sunny disposition blends easily with its fatalistic, dark humor as revealed in its plays, dialect, and street scenarios. Shoppers will find streets that have plenty of pizzazz in window displays. Gourmets prize its cuisine, among Italy's best, down to its bargain street food. Wines come from vineyards in nearby hills, mountains, and volcanic slopes that result in flavors that range from subtle and light to elegant and spicy. A world-class transportation system moves about complex terrain with great efficiency. You can go from palace to volcano, from archeological museum to steaming *fumaroles* in minutes.

Even Italians sometimes give warnings about getting around in Naples. Generally, apply precautions that are relevant to any big city in the world. Be attentive of your purse and personal belongings. This is not the city to wear a Rolex, it's a city to dress casually, elegantly, or even eccentrically without wearing objects that scream "money." Arrive unfettered by luxuries that you have to mind. The fun of Naples is to plunge right in and enjoy its color and vibrancy.

SIGHTS

Since the city is built on different heights of the mountain, an ideal map of Naples would be in 3-D. Naples' tourist attractions are spread out, so the best way to approach the city is on foot, making use of its efficient public transportation system. Some sights like Castel Nuovo, Piazza Plebiscito, and the San Carlo Opera are near the Bay of Naples and the port, while others like Certosa di San Martino and Museo di Capodimonte are up on the steep mountainside.

Fortunately, you can hop the funicular to move yourself uphill and downhill quickly and to get a sense of how the neighborhoods are laid out. You can then take one of the buses that wind around the hills in the direction you need to go. The subway does not serve all sections of the city, but it covers a vast territory. Unless you are very comfortable with driving in Naples, leave the car in a locked garage.

The city is multi-layered in other ways too. It's built on Greek, Roman, and medieval foundations, so don't forget to take a tour of subterranean Naples.

Piazza del Plebiscito and Piazza Municipio

Piazza del Plebiscito, one of Europe's grand squares, is only a short distance from Naples' port at **Molo Beverello.** Its dignified expanse is embraced on one side by the 1817 church of San Francesco di Paola, whose proportions recall Rome's Pantheon. The Royal Palace on the opposite side dates from 1600. A pinkish-orange facade adds warmth to the square and accentuates its majestic proportions.

PALAZZO REALE

Palazzo Reale (Piazza del Plebiscito, tel. 081/741-0067, Thurs.–Tues., 9 A.M.–8 P.M.) features the **Royal Apartments** with opulent furnishings and the 1768 **Teatrino di Corte** court theater. Researchers often use the palace library, **Biblioteca Nazionale,** one of the most important in Italy with over two million books plus rare manuscripts. If the upstairs terrace is open, there's a sweeping view of the Bay of Naples.

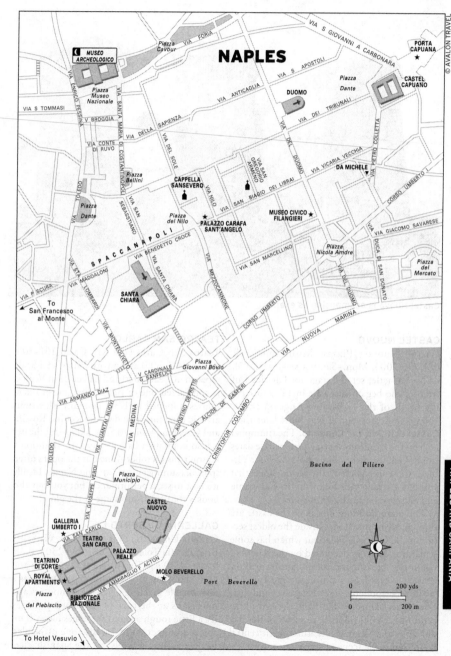

© AVALON TRAVEL

NAPLES AND CAMPANIA

© ALESSIA RAMACCIA

Castel Nuovo is as imposing as ever.

CASTEL NUOVO

Castel Nuovo (Piazza Municipio, tel. 081/795-2003, Mon.–Sat. 9 A.M.–7 P.M., €5), or New Castle, set the stage for Charles I of Anjou, who began the castle in 1279 to serve the needs of the expanding Angevin court. "New" indicates that it was built later than **Castel dell'Ovo** and **Capuano.** The triumphal arch on the facade in ivory-colored marble dates from 1443; the niches above hold the Four Virtues. Archangel Michael, the warrior angel that still has a strong cult following in Campania and Abruzzo, is on the tympanum.

The main building blocks of the castle are tufo, gray volcanic stone. Inside the oldest section is the Cappella Palatina, which has some remaining frescoes decorated by the school of Giotto. Its museum is especially strong in 19th-century Neapolitan paintings, a great way to see how Neapolitans view themselves and their city. Other paintings date from the 14th–19th centuries. Upper floors have views of the Bay of Naples and Vesuvius. Its atmospheric central courtyard is the scene of summer concerts.

TEATRO SAN CARLO

Teatro San Carlo (Via San Carlo 101–103, tel. 081/416-305) along with Milan's La Scala (opened 40 years later) and La Fenice in Venice, is considered one of Italy's three major opera houses. Opened in 1737, its many illustrious artistic directors included Gioacchino Rossini and Gaetano Donizetti. The 3,000-seat theater is also home to a ballet school. Its traditional season runs October–June but the opera often sponsors summer events around Naples. Ideally it's best to see a performance, but you can also book a tour to absorb some of the glory.

GALLERIA UMBERTO I

Galleria Umberto I (Via San Carlo, Via Santa Brigida, Via Toledo, tel. 081/797-2303, daily 9 A.M.–1:30 P.M. and 4–8 P.M.) is an iron and glass shopping arcade built in 1884. It was a fashionable meeting place for composers and musicians at the turn of the century. Today it's a little rough around the edges but still inspires architects. **Via Toledo,** one of Naples' longest streets, is named for the Spanish Vice-

CONTEMPORARY ARTS SCENE

In this city of super-charged energy above and below the earth's crust, Neapolitans are proud of their contemporary arts scene. After Turin, Naples has Italy's best gallery scene, which centers around Piazza dei Martiri in the elegant Chiaia district. Galleries pop up in other places, such as Pozzuoli. If you're not quite sure where to begin or if you want an overview to get in the right frame of mind, make your first stops in **MADRE** and **PAN** for an art sweep. At MADRE's already-made-it-big club, you can see major international artists. MADRE also is a good spot to have a coffee or creative light lunch. Stop by PAN to see what's been doing for the past half-century or so. Then go gallery hopping. Watch for openings, a great chance to see the elegant, stylish, creative, and eccentric side of Naples clustered together before they burst forth and explode back into the streets. Your hotel might have an interesting display, too. San Francesco al Monte, for example, has exhibited Robert Rauschenberg, while Costantinopoli 104 has nice contemporary art hanging in the salons and in some of the guest rooms. Even some of Naples' subway stops have been redesigned by modern architects. You can pick up a map and information at the tourist office.

- **Alfonso Artiaco** (Piazza dei Martiri 58, tel. 081/497-6072)

- **E-M Arts** (Via Calabritto 20, tel. 081/763-3737)

- **Galleria Fonti** (Via Chiaia 229, tel. 081/411-409)

- **Galleria Lia Rumma** (Via Vannella Gaetani 12, tel. 081/764-3619)

- **Galleria Raucci/Santamaria** (Corso Amedeo di Savoia 190, tel. 081/744-3645)

- **Mimmo Scognamiglio Arte Contemporanea** (Via Mariano d'Ayala 6, tel. 081/400-871)

- **Museo d'Arti Contemporanea Donna Regina Napoli or MADRE** (Via Settembrini 79, tel. 081/562-4561)

- **Palazzo delle Arte Napoli or PAN** (Via dei Mille 60, tel. 081/795-8605)

- **Studio Trisorio** (Riviera di Chiala 215, tel. 081/414-306)

- **T293** (Piazza Amendola 4, tel. 081/1972-8116)

roy Don Pedro de Toledo. It's lined with shops of all types. Look out for **Gay-Odin** chocolates and **Pinatauro's** pastry shop; both are Neapolitan traditions.

PALAZZO DELLE ARTI NAPOLI

Palazzo delle Arti Napoli (PAN, Via dei Mille 60, tel. 081/795-8600, Wed.–Mon. 9:30 A.M.–7:30 P.M.) is dedicated to contemporary art and the avant-garde. Don't be surprised if on your way here you see art restorers, furniture repairers, bookbinders, and papier-mâché sculptors restoring antiquities or continuing ancient traditions. A city teeming with experts sets a high bar for new arrivals. If you catch an opening, it's a great scene for mingling.

Spaccanapoli

Spaccanapoli, as the name suggests, slices Naples in two and has done so for thousands of years. Its origin dates from Greco-Roman times. What really holds the most fascination are the myriad of narrow side streets that feed into it, with entrances and exits from the hillside above and below. There are countless small shops to explore, many practicing trades that are extinct in other cities.

◖ MUSEO ARCHEOLOGICO

Museo Archeologico (Piazza Museo 19, tel. 081/440-166, Wed.–Mon. 9 A.M.–8 P.M., €6.50) is one of the world's best archeological museums. It's huge, so plan on at least two hours. If you have a passion for antiquities, allow half a day or more. The museum puts on first-rate temporary exhibits, too, dedicated to themes such as ancient food, villa restorations, jewelry, and the influence of Egyptian cults in ancient Rome. Its popular Gabinetti Segreti ("Secret Cabinets") are dedicated to erotica, of which the Greeks and Romans were masters; those rooms are so popular that separate tickets are required, so be sure to inquire at the ticket office upon arrival. A core of works was collected by Alessandro Farnese and brought from Rome to Naples, like the Farnese Bull sculptural group from the Baths of Caracalla. Most sculpture comes from excavations of Pompeii, Herculaneum, and elsewhere in Campania. The museum has a vast collection of gems, mosaics, frescoes, ancient Egyptian artifacts including mummies, and even a scale model of Pompeii. A visit here is a perfect complement to all of the archeological sites in Campania, as many of the most valuable works were removed here for safekeeping and display. The museum also has kid-friendly attractions: mummies. Walk like an Egyptian in the Decumano Maggiore near Piazza Museo and Piazza Cavour to the appropriate museum section, then move on from there if they're still enthused.

SANTA CHIARA

Santa Chiara (Via Benedetto Croce, tel. 081/552-6280, Mon.–Sat. 9:30 A.M.–6:30 P.M., Sun. 9:30 A.M.–2:30 P.M., €4) is named for Chiara or Clare, founder of the Poor Clares and the companion of St. Francis. Robert of Anjou began construction in 1310, not long after Clare's death. Royal Angevin tombs are located here. Ruins of Roman baths are near the outer courtyard, which can be seen at the church's **Museo dell'Opera.** The cloister's inner courtyard has a garden enclosed by octagonal pillars and benches that are colorful with 18th-century *majolica* tiles.

PALAZZO CARAFA SANT'ANGELO

Palazzo Carafa Sant'Angelo (Via San Biagio dei Librai 121, Tues.–Sat. 7 A.M.–1 P.M., 4–7 P.M.), is also known as the Palace of the Horse's Head for an ancient bronze sculpture of a horse's head that was a gift from Lorenzo de' Medici to Diomede Carafa in 1471. That housewarming gift now rests in the archeological museum, but the palace remains a fine example of Renaissance architecture in Naples.

MUSEO CIVICO FILANGIERI

Palazzo Como (Via Duomo 288, tel. 081/203-175, Tues.–Sat. 9:30 A.M.–2 P.M. and 3:30–7 P.M., Sun. 9:30 A.M.–1:30 P.M., €3), now Museo Civico Filangieri, was the Como family's residence built in the late 1400s. Converted to a monastery the following century and demolished 1879, it was rebuilt and houses Prince Gaetano Falangieri's art collection, which he donated to the city in 1888.

PIAZZA DEL MERCATO

Piazza del Mercato, the Market Square, could also be called Execution Square for all of the bloody events that have taken place here. A commercial center in the 13th century during the Angevins, in 1268 it also served as stage for the beheading the last Hohenstaufen king of Naples. It was the spot of the 1647 uprising against the Spanish, and the leaders of the short-lived Parthenopean Republic met their fates here in 1799.

CAPPELLA SANSEVERO

Cappella Sansevero (Via Francesco de Sanctis 19, tel. 081/551-8470, Mon.–Sat. 10 A.M.–6 P.M., Sun. 10 A.M.–1 P.M.) is the final magic act of alchemist, inventor, scientist, and Grand Lodge Master Prince Raimondo di Sangro. His two anatomical figures downstairs are of interest, but most visitors come to see the funerary sculpture. The marble sculpture of the *Veiled Christ* is so lifelike some Neapolitans suspected the alchemist prince used a real body to get the effect achieved by Neapolitan sculptor Giuseppe Sanmartino. Before you leave, be sure to look at the sculpture above the doorway: The subject is depicted climbing out of his coffin, evidently in haste to abandon his new lodging.

Via San Gregorio Armeno is named for the church erected here in the 8th century to St. Gregory. Its lavish Baroque interior includes frescoes by Luca Giordano. The entrance to **Napoli Sotterranea** is in the next block, where you can visit underground Naples and observe ruins that date back to Greek and Roman times.

Capodimonte

North of Spaccanapoli, the neighborhood of Capodimonte features the Museo Nazionale di Capodimonte that is to Naples what the Uffizi is to Florence, with masterpieces assembled by major collectors and benefactors of their day that expanded into world-class collections.

MUSEO NAZIONALE DI CAPODIMONTE

Museo Nazionale di Capodimonte (Via Miano 2, Porta Piccola, Via Capodimonte (Porta Grande), tel. 081/744-1307, Tues.– Sun. 9 A.M.–6 P.M., €7.50) is in a hilltop palace surrounded by a secluded park with expansive views. Its art treasures are first-rate and intelligently presented. Begin with a cappuccino at the bar in the courtyard. Upstairs the first room is dedicated to art collector Alessandro Farnese (he was catapulted to cardinal thanks to his sister Giulia being mistress of Pope Alexander VI). In his youth Farnese was painted by Raphael, in his twilight years by Titian; the entire room is a great study in power portraits of a single man. More of Titian's sensual art follows: *Portrait of Young Woman* (1576), perhaps a courtesan; and *Danae* with Jupiter who descends to her in a shower of gold. Luca Giordano's *Sleeping Venus* (1563) splendidly sleeps off her escapades: a satyr and cupid look on, her gold cup has tipped over with wine spilt on the floor. Move on to a bronze Cleopatra by Bandinelli (ca. 1420–1491). Guido Reni's *Atlanta e Ippomene* is an interesting departure from his many religious paintings, while Giovanni Lanfranco's *Assumption of Mary Magdalene* (c. 1605) is a subject rarely portrayed. Masters of the *chiaroscuro* technique, the dramatic use of light and shadow, are here including Caravaggio, Simon Vouet, Artemesia Gentileschi, and Jusepe de Ribera.

CATACOMBS OF SAN GENNARO

Catacombs of San Gennaro (Via Capodimonte 13, tel. 081/741-1071, Tues.–Sun., €5) began as a cemetery for the Christian community probably in the 2nd century and gained its fame after the body of martyr San Gennaro was buried here in the 5th century. The first morning tour begins at 9:30 A.M. and the final tour leaves at 11:45 A.M.

Tribunali and Capuana

One of the main streets in this neighborhood is Via dei Tribunali stretching from Castel Capuano on the east end to lively Piazza Bellini on the west end. Castel Capuana, which took its name from nearby Porta Capuana, was built in 1165 as the Norman castle of William I. Later enlarged by Frederick I of Swabia, Capuano remained the royal residence even after Castel Nuovo was constructed for Charles I of Anjou. In 1540, Don Pedro di Toledo ordered the palace to be transformed into law courts, a function that continues to this day.

The palace is usually called Tribunale, for the civil courts it houses, as well as for the Court of Appeals. For centuries the Tribunale has been the site of a great social scene. People of all classes met in court, spilling out into halls and stairways to watch the show of lawyers pleading cases and the court chambers full of law enforcement officers and the usual (and unusual) suspects. Many of the rooms are richly decorated with frescoes from the 16th century and later—some with religious subjects, others with allegorical stories of justice. Porta Capuana is one of the most beautiful gates of the Renaissance, with two cylindrical towers dating to 1484 representing honor and virtue.

CHIESA E QUADRERIA DEL PIO MONTE DELLA MISERICORDIA

Caravaggio was inspired by Neapolitan alleys for his use of space in his painting that hangs in Chiesa e Quadreria del Pio Monte della Misericordia (Via Tribunali 253, tel. 081/446-944, Thurs.–Mon. 9 A.M.–2:30 P.M., admission free). His masterpiece above the altar, *The Seven Acts of Mercy,* is an excellent opportunity to view the artist's work in the space for which it was commissioned.

DUOMO

Duomo (Via Duomo 147, tel. 081/449-097, Mon.–Sat. 8:30 A.M.–12:30 P.M. and 4:30–7 P.M., Sun. 8:30 A.M.–1 P.M. and 5–7 P.M., admission free), the cathedral built for Charles I of Anjou, has become most famous for the Miracle of the Blood. Neapolitans have gathered here since the late 1300s to watch the transformation of St. Gennaro's dried blood in vials that turn to liquid on the first Sunday in May and on September 19. If the blood does not liquefy, then disaster is imminent. The cathedral has an archeological area and the **Museo del Tesoro di San Gennaro** (Tues.–Sun., 9:30 A.M.–5 P.M., €5.50) with a gold bust of the saint.

MUSEO DI ARTE CONTEMPORANEA

Immersed in antiquities, visitors are sometimes surprised to see how vibrant and important the contemporary art scene is in Naples. Neapolitans are justly proud of it. A solid business in painting, sculpture, and other media makes Naples far more stimulating to gallery hop than Rome and is very different than the Milan scene. If you're not in the market as a buyer, there are major exhibits at Museo di Arte Contemporanea.

Museo di Arte Contemporanea (MADRE, Via Luigi Settembrini 79, Palazzo Donnaregina, tel. 081/1931-3016, Wed.–Mon. 10 A.M.–9 P.M., Sat. and Sun. open until midnight) features contemporary international and Italian artists in its permanent collection and temporary exhibits. In 2007, a new wing greatly expanded display space and a chic restaurant was opened.

PORTA CAPUANA

Porta Capuana is the gate redesigned in the 15th century with two towers, Honor and Virtue, a reference to the Tribunale or law courts that still operate in the Castel Capuano. Don Pedro de Toledo in 1540 converted the former royal residence to law courts, a function that remains today. The frescoed Court of Appeals is on the first floor.

SAN GIOVANNI A CARBONARA

San Giovanni a Carbonara (Via San Giovanni a Carbonara 5, tel. 081/295-873, Mon.–Sat. 9:30 A.M.–1 P.M., admission free) was founded in 1343 by Augustinian monks. It has the tombs of King Ladislas, his sister Joan II who succeeded him, and her lover Ser Gianni Caracciolo. The Caracciolo di Vico chapel dates from 1517 and is based on a design by Bramante, one of the architects of St. Peter's Basilica in Rome.

Greater Naples

Città della Scienza (Via Coroglio 104, tel. 081/735-260, Tues.–Fri. 9 A.M.–5 P.M., Sat.–Sun. 6:30–10 P.M. summer hours) is in a former industrial complex on the outskirts in the Bagnoli area (Bus C9 or C10). The first section is dedicated to everyday phenomena and great scientific discoveries, while the second for children has many hands-on exhibits.

Castel Sant'Elmo (Largo San Martino, tel. 081/578-4030, Thurs.–Tues. 8:30 A.M.–7 P.M. summer hours, €7) offers a castle to explore, occasional temporary exhibits, and a great view of Naples and the Bay from its position on the Vomero.

ENTERTAINMENT AND EVENTS

Entertainment has been going strong in the Naples since Emperor Nero performed his song and dance numbers. Some seats at the San Carlo Opera House may come with a steep price tag, but music permeates down every street. A fruit vendor or butcher could easily bust out with an aria. The performing arts are for everyone and participation is encouraged. Opera is still king and Naples' San Carlo theater competes with Milan and Venice for prestige and quality. The live arts are especially strong. Cities in other countries may have converted their stages to multiplex cinemas, but in Naples, the trend is the reverse. You'll find everything from ancient classics to plays in Neapolitan dialect and classical music in its many forms, from orchestra to chamber or solo recital. The lounge and jazz scene are ever present. And scattered stalwart groups vigilantly preserve traditional folk music, from Neapolitan songs to peasant ditties and shepherds' instrumental music from the hills who play their *tamburi*.

If your nightlife plans include street action, Naples is your place. *La Movida* (the movement) gets underway before the sun has set. Neapolitans use the term to describe their routine procession through favored neighborhoods: a drink here, finger food there, a chat in this piazza, a pose by a wall or perhaps gossip in a bar that by day doubles as a health spa or accessories store.

Festivals have their own themes, but most have religious origins linked to the Catholic church in celebration of some saint. Look closely at the Greek or Roman pagan calendar, though, and it's easy to see how many saints substitute for pagan rituals that had been celebrated for centuries. Others festivals are quite new, like film festivals in Capri. Don't overlook the possibility to see a performance on a hilltop above the sea or set in an ancient amphitheater, an event that is as memorable for the backdrop as for the performance.

Nightlife

Centers of nocturnal movement tend to be Via Giotto, Ruoppolo, Chiaia, and Piccinni in the Vomero. Lively piazze are centers of action, too, like Martiri or Dante. If you're nostalgic for the intellectual cafe scene, head for Piazza Bellini or **Intra Moenia** with its soundtrack of fusion and jazz. **Rising South** (Via San Sebastiano 19, tel. 339/794-6828) plays jazz and lounge music, live or recorded. Dancers head for **Chez Moi** (Via del Parco Margherita 13, tel. 081/407-526, Thurs.–Sun. 10 P.M.–4 A.M.) or **Keste** (Largo San Giovanni, tel. 081/526-2821, Mon.–Tues. 7:30 A.M.–8 P.M., Wed.–Fri. 7:30 A.M.–2:30 A.M., Sat.–Sun. 9 P.M.–2:30 A.M.). Jazz venues include historic **Otto Jazz Club** (Salita Cariati 23, tel. 333/918-4767). Try also **Notting Hill** (Piazza

Dante 88), **Queen Victoria** (Via Fornari Vito 15, tel. 081/422-334), **Ajahii** (Discesa Coroglio, tel. 081/617-1157), and **Around Midnight** (Via Bonito 32/a). Via Chiaia shopping district becomes as an upscale cocktail circuit. **Culti** (Via Carlo Poerio 47, tel. 081/764-4619) is a day spa that does double duty for drinks at night. **Kaligola** (Via Cappella Vecchia, tel. 081/658-2796) specializes in coral adornments, then morphs into a lounge. **Piazza Santa Maria la Nova** is a magnet for the young beer set. Contemporary art culture vultures can check MADRE (Museo D'Arte Contemporanea Donnaregina) and PAN (Palazzo delle Arti di Napoli) or adjacent spots for happenings. The public can be capricious: Expect the epicenter of cool to change or disappear at a whim and likewise for telephone listings.

Performing Arts

Naples was the Las Vegas of the ancient world. Even Emperor Nero entertained the public here with song and dance, although critics and judges rarely found flaws with his performances. The sophisticated audience in Naples expects the best and they get it. San Carlo is one of the world's best opera houses. As for the visual arts, one need only breeze through the Archeological Museum to see how skilled painters, sculptors, goldsmiths, potters, and glassblowers were in ancient times. Even earlier, the Etruscans had a major trade center in Greek objects, and there was big money to be made in copies, or even fakes. A solid tradition like that sets high standards and even two millennia later Naples maintains them in all categories.

Music still seems to be in the collective DNA, where arias might be sung on the street or a jilted crooner laments on the funicular. Take a walk on **Via Costatinopoli** and you'll see instrument makers and repairers; as a musician tries out an instrument in a music shop, others may join and form an impromptu duet or combo.

Theater seems more popular than cinema. In recent decades, even movie theaters were converted to stage use, a decidedly more interactive experience. They feature everything from experimental to various traditional forms, often in Neapolitan dialect. Even if you don't understand the language, on or off stage the whole scene will be interesting. Sophistication carries over to attire, so do dress up if you don't want to look like the reincarnation of a barbarian invader amidst this glamour.

Teatro San Carlo (Via San Carlo 101/3, tel. 081/416-305) is Naples' crowning glory for the performing arts. Its season begins in October and concludes in June, although the company sponsors outdoor performances around Naples in the summer. Most famous for opera, 3,000-seat San Carlo also offers classical music and ballet.

The instrument most associated with Naples perhaps is the mandolin. **Mandolin Ensemble** (www.mandolinensemble.it), formed in 1988 by Associazione Mandolinista Napoletana, preserves traditional Neapolitan music.

On stage, Naples often is featured in plays and musicals. *Scugnizzi* (Street Urchins) is an energetic, popular musical about the legendary Neapolitan street youth. **Mercadante** (Piazza Municipio 64, tel. 081/551-3396, www.teatrostabilenapoli.it) is beautiful and home of **Teatro Stabile di Napoli;** in 2006, an English-language production with John Turturro was performed and there are other occasional performances in English.

Teatro Trianon is the theater of Neapolitan Song. Neapolitan musicals are staged at the **Bellini** (Via Conte di Ruvo 14, tel. 081/549-9688, www.teatrobellini.it) and at the **Diana** (Via Luca Giordano 64–72, tel. 081/556-7527), while traveling musicals are usually at **Augusteo** (Via Toledo 262, Piazzetta Duca d'Aosta, tel. 081/414-243). **Sancarluccio** (Via San Pasquale a Chiaia 49, tel. 081/405-000) sometimes has English-language productions. **Totò** (Via Cavara Frediano 12, tel. 081/296-051, www.teatrototo.it) has variety shows. Fringe and experimental theater are at **Galleria Toledo** (Via Concezione A. Montecalvario 34, tel. 081/425-037, www.galleriatoledo.org) and at **Nuovo Teatro Nuovo** (Via Montecalvario 16, tel. 081/406-062, www.nuovoteatronuovo.it).

Chamber music is performed in the **Diana,** the **Bellini,** and citywide at churches, schools, museums, castles, and historic sites. **Teatro Palapartenope** (Via Barbagallo,115/Fuorigrotta, tel. 081/570-008) hosts rock concerts and other large-scale productions.

Good spots for performance information and ticket purchases are the **Box Office** (Galleria Umberto I, tel. 081/551-9188, www.boxofficenapoli.it) and **Concerteria** (Via M Schipa 23, tel. 081/761-1221).

Cinema

Plaza Multisala (Via Kerbaker 85, tel. 081/556-3555), **Institut Français de Naples Le Grenoble** (Via F. Crispi 86, tel. 081/669-665), **Modernissimo** (Via Cisterna dell'Olio 23, tel. 081/580-0254), **Warner Village Metropolitan** (Via Chiaia 149, tel. 081/4290-8225), and **Filangieri Multisala** (Via Filangieri 43, tel. 081/251-2408) all have occasional or regular screenings of English-language films. **Teatro Augusteo** has hosted a festival of films about contemporary art in original languages. Some cinemas have half-price films on Wednesdays. Summertime screenings outdoors in historic sites, squares, and parks are likely to be in Italian. Drive-ins offer a bit of retro entertainment outside in Pozzuoli, Caserta, and other spots.

Festivals and Events

Naples has many festivals dedicated to the arts. Themes like food or wine are also popular. But daily newspaper listings show that the majority of celebrations in Naples and outlying towns are religious. Major and minor saints are celebrated 365 days a year, not just Naples' patron saint, Gennaro. The Catholic Church established such measures in part to replace extremely popular pagan festivals related to other deities, and coincided with events like the harvest or solstice.

Like the rest of Italy, religious celebrations tend to have strong food and even wine components, when solemnity yields to festivity. Naples is a major center for the manufacturing of fireworks, so even small towns are likely to cap off the day's procession and events with an evening display.

Vitigno Italia is an annual exposition in May dedicated to promoting and tasting autochthonous or single-varietal wines, each made exclusively from one variety of grape rather than blends. Most wines come from Campania, but other Italian wines are represented.

Mostra di Arte Presepiale is an exhibit of various nativity scenes. Via San Gregorio Armeno is the most important area for purchasing complete nativity scenes or individual figures. **Certosa di San Martino** (Largo San Martino 5, tel. 081/578-1769, Thurs.–Tues. 8:30 A.M.–7:30 P.M.) stocks shelves full. St. Martin's Charterhouse in the Vomero neighborhood has a permanent collection of nativity scenes in the museum, some created by famous Neapolitan artists. Action picks up in November and continues through mid-January, but shops and museums have displays year-round.

San Gennaro, patron saint of Naples, has two major celebrations for the Miracle of the Blood: the first Sunday in May and on September 19.

The Dark Madonna is celebrated for saving the bell tower of **Santa Maria del Carmine.** Her Feast Day is July 16 in Piazza Mercato. The evening culminates in fireworks and the ritual "burning" of the tower that she saved from fire.

Santa Maria di Piedigrotta (Piazza Piedigrotta 24) feast day is observed in a procession on September 7, but celebrations are held the first half of September by this church that once faced a cave *(grotta).*

Culture until dawn is **La Notte Bianca** (The White Night), generally an October weekend (Rome's is in September). Museums and galleries are open with special events and concerts throughout the city.

Rare openings to archaeological sites and cultural institutions in Naples and throughout Campania take place during **Settimana della Cultura.** May visits are accompanied by special programs.

SPORTS AND RECREATION

Some 200 rides and attractions including Disney sets are at the **Edenlandia** (Viale J. F. Kennedy, tel. 081/239-4090) amusement park. **Bowling Oltremare** (Viale J. F. Kennedy, tel. 081/624-444) has ping-pong, soccer, bowling, and other games.

Soccer fans head for **Stadio San Paolo** (Via Claudio, tel. 081/239-5623), which packs in Neapolitans for games. The team returned to the first division recently and always gets animated against Rome or Milan. Ticket purchases require a passport or other identification as each spectator has an assigned seat by name.

Cave explorers can begin in **Pertosa** (tel. 0975/397-037 cave visits, or 0975/392-232-98 tourist information, www.grottedellangelo.sa.it, Mar.–Oct. 9 A.M.–7 P.M., Nov.–Feb. 9 A.M.–4 P.M., €10) at the **Museo di Speleologia,** then go explore caves in the **Grotte dell'Angelo** (Angel Caves, www.grottedellangelo.sa.it, Mar.–Oct. 9 A.M.–7 P.M., Nov.–Feb. 9 A.M.–4 P.M., €10), an easy guided trek suitable for amateurs. The caves are located near the Tanagro River east of Monti Alburni near the Vallo di Diano. From Salerno, take Autostrada A3 toward Reggio, exit Petina, then follow SS19 in the direction of Grotte dell'Angelo–Pertosa.

Cratere degli Astroni nature reserve on Vesuvius crater (Agnano exit on the *tangenziale* bypass road) is run by Naples WWF. Paths through the woods lead to stretches of water inhabited by herons and other birds. **Guide Alpine della Campania** offers tours in the park of Vesuvius. **Ente Parco del Vesuvio** (San Sebastiano al Vesuvio, Piazza Municipio 8, tel. 081/771-0911, www.parconazionaledelvesuvio.it) has information on various routes to Mount Vesuvius. The **Istituto Nazionale di Geofisica e Vulcanologia** (Via Diocleziano 328, tel. 081/610-8483, www.ingv.it) allows visitors to its center for geophysics and vulcanology by appointment only.

SHOPPING

Naples is a gold mine for crafts, which can be quite pricey when finely made. Look for papiermâché masks that have design origins back to the Renaissance and terra-cotta or wood figurines for nativity scenes, as well as musical instruments and custom-bound books. Antique restorers do a brisk business for the many dealers running small furniture shops. Food and wine are in no short supply, so look for local specialties like Taurasi, Aglianico, Lacrima di Cristi, and numerous other varietals. Local liqueurs made from walnuts, hazelnuts, and lemon work their way into the city from the hills and the coast. Coral is incorporated into all kinds of designs, from jewelry to small figurines. Ceramics can be quite nice, either particular designs specific to various towns, imitation antiques, or very contemporary. Simple housewares from an *alimentari* or other small shops might have just the cheese grater or espresso pot that you need. Hardware stores can turn up any variety of gadgets. Counterfeit kings are in their domain here, but beware that you can be fined if caught after you purchase knockoffs. For centuries, Naples has also been famous for its tailors. Until recent years, every Italian male had at least three suits in his life— for his confirmation, wedding, and funeral. Shirts made to order are still the norm.

Shops are generally open 9 A.M.–1 P.M. and 4–7 P.M., however some stores are closed Monday morning and Saturday afternoon.

Crafts

Ailing marionettes, porcelain dolls, nativity figures, and others are cured at **Ospedale delle Bambole** (Via San Biagio dei Librai 81, tel. 081/203-067), the doll hospital.

A hand-bound diary, custom album for photos, or handmade paper may be just the gift to pick up at **Gli Artigiani del Libro** (Calata Trinità Maggiore 4, tel. 081/551-1280). If a change of identity would be handy, try a Neapolitan mask at **Nel Regno di Pulcinella** (Via San Domenico Maggiore 9, tel. 081/551-4171).

Take a stroll on **Via San Gregoria Armeno** to see which artisan's nativity scenes most suit your style and budget. **Ulderico Pinfildi** and **Giuseppe Ferrigno** are popular. Check also the younger craftsmen who have branched out into *commedia dell'arte* and other non-religious figures. You could also bring your own design

and commission a papier-mâché sculpture they'll ship home to you.

Jewelry

If you want to pop the question in Italy or need a significant bauble to present, Italian-designed gold and dazzling gems are available at **Bulgari** (Via Filangieri 41, tel. 081/400-856) and **Damiani** (Via Calabritto 5, tel. 081/764-0734).

Art

Neapolitans are proud of their contemporary arts scene. After Turin, it's Italy's best. The scene centers around Piazza dei Martiri in the elegant Chiaia district and pops up in other places like Pozzuoli. If you're not quite sure where to begin or want an overview to get in the right frame of mind, drop into **MADRE** (Via Settembrini 79, tel. 081/562-4561) and **PAN** (Via dei Mille 60, tel. 081/795-8605) first for a sweep. At MADRE's already-made-it-big club, you can have a coffee or creative light lunch. Stop by PAN for a look at local artists from the past half-century. Then go gallery-hopping. Watch for openings, a great chance to see the elegant, stylish, creative, and eccentric side of Naples clustered together before they burst forth and explode back into the streets. Your hotel might have an interesting display, too. San Francesco al Monte had a Robert Rauschenberg in its exhibit space and Costantinopoli 104 has nice contemporary art hanging in the salons and in some of the guest rooms.

Gallery Navarra (Piazza dei Martiri 23, tel. 081/764-3595), **Lia Rumma** (Via V. Gaetani 12, tel. 081/764-3619), **E-M Arts** (Via Calabritto 20, tel. 081/763-3737), and **Studio Trisorio** (Riviera di Chiaia 215, tel. 081/414-306) are all worth checking.

Department Stores

Don't expect Italian department stores to have the variety and pizzazz of merchandise at Harrod's or Bloomingdales. Italian chains that have branches in Naples are **Coin** (Via Scarlatti 86/100, tel. 081/578-0111, Mon.–Fri. 10 A.M.–8 P.M., Sat.–Sun. 10 A.M.–8:30 P.M.),

La Rinascente (Via Toledo 343, tel. 081/411-5111, Mon.–Sat. 10 A.M.–8 P.M., Sun. 10 A.M.–2 P.M. and 5–8 P.M.), and **Upim** (Via A. Doria 40 and Via dei Mille 59, tel. 081/239-6360). Housewares or home furnishings sometimes are more interesting than fashions; clothing tends more toward mainstream or utilitarian rather than chic. If you have the patience, though, sometimes there are real finds hidden amidst middle-of-the-road style.

Designer Stores
Via Calabritto is the street to hit for **Prada** (Via Calabritto 9, tel. 08/764-1323) or **Valentino** (Via Calabritto 9/10, tel. 081/764-4262). **Emporio Armani** holds court at Piazza dei Martiri (tel. 081/406-363). Naughty **Versace** types head for the shop at Via Toledo 157 (tel. 081/551-0647). If you are on a tight budget but must have a designer gift or memento, Italian sunglasses are always the essence of cool. If you don't find your style at the designer's store, pop into an *ottica* (eyewear shop); usually there is a good designer section and you might find just the look. (This is also the spot to repair or replace glasses or contacts should the need arise.)

Markets
Market mavens can go antiquing for any size object on the last two weekends of each month at the antique fair, **Fiera Antiquaria Napoletana** (Villa Comunale, 8 A.M.–3 P.M.).

The market to root through for vintage and second-hand clothes is **Mercato del Ponte di Casanova** (Porta Capuana, Mon.–Sat. 8 A.M.–dusk). **Mercatino di Antignano** (Piazza degli Artisti, Mon.–Sat. 8 A.M.–1 P.M.) has textiles, clothes, and housewares.

ACCOMMODATIONS
Naples has excellent value accommodations. Some, like **Vesuvio,** have always been priced in the stratosphere. A number of accommodations are set in monasteries or villas that have been converted into lovely oases from the chaos. If you are noise-sensitive, factor that in and request a quiet room when you book, or at least one that doesn't face the street. Most hotels are well connected with public transportation. If you enter the city by train or plane, remember that base fares have been set for taxis between the airport and train station, so you need not worry about being overcharged.

Piazza del Plebiscito and Piazza Municipio
UNDER €100
Albergo Pinto-Storey (Via G. Martucci 72, tel. 081/681-260, www.pintostorey.it, €75€115 s/d) is in a Liberty villa and is well connected to public transportation.

Concordia B&B (Piazzetta Concordia 5, tel. 081/412-349, www.laconcordia.it, €80 d) is a small bed-and-breakfast with several large rooms and an owner who gives Neopolitans a good name. From Piazza del Plebiscito, take the funicular to Corso Vittorio Emanuele and your homey stay is a five-minute walk.

€100-200
Chiaja Hotel de Charme (Via Chiaia 216, tel. 081/195-73004, www.hotelchiaia.it, €115 d) near Piazza Plebiscito is on one of Naples most fashionable shopping streets. Rooms are furnished with antiques and half have whirlpool baths.

Steps from Piazza Plebiscito, **MH Design Hotel** (Via Chiaia 245, tel. 081/1957-1576, €120–180 d) is in a tranquil traffic-free area. Breakfast is served on a covered terrace and rooms emphasize modern design primarily in neutral tones.

A boutique hotel, **Micalo** (Riviera di Chiaia 88, tel. 081/761-7131, www.micalo.it, €150 d) is convenient to galleries and shopping. The Art bar on the ground floor serves cocktails until midnight and the front desk is open 24 hours.

◖ Hotel Vesuvio (Via Partenope 45, tel. 081/764-0044, www.vesuvio.it, €180 d) near the edge of Naples Bay remains the choice of visiting royalty and heads of state for its attentive service and elegantly furnished rooms (with terraces or balconies in many). There's also a spa and a rooftop restaurant.

€200-300

Set between the San Carlo Theater and Castel dell'Ovo, **Hotel Miramare** (Via N. Sauro 24, tel. 081/764-7589, €250 d) is a small hotel with a spectacular view from the terrace of Vesuvius and the Sorrento Coast. Breakfast is served outdoors in nice weather and there are two restaurants nearby that play live music.

Spaccanapoli

€100-200

Up the hill near the Botanical Gardens, **Hotel del Real Orto Botanico** (Via Foria 192, tel. 081/442-1528, €110–162 d), is away from the hubbub of the center with a view of Santa Maria degli Angeli a Tre Croce. The Archeological Museum, Cathedral, and Duomo are a short walk away. It's an ideal spot to take refuge immersed in a lush park and indulge in a lavish breakfast buffet.

Once a royal orphanage and conservatory, 18th-century **Palazzo Turchini** (Via Medina, tel. 081/551-0606, www.palazzoturchini. it, €125) near the Neptune Fountain has a roof terrace with a view of Palazzo Reale and Maschio Angioino, and a garden. Some guest rooms have private terraces.

A 19th-century noble villa lovingly restored in the historic center, **(** **Costantinopoli 104** (Via S. Maria di Costantinopoli 104, tel. 081/557-1035, www.costantinopoli104.it, €170–220 s/d) attracts sophisticated European guests and theater types for its homey elegance. There's a blazing fire in winter, a small swimming pool in the courtyard, art books in the library, and drinks set out in the afternoon. Modern art enlivens bedroom walls and the staff is exceptionally attentive.

Tribunali and Capuana

UNDER €100

AIG (Associazione Italiana Alberghi per la Gioventù, €20 pp d) **Ostello Mergellina** (Salita della Grotta 23, tel. 081/761-2346) near the train station has rock-bottom rates.

Terrazza Pignatelli B&B (Via Ascensione 8, tel. 081/408-351, www.terrazzapignatelli.

com, €22 s, €18.50 pp d) is an intimate spot near the Lungomare, Villa Comunale, shops on Via Chiaia, and Castel dell'Ovo.

€200-300

Only 200 meters from Stazione Centrale, **New Europe Hotel** (Via Galileo Ferraris 40, tel 081/264-344, www.neweuropehotel.it, €210 d) is a handy spot if you intend to move around by train to see other sights like Pompeii, Vesuvius, and still enjoy life near the center. The architecture is modern, and there is a decent restaurant. The hotel caters mostly to a business clientele and host small conferences.

Vomero

€100-200

Hotel Nesis (Via Nuova Agnano 5, tel. 081/762-0024, www.hotelnesis.it, €170 d) dates to the early 20th century and offers 39 comfortable rooms. It's just 50 meters from the train station, Ferrovia Cumana, which connects with Montesanto, the historic center, and Campi Flegrei.

Views of Vesuvius and Naples Bay abound from the elevated tranquility at **(** **San Francesco al Monte** (Corso Vittorio Emanuele 328, tel. 81/423-9111, www.hotelsanfrancesco.it, €165–210 s/d). The former monk cells now come with free minibars, sumptuous textiles, and large baths. There are frescoes in the hall, a contemporary art gallery, and a lovely terrace with its grotto and small swimming pool. The restaurant has attentive service and its cantina offers bargain late-night dinners.

OVER €300

A Naples tradition, **Grand Hotel Parker's** (Corso Vittorio Emanuele 135, tel. 081/761-2474, www.grandhotelpaerkers.it, €360 d) dates to the 19th century but has updated features like spacious rooms and a gym. Neapolitans come here for chef Baciòt's cuisine, enhanced by a view of the Naples Bay and Vesuvius; others puff away in a separate Cigar Room or book a private dining to watch the chef in action, an excellent gourmet crash course.

FOOD

Naples offers abundant cuisine at all price ranges. The local ingredients are bountiful thanks to mineral-rich volcanic soil and a long growing season. This is the home of buffalo, of Asian and African origin, that provide the rich milk for *mozzarella di bufala*. The fresh buttery-soft mozzarella balls or braids make for a delectable appetizer with tomatoes and basil with a swirl of olive oil, called *caprese*. The olive oil is made in the nearby hills of Campania, which also produce the prized plum-shaped San Marzano tomato, used primarily for sauces. Pasta is made from Durham wheat, also locally grown, with most commercial pasta-making companies centered around Torre Annunziata, where pasta dries in the sea air. Sauces will vary and are usually tomato based; generally they dress the pasta but don't drench it, so expect a lighter touch with the amount of sauce, but plenty of flavor.

Pizza purists claim that pizza must be made in a wood-burning oven and that there are only two "real" pizzas: the Napolitana with tomato sauce and anchovies, or the *margherita* with mozzarella cheese and fresh basil. Most pizzerias offer plenty of other options, some very creative. Neapolitans favor a crust that is thicker than the pizza in Rome.

Bread varies even from town to town. Every family table is set with *casareccia,* a crusty bread that also pairs well with local cheeses and salamis. Some bakers offer a great variety, including ground hazelnuts and olives. The flat focaccia (sometimes called *pizza bianca*) is fragrant with olive oil, and is a traditional late-morning snack that also is used to make sandwiches.

Some vegetable dishes serve as a main course, like eggplant *parmigiana* or *timballo,* which has layers of pasta and the cook's choice of fillings, including vegetables, mushrooms, and meat. Other vegetables are served as a *contorno,* the vegetable course served after the main course. Look for wild field greens typical of the area, like chicory or *friarelli* with their bitter flavor nicely balanced in some pasta dishes or with sausage. Fresh salads conclude a meal, to cleanse the palate for dessert.

Naples street food

Seafood is abundant. You can expect to find traditional favorites like clams, mussels, squid, and octopus, along with many varieties of fish, from the more humble sardines and anchovies to deep-sea fish with varying flavors. Some are found only in this region. Meat dishes are less typical of the city, but are more traditional fare in the hills of Campania, where lamb, pigs (including a local breed, Casertina), cattle, and game animals like wild boar and hare are plentiful.

The hills also yield excellent fruit, especially peaches, apricots, and figs; the area toward Avellino is famous for cherries. The lemons of the area are prized, especially along the Amalfi Coast, where they are used to make a traditional liqueur, *limoncello,* or for a refreshing lemonade, *spremuta.* The forests yield a variety of nuts, especially chestnuts and hazelnuts, which are made into delectable sweets.

Neapolitan desserts are delicious. A good *babà au rum* uses real rum, not rum flavoring. It's light, spongy, and boozy. The *sfogliatella* is made from pastry strands woven to look like a

© ALESSIA RAMACCIA

NAPLES AND CAMPANIA

clamshell then filled with ricotta cheese. Gelato is available everywhere and you can judge the quality by the color. It should be dense, not fluffy. Ices are refreshing and best made from fresh fruit like lemons or coffee.

Grapes grow in the entire region of Campania. Several varieties are unique to Campania or even to a specific zone like the slopes of Vesuvius. Most highly prized of the wines is the full-bodied red Taurasi, made from a specific variety of Aglianico grapes. Other reds include Falerno del Massico, Piedirosso, and Lacchryma Cristi. Whites wines include Falanghina, Fiano di Avellino, and Greco di Tufo

Many Italians say that the best coffee is in Naples due to the good brands used, the baristas' technique, and the water. After dinner a *passito* wine made from dried grapes or a liqueur is offered. Amalfi has its *limoncello,* Benevento has its *la Strega,* and other hill towns toward the interior come up with superb concoctions made of cherries or hazelnuts.

Piazza del Plebiscito and Piazza Municipio
NAPOLETANO
Set near the Castel dell'Ovo, **La Bersagliera** (Borgo Marina 10–11, tel. 081/764-6016, www.labersagliera.it, Wed.–Sun. noon–3:30 P.M. and 7:30–midnight, €9–14) specializes in fish and seafood with a nice view of Castel dell'Oro.

REGIONAL
The interior is warm and inviting at **Ristorante Amici Miei** (Via Onte Di Dio 78, tel. 081/764-6063, Tues.–Sat. 1–3 P.M. and 8–11:30 P.M., Sun. 8–11:30 P.M., €8–40) and good food keeps Neapolitan businesspeople satisfied. Its location is handy for pre- or post-opera at Teatro San Carlo. *Spigoli,* the house triangular-shaped pasta, with a creamy artichoke sauce is excellent. Meat is their specialty, so this is a good spot to try regional red wines like Aglianico.

PIZZA
Near San Lorenzo, the outside counter at **Antica Pizzeria Di Matteo** (Via Tribunali 94, tel. 081/455-262, Mon.–Sat. noon–1 A.M., €6) has

bargain Neapolitan street food with fried specialties. Try a *frittatina* (*maccheroni* in bechamel sauce with cheese bits), an *arancino* (rice ball), or a *croquette*. Inside, the pizza toppings begin with Naples' two traditional styles, *margherita* and marinara, but include many others.

Ernesto Cacialli at **Il Pizzaiolo del Presidente** (Via Tribunali 120–121, tel. 081/210-903, Mon.–Sat., €5) claims to have made pizza for President Clinton during his visit to Naples, thus the pizzeria's name. This is one place where you can order a small pizza with a limitless number of toppings. Beer and wine are available, but only by the bottle.

CAFÉS
Step into the Victorian era for a cappuccino or *aperitivo* at **Caffè Gambrinus** (Via Chiaia 1, tel. 081/417-582, daily noon–3 P.M. and 7:30–11 P.M.). Since 1860, this elegant historic coffee bar has attracted writers like Oscar Wilde to sip and dispense a wicked turn of phrase. Expand on the elegance with a visit to the Royal Palace across the street. By night this is a popular watering hole for the San Carlo set, who put on a nonstop show of glamour.

Chic locals alight at **Culti Spacafè** (Via Carlo Poerio 47, tel.081/764-4619, daily 10 A.M.–1:30 A.M., closed Sun.) for finger food before setting out on their night's adventure. Evenings are for the café and days for the spa.

DELICACIES
The same family has been hand making chocolates in Naples since 1894 at **Gay-Odin Cioccolateria Artigianale** (Via Toledo 427, tel. 081/551-3491, Mon.–Sat. 9:30 A.M.–1:30 P.M. and 4:30–7:30 P.M.). Try the Vesuvius chocolate volcano or have them create a chocolate bar with your own original love message. In cool months they will mail chocolate, too. There are eight other locations in Naples, but this is the original shop.

Spaccanapoli
NAPOLETANO
Port'Alba (Via Port'Alba 18, tel. 081/459-713, Thurs.–Tues. noon–4 P.M. and

7 P.M.–12:30 A.M., €8–10) is a traditional Neapolitan trattoria that's priced right. Gennaro claims they were one of the first to serve pizza. The eggplant parmigiana and fried shrimp and calamari platter are good, too. Wine is sold only by the bottle, but the list is interesting. In the 1960s, they opened a second restaurant in the more upscale Vomero neighborhood.

CAFÉS

Set on a street lined with shops that specialize in musical instruments, **Rising South** (Via San Sebastiano 19, tel. 339/794-6828, daily 3–8 P.M. and 11 P.M.–3 A.M.) is a hip spot where two young fellows preside over new trends in music including jazz and lounge. Its funky decor has cushy sofas with nice areas for conversation or listening, and a bar that doubles as an aquarium.

GELATO

Chocolate-maker **Gay-Odin Cioccolateria Artigianale** (Via Benedetto Croce 81, tel. 081/551-0794, Mon.–Sat. 9:30 A.M.–1:30 P.M. and 4:30–7:30 P.M.) also makes gelato here at this branch. Bittersweet with cocoa beans, chocolate laced with rum, chocolate with hot peppers, and a non-chocolate pistachio are among the delectable flavors.

QUICK BITES

Known for their pastries, **Scaturchio** (Piazza San Domenico Maggiore 19, tel. 081/551-6944, Wed.–Mon. 7:30 A.M.–8:20 P.M.) has excellent *babà* and *sfogliatella*, as well as good gelato. At midday the pastry shop is popular with locals for a light lunch. The artichoke *torta* is delicious.

Tribunali and Capuana
INTERNATIONAL

At **Eventi Restaurant & Lounge** (Via M. Schipa, 65–69) the owner's idea is to have fun with food. The menu changes weekly with different themes like soufflés, baked pasta, pork, or regional Italian cuisine. Don't arrive too late in the evening, as they may run out of food. Service sometimes is distracted, but the crowd

is lively. A good meal for under €20 in this upscale neighborhood is a find.

PIZZA

The best traditional pizza comes from the wood-burning oven at ◖ **Da Michele** (Via Cesare Sersale 1–3, corner Via P. Colletta, tel. 081/553-9204, Mon.–Sat. 10 A.M.–11 P.M., closed Aug., € 7). The white-and-green tile decor is no-frills, as are the two pizza options: *margherita* and marinara. Ask for any other toppings and you might be escorted to the door. When it's busy, which is almost always, prepare to wait and then share a table. Price varies not by size but by how much mozzarella is piled on top.

  Osteria la Chitarra (Rampa San Giovanni Maggiore, 1 bis, tel. 081/552-9103, Tues.–Fri. 12:30–3 P.M. and 8 P.M.–12:30 A.M., Sat. 8 P.M.–12:30 A.M., €7–9) has few tables, but the traditional Neapolitan food is a bargain.

Vomero
NAPOLETANO

Pizza and pasta are the specialties at **Acunzo** (Via Domenico Cimarosa 64, tel. 081/578-5362), with reasonable prices and located conveniently near the funicular that goes down to Via Roma.

  La Cantina de Sica (Via G. L. Bernini 17, tel. 081/564-2623) has wood tables and a wood-beamed ceiling to frame classic Neapolitan dishes from soups and pastas to dessert.

  A hilltop perch on the Vomero with a vista of the city is the star at **Il Gallo Nero** (Via Tasso 466, tel. 081/643-012, daily 12:30–3 P.M. and 7:30–11:30 P.M., €8–11), where the small but select Neapolitan menu and wines show off fish from the sea and meat from the hills of Campania.

  Named for two classic Neapolitan comic movie idols, **Toto, Eduardo e Pasta e Fagioli** (Corso Vittorio Emanuele 514, tel. 081/564-2623, Tues.–Sun. 12:30–3 P.M. and 7–11 P.M., €10–13) offers classic Neapolitan cuisine inside or on the terrace. Pastas are followed by a choice of meat or fish dishes, with plenty of desserts to cap it off.

INTERNATIONAL
Views of Vesuvius and Naples Bay are lovely from I **Barbanti** (Corso Vittorio Emanuele 328, tel. 81/423-9111) and its outside terrace. The formal dining room offers gourmet Mediterranean food served with international flair. The *degustazione* menu, €70, has a sophisticated variety. Downstairs **La Cantina,** the wine bar, offers a budget option after 10 P.M. for €25 that includes hot soup, a main dish, and dessert.

Chef Baciòt's cuisine in **George's** at Grand Hotel Parker's (Corso Vittorio Emanuele 135, tel. 081/761-2474) is enhanced by a view of the bay and Vesuvius. His style ranges from creative international to strictly mamma (especially for the pasta). His mini soufflé oozes liquid chocolate. At breakfast, *sfogliatelle* (clam-shaped pastry) arrive warm.

INFORMATION AND SERVICES
Tourist Information
A helpful tourist office is located within the central train station. Another next to the San Carlo Opera House is open in the mornings. Bus tours are offered at **City Sightseeing** (Piazza Municipio Largo Castello, tel. 081/551-7279, www.napoli.city-sightseeing.it, daily) in English. The tourist center, **Museo Aperto Napoli** (Via Pietro Colletta 89–95, tel. 081/563-6062, www.museoapertonapoli.com, Thurs.–Tues. 10 A.M.–6 P.M.) has an audioguide (€5) to 81 monuments throughout the city. **ArteCard** (www.artecard.it) will get you a discount on the entrance fee to many museums.

Government Offices
The **U.S. Consulate** (Piazza della Repubblica 2, tel. 081/583-8111, Mon.–Fri. 8 P.M.–1 P.M. and 2–5 P.M.) is near the port and is open weekday mornings for citizen services. It closes for both U.S. and Italian public holidays.

Hospitals, Police, and Emergencies
Hospitals that have a *pronto soccorso* (emergency room) are **Ospedale Cardarelli** (Via Cardarelli 9, tel. 081/747-1111), **Ospedale San Paolo** (Via Terracina 219, tel. 081/570-9761), and **Ospedale dei Pellegrini** in Pignasecca (Via Portamedia 41, tel. 081/751-2807). For medical emergencies, dial 118. To reach the police, dial 113. For boating or sea emergencies, call the **Coast Guard** (Guardia Costiera) at 1530.

Pharmacies
Pharmacies with continuous service 9 A.M.–8 P.M. are at Via Mergellina 35, Via Carducci 22, Gradoni di Chiaia 38, Via Cervantes 51/53, Via Santa Lucia 167, and various other locations. A *farmacia notturna* (night pharmacy) is at Piazza Municipio 54 and Via Carducci 21. These may rotate. To find more convenient locations, check the door of any pharmacy and *Il Mattino's* daily newspaper listings.

Banks and Currency Exchange
Naples has all of the major Italian banks. American Express (tel. 800/914-912), Thomas Cooke (tel. 800/872-050), and Visa offices are also conveniently located in the center.

Newspapers
Il Mattino, Naples' main daily newspaper, is a good source for concerts, films, and events. Other Italian newspapers publish a Naples edition with some event listings and local news. You can try *La Repubblica, Corriere della Sera,* and *Il Messaggero.*

GETTING THERE
Air
Capodichino Airport (tel. 081/789-6259) is served by Alitalia, Meridiana, and several European carriers, including budget airlines: Easy Jet, Eurofly, Virgin Express, and Transavia. A New York–Naples flight has been planned and may eventually materialize. U.S. carriers fly into Rome's Leonardo Da Vinci (Fiumincino); an airport train connects to Rome's Termini Station, which has direct trains to Naples.

Alibus (departures every 30 min., 6:30 A.M.–11:30 P.M.) connects the airport to the center at Piazza Garibaldi and Piazza Municipio. In 2005, *tariffa predeterminata* (flat rates) were established for taxi fares for specific routes. Special rates apply from the airport to Naples center hotels and various points. It's usually cheaper to ask for the flat rate.

Car

Most cars arrive in Naples directly from the A1 *autostrada,* which connects easily to the port and the ferries. The drive from Rome is under two hours with one toll along the way.

Bus

SITA (tel. 199/730-749, 7:30 A.M.–8:30 P.M.) serves outlying towns, Campania, and other regions. Various bus lines link Naples and Salerno with inland destinations like Benevento or the Adriatic Coast at Pescara, Bari, and Taranto. You can use **Curreri** (tel. 081/801-5420), Marino (tel. 080/311-2335), **Miccolis** (tel. 081/200-380), **Satam** (tel. 087/134-4969), or **Arpa** (tel. 087/142-431), depending on where you want to go. During peak season, buses may be the most hassle-free way to enjoy a ride along the Amalfi Coast.

Train

Ferrovie dello Stato runs local and national train routes (tel. 892/021, 7 A.M.–9 P.M., www.trenitalia.com) to Naples. Train-spotters will enjoy the newest line inaugurated in 2005. The high-speed, silent Alta Velocità connects Naples to Rome quickly (about 1.5 hours) and runs on its own dedicated track. If you prefer a slower pace, try circling around a dormant volcano in the **Circumvesuviana** (tel. 772/2444 or 800/0539-39), which serves volcano towns at the base of Vesuvius and beyond, including Sorrento, Baiano, Sarno, Torre Annunziata, and Porta Marino.

Italy's first train line was inaugurated in 1839 and went from Naples to Portiaci. Train history buffs will be pleased to know that plans are to expand the National Railway Museum, **Museo Ferroviario Nazionale** (Via Pietrarsa, tel. 081/472-0003), in Pietrarsa, where the railway works are located.

Boat

Sea shuttle **Metrò del Mare** (tel. 199/600-700, 9 A.M.–7 P.M.) connects Naples and other coastal towns by sea with eight metro sea lines that serve 22 ports north from Monte di Procida to the southern point at Sapri; full service runs June 30–September 9, then it's reduced. Charter boats are available at various ports, under Port of Naples Captain, **Capitaneria di Porto** (tel. 206-133). **SNAV** (tel. 081/428-5111, www.snav.it), **TTT** (tel. 800/915-365 or 0957/462-187), **Siremar** (tel. 892/1231), **Tirrenia** (tel. 720/1111) and **Ustica Lines** (tel. 081/551-7164 or 092/387-381, www.usticalines.it) sell tickets at the port; they serve Sicily, the Eolian Islands, Sardinia, as well as Tunisia. (Ships or ferries to Greece depart from Bari or Brindisi, and to Spain and Corsica from Civitavecchia, north of Rome.)

GETTING AROUND
Funicular

Songs are sung about the funicular (tel. 800/568-866, www.metro.na.it), which sometimes has itinerant musicians or singers aboard to add to the color. The train car moves riders on a dedicated track vertically up and down Naples' hills so you don't have to puff your way up to the Vomero.

Bus and Subway

Unico Napoli has several good offers. A regular bus ticket is valid for 90 minutes. The daily pass is good until midnight of the day it is issued. The weekend pass is valid for Saturday and Sunday. A weekly pass is valid from Monday until the following Sunday. A three-day pass for Campania serves the region, includes public transport in Ischia and Procida, and to the airport. Prices change periodically; check for current fares (www.unicocampania.it).

Sepsa operates the city bus system (tel. 800/001-616), while **Metronapoli** (tel. 800/568-866) runs a network of train and bus lines. Some stations have been redesigned by prominent architects and are worth a good look while you're there.

Taxis

Taxis are at designated stands near the train station, airport, and other central points, otherwise phone Radio Taxi (tel. 570/7070, 556/444, or 556/0202). Naples has established fixed flat rates that include trips from the airport, train station, port, and central hotels (get rate details from visitor information offices in those places).

Car, Motorcycle, and Bicycle

Car rentals are available from **Hertz** (tel. 081/761-6235), **Avis** (tel. 081/284-041), **Europcar** (tel. 081/595-6584), and other agencies. **ACI** (tel. 803/116), the automobile club of Italy, has excellent maps and some publications in English. Motorcycle and bicycle rentals are easily available at coastal towns; for the former, Italy enacted a helmet law in the past decade, which in Naples often goes ignored. Driving within Naples is best left to those with great agility and a sense of adventure: Dividing lines on highways and streets serve more of a decorative purpose than to maintain order, as do traffic lights. Leave no objects of value in the car and park it in a secure place.

Tours

City Sightseeing Napoli (Piazza Municipio Largo Castello, tel. 081/551-7279, www.napoli.city-sightseeing.it) offers two hop-on, hop-off itineraries. Bus A takes passengers to art sights, Piazza del Gesu, Decumani, Museo Archeologico, and Museo Capodimonte. Bus B is the Gulf View route that makes a panoramic sweep. Commentary is offered in eight languages, including English. The Napoli–Vesuvio D bus and Napoli–Pompeii–Vesuvio P bus run on Saturday and Sunday, respectively, or by reservation.

May is a big walking tour month for Naples, when Maggio dei Monumenti (Monument May) opens all kinds of sights usually closed to the public and offers many walking tours, some in English. The tourist office and many historic sights also provide free guided tours.

Vicinity of Naples

CAMPI FLEGREI

The ancients called the Phlegrean Fields the "burning land" because of the nature of its volcanic soil. The northwestern area of Naples is one of Southern Italy's most fascinating, thanks to eerie landscapes, fertile soil, craters, Bradyism, dormant volcanoes, and hot springs. The climate is mild and has natural sheltered ports. Averno Lake was the mythical entrance to the Underworld, where dead souls were escorted to the next world by Charon in his boat down the River Styx. Averno derives from the Greek for "without birds," due to the noxious vapors that would down them if they flew overhead.

Most of the action today centers around lively Pozzuoli, but the area extends to Cumae, Fusaro, Baia, Miseno, Bacoli, and Monte di Procida. It makes for some spooky hikes, a beach scene in summer months, funky cultural events, and thermal spa treatments that harness some of the seismic activity under the earth's crust for your enjoyment. All this fun, too, is without the crowds of Pompeii. Film star Sophia Loren is Puzzuoli's most famous native.

Sights

The Cuman Sibyl gave her prophecies at the cave in **Cumae,** a colony of Magna Grecia that kept the Etruscans but not the Romans at bay. Aeneas consulted the oracle here and, nearby, another grotto, **Cocceius,** connected Cumae to Lake Averno.

Water from the **Serino River** was brought via aqueduct to the Piscina Mirabilis that supplied the Roman fleet at **Miseno.** (Pliny the Elder, the commander of this fleet, perished in the A.D. 79 eruption of Vesuvius.)

The phenomenon of Bradyism, the movement of the earth's crust, continues to raise and lower the **Temple of Serapis** in **Pozzuoli.**

The temple is one of many indications that the ancient Egyptian kingdoms and their gods held no less fascination for the Romans than they do for us today. The influence of Egyptian religious cults was strong throughout ancient Rome. Unlike the Catholic Church, which later oppressed such cults and destroyed temples, Romans accepted them and often adopted their deities and rituals into their own pantheon of gods.

If you find rooms expensive or hard to come by in Naples, try Pozzuoli and zip by boat, subway, train, car, or bus into Naples or to other ancient sites. High season here is summer for the beach, but any other time you are likely to find rates reduced in hotels.

The **Anfiteatro Flavio e Serapeo** (Via Terracciano 75, tel. 081/526-6007, Wed.–Mon. 9 A.M. to one hour before sunset, €4 includes Temple of Serapis and the amphitheater) in the upper town is one of the most important ancient Roman theaters. It held 40,000 spectators and only the Colosseum in Rome and the amphitheater in Capua were larger. Nero, who fancied himself a great singer and musician, performed here in Puteoli (ancient Pozzuoli). The enlargement of an earlier theater was begun by Nero, although the date of its final completion is disputed. The burial of the underground parts left the entire arena mechanism intact. The current entrance is on the west side, Via Terracciano. The piperno pillars at the old entrance suggest the immense scale of the structure. The outside had 72 arches, three levels, walkways and passages in a vast network, and trap doors in the large pit to keep animals or stage sets contained in underground holding cells until they were raised to the stage to burst forth on the scene.

Spectators were seated according to social class and the entire amphitheater was embellished with hundreds of marble statues framed by elegant marble columns, porticos, and other decorative elements. Covered with volcanic and other matter accumulated by water, the amphitheater may have remained intact until the 16th century when excavations began.

Charles of Bourbon and Ferdinand IV ordered that marble and statues should be used to decorate the Reggia di Caserta, the Royal Palace in Caserta; 12 of the columns were used in its Court Theater. Under the A.D. 305 persecution of the Christians by Emperor Diocletian, several monotheists were to have been thrown to the animals here, but in the absence of the Governor of Campania they were decapitated at Solfatara instead.

A brisk 10-minute walk and you'll be at **Solfatara volcano crater,** which has more visible volcanic activity than Vesuvius and more vapors than Blanche Dubois. Nicknamed "Charonte" for Charon, the deity that escorted dead souls to the underworld, the caretaker presides over *fumaroles,* sulfur vapors, and bubbling mud all forced to the earth's surface from great pressure in the earth's core. Wave your newspaper or guidebook near some steam and watch what happens. Light a match and the earth below seems to reply in its own eerie language of fire, air, and steam. Stick your head in the little grotto (usually marked "no saunas") and see how the vapors relieve a headache or sinus distress.

Entertainment and Events

Active travelers can enjoy classes at funky **ArtGarage** (Pozzuoli, Via Solfatara, Parco Bognar 21, tel. 081/303-1395, www.artgarage. net), a low-budget arts space that occupies a former parking garage. Some weekends it offers master ballet and modern classes with dancers that have performed in Europe's most prestigious companies. Otherwise, just brush up on your judo or other martial arts skills.

Retro summer entertainment is in store at **Drive In Pozzuoli** (Pozzuoli, Via Contrada La Schiana 21, tel. 081/804-1175, night only, check newspaper listings for times). Watch a film from your car (Italian language, €4) or take in the action around you.

Sports and Recreation

Let those vapors work for you at **Terme Puteolane** (Pozzuoli, Corso Umberto I 195, tel. 081/526-1303, Apr.–Dec.). Take thermal mineral baths, *fanghi* (mud baths), inhalation therapy to relieve respiratory ailments, and massages. Price varies by treatment; mud wraps and thermal treatments are in the morning, with inhalation therapy and other treatments in the afternoon.

Accommodations

The only thermal resort in Naples is in Campi Flegrei. **Hotel delle Terme Di Agnano** (Via Agnano Astroni 24, tel. 081/762-2180, www. hoteltermeagnano.com, €100 d) is set in a green basin and is warmed with natural dry heat emitted from the "Burning Fields." The hotel is modern and the 62 rooms are set in a park designed centuries ago. Ruins of the Roman Thermae are nearby. Its parking is handy in an area where parking is not always easy to find and from where you can head off to an exhibit or trade show at Mostra d'Oltremare or the Citta della Scienza. It's also near the Campi Flegrei railroad stop.

Terme Puteolane (Pozzuoli, Corso Umberto I 195, tel. 081/526-1303) has rooms (€75 d) and a restaurant, so you can grab a snack before hitting the sack.

Hotel Tiro A Volo (Pozzuoli, Via San Gennaro Agnano 69a, tel. 081/570-4540, €45–75 d) became popular as a place where guests could take sailing lessons. Other hotels like **Circe** (Pozzuoli, Viale Sibilla 18, tel. 081/867-8215, www.hotelcirce.it, €95 d), **Girasole** (Via del Mare 76, Licola, tel. 081/804-4777, €47–65), and **Le Sirene** (Pozzuoli, Via Napoli 59, tel. 081/526-6566, €60–70 s/d) each have their own private beaches. **Grand Hotel Oasi** (Pozzuoli, Via Campana 253, tel. 081/303-1025, €150–250 s/d) has a swimming pool. **Agave** (Pozzuoli, SS 7/IV Domitiana km. 53,390, tel. 081/524-9961, www.agavehotel.it, €110 d), **American Gli Dei** (Pozzuoli, Via Antiniana 15, Agnano, tel. 081/570-5209, €145–180), **Villa Espero** (Pozzuoli, Via Scalandrone 12, tel. 081/854/9308, www.hotelvillaespero.it, €90 d), and **Villa Luisa** (Pozzuoli, Via Tripergola 50, tel. 081/804-2870, www.villaluisaresort.it, €90–120 s/d) are all considered the area's more deluxe options.

Food and Wine

Two young winemakers in Campi Flegrei had the kooky idea of carrying on the ancient winemaking tradition in today's Phlegrean Fields. Gennaro plants and harvests his grapes in a network of patches scattered above and around Monte di Procida. Each patch is wedged in behind an uncle's house here or a neighbor's garage there, all absorbing Neapolitan sun and sea air and making for a complicated harvest over rocky slopes. All are miraculously transformed into wine at **Cantine del Mare** (Azienda Agricola Cantine del Mare, Via Cappella IV 5, Monte di Procida, tel. 081/523-3040, www. cantinedelmare.it), where even pulling into the driveway requires finesse. But Gennaro loves to have visitors drop by and the twisting roads are worth the effort. His wines have an undertone of the soil's rich volcanic minerals, a taste that could only come from here. His 2006 Campi Flegrei Falanghina, bottled in September 2007, has an intense, sunny, fresh taste and is probably his best wine. Gennaro makes two good red wines with Piedirosso grapes and is perfecting his *passito;* he leaves Falanghina grapes to wither on the vine and absorb the salty sea air in winter before he picks and presses them.

Another local winemaker of Piedirosso and Falanghina dei Campi Flegrei is **Azienda Agricola Zasso Matilde** (Via Cuma-Licola 141, tel. 081/867-8112).

Getting There and Around

Campi Flegrei is easily reached directly by train (www.trenitalia.com) from Naples or other major cities and by Metro Line 2. The roads in the area are narrow, curve up and down hills, and are frequented by Neapolitan drivers. To reach Monte di Procida by bus, take the Linea Cumana rail line to Agnano stop, and then from there take the SEPSA bus marked Monte di Procida.

Bus 152 departs from Naples at Piazza Garibaldi for Pozzuoli. The Pozzuoli/Solfatara metro stop is a brisk 10-minute walk from Solfatara. There are ferry connections from Pozzuoli to the Island of Procida and other points along the coast.

Around Campi Flegrei

Baia Park has submerged villas and other ruins. Bacoli is lined with beach clubs and is at its most active in the summer. In ancient times the port was connected to Miseno Lake.

Once the site of an ancient spa dedicated to Venus and Mercury, excavations from the site are at **Museo Archeologico dei Campi Flegrei** (Via Castello, Baia, tel. 081/523-3797, Tues.–Sun. 9 A.M.–1 hour before sunset).

HERCULANEUM

Herculaneum can be combined as a half-day or full-day trip with Pompeii, although archeology and ancient history enthusiasts might want to dedicate a full day to Pompeii and a half-day to the site at Herculaneum. Inquire about a combined pass when you purchase your ticket. The modern neighborhood jumble varies from unattractive to rough-and-tumble. A lovely historic villa was renovated as a hotel in 2006 and a short walk away is an excellent *enoteca* (Viva Lo Re Restaurant) with good food, which now makes this a more attractive spot to spend a few days.

Sights

Different types of house construction in **Scavi Archeologici di Ercolano** (www.pompeiisites. org, Apr.–Oct. daily 8:30 A.M.–6 P.M., Nov.–Mar. daily 8:30 A.M.–3:30 P.M., closed Jan. 1, May 1, and Dec. 25, €10 or €18 for five sites over three days including Pompeii) are visible here, from the more humble trellis house of wood, reed, bricks, and tufa to more sumptuous dwellings like the **Villa dei Papiri** that served as J. Paul Getty's model for the museum villa that he constructed on a cliff in Malibu. The summer dining room in the **House of Neptune** and Amphitrite Mosaic shows Neptune and a favorite sea nymph in luminous detail.

Accommodations

The former Villa Aprile in Ercolano was converted in 2006 to the luminous white **Miglio d'Oro Park Hotel** (Corso Resina 296, tel. 081/739-9999, www.migliodoroparkhotel.

a Herculaneum fresco in the House of Neptune

© JUDY EDELHOFF

it, €109 d). Set right on the main street, it's a short walk to the ruins in Herculaneum and a block away from an excellent *enoteca*. Rooms are large and bright, and there's a nice garden out back.

Food

For good hearty food with nice wines in a cozy atmosphere and reasonable prices, head for **Viva Lo Re Restaurant** (Corso Resina 261, tel. 081/739-0207, Tues.–Sun., €10).

Getting There and Around

By train take the Portici–Ercolano line or Circumvesuviana Ercolano–Scavi, then take a taxi to the Scavi. By car take the A3 *autostrada* to the Ercolano exit.

Around Herculaneum

Southeast of Naples, situated on the coast between Herculaneum and Pompeii, is the town of **Torre del Greco,** known for its coral artisans. Mediterranean coral was highly prized in the ancient world and Torre del Greco is

NAPLES AND CAMPANIA

famous for its coral work. Apprentice gold-smiths, jewelers, and coral artisans study at **Museo del Corallo dell'Istituto State d'Arte** (Piazza I. Palomba 6) housed in an 18th-century Carmelite monastery. Tourists come by the busload to visit coral shops like **Giovanni Apa** (Via Enrico De Nicola 1, tel. 081/881-1155), in business since 1848, for museum-quality objects and moderately priced coral and cameo pieces. Collectors head to the private collection at **Basilio Liverino Coral Museum** (appointment only, some works for sale).

The archeological site of **Oplontis** (Via Sepolcri. tel. 081/857-5347, www.pompeiisites.org) is right in the town of **Torre d'Annunziata.** Oplontis has the Villa of Crassius Tretius, where a significant amount of jewelry and coins in gold and silver were found during excavations. After your Oplontis visit, stop by the pasta companies or their shops.

Torre del Greco and Torre d'Annunziata recieve a large volume of tourists that come to see coral shops and museums. Many stores are situated in buildings with electronic gates and armed guards, due to the volume of cash transactions and the value of the inventory. Keep in mind that this is an economically depressed area. Protect your personal belongings to avoid purse snatchings. Phone ahead to shops for advice about transportation or parking.

◖ MOUNT VESUVIUS

Mount Vesuvius remains one of the world's most dangerous volcanoes. Venting and tectonic activity continue in close proximity to densely populated areas. As you approach Naples from Rome, Vesuvius looms large over the city. Look at an aerial photograph of the Naples area from above and you'll see just how visible and dominant are the volcano and its crater. Activity on, under, and around Vesuvius is constantly monitored by land and satellite.

The famous eruption of A.D. 79 caused Pompeii and surrounding foothills to be covered by pumice, then by falling ash and debris from the column that shot up from the volcano, which could be seen from Rome. What the poison gases did not kill, tremendous thermal blasts

did, then falling ashes buried any procrastinators. Pliny the Younger's description, an eyewitness account that he wrote in a letter after his uncle perished, gives a portrayal of the column that rose up and spread out. What 21st-century eyes might compare to an atomic mushroom cloud he likened to an umbrella pine. He writes, "It is true that he [his uncle, Pliny the Elder] perished in a catastrophe which destroyed the loveliest regions of the earth, a fate shared by whole cities and their people, and one so memorable that it is likely to make its name live for ever…"

Pompeii, some five miles from the base of Vesuvius, and Herculaneum, even closer to the volcano's base, remained buried under ashes and debris for centuries. Vesuvius continued to erupt every 100 years or so, with an interruption in about 1037. The volcano erupted again in 1631 and killed about 4,000 inhabitants. Through the millennia, residents have baked bread, cooked meals, tended vineyards, or otherwise gone about their ordinary lives until the mountain blows.

The volcano that permeates the psyche of area inhabitants also makes for an interesting excursion. Some flora and fauna are unique to the area. Even species common to central European alpine regions make an appearance in this park. You have a spectacular view of the city and the sea on one side, and the crater on the other. The volcano may be dormant, but it certainly is not extinct as is evident from vapors that percolate up from the earth.

Vesuvius has two summits, **Mount Somma** and the cone of Vesuvius. The former is more humid, with vegetation unusual this far south, while the latter has Mediterranean plants. **Valle del Gigante** (Valley of the Giant) is divided into **Atrio del Cavallo** (Hall of the Horse) on the west and **Valle del Inferno** (Valley of Hell) on the east.

The West Face

Begin in Herculaneum (Ercolano) and follow directions to Vesuvius and the parking area. A shuttle will take you farther up or you can walk. The uphill walk is over a path of flattened cinders and lapilli, a desolate contrast to the fertile vegetation below. As you circle the summit's rim you'll have a view of the Bay of Naples with the Sorrento Peninsula to the south and **Cape Miseno** to the north. The opposite view inside the rim looks down into the gaping crater of the volcano with wafts of steam that drift up from among volcanic pebbles and rocks. Note that when vapor activity becomes too intense, park officials close access to the rim. From here you can descend southwest toward **Torre del Greco,** famed for its coral artisans and the school that trains them.

The South Face

Begin in **Torre Annunziata,** where you might want to first stop in the pasta factories. Take the road toward **Boscotrecase** until you have to get out on foot. This follows the track of ash and lapilli from the last eruption of Vesuvius in 1944. The view from here is of the **Sarno** plain and the coast south to **Sorrento.**

The land below Vesuvius is rich with vegetation and wildlife. Forests cover a large part. Land is still cultivated, although as part of Campania's plan for National Disaster Reduction inhabitants were instructed to live elsewhere but can continue to cultivate their vineyards and crops. Officially no one is supposed to reside on the slopes of Vesuvius and designated areas. Residential buildings are to be converted for the use of tourism, presumably a group that is smaller and easier to evacuate, rather than being expendable.

Unless you're a botanist or zoologist, you may not pick up on the incredible varieties of flora and fauna on the slopes of Vesuvius, which was made a national park in 1991. There are some 23 species of orchids and yellow broom. Mount Somma has birches as well as chestnuts, oak, alder, maple, and holm oak. The cone of Vesuvius has pine woods and holm-oak groves. You can ask about guided excursions through **Parco Nazionale di Vesuvio** (tel. 081/771-0911, www.vesuviopark. it). Or in Herculaneum, contact **Guide Alpine della Campania** (Piazzale di Quota 1000, tel. 081/777-5720) for guided tours in the park of Vesuvius. **Ente Parco del Vesuvio** (Piazza Municipio 8, tel. 81/771-8215) in **San Sebastiano al Vesuvio** has information on various routes to Mount Vesuvius. Usually the best activities are offered on weekends. **Istituto Nazionale di Geofisica e Vulcanologia** (Via Diocleziano 328, tel. 081/610-8483 www.ingv.it) conducts its main operations in Naples and Rome. The observatory founded in 1841 now has a permanent volcano exhibit at **Museo Vulcanologico dell'Osservatorio Vesuviano** (Via Osservatorio 14, tel. 081/777-7149).

◖ POMPEII

Pompeii is a moving experience—not only because it shows the remains of a port city in ancient Rome, but it's also a reminder of how precious everyday activities and daily life are when the world suddenly comes to a halt. After the August 24 eruption in A.D. 79, much of the population managed to escape under a shower of debris. It was the cloud of poisonous gases that shot up, fanned out, and descended some hours later that killed the people that had remained. Those unfortunate homeowners or thieves trying to carry off possessions, a child asleep, a wealthy woman resting in the gladiators' barracks, and so on did not escape and were frozen in time until they were rediscovered in the 16th century and excavations began in the 18th century.

Pompeii is a "living" site in that it's still being excavated (about one-third has not yet been uncovered), and new projects, like gardens and temporary exhibits, are in the works. The same dogs seem to patrol or laze about year after year. For the rest of us, it will take some strategy to get the most out of a tour of one of Italy's most visited sites.

The site of Pompeii is so vast that it's hard to cover it all in one visit. Be sure to wear good walking shoes, as you will be treading over streets paved with large, uneven volcanic basalt stones (very slippery when wet). There is no transportation once you enter the gate.

The site becomes crowded by 10 A.M., but thins out by mid-afternoon. Try to arrive either at opening time (8:30 A.M.), or before the last

THE ERUPTION OF VESUVIUS: AN EYEWITNESS ACCOUNT

Almost 2,000 years later, the most eloquent and vivid account of the destruction of Pompeii in August of A.D. 79 remains that of a teenager, Gaius Plinius Caecilius Secundus. Popularly known as Pliny the Younger, he was only 17 years old when he wrote what he had observed in his letters to Tacitus, a family friend and one of Rome's great historians.

Pliny's family home was in Misenum, on the northern rim of the Bay of Naples, where he lived with his mother and her brother. Commander of the naval fleet in Misenum, Pliny the Elder was a famous scholar and writer of the voluminous work *Natural History*, who brought up his nephew after the death of the boy's father. In his letters, Pliny the Younger described their experience in the days prior to and following the eruption of Vesuvius, an event that led to his uncle's death. He recalled the tremors of preceding days as "not particularly alarming because they are frequent in Campania." Residents of nearby Pompeii may have been more wary of a severe earthquake, since one had wrought major damage less than two decades earlier, around the time of Pliny the Younger's birth. But if tremors were that frequent, perhaps not.

Oddly enough, all this was happening just prior to the Vulcanalia, when on August 23, inhabitants around the Roman Empire held their annual celebration and sacrifice to the god of fire – and of volcanoes. The blacksmith god, Vulcan, was one of the major deities in the pantheon of Roman gods. Even the Forum in Rome had a temple dedicated to him. Vulcan's forge was said to be at the base of a volcano in the Aeolian Islands, but he could shift his foundry at will. Like the spouses of Elizabeth Taylor and Marilyn Monroe, perhaps Vulcan has the dubious distinction as being better known to some of us as "husband of." Vulcan, lame in one leg from a fall after he was flung from the heavens during a clash of the titans, was husband of Venus. (Venus, goddess of love, had her own temples and plenty of her own affairs to attend to.) During the Vulcanalia, mortals built bonfires and threw live fish on the fire to appease the god so that during the coming year they would have his protection from fire and volcanic eruptions.

On the afternoon of August 24, Pliny the Younger's mother brought her brother's attention to "a cloud of unusual size and appearance." A cloud column from the explosion of Vesuvius shot up into the sky for several miles and began to fan out. Pliny the Younger described it like "a pine tree" rising on a very long "trunk" with "branches" that spread. The cloud was full of ashes, pumice, stones, dirt, and other debris. "Some of the cloud was white, in other parts there were dark patches of dirt and ash." Some estimates put the speed of the clouds at 100 miles per hour.

"The sight of it made the scientist in my uncle determined to see it closer at hand." As he prepared to sail, Pliny the Elder had invited the Younger to join him, but the boy declined so that he could continue studying. That was the last he saw of his uncle alive. Pliny the Elder landed at Stabiae, on the southern rim of the bay below Pompeii, but later was unable to sail back out. In part, the wind was not in his favor. The shower of debris from the eruption of Vesuvius quickly filled the harbor with stones that raised the level of the sea bottom and pumice that floated on top and clogged the surface. Nature had blocked the sea vessels from departure.

During the night, Pliny the Younger reported that in Misenum the tremors were so violent that everything seemed to be "not only shaken, but overturned." Where his uncle slept in Stabiae (yes, "slept": eyewitnesses said he was able to sleep soundly), "buildings were rocked by strong tremors and seemed to have come loose from their foundations, sliding this way and that." The immediate dilemma was whether to remain indoors or to seek safer ground elsewhere. Inside the danger inside was from collapsing buildings. Outside the danger came not only from being pummeled by rocks, some "light and fire-consumed," but also from the panicked crowds trying to flee as they were engulfed by the dark cloud. "It was daylight elsewhere in the world, but there it was darker and thicker than any night." In broad daylight, people used torches to try to find their way in this sudden dark. They walked or ran with pillows strapped to their heads to protect them from the shower of rocks. Even away from the turmoil of crowds, outside rest was impossible for very long. Although the ashes were light in weight, they fell so rapidly and in such quantity that people would be crushed by their weight if they did not shake off the ashes and keep moving. Indoors they risked being buried alive. Like in a snowstorm, once the ashes reached several inches above a door or window, it became difficult – and later impossible – to open.

Pliny the Elder tried again to depart by sea with his crew, but the sea was blocked. When he was too tired to move on, he ordered the others to go ahead to try to save themselves. The smell of sulfur and the arrival of flames "sent others into flight, but revived him." Briefly. Pliny the Elder stood up and then collapsed – perhaps suffocated by noxious fumes, dust-laden air, or the intense heat of one of the volcano's fire surges. "When daylight arrived again two days after his death, his body was found untouched, unharmed, in the clothing that he had worn. He looked more asleep than dead."

Meanwhile, back in Misenum as they sought safer terrain, Pliny the Younger reported panic-stricken mobs and carriages that "began to run in different directions" and "would not remain stationary even when wedged with stones. We also saw the sea sucked away and apparently forced back by the earthquake . . . it receded from the shore so that quantities of sea creatures were left stranded on the dry sand." He reports that the black cloud "parted to reveal great tongues of fire, like flashes of lightning magnified in size." The cloud "sank down to earth and covered the sea: it had already blotted out Capri and hidden the promontory of Misenum from sight . . . Darkness fell, not the dark of a moonless or cloudy night, but as if the lamp had been extinguished in a closed room." When a glimmer of light did appear, it was from approaching flames, not from daylight. Then came more darkness along with more ashes that fell in heavier showers. "I could boast that not a groan or a cry of fear escaped me in these perils, had I not derived some poor consolation in my mortal lot from the belief that the whole world was dying with me and I with it."

When daylight finally broke through, Pliny the Younger said that the sun shone "yellowish as it is during an eclipse . . . We were terrified to see everything changed, buried deep in ashes like snowdrifts." Pliny and his mother returned to Misenum that night as earthquakes continued and "fear predominated" sometimes to the point of hysteria. They waited at home for news of his uncle. Later they heard the account of his final hours.

Pliny the Younger had studied under his uncle and had developed a keen sense of observation. Later he became a Roman senator under emperors Domitian, Nerva and Trajan. He lived long after the eruption and died ca. 112 or 113. His most famous works are his letters, including 121 to and from Emperor Trajan – bureaucratic paperwork that today gives us a window on Roman provincial administration. Although most of us depend on English translations, Pliny's letters show the importance of primary sources – and their power and beauty. No novel, play, or movie is likely to offer more drama or insight.

Scavi Archeologici di Pompei is €10. An €18 ticket good for three days has all five sites: Pompeii, Herculaneum, Oplontis, Stabia, and Boscoreale.

© ALESSIA RAMACCIA

the Amphitheater in Pompeii where gladiators once fought

entrance (3:30 P.M. in winter, 6 P.M. in summer). A late afternoon visit on a hot day might seem unappealing, but the crowds are gone, an afternoon breeze usually picks up, and photographers will find better lighting.

A minimum visit of 90 minutes will allow only the highlights of two major areas, the **Theater** and **Forum.** Budget your time carefully if you want to see the beautiful frescoes in **Villa dei Misteri,** the erotic frescoes in the **Lupanare,** or the grand **Amphitheater** that dwarfs the other theaters (two are at opposite ends diagonally and the other is in the middle of the site).

The newer entrance gate, Porta di Stabia, sets you into the site on flat ground. (Porta Marina is uphill on the way in.) Follow Via Stabiana to the theater complex with Teatro Grande and the Odeion (smaller theater). Then take Via dell'Abbondanaza to the Forum area, then exit downhill on Via Marina, the exit closest to public transportation. If you have time for the Lupanare (whorehouse), expect to wait until the previous visitors exit—just like in ancient times (only 10 or 15 are allowed in at a time).

Scavi Archeologici di Pompei entrance is €11. A combined ticket (about €20) is good for three days and has all 5 sites: Pompeii, Herculaneum, Oplontis, Stabia, and Boscoreale. When you buy your ticket, go to another window to pick up your free map in English, which has all the major sites shown in good detail.

Burial tombs that date from the 1st century B.C. line Via delle Tombe, situated just outside Porto Ercolano.

Sights

The largest and most aristocratic of the Pompeii homes is **Casa del Fauno** (House of the Faun), on Via della Fortuna. Its splendid mosaics of the victory of Alexander the Great over Darius is at Naples' Archeological Museum, as are most of the site's most valuable sculptures, paintings, and other decorations.

Leave it to the nouveau riche to go over the top. Evidently the freedmen that owned **Casa dei Vettii** decided to put Priapus, god of fertility endowed with a giant penis, at the center of their decorating plan. He's in the wall frescoes with their famous Pompeii red background color, weighing his enormous member on a scale. He appears, too, as a fountain statue that should have been in the garden, but was in the kitchen.

The main market, the **Macellum,** had a room in back at the right to sell meat and fish; the room on the left might have been used for banquets.

The family related to Nero's second wife may have owned **Casa di Menandro** (Menander's House), so named for the Greek playwright painted in the peristyle niches. The house is rich with frescoes and mosaics, including sea creatures, people of color, and a Nile scene.

Teatro Grande, the horseshoe-shaped Grand Theater, seated about 5,000 and was probably used for farces, plays, mimes, and pantomimes. It was restored with marble and statues after the A.D. 62 earthquake had damaged it. The Forum, or Foro, was the city's administrative, business, and religious center with citizens conducting business and nearby markets selling goods.

The more intimate **Odeion Theater** probably was used for music and poetry readings, with a roof that would have improved acoustics.

Via dell'Abbondanza was a central thoroughfare that passed the Stabian Baths and the Forum, but was lined with businesses like laundries that recycled urine to clean clothes, a wholesale bakery, inns that included Asellina's with popular foreign waitresses. Wagon wheels imprinted these hard stones with grooves on the streets. The stepping stones that crossed the street were of regular width so that wagons could pass but pedestrians could stay above the rain and slop.

The **Terme Stabiane** (Stabian Baths) are especially interesting for the floor heating methods used, from furnaces that forced heat to flow through ducts in walls. Its pool, rooms kept at various temperatures, gym, and dressing rooms for men and women would have been beautifully decorated with mosaics and stucco.

The trek to **Villa dei Misteri** (Villa of Mysteries) may add an extra half-hour to your visit.

It's worth every bumpy step to this getaway villa in a shady spot that contains a sublime room of frescoes with Pompeii-red backgrounds. In the main dwelling of this villa outside the main city walls, rooms have beautifully preserved frescoes. Walls provide a bold contrast to the delicately painted figures that suggest the initiation rites of a young woman to the cult of Dionysus, the god of wine—also associated with dance, music, and agriculture. In one scene a child reads from a text, perhaps the rites. Scenes of offerings and sacrifices follow. Another seems to be a flagellation, followed by the wedding of Ariadne and Dionysus. The dancing figures, bacchante, are associated with Dionysus or Bacchus. Dancers in bacchanalia sometimes became quite wild and frenzied. Another scene is the grooming and preparation of the bride. Perhaps the resident of the villa was a priestess in the cult of Dionysus. The actual interpretations remain a mystery today. The Naples Archeological Museum has other stunning examples of frescoes from Pompeii, but this is the best-preserved cycle that remains in the town. Other sections of Pompeii have magnificent sculptures or remains of temples and theaters, but if you want an idea of how splendidly some of the residents lived and how colorful the interiors were, this is a stop to savor.

Entertainment and Events

Night tours of Pompeii or musical concerts are offered some years, but not every year so check to see what's on (www.pompeiisites. org). Pompeii also has some experimental gardens, vineyards, and other sections that are periodically open for tours. Nearby Torre Annunziata, a pasta-making town, has a five-day **Pastafest** in October.

Accommodations

Although money pours into Pompeii's archeological site, this does not seem to have a trickle-down effect on the local economy, which shows evidence of dire straits. However, if you really want to comb the site you might want a base here for a night or two. Avoid the Vittoria on the edge of the site that at night is a desolate area, but a stay at a friendly bed-and-breakfast can be a pleasant experience.

The approach to **Pompei B&B** (Via A. Moro I Trav. 18, tel. 081/850-5011, www. pompeibedandbreakfast.com, €70–90 d) does not look promising on the outside, but once you are inside the security gate you have a comfortable, homey base with a cordial host. Breakfast is cheery and the living room is a welcome spot to meet other travelers and trade tips on visiting the area.

POMPEII'S LUPANARE REOPENED

The services of a *lupa* (prostitute or "she-wolf") in Pompeii's Lupanare on average cost the same as a glass of wine – at least that was the case in A.D. 79, the year that Vesuvius erupted. The Lupanare, Pompeii's only official house of prostitution, reopened in July 2006 to curious tourists. Restoration took a year in a project that also restored the Suburban Baths and cost €450,000, financed by Compagnia di San Paolo, a private company from Turin founded in 1563 as a guild to do good works.

Elsewhere in town there was sex for money, but the Lupanare was the only "indiscriminate" place for sex: all customers were accepted, and no membership was required. Graffiti on the walls represents some 150 customers plus up to an equal number of "workers" that might have added their own marks.

Walk through the main city gate that faces the Mediterranean, Porta Marina, head uphill on Via Marina (later Via Abbondanza), and then hang a left on Vicolo Lupanare. Sailors and other visitors would have entered town the same way, passing taverns with food and wine, shops with olive oil, and other necessities of daily life. Nearby are theaters and thermal baths. Wagon or chariot wheels have imprinted grooves on the large basalt street stones. Step inside the Lupanare and look above the doorway of each of the five rooms: The colorful fresco shows the specialty of the prostitute that occupied that room. Inside each room is a stone bed, approximately the height and width of a modern single bed but shorter in length (though adequate to replicate the position on the wall painting).

The upper floor of the two-story house presumably was for more exclusive customers. Upstairs (not open to the public) is bereft of frescoes, but like the downstairs has been architecturally renovated to correct problems with water seepage, cracks, weather, and other aging. Each floor has a toilet.

The Lupanare was discovered in 1862. While the United States was consumed with the Civil War, archeologists in Pompeii were digging out the house of easy virtue, shut down by ashes and debris from the ancient volcano eruption almost 2,000 years earlier. Its first restoration was around 1910 followed by another in 1949 that repaired damage suffered in World War II. The frescoes had darkened as a result of the previous restoration; waxy film was removed, as were the fake floors below. Lights were added and each picture now is covered with a polycarbonate shield that resembles Plexiglas.

Conservation requirements now limit visitor capacity to 10. However, that doubles the number of visitors permitted on the ground floor when the Lupanare was in business. (Calculations are based on the addition of images in the paintings: No act shows more than two people.) Various sources list the A.D. 79 population of Pompeii as 18,000–25,000, which probably does not include the sailors and others "just passing through." Now on a busy day Pompeii may have 5,000 visitors and their average stay is only an hour: improved odds for visiting the Lupanare, but minus the original services. Visits are not timed, but are self-regulated, which allows enough time for giggles and photographs (without flash) before the restless line of visitors outside encourages their exit – perhaps much like 2,000 years ago.

November and December are ideal for avoiding the spring and summer crowds at Pompeii. Stroll into Pompeii in the afternoon – morning is busiest. Golden autumn light, Vesuvius looms nearby, a sea breeze comes through town, and the place is more magical than ever. Hours are 8:30 A.M. to one hour before sunset.

Food

Ancient recipe books give us a good idea of what Romans ate. Authentic recipes of ancient times featured recipes such as quail eggs with *garum* (a fish-based sauce). Other dishes had peas with *seppie* (cuttlefish), meatballs, or pumpkin. Desserts were sweetened either with honey or a fruit base (sugar hadn't been discovered). The food variety was impressive, even without New World tomatoes, potatoes, coffee, or chocolate. As for beverages, wine was the choice. What grape varietals were used? The geographical point of origin was written on the amphorae (the ceramic vessels), like Falerno or Falernum, but did not identify specific grapes, which varied according to geographical zone.

Pompeii's Laboratory of Applied Research has been conducting years of study on ancient food and wines. The culinary and medicinal uses of Pompeii's plants and foods, as well as their preservation has involved the study of pollen samples through an electron microscope and taking samples from oil and wine jugs. While that study continues, **Mastroberardino Winery** (Via Manfredi 75/81, Province of Avellino, tel. 082/561-4111, www.mastro.it, by appointment only), based in Avellino, is studying how vines were cultivated: how plants were spaced, how vines were trained, and what countries may have traded or exported vines.

President (Piazza Schettino 12, tel. 081/850-7425, Mon.–Sat., €35–50) attracts well-heeled locals and politicians for its professional service and good food, especially fish and seafood. **Il Principe** (Piazza Bartolo Longo 8, tel. 081/850-5566, www.ilprincipe.com, Tues.–Sun. noon–3 P.M. and 7:30–11 P.M., €35–40) offers fine regional cuisine. Or opt for its ancient Roman menu, based on ancient recipe sources and using ingredients available at that time. Don't expect to find tomatoes or coffee on this menu.

Getting There and Around

From Rome by car take *autostrada* A3 toward Napoli/Salerno and exit at Pompeii. By train, FS Napoli–Salerno stops at Pompeii, as does the Circumvesuviana line.

◖ BENEVENTO

Benevento, the land of witches and magic, is both a city and a province. Legend attributes its founding to Diomedes, who arrived here after the destruction of Troy. The city has remarkable contrasts. Its ancient Roman Theater and Trajan's Arch are among the best-preserved monuments of their type anywhere. If all that antiquity is reducing you to ruins, try Benevento's contemporary art scene, Campania's most important after Naples.

The breezy town, easily reached by train, makes for a lovely stroll. Visit small churches built 1,000 years ago. Here Christians were busy converting the Longobard warriors that still worshipped the pagan deity Wohan. The yellow liqueur, La Strega (The Witch) takes its name from local legends. One story says Benevento's hills and riverbanks were where the witch consorted with the devil. You might prefer to be bewitched by the performing arts; the town has seven active theaters.

Sights

The Samnites settled here first, had a victorious battle over the Romans in 321 B.C., but fell under their control after the Third Samnite War in 290 B.C. Romans made Benevento an important trade center, situated along the Via Appia that connected to Brindisi and thus to the Orient. Built during the time of Hadrian, the **Roman Theater** could hold 20,000 spectators and originally had three levels, of which the first and part of the second remain.

The Senate and People of Rome (SPQR) built **Trajan's Arch** between A.D. 114–117 to honor the emperor and to mark the point where Via Traiana led to a shorter route toward Brindisi. The bas-reliefs refer to social works carried out by Trajan.

Local lore says that **Ponte Leproso** was named for a leper colony near the bridge and that witches congregated along the banks of the Sabato River under an old nut tree, which Bishop Barbato (the same trying to convert the Longobards) cut down to curtail their devilish powers.

The unusual floor plan, part circular and part star-shaped, helps give **Santa Sophia** its charm. The bell tower was built into an ancient city wall and its cloister has Moorish arches.

Piazza Papiniano is notable for its Egyptian obelisk erected in A.D. 88 under Emperor Domitian (one of the Colosseum's three builders). Another is in the **Museo del Sannio.** Egyptologists will find an extraordinary collection in the museum that shows how strong the cults of Isis and other Egyptian deities were in this area. The collection also reflects Samnite, Greek, and Roman influences in ancient times, as well as artifacts from later periods.

Raguzzini, the Neapolitan architect responsible for Rome's theatrical Piazza Sant'Ignazio, designed the chapel to San Michele in the San Bartolomeo Basilica, which he may also have designed to replace damage wrought by a 1688 earthquake.

A major investment in 2005 extended contemporary art well into the province. **ARCOS** (Corso Garibaldi 1, tel. 082/429-919), in Palazzo della Prefettura is a center for contemporary art exhibitions.

Entertainment and Events

Theater is a big scene in town. **Teatro Comunale** (tel. 082/421-848) on Via Garibaldi is a good resource for other events, too. The town holds an annual theater festival in late August/early September.

Il Premio Strega in June is the town's literary award. The first day is often dedicated to a literary film and on the second day a literary prize is awarded to contemporary authors.

Accommodations

Benevento has a shortage of chic boutique hotels, which means you can count on reasonable prices if not elegant decor. The province has many farms and wineries that rent out rooms, which are often quite charming and ideal for touring a bit of the countryside.

Hotel Villa Traiano (Viale dei Rettori 9, tel. 082/432-6241, www.hotelvillatraiano.it, €90–150 s/d) and **Grand Hotel Italiano** (Viale Principe di Napoli 137, tel. 082/424-111, www.hotel-italiano.it, €62–88 s/d) cater to business travelers and are in town. **Hotel D.G. Garden**

(Contrada San Chirico, tel. 082/425-331, www.dggarden.com, €45 pp) has a pool. The smaller **Hotel della Corte** (Piazza Piano di Corte 11, Via Papa Vittore II 9, tel. 082/454-819) is right in the center and has lower rates, parking, and allows dogs.

Thermal waters near Benevento are at Casamicciola Terme, Lacco Ameno, and Telesia, which offer accommodations and waters that claim to work magic on aches, pains, and other ailments that La Strega can't cure. In the Benevento countryside in Pescosannito, a stay at **Agriturismo Il Gelso delle Maitine** (Corso da Maitine, tel. 082/498-1157, www.ilgelsodellemaitine.it, €50 pp) is memorable not for the rooms, which are quite basic, but for the animals. The owner is a falconer, and raises and trains birds of prey. He also has talking parrots, peacocks, ducks, and many other birds, as well as sheep and chickens. The beautiful horses are perfect for scenic rides through the Benevento hills. The home cooking is good, too. If you don't stay overnight, come for lunch.

If you want chic and charming dwellings with a bit more of a romantic ambience, **Benevento Locanda Della Presuntuosa** (Contrada Fontanella 22, Pontelandolfo, tel. 082/485-1122, €140 d) has mini apartments in Il Chiostro and Il Pagliaio with wood beams, terra-cotta floors, sitting rooms, and fireplaces ready to get crackling. Southwest of Benevento the small **Cristina Park Hotel** (Via Benevento 104, tel. 082/483-5888, €120 d) has rooms with tasteful furnishings and nice textiles, plus a good restaurant and exercise room. Pretty sitting rooms make nice conversation or drink spots. You can opt for half- or full-board.

Food

Cuisine in the province shows a decided preference for meat and game, though it also includes river fish. The hearty cuisine pairs perfectly with the full-bodied red wine of the area, Aglianico, ruby in color and often with a spicy kick. The hillsides also yield the straw-yellow-colored Falanghina, a white wine with floral notes, and Fiano, a more intense white. If you can't visit a winery, seek an *enoteca* to taste these wines. La Strega, is a local liqueur that is sold internationally. Look for liqueurs made from nuts and fruit from the mountains. If you're lucky, some restaurant owner will pull out a bit of homebrew to try after the meal. **Nunzia** (Via Annunziata 152, tel. 082/29-431, Mon.–Sat. lunch and dinner, €20–25) is a simple trattoria with home-style cooking and reasonable prices.

Armando decided to expand his olive oil mill to a winery, **Terre Stregate** (Azienda Oleovinicola Pacelli Maria, Via Municipio 105, Guardia Sanframondi, tel. 0824/864-312, by appointment), to illustrate the family motto, "a vine is a bottle of wine." His elegant wines include three whites (Fiano, Falanghina, and Greco); reds are all Aglianico, each different in style and price to suit everyday or special occasions. In 2008, his new rosè comes on the market, also made from Aglianico grapes. Each wine is single varietal (made from one type of grape) and is a good way to taste differences between grapes, some unique to Campania. The oil, made from three types of olives, is tasty, too.

Information

The tourist office (Via Nicola Sala 31, tel. 824/319-911, www.eptbenevento.it) is especially helpful and provides updated information on the city and province.

Getting There and Around

Benevento is well connected to Naples, Caserta, and Rome by train (www.trenitalia.com) and by SEPSA bus (www.sepsa.it). All of the sights in town are easily accessed on foot. A car is handy if you want to visit wineries or stay in an *agriturismo* in the country.

Around Benevento

Two of Campania's major wineries are in Avellino. **Mastroberardino** (Via Manfredi 75/81, Province of Avellino, tel. 082/561-4111, www. mastro.it, by appointment only), founded in 1878, has a joint project with the Archeological Service of Pompei to research ancient grapes and growing systems. **Feudi di San Gregorio** (Sorbo Serpico, Via Cerza Grossa 1, tel. 082/598-6611) has a modern *cantina* of architectural interest designed in 2002 by Hikaru Mori; in 2006, its facilities expanded to receive overnight guests.

CASERTA

Grand Tour travelers in the 18th and 19th centuries were in no hurry to leave the Reggia's fashionable court. The palace and gardens are immense in size. You'll savor their beauty more if you don't rush. A full day in one of Europe's magnificent gardens is bliss and you can even catch an outdoor movie in them during the summer.

The palace that was built to match the glory of Versailles is rich with art and furnishings. This is a good stop, too, for traveling companions that have diverse interests: Divide in the morning to separate the outdoor types from the indoor culture vultures, meet for lunch, then decide where to continue. Caserta as a city does not look terribly prosperous, so its upscale designer shops, like Bulgari jewelers, may come as a surprise. Much of Naples and nearby cities have a social gulf between the rich and poor that seems to be widening, while the middle is diminishing in size. The city has a hotel to satisfy demands of well-heeled business travelers as well as smaller, more moderately price hotels.

◖ Reggia di Caserta

Charles Bourbon planned to transfer his court from Naples to Caserta, where he would rule the Kingdom of Two Sicilies from the Reggia (Royal Palace), which was built on a scale to rival Versailles. One of Europe's most popular and sophisticated courts, the grandeur of the architecture is matched by the immensity and enchantment of its gardens. In 1752, architect Luigi Vanvitelli began this 28-year construction, which was completed in 1780 by his son Carlo after his death.

A visit could be compressed into two hours, but that allows little time to see a fraction of the palace's 1,200 rooms, many of which are still lavishly decorated, on five floors with four

© ALESSIA RAMACCIA

The Reggia di Caserta has more than 1,000 rooms.

internal courtyards. Nor would you have time to savor the **Great Waterfall** that feeds three kilometers of fountains, pools, and streams, and the English Garden. It makes for an enchanting walk past rare plants and flowers (the first camellias in Europe), antiquities from Pompeii, fake ruins, brooks, thickets, the octagonal **Castelluccia** for the pleasure of young royals, and a landscape that has inspired poets.

In the palace itself in the lower left vestibule is the horseshoe-shaped **Court Theater** that was modeled after San Carlo in Naples, with 12 ancient columns that came from the great amphitheater in Pozzuoli. Five tiers of boxes are decorated with *putti* (cupids), shells, and flowers (the King's above the main entrance is decorated with a crown and drapes). Above alabaster columns support a ceiling vault frescoed with Apollo trampling a python. The most unique aspect is the stage: The back wall can collapse so that the royal park outside can become part of the set.

Back in the vestibule at the right, take the grand ceremonial staircase flanked by two imposing marble lions, symbols of royal power. The double vaulting enhanced the acoustics of musicians that would play in the niches upon the court's arrival. Upstairs from the octagonal shaped vestibule enter the **Palatine Chapel,** which the king intentionally had designed to resemble the one in Versailles. Stroll through royal apartments for full immersion in colored marble, stucco, elaborate furniture, plush textiles (some manufactured in nearby San Leucio), paintings and frescoes (landscapes of Campania and Southern Italy by Hackert are especially prized and are a pleasant mini-grand tour of the region). Queen Mary Caroline's apartment has a peculiar Swiss cage clock with its dial on the base and a small embalmed bird.

Once you've been wowed by the water spectacle in the Reggia, you'll probably want a peek at the engineering genius behind it. Head to the **Maddaloni Valley,** where Vanvitelli's **Carolino Aqueduct,** completed May 20, 1770, links Mount Longano with Mount Marzano. Three rows of arches of differing heights soar to 95 meters over the road, seen spectacularly from ground level on SS 265. Vanvitelli located a source high enough so that first the waters surged through San Leucio to power the king's silk mills before plunging into the Reggia's waterfall.

The Silk Road led from Reggia di Caserta to **San Leucio,** where the king expanded the silk industry in operation since the 16th century. His designs for an efficient, pleasant planned community for the court's silk manufacturing center were partly realized. Silk was spun, dyed, and woven into elegant textiles that also supplied a market well beyond Italy. San Leucio highlights include the Belvedere with its historic royal apartment and geometric Italian garden; the Museum of Silk Culture and Industrial Archeological Museum; and the Silk Weaver's House. San Leucio still produces silk textiles, of special interest to shoppers looking to update their interior designs.

Entertainment and Events

The Reggia's summer program (tel. 081/744-4149) includes outdoor movies in Giardini della Flora (Flower Gardens), light theater, and other events in the Reggia gardens. The Reggia di Caserta's **Sezione Didattica** (tel. 0823/448-084, 9 A.M.–4 P.M., call for days and advance reservations) offers special programs in English, each about 1.5 hours, to visit the Royal Apartments, park, English garden, and San Leucio's silk mill sites.

The World Buffalo Congress moves into Caserta for a few days in October. These aren't North American bison, they are descendants of Asian and African buffalo imported perhaps as early as the 15th century.

Shopping

A five-minute drive to the north, diggers for "white gold" will find buttery soft mozzarella balls at **Ponte a Mare** (Via Domitiana km. 34.07, tel. 082/385-1525, www.ponteamare.it), made right in back of the shop. If you head back south on the same road, on the left-hand side that expanse of brown earth is a large buffalo farm, not open to visitors, with the mud-hole near the barn being a favored spot to wallow.

Caserta has some upscale shops, including major jewelers and furriers, perplexing in a town that does not have a wealthy patina.

Accommodations

In Caserta, look for bargains during peak tourist seasons, as most area hotels cater to business travelers. This means that in August, December, and early January, you may almost have the run of the place. Only smaller hotels are likely to close for holidays. Rates increase when major conventions are in town.

Crowne Plaza Caserta (Viale delle Industrie, area ex Saint Gobain, tel. 082/352-3001, www.crowneplaza-caserta.com, €120–190 d) caters primarily to Italian business clients. Water sprites tempted by the pool at the Reggia will enjoy a splash in the courtyard's large outdoor pool. An excellent chef turns out sophisticated international cuisine upstairs; traditional dishes lure locals for bargain lunches in the lobby restaurant. Rooms are large with attractive modern furnishings. This hotel rarely discounts rooms, but you may be able to use Holiday Inn points here. The easiest route from the Reggia is to head toward San Nicola and follow the wall alongside the train tracks toward an attractive modern industrial park. There's underground parking.

In the San Marco Evangelista neighborhood's busy commercial street, **Grand Hotel Vanvitelli** (Via Carlo III, Via Carlo III, tel. 0823/217 111, www.grandhotelvanvitelli.it) has a lobby in step with Vegas, four restaurants with local and international cuisine, and Il Belvedere roof garden.

Near the hollow formed by the blast of the defunct Roccamonfina volcano, **◖ Agriturismo Terre di Conca** (Via Piantoli, Conca della Campania, tel. 339/592-8649) is set in pristine landscape so idyllic that the owner won't post a sign. This may take some effort to find (including assistance with Italian language), but it's only about 30 minutes by car from downtown Caserta and well worth the detour. The superb country dining features ingredients from local gardens and pastures, including the Bernardino's free-range nero Casertano black pigs that are transformed into excellent *lardo* and prosciutto. Vegetables are abundant and varied. Pet dogs and cats on the premises exchange pleasantries with a polyglot mynah bird. The interior is furnished with flair and an outdoor pool is beautifully landscaped.

Castel Volturno Holiday Inn Resort (Via Domiziana km. 35, tel. 081/509-5150) is hidden between a forest of graceful umbrella pines and the sea in Castel Volturno. This resort is an oasis just north of Naples on the Domitian Riviera. Europeans and Americans enjoy the golf course (18 holes, half set near the pine forest, the other half on sandier soil near the sea), tennis courts, and a large inviting pool. Summer offers outside dining. The funky Domiziana Road strip to its north is ramshackle, but the opposite side is lined with some of the earth's best mozzarella shops. Rooms are large and tastefully furnished with silk textiles from San Leucio (like Caserta, about a 30-minute drive). This lovely compound is an ideal spot to relax or play for several days; it's handy, too, for sightseeing with a free shuttle service to the airport, into Naples, and other points (seating is limited to eight). Nearby, **HyppoKampos Resort** (Via Fiumitello II, tel. 0823/762-106, www.hkresort.it) in Castel Volturno has sailboat lessons or rentals.

Food

Mozzarella is so important economically to the area that locals call it *l'oro bianco* (white gold). Along with Salerno's mozzarella, Caserta's is considered the absolute best. Each *bufala* cow is individually named and identified by her ear tag. Like hurricanes, each birth year names move on to the next letter in the alphabet (2008 is the year of the "P" and so on). Males, considered superfluous except for a lucky two or three, are quickly eliminated. When you buy mozzarella this fresh, don't put it in the refrigerator: leave it at room temperature in its own lightly salted brine and it will keep for five days or longer and will remain soft (refrigeration hardens it).

Caserta's province has a wide variety of superb local wines thanks to the variety of grapes grown here, some with roots back to ancient times. Falerno del Massico (DOC), Asprinio di Averso (DOC), Galluccio (DOC), Terre di Volturno (IGT), and Roccamonfina (IGT) are the most famous. Try them here as some are hard to find outside their hometowns, much less outside Campania or Italy. Look for Pallagrello and Casavecchia.

Crown Plaza (daily 6–10:30 A.M., noon–2:30 P.M., and 7–11 P.M., €10–17), Caserta's main restaurant in the cavernous lobby above the indoor waterfall offers economical lunches for nearby office workers, a good opportunity to dine well on a budget and see stylish locals.

Green Garden Gelateria and Bar (Piazza Gramsci 5, open 24 hours) is on the first street to the right as you face the Reggia (Royal Palace). Locals come here for ice cream, pastries, coffee, and other snacks to satisfy cravings at any time of day.

Oro Bruno Cafè (Via G. M. Bosco 18, tel. 082/332-3256, daily 7 A.M.–1 A.M. or later, closed mid-August) begins serving coffee and evolves into a sophisticated wine and cocktail bar. Packed in the wee hours, locals vie for position to sip well-made cocktails, plus good selections of wine, brandy, champagne, and prosecco.

Colonne (Via Nazionale Appia 7, tel. 082/346-7494, www.lecolonnemarziale.it, Wed.–Mon. noon–3:30 P.M., €8–12) is a spot to try local specialties at lunchtime.

Winemaker Nicola Trabucco, enologist and agronomist to other prestigious wineries in Campania and beyond, in 2003 decided to toss his hat in the wine ring, too, and opened his own winery, **Trabucco Winery** (Via Vittorio Emanuele, Santa Croce di Carinola tel. 082/373-7345, www.trabucconicola.it). He works in his small tufo (volcanic rock) wine cellar. Rapicano, his Massico Falerno red wine, is full and spicy; his Donnarosa made from Aglianico grapes pleases even those who usually overlook rosé; and his white Falanghina is elegant and refreshing. It's easy to find on Caranola's main drag, but phone ahead to be sure that Trabucco's not away dispensing advice. Production is limited but if you can't visit, he can tell you where to find his wine locally.

Sessa Aurunca on the slope of an extinct volcano once had temples dedicated to Mercury and Hercules. To its southwest toward the sea is Carano, about four kilometers south of the old Appian Way (SS 7) and **Masseria Felicia** (Azienda Agricola di Ruggiero Giuseppe, Via Provinciale Appia, Carano Loc. San Terenzano, tel. 082/393-5095, www.masseriafelicia. it), Alessandro's winery set in a tufo cellar set under the raspberry-pink country house. On a clear day you can see the sea and some of the islands. His 2003 Falerno del Massico Etichetta Bronzo is a spicy full-bodied red wine made from Aglianico and Piedirosso grapes and his white Anthologia made from Falanghina grapes is full of floral and fruit scents. On your way to or from Caserta, be sure to see Vanvitelli's aqueduct in the valley.

Getting There and Around

A car is essential for visiting wineries. Caserta is well connected to major towns by train.

The best approach is from the *autostrada* to Castel Volturno. You can take the M1N Bus to Baia Domizia from Piazza Garibaldi in Naples, but arrange for a pickup from the stop as this area has a vague sense of lawlessnes about it if you stray too far, especially to the north.

Around Caserta

An early Samnite settlement was followed by Romans, after which this perch above tufa cliffs was occupied by Goths who were clobbered in A.D. 553. The town of Goti remains named for them. The view of Sant'Agata dei Goti from below is beautiful, sometimes it seems suspended above the volcanic rock. Once inside, its medieval charm remains. The **Duomo** dates from 970 and you can dine right next to it, making this town an ideal stop for lunch or dinner when it is beautifully illuminated. The Sannio Film Festival is held in August.

Piazza Duomo (Piazza Duomo 6, tel. 082/371-7683, Wed.–Mon. lunch and dinner, €22–27) features traditional cuisine and wines of the region. **Le Cantine di Mustilli** (Via dei Fiori, tel. 0823/717-433, €22–38) is the place to taste local wines.

CASERTAVECCHIA

Casertavecchia, Old Caserta, sits on the slope of Mount Virgo in the Tifatini (from the Oscan word for hills covered with oaks) Hills. Constructed mostly of gray- and caramel-colored tufo typical of Naples, this medieval town has ancient roots. Once a popular trading area for Etruscans, Oscans, Samnites, and Greeks, later repeated Saracen raids in the valley, especially around 861, drove the Longobards up here to fortify a more defensible position. Eventually the settlement for warriors grew into a town that still shows clear religious and royal power divisions. The bishop presided over the Church from the Duomo, and the count looked after noble interests from the castle. Now casual restaurants attract locals for garden dining and sweeping views of Caserta in the valley and beyond.

Sights

A visit to Casertavecchia takes about an hour. The best sight is a walk through the town itself, with its narrow streets and the simple low houses made of tufo volcanic stone blocks. The dual division of power is clear between the castle and bishop's palace. Dedicated to the town's patron saint Archangel Michael, its 12th-century Duomo, the cathedral, inside has columns that probably came from the temple of Jupiter Tifatinus. Look also for the bishop's tomb that has a medieval view of Civitas Casertana, Caserta, sculpted on a panel. The feast day for St. Michael the Archangel is in September. The town's other major church, Chiesa dell'Annunziata is farther up the hill. The ruins of the **Castle** (Castello Longobardo, Sat.–Sun. 9 A.M.–1 P.M., 4–8 P.M.) are at the top of the hill and have a permanent exhibit on Frederick II and also host occasional temporary exhibits.

Accommodations

There are no accommodations in the *borgo* of Casertavecchia and cars must park outside the city walls. There are two relatively new

NAPLES AND CAMPANIA

hotels outside the town walls, **Casertantica** (Via Tiglio 41, tel. 0823/337-1158, www.ho telcasert-antica.it, €65–70) and **Park Hotel Castello** (Via Provinciale per Casertavecchia, tel. 0823/371-515, fax 0823/324-338, €65). Both hotels also have restaurants.

Food

Casertavecchia makes a good summer evening stop for dinner—it's cooler than Caserta in the valley and some of these restaurants afford a view or have a nice garden. Some good choices are **Ristorante la Castellana** (Via Torre 4, tel. 083/237-1230), **Ristorante gli Scacchi** (Via Sant'Annunziata 5, tel. 082/337-1086, Tues.–Sun.), and **Ristorante Mastrangelo** (Piazza Duomo 5, tel. 082/337-1377, Wed.–Mon.). All restaurants feature local specialties.

Getting There and Around

By car exit Caserta Nord and follow the signs for Casertavecchia, which is northeast of Caserta past Casolla. From the train station at Caserta, an ACMS bus departs hourly for Casertavecchia. Taxi service (tel. 082/332-2400) from Piazza Ferrovia to Casertavecchia or the reverse is €15 each way with no additional charge for the call.

Around Casertavecchia

If Urbino was making plans for the Ideal City in the Renaissance, then **San Leucio** was its 18th-century counterpart making plans to be an ideal village, a planned community based on silk manufacturing. Enlightened ideals and just laws were to be its foundation, but its creator did not live to see the experiment carried to its conclusion. Some of the housing and town was built, as was the silk mill.

Discuss your own enlightened ideals at **Antica Locanda** (Piazza della Seta 8–10, località San Leucio, tel. 082/330-5444) and see if you've landed in the ideal tavern, with local specialties and wines.

CAPUA

In the ancient world at the time of the Second Punic War, only Rome and Carthage were larger in size than Capua. When Hannibal cut a swath through Italy, he passed a winter here during his campaign. In 216, Hannibal had to leave one of his armies in Capua. The idleness, eating, drinking, womanizing, and wallowing in luxury was so legendary that to this day over 2,000 years later Italians frequently use the expression *gli ozi di Capua* (roughly "the idleness of Capua") to evoke that languid, sensual do-nothing state. Little surprise this army was trounced by the Romans while Hannibal, still considered one of the best military strategists of all time, was off fighting other battles.

Capua had been settled by Oscans about eight centuries before Hannibal arrived. Samnites, Greeks, and Etruscans left their marks, too. Some 150 statuettes, all of mothers carved from volcanic rock, were found here. Etruscans set up a major manufacturing and trading center to satisfy their avid demand for Greek pottery, for which they traded and even locally employed Greek craftsmen to imitate the imports. Capua for centuries remained a major production and commercial center for bronzes and ceramics, as well as wine, spelt, roses, spices, perfumes, and unguents. Early tombs have been discovered filled with Greek and Roman objects. Romans later moved in and routed the Appian Way through the city, making it seem that all roads led to Rome and to Capua, too, which remained a major power center.

The early Middle Ages brought Barbarian invasions and Saracen raids that reduced Capua's importance, although before the year 1000, the Benedictines established their headquarters here.

Sights

The ancient world's second-largest amphitheater is only slightly smaller than Rome's Colosseum. Despite having been plundered for building blocks, its remains are significant. The underground complex has passageways and openings for trap doors, which, unlike the Colosseum's, can be visited at close range.

Museo Campano (Via Roma, tel. 0823/961-402, Tues.–Sun. 9 A.M.–1:30 P.M.,

€4.50) has an extraordinary collection of antiquities, including 150 statues in tufa of mothers, each with a different pose and expression. During its Etruscan and Roman heydays, Capua traded and churned out copies of ancient Greek-style pottery and bronzes and original designs. Remarkable detail and skill is evident in the craftsmanship. Ceramic plates with bold fish designs show various species, accurate in detail. Here's your chance to see some of those objects that Hannibal's soldiers enjoyed, seduced into the world of Capua's luxury and leisure.

Benedictine monks knocked down and built over an ancient Temple to Diana to build their **Sant'Angelo in Formis** (Via Baia 120, tel. 0823/960-817, daily 9:30 A.M.–12:30 P.M. and 3–6 P.M., open until 7 P.M. in summer, admission free) that dates to 944 and has some medieval frescoes.

Accommodations
Downtown Capua bears little resemblance to its glory days, so you might prefer to stay in the tranquil countryside if you want to *oziare* (laze about) in a new *agriturismo*. Try **Masseria Giosole** (Via Giardini 31, tel. 082/396-1108, www.masseriagiosole.com, €45 pp), near the Volturno River. Rooms are comfortable and modern. The restaurant caters to locals and the farm operation produces a wide range of fruits and vegetables that you can purchase as jams and sauces.

Food
Linger too long and *gli ozi di Capua* may take effect at **Osteria dei Nobiluomini** (Piazza de Renzis 6, tel. 082/362-0020, www.osteria deinobiluomini.it, Tues.–Sat. 12:30–3 P.M. and 7:30–10:30 P.M., Sun. 12:30–3:30 P.M., closed for 2 weeks in Aug., €8–12), known for its good wine selection as well as regional cuisine.

Getting There and Around
Sepsa (www.sepsa.it) has bus service from Naples and **Trenitalia** (www.trenitalia.com) has the closest rail connection.

Islands of the Gulf of Naples

Each of the islands in the Gulf of Naples has its own distinct personality. Ideally, you'll try all three, but if time is limited you can easily pick the right fit. **Capri** faces the Sorrentine Peninsula and has Roman ruins, the Blue Grotto, fairy-tale looks, and jet-set hangouts where intellectuals once treaded. To experience Capri at its most authentic, you'll have to arrive in the late afternoon once the day trippers have left the island on the last ferry of the day. **Ischia** and **Procida** are the Phlegrean islands on the northern side of the Gulf. Ischia has island charm with a hefty dose of reality—people actually work here in trades other than tourism. It's the spot to take the thermal baths and rest weary bones. Procida is close to land, but has enough water to separate it from the bustle and plenty of laid-back spots to enjoy a slower pace of island life. If you are undecided, you can reach all three from Pozzuoli.

PROCIDA
Procida is the smallest of the three main islands of Naples Bay and the most laid-back. It's also the flattest, making this a good option for those not ready for the steep climbs (and prices) of Capri. Its picturesque multihued houses are supported by tufo, volcanic rock. Traditions and religious festivals remain more entrenched here, perhaps because it has had much less tourism than Capri or Ischia.

Sights
The Port of Sancio Cattolico, known as **Marina Grande,** sits on the north coast of Procida where boats dock from Naples and Pozzuoli. The town's architecture is primarily from the 17th and 18th centuries. Gardens and orchards lead down to quiet **Marina Corricella** on the northeastern coast. On the southwestern coast, the semicircular inlet at **Marina di Chiaiolella**

NAPLES AND CAMPANIA

is popular for swimming. On the southwest tip of Procida you can cross a bridge to the tiny island of Vivara and hike through the **Vivara Nature Reserve** (Villa Scotto Pagliara, Via Marcello Scotti 40, tel. 081/896-7400). Once the domain of rabbit hunters and olive groves, Vivara is now a delight for birdwatchers. Permission from the city of Procida is required to access the reserve, because the site is protected by the World Wildlife Federation. On the opposite side of the island, the road above Marina Corricella will take you to the northeast tip to visit Punta dei Monaci (Monks' Point) and the **Abbey of San Michele** (tel. 081/896-7612). The abbey dedicated to St. Michael Archangel was built in 1026, just after the turn of the first millennium, and sits near the town of Terra Murata, the highest point on the island. Plan on spending half a day to circumnavigate the island by car, or more if you prefer to linger. By boat you can see the island up close and enjoy its different shades of blue water.

Accommodations

La Tonnara (Via Marina di Chiaiolella 51b, tel. 081/810-1052, www.latonnarahotel.it, €145 d) and **Casa sul Mare** (Via Salita Castello 6, tel. 081/896-8799, www.casasulmare.it, €140 d) are the island's major hotels.

Ask for a harbor-view room at 10-room **Crescenzo** (Via Marina Chiaiolella 33, tel. 081/896-7255, €120 d), as some have balconies. **Hotel La Casa sul Mare** (Via Salita Castello 13, tel. 081/896-8799, €85 d) is in the center on the Bay of Coricella, five minutes from the port; most rooms have balconies with a view.

Food

Near Chiaiolella Harbor, **Crescenzo** (Via Marina Chiaiolella 33, tel. 081/896-7255) is considered to serve the island's best cuisine. **Gorgonia** (Marina Corricella 50, tel. 081/810-1060), named for a the local seaweed that suggests the Gorgon mythological monster, is set near the Corricella Harbor and offers fine seafood and local wines.

Located in Marina Grande, **Sent'Cò** (Via Roma 167, tel. 081/810-1120) buzzes with the atmosphere of a local trattoria and offers a daily catch that is plentiful and varied.

Information and Services

Stazione Marittima (tel. 081/810-7280 or 081/810-1968) and Ischia's tourist office (the same office for both) have information on sights, events, and accommodations. Residences and bed-and-breakfast accommodations may be the only options in August.

Getting There and Around

Caremar (www.caremar.it), **SNAV** (www.snav.it), **Procida lines** (tel. 081/8896-0328), and **Linea di Maio** (www.procida.net) connect Procida to the other islands and to the mainland at Naples and Pozzuoli. **Sepsa** (www.sepsa.it) provides bus service around the island.

ISCHIA

If Capri is an island dedicated unabashedly to leisure, Ischia is an island at work. The largest of the three main islands of Naples Bay still has car repair shops and normal work-a-day activity that seems almost absent from Capri. It's also a place to recharge in thermal baths, a feature that neither Capri nor Procida has. Its practicality and lower prices make the island popular with Germans, Swiss, and other Northern Europeans who make annual pilgrimages here.

The *acque termali* (thermal mineral waters) have been popular at least since the Greeks, Etruscans, and Romans sought their curative properties. Thermal baths and treatments are one of Ischia's main draws, in addition to its beaches. Whether you "take the cures" Italian-style, which is usually for 12–15 treatments over a period of 1–2 weeks, or you just want a good soak and massage to restore you upon arrival, it's easy to find here. If you decide to go the *terapeutiche* (therapeutic) route, you must have a physician's recommendation. This is easy, as all you need to do is make an appointment with the resident physician—all *stabilimenti* are required to have a physician present who is often multilingual—and a range of treatments will be prescribed. (Italian

© ALESSIA RAMACCIA

Castello di Ischia

national health insurance pays this cost and 10 days of treatment annually; all you have to do is pay the private visit fees.)

Treatments tackle all sorts of ailments, including old sports injuries and fractures to arthritis, gout, obesity, deafness, diabetes, anemia, sinusitis, as well as metabolic, circulatory, and respiratory disorders, and even complex issues resulting from stroke or heart attack. Therapy is not a do-it-yourself routine. The casual visitor should look for a *"centro estetico"* or *"benessere."* Categorized as beauty treatments, these don't require a physician's approval and are ideal if you just want a massage, mud pack, facial, or swim in the pool. Not all facilities have pools, since some waters are intended to be imbibed.

Sights

The town of Ischia is the island's most populous center. It stretches from the Aragonese castle, **Castello di Ischia** (tel. 081/992-834, www.castelloaragonese.it) at Ischia Ponte on Rocca del Castello, to the port formed by the sea that enters a volcanic crater. The castle rises from the sea and is linked to Ischia by a bridge. Inside the thick walls is a collection of weapons and macabre instruments of torture. The Lido is where you can book pleasure excursions to other beaches, towns, or hillside spots.

Even the center of the island at Serrara Fontana is endowed with hyperthermal water. Rural charm is matched with lovely panoramic vistas, which you may want to enhance by a trip to the summit of Mount Epomeo that has the St. Nicholas Hermitage. Joined by a narrow isthmus, you can go to the Sant'Angelo promontory to visit the fishing village, an ideal spot for dinner.

Linked to the Port of Ischia by a scenic road, **Casamicciola Terme** has been treating visitors since the 19th century (including Ibsen, who completed *Peer Gynt* here). Potters use its special clay to make ceramics. This town is more laid-back, informal, and has economical hostels and boarding houses that are less elegant than pricier Lacco Ameno. The salty *bomo iodo* waters claim to cure a multitude of ailments.

Barano has Maronti Beach, Ischia's largest, which also has hot spring waters bubbling beneath the sand, a phenomenon that also warms the sea water giving it the temperature and salty, iodic, or bicarbonate sulphate properties of a thermal spa.

Foro D'Ischia is especially popular with Northern European visitors who like the greenery and head for beaches like Citara and San Francesco, or take walks to the faro (lighthouse), Chiesa del Soccorso, Torrione, and the Gardens of Poseiden. This winemaking area is surrounded by vineyards and has a foreign artist colony. Thermal baths are chloride-sodium.

In addition to the archeological museum at Parco Termale Negombo di Lacco Ameno (see *Recreation*), there's also a marine museum at **Museo del Mare in Palazzo Orologio,** an archeological site at Monte Vico to explore, and the Basilica of Santa Restituta.

Recreation

Set on an inlet with a mushroom-shaped tufa rock, **Parco Termale Negombo di Lacco Ameno** is spa central, with numerous thermal baths, and an archeological museum in **Villa Arbusto Lacco-Ameno** (www.pithecusae.it) that has artifacts from excavations on Monte Vico.

The mineral sediments and crystallized salts from the spring mixed with natural radioactive water make for a thermal mud wrap that should leave you positively glowing.

Nightlife

On Ischia's main shopping drag, **Discoteca-Piano Bar Valentino di Ischia** (Corso V. Colonna, Fri.–Sun., €20) is decorated in Moorish style with walls painted with the island's favorite views of the island. It's equipped with two dance floors, three bars, and one live piano bar.

Accommodations

Set amidst a garden with a view of Mount Epomeo, **Hotel Grazia Terme** (Via Borbonica 2, tel. 081/994-333, €160 d) has tennis courts, a gym, fitness center, traditional and mineral water pools, whirlpool tub, a beauty center, and two restaurants, one near the pool.

Grand Hotel Punta Molino Terme (Lungomare C. Colombo 23, tel. 081/991-544, www.puntamolino.it, €230–360 d) has a thermal pool and spa facilities. In Lacco Ameno, **Hotel Grazia Terme** (Via Fango 2, tel. 081/994-333, www.hotelgrazia.it, €105 d) also has spa facilities.

If you want to kick back, **Residence Covo dei Borboni** (Via Borbonica 2, tel. 081/994-333, €570–970/week), has 12 apartments for weekly rental with kitchens, shady patios set in a nicely landscaped garden, and two swimming pools, one with mineral spa water. Guests use the spa facilities at Hotel Grazia Terme.

Food

On the Maronti Beach in Petrelle, carved out of a rock is Peppe's intimate **Aglio, Olio e Pomodoro** (Spiaggia dei Maronti, Località Petrelle, tel. 081/906-408, Apr.–Oct.). Other than the promised ingredients of garlic, oil, and tomato, the star is fish that changes daily depending on the catch. Try sautéed clams and mussels or perhaps fried sardines with grilled eggplant. For a grand finale after the meal, don't miss the cherry liqueur.

If you've been dying for an escape from fish and seafood, head inland through the vineyards to Barano d'Ischia's **Il Focolare di Loretta e Riccardo D'Ambra** (Via Cretajo al Crocifisso 3, tel. 081/902-944, Thurs.–Tues., closed most of Dec.). Begin with specialties like *crostini* with wild garlic or eggplant parmigiana, then try a hefty lamb or rabbit main dish. Desserts here have a floral spin, like *crème brûlée* with verbena or chocolate soufflé with geranium cream sauce.

Families of good standing in the South once had their *monsù*—local dialect for "monsieur," the household French chef that put an elegant, rich touch on Mediterranean cuisine. You'll find this sort of dining revived in Forio's **Il Cuoco Galante** (Via Casale 29, tel. 081/997-907, Wed.–Mon., closed Nov.). Expect a good wine with your meal, too, in this out-of-the-way spot.

An elegant Forio tradition, **Il Melograno** (Via G. Mazzella 110, tel. 081/998-450, Apr.–Dec.) turns out some of the area's most interesting dishes. **Il Saturnino** (Via Marina, tel. 081/998-296, Feb.–Dec. Wed.–Mon) is a Forio favorite for fish. Another Forio tradition for fish is **Umberto a Mare** (Via Soccorso 2, tel. 081/997-171, Apr.–Oct.), which serves only at night except on weekends when lunch is available, too.

Getting There and Around

Ischia bans cars for non-residents during summer months. In 2007, officials established flat rates to encourage use of taxis: Ask the driver to *non attivare il tassametro* (not activate the meter) and *applicare la tariffa predeterminata* (use the flat rate). English brochures with rates should be available on ferries and ticket offices. No additional fees are applied for holidays, baggage, animals, or driver's return, although a €3 supplement may be applied for night (10 P.M.–7 A.M.) fares. An island tour by taxi is a minimum of three hours including stops and cannot exceed €80. Typical fares range from the port to town for €12, up to €40 for the windy, 18-kilometer ride to Sant'Angelo. **Sepsa** (wwww.sepsa.it) and **Pegaso** (www.pesasospa.it) are the island's public bus lines.

CAPRI

Capri is dedicated to the art of leisure, as it has been for over two millennia. Its quiet streets wind through beautifully tended tiny gardens that are fragrant with lemons and flowers. Emperor Tiberius was seduced and swapped larger Ischia for this island. It became his infamous and treacherous headquarters where he retreated for the last years of his life and sunk into unchecked debauchery. Some have tried to follow in his footsteps but for depth of immorality he remains unmatched. It's been the playground of the rich and famous for decades, attracting intellectuals, writers, the film set, and shoppers with gobs of money to spend.

Visitors to the island are well advised to dress the part, expensive-casual, if you want to blend in with the rest of the fauna. Day-trippers that must be off the island by the departure of the last ferry rarely intersect with the privileged denizens, either on their boats or sleeping off a hangover from the previous night. They only come out at dusk, as a general rule, when the island has disgorged and the small main piazza once again becomes their salon.

Sights
PORTO MARINA GRANDE

Porto Marina Grande is where all the boats arrive, and it also has the last vestiges of the small fisherman's village. Take the Funicolare up to the **Piazzetta Capri,** the local name for Piazza Umberto 1 because it's more like a *salotto* (salon for conversation). Almost everyone has to pass through here, tourist or resident, but the latter is likely to frequent the piazza at night after the day-trippers have cleared out. Prices here are high, and people-watching is the game.

Tiberius pushed his lovers, of whom he quickly tired, off the cliff known as Tiberius' Leap. In the unlikely case one survived that, servants on boats below were ordered to harpoon survivors with boat hooks. That villa dedicated to kinky emperor pleasures is no more. The trek to the site is an arduous climb in a remote location. Pick up the tourist office map first, or hire a boat and look at the cliff from below.

◖ GROTTA AZZURRA

Although it seems to be illuminated by its own light source, the intensely bright Grotta Azzurra of Capri is a dazzling phenomenon of refracted light. The ride into the grotto is almost as much fun as seeing it. Navigating the entrance to the cave can be tricky. Passengers have to flatten to a prone position in the rowboat; when the sea is choppy, boats can't clear the low cave roof. Check at the marina to see which boats are going to the Grotto. Due to pollution, swimming is not permitted.

TRAGARA CAPRI

The most famous walk on the island passes elegant villas and finishes at the small park with a view of the Faraglioni rocks. It runs along the south side of the island toward Marina Piccola and can be picked up in Marina Grande.

FARO DI PUNTA CAREN

Anacapri's Faro di Punta Caren lighthouse has been operating since the mid-19th century and is the second-brightest in Italy. Nearby there is a chairlift up the mountainside that provides a stunning view of Naples and the Amalfi coast. There's a cafeteria and restroom at the top. Most people decide to take one of several paths back to Anacapri or Marina Grande.

Entertainment and Events

"They only come out at night" almost seems to be the theme song of residents, who assiduously avoid day-trippers on the island. Dance the night away at **Anema e Core** (Via Sella Orta 39e, tel. 081/837-6461) and **Musmè** (tel. 081/837-6011).

Capri has no thermal waters, but **Panta Rei** (Via Lo Palazzo 1, tel. 081/837-8898, www.pantareicapri.it) resolves that problem with its trendy spa, lounge bar, cafe, and tastings.

The **Capri Film Festival** generally takes place in late December between Christmas and the New Year. It features foreign and Italian films, with an emphasis on attracting major Hollywood celebrities.

Accommodations

The grand dame of the island is the 143-room 【 **Hotel Quisisana** (Via Camerelle 2, tel. 081/837-0788, www.quisi.com, €350 d). It's beautifully landscaped with a pool that looks toward the northern coast. The restaurant has a lovely garden overlooking the sea, with pampering service and a menu of updated Mediterranean cuisine.

Hotel Caesar Augustus Anacapri (Via G. Orlandi 4, tel. 081/837-3395, www.caesar-augustus.com, €430 d) has a spectacular view from its terraces and 56 guest rooms. The property so suited King Farouk of Egypt that he reserved a suite, now named for him, for an entire year.

Food

Island specialties include simple marinated anchovies for an appetizer, generally in a bit of white wine vinegar and olive oil with a dash of garlic and *peperoncino*. *Ravioli alla caprese* has *caciotta* cheese, *parmigiano*, and marjoram in its filling, and is served with a fresh basil tomato sauce. *Pezogna all'acqua pazza* is local fish poached in a broth of cherry tomatoes, *peperoncino*, onion, garlic, celery, carrots, white pepper, water, and white wine. Descendants of Austrian painter August Weber get the credit for *torta caprese*, a dense flat chocolate cake that dates from the 1930s and is made from ground almonds, bittersweet chocolate, and La Strega liqueur; some variations come very close to brownies.

Near the Piazzetta, **Aurora** (Via Furlovado 18, tel. 081/837-0181, daily) is one of Capri's classic restaurants for Neapolitan and Caprese cuisine, in its third generation with outside or inside dining. Celebrities favor **La Capannina** (Via Le Botteghe 14, tel. 081/837-0732, Wed.–Mon.) for its beautiful outside terrace dining, romantic setting, and local cuisine.

A small lemon grove is the setting for **Da Paolino** (Via Palazzo a Mare 11, tel.081/837-6102, daily), with traditional island cuisine that includes meat and fish specialties. **La Cantinella** (Matteotti 8, tel. 081/837-0616, Wed.–Mon.) offers a good selection of local wines and a limited daily selection of courses to show them off. A large terrace with lovely views and reliable local cuisine attract even locals to **La Pergola** (Traversa Lo Palazzo 2, tel.081/837-7414, daily).

Eduardo's **La Savardina** (Via Lo Capo 8, tel. 081/837-6300, Wed.–Mon. lunch only) attracts regulars for its orange trees, which grace the sea view. His linguini recipe is a local favorite and the main courses offer a good selection of meat and fish.

The setting for Anacapri's **Da Gelsomina la Migliara** (Via Migliara 72, tel.081/837-1499, Wed.–Mon. lunch only) is worth the walk along La Migliara; diners eat poolside in the garden. A good selection of well-prepared meat and fish dishes highlight local ingredients. The smart decor, superb service, fine wine selection, and creative cuisine that moves local ingredients to new heights make Anacapri's 【 **Capri Palace Hotel**

l'Olivo (Via Capodimonte 2b, tel. 081/978-0111, daily) a must for gourmet dining.

Information and Services

Capri's tourist information office, between the funicular and the **Piazzetta** (tel. 081/838-6246, www.cittadicapri.it) has especially good trail maps for hiking around the island. **Comune di Anacapri** (Via Caprile 30, tel. 081/838-6246, www.comune.anacapri.na.it) has additional information.

Getting There and Around

Getting around Capri is part of the fun, with plenty of transportation options, although some areas are accessible only on foot. When you arrive at the port, you have a choice of taking the funicular in its tube, a convertible taxi, a city bus, or various water taxis. Anacapri has a chairlift with a stunning view. **Unico Capri Card** provides three different daily options for combined transportation on the bus and funicular. It's on sale at the funicular ticket booth as well as in some *tabacchi* and newspaper stands.

The best way to travel around the island is to do what the locals do: go out on a boat for the day. Inquire at the tourist office or go directly to the port docks and chat up a local skipper; establish price, itinerary, and duration before you set out.

Amalfi Coast

The Amalfi Coast features some of Italy's most spectacular coastal scenery and its most charming hotels. Sheer cliffs overlook a Mediterranean blue sea. Netting is stretched to catch precious grapes, olives, and lemons, grown in vineyards, groves, and orchards wedged into some of the most improbable rocky spaces. Flowers brilliantly accent this derring-do, which makes agriculture seem like an extreme sport. The fragrance and views make for a heady mixture. After you dine you will be ready to cap off the night with a *limoncello,* the potent, thick lemon liqueur that is at its most authentic here. The original recipe calls for Amalfi lemons, some as big as softballs. The Coast of the Sirens is on the southern slope of the Sorrentine Peninsula and ends at the northern edge of the Gulf of Salerno. The area is full of bays and coves, plus its own Emerald Grotto at Conca di Marina to rival Capri's blue version. The fjords in Furore are another spectacle. All the villages have charm, each one distinct from the next. Positano lures shoppers with its boutiques, Vietri is known for its ceramics, and Amalfi has a bit of both.

SORRENTO

Down on the coast, more action is on boats than along beaches. Sorrento is ideal for leisurely strolls, shopping, and the cafe life. The air is fragrant with lemons and especially heady when the trees are in bloom. The fruit is destined to become *limoncello,* the thick liqueur sipped after dinner.

Sights

Take a walk through **Cataldo Lemon Orchard** (Giardini di Cataldo, Corso Italia 267, tel. 081/878-1888) to see local ceramics and other shops along the way. **Museo Correale di Terranova** (Via Correale 50, tel. 081/878-1846, Wed.–Sun. 9 A.M.–2 P.M., €6) is dedicated primarily to the decorative arts, displayed in a lovely villa converted into a museum. The **Duomo** (Cattedrale di San Filippo e Giacomo, Corso Italia 1, tel. 081/878-2248, daily 10 A.M.–noon and 4:30–7 P.M., admission free) was first constructed in the early Middle Ages and then remodeled in the 15th century.

Recreation

If you are coming from Naples and can't wait to take a dip in the water before you get to Sorrento, you might try **Bikini Vico Equense** (Stabilimento Bikini SS Sorrentino 145 km 13.9, www.ilbikini.it, tel. 081/801-5555), which is near sulfur springs on the coast.

NAPLES AND CAMPANIA

Nightlife

Dancers head to **Filou Club** (Via Santa Maria della Pietà 12, tel. 081/878-2083), **Matilda** (Piazza Tasso 8, 081/878-3236), **Kalimera** (Via Capo 53, tel. 081/807-3598), and **Artis Domus** (Via S. Nicola 56, tel. 081/877-2073). Many summer beach clubs along the Sorrento Peninsula often convert to discos at night, so ask around or look for postings for a *discoteca*.

The **Estate Musicale Sorrentina** festival is held throughout the entire summer in the cloister of Sorrento's San Francesco church.

Accommodations

Set right on the town's main square, the 100-room **Grand Hotel Excelsior Vittorio** (Piazza Tasso 34, tel. 081/807-1044, www. exvitt.it) gets you both a view from the top of the tufa cliffs and in the middle of the town action.

If you're hoping to absorb literary inspiration from previous guests like Milton, Byron, Shelley, Keats, Ibsen, and Longfellow, you might try **Imperial Hotel Tramontano Sorrento** (Via V. Veneto 1, tel. 081/878-2588, www.tramontano. com). This private home was converted into a hotel in 1812 and now has 105 rooms.

Built over a Roman villa by Count Mastrobuono in 1750, **Hotel Bellevue Syrene Sorrento** (Piazza Vittoria, tel. 081/878-1024, www.bellevue.it) has 73 rooms, 18th-century frescoes, and a terrace with lovely views of Naples Bay. It is considered one of Italy's finest historic hotels.

In 1822, Sant'Agnello di Sorrento's monastery was transformed into hotel. **Grand Hotel Cocumella** (Via Cocumella 7, tel. 081/878-2933, www.cocumella.com, Easter–Nov. 1, €330–760 d) has maintained its vaulted hall, once the cloister, and the chapel that is still used for weddings. Many of its 61 rooms have antique furniture and the bridal suite has a frescoed ceiling. The monks did not have a pool or a tennis court, which are now yours to enjoy.

Food

An old olive oil mill is the setting for **Antico Frantoio** (Via Casarlano 8, tel. 081/807-2959), which has a good selection of regional wines.

⟨ **Il Buco** (Rampa Marina Piccola 5, tel. 081/878-2354) is located in an old wine cellar and serves good specialties from land and sea, with some creative pairing of flavors.

Dedicated to the famous tenor, **Caruso** (Via Sant'Antonino 12) near Piazza Tasso offers elegant surroundings and refined cuisine. Down by the port where the ferries arrive and depart, **Sant'Anna da Emilia** (Via Marina Grande 62, tel. 081/807-2720) is simple in decor with a casual ambience. The friendly family serves fish and seafood pasta along with a half-dozen main courses.

Getting There and Around

On a summer weekend, drivers with their sights set on a lovely lunch often cannot find parking (pay or free) anywhere. If you are traveling during the summer, fill up the gas tank and plan accordingly to avoid disappointment. Or try the bus. (From Naples heading south, sit on the right for a view and photo-ops; if you dislike heights, sit on the left). The ferry offers good service, too, but you want to get that view from above at least once. The Circumvesuviana connects Sorrento with Naples. Ferries and hydrofoils arrive from Capri.

As you wind your way along the coast road, don't plan to be in a rush. Even in off-season the traffic can crawl along at a snail's pace during rush hour or when a vehicle blocks the narrow two-lane coastal road. That gives drivers a chance to enjoy the scenery instead of minding the road. Curves are tight, so allow buses and trucks plenty of room to maneuver. You may also need to occasionally reverse in order to let larger vehicles pass.

SANT'AGATA SUI DUE GOLFI

Sant'Agata Sui Due Golfi (not to be confused with the Sant'Agata of the Goths between Caserta and Benevento) is a must destination for epicureans, Neapolitans, and chic Europeans tempted by renowned restaurant Don Alfonso. Another attraction is the stunning view of the two gulfs. **Monastero del Deserto** (Via Deserto 23), or Monastero di San Paolo, is occupied by Benedictine nuns. The nuns do not permit visitors inside, however the **Belvedere** (Oct.–Mar. daily 3–4 P.M., APR.–SEPT. 3–8 P.M.) is open briefly thoughout the year and offers a beautiful observation point for visitors respectful of silence and contemplation. The walk to the monastery is lovely.

Accommodations

An extensive 2007 restoration of **❰ Don Alfonso 1890** (Corso S. Agata 11, tel. 081/878-0026, www.donalfonso.com, €280–380 d) has converted all the rooms to suites so guests can experience the same pampering that the restaurant delivers. Pastels echo the tranquil energy of the ground floor color scheme. Furnishings combine family antiques and modern pieces. Two suites on the second and third floors have views of Vesuvius and the bay. This unabashedly charming hotel is one of the most romantic, pleasure-filled getaways in Italy.

Food

When Livia passes by to ask, *"tutto bene?,"* everything is more than *"bene"* at **❰ Don Alfonso 1890** (Corso S. Agata 11, tel. 081/878-0026, www.donalfonso.com, Wed.–Sun. lunch and dinner), it's sublime. Food begins popping fresh from their garden on the precarious cliffs above the gulf. Then Alfonso, his sons, and an orchestra of chefs fine-tune the ingredients into the mythic experience of dining in one of Europe's best restaurants. Surrounded by vivid, joyous pastels, you can watch the action in the kitchen with its bright yellow appliances and ceramic-tiled walls. Gazpacho is made with their San Marzano tomatoes, ravioli filled with fresh *caciotta* cheese is fragrant with their herb garden marjoram and Vesuvian tomatoes, and red snapper is gently enhanced with a crust of "summer fragrances." It's hard to imagine anything outdoing the views of the two gulfs, but for gourmets this is the top sight. You can order à la carte or choose the tasting menu for €145.

Getting There and Around

Sant'Agata sui Due Golfi is served by SITA bus that connects from Sorrento, about 35 minutes without traffic jams.

POSITANO

Positano, Land of the Sirens, in ancient times was dedicated to pleasure villas of the Romans. Positano continues this dedication to pleasure, full of color in its local textiles, the *majolica* ceramic dome on its cathedral, its walls of cascading flowers, pastel houses, and the expanse of Mediterranean Sea below its dramatic cliffs. Near the sea is the scent of maritime fennel and citrus, as you go higher up the mountain the woods have chestnut trees and a vast range of flora. It's an area for bird-watchers, too, although more popular is the star-gazing when Italian celebrities show up in the port. From Positano you can amble through coastal towns on a Vespa.

Sights

The only ancient Roman villa remains are in nearby Minori. The town you see now developed in medieval times around the Benedictine abbey, a center of work and education, as well as medicine. San Vito, the patron saint, is popular throughout the Province of Salerno. The Church of Santa Maria Assunta is especially interesting outside for its bas-reliefs on the bell tower carved on the facade, with sea monsters and even a fox chasing a fish. Inside the church, everything is gold and white. Highlights are the sea view from the window near one of the right chapels and the Byzantine 12th-century Black Madonna. Near the last pew, note the glass cover over a Roman well.

Walk down to coast on foot to swim at one of the inviting beaches. **Spiaggia Grande** and **Fornillo** are both equipped with *stabilimenti* (beach establishments) where you can rent deck chairs and spend the day in the sun. In the port, fishermen will be delighted to take you to small inlets and lovely grottoes.

Shopping

As you walk around looking at shops or markets, keep in mind that if the prices seem too good to be true you are probably buying Chinese goods. Positano is known for its linen and cashmere, quality that isn't cheap. The swimsuit look for men here is paisley, which you find all over priced €15–20. If you're looking for a stunning evening gown or an updated, fashionable casual look, try **Sfizio** (Via del Saracino 55, tel. 089/875-358). The island's best buy is at the Il Mattino newsstand (Apr.–Oct. daily 8 A.M.–8 P.M.), where you can buy €1.50 postcards of Positano and other coastal towns painted by Ottavio Romano, an artist that lived here for years. Frame the card with a locally made ceramic or wood frame, and you have a splendid gift or memory for yourself.

Accommodations

Elegant **Hotel Sirenuse** (Via Colombo 30, tel. 089/875-5066, €150 d), graced with colorful bougainvillea and other colorful flowers, makes for a pleasant stay. A lovely atmosphere and good service keep guests coming back to **Hotel Poseidon** (Via Pasitea 148, tel. 089/811-111, €200 d).

Food

Don't shy away from hotel dining, which in Italy often has some of the most creative chefs. The international clientele in sophisticated hotels gives them the opportunity that they may not have in restaurants that cater to more tradition-bound local clientele. Try **Hotel Palazzo Murat** (Via dei Mulini 223, tel. 089/875-177, www.palazzomurat.it) and **Hotel San Pietro** (Via Laurito 2, tel. 089/875-455, www.ilsanpietro.it). There's also creative dining by candlelight in Hotel Sirenuse's **La Sponda** (Via Colombo 30, tel. 089/875-5066) restaurant.

Under an arbor of bougainvillea, a great place to start your morning with a cappuccino and sea view is **La Zagara Bar** (Via Mulini 5, tel. 089/811-210, Apr.–Oct. daily 8 A.M.–midnight), which is cozy in winter when they light up the fireplace. In the evening, locals pop in for an *aperitivo*. Set on the edge of the beach next to the port, **Buca di Bacco** (Via Rampa Teglia 4, 089/875-699, Mar.–Nov., €36–70) makes for good dining with cuisine that highlights bounty from the sea.

Getting There and Around

Before you arrive, be aware that Positano has posted notices about decorum in town: no swimsuits, resting, or singing (yes, that is what the sign says, perhaps the fear of Sirens runs deep) or you can be fined €25–500. By bike if you're fit or by Vespa if you need a motor, begin at Vietri sul Mare, past Cetara, Maiori, Minori, Atrani, Amalfi, Praiano and end 37 kilometers in Positano. See the *Salerno* section for bus and ferry information. Medieval cliff towns were not designed with parking in mind, so it can be tough to find a spot. Phone your hotel or restaurant in advance to see if they have parking. Narrow roads often have no shoulders even if you want to consider illegal parking.

AMALFI

Amalfi was once a sea power that rivaled Genoa and Venice. The only vestige of that is its lovely architecture and an annual regatta, **Regata delle Repubbliche Marinare.**

Sights

As you step onto land from the port, left of Porta Marina is the ex-Arsenal, where the stables once were. Now some of the stables are filled with nice shops that specialize in prints and antiques. In one of the stables, open only when an exhibit is on, you can see a full-scale model of a traditional regatta boat with Pegasus at one end, a reminder of the ancient republic's vast commercial empire. Trade took a triangular route to North Africa to sell hardwood, and from there to Constantinople to spend money on luxury goods. Amalfi's armory once housed some of the world's richest merchants—until the Amalfi's decline toward the end of the 13th century when Genoa and Venice remained dominant. These warehouses are all over town and in summer on Saturday nights you can take a tour that starts in Porta della Marina. The town's **Duomo** (Piazza del Duomo, tel. 089/871-324), constructed in the 9th century, is dedicated to St. Andrew. The bell tower is a curious hybrid of Moorish and Italian Romanesque architecture. A nice walk is to take routes toward Valle delle Ferriere or Cateri, toward the paper mills.

the ever-enchanting town of Amalfi

For centuries, Amalfi was famous for its fine paper production, centered in **Valle dei Mulini** (Valley of the Mills), which now is the site of **Museo della Carta** (The Paper Museum, Via Delle Cartiere, tel. 089/830-4561, www.museodellacarta.it, Mar.–Oct. daily 10 A.M.–6:30 P.M., Nov.–Feb. Tues.–Sun. 10 A.M.–3:30 P.M., €4).

As you walk uphill, enter the Duomo. Its museum has a mitre covered with 19,333 pearls, one held by the Bishop of Toulouse (you can see him holding it in Simone Martini's painting in Naples' Capodimonte Museum). This is where the silversmiths show their fine work on the chalices, pitcher, and even a 1713 silver altar. The cathedral is dedicated to St. Andrea (St. Andrew), whose feast day is November 30. On this occasion, swearing and even blasphemy are permitted because citizens believe that this angry action will help the miracle of the liquefaction of the blood to take place. Farther uphill is Via dei Mercanti, a covered street that has shops with ceramics and Amalfi paper, still made at the Cantiere in the Valle di Mull-

ini. The Supportico Rua Nova Mercantorum is a series of tunnels that once led to Arab baths in the 12th and 13th centuries.

Conca dei Marini, five kilometers from Amalfi, has a grotto with water that dazzles like that of Capri's Blue Grotto.

Shopping

Amalfi for centuries has been known for its locally made paper, prized by those who value quality for their correspondence, books, and art. Stop by **Cartiera Amatruda** (Via delle Cartiere 100, tel. 089/871-315) for a good selection that might lure you away from email and back to sending classy letters.

Pasticceria Panza (Piazza Duomo 40, www.pasticceriapansa.it) is famous for its pastry with lemon or orange cream or candied citrus fruits. They also make a good *limoncello*.

Accommodations

Santa Caterina (SS Costa Amalfitana 9, tel. 089/871-012, €335 d) has been run by the same family since 1880 and offers luxury that

© ALESSIA RAMACCIA

Piazza del Duomo in Amalfi

includes a spa, its own lido, and one of the town's best restaurants.

Set on a cliff by the edge of the sea, the 45-room **Luna Convento** (Via P. Comite 33, 089/871-002, www.lunahotel.it, €135 d) dates to the 13th century and in 1821 was transformed into a dreamy hotel with a splendid sitting area in its Moorish-inspired cloister, terrace, pool, and nearby Saracen tower. The formal Luna restaurant has views of the sea, and the bar will serve you where you wish, in case your perch in the cloister or terrace is too lovely to abandon.

Food

Amalfi's best restaurant is **Trattoria da Gemma** (Via Fra Gerardo Sasso 9, tel. 089/871-345, Thurs.–Tues. 12:30 P.M.–2 A.M., €49–65) in business since the 1800s. Set a few steps up from the main street in the center, it's

open for lunch and dinner. **The Gran Caffe Tea Room** (Viale delle Repubbliche Marinare 37, tel. 089/871-047, daily, closed Mon. in winter) dates from 1936, is open seven days, and an ideal spot for a cappuccino and a read of the local newspapers.

The former convent now caters to clientele that seek out superb wines to pair with good local food at **Cantina San Nicola** (Salita Marina Sebaste 8, tel. 089/830-4549, Sat.–Thurs. lunch and dinner, €20–25).

Its few tables make for an intimate dining experience at **Eolo** (Via Comite 3, tel. 089/871-241) where fresh fish and seafood are the specialties.

Set in Pogerola above Amalfi, **Trattoria Rispoli** (Via Riolo 3, tel. 089/830-080, Fri.–Wed. lunch and dinner, €20) serves traditionally prepared fish or meat dishes.

Hotel Luna Convento (open daily for lunch and dinner) has a menu that tends toward classic dishes, a bit retro even, but at reasonable prices. Pasta ranges €12–16, mixed fried fish is €20, and a fish casserole for two is €48. The service is formal and the setting offers a lovely view of the port.

Information and Services

Comune di Amalfi (tel. 089/873-6211, www.comune.amalfi.sa.it) and the **tourist office** (tel. 089/871-107, www.amalfitouristoffice.it) can provide hotel and transportation information.

Getting There and Around

Most of the sea towns provide excursions by boat. **SITA** (www.sitabus.it) buses serve Amalfi and other coastal towns. Service to Vietri and some smaller towns is provided also by a consortium (www.cstp.it).

◖ RAVELLO

Long past its medieval heyday when it was a trading center with Sicily and the Orient, Ravello now offers a picturesque town with Moorish influences, and narrow streets and alleyways to explore. Beloved home for many years of American writer Gore Vidal, this town has a sophisticated performing arts scene, especially during its summer festival. Off the beaten track above the main coastal road, it offers more seclusion than other coastal towns.

Sights

San Pantaleone, the town's patron saint, has the **Duomo** (Piazza del Vescorado, tel. 089/858-311, €2 museum) dedicated to him where his blood is kept in a vial in the San Pantaleone Chapel. Built in 1086 by the first Bishop of Ravello, the church was adorned in 1179 by a magnificent bronze door by Barisano da Trani that shows 54 panels with saints and other designs. The bell tower next to the church dates if from the 13th century.

Villa Rufolo (Piazza Duomo, tel. 089/857-657, 9 A.M.–8 P.M., €5) has had a number of illustrious occupants, including Nicholas Breakspeare, an English pope, Hadrian IV (1154-59), Charles II of Anjou, and King Robert. The villa is full of fantasy and magical spaces. There is a squared tower and a room that has a bathroom topped by a small cupola. The terrace has a view of Capo d'Orso. The tropical garden is where Richard Wagner is said to have set Klingsor's dream in the opera, *Parsifal*. The garden is lush with exotic plants, pines, and cypresses, and concludes in a ravine. Concerts in the villa are organized by the Ravello Festival.

Near the 1333 Church and Convent of Santa Chiara (St. Claire) is the **Villa Cimbrone** (Via Santa Chiara 26, tel. 089/858-072, www.villacimbrone.com), built in the Victorian era by English Lord Grimthorpe. Now a small hotel, the building is worth a visit for its spectacular views and dinner or a drink on the terrace.

Entertainment and Events

Ravello Festival (tel. 089/858-422 or 199/109-910, www.ravellofestival.com) is known as much for the beauty of its setting as for the quality of its chamber music, orchestras, films, dance, and art exhibits that run from early July to mid-September. Save your festival ticket to receive a discount at select restaurants (check the festival program for more information).

Accommodations

Built by a Roman nobleman in Ravello's historic center, **Hotel Villa Maria** (Via S. Chiara 2, tel. 089/857-071, €185–225 d) is an intimate family villa with 17 rooms, a splendid view, and a pool. It is open year-round. Its organic garden supplies the restaurant's kitchen with the freshest produce, which diners can enjoy in creative cuisine served under lime trees in nice weather.

Music lovers will enjoy **Hotel Giordano's** (Via Trinità 4, tel. 089/857-071, €150–175 d) close access to Villa Rufolo and the Cathedral. The swimming pool makes for a refreshing dip or lounge near the arbor.

Renovated in 2005, **Hotel Caruso** (Piazza San Giovanni del Toro 2, tel. 089/857-111, www.hotelcaruso.com, €530 d) has frescoes in the halls, antique furniture, and a garden perfect for a romantic stroll, which has charmed guests for more than a century.

Down below Ravello near the sea, a 15th-century paper mill was converted into the 37-room **Hotel Marmorata Best Western** (Via S.S. Amalfitana 163, tel. 089/877-777, www.marmorata.it, €230 d). A hotel shuttle and city bus connect it with Ravello.

For a pull-out-all the stops stay, guests head to **Rossellini's Palazzo Sasso** (Via San Giovanni del Toro 28, tel. 089/818-181, www.palazzosasso.com, open Mar.–Oct. 31, €429–715 d) to be pampered. Amenities include a perfectly heated pool, two hot tubs, a sauna, steam baths, and a choice of 20–30 spa treatments. The rooms feature colorful tiles and porcelain bathrooms. Guests can enjoy the convenience of being near the main square and gourmets will especially love the hotel's Rossellini Restaurant, which regularly wins major dining awards.

Food

A wine shop evolved to a lovely restaurant that excels at pasta and meat courses at **Cumpà Cosimo** (Via Roma 42, tel. 089/857-156, daily 12:30–3:30 P.M. and 7:30–midnight, €10–40). Order individual courses for a light bite or enjoy a full meal, but don't forget the wine—the choices here are good.

Getting There and Around

By car from Rome or Caserta, the fastest route is the Autostrada A30, exit Nocera-Pagani, follow Valico di Chuinzi and Costiera Amalfitana signs. For a more scenic route take the Vietri sul Mare exit, follow Costiera Amalfitana signs that pass by Cetara, Maiori, and Minori, a road that is heavy with sightseer traffic on weekends and holidays. By train to Naples or Salerno, connect via SITA bus. Or by water take the *aliscafo* (hydrofoil) to Amalfi, then connect to Ravello (7 km) by bus or taxi.

Gulf of Salerno

The Gulf of Salerno stretches from the Amalfi Coast in the north down past Paestum and towns on the Cilento Coast. Salerno was the Longobards' most important territory in Southern Italy. The area came under feudal domination by the Normans (1076–1189) and the Wabians (1190–1286) before Saracen and Byzantine sea merchants swept through. Salerno has been ruled by the Kingdom of Naples, the French, and the Spaniards. The area inland has some of Italy's most important caves in Pertosa and Castelcivita.

SALERNO

After a series of spectacular coastal or hilltop towns, the sight of a bustling city is a jolt back to reality. Therefore, Salerno, capital city of its province, is likely to be passed over by visitors that find that transition unwelcome after a series of dreamy towns. Salerno's modern construction offers little of aesthetic interest, but its medieval center and 19th-century boulevards lead to interesting sights. One of Italy's first medical schools for surgeons was founded here. Salerno makes a good base if you are on a tight

pleasure boats docked in Salerno's port

© ALESSIA RAMACCIA

budget. Hotels here cost less and you can connect to the Amalfi Coast easily and reasonably by public transportation on land or water. The train pulls up not far from the port, so it's easy to get oriented. When you return in the evening, you have good, economical restaurants, stores where locals shop, historic buildings to admire, and the movement of ships in the port. If you get out and walk, you'll see a swan begin to emerge from the ugly duckling.

Sights

One of Salerno's pleasant surprises is that so much is free, even museum entrances. You'll see lovely shops and historic bars in the old quarter, the cathedral, a Benedictine abbey, the funky local archeological museum, a museum of church treasures that includes some of the world's most impressive carved ivory, and a magical medieval herb garden. Pick up a map at the tourist office. A walking tour can begin at **Porta Nova.** As you reach **Piazza Largo Campo,** note the fountain that brought fresh water to the city in the 18th century and a point to refresh yourself or fill your water bottle. You'll see **Castello di Aredi,** with a mixed influence of Byzantine, Lombard, and Norman styles. **La Bastiglia** is the defensive tower above a medieval garden. You can visit its courtyard and see the panorama of sea and mountains from here.

On top of the hill that looks as if a shark has just risen up from the sea is the **San Liberato Monastery,** under restoration in 2008 but still a good place for a walk for its marvelous view. **Villa Comunale** was designed in the mid-19th century to complement the elegance of **Teatro Verdi** (Via Porta Caterina, www.teatroverdis alerno.it), still Salerno's focus for dramatic and musical performances. You can follow the stairway to Minerva, or conserve some energy by taking the town elevator, Ascensore Comunale, up where next you are going to head for **Giardino della Minerva** (tel. 089/252-2423, www.giar dinodellaminerva.it, daily 10:30 A.M.–1:30 P.M. and 5:30–8:30 P.M.), a magical spot that recreates the medieval medical botanic gardens that were essential in the 13th and 14th centuries here. The first section of the garden is classified by plants and herbs relating to the four elements (air, earth, fire, and water) and their corresponding qualities (warm, moist, dry, and cold). The garden is built on five levels, so be sure to see them all so that you can also observe the intricate series of ceramic pipes that moves water up and down from two springs, each level with its own channels and fountains. One level has a pool with goldfish. Each patio has a lovely view of the sea beyond the medieval walls. Stop in its **Tisaneria** (€3–5) to refresh yourself, see what ailments the herbs claim to cure, and buy some herb tea or biscuits to take home. From here you could take a walk on Via Tasso, a scenic street under renovation in 2008. Via Troula de Ruggiero is named for Salerno's first female surgeon, also from medieval times. Largo Montoro becomes the site for outdoor theater performances in the summer.

The **Duomo of San Matteo** (Piazza Alfano I, tel. 089/2231-387, daily 10 A.M.–6 P.M., closed during mass, admission free), commissioned by Robert Guiscard (1076), has a bell tower and medieval courtyard with 28 ancient Roman columns. The bronze door was cast in the 11th century in Constantinople, and nearby you can see graffiti of pilgrims from centuries past. Inside, the ciborio dates to 954. St. Matthew's crypt is particularly interesting for the two views of Salerno painted, restored by the Spanish viceroy in the 1600s, a reminder that until the 13th century Salerno was more important than Naples.

As you head toward the Duomo, stop first in **Museo Diocesano** (San Matteo, 9 A.M.–1 P.M.), once a seminary that now has an impressive collection of Roman and medieval coins, parchment documents, but most of all of intricately carved ivory panels. The 37 panels date to the late 11th or early 12th centuries and tell 18 stories from the Old Testament and 19 from the New. Note the fine details of the church door on one, down to its lock and wall panels. In the King Herod panel knights wear finely rendered mesh armor

The **Museo Archeologico Provinciale** (Via San Benedetto 38, tel. 089/231-135, Tues.–Fri.

8 A.M.–7:30 P.M., Sat.–Sun. 9 A.M.–1:30 P.M., admission free) has extraordinary artifacts from various ancient civilizations, including a life-size bronze sculpture, miniature bronzes, and ceramics; unfortunately, the displays suffer from neglect, poor placement, and you may even have to ask the attendant to turn on the lights, dim as they are.

The **Medieval Aqueduct** (Via Velia) is fascinating for its construction of stone, a marked difference from the precision of the ancient Roman brickwork. Unless you are determined to become acquainted with lesser-known artists of Campania, you can give the **Pinacoteca** (Palazzo Pinto, Via Mercanti 63, Tues.–Sat. 9 A.M.–1 P.M. and 4–7 P.M., Sun. 9 A.M.–1 P.M.), the town art museum, a miss. It's free, though, so maybe Nicola Maria Recco's *Still Life Kitchen Interior* will amuse you with 18th-century traditions that you still see in some country scenes today.

Nightlife

Like Naples, Salerno has its own *movida,* where groups of young friends tend to move from one piazza and bar to the next. Most activity radiates from Via Roma, Via da Procida, and Largo Campo.

Accommodations

Across from the tourist office next to the train station, **Hotel Plaza** (Piazza Vittorio Veneto 42, tel. 089/224-477, www.plazasalerno.it, €100 d) is a modern, functional hotel that isn't glamorous but serves as a handy base.

Salerno has converted a historic monastery into the large, white **Ostello Ave Gratia Plena** (Via Canali, tel. 089/234-776, €14 pp) with private rooms that are pleasant, economical, and have private baths, a model for other cities.

Just below the walls of the Giardini di Minerva, **B&B Villa Avenia** (tel. 089/252-281, www.villaavenia.it, €45 pp) offers a tranquil spot in the upper part of historic Salerno.

Food

The area is famous for its San Marzano tomatoes. The plum-shaped tomatoes, favored especially for sauces, are a major export industry, canned and shipped worldwide. Try them here fresh from the plains beyond the Lattari Mountains.

The pastries at **Antica Pasticceria Chianese dal 1860** (Via da Procida, tel. 089/231-1767), have been a favorite of Salernitans for almost 150 years.

When you are near Villa Comunale, do what the locals do and buy a lemon granita and have your ice as you walk through the exotic garden or sit on a bench. **Bar Umberto** (Via Roma, tel. 089/877-393) serves little snacks and appetizers at lunchtime.

The **Tisaneria** in Giardini di Minerva operates during garden hours, with herbal teas to relax or stimulate you, and expansive views of the sea.

Book an outdoor table in the lovely piazza at **Trattoria del Padre Eterno** (Piazza Flavia Gioia 12, tel. 089/239-305, Wed.–Mon., €10–12). The decor is rustic kitsch and the staff is friendly. The menu is all fish, from fried zucchini flowers with ricotta and anchovies, to boiled sliced potatoes with garum, or *zitia* pasta with *cannolichi* (long, flat, tubular clams). Finish the meal with *liquore di finochetto,* a liqueur made from wild fennel. It's a lively, friendly spot that closes at 1 A.M.

Just like traditional pizzerias, **Antica Pizzeria Vicolo della Neve** (Vicolo della Neve 24, tel. 089/225-705, dinner daily) opens only at night when it's cooler and comfortable enough to fire up the oven. In fact, everything here pops out of the oven. Traditional dishes from Salerno (like lasagna, eggplant, and sausages) are featured and they are all baked with the type of heartier, spicier tomato sauce that maybe you expected to find in Italy. In cooler weather, try heartier dishes like pork liver wrapped in laurel leaves and baked. The prices are good value, including Aglianico red wine that ranges €6–8 for a bottle. The same family has been running things for the last 200 years.

Symposium (Corso Garibaldi 29, tel. 089/233-738, Mon.–Sat.) is one of the area's most celebrated restaurants and features an excellent wine selection to complement its sophisticated cuisine. The owner moves his operation to Sardinia in the summer.

On top of the hill near San Giovanni, **Osteria al Brigante** (Via Linguiti 4, tel. 089/226-592, Tues.–Sun. 1:30–2:30 P.M. and 9–11 P.M., €9–13) has specialties like spaghetti with fresh anchovies or broccoli, pine nuts, and goat cheese. Main courses are fish or lamb and a good selection of *antipasti* will satisfy vegetarians.

Ristorante Sant'Andrea (Largo Campo, tel. 089/234-068, Tue.–Sun. 12:30–3:30 P.M. and 7 P.M.–midnight, €10–12) specializes in fish. For after the theater, or snacks at lunch and dinner, try **Café Bistrot** on Corso Vittorio Emanuele.

Information and Services

As you step out of the train station, Salerno's tourist office is conveniently located to your immediate right (Piazza Ferrovia). Pick up a city map, and the helpful staff will help plot a route. The maps and brochures are useful for the city or province. They can also find a guide for you. Salerno guide Paola Valtutti (tel. 329/460-7701) knows the historic center, coastal towns, and archeological sights well into the Province of Salerno. Another tourist office is located a few blocks away (Via Roma 58, tel. 089/224-744).

Getting There and Around

Salerno's **CSTP** (tel. 800/016-659) is the city bus line, while SITA serves locations out of town. Train and Metromare are other options. Taxi stands are at Piazza Ferrovia, Piazza Amendola, and Piazza Vittorio Veneto.

Salerno has two ports. The ferry is a scenic, economical way to see the Amalfi Coast and avoid car traffic and parking problems on land. By ferry, Salerno to Amalfi is 20 minutes, Amalfi to Positano is 30 minutes, Positano to Sorrento is about 45 minutes. The Salerno–Bacoli Metró del Mare (www.metrodelmare. com) ferry departs from the port Molo Manfredi MM3 and serves Amalfi, Positano, Sorrento, Fico Equense, Ercolano, and Naples. The MM5 goes from Salerno to Amalfi with stops in San Marco, Agropoli, Positano, and Amalfi. By sea, Salerno also links to Messina in Sicily on Caronte & Tourist (tel. 800/627-4141) or to Tunisia on Grimaldi Ferries (tel. 081/496-444).

By SITA bus, Salerno to Amalfi is about an hour and 15 minutes, Amalfi to Positano about 40 minutes. Salerno has direct one-hour bus service to Naples Capodichino Airport, to Naples downtown (1 hr), to Rome (5 hrs) and even Kiev (48 hrs) with stops in Venice and Udine. If you need help with complex bus routes, stop by **Buoncore Travel** (Via Torrione 91/93, tel. 089/795-068).

◖ PAESTUM

Paestum has three magnificent Greek temples, named for the gods Ceres, Neptune, and Hera. **Tempio di Ceres** (500 B.C.), dedicated to the goddess of agriculture and fertility, later became the site of an early Christian community. **Tempio di Nettuno** (450 B.C.), also sometimes called the Temple of Posidonia, has imposing lines, and may have actually been dedicated to Zeus. Paestum's **Basilica** (550 B.C.), a temple dedicated to the goddess Hera, is the best preserved, with nine tapered columns in the front and 18 on the side.

An encased tomb was found here in 1968 with frescoes that represent scenes from a symposium, as well as **Tomb of the Diver,** with a man diving towards the water, as he exits from this world to the next. They are in the **National Museum of Paestum** (Area Archeologica, Via Magna Grecia 919, tel. 0828/811-023, Nov. daily 9 A.M.–3:15 P.M., Jun.–July daily 9 A.M.–7:30 P.M., admission to temples €4 or €6.50 with museum admission), opened in 1952, where early sculptures of Hera and Zeus are also displayed along with artifacts that range from prehistoric to medieval times.

Paestum's temples are among Italy's Greek treasures and are better preserved than most of those that remain in Greece. The seacoast is where Aeneas' boatman drowned in Virgil's *Aeneid,* buried by the local inhabitants. Greek Achaeans came from Sybaris in the 7th century B.C. to settle along the Sele River, where they

© ALESSIA RAMACCIA

Tempio di Nettuno, one of the three Greek Doric temples at Paestum

first erected a sanctuary, the Heraion, dedicated to the goddess Hera from Argo. The religious function was probably matched by a defensive strategy against the Etruscans that had settled on the opposite side of the river. The sanctuary's fame spread widely, and took on its own mythology as having been constructed by Jason and the Argonauts.

Accommodations

Near the Greek temples of Paestum, a cow-punching countess at **Azienda Agrituristica Seliano** (Via Seliano, tel. 082/872-3634, www.agriturismoseliano.it, €120 d) runs this *agriturismo*, a working *bufala* farm that raises buffalo cows that produce milk destined for delicious mozzarella. They can also set you up for horseback riding.

An easy base to explore Paestum and the Cilento Park is from **Santa Lucia di Battipaglia, Antica Masseria La Morella** (Strada Provinciale 8, tel. 082/852-008, www.la-morella.it, €70–136 d), which specializes in *rughetta* that

it exports to England and other Northern European countries. They grow tomatoes, herbs, and other vegetables and fruits for their restaurant. This butter-yellow complex of buildings dates to the mid-1700s and has a swimming pool. Rooms and their apartments with kitchen tend to book up months ahead. The area is flat and nearby dirt roads make for good bike riding away from traffic.

Food

The town has several good *enoteche* (wine bars) that serve hearty food. Gourmet meals range from recipes based on ancient Greek or Roman dishes to contemporary regional cuisine. The moderately priced fare at **Oasi** (Via Magna Grecia 72, tel. 0828/811-935, Apr.–Sept. daily lunch and dinner, Oct.–Mar. Tues.–Sun. lunch and dinner, €18–40) includes pizza and the traditional food of Campania.

Pay tribute to the god of the sea at **Ristorante Nettuno** (Paestum Archeological site, tel. 0828/811-028, summer daily, lunch only, €30–40), near Neptune's temple. Run by the same family since 1929, the restaurant serves a complete seafood lunch (including antipasto, pasta, and *secondo*) and local wines. Outside tables offer temple views and well-prepared meals served by statuesque waiters.

Getting There and Around

The best way to get to Paestum is by car via SS18 south. From the Autostrada A3, exit Battipaglia and follow SS18 south to Paestum. Paestum is 96 kilometers south of Molo Beverello at the Port of Naples, or 35 kilometers south of Salerno. By train, get off at the Capaccio Scalo/Paestum stop, then connect by taxi or bus to Paestum. The **tourist office** in Paestum (Via Magna Grecia 887, tel. 0828/811-016) has bus and train schedules.

Around Paestum

Along the coast of **Agropoli** is where sailors in *The Odyssey* met up with Sirens, like the lovesick Licosa, who turned herself into a rock. Ernest Hemingway was a regular visitor in the 1950s and caught some of his biggest fish here. The historic center of Agropoli is worth a stroll. The town has a castle and its most significant churches are dedicated to the Madonna of Constantinople and to Peter and Paul.

Velia, formerly Elea, was a Greek Focae colony and the seat of the prestigious pre-Socratic school and home of poet Parmenides, a resident at the time of the Roman conquest. The Greek colony was prosperous enough that it minted its own coins. Evidence of this golden age remain in the street that leads to the **Porta Rosa** stone arch, a typical round arch of 4th century B.C. Greek construction.

PUGLIA

Puglia has tempted travelers since the Greeks spotted the rocky coast and decided to plant their civilization in these parts. The region marks a point between East and West where cultures have ebbed and flowed for centuries. You'll hear it in the accents and taste it in the food. It's not your average southern outpost. Puglia is well heeled and well off compared to its neighbors.

The plains and rolling hills that run parallel to the sea are covered in olive groves and vines and it tops the list in extra-virgin production. But this is also where they manufacture fuselages for Boeing Dreamliners and locals are as interested in the future as the past. Visitors are attracted by the long coast, *trulli* houses, and surplus of castles that protect nearly every seaside town.

Here it's possible watch the sunrise over the Adriatic and see it set in the Ionian Sea. In between are Baroque masterpieces like Lecce, blessed with a soft, local limestone that has given sculptors and architects new artistic possibilities. Fishing villages like Otranto and Gallipoli have remained faithful to their origins and provide an opportunity to step into a Byzantine and Norman past.

The exchange of culture is especially present in the region's kitchens, which rely on simplicity rather than over-elaboration. Fish is present on nearly every menu and the durum wheat grown throughout the interior is rolled and cut into dozens of original shapes. Anyone with an appetite can turn the local saying *"qui paga molto, mangia poco"* ("he who spends much, eats little") into a delicious mantra that is easy to follow in Puglia.

© ALESSIA RAMACCIA

HIGHLIGHTS

Castel del Monte: Pictured on the Italian one-cent coin and named as a World Heritage site, this gem of a fortress at the foot of Le Murge Mountains is one of Italy's finest castles, with eight towers overlooking hectares of olive groves and vineyards (page 670).

Lucera: Lucera has the looks of a movie set, but here the Roman amphitheater, castle, and sanctuary are all very real. The town is full of bed-and-breakfasts located inside historic palazzos where it's easy to forget about the 21st century (page 672).

Parco Nazionale del Gargano: Puglia's largest park has a supreme position in the center of the Gargano Promontory. Hundreds of mammals call it home and migrating birds make it an annual pit stop between hemispheres. Nearly every town bordering the mountainous terrain has a park office from where visitors can set off by foot, bicycle, or horseback (page 674).

Alberobello: This town is worth a visit to admire the unique skyline dominated by circular whitewashed *trulli* houses with high conical roofs. Many of the *trulli* houses can be visited and one of the best is the Trullo Sovrano (page 676).

Lecce: There is no one church or palazzo more beautiful than in Lecce. Anyone with a passion for Baroque architecture must make a pilgrimage to the city. At night, all the facades are illuminated and become the backdrop for a *dolce vita* southern style (page 682).

Otranto: This town sits on one of the most scenic bays in the country, but the real highlight here is its largest building, the Cattedrale di Otranto. The mosaic floors inside this church cover nearly 1,000 square meters and are the largest of their kind. It's almost a shame to walk on them (page 684).

LOOK FOR **(** TO FIND RECOMMENDED SIGHTS, ACTIVITIES, DINING, AND LODGING.

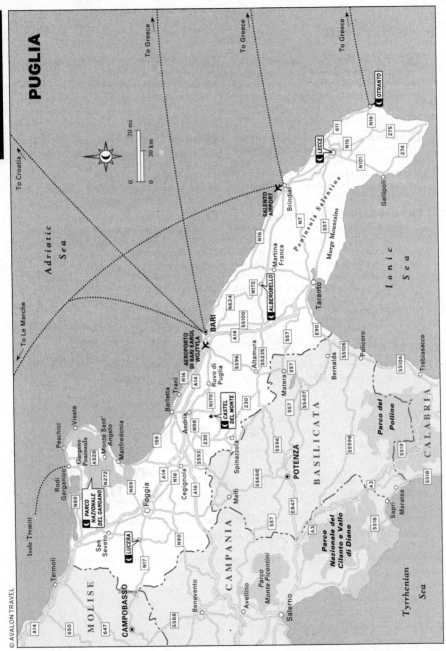

PUGLIA

PLANNING YOUR TIME

Puglia is shaped a little like Florida, minus the panhandle. Most of its 800-kilometer coast faces the Adriatic Sea and waters here are particularly clean. At the northern edge near the border with Molise is a vast promontory with two seaside lakes and 1,000-meter peaks in the center. There are hills inland, most notably Le Muraghe, that run north–south through western Puglia. The rest is flatland that has been a boon for grapes and especially olives. If your oil says "Made in Italy," chances are it comes from here and rows of twisted trees line the roads from Bari to Brindisi.

The climate and geography are also similar to the Sunshine State, and in the Salentina Peninsula only 50 kilometers separates the Adriatic from the Ionian Sea. Roads are relatively slow along the coast and the Autostrada Adriatica (A14) runs from Foggia to the outskirts of Taranto, where it remains to be completed. Eurostar train service between Foggia, Brindisi, and Bari is quick, but local trains make many stops and haven't run on time since Mussolini was in charge of things.

Unless you're planning on seeing it all or have a week to spend exploring the entire coast, you may have to choose between heading north or south from Bari. It's a tough choice between the natural wonders of the Gargano Promontory or the cultural ones of the Salentina Peninsula.

Lecce is the most beautiful city and should be circled on your map. Although it's not centrally located it can make a good base from which to absorb the region. It's close to the beaches and many roads lead from the city to surrounding countryside that provide endless opportunities for daily excursions.

Tourism is well developed and there is no lack of *masseria,* the Puglian version of *agriturismo* accommodation. On many of these farms, visitors can roll up their sleeves and give locals a hand transforming the fruits of the earth into *orecchiette* pasta, Altamura bread, and Negroamaro wine. August is crowded and the weather is as good in June. In recent years, forest fires have ravished vast swathes of land and it's wise to check the news before your arrival.

HISTORY

Greek colonists from Laconia and Sparta first reached the shores of Puglia in the 8th century B.C. They founded the cities of Gallipoli,

THE BATTLE OF CANNAE

In 216 B.C., Hannibal led Carthaginian forces from Spain across the Alps in an attempt to invade the Italian Peninsula and destroy Rome once and for all. Although the general ultimately failed to win the Second Punic War, he did manage to win its greatest battle. At Cannae he was confronted with eight Roman legions totaling 90,000 men and had less than half the number of troops in his ranks. The Romans set their cavalry on the flanks and advanced with their heavy infantry in deep formations in the center. Their plan was to use their numeric advantage to smash the enemy the tried and tested way.

Hannibal, on the contrary, knew his weakness and positioned his most unreliable troops in the center, with Libyan cavalry on either flank. Seasoned troops remained in the rear and formed a long arc. The center of this line slowly retreated as the Romans marched over the flat plain that separated the two armies into the expanding arc. They advanced so far that Hannibal's heavily armed troops on either wing faced the side of Roman legions who were caught between two hostile lines.

The Romans were eventually encircled and an estimated 60,000-70,000 legionnaires were killed or captured. The battle remains one of the deadliest conflicts over a single day in military history and the greatest defeat ever inflicted upon the Romans. The double encirclement, or pincer tactic, that Hannibal employed was successfully repeated by the Germans on the Russian front during World War II and is still studied today.

Otranto, and Taranto, where *Magna Grecia* prospered and managed to overcome fierce resistance from native Iapigi tribes who didn't welcome the newcomers with open arms. Roman interest in the area began after the second Sannitica war when bases were established in Lucera and Venosa. Taranto fell in 272 B.C. and began a long decline as Romans favored the port of Brindisi, which was later connected to Roma by the Via Appia and provided a convenient sea link to Macedonia, Greece, Egypt, and Syria.

Christianity began to play a role in the region during the third century A.D. and was firmly established by the time the archangel Michael was spotted on Monte Gargano. The fall of the Empire caused less chaos than in other regions and the real dark ages came during the years of fighting between Byzantines and Goths. Lombards and Saracens followed and it wasn't until the Normans arrived that things settled down.

Thanks to the first crusade, many of the coastal cities were revived and received both an economic and architectural lift. Frederick II was responsible for building more castles and churches than anyone else and managed to unify the land. Spanish occupation with brief intervals of Austrian and Napoleonic troops led to a steady decline, which the Bourbons had little interest in reversing. Things only began to improve after World War I when the economy began to diversify from agriculture into heavy industry. Today Puglia remains distinct from its southern neighbors and can look forward to the future with optimism.

Bari and the Adriatic Coast

Founded on a small promontory overlooking the Adriatic in the center of this region, Bari has been the most important city in Puglia since the French made it the capital in 1808. Its old town is a compact maze of buildings that contrast sharply with its newer neighborhoods organized in Manhattan-style blocks. The coastal road surrounding Bari is flat and runs along the sea. Beach establishments are plentiful here and divided by small inlets and picturesque dunes. Industrialization hasn't affected the color of the water in this area, which remains a delightful aquamarine and remarkably clean.

BARI

Bari is a bustling city of 400,000 in the center of the Adriatic coast. It has been the regional capital since 1808, when the French rewarded residents for their loyalty to republican ideals. Fishing is a major occupation and Horace's description of the city as being "rich in fish" remains as true today as it was when the town was known as Barium by the Romans. The most interesting parts are concentrated in the triangular neighborhood near the old port, where women still roll pasta outside their front doors and archways are too numerous to count.

Sights

Corso Vittorio Veneto divides the new city from old Bari. The difference is evident in the straightness of the roads and once you pass through the ancient walls the grid pattern gives way to a maze of intriguing alleys and piazze.

San Nicola (Piazza San Nicola, Sun.– Tues. 7:30 A.M.–7:30 P.M. and Wed.–Sat. 7:30 A.M.–12:30 P.M. and 4:30–7:30 P.M.) is easier to stumble upon than find by making a conscious effort. The Romanesque cathedral was built to preserve the remains of Saint Myra and Nicholas, the patron of the city, whose remains are buried in the crypt. The limestone facade is blinding on a sunny day and especially amusing are the two hippopotamuses supporting the columns of the central portal. Inside are more examples of fine medieval sculpture, including the marble Episcopal throne near the altar held aloft by three grotesque figures. Floor mosaics are the work of 12th-century craftsmen and show signs of Eastern influence.

Behind the church, **Via Venezia** runs along the ancient bastions parallel to the sea and leads towards **Piazza Mercantile,** where the town comes to celebrate. The stone column next to a sculpted lion is where debtors and thieves were tied up in the Middle Ages. Nearby is Piazza del Ferrarese and a lively local market. From here you can exit the old gate and stroll along the Augusto Coastal road built in the 1930s. The long promenade provides lovely views of the port and old town, and leads to **Fortino di Sant'Antonio,** where animals are blessed on January 17.

Castles in Puglia don't get much bigger than **Castello Svevo** (Piazza Federico II, tel. 080/528-6219, Tues.–Sun. 9 A.M.–7 P.M., €2). Frederick II used it to demonstrate his power and in 1233 added the monumental entrance to the existing fortifications. The rough hexagon shape is accentuated by corner bastions typical of military engineering of the time. They guard a shallow moat that prevented an approach from the sea. Inside it's a different story, and Isabella of Aragon held court here in the 16th century. She enjoyed a life of luxury in the Minorenni tower where her guests included a long list of writers, artists, and playboys. In the 18th century, it was transformed into army barracks and now houses a cultural center that frequently organizes temporary exhibitions.

The **botanical garden** (Via Orabona 4, tel. 080/544-2152) dates from the time of Gioacchino Murat, who built much of the new city that extends Manhattan-style south of Corso Vittorio Emanuele II. Buildings are a mix of 18th-century *palazzi* and neoclassical structures—like **Teatro Piccinni** (Corso Emanuele I, tel. 080/521-2484, www.teatropubblicopugliese.it), inaugurated in 1854, and **Museo Archeologico** (Piazza Umberto I, tel. 080/524-2361), with 30,000 prehistoric and Greek remains that can't be seen until restoration of the museum is complete in late 2008. New opening hours to be announced then.

Entertainment and Events
Procession of Mysteries is a tale of two moods. On Good Friday, the procession winds its way mournfully from Chiesa della Vallissa through the old town accompanied by a funeral march. Two days later, locals are smiling again and Easter songs are sung with gusto and *scarcedde* sweets are exchanged. If no one offers you any, just stop into the nearest *pasticceria* and buy your own.

The evening before **Festa di San Nicola,** the relics of the saint are symbolically returned from the sea. On May 8, a fisherman is chosen at random and rows the statue of the saint out into the port, where the faithful come to pay their respects. In the evening, pilgrims from Abruzzo carrying a liquid said to be derived from the bones of the saint celebrate the miracle man in his church.

Shopping
Via Sparano, which leads from the train station to the old town, is the main commercial thoroughfare. It's lined with elegant shops and is blissfully traffic-free.

Libreria Laterza (Via Sparano 136, tel. 080/521-1780, daily 9 A.M.–8:30 P.M.) is a historic bookstore that just received the 21st-century treatment. Crystal, wood, and steel now surround the books, which cover every genre from Arab literature to zoology. A high-speed Internet point, small cafeteria, and children's theater have also been added, making Laterza a pleasant pit stop. If books are a passion, drop by the **Biblioteca Nazionale** (Via Pietro Oreste 45, tel. 080/217-3111, daily 9 A.M.–1 P.M.), housed in two wonderfully restored buildings.

The name says it all. **Artelier** (Via Melo 195, tel. 080/528-9374) creates original sculptures from recycled materials that will give your other conversation pieces something to talk about. They also design clothes that take a lot of character to wear. For a more vintage look, visit **Les Trois Marchès** (Via XXIV Maggio 32, tel. 328/931-1846). This neatly organized store stocks ties, hats, shirts, and trousers first worn in the 1940–1980s.

© ALESSIA RAMACCIA

the pristine Adriatic Sea

Bari has a healthy number of stores selling art, antiques, and housewares. **Misia Arte Antiquariato** (Via Niccolò Putignani 153, tel. 080/521-2826, www.misiarte.com, Tues.–Sun.) is split into four sections: art deco, neoclassical, 17th century, and modern. During the summer, the small garden is used to stage concerts. For more design-oriented objects, try **Rouge** (Via Salvatore Cognetti 36, tel. 080/528-9597, Mon.–Sat. 10 A.M.–1 P.M. and 5–8 P.M.) or **Tarshito** (Via de Rossi 9). If you want something to hang on your walls or are searching for sculpture, **Galleria d'Arte Bonomo** (Via Niccolò dell'Arca 19, tel. 080/521-0145, Mon.–Sat. 11 A.M.–1 P.M. and 5–8:30 P.M.) and **Laterza** (Via Sparano) can help.

Accommodations

◖ **Scandic by Hilton** (Via Don Guanella 15, tel. 080/502-6815, €90 d) isn't an average hotel. It's a mix of contemporary art, design, and Mediterranean hospitality. Innovation is present in all 88 rooms, with lamps that dim or brighten by touch and the best showers in the region. The ground floor hall is the place to admire sculpture, check the Internet, or quench your thirst before entering the bright restaurant overlooking the garden. A beauty center and swimming pool are also available for guests.

Immersed within two hectares of olive trees, a short way from the center, **Terra Nobile** (Via Bitritto 101, tel. 080/506-1529, €180 d) is for people who take relaxation seriously. All 15 rooms of this charming hotel located within an 18th-century palazzo are decked out in period furnishings that help guests forget what year it is. If that doesn't work the underground spa with hammam, sauna, and swimming pool usually does. For lunch or dinner, the restaurant calms any remaining nerves with an impressive number of regional and national wines.

Food

Bari may seem like a synonym for bedlam, but once you enter **Al Focolare da Emilio** (Via Principe Amedeo 173, tel. 080/523-5887, Tues.–Sun. noon–3 P.M. and 7–11:30 P.M., closed Aug., €8–12) the chaos will be a distant memory. The Veronoli family put diners at ease with their good humor and excellent cooking. Dorotea prepares grilled vegetables, *frittatine*, and other antipasti that relieve hunger fast and prepare stomachs for the *tagliatelle ai frutti di mare* or fish specialties. There are few wine and dessert options, but they roll a good pizza after 7 P.M.

It's a lovely walk to **La Locanda di Federico** (Piazza Mercantile 63, tel. 080/522-7705, Tues.–Sun. noon–2:30 P.M. and 7–10:30 P.M., €7–9) along Corso Vittorio Emanuele, around Piazza Ferrarese (where fishmongers gather daily), and into the sumptuous Piazza Mercantile that smells of the old town. Gianluca hasn't removed his smile in years and escorts diners to outside or inside tables where *calzone di cipolla* (onion calzone), stuffed squid, and seafood specialties are waiting. This is the place to dig your spoon into *sporcamusi alla crema* (cream-filled pastry) and ponder how sweet life can be.

Not far from Piazza della Libertà and the animated narrow streets that supply old Bari with its charm is where traditionalists gather for lunch and dinner. ❖ **Osteria delle Travi** (Largo Chiurlia 12, tel. 339/157-8848, Tues.–Sun. noon–3 P.M. and 7–11 P.M., €8–11) is a large, functional *osteria* with high ceilings, lots of light, and an amazing floor. The Mastro brothers keep service running smoothly and the stuffed eggplants are legendary. First courses change according to what's on sale in the market and *orecchiette salsiccia e funghi* (sausage and mushroom pasta) appears in autumn and winter while the *frittura* (fried fish) platter is an annual that easily feeds two. Try the *cavallo* (horse) *al ragù* before you write it off. You may never eat another cow again. Wines are limited but the house red is worth a sniff.

For a taste of Bari's version of pizza by the slice, focaccia, or bread, visit **Panificio Veneto** (Via Corso Cavour 125, tel. 080/521-1431, Mon.–Sat. 8 A.M.–2:30 P.M. and 5:30–8 P.M.) or **Panificio Marazia** (Via Manzoni 217, tel. 080/521-9164, Mon.–Sat. 9 A.M.–2 P.M. and 4–8:30 P.M.). Cured meats and other gastronomic specialties from Puglia, Basilicata, and Calabria are waiting behind the counter of **Il Salumaio** (Via Piccinni 168, tel. 080/521-9345, Mon.–Sat. 8 A.M.–1:30 P.M. and 4:30–9 P.M.).

There is some debate but many say **Pasticceria Gelateria Stoppani** (Via Roberto da Bari 79, tel. 080/521-3563, Mon.–Sat. 7 A.M.–2 P.M. and 3:45–9 P.M.) serves the best espresso in town. They also do pastries, *panini*, and *aperitivi* after 4 P.M. **Caffè Sotto il Mare** (Via Venezia 16, Tues.–Sun.) and **DolceAmaro** (Via San Francesco d'Assisi 9, tel. 080/528-9368, Tues.–Sun. 4 P.M.–midnight), a literary coffee bar with a Paris feel, are also worth stopping by for a sip. Gelato fans can find naturally made flavors within an Asian-style atmosphere at **Barcolla** (Piazza Mercantile 70, daily). You can take the weight off on one of the red couches where locals and visitors gather to lick their cones.

La Puglia è Servita (Via Imbriani 17, Mon.–Sat.) is a gastronomic superstore stocked with oils, pasta, and cheese produced in the region. They also offer short cooking classes and can teach you how *orecchiette* should be served. It's hard to walk out of **Enoteca Cucumazzo** (Viale Japigia, Mon.–Sat.) without a bottle of wine. They have over 3,000 bottles on their wooden shelves and frequently run tastings that will help palates appreciate Puglian vintages.

Information and Services

There are information points in the arrival terminal at Bari airport, the ferry terminal, and at the train station. Each is open daily 9:30 A.M.–7:30 P.M. Free tours are organized from the train station office in Piazza Moro on Mondays and Tuesdays 2:30–7:30 P.M. Participants must register one day in advance at any of the tourist offices. Itineraries include archeological, biological, and cultural tours.

Getting There and Around

Bari International airport was recently renamed **Aereoporto di Bari Karol Wojtyla** in honor of the late Pope John Paul II. It's small and efficient, and has daily flights to Rome Fiumicino and both Milan airports. City bus 16 (daily

5 A.M.–11 P.M., €0.77) stops once an hour and gets passengers to the center in 40 minutes. Autobus Tempesta (5:30 A.M.–11:30 P.M., €4.15) is reliable, faster, and more expensive.

The A14 highway was routed specifically towards Bari and connects the city to the eastern side of the country. Drivers coming from Rome can head south on the A1 and pick up the A16 near Naples, which eventually joins the A14 near Canosa. It's a good seven-hour drive without traffic. Eurostar train service from the capital leaves before 8 A.M. and mid-afternoon. The journey costs €38 and takes under five hours. From the port, ferries regularly depart in the summer for Croatia and Greece.

AMTAB (Corso Italia 54, tel. 080/528-9587) operates city transportation and recently launched a "Bari in Bici" bike-sharing initiative. For €10, visitors can pick up a bicycle in one of five locations, including the train station, and explore the center and seaside promenades on two wheels. To receive the Bici card and a lock, stop by the AMTAB office. A single bus ticket costs €0.80 and a daily pass is €1.80.

TRANI

Trani is a whitewashed port founded in the third century B.C. Trade with the maritime republics of Genova, Pisa, and Amalfi helped shape the character of the town during the Middle Ages when a large Jewish community made the historic center their home. The town is famous for the Romanesque cathedral overlooking the sea that has been a landmark for sailors since the 11th century.

Sights

Trani should be savored slowly, and the old Jewish neighborhood is a good place to start. It houses four synagogues including **Sinagoga di Scolanova** (Via Scolanova 23, tel. 088/395-0639, opened upon request, admission free), which is the oldest temple in Europe. **Piazzetta Sinagoga** is the center of the area and all five streets leading from the square are tempting.

The **Cattedrale di Trani** (Piazza Duomo, tel. 088/348-0557, daily 9 A.M.–8 P.M., admis-

sion free) sits in a unique position by the sea uncluttered by other buildings. It was built over two previous churches and according to legend dedicated to Saint Nicola, a Greek shepherd carried to town by dolphins. The bronze doors of the central portal have 32 sculpted panels and are reached by a staircase that gives the church added height. Inside, the three naves supported by 22 marbles columns have recently been scrubbed to their original whiteness and lead to the **Museo Diocesana** (Palazzo Arcivescovile, Piazza Duomo 8/9, tel. 080/521-0064, Thurs. 9:30 A.M.–12:30 P.M. and 4:30–6:30 P.M., Sun. 9:30 A.M.–12:30 P.M., opened upon request on other days, €2) where a number of Middle Age paintings, sculptures, and religious relics are on display.

Castle Svevo (Piazza Federico II di Svevia 2, tel. 088/350-6603, Tues.–Sun. 8:30 A.M.–7:30 P.M., €2) next door was built by Frederick II between 1233 and 1249. It's reached by a long stone bridge and has been used as a courthouse and jail. In 1998 it was converted into a cultural center and now houses a small museum and permanent photographic exposition.

The **port** was the most important in the Adriatic between the 10th and 11th centuries, and the first medieval rules of the sea, *Ordinamento Maris,* were devised here. The pentagram-shaped basin faces several piazze from where fishermen can still be observed transporting their haul to market. On the opposite side of the cathedral are the communal gardens, which border the sea and provide clear views of the old town.

Accommodations

Located in a 15th-century palazzo in the Jewish quarter, **Porta Antica** (Via La Giudea 56, tel. 347/597-6656, €50 d) is a small bed-and-breakfast with two double rooms, a breakfast room, and apartment. The owners are quick to make guests feel at home and the small garden is ideal for ending a long day spent on the nearby beaches.

Hotel Regia (Piazza Mons, tel. 088/358-4444, €130 d) is near the cathedral and all 10 rooms have a view of the sea. An elegant decor and quality restaurant make it a good base from which to explore the town.

Food

The two dining rooms inside **Cafè Moliere** (Via Scolanova 7, tel. 347/946-7762, Mon.–Fri. 9:30 A.M.–noon, Sat.–Sun. 9:30 A.M.–2 P.M., €8) are surrounded by exposed brick walls and vaulted ceilings. The restaurant is perfect for a quick lunch or *aperitivo*. Besides a wide selection of cheeses, they serve a number of cold platters, including *bresaola* and smoked salmon that can be accompanied by good regional wines. **Corteinfiore** (Via Ognissanti 18, tel. 088/350-8402, Tues.–Sun. noon–3 P.M. and 7–11 P.M., €9–13) is more on the romantic side and is especially pleasant on summer evenings when the fruit trees are lit up and couples dine in relative intimacy. The menu has a strong Mediterranean influence and the fish soup and lobster Catalan-style are especially appetizing. Another seafood option near the castle is **I Vizi del Re** (Piazza Re Manfredi 12, tel. 088/350-6809, Thurs.–Mon. noon–3 P.M. and 7:30–10:30 P.M., €8–12), which serves grilled fish and *spaghetti allo scoglio* (seafood and pasta).

Getting There and Around

Trani lies on the Adriatic 42 kilometers north of Bari. It can be reached along the N16 coastal road that passes through Molfetta and Bisceglie or those towns can be bypassed with the freeway that runs slightly inland. The driving is slower on the coast but the views are better. Trains leave every hour from Bari central station and take 30 minutes.

RUVO DI PUGLIA

Ruvo lies at the foot of the Murge Mountains between vineyards and olive groves. The town has a 2,000-year-old reputation for producing *àpule* ceramics that can be seen at Museo Nazionale Jatta. The Romanesque cathedral is built from limestone and also deserves a visit.

Sights

The somber facade of the **cathedral** is pierced by a colorful rose window and a finely sculpted portal. Naves are higher than you'd expect from the exterior and if you stick to the right of the church you can see traces of an earlier church, mosaics, fragments of Roman dwellings, and an ancient well.

Museo Nazionale Jatta (Piazza Bovio 35, tel. 080/361-2848, www.palazzojatta.org, Mon.–Thurs. and Sun. 8:30 A.M.–1:30 P.M., Fri.–Sat. 8:30 A.M.–7:30 P.M., admission free) possesses a collection of 2,000 antique vases, including the superb *Cratere di Talos* in the last room that's painted black and decorated with red figures.

It's a nice stroll up **Via Gaspari** towards the 16th-century clock tower and Palazzo Caputi. The nearby **Piazza Matteotti** is a popular gathering spot for locals and is surrounded by beautiful buildings and the remains of a medieval castle.

Accommodations

Thirty meters from the cathedral in a tiny square, **La Torretta** (Via Sant'Arcangelo 29, tel. 349/723-2365, €80 d) provides two comfortable rooms within a medieval-era setting. The owners will happily suggest itineraries and point out what's worth visiting from the roof terrace. They serve breakfast on the first floor that includes locally produced jams and fresh breads. Those who like large rooms may find themselves a little cramped.

Food

The Saule family run a pleasant little *ristorante* that serves food grown and raised in the adjacent hills. Mother and father do the cooking while their two sons keep diners happy with plates of *focaccia farcita* (thin local bread made with flour, milk, and corn oil) and *burratine* (mozzarella-like cheese). They make a good *purè* and flavorful *fettuccine con ragù di anatra* (duck). The lamb is roasted with mountain herbs and the cellar is stocked with fine local wines. Given the small number of tables at **Ristor** (Via Alberto Mario 36, tel. 080/361-3736, Tues.–Sun. noon–3 P.M. and 7:30–10:30 P.M., €9–12) reservations are wise during the summer and on weekends.

PUGLIA

For extra virgin oil that can be drunk by the glass, visit **Elaiopolio Cooperativo** (Via Scarlatti 25, tel. 080/361-1619, daily 8:30 A.M.–1 P.M. and 4–7 P.M.) and take home some certified-organic olives that will transform salads and anything else they touch. **Pasticceria Petrarota** (Piazza Garibaldi 12, tel. 080/361-1022, Fri.–Wed. 8:30 A.M.–1 P.M. and 3:30–9 P.M.) was founded in 1870 and five generations later they still produce the best gelato in town. The pastries are equally good, but anyone allergic to almonds should beware.

Getting There and Around

Ruvo di Puglia is the kind of detour you take when time is on your side and you want to see some countryside. Roads to town are straight and you can either take the N98 or turn left at Molfetta. Train service is sketchy and after Ruvo runs on a single track.

Around Ruvo di Puglia
CASTEL DEL MONTE

Fifteen kilometers northwest of Ruvo on the N98/N170 is one of the finest castles in all of Italy. Castel del Monte (tel. 080/528-6238, daily 10 A.M.–6:30 P.M., €3) fully deserves its place on the Italian one-cent coin. It's an octagonal bastion with eight towers overlooking acres of olive groves and vineyards. It was built by Frederick II in the 13th century and used by the emperor as a hunting lodge and personal retreat. The eight rooms on the second floor are decorated in marble and benefited from a sophisticated plumbing system that recycled rainwater into an underground cistern. UNESCO recognized the castle as a World Heritage Site in 1996 for its symmetry. To fully appreciate the geometric form, visitors should circumnavigate the 24-meter-high walls before entering the Roman-style triumphal entrance.

Foggia and the Tavoliere

Puglia's fourth-largest city, Foggia, was flattened during World War II but fortunately many good parts were spared. It lies in the center of the wide Tavoliere Plain that stretches from the Adriatic to the Apennines. The roads leading out of the city are dotted with Romanesque churches and castles left behind by the Normans. There's an excellent example in Lucera where it's hard to eat a bad meal and the mozzarella is on par with Campania's.

FOGGIA

Puglia's capital wasn't blessed with the good looks of Lecce or Alberbello. The eyesores on the outskirts of this medium-size working-class city eventually give way to a compact historic center that has yet to catch the imagination of tourists. Still the town's location off the A14 and good road connections to a half-dozen interesting villages in the interior make it worth stopping for a couple of hours.

Sights

Signs to the *centro storico* lead to Piazzetta Cattedrale and the town's oldest street. Via Arpi was once the center of action and a walk up and down the cobblestones from Porta Arpi to Via Fuiani takes you past Foggia's finest palazzos and churches, many of which are open to the public.

The **Duomo** (Piazzetta Cattedrale, tel. 088/172-3141) is a mix of styles that was begun under the orders of Roberto il Guiscardo in 1080. It survived the earthquake of 1731 and heavy World War II bombings. Royal weddings were celebrated inside and if you look closely on the right wall you'll find the spot where Charles of Anjou's heart is buried. The Baroque angels and sculptures that cover the single nave are currently under restoration, along with the facade. Restoration efforts are expected to continue through early 2009.

Museo Civico (Porta Grande, Palazzo Negri, tel. 088/172-6245, Tues.–Sun. 9 A.M.–1 P.M., Tues. and Thurs. also 4–7 P.M., €2) was created in 1931 and recounts the history of the town and surrounding province. The museum is located inside an old villa near the imperial residence of Federico II, of which only an arch remains. On the ground floor are relics from the city's past and the tombs of prominent knights who once defended the area. Upstairs the guard has a scale model of a Puglian village and 19th-century ceramics all to himself. There is also a small archeological section with Roman remains and a gallery filled with local painters.

Entertainment

Foggia comes alive dark and nightlife during the summer gets going at midnight when Piazzetta Cattedrale fills up with a young crowd intent on having a good time. There's a high concentration of pubs, wine bars, and restaurants in the narrow streets around the area that remains buzzing until late. An acrobatic barman serves fruit cocktails to an eager clientele at **Touba** and a good selection of beer is available from **Nessun Dorma. Via Bruno** next to the Duomo has something for everyone from the Latin music of Nuevo Mundo to the refined Italian pub of **AlPachino** that also serves fabulous eggplant dishes. Nearby the cultural center of **La Table du Petit Chateau** (Via Bruno 12, Tues.–Sun.) organizes concerts and poetry readings accompanied by fusion recipes created by an Italian-Canadian chef who takes his artichokes seriously.

Teatro Umberto Giordano with its pretty neo-classical facade is the pride of town. Unfortunately, like the duomo, it's also undergoing a facelift and covered in scaffolding but the interior remains operational. Concerts are usually classical and tickets can be purchased on the day of an event from the box office. There's usually no problem finding a red velvet seat in one of the three balconies.

Shopping

On the second weekend of every month, Via Duomo fills with market stalls selling antiques and collectibles. There's a lot of old farm equipment that could look good hung up on a wall or resting on a mantle. At all other times, stop by **Paolo Antonio** (Via Arpi 3, tel. 088/172-5063, daily) for antiques hailing from the Gargano promontory. He also sells a range of ceramics, stamps, and assorted oddities that fill the shelves of this small shop on the town's most lively street. **Terra e Fuoco** (Piazza Federico II 13, tel. 088/172-3626, Mon.–Sat.) is a workshop where old mapmaking techniques are faithfully preserved. Most are produced on wooden panels and show the ancient transhumance routes once used by local sheepherders.

Accommodations

White House (Via Sabotino 26, tel. 088/172-1646, €100 d) is a four-star hotel with 39 rooms walking distance from the train station. Rooms are large and walls are covered in bright floral patterns. Staff is friendly and there's a free Internet point at reception, along with Wi-Fi coverage.

Also close to the station is **Cicolella** (Viale XXIV Maggio 28, tel. 088/156-6111, www.hotelcicolella.it, €170 d). It's elegant by Foggia's standards and the 102 rooms are all spacious, with king-size beds and marble-clad bathrooms. Some on the top floor have views of the city. The restaurant is excellent and the €35 tasting menu provides a range of local specialties.

Food

Dal Cacciatore (Via P. Mascagani 12, tel. 088/177-1839, www.albergodelcacciatore.it, Mon.–Tues. Tues.–Sun. noon–3 P.M. and 7:30–10:30 P.M., €8–12) is a pleasant trattoria inside a 16th-century palazzo with two rooms under vaulted ceilings. Food is simple and derives from traditional local recipes, with lots of mushroom- and ricotta-based options. Pasta and desserts are all made in-house. They also have 12 rooms where diners can spend the night after stuffing themselves on roasted lamb.

Near Teatro Giordano, **Pompeo** (Vico al Piano 14, tel. 088/172-4640, Mon.–Sat. 12:30–2:30 P.M. and 7:30–11 P.M., €15–17, cash only) has an open kitchen where you can watch the chefs turn fresh ingredients into elaborate local dishes like the *fagioli di Monteleone* (stewed beans) and fava puree. Tables are carefully set and there's just the right distance between diners, many of whom are on their way to the theater. Dessert ranges from pineapple to pizza with a sweet ricotta topping.

There's great gelato waiting at **Marcicangela** (Via Torelli 9, tel. 088/172-2069, Mon.–Sat. 7 A.M.–7 P.M.) along with pastries, a buffet, and rotisserie for anyone who prefers a quick snack.

Getting There and Around

Foggia is a regional rail hub and trains from Rome and Naples make regular stops in the capital. The station is northeast of the center and there are taxis and buses waiting in the piazza. The city is just off the A14 highway and there are several well-indicated parking lots where cars can be left overnight.

◖ LUCERA

Although it may look like just another sleepy Italian town, Lucera has a glorious past. If the ancient stones could talk, they would tell of Roman, Longobard, and Episcopalian eras. Until 1806, Lucera was capital of Capitanata and Molise. The amphitheater dates from Augustus' days and still stages performances during the summer. Frederick II built the impressive castle that later housed 20,000 Saracens during the town's Islamic period.

Sights

Lucera is a good town to explore without a map. The medieval streets lead to a succession of churches, *palazzi,* and piazze, and instinct is usually the best guide. A visit should include the old town as well as the castle and amphitheater that lie slightly outside the center.

The *centro storico* can be entered from a number of gates but **Porta Troia** is the oldest and best preserved. It leads to the 13th-century **duomo** that lies on a beautiful square where natives spend their afternoons exchanging gossip and ancient Romans once met. Under-

ground are remains of a mosque that was destroyed after the Saracens were exterminated. Both local and French craftsmen contributed to the Gothic facade and interior. Nearby **Museo Civico G. Fiorelli** (Via De Nicastri 74, tel. 088/154-7041, Apr.–Sept. Mon.–Sat. 9 A.M.–1 P.M. and 4–7 P.M., Sun. 9 A.M.–1 P.M., Oct.–Mar. Tues.–Sat. 9 A.M.–1 P.M. and 3:30–6:30 P.M., Sun. 9 A.M.–1 P.M.) is currently being restored (scheduled for completion by the end of 2008), which should help bring the building back to its former splendor. Inside is a Roman replica of Venus sculpted in marble and showing little signs of wear or tear.

The **Castello di Lucera** (Zona Castello, tel. 088/154-8626) is 500 meters from Piazza Matteotti at the end of Viale Castello. It was erected in the 13th century and has a perimeter of nearly one kilometer. There are 24 towers, one of which was for the Queen. If you walk around the fortification it becomes apparent how difficult it would have been to scale the high walls. It's much easier to walk through the gate and admire the view of the Tavoliere River from the ramparts.

The amphitheater (at the end of Viale Augusto, tel. 088/152-2762 or tel. 088/154-8626 for guided tours) is in the opposite direction. It was built in the usual elliptical shape and measures 130 by 90 meters. Archeologists fully unearthed the theater in 1932 and reconstructed the two main entrances visible today. Both use architraves rather than arches and Ionic pillars that indicate Greek influence. Many of the seats are the same used by Roman audiences and make a good place to pause for a picnic or afternoon nap.

Accommodations

Mimosa (Via De Nicastri 36, tel. 088/154-6066, www.mimosaluvera.it, €60 d) consists of two mini-apartments that sleep up to four and one double. Decor is simple yet tasteful and the former stable has been converted into a large lounge where guests regularly convene. The Egyptian owner of the antique store opposite the bed-and-breakfast sells a variety of interesting collectibles.

C **Palazzo D'Auria Seconda** was built in the 15th century on Roman foundations. It now houses a restaurant and five charming rooms on the first floor. Each is spacious and adorned with period furniture that includes antique wooden beds, wrought-iron candelabras, and frescoed ceilings. Downstairs the kitchen serves roast lamb and wild boar *ragù*. The wine list is long and choosing a bottle is a pleasant conundrum.

Food
Tucked inside a 17th-century palazzo where a noble family once lived, **Il Cortiletto** (Via De Nicastri 26, tel. 088/154-2554, Mon. dinner–Sun. lunch, €10–12) benefits from a lovely courtyard where lunch and dinner can be enjoyed most of the year. Paolo looks after the kitchen and serves gourmet dishes that don't leave you hungry. *Sformato di pancotto* (baked pasta dish) and *cicatelli* (local hand-rolled pasta) may be beyond translation but most stomachs will understand.

For pizza or roast chicken, stop by **Le Delizie di Bacco** (Via L. Zuppetta 27, tel. 329/029-4355, Wed.–Mon. noon–3 P.M. and 7–10:30 P.M., €5–10). They have a good selection of regional wines and serve locally brewed beer.

Getting There and Around
Lucera is five kilometers northwest of Foggia on the N17. There is no train service to town but SITA buses make the 20-minute journey from Stazione di Foggia to Lucera daily.

Around Lucera
The road to Troia weaves through a sea of gentle hills and fields of wheat that disappear into the horizon. This little agricultural town of barely 10,000 is home to one of the prettiest Romanesque churches in Puglia.

Cattedrale di Troia (Piazza Cattedrale, tel. 088/197-0064, daily 8 A.M.–1 P.M. and 4–8 P.M.) changes depending on the color of the sky. On a grey day it appears somber, when the sun is shining it seems nearly alive, and at night the facade becomes a mystery. The original church was completed in 1120 after only 27 years of labor and was later adjusted to its current Latin cross layout. Like most churches of the day, there is only one door and this one was cast in bronze and recounts the stories of saints. Above the portal is a unique rose window divided by 11 thin columns.

Museo del Tesoro (tel. 088/152-0882, Tues. and Thurs. 5:30–8:30 P.M., Sat. 10 A.M.–1 P.M.) in Piazza Episcopio contains the church treasures and is divided into four parts, including objects in silver, bronze, and ivory. Nearby in **Corso Regina Margherita** are many of the most elegant palazzi in town. **Chiesa di San Basilio** (Via San Basilio Magno, tel. 088/197-0054, daily 7:30 A.M.–1 P.M. and 6–9 P.M.) is the oldest church, notable for a 16th-century fresco depicting the baptism of Christ.

Gargano Peninsula

The Gargano Peninsula is different from the rest of Puglia and a worthy detour. The coast is lined with small fishing villages and rocky cliffs that are unusual for a region that's primarily flat. The entire area is practically mountainous parkland covered with pine forests and wild orchids. During the summer, the population rises significantly but there's enough sand for everyone and plenty of solitude along the trails across the interior. Less than 20 kilometers offshore are the Isole Tremiti, one of the rare archipelagos on Italy's Adriatic coast.

Leave it to geography teachers to argue whether Gargano is a peninsula or a promontory. The protrusion that juts out into the Adriatic at the northern edge of the region has it all. There are salt lakes along the coast, islands offshore, and a rough mountain interior that's home to Puglia's largest protected area. Along the way are whitewashed towns, sandy beaches, Doveresque cliffs, and some of the cleanest water in the Mediterranean.

RODI GARGANICO

The Greek influence on the northern coast is evident the moment you spot Rodi Garganico in the distance surrounded by olive trees and neatly cultivated fields. Houses are white and stacked on top of each other in a mesmerizing heap. The two neighborhoods of Castello Aragonese and Vuccolo are a labyrinth of narrow streets where fishermen's wives still call their husbands back to shore the old-fashioned way. Among the small shops are **Chiesa di San Nicola di Mira** and **San Pietro e Paolo,** the oldest church in town, completed in 1216. The Baroque sanctuary of **Madonna della Libera** is worth a look for the Byzantine-era paintings, including several colorful depictions of the Virgin Mary.

Rodi Garganico is architecturally homogenous with whitewashed houses and a labyrinth of streets that resemble Greek towns. There are two ancient neighborhoods to explore and stuffed peppers to sample. Olive groves and fruit trees grow up the hills behind town, and the sea lies enticingly in front. During the summer ferries sail daily from the small port to the Isole Tremiti.

ISOLE TREMITI

The four islands of this tiny archipelago are part of a marine reserve and best appreciated with a boat tour around the steep, rocky inlets where clear water is ideal for snorkeling and scuba excursions. Expect to run into grouper, red snapper, moray eels, and octopus hiding among the coral. Traffic is unknown and getting around on foot or moped is a pleasure. From the port of Rodi, the Isole Tremiti can be reached in under an hour. San Domino, San Nicola, and Capraia have been on the map since Homer imagined Ulysses shipwrecked there. The islands are part of Parco Nazionale del Gargano and a boat ride to any of them will help appreciate many rocky inlets where gulls nest and sailboats anchor in relative seclusion.

VIESTE

The westernmost town on the peninsula is also the largest and a magnet for beach lovers who spend days under the sun and nights strolling a historic center filled with restaurants and artisan boutiques. The old town stretches out on a thin strip of land that ends with the castle built by Federick II to prevent the frequent assaults by pirates. One of the fiercest of these decapitated the heads of hundreds of locals on a slab of limestone that's still visible today near the cathedral. Anyone who collects shells will appreciate the 14,000 examples on display at **Museo Malacologico** (Via Pola 8, tel. 088/470-7688, Apr.–Oct. daily 9:30 A.M.–12:30 P.M. and 4–8 P.M., admission free). The beaches on the edge of town get progressively more crowded until August, when barely a grain of sand is left uncovered. Just south are the *faraglione* rock formations that tower majestically off the coast.

MONTE SANT'ANGELO

Monte Sant'Angelo is 30 minutes from the coast up a scenic winding road. The town developed around **Santuario di Monte Sant'Angelo,** where, according to tradition, the archangel Michael was spotted in A.D. 490. Since then a steady stream of pilgrims and crusaders on their way to the Holy Land have paid their respects. Inside the sanctuary are a statue of the angel, the Episcopal throne, and an octagonal tower reminiscent of Castel del Monte. Hikers can pick up the Via Sacra Langobardorum, which leads to many Eastern-influenced convents and churches in the area. A grotto near the center of town contains the fountain where San Michele quenched his thirst. Nearby are the remains of the Longobard-Norman castle built in the 11th century and equipped with a moat that's now dry. On a clear day you can see much of Gargano, the Gulf of Manfredonia, and the coast all the way to Bari.

◖ PARCO NAZIONALE DEL GARGANO

Puglia's largest park is home to a diverse habitat and one of the last remaining old-growth forests in Italy. The area is crisscrossed with scenic, winding roads and it takes less than an hour to drive from one coast to another. There are few towns in between and wild boar are a likely sight for anyone who decides to get out and hike.

In the center of the promontory, the 120,000 hectares of Parco Nazionale del Gargano (Monte Sant'Angelo, Via Sant'Antonio Abate 121, tel. 088/456-8911, www.parcogargano.it) provide an exceptional variety of habitats for foxes, deer, wild boar, porcupines, and many other mammals. The rich flora includes 56 species of orchids that can be found nowhere else in Europe. The park provides dozens of itineraries, including mountain bike excursions from Vieste with **Explora Gargano** (Via Santa Maria di Merino 62, tel. 088/470-2237, www.explor agargano.it) and hikes through an old-growth forest with **Ecogargano** (Monte Sant'Angelo, Largo Guiscardo 2, tel. 088/456-5444). Both lakes are vital staging points for birds transiting between winter and summer nesting grounds and one of the last remaining wetlands in Italy.

Tremiti Diving Center (tel. 088/246-3765 or 336/829-746, www.marlintremiti.it) on the island of San Domino provides a full range of scuba services. A 70-minute underwater tour costs €55 and includes transportation, equipment, and oxygen. If you prefer snorkeling, you can rent fins and a mask for €6. There's a lot to see below the surface, especially around the small rock formations near Capraia where fish love to feed.

ACCOMMODATIONS

Pizzomunno Palace (Vieste, Lungomare Enrico Mattei, tel. 088/470-8741, €110 d) is a large hotel surrounded by bougainvillea, fruit trees, and pine growing in the Parco Nazionale del Gargano. Comfort is a common denominator of the rooms, restaurant, and health spa. There's a private beach with many water sports options as well as organized excursions into the park.

◖ Hotel Baia delle Zagare (Baia delle Zagare, tel. 088/455-0155, www.hotelba iadellezagare.it, €150 d) lies on a dead-end

road halfway between Vieste and Monte Sant'Angelo. It's a magical location on a cliff overlooking the sea from where guests can descend by elevator to one of two unspoiled beaches. Boats are available to explore the rocky inlets along the coast and the large hotel offers sports and entertainment activities worthy of a holiday village.

Accommodation options on the Isole Tremiti are limited and **Villaggio Turistico Internazionale** (Punta del Diamante, tel. 088/246-3405, www.puntadeldiamante.it, €75 d) is more of a campground than hotel. The village lies near the shore on San Domino island and offers all-inclusive *villette* and more spartan *casa tende* (tent houses) under a grove of pine trees. Scuba, canoeing, and boat excursions are all available nearby.

FOOD

Near the cathedral in Vieste, the chef at **Al Dragone** (Via Duomo 8, tel. 088/701-212, Wed.–Mon., €11–13) mixes locally produced ingredients into traditional dishes. They are strong on seafood and the interior provides a cave-like dining experience. If wine is all you're after, **l'Enoteca Vesta** (Vieste, Via Duomo 14, tel. 088/470-1212, daily) has over 300 local labels that are served by the glass or bottle in a suggestive 12th-century palazzo.

Pasquale Mazzone always goes the extra kilometer to get the freshest vegetables, fish, and locally fermented cheese. *Salumi* at **◖ Medioevo** (Monte Sant'Angelo, Via Castello 21, tel. 088/456-5356, Tues.–Sun. noon–3 P.M. and 7–10:30 P.M., €8–11) are produced from pigs on nearby farms and the handmade pastas are all flavored with rich earthy sauces. On a good day, when the fishermen have brought in an abundant haul, try the seafood platter grilled or fried in virgin oil that McDonald's french fries only dream about. The meat options are just as good and roasted lamb or *turcinieddi* will satisfy most hungers. Save room for the grilled cheese, almond desserts, and Montepulciano wine that Pasquale produces himself.

Monte Sant'Angelo is full of mouthwatering shops where visitors can sample the local bread, cheese, and pastries. **Forno Frisoli** (Via Manfredi 86) and **Taronna** (Corso Garibaldi 31) supply the town with dozens of baked goods and **La Montanara** (Corso Vittorio Emanuele 36) sells delicious hard and soft cheese.

INFORMATION AND SERVICES

Ente Parco Nazionale del Gargano park headquarters (Via S. Antonion Abate 121, tel. 088/456-8911, www.parcogargano.it) are located in Monte Sant'Angelo. There are also tourist offices in **Rodi Garganico** (Piazza Luigi Rovelli 12, tel. 088/496-5576) and **Vieste** (Piazza Kennedy 1, tel. 088/470-7495). The post office in Rodi is on Corso Madonna Della Libertà and there's a San Paolo bank with an ATM machine on Via Carmine Grossi 3. There are a dozen banks in Vieste, including three on Via XXIV Maggio. The post office is on Via V. Veneto.

GETTING THERE AND AROUND

Most of the roads on the promontory are scenic and the N89 hugs the coast from Rodi to Manfredonia. Car and motorcycle are the best ways to fully explore the area and allow visitors to discover the interior using panoramic routes like the N528 or N272. During the summer, ferry service connects Rodi with Peschici, Vieste, Pugnochiuso, and Manfredonia. Rodi is also where boats leave hourly for Isole Tremiti. Train service is limited to the northern coast and passengers must transfer at San Severo in order to reach Rodi and Peschici.

The Trulli District

Between the bustling ports of Brindisi and Taranto lies the olive heartland of Italy and some of the best extra virgin available anywhere. Peasants in the Itria Valley are famous for their distinctive *trulli* houses that are now visited by thousands but haven't lost their charm. Many have been converted into bed-and-breakfasts and Alberobello has the looks of a fairy-tale town. Craftsmen weave away in the streets and wine bars serve white Locorotondo that's grown nearby.

◖ ALBEROBELLO

If Bilbo Baggins moved to Italy, he'd settle down in Alberobello. The circular whitewashed *trulli* houses with high conical roofs made of slate are scattered around town and would make any hobbit happy. The unique skyline attracts many tourists and has been recognized as a national monument since 1930. It's natural, therefore, that visitors outnumber natives on the steep climb to the **Monti** neighborhood, but fortunately there are enough narrow lanes, back alleys, and *piazzettas* to have a tête-à-tête with this amazing town.

Sights

Many of the *trulli* can be visited in Alberobello and the largest one in town is the **Trullo Sovrano** (tel. 080/432-6030, daily 10 A.M.–6 P.M., €1.50) in Piazza Sacramento. It has two floors and 12 cones that were begun in the 16th century and initially used as a place of worship. If Monti seems too crowded, try the **Aia Piccola** neighborhood along Via Brigata Regina, which has fewer houses but where residents still go about their business without the glare of the tourist spotlight.

Museo del Territorio di Alberobello (Piazza XXVII Maggio, tel. 080/432-2580, Mon.–Fri. 10:30 A.M.–7:30 P.M., Sat.–Sun. 10:30 A.M.–10 P.M., €2) recounts the history of the community in nine rooms inside a large *trulli* that dates from the 18th century.

Entertainment and Events

Alberobello Jazz (www.alberobellojazz.it) is an innovative festival in September that gives equal space to veteran performers and local talent on the rise. Concerts are held in Piazza del

© ALESSIA RAMACCIA

distinctive *trulli* rooftops

Popolo, which also provides the best views of town and the surrounding plains.

Shopping

The Itrea Valley is rich in arts and crafts, and there are dozens of shops where skilled artisans turn simple materials into elaborate objects. Many are located inside *trulli,* so it's also a good opportunity to see some fascinating interiors. **De Alfa Artigianato** (Via M. S. Michele 40, tel. 080/432-1751, daily) is a small leather workshop with a unique method for treating hides that leaves wallets soft and smellingsweet. They also make bags, belts, and masks used by theater companies around the country. Located in the historic center, **Artigianato Artistico** (Via Duca d'Aosta, tel. 333/974-8298, daily) weaves locally spun wool into ponchos, blankets, and colorful carpets that come in all sizes. For hand-painted Puglian vases that can be used outdoors or inside, visit **Impronte Laboratorio Ceramiche d'Arte** (Viale Putignano 83, tel. 080/432-5988, Tues.–Sun.). The shop is full of terra-cotta ob-

jects, including napkin holders, wind chimes, and lampshades, many of which can be conveniently transported.

Accommodations

The best way to experience Alberobello is to spend the night inside a *trullo*. **❮ B&B Trulli per Vacanze** (Via Monte San Michele 58, tel. 080/432-4376, www.trullipuglia.com, €88 d) provides the opportunity to sleep within eight separate houses dating from the 16th century that have been modernized without sacrificing charm. All rooms have their own entrance, air-conditioning, mini-fridge, and cooking area if you prefer a DIY dinner.

Food

Domenico Laera opened an *osteria* halfway up to Monti in a group of *trulli* that are hard to resist. The menu at **L'Aratro** (Via Monte San Michele 25, tel. 080/432-2789, Tues.–Sun. noon–3 P.M. and 7–11 P.M., closed Jan., €9–13) has remained local and generations of out-of-towners haven't managed to dent the quality.

Antipasti include *sformati di ortaggi* and *burrate* (mozzarella-like cheese). There are some sea specials but if you're in the mood to be filled, order the roasted lamb and potatoes. The cellar is slanted towards red wines and no one should leave without tasting the almond mousse.

It's no coincidence the street name is the same as the family who have run **(La Cantina** (Vico Lippolis 8, tel. 080/432-3473, Wed.–Mon. 12:30–3 P.M. and 7:30–11 P.M., closed Jul., €8–12) for the past 50 years. They do it in a small *ristorante* that has remained as simple as some of the dishes Francesco Lippolis prepares in full view of diners. There's a good selection of hot and cold starters and it's wise to sample them all. *Orecchiette* and *ragù di cavallo* are the classic firsts; seconds consist of grilled and skewered meats, of which the sausages are notable. The wine list is an afterthought and the house version is more than acceptable.

There's a lot of fresh cheese inside **Artelat** (Via Traversa Colucci, tel. 080/432-5202, daily 8 A.M.–7 P.M.), which is a play on words of "art" and "milk" and indeed it takes great milk to make the great *mozzarelle, ricotta,* and *caciocavallo* they dish out. For gastronomic company, try the *taralli* bread baked at **Tarallificio dei Trulli** (Viale Einaudi, tel. 080/432-1358) with oil, wine, or spices.

Getting There and Around

Alberobello is 55 kilometers south of Bari on the SS 100 then the 172 or 634. There is frequent direct train service from Bari and Brindisi. The journey takes a little over an hour and a second-class Eurostar ticket from the regional capital costs €11. **Trulli e Natural** (tel. 080/432-3829) organizes excursions on foot, horseback, and mountain bike from **Museo dell'Olio** (Piazza XVII Maggio 22).

MARTINA FRANCA

Martina Franca occupies a hilltop on the Murge Mountains halfway between the Adriatic and the Ionian Seas. The vast maze of the old town is a picturesque mix of Baroque and Rococò that is far more somber than the Sicilian versions.

Sights

Although the original walls protecting the city were destroyed in 1861, it's still possible to enter town through the **Arco di Santo Stefano** that leads to **Palazzo Ducale** (Piazza Roma, tel. 080/483-6283, daily 8:30 A.M.–1:30 P.M. and 2:30–7:30 P.M., admission free). This grand building was designed by Bernini and the 300 ornate rooms include a chapel and theater.

Corso Vittorio Emanuele leads to Piazza Plebiscito, dominated by the white facade of **San Martino,** on which several saints are depicted. Inside, the altar is flanked by two marble sculptures representing Hope and Charity.

Accommodations

(Il Gallo Felice (Via Crispiano 101, tel. 099/375-992, www.scandic-hotels.com/bari, €60 d) is composed of five *trulli* facing a small courtyard. Rooms are decorated with style and none of the furniture is under 100 years old. The owners are a dynamic couple who organize cooking lessons, tastings, and massages upon request. They use olive oil for the massages and although they don't accept credit cards they happily welcome guests traveling with pets.

For a more luxurious stay, **Villa San Martino** (Via Taranto 59, tel. 080/480-5152, www.relaisvillasanmartino.com, €240 d) provides elegant rooms and suites within a 19th-century country house surrounded by a large park. Besides the outdoor swimming pool and gym, a small hammam and health center is available for guests.

Food

Near the Baroque center of town, **(Al Ritrovo degli Amici** (Corso Messapia 8, tel. 080/483-9249, daily noon–3 P.M. and 7–11 P.M., €10–15) provides elegant surroundings in which to enjoy lunch or dinner. Owner and chef Anna Ancona loves her job and it shows. Meals start with warm olive bread and an enticing array of appetizers that includes mushroom-stuffed crepes. Mashed potatoes here are called *purè* and many vegetables are used. There are a range of pastas covered in red sauces that can be followed by lamb cutlets or steak. Wines run the geographical gamut from Venice to Sicily.

Martina Franca has several *fornelli* where oven-roasted meats can be savored. Stefanuccio began as a butcher and started cooking his cuts at **Lisi** (Via Verdi 57, tel. 080/480-1547, Tues.–Sat., €10) next door several years ago. His daughter serves plates of salami, *bombette* (small donut), and freshly ground sausage spiced with a mixture of local herbs. Wine was recently added to a menu that will send vegetarians running.

The oven at **Serio Vito** (Via Ferrucci 20, Tues.–Sat., no phone) has been satisfying stomachs for over 90 years. There is very little waiting here and minutes after you've ordered the shish-kabob, *gnumarieddi* (lamb), or *straccetti* (beef) it's in front of you waiting to be devoured. Corso Italia is a good destination for dessert and **Partenopea** bakes the *bocconotti* (chocolate pastry) that the town is famous for. Gelato is waiting in **Bar Adua** in Via Mercadante.

Getting There and Around

Every road to Martina Franca is scenic. From Alberobello, the N172 is the fastest approach but there's also SP58 (also called Strada Alberbello)—a 15-kilometer alternative through the valley that offers plenty of panorama. It's a good place to stop for a picnic and starts on the outskirts of Alberobello. Trains from Brindisi require a transfer at Fontana or Taranto and usually take 90 minutes.

BRINDISI

Brindisi is place of departure and arrival. It was here that the Via Appia and Via Francigena ended, where Caesar landed after his sojourn with Cleopatra, and medieval knights set sail for Jerusalem. The sea is ever present and there's no escaping the *scirocco* winds that cover the narrow streets of the center with sand and salt. Roman shipwrecks testify to a long maritime history that can be admired in the archeological museum and ferries still regularly depart for all points east of the horizon.

Sights

Cattedrale di San Giovanni Battista in the heart of Brindisi has partaken in its fair share of history. Knights gathered within its walls prior to departing for the Holy Land on crusades, Ruggero was coronated King of Sicily in 1191, and Frederick II tied the knot in 1225. The treasury contains many relics brought back from the Middle East, including the Arca di San Teodora. Much of the church was rebuilt after the earthquake of 1743 and the colorful marble and bell tower are all new additions.

The two **Colonne Romane** near the port are symbols of the city's golden age. Only one of the columns is still standing and the remains of the second were given to Lecce in gratitude to Saint Oronzo for protecting inhabitants from the plague of 1528. They mark the spot where Via Appia ended, and, at 19 meters high, helped ancient sailors spot the town from a distance. Some historians believe they may have also been a gift from the Romans for resisting Hannibal's advances in 214 B.C.

San Giovanni al Sepolcro (Via del Tempio, tel. 083/122-9329) was built in the 11th century by the Knights of Templar. The semicircular structure is made of large stone blocks and the entrance pillars are supported by two marble lions. The inside is covered in medieval frescoes and can only be visited upon request. For many years it was used as a cultural center, and figures such as Mahatma Gandhi and Indian poet Tagore spoke here.

Rione degli Schiavone lies between Via Tarantini and Via Duomo, and is one of the most interesting areas in the city. In 1964, archeologists discovered the remains of a thermal bath, ancient houses, and the remains of a Roman road. The area is dominated by Nuovo Teatro Verdi and the antiquities can be viewed thanks to a suspended passegeway on Via Casimiro. The archeological zone is open daily 8 A.M.–2 P.M. On the other side of the port is the **Sciabiche** quarter where fishermen still repair their nets by hand and boats are made of wood rather than fiberglass. The name of the neighborhood derives from the Arab word for fishing.

Accommodations

Hotel Colonna (Corso Roma 83, tel. 083/156-2557, www.albergocolonna.it, €85 d) is on a main artery of the city close to the train station. The 43 rooms are spread out on seven floors and several at the top have views of the port. They all come with satellite TV, minibar, bathtubs, and safes. The front desk is active 24 hours a day and breakfast is served in the first-floor dining room.

The more upscale option is **Grande Albergo Internazionale** (Lungomare Regina Margherita 23, tel. 083/152-3473, www.albergointernazionale.it, €250 d), built by an English company in the 19th century for business travelers commuting between London and Bombay. The elegant hotel is directly in front of the port and it was here Vittorio Emanuele III held parliamentary meetings when the city was briefly the capital of Italy in 1943. Rooms are spacious with high ceilings and lots of red and gold furnishings.

Food

Diners should always beware of a town crawling with tourists and sailors looking for a quick meal. Fortunately some restaurants haven't let standards slip. In fact, the standards at **Pantagruele** (Via Salita di Ripalta 1, tel. 083/156-0605, Mon.–Fri. noon–3:30 P.M. and 7–11 P.M., €10–14) have been rising for years and the *osteria* is a reliable address for lunch or dinner. The fish here would start swimming if it were thrown back into the sea. Primary flavors aren't covered with distractions but are celebrated in their simplicity. Fresh mussels make a good opener and quality local meats and cheeses are always an option. The wine list is extensive and service is professional.

In the historic center, **Il Giardino** (Via Giovanni Tarantini 14, tel. 083/156-4026, Tues.–Sun. lunch, €8–12) benefits from a delightful garden with fruit trees that provide shade on hot summer days. The cooking is typical and offers both meat and fish options. Since this is a seafood town, you might as well try the fried seafood platter that comes with seven types of fish. Carni-vores, however, won't be disappointed with the Angus that's grilled to perfection.

There are many places to have a quick bite or order some take-out. **Pizzeria Luppolo e Farina** (Via Pozzo Traiano 22, daily, €8) serves 40 types of pizza underneath vaulted ceilings and ceramic-covered walls. To taste Brindisi's version of a calzone, visit **Friggioria Romanelli** (Via Santa Lucia 22, tel. 083/159-0496, daily, €1.50), which has been baking the tomato and mozzarella masterpieces since 1949. They also fry up a variety of fish and vegetables.

Almond-based pastries are a specialty of the area and can be sampled at **Esmeralda** (Via De Leo 42, tel. 083/152-3842) and **Rouge et Noir** (Via Santi 15, tel. 083/152-1939).

Getting There and Around

Aeroporto del Salento (tel. 083/141-6516, www.aeroportidipuglia.it) is the region's largest airport. A new terminal was built in 2007 that connects the city with Roma and Milano several times daily. **SITA** (www.sitabus.it, €3) runs buses from the arrivals terminal to the city center and car rentals are available from **Avis** (tel. 083/141-8826), **Europcar** (tel. 083/141-2061), or **Sixt** (tel. 083/141-1253) inside the terminal.

Brindisi is an hour from Bari by train and six hours from Roma on the Eurostar that leaves three times a day from the capital. The A14 highway may eventually reach Brindisi but until it does drivers can use the E55 from Bari or the E90 from Taranto.

TARANTO

The immense industrial area leading to Taranto doesn't provide a good first impression. This ancient city, founded by Greek colonists from Sparta in A.D. 706, becomes more appealing once the Aragonese castle comes into view.

Sights

The historic center of Taranto is an island connected to solid land by two bridges. The Aragonese castle guards the entrance to the drawbridge and overlooks the canal that connects Mare Piccolo to Mare Grande. The seaside promenade of Lungomare Vittorio

Emanuele II is a scenic approach flanked by elegant *palazzi* and palm trees.

Cattedrale di San Cataldo (Via Duomo, tel. 099/470-7545) was completed in 1070 on the foundations of a previous church destroyed by Saracen invaders. Much of the exterior was rebuilt following damage during World War II, while the interior fared much better. The three naves are divided by 16 columns and on the left side sits a Byzantine-era baptismal font. Much of the original mosaics are still visible. On the opposite side is an elliptical chapel covered in frescoes.

Founded in 1870 in a convent, **Museo Archeologico Nazionale** (Via Cavour 10, tel. 099/458-1715, www.museotaranto.it, daily 8:30 A.M.–7:30 P.M., €5) is the most important archeological museum south of Naples. Most of the sculptures have been unearthed in the area and recount the *Magna Grecia* past. On the second floor are classical statues such as Poseidon, found in Ugento, and a bronze figure of Zeus clutching a thunderbolt. There is also an extensive collection of ceramics and gold jewelry.

Accommodations

Located in a small alley in the center of the *centro storico*, **Hotel Akropolis** (Vico I Seminario 3, tel. 099/470-4110, www.hotelakropolis.it, €135 d) provides a comfortable retreat. The dozen rooms are elegant, if a little old-fashioned, but Liberty-style furniture and colorfully tiled floors make up for any decorating oversights. Sea excursions and visits to the necropolis are organized by the hotel. Drinking local wines and listening to live music at the underground wine bar is a pleasant way to end the evening.

Recently inaugurated **(Relais Culti** (Circummarpiccolo, Via Sant'Andrea, tel 099/472-1188, €220 d) is a luxurious hotel in a small *borgo* just outside of town, from where the sea is less than five minutes away. White is the major theme, from the pillowcases to the lampshades, and it's hard not to relax in this peaceful environment. The 46 rooms are surrounded by olive groves, flowered streets, and thermal baths. A restaurant proposes Mediterranean specialties and "Do not disturb" is the management's principal philosophy.

Food

With a name like **Gesù Cristo** (Via Battisti 8, tel. 099/477-7253, Tues.–Sun. lunch, €8–13), the food has to be good. Grandpa Caso founded the trattoria 70 years ago and his two grandsons now look after the place. Walls are covered with pictures of the chosen one and moments after you've sat down in one of three small rooms Pasquale or Alessandro bring the house appetizers to your table. Fish dominates the menu and it comes fried, grilled, or mixed with risotto. Desserts and service are less than memorable, but the kitchen keeps locals coming back.

Gatto Rosso (Via Cavour 2, tel. 080/930-6842, Tues.–Sun. €9–13) serves traditional dishes with a gourmet twist. The creativity is supplied by Agostino Bartoli, whose *gnocchetti di patate con gamberetti* are too good to share. The cellar is well stocked but if all you're interested in is drinking a good bottle of red or white grab a table at **Taverna le Fogge** (Via Ciro Giovinazzi 18, tel. 099/459-3733, Thurs.–Tues., €8). This *vineria* near the cathedral is carved into the rock and is a good place to fill up on local cheese and cured meats.

Don't let the crowds outside **Cremeria Vienna** (Via D'Aquino 120, tel. 099/459-6953, daily) put you off. This tiny *gelateria* produces some of the best ice cream in town and their *crema pasticcera* and *bacio* are both worth waiting for. **Marzulli Coloniali** (Via Anfiteatro 174, tel. 099/452-008, Tues.–Sun.) has been making pastries for over 65 years and the recipes have remained the same. They also create their own *limoncello* that's the perfect after-dinner drink on a hot summer evening.

Getting There and Around

If the A14 is ever completed it will eventually reach Taranto. As things stand now, the highway ends 17 kilometers outside the city and the N7 completes the journey. The more pleasant approach is along the coast road from Santa Maria di Leuca at the tip of the peninsula. Trains from Brindisi run hourly and the trip lasts one hour.

Lecce and the Salentine Peninsula

Few towns are associated with a single architectural style, but if you mention Lecce to any Italian the first association is usually Baroque. The city is full of marvelous buildings and is perfectly positioned for exploring the Salentine Peninsula. The coast road winds its way from the Adriatic to the Ionic Sea and is guarded by over 80 medieval towers that were once on the look-out for pirates. Every few kilometers are fortified towns steeped in Eastern traditions and many, like Otranto and Gallipoli, were founded by ancient Greeks. Water is enticingly transparent and could double for the Caribbean. There are plenty of beaches where the party goes on until after sunset and kiosks grill fresh seafood and serve strong negroamaro wine.

◖ LECCE

Lecce is synonymous with elegance and is a treat for the eyes. It is like a Monet study and changes appearance throughout the day as light alters the appearance of the beautiful Baroque buildings. At night the historic center is illuminated and the city transforms itself once again.

The 17th century left the greatest mark and many of the ornate facades date from this period. None of it would have been possible without the abundance of honey-colored limestone that is easily carved and that was mastered by artists such as Giuseppe Zimbalo.

Sights

Basilica di Santa Croce (Via Umberto I, tel. 083/224-1957) is the pinnacle of Baroque with a facade covered in fruit, flowers, and mythological figures. Work started in the church in 1353 and the final stones weren't laid until 1646. Generations of architects contributed to the project, from Gabriele Riccardi who began the facade, to Zimbalo who designed the three portals. The white interior is far more sober

the ornate rose window of the Basilica di Santa Croce

and relies on a medieval layout with a cupola in the center and wooden roof on either side.

The **Anfiteatro Romano** (Piazza San'Oronzo, tel. 083/224-7018, daily 24 hours) was discovered in 1901 and partially restored in 1934. It once held 20,000 spectators and now is a popular meeting place for locals. Concerts are staged during the summer and around Christmas it is the site of a life-size nativity scene. Nearby in **Piazza Sant'Oronzo** is a column topped with Saint Oronzo, who was the first bishop of the city and later martyred by emperor Nero. Zimbalo created the monument from a column given to the city by Brindisi.

Entertainment and Events

Anyone who prefers conversation over pounding beats can enjoy a chat at **Wine Bar** (tel. 083/224-5612, Wed.–Mon. 7 P.M.–1 A.M.) on the characteristic Piazza Orsini. The jazz lounge with soft lighting offers 300 labels from around the world and attracts a young crowd of locals and tourists who enjoy the external courtyard from May until September.

Misvagio (Piazza Sant'Oronzo 22, tel. 328/056-7079, daily 8 A.M.–2 A.M.) is open morning, noon, and night but this multifunctional hangout near the amphitheater is especially popular around *aperitivi* time when Giuseppe and Dario shake rum cocktails faster than they can be ordered. It's an excellent address for a quick bite and the DJ assures that people are dancing until late.

Trends fade but **Cagliostro** (Piazzetta Cairoli 25, tel. 083/230-1881, daily 7 P.M.–2 A.M.) has remained. The two small pastel-colored rooms fill up with a stylish crowd who come for the mojitos and the rum shots that are dispensed for free. During the summer, tables are set out in the typical courtyard underneath the stars. On weekends, chances are good there'll be some live music.

Baroque is not limited to church and palazzo facades in Lecce. It's also evident in dozens of courtyards and **FiordiBarocco** (tel. 083/234-3493) is an occasion to admire these on the third weekend of May. Palazzo Morisco, Palazzo Palombi, Castello di Carlo V, and other historic interiors are handed over to gardeners who create large-scale flower arrangements based on an annual theme.

Every year the basilica of Santa Croce becomes the headquarters of **Jazz in Puglia** (tel. 083/239-2629). For five days in mid-September, the marvelous Baroque interior reverberates with jazz, soul, gospel, and mambo. Concerts start at 9 P.M. and cost between €11–16.

From December 13 to Christmas Eve, the piazze of the city are filled with **Fiera dei Presepi e dei Pupi** stalls selling nativity scene characters, puppets, and local sweets.

Shopping

I Mestieri della Memoria (Via Pertini 2, tel. 080/239-4172) is a museum-workshop dedicated to *cartapesta* (papier-mâché). It's an old art in Lecce still practiced by a handful of artisans who have inherited the skills of their forefathers. In the little shop next door you can buy religious icons, Christmas decorations, and other figurines.

Local sculptor and designer Renzo Buttazzo sells his handmade creations inside **Petre** (Via Palmieri 47, tel. 083/233-1388). Works are highly original and constructed from a variety of materials.

Accommodations

There are a number of bed-and-breakfasts in the historic center that provide friendly service. **Chiesa Greca** (Piazza Chiesa Greca, tel. 083/230-2330, €70 d) is located on a lively square and has six elegant rooms in a 13th-century setting. The interior balances modern and antique furnishings and many original frescoes have been preserved. If you prefer a tower surrounded by orange trees, try **L'Aranceto** (Corte dei Carretti 7, tel. 083/227-7736, €80 d). There are three immaculate rooms and one suite with vaulted ceilings over 500 years old. Breakfast includes orange marmalade plucked from the garden and a host of delicious local cakes and breads. Each of the five stylish rooms at **Anfiteatro** (Via XXV Luglio 51, tel. 083/227-7622, €90 d) oozes charm. The bed-and-breakfast overlooks the public gardens and guests tend to linger on the terrace admiring the view. First-time visitors receive a discount and everyone can expect lots of *pasticciotti* pastries for breakfast.

Food

Food and interior decor are in perfect harmony at ◖ **Cucina Casareccia** (Via Costadura 19, tel. 083/224-5178, Tues.–Sun. noon–3 P.M. and 7–10:30 P.M., €8–11). Both are simple and have a family feel that's reinforced by Anna Perrone's greeting. Take her advice on what to eat and how to eat it. The extra virgin oil on tables is for flavoring the numerous grilled vegetables on the menu. In spring, try the artichoke soup and in winter the *zuppe di grano*. There are many pork and horse options for seconds and the red wine by the carafe may require a refill.

Halfway between Porta Napoli and Santa Croce, **Alle due Corti** (Via Leonardo Prato 42, tel. 083/224-2223, Mon.–Sat. noon–3:30 P.M. and 7:30–11 P.M., €9–12) preserves traditional Leccese flavors. The *osteria* consists of three small rooms and a low-key environment that doesn't distract from the food. The menu changes every 15 days according to the harvest and anyone dining in summer can taste historic dishes like *cocule* (eggplant meatballs) or *monicedde* (snails sautéed with wine and onions). The pies are all homemade and the cellar stocks regional bottles.

For bread, pizza, or a traditional snack, visit **Osvaldo** (Via Cosatadura 28) and **Furnu de Petra** (Via Casetti, tel. 083/234-8882). When locals get a craving for chocolate they head for **Maglio Arte Dolciaria** (tel. 083/224-3816) on Via Templari 16.

Information and Services

There are several tourist offices around the city, including the **Info Point** (9 A.M.–1 P.M. and 4–8 P.M., tel. 083/224-6517) in Castello Carlo V and **APT offices** (Mon.–Fri. 8 A.M.–2 P.M., Tues. and Thurs. 3–6 P.M.) in Via Monte San Michele 20 and Corso Vittorio Emanuele II. All three can assist with finding accommodation and obtaining transportation tickets.

The local police have recently added a section devoted entirely to assisting visitors. Sezione Turistica is based in Palazzo Carafa (Piazza S. Oronzo, tel. 800/524-337, daily 9 A.M.–1 P.M. and 4–9 P.M.).

Getting There and Around

By car from northeastern Italy, follow the A14 highway towards Bari and continue on the E55 until Lecce. It's an eight-hour drive from Rome along the A1 and A16 that runs into the A14. Lecce is the major rail hub of the Salenta Peninsula from which most of the area can be reached. The nearest airport is in Brindisi (tel. 080/580-0200, www.aeroportidipuglia. it) and a **SITA bus** (tel. 083/224-7882) from the arrivals terminal departs six times a day. The journey costs €5 and lasts approximately 45 minutes.

◖ OTRANTO

Otranto is as far east as you can get in Italy and if you listen carefully to the locals you'll recognize the Greek influence in their dialects. The town sits on one of the most scenic bays in the country, which has won many awards for the cleanliness of its waters. It was an important port for the Romans and one of the Byzantines' last possessions in Italy. The town's walls are as thick as ever and the castle built by the Aragonese adds to the charm of the town. In August it is overrun with tourists exploring the narrow streets and gazing over the immense mosaic of the cathedral.

Sights

The **Cattedrale di Otranto** (Via Duomo, tel. 083/680-1436, June–Sept. daily 7 A.M.–noon and 3–8 P.M., Oct.–May daily 7 A.M.–noon and 3–5 P.M.) is the largest building in this walled town and dates from the 11th century. Although the Roman-Gothic interior is impressive, what grabs the attention more than anything else are the mosaic floors completed in three years by some very skilled monks. The images are simple but the vivid colors and design keep eyes glued to the ground. There are several depictions of the tree of life, as well as

© ALESSIA RAMACCIA

downtown Otranto

representations of heaven and hell. In the crypt are the bones of 800 martyrs who refused to renounce their religion and were subsequently slaughtered by invading Turks in 1480.

Basilichetta di San Pietro (Via Padre Scupoli, tel. 083/680-1436, July 15–Sept. 15 10 A.M.–noon and 3:30–8 P.M., winter open upon request) is in the Byzantine style with frescoes of the Last Supper and the washing of feet. According to legend, it was founded by Saint Peter himself on his way to Rome.

Accommodations

Palazzo de Mori (Bastione dei Pelsagi, tel. 083/680-1088, www.palazzodemori.it, €100 d) is an old noble residence transformed into a hotel with a roof terrace overlooking the port. All 10 rooms come with plenty of space and large windows that let in the cool sea breeze. Decoration is essential but stylish and the welcome is warm.

Two kilometers from town, ◖ **Masseria Montelauro** (Località Montelauro, tel. 083/680-6203, www.masseriamontelauro.it, €155 d) has seen its share of honeymooners. This former Byzantine hermitage has been converted into a charming *relais* with 29 rooms near the sea, surrounded by a Mediterranean garden. Breakfast is served outside and at night the grounds are lit by candlelight.

Food

The streets of Otranto are lined with tempting restaurants, *osterie,* and artisanal food shops. **Da Sergio** (Corso Garibaldi 9, tel. 083/680-1408, Thurs.–Tues. noon–3:30 P.M. and 7–11 P.M., €9–15) is one of the oldest *trattorie* and has always been dedicated to fish. Many of the appetizers are served raw or marinated with oil and onions. First courses include linguine or risotto flavored with *frutti di mare* and spaghetti with shrimp. The catch of the day rolls by on a cart and diners can choose how they want their fish cooked. The restaurant has tables inside and out that are nearly always occupied. Make a reservation or arrive early to beat the rush.

Getting There and Around

From Lecce, drivers should head south on the N16 that makes a sharp left after Maglie. The N611 is the coast road that connects the town with Brindisi. There is no direct train service from Brindisi or Lecce and passengers must transfer in Maglie, which could be a good excuse to try the gelato at Gelateria Maglio in Corte San Giovanni while you wait. During the summer, ferries regularly depart for Greece as they have done for centuries.

GALLIPOLI

If you repeat Gallipoli 10 times fast it sounds like Kalle Polis, which means beautiful city, and is what the Greeks called this walled town surrounded by the sea. Today locals refer to the historic center as *l'isola* (island); it is connected to the modern town by a bridge. The fortifications were built by the Byzantines, strengthened by Normans, and reinforced by Aragonese. There's a surplus of churches and more pews per person than anywhere else in the region. On summer days, residents and anyone carrying a towel descend the ramparts and stretches out on Purità beach.

Sights

The **cathedral** (Via Duomo 1, tel. 083/326-1987) lies in the center of town and was given a Baroque makeover in the 17th century. The interior has a classic Latin cross design and contains many frescoes by local artists.

Entertainment

Beyond the city walls are kilometers of beach and the *stabilimenti* where vacationers go to spend a day by the sea. **Samsura** (Litoranea Sud, tel. 328/115-4455, daily 8:30 A.M.–2:30 A.M.) is one of the nicest of these. You can spend the day under an umbrella and the evening sipping cocktails and enjoying the sunset from the restaurant on the sand. Every Thursday night during the summer, live jazz, soul, and salsa serenades the tanned bodies mingling around the bar.

Accommodations

Located in a freshly painted 17th-century palazzo 50 meters from the beach, **Il Palazzetto** (Riva Sauro, tel. 335/599-7171, www.salentonascosto.it, €120 d) is an ideal place to stop and take in the atmosphere for a couple of days. The couple that run the hotel

are also film producers and the four rooms look like they could be the set for a romantic thriller. Each is named after a wind, and has high vaulted ceilings and delightful frescoes. The first-floor lounge is perfect for unwinding and sharing impressions of the old town with the hosts, who can arrange walking and boat tours of the area.

Food

Don't be tempted by the first restaurant or snack bar you pass in the narrow, winding streets of the old town. Many will have new owners by next year and care less about food than attracting tourists. That's not a problem at **Angolo Blu** (Via Muzzio 45, tel. 083/326-1500, Tues.–Sun. noon–3 P.M. and 7–10:30 P.M., closed Nov., €9–13) near Cattedrale di Sant'Agata, where the price-quality ratio is way above average. They serve an excellent seafood cocktail and prepare shrimp in a handful of ways. The fish soup is also very good.

   La Puritate (Via Sant'Elia 18, tel. 083/326-4205, Thurs.–Tues. noon–3:30 P.M. and 7–11 P.M., closed Oct., €10–15) is located in the center of *l'isola* and benefits from a gazebo that protects diners from the midday sun. It's a fish restaurant, so mussels, clams, and other crustaceans embellish many of the pasta dishes. For the second course, just pick the species that catches your eye from the fish cart and specify if you want it roasted, grilled, boiled, or cooked in salt. Less attention is given to desserts and it's worth strolling along Via De Pace and Via Roma to find something sweet.

   If you prefer a sea view, try **Marechiaro** (Lungomare Marconi 25, tel. 083/326-6143, daily, €10–15), which has a splendid veranda just outside the old town. The interior is covered in wood and the *pesce crudo* (raw fish) and *spaghetti con aragosta* (lobster) are the dishes to remember.

Getting There and Around

Gallipoli lies on the Ionian coast and is well served by road. The N101 connects the city with Lecce, while the N459/16 is the shortcut to Otranto. The train from Brindisi takes two hours and requires a transfer in Lecce.

BASILICATA AND CALABRIA

Italians might smirk or sneer if you reveal your intentions of visiting Basilicata or Calabria. These two regions can't compete with Tuscany, but there's still plenty to love about them. Both regions boast unspoiled landscapes throughout their rugged interiors and deserted beaches. And all of it has been touched by history with scattered Greek ruins, Norman castles, and hill towns.

Basilicata is the only region in Italy that has two names; if you call it Lucania locals will know what you mean. The older moniker derives from Latin and is a reference to either the woody landscape or the ancient Liky people who passed through these parts long ago. Basilicata was first written in a document dating from 1175 and originates from Basiliskos who ruled in those days.

Multiple names is just one of the contradictions of the region summarized so well in Carlo Levo's *Christ Stopped at Eboli*. Part of the explanation has to do with the seas on either side of a mountainous interior that doesn't encourage communication. Some of the most isolated villages in Italy are here, and cartographers have always procrastinated when asked to map the region. It's no wonder parents worry when their children announce intentions of visiting the area.

This is Mel Gibson territory and you'll need a little of that *Mad Max* spirit. There is a payoff, however, that's beyond the perseverance of most camera-happy tourists. It consists in natural beauty and timeless traditions. Travelers can expect breathtaking and unusual panoramas, cities crammed with history, and

© LETIZIA RAZZINO

HIGHLIGHTS

 **Melfi:** The magnificent 11th-century castle in this historic town, the Castello di Melfi, is the most famous fortress in Basilicata (page 696).

 **Matera:** The city of the Sassi is a settlement completely carved out of rock by the Christian Basilian monks who took refuge here. The environment is so suggestive and unique it's been listed as a UNESCO World Heritage site (page 700).

 **Maratea:** Maratea is a charming town on Basilicata's Tyrrehnian coast that is a less crowded alternative to the Almafi Coast. On the way to the town, you can't miss the Statua del Redentore on the top of Monte San Biagio, a 22-meter-high sculpture with arms outstretched towards the city and the bay (page 705).

 **Parco Naturale del Pollino:** The largest natural park in Italy is accessible from Basilicata and Calabria. The landscape varies greatly and it's a good alternative to sitting on a beach (page 707).

 **Tropea:** Tropea is one of the most picturesque towns on the Tyrrhenian coast of Calabria and a favorite destination during the summer period due to its beautiful sand and clear waters (page 718).

 **Museo Archeologico Nazionale della Manga Grecia di Reggio Calabria:** The most-visited sight in Reggio Calabria houses the world-famous Bronzi di Riace (Riace Bronzes), life-size bronze statues of Greek athletes (page 721).

LOOK FOR  TO FIND RECOMMENDED SIGHTS, ACTIVITIES, DINING, AND LODGING.

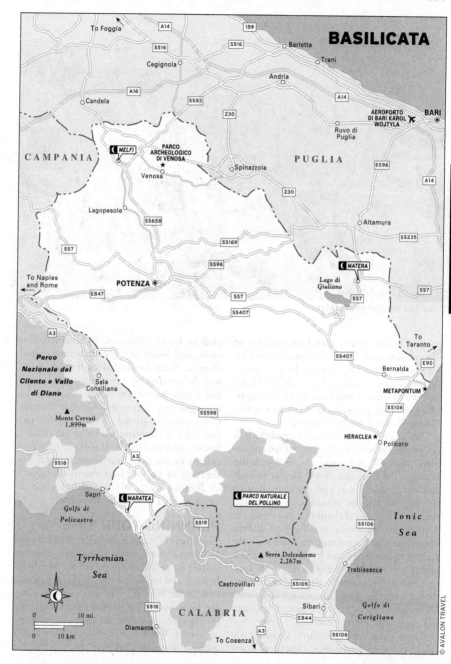

BASILICATA AND CALABRIA

cave-like dwellings in Matera

pristine seaside towns with long stretches of fine, golden sand. Here travelers earn each kilometer the hard way, but old Roman towns such as Venosa, medieval meccas like Melfi, and the Baroque Matera are worth the rigors. More relaxing pleasures do exist by the sea: Policoro is one town to remember.

Calabria is the southernmost tip of the Italian peninsula between the Tyrrhenian and Ionian coasts. Often described as the mountains between the seas, this area is almost entirely covered by highlands and plateaus. Besides sharing the Pollino massif with Basilicata, there's a long coastal chain that ends with the Aspromonte Mountains near Reggio Calabria. Forests and wide pastures alternate with the scanty vegetation caused by extensive periods of drought. Although nature is rich in the interior, tourists are generally attracted to the wonderful coastline made up of high cliffs with sheer drops into crystal-clear waters, enchanting coves, and golden beaches.

There's also a lot of history. Calabria was inhabited since prehistoric times and occupied by Greek, Romans, Byzantines, Normans, and Bourbons. It experienced periods of great splendor and decadent abandon, was devastated by invading populations, and struck by natural calamities, but it has managed to preserve its immense heritage. Calabrians are proud of their mythic past and enjoy recounting stories of grandeur to anyone who will listen. If you prefer to taste culture rather than hear about it, there's no shortage of age-old ingredients like *cipolla di Tropea* (sweet onion) and *liquirizia* (liquorice) used to surprise the mouth.

PLANNING YOUR TIME

The variety of things to do makes Basilicata and Calabria a good choice year-round. Summer is the best period to appreciate the wonderful beaches and the blue waters of the Tyrrhenian and Ionian seas. It's also nice to travel along the Ionian coast and visit Magna Grecia sites during spring and autumn when temperatures are cooler. Winter is optimal for skiing on the mountains of Sila and Aspromonte, which are

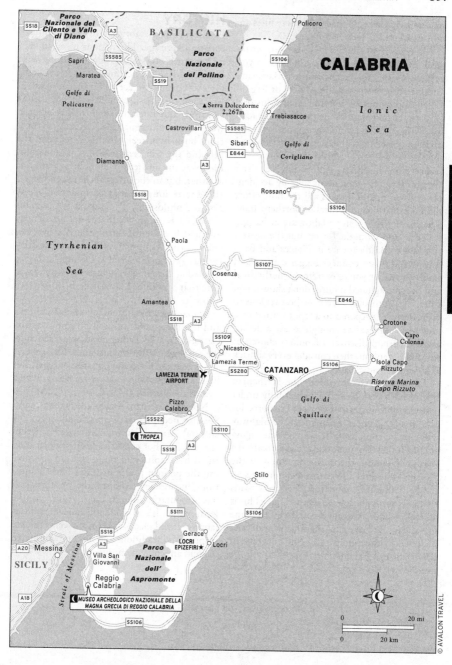

increasingly well equipped and where lines are non-existent.

Many tourists choose to spend an entire week in one of the coastal resorts, but if you prefer to visit the ancient ruins of Basilicata and Calabria, a weekend in Matera or Reggio Calabria provides a satisfying dose of history. Perhaps the best approach is a week on the road following the traces of Greeks and breaking up the sightseeing with a swim every now and then.

Traveling in either region, however, isn't always easy. You don't come here by accident or on a whim, and it takes a little more effort than destinations in central or northern Italy. The main airports in Calabria are at Reggio Calabria and Lamezia Terme, but the nearest runways to Basilicata are in Naples and Bari. Trains and buses connect bigger centers and small towns. If you're extremely methodical and become agitated if buses don't show up on time, these probably aren't the best regions to visit. If you're prepared to adapt to situations, however, and flexible enough to use a detour as an excuse to discover a fabulous church or seafood restaurant, then consider every setback as a potential adventure.

The A3 highway runs along the Tyrrhenian side of both regions and is perpetually under construction. Instead of weather or sports, locals small talk about when and if the highway will ever be completed. It's often more enjoyable to follow the panoramic coast roads. To reach the Ionian, the most convenient is the SS 106. You could also cross the mountains on the SS 280, but be prepared for narrow roads that pass through isolated countryside. This is where 24-hour roadside assistance can come in handy, just make sure the fine print doesn't include any exceptions regarding coverage in Basilicata and Calabria.

HISTORY

Basilicata and Calabria share a common history and heritage. The regions were, in fact, united until not so long ago and along with Sicily and Puglia once formed part of Magna Grecia (Greater Greece). The ancient cities of Metaponto in Basilicata, as well as Crotone (Kroton) and Locri Epizephiri in Calabria, were important centers of ancient civilization, built by Greek colonists between the 7th and the 6th centuries B.C. These colonies were in conflict for a long time with one another, but in the intervals between battles there were long periods of splendor in the arts and philosophy. Pythagoras founded his school in Kroton, while in Locri, Zaleucus dictated his laws, creating the first written code in the Western World. The most prestigious gymnasiums where Olympic athletes trained at the time were in Sibari and it was here that Strabo began writing history as we know it.

Romans and Byzantines followed the Greeks and left their mark in such buildings as the Cattolica in Stilo. Other mystic places include the religious establishments and caves of Matera, which testify to the presence of Christian Basilian monks who took refuge here and cultivated their souls.

Norman, Svevian, Angevin, Aragonese, and Spanish occupations have also added to the cultural mix evident in architecture, speech, and cuisine. For centuries both regions were ruled by Naples and marginalized, becoming the poorest places in Italy. These conditions encouraged banditry and Calabria still has a reputation due to the 'ndrangheta (the local mafia). It's no wonder Basilicata and Calabria are wild places where time seems to have stopped and traditions and folklore originated beyond anyone's memory.

Potenza and Vicinity

POTENZA

Every region has a capital and in Basilicata it's Potenza. The word means "power" in Italian and that's the impression you get approaching this hilltop town. At the apex is the oldest nucleus overlooking the Basento River. Around the historic center are 18th-century additions best exemplified in **Piazza Pagano**. This may be the only piazza in Italy named after pagans, who can be forgiven for deifying earthquakes. They happen a lot around here. In any case the Catholic church eventually arrived and the cathedral built for the town's patron saint would be impossible to build today. Engineers and bungee jumpers will also appreciate the bridge constructed in 1969 by Musumeci that is as modern as Potenza gets.

Sights

The historic center is reached by the narrow and cozy **Via Pretoria** that cuts the town in two and once led to a castle of which only a tower remains. Parallel (if such a word could be used in Potenza) to this street is the so-called sacred road of churches. Travelers with a long arm span can touch almost either side while they weave their way to the Romanesque pearl of **San Michele** and the imposing **Duomo di San Gerardo** (Corso XVIII Agosto, tel. 097/122-488, daily 7:30 A.M.–1 P.M.).

According to the man standing outside, it was built back in the 8th century, though some more reliable sources date it even earlier. A wide semicircular flight of steps leads to the entrance. San Gerardo is represented in the center of the portal surrounded by Evangelist symbols. Other sculptures in the sober facade recount the town's history since the saint was proclaimed Bishop in 1111.

For more insight into ancient aspects of Basilicata, have a look inside the **Archaeological Museum** (Via Ciccotti, tel. 097/144-4433, www.provincia.potenza.it/museo/, Tues.–Sun. 9 A.M.–1:30 P.M., Tues. and Thurs. 4–7 P.M., admission free). There are traces of history from the Paleolithic Age to Roman antiquity. Relics come from several zones around the region, in particular the Metaponto area, and include bronze objects, small statues, Greek and Latin inscriptions, ceramics, and weaponry. If you enjoy the past as much as the present, visit **Museo Archeologico Nazionale** (Largo Duomo 1, tel. 097/121-719, Tues.–Sun. 9 A.M.–8 P.M., €2.50). A walk through the galleries does more than any book to illustrate Greek colonization and Roman everyday life. Information is in Italian and English and panels clearly explain what was going on here while buffalo still roamed the Midwest. Highlights include refined armor from the warrior tombs of the Peuketiantes buried in the nearby ruins of Serra di Vaglio. There's also precious gold and amber jewelry that's never gone out of fashion. Guided visits are a good idea and can be booked in advance. They don't get many requests and are happy to show outsiders around the beautiful palazzo that houses the collection.

Entertainment and Events

Maggio Potentino is the major festival and takes place every year between May and June. It involves locals and tourists in a variety of cultural and leisure activities. For many Italian actors it's the equivalent of off-off Broadway and they learn their lines in the small theaters that host evening events. Food is the main reason to celebrate and restaurants offer special menus based on traditional cookery.

The climax of the festival is the **Sfilata dei Turchi** (Turkish parade) on May 29. It's based on an old legend about a band of Saracen pirates who attacked the city while everyone slept. The startled inhabitants were about to be massacred when the sky suddenly lit up and a row of angels appeared. The speechless Saracens were routed and the city saved. The miracle was attributed to San Gerardo and the procession honors him with reenactments of that long-ago night.

Fireworks are always exciting and are why locals look forward to the first Sunday in September. The pyrotechnics competition (www. fuochisulbasento.com) is held in **San Luca Branca**, a small village a few miles from Potenza. There's music, dancing, food, and a lowdown feeling that's contagious.

Accommodations

Tourist Hotel (Via Vescovado 4, tel. 097/125-955, www.touristhotelpotenza.com, €82–100 s/d) sounds like a place to avoid, but just because the owner lacks imagination doesn't mean it's a bad hotel. The name actually grows on you, and after awhile you'll enjoy telling people you stayed at the Tourist Hotel in Potenza. Besides it's bang in the center and a good starting point for a walk.

For more ambitious couples, there's always **B&B Al Convento** (Largo San Michele 21, tel. 348/330-7693, www.alconvento.eu, €80–90 s/d). The former convent where monks slept has been transformed into an intimate bed-and-breakfast. There are only two rooms, both elegant, both comfortable. It's just the place to wash off that Basilicata dust and slip into something romantic.

L'Albergo la Primula (C.da Bucaletto 61–62a, tel. 097/158-310, www.albergolaprimula.it, €135 d) is outside the center, near the train station, which makes it popular with business travelers and families alike. You get comforts here like bright rooms and handmade furniture and bed linen. There's no embroidery like this at the Howard Johnson. You can also choose to dine in the small restaurant that fills up most evenings with diners attracted by the large portions.

Food

Calling (**Trattoria Zi Mingo** (Via de Coubertin 43, tel. 097/144-2984, www.trattoriazimingo.com, Tues.–Sun. 12:30–3:30 P.M. and 7:30–11:30 P.M., €8–11) a culinary institution is an understatement. It's more like a gastronomic legend founded by uncle Domenico, better known as Zi Mingo, over 40 years ago. Although the legendary owner passed away, his nephew and niece have maintained the tradition of a simple and flavorful menu created from local ingredients. Start with *bruschette* on toasted Abriola bread and continue with any of the fresh pasta mixed and shaped by hand. The mushroom sauce and *ragù* are excellent, as is the house wine. Both dining rooms are as rustic as the food and the outdoor space may require reservations on weekends.

Due Torri (Via Due Torri 6–8, tel. 097/141-1661, Mon.–Sat. 12:30–3:30 P.M. and 7:30–11:30 P.M., €9–13) is in the heart of the old center, in one of the Aragonese towers. In spite of a prime location, the atmosphere inside lacks pretension. Silvia recites the menu orally and she'll happily repeat any of the delicious options. Food is ultra-traditional with dozens of starters and a different soup every day.

Next door the walls of **La Tettoia** (Via Due Torre 1, tel. 097/124-123, Mon.–Sat. 12:15–2:45 P.M. and 7:15–10:45 P.M., €10–14) are covered with famous diners and their words of accolade for the Lo Russo family. Vegetarians and fish lovers are especially spoiled for choice and meat and potato people can sink their teeth into *costatelle di agnello alla contadina* (lamb cooked country-style). The canteen in this large restaurant is well stocked with local labels and after-dinner spirits that are better sipped than swallowed in a single go.

Ristorante Pizzeria Fuori le Mura (Via IV Novembre 34, tel. 097/125-409, Tues.–Sun. 12:30–3:30 P.M. and 7:30–11:30 P.M., €10–12) is a good place to sample a selection of first courses or get reacquainted with pizza. They also grill a very tender steak.

Big-name wines are available to savor immediately or buy for a future occasion at **Laboratorio Divino** (Via Scafarelli 20, tel. 09/712-6396). They also carry many Slow Food products. Besides pizza and *panzarotti*, **Pizzeria Montesano** (Via Verdi 12, tel. 09/713-5355) dispenses the must-taste *oss di mort*. They'll tell you this special bread flavored with wild fennel is the best in the region and after you've tasted some in the surrounding towns you may agree.

To fill up a rucksack or suitcase with some

typical products, stop by **Piaceri Lucani** (Via Caporella bis, tel. 097/137-447) in the historic center. You'll find typical salami and cheeses like *pecorino di Filiano* and *canestraio di Moliterno*. If you can't decide, they'll be happy to let you sample a slice before you commit to goat, cow, or sheep.

Information and Services

Sportello Turistico Tourpass Basilicata (Piazza Vittorio Emanuele, tel. 097/141-5150) offers historical, cultural, and general information. The office provides brochures, thematic guides, and maps in several foreign languages, including English. For further information, you can also inquire at the **Associazione Pro Loco** (Vico Stabile 10, tel. 097/123-964, www.prolocopotenza.it).

Getting There and Around

To reach Potenza by car from the Tyrrenian coast, take the A3 Salerno–Reggio Calabria highway and exit at Sicignano. It's 48 kilometers to town on the Basentana SS 407 state road. From the Adriatic coast, use the A14 Bologna–Taranto highway (Autostrada Adriatica), at Foggia follow the signs for Candela (where you can also pick up the A16 Naples-Bari highway) and continue towards Melfi and Potenza.

If you prefer to ride the rails, Potenza is easily reached from Naples, Foggia, or Taranto. The Naples–Reggio Calabria line is particularly scenic and cuts through the center of the region to the Ionian Sea. The closest airports are Bari-Palese (55 minutes) and Napoli Capodichino (1 hour). It's possible to get around Potenza on **CO.TRA.B.** (tel. 800/064-500) buses or using the taxis waiting outside **Stazione Potenza Inferiore** (Viale Marconi, tel. 097/154-669).

LAGOPESOLE

Lagopesole is another town famous for its castle. It comes in and out of view as you approach from Potenza. During the Middle Ages, it played a vital role in protecting the Heraclea road and houses huddle safely under its shadow. Those with Melfi on their minds should drop in for a look.

Sights

Melfi may get more attention but **Castel Lagopesole** (Via Castello, tel. 097/186-083, daily 9:30 a.m.–1 p.m. and 4–7 p.m., €1.55) remains the most magical. The spirit of the great Swabian Emperor Frederick II is strong. This was one of the last castles he built and used as a hunting lodge. The rectangular walls deviate from the classic, hexagonal design generally used by Frederick's architects. The interior is as fascinating as the exterior, and the royal apartments and chapel merit a visit.

Entertainment and Events

Le Rosse al Castello ("Reds at the Castle") makes sense once you see the Ferraris. There are over 40 kinds from all years, including several rare 1950s models and some sleek Testarossas. It's not just the racing cars that are red, for two days in June the entire town is covered with flags and Ferrari gadgets. Don't resist staring and etting close to these jewels of Italian engineering. When they're not parked in front of the castle they're performing a variety of driving demonstrations.

Food

After Garibaldi united Italy, not everyone's life got better. **La Taverna dei Briganti** (Via Federico II 7, tel. 097/186-110, Sat.–Thurs. 12:30–3 p.m. and 7:30–11:30 p.m., €9–12), or the tavern of the brigands, was where rebels met to plan their next "operation." Today people meet to eat and any whispered conversation is harmless chitchat. The old building lies at the foot of the castle used by the *briganti* throughout the 19th century. It would be a crime to serve anything but large portions of local favorites and fortunately the chef is innocent.

Getting There and Around

Lagopesole is 30 kilometers from Potenza on the SS 658, which snakes across peaceful countryside. It's a half-hour by train (€2) from

Potenza to Castel Lagopesole station, from where you can take a bus to town.

◖ MELFI

If you believe history repeats then Melfi is probably only a few centuries from a comeback. It's just a question of time. The city's greatness began with the Normans and continued under the reign of Frederick the Second of Svevia. They left a magnificent castle behind and liked the town so much they made it their capital. Today it's a ghost of its former self and you can hear a pin drop inside the **Museo Nazionale del Melfese** and the fast-deteriorating Duomo. There's no need to put out a Do Not Disturb sign here and even the guard dogs are too lazy to bite.

Sights

Castello di Melfi (Via Castello, tel. 097/223-8726, Mon. 2–8 p.m., Tues.–Sun. 9 a.m.–8 p.m., €2.50) is the most famous fortress in the region. Normans laid the first stones and the oddly shaped profile is a clear signs of

later additions. Swabians and Angevins were especially busy redecorators and it was here, in 1231, that Frederick II enacted the Augustales Constitution of the Kingdoms of Sicily.

The external courtyard with its square and polygonal towers characterizes Angevin alterations. There's also a surprising lack of cylindrical forms. In the 16th century, it passed into the hands of the Dorians who transformed the central structure. Today it houses the **Museo Nazionale del Melfese** that occupies three halls on the ground floors. Several archaeological finds concerning local populations during the Prehistoric, Roman, Byzantine, and Norman periods are on display. There is also a collection of Byzantine jewelry.

The **Duomo** (Piazza Duomo, daily 9 a.m.–12:30 p.m. and 4–7:30 p.m.), is dedicated to Santa Maria Assunta and was built around 1100. The Norman bell tower was added by Noslo da Remerio in 1153 and looms above town. It is the oldest part of the church that was nearly completely rebuilt in Baroque style less than 300 years ago.

Castello di Melfi was the former home of the Normans.

© LETIZIA RAZZINO

Entertainment and Events

Varola Chestnut Festival (Sat. 4–11 P.M., Sun. 9 A.M.–11 P.M.) is a popular event with ancient origins. It takes place on the last two weekends of October in Piazza del Duomo and spreads to all the streets in town. There's a big influx of tourists during the festival and it's nice to see Melfi at its vibrant best. Visitors come primarily to taste and buy dozens of typical products derived from chestnuts. The most classic of these are *caldarroste,* roasted chestnuts cooked on the street while you salivate.

Night festivals always have a different aura about them and **Festa dello Spirito Santo** (Pentecost, tel. 097/225-1305) is particularly moving. It begins with girls and nubile women transporting the Holy Spirit (represented by a sculpture of a bearded man, dove, and the sign of the Trinity) to a cave-chapel in a nearby mountain before returning to town. The spirit is then placed on a highly decorated cart and pulled through the streets behind the Madonna and archangel San Michele. The pace of the procession is slow and steady with plenty of locals dressed in historical costumes. You can watch from the narrow sidewalks or actually take part.

Accommodations

Il Tetto (Piazza IV Novembre, tel. 097/223-6837, www.albergoiltetto.com, €50 d) is the latest hotel located in a defunct monastery. It's a sign fewer men choose to lead a monk's life and an opportunity to sample that life. In this case the building dates from the 7th century and restructuring has altered little. The accommodation is made up of 26 rooms with single, double, triple, and quadruple options occupied by groups of friends and families.

They couldn't have found a better place to build **(Relais la Fattoria** (SS 303, tel. 097/224-776, www.relaislafattoria.it, € 57–95 s/d). Everything about the landscape suggests serenity and sweetness. Rooms are a mix of rustic peasant furniture, antiques, prints, and paintings. Vineyards, orchards, woods, and sunflowers surround the small hotel, which makes an ideal starting point for a walk through the countryside.

Il Tratturo Regio (Contrada Casonetto, tel. 097/224-120, www.iltratturoregio.net, €25 pp) is a friendly farmhouse with an authentic *agriturismo* welcome. Here the olives and cows aren't just for show. They make delicious things that guests can taste in the restaurant and purchase. Visitors can also observe firsthand how cheese and oil are made. The house is four kilometers from Melfi and the Vulture Mountains, a landmark for anyone who enjoys nature, history, or good cooking.

Food

Novecento (SS 401, Contrada Incoronata, tel. 097/223-7470, www.ristorante-novecento.it, Tues.–Sat. 12:30–3:30 P.M. and 7:30–11.30 P.M., Sun. 12.30–3:30 P.M., €8–12) is a family restaurant near the entrance to Melfi. The Lamonts are gracious hosts who know the meaning of hospitality. Besides, any place with a cheese cart and a wine list this extensive is a good find. Specialties include: *maccheronata alla trainiera* (long homemade pasta seasoned with fresh tomatoes and basil), *lagana e noci* (rough-cut *tagliatella* with hazelnuts and cod), and *agnello a cutturiedd* (lamb stewed in a *terra-cotta* pot with onions and tomatoes). Don't forget the thick ricotta mousse for dessert.

Michele Sonnessa revitalizes old dishes at **La Villa** (Contrada Cavallerizza, tel. 097/223-6008, Tues.–Sat. 12:30–3:30 P.M. and 7:30–11:30 P.M., Sun. 12:30–3:30 P.M., €8–10). He's particularly fond of *antipasti* and has made choosing one difficult. It's best to share a couple or go for the mixed selection. *Maccheronata con ragù* is made with a unique pasta shape that deserves a patent. The wine menu is a chance to taste local wines produced in the DOC certified Aglianico del Vulture area.

Information and Services

You can get answers about Melfi and the surrounding towns at the **Associazione Pro Loco** (Piazza Umberto I 14, tel. 097/223-9751). To contact a medic (guardia medica) 24 hours a day, call 097/195-5196.

Getting There and Around

Melfi is 50 kilometers north of Potenza. It's a pleasant drive on the SS 658. The town is also in the middle of the Foggia–Potenza train line and makes a nice morning or afternoon stop. There a dozen departures every day and a ticket costs €3. It's about 700 meters from the *stazione* to the entrance of town up Via Santa Sofia. If you prefer bus, **Autolinee Moretti** (Via Foggia 16, tel. 097/224-590) makes the journey daily from Potenza in under an hour. Once there, the city is best appreciated on foot and the walk up to the castle helps work up an appetite.

VENOSA

Theories abound about Venosa. Some say it was founded in honor of Venus, others are convinced the name refers to the village's delicious Vinosa wine, and a few believe the answer lies with the town's windy or *ventoso* climate. What is certain is that the great Latin poet Orazio (Horace) was born here in 65 B.C. The Appia and Herculia roads intersected in Venosa, making it an important Roman town with sizable bathes and amphitheater. Another golden age arrived with the Normans, who left behind a handful of churches and palaces. Little has changed in the urban fabric since then and the town remains a set designer's dream.

Sights

The **Castello** (tel. 097/236-095, Wed.–Mon. 9 A.M.–8 P.M., Tues. 2–8 P.M., €2.50) treats foreigners better than in the past; thankfully they've stopped hurling boiling oil from the ramparts. It was erected in 1470 by Pirro del Balzo and retains classic defensive characteristics like the moat and drawbridge. Prisoners were kept in the towers and inscriptions on the cell walls are original.

Via Vittorio Emanuele II is the main street and takes you past piazze and near Horace's home. If you continue past Piazza Don Bosco, you'll reach **Parco Archeologico di Venosa** (tel. 097/236-095, Wed.–Mon. 9 A.M.–sunset, Tues. 9 A.M.–1 P.M., admis-

sion free). Within the park are remnants of an amphitheater, bathing complex, *domus* (house), and partially crumbling **Santa Trinità** church. It's a wonderful walk and a good look at some well-preserved Roman and medieval heritage.

The **Amphitheater** dates from the 1st century B.C. and played a major role in town. Spectacles, venations, and executions were all held inside the elliptically shaped theater where thousands of citizens and non-citizens once gathered for the show. If we call it an arena today, it's because of a thin layer of *rena* (sand) Romans used to prevent gladiators from slipping.

Across the way are the baths, today's equivalent of a fitness and beauty center. People came nearly every day (usually in the afternoons) to work out, relax, and socialize.

SEIZE THE MOMENT

People think Latin is dead, but when someone says *"carpe diem"* the meaning is clear. This often repeated piece of advice originated with Venosa's hometown poet Quinto Orazio Flacco, better known as Horace. He was also something of a philosopher and the meaning of his words has lost its edge over the years, although they're still fun to say.

A day was too long for Horace, he was more interested in moments, and enjoying whatever might occur in a succession of instances. He believed that those instances make up a lifetime, and that once you appreciate each single one you free yourself of the relentless search for pleasure, wealth, or fame.

"Autarkeia" was another favorite expression of Horace's; it means to be enough for oneself. His approach to a fleeting life was to be happy for the things you have and care not for the things you don't have. Whether he had many followers is unknown, but at least part of his thinking has stuck.

Generally you started with a sweat-inducing sauna, moved to a warm pool, and ended with a splash in the *frigidarium*. Nearby is an example of a **Roman *domus*** (house) decorated with the propitiatory symbols of the former owner. In the center of the villa is the atrium decorated with frescos and mosaics inhabitants admired while moving from one room to another.

The strangely shaped **Trinità Abbey** is hard to miss. It was built over a pagan temple and consists of two churches, one completed and one known as the **Incompiuta** (Unfinished). For a tour of the Abbey, contact the **La Quadriga** cultural association (tel. 09/723-6542, www.venosamelfiturismo.it). On the way back to town, bear right on Via Roma to see the **Fontana di San Marco** and two lovely churches near **Piazza Ninni.**

Entertainment and Events

Aglianica Wine Festival (tel. 097/272-0166, www.aglianica.it) occurs each summer in villages around the Vulture Mountains. Exhibitions, seminars, tastings, and expositions are organized to celebrate and promote the Aglianico grape. One taste could make you forget Chianti. Sommeliers from around the world show up to examine the latest harvest and local wineries open their cellars for the general public to discover.

Accommodations

Hotel Orazio (Corso Vittorio Emanuele II 142, tel. 097/231-135, www.hotelorazio.it, €50 d) is located in the historic center of town within a distinguished 16th-century palazzo. Service may be a little less distinguished but the price is good and they'll practically pay you to stay here during the early spring when the town is deserted of tourists.

A bit outside the old town walls is **Hotel del Sorriso** (Via Appia 135, tel. 097/235-975, www.hoteldelsorriso.com, info@hoteldelsorriso.com, €70 d). It's a modern, quiet hotel run by a nice family who chose simple, functional furniture in all the rooms. In the height of summer you may need to spend the siesta hours inside with the air-conditioning on.

Carpe Diem (Contrada Boreano, tel. 097/235-985, www.agriturismocarpediem.it, €50 pp) is an *agriturismo* near Venosa. There are eight double rooms and three self-catering apartments. The large farmhouse also has a good restaurant with regional specialties and lots of advice from the waiter on what to see and do in the area. Many of the organic products on the menu are from the farm and can be purchased. There are mountain bikes for rent and stables nearby where horses can be saddled up and taken for a trot.

Food

◖ Al Frantoio (Via Roma 211, tel. 097/236-925, Tues.–Sun. 12:30–3 P.M. and 7:30–11:30 P.M., €10–13) may be in the center of town but they've managed to keep things very calm. The olive trees help and the building was in fact home to an olive press for many years. Inside it's possible to taste the classics revisited according to the chef's humor that day. If he's angry, expect spicy; if he's in a good mood, bank on the desserts.

Il Ghiottone (Via Accademia dei Rinascenti, tel. 097/236-935, www.ristoranteghiottone.it, Tues.–Sun. 12:30–3 P.M. and 7:30–11:30 P.M., €7–10) is a modern and comfortable restaurant just outside the center. Fusion is in the air and many Mediterranean flavors are introduced to each other for the first time. *Fascine ceci e porri, pasta al torchio con cicerchie* (pasta with chickpeas), and *orecchiette alla contadina* (traditional tomato and goat cheese pasta) are all notable. Portions are generous and the cellar stocks local Agliano DOC and national labels worth uncorking.

To taste the same flavors Horace once enjoyed, visit **La Taverna Ducale** (Piazza Municipio 2, tel. 097/237-100, Tues.–Sun. 12:30–3 P.M. and 7:30–11 P.M., €12–15). The 15th-century palazzo is the perfect setting for palates to experience a culinary flashback. The poet's favorite dish is on the menu as well as many vegetables that taste better than they look.

Information and Services

There's a tourist information office in Piazza Municipio 7 with plenty of leaflets on local initiatives and an **Associazione Pro Loco** in Piazza Castello 47 that can get you out of any cultural jam. **Associazione La Quadriga** (tel. 339/480-7431) provided guided tours of town including Horace's home.

Getting There and Around

Reaching Venosa from Potenza by car takes an hour. The easiest route is SS 658 through Rapolla and then following the signs. The closest train station is Venosa-Maschito several kilometers from town. A taxi is usually waiting outside but you can also call **Venusia Travel** (tel. 097/232-012) to order one.

Matera and Vicinity

◖ MATERA

Sassi isn't a word you associate with Matera until you discover it's what locals call the hundreds of house-caves carved into the soft tufa rock. No one has lived in these since 1952 and the neighborhood is a tranquil contrast to the hustle and bustle in the new town. Many of the Middle Age dwellings have been restored to Flintstone quality and could make you rethink your dream house.

Besides spending a night underground, it's possible to taste the local red wines in a 9,000-year-old restaurant, walk a wild landscape, and visit more than 150 chapels built in the surrounding hillsides. Take the **Strada Panoramica dei Sassi** to get the best view of the caves UNESCO recently named as a World Heritage site.

Sights

Since the beginning, Matera has been populated by a variety of religious communities. Benedictines and Basil monks, escaping Ottoman Turks, have both prayed here. Their presence over the years led to the construction of all sorts of places to worship. These holy spaces were dug directly into the rock in the mountains around Matera.

Between the Agri Valley and the town, it's possible to admire countless of these **rock churches** (Sassi Tourism, Via Lucana 238, tel. 083/531-9458, www.sassitourism.it, daily Apr.–Oct. 9 A.M.–1 P.M. and 3–7 P.M., Nov.–Mar. 9:30 A.M.–1 P.M. and 2:30–4:30 P.M.). Many are frescoed and located along ravines—

LIGHTS, CAMERA, ACTION!

Chances are you've already seen Matera. It's a popular backdrop with directors who appreciate the resemblance to the Holy Land. Mel Gibson fell in love the moment he saw it and knew it would be the perfect location for *The Passion of the Christ* and save him the trouble of shooting in Jerusalem. It also provided atmosphere for *The Nativity* and *Omen 666* and deserves an Oscar for best set design. You can take a tour (www.sassiweb.it) of Gibson's set during the summer and see exactly where the Crucifixion, Last Supper, Jerusalem Gates, market, and Via Crucis scenes were shot. Legend has it a lock of Monica Bellucci's hair is kept in the cathedral. It's best to come armed with a camera and do a little filming of your own.

hard to reach except for the faithful. Notable examples include: **Madonna dell'Idris, San Giovanni in Monterrone, Santa Maria de Armenis,** and **Madonna delle Tre Porte.** There are several organized tours. The short one (€2.50) is a single church, the medium length (€5) takes in three caves and the long walk (€6) brings you everywhere.

Matera's **cathedral** (Piazza Duomo, www.matera-irsina.chiesacattolica.it, Mon.–Sun. 9 A.M.–1 P.M. and 4–7 P.M.) is located in the *civita,* a spur of land between the Sassi. It

© LETIZIA RAZZINO

white-washed houses in Matera

was Archbishop Andrea's idea and completed in 1270. The interior is full of anonymous sculptures and paintings like *Madonna della Bruna,* the town's patron saint. **Via Duomo** leads to **San Francesco** (Piazza San Francesco D'Assisi, tel. 083/533-2908, Mon.–Sun. 10 A.M.–12:30 P.M. and 4–8 P.M.), a second-generation church built on the ruins of St. Pietro and Paolo. Saint Francis himself is said to have walked all the way from Umbria to see it. There's an interesting fresco inside showing Pope Urbano II's 1093 visit to town. Surprisingly little has changed.

Museo Nazionale Ridola (Via Ridola 24, tel. 083/531-0058, Tues.–Sun. 9 A.M.–8 P.M., Mon. 2–8 P.M., €2.50) was founded in 1911 thanks to the tireless work of a senator with an interest in archeology. The collection includes many prehistoric materials from Neolithic trench villages that demonstrate there's a lot of surface to scratch in Italy. Another respite from the heat or cold is the **Museum of Peasant Culture** (Via S. Giovanni Vecchio 60, tel. 083/534-4057, www. museolaboratorio.it, summer daily 9 A.M.–1 P.M.

and 4–8 P.M., €2). If you never could imagine the realities of a peasant lifestyle, this is where to set the record straight. The museum reconstructs how residents of the Sassi lived for centuries. During the winter, visits to the museum must be arranged in advance. **Casa Grotta** (tel. 083/531-0118, daily 9:30 A.M.–until late, €1.50) on Vico Solitario, in the Sasso Caveoso, is another example hollowed out in the 1700s. There's a masonry kitchen, cistern for collecting rainwater, stable, and manger. All the furniture is original including the large double bed, wooden cradle, chest of drawers, and storage cabinets.

Entertainment and Events

July 2 is the day to thank **Madonna della Bruna.** The festival has been held for over 600 years and originates from an old legend. The story goes that a beautiful, impoverished woman asked a peasant, traveling by cart, for a lift into town. The peasant agreed but at the entrance to the village the woman transformed herself into a wooden sculpture of the

Holy Virgin. Astonished citizens divided it into pieces so they each possessed a fragment.

The celebration begins at dawn with a procession of shepherds. A triumphal carriage is then escorted by knights through the streets and the festival culminates in the evening with the destruction of the cart. The demolition represents everyone's hope for a prosperous harvest and anyone able to grab a piece can expect lady luck's company for an entire year. Fortunately there's enough to go around but getting into the scrum is good fun.

Shopping

People have been working stone for a long time in Matera. Although tufa is soft, it's also very brittle and takes great skill to sculpt. It's used to make household accessories and small objects like terra-cotta cuckoos or the famous *fischietti* whistle painted in bright colors. You can find these unique items in the crafts shops around town. **Pietro Gurrado** (Via Duomo 3–5, tel. 083/533-0447) is one of the best artisans. He produces incredibly detailed holiday scenes and miniature statuettes of typical Basilicatan characters.

Matera is also a good hunting ground for antiques. On the first Sunday of each month, Piazza Vittorio Veneto hosts a market with 80 stands selling vintage furniture, ceramics, bed linens, and vinyl records. It's a real treasure trove.

Accommodations

Casa d'Imperio (Via d'Addozio 39, tel. 083/533-0503, www.casadimperio.it, €65 d) is in the historic Sassi di Matera neighborhood. The 15th-century structure has a classic internal courtyard and terrace. During the summer, breakfast is served outside and two of the four rooms are equipped with kitchens for anyone with intentions of a long stay.

Life in a cave is hard to imagine until you've stayed at **Locanda di San Martino** (Via Fiorentini 71, tel. 083/525-6600, www.locandadisanmartino.it, €85 d). The 22 rooms are situated on four levels and are the same type of cave dwellings locals have used for years.

These, however, have been adapted to modern living and comforts like private plumbing and electricity have been added. Through a series of balconies it's possible to enjoy an evocative view of the Sasso Barisano. **Residence San Pietro Barisano** (Rione San Biagio 52–56, tel. 083/534-6191, www.residencesanpietrobarisano.it, €85 d) is a similar structure in the center with elegant rooms and attention to detail.

Close to the Cathedral and main piazza is **Le Monacelle** (Via Riscatto 10, tel. 083/534-4097, www.lemonacelle.it, €85 d), a hotel, hostel, and meeting center. It was once a music school and hospitality house that now offers panoramic views of Matera. The hotel has nine rooms and the hostel has two with plenty of bunk beds in each. It's central, quiet, and popular with backpackers from around the world.

❰ Hotel Sant'Angelo (Piazza San Pietro Caveoso, tel. 083/531-4010, www.hotelsantangelosassi.it, €120 d) is the result of painstaking preservation and renovation of over 1,400 square meters of caves, passages, stairways, and courtyards. It can accommodate up to 45 guests in 16 historical rooms. There's a very nice restaurant with a warm rustic atmosphere perfect for enjoying Lucanian specialties.

Food

Basilicata's cuisine gets its trademark flavor from strong, spicy ingredients. Dishes are perfumed with wild herbs and tomatoes, silvery olives, and prickly pear cacti. Red peppers are a staple of every kitchen and sheep and goat cheese are popular ingredients. Recipes are simple and generally require some baking or grilling. *La Pignata,* a traditional lamb-based dish, is on many menus. The name comes from the terra-cotta container in which it's baked for several hours. *Cialledda,* on the other hand, is a light summer mix of bread, tomatoes, cucumbers, onions, and olive oil seasoned with oregano or basil. There are many places in town to try these and other typical recipes.

Seclusion from the outside world has been a good thing for **Lucanerie** (Via Santo Stefano 61, tel. 083/533-2133, Tues.–Sat.

12:30–3 P.M. and 7–11 P.M., Sun. 7–11 P.M., €7–12) and the people who regularly dine there. The traditional recipes are untainted by Jamie Oliver and modern theories of cooking. Nothing is prepared by the book but by word of mouth; the *antipasti* is edible history. Pasta is handmade and comes in uncommon shapes like *ferricelli* and *rashcatielli*. The barley soup with porcini mushrooms is a classic peasant dish that could make you switch careers. If you're in town around Christmas, the *cartellate* dessert with honey is a must. A few meters away is **Perrone** (Via Giovanni Maria Trabaci, tel. 083/538-8335), which sells bread, *taralli,* and sweets baked in their wood oven.

⟨ Don Matteo (Via San Biagio 12, tel. 083/534-4145, Mon.–Sat. 7–11 P.M., Sun. 12:30–2:30 P.M. and 7–11 P.M., €10–13) gets an A for ambiance. The restaurant is down a flight of well-worn stairs inside a Paleolithic-era cave. There's an open kitchen that is like being at grandma's house and a wonderful view of the Sassi. The chef combines a touch of creativity with tradition and his *ricotta alla stazzona* dessert has won several awards. It was especially popular in the 18th century and served in aristocratic households. Reservations are recommended.

In the heart of the Sassi, **Baccanti** (Via Sant'Angelo 58–61, tel. 083/533-3704, www.baccantiristorante.com, Mon.–Sat. 7–11 P.M., Sun. 12:30–2:30 P.M., €9–12) is a small rustic restaurant, full of atmosphere. It's dug out of tufa and has a pleasant terrace that makes for a romantic evening. Food is an update of regional dishes and changes frequently according to the season.

Le Botteghe (Piazza San Pietro Barisano 22, tel. 083/534-4072, daily 12:30–2:30 P.M. and 7–11 P.M., €8–12) is in a lovely piazza that attracts curious tourists. Pino welcomes guests into the large interior with tufa floors and vaulted ceilings. The grill is Angelo's domain and he cooks all sorts of meat to perfection. *Pignata* takes a while but this sheep and potato dish is worth the wait. Even the oil is good here and it's been pressed locally by hand.

In summer there are many tables outside with charming views of town.

Caffè Tripoli (tel. 083/533-3991, daily 7 A.M.–7 P.M.) in Piazza Vittorio Veneto is ideal for an *aperitivo* or an after-dinner taste of gelato made the old-fashioned way.

Information and Services

The **APT office** in Matera is on Via Spine Bianche 22 (tel. 083/533-1817). For a medical emergency, call **Pronto Soccorso** (tel. 083/524-3212) or **Guardia Medica** (tel. 083/526-2260).

Getting There and Around

The closest airport is Bari Palese, 64 kilometers away. There are many national connections and you can catch a train the rest of the way. They're more frequent from the **FAL** (www.fal-srl.it) than the Central Station and run about every hour. Just pay attention if it's a direct service or whether you need to change at Altamura. Matera is also well connected by bus from many Italian cities and the APT office can provide a list of companies and timetables.

Rome is only four hours away by car. From the Tyrrhenian coast, travel along the A3 Salerno–Reggio Calabria highway until Sicignano and take the Basentana SS 407 for 120 kilometers, then the SS 7 all the way to town. From the Adriatic coast, use the A14 Bologna–Taranto highway and exit at Bari Nord. It's then 60 kilometers on the SS 96 in the direction of Altamura.

Once in Matera, walk or hop on one of the orange buses run by **CASAM** (www.casam .it) that mostly cover the new town. **Taxi service** is available in Via XX Settembre (tel. 083/533-3472) and Piazza Matteotti (tel. 083/533-4348).

MURGE MOUNTAINS AND BASILICATA VALLEYS

Matera is surrounded by the Murge Mountains and Basilicata Valleys, well known for their wheat. *Masserie* (farms) are a common sight but have an unusual appearance. These solid structures sheltered large extended families and protected them from bandits. Fortifications include towers, boundary walls, and patrol bays to defend barns and herds. Most are located on hilltops where threats could easily be seen coming. You can arrange guided visits of the fortress-farms at the **Parco Murgia** office in Matera (Via Sette Dolori 10, tel. 083/533-6166, www.parcomurgia.it, Mon.–Fri. 8 A.M.–2 P.M., Tues. and Thurs. also 4–6 P.M.). It's possible to see **Torre Spagnola, Casino Venusto,** and **Masseria Malvezzi.**

ALIANO

Another interesting place is the town of Aliano. Travelers tracking literary heroes shouldn't miss the **Parco Letterario di Carlo Levi** (Via Martiri d'Ungheria 1, tel. 083/556-8529, www.aliano.it, Thurs.–Tues. 9 A.M.–12:30 P.M. and 4–6:30 P.M.). The park was created to honor the writer, doctor, and painter forced into exile by Italy's fascist government between 1935–1936. It's possible to visit the restored house where he lived, watch theatrical performances in the open, visit a permanent exhibition in the former town hall, and see the rebuilt set of the film *Christ Stopped at Eboli*. There's also the **Museo Storico Carlo Levi** (tel. 083/556-8074, Apr.–Sept. daily 10 A.M.–12:30 P.M. and 4–6 P.M., Oct.–Mar. Wed., Sat., and Sun. 10 A.M.–12:30 P.M. and 3–5 P.M.) in Via Cisterna with a collection of letters, documents, and drawings relating to his banishment. Original lithographs donated by the writer himself are particularly interesting.

The Basilicata Coast

METAPONTO AND VICINITY

Basilica's Ionian coast is a 40-kilometer stretch of sand between the Apulian and Calabrian borders. Greek colonists landed here close to 3,000 years ago and the area quickly became a hotbed of Hellenic culture. Metaponto is full of ancient treasures and traces of Magna Grecia glory.

History isn't the only draw and towns like **Policoro** and **Scanzano Ionico** are summer destinations on the rise. It's hard not to appreciate the long sandy beaches, transparent water, and wonderful pine groves that grow along the coast. In recent decades, new bathing establishments, campsites, holiday resorts, and hotels have helped revitalize tourism in the area.

Sights

Besides fantastic beaches, Metaponto has a great open-air **museum** (Via Aristea 21 Metaponto Borgo, tel. 083/574-5327, Tues.–Sun. 9 A.M.–8 P.M., Mon. 2–8 P.M., €2.50) that displays a wide range of archaeological finds. There are vases, weapons, and hundreds of personal ornaments imported from around the Mediterranean. Scale models show how the place looked from the first prehistoric beginnings to the arrival of the Greeks in the 5th century B.C. and eventual Romanization of town.

Evidence of prosperity in the city renamed **Metapontum** by the Romans can be found in several archaeological areas outside the center. On a nearby hill are the ruins of the **Tavole Palatine** (SS 106, tel. 083/574-5327, daily 9 A.M.–1 hour before sunset, admission free) temple probably dedicated to Hera. Built in the Doric style in 530 B.C., it's the only monumental building whose external colonnade has remained intact (they were partially restored in 1961). There are 15 columns left, arranged on two sides that support pieces of an *architrave*.

New Policoro was built on the site of ancient Heraclea, a Greek colony founded around 434 B.C. Before that, an Ionic group was completely destroyed by Metaponto and her allies. If that sounds complicated you'll want to visit the **National Museum of Sirtide** (Via Colombo 8, tel. 083/597-2154, Wed.–Mon. 9 A.M.–7 P.M., Tues. 2–7 P.M., admission free) and the archeological park that helps put the town's long history into context. There's also a lot happening on the beaches. Marine tortoises use the sand as a daycare center for their eggs and blue dolphins are often spotted swimming playfully offshore. The sand is an invitation to spread a towel or rent a deck chair and enjoy the sun. **Scanzano Ionico** is another small village with a reputation for a waveless sea and spacious beach.

Accommodations

Every once in a while it's nice to stay somewhere without a hint of rustic. **Hotel Club Orohotel** (Policoro, Via Lido, tel. 083/591-0190, €120 d) is that place and is only 500 meters from the beach. Rooms are modern without being stylish and provide all around good comfort for travelers tired of bed-and-breakfasts. **Camping Village Heraclea** (Spiaggia di Policoro, Via Lido 37, June–Sept., tel. 083/591-0168, www. campingheraclea.it) is the rough-and-tumble option. The grounds are located within a beautiful new-growth forest close to the sea. Lots are secluded and the camp's facilities include bar, restaurant, and bike rental.

Food

Mrs. Teresa is responsible for the cooking at **Antichi Sapori Lucani** (Scanzano Ionico, Via Novello 34, tel. 083/595-4644, Mon.– Sun. 12:30–3:30 P.M. and 7–11 P.M., €7–10). After you get through the mixed *salumi* starters, she'll be glad to prepare *frizzulli con mollica,* one of the oldest recipes in the region. If that doesn't tempt, there are always a variety of vegetable soups and deceptively simple pasta.

Information and Services

The area isn't entirely geared for tourism and a lot of towns provide only basic services. You can get some maps in Poliporo from the **Pro Loco office** (tel. 083/598-0998) in Piazza Eraclea. The library is also located there. **Guardia Medica** can be reached at tel. 083/598-6455 anytime day or night.

Getting There and Around

From the A14 Bologna-Taranto take the SS 106, towards Reggio Calabria until you reach

Metaponto and the other towns along the coast. Most can be visited in 15 minutes but observing daily life for a little longer is priceless.

◪ MARATEA

Mountains are rugged on the Tyrrhenian coast and descend steeply into sea. The coastline has been spared overdevelopment and much of it is in the hands of nature. Locals consider the area a cheaper, less crowded alternative to the Amalfi Coast with a town that rivals Positano in charm and good looks.

Sights

The road to Maratea is full of distractions. There are calm bays, small harbors, and a choice of sandy, stony, or black beaches. The biggest attention-getter is the **Statua del Redentore.** It stands on the top of Monte San Biagio and is hard to miss. The sculpture is second in size only to the one in Rio and the saint's face alone is three meters wide. His arms are outstretched towards the sea so as to protect the entire region. From the base of the statue, there's an unobstructed view of Maratea and the entire coast. The sighting towers (**Crini, Acquafredda, Apprezzami l'Asino,** and **Santa Venere**) in the distance were built by the Spaniards to defend the area against Saracen attacks and warn villages of marauding pirates.

Once the bells start ringing midday, you'll know why the town is known for its 44 churches. Many of these are scattered in the *centro storico* and contain fine works of art including Byzantine and Baroque frescos. Some are decorated with stone lions, old coats of arms, and wooden choirs from the 18th century. Among the most beautiful churches are **San Vito,** the oldest, **Santa Maria Maggiore,** in the adjacent piazza, and the **Annunziata** (Via Canalelli 1, www.parrocchiamaratea.it), where a marble relief and a bust of San Biagio are displayed.

Piazzetta Buraglia is full of small shops selling handicrafts and gastronomic products. It's a popular meeting point for locals and tourists exploring Maratea's back streets. In

BASILICATA AND CALABRIA

summertime, the *piazzetta* hosts a variety of art exhibitions, classical and jazz concerts, and traditional folk events.

Entertainments and Events

There are many things to do in Maratea, but perhaps the most enjoyable is just enjoying an *aperitivo* or gelato along the harbor. Otherwise, there are always the discos; the most famous one of these is **Santojanni** (Contrada San Giuseppe Maratea, SS 18 direction Praja a Mare, tel. 09/857-2076, www.santojanniclub. com, summer daily until 1 A.M., no cover). It's about seven kilometers from the center directly on the sea. DJs work overtime and dancing can be interrupted with a cocktail on the terrace.

Jazz resonates off the peeling walls of the old town every summer. **Marajazz** (Piazza del Gesù 32, tel. 097/3876-908) attracts a dynamic lineup of young musicians exploring the boundaries of the genre. There's a great deal of audience participation and the annual event is one of the most popular in the region.

The week between the first and second Sundays in May is devoted to **Festa di S. Biagio,** patron saint of Maratea. During the celebrations a silver bust of the Saint is covered with a red cloth and carried to the mayor's office. He takes off the cloth, and then the statue is blessed and transported to Chiesa Madre for a special mass. On the last Sunday the bust is returned to the Basilica by way of a path that passes the Castle and Via Nuova.

Shopping

La Farmacia dei Sani (Via Cavour 10, tel. 097/387-6148) sells gourmet foods that would cost three times as much anywhere else (assuming you could find these delicacies anywhere else). *Palloni di fichi* (fig balls) consist of semi-dried fig packed inside dried fig leaves. Cut the strings that hold the baseball-size treat together and enjoy. *Salami di fichi* is a sweetmeat sausage made with figs, chocolate, orange, spices, and rum. It tastes better than it sounds and looks like a normal salami. You'll also find olive oils, grappa, sweet chestnuts

in honey, and *Dolceria d'Uva*. The store gift wraps purchases upon request and can put together a custom assortment of products in a traditional reed boxes.

For over a century, **L'Antica Casa del Tessuto** (Piazza Muraglia 15, tel. 097/387-6520) has been weaving and selling cloth in a small, central shop. Fabric like this isn't made in China and the tablecloths, sheets, and towels are all highly refined. If you bring along the measurements they will happily custom-make curtains or anything else you like and ship it to your home.

Accommodations

((La Locanda delle Donne Monache (Via Carlo Mazzei, tel. 097/387-7487, www.locan dadelledonnemonache.it, €80–200 s/d) is in the old monastery of the Visitandone. The 11 rooms that were once dedicated to meditation and prayer haven't lost their sense of tranquility. Decoration is refined and unique in each. Some of the suites were hollowed out in the rock and come with canopy beds or hydromassages. If you prefer something closer to nature in a relaxing location, consider **B&B Nefer** (Via Cersuta, tel. 097/387-1828, €50–65) your oasis. **Villa Cheta** (Via Timpine 46, tel. 097/387-8134, www.villacheta.it, €130 d) in nearby Acquafredda is the romantic option, or for five-star service stay at **Hotel Santavenere** (Loc. Fiumicello, tel. 097/387-6910, www.ho telsantavenere.it, €150–400 s/d), which has a very soothing solarium and spa.

A night at **Villaggio Camping Maratea** (Fraz. Castrocucco 72, tel. 097/387-1680, www.campingmaratea.it, €5 and up) is like camping on the beach. The ground is in a eucalyptus grove moments from cobalt-blue water. Ruins of 13th-century **Castrocucco** castle loom above the campsite and give moonlight walks added value.

Food

((Taverna Rovita (Via Rovita 13, tel. 097/387-6588 Wed.–Mon. 7–11:30 P.M., €9–13) is another converted convent that hasn't lost the atmosphere. They serve typical local dishes and are adept at cooking both meat and fish. The menu changes daily according to the morning haul. Specialties include red *strascinati* with swordfish, snails in creamy truffle sauce, and king prawns *alla Rovita*. Don't miss the ricotta and pear cake desserts.

If you're looking for comfort food and a friendly face, the **Lanterna Rossa** (Via Arenile, tel. 097/387-6352, Tues.–Sun. 12:30–3 P.M. and 7–11:30 P.M., €12–15) may fit the bill. It has a wide terrace near the port with views that get better with every chew. **Za' Mariuccia** (Maratea Porto, tel. 097/387-6163, Mon.–Sun. 7–11:30 P.M., €10–13) is also very characteristic and overlooks the harbor. It's possible to taste many delicious fish platters here, including grilled or fried calamari.

Ristorante 1999 (Maratea Porto, Via Tocia 15, tel. 097/387-7580, Tues.–Sun. 12:30–3 P.M. and 7–11:30 P.M., €9–14) is a refined and fashionable restaurant that provides a breath of modernity to a meal. A candlelight dinner is hard to forget and even the background music is at the right decibel. Reservations are wise and it never hurts to mention it being your birthday or honeymoon.

Getting There and Around

The quickest way to reach Maratea is by car. It's about three hours from Naples on the A3. Exit the *autostrada* at Lagonegro Nord/Maratea and follow the road to town.

The coast road (Via Nazionale) is a more scenic possibility. Drivers should remember that most roads are single-lane affairs with many blind curves. They're in good condition and equipped with guardrails and reflectors. Take it slow and don't let tailgaters distract you.

Maratea is a little over three hours from Naples Central Station on the regional train or two hours on the InterCity. The latter is infrequent but there's also a Eurostar that stops in nearby Sapri twice a day and connects Genoa with Reggio Calabria.

Santavenere, Locanda della Donne Monache, and **Pianeta Maratea** operate a free shuttle bus between the hotels, historic center, and port. For a taxi, contact **Eurotravel**

(tel. 0973/876-077 or 339/699-1878) on Via Brefaro 18d.

Around Maratea
BEACHES

Beaches in the area each have of a personality their own. **Cersuta** has fine, white sand with rich vegetation directly behind the beach. **Cala Sannita** is entirely black and **Aquafredda** has a rocky seabed that gets deep meters from shore. It's ideal for snorkeling and scuba diving. All three are located within 10 kilometers of Maratea.

◆ PARCO NATURALE DEL POLLINO

Parco Naturale del Pollino (tel. 097/366-9311, www.parcodelpollino.it) is by far the largest national park in Italy. It's located between Calabria and Basilicata and forms a natural border between the two regions. There's a great variety of landscapes and wilderness where cuirassed pine, the emblem of the park, clings to rocky slopes. Rolling hills and mountains alternate with lush valleys full of wildflowers in spring, and upland plains where sheep have grazed since antiquity. Among the most typical animals are the *capriolo* (roebuck), wolf, and golden eagle.

In addition to catching some enchanting sea views, it's also possible to visit tiny villages with remnants of *arbë reshe* culture that can be traced back to the Balkans. The customs and folklore of these towns has survived for centuries within a spectacular natural backdrop that provides visitors with a dual attraction.

There are several entrances to the park from either region, and daily excursions with skilled guides or trekking adventures lasting several days can be organized. It's a good idea to pick up a map from any of the park offices and become familiar with the itinerary you plan to follow before setting off into this great unknown. Water, layered clothing, knapsack, binoculars, and camera will come in handy.

It's also a great place to hike or practice water sports. The Lao River's gentle current makes is good for rafting, canoeing, or hydrospeed (riverboarding). Equipment can be rented from **Canoa Club Lao Pollino** (Laino Borgo, tel. 098/185-673, www.laocanoa.it). They also run half-day tours on the river. You can rent a boat in the harbor or join one of the guided excursions around the gulf. **Infopoint Maratea** (tel. 097/387-6439 or 347/802-1537) runs night tours that include dinner and *pesca al Totano*.

Ionian Coast

This side of Calabria is windy and wild. Tourism in the area has some catching up to do compared to other regions but places like **Capo Rizzuto** are starting to show signs of improvement. Less five-star resorts means more authentic travel experiences and the possibility to appreciate genuine Calabrian scenery.

ROSSANO

Rossano is a compact town six kilometers from the coastal highway. The center was built on a rocky spur and is one of the best examples of medieval urban development in Southern Italy. Bring a good pair of walking shoes and prepare for blistering heat in July and August. There are *palazzi,* piazze, underground passageways, and nearly 50 churches scattered around town.

Sights
Corso Garibaldi is a good place to start. It winds its way from San Nilo to San Marco, the oldest church in town. Along the way are noble residences built between the 17th and 18th centuries. In Piazza Steri you can visit **Museo Diocesano** (Palazzo Arcivescovile, tel. 098/352-0282, daily 9 A.M.–1 P.M.), which contains the *Codex Purpureus Rossanensis,* an extremely rare work from the 6th century. The Codex is one of the oldest illustrated manuscripts in the world, featuring 15 miniature pages that are among the earliest examples of Byzantine art.

Next door is the **Cattedrale,** whose facade was badly damaged in the earthquake of 1836 and was not restored until 80 years later. The Baroque altar inside is attached to a pillar on the north end of the church near the nave with an ancient Byzantine Madonna and beautiful wooden ceiling.

About 600 meters outside of town is the isolated **Santa Maria del Pathirion.** This Norman-Basilian church has remained unaltered since it was built in 1095 and offers wonderful views over the Sibari plain.

Entertainment and Events
Although it's relatively new, the **Marco Fiume Blues Passion** (Torre Stellata, Lido S. Angelo, tel. 333/232-6153, www.myspace.com/marcofiume) festival in the third weekend of July attracts veteran players like Louisiana Red and his all-star band. Chances are you haven't heard of the musicians strumming on the outdoor stage but you may want to memorize a few names after the concert. Shows start at 8:30 P.M. and generally end with a jam session.

Throughout the summer, **Estate Rossanese** organizes musical events and open-air cinema in the piazze. The first Sunday of August is dedicated to Madre Maria Stella del Mare. A procession of boats makes its way around the port followed by fireworks.

Accommodations
There are several bed-and-breakfasts in town and many *agriturismo* beyond the walls to spend a relaxing couple of days exploring the area. **Il Giardino di Iti** (Contrada Amica, tel. 098/364-508, www.giardinoiti.it, €45, pp) is a converted farmhouse that has retained its old terra-cotta floors and a fireplace that's used in winter. The beach is three kilometers away and the owner will serve breakfast to late risers, who can go for a pleasant bike ride afterwards.

Le Colline del Gelso (C.sa Gelso-Mazzei, tel. 098/356-9136, www.lecollinedelgelso.it, €76–116 s/d) is an elegant, ivy-covered country house a short distance from town. The residence is surrounded by 55 hectares of olive and fruit trees harvested by Alessandra Mazzei and her family. Many of the 10 rooms have sea views and furniture that's been made to last. **Zefiro** beach is easily reached on foot past wheat fields and poplar trees. You can also explore the countryside by bicycle or horseback and enjoy *risotto agli asparagi* and local cheeses in the restaurant.

The choice at **Marina di Rossano Club Village Camping** (Contrada Leuca-Rossano scalo, tel. 098/351-6054, www.marinadirossano. it, €6 and up) is between sleeping on the ground or in one of the comfortable bungalows. The village is immersed in nature and suits backpackers and service-oriented travelers alike. Grounds extend all the way to the sea and there are 250 spots that are often filled with Northern Europeans nursing fresh sunburns.

Food

Carmen makes sure no one leavse hungry from **Ristorante San Marco la Bizantina** (Corso Garibaldi 246, tel. 098/352-5340, www.labizantina.net, Tues.–Sun. 12:30–3 P.M. and 7–11:30 P.M., €8–10). Her eggplant dishes are unbeatable and the fireplace, exposed stone walls, and checkered tablecloths make for a pleasant lunch or dinner. In the summer, ask for a table on the veranda with panoramic views of town.

The interior may be new, but the recipes at ◖ **Paridò** (Rossano Stazione, Via dei Normanni, tel. 098/329-0731, www.paridoristorante.it, Mon.–Sat. 12:30–3 P.M. and 7–11:30 P.M., €8–12) are old and Pietro Rizzuti is always on the lookout for ancient flavors that need reinterpretation. The vegetable and fish *antipasti* make good starters and the first courses change according to the season. There's gnocchi with porcini mushroom sauce in autumn and many types of soup in winter. House wine can be ordered by glass or carafe.

Information and Services

The information office (tel. 098/352-1137) is located near the cathedral. They provide a detailed brochure and map specifically for visiting the numerous churches.

There are several pharmacies along Corso Garibaldi and either Rizzo (tel. 098/352-0432), Barone (tel. 098/352-0725), or Pappalardo (tel. 098/353-0300) is open. Ospedale Civile (tel. 0983 5171) is just outside of town and they can send an ambulance if necessary.

Getting There and Around

Arriving by car can be a little tricky. Follow the signs for *centro storico* and *chiese Byzantine*. You can use the SS 106 or A3 highway, which is considerably faster. If you choose the highway, exit at Sibari-Firmo.

The principal train stations are in Rossano and Sibari and provide local service along the coast. The Rossano station is four kilometers from town and there's a bus that completes the journey. **Scura** operates buses between Rossano and major towns in the region.

Around Rossano

Rossano is famous for licorice and **Museo della Liquirizia** (SS 106, Contrada Amarelli, tel. 098/351-1219, www.museodellaliquirizia.it, summer daily 9:30 A.M.–1:30 P.M. and 6:30–8 P.M., winter daily 9 A.M.–1 P.M., admission free) is a Willy Wonka dream. The small museum recounts the candy's history with the machinery once used to make it and old advertising campaigns that helped popularize it. The central gallery illustrates the production process from basic ingredients to commercialization and packaging that can be admired and purchased in the reconstructed 19th-century store. Tours are available but must be reserved in advance.

ISOLA CAPO RIZZUTO

Despite its name, Isola Capo Rizzuto is not an island; it's actually four kilometers inland. According to legend, it was founded by Astiochena escaping from Troy, along with her father and two sisters. The town prospered during the Magna Grecia period and was gradually dominated by nearby Kroton. It's the site of the Pythagorean and Alcmeon medical schools and was the home of revered athletes like Milo, who triumphed in the original Olympic games.

The town continued with mixed fortunes in the Middle Ages, becoming an important center for the propagation of Catholicism in Southern Italy and was an Episcopal seat until 1818. Today it's possible to admire some of the buildings of that period and nearby gems like the Aragonese castle of **Le Castella.** There are also numerous coastal lookout towers such as **Torre Vecchia** and **Torre Nuova** with military garrisons and cannons. In the last decade Isola Capo Rizzuto has started to take full advantage of its glorious past and beautiful marine area.

Sights

There's no single color to describe the water in the **Riserva Marina Capo Rizzuto** (Capo Rizzato, Piazza Santuario, tel. 096/279-6019, www.riservamarinacaporizzuto.it). It varies from aquamarine some days to emerald green on others. The protected area stretches for 36 kilometers between Crotone to Praialonga and includes 15,000 hectares of sea where history and nature meet.

There are many different ways to approach the park. From **Le Castella,** it's possible to discover the remains of mythic islands like **Ogigia,** home of a witch described in the Odyssey. The scuba itinerary takes divers to the principal monuments around **Capo Donato** where a 12th-century ship lies on the seabed. On the mountainside of **Capo Colonna** are the remains of marble columns erected by the Romans in the 3rd century A.D.

The marine park is divided into three zones. These correspond to: the sea around Capo Colonna (B), Capo Cimiti (B), and Capo Bianco (A) where strict conservancy measures are enforced. In Zone A, swimming, scuba diving, sailing, and fishing are restricted. In Capo Cimiti guided tours are organized by the Provincial Board of Crotone, which also conducts surveillance and scientific research.

In the General Reserve, or Zone B, bathing, scuba diving accompanied by local centers, and sailing (less than 5 knots per hour) are permitted. You'll need a license to fish or will have

find a local who will take you on board. Zone C, or Partial Reserve, runs along the perimeter of the park and bathing and scuba diving are allowed. If you're worried about breaking the rules, just read the signs carefully or pick up a brochure at any of the three capes.

Linked to the Riserva Marina Capo Rizzuto is the **Acquarium** (Capo Rizzuto, Piazza Santuario, tel. 096/279-6019, Mon.–Fri. 9 A.M.–4 P.M., €2.50). Within the 22 tanks, 22,000 liters of water are home to marine animals and plants native to the park. Highlights include the jellyfish, octopus, and starfish clinging to the side of their glass homes. A theater regularly projects films with an environmental consciousness and visitors are encouraged to make contact with the sea's inhabitants in the touching pool.

In addition to marine treasures, there are inland sites like **Le Castella,** with its millenary history of glory and misfortune. The castle originated from a treaty drawn up between Rome and Taranto in 304 B.C. that established boundaries of navigation for their respective fleets. The inhabitants of Taranto constructed a tower later enlarged by Hannibal, who used it as a lookout post. The commander had many friends among the Bruzi, who were intolerant of Roman supremacy. After the Arab occupation in the 11th century, the town grew undisturbed until the ferocious war between the Angevins and the Aragonese. It's worth taking a guided tour of the **Castle** (Via Duomo, tel. 09/6279-5320, daily 9:30 A.M.–noon and 4:30–7:30 P.M., Jun. 15–Aug. daily 9 A.M.–1 A.M., €3) that can also be booked at night.

Capo Colonna (Località Capo Colonna, tel. 096/293-4188, Tues.–Sun. 9 A.M.–one hour before sunset, admission free) is a vast archeological site, national park, and wildlife preserve on a narrow promontory with dry headlands. Visitors may roam around the columns and take a close look at the archaeological excavations that are ongoing and regularly turn up traces of Greek culture. Access to some parts of the site requires special permission that can be obtained with a phone call (tel. 096/293-4188).

Entertainment and Events

Aurora is a charming music show performed at 4 A.M. among the ancient ruins of the Hera temple, built in 5th century B.C. It's the last day of a festival that runs the entire month of May and offers a string of classical recitals by small international orchestras.

The center of attention during the **Processione della Madonna Greca** is an icon that was brought to town by a group of Greek monks. The celebration starts at sunrise on the first Saturday in May. There's a procession to a nearby church and lots of singing. Fireworks light up the sky and special delicacies are served.

Sports and Recreation

Boats with transparent hulls have been a huge hit with tourists and are the best way to view the multicolored fish without getting wet. Tours on the *Eranusa* (tel. 096/279-5353 or 339/392-0514) last one hour and leave day and night. On hot days, the captain usually stops in one of the coves to let passengers refresh themselves in the cool waters.

Pescaturismo is the marine equivalent of *agriturismo* and provides visitors with a taste of what it means to earn a living from the sea. It's also a good chance to reel in some fish and discover traditions preserved in the boats that line nearly every port. **Cooperativa di Pesca Poseidon** (Le Castella, Via Porto, tel. 339/210-8059) and **Cooperativa Le Castella** (Le Castella, Via Fosso, tel. 096/279-5071) both provide rods and guarantee a good catch.

The high number of sunken ships has made archeological scuba diving quite popular. The water south of Le Castella is particularly rich and there's a 400-meter-long underwater itinerary with 15 sights. Each has a plaque with a brief explanation, and visibility depends on the season. The circuit can be completed in 30 minutes, and given the shallowness, is also suitable for snorkeling. Gear is available from **Tiris Diving Center** (Le Castella, tel. 096/279-5483, www.tiris.it) and **Hera Sub** (Crotone, tel. 096/221-553).

Accommodations

◖ **Villaggio Valtur** (Isola Capo Rizzuto, tel. 096/290-7486, www.valtur.it/villaggio/caporizzuto, €600 per week) is at the end of a scenic road that leads to the sea. It's a perfect place to relax and once you arrive there's no reason to leave. The resort is surrounded by olive groves and palm trees border the large pool. The restaurant is part of an all-inclusive package and offers a buffet that's hard to resist. A flight of steps leads to a beach equipped with lounge chairs and umbrellas. Cars can be rented and a disco keeps the young crowd occupied until late.

Cheaper accommodation is waiting at **Villaggio Camping Marinella** (Marinella, tel. 096/279-9810, www.villaggiomarinella.com, from €5). The camping ground is situated in the heart of the marine reserve and surrounded by tropical vegetation. Nearby beaches are favored by families and water-sports enthusiasts. Sailboats, surfboards, and other equipment can be rented directly from the village.

Fattoria Il Borghetto (Capo Bianco, tel. 096/279-6223, www.fattoriailborghetto. it, €70–100 s/d) is a medium-size hotel immersed in 10 hectares of vineyards, pastures, and farmland. Rooms are comfortable and the only thing you'll hear in the morning is the rooster. The restaurant serves locally cultivated ingredients and especially good meat.

Food

Ristorante l'Ancora (Via Faro, tel. 096/279-9253, www.ristorantelancora.it, Tues.–Sun. 12:30–2:30 P.M. and 7:30–11 P.M., €8–13) is a stone's throw from the sea. There are three dining rooms and a panoramic terrace that gets a little hot during the summer. Service is courteous and waiters incredibly patient. Ask about the fish of the day or try the *antipasti di mare* that's as fresh as you can get. First courses include *linguine ai frutti di mare, rigatoni alla rana pescatrice*, and *risotto ai frutti di mare*. Reservations are advisable in July and August.

For an alternative to fish, there's **Ristorante Il Pino** (E90 km. 232, tel. 096/279-4426, Tues.–Sun. 12:30–2:30 P.M. and 7:30 P.M.–11 P.M., €15). The dining room is impressively laid out with columns between the tables that provide intimacy. Local cheese, vegetable fritters, homemade pasta, rabbit *alla cacciatora,* and lamb with potatoes characterize the cuisine.

'Zza Rosì (Crotone, Via Tedeschi 81, tel. 096/290-0422, Mon.–Sat. 12:30–2:30 P.M. and 7:30–11 P.M., €7–10) is an informal restaurant with a Mediterranean menu that changes every day according to what the fishermen have brought in that morning. The wood-oven pizza is also very good and the same method has been used for making the dough since 1953.

Information and Services

Tourist information is available from the **APT** office in Crotone (Via Torino 148, tel. 096/223-185) or the **Riserva Marina di Capo Rizzuto** (tel. 096/795-511).

Getting There and Around

By car take the A3 and exit at Sibari (from the north) or Catanzaro Lido (from the south) and then follow the SS 106. Smaller roads lead off the 106 towards Le Castella, Capo Rizzuto, and Capo Colonna. If you are traveling by train, the nearest station is in Crotone. The busiest lines are the Taranto–Reggio Calabria and Catanzaro Lido–Lamezia Terme. For a taxi and reliable driver, call Perri Pasquale Servizio Taxi (tel. 096/225-168).

STILO

Don't expect much fanfare in Stilo. On a summer afternoon the shops will be closed, shutters downs, and locals napping. Stick to the shaded colonnades in this earthquake-prone town built on the side of Monte Consolino. For the best view, climb up to the Cattolica church, a remnant of the town's golden age when Basilian monks lived and worshipped here.

Sights

The **Cattolica** (Via Cattolica, www.cattolicadistilo.it, daily) is a well-preserved Byzantine church built in the 10th century. The five terra-cotta domes are a reflection of Greek in-

© LETIZIA RAZZINO

the five-domed Cattolica in Stilo

fluences and the same style can be found in Georgia, Armenia, and Anatolia. There are three apses facing east and mismatched columns that divide the interior. The monks of St. Basil (Basilians) found refuge in Calabria and pursued their ideals of poverty and detachment from worldly concerns. What is most striking inside is the light, almost blinding in the upper part but faint in the lower so as to encourage prayer and meditation. Immersed in rocks and vegetation, the small cube of the Cattolica seems suspended, with its little forest of domes, between the earth and sky.

Near the Cattolica in Via Tommaso Campanella is the medieval **Duomo,** as well as 17th-century ruins of the **Convent of San Domenico,** where the philosopher-friar Tommaso Campanella spent his younger days. **San Giovanni Theresti** is a Baroque-style church, decorated with stucco and dedicated by the Basilian monks to their saint, whose remains are preserved within. The **Norman Castle,** constructed on the summit of Monte

Consolino by Roger II, can be reached on foot via a scenic path that starts from the Cattolica. Arabic culture also left an imprint on the town and the Moorish sculptures of the **Fountain of the Dolphins** are worth visiting.

Accommodations

Set in the center of Stilo, **San Giorgio** (Via Citarelli 8, tel. 096/477-5047, €60 d) is a comfortable hotel located in a restored 17th-century palazzo and furnished with 18th-century antiques. Rooms are very quiet and the owners are happy to spend the afternoon rehashing legends.

Villa Vittoria (Contrada Butteria, tel. 096/786-751, www.villavittoria.net, €16 pp and up) is a converted farmhouse that has accentuated its links to the past. There are tools on the walls and a big fireplace around which breakfast is served in the winter. Hospitality is taken seriously here and many of the guests are second-time visitors with fond memories of their first stay. The other reason people come back is the simple country cooking.

Food

Partially located in a carved-out cave that once served as a warehouse, **Antica Taverna la Buca del Re** (Via XXI Aprile, tel. 333/720-5618, daily 12:30–3 P.M. and 7:30–11 P.M., €10–12) is on the main road through town facing a lovely *piazzetta*. Small windows on the inside provide rooftop views of San Domenico. The fettuccine is rolled in-house and served with porcinior wild boar sauce. If you like game meats, try the grilled deer served on terra-cotta plates in the traditional local shape.

An alternative with slightly more vegetarian options is **La Quercia** (Contrada Pannara, tel.096/477-5462, daily 12:30–3 P.M. and 7:30–11 P.M., €9).

Information and Services

For tourist information, go to the **Municipio** in Piazza San Giovanni (tel. 096/477-5031). The hours fluctuate but you'll generally find someone in the morning 9 A.M.–12:30 P.M.

Getting There and Around

By car, follow the SS 106 until Monasterace Marina then take the SS 110 for 10 kilometers until Silo. The SS 110 is a very scenic road that crosses from the Ionian to the Tyrrhenian coast. It may look like a short drive on a map but the road is very windy so every kilometer here should be multiplied by three. The nearest train station is in Monasterace Marina. A local bus leaves every half-hour for Stilo.

GERACE

Back in the 9th century, the Saracens were the most feared pirates in the Mediterranean and never ceased harassing towns and villages along the coast. Refugees from **Locri Epizefiri** founded Gerace to escape attack and this time they decided to settle slightly inland. The defensive walls were an added precaution and have survived many violent earthquakes. Houses in the center are dug into the rock and have internal courtyards that stay cool even when the temperatures rise.

Sights

The **Duomo** in Gerace comes as a surprise, like finding a skyscraper in South Dakota. It's one of the largest in Calabria and is a clue as to how important the town was up to the Middle Ages. Gerace was, in fact, a strong spiritual and cultural center in that period. The Duomo was built and rebuilt several times, with the last touches added in the 18th century. The crypt is the main attraction; it constructed from ancient marble and granite columns, probably recycled from Locri Epitefiri.

In **Piazza Tre Chiese** lies the monastery, Gothic church of San Francesco d'Assisi, and the 11th-century San Giovanni Crisostomo, which combines Byzantine and Norman styles. There are also ruins of a Norman castle from which you can walk a panoramic path known as the **Passeggiata delle Bombarde.**

Entertainment and Events

Festival Musica Architettura combines the stunning backdrops around Gerace with chamber music that begins at sunset during the first week of August. The two most important festivals are Maria del Carmelo in July and Sant'Antonio del Castello on August 23. Both involve parades of local women dressed in black and if you can wrangle an invitation into their homes your stomach will never stop thanking you.

Shopping

The town is famous for ceramics and weaving. They make wonderful clay masks that are painted in bright colors and hung on the sides of houses. **Aracne Cooperative** (Via Roma, tel. 096/435-6318) sells handmade textiles, including sheets, tablecloths, and other items made of wool and silk. **Ceramiche Condò** (Via Zaleuco 27, tel. 096/435-6663) and **La Lucerna Arte** (Via Nazionale 84, tel. 096/435-6060) are the best addresses for anything molded from clay.

Accommodations

From the terrace of **☖ Palazzo Sant'Anna** (Via Sant'Anna 1, tel. 096/435-5010, www. palazzosantanna.it, €100 d), Gerace is your oyster. The former convent of Basilean nuns has a rustic 700-year-old atmosphere and much of the furniture is nearly as old as the building. The outdoor restaurant is called **A Due Passi dalle Stelle** ("Two Feet from the Stars") and feels like you could reach a hand into the galaxy. The menu alternates national with regional meat and fish dishes.

La Casa nel Borgo (Via Nazionale 66, tel. 096/435-5150, www.lacasanelborgo.it, €70 d) is situated at the entrance to town and exemplifies the simplicity of the place. It's a reference point for Gerace hospitality, which is warm and spontaneous.

Le Macine (C. da Barbara, tel. 096/435-6492, €80 d) is a farmhouse encircled by vineyards and olive trees. It's two kilometers from Gerace and six from the sea. In the center of the farm is an oil mill made of rough-cut stone dating from the 18th century. The inside is now used to house and feed up to 15 guests. There's a great view from the top floor and locally produced cheese, *salumi*, and wine

in the restaurant below. The red and rosè are excellent and can be purchased directly from the owners.

Food

After 20 years in business, **La Terrazza** (Via Nazionale, tel. 096/435-6739, Tues.–Sun. 12:30–3 P.M. and 7–11:30 P.M., €10–12) is still going strong. Grab a seat on the spacious covered terrace and taste local specialties while admiring the view of the Gelsomini coast. All the *antipasti* are hearty and delicious, but if you've never tasted handmade salami prepare for heaven.

Lo Sparviero (Via Luigi Cadorna 3, tel. 096/435-6826, Tues.–Sun. noon–3 P.M. and 7–10:30 P.M., €7–9) is as fascinating as the town outside. Fabrizio offers a faithful menu of classics in three vaulted rooms that remain cool even when the asphalt is melting outside. *Friselle* is a popular starter and zucchini and *pecorino* cheese are star ingredients. *Macaruni* are a mandatory first course that can be ordered with an eggplant or red pepper sauce. House wine is practically free and goes down well with the grilled lamb steaks.

To pick up some of the cheeses and extra virgin olive oil used by the town's restaurants, visit **Francesco Femia** on Via Cavour.

Getting There and Around

The best way to reach Gerace is along the SS 111. It's about 10 Kilometers from Locri where the nearest trains stop. Park at the entrance to town and visit the numerous architectural gems on foot.

Around Gerace

Locri Epizefiri (the original Gerace) is nearby off the SS 106 and is a fascinating detour. It was the first Greek city with written a code of law (660 B.C.), but it was a losing battle getting the Saracens to respect it. There are temples, theaters, and tombs onsite, as well as a small museum (Contrada Marasà, tel. 096/439-0023, daily 9 A.M.–7 P.M., closed 1st and 2nd Mon. of each month) displaying Greek and Roman finds.

Tyrrhenian Coast

The A3 highway makes it faster to get around this side of Calabria, which has had an effect on tourism. It's much easier to find a decent hotel here, and if a restaurant is booked there's always another one waiting around the corner.

DIAMANTE

Diamante (diamond) lives up to its name and is one of the prettiest towns in Calabria. Clean waters make it a favorite summer destination and the **murals** can be admired all year long. The tradition was started in the 1900s by artists who wanted to paint but couldn't afford canvas. Today the narrow streets are covered in color and creativity. Hot peppers are the other claim to fame and hang from every balcony. *Peperoncini* are used in many local dishes, and *sopressata* sausage will satisfy anyone with a taste for spicy. If you've ever wondered what makes Southern Italian food special, this is the place to find out.

Entertainment and Events

After the peppers are harvested each summer, communities come together to celebrate. Diamante is at the center of the festival that climaxes September 5–9. More than 100,000 people show up from across Italy to participate in the event known as the **Carnival of the South.** There's dancing on every street, open-air bars, men on stilts, and traditional music played well into the night. Of course it's also the chance to burn your tongue with every sort of pepper dish imaginable.

Accommodations

Ferretti Hotel (Via Poseidone 4, tel. 098/581-428, €70–200 s/d) is located in one of the most delightful corners of Calabria, where ancient architects couldn't go wrong, and nearly every window has a sea view. Here you get your own patio and access to a private beach and swimming pool. Service is to the letter and staff have a good memory for names.

Hotel Airone (Via dei Mandorli 77, tel. 086/587-6699, www.airone-hotel.it, €40 pp) and **Hotel dei Focesi** (Contrada Monache, tel. 098/581-515, www.hoteldeifocesi.it, €50 pp) are good alternatives. The first has a terrace to die for and the latter is directly on the beach.

Food

The Perrone brothers devote a lot of their menu to fish and don't bother getting too elaborate with their cooking. **La Guardiola** (Via Stromboli 20, SS 18, tel. 098/242-8262, Mon.–Sun. 12:30 A.M.–3 P.M. and 7–11 P.M., €30) after all is a *trattoria di mare,* where old-time fishermen with stories that would impress Hemingway come to eat. *Diavolilli* is a house favorite and these little devils leave brave diners gasping for water. *Spaghetti alla Lucifer* continues the spicy theme, but there are also less hellish dishes for cautious palates. House wine comes dry or sparkling and the licorice-flavored liquor is a traditional way to end a meal.

To get your fill of hot pepper products, visit **L'Accademia del Peperoncino** in Via Amendola 3. A jar of their dried peppers could probably last a lifetime and will definitely put drug-sniffing dogs off any trail. **Pierino** on the *lungomare* serves classic *gelato* and *granite* flavors but it's his *peperoncino* that daredevils prefer.

Getting There and Around

By car drive along the A3 Salerno-Reggio Calabria highway and exit at Lagonegro Nord. Proceed along the SS 18 for 50 kilometers until you reach Diamante. From the south, on the A3, exit at Falerna. It's about 100 kilometers northbound on the SS 18. Arriving by train can be faster and the station in Diamante serves all cities along the coast.

PAOLA

Paola is located on the edge of the Tyrrhenian Sea, north of Lamezia Terme, and west of Cosenza. It's an airy town with an ancient *centro storico* and a modern *lungomare* with many seaside amenities. During the summer it's one of the busiest resorts on the coast and a popular destination with families and singles.

Sights

Local are proud of the fact that their city is the birthplace of **San Francesco di Paola** (1416–1507), founder of the Minims, the strictest order of the Franciscans. These guys never smiled and it took a special temperament to make the cut. Their **Santuario di San Francesco** (www.santuariosanfrancesco dipaola.it, Oct.–Mar. daily 6 A.M.–1 P.M. and 2–6 P.M., Apr.–Sept. daily 6 A.M.–1 P.M. and 2–8 P.M., admission free) is above town off the SS 18 and dates from 1435. There's a wide piazza in front of the austere building with a modern statue and obelisk in the middle commemorating the Holy Year of 1950.

Entertainment and Events

The biggest day of the year is reserved for San Francesco da Paola, who is said to have possessed divine powers. Faithful come from as far away as Sicily to spend May 1 around a campfire singing traditional folk songs. In the morning, a statue of the saint and the rowboat he used to cross the Straits of Messina are carried down to the sea and the fishermen are blessed.

Accommodations

Albergo Residence Blumentag (Viale Magna Grecia 8, tel. 098/261-3544, www.albergoblu mentag.it, €40 pp) is a favorite with German tourists but there's no reasons to let them have all the fun. The hotel is ideally located between the mountains and the sea, less than two kilometers from the historic center. Rooms are spotless and the breakfast buffet offers something new every day. If you prefer a bird's-eye view, the **Hotel Alhambra** (Via della Civiltà 56, tel. 098/258-2240, www.hotelalhambra.it, €40 pp) is up the hill overlooking town within walking distance of the sanctuary.

Ostello della Gioventù (Salita Immacolata 1, Vico Montevergine 6, tel. 098/258-5562, www.palazzoscorza.it, €22 pp) could make you rethink hostels. This one is inside the historic 17th-century Palazzo Scorza that's been recently scrubbed up and delights backpackers and travelers without preconceptions. All 14 double and triple rooms come with private bathrooms. Once outside, you're only minutes from the piazze and fountains of the old town.

Food

Not far from the center of Paola stands **Le Mimose** (Via Gaudimare 9, tel. 098/261-1563, Tues.–Sun. 12:30–3 P.M. and 7 P.M.–11 P.M., €9–13), a lovely rustic-style restaurant with five spacious rooms. You can eat outdoors or in the main hall, which has an attractive working fireplace. The chef has a love of mushrooms and grilled fish. It can sometimes be difficult to have a conversation on an August evening when the place is packed to the gills.

Another reliable address in Paola is **'U Trappitu da Mario** (Via San Salvatore 99, tel. 098/262-1448 Tues.–Sun. noon–3 P.M. and 7:30–11 P.M., €8–12). The old oil factory has conserved its original brick floors and stone walls that can't be beat for atmosphere. The owners are equally welcoming and propose a wide assortment of local dishes. The quality/price ratio is very good here and house wine is as drinkable as any of the expensive stuff.

Getting There and Around

Southbound drivers should exit the A3 at Lagonegro Nord/Marate, a then continue on the SS 585 that becomes the SS 18 and leads directly to Paola. Northbound, it's better to exit at Cosenza Nord and follow the SS 107. There should be no problem locating Paola, as it's well indicated and serviced by railroads and boat. Navigating the town itself can be difficult with a car and it's easier to park near the Sanctuary and walk down into town.

AMANTEA

Long before Greeks and Roman set foot in this seaside town, early settlers were using Bronze and Iron Age tools to make a living. They chose a spot near the Savuto River that makes a natural port. The Bruzi, Calabria's native warriors, resisted Greek incursions and there is very little Hellenic Greek architecture around. The Romans were another story and transformed the land around to provide food for a growing Imperial population. The city was later controlled by the Byzantines, who built an impressive castle to protect their borders. The **castle** is still prominent on the hill above town but it wasn't enough to keep the Arabs from overrunning the place and founding an emirate. Amantea is derived from the Arabic Al Mantiah (stronghold) and North African influences are still present today.

Sights

Amantea is divided into two sections. The old center is located on a hill above the new town where shops, restaurants, and piazze line a long promenade. It's a friendly place and almost impossible to get lost. If you do, a local is likely to walk you whereever you need to go or will just point to the castle that is the major historic destination.

The sandy beach of Amantea is one of the jewels of the coast. There are also two tiny islands 800 meters north of the port known as the **Oasi Blu dell'Isca.** The water is extremely clear around these and reaches a depth of 25 meters. Several glass-bottomed boats leave every day from the port for a tour of the fauna and the countless fish that have made this habitat their home.

Accommodations

Near the sea and four kilometers from Amantea is **Hotel la Tonnara** (Lungomare Tonnara 13, tel. 098/242-4272, www.latonnara.it, €40 pp). It's good for a multi-night stay and the modern rooms have been recently repainted and equipped with new fittings. There's a nice panoramic terrace and more satellite channels than you thought possible in Italy.

Hotel delle Canne (Via Stromboli 229, tel. 098/241-947, www.hoteldellecanne.it, €45 pp) is on the edge of town and has a private beach. A large dining room, living room, bar, and swimming pool are also available. The hotel

is popular with both business travelers and tourists. **La Ninfa Marina** (Via Firenze, tel. 098/242-8440, www.hotelninfamarina.com/, €40 pp) offers a wide range of facilities and good views of the historic center.

Food

The fish Maurizio serves at **Locanda di Mare** (Via Stromboli 20, tel. 098/242-8262, Tues.– Sun. 12:30–3 P.M. and 7–11 P.M., €10–15) was swimming less than 24 hours before it reached your plate. Seafood permeates every course and the life-size prow of a ship at the entrance emphasizes what this trattoria is all about. The mixed antipasto is a good way to start, otherwise Maria has some daily specials that may interest you. Pasta *con alici* is the ticket for anchovy lovers and seconds can be grilled or fried. The house white is served ice cold and goes down like water.

Gianluca Ganci had a good idea when he decided to transform his wine bar into a restaurant. It was a gradual change that began with appetizers and cold dishes. Now his partner cooks up a full range of dishes inside the kitchen at **⟨ Enoteca due Biccheri** (Via Dogana 192, tel. 098/242-4409, daily in summer 7–11:30 P.M., €7–10). The wine selection has remained first rate. Marinated anchovies go well with the Calabrian whites and wild boar *ragù* cries out for a full-bodied red. Tiramisù with fresh fruit is a novelty enjoyed on the halfdozen outdoor tables. The Ganci family specializes in salted and preserved fish they sell in a small shop 100 yards from the restaurant.

Getting There and Around

By car, follow the SS 18 coastal road or take the train directly to the center of town. During the summer, you can also arrive by boat from Reggio Calabria.

PIZZO CALABRO

Pizzo Calabro has a double personality. It's both a popular seaside resort and an important fishing town. The sea satisfies tourists and fishermen alike who cast their nets in the spectacular **Golfo di Santa Eufemia.** Pizzo, as locals call it, was built on the ruins of Napitia (Napitum), an old Phoenician colony destroyed in the 4th century A.D. by rampaging Saracens. Coral pickers from Amalfi arrived in the Middle Ages and erected several churches. Business has been good ever since.

Sights

The center of town offers picturesque medieval perspectives and exclusive villas from various ages. **Piedigrotta Church,** which is dug into tufa, and **San Giorgio Martire Church** are worth a visit. The latter is a Calabrian version of Baroque with many priceless sculptural works inside. There's a 17th-century wooden crucifix, a Madonna with Child by Gagini, and a captivating St. John the Baptist credited to Pietro Bernini.

Pizzo Castle (tel. 096/353-2523, daily 9 A.M.–1 P.M. and 3 P.M.–7 P.M.) was commissioned by Ferdinand I of Aragon in 1400 and later witnessed the intriguing death scene of Joaquin Murat. The castle has been declared a national monument and unlike the Disney version, there's a dungeon where prisoners were tortured until they snapped.

Accommodations

There are several moderately priced hotels in Pizzo. **Murat** (Piazza della Repubblica, tel. 096/353-4469, €35 pp) and **Marinella** (Via Riviera Prangi, tel. 096/353-4884, €35 pp) could be twins. Both are medium-size three-star hotels with clean rooms, floral wallpaper, and a restaurant. For something right on the beach, try **Casa Armonia** (Via Armonia 9, tel. 096/353-4183, www.casaarmonia.com, €40 pp). Leave the window open at night and fall asleep to the sound of waves.

Food

With 14 *gelaterie,* Pizzo is considered the ice-cream capital of Calabria. *Il tartufo di Pizzo* is one of the traditional flavors and scooped daily during the summertime. The name derives from the shape and the color rather than anything related to truffles. The actual ingredients are hazelnuts, chocolate, and a dusting of cacao that's hard to resist. You can sample a cone or cup at **L'Arte del Gelato** (Piazza della Repubblica, tel. 096/353-1149). Everything has been hand-churned since the 1970s at this common-looking bar that gets very crowded on August evenings.

Pizzo isn't just about dessert. You can also eat fresh fish (tuna in particular), taste the famous *'nduja* (a typical salami that's spread on bread), try *fileja* (homemade pasta), and end a meal sipping *zibibbo,* a sweet wine. Good restaurant options in the historic center are **Forte della Monacella** (Lungomare C.Colombo, tel. 096/353-1307, Tues.–Sun. 12:30–3 P.M. and 7–11 P.M. €9–13) and **Ristorante Medusa** (Via Marcello Salomone, tel. 096/353-1203, Mon.–Sat. 12:30–3 P.M. and 7–11 P.M. €10–14).

People come to **Go** (Strada Provinciale Sant'Onofrio, tel. 347/113-7854, Tues.–Sun. 12:30–3 P.M. and 7–11 P.M., €12–15) in part for the food and in part for the location overlooking the Tyrrhanean. Vittorio has a Zorba-like personality and doesn't need much persuading to pick up his guitar and start into a Calabrian folk song. Fortunately Maria isn't easily distracted in the kitchen and she turns out a great fish *ragù* and oven-baked eggplant plate.

Getting There and Around

To reach Pizzo by car, drive along the A3 as far as the Pizzo junction and follow the coastal road to town. If you prefer traveling by train, there are two stations: Lamezia Terme and Vibo Valentia-Pizzo. Lamezia Terme is the nearest airport.

◖ TROPEA

Tropea is a picturesque nutshell of a town that rises out of the Monte Poro promontory between the gulfs of Sant'Eufemia and Gioia. The town overlooks a crystal-clear sea with majestic rock formations where Benedictine monks chose to build their monastery. The area is surrounded by white, sandy beaches that snake along little grottoes and creeks covered with bougainvillea, verbena, jasmine, and other sweet-smelling Mediterranean plants.

Houses in the center have impressive en-

© LETIZIA RAZZINO

Santa Maria dell'Isola in Tropea

trances adorned with sculptures and frescoes that were once the pride of their owners. The Cathedral has been rebuilt several times and contains many sacred objects recalling local legends. Tropea isn't just a pretty face, however. It's also been awarded the highest rating from the *Legambiente* environmental group that has 128 parameters for its yearly quality test. The evaluation takes into account natural beauty, pollution, noise levels, and recycling.

Sights

The town has preserved its 16th-century grid pattern and **Porta Nuova** has been the main entrance since the earthquake of 1783. It leads to Corso Vittorio Emanuele, which runs the entire length of town. The **Cathedral,** at the end of via Roma, is of Norman origin, but it has been rebuilt each time the earth has moved and reflects many different styles.

Directly in front of Tropea is the town's most famous sight. **Santa Maria dell'Isola** lies on the top of a cliff and has served as a Benedictine sanctuary and church. The interior naves were remodeled during the Renaissance while the exterior portico is strictly Baroque. The entire facade was rebuilt in 1905 after another devastating earthquake. The church can be reached by way of a steep path. There is a wild garden behind the building with breathtaking views and a secluded stretch of beach below that's perfect for romantics.

Entertainment and Events

Festa del Cammello, on the first Sunday in May, recalls the town's victory over the Saracens. Back then they placed the Arabic commander on a camel and burned him alive. Today they carry a papier-mâché version of the camel around town accompanied by percussionists and dancers. Later that evening it's stuffed with explosives that light up Piazza Ercole.

Shopping

It takes less than a half-hour to walk through town but if you stop into every shop you could be here an entire afternoon. The small *botteghe* are generally run by craftspeople who produce objects out of wood, iron, cloth, and terracotta. Olive oil and wine is also well stocked on the shelves and the famous *nduja di spilinga* (red onion) is used to make marmalade and sauces that are a staple of the local diet.

Accommodations

In the middle of the green hills of Tropea, **Hotel Maddalena** (Drapia, Contrada Rizzina 12, tel. 096/366-7805, hotelmaddalena@tropea.biz, €40 pp) offers guests pleasant rooms, a delicious restaurant, and a warm welcome. The hotel operates a shuttle bus to Tropea and the beach that's five kilometers away. Private parking, a swimming pool, and tennis courts are available. There's also a Mini-Club that keeps underage guests occupied.

La Pineta (Via Marina 150, tel. 096/361-777, €40 pp) is a typical resort hotel open June–September. The decoration is fairly ordinary but there are good sporting facilities and a scenic tennis court. **Hotel Villa Antica** (Viale Stazione 15, tel. 096/360-7176, €70–200 s/d) is in the historical center, a few meters from the main square. The large rooms have high ceilings and antique furnishings worthy of the villa built by a wealthy family in the early 20th century. There are camping and bungalow options in **Camping Marina del Convento** (Via Marina del Convento, tel. 096/362-501, www.marinadelconvento.it, €8 and up).

Food

A few steps from Largo Galluppi, near the Duomo, is **Antico Borgo** (Via Aragona, Palazzo Cesareo, tel. 096/362-562, daily 9 A.M.–3 P.M. and 6 P.M.–midnight, €6–12). The pizzeria and restaurant is located in the cave-like depths of Palazzo Cesareo. Fish and other Tropean specialties fill a menu that has a vast choice of wines from the region and beyond. Not far away is the family-run **Osteria del Pescatore** (Via del Monte 7, tel. 347/531-8989, daily noon–3 P.M. and 7–11 P.M., €8–12). It's also focused on fish but here you can arrange to spend the morning with Gaetano in search of octopus and eat the

fruits of your labors as soon as you get back to shore. If that sounds like too much work, just scan the chalkboard for something tasty. 'Nduja and *insalata di polpo* are not spelling mistakes and the spaghetti with red onions is an edible masterpiece.

Getting There and Around

The nearest airport is Lamezia Terme 60 kilometers away. By car, drive along the A3 and exit at Pizzo Calabro (north) or Rosarno (south) and follow the SS 522 towards Tropea. The town is also reachable by train from Reggio Calabria.

Around Tropea

Continuing south along the promontory across small, winding roads you'll eventually reach **Capo Vaticano** and a lighthouse that has been guiding sailors for centuries. This is the last strip of land before the Straits of Messina and the waves get pretty high around here. Visitors come to lose track of time and fantasize about ancient shipwrecks scattered off the coast. Life in **Santa Maria** is dominated by the sea and the swordfish, tuna, and blue sharks that migrate past the village every spring.

REGGIO CALABRIA

Located along Italy's big toe, at the base of the **Aspromonte**, a long, craggy mountain range, Reggio Calabria is the largest city in the region. It lies in a splendid position on the eastern coast of the Messina Straits and enjoys an exceptionally mild climate all year-round that makes it popular with tourists. They don't come for the architecture, though. Most of the city was rebuilt after the earthquake of 1908 and the new buildings would make the Greek founders roll in their tombs. The real reason to brave the eyesores is the **Museo Nazionale della Magna Grecia,** which has a unique collection of Hellenic artifacts.

Greek settlers arrived in the early 8th century B.C. and named the town Rhegion. Until 280 B.C., the colony was allied with Athens before switching their allegiance to Roma. After the Empire evaporated, the town passed through

Visigoth, Ostrogoth, Swabian, Byzantine, and Arabic hands. Normans arrived in 1060 and incorporated most of Calabria into what became the Kingdom of the Two Sicilies.

Reggio was the first capital of Calabria, but lacks the charm of other Italian cities and there's hardly any historic center to speak of. The ancient walls, temples, Greek and Roman public buildings, and medieval heart have been nearly totally destroyed, either by armies of invaders or massive, pulverizing earthquakes.

Sights

Remnants of defensive walls built by early Greek colonists are visible from the water and near the ruins of the Roman baths along **Via Vittorio Emanuele.** On either side of the city are long sandy beaches with the usual complement of colorful lidos full of bathers. **Lungomare Matteotti** is a wide boulevard directly on the sea and on a clear day you can spot Sicily across the Straits. The writer Gabriele D'Annunzio called it the best kilometer in Italy. The botanical garden nearby preserves many local specimens and the beach can be easily reached. The promenade was recently repaved and new urban furnishings installed making it a great place to cap an evening and admire the lights dotting the opposite coast.

The center of town was rebuilt between the 19th and 20th centuries. There are a number of fashionable shops, restaurants, and cafes along **Via Corso Garibaldi** and the surrounding neighborhoods where historic palazzos will be hard to find. The **Aragonese Castle** may be the only exception but don't be fooled by the **Duomo.** It was completely destroyed in 1908 and rebuilt in an imitation Romanesque style. If you can spot the difference pretty soon you won't need a guide.

◖ MUSEO ARCHEOLOGICO NAZIONALE DELLA MAGNA GRECIA DI REGGIO CALABRIA

The most visited sight in Reggio Calabria is the Museo Archeologico Nazionale della Magna Grecia di Reggio Calabria (Piazza de Nava 26, tel. 096/581-2255, Tues.–Sun 9 A.M.–8 P.M.,

€4). It houses a fabulous collection of artifacts, including the world-famous **Bronzi di Riace** (Riace Bronzes). An entire room is dedicated to the life-size sculptures that look in better shape than most of the admiring visitors. What's especially interesting about the young, bearded warriors are the faces. Once you make eye contact it's difficult to turn away. Statue A (460 B.C.) has been attributed to Fidias. The artist was famous even in his day and this is the only example of his work in Italy. Archeologists think statue B (430 B.C.) was cast by Polyclitus and may have once resided in Delphi.

Near the bronzes is the **Head of the Philosopher,** one of the first sculptures of a life-like subject. Other displays include artifacts recovered in the Greek settlements of Caulonia, Sibari, Krimisia, Locri, and Crotone. If Magna Grecia is a new concept the information panels and brochures will get you up to speed.

Sports and Recreation

Believe it or not, the most popular sport Reggio Calabria is skiing. The Aspromonte Mountains dominate town after all and the slopes of **Gambarie** (www.gambarie.it) are only 30 minutes away. Downhill here is an unforgettable experience with a view of the sea that can be enjoyed from the lifts and coming down the half-dozen trails. These are suitable for beginner and mid-level skiers or snowboarders and if you've never paralleled before there is a school with very patient instructors.

Shopping

Reggio Calabria may lack beauty but it doesn't lack food and the pastry shops that you'll find on nearly every street are crammed with sweet and salty delicacies made from bergamot. For a gastronomic tour, start with the old recipes prepared at **Malavenda** (Via S. Caterina 85, tel. 096/548-638, www.malavenda.it). You can pick out something to eat immediately or have it wrapped to go.

Accommodations

For a single day in Reggio Calabria, **Hotel Palace Masoanri's** (Via Vittorio Veneto 95, tel. 096/526-433, €110 d) is perfect. Compared to many hotels on the coast the rooms will seem luxurious. Even by national standards they're comfortable and convenient for anyone without a car. Both the Bronzi di Riace and *lungomare* are nearby. For a five-star treat, there's always the **Altafiumara** (Loc. Santa Trada, Cannitello di Villa San Giovanni, tel. 096/575-9804, €260 d) just outside the city. The price includes a spectacular view of the Straits and afternoons lounging by the pool. Treatments in the spa are extra.

Grand Hotel Excelsior (Via Vittorio Veneto 66, tel. 096/581-2211, €200 d) is another extravagant choice on the city's main street. The hotel offers some of the best facilities in Southern Italy and appeals to business travelers as well as weary tourists. On the last floor is the **Galà** (€20) restaurant and the best view in town. Expect small portions of haute cuisine with a touch of tradition.

Food

The Riggio brothers and their wives run a pleasant seaside restaurant with a cozy little veranda. **Baylik** (Vico Leone 1, tel. 096/548-624, Tues.–Sun. noon–3 P.M. and 7–11:30 P.M., €9–14) has won awards for its pizza but if you're in the mood for fish order the *carbonara*. Aromatic bread is cooked in the wood-burning oven and *antipasti* can be a meal in itself.

The chef at **Ristorante Teatro i Tre Farfalli** (Via del Torrione 47–49, tel. 096/581-7667, www.itrefarfalli.it, Mon.–Sat. 12:30–3 P.M. and 7–11:30 P.M., €7–11) is stuck in the past. What was good enough to eat then is good enough to eat now. He serves it with traditional folk music and dancing that enhances the flavors. Everything is aimed at demonstrating the links between local culture and gastronomy. One of the house specialties is *fonduta di formaggio pecorino* and great to share with friends. **Trattoria al Focolare** (Via Anita Garibaldi 203, località Gallico Superiore, tel. 096/537-3661, Tues.–Sun 12:30–3 P.M. and 7–11:30 P.M., €8–14) is a favorite with carnivores. The roasted

---

BERGAMOTTO: ONE FRUIT, 1,001 PRODUCTS

The bergamot (Citrus bergamia) originated in Persia and the name is a descendant of an old Turkish epithet *Bergàrmundi*, meaning pear tree of the Lord. It's an accurate description considering the number of uses for this fabulous fruit. Nowadays the plant is only cultivated in Calabria, along the coast of Reggio Calabria, in clay and calcareous soil. The first tree was planted in 1750 by Nicola Parisi, who extracted the essence by pressing it into sponges before squeezing the precious substance into glass vials.

The peel is smooth and yellow and rich in an essential oil that's vital for making perfume. It has an incredible stimulating power and an unmistakable smell. Bergamot is helpful in relieving anxiety, stress, tension, depression, and stimulates the central nervous system. That's why it's often used in aromatherapy. It's also said to prevent hair loss. Pharmaceutical companies value bergamot for its antiseptic and antibacterial properties. The essence is also the principal ingredient of well-known Calabrian sweets and one of the most appreciated flavors of Earl Grey tea. If you include candy, ice cream, liqueur, jam, soap, and whatever local minds can come up with it, soon it becomes obvious there's no stopping this versatile fruit.

---

lamb dishes and meat *ragù* are delightfully good. To prepare a picnic or stock up on sausage before the next train leaves, stop in at **Specialità Pazzimenti** (Via Fata Morgana 46, tel. 096/533-1604). Shelves are bursting with Calabrian cold cuts, cheeses, and wine.

Gallina may seem like a long way to go for gelato but once you've tasted a cone at **Gelateria il Bergamotto** (Via F. di Sales, Gallina, tel. 096/5682-555) you'll be glad you made the 20-minute trip. The must-taste flavor is, of course, bergamot.

Information and Services

The main **APT office** is on Via Roma 3 (tel. 096/521-171), however, there are smaller information points at the airport and train station. All three provide maps and a useful events calendar.

Getting There and Around

Reggio Calabria is easily reached by air, especially from Rome or Milan. A train from the capital takes seven hours and unless you like long journeys you'll want to book a bunk on the overnight service. The A3 highway ends in Reggio Calabria and the first exit after the *porto* heads directly into town.

The harbor connects the city with Naples, Malta, and many destinations along the Sicilian coast. It's busy and crowded during the summer and a popular destination for petty criminals. Not all the ferries carry automobiles and if you want to get straight across to Sicily with a car you're better off boarding at Villa San Giovanni, 15 kilometers north of town.

Around Reggio Calabria

According to the Odyssey, ancient **Scilla** was inhabited by monsters and dreaded by sailors. There's nothing threatening about the town today unless you have a fear of wide, sandy beaches. By day it's crowded with bathers and by night it becomes a small Daytona. At the northern end of the bay is a **castle** that now houses a youth hostel where young party animals stay. By the time they wake up, the tall masted swordfish boats that patrol the Straits have already returned to port. The restaurants and cafes lining the *lido* make the town a convenient rest stop to or from Reggio Calabria. **La Pescatora** (Lungomare Colombo 32, Scilla, tel. 096/575-4147, Tues.–Sun. 12:30–3 P.M. and 7–11:30 P.M., €9–15) is on the hill where fresh fish comes with a spectacular view.

BASILICATA AND CALABRIA

SICILY

Sicily doesn't feel like Italy. Step off the plane, train, or boat, and it's clear you're somewhere else. The air smells sweeter, the sun shines brighter, and the sea is bluer. Early Greek sailors must have thanked their gods for landing them here. The only other thing you could ask for is an active volcano, some stunning archipelagos, and enough fertile soil to intoxicate an empire.

The biggest island in the Mediterranean has those things, too—and before all roads led to Roma, many boats were anchoring here. The civilizations that disembarked over the centuries spread themselves around the island and blended into and out of each other both peacefully and violently. The cultural enigma that emerged is an inheritance that's not easy to untangle.

Across the island, history has left its stamp — from the temples in Segesta and Agrigento to the Baroque facades of Ragusa and the mosaics of Villa Imperiale. Cultures are so intertwined that locals have lost track of their blood type and mainland Italian ears are at a loss to understand the meaning of entire sentences.

Palermo, with its multiple Euro-Afro-Asian personality, is the pinnacle of this exchange. A walk in the city's markets or a careful gaze at church domes are vivid reminders that globalization started long ago. The wrinkled women selling cucumbers, teenagers hawking pirated CDs, and butchers displaying cuts of beef would be more at home in a Middle Eastern souk than in any suburban shopping mall.

The difference is also evident on Sicilian tables. The island is home to more calories than

HIGHLIGHTS

◖ **Palermo's Street Markets:** Don't miss the vibrant Ballarò and La Vucciria street markets. Anthropologists would have a field day analyzing these animated markets in the center of Palermo. It's not so much the variety of articles on display but the colorful buyers and sellers that are endearing (page 733).

◖ **Monreale:** Seven kilometers south of Palermo in the town of Monreale is the most impressive cathedral ever built by the Normans. There are more mosaics inside the Duomo than anywhere else on the island, and attached to the church is a cloister with 228 columns that was once part of a royal palace (page 739).

◖ **Stromboli:** Stromboli would be worth visiting even if there wasn't an active volcano dominating the small island. Nighttime pyrotechnics occur with regularity every 10-15 minutes, and a climb to the crater is much more than a photo opportunity (page 747).

◖ **Taormina Arte Festival:** Frankly, with a Greek theater overlooking Mount Etna,

it doesn't matter who is playing on stage. Taormina Arte Festival, however, attracts performers who can match the beauty of the surroundings, and seeing Bob Dylan sing "Blowing in the Wind" here gives the song an entirely new meaning (page 750).

◖ **Mount Etna:** The best views of the highest and most active volcano in Europe are from onboard the Circumetnea Railway that circles the entire volcano. A journey in one of the vintage diesel cars reveals a complete range of landscapes (page 752).

◖ **Valle dei Templi:** This 4,500-acre park offers some of the best preserved ancient temples anywhere, including the Concordia, which has remained virtually intact for over 2,400 years (page 763).

◖ **Erice:** Erice is the Sicilian version of a hill town and can be reached by a scenic cableway journey. From the top, all of western Sicily is visible and along the streets, *pasticceria* display the pastries that the town is famous for and keep gourmets coming back (page 770).

SICILY

LOOK FOR ◖ TO FIND RECOMMENDED SIGHTS, ACTIVITIES, DINING, AND LODGING.

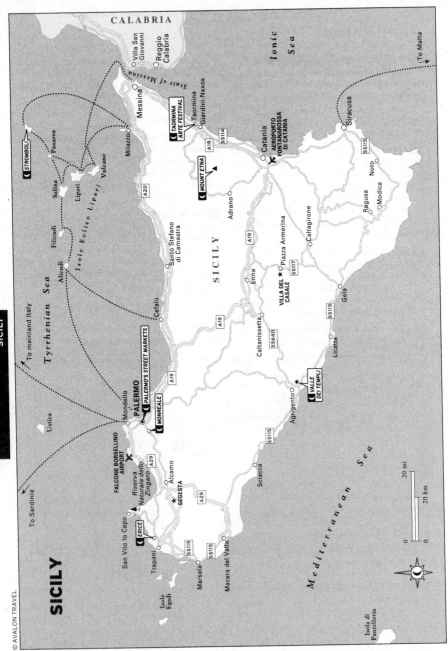

SICILY

© AVALON TRAVEL

any other region in Italy. Couscous competes with pasta on menus and dishes are spicier than what Venetian or Tuscan tongues are used to. Fruits and vegetables have tropical dimensions and if you don't taste at least one orange (season permitting), one lemon *granita*, and one dessert from Modica, your taste buds will regret it. Honey has been used since the Greeks arrived and is combined with almonds, pistachios, and cacao. Cannoli may be renowned but every town has its own unique recipe and some, like Marsala, even have their own wine.

Fortunately there are unlimited ways to work off those calories. Hiking to the top of a volcano or climbing to a Greek amphitheater are great fat-burners and the cobalt sea is always glistening invitingly. Hills and mountains prevail, with the highest running along the northern coast towards Mount Etna, which humbles everything else. Thirteen percent of Sicily is protected parkland and the Aeolians and Etna are UNESCO World Heritage sites for a reason.

Although the past is present in Sicily, it's also fading. Old-timers lining the Syracuse shorefront can testify to that. Some traditions have been lost or are reproduced only for annual festivities. The brightly painted horse-drawn carriages common in Palermo 50 years ago have nearly all disappeared and puppetry that entertained a pre-cinematic public has suffered a decline. Few Sicilians complain that the salt flats have closed or that tuna fishing isn't what it once was. Today agriculture, heavy industry, and especially tourism represent the future of an island unlike any other.

PLANNING YOUR TIME

Although it's perfectly feasible to break up a week in Rome with a weekend in Palermo, Sicily demands more time to be fully appreciated. You can arrive by land, air, or sea to all the major cities but Palermo is the only one where several days can be justified. Then it's best to rent a car and hit the road or catch a train that skirts the coast.

On the map, Sicily looks big. It is the biggest island in the Mediterranean, but get-

THE ITALIAN MAFIA

Sicily has always been associated with the Italian mafia. In some ways the Italian mafia was a French revolution in disguise and a struggle for a better life. It started out 150 years ago in a region that was desperately poor, governed harshly, and discarded by nobility. Although ideals proved self-serving in the end, the name translates to "hostility to the state." As things got more organized that meant extortion, property speculation, and drug trafficking.

Modern Italian administrations have spent millions trying to eradicate organized crime, and to some extent their efforts have paid off. Tommaso Buscetta and Toto Riina are behind bars and the mafia keeps a low profile these days. You won't see anything unusually fishy going down in the back streets of Catania or Messina. There's more violence on screen than in Corleone, and Sicilians prefer you remember them for their hospitality rather than the St. Valentine's Day massacre.

ting around is actually quite easy by car and highways are surprisingly smooth. The fastest stretches are those along the northern coast from Palermo to the Corno D'Oro and down to Catania. Rail surrounds nearly the entire island, but most lines only have a single track, which can make service slow.

If you have more time you can plan a journey to one of the archipelagos off the coast of Sicily. The three Egadi Islands, 20 minutes from Trapani, can be a day or overnight detour on the way to Agrigento. The Aeolians are farther from the coast and shouldn't be rushed. With seven islands to choose from, you can island-hop or take the more relaxing option of lying low in one of the comfortable hotels.

Sicily's interior is quite scenic and can be crossed relatively quickly. It takes less than three hours to travel from Agrigento to Cefalù, both of which should be avoided during the summer when parking becomes impossible and crowds disturbing. Spring is the best time to visit; once the April rains have passed, the entire island starts to blossom in red, yellow, and blue. Most of the cities are compact with sights concentrated around the historic center. Palermo has a well-deserved reputation for heavy traffic but once outside the center jams are rare.

Most of Sicily is safe but you should be careful after dark in the larger towns and avoid any unlit streets in Catania or the waterfront of Messina, where civility may be lacking. Purse-snatchers generally work in pairs. One drives the scooter close to the victim while the other does the snatching.

HISTORY

An island as big as Sicily doesn't go unnoticed for long. For early seafaring civilizations it was a convenient stop in the center of the Mediter-

ranean with deep harbors and potential trade. Greeks colonizers first landed in Sicily in A.D. 800. They found the island inhabited by Sicani and Siculi tribes and eventually expelled their Carthaginian rivals. By the 5th century A.D., they reached the height of their success and Syracuse rivaled Athens in beauty and wealth. The Romans put an end to all that and after the first Punic war in A.D. 241 gained complete control of the island. After the empire disintegrated there were several waves of barbaric invasions, and it wasn't until the Arabs arrived in the 9th century that civilization returned. The Norman invasion that followed continued the island's golden age and lasted until Carlo d'Anjou was dethroned in favor of Aragonese nobility who united the island's fortunes with the Bourbons of Napoli. Garibaldi and the 1,000 ushered in the modern age in 1860 when Sicily was incorporated within the new Italian state.

Palermo and the Tyrrhenian Coast

Italians talk with their hands and nowhere do they talk louder than Palermo. It's a dusty town with traces of World War II explosions and roosters crowing in the morning. The historic center could be Barcelona or Marrakech. Narrow streets and alleys invite the curious to explore. Monuments vary in style and there are dozens of noteworthy Norman churches, puppet theaters, and ancient trees. Some sights, like the **Duomo,** are the result of many layers of history and can only be classified as unique.

Quattro Canti marks the center of the historic district where Via Maqueda and Corso Vittorio Emanuele intersect. Neither of these avenues is particularly beautiful and the minuscule sidewalks are where locals play "dodge the tourist." It's more gratifying to stick to side streets like **Via Biscottai** or **Via Bandiera** that run roughly parallel to the Corso during the day. At night these take on a slightly menacing appearance while the avenues remain crowded until 11 P.M.

PALERMO
Sights
PALAZZO DEI NORMANNI

Nearly everyone who ruled Palermo has resided inside Palazzo dei Normanni, also known as Palazzo Reale (Piazza Indipendenza, tel. 091/705-4317, daily 8:30 A.M.–5 P.M., €6). The fortress is not particularly impressive unless you were trying to attack it, in which case you'd find the high walls impregnable. The building lies on the edge of the old town and provides commanding views over the city and port. Contrary to what the name suggests, Byzantines and Arabs built the initial structure. Normans enlarged the complex and the royal apartments from where they ruled, dined, and slept can be visited. **Cappella Palatina** was another Norman initiative. The stunning chapel inside the palace demonstrates how receptive the Normans were to outside influences and contains a mixture of Islamic and Norman craftsmanship. It is almost completely covered

Palermo's Duomo

in mosaics and gold seems to have been the favorite color. Today laws are still being passed inside the >palazzo, although now it is the Sicilian Assembly that calls the shots.

SAN GIOVANNI DEGLI EREMITI

The four red domes are the most obvious sign that San Giovanni degli Eremiti (Via dei Benedettini, tel. 091/651-5019, Mon.–Sat. 9 A.M.–7 P.M. and Sun. 9 A.M.–1 P.M., €4.50) isn't an average church. Ruggero II hired Arab architects for the job in 1132 and the building looks more like a mosque than a church. It is one of the best examples of Norman-Arabic architecture in Palermo. The entry fee includes access to the grounds that surround the grey, austere walls and provide a welcome escape from traffic. There's also a tranquil garden within the adjacent cloister where palms and the bell tower can be admired. If you think this would be a good place to get married, think again: The church was deconsecrated a long time ago. Part of the building is covered in scaffolding and restoration is ongoing.

DUOMO

It's difficult to classify the Duomo (Piazza della Cattedrale). There have been countless additions since it was built in 1184 and the overall effect is disorienting to the eye. Geometric patterns recall the orient while the two bell towers are a Sicilian take on Gothic. To see the Catalan contribution, walk around to the southern portico. The interior is less impressive but many of the Spanish kings who influenced how the city looks today are buried there. Some of their belongings are visible in the **Treasury** (tel. 091/334-3763, Mon.–Sat. 8 A.M.–6 P.M., €2). The most impressive object is the imperial crown and the 23 sarcophagi in the crypt below.

PIAZZA BELLINI

Piazza Bellini contains two small churches that are a contrast in style. **La Martorana** (tel. 091/616-1692, Mon.–Sat. 8 A.M.–1 P.M. and 3:30–6:30 P.M., Sun. 8:30 A.M.–1 P.M.) combines a Baroque facade and Norman bell tower. Inside the smell of incense fills the air and time seems to have stopped. Mosaics are encrusted in the ceiling and recount the life of Christ. Tour groups alternate positions underneath the narrow dome and guides point out the stories from the Old Testament to admiring tourists.

A few meters away **San Cataldo** (Mon.–Sat. 9:30 A.M.–12:30 P.M. and 3:30–6:30 P.M., €1) has retained its tranquility. The three red cupolas and squatness of the building are the work of Islamic hands. The small fee puts off enough people to keep the interior relatively peaceful. Here the walls are bare and the only color is provided by the Knights of Malta. A photocopy of the church's history is distributed by staff, who are happy to answer questions. Unless you don't mind overpaying for a cappuccino, avoid the bar in the piazza next door.

MUSEO ARCHEOLOGICO REGIONALE

Museo Archeologico Regionale (Piazza Olivella 24, tel. 091/611-6805, daily 8:30 A.M.–6:30 P.M., €4.50) contains remnants of Sicily's ancient visitors. The sculpture, ceramics, glassware, and weaponry come from across the island and are displayed within a former monastery. On the ground floor are two Phoenician sarcophagi discovered in Selinunte. Bronze and marble statues—including *Ariete,* unearthed in Syracuse—recall Greek roots. The museum is pleasantly free of crowds and accessible to all. A special combination ticket can be purchased with the **Galleria Regionale della Sicilia** (Via Alloro, tel. 091/623-0011, daily 9 A.M.–1:30 P.M., Mon.–Fri. also 2:30–7:30 P.M., €8) for €8. The gallery is notable for the beautiful Palazzo Abatellis and the manner in which Carlo Scarpa designed individual displays. Each of the most important works of art was given its own particular frame and background. Natural lighting also helps bring out the beauty of the paintings. The *Trionfo della Morte* fresco and *Vergine Annunziata* by da Messina never looked better.

LA ZISA

La Zisa (Piazza Guglielmo il Buono, tel. 091/696-1319, Mon.–Sat. 9 A.M.–6:30 P.M. and Sun. 9 A.M.–1:30 P.M., €4.50) derives its name from the Arabic word for "splendid" and demonstrates what can happen when West meets East. The castle was erected by William II in 1160 along Muslim principles. It was recently restored and transformed into an Islamic art museum. The ground floor **Sala della Fontana** is covered in mosaics, with hunting scenes providing the main motif. Upstairs are the six royal apartments where kings slept without fear of being disturbed. The area around La Zisa isn't particularly beautiful, but the park surrounding the fortress provides refuge from the urban chaos. There are some wonderful fountains and frequent concerts during the summer.

CATACOMBE DEI CAPPUCCINI

Catacombe dei Cappuccini (Via dei Cappuccini, tel. 091/212-117, daily 9 A.M.–noon and 3–5 P.M., €1.30) isn't for the faint-hearted. It's probably the only place in the world to see 8,000 mummified corpses. Monks started the tradition when they discovered that the extremely dry air was perfect for preserving dead bodies. They were soon joined by local residents who were dressed in their finest gear before being laid to rest in the long underground passages. The catacombs are at the end of Corso Vittorio Emanuele and can be reached on bus 327 from Piazza Indipendenza near Palazzo dei Normanni.

Entertainment and Events
DANCE CLUBS

You can have a romantic dinner or spend the night dancing at **Vicolo delle Stelle** (Via Pietro Bonanno 42b, tel. 091/637-1186, Tues.–Sun. 7 P.M.–2:30 A.M., no cover). This elegant nightspot is a restaurant, pub, and disco all in one—with fantastic views of the city and stars. Candles illuminate tables on the third floor terrace while local DJs operate the consoles down below on weekends. Music is a mix of soft house and commercial. If you plan on drinking the night away, the drinks card will save you a euro or two.

It only took a couple of months for **Sesto Senso** (Vicolo Fonderia 3–5, Fri.–Sun.

7:30–3 A.M., no cover) to become one of the coolest spots in the city. The location within an old palazzo near Piazza San Domenico is decorated in warm colors and modern lounge furniture. On the ground floor is a bar, small tables, and enough space for a little dancing. You can observe the scene from the balcony, equipped with comfortable sofas and armchairs, while sipping the house cocktail. Two giant screens play a succession of videos and on Sunday nights (7:30–10 P.M.) the *aperitivo* comes with a shiatsu massage. Arrive early if you want to get rubbed.

In Palermo even nightclubs serve good food; although dancing on a full stomach may seem risky, the menu at **Tina Pica** (Via Giovanni Meli 13, tel. 091/612-3934, Tues.–Sun. 7:30 P.M.–3 A.M., no cover) is hard to resist. *Spaghetti chitarra con ricci* (pasta with sea urchins) is what most of the locals choose to get evenings started inside this modern club. Music has a high bpm count and live performances are frequent. There's air-conditioning in the summer, when this legendary locale fills up early.

LIVE MUSIC

Zsa Zsa Mon Amour (Via Francesco Angelitti 32, Wed.–Sun. 9:30 P.M.–3 A.M.) is a former disco now dedicated to live music. The large stage hosts local and international acts performing everything from reggae to metal. After the concert on Saturday nights a DJ keeps audiences dancing with hip-hop, rock, and pop. Chances are that Mr. Sinclair will be on the mic, which means anyone with fond memories of the '80s will get their fill of revival hits. Making eye contact with the barman isn't easy, so when you do get his attention be sure to be ready with your beer, wine, or cocktail order.

Something's always happening at **Candelai** (Via Candelai 65, tel. 091/327-151, Tues.–Sun. 7 P.M.–3 A.M.). It could be live music, theater, or an exhibition. This large venue in the center of town contains a performance space, snack bar, and pub on the second floor. In the summer, the courtyard is where the young crowd mingles between sets and en-

joys the daily happy hour. Music alternates between R&B, Latin, and rock.

Palermo is a jazz town and aficionados of be-pop meet at the **Open Music Club** (Via Niccolò Turrisi 51–53, tel. 091/582-513, Thurs.–Mon. 8 P.M.–1 A.M., concerts at 9:30 P.M.). If you can get a seat at one of the tables, there's a concert every night. Otherwise the wine bar next to the concert space is equipped with a piano and someone is generally improvising something. Special events are common and Monday night is reserved for the local jam session. Membership to the club is €5.

THEATER

Teatro Massimo (Piazza Verdi, tel. 800/907-080, www.teatromassimo.it) is the cultural heart of the city on the edge of old and new Palermo. The theater was built in 1897 and is impressive both inside and out. After a centennial restoration, project acoustics have been improved and the program varies between opera, ballet, and orchestral music. **Teatro Politeama** (Piazza Ruggero Settimo 2, tel. 091/588-001, box-office open Tues.–Fri. 9:30 A.M.–1 P.M. and 4–7 P.M.) nearby is the home of the Sicilian Symphonic Orchestra, which performs most weekends throughout the year (except for a short break in July and August). On the top floor of the theater is the modern art gallery. Theater, dance, and music alternate nightly at **Teatro Libero** (Piazza Marina, tel. 091/617-4040, www.teatroliberopalermo.it). Experimentation and innovation are the common themes of each performance.

For a more intimate experience, try **Teatro Ditirammu** (Via Torremuzza 6, tel. 091/617-7865, www.teatroditirammu.it) near Piazza Kalsa. There are only 52 seats, so book tickets in advance or arrive early. Most nights, folk groups performing popular Sicilian song and dance occupy the stage. There's also a small museum open daily 4:30–7 P.M. that provides a behind-the-scenes look at the theater.

Traditional puppet theater can be experienced at **Teatro Ippogrifo** (Vicolo Ragusi 6, tel. 091/329-194), where puppet masters pull the strings every Friday, Saturday, and

Sunday. **Teatro dei Pupi di Enzo Mancuso** (Via Collegio di Maria 17, tel. 091/814-6971) and **Cuticchio Mimmo** (Via Bara all'Olivella 95, tel. 091/323-400) also preserve this unique art form.

FESTIVALS AND EVENTS

Rosalia became patron saint of Palermo soon after she saved the city from the plague four centuries ago. Her festival is as popular as it gets and one of the highlights of the weeklong extravaganza is a parade from the Quattro Canti to Piazza Marina where an orchestra in typical Sicilian dress keeps crowds of followers dancing. The festival concludes with fireworks on July 15 and a citywide theatrical performance that includes storytellers, acrobats, and tightrope walkers that leave spectators gaping. A second part of the celebration takes place on September 3 and 4 when the city's faithful undertake a pilgrimage to Mount Pellegrino on foot. It's a steep 14-kilometer climb to the sanctuary, but the views are good and the mood of the pilgrims is cheerful.

Il Genio di Palermo (Genius of Palermo) is an opportunity to discover the creative process of over 30 local artists during the last week of September. The event is centered around Piazza Rivoluzione, where exhibitions and films are projected. You can pick up a map showing where this year's participants are located. Most studios are in the center and as long as you turn up at a decent hour the painters, sculptures, and photographers will happily demonstrate how they keep artist's block at bay.

Everything is possible during the **Festival di Morgana**, which runs November 8–December 10. The protagonists of this unique festival are traditional Sicilian puppets and their cousins from Vietnam, Bali, and Myanmar. Expert puppeteers from Italy and Asia demonstrate their skills within **Museo Internazionale delle Marionette** (Via Butera 1, tel. 091/328-060, Mon.–Fri. 9 A.M.–1 P.M. and 3:30–6:30 P.M., €5). If you miss the Vietnamese water puppets or the shadow puppet performances of the Balinese troupe, the 3,500 marionettes hanging within the museum are still worth a visit. They also put on shows every Tuesday and Friday in October.

Shopping

Souvenir hunters have a lot to choose from in Palermo but it's the characteristic *pupi* marionettes that are most strongly associated with the city. Production hasn't been exported to China just yet and a handful of families continue to demonstrate their puppet-making skills along Corso Vittorio Emanuele. Cost varies depending on size and quality of the armor worn by the puppets, which can weigh up to 15 kilograms. The Sicilian cart is another typical product; it's decorated in bright colors depicting the heroic feats of valiant knights. If long hours with a paintbrush don't impress you, the shops on Via Liberty are probably more your style. All the trendiest brands, like Tod's, Dolce & Gabbana, and Cartier, can be found there.

ARTS AND CRAFTS

Mimmo Cuticchio has been making and repairing *pupi* since he can remember. If you're lucky you'll have a chance to see him in action inside **Figli d'Arte Cuticchio** (Via Bara all'Olivella 40, tel. 091/323-400, Sat.–Sun. 10 A.M.–1 P.M. and 4–7 P.M., performances 6:30–8 P.M.). It's a job that requires the skills of a carpenter, painter, and actor. Mimmo has all three and the expressions of his puppets, some of which are 80 centimeters tall, speak for themselves. If you want to adopt one, be prepared to pay cash.

Casa Merlo (Via Merlo 44, tel. 09/1623-0647, daily 10 A.M.–3:30 P.M. and 5–8:30 P.M.) is a bit like a ceramics museum without the guard. Here you get a delightful explanation of the work on display by the owner, who has selected the artists and pieces herself. There is a mix of practical and artistic in varying sizes that illustrate the Sicilian take on the art of ceramics. Prices start at €5 for an egg holder and get up into high triple digits for some of the abstract pieces. The store is divided into three bright rooms and overlooks the church of San Francesco.

If a single tile is all you're after, **L'Angolo del Cotto** (Via Alloro 25, tel. 091/610-1176, Mon.–Sat. 9 A.M.–1 P.M. and 3–7 P.M.) has hundreds to choose from. The hand-painted ceramics can be displayed on a wall or used more functionally as a hot plate. The designs are reproduced from 16th-century palazzi.

ANTIQUES
Corimbi (Via Principe di Belmonte 12, tel. 091/589-426, Tues.–Sun. 9 A.M.–noon and 2:30–6:30 P.M.) is a riot of different eras all mixed together. You need a good eye to distinguish between the truly antique and the more recent objects that crowd the small shop. There is an extensive collection of 20th-century fabric that deserves to be framed and 1950s desk lamps that haven't gone out of style.

BOOKSTORES
Libreria Dante Quattro Canti di Città (Via Maqueda 172, tel. 091/585-927, daily 9 A.M.–1 P.M. and 4:15–7 P.M.) is the oldest bookstore in the city. They specialize in architecture and if it's Bauhaus or Le Corbusier you're after, you'll find it on these well-stocked shelves. Unfortunately there is very little seating.

SHOES AND ACCESSORIES
La Coppola Storta (Via dell'Orologio 25, tel. 09/1743-4745, daily 9 A.M.–1 P.M. and 3–7:30 P.M.) sells the kind of caps worn by old-time Sicilians chatting in the piazzas of Palermo. They have been updated for a new generation and the variety of colors and patterns is immense. Feel free to try as many of the hats you like and have store assistants take your measurements if in doubt about your cranial dimensions. A *coppola* should fit snuggly at any angle. **LUAN** (Via Bara all'Olivella 113) is another good address for finding stylish headgear.

HOME
Officina Achab (Via Alloro 13, tel. 091/616-1849, Mon.–Sat. 9:30 A.M.–1 P.M. and 3–7 P.M.) has the entire house covered. They sell handmade sheets and pillows for the bedroom, bookends to keep shelves in order,

© ALESSIA RAMACCIA

a colorful Palermo wagon wheel

SICILY

and tapestries that could hang anywhere. The owner also produces his own line of clothing and accessories that are only sold here.

◀ STREET MARKETS
The most vibrant places in Palermo are the markets. **Ballarò** (Piazza Ballarò) is a chaotic mix of vegetable, fish, and dry good stalls where few tourists venture. Eggplants and fava beans are unusually large and Roma accordion players serenade vendors shouting unintelligibly to passersby. Keep a hand on your wallet and refrain from taking too many photos, as locals don't always appreciate being captured in pixels. **La Vucciria** (between Via Roma and Corso Vittorio Emanuele) is the largest market in Palermo and equally lively. Both markets are held every day except Sunday from early morning until 2 P.M.

If the Ballarò and Vucciria have whet your appetite for Palermo's markets, you'll find more colorful stalls selling housewares, clothing, and second-hand objects at **Il Capo** (Via Sant' Agostino) and **Casa Professa** (Piazza Casa

Professa) on weekday mornings. There's also a flea market selling antiques and handmade local products near Palazzo dei Normanni. Every weekend, bric-a-brac and crafts fill Piazza Marina and on the first Sunday of every month Piazza Unità d'Italia is the place to find old keys, out-of-date globes, and tools that have little use nowadays except for collectors. ·

Sports and Recreation

Skybrothers (Via Salvatore Spinuzza 51, tel. 091/662-2229, www.extremeplanet.biz) have one goal and one goal only: to raise your adrenaline. How they do it is up to you and can mean rock climbing, parasailing, or bungee jumping. Experienced climbers leave every Sunday for the mountains behind Palermo; the cost of joining the four person expedition is €15. A full climbing course that includes equipment, theory and practice, and insurance is also available for novices.

Orto Botanico (Via Abramo Lincoln, tel. 091/623-8241, daily 9 A.M.–5 P.M., €3.50) has one of the best collections of Mediterranean and tropical plants in Europe. There are rare examples of aquatic species that would have inspired Monet and a giant *Ficus magnolioides*. A botanical school is also located in the gardens and can be visited.

Parco della Favorita (Viale Diana) is a popular weekend destination for Palermitans looking for a little greenery. The former hunting reserve was home to Ferdinand III after he was expelled from Naples by Napoleonic troops. The Chinese Palace where he resided is an odd-looking building commissioned at the end of the 19th century when everything Asian was in fashion. The palazzo now contains the **Museo Etnografico Pitrè** (tel. 091/740-4893, Sat.–Thurs. 7:30 A.M.–7:30 P.M., €5) with a large collection of everyday Sicilian objects documenting how the island's inhabitants once lived.

Accommodations
UNDER €100
Hotel Ambasciatori (Via Roma 111, tel. 091/616-6881, www.ambasciatorihotelpalermo.

com, €70–90 s/d) is convenient for anyone arriving by rail. It's also close to most of the monuments of the historic center and allows visitors to get a sense of Palermo's grittiness without sacrificing comfort. The 18 rooms are completely non-smoking and decorated in a generic modern style. Guests are a mix of Italian and foreign visitors attracted by price. Breakfast is served in the small dining room on the first floor and the front desk is available 24 hours a day.

A slightly smaller hotel also in the center is the **Gardenia** (Via Mariano Stabile 136, tel. 091/322-761, www.gardeniahotel.com, €65–95 s/d). Most rooms have a tasteful green decor and some come with terraces and plastic garden furniture. Breakfast is €5 and includes all the coffee and pastries you can eat.

€100-200
Posta (Via Antonio Gagani 77, tel. 091/587-338, www.hotelpostapalermo.it, €100 d) has a film noir atmosphere that would make Bogart feel at home. Rooms are essential and heavy curtains keep things dark. Guests are treated with extreme politeness by the family that has run the hotel since the 1930s. Walls of the ground floor bar and breakfast area are covered with photos of famous Italian film stars who spent their nights here.

Mediterraneo (Via Rosolino Pilo 43, tel. 091/581-133, www.abmedpa.com, €120 d) resembles an English country club transplanted to a residential Palermo street. Communal rooms are large and the leather sofas could easily fit five. The elegant bar is a good stop before or after strolling Palermo's cultural quarter. Theaters are a moment away but if you prefer to call it an evening, the hotel restaurant is exclusively for guests and serves wonderful regional specialties.

Hotels like **Grand Hotel des Palmes** (Via Roma 398, tel. 091/602-8898, www.grandho teldespalmes.it, €160 d) are from a different era; the ceiling decorations in the main hall alone make a visit worthwhile. The 177 rooms haven't been abandoned to history, however, and aristocrats who once frequented the hotel wouldn't recognize the light wood furniture, beige carpets, and marble-covered bathrooms that now predominate. La Palmetta serves local and international dishes and indoor parking is available upon request.

€200–300

Hotel Plaza Operà (Via Nicolò Gallo 2, tel. 091/381-9026, www.hotelplazaopera.com, €170–200 s/d) combines antique furnishings with modern design. The minibar is complimentary and there are 18 satellite channels on the LCD TVs equipped with Internet and wireless keyboards. Shopping and art are just around the corner and suites come with glass-enclosed whirlpool tubs and a private solarium. The breakfast buffet is a feast for the eyes and laundry service is available.

FOOD

It's no coincidence that the first Western cookbook was written in Sicily. The island supplies a cornucopia of ingredients and Palermo serves up some wonderful combinations. *Pasta con le sarde* can be found in the most humble or elegant restaurants and consists of wild fennel, fresh sardines, anchovies, saffron, sultanas, and pine nuts. Aromas are everywhere and the city's streets are full of temptations. *Panelle* is the equivalent of a New York pretzel made from chickpea flour, salt, pepper, and parsley, fried in vegetable oil and served in open-air kiosks. The ones near the old Arabic quarter of la Kalsa are particularly good. Other street snacks are *sfincione,* a kind of pizza topped with tomato, anchovies, and onion, and *pani c'a meusa* (spleen sandwich), with ingredients that make some visitors squeamish. Sicily has a particularly strong reputation for desserts and Palermo is chock full of *pasticcerie* selling *cassata* (ricotta-filled cake) and *frutta di martorana* (fruit-shaped pastries) that are as attractive to the eye as they are to the stomach. Many Sicilian restaurants don't accept credit cards, so have cash ready in order to avoid washing dishes in a Palermitan kitchen.

SICILIAN

Ru Fila Ri Pasta (Via Salinas 16–18, tel. 091/730-3059, Tues.–Sun. 12:30–3 p.m. and

---

FRUTTA DI MARTORANA

Marzipan is a traditional Arabic concoction imported to Sicilia during the 12th century. It's prepared by crushing almonds, adding a little sugar, and flavoring the mixture with orange water and vanilla. Then it's heated over a low flame and shaped into *frutta di Martorana*. The name comes from the convent where nuns first began turning marzipan into imitation fruit and vegetables. Palermitan families would visit the convent during festivals to buy the dessert that quickly spread across Sicily.

Pasticceria took the idea even further, creating sweets that resemble sausage, chicken, pasta, and more. It takes creativity and good technique to create *martorana* but more than anything bakers must be fast. If the dough isn't kneaded quickly, the almond oil comes to the surface and ruins the taste and look of the pastry. Color is the last touch and is traditionally obtained from gum plants. The resulting sweet is deceiving to the eye and pleasing for the stomach. It can be tasted in all its incarnations in Palermo at **Pasticceria Amato** (Via Alberto Favara 14, tel. 091/321-897, daily in summer 7 A.M.–9 P.M., closed Sun. rest of the year) and throughout the island.

7–11 P.M., €6–8) is Palermitan for *due fili di pasta*—the two strands of spaghetti Italians say they could eat when they were extremely hungry. It's no wonder portions are generous at this restaurant near Via Terrasanta. Dishes are prepared the traditional way without fuss and are on your table in no time. The veal meatballs should not be overlooked. Prices here are from another century and three courses at lunch barely adds up to €10. The lack of an extensive wine list may be the only drawback, but after the first bite of *cannoli* or *crostate* everything is forgiven.

Simplicity is a good sign in Palermo's restaurants and the Riccobono brothers haven't gone out of their way to decorate the five rooms that make up **Ai Cascinari** (Via d'Ossuna 43–45, tel. 091/651-9804, Tues.–Sun. noon–3:30 P.M. and Fri.–Sat. 7:30–10:30, €7.50–10). Instead they've concentrated on the classics, reinvigorating after a walk through the nearby Capo market. There's good anchovy spaghetti, stuffed calamari, and a mix of meat and fish dishes. Eavesdropping is nearly impossible given that most tables are occupied by locals speaking in heavy dialect.

Cambio Cavalli (Via Pataria 54, tel. 091/581-418, www.cambiocavalli.com, daily noon–3 P.M. and 7–11 P.M., €8–11) is a favorite with couples who sit in the 16th-century courtyard surrounded by wrought iron and wooden beams where horses once passed. Dario Aloisa is the chef and doesn't like to offer the same menu twice. He experiments every week with new creations based on fresh ingredients. One dish that keeps coming back by popular demand is the *passatine di piselli ai crostacei* (pea and shellfish soup).

SEAFOOD

Osteria Paradiso (Via Serradifalco 23, Mon.–Sat. 12:30–3 P.M., €8–10) is a neighborhood joint that hasn't changed much since the Corona family opened the restaurant in 1967. They still don't have a telephone and they still don't accept credit cards. You can choose the fish you want to eat from the tank and can select from a number of original first courses. Spaghetti with clams and anchovy lasagna is the house specialty. Fresh fruit is the only dessert and coffee is available at the bar across the street. Since there are only six tables and reservations are impossible, it's wise to arrive early and be prepared to make new friends if necessary.

Simple ingredients, traditional recipes, and courtesy are what keep locals coming back to **Piccolo Napoli** (Piazzetta Mulino a Vento 4, tel. 091/320-431, Mon.–Sat. noon–3:30 P.M. and Fri.–Sat. 7–10:30 P.M., €9–11). Seafood is the protagonist and the buffet prepared by Gianni and Pippo features fried calamari, roasted vegetables, and *polpo lesso* (octopus). An opportunity to try this many flavors in one sitting is rare. *Bucatini con le sarde* is hard to resist and the oven-baked swordfish is an old recipe that includes a little milk. The *cassatta* served for dessert comes from a nearby *pasticceria;* if none of the desserts catch your fancy, then a visit to **Scimone** (Via Miceli 18b at the corner of Via Imera) provides many tempting ricotta- and fruit-based sweets.

FUSION

 Cucina Papoff (Via Isadora la Luma 32, tel. 09/158-6460, Mon.–Fri. noon–3 P.M. and 8–11 P.M., €8–10) is a dining experience that's hard to forget. The interior is unexpected considering the smoked glass windows on the outside. Ring the bell to enter and discover high wood ceilings, stone walls, music at just the right volume, and a couple who take food very seriously. They greet everyone at the door personally and if you haven't made a reservation you're likely to be turned away. The menu is decidedly fish-focused and citrus fruits are used to surprise the palate in many of the appetizers. Smoked salmon with pears and oranges followed by fettuccine with swordfish and zucchini is a highly gratifying one-two combination. Both risotto options are delicious and there's a superb selection of wine by the bottle and glass.

QUICK BITES

Someone is always waiting to serve clients behind the large counter filled with trays of pizza and *focacce* at **Focacceria Basile** (Via Bara all'Olivella 76, tel. 091/335-628, Mon.–Sat. noon–3:30 P.M., €5–7). Just choose a flavor and use sign language to indicate how big a piece you want. Have lunch wrapped to go or sit down in one of two spartan rooms where a basic rotisserie menu is also available.

The little piazza in front of San Francesco is a great stop for lunch and fortunately **Antica Focacceria S. Francesco** (Via A. Paternostro 58, tel. 091/320-264, daily 12:30–3 P.M. and 7:30–11 P.M., €3–8) provides indoor and outdoor seating options. The Liberty-style interior covers three floors and the food is what peasants have been digesting for years. *Pani ca' meusa* is the house specialty, but if a spleen sandwich doesn't tempt you steer towards the fixed-price buffet. If you do develop a taste for *meusa*, try **Pani Ca' Meusa** (Porta Carbone, Via Cala 48) near the tourist port and **Focacceria Politeami Giannettino** (Piazza Ruggero Settimo 11).

CAFÉS
Bar Touring (Via Alcide De Gasperi 237, tel. 091/517-682, daily 6 A.M.–10 P.M.) is a daily rite of passage for hard-core Palermitans. They come for one thing in particular and that's the *arancia bomba* (orange bomb)—an orange-flavored doughnut that's stacked in neat rows behind the glass counter. The other pastries are equally enticing and could turn anyone into a regular customer of this friendly bar that serves strong espresso at inflation-free prices.

   Antico Caffè Spinnato (Via Principe di Belmonte 111, tel. 091/329-220, daily 7 A.M.–2 A.M.) is a great place to linger. In the morning you can enjoy a pastry in the marble-clad interior that's been serving cappuccino since 1860. Outside on the pedestrian boulevard, tables fill up fast in the afternoon and elegantly dressed waiters serve cannoli and *torta al pistacchio* to aspiring socialites. The *rosticceria* satisfies appetites during dinner and a pianist plays jazz standards while couples and groups of friends enjoy their nightcap.

   Aluia (Via Libertà 27, tel. 091/730-8688, daily 7 A.M.–9:30 P.M.) is ideal for breakfast, a quick lunch, or a cocktail. You can sit outside and study the Palermitan characters passing on Via Libertà or opt for a quiet table on the side street. Cheesecake and *tre cioccolati* provide added energy for browsing designer boutiques and exploring the Art Nouveau buildings in the area. The vegetable couscous and paella are equally noteworthy, as is the vast array of gelato.

SPECIALTY FOOD SHOPS
All of the savory Palermitan breads like *torcigliato* and *fioni,* along with an assortment of traditional biscuits, can be found at **Fraterrigo**

(Via Panieri 26) and **Tuttoilmondo** (Via Nebrodi 43). Both bakeries get crowded in the morning and lines are not always respected.

Information and Services
TOURIST INFORMATION
There are APT tourist offices at the airport arrivals hall, **Stazione Centrale** (Piazza Giulio Cesare, tel. 091/616-5914, www.palermotourism.com, daily 8:30 A.M.–2 P.M. and 2:30–6 P.M.), and in the center of town (Piazza Castelnuovo 34, tel. 091/605-8351). Pick up a copy of the **Agenda Turismo** booklet that provides detailed information about the city and province. Visitors can choose from five combination tickets that allow entrance into several museums over a period of two days.

BANKS AND CURRENCY EXCHANGE
Most banks are clustered along the avenues of Via Roma, Maqueda, and Libertà. They are open on weekdays, but take a one-hour pause for lunch and close mid-afternoon. If you must go, remember to deposit large metal objects in the lockers outside and try to make it there by 11 A.M. in order to avoid the rush. Many provide exchange services, as do the **post office** on Via Roma (Mon.–Sat., 8:15 A.M.–1:20 P.M.) and **BDS** (Mon.–Fri. 8:20 A.M.–1:20 P.M. and 2:45–3:45 P.M.) and **MAA** (Mon.–Sat. 9 A.M.–4:30 P.M.) at the airport. Currency can also be swapped at Ufficio Informazione inside the train station, open daily 8 A.M.–8 P.M.

GOVERNMENT OFFICES
The **U.S. consulate** (tel. 091/305-857) is located on Via Vaccarini 1 and is open weekdays 9 A.M.–12:30 P.M.

NEWSPAPERS AND INTERNET
Day-old foreign newspapers are available at Edicole a Palermo, which operates kiosks in Piazza Castelnuovo, Verdi, and Vittoria. Email can be checked for free at the public libraries in **Villa Travia** (Via Salinas 3, tel. 091/740-5941, daily 9 A.M.–7 P.M.) or **Villa Niscemi** (Piazza Niscemi, tel. 091/740-4805, Mon.–Sat. 9 A.M.–3 P.M. and 3:30–7 P.M.). You can also

pay to surf at Navigando on Via Libertà 73 and Accademia Internet in Via Cala 64.

Getting There

Palermo may be closer to Tunis than Rome but that doesn't make it hard to reach. Alitalia flights arrive from around the country, ferries anchor daily, and trains connect other Sicilian towns. Highways to the city deserve a much better reputation and drivers will be surprised at how easy it is to reach the capital.

AIR

Falcone Borsellino airport is 30 kilometers west of Palermo off the A29 highway. There are direct flights from all major Italian cities and low-cost links to European destinations. An express train from the airport departs for Stazione Centrale in Palermo every hour 5 A.M.–midnight and costs €4.50. Buses are also available to the center every 30 minutes from 5 A.M. until the last flight. The journey takes 50 minutes and costs €4.80. A taxi ride is €35–45 depending on the address. For car rentals take the airport shuttle to the first stop, where a dozen companies are located.

CAR

From continental Italy, take the A3 Salerno–Reggio Calabria highway south and exit at Villa San Giovanni to reach the ferries. Once you've crossed over to Messina follow the A20 and A19 highways along the coast all the way to Palermo. From Taormina or Syracuse, drive to Catania and pick up the A19 Palermo–Catania. It's a 260-kilometer drive between the two cities. From Agrigento, take SS189, which cuts across the island and reveals some beautiful countryside.

TRAIN

Palermo can be easily reached by train from Taormina, Catania, and Syracuse. From other more remote locations, a transfer is required. If you think that the idea of a 12-hour journey has a romantic ring to it, you can catch a train from Rome to Palermo. Night trains leave daily at 8:02 P.M. and 8:47 P.M. and pull into Palermo a little after 8 A.M. There are a number of sleeping options and a *couchette* in a double compartment costs €95 one-way.

The ticket office is open daily 5:30 A.M.–8:40 P.M. and there is baggage deposit service available if you only plan a brief stay in the city.

BOAT

By far the slowest way of reaching Palermo is by boat. There are daily **Grandi Navi Veloci** (www.gnv.it), **SNAV** (www.snav.it), and **Tirrenia** (www.tirrenia.it) ferries from Genoa (20 hours), Rome Civitavecchia (12 hours), and Naples (10 hours). Cars are welcome on board and cabins are available.

Getting Around

BUS

AMAT (Via Stabile, tel. 091/729-1111, www. amat.pa.it) runs the buses in the city; a single ticket valid for 60 minutes costs €1. A day pass is €3.35 and can help take the weight off. A good way to get an overview of the city is the **Linea Gialla** and **Linea Rossa** (AMAT Palermo, Stazione Centrale, tel. 09/350-111 or 848/800-817, www.amat.pa.it, €0.52) that loops around the historic center, departing every 15 minutes from Stazione Centrale. The 806 goes to Mondello and the 389 terminates in Monreale.

Buses to Cefalù and Agrigento leave from Piazza Maggione. **Costanzo & Todaro** (tel. 091/821-4122) is one of a handful of companies that make the journey. To reach Segesta or San Vito Lo Capo go to Piazza San Marina.

TRAIN

The **Metropolitana** consists of one line and makes 13 stops from Stazione Centrale to Punta Raisi. It runs daily 6:10 A.M.–8:35 P.M. and tickets cost €1. Exploring the historic center, however, is better done on foot or by bus.

CAR

Unless you like traffic jams and spending hours searching for a parking, don't drive in Palermo. The best chance of finding a spot is on Via

Lincoln near the Orto Botanico or in one of the large lots outside the city center. It's also wise to rent a car from **Avis** (tel. 091/591-684) or **Sixt** (tel. 091/651-1393) at the airport rather than risk getting lost in the center.

TAXI
There are taxis ranks in all the major squares, the train station, and on Via Roma. Cabs can also be ordered by calling **Radio Taxi** (tel. 091/225-455) or **Autoradio Taxi** (tel. 091/512-727). Fares start at €3.81 during the day and cost roughly €1 per kilometer.

BICYCLES AND SCOOTERS
Bicycles aren't very common in Palermo but can be rented from **Cannatella** (Via Papireto 14, tel. 091/322-425). Much more common are scooters. Natives tend to enjoy riding without helmets and coming dangerously close to pedestrians. **Rent a Scooter** Via E. Amari 63, www.rentascooters.com) charges €27 per day for a 50cc Vespa.

BOAT
From Palermo it's possible to catch a ferry to the Aeolian Islands (Ustica Lines, www.usticalines.it), Ustica (Siremar, www.gruppotirrenia.it/siremar), and Cefalù (Ustica Lines). Most ferry companies have a ticket office near the port and there are frequent daily departures during the summer.

TOURS
City Sightseeing Palermo (Piazza Castelnuovo 6, tel. 091/589-429, www.city-sightseeing.it) operates a nine-kilometer circuit around the city in double-decker buses. There are 10 stops, including Quattro Canti, Stazione Centrale, and Teatro Massimo. The €20 ticket can be purchased onboard and at many hotels. **AMAT** (Piazza Ruggero Settimo, tel. 091/674-2163, www.amat.pa.it) runs a similar service without commentary. Tickets are €10 and children under 12 ride free. **Sicilia & Dintorni** (Via Castello 8, tel. 339/372-1811, www.siciliaedintorni.it) leads half-day, in-depth tours of Arab-Norman or Baroque Pal-

ermo that includes lunch. They also offer a three-hour Palermo by Night tour that departs nightly at 8:30 P.M. **Riciclando** organizes bike tours of Palermo and the island. A three-night all-inclusive trip is less than €400.

Around Palermo
◖ MONREALE
Monreale is perched eight kilometers southeast of Palermo in the shadow of Mount Caputo. The town is famous for the Duomo the Normans left behind and tourists flock to the vast complex in droves, often ignoring the late medieval and Baroque churches sprinkled around town. A complete visit requires half a day. There's only one road up the mountain and it's often clogged with traffic.

The origin of the **Duomo** (tel. 091/640-4413, daily 8 A.M.–6 P.M.) lies in a power struggle between the Archbishop of Palermo and William II, who wanted to consolidate his powers. What began to take shape in 1174 soon became the most imposing church on the island, with Lombard, French, Islamic, and Byzantine contributions. Inside, 20,000 square meters of ceramics from ceiling to floor recount the Old and New Testaments. You can walk down the three naves supported by granite columns or take a seat in the center of the church to better observe Noah building his arc, loading the animals on board, and persevering through 40 days and 40 nights. There are plenty of distracted children on field trips and tour groups, and a priest regularly uses the PA system to remind visitors where they are. Christ with his arms outstretched occupies the dome above the altar and it's here that the sarcophagi with the bodies of Kings William I and II lie. Before you leave, take a look at the bronze doors. Each has a different number of panels depicting saints; the door on the left was signed by Barisano da Trani. If you have the energy, climb up the steps to the terrace (9:30 A.M.–5:45 P.M., €1.50) for a bird's-eye view of the cloister and Conca d'Oro.

On the immediate right of the Duomo is the **Benedictine monastery** (Mon.–Sat. 9 A.M.–7 P.M. and Sun. 9 A.M.–1 P.M. and 3–7 P.M., tel. 091/640–4403, €4.50). Inside

SICILY

are the cloisters, made up of a vast quadrangle surrounded by Islamic-inspired arches. Each is supported by a twin column with a unique pattern. The capitals are intricately carved with figures of animals, plants, and humans captured delicately in stone. In the center, a palm-shaped fountain lets out a slow stream of water.

Driving to Monreale is a risky proposition, even for the locals. Parking spaces are in short supply and the *vigili urbani* are on constant lookout for offending vehicles. Bus 389 from Piazza Indipendenza is the less stressful option. The ride isn't particularly scenic but gets you there in around 30 minutes.

MONDELLO

When Palermitans want to go to the beach, they go to Mondello. What started out as a few huts was transformed into a playground for wealthy families during the Belle Epoque and is now full of restaurants and hotels. **Kursaal** (Foro Umberto I 21, tel. 091/616-2282, 1–3:30 P.M. and 8–11:30 P.M.) and **Bye Bye Blues** (Via Mater Dei 23, tel. 09/1684-1415, Wed.–Mon. 7–11:30 P.M.) have maintained the 19th-century elegance and provide great scenery and fresh fish.

Each May, champion windsurfers turn up for **World Festival on the Beach** (www.wwfestival.com) and compete in a variety of categories. There are also volleyball, skydiving, and kitesurfing demonstrations along with a full lineup of concerts held each night on the beach.

CEFALÙ

Cefalù is an enchanting fishing village straddling the sea and a high peak known as **La Rocca.** If the name sounds Greek, it's because Athenians were the first to recognize the natural beauty of the area. Today the good beaches and high concentration of wine bars hasn't gone unnoticed by tourists who fill **Via Re Ruggeria** to bursting during the summer. Ceramic and souvenir shops are plentiful and if you forgot anything at home, the clothing stores on **Via Vittorio Emanuele** stock racks of bathing suits, sandals, and towels.

the Duomo in Cefalù

© ALESSIA RAMACCIA

The center is compact and can be explored in a couple of hours, after which the cafes in **Piazza del Duomo** are an excellent place to admire the twin-towered facade of the Duomo and try a refreshing iced cappuccino or granita. Finding a restaurant in the old town or along the beachfront takes little effort; fish is usually the star ingredient. There are abundant bars overlooking the sea and legions of young, tanned Italians heading for the discos.

Sights

The **Duomo** (Piazza del Duomo, tel. 092/192-2021, 8 A.M.–noon and 3:30–7 P.M.) sticks out above everything else in Cefalù and has been the symbol of the town since it was completed in 1240. Ruggero II wanted the church to be the religious center of the island; although it never fully achieved that role, its beauty has never been overshadowed. The facade is divided into two levels and bordered by massive twin towers that are not exactly identical. The real wonders, however, are inside. The three naves are covered in Byzantine mosaics similar to those in Monreale. Gold and emerald green dominate the scenes of apostles and angels and it's best to visit the church mid-afternoon when the light is strongest. Take a moment to examine the columns and Baroque works of art that were added later. On the side of the Duomo is the monastery.

The other unmistakable landmark in Cefalù is La Rocca, visible from nearly everywhere in town. More ambitious travelers can make the climb to the top. The trail passes by the remains of **Tempio di Diana,** built in the 5th century B.C., and ends at the Byzantine castle. On a clear day, Palermo and the Aeolian islands can be spotted in the distance, making all the effort worthwhile. To reach the path from the center, take the **Salita dei Saraceni.** It's a good 40 minutes to the top and better confronted when temperatures are at their lowest. A bottle of water goes without saying.

Museo Mandralisca (Via Mandralisca 13, tel. 092/142-1547, daily 9 A.M.–7 P.M., €4.20) contains a collection of ancient coins, ceramics, vases, and shells. Displays haven't been modernized in a while but are interesting nonetheless. The star attraction is *Portrait of a Man* by Ignoto di Antonello da Messina. What is most interesting about the painting is the enigmatic smile reminiscent of a more famous picture hanging in the Louvre. Outside the museum are the remains of the stone washbasins women of Cefalù used until a couple of decades ago. In those, days most of the men made their living from the sea. The little port is a nice place to watch the sunset.

Entertainment

Tons of bars line the seaside but **Sottozero** (Lungomare, Punta Arenas entrance, admission free) has a prime spot near the Punta Arenas lido. In the late afternoon the flight of stairs leading past the bar gets covered in carpets, cushions, and small tables where the after-beach crowd meet. The place is packed by 8 P.M. and it takes a while to get served, but with a view this good no one really cares.

It's better to arrive early at **Malibu** (Lun-gomare Giardini, tel. 347/040-5132, summer Tues.–Sun. 10 P.M.–3 A.M., Sept.–Apr. Wed. and Sat. 10 P.M.–3 A.M., €10, women free before 1 A.M.) if you want to avoid the lines. This disco at the end of the *lungomare* is populated by a young crowd eager to prolong the evening. There are two dance floors and two bars, one of which is a VIP section where conversation is possible. If you can't make it past the ropes, try the chill-out area in the garden near the entrance. Different DJs perform every night so the style and sound changes according to who's manning the decks. Women enter for free until 1 A.M.

Le Calette (Via Presidiana, tel. 092/142-4144, www.lecalettediscoclub.it, Wed.–Sun. 10 P.M.–3 A.M., €10) is the thinking man's disco, located midway between the old port and Caldura. It's a 10-minute walk from the historic center and worth the trip. The entire club is outdoors and nature plays a big part in the ambiance. Music is lounge and DJs steer clear of commercial tracks. Cocktails are as refined as the surroundings and acne is absent from the faces of revelers.

Sports and Recreation

Part of Cefalù's attraction are the beaches along its coast. These alternate between long sandy stretches fully equipped with facilities and more intimate coves removed from the throngs of bathers. **Il Lungomare** is the closest beach to town and the *stabilimenti* rent lounge chairs and umbrellas. On weekends in July and August there's hardly any room to lay a towel down. The sea isn't very deep here, making it ideal for Italian families who spend the entire morning or afternoon enjoying the sand. **Le Salinelle** is a long beach seven kilometers from town towards Palermo. In summer, a bar opens and the strong winds make the area ideal for windsurfing. **Mazzaforno** is a small locality west of Cefalù with dozens of small beaches (or *spiaggette*, as they're called) that can be reached on small dirt tracks from the coastal road.

Less than 20 kilometers inland lies **Piano della Madonie** (tel. 092/192-3327 for guided

SICILY

tours, www.parcodellemadonie.it) national park and ski resort. The highest peaks reach an altitude of 1,572 meters. Two lifts operate in winter and skiers choose from seven trails. Beginners can get the hang of things at the ski school and there are several places to rent equipment. Cross-country skiing is also possible at the **Carbonara** and **Piano Cervi** (tel. 092/164-9994) ski resorts. These are some of the most scenic routes in Sicily, and the forests are populated by spruce, fir, and pine trees rarely seen this far south. **Club Alpino Italiano** (tel. 092/164-9994) is based nearby and organizes walking excursions in the area year-round.

Accommodations

Many of the small hotels in the center are quite frankly disappointing and merit negative stars. Honeymooners, couples, and families would be better off staying at **Valtur** (SS 113 Settentrionale Sicula, Finale di Pòllina, tel. 092/142-6243, www.valtur.it), on the coast nearby. The rooms are huts and the buffet keeps guests occupied for hours. Water activities abound and a shuttle regularly travels to Cefalù, which is less than 20 minutes away. Prices vary from €500 (per person per week) in May to €1,200 in August and includes all meals and sporting facilities.

If you don't mind the ringing of bells **Appartamenti Palazzo Maria** (Piazza Duomo 18, tel. 092/192-5060, www.palazzomaria.it €80 d) is a convenient place to stay. This guesthouse overlooking the main piazza offers six rooms that are clean and as central as you can get. The waterfront is a short walk away and the terrace offers a close up view of the duomo.

Food

La Botte (Via Veterani 6, daily, noon–3 P.M. and 7–10:30 P.M., €7–10) is a small restaurant on a typical cobblestoned street near the Duomo. The menu offers quality over quantity and homemade dishes with a long tradition behind them. There's outside dining in the summer and a wine list with a notable preference for Sicilian grapes.

Before you've reached the last step leading down to **La Brace** (Via XXV Novembre 10, tel. 092/142-3570, Wed.–Sun. 1–3:30 P.M. and 7–11:30 P.M., €8–12), someone has already greeted you and is gesturing to one of the tables in the large dining room. Appetizers include something for artichoke and eggplant lovers. They have a special way of preparing swordfish here and waiters are happy to reveal the secret recipe. Diners are a mix of loyal locals and travelers making a memorable gastronomic discovery.

An aquarium full of crustaceans and sea bass is the obvious clue that **La Marina Vecchia** (Via Vittorio Emanuele 73–75, tel. 092/142-0388, Wed.–Mon. noon–3 P.M. and 7–11 P.M.,€9–11) serves fish. In the summer they do it on the small terrace with a beautiful view of the sea. If traditional is what you're after, this is the place to try it. Prices are reasonable and friendliness is always included. Reservations are essential in the high season.

Getting There and Around

Cefalù is off the A20 highway and easily reached by car. It's less than an hour drive from Palermo and about twice as long from Messina. There are plenty of daily train departures (tel. 892-021, www.trenitalia.it) from both cities and rail avoids unnecessary time hunting for a parking spot. Trains from the capital take under an hour and cost €7.50.

Ustica Lines (tel. 092/387-3813, www.usticalines.it) operates a hydrofoil service between Palermo and Cefalù that arrives in 70 minutes. Winter ferries leave once every Monday, Friday, and Sunday. During the summer, there's a daily early-morning departure. Ticket prices vary according to the season.

Scooters are a good way of reaching the outlying beaches and are available from **Scooter for Rent** (Via G.Matteotti 13 bis, tel. 092/142-0496, www.scooterforrent.it). A 50cc Vespa for the day costs €35 and includes 24-hour assistance. They also have motorcycles that can be delivered directly to your hotel if you're staying outside of town.

Aeolian Islands

The Aeolian archipelago is made up of seven islands spread out in a "Y" shape off the coast of Milazzo. The seven "pearls" or "sisters," as they're known, may have similar volcanic origins but each has a unique character. **Lipari** is the largest and contains the most ancient remains. **Vulcano** and **Stromboli** remain geologically active and are best explored on foot. **Panarea** has been colonized by the international jet set and **Salina** is the greenest one famous for its Malvasia wine. **Filicudi** and **Alicudi** are off the trodden trail and mules are used in the latter, where roads barely exist.

All seven have been declared World Heritage sites by UNESCO and it's easy to understand why after a dip in the cobalt blue waters. If you have the time, this is the place to relax and enjoy nature. You can sail, scuba dive, or just lie on a black sandy beach. Of course anyone with a fascination for lava can get a close up look at extinct and active craters. Walking and cycling are the preferred means of transportation but cars can be ferried to Lipari. During winter, service is limited and many restaurants and hotels close for the season.

LIPARI

Lipari is the largest and most populated of the islands. It's the administrative headquarters and where most of the history has taken place. In the summer the streets are closed to traffic and **Corso Vittorio Emanuele** fills with strollers. The most scenic part of town is the old fishing port of **Marina Corto.** There are dozens of restaurants, bars, and *gelaterie* with outdoor tables where the island's granita can be sampled.

Sights

It's hard to believe that such a small island contains one of the most important archeological museums in the world. **Museo Archeologico Eoliano di Lipari** (Via Castello 2, tel. 090/988-0174, daily 9 A.M.–1:30 P.M. and 3–7 P.M., €6) is divided into five sections that illustrate a history stretching from the Stone Age to Roman antiquity. The 250 miniature Greek theater masks are particularly fascinating and were once sold as souvenirs to ancient travelers. Outside of the museum there's a park containing finely carved Greco-Roman tombs from the 4th–2nd centuries B.C.

Much of the western half of the island is inaccessible by car, and only a boat tour can reveal the *faraglioni* (rock formations near the coast) of **Pietra Lunga** and **Pietra,** the lava arch of **Punta del Perciato,** and the aquamarine grottoes. There are a dozen tour operators in Marina Corta with hourly departures around the island.

Shopping

In summer Marina Corta is chock-full of small shops selling artisan goods to the hundreds of tourists milling the streets. **Ceramiche Stefano** (Via Roma 1, tel. 090/981-2021) creates plates and accessories for the table using the traditional Aeolean methods of sculpting. Colors are inspired from the sea and the rock, and Stefano is happy to ship items overseas if you prefer to travel light.

All the jewelry inside **I Gioielli del Mare** (Via Garibaldi 8, tel. 090/988-0857, daily in summer) is inspired from the sea. White coral and pink shells are transformed into one-of-a-kind earrings and necklaces. They also carry the particular engagement rings used by locals to demonstrate their affection.

Accommodations

Hotels on the island generally have a price for each season. These vary considerably and even the fanciest boutique lodging is quite reasonable in late autumn or early spring when waters are still warm.

Hotel Poseidon (Via Ausonia 7, tel. 090/981-2876, www.hotelposeidonlipari.com, €100–150 s/d) is conveniently located 100 meters from the port and 50 meters from a bus stop that services Canneto and all the island's best beaches. Blue and white dominate the recently restructured villa that has preserved typical Aeolean finishings. The Sicilian theme continues inside the 18 rooms. Breakfast is served in the bright, airy bar, or outside on the terrace.

Surrounded by a large garden, the **Tritone** (Via Mendolita, tel. 090/981-1595, http://tritone.hotelsinsicily.it, €150–200 s/d) is a luxury four-star hotel. Each of the 38 rooms comes with a view of the sea. The highlight is the pool with naturally heated water. Portinente beach is 500 meters away but the beauty and fitness center is open all day if you prefer yoga.

Food

There are two historic restaurants in Lipari. One is **Filippino** (Piazza Mazzini, tel. 090/981-1002, summer daily noon–2:30 P.M. and 7 P.M.–midnight, winter Tues.–Sun. noon–2:30 P.M. and 7 P.M.–midnight), where the chefs wear white hats and have been specializing in fish since 1910. The ravioli and *mupa al sale* (fish cooked in salt) are absolute musts. The sesame desserts go perfectly with the Malvasia wine. For typical Aeolian cooking on a vine-covered terrace, **E Pulera** (Via Isabella Conti, tel. 090/981-1158, summer daily, winter Fri.–Sun.) is ideal. There are no weak links on the menu, which features fish balls made from pine nuts, olives, breadcrumbs, and swordfish.

Le Macine (Via Stradale 5, tel. 090/982-2387, Wed.–Mon., daily in summer 12:30–3 P.M. and 7–10:30 P.M., €7–11) is on the road to *terme di San Calogero,* an ancient therapeutic spa. The inside is decorated with farm objects and Tina and her son Emiliano prepare a surprising array of seafood platters. The buffet is the quickest way to fill your plate with stuffed zucchini and tuna tartare. House wine is courtesy of Giovanni, who can arrange free transport back to town if necessary.

Behind the curtains of the **Kasbah Café** (Via Maurolico 25, tel. 090/981-1075, daily 6 P.M.–3 A.M., €8–12) lies a citrus garden perfect for drinking an after-dinner cocktail. There are plenty of comfortable couches in this exotically decorated locale. For dinner, opt for a well-anointed pizza or three-course meal beginning with an antipasto buffet where grilled vegetables and marinated shellfish await.

Getting There and Around

The quickest way to the Aeolians is from the port of Milazzo, 20 minutes from Messina. In summer there are high-speed hovercraft and ferry departures every 30 minutes. **Ustica Lines** (www.usticalines.it) and **Siremar** (www.siremar.it) connect the islands and most boats make multiple stops around the archipelago.

There are two daily departures from Palermo to Salina, Alicudi, and Filicudi. A night ferry also leaves from Naples and stops in Salina and Alicudi only. Ferries also depart from Cefalù and Reggio Calabria. The ferry ride to these towns takes about six hours.

Lipari is the only Aeolian island you'd want to bring a car to, and a single sporadically paved road connects the seven small towns.

VULCANO

Although it's the closest to mainland Sicily, Vulcano has never attracted many settlers. Ancient civilizations were wary of active volcanoes and kept their distance. Today the island is inhabited primarily during the summer with young travelers looking for adventure and older ones hoping to soothe their aches in the therapeutic mud bath. The smell of sulfur is ever present, and although the last eruption was in 1888, the Gran Cratere that towers in the center of the island is still smoking.

Sights

Pozza dei Fanghi was created in the 1970s when tourism first kicked off. The little pond lies between **Porto di Levante,** where ferries dock, and **Porto di Ponente,** where bikinis lie on black sand. The water is 50 centimeters deep and remains 34°C all year long thanks to the volcanic activity deep underground. If you can resist the acrid odor, the water is said to benefit joints and skin.

Gran Cratere is good training for anyone with their sights set on Stromboli. It's a two-hour walk up a zigzag path that can be scaled with ease. The crater is 500 meters in diameter and 200 meters deep. A wet handkerchief is useful for protecting your nose and mouth from the stench that grows stronger the farther you climb. From the border of the crater there's a clear view of Vulcanello below and the island of Lipari.

Accommodations

All the Aeolians can be seen from the terrace of the **Therasia Resort** (Vulcanello, tel. 090/985-2555, www.therasiaresort.it, €220 d). This whitewashed hotel on the Vulcanello promontory was renovated using molten rock from Mount Etna, terra-cotta, and olive wood. The typical Mediterranean-style rooms are equipped with bathrooms finished in lava stone and multi-colored Sicilian tiles. It's one kilometer to the nearest beach and a minibus shuttles guests to and from the port.

Food

James Stevenson bought Vulcano in 1860. The Scottish entrepreneur extracted minerals and produced wine here until the eruption of 1888 rattled him. The memories of those days are alive at **Cantine Stevenson** (Porto di Levante, tel. 090/985-3247, summer daily noon–3 P.M. and 7 P.M.–1 A.M., €9–13). Today the old factory is a popular pub overlooking the port. Light dishes are accompanied by a refined list of wines and beers.

Da Vincenzino (Porto di Levante 25, tel. 090/985-2016, summer daily 12:30–3:30 P.M. and 7–11 P.M., €10–12) is a stone's throw from the sea and a splendid panorama can be admired from nearly every table on the large terrace. The menu of meat and fish dishes isn't bad either and the *tagliatelle alla vulcanara* (volcano pasta) should come with a warning for your tongue.

Getting There and Around

Vulcano is the closest island to Milazzo and 10 minutes by hydrofoil from Lipari. A bus from Porto di Levante links the town to Piano on the other side of the island and most people travel by bicycle or scooter, available in the port.

SALINA

Salina is in the center of the archipelago and the greenest of the bunch. **Monte Fossa delle Felci,** the highest mountain of any of Sicily's outlying islands, and **Monte dei Porri** capture humidity and allow grapes and capers to be grown in abundance. **Santa Marina** is the main port from where a tortuous road reaches the other towns on the island. The beach at **Pollara** is formed from an ancient crater. On the hillside above is the house where Massimo Troisi delivered mail in *Il Postino*. The island is popular with families and couples staying in the many romantic hideaways.

Sights

Salina was the first island to have a natural reserve. The **Riserva Naturale** was established back in 1981. In its center is 962-meter Monte Fossa delle Felci, which can be reached in a couple of hours of strenuous walking. There are 13 trails varying in difficulty and ranging 2–5 kilometers in length. Most are accessible from the road that circles the island. The reserve has over 400 types of plants, of which half are endemic to the island. Falcons circle the pines overhead looking for something good to eat.

Accommodations

Any hotel room that comes with a hammock on the terrace deserves an extra star. A few swings are all it takes to slow down and get into the Salina frame of mind. **Mamma Santina** (Via Sanità 26, tel. 090/984-3054, www.mammasantina.it, €180 d) is wonderful down to the doorknobs. The restaurant perpetuates the island's traditions by using ingredients from the garden out back. The hotel catamaran leaves every day at 10 A.M. for the coves around Salina or any of the nearby islands you and your fellow passengers choose to visit.

Tre Pini (tel. 090/980-9155, www.trepini.com, €6 pp) campground is near the village of **Rinella** surrounded by olive groves and umbrella pines. Each spot is well shaded and has electricity nearby. Days start with granita and brioche from the bar before deciding whether to climb up the volcano or take it easy and relax by the beach. Nights are spent near the piano congratulating the creativity of the barman.

Food

There's only one place to try *insalata di capperi* and if you've never tasted fresh capers before **Da Franco** (Via Belvedere, tel. 090/984-3287, daily noon–3 P.M. and 7–10:30 P.M., €8–11.50) is a must. This award-winning restaurant also turns out a *maccheroni* that never saw the inside of a box. The restaurant is open all year long. For a view and a massive selection of Malvasie wine, **Portobello** (Lungomare, tel. 090/9843-1525, 12:15–2:45 P.M. and 7–11 P.M., closed Nov.–Mar., €10–13) along the waterfront is an excellent choice. You can eat inside or out and taste a creative take on the local standards.

Getting There and Around

There are two daily departures from Palermo to Salina. Ustica Lines (tel. 09/2387-3813, www.usticalines.it) runs a Palermo to Alicudi, Salina, and Vulcano ferry service that takes 4.5–5 hours. Milazzo (40 kilometers west of Messina) is the main jump-off point to the islands; Ustica operates boats throughout the year. Hydrofoils take 1.3 hours to reach Salina while the ride on a ferry is about twice as long. The quicker option is from Milazzo onboard the Ustica or Miremar ferries that depart every half-hour and usually stop in Lipari before reaching Salina. Cars can be taken across, but mopeds are more suited to the small roads and can be rented directly from the port upon arrival.

PANAREA

Panarea is the smallest of the Aeolians—with barely 300 residents occupying three square kilometers. It was popular with artists and intellectuals in the 1970s and eventually attracted a trendier crowd that now regular descends upon the island. In August, maxi-yachts fill the **Cala Zimmari** and VIPs from all over the world rub shoulders inside the island's nightspots. Bottled water here costs more than anywhere else

in Sicily and it's best to come before or after the millionaires arrive.

San Pietro is the only port, where all the hotels, restaurants, and bars are concentrated. The entire town is Lilliputian in scale and nature has suffered little manmade damage. There are no banks, but there are a few ATMs for buying the next round of granita.

Sights

Punta Milazzese is the perfect spot to found a village and is exactly where Bronze Age settlers pitched their camp. The structures they built were circular and the foundations of 23 of these prehistoric homes can still be seen. Excavations have turned up amulets, cooking utensils, and vases that have helped date the site. The promontory is a 30-minute walk from San Pietro along a beautiful path. At **Drauto** you might be tempted to forget the ancient village and descend to the magnificent beach below. Panarea isn't particularly blessed with beaches and what does exist is very rocky except for Cala Zimmari. **Club Alpino Italiano** has marked a trail in red from the port to Punta Corvo, the highest peak on the island. It's 420 meters to the top but you do get a view of the entire archipelago for the endeavor.

Entertainment

Panarea is hands down the most fashionable of the islands. Jet-setters go yacht-hopping from party to party and everyone else enjoys the innumerable happy hours on dry land. One of the trendiest of these is held at the ex-bridge club now known as the **Bridge Sushi Bar** (Via Porto, tel. 339/217-2605, 1–3:30 P.M. and 7 P.M.–1 A.M., admission free). There's a fabulous view from the terrace and this is the only chance you'll get to satisfy a craving for teriyaki. Nights usually end at **Nirvana** (Contrada San Pietro, tel. 090/983-014, 7 P.M.–2 A.M., €10) or the **Raya** (Punta Peppe e Maria, tel. 09/098-3013, 10 P.M.–5 A.M., €10), where paparazzi stake out film stars and wealthy players get their kicks sipping champagne cocktails and listening to Café del Mare remixed by international DJs flown in for the occasion.

Sports and Recreation

The waters around Panarea never stop bubbling and sometimes it looks like the sea is boiling. There are dozens of small rock formations on the eastern side of the island and **Amphibia** (Via San Pietro, tel. 06/592-4692 or tel. 335/124-5332, silvia@amphibia.it) takes divers down to explore craters, some of which are 30 meters deep. Underneath the miniature islands of Dattilo and Lisca Bianca are remains of Roman walls that confirm the island was once much larger. They also have a diving center in Salina and organize trips across the Aeolians according to your interests.

Accommodations

Hotel Oasi (Via San Pietro, tel. 090/983-032, www.dapina.com, €140 d) is a friendly three-star hotel with 11 rooms five minutes from the port. Each of the uniquely decorated doubles comes with air-conditioning, minibar, and TV,. Outside there's a geothermal pool, two restaurants, and a small supermarket. You can rent scooters and electric golf carts directly from the hotel.

Raya (Via San Pietro 1, tel. 090/983-013, www.hotelraya.it, €285 d) is not a typical hotel. There are no TVs, elevators, parking, or anything that might distract a guest from nature. It's more like an oasis where every room has a view. Owner Myriam Belrami is attentive to the impact the hotel has on the environment and strives for the smallest footprint possible. The restaurant uses simple Mediterranean cooking methods to conjure extraordinary flavors.

Food

A desire for meat can strike even on an island and fortunately **Da Antonio il Macellaio** (Via San Pietro, tel. 090/983-033, daily 8 A.M.–1 P.M. and 5–7:30 P.M., €8–11) is waiting for you. The owner lived in Argentina and learned the secrets of grilling a good steak. Meatballs may sound mundane but these are spiced to perfection. Chicken is roasted slowly on an open flame and basted until the skin crackles.

For local recipes eaten under the stars, there's **La Nicchia** (Corso da Scauri Basso, tel. 092/391-6342, Mar.–Nov., daily 7–11:30 P.M., €10–12). The Arab garden is an especially romantic way to cap an evening and get a healthy dose of fish. Reservations are almost always necessary and you should wear something nice if you don't want to stand out.

Getting There and Around

Cars aren't allowed on the island, but there are a few electric taxis shuttling visitors from port to hotel to bar and back again. The island's crystal-clear waters can be circled in under an hour and **Nautilus** (Via Drautto, tel. 090/983-074, www.panarea.com) rents small and medium-size boats that don't need a license to captain.

STROMBOLI

Stromboli isn't for the casual tourist. There are no palm trees here, just one immense volcano that lets out a good rumble nearly every hour. Houses are mostly white, and are cube-shaped in order to resist the periodic rumblings. **Iddu**, as local residents call their volcano, is the most active volcano in Europe and is one of five perennially active volcanoes in the world. The last major eruption was in March 2007 when many full-time residents decided it was time to pack their bags. Once the lava had cooled, however, they returned. Once adventurous visitors have experienced climbing the volcano they may find it is hard to leave the island.

Sights

Active volcanoes should always be approached with caution. Since the last eruption, the civil protection agency has limited solo expeditions to 290 meters up the mountain. They recommend hiking boots, extra water, a flashlight, and windbreaker. Wearing contact lenses is discouraged. If you want to get any closer, you'll need to hire a professional guide from **Magmatrek** (Via Vittorio Emanuele, tel. 090/986-5768) or the **Ufficio Guide** (Piazza San Vincenzo, tel. 090/986-211). A trek up lasts three hours and vegetation changes as the altitude does. Groups generally leave in the afternoon and are required to return by midnight. Spending the night on the mountain is not permitted. You can get a good look and excellent photos from the observation deck.

Accommodations

Il Giardino Segreto (Via Francesco Natoli, tel. 090/986-211, www.giardinosegretobb.it, €120) is high on the hillside with excellent views of Stromboli and Iddu from the panoramic terrace. The owners of this small bed-and-breakfast enjoy gardening and have cultivated quite a bit of land around the house. Fresh fruit at breakfast comes from the nearby trees. Rooms all have their own particular character; *Cisternino,* with its cast-iron bed and garden entrance, may be the best of the lot.

Ossidiana (Via Marina 18, tel. 090/986-006, www.hotelossidiana.it, €170) is the only hotel open year-round on the island. The three-story elegant whitewashed building is near the port and in front of the beach. Rooms are decorated in natural wood and guests can choose between a view of the sea or the volcano. Breakfast buffet is included in the price and served in the bright dining room on the ground floor.

Food

The fish is always fresh at **Punta Lena** (Via Marina 8, tel. 090/986-204, Apr.– Oct. daily 12:30–3 P.M. and 7–10:30 P.M., closed Nov.–Mar., €8–12) but if chef Stefano's grilled sea bass and shrimp aren't enough, then keep in mind that everything is served under a shaded arbor with splendid views of the sea. It's also a good chance to see an old Aeolian house from the inside and get your fork around a plate of *spaghetti stromboliani.*

La Tartana (Via Marina, Ficogrande, tel. 090/986-025, May–Oct. daily 12:30–2:30 P.M. and 7:30–11 P.M., closed Nov.–Apr., €26) proves that chic does exist in Stromboli. This elegant restaurant has more silverware than usual laid out on carefully set tables and a prix-fixe menu that provides a taste of all the island's favorites, including *cernia* (grouper) grilled in lemon leaves.

Getting There and Around

Boats and hydrofoils dock at Scari near the black beaches and countless sailboats. Cars aren't allowed so if you want to move you'll have to walk or rent some wheels. **Sabbia Nera** (Via D. Cincotta, tel. 09/098-6390, www.sabbianerastromboli.com) rents bicycles, scooters, and runs guided tours of the volcano and lava slope on foot or by helicopter. The office is 50 meters from the disembarkation point on the left and is open from 7 A.M.–11 P.M. in the summer.

Ionian Coast

The real show stopper on Sicily's Ionian Coast is Mount Etna, which is visible from hundreds of kilometers in every direction and can be circled by car or train from Catania. Some of the region's best beaches are nearby the mountain which are fairly crowded during the summer and the widest stretch of sand is just outside of Taormina. Highway A18 ends abruptly just south of Catania after which single-lane roads skirt the coast and the flatlands toward Syracuse.

MESSINA

Messina is the 13th-largest city in Italy, which may explain the frequent bouts of bad luck. The town suffered a seaquake in 1908 and was heavily bombed in 1943. Misfortune isn't new as the inscription on the column at the entrance to the port indicates. According to legend the Virgin Mary sent a letter blessing the city after yet another catastrophe. Nevertheless, there's a certain thrill in landing here and feeling Sicily under your feet for the first time.

Sights

The **Duomo** may look new but it's actually been rebuilt twice. Only the portal is original. **Al Campanile** (Piazza del Duomo, tel. 090/675-175, daily 9 A.M.–1 P.M. and 4:30–7 P.M., €3.50) on the side is one of the tallest mechanical clocks in the world and looks like it would be at home in Munich or Prague. If you're around at midday or midnight you'll a see the automats recounting biblical stories. Facing the church is **Fontana di Orione,** constructed in 1547 to celebrate the building of the city's first aqueduct. It miraculously survived repeated bombing during World War II.

Museo Regionale (Viale della Libertà 465, tel. 090/361-292, Mon. and Fri. 9 A.M.–1:30 P.M., Tues., Thurs., and Sat. 9 A.M.–1:30 P.M. and 4–6:30 P.M., Sun. 9 A.M.–12:30 P.M., €5) is accessed through a garden filled with sculptures, including one of Neptune recovered from a building that collapsed during the earthquake. A dozen rooms contain several triptychs of the Sienese school, works by the city's native son Antonello da Messina, and two paintings by Caravaggio completed in 1608 and 1609 when the artist was on the run. **Acquario Comunale** (Villa Mazzini, Piazza Unità d'Italia, tel. 090/48897, Sun.–Thurs. 9:30 A.M.–12:30 P.M., Fri. 4–7 P.M., admission free) is on the way to the museum and numbers 22 tanks with 100 species of Mediterranean fish. It's a good preview for scuba divers and something fun for children.

Shopping

Along the ancient artery of the *corso,* **Fabbro dell'Oro** (Corso Cavour 72, tel. 090/662-200) stands out for the original gold and silver creations displayed in the window. The unique pieces are all based on ancient Egyptian, Greek, and Etruscan designs that are generally only found inside museums. Old and new stones are used.

Accommodations

Situated near the train station and ferry terminal, the **NH Liberty** (Via I Settembre 15, tel. 090/640-9436, www.framonhotels.com, €102 d)

hasn't lost its character since the recent renovation brought it up a notch or two in style. It's popular with business travelers and tourists who relax at the bar on the roof terrace after a day of sightseeing. All rooms are non-smoking and reception can arrange car rental upon request.

Food

Al Padrino (Via Santa Cecilia 54–56, tel. 090/292-1000, Mon.–Sat. noon–3 P.M. and 7:15–10:45 P.M., €7–10) is popular with locals who work in the area and occupy the 12 tables at lunchtime. Pietro Denaro greets them with his ironic humor and has a joke each time he delivers a plate to his amused customers. Don't worry if none of it makes sense, as he's equally funny in English and the *pasta con ceci* (pasta with chickpeas) is really all you need to understand. The meat shish kebab is good if you're tired of fish and the house wine helps wash everything down.

For something sweet, try the *bignè fritti* (deep-fried pastry with cream) or *torroncini* (milk chocolate with hazelnuts) at **Antica Pasticceria Irrera** (Piazza Cairoli 12, tel. 090/673-823, daily 7 A.M.–7 P.M.), where the waiters wear bow ties and the selection of pastries is endless. If granita is more your thing, give the ones next door at **Bar Billè** (Piazza Cairoli 7, tel. 09/071-8311, daily 9 A.M.–9 P.M.) a taste and enjoy your treat at one of the tables overlooking the piazza.

Getting There and Around

Until the controversial bridge connecting Messina with the continent is built, the best way to cross the strait is by ferry. The journey from Reggio Calabria takes 30 minutes with **Tirrenia** (www.tirrenia.com) or any of the other companies that regularly make the trip. Cars can be taken onboard and special boats are used for shuttling trains across.

TAORMINA

Taormina is Sicily's most famous destination and has been on the tourist trail since Kaiser William raved about the town in 1896. D. H. Lawrence and Oscar Wilde publicized

SICILY

the sandy beaches and ancient remains with their pens and it was only a matter of time before the masses arrived. From April to September, the town is bloated with visitors yet the ancient Greek theater and narrow lanes of the medieval center is a must for anyone on the modern grand tour.

Sights
TEATRO GRECO

The horseshoe-shaped Teatro Greco (tel. 094/223-220, 9 A.M. until 2 hrs. before sunset, €2) was built in the 3rd century B.C. and does not disappoint. It uses the natural contours of the hill and was later transformed by the Romans to stage gladiatorial contests. Climb to the last row to get the best view of Mount Etna and the Ionian coast. Today seats are filled in the summer with people enjoying music, cinema, and theater.

Festivals and Events
(TAORMINA ARTE FESTIVAL

Teatro Greco isn't just an ancient site; it's still used as the Greeks once intended. Every summer (June–Aug.), Taormina Arte Festival (Corso Umberto 19, tel. 094/221-142, www.taormina-arte.com) invites international stars to perform here. Past guests have included Caetano Veloso, Bob Dylan, Goran Bregovic, and Diana Ross. Audiences can also listen to classical and opera performed by the world's premier musicians. WOMAD in Taormina is a parenthesis within the festival in mid-July dedicated to three days of ethnic music from around the globe.

Accommodations

Many villas in or near Taormina have been converted into hotels and provide an idea of how 18th-century aristocrats once lived. **(Villa Carlotta** (Via Pirandello 81, tel. 094/262-6058, €150 d) hasn't lost any of its splendor, and the Quartucci family has worked hard to make sure each of the four stars is deserved. All 27 rooms have a wonderful view of the sea and cherrywood antiques purchased from local fairs. You'll want to take your shoes off when you see the terra-cotta and lava floors typical of Sicilian houses. If you're traveling

Taormina's Teatro Greco with Mount Etna in the background

with small pets, they'll be welcome as long as they stay out of the pool.

You don't have to leave your room at the **Villa Ducale** (Via Leonardo da Vinci 60, tel. 094/22815-328154, www.villaducale.com, €170 d) to admire the panorama that Goethe called paradise. Just step out onto the private terrace. The hotel successfully combines traditions like wrought-iron beds and modern amenities like Wi-Fi. Although the hotel is refined, the staff are never stuffy and friendliness is preferred over formality. Parking is free and the center of town is easily reached on foot.

Food

◖ **Al Duomo** (Vicolo Ebrei 11, tel. 094/262-5656, Thurs.–Tues. noon–2:30 P.M. and 7–10:30 P.M., €8–11) is as magical as the town that surrounds it. The bright dining room filled with colorful chairs makes a good first impression that lasts throughout the meal. Flaviani Ferri has been serving traditional recipes from the region for the last 10 years and taken hundreds of photos of happy diners enjoying *insalata di stocco* (fish salad) and *pasta col novellame* (fish pasta) inside at on the little piazza flanking the cathedral of San Niccolò.

A'Zammàra (Via Fratelli Bandiera 13–15, tel. 094/224-408, www.zammara.it, Thurs.–Tues. 12:30–3 P.M. and 7–11 P.M., €7–10) is the rustic option surrounded by a splendid orange garden. None of the ingredients have traveled more than 100 kilometers and the *antipasto rustico* can easily feeds two. The meatballs and fish are all good but the almond and chocolate desserts are what leave the most pleasant aftertaste.

Pietro d'Agostino is a chef on the rise and his reputation has grown ever since he opened **La Capinera** (Via Nazionale 177, tel. 094/262-6247, Tues.–Sun., €9–12). Most of the tables are on the terrace and you may not want to sit face-to-face with a view this good. Traditional dishes have been shaken up and stirred in new ways—from the breads served irresistibly hot all the way to the chocolates waiting to cap a meal. Wine is a problem. There are over 800 labels and if you find one you like, you'll want to write down the name. It's possible to buy the same bottle, as well as many pistachio-based specialties, at **La Torinese** (Corso Umberto 59, tel. 094/223-321, daily 9:30 A.M.–1 P.M. and 4–8 P.M.).

They serve 18 flavors of granita at **Bam Bar** (Via Di Giovanni, tel. 094/224-355, Wed.–Mon. 8:30 A.M.–midnight), including fig, peach, and the classic almond that usually calls for seconds. **Wunderbar** (Piazza IX Aprile 7, tel. 094/262-5302, Wed.–Mon. 8:30 A.M.–2 A.M., closed Jan. 15–Mar. 1) is the place to take a load off and breathe in the history. The salon inside is full of elegant fixtures. You can choose which pastry you want at the bar, or wait to be served on the large terrace where Liz Taylor and Richard Burton once sat drinking cocktails.

Getting There and Around

It takes 30 minutes to reach Taormina by car from Messina or Catania. The exit is clearly indicated off the A18 highway. Finding parking is a game of roulette in the summer, but start by trying the two parking silos at the north and south ends of town. Otherwise, leave the car in Mazzarò and take the cableway up.

The train station is both practical and beautiful. It's four kilometers from town and there's regular service from across the island as well as from Milan, Rome, and Naples. Taxis and buses are outside. There's also a modern bus terminal just outside the walls and **Interbus** (tel. 094/262-5301, www.interbus.it) connects the city with Palermo, Catania (including the airport), and Messina.

All of the inner town can be reached on foot, but **public buses** (www.taorminaservizipubblici. it) do run in the center and outlying areas. A ticket costs €0.50 and **linea beachbus** (€1) runs along the shore. The cableway (daily 8 A.M.–1 A.M. in summer) is just plain fun and the fastest way of reaching the beach from town or vice versa. It's on Via Pirandello just outside Porta Messina and drops passengers off in Mazzarò, from where the beaches of Isolabella, Spisone, and Mazzeo can be reached on foot. One-way is €1.80, round-trip €3, and if you'll be in Taormina for a while you can get 14 tickets for €20.

© LAURIE ELIE

Mount Etna is Europe's most active volcano.

◀ MOUNT ETNA

It's no wonder the Romans thought the God of fire worked inside Mount Etna. It's the highest (3,323 m) and most active volcano in Europe. That activity has been great for the soil, and everything grown on the hillside and nearby plains has a unique flavor. A pistachio or olive here is unlike anything on the mainland.

Parco Regionale dell'Etna covers a territory of 60,000 hectares around the volcano. It's possible to make it almost to the pinnacle of Etna and in the winter you can experience the emotion of skiing with a view of the sea. The mountain is in fact covered with snow for many months and has become the most renowned winter sports center in Sicily. You don't need to be a super athlete to enjoy the mountain, and there are valleys, canyons, and lava fields for every level of hiker.

Sights

The volcano can be approached from the north or the south, with each approach revealing strikingly different landscapes. Scenery is never

the same as the **great gorge** and **new mouth** craters that are continually altering the mountainside. It's a good idea to contact the visitors center before planning an excursion. Hikers are advised to wear heavy clothing and rugged hiking boots when climbing the mountain.

Linguaglossa is the main departure point from the north and **Gruppo Guide Alpine Etna Nord** (Piazza Santa Catarina 24, tel. 095/647-833) organizes daily Jeep excursions (€35) to the new observatory with views of smoking lava pits. Upon request, guides can organize alpine skiing, trekking, and visits to the volcanic grottoes dotting the side of the mountain.

You can get even closer to the top from the south. **Nicolosi** is the main departure point. Serious volcanologists or anyone with a love of lava will appreciate the displays inside the **Museo Vulcanologico dell'Etna** (Nicolosi, Via C. Battisti 28, tel. 095/791-4589, Tues.–Sun. 9:30 A.M.–12:30 P.M.), which provides a geologic introduction to the mountain. **Gruppo Guide Alpine Etna Sud** (Via Etnea 49, tel. 095/791-4755) takes small groups to the top on foot or on 4x4 excursions that last two hours. Itineraries vary depending on the conditions but generally include a stop at the **Rifugio Sapienza** (1,900 m) and the **Silvestri** crater formed in 1892. From here there is a cableway that takes visitors even farther up. It was near here that the Greek philosopher Empedocle conducted the first scientific observations of the mountain.

Festivals and Events

All the small towns surrounding Etna have something different to offer and are famous for their produce. The town of Bronte hosts the **Sagra del Pistacchio** (tel. 095/774-7213, www.comune.bronte.ct.it) at the end of September with a chance to taste the famed Bronte pistachios. Streets are filled with stalls selling all sorts of derivatives of this tasty nut. Zafferana Etnea on the eastern side of the volcano—a good base for both winter and summer excursions up Mount Etna—celebrates **Ottobrata** (www.zafferana-etnea.it) every Sunday in October; honey, grapes, mushrooms, and hazelnuts are freely distributed to visitors. Tourists from all over the world turn up to participate in the 10 highly animated days of **Carnevale di Acireale** (www.carnevalediacireale.it). Festivities include street poets reciting in Sicilian dialects, popular games, gastronomic competitions, and music from dusk until dawn. The event terminates on Tuesday night with a huge bonfire.

Sports and Recreation

If you slice badly at the **Il Picciolo Golf Club** (Castiglione di Sicilia, tel. 094/298-6252, www.ilpicciologolf.com), your ball risks ending up in an ancient lava flow. This 18-hole course is unforgettable and it's difficult not to let Etna and the forests distract you from your game. The resort also includes a luxury hotel.

Accommodations

Brunek (Etna North, Bosco Ragabo, Via Mareneve, tel. 095/643-015, €52 d) is a Swiss-like chalet with small comfortable rooms and a restaurant serving mushroom-based dishes.

It's convenient for motorcyclists. Credit cards are not accepted.

Rifugio Sapienza (Etna South, Nicolosi, Piazzale Funivia dell'Etna, tel. 095/915-321, €98 d) is a small hotel near the cableway run by the Club Alpino Italiano. The hot chocolate they serve is reinvigorating after a day skiing or walking the slopes. The 24 rooms fill up fast, so it's best to book early if you want to stay near the top.

Food

Walking up Etna is the surest way to build an appetite, and **Ristorante Antico Orto dei Limoni** (Via Grotte 4, tel. 095/910-808, Wed.–Mon. noon–2 P.M. and 8–11:30 P.M., €8–11) is a welcome sight. The interior of this former farm is covered in lava decorations. The small dining room is full of instruments for making oil, and the flavors served are purely Sicilian.

Information and Services

Ente Parco dell'Etna (Nicolosi, Via del Convento 45, tel. 095/821-111, www.parcoetna.it) is the main visitors center and provides good maps, the latest geological forecasts, and a list of all the registered guides in the area. There is also an information office in Linguaglossa (Piazza Annunziata 7, tel. 095/643-094) and Zafferana Etnea (Piazza Luigi Sturzo 3, tel. 095/708-2825).

Getting There and Around

Catania is the closest airport to Etna and if you sit on the right side of the plane you'll get a great view of the volcano. The mountain can be reached from the A18 or A19 highways and a series of scenic roads, including the N284 and N120, circle the park.

Etna is hard to miss and can be entirely circled by car. The most scenic route around the mountain, however, is onboard the **Circumetnea Railway** (tel. 095/541-250, www.circumnetnea.it, Mon.–Sat. 6 A.M.–9 P.M., €3.10) that leaves from Catania Borgo or Stazione di Giarre near the Catania Stazione Centrale and is convenient for anyone arriving from Taormina. The train has been running since 1859 and circumnavigates the base of the volcano. It's a 114-kilometer ride through olive groves and cultivated fields that offer a different angle of the mountain around every curve. On Sundays, **Associazione Strada del Vino dell'Etna** (tel. 899/908-069) organizes wine-tasting tours of the areas wineries onboard a vintage 1937 diesel engine.

CATANIA

Etna has been a blessing and a curse for Catania. The city was completely destroyed during the eruption of 1693 and subsequently rebuilt using solidified lava and a new urban plan with wider streets and large piazzas to permit escape should the mountain strike again. Baroque was the fashion of the day and a walk down **Via dei Crociferi** reveals the best examples of the movement.

Catania is one of the hottest cities in Sicily and temperatures can rise to 40°C during the summer. If you are visiting in summer, avoid walking around at midday.

Sights

Piazza del Duomo is the center of the city and Baroque is everywhere—from **Fontana dell'Elefante,** constructed in black lava, to **Palazzo Senatorio,** which houses the municipality. The **Duomo** is dedicated to Saint Agata, the patron saint of the city, who may have neglected her duties during several earthquakes and eruptions. Several blocks west are the oldest remains. **Teatro Romano** (Via Vittorio Emanuele, tel. 095/715-0508, daily 9 A.M.–1:30 P.M. and 3–5 P.M., €3) lies on top of a Greek theater and is the third largest after the Colosseum in Rome and Arena in Verona. **Teatro Odeon** immediately adjacent is the only example of the enclosed theaters once used by Romans to stage music and dance.

Entertainment and Events

Nightlife enthusiasts have a habit of gathering between the Baroque monuments on Via Crocifera. There are a number of bars and pubs populated by students and **Nievsky** (Scalinata Alessi 15/17, tel. 095/313-792, Tues.–Sun.

6 P.M.–1 A.M.) is the epicenter of happy hour. Grab one of their lemon or orange cocktails and have a seat on the steps leading to Chiesa di San Benedetto. On weekends it's packed and the lively atmosphere continues all the way to Piazza Asmundo around the corner.

Accommodations

Catania Centro (Viale Regina Margherita 2d, tel. 095/716-4085, www.hotelcataniacentro. it, €90 d) is at the crossroads of Via Etnea and Viale Regina Margherita, from where both new and old parts of the city are easily accessible. The hotel occupies one wing of an 18th-century palazzo and provides comfortable rooms on the first floor. The sober style is lightened by staff who enjoy helping guests discover their city. Parking is available upon request.

Food

To spend more time in Piazza Duomo, just enter **Ambasciata del Mare** (Piazza Duomo 6, tel. 095/341-003, Tues.–Sun. noon–2:30 P.M. and 7–10:30 P.M., closed September, €8–12). Valestro and Ciro run the dining room, while Francesco governs the kitchen. Fish is the main attraction here and if you want to try a little of everything order the *antipasto della casa* as a starter. Pasta with tuna *ragù* is made fresh every day, as are the tarts and cannoli on offer for dessert.

The atmosphere at **Osteria Antica Marina** (Via Pardo 29, tel. 095/348/197, Thurs.–Tues. noon–2:30 P.M. and 7–10:30 P.M., €8–10) hasn't changed. It's still lively and popular with neighborhood residents who fill the two rooms covered with black-and-white photographs illustrating how the neighborhood once looked. Ingredients come from the covered fish market next door, which remains one of the most authentic parts of the city. The grilled fish platter is delicious and the fish soup is a meal in itself. Lemon- or almond-flavored sorbet is what waiters recommend for dessert.

For something refreshing, try the kiosk in **Piazza Spirito Santo** selling different ice-cold syrup-flavored drinks. The lemonade here can cool you down even on the hottest days and is served with a dash of seltzer water.

Getting There and Around

Catania is midway down the Ionian coast. **Aeroporto Fontanarossa di Catania** (www. aeroporto.catania.it) is the second-largest airport on the island and Alitalia and other airlines connect the city with mainland Italy and Europe. It's possible to catch an **AST** (tel. 095/723-051, www.aziendasicilianatrasporti. it) bus from the arrivals terminal and get to the center or head to other destinations along the coast. There is frequent train service from Messina and Taormina and **TTT Lines** (tel. 095/746-2187, www.tttlines.it) operates a ferry from Naples.

The streets may have been widened after the earthquake but they still aren't large enough for all the traffic. There are five parking lots around Piazza Repubblica, from which the old town is less than 15 minutes away.

SYRACUSE

Syracuse was a colonial success story. Founded by Corinthian Greeks in the 8th century B.C., the town soon fell under the control of tyrants who enriched the city and eventually managed to defeat Athens. The walls of the city were 22 kilometers long and it took a six-month siege for the Romans to capture the city. Today all that remains from the glory days are the old entrance and a temple on the **Isola di Ortigia** among a labyrinth of medieval and Baroque palazzi.

Sights

A few hundred yards from the bridge leading to Isola di Ortigia are **Porta Urbica** and **Tempio di Apollo.** Porta Urbica is the last sign of the Greek fortifications that once surrounded the island. The temple is within a small park and is the oldest Doric building in Sicily. All that remains are four steps leading to the entrance, two entire columns, and several others that have suffered the wear and tear of time. There's a daily market nearby in **Piazza Cesare Battisti** with fish still gasping for air and tuna so big it takes a saw to slice a piece off. **Piazza Duomo** is down Corso Matteotti and contains the Baroque masterpieces of the city. The Duomo began as a temple dedi-

The Greeks carved Syracuse's Teatro Greco into the hillside.

cated to Athena. The columns were incorporated into the Byzantine church and are best observed from Via Minerva. It had a brief stint as a mosque, and after the devastating earthquake of 1693 Andrea Palma added the current Baroque facade.

The largest ruins can be found in the **Parco Archeologico della Neapolis** (Via Paradiso or Via Rizzo, tel. 093/148-1111, daily 9 A.M.–6:30 P.M., €6). The park provides a pleasant walk under cypress and pine, especially if you can avoid the tour groups that tend to arrive in the mornings. **Teatro Greco** was built into the hillside and divided into nine sections with 46 rows each. It's the biggest Greek theater in Italy and was given new life in 1914 with the inauguration of the festival del'Inda. The **Roman amphitheater** was also carved from the rock and is where gladiators fought each other and the wild animals imported from Africa. Nearby is the manmade cave of **Orecchio di Dionisio,** formed by the extraction of stone over the centuries. It's 23 meters high and 65 meters long, with some wonderful acoustics.

Entertainment

Few people aspire to be puppet masters these days and if they do it's generally because the profession runs in their family. That's the case with the Mauceri brothers, related to the great Alfredo Vaccaro—who made more children smile than Santa Claus. The young Siracusans decided they wanted to follow in their uncle's footsteps and opened **Il Piccolo Teatro dei Pupi** (Via della Giudecca 17, tel. 093/146-5540) in 2003. There are barely 35 seats in this little gem of a theater where a classic *paladini* repertoire is regularly staged. The brothers never tire of pulling the strings and bringing the puppets to life, and they created many of the wooden stars themselves.

Shopping

Where Greeks settled there was writing and where there was writing 2,500 years ago there was papyrus. It was the computer of its day and allowed records of all kinds to be kept: a very useful thing when you were sailing to distant and sometimes unknown parts.

Papyrus stalks are still growing near the Fountain of Aretusa, where the first Greeks set foot. They couldn't pass up a natural spring that runs during a drought and Nelson couldn't resist a drink before his rendezvous with Napoleon. Papyrus is also on sale inside **Galleria Bellomi** (Via Capodieci 15, tel. 093/161-340, daily 9 A.M.–1 P.M. and 3–7 P.M.). Flavio Massara creates souvenirs from the thick paste he dries into sheets using a technique described by Pliny the Elder. It can be easily rolled and is something future generations will surely wonder about.

The unexpected is waiting at **Bazar delle Cose Vecchie** (Via Consiglio Regionale 7/30/40, tel. 093/124-191, daily 9 A.M.–12:30 P.M. and 2:30–7 P.M.). The bric-a-brac count is high and there are hundreds of dusty collectables. It's actually three stores crammed with Sicilian ceramics, hanging oil lamps, puppets, coral jewelry, and walking canes that Snoop Dogg would love.

TYRANTS AND THINKERS

The Greeks may have invented democracy, but they were also pretty good at dictatorship. Many cities, like Syracuse, fell under the control of tyrants whose personal whims became law. **Dionisio il Vecchio** (405-367 B.C.) was the most famous ruler during this period and was extremely distrustful. He spent most of the time safe in his castle on the island of Ortiga, wore armor under his clothes, and changed bedrooms every night. Plato visited Syracuse to study the reign of Dionisio but was kicked out of the city after a couple of weeks.

A more intellectual native of Syracuse was **Archimade**, born in 287 B.C. and often so distracted with his calculations that he forgot to eat and drink. According to legend he discovered the theory that carries his name while in his bathtub and ran around the city half-naked yelling *"Eureka!"* ("I found it!"). During the Roman siege of the city, he devised a mirror for burning enemy ships. When the Romans finally entered Syracuse he was surprised in his workshop by a legionnaire and killed.

Accommodations

[**Palazzo del Sale** (Via Santa Teresa 25, tel. 093/165-958, www.palazzodelsale.com, €80 d) once belonged to a salt merchant back when salt was a good investment. He could afford a palazzo with all the trimmings and now you can sleep inside his mansion. There are six rooms to choose from and not a bad one in the bunch. Stone walls and wood beams are exposed and furniture is many times older than the young, energetic guests. Breakfast on the terrace overlooking Isole di Ortigia is all the inspiration needed to start the day.

If design matters and you prefer pillowcases to match the color of the walls then only **Caol Ishka** (Pantanelli, Via Elorina 154, tel. 093/316-9057, www.caolishka.com, €190 d) will do. This small 10-room hotel on the shore of the Anapo River is proof that boutique hotels exist in Syracuse. Everything is comfortable and relaxing to the eyes. You can wind down or begin the day with a swim. Fish, meat, and vegetarian dishes are available at the restaurant. A hydro-taxi brings guests to town in five minutes.

Food
If the tomatoes taste better in Syracuse it's because they're near the source. Less than 30 kilometers away is Pachino, which is visible from space. The place is vine-to-vine tomatoes inside hundreds of football field–length nurseries.

To get an idea of how these tomatoes might taste with *lumache* (snails), give **Da Mariano** (Vicolo Zuccolà 9, tel. 093/167-444, Wed.–Mon. 12:15–3:15 P.M. and 7:15–11:15 P.M., €6.50–9) a try. If you've never tasted snails, then it's time you mustered the courage. Besides, Paolo serves lots of other delicious things and the view is too good to pass up.

Getting There and Around
Syracuse is in the extreme southeast of the island 60 kilometers from Catania. From Taormina, take the A18 then the SS114 south until you reach the city. It's about four hours by car from Palermo on the A19 followed by the SS114. Train service (trenitalia, tel. 892-021) from Catania and Taormina departs every hour and requires a transfer from Palermo. There's a night train from Rome that takes 12 hours.

Around Syracuse
Riserva Naturale Orientata Oasi Faunistica di Vendicari is a must for bird-watchers. The nature reserve also boasts rocky coasts and peaceful marshes. Information about the park is available from the tourist office in Syracuse (Via Maestranza 33, tel. 093/146-2452).

NOTO
The year 1693 was difficult for towns in southeast Sicily, and none suffered more than Noto. The earthquake flattened everything and prospects of rebuilding were so bad that officials decided to start over on a hill 10 kilometers away. The stone they used was white tufo and the style was Baroque. The lower town is the religious center, where you'll find the most churches, and Corso Vittorio Emanuele and Via Corso run east to west past the Duomo and other churches turned golden brown by the sun.

Sights
Piazza Mercato and the **Duomo** form the center of the reconstructed town and the grid pattern that was followed is dotted with Baroque palazzi. The style is unlike other towns in the area and reflects the personal tastes of the guild workers who rebuilt the town.

The Duomo was completed in 1770 and suffered a second mishap when the dome collapsed in 1996. It was a wake-up call for local officials, who realized much of Noto was in need of restoration. Scaffolding has been a common sight ever since. The facades of **Palazzo Villadorata** on Via Nicolaci (with balconies supported by lions) and the concave surface of **Montevergine,** on the same street, have benefited from the added attention. A small library with the original plans of the reconstruction are housed inside the Palazzo Villadorata.

Entertainment and Events
There's nothing like listening to Baroque music surrounded by Baroque architecture and that's the whole idea behind **Magie Barocche** (July–Sept., tel. 093/157-3779, www.magiebarocche.com). The festival takes place simultaneously in all eight towns in the Noto Valley. Concerts are outdoors and in Noto the main stage is set up in front of Palazzo Ducezio. A more olfactory event is the **Infiorata di Noto** on the third Sunday in May, when the steep streets are covered in designs made from petals. For information, contact the tourist office in Piazza Municipio (tel. 093/183-5201, www.comune.noto.sr.it or www.infioratadinoto.it).

Teatro Comunale Vittorio Emanuele III (Piazza XVI Maggio, tel. 093/183-5073) is the cultural heart of town and organizes music and dance events throughout the year. The theater deserves a visit even when the curtain is down to see the frescoes and the rows of box seats adorned in gold and red. During the summer concerts are held outdoors.

Accommodations
Terra di Solimano (Contrada Busulmone, tel. 093/183-6606, www.terradisolimano.it, €35 pp) is a couple of kilometers outside of Noto on a working farm that sells the olive oil and marmalade produced from the trees nearby. The six double rooms all have entrances on a cobblestoned courtyard and the dining hall consists of long tables where travelers exchange stories. Meals are entirely based on Sicilian food and are reasonably priced. Mountains bikes can be rented and cycling to town only takes 10 minutes.

Food
Ⓒ Trattoria del Crocifisso da Baglieri (Via Principe Umberto 46–48, tel. 093/157-1151, Thurs.–Tues. 12:30–3 P.M. and 7:30–10:30 P.M., €7–9) in the upper town is one of the best places to satisfy your appetite. The interior decoration lacks the fantasy of the Baroque outside, but once you've sampled Mamma Corradina's dishes the starkness won't matter. A good start is the *antipasto rustico*, served in many trattorias in the area. This version comes with potato meatballs, fried onions and peppers, grilled vegetables, olives, and sun-dried tomatoes. The bread is dark and you shouldn't be embarrassed to use it to soak up the sauces on your plate. That's what locals call *scarpetta* and generally ingratiates you with whoever is doing the cooking. The odd shape of the pasta is a sign it hasn't come from a box and the ravioli and *spaghetti sarde* are equally tempting. For a traditional dessert, order the *'nfigghiulata* made from ricotta and a glass of limoncello to wash it all down.

If you can't get a table at Trattoria del Crocifisso da Baglieri, **Trattoria del Carmine** (Via Ducezzio 1, tel. 093/183-8705, Tues.–Sun. noon–3:30 P.M. and 7–11:30 P.M.,

€8–10) and **Trattoria Mannarazzi** (Via Cavour 116, same phone number and hours) are good alternatives.

Noto is the origin for many of Sicily's pastries and **Caffè Sicilia** (Corso Vittorio Emanuele 125, tel. 093/183-5013, Tues.–Sun. 7 A.M.–8 P.M., closed Jan. and Feb.) is responsible for half the town's cavities. The Assenzo brothers who run the *pasticceria* have become minor celebrities thanks to the traditional and rare specialties behind the glass counters. *Cioccolati, croccanti,* and *torroni* are all waiting to be sampled and gung-ho palates should try one of each. If country bread and foccacia are more your thing, **Sarta** (Via Manzoni 1, tel. 093/189-4557, Mon.–Sat. 7 A.M.–7 P.M.) sells fresh loaves by the kilo.

Getting There and Around
Although most roads in Sicily are good, half-completed highways and off-ramps that lead to nowhere are not uncommon in this part of the island. Augustus would be shocked and no doubt have the governor recalled to Rome and severely punished. Today's politicians are a bit more lenient and it's up to drivers to keep an eye on potholes.

Noto is off the SS115, 32 kilometers from Syracuse and 300 from Palermo. To arrive by train, travel to Syracuse and transfer to the local service, which takes 30 minutes to reach town. The station is open 7 A.M.–9 P.M. **AST** (tel. 093/146-4820) and **Interbus** (tel. 093/166-710) also make the journey. Information and tickets are available from Bar Efirmedio in Largo Pantheon where buses terminate. Interbus also has a service to the Riserva Naturale Orientata Oasi Faunistica di Vendicari. In general, orange buses provide local service and the blue ones are for interurban journeys.

Tours around the popular quarters of Noto can be arranged with **Allakatalla** (tel. 093/183-5005). The friendly guides have something to say about nearly every house, piazza, and fountain. They can also lead you on a wonderful gastronomic visit of the town's bakeries.

Inland Sicily

Venturing into the interior of Sicily is as exciting as exploring the coast. Here lie the deeper secrets, the tragedies, and the ruins that prove you aren't the first to tread these tracks. Landscapes in spring and early summer are not harsh and dry but supple and verdant. The land is alive with color and towns sit blindingly bright on the hilltops—beacons for anyone who wants to lose track of time.

MODICA

Modica has something of Havana about it. The same palm trees, the same slightly crumbling houses, and the same old wrinkled men in the piazza rehashing their stories. What's missing is the sea. Modica lies at the edge of a canyon and unlike Noto was rebuilt in the same location after the earthquake of 1693. **Modica Bassa** is the center of the old town and Corso Umberto runs the length of the Baroque neighborhood. **Modica Alta** is reached by way of steep streets leading to the cathedral.

Sights

At one end of Corso Umberto stands **Chiesa di San Pietro** and 12 life-size sculptures of the apostles. Behind the building is **San Niccolò**, which hardly qualifies as a church and is more like a chapel filled with medieval frescoes. The stairs nearby lead to the house of Modica's most famous poet. **Casa Salvatore Quasimodo** (Via Posterla) is covered with his poems and every August a group of actors lead visitors on a tour of Quasimodo's Modica.

Reaching Modica Alta requires a little endurance and good calves. **Duomo di San Giorgio** is dedicated to the fighting saint, as he's called, and the tower is the tallest in town. The stairs leading to the cathedral are the real attraction and should be approached with caution.

Events

Eurochocolate Modica (tel. 093/294-8203) is held in March and is a chance to visit the town while participating in dozens of cacao-inspired events. Gastronomic tours are organized to taste the local specialty in its traditional or more innovative incarnations.

Accommodations

Talia (Via Exaudinos 1–9, tel. 093/275-2075, www.casatalia.it, €120 d) in Sicilian dialect means "look," and is an apt name for a bed-and-breakfast immersed in olive and lemon groves. The four rooms inside the typical rural structure are inspired by the cultures that have left their mark on the island. Each has a separate entrance onto a peaceful garden. Modica is on the hillside opposite and Baroque is only five minutes away.

The high part of town is where nobles once lived and **Palazzo Failla** (Via Blandini 5, tel. 093/294-1059, www.palazzofailla.it, €130 d) provides a taste of their 18th-century lifestyle. The hotel has preserved the elegant frescoes and ceramic decorations while adding modern conveniences like hydro-massage bathtubs. The breakfast buffet is sweet or salty and all the bread is made in-house. Tours of the town can be organized upon request.

Food

Concetta Nicastro is the mastermind behind the kitchen at 🄲 **Taverno Nicastro** (Via Sant'Antonio 28, tel. 093/294-5884, Tues.–Sat. 7–11 P.M., €6–9) and has been since she opened the restaurant with her husband in 1948. Their son now welcomes guests in the large rustic dining room. In the summer, tables are set up near a panoramic flight of steps while inside Concetta works her magic on the dough. The antipasto is practically an entire meal and if you don't come with an appetite you'll be doing your stomach a disservice. All the seconds are robust and the digestive liquor that's made in-house is strong.

Fattoria delle Torri (Vico Napoliano 14, tel. 093/275-1286, www.fattoriadelletorri.it, Tues.–Sun. 12:30–3 P.M. and 7:30–11 P.M.) is an elegant alternative within the splendor of an antique palazzo. Chefs mix creativity with tradition using select ingredients served with great professionalism. *Mpanatigghe* (pronounced Pa-Na-TEA-Gee) is all you'll need to memorize for dessert.

There are more delicious things to taste per square meter in Modica than in most metropolises. Gluttony is hard to resist and **Antica Dolceria Bonajuto** (Corso Umberto I 159, tel. 093/294-1225, www.bonajuto.it) isn't for anyone counting Weight Watchers points. Locals say Modica's famous chocolate originates from an Aztec recipe. It comes mixed with cinnamon, vanilla, or hot peppers at **Donna Elvira** (Via Risorgimento 32, tel. 092/394-1444, Mon.–Sat. 7:30 A.M.–1 P.M. and 4–8:30 P.M., closed Wed. 4–8:30 P.M.) and **Don Puglisi** (Vicolo De Nari 9, tel. 093/275-1786) gets his cacao directly from Ecuador. The honey that serves as a base ingredient for many pastries can be purchased at **Apicoltura Iblea** (Via Passo Gatta 36a, tel. 093/275-6011, www.apicolturaiblea.it). On a hot day, cool granita slushes are prepared at **Gelateria Ciacheria** (Corso Unmerto I 28).

Getting There and Around

From Catania, take the SS114 and then a right onto the SS194 in the direction of Lentini–Ragusa until the exit for Modica. There's **AST** (tel. 095/723-051, www.aziendasicili-anatrasporti.it) bus service from Catania airport (www.aeroporto.catania.it) every hour and a half 8:45 A.M.–7:45 P.M. The journey time is under two hours. There are also departures from the Catania train station 8:30 A.M.–7:30 P.M.

RAGUSA

Ragusa is actually two towns in one. **Città Alta** is relatively modern and streets follow a rectangular plan. **Ragus Ibla** is at the base of the hill and contains a labyrinth of medieval alleys that can only be explored on foot. **Piazza Duomo** is in the center and a reassuring landmark for anyone with a bad sense of direction. **Santa Maria delle Scale** is where the two towns meet and the 340 steps keeps locals fit.

© LAURIE ELIE

Ragusa's Duomo di San Giorgio

Sights

Rosario Gagliardi rebuilt the **Duomo di San Giorgio** in the 18th century. He divided the Baroque facade into three orders using cornices and columns. The interior continues the theme and the Treasury preserves sacred gold and silver objects of worship. It's worth attending mass to hear the monster Serassi organ being played.

Around the corner from the Duomo is **Circolo di Conversazione** (Via Alloro 5, daily 10 A.M.–1 P.M. and 3:30–9 P.M., admission free), the conversation club built by nobles in 1815. The seven rooms where members spend the day chatting haven't changed and provide an immediate idea of 19th-century Sicilian tastes.

It doesn't often rain in Ragusa, but if it does **Museo Archeologica Ibleo** (Via Natalelli, tel. 093/262-2963, daily 9 A.M.–1:30 P.M. and 4–7:30 P.M., €2) is an interesting way to stay dry. The museum houses a collection of artifacts dug up from around the province. There are prehistoric, Bronze Age, Hellenistic, and Roman finds divided into five sections. A Greek kiln for glazing ceramics has been reconstructed.

SICILY

Accommodations

Locanda Don Serafino (Via XI Febbraio 15, tel. 093/222-0065, www.locandadonserafino.it, €150 d) was rebuilt after the earthquake of 1693 using material from fallen buildings all around Ragusa Ibla. The result is a collage of styles that makes the hotel's interior unique and raises the romance factor exponentially. Some of the 10 carefully decorated rooms look out onto the valley, while others have a rooftop view that includes the cupola of San Giorgio.

Food

In one of the lost corners of Ragusa Ibla, you'll find **Cucina e Vino** (Via Orfanotrofio 91, tel. 093/268-6447, Thurs.–Tues. noon–3 P.M. and 7–11 P.M., closed Feb., €7–9) inside an early 18th-century palazzo with stone vaulting that was earthquake proof. Tables are arranged in three rooms and a small courtyard during summer. Luigi Grasso and his son Luca offer a classic Sicilian menu with few deviations. *Frittata di asparagi* is a good opener if you like asparagus and the *insalata di arance* is refreshing when the mercury rises.

Dishes are more refined and more expensive at **Duomo** (Via Capitano Bocchieri 31, tel. 093/265-1265, www.ristoranteduomo.it, Tues.–Sun. 12:30–3 P.M. and 7:30–10:30 P.M., €14–20), where chef Ciccio Sultano serves a warm seafood cocktail on a cuttlefish wafer. Flavors that have never met are regularly combined.

Antica Drogheria (Corso XXV Aprile 57, tel. 093/265-2090, daily 10 A.M.–8:30 P.M., closed in winter) sells all the basic ingredients for a picnic. They carry local *ragusani* cheeses, *salumi,* and good red wine, which they'll happily uncork. Honey and chocolate are also available in many varieties and souvenir hunters can browse the collection of ceramics. Scoops of wine- and honey-flavored gelato are served daily at **Gelati Divini** (Piazza Duomo 20, tel. 093/222-8989, Wed.–Mon. 10:30 A.M.–midnight). *Moscato* merits a toast.

Getting There

Ragusa is 90 kilometers from Catania and can be reached along the coast via the N115 or inland on the SS194 and SS514. Train service is painfully slow and requires several transfers. A second-class ticket from Catania is €9.45 with departures every two hours.

VILLA IMPERIALE DEL CASALE

Mosaics are a key to understanding Roman life and nowhere are they better preserved than Villa Imperiale del Casale. The scenes are incredibly diverse and illustrate all sorts of activities that transpired during Imperial times. An ancient flood covered the complex and protected the floors for centuries until 19th-century archeologists rediscovered the area. The vibrant mosaics they unearthed are further proof that the more things change the more they stay the same, especially when swimwear is concerned.

Sights

It takes about 1.5 hours to wander around the villa and raised passageways have been built to facilitate examination of the floors. **Ambulacro della Grande Caccia** shows wild boar, lions, and tigers being hunted for export to arenas around the empire. **Sala delle Dieci Ragazze in Bikini** is a fashion flashback familiar to modern eyes. The 10 girls dressed in two-piece bathing suits are all engaged in different gymnastic exercises. One muscular blonde is busy lifting free weights. Mythology and Roman legends dating from the time of Constantino are also widely depicted.

It's best to arrive at this World Heritage site early, as it can get uncomfortably hot under the plastic roof that protects the mosaics. Specialized guides can be hired at the entrance otherwise the audio ones help decipher Roman habits.

Accommodations

Gigliotto (Contrada Gigliotto, tel. 093/397-0898, www.gigliotto.com, €45 pp) is a short drive away on the SS117 along hills that undulate like waves. This *agriturismo* is very much active and the olives and vines aren't just for show. Guests stay in 14 fully equipped rooms that were once part of a monastery.

Half-board is a good idea considering the grilled meats and vegetables served in the restaurant. Bicycles can be rented on-site and horseback riding and walking tours are organized upon request. Doing nothing by the pool or taking a Sicilian cooking lesson is also possible.

Food

About half a kilometer from Villa del Casale, an old mill has been transformed into **La Ruota** (Contrada Paratore-Casale, tel. 093/568-0542, daily noon–3:30 P.M., €7.50–9). The family atmosphere is strong and you get the sense people are happy here. There's a good selection of pasta and all the meat is locally raised. Deciding between sausage, lamb, or rabbit is difficult. There's less choice with wine but the bottles that are available are all well priced. For a gourmet dinner or a glass of superb Sicilian wine visit the whitewashed stone interior of **Locanda Don Serafino** (Via Orfanotrofio 39, tel. 093/224-8778, Wed.–Fri. 12:30–3 P.M. and 7–11:30 P.M.).

Getting There

The only way reach the villa is by car. Take the A19 highway from Catania or Palermo and exit at Mulinello onto the N192 towards Piazza Armerina. The mosaics are just south of town along the SS117 bis. There's plenty of parking out front.

Around Villa del Casale

Piazza Armerina is situated in the middle of a green valley five kilometers northeast of the villa. The medieval center makes a good pit stop and local trattorias are famous for ricotta, goat cheese, and roasted pork. **Al Fogher** (Corsa da Bellia, SS117 bis, tel. 093/568-4123, www.alfogher.net, Tues.–Sun. 12:30–2:30 P.M. and 7:30–10:30 P.M., €12–16) on the outskirts of town is a meat-and-potatoes kind of place with Sicilian flare. The renovated railway building hasn't lost its character and the second floor is for more intimate dining.

ENNA

"Belvedere di Sicilia" is a fitting nickname for a town 1,000 meters above sea level. Etna, Noto, and Erice are all visible and there seems to be

more stars in the night sky. Watchtowers would appear unnecessary with views this good, yet they were constructed in great numbers. Six are still standing inside **Castello di Lombardia,** where all of Sicily is laid out before you.

Sights

Sunsets from Enna are spectacular and the best place to watch the last rays of light transform the horizon into different hues of orange, pink, and blue is **Castello di Lombardia** (tel. 093/540-347, 8 A.M.–sunset, admission free). Climb the highest tower and let nature do the rest.

Most of the old town is clustered around **Via Roma** and at the end of this long street is **Torre di Federico.** The octagonal tower was built by Federick II to defend the city and is now surrounded by a small public garden. **Piazza Crispi** also has good views and **Museo Alessi** (Via Roma 465, tel. 093/550-3165, Tues.–Sun. 8 A.M.–8 P.M., €2.60) contains the cathedral's treasures and a fine coin collection.

Accommodations

Just south of Enna overlooking Lake Pergusa, **Masseria Bannata** (Corso Bannata, SS117 bis km. 47, tel. 09/3568-1355, www.agriturismobannata.it, €90 d) is an old farmhouse with three lovely rooms covered in local stone and antique beams. The owners have created several itineraries to nearby archeological sites that can be reached by car or bike. Make sure however you get back in time for dinner, which consists of ingredients grown on the farm. Anyone with an artistic streak can borrow an easel and seek inspiration from the hills that surround the *agriturismo*.

Food

Michele Bonaccorso serves Sicilian comfort food in a two-room trattoria he runs with his wife Rita. The locally inspired recipes at **Antica Hostaria** (Via Castagna 9, Wed.–Tues. 12:30–3 P.M. and 7–10:30 P.M., €8–12) include stuffed artichokes and *pasta col ragù all'ennese*. Seconds are more abundant in winter and fish is only prepared on weekends, when Michele scouts the markets of Licata looking for swordfish. During the summer, five tables with checkered tablecloths are set up outside.

Getting There and Around

Enna is in the center of the island along the A19. It's about a two-hour drive from Palermo and a little over an hour from Catania. The last 100 yards to Enna are the steepest and the curves should be taken with caution. Park near the highest part of town. Train service is slow and let's passengers off several kilometers from the center. Buses (€1) from outside the station make the slow climb up to Via Roma every 15 minutes.

Mediterranean Coast

The Mediterranean Coast is the least populated in Sicily and the only coastal area not served by a highway. Towns are small here and the dusty, dry landscape could be mistaken for Mexico if it weren't for the olive groves and ancient Greek temples. There are columns still standing at Selinunte, but Agrigento is the main draw and should be a mandatory stop. Nearby, Golf of Gela has plenty of sandy beaches and very few tourists.

AGRIGENTO

Agrigento has a reputation for ugliness and the drab 20th-century architecture is a stark contrast to the monuments in the valley below. Only the extremely curious and those on literary pilgrimages make it into the town where Pirandello was born. Everyone else makes a beeline for the nine Greek temples that are still visible today.

The archeological zone is dived into two parts. The first includes temples, gardens, and an early Christian necropolis. The second is made up of the **Museo Archeologico** and the Greco-Roman quarters. Most people start with the temples because that's what's most impressive, and never get to the museum. It takes over a half-day to see both and it's better to arrive without any time limits.

Sights

◖ VALLE DEI TEMPLI

Valle dei Templi (Via Passeggiata Archeologica, tel. 092/262-1620, www.lavalledeitempli.it, daily 9 A.M.–sunset, €6–10) is what keeps people coming to Agrigento and in antiquity was considered the most beautiful city

SELINUNTE

The westernmost Greek colony in Sicily was founded in the small coastal town of Selinunte (located off the SS115, tel. 092/446-277, summer daily 9 A.M.-6 P.M., winter daily 9 A.M.-4 P.M., €6) in 628 B.C. It was a bit too close to Carthaginian settlements and destroyed by the forces of Hannibal. A violent earthquake in A.D. 1000 convinced any lingering inhabitants they where better off somewhere else and the site was completely abandoned. Today it's the largest archeological park in Europe and deserves a visit for its proximity to the sea as well as the remains. Many remnants are a jigsaw of scattered marble, so it takes imagination to picture how the city once looked. The best-preserved parts are the defensive wall around the Acropolis and five temples. **Tempio G** was probably dedicated to Zeus and dates from 530 B.C. The stone used was quarried eight kilometers away in the caves of Cusa. More complete is **Tempio E,** which was rebuilt in 1960 after its Doric columns collapsed. The 250-hectare park also contains a sanctuary and necropolis. **Ecotour** (Via Megara Nysea 24, tel. 092/494-1208 or 347/164-5862) rents electric carts that are useful for getting around the vast site and to the nearby beaches.

ever built. The famed Doric temples lie on a low ridge overlooking the sea on either side of the main visitors center. The better preserved

SICILY

Valle dei Templi in Agrigento

temples, or those that have been painstakingly rebuilt, are along the **Via Sacra.** This is also where you'll find battalions of tourists listening to their guide recounting history.

Fortunately, parallel to this there's a dusty path along the ancient walls that's a little more serene. **Tempio di Concordia** is the most majestic and best-preserved temple in Sicily. It was built in 430 B.C. using the classical 6-by-13 column layout. It was converted to a Christian church in the 4th century A.D., which saved it from destruction. Some of the Catholic alterations can be seen. Unfortunately, it's surrounded by a fence and the ancient steps are the closest you can get.

Seven hundred meters farther away in the highest part of the ridge is **Tempio di Giunone.** Of the 34 original columns, 25 are still standing. In the 18th century, archeologists repaired damage caused by Carthaginians and early Christians. Just east of the temple is an altar once used for ceremonial sacrifice and behind it a cistern.

Temples weren't as empty as they appear

and **Museo Archeologico** (Via Passeggiata Archeologica within walking distance of temples, tel. 092/240-1565, daily 9 A.M.–7 P.M., €6–10) conserves vases like the Cratere di Dionisio, painted on a white background. A room is reserved for the gigantic column from the **Tempio di Zeus,** which would have been the biggest temple ever built had it been completed. Rooms 10 and 15 contain Hellenic sculptures, including the slightly handicapped *Efebio*.

Entertainment and Events

San Calogero isn't the patron saint of Agrigento, but this black-skinned miracle worker and protector of crops is very popular anyways. His feast is held in the first week of July when the faithful offer wheat, play the tambourine, and parade donkeys and horses around town. During the final procession, hundreds kiss a wooden sculpture of the saint and pieces of sesame bread are thrown at him in memory of his generosity. The honor of carrying the saint's statue is hereditary and passed down from father to son.

In February, Valle dei Templi becomes an open-air theater for **Sagra del Mandorlo in Fiore** (Almond Blossom Festival, tel. 092/220-454, www.mandorloinfiore.net). Acclaimed folk musicians from around the world turn up to celebrate almonds and give their instruments a workout.

Accommodations

There's a bed-and-breakfast next to the second parking lot with a lot of dogs in the garden but there are also some wonderful villas and farmhouses near the temples that can accentuate a visit.

Domus Aurea (SS640 Maddalusa, tel. 092/251-1500, www.hoteldomusaurea.it, €180 d) is near the sea 10 minutes from Agrigento. Furniture is classic and the elegant rooms all come with a balcony overlooking the garden. From the superior, deluxe, and junior suites you can see the Valle dei Templi. Between May and October the restaurant is open serving Sicilian favorites. Five hundred meters from the hotel is a private guest beach equipped with umbrellas and sun beds.

Near Casa Pirandello, surrounded by olive trees, is a 15th-century villa that exudes charm. **Hotel Kaos** (Villaggio Pirandello, tel. 092/259-8622, www.athenahotels.com, €130 d) is full of mirrors and marble. Rooms are functional and outside there's a pool with a panoramic view.

Food

Valle dei Templi provides a memorable backdrop for a picnic, but if you aren't packing a bottle of red, a loaf of sesame bread, and cheese, then you should skip the snack bars and head to **Leon d'Oro** (Viale Emporium 102, tel. 092/241-4400, Tues.–Sun. lunch and dinner, €8–12). Vittorio and Totò put everyone at ease inside their convivial restaurant by the sea. *Pasta con sarde* is done the Agrigento way and sardine lovers will be happy. The selection of wine is wide.

Information and Services

The main visitors center is located near the temples and parking lots. A map, audio guide (€5), postcards, and snacks are available. Toilets are next door and also at the bar in the park itself. In summer, it can get a little messy and the policeman directing traffic has his hands full.

Getting There and Around

Via dei Templi divides the park and parking near the visitors center fills up quickly. There's a second lot on the left in the direction of Agrigento. A man at the entrance solicits euros and it's probably best to pay him. Trains from Palermo arrive daily and there's a shuttle bus (€1) from Stazione Centrale in Agrigento down to Valle dei Templi.

Around Agrigento

It's a long way from Villaseta to the Nobel Prize for Literature, but Luigi Pirandello took that journey. If literary tourism is your thing or Jim Morrison's grave gave you goose bumps, than steer towards **Casa di Pirandello** (Villaseta, tel. 092/251-1826, daily 9 A.M.–1 P.M. and 2–6:30 P.M., €2).

The house where the great dramatist was born is now a little museum preserving odds and ends of Pirandello's legacy. Autographed letters, awards, photographs, and first editions all line the shelves. Pirandello liked his hometown and always wanted to end his days there. His ashes rest outside under a big pine tree in the Greek urn he found on the property. Serious readers will enjoy a moment inside the multimedia library.

The house is 10 minutes from Valle dei Templi. Take the first right at the roundabout just south of the visitors center and continue along the SS115 until you see the sign.

MARSALA AND VICINITY

Marsala is a sleepy town with Phoenician origins and an Arab name *(Mars Allah)* that stuck. The Woodhouse family made it famous for wine and the archeological museum contains the only remains of a Punic vessel. This is where Garibaldi landed in 1860 and started his famous quest to unite Italy.

Sights

Next to the sea in a former wine warehouse is **Museo Archeologico** (Via Boeo, daily

9 A.M.–2 P.M. and 4–7 P.M. on weekends, €4). The Punic warship fills an entire hall, although most of the wooden planks have remained under water. There are also a great variety of amphorae and vases that helped move olive oil, grain, and wine around the Mediterranean.

The center of town revolves around **Piazza della Repubblica.** Residents in their Sunday best chat idly on the little square in front of the cathedral while children chase pigeons. A walk down the main thoroughfare leads to the sea.

Entertainment and Events
The Thursday before Easter there's an elaborate procession towards the church of Sant'Anna (Via XIX Luglio 81). Groups dress up as Romans and early Christians in a reenactment of the passion of Christ. A large wooden cross and children imitating sacred characters lead the parade, which was initiated during Spanish rule of the city.

Accommodations
Hotel delle Palme (Via Trapani 330, tel. 092/373-9044, www.classicahotels.com, €85 d) is an ideal place to spend a couple of days exploring the western tip of Sicily. There's an excellent view of the Egadi Islands and the ruins of Mozia are within a short drive. Rooms have preserved their 18th-century appearance and service is highly accommodating.

Baglio del Marchese (Litorale Sud, tel. 092/395-1115, www.bagliodelmarchese.com, €90 d) was once a hunting lodge where nobles practiced their favorite hobby. Today gunfire is the last thing you'll hear at this luxury *agriturismo* immersed in a beautiful garden minutes from the beach. Rooms are all air-conditioned and furniture is antique. The wine served in the restaurant is produced from the vineyards outside.

Food
Davide and the cooks decide each morning what the menu will be at **Il Gallo e l'Innamorata** (Via Stefano Bilardello 18, tel.329/291-8503, Wed.–Mon. 7 P.M.–late, €7–9). The select number of dishes are re-

---

LUCKY WINE

The first Italian wine to receive *denominazione d'origine controllatta* (DOC) status was from Sicily. The honor went to Marsala and the liquor of the same name that became famous by chance. It happened back in 1773 thanks to an Englishman named John Woodhouse who was forced to take refuge in the city during a storm. Locals offered him some marsala, and several bottles later he was planning an export business. The first cases sent back to Liverpool were a big hit and Nelson adopted the "victory wine" as the official beverage for his fleet. Even today, the cellars of Buckingham Palace are stocked with marsala.

The distinctive port-like flavor is a result of the high sugar content of the grapes. Depending on the fermentation process, a dry, semi-dry, or sweet variety can be produced. To find out which type you prefer, visit **Florio Vinicola** (Marsala, Via Florio 1, tel. 092/378-1111, Mon.-Fri. 10-11 A.M. and 3:30-4:30 P.M., €3) or **Cantine Pellegrino** (Marsala, Via del Fante 39, tel. 092/371-9911, €2) for a guided tour of the cellars and a tasting.

---

lated to local tradition and seafood couscous is nearly always on the tables of this small trattoria that metamorphosis's into a wine bar after dinner. The *torta della nonna* (grandmother's tart) is an old family recipe.

For good outdoor dining on a small *piazzetta* near the center of town, try **Garibaldi** (Piazza dell'Addolorata 35, daily lunch and dinner, closed Sat. lunch and Sun. dinner, €9–12). Fish comes from the market next door. There's a good selection of local desserts at **Gianfranco Vivona** (Via Bilardello 21).

Around Marsala
Ten kilometers north of Marsala on the island of San Pantaleo is the ancient Phoenician city of **Mozia.** It's a short boat ride (daily 9 A.M.–1 P.M. and 3 P.M.–1 hour before sunset,

€3) across the **Laguna dello Stagnone** to the ruins founded in the 8th century B.C. Visitors should follow the path counterclockwise to get the best views of nature and the houses, temples, and gateways that still stand. The museum (€6) contains 10,000 artifacts including the life-size *Efebio di Mozia* sculpture.

TRAPANI

Buildings in Trapani are a creamy yellow reminiscent of Beirut or Baghdad. The city was less damaged in the last war and the center is better preserved than Palermo. Things start to get interesting after Piazza Vittorio Emanuele. Every morning along the Pescheria waterfront an animated fish market is held. According to locals, freshness can be seen in the eyes.

Sights

Old Trapani is clustered on a narrow peninsula and much of the area is closed to traffic. The palazzi and churches along Via Garibaldi display the particularities of Sicilian Baroque and gets lively at night and on weekends when shoppers turn out in mass.

Biblioteca Fardelliana (Via San Giacomo, tel. 092/355-3108, Mon.–Fri. 9 A.M.–1:30 P.M. and 3–7:30 P.M., Sat. 9 A.M.–1 P.M.) isn't for everyone. It's a good place to add a new entry in the diary or author a few postcards. The library was founded in 1830 by Enrico Fardella and now contains 140,000 volumes. Among the interesting reads are the 14th-century manuscripts, codices, and a book by Samuel Butler that contends that the *Odyssey* was written by a Trapanese woman.

Santaria dell'Annunziata (tel. 092/353-9184, daily 7 A.M.–noon and 4–7 P.M.) was built in the 13th century and transformed in the 16th. On the left side is the **Cappella dei Marinai,** a reminder that the Renaissance also reached Trapani. Inside the **Cappella della Madonna** is a beautiful arch covering the statue of the *Madonna of Trapani,* revered by sailors and fishermen. The gardens invite reflection.

Nearby is **Museo Pepoli** (Via Conte Agostino Pepoli 180, tel. 092/355-3269, daily

9 A.M.–1:30 P.M., €4) and a collection of just about everything. The former convent contains ceramics, paintings, artifacts, jewelry, and coral. Don't miss the chandelier, the wooden angels, and the Tiziano portrait of *San Francesco.* Both the sanctuary and museum are outside the old town center.

Festivals and Events

Every year the city holds a handful of **Giornate Ecologiche** or Ecological Days (www.comune.trapani.it). Streets in the center are closed to cars, spectacles are organized, and ecological groups inform citizens about what part they can play in healing the planet. It's a good time to rent a bike or walk along the walls undisturbed by motorists.

Shopping

The seabeds off Trapani are full of pink and white coral that has been used to make jewelry for centuries. **Platimoro Fiorenza Coralli** (Via Osorio 36, tel. 092/320-785, Mon.–Sat.) works the underwater material into earrings, necklaces, and bracelets. Many of the pieces are inspired from antique designs you may have spotted in one of the archeological museums. Less elaborate souvenirs are on display at **Ceramiche Perrone** (Corso Vittorio Emanuele 102). This ceramic institution sells jars, plates, and many other terra-cotta objects, all decorated with images from the city. Around Christmas they also make nativity scene decorations.

Accommodations

Trapani can be seen in less than a day but if you do decide to stay longer **Ai Lumi** (Corso Vittorio Emanuele 75, www.ailumi.it, €60–100 s/d) is the place to hole up. The 18th-century palazzo is five minutes from the train station and the courtyard is a peaceful oasis in the center of the old town. Pubs and restaurants beckon nearby and once you've had your fill of Trapani nightlife a comfortable room with modest furniture is waiting. Apartments are also available and staff will happily arrange car rental if necessary.

SICILY

Food

Over the last 40 years, Pino Maggiore has worked his way up from bus boy to cook to owner of **Cantina Siciliana** (Via Giudecca 32, tel. 092/328-673, daily noon–3 P.M. and 7–10:30 P.M., €7–10). His charisma, as well as the food, is instantly appealing. Appetizers are numerous and most have one or more ingredients from the sea. The Tunisian cook prepares a superb seafood couscous but is equally adept at pasta or grilled fish. There are 300 wines from Sicily and other regions, many of which can be purchased at the shop next door.

Muna Café (Via Garibaldi 52, tel. 329/166-8547) is decked out in Sahara style with tapestries, pillows, and candleholders reminiscent of Morocco. On summer nights, live music is played on the terrace and the town's hipsters turn out to drink wine and be seen. The oldest *pasticceria* in Trapani is also the best. In winter, **La Rinascente** (Via Gatti 3, tel. 092/323-767) serves *cassata* and in summer they whip up slices of ice-cream cake. **Pasticceria Colicchia** (Via delle Arti 6, tel. 092/354-7612, Mon.–Sat. 7 A.M.–6 P.M.) is famous for their ricotta-based desserts and the granita locals enjoy with a brioche outside on the terrace.

Getting There and Around

Trapani is 25 kilometers north of Marsala and directly linked to Palermo by way of the A29 highway. It's a little over a one-hour drive from the capital. Train service is very efficient and lets passengers off a short distance from the historic center. **Autoservizi Segesta** (tel. 092/320-066) operates buses between the two cities and also links Trapani with Rome. The port is very active and ferries arrive daily from Tunis (Linea Tirrenia, www.gruppotirrenia.it), Cagliari (Tirrenia), Naples (Ustica Lines, www.usticalines.it), and the Egadi Islands (Ustica Lines). Cars can be transported on most boats and booking in advance saves you money.

EGADI ISLANDS

The Egadi Islands are a small archipelago off the coast of Trapani. **Favignana, Levanzo** and Marettimo are part of the largest marine park in Europe and have retained a wildness that's getting harder and harder to find. Favignana is the biggest and most touristy, Levanzo is the smallest, and Marettimo is where fishermen welcome you into their homes.

Sights

Favignana gets its name from the warm wind that blows in from the west. It takes less than 20 minutes to reach **Porto di Favignana** from Trapani. The town is dominated by **Forte San Caterina,** built by the Saracens and later transformed into a prison by the Bourbons. There are four pretty piazzas to explore and in the summer no shortage of boats to be hired out. A trip around the island reveals many intimates inlets and coves, such as the **Grotta Azzurra.**

Levanzo is mostly mountainous and lacking in roads. **Cala Dogana** is the only port, and consists of a scattering of white houses and a little less than 200 inhabitants. The island is famous for prehistoric drawings inside **Grotta del Genovese.** The cave is 35 meters long and can be reached by boat, Jeep, or on foot in one hour. Be careful not to hit your head at the entrance. Primitive images depict hunting and fishing scenes over 11,000 years old. Visits can be arranged by calling **Natale Castiglione** (tel. 092/392-4032 or 339/741-8800, www.grottadelgenovese, €15). The fee includes transportation to and from the site.

Marettimo is the most remote of the three islands. Blue and white are the official colors of the only town, which is populated almost exclusively by fishermen. Many residents become tour guides in the summer and can point out over 400 caves along the coast. **Pizzo Falcone** (685 m) is the highest mountain in the archipelago and is a source of fresh water that nourishes plants and animals living on the hillside.

Sports and Recreation

It's worth picking up some snorkeling gear in Trapani. The cobalt blue waters around the islands are extraordinarily clear and visibility is good. The sea is home to many fish, and divers who prefer history can find remnants of a Roman fleet near **Capo Grosso** (Levanzo).

Accommodations

Aegusa Hotel (Favignana, Via Garibaldi 11, tel. 092/392-2430, www.aegushotel.it, €80 d) is conveniently reached from the port. Its 28 large, airy rooms are located in two 18th-century buildings. Fully equipped apartments can be rented from **Il Baglio del Piffero** (Favignana, Via Pascoli, tel. 340/791-0967, www.favignanaweb.it, €350 per week) and can accommodate up to seven. For something a little more secluded on the other side of the island try **Villa Margherita** (Favignana, Corso Bue Marino, tel. 092/392-1501, www.villamargherita.it, €60 d). The owner of this enchanting bed-and-breakfast has cultivated a secret garden where lemons, pines, cactus, palm, and even bananas grow. You can choose to swim in the large pool or descend the rocky path and immerse yourself in the clear blue sea.

L'Albergo dei Fenici (Levanzo, Cala Dogana, Via Calvario 18, tel. 092/392-4083, €60 d) is a simple hotel with a good restaurant. The entire town is visible from the terrace. Rooms are clean and the sound of waves is never far away. The front desk organizes fishing expeditions for anyone who wants to try reeling in some sea bass.

The Guerra sisters provide a warm welcome in an old house that's full of character. The 10 rooms at **La Perla** (Marettimo, Via Scalo Vecchio 13, tel. 092/392-3206, www.marettimonline.it, €60 d) come with iron beds and shutters that keep heat and light at bay. There's a solarium upstairs and pictures of famous former guests by the entrance. The sisters accept only cash. Slightly up the hill in a panoramic position overlooking the port, **Isola del Miele** (Marettimo, Via Chiesella 3, www.isoledelmiele.it, €50 pp) has four doubles and two suites. They may not be the most elegant accommodations, but they are comfortable and a favorite with hikers. In addition to lodging, the residence keeps visitors busy with organized diving, sailing, and hiking excursions all around the island led by lifelong residents.

Food

Favignana, the most crowded in the summer, can occasionally leave diners feeling like they paid too much and ate too little. That's never the case at **La Bettola** (Via Nicotera 47, tel. 092/392-1988, daily in summer 12:30–3 P.M. and 7–11 P.M., €8–10.50), where Bastiano and his wife guarantee satisfaction. During the tuna season the island's favorite fish is served grilled, sweet and sour, with pasta, or in fish balls. *Couscous alla Trapanese* can be ordered with or without lobster and washed down with a good selection of Sicilian wines. It's best to reserve as the outdoor tables fill up fast. **Bar 2 Colonne** (Piazza Madrice) is great for light snacks and after dinner drinks. For any products related to tuna or swordfish, visit **Conservittica Sammartano** (Via Garibaldi 8 or Strada Comunale Madonna 4, tel. 092/392-1054, daily). A jar of *bottarga* makes a delicious souvenir.

◖ **Il Timone** (Marettimo, Via Garibaldi 18, tel. 092/392-3142, daily noon–2:30 P.M. and 7:30–11 P.M., closed Nov.–Mar., €7–10) is one of the best restaurants in the Egadi Islands. Service is attentive, efficient, and fast. Maria Citrolo prepares hot and cold appetizers; the mussels are her specialty. She also makes fresh pasta and stirs up a great lobster sauce while her husband Nino and the kids serve eager customers in the small dining room and outside on the terrace. Nearby in Piazza Umberto, **Baia del Sole** (tel. 339/769-8788) makes great gelato from scratch and sells a variety of Sicilian pastries.

Getting There and Around

There are departures every half-hour between Trapani and Favignana during the summer. The hydrofoil takes 20 minutes and the ferry lasts one hour. Both **Siremar** (www.siremar.it) and **Ustica Lines** (www.usticalines.it) operate boats, some of which also stop at Levanzo and Marettimo.

Cars can be taken to Favignana, but it's more

SICILY

fun to rent a scooter or bicycle if you're staying near the port or if you aren't weighed down with luggage. There are also small public buses that cover various routes around the island. Cars are not welcome on Levanzo or Marettimo.

◖ ERICE AND VICINITY

Many towns in Sicily suffer from urban sprawl that's unpleasant to the eye. That's not the case in Erice where medieval churches are undisturbed by the passing of centuries and the intricately cobbled lanes are traffic-free. The town is still surrounded by 750-meter thick walls reinforced over the years by Phoenicians, Romans, Arabs, and Normans. Here you will find an abundance of pastry shops filled with local specialties and merchants selling the distinctively patterned tapestries unique to the town. From **Castello di Venere,** where the goddess Venus was once worshipped, the Egadi Islands and Tunisian coast are visible. In winter, the medieval town is covered in fog.

Sights

Erice is triangular shaped and nearly every square centimeter is covered in stone. **Porta di Trapani** leads to the **Duomo.** For a good view of the town and surrounding countryside, climb the adjacent **Campanile.** Farther down Via Vittorio Emanuele is the main square and the **Museo Comunale** (Piazza Umberto I, tel. 092/386-9258) contains a collection of classical remains.

Castello Normanno lies on the highest point of the mountain and has been transformed into a luxury hotel. The **Giardini de Balio** gardens are a nice place to sit admiring the castle and the view of western Sicily. Some of the stone used to build churches like **Chiesa Matrice** was removed from here.

Shopping

The tapestries hanging outside **Pina Parisi** (Viale Pepoli 55, tel. 092/386-9049) and **Vario Francesca** (Via Vittorio Emanuele 56, tel. 092/386-9049) come in all colors and sizes. The intricate geometric designs are strangely reminiscent of Latin American patterns and may have been inspired by Spanish rulers. They

are all woven by hand using natural cotton fibers and are easily transported. The ceramic tradition is also strong in Erice and pottery can be purchased at **Ceramica Ericina** (Via Guarnotti 15, tel. 092/386-9440).

Accommodations

Cobblestones are a nightmare for wheeling luggage around and the journey to **Il Carmine** (Piazza del Carmine 23, www.ilcarmine.com, €70 d) may seem to last an eternity. For anyone arriving by car, the shortcut to this well-kept monastery is up Viale delle Pinete and through Porto Carmine. Interiors are spartan but spacious and some rooms accommodate larger groups. Service is friendly and the breakfast leaves room for the pastries ahead.

Hotel Moderno (Via Vittorio Emanuele 63, www.hotelmodernoerice.it, €90 d) is a comfortable option spread out on two floors near the entrance of town. The panoramic terrace has a solarium and the restaurant serves crustaceans like there's no tomorrow.

Food

In the morning and late afternoon, the pastry shops of Erice never cease to entice with ancient recipes rolled in the back room. A pastry crawl of the town should begin with **Maria Grammatico** (Via Vittorio Emanuele 14, tel. 092/386-9390, summer daily 7 A.M.–7 P.M.). Her *Seni di Vergine* were handed down by local monks who worshipped good flavor. **Antica Pasticceria del Convento** (Via Guarnotti 1) is another mandatory stop.

For a good lunch on a pleasant terrace within a lovely garden, look no further than **Monte San Giuliano** (Vicolo San Rocco 7, Tues.–Sun. noon–3 P.M. and 7–11 P.M., €8–10). Count on Andrea and Matteo to serve *busiati* pasta and perch in the *maccarruni* manner. Many of the best wines in Sicily can be ordered from the cellar and the *semifreddi* was made for summer nights.

Getting There and Around

Erice sits on the San Giuliano mountain overlooking western Sicily. It's a windy drive up a panoramic road. If you prefer to keep your eyes on the view, take the **funicular** (Piazza Umberto I, tel. 092/386-9720, www.funivi aerice.it, Mon.–Fri. 7:30 A.M.–8:30 P.M. and Sat.–Sun. 9:30 A.M.–midnight, closed Mon. morning for maintenance, €5 round-trip) that connects the town with Trapani. There's a parking lot at either end and it's best if you don't have heavy luggage.

Around Erice

There may only be one temple in **Segesta** (located between Palermo and Trapani off A29, Comune di Calatafimi Segesta, tel. 092/495-2356, www.calatafimisegesta.it, daily 9 A.M.–7 P.M.), but it's as impressive in size and location as anything in Agrigento. In some respects it's better than the famous valley. Here you can walk inside a mammoth temple that stands largely intact. All around is rolling countryside and on the next ridge are the remains of the theater and town that once rivaled Selinunte.

It costs €6 to climb up to the temple and the bus to the amphitheater is €1.50. It's only two kilometers away but it's all uphill and can be grueling if you haven't trained. The view, especially from the top rows of the theater, is beautiful and would surely have distracted from any performances being staged.

SAN VITO LO CAPO AND VICINITY

If you've made it around Sicily in one go and need a rest then it's time for San Vito Lo Capo. The crescent bay and long sandy beaches are an oasis for weary travelers and fun-seekers. The mountain in the background could be a twin of Gibraltar and it's easy to settle into the beach town pace. Water is warm in June and September and the main street is full of flip-flops in August.

Festivals and Events

Couscous is a common denominator to many cultures, and each September, unique flavors are exchanged at San Vito Lo Capo's *Cous Cous Fest*. Chefs from Israel to Morocco by

© ALESSIA RAMACCIA

Greek temple in Segesta

SICILY

way of Brazil turn up to celebrate this versatile ingredient. In addition to the gastronomic competition there are international food tastings and musical events. Cous Cous Fest runs for an entire week and attracts crowds of open-minded people.

Accommodations

San Vito Lo Capo is full of small rooming houses and a couple of larger hotels along the beach. **Ai Dammusi** (Via Savoia 83, tel. 092/362-1494, www.aidammusisanvito.it, €70 d) is close to all the action in town and five minutes from the sand. Rooms are cozy and clean. Breakfast is served at the bar across the street and the family that runs the bed-and-breakfast are quick to satisfy any requests. **Hotel Capo San Vito** (Via San Vito 1, www.caposanvito.it, €130 d) is a more elegant option with unobstructed views of the bay. You can dine in bare feet outside in the ground-floor restaurant that serves excellent seafood couscous. Spa service is also available. Campers and anyone packing a tent can bed down at **Camping la Fata** (Via Bino Napoli 68, www.trapaniweb.it/lafata, €5.50).

Food

The main street is lined with restaurants, all of which have outdoor terraces and prix-fixe menus. Couscous figures heavily but if Arabic flavors are what you're after, head to **Tha'am** (Via Duca degli Abruzzi 32, tel. 09/2397-2836, summer daily 12:30–3 P.M. and 7–11 P.M., €12). The interior is decorated with Middle Eastern tapestries and lamps that light up the gazebo during the summer. There's a choice of fish, meat, or vegetarian couscous and other hard-to-pronounce plates that combine Sicilian and Arabic influences.

There's a great view of the bay from **Alfredo** (Corso Valanga, tel. 09/2397-2366, summer daily noon–3 P.M. and 7:30–11:30 P.M., €10–14), where fish is the main attraction. It's added to tagliatelle and stuffed inside ravioli for the first courses and comes grilled and fried for the seconds. A walk along the nearby beach can counteract any overeating.

Getting There and Around

San Vito Lo Capo is 29 kilometers north of Trapani along the coast road. There is free parking on Via Faro. **AST** (tel. 092/323-222) and **Russo** (tel. 092/431-364) operate buses from Trapani and Palermo. They terminate near the port where **Siremar** and **Ustica Lines** run ferry service to various islands during the summer.

Around San Vito Lo Capo

Riserva Naturale Orientata Zingaro (www.riservazingaro.it, €3) is a break from the man-made and an immersion into one of Sicily's last remaining stretches of unadulterated coastline. The park can be approached from San Vito or Scopello. Staff at each entrance provide visitors with maps and can suggest one of several routes along the sea or up into the mountains. Along the way are a couple of museums where park personnel recount 19th-century farming and fishing techniques. There are also two picnic grounds on either end of the park where barbecuing is allowed and shaded benches look out over the sea. Donkeys graze nearby. Small lizards scuttle along the gravel trails that blend into the cactus landscape. If you get tired, descend to the rocky inlets and take a dip in pristine waters. **Cetaria** (Scopello, Via Marco Polo 3, www.cetaria.com) organizes diving, snorkeling, and sea excursions along the coast. They rent mask and fins, and can get your scuba career off to an excellent start.

SARDINIA

Although Sardinia is commonly listed last in guidebooks and treated with the respect of an afterthought, it is arguably the best region in Italy. Visiting the island is almost like visiting a separate country. Even though it was the first overseas conquest of Republican Rome and has absorbed many cultures through the centuries, it has managed to retain an identity distinct from the mainland. In fact, older Sardinians often refer to the rest of Italy as the continent.

Part of that character is a result of the land, which is wild and could easily be mistaken for the American Southwest or North Africa. The other is the sea, which has carved out postcard-perfect coastlines and an abundance of splendid beaches. In July and August, Stintino and Baia Chia are covered with bathers, especially Italians, for whom Sardinia is a favorite summer destination. Spring is less crowded and a good time for driving coastal roads like the N127 from Alghero to Bosa or interior routes like the N125 east of Cagliari.

The main arrival point is Olbia in the northeast, which began to exploit the potential of tourism in the early 1960s. Luckily most of the holiday construction is well regulated and much of the architecture preserves the traditional aesthetics of the island. From Olbia, visitors are within a short distance of the Costa Smeralda, named after clear emerald waters that don't disappoint. This is where billionaires come to park their mega-yachts before heading back to St. Tropez and where everyone else comes for a spot of sun and glamour.

© CRISTIANA LOMMI

HIGHLIGHTS

◖ Arcipelago della Maddalena: Garibaldi knew a good thing when he saw it and purchased one of the islands in this small archipelago off the coast of Sardinia before prices skyrocketed. Today it's a paradise for nature lovers, who can tour La Maddalena in a day or spend a week beach-hopping (page 781).

◖ Capocaccia: The views from Capocaccia are some of the best on the island but it's what's inside this rock overlooking Alghero that's most impressive. La Grotta di Nettuno is a 2,500-square-meter network of caves that can be reached by land or sea and that reveal some very interesting things about the planet (page 787).

◖ Tharros: You can explore the oldest Phoenician ruins in Sardinia in Tharros. The solid stone remains overlook the sea and are invitingly close to the beach (page 790).

◖ Trenino Verde: Sardinia has a half-dozen historic train lines where vintage diesel engines take passengers into the wild interior of the island. The Arbatax-to-Mandas line is the longest and extends from the sea to the mountains with many interesting stops along the way (page 795).

◖ Carnevale di Mamoiada: Few Sardinian traditions are as bizarre as the Carnevale di Mamoiada in Nuoro. You'll hear the cow bells before you see the locals dressed in animal skins representing a distant history and performing ancient rituals that have withstood the test of time (page 796).

LOOK FOR ◖ TO FIND RECOMMENDED SIGHTS, ACTIVITIES, DINING, AND LODGING.

SARDINIA

© AVALON TRAVEL

PLANNING YOUR TIME

Sardinia is the second-largest island in the Mediterranean after Sicily. It's surrounded by the Tyrrhenian Sea in the east and the Sardinian Sea in the west. The Straits of Bonifacio separate the island from Corsica 20 kilometers north of La Maddalena. All that water attracts a lot of tourists and it's a favorite holiday destination among Italians, who debark on the island by the thousands every day in July and August.

Another good reason to avoid peak summer season is the heat, which borders on stifling at times and will get even the most adamant environmentalists to turn the air-conditioning full blast. Spring is much milder and a chance to see the landscape transformed by colorful aromatic plants and scented flowers. By May, you'll need a bathing suit and will be in time to see one of the intricate Easter festivals that are celebrated in nearly every town.

The island deserves a week and anything less will be like limiting yourself to a spoonful of *seadas* (fried cheese dessert covered in honey).

Most of the ferries that leave from Genoa, Livorno, and Civitavecchia (north of Roma) carry motor vehicles, but you can also fly into Olbia, Alghero, or Cagliari and rent a car on the spot. Roads are good and in half a day it's possible to cross the island from the trendy beaches of Costa Smeralda to the more laid-back life of Alghero. If you do plan on driving, keep an eye on the fuel tank as gas stations can be rare in the interior.

Train service is limited to the major towns and most travel on single tracks, making journeys relaxing rather than rapid. Routes are often quite secluded and provide an eyeful of relatively virgin landscape. You can also get a good look of the island on the panoramic railroads that run up and down the hillsides of Bosa and Arbatax. Blue urban buses connect the major towns and run to schedule although you may not want the window seat facing the ocean on some of the cliffside roads around Alghero.

The alternative to a Sardinian road trip is simply to remain sitting on the beach. There's

Costa Smeralda

a prehistoric *nuraghe* tower in Su Nuraxi

a major surplus of sand and many resorts where the toughest decision you'll make is whether to sit by the pool or the ocean. Most restaurants, bars, and shops are open daily during the summer holiday season and reduce their hours or close in winter when the warmth of the sun is a distant memory and snow covers mountain tops in the center of the island.

HISTORY

Sardinia is haunted by the Nuragic civilization, which flourished from 1800 B.C to 500 B.C. Evidence of their presence is on nearly every hilltop in the form of cone shaped stone towers. There are nearly 7,000 of these *nuraghi* structures on the island, built without cement and used as dwellings, watchtowers, and fortresses.

History after the Nuragic people has been marked by one invasion after another. The Phoenicians planted their flag in Tharros and

Cagliari in the 8th century, followed by Romans, Vandals, and Byzantines. Saracen pirates harassed the shores during the Dark Ages, which were especially dark here, and led the local population to retreat to the mountainous interior.

In the Middle Ages, the maritime republics of Pisa and Genoa contested the island. Spain dominated the western coast long enough to erect dozens of towers from Stintino to Arbatax and leave Alghero residents with a distinctive dialect all their own.

Vittorio Amedeo II di Savoia established the Kingdom of Sardegna in 1718, which greatly increased the island's ties with the mainland. In 1861, Sardinia joined the unification boat and 90 years later was granted special autonomous status. After years of decline, malarial marshland was reclaimed after World War II and tourism has thrived ever since.

SARDINIA

Northern Sardinia

Crystal clear waters and small beaches hidden within beautiful inlets is what Sardinia is famous for and what attracts visitors to the northern half of the island. Along the northeast coast are its most famous resorts and the islands of the Maddalena Archipelago, which has successfully resisted the onslaught of mass tourism. Here herring gulls and moray eels still thrive and Garibaldi was so taken with the scenery that he bought one of the islands.

The northwestern coast has a distinctive Spanish feel. The towers they built are still standing and street names in Alghero and Bosa are written in Italian and Catalan. Ask one of the old-timers sitting by the port for directions and chances are the reply will be barely intelligible even to a Roman.

Marshland along the sea was drained in the 1930s and is now some of the most fertile on the island. Grapevines are a common sight on the hillsides near Capocaccia and the native Cannonau and Vernaccia white wines go perfectly with the grilled fish and roast pork that are a mainstay of Sardinian diets, along with the thin *carasau* bread that is addictive.

OLBIA

The last 30 years have seen Olbia develop more than in the previous 300. Tourism is the major stimulus of the boom and the town is one of the major entry points by air and sea into Sardinia. Its excellent position on a wide gulf overlooking the islands of Tavolara and Molara provides a good place to stretch your legs after a five-hour ferry crossing.

Sights

Olbia is generally ignored by visitors on their way to other points along the Costa Smeralda but that doesn't mean there's nothing to see. In Piazza Margherita there are traces of a Roman-era cistern. Nearby is the Romanesque church of **San Simplicio** that was started in the 11th century and significantly enlarged in the 13th.

The interior is raw and a sure place to find tranquility before hitting the beaches.

Four kilometers northeast of the port is an opportunity to discover the first inhabitants of the island. **Cabu Abbas** is past the train station, up Via d'Annunzio and down a dirt road. A brown sign indicates the way to the Nuragic complex and the last 500 meters can only be covered on foot. The payoff is a great view of the gulf and remains of a prehistoric tower where human sacrifices kept the god of water satisfied.

Accommodations

Janas (Via La marmora 61, tel. 339/109-2836, www.janasaffittacamere.com, €75 d) is a three-room bed-and-breakfast in the historic center close to the train and bus stations. Rooms are plain but immaculate and look out onto a garden with lemon trees where breakfast is served. The owner enjoys quoting D. H. Lawrence's **Sea and Sardegna** and takes hospitality seriously.

Food

Da Gesuino (Via Garibaldi 3, tel. 07/892-2395, Mon.–Sat 11:30 A.M.–3 P.M. and 7–11:30 P.M., €10–14) has been a family affair for over 50 years. Sebastiana handles the fish in the kitchen while her brother Gesuino looks after diners. He's likely to suggest the *insalata di mare* or the *zuppa di pesce* and both are good tips. It's a toss-up between the ravioli stuffed with fish or *penne alla sarda* and the fried or grilled fish platter is mandatory after a day on the beach. They offer a surprisingly wide range of cheeses and some of the best regional bottles are waiting to be sampled from the cellar.

There's an alternative to seafood in Olbia. It's called **Barbagia** (Via Galvani 94, tel. 07/895-1640, Thurs.–Mon. noon–3:30 P.M. and 7–11 P.M., closed Jan., €9–13) and it's dedicated to traditional meat dishes. The Loddo cousins serve classic starters in their large restaurant/pizzeria that sits 100 indoors and out.

antipasto sardo is a generous sample of cured meats that is best shared. The roast pork *(porcetto)* or lamb is a hearty follow-up that can be accompanied by a bottle of local wine.

Getting There and Around

Aeroporto Costa Smeralda (tel. 07/895-2634, www.aeroportodiolbia.com) established the area as one of Italy's premier holiday destinations. The runway lies five kilometers southeast of Olbia and Meridiana (tel. 199/111-333, www.meridiana.it) flies several times daily from Roma and Milano. A round-trip ticket from the mainland is €120 if purchased in advance. Less frequent service is also available from Genova, Catania, and Venezia with Airvallee (tel. 016/530-3303) and AlpiEagles (tel. 899/500-058). A taxi ride into the center is €13, or you can wait for the Linea 2 or 10 bus that runs 7 A.M.–7 P.M.

Moby Lines (tel. 199/303-040, www.mobylines.it) and **Tirrenia** (tel. 892-123, www.tirrenia.it) are the two largest ferry operators and connect Olbia (and Golfo Aranci nearby) with Genoa, Civitavecchia, and Livorno. There are a variety of boats, some of which make the crossing at night and for which a cabin can be reserved. Most also carry cars and the trip from Civitavecchia north of Roma is around five hours. Both companies provide discounts for advance booking and prices can be as low as €1 if booked far enough in advance.

Both the train and bus stations are conveniently located in the center. It's a three-hour train journey to Alghero via Sassari through an arid landscape that looks like the set of a spaghetti western. Trains also depart a half-dozen times a day for Golfo Aranci, Oristano, and Cagliari at the southern tip of the island.

Ticket prices on **ARST** (tel. 800/865-042, www.arst.sardegna.it) buses are based on distance. A 50-kilometer journey is €4 and a round-trip is €7. A prepaid book of 10 trips can be purchased at the airport and other locations in town. The bus to Bosa leaves daily from the port at 8:10 A.M. and arrives on the western coast three hours later.

Cars and motorcycles can be rented from **Unieurope Auto Moto Noleggio** (Stazione Marittima, tel. 07/892-3950) directly at the port and a Fiat Punto or similar compact averages about €35 per day.

COSTA SMERALDA

Before 1962, the 88 kilometers of picturesque coastline from **Porto Rotondo** to **Baja Sardinia** was known as Monti di Mola (millstone). It was a quiet stretch of promontories, islets, and coves inhabited by more seagulls than bikinis. That all changed when Prince Ismaelita Karim Aga Khan spent $1 billion transforming the area into a luxury playground. He renamed it Costa Smeralda (Emerald Coast) and VIPs have been arriving ever since.

Porto Cervo is the center of the holiday action. It's in full swing in June, July, and August, when the mega-yachts are too numerous to count and the probability of bumping into Naomi Campbell or Mrs. Guy Ritchie are high. During the day there is no end to the water sports available on most beaches and at the many seaside resorts. At night the beautiful and tanned migrate to the clubs, where entry is assured only for soccer players, ex-politicians, and showgirls. Rejection can be dealt with at the many pubs that cater to the masses and have a spring break atmosphere.

Sights

Porto Cervo is the uncontested heart of Costa Smeralda. Everything here was built to perfection in a Neo-Mediterranean style using traditional local stone, tiles, and brick. If you take a deep breath you can smell the money. The bay is a natural port where hundreds of boats are berthed and visitors come to see how the other 3 percent live. *La passeggiata* (the walk) begins in the little central square surrounded by cafes where the price of a drink includes a view of the rich and sometimes glamorous.

Cannigione, like many of the little hamlets dotting the coast, was once a small fishing village. Although tourism has altered things greatly, restaurants still serve fresh fish and hand-rolled Sardinian desserts any octogenarian would recognize. The narrow streets of the old town lead to a port where excursions to the La Maddalena depart daily in summer.

Battistoni was dubbed **Baja Sardinia** by a group of Italian businessmen who saw the potential of crystalline waters, fine sand, and a view of Caprera Island. All that was missing were the hotels and it didn't take long for a string of holiday resorts to appear. Fortunately the architects respected the natural surroundings and were not inspired by Cancun. The town comes alive at night when shoppers browse the boutiques until midnight, amateur concerts are held in the main square, and discos remain packed until dawn.

Entertainment and Events

There's no lack of nightlife along the Costa Smeralda, from the swanky clubs in Porto Cervo to the *stabilimenti* along the beaches where a young international crowd lingers hang out. **Billionaire** (Porto Cervo, tel. 07/899-4192) is the disco of the moment and the two tuxedo-clad doormen standing outside have mastered the art of turning people away without bruising egos. The most common excuse they use is the private party inside and P. Diddy and Paris not wanting to be disturbed.

Women will have a better chance of getting into clubs and may be excluded from paying cover charges that can be as much as €50 with one or more drink included. Dress code is stylish and if all you packed are shorts and a pair of old jeans you're better off grabbing a stool in one of the English-style pubs and piano bars in Baja and Porto Cervo, where everyone is welcome. Sitting in the little square can be as fun as dancing the hours away and provides an instant idea of where fashion is heading.

Most clubs, bars, and discos are open daily May–September. After that, DJs migrate back to Milan and Rome and revelers will have to entertain themselves. If you do intend to party, be aware that petty criminals are more likely to target anyone stumbling through town or hugging a mailbox.

Sports and Recreation

Besides all the windsurfing, scuba, snorkeling, Jet Skiing, and beach volleyball options readily available along the coast you can also play a round of golf on one of the most spectacular courses in the world.

Circolo Pevero Golf Club (Cala di Volpe, tel. 07/8995-8000, www.golfclubpevero.com) is an 18-hole, 72-par course overlooking the sea. It takes a lot of concentration to block out the scenery and attempt to avoid the sand traps and bunkers that prey on distracted golfers. The high-season green fee is €110 and one non-player may accompany each golfer. Cellular phones are pleasantly banished from the clubhouse, which serves lunch and light snacks throughout the day.

Accommodations

Hotel Romazzino (Romazzino, tel. 07/8997-7111, www.starwoodhotels.com, €250 d) lies four kilometers south of Porto Cervo near Cape Capaccia. This is the place to sample the good life for a couple of days. All 78 rooms and 16 suites come with terraces facing the sea or the splendid gardens that surround the hotel. Many have floor-to-ceiling windows and twin wash basins, and are decorated in Costa Smeralda pink and blue. The restaurant prepares regional specialties and Bar Ginepro shakes cocktails guests happily sip while listening to live piano music every evening.

Aquamarine is the theme color of **Hotel Tre Monti** (Baja Sardegna, tel. 07/899-9578, www.hoteltremonti.it, €150 d). Although the 22 rooms are well appointed with modern comforts like air-conditioning and minibar, what really sets it apart is location. Guests have access to a wonderful beach on Golfo di Arzachena with dozens of small inlets to explore. Whatever your water sport, it can practiced within 50 yards of the hotel. Zodaics are available for rental nearby and are the best way to explore the islands offshore.

You don't have to be a millionaire to afford a room on the Costa Smeralda, and reasonably priced *agriturismi*, bed-and-breakfasts, and campsites are plentiful. **Centro Vacanze**

Isuledda (Località La Conia, Cannigione di Arzachena, tel. 07/898-6003, www.isuledda. it, bungalow €110) offers low-cost options for travelers with tents and bunk bed–equipped bungalows that sleep up to four. The site is positioned under umbrella pines and Mediterranean brush that provide plenty of privacy. If water sports are the reason you came to Italy, Isuledda delivers them all. Italy's first sea kayak school is within walking distance as is **La Compagnia dell'Avventura,** which organizes excursions to La Maddalena onboard a sleek sailing boat. Of course if you prefer a game of beach volleyball against the locals, just join the line to face the winners.

The mule outside **Ca'la Somara** (Località Sarra Balestra, tel. 07/899-8969, calasomara@ libero.it, closed Jan.–Feb., €45 pp) is the first sign you've left luxury far behind. This small *agriturismo* in the hinterland 12 kilometers from shore is a calm place to bed down after a day under the hot sun. If you make it back before 8 P.M. you can enjoy a Sardinian or vegetarian meal accompanied by bottles of local wine. The surrounding countryside is full of half-day walking excursions for anyone who wants to avoid the paparazzi.

Food

Travelers should check menus carefully before sitting down to eat in towns along the Costa Smeralda. Some restaurants, especially those with a good view or on a central square, can be quite expensive and you are likely to eat as well a few streets over. **Gianni Pedrinelli** (Località Piccolo Pevero, tel. 07/899-2436, daily 7–11 P.M., €11–13) serves mainly fish and depending on the catch you'll find mussels, clams, spaghetti with lobster, and homemade gnocchi. During the summer, suckling pig is roasted on the spit outside;it goes well with the house white wine. **Il Baretto** (Porto Rotondo, Piazzetta Rudalza, tel. 07/893-4018, daily noon–3:30 P.M. and 7–11:30 P.M., €10–14) is open from Easter to the end of September when the weather is good and diners can enjoy the outdoor dining. If you can't take the heat, there's air-conditioning inside but there's far

less atmosphere. Ravioli stuffed with fish is the classic first course, and can be followed by a nice plate of grilled calamari. Service can be a bit slow in the summer but the *coccoi* bread soothes grumbling stomachs.

Getting There and Around

The N125 north of Olbia runs inland parallel to the coast. Any right turn off this road leads to the Costa Smeralda and a scenic seaside route that is bumperto bumper in August. Signs to Porto Cervo are clear and there is paid parking near the port. Traffic wardens make frequent rounds and it's better to drop another euro into the meter than risk a €35 ticket. The closest train stations are in Olbia and Palau, from which buses regularly depart for the towns along the coast. There's also direct bus service to Porto Cervo from the airport in Olbia.

◖ ARCIPELAGO DELLA MADDALENA

The Maddalena archipelago is made up of seven small islands near the Straights of Bonifacio in northeast Sardinia. They were acquired by the Kingdom of Sardegna in 1767 and became a national park in 1996. **Maddalena** is the largest and the center of tourism. It is connected by a bridge to **Caprera** where Italy's George Washington is buried. The other islands are inhabited only by seabirds and the humans who come to watch them. Waters around the archipelago are popular with sailors who can count on steady west winds and scuba divers who enjoy the underwater life. It's quiet compared to the summer madness of the Costa Smeralda and perfect for travelers who want to swim away from it all.

Sights

La Maddalena is the main town on the island of the same name. It was used as a naval base by the Kings of Savoia, but pleasure boats now outnumber warships in the harbor. Via Garibaldi is lined with 19th-century palazzi and is a favorite destination with locals taking their after-dinner stroll.

© CRISTIANA LOMMI

view of the Arcipelago della Maddalena

A drive around Maddalena's 20 kilometer **scenic route** passes through the bays of Spalmatore and Trinità, which will be hard to resist on hot summer days. It also goes past the two forts on the island, and **Museo Archeologico Navale** (Località Mongiardino, tel. 07/8979-0660, Tues.–Sun. 8 A.M.–1:30 P.M., €2) displays the cargo of an ancient Roman ship discovered on the seabed nearby.

Caprera is connected to Maddalena by a bridge and no visit is complete to this small island without paying one's respects to Italy's greatest national hero. It was Garibaldi's tireless efforts that helped unite Italy in 1861. He bought the island in 1856 and personally built the house, which is now a museum. Inside are his belongings, including the red shirt he wore in many battles. In the salon, calendar and clocks have not been disturbed since the moment of his death at 6:20 P.M. on June 2, 1882. His tomb is outside.

Garibaldi liked to walk up the 212 meters of Monte Teialone from where all the islands in the archipelago are visible. **Santo Stefano** and **Budelli** can be reached by ferry from La Maddalena and the latter is famous for its pink sand and unspoiled beaches. Facilities are non-existent so if you don't come with an organized tour bring enough water, suntan lotion, and *pecorino* to last the day.

Sports and Recreation

Winds consistently reach 40 kilometers per hour (25 mph) in the Straits north of the archipelago, making it a natural place to hold regattas. In even years, the Costa Smeralda Yacht Club organizes the Sardegna Cup; on odd ones, vintage schooners sail around the islands for old time's sake. Both events, along with the world yacht championships, are held throughout the summer. The fleets are an impressive sight and a good ambience reigns around the ports.

Palau is the main center for scuba excursions in and around the Parco Nazionale della Maddalena. **Nautilus** (Piazza G. Fresi 8, tel. 07/8970-9058, www.divesardegna.com) provides gear and takes divers out to depths pop-

SARDINIA

ulated by dolphins, moray eels, and hundreds of other species. They can also film your underwater adventures and burn memories onto DVD. If you'll be staying in La Maddalena, you can also rent equipment from **Acqua Pro Scuba Center** (tel. 07/8973-5385), located near the ferry dock. The best places to windsurf on La Maddalena are the beaches of Monti d'Arena and Porto Massimo on the northern tip of the island. Sand is fine and rocks have been smoothed by the wind.

Accommodations

Frank Zappa would be happy to stay at **(Sa Bertula** (La Maddalena, Via Indipendenza, tel. 340/895-7882, www.lamaddalena.com, €55 pp). This little bed-and-breakfast with hand-painted murals in the rooms and public areas is the most original place to spend the night on the island. The rustic farmhouse with exposed brick and do-it-yourself furniture is near town and there are several beaches nearby. Boats, guided excursions, and horseback riding can be arranged directly with the friendly hosts. Besides breakfast, the small kitchen also prepares excellent lunches and dinners with ingredients supplied by the sea.

Cala Lunga (Isola Maddalena, Porto Massimo, tel. 07/8973-4042, €125 d) is a small resort hotel overlooking a bay six kilometers from the ferry landing. The advantages are the private coves and pristine beaches that are the cure for any ailment. It's almost a travesty to swim in the pool.

Food

Along the road that leads to Giardinelli, **Da Raffaele** (La Maddalena, località la Ricciolina, tel. 07/8973-8759, Tues.–Sun. 12:30–3:30 P.M. and 7–10:30 P.M., €9–12) serves roast pork, *zuppe gallurese,* and a fish of the day that varies from red mullet to striped sole. Most of the wines are island vintages and the whites are particularly good served cold on a hot summer afternoon. Located inside a former fish market, **La Grotta** (La Maddalena, Via Napoli 1, tel. 07/8973-7228, www.lagrotta.it, Tues.–Sun. noon–3 P.M. and 7–11 P.M., €10–18) is dedi-cated entirely to seafood. The prices can be steep but the ingredients and the atmosphere are congenial and welcoming.

There are also many dining options in Palau for day-trippers who prefer to eat on the mainland. **Robertino** (Palau, Via Nazionale, tel. 07/8970-9610, €8–12) serves all the flavors of the sea (stuffed clams, fried calamari, boiled lobster, etc.) at some of the best prices around. **La Gritta** (Palau, Porto Faro, tel. 07/8970-8045, Mar.–Oct., €9–13) is famous for its terrace, from where diners can gaze at the archipelago and sample traditional Sardinian dishes like *malloreddus gnocchi* served with fresh tomato sauce and flavored with saffron.

Information and Services

Azienda Autonomia Soggiorno (Via XX Settembre 24, tel. 07/8973-6321) in La Maddalena is the central tourist office for the entire archipelago; it provides maps and tour information, and can help with last-minute accommodation if you decide to turn a day trip into an overnight stay.

Getting There and Around

During the summer, ferries leave every 20 minutes from Palau. Some of these also carry cars, but bicycles and scooters can be rented in La Maddelena and get you closer to nature. A dozen companies run tours around the Archipelago and most have a stand in front of their boat with information in English describing specific itineraries. Motorboats and sailboats can also be rented but novice sailors should think twice before confronting the often-choppy waters. Caprera is reached via the Passo Moneta footbridge from La Maddalena.

Several companies provide all-day excursions directly from Palau. **Palau North Light** (Porto Turistico di Palau, Pontile F, tel. 347/817-2298, Apr.–Oct.) offers three itineraries to the most beautiful beaches and coves around the archipelago and Corsica. The seven-meter open boats carry a maximum of 10 passengers. They depart daily at 9:30 A.M. and return to port at 6 P.M.

STINTINO

Once you see the wind turbines, you'll know you're getting close to Stintino on the northwestern tip of Sardinia. The small town of barely 1,000 has two harbors from where tuna fishermen once set off to cast their nets. Today **Portu Mannu** and **Portu Minori** cater to tourists and there are dozens of aquatic expeditions to choose from. The big attraction, though, is the beach, which is one of the most photographed on the island.

Sights

Old Spanish towers, tropical-like waters, and three kilometers of smooth white sand make **Spiaggia la Pelosa** a shoe-in for Sardinia's top-10 beach list. Paradise is just north of town in front of tastefully built resorts and condos that don't interfere with the scenery.

During July and August, it's best to arrive early or you may risk finding little room for your towel. If you aren't interested in a tan, walk north towards **Capo Falcone** and explore the inlet of Fornelli, where three Spanish fortifications protected the coast from pirates. Across a narrow straight is the inhospitable island of Asinara, where Italian convicts do their time.

During the summer, regattas (www.regatadellavelalatina.it) are held on antique Vela Latina boats that have changed little since they were first conceived in the Middle Ages. The most popular race takes place on the second to last weekend in August when over 100 vintage sail boats compete for the **Trofeo della Repubblica.**

Accommodations

Geranio Rosso (Via XXI Aprile 4, tel. 07/952-3292, €85 d) is a cheap and cheerful hotel with five rooms and a decent restaurant that runs the surf-to-turf gamut. If you can't forgive a little kitsch, you'd better steer clear, but otherwise this is a comfortable option within walking distance of the sand. For air-conditioning, a swimming pool, and luxury, there's **Rocca Ruja** (Capo Falcone, tel. 07952-9200, €175 d). This modern resort

© ALESSIA RAMACCIA

August in Stintino

complex overlooks Asinara and you can get to the beach in minutes. The restaurant and bar are lively at night and most guests fall into the family or couples category.

Food

People have been coming to **Silvestrino** (Via Sassari 12, tel. 07/952-3007, Tues.–Sun. noon–3 P.M. and 7–10:30 P.M., €8–12) for lobster soup and grilled fish for over 50 years and the owner has yet to receive a complaint about the quality or the prices. The large restaurant is on the ground floor of a hotel and fills up with families during the summer. It can get a little loud but everyone is generally in a good mood after a day on the beach and children at different tables are quick to become friends. There is seating outside and a fixed-priced menu for anyone who wants to taste a variety of Sardinian flavors.

Getting There and Around

The closest train station to Stintino is in Porto Torres from where a local bus makes the short journey every hour. Drivers can use the coast road that runs along northern Sardinia or the SS 131 highway if approaching from the south. The coast road can be very congested during the summer and it's important to travel when the masses are still sunning themselves rather than when everyone is rushing home to wash the sand from their toes.

Parking near Pelosa can also be a problem during peak season and another good reason to arrive early or walk to the beach from town. Parking attendants should have an official identification badge and will generally charge drivers as they leave based on the amount of time parked.

ALGHERO AND VICINITY

Alghero has it all: a historic center, port, and beach. It's the main town on the northwestern coast, also known as the **Riviera del Corallo,** and has a distinctly Spanish flavor. The *centro storico* is covered with remnants of Gothic-Catalan architecture, and most of the streets are too narrow for cars.

The port has fewer and fewer fishing boats

but pleasure boats docked by the hundreds. In August, the yachts pull in and provide entertainment for locals and visitors enjoying their evening stroll around the ramparts overlooking the sea. During the day, tourists flock to the long stretch of beach on the edge of town or ride out to visit the **Grotte di Nettuno** caves.

Sights

For dramatic effect, it's best to enter Alghero through the gate in front of the port that leads to **Piazza Civica.** There's a bar with outside tables from where you can relax and admire this beautiful square teeming with life from dusk until after dawn.

Nearby is the **Duomo,** with a carved portal from the 14th century and a **bell tower** (Tues., Thurs., Sat. 7–9:30 P.M., €2) that is open to the public during the summer. A climb to the top reveals the rooftops of the old town and cape **Capocaccia** in the distance. The other side of the cathedral is more recent and looks like an entirely different church. On weekends you can hear the local band rehearsing inside.

The old town is surrounded by massive walls and a series of watchtowers. Once you've explored the cobblestone streets, it's nice to walk along the ramparts and enjoy the sea air. The sun sets over the hills in the distance and there is no shortage of bars from which to watch the changing colors of the sky. **Torre dell'Espero Real** (Piazza Sulis) is the most impressive tower and occasionally hosts cultural events. Inside the multiple levels of the 16th-century structure is connected by a 23-meter-high spiral staircase.

Shopping

The center of Alghero is filled with boutiques selling jewelry, shoes, and fashionable clothing. Coral is still handcrafted into necklaces and earrings that can be purchased at reasonable prices. There's also a handful of souvenir shops selling Sardinian branded t-shirts. On August evenings **Via Carlo Alberto** is wall-to-wall people walking off their fish dinners, pushing strollers, holding hands, and enjoying gelato.

During the summer, the street along the sea heading towards Bosa is lined with crafts stalls

ALESSIA RAMACCIA

The Torre dell'Espero Real in Alghero overlooks the sea.

that start selling their wares in the early evening and go on doing business until after midnight. Many of these are manned by locals who spend half the year in India collecting jewelry and clothes and the other half selling it in Alghero.

Antonio Marras may be a big-time stylist these days and the creativity behind Kenzo but he hasn't forgotten his roots. In 2006, the Alghero native opened a large boutique on the corner of Piazza Civica that would be equally at home in New York or Paris. The store is full of found objects—like old mirrors, lost luggage, and discarded shoes—that give it a bohemian feel. The clothes are divided into men's and women's section and are all originally tailored. The only problem is the price but it's still worth a look for the interior alone.

Sports and Recreation

The closest beach is within walking distance of the old town and a new promenade with palm trees and modern lighting makes it a pleasant journey. All along this stretch are *stabilimenti*, cafes, restaurants, and bars where you can take a break from lying in the sun. Although most

of the hotels are located in this area the beach is long enough to absorb the crowds. Locals generally tend to drive north to **Le Bombarde,** which has suffered severely from erosion and is usually packed. **La Speranza,** in the opposite direction towards Bosa, is set between the mountains and the sea. There's a good fish restaurant and remnants of World War II bunkers from where fishermen now cast their lines. **Porto Ferro** off the N291 is popular with surfers as the waves can reach several meters in height. The crescent-shaped beach is quite long and the old Spanish tower makes for a nice excursion along the rocky inlets. The far end is the designated nudist area.

Accommodations

Hotel San Francesco (Via A. Machin 2, tel. 07/998-0330, www.sanfrancescohotel.com, €90 d) is on the second floor of a 14th-century monastery in the heart of Alghero. The 22 rooms haven't lost touch with their origins and, besides the air-conditioning, things are pretty much the same as when the monks lived here. Breakfast is served on the outdoor terrace overlooking the courtyard where concerts are frequently held during the summer months.

Larger luxury hotels are located south of the old town facing the sea on the road towards Bosa. **Carlos V** (Lungomare Valencia 24, tel. 07/9972-0600, www.hotelcarlosv.it, €175 d) is one of the nicest of these and the 179 rooms were all recently renovated in an international style. If the beach seems too far you can enjoy the large pool surrounded by deck chairs and umbrellas. The restaurant serves a buffet for breakfast, lunch, and dinner, and half-board is available.

Food

There are plenty of places to eat outside along the ramparts with a view of Capocaccia in the distance. It's especially pleasant at night but if you prefer pizza and Italian accents rather than English ones try **El Pultal** (Via Columbano 40, tel. 07/997-4720, daily lunch and dinner, €8) down a quiet street most tourists miss. Watching the *pizzaiolo* pull the pies from the woodburning oven is half the fun. The seafood pasta

SARDINIA

is also good but this place is primarily about pizza and cold Peroni from the tap.

Al Tuguri (Via Maiorca 113, tel. 07/997-6772, Fri.–Wed. lunch and dinner, €9–14) serves fish and Catalan-style dishes in a refurbished 15th-century palazzo decorated with old maps and pictures of boats. Most of the menu is seasonal but there is usually lobster waiting to be picked from the large tank near the entrance. The onion soup is good and the tables upstairs provide intimate dining.

◖ Da Bruno (Località Fighera frazione Fertilia, tel. 079 373104) took off with the arrival of the pilots from the nearby Alitalia flying school. These guys could really eat and Bruno spent his time making sure they were filled. Today this restaurant with indoor and outdoor rooms includes a hotel and is a reliable address for pasta and fish dishes. You don't have to wait for the waiter to fill up a plate at the buffet stocked with shrimp salad, crabs, roasted vegetables, artichokes, and everything else that helps calm a hearty appetite. Fish platters can be grilled or fried to perfection and out back Bruno roasts whole pigs around Christmas and Easter. The restaurant is five kilometers outside of town and drivers should take the first left after the bridge leading to Fertilia. Look for the blue neon sign.

Jamaica Inn (Via P. Umberto 57, tel. 079/973-3050, summer daily noon–1 A.M., €5) is an English-style pub with wooden booths that have been carved with the initials of generations of tourists. There are several bars along the walls that serve good mojitos and that get crowded around midnight. Gelato is a favorite after dinner treat and the most popular *gelateria* is at the entrance to town near the port. It's usually very crowded and if you don't defend your place in line you may never get served.

Information and Services

General info about Sardinia is available at the airport. There are also two tourist offices in Alghero. The one in Piazza Porta 9 is inside an old Spanish tower and provides books and videos about the town in several languages. In Via Columbano 6 you can purchase tickets to local events, book hotels, and receive a map of town.

Getting There and Around

Alghero Aeroporto (tel. 07/993-5124, www.algheroairport.it) is another major entry point to the island with daily flights from Rome, Bologna, and Milan, as well as many European destinations served by low-cost carriers like Ryanair. Buses to Alghero leave from outside the arrivals hall and tickets cost €0.70 for the 20-minute ride.

Even if you don't plan on buying fish, it's worth walking through the covered market in the morning just outside the old town near the tourist office. The stands are covered with the daily haul and fishmongers proclaiming the freshness of their product. Across the street is the fruit and vegetable market. A taxi into town is €10 and there are usually several waiting out front. All the major car rental companies have offices inside the main terminal, including Europcar (tel. 07/993-5032), Hertz (tel. 07/993-5054), and Maggiore (tel. 07/993-5045).

The fastest way to reach Alghero by car from the northeast coast is along the N199 that cuts through the interior and joins the SS131 highway near Sassari. From there, take the N291 and follow the signs into town. It's about a three-hour journey from coast to coast.

Stazione Autobus Alghero (Via Catalogna 1, tel. 07/995-0179) serves many towns around the island and there are several daily departures to Olbia, Sassari, and Bosa. All the interurban buses are blue and destinations are clearly marked on the front. The train station on Via Don Minzoni is small and connects the city to the provincial capital of Sassari from where passengers must transfer in order to reach other destinations on the island.

A tourist train and horse-drawn carriage parked near the port take visitors around the *centro storico,* but the best way to discover the old town is on foot.

Around Alghero
◖ CAPOCACCIA

The caves underneath Capocaccia were first explored in the 18th century and quickly began to attract the attention of kings, princes, and those interested in nature. The 2,500 meters of

SARDINIA

galleries, lakes, and stalactite formations inside **La Grotta di Nettuno** (tel. 07/994-6540, Apr.–Sept. 9 A.M.–7 P.M., Oct.–Mar. 9 A.M.–5 P.M., €10) resemble the interior of a cathedral. It's best not to stray from the narrow path that looks like it could lead to the center of the earth. In sections there is a black line that indicates the sea level in prehistoric times. It's four meters above current levels and has helped researchers studying climate change.

There are two ways of reaching Capocaccia and the caves underneath the promontory shaped over the last 135 million years. Many boats make the journey by sea and **Traghetto Navisarda** (tel. 07/995-0603, Mar.–Oct. daily 9 A.M.–5 P.M., €13) leaves every hour from the port. The entire trip lasts 2.5 hours and includes a guided visit. By land you can either take the bus (€3.50 round-trip) from the train station that leaves at 9:15 A.M. and 3:10 P.M. or drive 26 kilometers along the N127 coastal road. If you choose the land approach, be prepared for 654 steps on a staircase built into the side of the cliff that leads down to the cave entrance.

BOSA

Bosa, like many Sardinian seaside towns, leads a double life. Most of the year it's a quiet town of barely 8,000 that snaps out of its lethargy around June when the population of pale faces increases incrementally. The wide beach tucked between two mountains is the main attraction, but the pastel-colored houses of the old town and Malaspina castle overhead draw a stream of curious visitors.

The town was founded by Phoenicians on the left bank of the Temo River and moved to the opposite side during the Middle Ages when the threat of pirates forced the citizens to seek the protection of the Malaspina family. Bosa became a royal city under the Spanish, whose influence can still be seen in the architecture and rooftops today.

Sights

Much of Bosa has been recently restored although there's always a facade that needs fix-

ing. The cobblestones of the medieval **Sa Costa** neighborhood in the center lead to narrow side streets where locals sit chatting to each other from second-story windows. The center can be covered in under an hour before or after relaxing on the Bosa Marina beach that lies two kilometers away.

The **cathedral** (Piazza Duomo, tel. 07/8537-3286, daily 7 A.M.–7 P.M.) will look familiar to anyone who has visited Alghero. It was rebuilt in the 19th century in a laid-back Baroque style and is usually empty. Alternating black and white tiles lead to a statue of the *Madonna and Child* to which the church is dedicated. It may not be the grandest church on the island but the cool interior is a reprieve from the summer heat and the allegory of two marble lions near the altar struggling with dragons provides something to think about.

Unless the locals invite you into their homes, the only way to get an inside look of Bosa is at **Pinacoteca Civica** (Casa Deriu, Corso Vittorio Emanuele II 59, Mon.–Sat. 10 A.M.–1 P.M. and 6–9 P.M., Sun. 10 A.M.–1 P.M.). The museum is housed inside a typical 19th-century palazzo that is dedicated to preserving local culture. On the ground floor, traditional desserts, breads, and wines are on display, along with a number of photographs that show what the town and locals looked like several generations ago. Upstairs are the vaulted ceilings and olive wood floors that provide an idea of how middle-class residents once lived. The third floor is an art gallery with works by hometown artist Melkiorre Melis, who spent his youth in Tripoli, which inspired many of his paintings.

The Malaspina family were the big shots in town and after they built their castle in 1112 everyone wanted to stay on their good side. Although only the outer walls and a tower have survived, **Castello Malaspina** (Via Ultima Costa 14, tel. 07/8537-3030, daily 10 A.M.–1 P.M. and 3–6 P.M., €2) is still impressive. Inside the structure all that remains is a chapel with rare series of Catalan frescoes. The best reason to climb the steps up to the red ochre fortress, however, is the view of the Temo Valley and the rooftops of the town below.

If you're not in a hurry and enjoy train rides, board the **Trenino Verde** (tel. 800/460-220, www.treninoverde.com, €8), which departs from the station near Bosa Marina and weaves its way up to Macomer. It's a 95-minute round-trip to Tresnuraghes along the sea and across the Rio Abba Mala Valley. The two vintage diesel cars keep well under the speed limit and refreshments on board are strictly BYOB. Trains leave on Saturdays at 11:20 A.M. and Sundays at 9:20 A.M.

Entertainment and Events

In February, during the last week of **Carnevale,** masked groups often equipped with guitars and other instruments make their way from house to house singing satiric songs. Many of these original compositions are inspired by local gossip or political intrigue. Sausage, wine, and sweets are handed out to the players, who continue their rounds until late. On **Martedi Grasso** (Tues. before Ash Wed.), a procession of men in mourning carry a broken doll that represents a woman who has enjoyed herself too much. At nightfall the distinction between spectators and participants ends. The Gioldzi mask is worn by men and women of all ages who chase each other around town until late.

Shopping

Corso Vittorio Emanuele II is the main street in town and has the highest concentration of shops selling jewelry, crafts, and local delicacies. **Vadilonga Arte Orafa** (Corso V. Emanuele 84, tel. 07/8537-3148) has a wide selection of pink coral that's been transformed into earrings and necklaces. You'll also find the traditional *lasu* pendant in the shape of a butterfly and the traditional Sardinian engagement ring, which can be worn even if you're traveling alone.

Accommodations

Hotels in the center are limited and it may be more convenient to stay near the shore. **Toras** (Località Turas, tel. 07/8535-9230, €90 d) overlooks the sea and if you can stand the 1970s decorating scheme it's a pleasant place to spend a night or two. Many of the 38 rooms have good

views and the beach is just minutes away. The restaurant on the ground floor is reasonably priced and open for lunch and dinner.

Also facing the sea is **Hotel Al Gabbiano** (Viale Mediterraneo 5, tel. 07/8537-4123, gabbianohotel@tiscali.net, €85 d), where guests have access to a private beach. Rooms contain only the essentials and groups of four or more can opt for an apartment in the adjacent Liberty-style villa. The all-you-can-eat breakfast is an additional €6 and on summer nights the pizzeria downstairs is full.

Food

A short walk from Ponte Vecchio and the *centro storico* you'll find **Sa Pischedda,** a hotel founded in the 18th century that now possesses an excellent fish restaurant. During the spring and summer, diners sit out on the veranda and enjoy views of the Temo River. If fish eggs aren't a problem, the *bottarga di muggine* is a chance to taste a traditional starter. There's a wide choice of classic pasta dishes and *tagliatelle alla granseola* has never disappointed. The fish soup is another tasty option and can be accompanied by a large selection of Sardinian wines from the cellar.

La Margherita (Via Parpaglia, tel. 07/8537-3723, Thurs.–Tues. 7–11:30 P.M., €8–12) runs the gamut from *risotto alla marinara* to *porcetto arrosto*. Antonio Fiorelli's restaurant is a pleasant place to pass the evening and fills up with families and young couples with a craving for pizza. Pasta is equally tempting, and the desserts include *seadas* and *pabassinos.* The wine list may lack depth but they also have local Sardinian beer on tap that's served ice cold.

Getting There and Around

Bosa is 30 kilometers south of Alghero, along one of the nicest roads on the island. The N127 hugs the coast and there are many places to pull over and admire the sea on one side and the mountains on the other. ARST buses depart regularly from Olbia and Alghero, but arriving by train requires patience and a transfer at Macomer.

SARDINIA

Southern Sardinia

Sardinia's most impressive prehistoric and ancient sights are located in the south. Although you'll probably pass dozens of Nuragic towers built by the island's original inhabitants the remains at **Su Nuraxi** are the most impressive and demonstrate that civilization existed before the arrival of the Romans. Phoenicians, Pisans, and Aragonese all contributed to the development of Cagliari, the island's capital, that's built on a limestone port and still has a very busy port.

The interior is rugged and sparsely populated. News travels slowly and many traditions like the **Mamuthones** carnival have endured to the present day. Residents are fiercely independent and even Christianity took a while to spread throughout the mountainous terrain where shepherds still tend to their flocks and adventurous trekkers follow the unbeaten track to Tiscali. The old way of life is preserved in Nuoro's Museo Etnografico and the scenic trains from Cagliari and Arbatax provide access to cliff top villages and ancient forests.

◖ THARROS

Sardinia is full of places where you don't have to choose between culture and pleasure. At Tharros you can enjoy both a Phoenician city founded in the 8th century B.C. and the beach. The ancient remains lie on a gentle slope on the edge of the Sinis peninsula overlooking the bay of Oristano. It was an active port and provided a convenient stop for merchant ships transiting between Carthage and Marseille. The town was abandoned spontaneously around 1,000 A.D. and covered in sand until archeologists unearthed the site in the 19th century.

Sights

Although most of Tharros (tel. 078/337-0019, Tues.–Sun. 9 A.M.–sunset, €4) is still underground, what has been excavated provides a clue about how Phoenician and Roman inhabitants once lived. The remnants of large basalt blocks near the entrance is a good example of Punic building techniques and was once part of a four-meter-thick wall. At the highest point of town is the circular *arena* and sanctuary from where all the ruins are visible. The road towards the sea is in remarkably good condition and includes a drainage system in the center that provided houses with an early version of plumbing. It ends in a small square where a sandstone cistern collected the water that was used for sacred rights in the temple nearby.

The Corinthian columns close to the sea are the only ones still standing and were reconstructed in the last century. On both sides are bathing complexes and on the way back there's an ancient oven used by Roman bakers. The millstone turned by slaves and basins used to knead the dough are still visible.

Many of the oil lamps, jewelry, and sculpture uncovered here are on view at the archeological museum in Cagliari. The monuments themselves are poorly indicated, but a map of the area is included with the ticket price. Organized tours are available on occasion.

Sports and Recreation

Phoenicians may not have been sun worshipers but that hasn't stopped modern visitors from spreading their towels on the white sands of **San Giovanni di Sinis** near Tharros. After visiting the ancient ruins, a splash in the clear Mediterranean waters is the perfect remedy to the heat. There's no shortage of space near the Spanish tower and a refreshment stand along the dirt road leading to the beach can also keep you cool with ice cream and cold drinks. Kite sailing is big in these parts however the closest rental shops are in Oristano. If you want to combine shopping with improving your tan, just wait for one of the itinerant salesmen who pass by regularly with their collection of trinkets. These guys can be unrelenting, so if you don't want anything be firm and if you do want to buy make sure to negotiate.

Winter and spring are the best times to visit the **Sale Porcus** marshes that lie several kilometers behind Tharros. Seasoned bird-watchers will have no trouble recognizing the flamingos, cranes, wild geese, and mallards that stop to feed here on their way to and from Africa. In summer the salt flats dry up and visitors can cross this natural reserve on foot. All paths start from the **Oasi LIPU museum** (S. Vero Milis, tel. 07/835-2200, daily), where an exhibit explains the life cycle of the marshes' temporary residents. The park can also be explored on horseback with **GEA** (tel. 07/8352-8100) equestrian guides, whose stables are near the entrance.

Accommodations

Unfortunately sleeping on the beach is not an option but after the sun goes down you can expect a warm welcome and four simple rooms at **S'Ungroni**. The *agriturismo* is in the center of the Sinis peninsula between Tharros, marshlands, wineries, and the provincial capital of Oristano. Half-pension is available and the owners never hesitate to fire up the barbecue and cover the grill with pork chops. The 18 hectares of land are dotted with olive and fruit trees and if you're interested in local farming techniques they'll be happy to show you around.

Food

There are no full-scale restaurants at the site but there are several snack bars near the ticket office and on the beach below. On a hot day it's worth grabbing a bottle of water and panini for an impromptu picnic along the ancient port. For a proper si-down meal, drive to Oristano 10 kilometers away.

Grapes have been cultivated in the area since the Phoenicians arrived and the land is quite fertile. Vernaccia is the grape of choice grown in great quantities in the towns of Cabras, Riola, and Baratili. At 15 percent alcohol it's potent stuff, and a bottle's worth at lunch could lead to an extended nap. Many wineries are open to the public and **Cantina Sociale della Vernaccia** (Rimedio, Via Oristano 149, tel. 07/833-3155, www.vinovernaccia.com) provides tours of their vineyard and the cellar where newly pressed grapes ferment in large wooden casks.

Getting There and Around

Tharros can be reached from northern or southern Sardinia byway of the SS 131 highway that connects Olbia with Cagliari. Exit at Oristano and drive the remaining 15 kilometers towards the sea. The closest train station is also in Oristano, however there is no public transportation to the ruins and a taxi costs €12. Getting back could be a problem.

SU NURAXI

Near the high basalt plateau of Giara di Gesturi 500 meters above sea level lies the ancient fortified village of Su Nuraxi. The settlement dates from 1500 and is the largest and best-preserved Nuragic sight on the island. The central tower is 20 meters tall and was the home of a succession of local "kings" who inhabited the complex right up to the time of the Roman invasion.

Today the ruins resemble a maze of circular foundations that can be thoroughly explored. The town's remote location keeps many tourists away and the surrounding open countryside adds to the appeal of the location.

Sights

The central fortification was built on a hill that prevented any surprise attacks. Defenses consisted of four towers connected by a central courtyard and a keep that was the safest place to be during a Carthaginian raid. Outside of this central bastion is an outer wall added in the 7th century B.C. All the blocks of stones used are irregularly shaped and held in place without mortar.

Beyond the fort are the ancient dwellings and circular assembly hall where elders sat and solved the problems of the day. Two hundred houses were once clustered together here and from the foundations it's clear that some people lived larger than others.

A flour mill and bakery that supplied the village with food are still recognizable but the bronze weapons, pottery, and other objects were transferred to the archeological museum in Cagliari.

Accommodations

Five-star accommodation is rare in these parts and an *agriturismo* is usually the best way to go. **Sa Scrussura** (Sini, Località Padrosu, tel. 07/8393-6167, €23 pp) is simple but the hospitality is warm. There are four rustic doubles and a self-catering apartment that can be rented by the week. Half-board is available for an extra €12 and the restaurant is a nice place to come home to after a day of hiking. The owners are happy to show visitors around the farm that includes beehives and the honey they produce is served at breakfast.

Food

There are no restaurants near the site and the ancient bakery stopped working a long time ago. The closest town is Barumini, one kilometer away where a bar and several *osterias* cater to hungry stomachs. Otherwise if the weather is good, spread your picnic blanket on the grass that surrounds the entire site and enjoy a panini while imagining Su Nuraxi in its heyday.

Getting There and Around

From the south, drivers should exit the SS 131 at Villasanta and proceed on the SS 197 for 20 kilometers until Barumini. Follow the signs for "Complesso Nuragico" to reach the ancient site. **ARST** (Piazza Matteotti, tel. 070/409-8324, www.arst.sardegna.it, daily 6 A.M.–8:30 P.M.) buses make the one hour and forty minute journey three times a day from Cagliari, with the first departure at 2:30 P.M. From the bus stop in Barumini the ruins are one kilometer east of town and easily accessible by foot.

Around Su Nuraxi

The **Giara di Gesturi** plain four kilometers north of Su Nuraxi is free of manmade incursions and full of wildlife. There's plenty low Mediterranean vegetation and several ponds that attract Sardinian ponies. They graze in small herds and are likely to be spotted in early spring.

CAGLIARI AND VICINITY

Sardinia's capital and largest city lies in the center of a wide gulf surrounded on three sides by sea and marshes. The Phoenicians called it Karalis (rocky city) and used the port as a rest stop for sailors traveling between the Spanish Peninsula and Lebanon. Carthaginians and Romans laid the foundations of the town and entertained themselves in the large **amphitheater** where concerts are still staged during the summer.

Most of what's visible today was built by Pisans who fortified the **Castello** district during the Middle Ages. Around **Su Casteddu**, as locals refer to the castle area, are four neighborhoods once separated by walls that now constitute modern Cagliari. Many of the fishermen and merchants have disappeared but the back alleys in the Marina quarter still provides plenty of charm.

Although Cagliari suffered considerable damage during World War II, bombs did not destroy what D. H. Lawrence considered an un-Italian city and it's still as steep as it's always been.

Sights

There's no escaping the sea in Cagliari and if you arrive by ferry the 19th-century buildings lining Via Roma are a welcome sight. This is where locals come to shop and chat under the arcades, and eat in one of the many trattoria in the back streets of the **Marina** neighborhood. The information office is close by and if you walk up the tree-lined Largo Carlo Felice you'll reach the **Castello** district on top of a hill. It's the oldest part of the city and most of the Pisan-built fortifications are intact. **Piazza Palazzo** is the center of the quarter and a good place to begin a visit.

The **cathedral** (Piazza Palazzo, tel. 07/066-3837, daily 8 A.M.–noon and 4–7 P.M.) was built in the 12th century in Pisan style. The exterior is relatively plain compared to the two pulpits sculpted by Guglielmo da Pisa on the inside. The panels covering these recount the life of Christ and are more informative than many history books. The small doorway on the right of the church leads to the sanctuary and crypt redecorated in the 16th century. Along the walls are urns containing the garments of Christian martyrs. Farther down on the right is tomb of Maria Luisa di Savoia, who was the sister of the King of Sardegna.

Cittadella dei Musei (Piazza Arsenale) is five museums in one located in a former armory. It's home to **Museo Nazionale Archeologico** (tel. 07/065-5911, Tues.–Sun. 9 A.M.–9 P.M., €4), which has the island's best collection of prehistoric finds, weapons, and Bronze Age tools. The Pinacoteca next door displays furnishings and paintings from the 13th–19th centuries. There are single and all-inclusive ticket options for anyone who wants to see the Thai objects and anatomic wax models at Museo Cardu.

The best views of the gulf and seafront are from **Bastione San Remy** at the end of Via Cannelle. The bastion was created in the 1900s when Spanish defensive walls were transformed into a panoramic terrace. When entering or leaving Castello, have a look at the towers and gates that once kept Saracens at bay. Names are usually quite literal. **Porta dei Leoni** is named after the two lions embedded above the arch while **Torre dell'Elefante** has a statue of an elephant and a gate-opening mechanism that's still visible.

The **Amphitheater** (Viale Fra Ignazio, daily 9 A.M.–1 P.M. and 5–7 P.M.) north of Castello is the most important Roman structure on the island. Unlike the version in Rome, this one was carved out of the rock in the same way ancient Greeks built their theaters. It was plundered for stone to build other parts of the city during the Middle Ages and what remains are underground passageways, pits where exotic animals were kept, and some seating. All it takes is a little imagination to conjure up the roar of the crowd and the sea battles that were recreated here using a canal system that filled the arena with water.

Entertainment and Events

Saints aren't forgotten easily in Italy and Sardinians have a good reason to remember Sant'Efisio. He saved the island from the plague and has been celebrated for the last 350 year. After mass on May 1, a large procession assembles led by mounted *carabinieri* and locals in traditional costumes riding horse-drawn carriages. A band plays an ancient flute-like instrument called the *launedda* and the statue of the saint is carried to Nora where it remains for three days. Sant'Efisio returns on May 4 accompanied by an army of torch-bearers who light his way. Anyone who wants good luck for an entire year need only touch the chariot carrying the saint.

Shopping

Via La Marmora is home to a dozen or so antique and craft shops. **La Siliqua** (Via La Marmora 41, tel. 07/065-1483) is a jewelry store that sells many of the necklaces and bracelets superstitious Sardinians wear to keep evil away. If you prefer ceramics visit **Cristina Di Martino** (Scalette Santa Teresa 2, tel. 07/065-3898) or **Le Ceramiche di Anna Pellegrini** (Via Cardano 8, tel. 07/040-1471), both of whom create original table and housewares.

Every Sunday morning, an animated **flea market** is held on the terrace of Bastione San Remy. In November, the **Mostra dell'Antiquariato** (tel. 07/034-961) antiques fair is set up in different locations around the city. It's a good chance to get acquainted with 19th-century Sardinian country furniture and many other collectables.

Accommodations

Regina Margherita (Viale Regina Margherita 44, tel. 07/067-0342, €90 d) is a short distance from the Castello district. It's a big hotel with 100 rooms and an attentive front desk that can answer most queries. There's parking and a terrace bar from which to enjoy the view.

[**T-hotel** (Via Dei Giudicati, tel. 07/047-400, www.thotel.it, €99 d) is a sharp contrast to the city outside. It's pleasantly modern and located within an unfinished skyscraper near Teatro Lirico and its fabulous S'Apposentu restaurant. The hotel lobby is spacious and the adjacent bar is a popular meeting place with guests and locals. Rooms are furnished with contemporary furniture in beiges and pastels. The ones near the top have good views and benefit from what D. H. Lawrence described as Cagliari's "enchanting light."

If leisure is a priority, **Chia Laguna Resort** (Località Chia Laguna, Domus de Maria, tel. 07/092-391, €95 d), 25 kilometers southeast of town on the SS 195, is the ideal place to spend a couple days with your feet in the sand. This holiday village is near one of the island's best beaches. Half- and full board is available, as are excursions to the nearby park and golf club.

Food

Stampace is one of Cagliari's oldest neighborhoods and Via Azuni is one of its most characteristic streets. Across from the former military hospital lies ◖ **La Vecchia Trattoria** Via Azuni 55, tel. 07/065-2515, Mon.–Sat. noon–3 P.M. and 7–10:30 P.M., €8–12) where regulars outnumber tourists for a reason. On the left is the kitchen where Claudio Ara prepares slabs of beef for grilling and stirs *ragù* with passion. On the right are the two dining rooms, one a bit cramped, the other spacious. The fixed price €25 menu is a good introduction to regional flavors and the *tiramisu* should not be missed.

Quirinus (Via Angioj 82, tel. 07/067-0702, Mon.–Sun. dinner, noon–3:30 P.M. and 7–10:30 P.M., €8–11) is an elegant restaurant with a large dining room decorated with period furnishings. The menu provides many fish and meat options that occasionally divert from tradition. *Filetto di cavallo al gorgonzola* is one of the chef's gastronomic detours as are the vegetable packed salads that can be a one-course meal. The catch of the day is served grilled or fried and wine is very reasonably priced.

Getting There and Around

Aeroporto Di Cagliari-Elmas (Via dei Trasvolatori, tel. 070/211-211 www.cagliariairport.it) is seven kilometers north of the city and there are daily flights from Rome and Milan with Alitalia, Airone, and Meridiana. ARST shuttle buses connect the airport with the center daily 8:40 A.M.–11:30 P.M. and taxis

(tel. 07/040-0101, www.cagliaritaxi.it) make the journey in under 15 minutes. Cars can be rented from **Thrifty** (tel. 07/021-2096, www.thrifty.it) or **Budget** (tel. 07/024-1149, www.budgetautonoleggio.it) in the arrivals hall.

Cagliari is reachable by train from all the major towns across Sardinia. The trip from Olbia takes four hours and costs €15 for a second-class ticket. ARST buses leave from Piazza Matteotti and connect smaller destinations. Tickets can be purchased at the office in the square next to the tourist bureau or wherever the ARST logo is displayed. Moby and Tirrenia ferries connect Sardgena's largest port with Palermo, Naples, and Civitavecchia. Cars can be transported on all of these.

The SS 131 highway is the principal north–south artery on the island and connects the capital with Oristano, Nuoro, Sassari, and Olbia. It's a two-lane road for the most part and generally less congested than coastal routes. Much of the center is a limited traffic zone (ZTL) and cars can be left near the port. CTM runs local buses and visitors can choose between a 90-minute €1 ticket or €2.30 for a daily pass. Most lines stop at the train station in Piazza Matteotti.

Around Cagliari

The SS 125 **Strada di Muravera** is one of the most scenic routes on the island. The 30-kilometer single-lane road winds its way northeast from the capital to the beach town of **Muravera.** Spring is a good time to picnic along the red rocks and enjoy the perfume of the oleander and fichus that grow all around.

In the other direction, the N195 runs along the southern coast towards the Phoenician ruins of **Nora** and **Baia Chia**—popular with tourists and migrating aquatic birds who use the marshlands as a mating ground. If you don't have a car, the closest beach to Cagliari is **Il Poeta,** an animated stretch of sand where locals go to get tan.

ARBATAX

Arbatax is a small town on Cape Bellavista on the southwest coast. Ferries and pleasure boats regularly pull into the small port and a lighthouse at the tip of the promontory can easily be reached on foot. A Spanish-made tower still stands near the small train station that's used by visitors more than commuters. Most people come to enjoy the clean beaches that are less crowded and see the red and grey granite rock formations that jut into the sea.

☾ Trenino Verde

The longest Trenino Verde historic train line (tel. 800/460-220, www.treninoverde.com) in Italy runs from Arbatax to Mandas deep in the Sardinian interior. It's a 159-kilometer journey that crosses the Gennargentu Massif and many wooded landscapes. The full trip to Mandas (one-way €17.50) is five hours, and passengers remain glued to the windows of the diesel trains most of the time. There are daily departures (except Tuesday) at 7:50 A.M. and 2:35 P.M. If train sickness is a problem you can always get out at one of the small towns along the way and visit the area on foot. **Tortoli** is the first stop and provides a good view of the gulf. **Villagrande** and **Palarana** are both located near lakes.

Entertainment

The most important festivals are religious in nature and generally involve saints. Santa Lucia is celebrated on May 29 and 30, Sant'Anna is remembered on July 26, and San Salvatore is rejoiced on September 10. Each holiday involves a parade of the faithful and those who enjoy a good meal. For non-believers these events are a chance to see inhabitants carrying out age-old rituals in their Sunday best.

Sports and Recreation

Beaches around Arbatax are far less crammed than on the Costa Smeralda, or any other part of Sardinia for that matter. Ten kilometers north of town on the N125 are the *stabilimenti* of **Lotzorai,** where umbrellas and lounge chairs can be rented by the day. A little farther on is the charming beach town of **S. Maria Navarese. Lido Orri,** just south of Arbatax, has the area's finest sand that's soft to the touch and perfect for burying fellow

travelers. Water is very shallow and generally calm. Nearby are the red rocks and pebbled beaches of **Scoglius Arrubius.**

Accommodations

Sa Contonera (Viale Arbatax 148, tel. 07/8266-5021, www.sacontonera.it, €65 pp) is a medium-size three-star hotel near the beach. All rooms have wood-beamed ceilings, satellite TV, air-conditioning, and minibar. A breakfast buffet is included in the price and is served in a cheerful dining room on the ground floor or outside overlooking the swimming. Bicycles and mopeds can be rented directly from the front desk, which can also advise you about sightseeing options in the region.

Food

Del Porto (Via Bella Vista 14, tel. 07/8266-7226, closed Dec.–Mar., Tues.–Sun. noon–3 P.M. and 7–11 P.M., €10–13) is conveniently located near the port and after a long drive or ferry trip is just the place to recuperate. Sit outside if there's room to enjoy the view of the seafront and activity along the docks. Fish is the main draw, and the risotto is thick and creamy. There are several tasty vegetarian options and a wide selection of Sardinian reds and whites from the cellar.

Getting There and Around

From Cagliari or Olbia, drivers can take the scenic N125 that runs along the western edge of the island. Train service is limited to the Trenino Verde and not the fastest way to get to town. ARST buses arrival daily from the provincial capital of Nuoro and Tirrenia (www.tirrenia.it) ferries dock twice a week from Civitavecchia. It's also possible to catch a boat from Cagliari and Olbia.

NUORO AND VICINITY

From a distance, Nuoro could be mistaken for Bogota or some other South American city high in the Andes. The city lies on a plateau surrounded by the Ortobene Mountains that provided a geographical barrier with the outside world. There are fewer tourists here than along the coast, which has helped local traditions survive. The Museo Etnografico is the place to relive the islands' past and understand where Sardinians get their independent streak. Rebellion has never been a dirty word in these parts and not even the Romans fully managed to control the area's inhabitants. In the 20th century, the city became a hotbed of local artists, including Grazia Deledda, who won the Nobel Prize in Literature for her portraits of Sardinian life.

Sights

Like Bogota there are plenty of mid-rise buildings that would make Frank Lloyd Wright spin in his grave. Most of these are located on the periphery and the *centro storico* has managed to preserve some picturesque streets. Many of these can be found along Corso Garibaldi and the white-washed Piazza Satta in the San Pietro neighborhood that is home to the pink neoclassical cathedral.

Museo Etnografico (Via A. Mereu 56, tel. 07/8484-2900, Tues.–Sun. 9 A.M.–1 P.M. and 3–7 P.M., €5) recreates a typical Sardinian village with objects and costumes representing the island's colorful history. It isn't likely to be teeming with visitors except when schoolchildren make the annual field trip to see how their ancestors lived, worked, and played. The museum is slightly outside the historic center but well within walking distance.

To see the humble origins of the island's only Nobel laureate, visit **Museo Deleddiano** (Via Grazia Deledda 28, tel. 07/843-4571, €3). Grazia Deledda's birthplace is a flash from the 19th-century past and decorated exactly how she described the home in her novel *Cosima*. The courtyard occasionally hosts cultural events and the three floors contain her contributions to literature, as well as a copy of her Nobel Prize diploma.

The mountains east of town are a favorite weekend destination for locals who gather on the slopes by the hundreds on the first Sunday in August for the **Sagra del Redentore** procession.

Entertainment and Events
ASCENSION

As in many towns in Sardinia, the year really starts on January 17 with the Ascension and the way islanders ring in the new is to burn the old. Bonfires are built in various neighborhoods several days in advance when locals add their broken chairs and unwanted crates to the pile of wood used to heat things up. Banquets are organized and residents contribute to the long established meal of *fava 'e lardu* (fava beans and pork) that's washed down with local red wine. After dinner, participants go from fire to fire and follow the tradition of circling each three times before reciting a New Year's resolution aloud. It's a memorable evening and a good excuse to give up smoking.

◖ CARNEVALE DI MAMOIADA

Mamuthones look a little like Big Foot at a Halloween party. They're a scary sight for first-timers of the Carnevale di Mamoiada and it's only natural they represent Moorish prisoners captured in battle. The masked figures are covered in long-haired animal skins and walk slowly through the streets to the beat of heavy cow bells carried on their shoulders. The procession is a cross between a parade and a dance that's witnessed by thousands in early February. Prisoners are led by *Issokadores,* who represent the victorious Sardinians. They jump and skip about and periodically send their captives into the thick crowd of onlookers. Throughout the three days of celebration that culminate in *martedi grasso,* great amount of roast pork and *vinu nigheddu* wine are consumed.

PIAZZA VENETO

The communal amphitheater in Piazza Veneto is the cultural center of the city where music, dance, and other spectacles are regular staged. Look for posters plastered around town to see what's on or visit the tourist office in Piazza Italia 19.

Accommodations
Agriturismo Testone (Via Verdi, tel. 07/8423-0539, matteo.secchi@tiscali.it, €41 pp with half-board) lies on 350 hectares in the

surrounding countryside and feels like it's in the middle of nowhere. The animals and vegetables raised on the farm supply a kitchen that never strays from tradition. Even the wine is home-pressed, and the eight rooms were all lovingly restored using local stone. Bikes and canoes are available for exploring the lakes and mountains in the vicinity and cooking classes are organized upon request.

Food

(€ Il Rifugio (Via A. Mereu 28, tel. 07/8423-2355, Thurs.–Tues. noon–3 P.M. and 7–10:30 P.M., €8–11) is near the duomo and all three of the town's museums. The informal atmosphere offers a variety of turf specialties that originate from the stalls of the local market. *Antipasti* includes *salami di pecora* (goat), smoked sausage, and grilled vegetables. If you want to try the local pasta, order the *malloreddus alla nuorese* and make sure to end a meal like the natives with a glass of *liquore di mirto* or *filuferru*.

Getting There and Around

Nuoro can be reached from Cagliari or Olbia via the SS 131. The city is three kilometers from the nearest exit; however, if you prefer a scenic route and are approaching from the south get off on the N129. There are two departures a day by train from Cagliari and both require a transfer at Macomer. **ARST** (www .arst.sardegna.it) buses are somewhat faster and also arrive from Alghero and Olbia.

Around Nuoro

The prehistoric village of **Tiscali** was discovered in the 19th century by a couple of lumberjacks. What they found is a large chasm that once contained numerous stone huts and was occupied up to the time of the Romans. The site is 500 meters above sea level but even less seasoned hikers can reach the Nuragic-Nuragic remains within an hour. Although most of the dwellings are barely recognizable the journey up the rocky trail makes it all worthwhile.

The village is southeast of Nuoro towards **Oliena** (tel. 07/8428-8363) and **Dorgali** (tel. 07/649-6113), from where tours regularly depart. Do-it-yourselfers should follow the red and white markings that begin in the Lanaittu plain.

BACKGROUND

The Land

No country is as closely associated with its shape than Italy. The instantly recognizable "boot" extends over 1,000 kilometers from the underbelly of the European continent to the "heel" and "toe" in the center of the Mediterranean. To the west lies the Tyrrhenian Sea and to the east the Adriatic. Neighboring countries include France, Switzerland, Austria, and Slovenia. The Apennine Mountains form the peninsula's backbone (or zipper if you want to stretch the metaphor) that runs down the center of the peninsula and divides the coasts. The Alps form the country's northern boundary and feed Italy's largest lakes and longest river.

GEOGRAPHY

Italy is 301,338 square kilometers in size or a little larger than Colorado. Yet within this small space is a tremendously varied landscape. It was all formed millions of years ago in the Cenozoic Era when the continental plates dividing Europe and Africa collided and transformed the earth inch by inch. Over the last million years, alternating warm and glacial periods shaped the terrain and formed mountain ranges, hillsides, lakes, and rivers. If you travel the length of the country you will pass from year-round snow in parts of the Alps to near-subtropical conditions in Sicily.

It's a land of active volcanoes and frequent

Italy's alpine lakes are remnants of the last ice age.

earthquakes that regularly alter the landscape. Most of Italy, however, is made up of mountains and hills with only 23 percent of perfectly flat terrain. Much of this has been altered by humans who have replaced low-lying flood-lands with crops. Northern Italy is characterized by the Alps, which form an arc from Liguria to Friuli. They're divided into a dozen ranges with valleys that lead south towards the Pianura Padana. The Po River and its tributaries wind across this vast plain that supplies food for much of the country.

The Apennine Mountains are never out of sight in Southern Italy. The long rugged chain cuts through the center of the country from Liguria to Calabria. On either side are 7,375 kilometers of coastline that alters from sheer cliffs that could be mistaken for Dover in Le Marche to long stretches of sand around the islands of Sicily and Sardinia. The Maremma in southern Tuscany and northern Lazio and the Tavoliere plain across Puglia are the only flatlands covered with vines and olive groves for as far as the eye can see.

Mountains

The Alps are Italy's Rockies. Monte Bianco (4,807 meters) on the French border is as high as it gets in Europe and 23 peaks are over 3,000 meters. Temperatures drop into negative territory frequently and snow covers the area eight months out of the year. Courmeyer and Cortina have become world-renowned ski resorts but finding a lift in these parts is easy. The world's first cable car was built in Trentino. Many of the glaciers from the last ice age are still visible (although disappearing fast) and the ones that already retreated have left behind lakes Maggiore, Como, Garda, and Iseo. The mountains are equally stunning in spring and summer when valleys are in full bloom, and Gran Paradiso and Stelvio national parks provide spectacular hiking.

The Apennines are smaller than the Alps but run through nearly every region south of the Po. They are divided into three sections that form a near-continuous chain where many of Italy's rivers begin. The Arno and Tiber both start as a trickle high within these mountains,

THERMAL SPRINGS

Volcanic activity in Italy over the millennia has created thermal springs that provide opportunities for unwinding. The Romans exploited the use of warm, running water, and enjoyed it in thermal areas across the country. Today spas have regained the status they once had. The naturally heated waters can be enjoyed throughout the year and most resorts include a full range of dining and hotel facilities.

CARAMANICO TERME (ABRUZZO)

Immersed within **Parco Nazionale della Maiella,** this thermal area has been known for its healing waters since the 16th century. Spas in the area are big on mud baths and a dip in the sulfuric pools helps remove every last ounce of tension. **La Reserve** (Via Santa Croce, tel. 085/923-9502, www.lareserve.it) also has a vapor tunnel where sinuses are instantly cleared.

TERME DI BAGNO VIGNONI (TUSCANY)

Val d'Orcia was declared a World Heritage Site in 2004. In the center of San Quirico d'Orcia is the thermal pool where Saint Catherine of Siena and Lorenzo Medici took their baths. The **Adler Thermae Spa and Wellness Resort** (San Quirico d'Orcia, tel. 05/7788-9001, www. adler-thermae.com) is also in this square.

TERME DELLA SALVAROLA (EMILIA ROMAGNA)

In **Salvarola** (Via Salvarola 131, tel. 05/3687-1788, www.termesalvarola.it), outside of Modena, the earth delivers four variations of water that differs in temperature and mineral content. Each type is said to cure different ailments.

TERME EUGANEE (VENETO)

Petrarch, Byron, and Shelley all found inspiration here surrounded by castles, villas, and botanic gardens. The spa **Al Relilax** (Montegrotto Terme, tel. 049/891-1755, www.relilax. com) provides nutrient treatments that regenerate skin and have everyone glowing. Outside the spa are clearly marked trails along the **Parco Regionale dei Colli.**

TERME DI MÈRANO (TRENTINO-ALTO ADIGE)

The spa here is protected by an immense glass cube that provides views of snow-covered Alpine peaks. There are 25 pools containing salt- and freshwater, and the brave will alternate between cold and hot. A tunnel underneath the modern complex connects the spa to **Albergo Steigenberger** (Piazza Terme 1, tel. 04/7325-9000, www.meran. steigenberger.it).

---

which alternate between limestone and granite formations. Gran Sasso in Abruzzo is the highest peak at 2,192 meters.

Islands

Sicily and Sardinia are the two largest islands in the Mediterranean. Both lie in the Tyrrhenian Sea and each has a number of postcard-perfect archipelagos, some of which, like Stromboli and Vulcano in the Eolians, are volcanic in nature. Elba, off the coast of Tuscany, is Italy's third-largest island, and there are a dozen of smaller islets from Gorgona off the coast of Livorno to Capri overlooking Naples. The Adriatic coast is far less endowed and only the Tremiti Islands

and Pianosa near the Gargano Promontory provide any opportunity to get lost.

Rivers

As with all Mediterranean coasts, river estuaries are hazardous for shipping. The sea has no strong tides to scour away the fluvial deposits and entrances are commonly blocked with banks of silt. Neither the Po (652 km) nor the Tiber (405 km) has ever been accessible to large vessels and Mark Twain once wryly remarked the Arno (241 km) would be a river "if they pumped some water into it." Droughts are increasingly common and lack of water may become a major environmental issue in the near future. Of Italy's best harbors, Genoa and La Spezia are dead-ends in the Maritime Alps, and lay almost unused in ancient times; two other large basins at Brindisi and Taranto open on to the same hinterland.

CLIMATE

Italy has three different types of climate: continental in the north, temperate inland, and Mediterranean along the coast. Weather still follows a predictable pattern even if global warming occasionally disrupts Mother Nature's old habits. Here the winds have names (*bora, scirocco, maestrale*) and seasons are relatively well defined. Temperatures vary considerably from north to south and Milan has a reputation for being grey much of the year.

The fact most Italians don't own dryers and hang their clothes in the sunshine provides a clue about the weather. Overall summers are hot and dry, and skies are patented blue. Winters are mild except in the Alps where thermometers hit -20°C and Eskimos would feel at home. Liguria is the exception and remains perennially balmy due to the thermal effect of the sea and the mountains that protect the region from cold northern winds.

Along the peninsula climate varies from coast to coast. Temperatures are generally higher along the Tyrrhenian than the Adriatic, which is exposed to cold streams from northeastern Europe. Elevation plays a part in conditions and a city like L'Aquila that's on the same latitude as Rome but 500 meters higher may require a jacket and scarf even in early spring.

Altitude also determines whether you'll need to pack an umbrella or not. Alpine regions

THE FATA MORGANA MIRAGE

Fata Morgana is an optical phenomenon that results from a temperature inversion over the Straits. Objects on the horizon – such as islands, cliffs, and ships – appear much closer than they really are and seem to float above the water. The legend goes that an invading king who didn't know about the occurrence was fooled by a local girl into thinking Sicily was only an arm's length away. The excited king rode out on his horse and eventually drowned. The girl has been known ever since as the Fata Morgana or Morgana Fairy.

Today you can experience this strange illusion in summer when the sea is very calm. Warm winds over the cold dense air near the surface act as a refracting lens and produce an upside-down image of objects that hover in space. Fata Morgana is usually seen in the morning after a cool night and is nearly impossible to photograph.

1,000 meters above sea level average over 110 centimeters of rainfall per year. The number of drops decreases as you travel south and to lowlands along the coast. The driest parts of Italy are Sicily and Sardinia, which receives a record low 55 days of rain per year. November can seem like monsoon month in Rome when torrential downpours go on for days. As far as snow is concerned, there are heavy falls above 2,000 meters in all the mountainous regions from Etna to the Dolomites.

Flora and Fauna

Italy's varied climate and terrain provide a wealth of habitats for plants and animals. Humans, however, have altered nature over the centuries favoring cereals, fruit trees, rice and wheat production that has gradually reduced the number of species living on the peninsula. There are now few areas where flora remains in its original state and you'll have to climb pretty high or swim very deep to see truly virgin landscape.

The Italian conservation movement has done its best to reintroduce endangered animals into reserves and parks that make up 10 percent of the country and can be found in every region. It's in part thanks to this that Italy boasts the highest level of biodiversity in Europe.

FLORA

Italy can be roughly divided into several floral zones. Much of the peninsula as well as the islands is classified as Mediterranean and contains a mixture of deciduous trees such as pine and many types of oak. Travelers will find juniper, thyme, and rosemary growing in the wild. On forest floors, myrtle and lavender are common as are many species of mushrooms and the prized white and black truffle. If you stumble across one of these you could earn enough to pay for the flight over. Some regions are particularly associated with a specific tree. Tuscany's rolling hillsides would be bare without the cypress that grows over 50 meters tall and was first planted in the area by the Romans. Rome would be unimaginable without its umbrella pines that provide shade and the nuts used in dozens of local dishes.

Palms can be seen throughout the south and in Liguria, and cacti turns much of Sicily and Sardinia into a Far West lookalike. Late spring is the best time for wildflowers, especially in the Alps and mountainous regions of the south where roads are flanked by bright blues, yellows, and greens.

© ALESSIA RAMACCIA

Cacti grow throughout Southern Italy.

FAUNA
Mammals

Large predators that once stalked the peninsula have disappeared thanks to the Romans, who slaughtered thousands of animals for entertainment. The largest remaining mammal is the Marsican brown bear, which leads a precarious life in Abruzzo. Only 100 now roam the park and two were recently found poisoned by disgruntled farmers. Apennine wolves are equally scarce and there's a better chance of seeing chamois or roe deer. Wild boar are also common along the coastline and forests, where they travel in small groups consisting of a mother and her offspring. In the Po Valley and other lowlands, harvest mice, rabbits, and moles keep a low profile during the day and come out at night to feed.

Sealife

Italian rivers lack substantial vegetation and have a relatively low oxygen count yet they support a large number of fish. Eels can be spotted swimming in the Tiber along with perch that were introduced in the 1960s and have begun to threaten older species like carp, another Roman legacy. Catfish thrive in great numbers regardless of the pollution that has affected less robust species.

In Naples and especially Sicily, large shoals of tuna and swordfish have sustained fishermen for generations. Much of the water, however, along the peninsula and Sardinia has been transformed into marine reserves and the return of monk seals in recent years is one of the most prominent success stories.

Scuba divers will be pleasantly surprised by Italy's underwater landscape. Neptune grass and red algae provide the color while invertebrates along the rocky shores attract seabream, mullet, rainbow wrasse, scorpion fish, and the sea peacock. Octopus and sea urchin are also tucked away along the seabed and there has been an influx of tropical fish that have migrated from the Indian Ocean into the Mediterranean by way of the Suez Canal. Dolphins and whales populate the

© ALESSIA RAMACCIA

Sicilian donkeys grazing near San Vito Lo Cap

deeper waters of the Tyrrhenian and tours regularly depart from Liguria on the lookout for fins.

Birds

Italy has a wide range of birds divided between permanent residents and migrating species just passing through. Binoculars are especially handy in spring when populations soar. Italian birds aren't restricted to the countryside and St. Mark's Square in Venice isn't the only place breadcrumbs will come in handy. Besides crows and pigeons the skies above Italian cities are filled with grey wagtails, blue rock thrushes, kestrel, and owls. Many of these nest in bell towers and ruins out of sight from tourists and feed on insects and small rodents.

Along rivers and coast, herring and black-headed gulls scour the water for fish and mallard and grebe ducks lead a tranquil life among the reeds. Larger birds like the great cormorant and grey heron spend their time fishing in Italy's lakes. The spotted flycatcher arrives in mid-May from Africa and the Italian sparrow, recognizable by its brown cap, is found all over the country. These along with starlings, blackbirds, and orioles are part of the welcoming committee that serenade visitors with song and are a wonderful way to start the day. Less accommodating is Italy's golden eagle, which flies above the foothills of the Alps in search of small mammals to snack on.

History

History is everywhere in Italy and every stone tells a story. The Romans are usually mentioned and the foundations they laid have been built upon for the last 2,000 years. Distinguishing between one age and the next isn't easy and historians often spend a lifetime on a single period. To understand it all is impossible, yet learning just a little about Etruscans, Medicis, or Garibaldi (or better yet seeing what they left behind) creates a desire to know more about the events and peoples that helped shape Italy.

PREHISTORY

The first visitors to the peninsula looked different from those of today and probably needed a shave. Neanderthals arrived 50,000 years ago when the Alps were covered in ice and herds of large mammals encouraged small groups of hunters to make the difficult journey. Remains from this period are found scattered around Liguria and Lombardy, where man's predecessors spent their free time recounting their exploits on cave walls.

The biped story, however, may have started much earlier and scientists have recently discovered remains of *Homo Aeserniensis,* the first-known inhabitant of Europe, who lived about a million years ago in the area of Isernia in Molise. Italy was a natural bridge between Africa and Europe that allowed a permanent flow of prehistoric traffic. These inhabitants did not leave much in the way of art and culture and it wasn't until the 8th century that anything resembling civilization arrived. At that time the Italics lived in small tribes across the peninsula and spoke a number of different variants of the same language. Meanwhile across the Tyrrhenian, two of Italy's most sophisticated ancient peoples were assembling the boulders that still stand today. Much remains of early Sicilians and Sardinians, who were skilled bronze craftsmen and whose Nuraghe towers still dot the landscape.

ETRUSCANS AND GREEKS

The Etruscans were the first major civilization in Italy. Recent DNA testing indicates that they emigrated from the Near East and probably originated somewhere in Turkey. They began to spread through the center of the peninsula in the 9th century B.C. and their territory included Lazio, Tuscany, and parts of Umbria. Although their language remains a mystery, archeologists have learned a lot from the thousands of tufa rock tombs that testify to their existence. At one point in the 6th century B.C., Etruscan kings ruled over Rome, and although the city later superseded them much of their culture and artistry was absorbed into Roman tradition.

At the same time farther south, Greek colonists were busy settling the coasts. They were especially active in Puglia, Calabria, and Sicily, where they founded dozens of cities. Syracuse and Akragas eventually dominated central Mediterranean trade routes and became wealthy as a result. The temples at Agrigento and Paestum are nearly as impressive as anything built in Athens and have remained in much better shape. Power struggles between individual cities and the rise of the Romans led to a slow decline but like the Etruscans (who were both rivals and trading partners) a great deal of Greek culture and philosophy became the root of Roman thinking.

ROME

No Greek soothsayer ever predicted that Rome would become an eternal city. At its founding in 753 B.C., it was little more than a backwater on the banks of the Tiber. Yet in the centuries that followed village evolved into town and town grew into city. There are in fact three distinct periods in Rome's ancient history: Kingdom, Republic, and Empire. The first was the shortest and a time in which the city was subjugated. Etruscan Kings, however, were overthrown in 509 B.C. and a Republic was established that eventually conquered the entire peninsula. Roman customs, language, and law were imposed on enemies who were integrated into the new society. It wasn't until the turn of the millennium that social tensions allowed Julius Caesar the opportunity to take absolute power and do away with the old checks and balances.

Rise

Anyone familiar with Risk or Age of Empires has some idea of how the Romans beat the odds. It took a little luck and unrivaled organization on and off the battlefield. After the Etruscans were expelled, Rome spent 100 years at war with various cities of Etruria, while gradually subjugating the rest of the Latins and neighboring tribes.

Most tribes were allowed to remain independent as long as they accepted Roman hegemony and new colonies were set up in strategic locations so that conquered lands would remain within the fold. Attention was then turned to the only power left in Italy: the Samnites, who were defeated along with their Etruscan and Celtic allies. By 283 B.C., nearly the entire peninsula was in Roman hands and Greek cities could be easily picked off one by one.

Punic Wars

Once Rome had domesticated the peninsula it turned its attention overseas. Carthage was another rising power at the time and the Mediterranean wasn't big enough for both of them. They faced off in three epic wars that kept the Senate in nonstop suspense. In the first

a portrait statue of Augustus as a general, Musei Vaticani

© ALESSIA RAMACCIA

(264–241 B.C.), Rome secured Sardinia, Corsica, and parts of Sicily. The defeat never went down well with the Carthaginians, who broke the peace accords and sent their best general to stomp out the Romans once and for all.

Hannibal was one of the greatest military strategists of all times and nearly succeeded in crushing Rome. He inflicted the greatest defeat on the Roman army at Canae and with proper reinforcements might have altered history. As it turns out, Roman society held firm and the legions eventually made a dramatic comeback at the battle of Zara. Afterwards heavy sanctions crippled Carthage and the third war was the excuse Rome was looking for to annihilate their old enemy and become masters of the Mediterranean.

Empire

Until Caesar came along, the Republic had been governed by two consuls elected to one-year terms by the Senate. Not everything was rosy in Italy and although new territories meant wealth for a few, many Romans were having a tough time surviving. Cheap grain imports from Egypt put Italian farmers out of business. Famines were frequent and the ruling class was deaf to calls of reform. Populist statesmen who did advocate change met a brutal end.

Times were volatile and slave revolts like the one Spartacus led in 73–71 B.C. not uncommon. At the same time each new conquest gave more power to Roman generals who could count on the support of their troops. Caesar was the most successful of these and after he prevailed over the Gauls returned to Rome in 49 B.C. to defeat the competition.

Caesar's assassination four years later marked the end of Republic and a new golden age in which the Senate was reduced to insignificance and emperors called the shots. The first of these was Augustus, the adopted son of Caesar, who ushered in a long period of stability. The empire eventually stretched from the Red Sea to Great Britain and although some emperors like Nero favored debauchery, the wisdom of Trajan, Hadrian, and Marcus Aurelius in the 2nd century A.D. led to higher living standards for all. Slaves performed much of the heavy work, wheat was free, and entertainment was only as far as the amphitheater.

Nearly every large town has the remnants of an arch, aqueduct, or temple from the period. The Colosseum and Pantheon are the most famous monuments and Pompeii and Ostia the best-preserved Imperial-era cities.

Decline and Fall

No empire lasts forever, though the Romans did come close and have left an indelible trace on language, customs, and ideas. Over the centuries the legions lost their edge and had to rely on an influx of foreign recruits who were no longer the cream of the crop. Equipment became obsolete and tactics were superceded by new forces that threatened northern borders.

Constantine moved the capital to Constantinople (modern-day Istanbul) in A.D. 312, which led to the split of the empire into a Western and Eastern half. While the latter survived for another thousand years in the guise of the Byzantine Empire, the west could not hold back the

Trajan's Forum in Rome

© ALESSIA RAMACCIA

hordes of Franks and Alemani invading Gaul. The last emperors kept their courts in army headquarters in Medilanum (Milan) and then in Ravenna on the Adriatic.

Rome fell on hard times and was sacked in 410 B.C. by Aleric and his Visgoths. Saint Augustine announced the end of the world and Attila the Hun obliged him with years of chaos when it was no longer possible to distinguish Roman from Barbarian. The Dark Ages had begun and Italy would have to wait a thousand years to regain its place at the center of the world.

MIDDLE AGES

After the fall of the Western Empire in 476 A.D., foreign invasion became the rule in Italy. Lombards arrived and founded their capital in Pavia, only to be replaced by the Franks and Charlemagne, who was crowned Holy Roman Emperor in St. Peters. In the south, Saracen pirates were landing in Sicily followed by Normans who went on to build some of their most impressive fortifications in Puglia.

In the fray many cities managed to break free of their feudal lords and win independence. Venice was the most successful and grew rich importing silk and spice from the Orient and shipping crusaders off to the Holy Land. In 1271, Marco Polo set off with his father on his famous journey to China and returned 25 years later with enough stories from the court of Kublai Khan to fill several diaries. Genoa and Pisa also rose to prominence and were the other great maritime republics on the Tyrrhenian.

Inland Milan and Florence took advantage of conflict between the Papal States and Holy Roman Empire to flex their muscles. Bands of mercenaries were paid by towns to conquer their rivals. Competition was not just about winning on the battlefield. Perugia wanted to outdo Siena in architecture as well. Florence had to have grander Cathedral doors than Pisa. The piazze present in nearly every Italian town today were built for the most part during the Middle Ages. A sense of civic pride was born which along with a skilled class of tradespeople paved the way for the Renaissance that was to come.

RENAISSANCE

No one knew they were living in the Renaissance and the word itself was coined much later. What they knew was that things were happening like never before. The plague was just a bad memory and the new churches that were slowly rising above the skylines greatly over shadowed the old ones.

Business was good and much of it was handled by newly founded Venetian and Florentine banks. Economic expansion required investment, which in turn encouraged greater productivity. The practice of charging interest became standard compensation when lending or investing. A check was used for the first time in Pisa in the 14th century and was commonplace by the middle of the 15th. Modern capitalism spread fast and once money was available people needed something to spend it on.

The wealthy merchants who vied for control began to take interest in the arts. The Medicis in Florence and Sforzas in Milan wanted to make a statement with their *palazzi* and interior decoration became important again. Art and culture mattered like never before. Antiquity was rediscovered and an incredible generation of artists was born in the right place at the right time.

Leonardo da Vinci, Michelangelo, Raphael, and Titian were all contemporaries who managed to make the incredible jump from craftsman to artist and subsequently genius. Painting and sculpture became vital to city life and people were as likely to gossip about Michelangelo's latest sculpture than charges of sodomy against the archbishop. Competitions were held for important commissions and Brunelleschi's scale model of Florence's cathedral dome is still on display in the duomo museum. The signs of Renaissance Italy are everywhere and although Florence was the epicenter of the movement the historic centers of Mantova, Urbino, and Bologna all recall the second of Italy's golden ages.

POST-RENAISSANCE

In the 15th century the economic boom was put on hold. Northern financiers miscalculated their investments and preferred to invest in land rather than risk their money on new ideas. Lack of imagination and vision in developing new ventures was greatly responsible for the slowdown. At the same time the waves of crusaders, who had been a goldmine for merchants, had stopped arriving. In 1566, the defeat of the Turks at Malta by Christian forces pretty much ended the crusades. The Portuguese discovered new routes to the Indies that bypassed the Mediterranean and cut into profits. Venice lost the spice trade and the textile industry took a dramatic hit. Old ports were deserted and only Genoa continued any substantial trading. By 1650, Italy had stopped playing an important role in European affairs. Banks could no longer compete with emerging powers and foreign influence would once again be the rule.

Southern Italy got the brunt of the bad news. People were already very poor and the Aragonese forces who governed weren't motivated by kindness. They needed funds to finance their wars. Taxes were high and brutality the consequence of not paying. When the Spanish contemplated a tax on fruit they sparked a rebellion that lasted over a year. It was a minor revolution with militias and peasant councils controlling many areas. Thousands were massacred by a Spanish regime determined to use the iron fist approach.

Impoverished, humiliated, and bullied, 17th-century Italy tried in vain to hold on to lost glory and former prominence in the arts and sciences. Galileo Galilei utilized telescopes, Monteverdi composed his first operas, and Palladio went on a building spree. Bernini and Borromini turned Rome into the capital of Baroque. The ornate style with little substance was the perfect sign for an age of political repression when free thinking was heavily frowned upon. Galileo later renounced his theory that the earth revolves around the sun and scholars wrote hundreds of books without really saying anything significant for fear of offending government, church, and the Inquisition. Carnivals and state celebrations distracted people and manners became extravagant. Clothing was more flamboyant than it

ever had been and titles of nobility were for sale. Revolutionary spirit was dampened and the country divided by the Papacy and foreign powers that would continue to pull the strings for several centuries.

RISORGIMENTO

Modern Italy began in the 1750s with the birth of a Republican movement determined to unite a fragmented territory. The *risorgimento* (resurgence) was a difficult endeavor and required unusual men doing extraordinary things. One of the greatest leaders of the period was Giuseppe Garibaldi. Anywhere you go in Italy you're likely to find a piazza or via named after this patriot who surmounted endless hurdles to bring about the Italy of today.

The first obstacle was Austria, which after the Treaty of Vienna in 1815 occupied northeastern Italy from Lombardy to Friuli. Garibaldi fought three wars against the Austrians. He lost two and was on the verge of winning the third when the Austrians surrendered to Prussia, thus avoiding any territorial loses. To this day one of the worst names you can call someone in Northern Italy is a Croato, a reference to the Croatian soldiers conscripted to fight for the Austrians.

Garibaldi's other problem was further south and the Kingdom of Two Sicilies that consisted of Bourbon monarchs who ruled over Southern Italy from their capital in Naples. In 1860, Garibaldi set off from Genoa with 1,000 volunteers. They used hand-me-down weapons and their red shirts were the only sign of a uniform, but what they lacked in training they made up for with spirit. After landing in Marsala, they took Palermo and the rest of Sicily with little bloodshed. The going was tougher in Campania but the Bourbons eventually surrendered Naples and retired to France.

Italy was a little closer to unification but there was still the matter of the Papal State that controlled Rome and much of Central Italy. The real problem was Napoleon III, who supported the Vatican and had sent troops to guard the city. Later that decade however the

Prussians defeated the French who were forced to pull out, thus opening the way for Garibaldi's red shirts. The Aurelian wall was pierced at Porta Pia and a statue later erected on the historic spot. Resistance was light and the Swiss Guard didn't put up much of a fight. An accord was drawn between the new state and the church that recognized the new Republic.

Even after the events of 1870 the Italian map was not complete and it wouldn't be until the end of World War I, when Austria ceded Trentino, that Italy reached her current territorial state.

THE 20TH CENTURY
World War I

Italy entered the 20th century united but still in search of itself. The country was not threatened and there was little necessity to go to war yet politicians and intellectuals alike succumbed to the fervor of conflict. Nationalism took hold and the unsettling tide of events that was rocking other European capitals spread to Rome. Which side Italy actually joined wasn't settled until the last minute, when the Allies made a better offer and victory would mean expanding borders and regaining Trieste from Austria.

And so with little preparation and less forethought, the Italian war machine mobilized for what everyone predicted would be a short war. The army set off badly equipped and ill commanded. Reality set in after the Battle of Caporetto and a long-hard fought campaign ensued that saw very little progress. By 1919, about 650,000 Italians had died and over a million were wounded in the fighting.

Fascism

Post-war Italy was greatly deprived and it was in this period that many peasants packed their bags and headed for the United States, Argentina, and Australia. Those that remained often lived from day to day and survived on a meager diet. There was a feeling of disappointment in the air. The promise of war had not been fulfilled and territorial additions seemed small compared to the suffering now spreading. The economy was weak and the revolution in Russia gave many workers something to think about. Extremes began to form and both sides were convinced liberal policies of the government were outdated.

One proponent of change was Benito Mussolini. Before the war, he had been an editor of the socialist party newspaper, *Avanti*. He had a talent for increasing readership and postwar confusion provided the opportunity to assert himself.

His idea of Fascism developed slowly and remained heavy on propaganda and light on philosophy. Economic hardship made recruiting easy and a private police of black shirts was soon protecting landowners, battling communists, and beating Slavs. In October 1922, Mussolini announced he would march on Rome. King Enamuele III refused to sign a decree of martial law that might have stopped the Fascists and had no choice but to appoint Mussolini as prime minister. Order was restored, trains started arriving on time, and opponents of the party could still show their faces. Things changed after the elections of 1924 and the assassination of Giacomo Matteotti, who was a rare politician not intimidated by black shirts. Over the next years Fascists used parliamentary means to convert Italy into a virtual dictatorship. Mussolini started giving his famous speeches from the balcony in Piazza Venezia and a love affair with the Italian people began in earnest. He used large-scale public work projects as well as the new medium of cinema to glorify every accomplishment.

World War II

One of Il Duce's favorite slogans was "whoever stops is lost." Mussolini could not stop and Italians could not stop Mussolini. He invaded Ethiopia and joined the Spanish Civil War on the side of Franco in 1936. This endeavor forged an alliance with Hitler that would later be fatal. Once again Italy was led unprepared into a world-shattering conflict. The results were even worse than World War I and even the magic of Cinecittà could not candycoat defeats in North Africa and the Balkans.

General Patton and Montgomery reached Sicilian shores in July 1943, by which time it was clear the tide had turned against Mussolini. An armistice was hastily drafted and signed in Brindisi, but this did not end the conflict. German divisions held very firm and made the Allies pay a heavy price for every muddy inch they advanced. The Battle of Monte Cassino was especially bloody and a throwback to the futility of trench warfare. Italian resistance behind the lines organized quickly. Partisans hampered German movement and managed to liberate many parts of Northern Italy before Sherman tanks rolled in at the end of the war.

Mussolini was caught trying to escape to Switzerland in April 1945. He and his mistress were shot and hung up for all to see in Milan. He remains popular with modern-day extremists, and his granddaughter has tried her best to follow in his footsteps.

1945 to the Present

Postwar Italy was a time of rationing and hunger. The *dolce vita* and miraculous economical recovery were still decades away and it took a while to pick up the pieces. In 1946, a referendum narrowly chose the Republican path over a return to monarchy and a new constitution was adopted. Government at the time was dominated by Christian Democrats and a revitalized Communist party.

In the 1950s, Rome made another memorable comeback. Italian style and cinema caught the attention of the world. Rossellini, De Sica, and Fellini shot gritty realism as the economy slowly rebounded. Factories in the north began to increase production and Fiats rolled off the assembly lines in Turin at unprecedented speed. Roads were built, the Vespa was born, and people were smiling again. Poverty still existed but it was concentrated in the south, where it remains to this day.

Government

Anything written about the Italian government is likely to be obsolete before it's printed. There have been over 60 governments formed since the end of World War II and that number seems destined to rise. In 2005, the center left led by Romano Prodi won a very slim majority over the center right of Silvio Berlusconi. The lack of a strong majority has meant a fragile government that could be dissolved at any moment. Laws are regularly passed by slim margins, after which one party breathes a sigh of relief while the other prepares its next offensive.

On the surface of things, there is very little constructive dialogue and politicians on the evening news compete for the best sound bite. Low blows are permitted and talk of armed uprisings and taking it to the streets are all part of the Italian political show.

One of the fundamental problems of the current system is the electoral process and imbalance of parliamentary power. Voters elect parties who in turn assign seats within the government. It's like buying a car without specifying the model you want and guarantees that the same old faces remain ever-present. Both sides know there is a problem, but getting politicians to agree on a reform that will affect their livelihood isn't easy.

ORGANIZATION
President of the Republic

The President of the Republic is elected for a seven-year term by a two-third majority of both chambers of parliament. The current President is Giorgio Napolitano. He heads the armed forces and has the power to veto legislation, dissolve parliament, and call for new elections. It's a difficult job that requires tremendous neutrality. Once elected, the President nominates the first Government Minister or *Presidente del Consiglio*.

Presidente del Consiglio handles the day-to-day running of the state. He selects ministers who are formally appointed by the President and in the case of Romano Prodi does the best to preserve the unanimity of his coalition.

Parliament

Parliament consists of two chambers: Chamber of Deputies and the Senate. According to the Constitution of 1948, both chambers have the same rights and powers. They are independent of each other and joint sessions are rare. The main business is the enactment of laws. For a text to become law, it must receive a majority in both houses. A bill is discussed in one house, amended and approved or rejected. If approved, it is passed to the other house, which can amend it and approve or reject it. If everything runs smoothly, the text is proclaimed law by the President of the Republic and enacted.

The Parliament is also responsible for the vote of confidence, which every government must pass in order to begin its mandate. It can also request such a vote at any time if a quota of any house is reached. Should a government fail a vote of confidence it must resign, at which point a new government is formed or the President of the Republic calls for new elections.

Chamber of Deputies

The Chamber of Deputies is located in Palazzo Montecitorio and has 630 members elected by all Italian citizens over the age of 18. Deputies are elected for five-year terms unless the President dissolves parliament. Reforms in 2005 significantly complicated things. The electoral system combines proportional representation with priority for the coalition securing the largest number of votes, so the emerging government has a stronger basis and can achieve its agenda. That hasn't been the case and there is now talk of further electoral reform that would implement a system similar to the one used in Germany. Anyone can be elected to Parliament and over a dozen members have been convicted of some crime or other.

Senate

The Senate is located in Palazzo Madama. The Senate has 315 members, elected for five-year terms by Italian citizens over the age of 25. Members are elected by proportional representation based on party lists from each of Italy's 20 regions. Six Senators represent Italians living abroad and seven are members for life.

POLITICAL PARTIES

Italy is as far as you can get from a two-party system. There are well over 74 officially organized groups that run the gamut from hardcore communist to right-wing separatist. In between are small and medium-sized groups, none of whom are large enough to govern on their own.

Coalitions are therefore a necessity. Unione consists of liberal-minded parties such as Olive and Margherita, and Casa della Libertà is a conservative-oriented umbrella group under which Forza Italia, Allenza Nazionale, and UDC are more or less united.

Consolidation is the latest trend on the left and the Partito Democratico was created to assimilate smaller parties into a large political force capable of winning a substantial majority in parliament. The leader of the group is the current mayor of Rome, who many consider the likely successor of Prodi. The real test will come at the next elections.

To get a sense of Italian politics, just look for the posters pasted on nearly every wall. Most are simple enough to understand and remind passersby about the shortcomings of the adversary.

ELECTIONS

On December 14, 2005, a new electoral system was approved and put into place. The system is based on proportional representation with a series of thresholds to encourage parties to form coalitions. To be part of a coalition a party must have a program and specify a candidate as possible President del Consiglio.

The country is divided into constituencies in which seats are distributed according to the share of votes received by a party. Lists of candidates within each party must be announced beforehand and electors vote for their preferred list rather than individual candidates. If a party wins 10 seats, the first 10 candidates on its list are elected.

JUDICIAL SYSTEM

The Judicial branch of the Italian Government is represented by the Constitutional Court of Italy. This is Italy's Supreme Court. It is composed of 15 judges. One-third are appointed by the President, one-third elected by the Parliament, and the remainder are elected by lesser courts. They have their work cut out for them and a tremendous backlog of cases waiting to be heard.

Economy

Italy is the sixth-largest economy in the world with a GDP of $1.5 trillion. The average income per family is over $25,000 and Italian politicians regularly attend G8 meetings. The introduction of the euro, however, has taken its toll on disposable income and while prices have gone up salaries haven't. Growth is beneath the European average and stagnant at best. The country's main trading partners are Germany, France, the Netherlands, and the United States. Unemployment hovers around 7 percent and avoiding taxes is a national obsession.

INDUSTRY

Northern Italy is the traditional home of the country's industrial sector. From 1951 to 1963, the economy grew over 6 percent per year and cities like Turin nearly doubled in population within 20 years. Fiat led the economic postwar recovery and its cars still make up the largest slice of the domestic market. Other goods include precision machinery, pharmaceuticals, home appliances, luxury items, textiles, clothing, and ceramics.

There are no deposits of iron, coal, or oil. Natural gas reserves can be found in the Po

business as usual in Milan

© PURESTOCK

valley and offshore in the Adriatic Sea. Most raw materials for manufacturing and more than 80 percent of the country's energy sources must be imported.

One of Italy's strengths is small and medium-size family-owned businesses. Over 90 percent of all companies employ less than 10 people. These take pride in their work and have managed to maintain traditional methods of craftsmanship even the Chinese can't imitate.

ECONOMIC FUTURE

The Minister of Finance has the hardest job in Italy (although he does earn over €30,000 per month). The country faces a rising trade defi-

cit, high labor costs, and a substantial national debt. "Reform" is a dirty word and higher taxes could set off a revolution. Italian companies are already at a tax disadvantage compared to their European rivals and competition from Asia is starting to hurt.

The challenge will be to find new markets for Italian goods and increase production and exportations. Investment in research and development is dangerously low and the strong euro increases the price of exports and prices the country out of many markets. Italians, however, are ingenious and companies like Benetton and Luxottica have managed to make Made in Italy one of the most desirable labels in the world.

People and Culture

DEMOGRAPHICS

Italy is one of the most densely populated countries in Europe, with over 58 million inhabitants. Rome is the largest city, with a population of 2.5 million, followed by Naples and Milan. The average life expectancy is 83 years for women and 77 for men. There are also plenty of people pushing 100 and close observation of any bus or street corner reveals that age greatly outnumbers youth. Birth rates are low and it's only through immigration that the country has managed to keep its population from declining.

IMMIGRATION

Immigration is a new phenomenon in Italy. Until 1989, more people left the country than arrived and foreign faces were rare. The official number of immigrants is around two million but the real number is probably closer to three. It's estimated that 6 percent of the population was born outside the country and in Europe only Germany and Spain have higher immigrant populations.

The largest communities are made up of Moroccans, Albanians, Romanians, Chinese, Tunisians, Serbs, and Senegalese. Most are attracted to northern industrial cities where

the chances of finding a job are better than down south. Many work as day laborers on farms, in construction, or as caretakers for the elderly. Today it's not uncommon to see a Pakistani chef preparing pasta and Nigerian schoolchildren speaking perfect Italian.

Native Italians are still coming to grips with the changing ethnic landscape, and a recent crime wave committed by foreigners, or *stranieri* as they're called, has led the government to take a tougher stance on who enters Italy. As with all Mediterranean countries, illegal immigration from North Africa is a problem and boats regularly reach the shores of Sicily packed with desperate people looking to start a new life abroad. For some, Italy is the promised land, while for others it's only part of a journey that may eventually end in the United States or Canada. Many immigrants also return to their native country after earning enough to start over again. Life is difficult for newcomers who live on the margins of society with little hope of integration.

YOUNG ITALIANS

Very little distinguishes an Italian teenager from any other crisis-prone youth in the

Western hemisphere. The jeans are the same, the music is the same, and the movies are the same. The greatest difference is the moped young people start to ride at 14, which provides an instant sense of freedom.

Real freedom, however, is a long way off for young people and a large proportion of twenty-somethings live with their parents. Most attend universities in the same city and the lack of well-paying jobs means financial independence isn't attained until well into the 30s. Contracts are usually short-term and don't provide the stability needed to make too many plans for the future. The cost of housing is another obstacle to breaking away from the family nest and rents are high. It usually takes a long period of saving before young people can purchase a home of their own, which explains why the term *ragazzo* (boy) is often used for someone well past their 30th birthday.

RELIGION

Peter was the first apostle to reach Italy and although he was martyred by the Romans the message of monotheism he preached stuck. When the empire crumbled, Christianity survived and for centuries was the only thing going. Priests kept Latin alive in a world where scholarship took a back seat to survival. The Papal State grew wealthy and its influence spread throughout central Italy. Popes commissioned churches and art became a way of promoting the Bible. Religious ceremonies were not only held on Sundays and mass could go on for hours. Every town has a patron saint that is still celebrated with feasts and festivals.

The vast majority of Italians are Catholic, although the numbers regularly attending church is on the decline. The Lateran Agreement of 1929 officially formalized the relationship between the Italian State and the Vatican, which continues to benefit from substantial tax breaks. Although church and state are divided in the constitution it's not uncommon to see crucifixes in police stations, hospitals, and schools.

Islam, Buddhism, and Orthodox Christianity are the fastest growing religions. Many Muslims face Mecca inside homemade mosques and some Italian cities have been reluctant to provide building permits for new Mosques. Jews have been present in Italy nearly from the beginning and the oldest synagogue in Europe is in Ostia Antica. Treatment varied through the ages and many towns have the remnants of ghettos where Jews were forced to live.

LANGUAGE

Italy's national language derived from Latin and owes a great debt to Dante, who was the first to codify and utilize the dialects spoken on the Renaissance streets of Florence in his tales of heaven and hell. Not all Italian is equal and a trained ear can detect the difference between a Neapolitan and a Venetian accent. Besides regional differences, there are also minority languages such as Sardo, spoken by over a million people in Sardinia, and Friulano, widely used in Friuli. Ladino and Catalan are the smallest linguistic enclaves spoken in the Alps and on the northwestern coast of Sardinia. Both are remnants of foreign occupation and gradual contact with Italian has led to colorful words and expressions missing from dictionaries.

Aosta is officially bilingual and most residents speak both French and Italian. German is common in Alto Adige and towns in the region have both Italian and German names. Many people on the eastern border of Friuli speak Slovanian and you're unlikely to hear any Italian in the Val di Resia. Farther south Albanian immigrants from the 19th century left behind linguistic pockets throughout Calabria and Molise.

Thornton Wilder once said everyone should travel to a country where English isn't spoken and they don't even want to speak it. Italy isn't that country and language schools have no problem filling seats. Most Italians have a basic understanding of English and whatever vocabulary they lack they can usually express with their hands.

Art and Architecture

Art is everywhere in Italy and if you could put a price tag on all the frescoes, paintings, and sculptures you'd be close to infinity. The Borghese Gallery alone is stuffed with more beauty than some cities. Fortunately you don't need to be an art historian to appreciate the mosaics of Ravenna or the inlaid marble of Florence's campanile. All it takes is an open eye. A stroll in any town is a walk through a patchwork of styles, from ancient stadiums to Gio Ponti's Pirelli skyscraper. Don't worry if you can't recognize Gothic from Baroque: Just notice the slant of a roof and particular shade of brick, and the eras will eventually fall into place.

STYLES
Classical
The first architects in Italy were Greek, and the temples they erected inspired Romans to lay foundations that remain visible today. The most distinguished feature of these buildings is the column. Often it's the last thing standing. Columns came in three orders: Doric (flat), Ionic (curved), and Corinthian (flowery) can all be spotted on the Colosseum and were recycled by Renaissance designers hundreds of years later. Structures that remain from this period include amphitheaters, triumphal arches, and public baths. Advances in the casting of concrete and the use of the arch allowed Roman builders to think bigger than ever before and impress even modern eyes. The dome was perfected, exteriors adorned with marble, and interiors decorated with elaborate mosaics and frescoes that have survived in Ostia Antica and Pompei.

Romanesque
Churches are the great architectural legacy of the Middle Ages. The first paleo-Christian places of worship were small and appeared towards the end of the empire. There was a boom in baptisteries around 1000 A.D. and each region had its own take on the style. Buildings in this era had simple facades and small windows that were later enlarged once glass became widespread. It was common to make alterations throughout the centuries as fashion and tastes changed, and few buildings from the period escaped some form of remodeling. Greater wealth allowed more ambitious building programs. Pisa got the ball rolling with its cathedral, which recaptured the greatness of the ancient world. A black and white style was developed in Siena and Florence and competition between cities helped spur on the movement. Noble families in San Gimignano and Ascoli went vertical with urban towers that dotted the skyline. Byzantine and Muslim influences in southern Italy introduced complex geometrical patterns. Church ground plans were generally in the form of a crucifix and consisted of single naves. Interiors weren't fancy and nothing was meant to distract worshippers from salvation. Many basilicas like St. Francis in Assisi were decorated with frescoes recounting the Bible. Mosaics were especially popular in Venice and Sicily, where Norman churches like the cathedral of Monreale took the technique to new heights.

Gothic
Architecture eventually exploded beyond the confines of rigid shapes and traditional forms. Gothic emerged in the 12th–16th centuries and seeped down the peninsula from the north. Groups of masons, like the Campionese Masters, built cathedrals and basilicas from Milan to Assisi. In Venice, the style combined with Asian influences, giving the city a look of its own. Ornament was added to churches and archways pointed the way to heaven. Cathedrals rose higher than ever before supported by rib vaulting. This meant that walls could be thinner, which allowed for the introduction of stained glass and rose windows imported from France. Orvieto's cathedral is one of the finest examples of the movement. In Rome, many Gothic buildings were given a Baroque makeover and reveal their true identity in the mosaics and paintings that were spared.

Renaissance

Renaissance architecture was less spectacular than the art that emerged from the period. There were certainly outstanding achievements—like Brunelleschi's dome in Florence and Michelangelo's cupola in St. Peter's—but it was also a time of confusion and aesthetics that failed to take off the way sculpture and painting did. Antiquity was still admired over creativity and the imagination of the previous eras was abandoned in favor of austerity. Practioners like Bramante and Codussi left behind marvelous palaces financed by a growing upper class eager to outdo its neighbors.

Baroque

Baroque architecture is easier to identify than Renaissance architecture. A Baroque building wants to be noticed and catches the eye with elaborate lines and unusual flare. It's a love-it-or-leave-it style that grew out of the ideals of the Counter-Reformation in the 17th and 18th centuries. Many church interiors were remodeled during that time, which explains why you can't always judge a cathedral by its facade. Rome led the way in the movement thanks to the genius of Bernini and Borromini. Popes indulged themselves on irreverent designs that were not universally adopted. Florence and Venice passed on the movement and the southern Italian incarnation took the studied excess in a new direction. Some towns like Lecce are crammed with Baroque and became forever associated with the movement. Italian gardens also sprang up in this era and examples at Tivoli and Isola Bella matched the splendor of the palazzos they were meant to accentuate.

Neoclassicism

Baroque wasn't easily replaced and Italy lost her supremacy on the art and architecture front during the 18th century. Neoclassicism dusted off Romans designs and gave them an updated treatment. Symmetry and the use of architectural standards of the past are its notable characteristics. Grand opera houses sprung up in major towns and enclosed shopping galleries were built in Milan and Naples. Public buildings became extravagant and for a while the Mole Antonelliana was the tallest building in the world. Fading dynasties also got into the act and a neoclassical palace was built in Caserta to rival Versailles. Towards the early 19th century the movement evolved into Umbertine, best expressed in the massive Vittorio Emanuele II monument in Rome that Caesar would have loved but is generally dismissed by modern residents. Harder to find and on a much smaller scale are examples of Art Nouveau, which spread from France; although short-lived, it marked the beginning of modern architecture. The best examples are usually related to the burgeoning tourist industry and many luxurious hotels, spas, and casinos on the Italian Riviera adopted the distinctive style.

Modern

Modern architecture evolved late in Italy and steel and glass never replaced reinforced concrete as the material of choice. With the rise of Fascism, a stark, monumental style was promoted that's visible in EUR and in many cities in the south, some of which were built from scratch. After World War II, trends mixed and postmodernism slowly snuck into a few skylines. Pier Luigi Nervi was one of the only 20th-century architects who combated dreariness with skyscrapers—like the Pirelli tower in Milan, a rare modern construction that still looks good.

Today

Getting a building permit is difficult, and even homegrown stars like Fuksas and Piano have trouble realizing their visions. Today's buildings often look obsolete before the last nail is hammered. There was no shortage of controversy when Richard Rogers completed his Ara Pacis museum in Rome and Calatrava installed a new bridge in Venice. New is often shunned in favor of conventional and downright ugly. Hundreds of buildings could do with a little dynamite and the rationalist mistakes of the 1960s eradicated for good. More than one architect, in fact, has secretly prayed for Etna to erupt again.

VISUAL ARTS

Medieval

When the Empire fell, creativity wasn't extinguished. Creativity flourished in Ravenna, where Byzantine craftsmen adorned churches with mosaics. Lombard art supplied new talent in the 7th–9th centuries and spread to Cividale del Friuli and Spoleto. Most painting and sculpture was intended for religious purposes and inspiration came directly from the Bible.

Renaissance

The name says it all. The Renaissance was a time of artistic leaps and bounds. Artists were capable of miracles and the imagination was set free like never before. Tuscany was the epicenter of this golden age and Da Vinci, Raphael, and Michelangelo rubbed shoulders in Florence. Rather than just copy ancient works, they expanded upon medieval art traditions and explored new possibilities of expression. Many artists began as apprentices under fine craftsmen or other artists before leapfrogging their masters. Florentine style was exported beyond the region by its purveyors, who went on a creative binge throughout Europe. Painting and sculpture lost its stiffness and began to look lifelike. Space on canvas and walls was redefined and the world was accurately reflected like never before. Giotto nearly single-handedly invented 3D and put it to work in Assisi. During the Early Renaissance, artists in Siena painted brightly colored scenes with thousands of details. Venice had its own distinct school led by Mantenga and towns from Mantua to Perugia contributed to the advancement of art.

Mannerism

Mannerism developed in the mid-16th century and was a response to the High Renaissance and new political realities. Rome was sacked, freedom restrained, and religion was splitting at the seams. Artists became less interested in the observation of nature but in the style or manner in which they painted. Compositions were unordered and focal points disappeared. Proportions were exaggerated and figures elongated or twisted into graceful or bizarre postures. Colors often clashed and instability was favored over the balance depicted by previous generations of artists.

Baroque

The Council of Trent (1545–1563) did more than reform Catholic dogma. It started a re-evaluation of art, of which the church was a major sponsor, and began a return to spirituality and tradition. Art was no longer just for the well-to-do but was intended to stir everyone's soul. Inspiration came from the saints, Virgin Mary, and the Old Testament. Rome was the center of the movement and Caravaggio and the Carracci brothers took turns innovating church interiors, fountains, and living rooms around the city. Drama is the common denominator and Bernini emerged as the greatest exponent of the period. His battling Baroque *David* stands in stark contrast to Michelangelo's contemplative version. Viewers could not help be moved and no one could pass the Fontana di Trevi with indifference. Sculpture gained multiple viewing angles and ressembled actors on a stage. There was a return to group figures and all sorts of props were used to add to the drama.

Futurism

Futurism was the last great Italian contribution to the art world. It was a response to Cubism with three principal elements: speed, technology, and modernity. The movement was born in the early 20th century with Filippo Marinetti's avant-garde manifesto calling for the burning of libraries. Artists gradually followed in his intellectual footsteps and began portraying sensations and capturing the essence of objects. Canvases and sculpture moved just as fast as the world on the verge of war. Factories and machines were idealized and artists unknowingly paved the way towards Fascism. The movement merged with others around Europe and shared many traits with Russian Constructivism. Good examples of the genre are hanging in Rome's and Milan's modern art museums. The only other art to attract international attention during the 20th century was the mysterious, metaphysical work of De Chirico and the oddly thin sculptures of Giacometti.

MAJOR ARTISTS
Giotto

If anyone deserves the title of "godfather of painting," it's Giotto di Bondone (c. 1266–1337). He was lucky enough to be born near Florence and to have studied under Cimabue, who according to legend discovered Giotto drawing on a rock. By 1312, he had joined a guild and spent three years working for the King of Naples before becoming responsible for the building of the Cathedral of Florence. Identifying his works has always been tricky as only three were signed; debates still rage over authenticity. The most famous attributed works are the Arena Chapel frescoes in Padova and the 28 panels illustrating the life of St. Francis in Assisi. Giotto was particularly concerned with figures and the challenge of accurately representing them on a flat surface. He developed the three-dimensional space that is now so familiar but was revolutionary then. His genius was immediately recognized by peers, who gradually gave up the old forms of art and adopted the new way. He was buried in Florence with full honors and the city paid for the funeral.

Donatello

Donato di Bardi (1386–1466), known as Donatello to his friends, was born in Florence. He was an excellent sculptor and his statues were rarely surpassed for their grace or beauty. The popular artist was also highly regarded as an architect and could work miracles with stucco. His work shows an understanding of Greek and Roman precedent and could easily be confused with antique sculptures if it weren't for his inventive poses and innovation of low relief.

Mantegna

Andrea Mantegna (c. 1431–1506) was an early Renaissance artist. He spent a great deal of time studying Roman ruins and constantly experimented with perspective. The workshop he opened produced thousands of prints but his lasting legacy are frescoed ceilings and paintings like the *Lamentation over the Dead Christ*. The style he developed borrowed a lot from the principles of sculpture and his figures appear rock solid.

Botticelli

The son of a Florentine tanner, Alessandro Botticelli (c. 1444–1510) was apprenticed to a goldsmith and studied painting under Fra Filippo Lippi. At the age of 25, he was running his own studio and producing an impressive number of small religious canvases. His big break came in 1474, when he was commissioned to paint St. Sebastien for the church of Santa Maria Maggiore. It caught the attention of the Medicis, who hired Botticelli to paint dozens of family portraits. The artist, however, is most famous for the many depictions of the Madonna and later works became influenced by the asceticism preached by the Dominican monk Girolamo Savonarola. Faces became more severe and his illustrations for Dante's *Inferno* are as frightening as the text.

Leonardo da Vinci

Leonardo da Vinci (1452–1519) defies categorization, as he was equally gifted as a painter, sculptor, architect, and inventor. Everyone knows *Mona Lisa* and yet no one could have predicted such a brilliant career for the illegitimate son of a Tuscan peasant woman. At the age of four, he went to live with his father's family, who moved to Florence, and as a teenager he studied under Andrea del Verrocchio. It wasn't long before pupil surpassed master and many of his early works were portions of Verrocchio's compositions. In search of patronage he moved to Milan and won dozens of commissions, including *The Last Supper* inside Santa Maria delle Grazie. Unfortunately his love of experimentation led him to try a new technique that did not prove as resilient as he had hoped. At the same time he studied science and medicine and the notebooks he left behind demonstrate his interest in nearly everything that was cutting edge at the time. His last years were spent imparting knowledge to a young French king.

Raphael

Raffaello Sanzio (1483–1520) was the last of the Renaissance superstar painters. He was born in Urbino and inherited the love of brushes from his father, who was a small-town painter. As a teenager, he moved to Florence and studied under Perugino. Michelangelo and Leonardo da Vinci were his heroes, but he developed his own style. He used rich, strong colors, and always managed to balance his canvases. In 1508, he moved to Rome, where talent and personality made him popular and successful. Pope Julius II selected Raphael to paint his private rooms and appointed him as one of the architects of St. Peter's. He was also superintendent of excavations for ancient Rome and designed the tapestries within the Sistine Chapel. Wealthy families hired him to paint their portraits and his studio was one of the busiest in Italy. Although he had plenty of assistants, Raphael was a workaholic and the strain led to a premature death.

Michelangelo

Michelangelo di Lodovico Buonarroti Simoni (1475–1564), known universally as Michelangelo, was a painter, sculpture, architect, and poet. After an apprenticeship with Bertoldo di Giovanni, Michelangelo began a series of prestigious commissions in Florence and Rome. He led art in a new realistic direction that eventually became synonymous with the Renaissance. His work in the Sistine Chapel and the statue of *David* are some of the most visited artworks in Italy and both took several years to complete. But these famous works are really just a taste of what this artist accomplished. Most churches in Florence boast at least one of his sculptures and he left behind many unfinished works that demonstrate his unrivaled technique. Although the personal details about his life are unreliable, art historians generally portray him as solitary and ill-tempered with few social graces. (See *Following Michelangelo* in the *Discover Italy* chapter for more information on the artist.)

Caravaggio

Michelangelo Merisi da Caravaggio (1573–1610) took painting on a new revolutionary path. His talent was revealed from an early age and his apprenticeship was brief. Although his style ressembled Mannerism, he was one of the first painters with a social consciousness. Models were average people and set in everyday surroundings that were infused with spirituality. Light in his canvases is unreal and creates great contrast that adds emotion and drama to his subjects. His irreverence to artistic trends made him unpopular during his lifetime and a bohemian lifestyle set the tone for generations of aspiring artists. After killing a man, he was forced to flee and eventually died from malaria at an early age. Nevertheless his influence on 17th-century art is unquestionable and his approach spread quickly throughout Europe.

ESSENTIALS

Getting There

AIR

Rome Fiumicino, Milan Malpensa, and Pisa Galileo Galilei are the main international airports with daily flights from North America. Where you land depends on whether you're headed for northern, central, or southern Italy. That said, distances will seem greatly reduced especially if you're from Alaska, Texas, or Montana. Price therefore may be a decisive factor on which airport you choose.

You can transfer from all three to dozens of smaller airports around the country and the islands of Sicily and Sardinia. A new aviation agreement between the EU and United States has also relaxed some of the old regulations and may soon make Pittsburgh to Palermo a reality.

Rome Fiumicino (Leonardo da Vinci) and Roma Ciampino are managed by ADR S.p.A. (Aeroporti di Roma, www.adr.it). The website provides information on routes, flight times, and car rentals. SEA (www.sea-aeroportimilano.it) provides similar services for Milan's airports.

Most major airports in Italy have convenient train service that gets passengers into city centers quickly and are the best way to avoid starting your holiday with a traffic jam. Fares are cheaper than taking a cab.

© PURESTOCK

Airlines

Flights from the east coast take slightly over eight hours and a little *more* on the way back if the trade winds are blowing. Nonstop flights are preferable unless you're curious about Amsterdam, Zurich, or London, or looking to save money. **Alitalia** (www.alitalia.it) is the Italian national carrier and there's been a lot of speculation about a takeover in recent years. They serve good food and flight attendants wear Armani-designed uniforms. They fly from Boston, New York, Chicago, and Miami. **Delta** (www.delta.com), **American Airlines** (www.aa.com), **Continental** (www.continental.com), and **United Airlines** (www.united.com) connect Atlanta, Los Angeles, Chicago, and Newark with Rome and Milan daily.

If the thought of a three-hour layover and another crack at the duty free shops doesn't frighten you, try New York JFK to Rome via Zurich with **SwissAir** or **KLM** to Rome from Newark via Amsterdam. There may be other attractive layover alternatives with national European carriers like **British Airways, Air France,** or **Lufthansa.** Just ask your travel agent or compare prices on the Internet.

Costs

Besides the airline websites, it's worth browsing www.opodo.com, flightscanner.net, and www.expedia.com to get a rough ideas of prices. Many sites provide fare alerts based on your preferences, and www.travelzoo.com or www.airfarewatchdog.com will let you know the best deals as soon as they are available.

There are usually significant variations around summer and during the Christmas and Easter holidays. If Italy has been on your mind for awhile, you can save by booking three or more months ahead of time. If it's a-spur-of-the-moment thing, you might also save with a last-minute fare. In between is when the airlines make their money. Keep in mind that every seat is priced differently and the guy sitting next to you may have paid outrageously more or less than you did. Also, passengers are superstitious and departures on the 13th of each month, as well as September 11, are up to 40 percent cheaper.

If you're flexible with departure times or can travel in March or October you could shave some dollars off the cost off a ticket. Look for midweek flights in the early morning or late evening. You might reach your destination with a little more jet lag but there's an espresso waiting that will wake you up.

Italy is also well connected with other European cities and the boom in low-cost aviation has led to very attractive prices. If time is on your side you can fly **Ryanair** (www.ryanair.com) or **Easyjet** (www.easyjet.com) from Berlin, London, Paris, and Madrid. Other budget carries worth checking if Italy is a second or third stop on a European tour are Germanwings, TuiFly, and Air Berlin.

Insurance

Ninety-nine times out of a hundred you won't need travel insurance. It's that one time however that could make a policy worthwhile and reimburse a missed flight, stolen luggage, or a medical emergency. You may already be covered, so check with any existing policies you have and make all your purchases with credit cards that often cover flight and rental insurance. Most gold or premium cards include these services, as does American Express, but it's worth checking with your credit card company before making a purchase. Travel agents also sell insurance but their prices may include a commission and you can often get a better deal online with companies like **Travel Insured** (www.travelinsured.com), **Travelex** (www.travelex-insurance.com), or **World Nomads** (www.worldnomads.com), which offers good rates for backpackers and budget travelers.

LAND

Since the Schengen Agreement, traveling between EU countries has become hassle-free. Border controls are a thing of the past and entering Italy by car from France, Switzerland, Austria, or Slovenia is a breeze. It's 200 kilometers from Nice to Genova on the A10 highway,

140 from Genova to Aosta on the A5, 500 from Munich to Milan on the A9, and 120 from Innsbruck to Bolzano on the A22.

You may need to pay a toll when entering the country. As most of the highways into Italy are at fairly high altitudes, snow and fog can lead to some delays. Smaller roads that cross the Alps are full of curves and best driven during the day at slow speeds.

Arriving by train from other European destinations often requires a long and tortuous journey. There are daily departures from Paris to Rome onboard the **Artesia** service that leaves early evenings and arrives at Termini in the morning. If you want to avoid a neckache it's worth purchasing a berth in one of the sleeping cabins (*couchettes*). There are also many trains from Northern European cities to Milan, Turin, Venice, and Verona. Single tickets can be purchased through www.trenitalia.it or if you are on a European vacation and will be visiting many countries it may be cheaper to purchase a railpass from **Eurail** (www.eurail.com) or **Rail Europe** (www.raileurope.com).

Bus service is the cheapest and least comfortable way to reach Italy. **Eurolines** (www.eurolines-pass.com) operates service from many European capitals and the trip from London Victoria is 28 hours to Milan and 36 hours to Rome. Drivers make regular stops where you can stretch your legs and grab something to eat.

SEA

It's possible to reach Italy by sea from many Mediterranean countries. During the summer, there are frequent links from the Greek ports of Corfu and Patras to Brindisi on the Adriatic coast. Ferries also operate from Spain, France, and Tunisia to Genoa, Livorno, Cagliari, and Palermo. It takes two days to reach Civitavecchia from Barcelona and cabins are available. Boats on longer routes are equipped with entertainment and dining facilities that help pass the time.

Getting Around

AIR

Low-cost aviation has arrived in Italy and provides the quickest way of getting from city to city, although you'll miss the scenery that sometimes makes a slower journey worthwhile. Rome–Milan is the busiest route and both cities fly to many smaller destinations. New budget airlines are launched every year and competition keeps prices attractive. **Meridiana** (tel. 199/111-333, www.meridiana.it) is one of the most reliable and recently advertised Rome–Palermo fares for under €20. It's an ideal way to jump from north to south if time is limited and get an instant change of scenery. **Air Vallee** (tel. 016/530-3303, www.airvallee.com), **Airone** (www.flyairone.it), and **Alpi Eagles** (www.alpieagles.com) are also worth investigating.

TRAIN

Trains haven't run on time since Mussolini was in charge, but that shouldn't stop you from getting on board. There are several different types of trains, as well as first- and second-class service, and sleeping cars on overnight journeys.

Eurostar (ES) trains are the fastest and connect major cities. Reservations are mandatory but there are usually hourly departures from Rome towards Florence or Naples. The Eurostar between Milan and Naples takes 6.5 hours. **Intercity** are slightly slower but you can usually get a last-minute ticket without a problem. **Direct** and **Inter-Regional** trains are generally the most crowded as they make local stops and it can be worth buying a first class ticket for a slightly larger seat and more leg-room.

The train network in Northern Italy runs north–south and east–west, while lines farther down the peninsula are impeded by the Apennine Mountains and consist of two major tracks that run up and down the eastern and western coasts. Rome is the center of the network and from Termini station you can get to any location in Italy, although it may require a transfer or two.

Before boarding any train, make sure to validate your ticket. Validation boxes are yellow and near the platforms. They print the time and date of your journey. If you do forget, pleading ignorance might get you off the hook and avoid a stiff fine. Hold on to your ticket until the journey is completed. When sitting down next to other passengers, it's customary to say *"buongiorno"* (good day), which more often than not leads to a memorable conversation.

Train stations, especially in large cities like Milan and Rome, often attract dubious characters who prey upon distracted tourists. Keep your senses peeled and don't linger more than you have to.

Trenitalia (tel. 892-021 or 06/44101, www.fer roviedellostato.it) operates all trains in Italy.

Travel Passes

Trenitalia offers a variety of passes and discounts for passengers under 26 years of age **(Carta Verde)** and over 60 **(Carta Argento).** All their deals are outlined on the website (www.ferroviedellostato.it) which is also in English. Eurail (www.eurail.com) and Rail Europe (www.raileurope.com) provide the classic passes that aspiring backpackers dream about. These often provide a fixed number of days or countries per month and unless you are certain of your routes it can often be cheaper to buy your tickets upon arrival.

Local Trains, Trams, and Subways

Most Italian cities have a network of commuter trains that serve the suburbs. These are also operated by Trenitalia and often depart from secondary stations. They can be quite crowded during the week as people make their way to and from work.

Rome, Milan, Naples, and Turin are the only cities with subways *(metropolitana).* All four networks are relatively small and provide a cheap way of avoiding traffic on the streets overhead. Tickets can be purchased at *tabacchi*

(newsstands) or at stations, where you can also get a map. In Rome there are only two lines (A and B) that intersect at Termini. Stations in the capital are currently being remodeled and a third line is under construction. Milan's network is color-coded red, green, and yellow. Tickets cost €1 and provide 75 minutes of travel that includes transfers to buses or trams. Daily and weekly passes are also available and usually well worth the price. Although there are cameras and subway police, pickpockets are common and too much map-reading will single you out as an easy target.

BUS
National

Wherever trains can't go buses usually operate and there are dozens of regional companies that connect Italy's harder-to-reach destinations. Most depots are located near train stations or large squares and service is generally more reliable on weekdays as they cater for commuters and students. Tickets can be purchased on board or at the station and many companies offer passes for anyone who plans on making buses their primary means of travel. **Lazzi** (tel. 05/521-5155) and **SITA** (tel. 05/521-4721) are two of the largest companies and run many routes between Lazio and Tuscany. To see a complete list of operators, visit www.busstation.net.

Local

Local buses are usually orange, while interurban buses are blue. A single ticket is usually €1 and can be purchased from news agents or *tabacchi.* Like train tickets, these must be validated and inspectors are out hunting fare-dodgers on a regular basis. Buses are a great way to explore a city, gazing out the window and observing fellow passengers. Don't get too distracted though, as pickpockets are not uncommon.

TAXI

Taxis are convenient for travelers with lots of luggage or groups who want to split a fare. Prices to and from airports can be very expensive and it's usually cheaper to stick to

Taxis are usually waiting in large piazzas.

mass transit (Pisa and Milan Linate are the exceptions, as they are located very close to the center).

Most cities have dedicated bus and taxi lanes that make cabs useful if you are in a hurry. For the most part, cabs are not randomly hailed at street corners but picked up at taxi stands located on the larger piazzas. There's usually a few waiting outside any train station. They can also be ordered by phone for direct pickup. Taxis in Italy are white and by law must display their prices. If you notice the driver hasn't started the meter make sure to remind him.

Fares vary from city to city but are usually based on a combination of distance and time. There are surcharges for nighttime travel (10 P.M.–7 A.M.) and extra baggage. Some cities, like Rome, have a fixed price for travel to and from airports but you are better off establishing a fare before entering a cab in Naples. Drivers may not have change for a €50 so make sure you have smaller bills. Tipping is not required but it's usual to round up a euro or two.

CAR

Italy has fewer stop lights per kilometer than any other country in Europe. The yield sign is king and rolling stops are the rule. Driving really varies from region to region and road by road. Sardinians tend to drive slower than Romans, seatbelts are rarely worn in Palermo, and anything usually goes in Naples.

Motorists are in a hurry and they're generally annoyed because someone is ahead of them. Someone is always ahead and the trick is getting into the Italian rhythm without losing your calm. Don't worry about tailgaters, ignore the mopeds swarming around you, and don't forget to use your turn signal. Less than half of Italians signal but they'll be on their horn in half a nanosecond if you haven't moved when the light turns green. Take a deep breath and relax, it's actually fun driving here especially if you've rented a Smart or new Fiat 500 that will feel like a toy compared to the SUV back home.

Rentals

The no-hassle and low-risk way to guarantee yourself a car is to reserve one prior to departure. You might, however, get a better deal as a walk-up customer so if price matters hedge your bets with a reservation and check fees with other companies upon arrival. All the major companies (Avis, Budget, Hertz) have offices in airports and major cities. Big European outfits like Europcar and Maggiore may also have good deals and Sixt advertises Smart cars for €5 a day.

Subcompacts are great for moving around cities but on the highway or open countryside a little extra horsepower helps. Most fleets include a range of models and you can choose from automatic or standard versions. Rentals run about €250–350 per week depending on the type of car and whether you have limited or unlimited mileage. It's worth calculating the distances you plan to travel on a map before deciding one way or the other.

Campers

Campers are quite common in Italy and although they may be a little intimidating at first are a great way to discover national parks and Italy's less-traveled regions. There's a well-organized network of campsites that has areas specifically designated for campers as well as many free parking areas *(sosta camper)* that are very often located in scenic areas. A four-berth vehicle in high season is around €1,500 a week with unlimited mileage. **Blu Rent** (tel. 017/160-1702, www.blurent.com), **Comocaravan** (tel. 031/521-215, www.como caravan.it), **DueDi** (tel. 045/956-677) and **Maggiore** (tel. 840/008-840, www.maggiore-camperrent.it) provide modern vehicles with a wide range of comforts.

Insurance

Driving without insurance is a risk you don't want to take in Italy. Collision Damage Waiver insurance however can often double the price of a rental and may already be provided by your credit card company. American Express offers the service and it's a good idea to check before your departure. If you do get into an accident remain calm and congratulate yourself for having gotten insurance. All rental cars have the necessary paperwork you are required to fill out. Other drivers upon hearing your accent may try to shift the blame and it's wise not to sign any documents you don't understand until the police arrive.

Legal

Drivers must be at least 21 years of age and have a valid license. A *carabiniere's* favorite pastime is pulling cars over, so having an International Drivers License may help avoid confusion. These cost $15 and are issued from any branch of AAA on the spot. All you'll need to provide are two passport-size photos and a license.

Rules

Rules may seem like a contradiction in Italy, but they do exist and may one day be enforced. Drivers must wear their seatbelts and give way to traffic on the right whenever in doubt. Speed limits in towns and cities are 50 kilometers per hour and 110 on highways, where headlights

© PURESTOCK

Red traffic lights are sometimes ignored in Italian cities.

must remain on at all times (this was recently proven to reduce the number of accidents). Not all road signs will be familiar so if you want to recognize a "No Stopping" sign from a "No Parking," ask your rental company to provide you with the appropriate guide.

Police have recently begun to crack down on drunk drivers and the alcohol limit is 0.05 percent blood alcohol level (about two glasses of wine). You are not legally required to take a Breathalyzer test but refusal will probably lead to a fine.

Roads and Highways

Italy has a decent network of roads, although the ancient Romans would probably be shocked at the condition of some of the asphalt. *Autostrada* (highways) are indicated in green and the letter "A". The A1 and A14 are the longest stretches that run north to south. Most highways have tolls that are paid at the end of your journey. Fees are expensive by North American standards and a trip from Rome to Milan costs around €20. There are separate booths for paying by cash, credit card, or prepaid cards. There are rest stops or *Autogrill* every 40 kilometers where tanks and stomachs can be filled.

Secondary roads are blue and either Nazionali (N) or Statali (SS). These are generally single lane and vary in quality. Very often the same road will have two names, which adds to the confusion of signs that are either non-existent or too small to read. Many smaller roads are steep and winding, which can turn a mere 10 kilometers into a 30-minute drive.

Traffic

Three-lane highways are rare in Italy and most only have two which leads to a lot of congestion during the mass departures of August when millions of drivers hit the road simultaneously. If you must drive during these periods consider an early morning or midnight departure. Traffic is quite intense in cities and a good chance to improve your vocabulary of "dirty" words. The trick to avoiding traffic is doing the exact opposite of what Italians do. When they are sitting down for lunch (1–3 P.M.) or dinner (8–10 P.M.) you should be sailing along without a car in sight. When they are stuck in a jam, you should be enjoying a meal.

Gas

Italy has some of the most expensive gas in Europe and the government has recently launched an inquiry into possible price-fixing by oil companies. There is some regional variation and you can usually get the best deals on the highway. Americans shocked at paying over $2.50 back home will have a heart attack when they see the prices here.

A full tank costs around €60 and a liter of unleaded is €1.30. Diesel is only slightly cheaper. Most stations offer self- and full-service for a few cents more. With the exception of highway rest areas, most stations keep standard Italian hours with a break at lunch and quitting time at 7 P.M., after which you'll need to serve yourself.

During off-hours, many gas stations are manned by immigrants who fill up tanks for a living. Sri Lankans seem to dominate this sector and have no interest to rip you off. Just hand them some cash and keep an eye on the counter. When they're finished, give them a coin. If you're paying by credit card or prefer to pump your own gas, the machines are self-explanatory and operate pretty much as they do everywhere else.

Parking

Parking is a national dilemma in a country where drivers tend to get very creative with where they leave their cars. This is one occasion you shouldn't do as the Romans do as *vigili* (traffic police) are quite active and have no qualms about towing cars. In most towns, painted blue lines are a safe place to park and operate on a pay-and-display basis. Tickets are purchased at machines with coins and the ticket must be left on the dashboard. Parking is often free after 8 P.M. and on Sundays but it's always better to read the signs or ask. Whites lines are free and yellow are reserved for residents. Garages are generally expensive but can be a necessity in large cities where spaces are lacking. Chances of finding a spot at night are usually better than during the day, but if your car is the only one on the street there's probably a reason. Always lock your car and don't tempt thieves with bags or cellular phones left lying on the seat.

BOAT

Sicily and Sardinia as well as Italy's smaller islands are connected to the mainland by an efficient network of ferries and hydrofoils. Genoa, Livorno, La Spezia, Civitavecchia, Fiumicino, and Naples are the main ports where cars can also be transported. All the northern lakes are also well served by boats that run nearly as frequently as buses during the summer and require a little more patience during the winter.

Fares are quite reasonable and booking in advance over the Internet can save you a considerable amount of money, especially if you

© PURESTOCK

Cyclists have an advantage on Italy's narrow streets.

plan on transporting a vehicle. Showing up without reservations in peak summer months is risky. For a list of all the main ferry companies, visit www.traghetti.com.

BIKE
Bicycles

Cycling paths may not be as common as in Northern Europe but certain regions like Tuscany and Trentino Alto-Adige are especially adapted to travelers who prefer pedaling from town to town. It's also a great way to explore islands where car traffic can be limited or nonexistent. Rental shops are frequent in large cities and tourist areas, and there are a growing number of hotels with facilities especially suited for cyclists. For a complete list of these accommodations, visit www.italybikehotels.it or call 05/4166-0410.

Mopeds

Mopeds are another enjoyable way to see Italy. Although they aren't especially adapted for long distances, renting one in a city or on an island increases mobility and gives you an idea of how the natives live. Helmets are mandatory although south of Rome the law is often ignored.

Visas and Officialdom

VISAS AND PASSPORTS

Visitors from the United States and Canada do not need a visa to enter Italy. All that is required for stays under three months is a valid passport. EU travelers can enter the country with any valid ID.

ITALIAN EMBASSIES AND CONSULATES

The **Italian embassy** (3000 Whitehaven St. NW, tel. 202/612-4400, www.ambwashing tondc.esteri.it) in the United States is located in Washington D.C. There are also consulates in **Boston** (tel. 617/722-9201), **Chicago** (tel. 312/467-1550), **New York** (tel. 212/737-9100), **San Francisco** (tel. 415/931-4924), and other cities nationwide.

Canadians can contact the Italian embassy in **Ottawa** (275 Slater St, Ottawa, tel. 613/232-2401, www.ambottawa.esteri.it) or consulates in **Montréal** (tel. 514/849-8351) and **Toronto** (tel. 416/977-1566).

FOREIGN EMBASSIES

Hopefully you will never need to contact the embassy in Italy. If you have lost your passport, are a victim of a serious crime, are arrested, or require emergency medical attention they should however be alerted immediately. The U.S. Embassy (Via Veneto 119a, tel. 06/46-741) is in Rome and there are consulates in Naples, Florence, and Milan. The Canadian embassy is in Rome on Via Zara 30 (tel. 06/445-981). Offices are usually open on weekday mornings 8:30 A.M.–1 P.M.

CUSTOMS

Customs is a straightforward affair with an official glancing at your passport, making sure you're not on the Interpol most-wanted list, and waving you forward towards baggage claim. After that it's usually smooth sailing unless you happen to attract the attention of sniffer dogs that regularly patrol Italian airports. Most travelers won't have a problem and luggage is rarely controlled. Do keep in mind that you are expected to declare an amount over €6,000 in cash and are prohibited from importing animal-based food products into the country. Duty-free imports for passengers from outside the EU are limited to one liter of liquor, two liters of wine, 200 cigarettes, 50 cigars, and 50 milliliters of perfume.

Bags are more likely to be heavier upon leaving Italy than on entering and sausage smuggling is frequent. U.S. citizens are limited to $800 worth of goods deemed for personal use. Anything over that amount must be declared and will be taxed by Uncle Sam. Fresh fruits and vegetables, cheeses, and animal-based products are not allowed into the United States.

Things are more relaxed for EU citizens, who can purchase and transport whatever they like as long as it's for personal consumption and is legal.

POLICE

Even though Italy is a relatively safe country, there's always a robbery, murder, or abduction making headlines on the evening news. In an emergency dial **112** from any phone. Operators are multilingual and can provide immediate assistance.

There are several branches of police in Italy with separate jurisdictions. **La polizia** is the state police who deal with most crimes. They wear blue uniforms and drive Alpha Romeos. **Carabinieri** are military police and usually carry machines guns. You'll see them at airports and on the road where they conduct random searches of vehicles. They wear dark blue uniforms with red-striped pants. **Vigili urbani** (urban vigils) are the most feared by drivers, as they direct traffic and hand out parking tickets. They're recognizable from the white hats and light blue shirts.

If you are pulled over, being a foreigner usually gets you off the hook. Don't assume anything, however, and provide whatever documentation an officer may want to see. To report a crime, go to the nearest police station. If all you need are directions, any member of the police will be able to help.

Accommodations

An influx of tourists over the years has produced a great range of accommodations, from five-star luxury to clean and comfortable youth hostels. Prices must be displayed in every room by law and there is great variation throughout the year. High season in art cities like Rome, Florence, and Venice runs from Easter to October while along the coast the busiest months are July and August. In winter, ski resorts are crowded during the February *settimana bianca* (white week). Christmas is another peak time and special events like the film festival in Venice or Palio in Siena can substantially increase the price of a room. During these periods, reservations should be made in advance. Prices are also affected by geography and a room in Southern Italy costs less than it does in Northern Italy. About €100 usually gets you a decent room with private bath, although you'll need to spend more if you're after local charm and facilities like a pool or spa.

HOTELS

Italian hotels are graded on a system of stars that ranges from one to five. How many stars an establishment has depends on facilities like maid service, minibar, air-conditioning, and other extras. Criteria vary from region to region, but a three-star establishment is usually a safe bet. Reservations can be made online and most hotels now have websites with English-language pages.

All the big international chains like Hilton, Sheraton, and Best Western operate in Italy as well as home-grown hotels like **Jolly** and budget accommodations like **Ibis.** Service may be better in these hotels and rooms slightly larger but they often lack character and could be located anywhere in the world. You're often better off staying in smaller boutique hotels that have become more common or with chains like **Relais et Chateux** that are located inside historic villas, castles, and monasteries.

HOSTELS AND PENSIONES

There is no age limit to staying in Italian youth hostels *(ostelli),* which are located in most large and medium-size cities and provide affordable accommodation. Many are less sparse than you might imagine and include single, double, and quad options in addition to the classic dormitory-style rooms. A bed usually costs €20 per person and may include breakfast. The other good thing about hostels is the ambiance. They are very often filled with students and post-graduates at various stages of a round-the-world trip. All hostels are overseen by **Associazione Italiana Alberghi per la Gioventù** (tel. 06/487-1152, www.ostellionline. org). You can also get information at www.ital iayhf.org and www.hostels-aig.org.

Pensioni is another term for small, lower-grade hotels that are often family-owned. Rooms are generally clean and functional although you may be required to share a bathroom. They are often located near train stations or city centers in older buildings that may or may not have elevators. You should also check about any curfews as front desks are not always manned 24 hours a day and ensure that heating will be operational if you visit in winter.

AGRITURISMI, CAMPING, AND RIFUGI

Agriturismi are a wonderful Italian invention that combine bed-and-breakfast type accommodations with rural living. Most of these are located in converted farmhouses on land that is still used to grow crops and raise animals. Decor is rustic and rooms are limited to a half-dozen or so. Meals are often available and consist of local ingredients. Owners are happy to show you around the ranch and the proximity to the countryside allows guests to spend time surrounded by nature.

Italy has over 2,200 campsites that are generally open April–September. Many sights are located in pristine natural settings where it would be impossible to build a hotel, such as national parks, on many islands, and along the coast. Facilities vary but usually include a bar or restaurant, showers, and telephones. You can rent equipment from some campsites if you've forgotten your tent at home. A full list of sites is available from the **Italian Campsite Federation** (tel. 05/588-2391, wwwfeder campeggio.it).

In higher altitudes throughout the Alps, hikers can spend the night in mountain refuges (*rifugi*). These are similar to hostels and often close during the winter when trails are covered with snow. It's a good idea to check with **Touring Club Italia** (Milan, Corso Italia 10, www.touringclub.it) before setting off and finding yourself stranded on a mountain.

VILLAS

Travelers who prefer to get a more authentic feel of the country or just want to relax in one location can rent a villa or apartment. You can contact owners directly through www.home-away.com and www.rentalo.com.

Food

Italian may be one of the most popular foods in the world, but the pizza and pasta from your favorite restaurant back home are just the tip of the culinary iceberg in a country where every town, province, and region has its own flavors. Letting your palate loose is part of the fun of traveling and the best way of getting to know Italy.

MENUS

Menus may seem hard to decipher at first but if there is an English translation you're probably in the wrong place. The thing to remember is that there's an order to dining in Italy and it exists for a reason. *Antipasti* (starters) are the first thing you'll see and can be as simple as *bruschette* (toasted bread topped with tomatoes) to *fiori di zucchine* (fried zucchini flowers stuffed with anchovies). The point of an *antipasto* is to relieve your stomach of any immediate hunger and introduce it to the meal ahead. House starters (*della casa*) offer a number of different cold cuts and cheeses that can be shared among several diners. Next comes the first (*primo*) course, which is either pasta, polenta, or risotto. There are hundreds of traditional pasta shapes, all of which are combined with particular sauces that may include vegetables, meat, or fish. Not everything can be translated and this is a chance to get adventurous. Many people stop after the first course but

cappuccino

© ALESSIA RAMACCIA

a complete dining experience always includes seconds (*secondo*) that are based on meat or fish. What you choose depends on the season and location. Most seaside restaurants serve a good mixed seafood platter that can be ordered grilled or fried. Mountainous and landlocked regions like Umbria are well known for their beef and lamb as well as more exotic game like wild boar. Unless you order a side *(contorno)*, your steak will be a little lonely. Let your waiter know if you want it rare *(al sangue)*, medium rare *(cotta)*, or well done *(ben cotta)*. No meal is complete without dessert and coffee or an after-dinner liqueur that facilitates digestion and is very often offered on the house.

Drinks

The selection of wines can be dizzying and can be served by the glass or bottle. House wine is locally produced and comes in carafes of different dimensions. If you want something more refined, it's usually wise to go with a regional vintage. In restaurants, prices can vary widely and waiters make a great show of opening bottles.

Tap water *(acqua del rubinetto)* is excellent in Italy yet the country is the number-one consumer of mineral water in the world. It comes either sparkling *(frizzante)* or still *(naturale)* and there are hundreds of brands to choose from.

TYPES OF RESTAURANT

The differences between trattoria, *osteria*, and *ristorante* are less defined these days than they used to be, however the former are generally cheaper and serve a simpler style of food. Service is often ad hoc in trattorias where owners exchange banter with customers and act like they own the place. There may also be fewer items on an *osteria* menu but what you will find is likely to be traditional local recipes like *cacio e pepe* in Rome and tortellini in Bologna.

Although there are no official dress codes, Italians tend to dress up when they go out and fitting in means avoiding anything that's overly casual. Smoking has been banned since 2005 in all restaurants and if you want a puff you'll need to step outside or ask for an outdoor table. A satisfying lunch or dinner with antipasto, *primo*, wine, dessert, and coffee runs around €20–25. Many restaurants also offer a fixed-price option that's both economical and delicious.

Italian stomachs are well regulated and lunch is eaten between 1–2:30 P.M., while dinner is served 8–10 P.M. Meals are savored in Italy and

WINERY VISITS

Much like the way Italian museums were run through the 1990s – and in some cases still are – many winemakers and wineries don't see their role as educators. They assume visitors know their subject, have done their research, and are there for a specific purpose, like distribution, bottling, or importing. Family-run operations often don't have time to explain their wines to visitors. Always phone first and assume that even with an appointment any of the above or other factors can affect your visit.

Some wineries will charge for tastings and many will just send you off to the local trattoria or *enoteca* to sample the wines there. Large wineries are more likely to be set up for tourists, and are often in stunning settings with an English-speaking staff. Don't overlook the small operations, though, where you'll find real personality and art in the final product.

Seek out a good sommelier or wine shop owner that can introduce you to these wines. They are a great source of information and often can tell you about the winery, even if you can't visit it. Some hotel owners or concierges are also well connected with local wineries and various wineries will prefer that the hotel set up a tasting.

usually last over an hour. If you're in a hurry or get a craving outside opening hours, head to a bar for a panini (sandwich) or to a pizzeria that sells pizza by the slice. *Tavole calde* offer buffet-style food that's already prepared and popular with lunchtime crowds. If wine is your priority, there are usually hundreds of bottles that can be sampled inside the country's many *enoteche* (wine bars). These also generally serve a selection of cured meats and cheeses.

Breakfast is not the most important meal of the day in Italy and if you're used to bacon and eggs you'll probably be disappointed with the cappuccino and *cornetto* (croissant) served in bars. Large hotels however offer abundant breakfast buffets where cereal addicts can get their fix.

TIPPING

Americans love to tip and feel guilty if they don't, but this is Italy—where waiters aren't aspiring actors but real pros. Besides, the bill already includes a charge *(coperto)* that covers bread and service. Still no one refuses money and leaving €3–5 behind after a good meal is the obvious way to show your appreciation.

Conduct and Customs

SOCIAL BEHAVIOR

There's no better place to study the Italian character than from a cafe table in a small square. The first thing you may notice is how social locals are. You don't need to hear a conversation to understand what people are expressing. Body language is as important as words and hands often say more than lips. It's a touchy-feely country where friends of the same sex walk arm in arm and kisses are distributed generously. Given the size of the country, space is perceived differently. People get close to each other and you'll probably be bumped more than once when standing on a bus or subway. *"Permesso"* is a useful word that let's someone know you need to get by.

In general Italians are very polite but this varies and modern life has taken a toll on gallantry. Still, "good morning" *("buongiorno")* and "good evening" *"(buonasera)"* can frequently be heard among shop owners and their clients or passengers on an elevator. As in all Romance languages, there is a formal form of the singular "you" that's used between strangers and creates a division between friends and family and everyone else. Garibaldi, Italy's national hero, only used this form with the king and unlike most Italians he cared little about what people thought of him.

Many Italians are concerned about how they look and a mirror is the opportunity to put a curl back in place or check that lipstick hasn't smudged. The overall impression of free spiritedness can be deceptive but it would take a lifetime to get to the root of the Italian character. Just enjoy the show and look out for the faces that so fascinated Fellini.

Meeting people is easy and foreigners are treated with friendliness. If you are lost more often than not someone will offer to show you the way. If you ask a question you are likely to get the long response. Italians are naturally curious and fond of Americans. They will ask where you are from and want to know what you like about their country. If you want to surprise them don't include food and wine in your answer. Perhaps style is their greatest asset. Italians can accomplish the most mundane things like taking out the garbage or lighting a cigarette with Marcello Mastroianni finesse no one else in the world possesses.

ETIQUETTE

Most of the things considered rude in North America are also considered rude in Italy. One exception is lines, which rarely form in any organized way and generally resemble a fumble recovery. If you do not say something *(scusi* or a loud cough will do) you may be waiting all day for that cappuccino or slice of prosciutto. Fortunately ticket machines are in operation at post offices and pharmacies.

Meals are usually divided *alla Romana* (dutch) between friends but no one will take offense if you offer to pay. Although Italians are generous, rounds of drinks are generally not purchased as they are in England or the United States. Drinking in general is done over dinner rather than with the purpose of getting smashed, and displays of public drunkenness are rare.

Remember not to wear shorts inside churches or sacred buildings. Also, don't remove your shirt except if you are at the beach where staring too long at topless sunbathers will mark you out as a debutant tourist.

GREETINGS AND GOODBYES

Kissing is as Italian as pizza and the way individuals demonstrate respect, friendship, and love. The most common form is the double-cheek kiss as made famous by *Borat*. It can be uncomfortable to some people but no one will impose this greeting on you and a handshake is equally acceptable, although far less intimate.

In Italy, women kiss women, women kiss men, men kiss men, and everyone kisses children. Men who kiss men are good friends, relatives, or gay. Kisses are exchanged at the beginning and end of most social encounters. Italian men introduced to Italian women for the first time (or vice versa) will generally exchange kisses. Men will shake hands and women may kiss or shake hands. Non-Italians can greet however they please.

Italians love to linger. The Italian goodbye is a phenomenon that has puzzled sociologists for years. The average time between verbal indication of departure and physical departure fluctuates between 7–12 minutes. This uniquely Italian span of conversation is dedicated to discussing the next day and making preliminary arrangements for a future meeting.

Tips for Travelers

STUDY, EMPLOYMENT, AND VOLUNTEERING

Anyone who falls in love with Italy and wants to stay over the three-month limit will require a *permesso di soggiorno* (permit of stay). Getting your hands on this document provides a good introduction to Italian red tape, but theoretically it's very straightforward. There are two types of permits, which can be applied for at any police station. The *permesso di lavoro* allows visitors to work, while the *permesso di studio* is for students. For both you will need to fill out an application, provide passport-size photos, and a photocopy of your passport. For a work permit you must provide proof of future employment (a letter from the employer on company stationery is fine) or demonstrate your financial independence.

Students must provide a letter from the institution where they plan to study with details of the course they will follow. This should be sent to the consulate in your home country, which will in turn officially validate your declaration. Students will also be required to demonstrate they are covered by health insurance.

All of this usually boils down to a few days waiting in line and going back and forth between consulates, immigrations offices, and the copy shop. If you want to avoid bureaucracy and still build up a sweat consider volunteering. There is no shortage of archeological sights and vineyards where you can lend a hand and be paid with a good meal.

ACCESS FOR TRAVELERS WITH DISABILITIES

Curbs are high in Italy and sidewalks can be an insurmountable obstacle for anyone using a wheelchair. Most large hotels, however, have special accommodations, though it's always worth confirming before your departure. To receive information about the accessibility of specific sights, contact **Associazione Italiana Disabili** (Milan, Via S. Barnaba 29, tel. 02/800/810-810) or www.italiapertutti.it (Italy for everyone) that provides information about hotels, restaurants, and monuments.

TRAVELING WITH CHILDREN

Italians go crazy for kids and their love could have kept Freud busy for decades. If you're traveling with a toddler, expect people to cross the street to take a peek inside the stroller or stop you to ask the name, age, and vital statistics of your child. Restaurants and hotels generally welcome young travelers and some high-end accommodations offer babysitting services for parents who want to do a little sightseeing of their own. Parks are usually equipped with playgrounds and beaches are perfect for summer fun. Children under 12 pay reduced rates to museums, amusement parks, and on board public transportation that is very often free.

WHAT TO BRING

The contents of your suitcase should depend on the season and the length of your stay. Beware of overpacking and select comfortable clothing that can easily be mixed and matched. Layers are important in spring and fall when mornings are chilly and temperatures vary throughout the day. A bag with wheels will make it easier to get around airports and to the next hotel. Backpacks or handbags are good for storing items you'll take on daily excursions and should have zippers to dissuade pickpockets. It's probably best to leave expensive watches at home and travel without any flashy jewelry. A money belt can be useful for storing necessary valuables and cash.

Some formal clothes may be necessary if you plan on any fine dining or clubbing. Italians generally like to dress up and rarely let down their fashion guard. Flip-flops are fine for the beach, but the Swiss Guard won't permit them inside the Vatican. Keep in mind that knees and shoulders must be covered when entering religious buildings. Sunglasses are essential during the summer, especially if you'll be doing any driving, and baseball hats are useful – even if Italians don't often wear them. A high-SPF sunscreen is vital if you're heading for the beach, and bug repellent will come in handy in the countryside or sitting around a campfire.

You'll probably do more walking in Italy than at home and it's hazardous for your feet to break in a new pair of shoes on cobblestoned streets. Bring at least two comfortable pairs of shoes, especially if you'll be hiking. If you're only traveling for a week, it might be useful to buy sample-size shampoo, toothpaste, and soap to keep weight down (and they'll cause less damage if they accidentally open). If you forget something, you shouldn't have a problem finding it in Italy; pharmacies are especially useful for replacing lost toiletries or picking up aspirin. If you take prescription drugs, make sure to bring enough and have a copy of the prescription in case you need a refill.

Most hotels provide hairdryers but if you are staying in a bed-and-breakfast or camping you may want to pack a small one. It should be adaptable to Italy's 220 voltage. A European plug converter is useful for recharging MP3 players, digital cameras, and cellular phones. Adapters can be hard to find in Italy and airports are usually the best place to pick them up. If you're taking photos the old-fashioned way, stock up on film before you leave as it's more expensive in Italy. An extra memory card is useful for digital photographers planning on documenting every moment of the journey.

Items like binoculars are helpful for observing the ceiling of the Sistine Chapel, church facades, and wildlife. Pack a pen if you plan on writing any postcards and a notebook for jotting down impressions of hill towns and memories of seaside lunches. Even if you aren't an artist, try sketching the sights or making souvenir rubbings of the ruins you encounter. A good book will help pass the time on long-distance train or bus trips or while waiting your turn at the post office.

You'll need your passport and a driver's license if you plan on renting a car. An international license is not required, but it can avoid confusion if you are pulled over. It only costs $15 and is available from any AAA office in the United States. Making a copy of vital documents facilitates replacing them should they be lost or stolen. You can also email yourself any important credit card codes or customer service numbers to report stolen cards.

Most of all, don't forget to pack your curiosity.

WOMEN TRAVELERS

Women are nearly as popular as kids and attract the curiosity of Italian men whether traveling alone or in groups. For the most part advances are good-natured and anything beyond that can simply be ignored. If you do feel threatened, enter a shop, bar, or public space where people are around. Should harassment persist, call the police and remain in a crowded location. At night it's best to avoid unlit streets and train stations. If you must pass through these areas walk quickly and keep your guard up. Having a cell phone is a wise precaution and keeping in touch with family back home never hurts. Hotels often go out of their way to assist single travelers and will be happy to order you a cab when going out at night.

SENIOR TRAVELERS

Italy is the place to feel young again while taking advantage of many of the same benefits you enjoy back home. Anyone over 65 can benefit from reduced entry into museums, theaters, and sporting events as well as discounts on public transportation, hotels, and many other services. A passport or other valid ID is all you need to prove your age. **Carta d'Argento** (Silver Card) is available from Trenitalia for over 60s and provides 15 percent discounts on first- and second-class seats on all trains. The card costs €30, is valid one year, and can be purchased at any train station.

It's wise to bring any medications you may need on your journey as well as prescriptions should you run out or lose your luggage. Most pharmacists can help diagnose minor problems and will able to offer sound advice. For any serious medical problems, call **118** or go to the nearest hospital.

GAY AND LESBIAN TRAVELERS

Italians are pretty accepting in general and, regardless of what the Vatican says, gay and lesbian travelers are as welcome as anyone else. After all, this is the land of Dolce & Gabbana, Armani, and Valentino. Even Michelangelo was recently outed. Same-sex heterosexual couples often walk arm-in-arm and only the most outrageous behavior will even get you a second glance.

Nightlife is not as developed as in the United States but bar, sauna, and resort alternatives are on the rise. Bologna is the closest Italy gets to San Francisco and most large cities have a well-established scene. These tend to be spread out and there is no predominantly gay neighborhood in Rome or Milan as there is in London or New York. Away from big cities, activity tends to be more covert and cruising tends to be done in remote parks and beaches late at night. **Arci Gay** (tel. 051/649-3055, www.ar cigay.it) is the Italian gay organization with branches across Italy. For information on clubs, events, and gay-friendly accommodations, visit **www.gay.it.**

Health and Safety

Italian medical and emergency services are relatively efficient and modern. *Farmacie* are the first place to turn if you have a tooth or stomach ache. For anything more serious you can dial **118** or go directly to the *pronto soccorso* (emergency room) located in most hospitals. Italians themselves can be quite helpful and are usually eager to help a tourist in need.

BEFORE LEAVING

If you suffer from a serious ailment, make sure your medical information is up-to-date and consult your doctor regarding any specific precautions to take. Medication should be carried in original containers to avoid any trouble with customs and make a pharmacist's job easier in case you require a refill. Anyone with food allergies should memorize or write down the

Italian equivalents and let waiters know to take it easy on the Parmesan or peanuts.

Health Insurance

Check with your health provider what if any coverage you can expect while overseas. If you don't like their answer, there are dozens of companies dedicated entirely to insuring travelers like **Travel Guard** (www.travelguard.com) and **STA Travel** (www.statravel.com), which is specifically geared to students. Most companies will require you to pay for treatment up front and refund you once you get home. That's not as bad as it sounds as most treatments are much cheaper than they are in the United States. Public hospitals in Italy cannot refuse a patient and will treat you free of charge.

Vaccinations

Malaria, which literally means "bad air," was once a serious problem in Italy. It's been eradicated since the early part of the 20th century and no specific inoculations are required when entering the country. Updating tetanus and polio vaccinations, however, never hurts.

HEALTH MAINTENANCE
Pharmacies

Pharmacies are recognizable by their green cross sign and are common in city centers. Many now operate non-stop hours and remain open during the traditional lunch break. If a pharmacy is closed, you can always find a list of the closest open drugstores posted in the window. In larger towns and cities at least one pharmacy remains open overnight and some 24-hour pharmacies are located within train stations. If all you need is a condom, many pharmacies have automated vending machines out front.

Pharmicists are very helpful in Italy and can offer lots of advice for treating any ailment you may have. You'll also find more practical items like toothbrushes and sunscreen if you happen to misplace the one you brought from home.

Medical Kit

If you're traveling over a long period of time or with children, it's a good idea to pack a small medical kit with items you'll need to handle minor scrapes and headaches. It should contain

Italy's military police

©ALESSIA RAMACCIA

aspirin or some form of pain relief, Imodium for stomach problems, Band-Aids, bug repellent, sun protection, and tweezers.

CRIME

Although violent crime in Italy is rare, petty criminals thrive in large cities like Rome and Milan making a living off unaware tourists. Should you be the victim of a pickpocket or have your bag snatched, report it within 24 hours to the nearest police station. You'll need a copy of the *denuncia* (police report) in order to make an insurance claim.

Don't tempt thieves with open knapsacks or wallets dangling enticingly from your back pocket. Keep jewelry, MP3 players, and cameras out of sight and always count your change before leaving a store rather than on the street. Make a photocopy of your passports and any other vital documents should the worst happen and call your credit card company immediately if your wallet has been stolen.

Information and Services

MONEY
Currency
The euro has been Italy's currency since 2000. The colorful bills come in different sizes and denominations of 500, 200, 100, 50, 20, 10, and 5. There are eight coins including 2 and 1 euros, 50, 20, 10, 5, 2, and 1 cents. As the currency is shared between 13 nations in the EU, you may find yourself with coins minted in France, Germany, or Austria. There's even a Vatican edition that is a must for collectors.

Exchange Rates
The dollar isn't what it used to be and the disappearance of the lire has meant it's no longer possible to feel like a millionaire after changing your money. Since the launch of the new currency when the euro was valued at $0.80 the monetary tide has turned and one dollar only gets you about €0.70. The trend is likely to continue as the price of oil rises and governments switch their currency reserves to euros.

Changing Money
The best rates are usually at banks back home but if you do wait to change your money at the airport shop around. Rates vary and even a fraction can have a significant impact on your budget. Do ask about commission fees, however, which very often wipe out any conversion advantages. Most Italian banks in large cities provide exchange services (cambio).

When changing money ask for both large and small denominations and count your money at the counter before leaving. Some hotels also provide conversion services but usually charge a higher fee for the convenience.

ATMs
The majority of bank branches are equipped with ATM machines where travelers can use debit or credit cards to withdraw cash. Exchange rates are set by the market and offer the best bang for your buck. You should, however, check with your bank or credit card company to determine what withdrawal fees they charge. Some smaller banks like Commerce Bank in the mid-Atlantic waive all fees while most others charge 1–3 percent.

The maximum you can withdraw per day in Italy is €250 and most machines offer instructions in English. Be aware of your surroundings when withdrawing cash late at night or on a deserted street. If the card doesn't work try another bank before contacting your bank. Also it may be worth calling your bank and informing them of your travel plans as many institutions will block a card that has never been used overseas.

Banks
Italian banks still have some consolidating to do and most branches are regional rather than national. Hours are normally weekdays

8:30 A.M.–1:30 P.M. and 2:30–4 P.M. Security is tight and you'll need to leave keys, phones, and other metal objects in the lockers at the entrance in order to avoid setting off the metal detector.

Credit Cards

Don't leave home without American Express (tel. 800/874-333), Visa (tel. 800/877-232), or Mastercard (tel. 800/870-866), which are widely accepted in Italy. AmEx has an office in Rome in Piazza di Spagna. Discover and Diners Club are uncommon and many shops and some bed-and-breakfasts in rural areas only accept cash.

Credit cards are convenient, but there can be some hidden fees when using them abroad. It's worth calling to check what surcharges may be applied. If there is a fee see if the gold or premium version of the card will waive such charges.

If a shop offers to charge your card in dollars, you're better off refusing as exchange rates are likely to be above international rates. If you don't already have a credit card that charges no fees for foreign transactions, get one that does. Amalgamated, Capital One, and Tompkins Trust all offer this service standard. A Capital One card also has no annual fee and uses standard exchange rate. Some cards like MBNA could earn you a net profit when you make overseas purchases. It may seem like a detail but a little investigative work could rack up considerable savings.

Sales Tax

All visitors who reside outside the EU are entitled to get refunded on tax, which varies depending on the type of good you are buying. Just look for the Tax Free Shopping logo that is displayed in over 26,000 stores and outlets. The only catch is that items must total over €155 in a single store and be exported within three months of purchase. The paperwork is straightforward and staff are happy to help you save.

COMMUNICATIONS AND MEDIA
Mail

Poste Italiane (tel. 800/160-000, www.poste. it) offices are yellow and large branches are usually open weekdays 8:30 A.M.–7:30 P.M. and

Saturdays 8:15 A.M.–12:30 P.M. Post offices in smaller towns are open only in the morning, but stamps (*francobolli*) can also be purchased at *tabacchi*. A postcard to anywhere in the EU is €0.45 and €0.60 for all other destinations. Letters vary according to weight and can be sent *posta prioritaria* (express) for a few cents more. Mailboxes are red and have a slot for international and local mail.

Public Telephones

Italians have a love affair with their phones and spend great parts of the day chatting away. The advent of cell phones has led to the decline in public phones. Most now operate with phone cards that can be purchased at *tabacchi* or news agents. Ask for a *scheda telefonica*, which are inserted into a slot in the machine. International calls are expensive and you can cut costs by purchasing a phone card for as little as €5. Just dial the number and PIN on the back then whatever number you want to call. The access code for the United States and Canada is 001 followed by the area code and number.

Numbers in Italy are not standardized and regions have different length area codes. You may also find yourself dialing a six-digit number in one town and an eight-digit number in the next. That's just one of Italy's mysteries. Numbers that start with 800 are toll-free, 170 gets you an English-speaking operator, and 176 is international directory assistance.

Cell Phones

If your cell phone operates on a GSM network, used by most European countries, all you'll need is a local SIM card, a removable chip that determines the phone's network and number. These can be purchased in any electronic store. Local calls are inexpensive this way and incoming calls are typically free. Telestial sells a $49 Passport SIM card that includes $10 of airtime. Rates to call the United States start at $0.49 a minute.

If you don't have a GSM phone, it can be far cheaper to buy a cell phone in Italy than rent one. This also allows you to re-use it on return visits. Prices are very competitive and

public telephones

the least-expensive Nokia model is under €50. Phones can be purchased at media stores like Euronics or UniEuro, or directly from network providers like Vodafone and 3, which have shops in all major cities. You'll need to show your passport when buying a phone and most run on a pay-as-you-go system with top-ups available from news agents or through ATM machines.

Internet Access and Wi-Fi

You can avoid telephone charges altogether if you have a computer and access to broadband or Wi-Fi. Many hotels have Internet points and using Skype or other VOIP providers costs a fraction of a standard telephone call. Internet facilities are not as common as they are in the United States but every town has at least one cybercafe where you can upload photos and share your adventures with friends. These are usually a good place to meet other travelers and learn about upcoming events.

If you're packing an MP3, downloading podcasts can help make a visit more interest-ing and guide you through a museum, church, or street. Italy Guides (www.italyguides.it) provides free audio tours of Rome, Florence, Venice, and Naples. A search on iTunes will also turn up more out of the way destinations.

English-Language Press

The *International Herald Tribune* and *USA Today* are the newspapers you're most likely to see on newsstands. In Rome and Milan they can be found on the day of publications and in most other cities are a day or two late. Old news costs several times more than what you'd pay back home.

Italian Press

Italian newsstands are crammed with newspapers and magazines on everything from knitting to military aviation. *La Repubblica* and *Corriere della Sera* are the two most popular papers and both print local editions. Newspapers in Italy and journalists in general don't seem to be familiar with objectivity and most have some political agenda. *L'Unità* represents the Communist Party, while *La Padania* serves the interest of the right-wing Lega Nord party. Both are better for wrapping fish than reading. What Italians really care about is sport and the best-selling broadsheets are the *Corriere dello Sport* and the pink *Gazzetta dello Sport*. Many papers in cities have an events listing that comes out midweek with some sections in English. When in doubt, ask the newspaper attendant.

MAPS AND TOURIST INFORMATION
Tourist Offices and Websites

Tourism is well organized in Italy and each region, province, and many cities have their own **APT** (Azienda Promozione Turistica) or **IAT** (Ufficio Informazioni Accoglienza Turistica) office that distributes brochures and maps and helps visitors find suitable accommodation. Staff is usually multilingual and friendly. Information can be sent overseas if you prefer to start to study your itinerary in advance; otherwise, you can contact the **Italian State Tourist Office** (630 Fifth Avenue, Suite 1565, New York, tel. 212/245-4822, www.enit.it), which has several locations in the United States and Canada.

Local offices are open Monday–Saturday 9 A.M.–1 P.M. and 4 P.M.–7 P.M. They can usually be found in the center of town on a main square or main street and signage usually points the way. If they are closed or do not exist, hotels and bars often have maps or local directories that can help figure out a location.

WEIGHTS AND MEASURES

Italy uses the metric system, which bases everything on multiples of 10. Ten millimeters equals a centimeter, 100 centimeters equals a meter, and 100 meters equals a kilometer. Voltage (discovered by the Italian inventor Volta) is 220 volts and plugs have round prongs. If you're bringing electronic equipment that needs to be recharged, you'll need an adaptor. It's safer to buy these before your departure or in the airport, as they can be hard to find in Italy.

Italy is in the Central European time zone, six hours ahead of the U.S. East Coast and nine of the U.S. West Coast. Military time is frequently used to avoid the necessity of A.M. and P.M. and takes a quick calculation to figure out. After midday, subtract 12 from any number you see. 1300 is 1 P.M., 1700 is 5 P.M., etc. Italians also use commas where decimal points are used back home (€10,50 is €10.50, 1.000 is 1,000).

RESOURCES

Glossary

abbazia abbey
aeroporto airport
agriturismo a working farm combined with a bed-and-breakfast
albergo hotel
alcolici liquors
alimentari grocer's shop
amaro bitter
ambasciata embassy
analcolico non-alcoholic
aperto open
aperitivo appetizer or Italian happy hour that generally includes finger food
appetito appetite
arrivo arrival
autista driver
autobus bus
autostrada motorway
bagaglio luggage
bagno bathroom
banca bank
benvenuto welcome
bibita soft drink
biglietteria ticket office
biglietto ticket
buono good
calcio soccer
caldo hot
cambio change/exchange
camera room
cameriere waiter
campeggio camping
cappuccino coffee with foam milk
cartolina postcard
cascata waterfall

cassa cash desk
castello castle
cattedrale cathedral
centro benessere beauty center/spa
centro storico old town center
chiesa church
chiuso shut
cincìn cheers
città city
climatizzato air-conditioned
coincidenza connection
consolate consulate
contante cash
conto check
crociera cruise
destinazione destination
destra right
discoteca disco
dogana custom
donna woman
dopo after
dove where
drogheria grocery shop
duomo cathedral
economico cheap
edicola newsstand
entrata entrance
enoteca wine bar (plural *enoteche*)
escursione excursion
estat summer
farmacia chemist
fermata stop
ferrovia railway
fontana fountain
francobollo stamp

gita trip
gratuito free
grazie thank you
lago lake
letto bed
libreria bookshop
lontano far
luogo place
lungomare boardwalk
macchina car
macelleria butcher
mare sea
marmo marble
mercato market
metropolitana subway
moda fashion
moneta coin
montagna mountain
monumento monument
mostra show
municipio mayor's office
museo museum
nave ship
negozio shop
orario timetable
ordinazione order
ospedale hospital
ostello youth hostel
paese country
paio pair
palazzo building
panetteria bakery
panino(i) sandwich(es)
parcheggio parking lot
parco park
partenza departure
passeggiata walk
pasticceria cake shop

pasto meal
perchè why
periferia outskirts
piazza square
piccante spicy
più more
pochi few
polizia police
ponte bridge
porto port
prenotazione reservation
prezzo price
quartiere district
rione neighborhood
ristorante restaurant
sci ski
sconto discount
soccorso assistance
spiaggia beach
spuntino snack
stanza room
stazione station
strada road
stabilimenti seaside resort
tabaccherie tobacco shop
teatro theater
torre tower
traghetto ferry
tramezzino triangular sandwich
trattoria restaurant
treno train
ufficio bureau
uscita exit
valigia suitcase
via street
viaggio journey
viale avenue
vicino near

Italian Phrasebook

When in Italy, do as the Italians do. More than anything that means speaking the language. It's much better to make an attempt in rudimentary Italian than to start off directly in English. You'll find you get a warmer reception and more often than not Italians will be happy to speak English after listening to your good-natured attempt at their language.

Try not to be intimidated and listen to people speaking in bars or cafes. Turn on the TV or radio (102 Monte Carlo or 106 Lifegate) in your hotel room as you plan the next stage of your trip. Pretty soon you'll start to recognize words and expressions and what seemed like a mystery will start to sound familiar. Besides you already speak more Italian than you think (*ciao, pizza, jacuzzi, grazie*).

PRONUNCIATION
Vowels

There are seven Italian vowel sounds (one each for a, i, and u and two each for e and o) compared to 15 in English, but the most striking difference is the purity of Italian vowels. A sound written with a single letter has a single, unchanged value, whereas in English the sound often changes arbitrarily (think of the word "read" in present tense and "read" in past tense).

a	long like a in father
e (è)	short like e in set, or (è) long like a in way
i	like ee in feet
o	short like o in often, or long like o in rope
u	either like oo in foot or w in well

Consonants

b	like b in boy, but softer
c	before e or i – like ch in chin
ch	like c in cat
d	like d in dog, but softer
f	like f in fish
g	before e or i – like g in gymnastics or like g in go
gh	like g in go
gl	like ll in million
gn	like ni in onion
gu	like gu in anguish
h	always silent
l	like l in lime
m	like m in me
n	like n in nice
p	like p in pit, but softer
qu	like qu in quick
r	rolled/trilled similar to r in Spanish or Scottish
s	between vowels – like s in nose or s in sit
sc	before e or i – like sh in shut or sk in skip
t	like t in tape, but softer
v	like v in vase
z	either like ts in spits or ds in pads
zz	either like ts in spits or ds in pads

Accents

Acute (á, é, í, ó, ú) and grave (à, è, ì, ò, ù) accents are used in Italian, and called *accento acuto* and *accento grave*. Only grave accents are used to stress open vowels while acute accents are used for closed vowels. There are some exceptions when a grave accent is used on closed vowels. Accents are used to indicate that the stress falls on the last vowel in a polysyllabic word.

ESSENTIAL PHRASES

Hello. *Ciao.*
Goodbye. *Arrivederci.*
Good morning. *Buongiorno.*
Good evening. *Buonasera.*
Good night. *Buonanotte.*
How do you do? *Piacere?*
Thank you. *Grazie.*
You're welcome. *Prego.*
please *per favore*
yes *si*
no *no*
I don't know. *Non lo so.*
Do you speak English? *Parla inglese?*
I don't understand. *Non capisco.*

I am in trouble. *Ho bisogno di aiuto.*
I have lost my way. *Mi sono perso.*
Where is the American consulate? *Dovè il consolato americano?*
What's your name? *Come ti chiami?*
My name is Martin. *Mi chiamo Martin.*
This is Caterina. *Le presento Caterina.*
How are you? *Come sta?*
I'm fine, thank you. *Sto bene, grazie.*
Pleased to meet you. *Piacere.*
It was nice to meet you. *È stato un piacere conoscerla.*
Excuse me, what did you say? *Scusi, che cosa ha detto?*
Could you speak slowly? *Può parlare lentamente?*
I'm sorry, I don't speak Italian very well. *Mi dispiace, ma non parlo bene l'italiano.*
Have a nice day! *Buona giornata!*
My address is... *Il mio indirizzo è...*
I come from... *Vengo da...*
I live in Rome. *Abito a Roma.*
I'm here on holiday. *Sono qui in vacanza.*
Where do you come from? *Da dove viene?*
Would you like a drink? *Vuole qualcosa da bere?*

TRANSPORTATION

Where is...? *Dov'è...?*
How far is to...? *Quanto è distante...?*
Where? *Dove?*
Which? *Quale?*
the bus station *la stazione dell'autobus*
the bus stop *la fermata dell'autobus*
Is there a bus to...? *C'è un autobus per?*
Which bus goes to...? *Quale autobus va...?*
Does this bus go to...? *Quest'autobus va a...?*
Where do I get off? *Dove devo scendere?*
What time does the bus leave/arrive? *A che ora parte/arriva l'autobus?*
Where is the nearest subway station? *Dov'è la stazione metro più vicina?*
Where can I buy the ticket? *Dove posso comprare il biglietto?*
Is this the train for? *È questo il treno per?*

When is the next train to...? *Quando parte il prossimo treno per...?*
What time does it get there? *A che ora arriva?*
A roundtrip ticket/A single ticket to... *Un biglietto di andata e ritorno/andata per...*
first/second class *prima/seconda classe*
Where do I change for...? *Dove devo cambiare per...?*
I have a seat reservation. *Ho un posto prenotato.*
What is the dish of the day? *Qual è il piatto del giorno?*
Can I have the check please? *Mi può portare il conto per favore?*

FOOD

artichoke *carciofo*
beef *manzo*
beer *birra*
bottle *bottiglia*
bread *pane*
breakfast *colazione*
butter *burro*
cheese *formaggio*
chicken *pollo*
chili pepper *peperoncino*
chocolate *cioccolata*
coffee *caffè*
coffee with a dash of milk *caffè macchiato*
decaffeinated coffee *caffè decaffeinato*
digestive *cigestivo*
dinner *cena*
dish *piatto*
dressing *condimento*
duck *anatra*
extra-strong coffee *caffè ristretto*
fish *pesce*
fork *forchetta*
fruit *frutta*
fruit salad *macedonia*
glass *bicchiere*
ham *prosciutto*
hors d'oeuvre *antipasto*
ice *ghiaccio*
ice cream *gelato*
ice water *granita*
jam *marmellata*

lamb *agnello*
lemon *limone*
liqueur *liquore*
lobster *aragosta*
lunch *pranzo*
meat *carne*
oil *olio*
olives *olive*
onion *cipolla*
orange *arancia*
parmesan *parmigiano*
pineapple *ananas*
raw *crudo*
rice *riso*
salad *insalata*
sauce *sugo*
shellfish *crostacei*
soup *minestra*
squid *calamari*
steak *bistecca*
strawberry *fragola*
tomato *pomodoro*
vegetables *contorno*
water *acqua*
watermelon *anguria*
weak coffee *caffè lungo*
wine *vino*

SHOPPING

money *soldi*
shop *negozio*
What time do the shops close? *A che ora chiudono i negozi?*
How much is it? *Quanto costa?*
I'm just looking. *Sto guardando solamente.*
What is the local speciality? *Quali sono le specialità locali?*

HEALTH

drugstore *farmacia*
pain *dolore*
fever *febbre*
headache *mal di testa*
stomachache *mal di stomaco*
toothache *mal di denti*
burn *bruciatura*
cramp *crampo*
nausea *nausea*

vomiting *vomitare*
medicine *medicina*
antibiotic *antibiotico*
pill/tablet *pillola/pasticca*
aspirin *aspirina*
I need to see a doctor. *Ho bisogno di un medico.*
I need to go to the hospital. *Devo andare in ospedale.*
I have a pain here... *Ho un dolore qui...*
She has been stung/bitten. *È stata punta/morsa.*
I am diabetic/pregnant. *Sono diabetico/incinta.*
I am allergic to penicillin/cortisone. *Sono allergico alla penicillina/cortisone.*
My blood group is A positive/negative. *Il mio gruppo sanguigno è A positivo/negativo.*

NUMBERS

zero *zero*
one *uno*
two *due*
three *tre*
four *quattro*
five *cinque*
six *sei*
seven *sette*
eight *otto*
nine *nove*
10 *dieci*
11 *undici*
12 *dodici*
13 *tredici*
14 *quattordici*
15 *quindici*
16 *sedici*
17 *diciassette*
18 *diciotto*
19 *diciannove*
20 *venti*
21 *ventuno*
30 *trenta*
40 *quaranta*
50 *cinquanta*
60 *sessanta*
70 *settanta*
80 *ottanta*

90 *novanta*
100 *cento*
101 *centouno*
200 *duecento*
500 *cinquecento*
1,000 *mille*
10,000 *diecimila*
100,000 *centomila*
1,000,000 *un milione*
one-half *metà*
one-third *un terzo*
one-fourth *un quarto*

TIME
What time is it? *Che ora è?*
It's one/three o'clock. *È l'una/sono le tre.*
four thirty *quattro e mezza*
a quarter to seven *un quarto alle sette*
a quarter past eight *le otto e un quarto*
midday *mezzogiorno*
midnight *mezzanotte*
morning *mattino*
afternoon *pomeriggio*
evening *sera*
night *notte*
after *dopo*
before *prima*

DAYS AND MONTHS
today *oggi*
tomorrow *Domani*
yesterday *ieri*
week *settimana*
month *mese*
Monday *lunedi*
Tuesday *martedi*
Wednesday *mercoledi*
Thursday *giovedi*

Friday *venerdi*
Saturday *sabato*
Sunday *domenica*
January *gennaio*
February *febbraio*
March *marzo*
April *aprile*
May *maggio*
June *giugno*
July *luglio*
August *agosto*
September *settembre*
October *ottobre*
November *novembre*
December *dicembre*

VERBS
to have *avere*
to be *essere*
to go *andare*
to come *venire*
to want *volere*
to eat *mangiare*
to drink *bere*
to buy *comprare*
to need *necessitare*
to read *leggere*
to write *scrivere*
to stop *fermare*
to get off *scendere*
to arrive *arrivare*
to return *ritornare*
to stay *restare*
to leave *partire*
to look at *guardare*
to look for *cercare*
to give *dare*
to take *prendere*

Suggested Reading

CULTURE

Barzini, Luigi. *The Italians: A Full Length Portrait Featuring Their Manners and Morals.* Simon & Schuster, 1996. This classic, first published in the 1960s, provides comprehensive insight into what it means to be Italian. Barzini is a great observer and the behavior he describes in great detail will all become clear after a visit to the country.

Cellini, Benvenuto. *Autobiography.* Penguin Classics, 1998. Cellini was a skilled Renaissance goldsmith and highly regarded sculptor. His fame rests on an autobiography that recounts the triumphs and trials of his own life and the wars and political struggles during one of Italy's golden ages.

D'Epiro, Peter, and Mary Desmond Pinkowish. *Sprezzatura: 50 Ways Italian Genius Shaped the World.* This book provides a penetrating panorama of Italian contributions to the world—an extraordinary cultural legacy that has enhanced nearly every field of human endeavor. It quickly becomes evident the world would be a different place without Italian inventiveness.

Hofmann, Paul. *That Fine Italian Hand.* Henry Holt and Company, Inc. 1990. In this wryly affectionate book, Paul Hofmann reveals his adopted countrymen in all their marvelous and remarkable paradoxes. The national pastimes of dodging taxes, double dealing, working only as hard as one must—is balanced by Italian inventiveness, gusto for life, fierce individuality, deep family bonds, and cultural sophistication.

Severgnini, Beppe. *La Bella Figura: A Field Guide to the Italian Mind.* Broadway Books, 2006. Toss out your stereotypes about Italy. Severgnini is out to prove that 21st-century Italians are more complicated than anyone ever expected. He takes readers on an adventure through a country that has "too much style to be hell" but is "too disorderly to be heaven."

St. Aubin de Teran, Lisa. *A Valley in Italy: The Many Seasons of a Villa in Italy.* HarperCollins, 1994. Lisa's dream to live in a castle was rooted in her until she caught a view of the Villa Orsola deep in the Umbrian hills. "It was standing like a jilted beauty still dressed in its ancient best." She later purchased the property only to discover her dream house was a vast ruin. The book is an account of the restoration that followed and the charms of village life.

HISTORY

Astarita, Tommaso. *Between Salt Water and Holy Water: A History of Southern Italy.* W. W. Norton and Company, 2005. Southern Italy is very often neglected by history books. Astarita rectifies the matter and explains the historic and geographic factors that created a different Italian experience for southerners. Readers are introduced to dynamic historical figures, diverse populations, ancient ruins, beautiful landscapes, sweet music, and magnificent art—all of which inspired visitors to claim that one had to "see Naples, and then die."

Bosworth, R. J. B. *Mussolini's Italy: Life Under the Fascist Dictatorship, 1915–1945.* Penguin Classic, 2007. This book vividly brings to life the period in which Italy participated in one of the 20th century's most notorious political experiments. Il Duce's Fascists were the original totalitarians, promoting a cult of violence and obedience that inspired many other dictatorships including Hitler. But as Bosworth reveals, many Italians resisted its ideology, finding ways, ingenious and varied, to keep Fascism from taking hold as deeply as it did in Germany. Mussolini's Italy is a sweeping chronicle of struggle in Italy's darkest hour.

Heiken, Grant, Renato Funiciello, and Donatella De Rita. *The Seven Hills of Rome: A Geological Tour of the Eternal City.* Princeton University Press, 2005. *Seven Hills* contains plenty to interest geology and history buffs and travelers alike. It demonstrates the important link between the history of Rome and its geologic setting. Chapters are arranged geographically, based on each of the seven hills, the Tiber floodplain, ancient creeks that dissected the plateau, and ridges that rise above the right bank. As a bonus, the last chapter consists of three field trips around the center of Rome, which can be enjoyed on foot or by public transportation.

Hibbard, Howard. *Bernini.* Penguin Books, 1990. More than one contemporary thought Bernini was not merely the greatest artist of the century but the greatest man. He was not only a uniquely talented sculptor but also an architect, painter, playwright, and stage designer. A great many of his works are illustrated in this book. He gave a public opera in which he did it all: painted the scenes, cut the statues, composed the music, wrote the comedy and built the theater. Bernini was the last of the "dazzling universal geniuses who made Italy the artistic and intellectual center of Europe for more than three hundred years."

Katz, Robert. *The Battle for Rome: The Germans, The Allies, The Partisans, and The Pope September 1943–June 1944.* Simon and Schuster, 2003. This is a nearly day-to-day episodic reconstruction of the nine months when Rome was caught between the Nazi occupation and the Allied drive to free the city. The Allies were about to open a second front in Italy, south of Rome. The Italians deposed Mussolini and signed a peace treaty with the Allies. This caught the Germans by surprise. At the same time the Italian resistance movement, Partisans, made the largest attack against the Germans, to date, of any of the occupied European countries. In response, the Germans launched a determined fight to punish the Italians and push the Allies into the sea. Hitler's plan should the Allies capture Rome was to "level the City."

Levey, Michael. *Florence: A Portrait.* Harvard University Press, 1998. Florence has an amazing mix of great art and literature, natural splendor, and remarkable history. This scholar-author offers a wide-ranging coverage, in which he diagnoses it all. He weaves, with clarity, the threads of politics and the strands of cultural history. His focus is on Florence after the high Renaissance. A period he contends has considerable creative beauty and merits close examination that will stimulate your treasure-hunting instincts.

Martines, Lauro. *April Blood: Florence and the Plot Against the Medici.* Oxford University Press, 2003. The title of this book comes from a failed conspiracy in April 1478 to kill the two heads of the Medici family: Lorenzo the Magnificent, unofficial head of state, and his younger brother Giuliano. Known as the Pazzi Conspiracy, the plot only managed to assassinate the younger brother. While the Pazzi clan led the conspiracy, others throughout Italy were secretly involved: bankers, mercenaries, a duke, a king, even a pope. Revenge came quickly, with violence. "Plotters were hanged or beheaded, accomplices were hacked to pieces, and bodies hung out to dangle from government palace windows." This was a world of political maneuvering with the gloves off. At the center of this intrigue was Lorenzo, who survived as "boss of bosses."

McGregor, James H. S. *Rome: From the Ground Up.* Harvard University Press, 2006. This fascinating book describes how Rome slowly evolved into a city. In each epoch there has been a center, and that center remained even while a new center rose in importance. The book's clear prose, color photos, engravings, historical maps, architectural plans, and drawings bring Rome's past to life. The same author also wrote *Venice: From the Ground Up.*

Romano, Dennis. *The Likeness of Venice: A Life of Doge Francesco Foscari*. Yale Press, 2005. Francesco Foscari reigned as the powerful doge of Venice during tumultuous years of 1423–1457. His life was marked by political conflict, vengeful enemies, family heartbreak, and, at the end, the forced removal from the ducal throne. Since he left no personal records, a complete biography had not been until now. Romano reconstructed Foscari's life through careful reading of governmental records and chronicle sources. Romano analyzes how art and power intersected in Renaissance Italy and how the doge came to represent and even embody the state.

Scirocco, Alfonso. *Garibaldi: Citizen of the World—A Biography*. Princeton University Press, 2004. Garibaldi was one of the most extraordinary figures of the 19th century. The revolutionary, soldier, politician, and greatest figure in the fight for Italian unification, Garibaldi (1807–1882) was a much beloved hero. He was also a contradictory figure: a pacifist who spent much of his life fighting; nationalist who advocated European unification; and republican who served a king. He always however refused honors and wealth and spent his last years as a farmer.

Wills, Garry. *Venice: Lion City*. Simon and Schuster, 2002. Since its creation in the 1400s and 1500s the city has been a magnet, attracting writers, artists, lovers, and curious travelers. Wills relates the history of this fascinating and multifaceted city through its splendorous art (more than 130 works of art, 30 in full color) and, in turn, illuminates the art through the city's history. He portrays all the many Venetians who created a city that is "the greatest art museum in the world."

ART AND ARCHITECTURE

Brooks, Julian. *Taddeo and Federico Zuccaro: Artist-Brothers in Renaissance Rome*. Getty Publications, 2007. Never fully published until now, the series shows Taddeo's trials and tribulations as a young artist trying to achieve success in Renaissance Rome, and his eventual triumph. The drawings contain charming details of the life of a struggling artist and reveal much about the younger brother, Federico, a successful artist in his own right. Of particular importance is its examination of the role of the copying of masterworks in the training of young Renaissance artists.

da Vinci, Leonardo. *A Treatise on Painting*. Prometheus Books, 2002. If you would like to get started painting, let Leonardo get you off on the right path. This is his primer for those interested in learning the craft of drawing and painting. He leads by example revealing how he accomplished his great works of art. Starting with the anatomy of the main features of the human body and techniques for creating motion and perspective, he discusses aspects of good composition and artistic form. Throughout Leonardo stresses two highly important criteria—detailed and complete study of your subject and careful, concentrated, continuous practice.

Kemp, Martin. *Leonardo da Vinci: The Marvelous Works of Nature and Man*. Oxford University Press, 2004. This book is considered the classic treatment of the Renaissance giant, offering penetrating insight into Leonardo's intellect and vision at every stage of his artistic career. Kemp takes us on a fantastic journey through the whole span of the great man's life, describing an integrated picture of his artistic, scientific, and technological achievements.

King, Ross. *Michelangelo and the Pope's Ceiling*. Penguin, 2003. King portrays the epic struggle between Michelangelo, as egotistical genius and Pope Julius as brilliant manipulator. King's political background to the period shows how the ebb and flow of Julius's military campaigns affected the artist's work. Competition between Michelangelo and young Raphael offers even more drama. We are reminded that while they were brilliant artists, Renaissance masters were challenged by the same personal and professional problems that confront artists today, that creativity and performance has as much to do with opportunity as it does talent.

Morrissey, Jake. *The Genius in the Design: Bernini, Borromini and the Rivalry that Transformed Rome.* Harper Perennial, 2006. The artistic passions and ambitions of two of the greatest architects in Western history fueled a rivalry that culminated in their designing some of the most beautiful buildings in the world. Many of the innovative ideas of these two brilliant designers are clearly described, as well as their fierce competition that resulted in bitter animosity between them.

Murray, Peter. *The Architecture of the Italian Renaissance.* Schocken Book Inc., 1986. This is a clear, comprehensive coverage of a seminal period in art and architecture history. From Leonardo, Raphael, Michelangelo, Palladio, and Brunelleschi to St. Peter's in Rome, the palaces of Venice, and the Medici Chapel in Florence, Murray's elaborately illustrated book shows everything you need to know about the architectural world of Italy in the 13th–16th centuries.

Vasari, Giorgio. *Lives of the Artists* (in two volumes), Penguin Classics, 1987. While Vasari (1511–1574) was a well-known painter and architect, his book, *Lives of the Artists* made him famous, even in his own time. These short biographies of renowned Italian artists, traced the development of art and architecture across three centuries. He traveled all about Italy to view art and speak to artists. He asked about technique, tools, and materials and what they were trying to achieve through their art. He

managed to infuse his work with the passion for the creative process that he saw exhibited by these artists.

FOOD

Riley, Gillian. *The Oxford Companion to Italian Food.* Oxford University Press, 2007. This book will set your mouth watering, as it describes a rich and complex culinary culture: the Italian. Gillian covers all aspects of the history and culture of Italian gastronomy, from dishes, ingredients, and delicacies to cooking methods, and implements, regional specialties to the universal appeal of Italian cuisine. Following the footsteps of "princes and popes, vagabond artists and cunning peasants, generations of unknown, unremembered women who shaped pasta, formed cheeses, and lovingly tended their cooking pots," Gillian creates an inspiring celebration for one of the world's favorite cuisines.

FICTION

Silone, Ignazio. *Bread and Wine.* Signet Classics, 1986. In 1936, when *Bread and Wine* first became available, it shocked the world with how Mussolini's fascist state was treating the Italian people. Silone was one of the major voices of his time, and this is his greatest novel. "In this masterpiece, he brings to life: priests and peasants, students and revolutionaries, simple girls and desperate women in a vivid drama of one man's struggle for goodness in a world on the brink of war." The book speaks to anyone, of whatever age, "who tries sincerely to reflect upon man's fate in our century."

Suggested Films

Open City (1945)

This film directed by Roberto Rossellini about the Italian Resistance was scripted in the days of the underground battle against the Nazis. It is the story of the solidarity of Rome as a city that anticipates a final victory against the invaders. Some of the film's heroes will forever remain in the hearts of viewers. Who can forget the sight of a pregnant Pina (Anna Magnani) running through bullets or the kind priest shot before the frightened eyes of the children? The story is just as moving today as it was then. No surprise, after her role, Magnani became one of the greatest actresses of the Italian screen. This film won the Grand Prize at the Cannes Film Festival.

The Bicycle Thief (1948)

In the *The Bicycle Thief* directed by Vittorio De Sica, Antonio Ricci, an unemployed worker in postwar Rome, finds a job putting up movie posters after his wife pawns the family's bedsheets to get his bicycle out of hock. But right after he starts work the bike is stolen, and with his little boy Bruno he crisscrosses the city trying to recover it, encountering various aspects of Roman society including some of the more acute class differences, in the process. The movie contains possibly the greatest depiction of a relationship between a father and son in the history of cinema, full of subtle fluctuations and evolving gradations between the two characters in terms of respect and trust, and it is a wondrous heartbreaker. The film won the Oscar for Best Foreign Language Film.

La Dolce Vita (1959)

Federico Fellini shot *La Dolce Vita* in 1959 on the Via Veneto, the Roman street of nightclubs, sidewalk cafes, and the parade of the night. His hero is a gossip columnist, Marcello, who chronicles "the sweet life" of fading aristocrats, second-rate movie stars, aging playboys, and women of the night. The role was played by Marcello Mastroianni. The two Marcellos—character and actor—flowed together into a handsome, weary, desperate man, who dreams of someday doing something good, but is trapped in a life of empty nights and lonely dawns. The movie leaps from one visual extravaganza to another, following Marcello as he chasses down stories and women, in his search for the sweet life. This won Best Foreign Language Film.

Spartacus (1960)

Stanley Kubrick brought Howard Fast's tale of a slave revolt in ancient Rome to the screen, with scenes of the power struggle in the senate and brotherhood between the slaves. Spartacus (Kirk Douglas) is the slave at the center of the action, who inspires many like him to rise up against their oppressors. The revolt and battle sequences are riveting, but the biggest surprise is the final heart wrenching moments as Spartacus's love Varinia (Jean Simmons) holds up their child for him to see as he dies, crucified alongside the men who followed him.

The Garden of the Finzi-Continis (1970)

The film directed by Vittorio De Sica is based on Gorgio Bassani's novel of Italian Jews slowly adapting to the coming fascist oppression. As the political atmosphere becomes increasingly hostile to Jewish citizens, they turn their home into a refuge for other Jewish friends and families. The instability of their situation spirals into tragedy as Fascism gradually descends upon their world. This is a touching parable about the interrelation of personal and political, private, and public drama. Winner of 26 International Awards.

Cinema Paradiso (1988)

This is not only a nostalgic evocation of the director's (Giuseppe Tornatore) childhood days, but of those happy times before television when people used to go the cinema. It tells the story of a filmmaker who, after being told by his mother that "Alfredo died," starts to remember the 1950s, when as a boy living in a small Sicilian village, he spent almost all his time at the Cinema Paradiso. While there he becomes friends with the projectionist Alfredo. Everything in their village spins around the cinema, a place of entertainment, but also of meeting and chatter.

Internet Resources

The Web is a vital tool for hitting the road and it's hard to imagine how anyone ever traveled without it. Gone is the risk of an unsightly hotel or the disappointment of missing the cheese festival. Nowadays train tickets and seats at La Scala can be purchased online. Bookmark a few good addresses and spend lunch hour mastering the Italian highway system or Calabria's best beaches. The Web is ideal for getting real-time ski conditions and deciding in a few clicks whether a bed-and-breakfast is suitably romantic. Most sites have an English version and the following may prove useful in planning a getaway.

GENERAL INFORMATION

Italian Tourism
www.italia.it

This is one of several official websites and a good place to be inspired if you're still wavering between destinations. There's comprehensive hotel and travel information along with an overview of Italian culture and history. Images are tempting and the "Visit Italy" section provides links to regional websites that go into even greater depth. Two of the best are **www. turismo.toscana.it** for Tuscany and **www. suedtirol.info** for Alto Adige.

www.enit.it

Enit is operated by the Italian tourist board and provides regional, provincial, and local travel information. It's not very polished but there are alluring itineraries, a calendar of events, and an extensive database where travelers can search for museums and sights based on interest.

PARKS AND RECREATION

Nature
www.parks.it

Italy's 22 national and hundreds of regional parks are described in this naturalistic portal. Accommodations and services are listed near the protected areas, along with details about trails and what sports are available where.

Trekking
www.cai.it

The Alpine Club is an association of outdoor types with a passion for walking. There's an office in nearly every mountain town and they have the lowdown on all the trails and paths throughout the peninsula. They also list refuges where hikers can spend the night and offer a membership card that provides discounts to hotels and restaurants.

Camping
www.camping.it

This site lists hundreds of campsites where travelers can pitch their tents or park the caravan.

Winter Sports
www.skiinfo.it

Anyone packing skis or planning on renting them should log on to this site before setting off. It covers resorts in every region and provides updated snow conditions, trail info, lift prices, and webcams.

www.dolomitisuperski.com

The Dolomites in Trentino are a paradise for skiers and all of the valleys in the area are made accessible to prospective visitors on this site.

FOOD AND WINE

www.deliciousitaly.com

When food matters just as much as the monuments, this is the place to browse. Find out about typical products, gastronomic itineraries, and specialty festivals, or go all out and book a culinary holiday.

www.movimentoturismovino.it

This is a great resource for anyone who wants to combine a visit to Italy with a taste of the country's best grapes. Vineyards are listed in each region along with recommended itineraries along scenic wine routes. Although there is an English section, more information is offered in Italian.

ACCOMMODATIONS

Bed-and-Breakfasts
www.bed-and-breakfast.it

A vast list of bed-and-breakfasts with photos, contact information, and prices. All regions are listed and nearly every town covered.

Agriturismi
www.agriturismoitaly.it

If you're looking for a place to lie low for a couple of days and are curious how olive oil or honey is made, visit this site. The *agriturismi* listed provide great accommodations and most double as working farms.

Hostels
www.ostellionline.org

Budget travelers and backpackers will find suitable accommodations organized by city and region. Reservations can be made online and basic information regarding local sights is provided.

Advice
www.tripadvisor.com

A hotel website may look good, but feedback from people who have recently stayed there can be even more insightful. Comments are detailed and often highlight inconveniences like a bad view or small bathroom.

PRACTICALITIES

Airports
www.adr.it and www.sea-aeroportimilano.it

Plane spotters can check on departures and get the latest flight information for airports serving Rome and Milan at these sites. Each also lists airlines and specifics for reaching the city center.

Trains
www.ferroviedellostato.it

A few minutes on this site operated by the Italian national rail service can help avoid a long wait later on. Just type in a destination and departure times and ticket prices appear for local and express trains. Passes can be purchased and discounts are available for young and mature travelers.

Highways
www.autostrade.it

This is the place to get familiar with Italy's highways. Meticulous drivers can calculate mileage (in kilometers) and toll costs. Rest areas are listed, as are the cheapest gas stations along any itinerary. It's also useful for learning about roadwork and brushing up on the Italian rules of the road.

ENTERTAINMENT

Nightlife
www.2night.it

Clubs, bars, and music venues in all of Italy's major cities. Most reviews are in Italian but photos and contact information needs no translation.

Children
www.travelforkids.com

Keeping kids happy is what this site is all about. It lists many alternatives for preventing tots and teenagers from yawning.

Index

WXYZ

Map Index

Acknowledgments

Thanks to Italy. Without her there wouldn't be a book. She has revealed an astonishing history, culture, and land. Capturing it all on paper has been a challenge and would have been impossible without a surplus of helping hands. Over the last year I have met many good people who have generously shared their experiences and to whom I am grateful.

Thanks to the writers. If it comes to kilometers clocked, the award goes to Judy Edelhoff, who tracked more vineyards than anyone can count and regularly journeyed off the map. Kristine Crane tirelessly ran across Emilia Romagna, and Letizia Razzino earned the nickname Ms. Basilicata. The *Background* chapter was made wiser with Charles Lee's contributions on film and literature, and Cecile Detre successfully deciphered Italian politics. Holger Engelhart put his plane-spotting skills to good use throughout, and Fabrizio Ramaccia could never resist a golf course or trattoria.

Photographers also went out of their way. Laurie Elie and Mario took wonderful shots of Sicily and Liguria, Cristiana Lommi captured the beauty of Sardinia, and Judy snapped every place she traveled. Thanks also to persistent volunteers who made thousands of phone calls, checked facts, researched, and proofread every line.

Italians have a lot to say and one question gets plenty of answers. Thanks therefore to all the public officials and townspeople who gladly pointed the way. Franco provided the low-down on Lazio and the joy of a seasonal diet. Massimo de Palo made sense of the *Risorgimento* and supplied dozens of maps. Genova, Tuscany, and the Roman Empire were Livio Livi's domain, and Giuseppe Galiani's passion for grapes was contagious. Thanks also to Marc Bush's tireless quest for exceptional gelato and Carlo Luzzi's lessons in bocce. Antonello Minieri was vital in Milan and never tired of shopping for the cause. Letizia Rossi and Laura Tellarini scouted the best valleys in Val d'Aosta and fearlessly rode cable cars across the Alps.

There are too many stomachs to cite that suggested pizzerias and *osterias* up and down the peninsula. Special credit, however, goes to Franca, who fed the author on many occasions and whose artichokes *a la romana* are legendary. Thanks also to the support of friends and family—in particular, Eric Lommi and Simone Dovigo, who supplied endless enthusiasm and kept everyone's spirits high.

Applause to the energetic team at Avalon Travel. Grace Fujimoto for believing and Erin Raber for the patience and thoughtful suggestions that made this a better book. Hats off to Editorial, Cartography, and everyone who worked behind the scenes to make this guide a reality.

Thanks to Alessia for proofreading, translation, photography, art direction, research, and infinite encouragement. The adventure wouldn't have been possible without you.

This book is dedicated to Sacha, who has yet to discover Italy, and Julien, who never had the chance.

Contributing Writers

Kristine Crane

Kristine Crane wrote the *Emilia Romagna* chapter for this edition of *Moon Italy*. She fell in love with Emilia Romagna after studying history and literature at the University of Bologna and has rediscovered the region as an amateur runner and expert eater. She served as a news assistant for the *Wall Street Journal Europe's* Rome bureau and the Dow Jones Newswires Rome bureau and worked as a researcher on immigration issues in Rome after studying immigration as a Fulbright scholar. Kristine is currently studying for a Masters in Arts in science reporting at the Columbia University School of Journalism.

Judy Edelhoff

Judy Edelhoff wrote the *Venice, Veneto, and Friuli-Venezia Giulia, Le Marche, Abruzzo and Molise,* and *Naples and Campania* chapters for this edition of *Moon Italy.* Judy has written about art, food, archaeology, wine, theater, film, and customs in Italy for *Italy Daily* (by the *International Herald Tribune*) and *The American Magazine,* where she is the chief restaurant critic. She has broadcast live from Rome for CNN on Italian law and politics, was a contributing writer for *Moon Metro Rome,* and has written about Umbria, Tuscany, and Sicily for other travel publishing companies.

www.moon.com

For helpful advice on planning a trip, visit www.moon.com for the **TRAVEL PLANNER** and get access to useful travel strategies and valuable information about great places to visit. When you travel with Moon, expect an experience that is uncommon and truly unique.

HANDBOOKS | METRO | OUTDOORS | LIVING ABROAD

MAP SYMBOLS

▤▤▤ Expressway	◖ Highlight	✗ Airfield	⌖ Golf Course
▭▭▭ Primary Road	○ City/Town	✈ Airport	▣ Parking Area
▭▭▭ Secondary Road	◉ State Capital	▲ Mountain	▰ Archaeological Site
▭ ▭ ▭ Unpaved Road	⊛ National Capital	✛ Unique Natural Feature	♠ Church
- - - - Trail	★ Point of Interest		⛽ Gas Station
⋯⋯⋯ Ferry	• Accommodation	≈ Waterfall	Glacier
┼┼┼┼ Railroad	▼ Restaurant/Bar	♠ Park	Mangrove
▤▤ Pedestrian Walkway	▪ Other Location	◨ Trailhead	Reef
▥▥▥ Stairs	Λ Campground	⛷ Skiing Area	Swamp

CONVERSION TABLES

°C = (°F – 32) / 1.8
°F = (°C x 1.8) + 32
1 inch = 2.54 centimeters (cm)
1 foot = 0.304 meters (m)
1 yard = 0.914 meters
1 mile = 1.6093 kilometers (km)
1 km = 0.6214 miles
1 fathom = 1.8288 m
1 chain = 20.1168 m
1 furlong = 201.168 m
1 acre = 0.4047 hectares
1 sq km = 100 hectares
1 sq mile = 2.59 square km
1 ounce = 28.35 grams
1 pound = 0.4536 kilograms
1 short ton = 0.90718 metric ton
1 short ton = 2,000 pounds
1 long ton = 1.016 metric tons
1 long ton = 2,240 pounds
1 metric ton = 1,000 kilograms
1 quart = 0.94635 liters
1 US gallon = 3.7854 liters
1 Imperial gallon = 4.5459 liters
1 nautical mile = 1.852 km

°FAHRENHEIT / °CELSIUS thermometer:
230 — 110
220 — 100 WATER BOILS
210 — 100
200 — 90
190 —
180 — 80
170 —
160 — 70
150 —
140 — 60
130 —
120 — 50
110 —
100 — 40
90 — 30
80 —
70 — 20
60 —
50 — 10
40 —
30 — 0 WATER FREEZES
20 — -10
10 —
0 — -20
-10 —
-20 — -30
-30 —
-40 — -40

Clock face: 12/24, 1/13, 2/14, 3/15, 4/16, 5/17, 6/18, 7/19, 8/20, 9/21, 10/22, 11/23

INCH ruler: 0 1 2 3 4

CM ruler: 0 1 2 3 4 5 6 7 8 9 10